TORTS:
CASES, PROBLEMS, AND EXERCISES

RUSSELL L. WEAVER

Professor of Law & Distinguished University Scholar
University of Louisville
Louis D. Brandeis School of Law

JOHN H. BAUMAN

Professor of Law
South Texas College of Law

JOHN T. CROSS

Professor of Law and Wyatt, Tarrant & Combs Fellow
University of Louisville
Louis D. Brandeis School of Law

ANDREW R. KLEIN

Associate Dean for Academic Affairs and
Paul E. Beam Professor of Law
Indiana University School of Law—Indianapolis

EDWARD C. MARTIN

Professor of Law
Samford University
Cumberland School of Law

PAUL J. ZWIER, II

Professor of Law
Emory School of Law

LexisNexis™

LCCN: 2005920019

ISBN: 0-8205-6331-5

Editorial Offices
744 Broad Street, Newark, NJ 07102 (973) 820-2000
201 Mission St., San Francisco, CA 94105-1831 (415) 908-3200
701 East Water Street, Charlottesville, VA 22902-7587 (804) 972-7600
www.lexis.com

(Pub.3618)

DEDICATIONS

To Ben and Kate, with love. **RLW**

To Kathee, and to Mary, Hannah and Clare. **JHB**

To my Parents, who convinced me
anything is possible. **JTC**

To Diane, Timothy & Jason. **ARK**

This book is dedicated to all of my former Torts students through
the years who have made teaching this subject such a joy!
Thank you. **ECM**

To my Torts Students. And to Marlene with Love. **PJZ**

PREFACE

As we move to a second edition of this torts casebook, our goal remains the same: to create a "teacher's book." As with the first edition, the second edition contains thought-provoking problems designed to stimulate thought and produce interesting classroom discussion. The problems are woven throughout each chapter and are designed to help students learn doctrine, illuminate trends in the law, and ultimately produce better learning.

A secondary goal was to includes a "skills" component. Some of the problems place students in practical situations that they are likely to encounter in practice, and therefore encourage students to think about how they might handle these situations.

In any book, tradeoffs are necessary. In this book, we have chosen not to include encyclopedic notes and references like those found in other books. In the torts area, students have numerous high-quality secondary sources available to them, and students can consult these sources for expanded scholarly discussions of the law. Consistent with our goal of producing a "teacher's book," we opted to limit the scope of our notes and to substitute problems.

We are thankful to our research assistants and secretaries for their help in producing this book. In addition, we want to thank the many students who were subjected to early drafts of this book and ultimately helped us produce a better product.

We welcome input from faculty and students who use this book. You can contact us at the following e-mail addresses: Professor Russell Weaver (russ.weaver@louisville.edu); Professor John Bauman (jbauman@stcl.edu); John Cross (john.cross@louisville.edu); Professor Andrew Klein (anrklein@iupui.edu); Professor Ed Martin (ecmartin@samford.edu); Professor Paul Zwier (zwier@law.emory.edu).

RLW, JHB, JTC, ARK, ECM, PJZ

December, 2004

ACKNOWLEDGMENT

Permission from the American Law Institute to reprint the following Restatement materials is gratefully acknowledged:

Restatement (Second) of Agency

Copyright 1958 by the American Law Institute. All rights reserved. Reprinted with permission.

Restatement (First) of Torts

Copyright 1938 by the American Law Institute. All rights reserved. Reprinted with permission.

Restatement (Second) of Torts

Copyright 1965, 1977, 1979 by the American Law Institute. All rights reserved. Reprinted with permission.

Restatement (Third) of Torts: Products Liability

Copyright 1998 by the American Law Institute. All rights reserved. Reprinted with permission.

Restatement (Third) of Torts (Tentative Draft No. 1 2001)

Copyright 2001 by the American Law Institute. All rights reserved. Reprinted with permission.

EDITING NOTE

Many torts cases are far longer than can be included in a book of reasonable length. In addition, many cases include multiple issues, some of which are irrelevant to the torts issues in this case. In creating this book, we have consistently tried to be faithful to the deciding court's language and the spirit of the opinion. However, although we have indicated some changes (usually by brackets or an ellipses), we generally do not note omissions from the edited opinions in this book

TABLE OF CONTENTS

Chapter 1

INTRODUCTION TO THE STUDY OF TORT LAW

A. WHAT IS A TORT?

In this course we will be studying the law of "torts." Basically, a tort is defined as a civil wrong for which the law recognizes a legal remedy on behalf of a private individual. In the vast majority of tort cases, this legal remedy exists in the form of monetary damages. In some cases, other remedies, including injunctive relief also may be available. Look closely again at the definition of a tort. Notice that it pertains only to a *civil* wrong, as opposed to a *criminal* wrong.

How does tort law differ from the criminal law? In fact, although the same conduct may give rise to both tort liability and criminal liability, tort law handles this conduct quite differently. While criminal misconduct certainly does produce individual victims, the focus is on the wrong against society at large. Individual violations of criminal law are brought against the accused by official representatives of the state for the purpose of punishing the guilty individual for his or her criminal misconduct, as well as to deter similar misconduct by other members of society. Punishment is accomplished through the imposition of a monetary fine, incarceration in jail (*i.e.*, a deprivation of the individual's personal freedom), or the loss of life (capital punishment). Usually, the individual victim of criminal misconduct remains personally uncompensated for any monetary losses that may have resulted from the crime. By contrast, the primary purpose of a tort action is to provide a legal mechanism whereby the individual victim of the tortious misconduct can recover monetary damages to compensate him or her personally for actual injuries. In a tort action, the victim must personally and individually pursue the action against a defendant accused of committing a civil wrong. The victim, at least initially, also must bear the entire cost of bringing his or her own tort action.

Tort law and other civil wrongs. Tort law compliments other areas of civil law. For example, a person might intentionally enter into a written contract with another and then knowingly breach that contract by not performing in accordance with the previously agreed-upon terms. Such conduct would arguably be considered "wrong" by many members of our society, yet it is not likely to be found either tortious or criminal by the courts. The law of Contracts addresses such matters by providing specific remedies to the aggrieved party. For this reason, the defendant's conduct in breaching the contract, although perhaps a "wrong," is not a tort. Tort law developed as a way of remedying those unique wrongs that do not rise to the level of truly criminal misconduct at one extreme, nor for which the common law provided a remedy under other causes of action.

B. THE CASEBOOK METHOD OF STUDYING TORTS

The majority of American tort law is derived from common law court decisions. Therefore, our system of tort law is still almost entirely construed and applied according to traditional common law principles. For this reason, many first-year law school courses, including this one, are taught utilizing the "casebook" methodology. In casebooks, students are presented with a series of edited judicial opinions that have been written by appellate courts in their resolution of actual legal disputes. Typically, these appellate decisions represent the final stage in a long litigation process that actually began years earlier. As this dispute made its way into the courts and through the judicial system, pleadings were filed with the trial court; the parties then made numerous pre-trial motions; they engaged in a process of "discovery" to learn as much as they could about the specific details of the other party's case; they collected, and then presented, evidence in support of their respective legal claims. If the case made it to trial, they then examined and cross-examined each other's witnesses; they made numerous motions throughout the course of the trial itself; they requested specific jury instructions at the end of the trial; and they made additional motions even after the jury reached its verdict in the case. At any number of times throughout this often lengthy litigation process, errors may have been made by the trial judge who was required to make legal rulings at each stage of the proceedings. All of the trial court's rulings are reviewable by an appellate court, and any one erroneous ruling, if properly preserved by the affected litigant, can provide the basis for a successful legal challenge on appeal. In most cases the appellate decision is written specifically in response to some legal question that has been presented by one or both of the parties from the earlier litigation. Thus, either party may prevail on an appeal without ever really "winning" the underlying case on its actual legal merits.

Our purpose in studying these appellate decisions is to understand the precise process by which appellate courts resolve legal disputes. Sometimes the answer to these questions will relate to how the appellate court interprets some specific legal rule or doctrine of tort law. Often, the answer involves a purely procedural or technical question that has little, if anything, to do with the substantive legal controversy involved in the underlying litigation. Occasionally, the outcome of an appeal may even depend upon whether or not the appellate court chooses to recognize or apply some policy intended to influence or direct how future tort cases will be resolved.

C. PROCEDURAL STAGES OF A TYPICAL TORT CASE

Even though our primary emphasis in studying appellate case decisions will focus upon the individual cases themselves, it is imperative that students understand the entire procedural process involved as each case makes its way through the judicial system.

The litigation process is designed primarily as a means of resolving disputes between two or more opposing parties. In most litigated cases, these disputes involve both factual and legal issues. The basic process by which these disputes are resolved by courts and attorneys often seems mysterious, even incomprehensible to the beginning law student. Indeed, one court, in comparing this process to some kind of arcane religious ritual, described it in the following colorful terms:

> "The lay litigant enters a temple of mysteries whose ceremonies are dark, complex and unfathomable. Pretrial procedures are the cabalistic rituals of the lawyers and judges who serve as priests and high priests. The layman knows nothing of their tactical significance. He knows only that his case remains in limbo while the priests and high priests chant their legally arcane pretrial rites."

Daley v. County of Butte, 227 Cal. App. 2d 380, 392, 38 Cal. Rptr. 693 (1964).

While the various procedures and processes involved in a typical tort litigation may not be quite so daunting as the foregoing quote implies, they still seem somewhat overwhelming to the uninitiated. Nevertheless, once the specific purpose for and function of each individual step involved in the civil litigation process is understood, the mystery is comprehensible.

The following materials provide a brief summary of the major elements that are usually present in a litigated tort case. Initially, each step of a typical civil litigation (indicated in these materials in **boldface** captions) is briefly explained. Then, at the appropriate stage throughout the litigation process (An interactive chart showing the litigation timeline can be found on the internet at: http://www.samford.edu/schools/netlaw/dh2/casetutorial/Figure1.htm), the nature and function of various typical procedural devices (*italicized* in these materials) are also explained.

Initially, assume that the aggrieved party has consulted with an attorney who has investigated the alleged claim and determined that it is one for which some relief might properly be permitted under our existing body of tort law. Assume further that the attorney next exhausts any appropriate alternatives to litigation by making reasonable efforts to resolve the aggrieved party's dispute through various informal processes. Assuming that all of these other available alternatives have failed, the attorney has then proceeded to present the aggrieved party's case to a court for adjudication. For purposes of this discussion, you may assume also that the aggrieved party's legal claim has been contested by the opposing party.

Step 1: A Complaint Is Filed. This is a formal legal document stating the relevant factual and legal bases in support of the claim by one party (now designated as the plaintiff) for relief against another party (designated as the defendant) alleged to be responsible for causing the legal harm about which the plaintiff is complaining. The purpose of the "Complaint" is to put the defendant on notice as to the specific facts and circumstances of the plaintiff's claim, as well as what type of relief the plaintiff is seeking to obtain from the court. In a tort case this relief usually takes the form of a demand for monetary damages. After the Complaint is officially *filed* with the clerk of the court in the jurisdiction where the lawsuit has been brought, a copy is also personally delivered to the defendant (known as "*service of process*") by the sheriff or some other authorized official of the court.

Motion to Dismiss. The Motion to Dismiss (also referred to as a "Demurrer" in some jurisdictions) is a formal request for the court to dismiss the Complaint without the necessity for filing any further pleadings in a case. This motion is made when the moving party (usually the defendant at this stage of the litigation) believes that there is no legal basis for the case to continue. Specifically, this motion says that even if the facts as alleged in the Complaint are found to be true, the law simply does not recognize the asserted cause of action. Thus, the purpose of a Motion to Dismiss is to prevent the case from progressing any further when there is absolutely no legal possibility that it can ever succeed. In a Motion to Dismiss, there can be no dispute about any facts that are deemed material to the outcome of the lawsuit, because the case has not yet proceeded to a jury. In ruling on a Motion to Dismiss, therefore, the trial court must accept as true non-movant's version of the facts as set out in the pleadings. If the Motion to Dismiss is granted, the court can either permit the plaintiff to amend the Complaint by adding additional allegations that would make the Complaint sufficient to state a proper legal claim and then allowing the plaintiff to start all over again, or the court can simply grant the Motion to Dismiss without leave to amend. Courts adopt the latter course only when there are no additional material facts whatsoever that could be added to the Complaint to make it legally sufficient to state any cause of action. If the Motion to Dismiss is denied by the trial court, then the case will proceed to the next step of the litigation. Depending upon the jurisdiction, the Motion to Dismiss may be filed by the defendant prior to the filing of a formal Answer. However, it is commonly filed by the defendant at the same time as the filing of the Answer and as a part of the Answer itself.

Step 2: The Answer Is Filed. After a *Complaint* has been served against the defendant, that party has a specified period of time within which to file a formal written response to the plaintiff's Complaint with the court. In most jurisdictions, this period of time is about thirty days, as measured from the date of service. The most typical form of written response to a Complaint in a tort case is referred to as an *Answer*, whereby the defendant formally must either admit or deny each specific allegation asserted in the plaintiff's Complaint. Rules in most jurisdictions also require that certain types of legal defenses be asserted in writing with the defendant's first responsive pleading. For example, if the plaintiff alleges in a Complaint that the defendant "kicked the plaintiff's dog, causing injury to the animal," the defendant might file an Answer simply denying such allegations altogether. Conversely, the defendant's Answer might admit the allegations in the plaintiff's Complaint, but nevertheless assert some proper legal excuse or justification (typically referred to as a *defense*) for the challenged action. In addition, the defendant at this time may also wish to assert a *Counterclaim* (a separate Complaint against the plaintiff), or even a *Cross Claim* (a separate Complaint against some third party that arises out of the same factual occurrence). The allegations set forth in the plaintiff's Complaint, together with the responses to those allegations as contained in the defendant's Answer, allow both parties, as well as the court, to know precisely what specific issues (both factual and legal) will be involved in the litigation. Taken together, the plaintiff's Complaint and the defendant's Answer and all other related filings are commonly referred to as the *"pleadings"* in the case.

Step 3: Discovery. After the plaintiff's Complaint has been put "in issue" by the filing of the defendant's Answer or other responsive pleadings, both parties to the litigation have at least a general idea of the legal and factual issues that are likely to arise in the case. However, many specific details pertaining to those issues still remain uncertain. In most jurisdictions, both parties are then permitted to engage in a series of procedures (known generally as *Discovery*) during which they may seek further details about the opposing party's case. Each party may ask written questions (known as *interrogatories*) to which the other party must respond in writing and under oath. Each party is also permitted to ask questions in person to the other party and their witnesses to which the other party must also respond under oath. These questions and answers are often transcribed into documents called *depositions* that can then be used at the trial for a variety of different purposes. A party during discovery may request the opposing party for an *admission* of certain specific facts, and any such fact that is not specifically admitted or denied from that point on in the proceedings will be treated as if it had been admitted by the opposing party. Finally, during discovery each party may also demand that the other party produce certain specified documents or other physical evidence prior to the trial. The basic purpose of this period of "discovery" is to avoid situations where either party might be unfairly "surprised" at the actual trial by the introduction into evidence of some evidence or by the testimony of some "surprise" witness about which they were unaware. In theory, discovery allows the parties to narrow the issues that are in dispute in a trial, thus simplifying and shortening the actual trial itself. In practice, however, discovery in many cases is hotly contested by the parties, and it often results in additional pre-trial delays and expenses.

Motion for Summary Judgment. After all of the pleadings have been filed, and discovery conducted, by both parties, either party may file a Motion for Summary Judgment. This motion, like the Motion to Dismiss, again asks the trial court to rule in favor of the movant as a matter of law, without permitting the case to proceed to trial. Unlike the Motion to Dismiss which merely assumes the truth of all disputed facts in favor of the non-moving party, the Motion for Summary Judgment specifically adds additional facts to the pleadings in order to establish that there are indeed no disputed material facts whatsoever. Hence, the Motion for Summary Judgment is made in an attempt to avoid the expense and delay of a trial, by asserting that there are no disputed factual issues to be resolved by a jury. Usually, the additional facts necessary for the Motion for Summary Judgment are supplied through the discovery process described above. Thus, the Motion for Summary Judgment asserts that there is no need for a trial because there is no dispute as to any material fact issues in the case and the law is clear, demanding a judgment in favor of the moving party. If the trial court grants the Motion for Summary Judgment, the case ends at this point.

Motions in Limine. Once it has been determined that a case will proceed to trial, the focus of both parties' motions usually shifts to specific questions regarding the admissibility of certain types of evidence. Either party may file a Motion in Limine (*i.e.*, a Motion "on the verge" of the trial) at any time prior to the actual trial in order to request an "advance ruling" by the trial judge on a variety of issues that are likely to arise in the upcoming trial. The purpose of this motion is to limit or otherwise control the direction that the trial will take in regard to a particular issue or evidentiary matter that is anticipated. For example, a party may wish to file a Motion in Limine asking the trial judge to rule on the admissibility of a certain piece of evidence, or to limit the scope of a particular witness' testimony, in order to reduce the potential for unfair prejudice or surprise that might otherwise arise during the actual trial.

Step 4: Selection of a Jury. The first step in any jury trial involves the selection of the jury. Prospective jurors are initially selected (usually by the clerk of the court) from a pool of local citizens. These persons are questioned first by the trial judge, and then usually questioned further by the attorneys on behalf of each of the respective parties to the litigation. The purpose of this questioning (a procedure known as *voir dire*) is to identify any potential jurors who might be disqualified from service because of some personal interest or bias with respect to the specific litigation or the parties, witnesses, or attorneys involved in it. During this process, each party is also permitted to remove a limited number of potential jurors even without a showing of prejudice or other cause (in a process referred to as "striking" jurors). Eventually, when the process of *voir dire* is concluded, the entire jury panel (at this time often referred to as a *petit jury*) typically consisting of twelve or eight or even six persons, is given an oath. Once the jury is empanelled, the formal part of the trial begins.

Step 5: Opening Statements from Both Parties. Initially, the plaintiff's attorney begins the formal part of the typical jury trial in a tort case by presenting to the jury a brief summary or overview of what the case is all about. Known as an "Opening Statement," this oral presentation is intended to give the jury a brief preview of the plaintiff's case and to alert them as to what specific facts they should look for when the evidence is presented to them. Once the plaintiff's attorney has concluded with the opening statement, the opposing party's attorney is then given an opportunity to present a similar statement.

Step 6: The Plaintiff's Case. Since the plaintiff initiated the lawsuit by filing the Complaint, it remains the plaintiff's ultimate responsibility to satisfy the burden of proof with respect to establishing each and every legal element of any claim(s) that are alleged. For this reason, the plaintiff is entitled to go first in the presentation of witnesses and other evidence necessary to establish all of the facts pertaining to each part of the plaintiff's allegations. After each witness is questioned first by the attorney who called that particular witness (a process known as *direct examination*), the same witness is then subjected to further questioning by the attorney who represents the opposing party (in a process known as *cross examination*). These detailed examinations of each and every witness in a trial by attorneys who represent both parties are intended to eliminate any factual inaccuracies in the witnesses' personal observations and recollections, as well as to reveal any personal biases and other factors that might inappropriately influence or prejudice the outcome of the trial in favor of one party or another.

Step 7: The Defendant's Case. After all of the plaintiff's witnesses (and other evidence) have been presented and subjected to thorough cross-examination, the defendant's attorney then has an opportunity to present the other side of the case. As the defendant's witnesses are presented, they too are subjected to cross-examination, this time by the plaintiff's attorney. In this manner each party continues, in turn, offering evidence in support of their respective claims until all of the witnesses and other evidence have been presented before the jury. Ultimately, it is the jury's responsibility to weigh the credibility of each witness and to determine which version of any disputed facts to accept.

Motion for Directed Verdict (referred to in federal court as a Motion for Judgment as a Matter of Law). At the conclusion of each party's presentation of their evidence, a Motion for a Directed Verdict is often made on behalf of the opposing party. The purpose of this motion is to challenge the sufficiency of the evidence that has been presented in support of the non-moving party's claim. Since the jury has not yet had an opportunity to evaluate the evidence from the trial, the trial judge must consider this motion in the light most favorable to the non-moving party. After doing so, the judge may grant such a motion only if it determines that "no reasonable juror" could interpret the evidence in favor of the non-moving party. If there is any doubt as to how a reasonable juror might resolve some conflict with regard to any material facts in the case, then the Motion for Directed Verdict will be denied and the case will proceed for a final decision by the jury. The Motion for Directed Verdict is quite similar to a Motion for Summary Judgment in its legal effect, but it can only be made at the end of the trial, after all of the parties' evidence has been presented.

Step 8: Closing Arguments. Finally, after all of the evidence has been presented to the jury. Each party is given an opportunity to argue their version of the case to the jury in an attempt to persuade them in favor of one party's assertions or another. The plaintiff's *closing argument* is presented first, followed immediately by the defendant's argument.

Step 9: Jury Instructions. Before the jury is allowed to begin their deliberations in the case, they must be instructed (a process known as *"charging"* the jury) by the trial judge as to the relevant law which they are to apply in deciding the case. Although the jury is generally free to exercise their own judgment and discretion (subject only to review by the courts for abuse of that discretion) when determining each relevant fact in the case, they *must* follow the trial court's instructions when applying those facts to the applicable law in the case. Each party is permitted to propose jury instructions. Ultimately, however, the trial judge must decide which of these legal rules should be included in the jury's instructions and which should be left out.

Step 10: The Verdict. Once the jury has been instructed by the trial judge, they then retire to deliberate their verdict. A foreman (*i.e.*, leader) is chosen by the jury from among their own members and the jury's deliberations take place in secret. Neither party is permitted to present anything further to the jury, although the jury is given copies of all the pleadings in the case, as well as any documentary evidence that was presented during the trial. Individual jurors are also generally permitted to refer to their own personal "notes" that they may have taken during the course of the trial. When the jury reaches their decision, they then report their verdict to the trial judge. This verdict may take the form of a *general* verdict (*e.g.*, "We find in favor of the plaintiff on his claim of negligence against the defendant"), or it may be reported as a *special* verdict consisting of a series of answers to very specific questions that were submitted for determination (*e.g.*, "We find that the defendant violated statute 1-101 by running the stop sign at the intersection of Fourth and Main").

Motion for Judgment, N.O.V. (referred to in federal court as a Renewed Motion for Judgment as a Matter of Law). A Motion for Judgment, N.O.V. (*non obstante verdicto*, meaning in Latin, notwithstanding the verdict) is very similar to a Motion for a Directed Verdict, except that it is made only after the jury has returned a verdict that is unfavorable to the moving party. If the trial judge, for whatever reason, was unwilling to grant a party's Motion for a Directed Verdict at the end of the formal presentation of evidence in the case, this Motion gives the judge one last opportunity to do so now that the jury has rendered their verdict. Most of the time if the trial judge denies the movant's Motion for a Directed Verdict it is very unlikely that the judge will grant a Motion for Judgment, N.O.V. made by that same party after the jury has returned a verdict in the case. However, this Motion does give the judge one last opportunity to change his or her mind. Perhaps, for example, the trial judge simply chose to deny the earlier Motion for a Directed Verdict, believing (or even hoping) that the jury would return their verdict in favor of the movant. Likewise, the judge, although initially willing to allow the jury to return a small verdict against the movant, may be unwilling to support a verdict that was substantially higher than the judge thought appropriate for the case. In any event, the question presented by a Motion for Judgment, N.O.V. is whether the evidence at the trial was sufficient to support the jury's verdict. Obviously, a Motion for Judgment, N.O.V. can be made on behalf of either party.

Motion for New Trial. After the conclusion of the trial, either party may make a Motion for a New Trial. The purpose of this motion is to give the trial judge one last opportunity to correct any serious legal errors that may have occurred at any time during the trial. When the error originally occurred, the judge simply may have regarded it as harmless or insignificant under the circumstances as they were then perceived. However, upon further reflection after the outcome of the trial is now known, this Motion gives the judge a chance to correct such an error before the verdict becomes final. Once a verdict becomes final, the parties' only procedural recourse is to appeal the decision of the trial court in denying the Motion for a New Trial.

Step 11: Final Judgment. The verdict of the jury is not final until it has been formally approved by the trial judge. Typically, both parties are given at least a limited opportunity even after the verdict has been returned by the jury to review the case in order to decide whether any serious error has occurred at any point in the trial. Whichever party has prevailed in the trial will usually be asked by the trial judge to draft a "Final Judgment Order" which is then signed by the trial judge and becomes the official document that records the outcome of the parties' litigation. Neither party can "Appeal" the results of the trial until the trial judge has entered a Final Judgment Order.

D. THE DEVELOPMENT OF FAULT-BASED TORT LIABILITY

We now begin a substantive study of tort law. Scholars trace the roots of modern tort law to thirteenth century England, when the King conducted business by royal writ. Those who sought justice in one of the King's courts, therefore, needed to purchase the proper writ from the King's chancellor in order to pursue a claim. Perhaps the most important writ for purposes of civil justice was the writ of trespass. Trespass was used when a person was directly injured by another's conduct. Three forms of the writ evolved, each allowing a person to protect a different type of interest: (1) trespass vi et armis (with force and arms) to protect one's interest in physical integrity; (2) trespass de bonis asportatis (taking of goods) to protect one's interest in personal property; and (3) trespass quare clausum fregit (breach of the "close") to protect one's interest in real property. By the sixteenth century, the writ of trespass on the case developed as a supplement to the writs of trespass. Trespass on the case allowed individuals to seek justice when they were harmed *indirectly* by another's conduct. *See* W. PAGE KEETON ET AL., PROSSER & KEETON ON TORTS at 29 ("The classic illustration of the difference between trespass and case is that of a log thrown into the highway. A person struck by the log as it fell could maintain trespass against the thrower, since the injury was direct; but one who was hurt by stumbling over it as it lay in the road could maintain, not trespass, but an action on the case.").

In the United States, each state (except Louisiana) created its legal system by "receiving" the common law of England, including the writ system described above. For a long time, however, it was unclear whether these actions simply required a plaintiff to prove that the defendant invaded his interests, or whether the plaintiff needed to prove that the defendant did so with intent or through negligent conduct. If the plaintiff was not required to prove intent or negligence, liability was described as *strict*. If, however, intent or negligence was required, we say that the plaintiff must prove that the defendant was at *fault*. The following case is frequently cited as the leading American decision establishing that actions derived from trespass and case should be based on fault.

BROWN v. KENDALL
60 Mass. (6 Cush.) 292 (Mass. 1850)

This was an action of trespass for assault and battery, originally commenced [by plaintiff George Brown] against George K. Kendall, the defendant.

It appeared in evidence [at trial] that two dogs, belonging to the plaintiff and the defendant, respectively, were fighting in the presence of their masters; that the defendant took a stick about four feet long, and commenced beating the dogs in order to separate them; that the plaintiff was looking on, at the distance of about a rod, and that he advanced a step or two towards the dogs. In their struggle, the dogs approached the place where the plaintiff was standing. The defendant retreated backwards from before the dogs, striking them as he retreated; and as he approached the plaintiff, with his back towards him, in raising his stick over his shoulder, in order to strike the dogs, he accidentally hit the plaintiff in the eye, inflicting upon him a severe injury.

The defendant requested the judge to instruct the jury, that "if both the plaintiff and the defendant at the time of the blow were using ordinary care, or if at that time the defendant was using ordinary care and the plaintiff was not, or if at that time both plaintiff and defendant were not using ordinary care, then the plaintiff could not recover."

[The judge refused to give the instructions requested by the defendant. Instead, the judge instructed the jury that liability should turn on whether the defendant's conduct was a "necessary act." If so, the jury was instructed to find for the defendant if he acted with "ordinary care." If not, the jury was instructed that the defendant needed to exercise "extraordinary care." The judge further charged the jury that the defendant bore the burden of proving that he exercised extraordinary care, or lack of ordinary care on the part of plaintiff as a way to exculpate himself.]

The jury under these instructions returned a verdict for the plaintiff; whereupon the defendant alleged exceptions.

SHAW, C.J.

The facts set forth in the bill of exceptions preclude the supposition, that the blow, inflicted by the hand of the defendant upon the person of the plaintiff, was intentional. The whole case proceeds on the assumption, that the damage sustained by the plaintiff, from the stick held by the defendant was inadvertent and unintentional; and the case involves the question how far, and under what qualifications, the party by whose unconscious act the damage was done is responsible for it. We use the term "unintentional" rather than involuntary, because in some of the cases, it is stated, that the act of holding and using a weapon or instrument, the movement of which is the immediate cause of hurt to another, is a voluntary act, although its particular effect in hitting and hurting another is not within the purpose or intention of the party doing the act.

It appears to us, that some of the confusion in the cases on this subject has grown out of the long-vexed question, under the rule of the common law, whether a party's remedy, where he has one, should be sought in an action of the case, or of trespass. This is very distinguishable from the question, whether in a given case, any action will lie. The result of these cases is, that if the damage complained of is the immediate effect of the act of the defendant, trespass *vi et armis* lies; if consequential only, and not immediate, case is the proper remedy.

In these discussions, it is frequently stated by judges, that when one receives injury from the direct act of another, trespass will lie. But we think this is said in reference to the question, whether trespass and not case will lie, assuming that the facts are such, that some action will lie. These *dicta* are not authority, we think, for holding, that damage received by a direct act of force from another will be sufficient to maintain an action of trespass, whether the act was lawful or unlawful, and neither wilful, intentional, or careless.

We think, as the result of all the authorities, the rule is that the plaintiff must come prepared with evidence to show either that the *intention* was unlawful, or that the defendant was *in fault*; for if the injury was unavoidable, and the conduct of the defendant was free from blame, he will not be liable. In applying these rules to the present case, we can perceive no reason why the instructions asked for by the defendant ought not to have been given; to this effect, that if both plaintiff and defendant at the time of the blow were using ordinary care, or if at that time the defendant was using ordinary care, and the plaintiff was not, or if at that time, both the plaintiff and defendant were not using ordinary care, then the plaintiff could not recover.

The court instructed the jury, that if it was not a necessary act, and the defendant was not in duty bound to part the dogs, but might with propriety interfere or not as he chose, the defendant was responsible for the consequences of the blow, unless it appeared that he was in the exercise of extraordinary care, so that the accident was inevitable, using the word not in a strict but a popular sense. This is to be taken in connection with the charge afterwards given, that if the jury believed, that the act of interference in the fight was unnecessary, (that is, as before explained, not a duty incumbent on the defendant), then the burden of proving extraordinary care on the part of the defendant, or want of ordinary care on the part of plaintiff, was on the defendant.

The court are of opinion that these directions were not conformable to law. If the act of hitting the plaintiff was unintentional, on the part of the defendant, and done in the doing of a lawful act, then the defendant was not liable, unless it was done in the want of exercise of due care, adapted to the exigency of the case, and therefore such want of due care became part of the plaintiff's case, and the burden of proof was on the plaintiff to establish it.

New Trial ordered.

NOTE

The vast majority of tort law in America today is fault-based. We will begin our study of American tort law by looking at cases in which the defendant's fault is defined as intentional. (These are cases that largely grew from the writs of trespass). Later, we will study cases in which the defendant's fault is defined as negligent. (These are cases that largely grew from the writ of trespass on the case). Still later we will study surviving pockets of strict liability in tort.

Chapter 2

INTENTIONAL TORTS

A. BATTERY

Battery is the intentional tort that protects a person's interest in freedom from unwanted bodily contact. To maintain a battery action, a plaintiff must establish: (1) The defendant *acted*; (2) that the act was done with the *intent* to cause a harmful or offensive contact with another; and (3) that *harmful or offensive contact* actually resulted. *See* RESTATEMENT (SECOND) OF TORTS §§ 13, 18 (1965). We will now look at each of these elements in more detail.

1. Intent

GARRATT v. DAILEY
279 P.2d 1091 (Wash. 1955)

HILL, J.

The liability of an infant for an alleged battery is presented to this court for the first time. Brian Dailey (age five years, nine months) was visiting with Naomi Garratt, an adult and a sister of the plaintiff, Ruth Garratt, likewise an adult, in the backyard of the plaintiff's home, on July 16, 1951. [Plaintiff contends] that she came out into the backyard to talk with Naomi and that, as she started to sit down in a wood and canvas lawn chair, Brian deliberately pulled it out from under her. . . . The trial court, unwilling to accept this testimony, adopted instead Brian Dailey's version of what happened, and made the following findings:

"III. Brian Dailey, picked up a lightly built wood and canvas lawn chair [and] moved it sideways a few feet and seated himself therein, at which time he discovered the plaintiff, Ruth Garratt, about to sit down at the place where the lawn chair had formerly been, at which time he hurriedly got up from the chair and attempted to move it toward Ruth Garratt to aid her in sitting down in the chair; that due to the defendant's small size and lack of dexterity he was unable to get the lawn chair under the plaintiff in time to prevent her from falling to the ground. That plaintiff fell to the ground and sustained a fracture of her hip, and other injuries and damages as hereinafter set forth.

"IV. That the preponderance of the evidence in this case establishes that when the defendant, Brian Dailey, moved the chair in question *he did not have any wilful or unlawful purpose* in doing so; that *he did not have any intent to injure the plaintiff, or any intent to bring about any unauthorized or offensive contact with her person* or any objects appurtenant thereto; that the circumstances which immediately preceded the fall of the plaintiff established that the defendant, *Brian Dailey, did not have purpose, intent or design to perform a prank or to effect an assault and battery upon the person of the plaintiff.*" (Italics [by the court], for a purpose hereinafter indicated.)

It is conceded that Ruth Garratt's fall resulted in a fractured hip and other painful and serious injuries. To obviate the necessity of a retrial in the event this court determines that she was entitled to a judgment against Brian Dailey, the amount of her damages was found to be eleven thousand dollars. Plaintiff appeals from a judgment dismissing the action and asks for the entry of a judgment in that amount or a new trial.

The authorities [generally state] that, when a minor has committed a tort with force, he is liable to be proceeded against as any other person would be. . . . [But] Brian, whether five or fifty-five, must have committed some wrongful act before he could be liable for appellant's injuries.

It is urged that Brian's action in moving the chair constituted a battery. A definition (not all-inclusive but sufficient for our purpose) of a battery is the intentional infliction of a harmful bodily contact upon another. The rule that determines liability for battery is given in 1 Restatement, Torts, 29, § 13, as:

> "An act which, directly or indirectly, is the legal cause of a harmful contact with another's person makes the actor liable to the other, if
>
> "(a) the act is done with the intention of bringing about a harmful or offensive contact or an apprehension thereof to the other or a third person, and
>
> "(b) the contact is not consented to by the other or the other's consent thereto is procured by fraud or duress, and
>
> "(c) the contact is not otherwise privileged."

We have in this case no question of consent or privilege. We therefore proceed to an immediate consideration of intent and its place in the law of battery. In the comment on clause (a), the Restatement says:

> "Character of actor's intention. In order that an act may be done with the intention of bringing about a harmful or offensive contact or an apprehension thereof to a particular person, either the other or a third person, the act must be done for the purpose of causing the contact or apprehension or with knowledge on the part of the actor that such contact or apprehension is substantially certain to be produced."

See also, PROSSER ON TORTS 41, § 8.

We have here the conceded volitional act of Brian, *i.e.*, the moving of a chair. Had the plaintiff proved to the satisfaction of the trial court that Brian moved the chair while she was in the act of sitting down, Brian's action would patently have been for the purpose or with the intent of causing the plaintiff's bodily contact with the ground, and she would be entitled to a judgment against him for the resulting damages.

The plaintiff based her case on that theory, and the trial court held that she failed in her proof and accepted Brian's version of the facts rather than that given by the eyewitness who testified for the plaintiff. After the trial court determined that the plaintiff had not established her theory of a battery (*i.e.*, that Brian had pulled the chair out from under the plaintiff while she was in the act of sitting down), it then became concerned with whether a battery was established under the facts as it found them to be.

In this connection, we quote another portion of the comment on the "Character of actor's intention," relating to clause (a) of the rule from the Restatement heretofore set forth:

> "It is not enough that the act itself is intentionally done and this, even though the actor realizes or should realize that it contains a very grave risk of bringing about the contact or apprehension. Such realization may make the actor's conduct negligent or even reckless but unless he realizes that to a substantial certainty, the contact or apprehension will result, the actor has not that intention which is necessary to make him liable under the rule stated in this Section."

A battery would be established if, in addition to plaintiff's fall, it was proved that, when Brian moved the chair, he knew with substantial certainty that the plaintiff would attempt to sit down where the chair had been. If Brian had any of the intents which the trial court found, in the italicized portions of the findings of fact quoted above, that he did not have, he would of course have had the knowledge to which we have referred. The mere absence of any intent to injure the plaintiff or to play a prank on her or to embarrass her, or to commit an assault and battery on her would not absolve him from liability if in fact he had such knowledge. Without such knowledge, there would be nothing wrongful about Brian's act in moving the chair, and, there being no wrongful act, there would be no liability.

While a finding that Brian had no such knowledge can be inferred from the findings made, we believe that before the plaintiff's action in such a case should be dismissed there should be no question but that the trial court had passed upon that issue; hence, the case should be remanded for clarification of the findings to specifically cover the question of Brian's knowledge, because intent could be inferred therefrom. If the court finds that he had such knowledge, the necessary intent will be established and the plaintiff will be entitled to recover, even though there was no purpose to injure or embarrass the plaintiff. If Brian did not have such knowledge, there was no wrongful act by him, and the basic premise of liability on the theory of a battery was not established.

The cause is remanded for clarification, with instructions to make definite findings on the issue of whether Brian Dailey knew with substantial certainty that the plaintiff would attempt to sit down where the chair which he moved had been, and to change the judgment if the findings warrant it.

Remanded for clarification.

NOTES

1. On remand, the trial judge re-evaluated the facts of the case in light of the Washington Supreme Court's opinion and entered judgment in favor of the plaintiff. The Washington Supreme Court later affirmed the trial court's ruling. 304 P.2d 681 (Wash. 1956).

2. The Restatement of Torts, quoted in *Garratt*, is published by the American Law Institute ("ALI"). The ALI is an organization composed of prominent lawyers, judges, and legal academics. The Restatement does not itself have precedential value. Judges, however, frequently find the Restatement influential and cite to its provisions. Not long after the Washington Supreme Court decided *Garratt*, the ALI promulgated the Restatement (Second) of Torts, which defined intent as denoting that "the actor desires to cause the consequence of his act, or that he believes that the consequences are substantially certain to result from it." RESTATEMENT (SECOND) OF TORTS § 8A (1965). Most commentators find this provision consistent with the rule in *Garratt* by defining intent as encompassing both purpose (or desire) *and* knowledge to a degree of substantial certainty.

3. The ALI is in the process of revising the Restatement of Torts. A tentative draft of the Restatement (Third) of Torts: General Principles defines intent as follows:

A person acts with the intent to produce a consequence if:

(a) The person has the purpose of producing that consequence; or

(b) The person knows to a substantial certainty that the consequence will ensue from the person's conduct.

RESTATEMENT (THIRD) OF TORTS: LIABILITY FOR PHYSICAL HARM (BASIC PRINCIPLES) § 1 (2001). Does the proposed section significantly alter the rule in the Second Restatement?

4. Mental incapacity does not protect a defendant from intentional tort liability. Therefore, courts *do* hold children and those with mental disabilities liable for intentional torts. That being said, one should understand that a plaintiff still must establish that a defendant formed the requisite intent to succeed in an action. For example, a nine-month-old baby will not be liable for battery when she crawls into her uncle's ankle and causes him to fall. The rationale, however, will not relate simply to the child's age. Instead, it will relate to the baby's inability to form a conscious purpose (or knowledge to a substantial certainty) that she was going to cause the contact.

PROBLEMS

1. Does intent for purposes of battery require that the defendant intend to actually harm or offend the plaintiff? Is intent to touch, combined with resulting but unintended harm or offense, sufficient? Consider the following:

  a. Richard is at a crowded cocktail party in an unfamiliar home. He taps Jane on the shoulder so that he can gain her attention and ask the location of the bathroom. Jane takes offense at Richard's tap and sues him for battery. Can Jane prove intent?

  b. At the same cocktail party, Richard encounters Paul, a business acquaintance. Richard gives Paul a hearty slap on the shoulder as a greeting. Unfortunately, Paul was recovering from surgery, and the slap caused him a great deal of pain. Paul sues Richard for battery. Can Paul prove intent?

2. What if the defendant does not act volitionally? Consider the following:

  a. Richard is carefully walking on the sidewalk when he slips on a patch of ice. Richard falls and bumps into Peter, another pedestrian on the street, who also falls and breaks his arm. Peter sues Richard for battery. Can Peter prove intent?

  b. Assume similar facts as above, but suppose that Richard was extremely drunk and walking quickly on the icy sidewalk when he slipped. Does Richard's impaired condition impact Peter's ability to prove intent?

SHAW v. BROWN & WILLIAMSON TOBACCO CORP.
973 F. Supp. 539 (D. Md. 1997)

BLACK, JR., SENIOR DISTRICT JUDGE.

Robert T. Shaw was employed as a long distance truck driver with the Kelly-Springfield Tire Company from 1968 to 1991. From May 1, 1973 to November 14, 1984, Shaw routinely traveled in an enclosed truck with a co-worker who smoked Raleigh cigarettes, which are manufactured, produced, and distributed by Brown & Williamson. Shaw did not smoke cigarettes at any time during his employment with Kelly-Springfield. Nevertheless, Shaw was diagnosed with lung cancer in 1992. Shaw and his wife allege that he developed lung cancer as a result of his exposure to second-hand or environmental tobacco smoke (hereinafter "ETS") emitted from the Raleigh cigarettes. [Shaw brought claims against Brown & Williamson under several theories, including battery. Brown & Williamson moved to dismiss.]

Defendant challenges plaintiffs' ability to establish that Brown & Williamson had the intent necessary to commit a battery. Under Maryland law, "[a] battery is the 'unpermitted application of trauma by one person upon the body of another person.'" *Janelsins v. Button*, 102 Md. App. 30, 35, 648 A.2d 1039 (1994) (quoting *McQuiggan v. Boy Scouts of America*, 73 Md. App. 705, 714, 536 A.2d 137 (1988)).

"[T]he tort of battery requires intent by the actor 'to bring about a harmful or offensive contact. . . . [It is] confined to intentional invasions of the interests in freedom from harmful or offensive contact.'" *Janelsins*, 102 Md. App. at 35, 648 A.2d 1039 (quoting FOWLER V. HARPER, 1 THE LAW OF TORTS § 3.3, at 272-73, 276 (2d ed.1986)). Accidental contact does not constitute a battery because "[w]here an accident occurs, the actor would not have intended to invade the other's interest." *Janelsins*, 102 Md. App. at 35 n.5, 648 A.2d 1039. A defendant in a battery action need not have intended to do harm, however, as the crux of a battery claim is an absence of consent on the part of the plaintiff. *Ghassemieh v. Schafer*, 52 Md. App. 31, 38, 447 A.2d 84 (1982). Nevertheless, he must have done some affirmative act and must have known that an unpermitted contact was substantially certain to follow from that act. Indeed, it is this intent that separates battery from mere negligence:

> In negligence, the actor does not desire to bring about the consequences that follow, nor does he know that they are substantially certain to occur, or believe that they will. There is merely a risk of such consequences, sufficiently great to lead a reasonable man in his position to anticipate them, and to guard against them. If an automobile driver runs down a man in the street before him, with the desire to hit him, or with the belief that he is certain to do so, it is an intentional battery; but if he has no such desire or belief, but merely acts unreasonably in failing to guard against a risk which he should appreciate, it is negligence.

Id. at 41, 447 A.2d 84 (quoting PROSSER, LAW OF TORTS § 31, at 145 (4th ed.1971)).

Plaintiffs argue that the intent requirement is satisfied by Brown & Williamson's intentional manufacture, marketing, and distribution of Raleigh cigarettes, on the basis that such acts "set[ ] in motion the inevitable series of events leading to plaintiff Robert Shaw's injuries." The Court disagrees.

In *Pechan v. DynaPro, Inc.*, 251 Ill. App. 3d 1072, 190 Ill. Dec. 698, 622 N.E.2d 108 (1993), a plaintiff alleged that her former employer was liable for her exposure to second-hand cigarette smoke in the workplace. The appellate court affirmed the dismissal of plaintiff's battery count, finding that the employer could not, as a matter of law, have had the intent necessary to commit a battery. The *Pechan* court reasoned that "[s]moking is a legal activity and not an act of battery because, generally, smokers do not smoke cigarettes with the intent to touch nonsmokers with secondhand smoke." Similarly, Brown & Williamson does not manufacture, market, or distribute cigarettes for the purpose of touching non-smokers with second-hand smoke. Furthermore, Brown & Williamson did not know with a substantial degree of certainty that second-hand smoke would touch any particular non-smoker. While it may have had knowledge that second-hand smoke would reach some non-smokers, the Court finds that such generalized knowledge is insufficient to satisfy the intent requirement for battery. Indeed, as defendant points out, a finding that Brown & Williamson has committed a battery by manufacturing cigarettes would be tantamount to holding manufacturers of handguns liable in battery for exposing third parties to gunfire. Such a finding would expose the courts to a flood of farfetched and nebulous litigation concerning the tort of battery. It is unsurprising that neither plaintiffs nor the Court have been able to unearth any case where a manufacturer of cigarettes or handguns was found to have committed a battery against those allegedly injured by its products.

Accordingly, dismissal is appropriate with respect to [Shaw's battery claim].

NOTES

1. If Brown & Williamson was substantially certain that second-hand smoke from its product would cause a harmful or offensive contact with someone, why not allow an actual victim to maintain a claim? The court explains its conclusion, in part, by stating that "[s]uch a finding would expose the courts to a flood of farfetched and nebulous litigation concerning the tort of battery." Defendants frequently raise fear of a "flood of litigation" as an argument against expanding tort liability theories. Is such a fear a justifiable reason to deny liability where a defendant has actually caused a plaintiff harm? Consider this statement from the California Supreme Court: "To the extent that [defendants contend] claims should be denied because otherwise courts would experience a 'flood of litigation,' we point out that courts are responsible for dealing with cases on their merits, whether there be few suits or many; the existence of a multitude of claims merely shows society's pressing need for legal redress" *Dillon v. Legg*, 441 P.2d 912, 917 (Cal. 1968). Do you agree? Could this principle reasonably be followed in a case like *Shaw*?

2. The *Shaw* court also explained its decision by stating that "[w]hile [Brown & Williamson] may have had knowledge that second-hand smoke would reach some non-smokers, the Court finds that such generalized knowledge is insufficient to satisfy the intent requirement for battery." Be careful not to read this statement too broadly. In fact, it is *not* necessary for a plaintiff to prove that a defendant intended to cause contact specifically with her in order to prove a prima facie battery case. The principle that allows a plaintiff to prove intent when a defendant's action is directed at another is called *transferred intent*. For example, in *Davis v. White*, 18 B.R. 246 (Bankr. E.D. Va. 1982), White was arguing with Tipton, who attempted to flee on a motorcycle. White pulled a gun and shot at Tipton. White's shot, however, missed Tipton and hit Davis instead. The court concluded that White's action constituted a battery against Davis. "White's action cannot be excused solely because he missed his intended victim and instead hit someone else. The injury is not required to be directed against the victim, but includes any entity or other than the intended victim." 18 B.R. at 249. Intent, therefore, can "transfer" from intended victim to actual victim.

Transferred intent is addressed in more detail in *Holloway v. Wachovia Bank & Trust Co.* 428 S.E.2d 453 (N.C. Ct. App. 1993), which is the primary case in our section on assault.

PROBLEMS

1. Pete and Joe were arguing, standing face to face. Joe takes a deep drag on the cigarette he was smoking and blows a stream of smoke into Pete's face. Is this a battery? Would Joe need to have some specific reason to believe it was harmful or offensive, such as knowing that Pete had asthma, or was trying to quit smoking?

2. Consider the facts of *Scott v. Shepherd*, 2 Wm. Bl. 892, 96 Eng. Rep. 525, 525-26 (1773):

> On the evening of the fair-day at Milborne Port, 28th October, 1770, the defendant threw a lighted squib [firecracker], made of gun-powder from the street into the market-house, which is a covered building supported by arches, and enclosed at one end, but open at the other and both the sides, where a large concourse of people were assembled; which lighted squib, so thrown by the defendant, fell upon the standing of one Yates, who sold gingerbread. That one Willis instantly, and to prevent injury to himself and the said wares of one Yates, took up the said lighted squib from off the said standing, and then threw it across the said market-house, when it fell upon another standing, and then threw it to another part of the said market-house, and in so throwing it, struck the plaintiff then in the said market-house in the face therewith, and the combustible matter then bursting, put out one of the plaintiff's eyes.

Would the concept of transferred intent allow the plaintiff to prove intent in an action against the defendant? Why or why not?

2. Contact and Offensiveness

FISHER v. CARROUSEL MOTOR HOTEL, INC.
424 S.W.2d 627 (Tex. 1967)

GREENHILL, J.

This is a suit for actual and exemplary damages growing out of an alleged assault and battery. The plaintiff Fisher was a mathematician with the Data Processing Division of the Manned Spacecraft Center, an agency of the National Aeronautics and Space Agency, commonly called NASA, near Houston. The defendants were the Carrousel Motor Hotel, Inc., located in Houston, the Brass Ring Club, which is located in the Carrousel, and Robert W. Flynn, who as an employee of the Carrousel was the manager of the Brass Ring Club. Flynn died before the trial, and the suit proceeded as to the Carrousel and the Brass Ring. Trial was to a jury which found for the plaintiff Fisher. The trial court rendered judgment for the defendants notwithstanding the verdict. The Court of Civil Appeals affirmed. The questions before this Court are whether there was evidence that an actionable battery was committed, and, if so, whether the two corporate defendants must respond in exemplary as well as actual damages for the malicious conduct of Flynn.

The plaintiff Fisher had been invited by Ampex Corporation and Defense Electronics to a one day's meeting regarding telemetry equipment at the Carrousel. The invitation included a luncheon. The guests were asked to reply by telephone whether they could attend the luncheon, and Fisher called in his acceptance. After the morning session, the group of 25 or 30 guests adjourned to the Brass Ring Club for lunch. The luncheon was buffet style, and Fisher stood in line with [other guests]. As Fisher was about to be served, he was approached by Flynn, who snatched the plate from Fisher's hand and shouted that he, a Negro, could not be served in the club. Fisher testified that he was not actually touched, and did not testify that he suffered fear or apprehension of physical injury; but he did testify that he was highly embarrassed and hurt by Flynn's conduct in the presence of his associates.

The jury found that Flynn "forcibly dispossessed plaintiff of his dinner plate" and "shouted in a loud and offensive manner" that Fisher could not be served there, thus subjecting Fisher to humiliation and indignity. It was stipulated that Flynn was an employee of the Carrousel Hotel and, as such, managed the Brass Ring Club. The jury also found that Flynn acted maliciously and awarded Fisher $400 actual damages for his humiliation and indignity and $500 exemplary damages for Flynn's malicious conduct. [The trial judge granted judgment notwithstanding the verdict because Flynn did not make physical contact with Fisher, nor did Fisher apprehend physical contact. The Court of Civil Appeals affirmed.]

[I]t has long been settled that actual physical contact is not necessary to constitute a battery, so long as there is contact with clothing or an object closely identified with the body. 1 HARPER & JAMES, THE LAW OF TORTS 216 (1956); RESTATEMENT OF TORTS 2D, §§ 18 AND 19. In PROSSER, LAW OF TORTS 32 (3d Ed. 1964), it is said:

> The interest in freedom from intentional and unpermitted contacts with the plaintiff's person is protected by an action for the tort commonly called battery. The protection extends to any part of the body, or to anything which is attached to it and practically identified with it. Thus contact with the plaintiff's clothing, or with a cane, a paper, or any other object held in his hand will be sufficient;... The plaintiff's interest in the integrity of his person includes all those things which are in contact or connected with it.

Under the facts of this case, we have no difficulty in holding that the intentional grabbing of plaintiff's plate constituted a battery. The intentional snatching of an object from one's hand is as clearly an offensive invasion of his person as would be an actual contact with the body. "To constitute [a battery], it is not necessary to touch the plaintiff's body or even his clothing; knocking or snatching anything from plaintiff's hand or touching anything connected with his person, when done in an offensive manner, is sufficient."

The rationale for holding an offensive contact with such an object to be a battery is explained in 1 Restatement of Torts 2d § 18 (Comment p. 31) as follows:

> Since the essence of the plaintiff's grievance consists in the offense to the dignity involved in the unpermitted and intentional invasion of the inviolability of his person and not in any physical harm done to his body, it is not necessary that the plaintiff's actual body be disturbed. Unpermitted and intentional contacts with anything so connected with the body as to be customarily regarded as part of the other's person and therefore as partaking of its inviolability is actionable as an offensive contact with his person. There are some things such as clothing or a cane or, indeed, anything directly grasped by the hand which are so intimately connected with one's body as to be universally regarded as part of the person.

We hold, therefore, that the forceful dispossession of plaintiff Fisher's plate in an offensive manner was sufficient to constitute a battery, and the trial court erred in granting judgment notwithstanding the verdict on the issue of actual damages.

[The court then addressed the issue of whether the plaintiff could recover actual damages for mental suffering in the absence of physical injury.]

In *Harned v. E-Z Finance Co.*, 151 Tex. 641, 254 S.W.2d 81 (1953), this Court recognized the well established rule that mental suffering is compensable in suits for willful torts "which are recognized as torts and actionable independently and separately from mental suffering or other injury." Damages for mental suffering are recoverable without the necessity for showing actual physical injury in a case of willful battery because the basis of that action is the unpermitted and intentional invasion of the plaintiff's person and not the actual harm done to the plaintiff's body. RESTATEMENT OF TORTS 2D § 18. Personal indignity is the essence of an action for battery; and consequently the defendant is liable not only for contacts which do actual physical harm, but also for those which are offensive and insulting. We hold, therefore, that plaintiff was entitled to actual damages for mental suffering due to the willful battery, even in the absence of any physical injury.

The judgments of the courts below are reversed, and judgment is here rendered for the plaintiff for $900 with interest from the date of the trial court's judgment, and for costs of this suit.

NOTES

1. Note that in *Fisher*, the court found Carrousel Motor Hotel liable based on the conduct of its employee, Flynn, while he was on the job. This is an example of what the law calls "vicarious liability" — a theory under which one party can be found liable for the conduct of another based on the strength of their relationship. We address vicarious liability in detail in Chapter 13.

2. A primary purpose of tort law is to compensate those who have been harmed by the tortious conduct of others. Occasionally, however, the tort system permits juries to award "exemplary" or "punitive" damages, as the jury did in *Fisher*. Punitive damages are not designed to compensate plaintiffs, but rather to punish the defendant and deter others from engaging in similar conduct. To obtain punitive damages, a plaintiff must show that the defendant behaved in a particularly egregious fashion. Often, courts describe the standard with words like "willful," "wanton," or "malicious." The size of punitive damage awards, particularly in lawsuits against large corporations, has generated a great degree of controversy in recent years. The controversy has prompted some states to limit the size of punitive damage awards by statute. *See, e.g.,* IND. CODE § 34-51-3-4 (1994). In addition, some defendants have raised constitutional challenges to punitive damage awards (arguing that the size of punitive damage awards alone might violate the Due Process Clause of the Fourteenth Amendment to the United States Constitution). *See, e.g., BMW of America, Inc. v. Gore*, 116 S. Ct. 1589 (1996).

PROBLEMS

1. The *Fisher* court states that the contact element of a battery action is satisfied "so long as there is contact with clothing or an object closely identified with the body." Does this mean that the contact must be with something *physically* connected to the plaintiff's body? Consider the following:

   a. Suppose that Fisher had placed his plate on a table near the buffet line and Flynn knocked it away just as Fisher's hand left the plate. Is there a "contact"?

   b. What if Flynn touched something other than Fisher's plate — perhaps an item of jewelry that Fisher normally wore, but had momentarily set down. Would contact with such an item (say, Fisher's favorite watch or an heirloom pendant that Fisher wore every day) be contact with something "closely identified with the body," even if it were not at that moment physically connected to Fisher's body?

   c. Would your answer change as Fisher moved further away from the item of jewelry? Suppose that Fisher walked back to his table after setting his heirloom pendant on the ledge of the buffet. Suppose further that Flynn smashed the pendant while Fisher was watching from ten feet away. Do we still have contact with something "closely identified" with Fisher's body?

    d. Would your answer change if Fisher did not observe the contact? Suppose that Fisher was outside in the parking lot at the time. Can you argue that we still have contact with something "closely identified" with Fisher's body?

    e. Suppose Flynn kicked the leg of a chair on which Fisher was sitting? Or suppose Flynn kicked the tire of a golf cart in which Fisher was sitting?

2. *Fisher* also demonstrates that a plaintiff can maintain a battery action where the contact is "offensive," even if it is not harmful. *See* RESTATEMENT (SECOND) OF TORTS § 19 (1965) ("A bodily contact is offensive if it offends a reasonable sense of personal dignity.") Clearly, the contact in *Fisher* would offend a "reasonable sense of personal dignity" from any perspective. But what if the facts changed?

    a. Suppose that James has a phobia about having his elbow touched. Any elbow contact causes him to suffer from extreme emotional trauma. One day James is riding on the subway when Alexis enters his car and touches his elbow in order to get past him. Because of the touching, James becomes highly distraught. Is the contact "offensive" for purposes of battery?

    b. Would your answer change if Alexis *knew* about the phobia and brushed against the elbow for the sole purpose of bothering James?

B. ASSAULT

The previous section covered situations where a defendant's action caused a harmful or offensive contact with the plaintiff. Tort law also protects plaintiffs from the *apprehension* of such contact, even if contact never occurs. This protection is accomplished through the tort of assault. Like battery, assault developed from the writ of trespass and has a long history in the common law system. For example, some commentators cite *I. de S. & Wife v. W. de S.*, Y.B. Lib. Ass. f. 99, pl. 60 (1348), as a very early example of an assault case. In *I. de S.*, the defendant arrived at the plaintiff's tavern, looking for wine. Upset that the tavern was closed, the defendant beat on the door with a hatchet. The plaintiff's wife put her head out the window and told the defendant to stop hitting the door. The defendant then swung his hatchet again, although he did not strike the wife. Despite the lack of contact, the court ruled that he had committed a trespass by making an "assault upon the woman." A more modern example follows.

HOLLOWAY v. WACHOVIA BANK & TRUST CO.
428 S.E.2d 453 (N.C. Ct. App. 1993)

EAGLES, JUDGE.

In April 1985, plaintiff Hallie Holloway purchased a car financed by defendant Wachovia Bank & Trust Co., N.A. (hereinafter "Wachovia"). She defaulted on the loan. On 21 May 1986, defendant Jean Dawson, an employee of defendant Wachovia, attempted to repossess the car in the parking lot outside of a Durham laundromat. At the laundromat with Hallie Holloway were: 1) Sue Holloway, who is Hallie Holloway's mother; 2) Swanzett Holloway, who is Hallie Holloway's 10-year-old niece, and 3) Damien Holloway, who is Hallie Holloway's 4-month-old son. Plaintiffs left the scene driving the car defendant Dawson sought to repossess.

In their 27 April 1988 complaint, plaintiffs alleged that defendant Dawson aimed a gun at them in her attempt to repossess the car. Each plaintiff sought recovery for assault. Additionally, plaintiffs Hallie Holloway and Damien Holloway sought recovery for battery arising from defendant Dawson's touching them while "reach[ing] through the window of the car" to take the car keys from the ignition.

[The trial judge dismissed the claims of Hallie Holloway and Sue Holloway based on a previous determination that these claims were barred by the statute of limitations.]

At trial, directed verdicts in favor of defendants were entered on Damien Holloway's battery claim and both Swanzett Holloway's and Damien Holloway's assault claims. Plaintiffs appeal.

[P]laintiffs argue that the trial court erred by granting defendants' motions for directed verdict. As to Damien Holloway's assault claim, we affirm. As to Damien Holloway's battery claim and Swanzett Holloway's assault claim, we reverse and remand for a new trial on these two claims only.

Regarding the tort of assault, this Court has stated:

> The interest protected by the action for assault is freedom from apprehension of a harmful or offensive contact with one's person. In *Dickens v. Puryear*, 302 N.C. 437, 445, 276 S.E.2d 325, 330 (1981), our Supreme Court stated assault requires the plaintiff's reasonable apprehension of an immediate harmful or offensive contact. The *Dickens* Court further quoted the Comment to Section 29(1) of Restatement (Second) of Torts (1965): "[T]he apprehension created must be one of imminent contact, as distinguished from any contact in the future. Imminent does not mean immediate, in the sense of instantaneous contact . . . it means rather that there will be no significant delay."

At trial, plaintiff Hallie Holloway answered "yes" to the question "throughout this he [Damien Holloway] was either asleep or too young to understand what was going on throughout this confrontation; isn't that correct?" Plaintiffs have failed to show that the infant Damien experienced any apprehension of harmful or offensive contact. Accordingly, we find no merit in plaintiffs' argument.

However, there was sufficient evidence to permit a jury to consider the infant Damien Holloway's battery claim. "The elements of battery are intent, harmful or offensive contact, causation, and lack of privilege." As with assault, a showing of actual damage is not an essential element of battery.

Hallie Holloway testified that while she was sitting in the driver's seat of the automobile, she had the infant Damien "up on my chest." She further testified that as defendant Dawson reached to take the keys from the ignition on the right hand side of the steering wheel, defendant Dawson "had her elbow in my baby's back. She was trying to pull my hands off the key."

Defendants argue that the trial court "allowed a directed verdict on Damien Holloway's battery claim because there was clearly no intent to touch Damien. Rather his touching was inadvertent, incidental, and unintentional." However, "[t]he gist of the action for battery is not the hostile intent of the defendant, but rather the absence of consent to the contact on the part of the plaintiff." *See N.C. Farm Bureau Mut. Ins. Co. v. Stox*, 330 N.C. 697, 707, 412 S.E.2d 318, 324 (1992) (" '[t]he intent with which tort liability is concerned is not necessarily a hostile intent, or a desire to do any harm. Rather it is an intent to bring about a result which will invade the interests of another in a way that the law forbids.' " PROSSER, [LAW OF TORTS] § 8, p. 36 [(5th ed. 1984) (hereinafter "Prosser")]. Based upon the record before us, the issue of whether the infant Damien was entitled to recover upon a claim of battery should have been submitted to the jury.

Next, we address Swanzett Holloway's assault claim. "An assault is an offer to show violence to another without striking him." *Dickens*, 302 N.C. at 444, 276 S.E.2d at 330. "The elements of assault are intent, offer of injury, reasonable apprehension, apparent ability, and imminent threat of injury." Plaintiff establishes a cause of action for assault upon proof of these technical elements without proof of actual damage.

At the time that Jean Dawson had the gun in her hand, Swanzett Holloway was sitting in the back seat of the automobile. At trial, Swanzett Holloway gave the following testimony:

Q [Plaintiffs' counsel]: Did you see the gun?

A [Swanzett Holloway]: Yes.

Q: And how did you see the gun?

A: It was in her [defendant Dawson's] hand.

Q: All right. And where did she have — where was she when you saw her with the gun?

A: She was outside the car on the driver's side.

Q: On the driver's side. Where did she have it pointed?

A: Toward Hallie [Holloway] and her baby [Damien Holloway]. . . .

Q: Now, but for Hallie would the gun have been pointed at you the way you described it on here?

A: Yes. . . .

Q: Could you see the barrel of the gun?

A: Yes, I saw the gun, black and brown.

Q: . . . What did you think or what did you feel when you saw the gun?

A: I was scared.

Q: What were you afraid of?

A: She could have shot either one of us.

Q: . . . Were you afraid of being shot?

A: Yes.

Since Swanzett Holloway testified that the gun was not pointed directly at her, she relies on the concept of transferred intent to recover on this assault claim. The Restatement (Second) of Torts explains the concept of transferred intent as follows: "If an act is done with the intention of affecting a third person . . . but puts another in apprehension of a harmful or offensive contact, the actor is subject to liability to such other as fully as though he intended so to affect him." *Id.* § 32(2).

Our research indicates that the concept of transferred intent has not been applied in a civil case in North Carolina. However, at least four criminal cases have tacitly recognized transferred intent principles. *See generally* DAYE AND MORRIS, § 2.31.2, pp. 8-9 (stating three reasons why transferred intent should be applied in tort actions: "First, in the intentional torts area, North Carolina law tends to be consistent with the general rules of American jurisprudence. Second, North Carolina courts have applied transferred intent concepts in criminal cases. Third, the use of the concept of transferred intent in civil cases was originally adapted from the criminal law. As has been shown, courts have applied criminal concepts of intent to analyze civil liability.").

"North Carolina follows common law principles governing assault and battery. . . . Common law principles of assault and battery as enunciated in North Carolina law are also found in the Restatement (Second) of Torts (1965)." *Dickens*, 302 N.C. at 444-45, 276 S.E.2d at 330-31. Prosser notes that the concept of transferred intent existed at common law, first appearing

> in criminal cases at a time when tort and crime were still merged in the old trespass form of action. It represents an established rule of the criminal law, in cases in which shooting, striking, throwing a missile or

poisoning has resulted in unexpected injury to the wrong person. The criminal cases have been understandably preoccupied with moral guilt, and the obvious fact that if the defendant is not convicted there is no one to hold liable for the crime. *But the same rule was applied to tort cases arising in trespass* [which "was the progenitor not only of battery, but also of assault and false imprisonment"]. . . . It is quite probable, however, that the persistence of the principle has been due to a definite feeling that the defendant is at fault, and should make good the damage. The defendant's act is characterized as "wrongful," and the fault is regarded as absolute toward all the world, rather than relative to any one person. Having departed from the social standard of conduct, the defendant is liable for the harm which follows from the act, although this harm was not intended.

PROSSER, § 8, pp. 37-38 (emphasis added). Since the concept of transferred intent was recognized at common law, we hold that on the facts presented in this case, the issue of whether Swanzett Holloway was entitled to recover for a claim of assault should have been submitted to the jury.

Affirmed in part; reversed in part and remanded.

NOTE

During trial, the plaintiffs' lawyer elicited answers from Swanzett Holloway making it clear that her apprehension of being shot was both reasonable and immediate. "I saw the gun, black and brown," Swanzett said, and " I was scared." It is important that a plaintiff apprehend imminent contact if the plaintiff wants to maintain an assault action. Indeed, some courts are quite particular about this requirement. Consider, for example, *Vietnamese Fishermen's Ass'n v. Knights of K.K.K.*, 518 F. Supp. 993 (S.D. Tex. 1981), in which a group of Ku Klux Klan members attempted to intimidate local fishermen of Vietnamese descent. During a boat trip on Galveston Bay, more than a mile from the fishermen's docks, the Klan members hung a figure in effigy, and fired a cannon. Despite the fishermen's understandable fear, the court found that they could not maintain an assault action. "[T]he defendant's act must amount to an offer to use force, and there must be an apparent ability and opportunity to carry out the threat immediately. There is no assault where the defendant is too far away to do any harm." For similar reasons, courts generally find that words *alone* do not constitute assault. *See* RESTATEMENT (SECOND) OF TORTS § 31 (1965) ("Words do not make the actor liable for assault unless together with other acts or circumstances they put the other in reasonable apprehension of an imminent harmful or offensive contact with his person.").

PROBLEMS

1. It has been suggested that "every battery includes an assault." *See, e.g., Martin v. Yeoham*, 419 S.W.2d 937, 946 (Mo. Ct. App. 1967); *Narell v. Sasso*, 72 A.2d 432, 433 (R.I. 1950). Is this correct? Suppose that John sneaks up on Ed from behind and hits Ed on the back of the head. Surely Ed can maintain a battery action against John. Does the battery action also include an assault?

2. Defendant, in the grand Hollywood Western tradition, pats his holstered gun and tells Plaintiff, "You have until sunset to get out of town." Assault? Does it matter what time it is?

3. The *Holloway* court permits Swanzett to prove intent, even though Dawson's purpose in pointing the gun was to frighten Hallie. This use of "transferred intent" is consistent with the discussion in the notes after *Brown & Williamson* because it allows intent to transfer from intended victim to actual victim. But the *Holloway* court makes it clear that transferred intent can apply between torts, as well as between victims. Do you understand how this might work? Consider the following:

    a. Andy throws a rock with a purpose to hit Jason. Andy's throw, however, misses Jason by an inch. If Jason sues Andy for assault, can he prove intent?

    b. Andy throws a rock with a purpose to frighten Jason. Unfortunately, Andy's aim is poor and he hits Jason instead. If Jason sues Andy for battery, can he prove intent?

4. The *Holloway* court quotes Prosser in suggesting that the doctrine of transferred intent applies between all torts that grew from the old writ of trespass. This makes sense among the torts that are designed to protect one's physical dignity (battery, assault, and false imprisonment). But should transferred intent apply to prove one of these torts if the defendant had the intent only to invade one's property interests? Suppose that Carl is training to compete as a high jumper in the Olympics. He has decided that the most convenient way to practice his jumps is by leaping over a six-foot fence that separates his yard from his neighbor's yard. Carl does not have permission to do this, and he knows that his neighbor would probably disapprove. But Carl plans to practice during the day, while his neighbor is at work, and he assumes that his neighbor will never know. One day, Carl saw his neighbor leave for work. Carl went to his back yard, stretched out, and leapt over the fence. A perfect jump. Except for the fact that his neighbor's fiancé decided to spend the day sunbathing in the neighbor's back yard. Carl landed right on top of her. The fiancé sues Carl for battery. Can she prove intent?

C. FALSE IMPRISONMENT

False imprisonment is the third intentional tort that grew from the old writ of trespass to protect an individual's physical integrity. False imprisonment differs from battery and assault in that it does not protect against contact or apprehension of contact. Rather, it protects an individual's right to move freely from place to place as she sees fit. *See* EPSTEIN, TORTS § 1.9 at 19. The Restatement (Second) of Torts defines false imprisonment as follows:

> (1) An actor is subject to liability to another for false imprisonment if
>
>> (a) he acts intending to confine the other or a third person within boundaries fixed by the actor, and
>>
>> (b) his act directly or indirectly results in such a confinement of the other, and
>>
>> (c) the other is conscious of the confinement or is harmed by it.

RESTATEMENT (SECOND) OF TORTS § 35 (1965). As a practical matter, most false imprisonment cases turn on the issue of whether the plaintiff was truly "confined" to a bounded area. Consider the following case in deciding what factors courts use in resolving that issue.

TEICHMILLER v. ROGERS MEMORIAL HOSPITAL, INC.
597 N.W.2d 773 (Wis. Ct. App. 1999) (Unpublished Decision)

PER CURIAM.

Elaine Teichmiller appeals from a summary judgment dismissing her claims for wrongful discharge and false imprisonment. Because we conclude that summary judgment was appropriate, we affirm.

Beginning in September 1994, Teichmiller, a registered nurse, was an at-will employee of Rogers Memorial Hospital at its main facility. In the spring of 1995, Teichmiller began working as a nurse at the hospital's Racine clinic. Her immediate supervisor was Christine Hansburg-Hotson. Hansburg-Hotson reported to Debbie Bergerson-Hawkins, the Director of Clinical Services. Bergerson-Hawkins reported to Sue Otto, Vice President of Patient Care Services.

One of Teichmiller's responsibilities at the clinic was to perform patient intake and multidisciplinary assessments. Another of her responsibilities was to complete medical records or charts. In her amended complaint, Teichmiller alleged that she was directed to falsify medical records and that her refusal to do so resulted in her forced resignation. In effect, Teichmiller claimed that she was wrongfully discharged because she was forced to leave her employment after declining to falsify medical records. [Defendants Rogers, Bergerson-Hawkins, and Otto moved for summary judgment on Teichmiller's wrongful discharge claim. The trial court granted the motions, and the court of appeals affirmed. The court then discussed Teichmiller's false imprisonment claim.]

The [false imprisonment] claim arises from a confrontation between Teichmiller and her superiors at the September 12, 1995 meeting to discuss her impending departure. In her deposition, Teichmiller testified that she was asked to meet at the clinic with Hansburg-Hotson, Bergerson-Hawkins and Otto. The purpose of the meeting was to discuss Teichmiller's exit requirements, specifically the need to complete medical records before she departed. Teichmiller sat in the chair nearest the door, which remained open during the meeting. She was handed the exit requirements and was told that she would be assisted in completing her charts. Teichmiller refused to sign the form and stated that she had consulted an attorney. Bergerson-Hawkins and Otto became very excited and started shouting about Teichmiller's contact with an attorney.

When Teichmiller stated that she wanted to make a copy of the document, Otto and Bergerson-Hawkins left their chairs. Bergerson-Hawkins came to Teichmiller's right side and blocked the doorway. Otto came to Teichmiller's left side. Bergerson-Hawkins and Otto screamed at Teichmiller that she was stealing hospital property because she was going to take the exit requirements form to the copier in the conference room. Otto and Bergerson-Hawkins continued to stand on either side of Teichmiller and attempted to grab the form from Teichmiller's hands. Teichmiller felt caged and could not move left or right because Bergerson-Hawkins and Otto were on either side, her chair was behind her, and the office desk was in front of her. Bergerson-Hawkins and Otto held their hands approximately one-inch above Teichmiller's arms while they were trying to grab the form. Teichmiller felt that Bergerson-Hawkins and Otto were being aggressive and were dangerous.

Bergerson-Hawkins blocked Teichmiller's movement to the right toward the open door. Teichmiller was afraid that if she moved, they would think she was being aggressive. The standoff took three to four minutes and then on Teichmiller's third attempt to move to the right, Bergerson-Hawkins stepped aside and Teichmiller left for the copier. Bergerson-Hawkins and Otto "chased" Teichmiller to the copy room where they stood on either side of her as she unsuccessfully tried to use the copier, followed her to her office, and "guarded" her from outside of the women's restroom where she fled after her first attempt to use the copier. Teichmiller later permitted Otto to speak privately with her in Teichmiller's office after Teichmiller had photocopied the exit requirements form. Teichmiller testified that she did not feel free to move when Bergerson-Hawkins and Otto were standing next to her in the office and at the copier. Teichmiller concedes that she was not touched or threatened with physical contact, although she felt threatened physically and verbally because Otto and Bergerson-Hawkins were in proximity to her and were excited.

Although Teichmiller stated that Bergerson-Hawkins and Otto refused to let her leave, she testified that she never actually asked to leave the office.

Rather, she repeatedly stated that she needed to make a copy of the document and because the copier was not located in the office, she believes she made it clear that she had to leave the room.

Bergerson-Hawkins and Otto do not dispute most of Teichmiller's description of the confrontation in the office and at the copier. Nevertheless, they argue that Teichmiller's allegations do not rise to the level of false imprisonment.

[The record] does not support Teichmiller's claim that she was intentionally and unlawfully restrained. Teichmiller did not ask to leave her supervisor's office; at best, she obliquely requested to leave when she demanded access to the copier. Teichmiller also states that after three to four minutes, Bergerson-Hawkins moved out of her way and she left the office. In light of the cases discussed below, Teichmiller's false imprisonment claim cannot stand.

In *Herbst v. Wuennenberg*, 83 Wis.2d 768, 266 N.W.2d 391 (1978), political canvassers checking addresses against voting registration lists were approached in an apartment building vestibule by Wuennenberg, the area's alderperson. Wuennenberg demanded that they identify themselves, and when they refused, she directed her husband to call the police. Wuennenberg stood in front of the building's outer door and "[stood] there with her arms on the pillars to the door" which, the canvassers believed, blocked their exit. The canvassers sued for false imprisonment but conceded that Wuennenberg had not threatened or intimidated them and that they did not ask her permission to leave or make any attempt to get Wuennenberg to move away from the door. Each of the canvassers assumed that he or she would have to push Wuennenberg out of the way in order to leave the vestibule.

The central issue was whether the canvassers were confined by threat of physical force, *i.e.*, an apparent intention and ability to apply force as expressed in words or acts. The court noted that Wuennenberg did not verbally threaten the canvassers and none of them asked her to step aside. Therefore, it was speculation to conclude that Wuennenberg would have refused a request to step aside and would have physically resisted the canvassers' attempt to leave. The court concluded that the evidence at best supported an inference that the canvassers remained in the vestibule because they assumed they would have to push Wuennenberg out of the way in order to leave. The court found this assumption insufficient to support the false imprisonment claim.

The *Herbst* court distinguished *Dupler v. Seubert*, 69 Wis.2d 373, 230 N.W.2d 626 (1975), in which an employee claimed to have been falsely imprisoned by her employer when she was called to the office to be informed of her termination. The manager yelled at the employee, blocked the office door and told her in a loud voice to "sit down." The manager declined the employee's repeated requests to leave. The jury found false imprisonment. On review, the court held that the employee was intentionally confined by an implied threat of actual physical restraint.

In distinguishing *Dupler*, the *Herbst* court noted that the canvassers could not bring themselves within the purview of *Dupler* because they were not berated or screamed at by Wuennenberg, they outnumbered Wuennenberg three to one, and there was no evidence that they were frightened of Wuennenberg or that they feared harm. The canvassers "did not submit to an apprehension of force" and therefore were not imprisoned.

Teichmiller's deposition testimony indicates that she was yelled at, outnumbered and feared she would be harmed. However, she never actually asked to leave the clinic manager's office and was able to leave the office on her third attempt to move past Bergerson-Hawkins, who apparently was standing between her and the door. While Teichmiller claims she was afraid force would be used, it appears that this was speculation.

We conclude that there are no facts showing that Teichmiller was intentionally and unlawfully restrained, in an office whose door was open and from which she never asked to leave.

By the Court. — Judgment affirmed.

NOTES

1. Notice that the caption of this case indicates the opinion is "unpublished." Judges have discretion to decide whether to publish their written opinions in books that contain official reports of court decisions. A variety of reasons might support a decision about whether to publish an opinion. However, a decision not to publish frequently suggests that the opinion does not break any new ground in an area where the law is well-settled. *See* WIS. R. CIV. PRO. § 809.23(1) (Reasons for not publishing an opinion include that the "issues involve no more than the application of well-settled rules of law to a recurring fact situation."). Until recently, it was difficult to obtain unpublished decisions. Now, however, courts frequently make unpublished opinions available through electronic legal research tools. Despite this availability, unpublished opinions have limited precedential value. For example, in Wisconsin the rules of civil procedure provide that "[a]n unpublished opinion is of no precedential value and for this reason may not be cited in any court of this state as precedent or authority, except to support a claim of res judicata, collateral estoppel, or law of the case." WIS. R. CIV. PRO. § 809.23(3). For an interesting discussion of this issue, see Boyce F. Martin, *In Defense of Unpublished Opinions*, 60 OHIO ST. L.J. 117 (1999) and Daniel A. Berman & Jeffrey O. Cooper, *In Defense of Less Precedential Opinions: A Reply to Chief Judge Martin*, 60 OHIO ST. L.J. 2025 (1999).

2. Note also that no single judge took credit for writing the unpublished opinion in *Teichmiller*. Rather, the opinion was "per curiam." Per curiam is latin for "by the court." Short opinions or brief dispositions of cases are frequently issued per curiam, instead of by a single judge.

3. The Restatement indicates that a plaintiff seeking recovery for false imprisonment must prove that the defendant confined her "within boundaries fixed by" the defendant. Sometimes it is easy to recognize the bounded area (as in the the *Teichmiller* case, where the defendants blocked the plaintiff's exit from the room). Other times, however, the "bounded area" requirement is a bit more difficult to conceptualize. For example, in the famous case of *Whittaker v. Sandford*, 85 A. 399 (Me. 1912), a member of a religious sect in Jaffa (today Tel Aviv) decided to leave the sect and return to the United States. The leader of the sect offered the member passage to Maine (where the sect maintained another colony) on his yacht. The member accepted the offer. However, when the yacht arrived in port, the leader refused to furnish her a boat to go ashore. The plaintiff eventually freed herself, and she later sued the sect leader for false imprisonment. In affirming a jury verdict in favor of the plaintiff, the Supreme Judicial Court of Maine compared the plaintiff's plight to that of a person locked in a room:

> If one should, without right, turn the key in a door, and thereby prevent a person in the room from leaving, it would be the simplest form of unlawful imprisonment. The restraint is physical. The four walls and the locked door are physical impediments to escape. Now it [is] different when one who is in control of a vessel at anchor, within practical rowing distance for the shore, who has agreed that a guest on board shall be free to leave, there being no means to leave except by rowboats, wrongfully refuses the guest the use of the boat? The boat is the key. By refusing the boat he turns the key. The guest is as effectively locked up as if there were walls along the sides of the vessel. The restraint is physical. The impassable sea is the physical barrier.

Whittaker, 85 A. at 402.

4. With respect to the intent element of false imprisonment, it is only necessary for the plaintiff to prove that the defendant had a purpose to confine her, or that the defendant was substantially certain that his conduct would cause confinement. The defendant's motive for confining the plaintiff is irrelevant, at least so far as the prima facie case goes. The distinction between intent and words such as "motive," or "malice" can be difficult to sort out. In trying to understand the terms, consider the following passage from a South Carolina appellate court decision:

> Volition is the actor's willingness to do an act. Deliberation is the thinking out or weighing of the act before it is done. Purpose is the result desired by the actor. Motive is the actor's subjective reason for doing the act. Malice is the actor's feeling of ill will or hatred towards the victim of the act.
>
> Intent is proved by showing that the actor acted willingly (volition) and that he knew or [was substantially certain] the result would follow

from his act. Neither deliberation . . . nor motive nor malice are necessary elements of intent.

One reason [these terms] are often confused is that they are used synonymously in ordinary speech. This can be illustrated by considering the following sentences:

"He intentionally broke the dish."

"He deliberately broke the dish."

"He broke the dish on purpose."

"He meant to break the dish."

In common understanding, each of these sentences means the same thing: *i.e.*, the actor's purpose was to break the dish. Judges also tend to use [these terms interchangeably]. Unfortunately, these usages are so entrenched in judicial writing that they are unlikely to change. The result will be to continue to confuse what is meant in law by "intent."

Snakenberg v. Hartford Cas. Ins. Co., 383 S.E.2d 2, 7 & n.7 (S.C. Ct. App. 1989).

5. Suggesting that "motive" or "malice" are not relevant to a false imprisonment case is not the same as saying that a defendant is never privileged to detain another individual. One common fact pattern where such a privilege might exist is where a store owner (or a security guard on her behalf) detains a shopper suspected of shoplifting. If both the suspicion and the manner of detention were reasonable, the defendant's desire to protect her property might serve as a valid defense to the plaintiff's false imprisonment claim. *See K-Mart Corp. v. Washington*, 866 P.2d 264, 280 (Nev. 1993). A merchant can lose the privilege, however, if he uses excessive force to protect his property, or if the merchant detains a suspect for an excessive period of time. *See Gortarez v. Smitty's Super Valu, Inc.*, 680 P.2d 807 (Ariz. 1984); *Silvia v. Zayre Corp.*, 233 So. 2d 856 (Fla. Dist. Ct. App. 1970). "Defense of property" is among several defenses to intentional torts that will be discussed in Chapter 3, *infra*.

6. In general, the length of time that a defendant has confined a plaintiff is irrelevant to the plaintiff's ability to maintain a false imprisonment claim.

PROBLEMS

1. Can a defendant confine a plaintiff by means other than physical barrier or physical force?

  a. Burglar walks into Merchant's store. Without blocking the door or displaying a weapon, Burglar says to Merchant: "Don't move or I'll shoot you." Has Burglar confined Merchant?

  b. Burglar breaks into Homeowner's house and finds Homeowner and his small child in the living room. Burglar tells Homeowner that he is free to leave, but threatens to shoot the child if Homeowner does so. Homeowner stays put. Has Burglar confined Homeowner?

2. Assuming that threats to apply physical force can constitute confinement, how far does this push the concept of "bounded area?" What if Alice tells Bernice that she will "hunt her down and kill her" if she leaves the city? Has Alice falsely imprisoned Bernice to city limits? What if the threat related to an entire state? Or an entire country?

3. In light of the "intent" issues raised in Note 4 above, consider the following. Al and his twin brother, Barry, attend a party at Casey's house. Al does not drink any liquor, but Barry becomes highly (and visibly) drunk. At the end of the evening, Al is the last guest at Casey's house. Casey, however, mistakes Al for Barry and takes his car keys. "You're not going anywhere," Casey says to Al. "You're too drunk to drive!" Al (who, of course, is sober) spends the entire evening at Casey's against his will. Has Casey falsely imprisoned Al?

4. On a Sunday at 10:00 p.m., Margaret boarded a Golden Airlines flight in Los Angeles with non-stop service to San Francisco. The plane pulled back from the terminal, but stopped on the tarmac for 45 minutes. Finally, the pilot made an announcement: "Due to mechanical problems, we will need to change equipment. We apologize for any inconvenience, and we thank you for flying Golden Airlines." Shortly thereafter, flight attendants ushered Margaret and other passengers out of the plane and onto a waiting bus. Margaret assumed that the bus would take her to another plane. Within minutes, however, Margaret realized that she was wrong. The bus had left the airport and was driving to San Francisco! Margaret desperately wanted to get off the bus. But neither she, nor any other passenger, expressed such a sentiment to the driver. The bus finally reached San Francisco at 5:00 on Monday morning. Margaret has come straight to your office, asking that you file a false imprisonment claim against Golden Airlines. Evaluate the claim.

D. TRESPASS TO LAND

Up to now, we have considered intentional torts that protect a plaintiff's physical integrity. Intentional torts also can protect a plaintiff's property interests. In this section, we will discuss the intentional tort of trespass to land. The Restatement of Torts defines trespass to land as follows:

One is subject to liability to another for trespass, irrespective of whether he thereby causes harm to any legally protected interest of the other, if he intentionally

(a) enters land in the possession of the other, or causes a thing or third person to do so, or

(b) remains on the land, or

    (c) fails to remove from the land a thing which he is under a duty to remove.

RESTATEMENT (SECOND) OF TORTS § 158 (1965).

Note that the Restatement suggests the imposition of liability without regard to whether the defendant harmed the plaintiff. This reflects the fact that trespass to land developed as a mechanism to enforce property boundaries, not as an action to compensate individuals for actual harm. This development reflects the great importance that people in early England placed on possessory rights in land. Professor Richard Epstein, for example, traces the roots of the tort to the Crown's need to maintain social order. "One symptom of the high levels of disorder was the frequency with which owners were dispossessed — or as the older law said disseised — of their land by strangers." EPSTEIN, TORTS § 1.10 at 22. As one means to respond to attacks on property, according to Professor Epstein, "the common law developed the action trespass *quaere clausam fregit*, or trespass qcf: why did D break into P's 'close,' or land, *vi et armis* (by force and arms)? The reference to force and arms shows the close historical connection between trespass and civil order, and it reminds us that in early intentional trespasses, deliberate seizure and destruction of land were the chief targets of the versatile trespass action." *Id.* at 22-23.

Despite the ability to maintain an action without regard to damages, plaintiffs did need to demonstrate that the defendant's invasion of land was tangible — for example an invasion by the defendant's own body or by the building of a fence post. The tangibility requirement seems logical at first glance. But is it still a tenable requirement in modern times? Consider that issue (among others) in the following cases.

AMPHITHEATERS, INC. v. PORTLAND MEADOWS
198 P.2d 847 (Or. 1948)

BRAND, JUSTICE.

[Defendant built and operated a horse race track with lighting for night racing. Nearby, plaintiff built an outdoor movie theater.]

The plaintiff invested $135,000 in the construction of the outdoor theater and sums greatly in excess of that amount were expended by the defendant in the development of the race track and facilities. The lighting facilities alone involved an investment by the defendant of $100,000. The two tracts operated by plaintiff and defendant respectively are located just north of the city limits of Portland, Oregon. They adjoin and lie between two arterial highways, Denver Avenue and Union Avenue. The defendant's track consists of a mile-long oval extending in a general northerly and southerly direction. The auto race track which encloses the plaintiff's moving picture amphitheater lies between Union Avenue and the Northeast curve of the defendant's oval track. Union Avenue runs in a northwesterly direction along and parallel to the plaintiff's property of which it forms the northeasterly boundary. The theater screen, approximately 40 feet high and 50 feet wide, is backed up against the westerly line of Union Avenue and faces slightly south of west and directly toward the defendant's race track.

In installing outdoor moving picture theaters, it is necessary to protect the premises from outside light interference. For that purpose the plaintiff constructed wing fences for a considerable distance on each side of the screen and along the westerly line of Union Avenue for the purpose of shutting off the light from the cars traveling on that arterial highway. It was also necessary to construct a shadow box extending on both sides and above the screen for the purpose of excluding the light from the moon and stars. The testimony indicates that the construction of the shadow box was necessary if a good picture was to be presented on the screen. The extreme delicacy of plaintiff's operation and the susceptibility of outdoor moving pictures to light in any form was conclusively established by the evidence.

In order to illuminate the defendant's track for night horse racing, approximately 350 1500-watt lights are mounted in clusters on 80-foot poles placed at intervals of approximately 250 feet around the track. The flood lights are in general, directed at the track, but there is substantial evidence to the effect that reflected light 'spills' over onto the plaintiff's premises and has a serious effect on the quality of pictures shown on the screen. The nearest cluster of lights on the defendant's track is 832 feet distant from the plaintiff's screen. The light from the defendant's track not only impairs the quality of the pictures exhibited by the plaintiff, but there is also substantial evidence that plaintiffs have suffered financial loss as the result of the illumination of which they complain. On one occasion at least, plaintiffs felt themselves required to refund admission fees to their patrons on account of the poor quality of the picture exhibited. The evidence discloses that the light from the defendant's race track when measured at plaintiff's screen is approximately that of full moonlight.

Upon the opening of the racing season in September, 1946, the plaintiff immediately complained to the defendant concerning the detrimental effect of defendant's lights, and shortly thereafter suit was filed. In the fall of 1946 the defendant, while denying liability, nevertheless made substantial efforts to protect the plaintiff from the effect of defendant's lights. One hundred hoods were installed on the lights, and particular attention was given to those nearest to the plaintiff's property. In 1947, and prior to the spring racing season, which was to last 25 days, thirty louvers were also installed for the purpose of further confining the light to the defendant's property. These efforts materially reduced, but did not eliminate the conditions of which plaintiff complains.

[Plaintiff filed an action asserting that defendant's lights constituted both a trespass upon his land and a nuisance. The trial court directed a verdict in favor of defendant on both counts.] Plaintiff contends that the defendant, by casting light equivalent to that of a full moon upon plaintiff's screen has committed a trespass upon real property and error is assigned by reason of the failure of the court to submit to the jury the question of trespass. While the dividing line between trespass and nuisance is not always a sharp one, we think it clear that the case at bar is governed by the law of nuisance and not by the law of trespass. Under our decisions every unauthorized entry upon land of another, although without damage, constitutes actionable trespass. The mere suggestion that the casting of light upon the premises of a plaintiff would render a defendant liable without proof of any actual damage, carries its own refutation. Actions for damages on account of smoke, noxious odors and the like have been universally classified as falling within the law of nuisance. In fact, cases of this type are described in the Restatement of the Law as 'non trespassory' invasions. RESTATEMENT OF THE LAW OF TORTS, Vol. 4, Ch. 40, p. 214, et seq.

Many of the cases on which plaintiff relies in support of its theory of trespass involve the flight of airplanes at low level over plaintiffs' land. The modern law with reference to trespass by airplanes has developed under the influence of ancient rules concerning the nature of property. Ownership of lands, it has been said, 'includes, not only the face of the earth, but everything under it or over it, and has in its legal signification an indefinite extent upward and downward, giving rise to the maxim, *Cujus est solum ejus est usque ad coelum*'. 50 C.J. 752, PROPERTY, § 24. Harmonizing the ancient rule with the necessities of modern life, the Restatement of the Law declares that one who intentionally and without a privilege enters land, is a trespasser. RESTATEMENT OF THE LAW OF TORTS, Vol. 1, § 158, p. 359. Air travel over a plaintiff's land is still recognized as trespass prima facie imposing liability but the rights of airplane travel are established or recognized by the doctrine of privilege. RESTATEMENT OF THE LAW OF TORTS, §§ 158, 159, 194.

In support of its theory of trespass, the plaintiff cites [several cases, all of which] involve the flight of airplanes and which reflect the influence of the ancient rules of ownership *ad coelum* as modified by the rules of privilege set forth in the Restatement. The historical background of these cases distinguishes them from the non trespassory cases which are controlled by the law of nuisance. *Portsmouth Harbor Land & Hotel Co. v. United States*, 260 U.S. 327 [is similar]. The case involved a taking by the United States by means of the continuous firing of artillery over the petitioners' land. We need not argue the distinction between a cannon ball and a ray of light.

As its second assignment, the plaintiff asserts that the trial court erred in failing to submit the case to the jury on the theory of nuisance. [The court then discussed this issue and affirmed the ruling of the trial court.]

The trial court did not err in directing a verdict. The judgment is affirmed.

NOTE

In *Amphitheaters*, the Oregon Supreme Court applied the traditional rule requiring a tangible invasion of a plaintiff's land for purposes of a trespass action. Eleven years later, the same court considered a case in which an aluminum manufacturer caused invisible gases and particulates to settle upon a livestock owner's land. The livestock owner filed a trespass action against the aluminum manufacturer and won a verdict in the trial court. The Oregon Supreme Court affirmed the judgment:

> The view recognizing a trespassory invasion where there is no 'thing' which can be seen with the naked eye undoubtedly runs counter to the definition of trespass expressed in some quarters. 1 RESTATEMENT, TORTS § 158, Comment h (1934); PROSSER, TORTS § 13 (2d Ed.1955). It is quite possible that in an earlier day when science had not yet peered into the molecular and atomic world of small particles, the courts could not fit an invasion through unseen physical instrumentalities into the requirement that a trespass can result only from a direct invasion. But in this atomic age even the uneducated know the great and awful force contained in the atom and what it can do to a man's property if it is released. In fact, the now famous equation $E=mc2$ has taught us that mass and energy are equivalents and that our concept of 'things' must be reframed. If these observations on science in relation to the law of trespass should appear theoretical and unreal in the abstract, they become very practical and real to the possessor of land when the unseen force cracks the foundation of his house. The force is just as real if it is chemical in nature and must be awakened by the intervention of another agency before it does harm.

> If, then, we must look to the character of the instrumentality which is used in making an intrusion upon another's land, we prefer to emphasize the object's energy or force rather than its size. Viewed in this way we may define trespass as any intrusion which invades the possessor's protected interest in exclusive possession, whether that intrusion is by visible or invisible pieces of matter or by energy which can be measured only by the mathematical language of the physicist.

> We are of the opinion, therefore, that the intrusion of the fluoride particulates in the present case constituted a trespass.

> The defendant argues that our decision in *Amphitheaters, Inc. v. Portland Meadows*, 1948, 184 Or. 336, 198 P.2d 847, requires a contrary conclusion. In discussing the distinction between trespass and nuisance the court referred to a difference between 'a cannon ball and a ray of light' indicating that the former but not the latter could produce a trespassory invasion. The court also said 'The mere suggestion that the casting of light upon the premises of a plaintiff would render a defendant liable without proof of any actual damage, carries its own refutation.' We do not regard this statement as a pronouncement that a trespass can never be caused by the intrusion of light rays or other intangible forces; more properly the case may be interpreted as stating that the conduct of the defendant in a particular case may not be action-

able if it does not violate a legally protected interest of the plaintiff. The court states that the defendant is not liable without proof of actual damage. In that case the plaintiff contended that he had suffered damage in the form of a less efficient cinema screen due to the defendant's lights.

The *Amphitheaters* case [may] be viewed as a pronouncement that a possessor's interest is not invaded by an intrusion which is so trifling that it cannot be recognized by the law. Inasmuch as it is not necessary to prove actual damage in trespass the magnitude of the intrusion ordinarily would not be of any consequence. But there is a point where the entry is so lacking in substance that the law will refuse to recognize it, applying the maxim de minimis non curat lex. Thus it would seem clear that ordinarily the casting of a grain of sand upon another's land would not be a trespass. And so too the casting of diffused light rays upon another's land would not ordinarily constitute a trespass.

The broader and more diverse the possessor's protectible interests the more sensitive they are to violation by the defendant and the easier it is to find that his conduct, although apparently inconsequential, gives rise to liability. The scope of the possessor's legitimate interest in the exclusive possession of land is broad and difficult to define specifically. Once recognizing that actual damage need not be shown in making out an actionable invasion, the plaintiff's right to insist upon freedom from interference with his possession seems almost limitless.

Martin v. Reynolds Metals Co., 342 P.2d 790, 794-96 (Or. 1959). What do you think of the Court's discussion of *Amphitheaters*? Did the court sufficiently distinguish the case? Even if not, what does the outcome in *Martin* suggest about the old rule that one need not prove damages in a trespass to land action? On that issue, consider the following case.

BRADLEY v. AMERICAN SMELTING AND REFINING CO.
709 P.2d 782 (Wash. 1984)

CALLOW, JUSTICE.

This comes before us on a certification from the United States District Court for the Western District of Washington. Plaintiffs, landowners on Vashon Island, had sued for damages in trespass and nuisance from the deposit on their property of microscopic, airborne particles of heavy metals which came from the American Smelting and Refining Company (ASARCO) copper smelter at Ruston, Washington.

The issues certified for answer are as follows:

(1) Did the defendant have the requisite intent to commit intentional trespass as a matter of law?

(2) Does an intentional deposit of microscopic particulates, undetectable by the human senses, upon a person's property give rise to a cause of action for trespassory invasion of the person's right to exclusive possession of property as well as a claim of nuisance?

(3) Does the cause of action for trespassory invasion require proof of actual damages?

* * *

As a part of defendant's smelting process, the Tacoma smelter emits into the atmosphere gases and particulate matter. For the purposes of resolving the certified questions, the parties stipulate that some particulate emissions of both cadmium and arsenic from the Tacoma smelter have been and are continuing to be deposited on plaintiffs' land. Defendant ASARCO has been aware since it took over operation of the Tacoma smelter in 1905 that the wind does, on occasion, cause smelter particulate emissions to blow over Vashon Island where plaintiffs' land is located.

This case was initiated in state court and later removed to federal district court. Upon the plaintiffs moving for summary judgment on the issue of liability for the claimed trespass, the stated issues were certified to this court. The issues present the conflict in an industrial society between the need of all for the production of goods and the desire of the landowner near the manufacturing plant producing those goods that his use and enjoyment of his land not be diminished by the unpleasant side effects of the manufacturing process. A reconciliation must be found between the interest of the many who are unaffected by the possible poisoning and the few who may be affected.

1. Did the defendant have the requisite intent to commit intentional trespass as a matter of law?

The parties stipulated that as a part of the smelting process, particulate matter including arsenic and cadmium was emitted, that some of the emissions had been deposited on the plaintiffs' land and that the defendant has been aware since 1905 that the wind, on occasion, caused these emissions to be blown over the plaintiffs' land. The defendant cannot and does not deny that whenever the smelter was in operation the whim of the winds could bring these deleterious substances to the plaintiffs' premises. We are asked if the defendant, knowing what it had to know from the facts it admits, had the legal intent to commit trespass.

Addressing the definition, scope and meaning of "intent," section 8A of the Restatement (Second) of Torts says:

> The word "intent" is used . . . to denote that the actor desires to cause [the] consequences of his act, or that he believes that the consequences are substantially certain to result from it.

and we find in comment b at 15:

Intent is not, however, limited to consequences which are desired. If the actor knows that the consequences are certain, or substantially certain, to result from his act, and still goes ahead, he is treated by the law as if he had in fact desired to produce the result.

The defendant has known for decades that sulfur dioxide and particulates of arsenic, cadmium and other metals were being emitted from the tall smokestack. It had to know that the solids propelled into the air by the warm gases would settle back to earth somewhere. It had to know that a purpose of the tall stack was to disperse the gas, smoke and minute solids over as large an area as possible and as far away as possible, but that while any resulting contamination would be diminished as to any one area or landowner, that nonetheless contamination, though slight, would follow. In W. Prosser, Torts § 8, at 31-32 (4th ed. 1971), intent is defined as follows:

> The intent with which tort liability is concerned is not necessarily a hostile intent, or a desire to do any harm. Rather it is an intent to bring about a result which will invade the interests of another in a way that the law will not sanction. The defendant may be liable although he has meant nothing more than a good-natured practical joke. . . .

* * *

Intent, however, is broader than a desire to bring about physical results. It must extend not only to those consequences which are desired, but also to those which the actor believes are substantially certain to follow from what he does. . . . The man who fires a bullet into a dense crowd may fervently pray that he will hit no one, but since he must believe and know that he cannot avoid doing so, he intends it. The practical application of this principle has meant that where a reasonable man in the defendant's position would believe that a particular result was substantially certain to follow, he will be dealt with by the jury, or even by the court, as though he had intended it.

This has been the reasoning of the decisions of this State. *Garratt v. Dailey*, 46 Wash. 2d 197, 279 P.2d 1091 (1955) involved a 5-year-old boy who pulled a chair from under an arthritic woman as she was about to sit in it. The court held that to find liability for an intentional tort it had to be found that there was a volitional act undertaken with the knowledge and substantial certainty that reasonably to be expected consequences would follow.

It is patent that the defendant acted on its own volition and had to appreciate with substantial certainty that the law of gravity would visit the effluence upon someone, somewhere.

We find that the defendant had the requisite intent to commit intentional trespass as a matter of law.

2. Does an intentional deposit of microscopic particulates, undetectable by the human senses, upon a person's property give rise to a cause of action for tres-

passory invasion of the person's right to exclusive possession of property as well as a claim of nuisance?

Just as there may be proof advantages in a trespass theory, there may be disadvantages also. Potential problems lurk in the ancient requirements that a trespassory invasion be "direct or immediate" and that an "object" or "something tangible" be deposited upon plaintiff's land. Some courts hold that if an intervening force, such as wind or water, carries the pollutants onto the plaintiff's land, then the entry is not "direct." Others define "object" as requiring something larger or more substantial than smoke, dust, gas, or fumes.

Both of these concepts are nonsensical barriers, although the courts are slow to admit it. The requirement that the invasion be "direct" is a holdover from the forms of action, and is repudiated by contemporary science of causation. Atmospheric or hydrologic systems assure that pollutants deposited in one place will end up somewhere else, with no less assurance of causation than the blaster who watches the debris rise from his property and settle on his neighbor's land. Trespassory consequences today may be no less "direct" even if the mechanism of delivery is viewed as more complex.

The insistence that a trespass involve an invasion by a "thing" or "object" was repudiated in the well known (but not particularly influential) case of *Martin v. Reynolds Metals Co.*, [221 Or. 86, 342 P.2d 790 (1959)], which held that gaseous and particulate fluorides from an aluminum smelter constituted a trespass for purposes of the statute of limitations.

We hold that the defendant's conduct in causing chemical substances to be deposited upon the plaintiffs' land fulfilled all of the requirements under the law of trespass.

Having held that there was an intentional trespass, we adopt, in part, the rationale of *Borland v. Sanders Lead Co.*, 369 So. 2d 523, 529 (Ala.1979), which stated in part:

> Although we view this decision as an application, and not an extension, of our present law of trespass, we feel that a brief restatement and summary of the principles involved in this area would be appropriate. Whether an invasion of a property interest is a trespass or a nuisance does not depend upon whether the intruding agent is "tangible" or "intangible." Instead, an analysis must be made to determine the interest interfered with. If the intrusion interferes with the right to exclusive possession of property, the law of trespass applies. If the intrusion is to the interest in use and enjoyment of property, the law of nuisance applies. As previously observed, however, the remedies of trespass and nuisance are not necessarily mutually exclusive.

* * *

Under the modern theory of trespass, the law presently allows an action to be maintained in trespass for invasions that, at one time, were considered indirect and, hence, only a nuisance. In order to recover in trespass for this type of invasion [*i.e.*, the asphalt piled in such a way as to run onto plaintiff's property, or the pollution emitting from a defendant's smoke stack, such as in the present case], a plaintiff must show 1) an invasion affecting an interest in the exclusive possession of his property; 2) an intentional doing of the act which results in the invasion; 3) reasonable foreseeability that the act done could result in an invasion of plaintiff's possessory interest; and 4) substantial damages to the res.

3. Does the cause of action for trespassory invasion require proof of actual damages?

When airborne particles are transitory or quickly dissipate, they do not interfere with a property owner's possessory rights and, therefore, are properly denominated as nuisances. When, however, the particle or substance accumulates on the land and does not pass away, then a trespass has occurred. *Borland v. Sanders Lead Co., supra; Martin v. Reynolds Metals Co., supra*. While at common law any trespass entitled a landowner to recover nominal or punitive damages for the invasion of his property, such a rule is not appropriate under the circumstances before us. No useful purpose would be served by sanctioning actions in trespass by every landowner within a hundred miles of a manufacturing plant. Manufacturers would be harassed and the litigious few would cause the escalation of costs to the detriment of the many. The elements that we have adopted for an action in trespass from *Borland* require that a plaintiff has suffered actual and substantial damages. Since this is an element of the action, the plaintiff who cannot show that actual and substantial damages have been suffered should be subject to dismissal of his cause upon a motion for summary judgment.

The United States District Court for the Western District of Washington shall be notified for such further action as it deems appropriate.

NOTES

1. As *Bradley* makes clear, intent remains an element of a trespass to land action. This means that a plaintiff must prove that a defendant had the purpose to invade her possessory interest in land, or that the defendant was substantially certain that her action would do so. However, it is not necessary that a defendant be aware that she is on another's land for the plaintiff to succeed in her action. Rather, it is only necessary that the defendant enters the land in a volitional fashion. *See* RESTATEMENT (SECOND) OF TORTS § 163 comment b (1965) ("It is . . . immaterial whether or not [a defendant] honestly and reasonably believes that the land is his own, or that he has the consent of the possessor or a third person having power to give consent on his behalf, or that he has a mistaken belief that he has some other privilege to enter."). *See also* RESTATEMENT (SECOND) OF TORTS § 164 (1965). Is this a rule with any relevance? Why might a plaintiff even bring an action against a defendant who entered her property

mistakenly and without causing any harm? What kind of damages might she recover?

2. Is it unfair if a plaintiff cannot maintain a trespass action against a defendant who is obviously interfering with the plaintiff's ability to use her land, but not sufficiently invading the plaintiff's possessory interest in land? The *Bradley* court explains that such plaintiffs are not always without a cause of action because of the availability of a nuisance claim. Private nuisance law, for example, allows a plaintiff to recover when the defendant's intentional conduct causes a substantial and unreasonable interference with the plaintiff's use and enjoyment of land. The topic of nuisance is taken up in Chapter 15.

3. Another issue that courts have faced in modern times concerns the definition of "land" itself. For many years, the law took the position "*cujus est solum ejus est usque ad coelum*" or he who has the soil owns the upward unto heaven, and by analogy, downward to perdition. *See* RESTATEMENT (SECOND) OF TORTS § 159 comment g (1965); PROSSER & KEETON ON TORTS § 13 at 79. The advent of aviation, however, made application of such a rule impractical. Today, courts generally follow a rule of "effective possession," allowing property owners to protect the airspace above their land and the subsurface below their land only to an extent that the landowner can make practical use of the space. *Id. See, e.g., City of Newark v. Eastern Airlines*, 159 F. Supp. 750 (D.N.J. 1958).

PROBLEMS

1. Oscar and Bert are next-door neighbors in the small town of Hoosierville. Each Friday, Bert likes to cook spare ribs on a barbeque grill that he keeps on his front porch. The smoke (and accompanying odor) from Bert's grill wafts over Oscar's property, much to Oscar's chagrin. Can Oscar maintain a trespass to land action against Bert?

2. Jethro owns property in Texas on which he maintains oil wells. Jethro attempts to extract more oil from one of his wells by using a "secondary recovery" method that involves injecting water into the well at an irregular angle. The injection, however, causes water to flow underneath the property of his neighbor, J.R. J.R. alleges that the water is decreasing his ability to extract oil from his own property. Can J.R. maintain a trespass to land action against Jethro?

3. Sandra and Alice are jogging on a public street that runs alongside Pauline's property. Sandra shoves Alice, who stumbles and falls onto Pauline's property, damaging one of her shrubs. Pauline wants to file a trespass to land action to recover the value of the shrub. Will she succeed against Alice? Against Sandra?

4. Ed and Russell are next-door neighbors in a suburban village. Each evening, between 5:30 and 6:00, Russell stands on his front yard and repeatedly throws a boomerang toward Ed's front yard. Every time Russell throws the boomerang, it sails over Ed's yard, reverses course, and returns to Russell's

hands. Ed has filed a trespass to land action against Russell. Russell has moved to dismiss Ed's action for failure to state a claim upon which relief can be granted. Is Ed's inability to prove "substantial damages" fatal to his claim?

E. TRESPASS TO CHATTELS

Trespass to chattels grew from the common law writ of *trespass de bonis asportatis* — literally, the asportation or carrying away of chattels. Courts later expanded the action to include situations where the defendant did not literally take the chattel, but instead simply damaged it. Today, the law reflects a position that allows a plaintiff to maintain an action in a broad range of situations where a defendant dispossesses another of her chattel, or where a defendant "uses" or "intermeddles" with another's possessory interests in personal property. See RESTATEMENT (SECOND) OF TORTS § 217 (1965).

One can imagine a number of straightforward situations that would give rise to a trespass to chattels claim. For example, a vandal who purposely scratched your car would be liable for cost of repainting the vehicle. Or a classmate who purposely spilled coffee into the keyboard of your laptop would be responsible for subsequent repairs. In recent years, however, the advent of technology has forced courts to consider some interesting issues concerning the concept of what constitutes "property" itself. The following case is a good example of the difficulties that modern courts face in applying the old rules of trespass to chattels.

COMPUSERVE, INC. v. CYBER PROMOTIONS, INC.
962 F. Supp. 1015 (S.D. Ohio 1997)

GRAHAM, DISTRICT JUDGE.

This case presents novel issues regarding the commercial use of the Internet, specifically the right of an online computer service to prevent a commercial enterprise from sending unsolicited electronic mail advertising to its subscribers.

Plaintiff CompuServe Incorporated ("CompuServe") is one of the major national commercial online computer services. It operates a computer communication service through a proprietary nationwide computer network. In addition to allowing access to the extensive content available within its own proprietary network, CompuServe also provides its subscribers with a link to the much larger resources of the Internet. This allows its subscribers to send and receive electronic messages, known as "e-mail," by the Internet. Defendants Cyber Promotions, Inc. and its president Sanford Wallace are in the business of sending unsolicited e-mail advertisements on behalf of themselves and their clients to hundreds of thousands of Internet users, many of whom are CompuServe subscribers. CompuServe has notified defendants that they are prohibited from using its computer equipment to process and store the unsolicited e-mail and has requested that they terminate the practice. Instead, defendants have sent an increasing volume of e-mail solicitations to CompuServe subscribers. CompuServe has attempted to employ technological means to block the flow of defendants' e-mail transmissions to its computer equipment, but to no avail.

This matter is before the Court on the application of CompuServe for a preliminary injunction which would extend the duration of the temporary restraining order issued by this Court on October 24, 1996 and which would in addition prevent defendants from sending unsolicited advertisements to CompuServe subscribers.

For the reasons which follow, this Court holds that where defendants engaged in a course of conduct of transmitting a substantial volume of electronic data in the form of unsolicited e-mail to plaintiff's proprietary computer equipment, where defendants continued such practice after repeated demands to cease and desist, and where defendants deliberately evaded plaintiff's affirmative efforts to protect its computer equipment from such use, plaintiff has a viable claim for trespass to personal property and is entitled to injunctive relief to protect its property.

I.

Internet users often pay a fee for Internet access. However, there is no per-message charge to send electronic messages over the Internet and such messages usually reach their destination within minutes. Thus electronic mail provides an opportunity to reach a wide audience quickly and at almost no cost to the sender. It is not surprising therefore that some companies, like defendant Cyber Promotions, Inc., have begun using the Internet to distribute advertisements by sending the same unsolicited commercial message to hundreds of thousands of Internet users at once. Defendants refer to this as "bulk e-mail," while plaintiff refers to it as "junk e-mail." In the vernacular of the Internet, unsolicited e-mail advertising is sometimes referred to pejoratively as "spam."

CompuServe subscribers use CompuServe's domain name "CompuServe.com" together with their own unique alpha-numeric identifier to form a distinctive e-mail mailing address. That address may be used by the subscriber to exchange electronic mail with any one of tens of millions of other Internet users who have electronic mail capability. E-mail sent to CompuServe subscribers is processed and stored on CompuServe's proprietary computer equipment. Thereafter, it becomes accessible to CompuServe's subscribers, who can access CompuServe's equipment and electronically retrieve those messages.

Over the past several months, CompuServe has received many complaints from subscribers threatening to discontinue their subscription unless CompuServe prohibits electronic mass mailers from using its equipment to send unsolicited advertisements. CompuServe asserts that the volume of messages generated by such mass mailings places a significant burden on its equipment which has finite processing and storage capacity. CompuServe receives no payment from the mass mailers for processing their unsolicited advertising. However, CompuServe's subscribers pay for their access to CompuServe's services in increments of time and thus the process of accessing, reviewing and discarding unsolicited e-mail costs them money, which is one of the reasons for their complaints.

In an effort to shield its equipment from defendants' bulk e-mail, CompuServe has implemented software programs designed to screen out the messages and block their receipt. In response, defendants have modified their equipment and the messages they send in such a fashion as to circumvent CompuServe's screening software. Allegedly, defendants have been able to conceal the true origin of their messages by falsifying the point-of-origin information contained in the header of the electronic messages. Defendants have removed the "sender" information in the header of their messages and replaced it with another address. Also, defendants have developed the capability of configuring their computer servers to conceal their true domain name and appear on the Internet as another computer, further concealing the true origin of the messages. By manipulating this data, defendants have been able to continue sending messages to CompuServe's equipment in spite of CompuServe's protests and protective efforts.

Defendants assert that they possess the right to continue to send these communications to CompuServe subscribers. CompuServe contends that, in doing so, the defendants are trespassing upon its personal property.

Trespass to chattels has evolved from its original common law application, concerning primarily the asportation of another's tangible property, to include the unauthorized use of personal property:

> Its chief importance now, is that there may be recovery . . . for interferences with the possession of chattels which are not sufficiently important to be classed as conversion, and so to compel the defendant to pay the full value of the thing with which he has interfered. Trespass to chattels survives today, in other words, largely as a little brother of conversion.

PROSSER & KEETON, PROSSER AND KEETON ON TORTS, § 14, 85-86 (1984).

Both plaintiff and defendants cite the Restatement (Second) of Torts to support their respective positions. . . . The Restatement § 217(b) states that a trespass to chattel may be committed by intentionally using or intermeddling with the chattel in possession of another. Restatement § 217, Comment e defines physical "intermeddling" as follows:

> . . . intentionally bringing about a physical contact with the chattel. The actor may commit a trespass by an act which brings him into an intended physical contact with a chattel in the possession of another[.]

Electronic signals generated and sent by computer have been held to be sufficiently physically tangible to support a trespass cause of action. It is undisputed that plaintiff has a possessory interest in its computer systems. Further, defendants' contact with plaintiff's computers is clearly intentional. Although electronic messages may travel through the Internet over various routes, the messages are affirmatively directed to their destination.

Defendants, citing Restatement (Second) of Torts § 221, which defines "dispossession", assert that not every interference with the personal property of another is actionable and that physical dispossession or substantial interference with the chattel is required. Defendants then argue that they did not, in this case, physically dispossess plaintiff of its equipment or substantially interfere with it. However, the Restatement (Second) of Torts§ 218 defines the circumstances under which a trespass to chattels may be actionable:

> One who commits a trespass to a chattel is subject to liability to the possessor of the chattel if, but only if,
>
> (a) he dispossesses the other of the chattel, or
>
> (b) the chattel is impaired as to its condition, quality, or value, or
>
> (c) the possessor is deprived of the use of the chattel for a substantial time, or
>
> (d) bodily harm is caused to the possessor, or harm is caused to some person or thing in which the possessor has a legally protected interest.

Therefore, an interference resulting in physical dispossession is just one circumstance under which a defendant can be found liable. Defendants suggest that "[u]nless an alleged trespasser actually takes physical custody of the property or physically damages it, courts will not find the 'substantial interference' required to maintain a trespass to chattel claim." [However, it] is clear from a reading of Restatement § 218 that an interference or intermeddling that does not fit the § 221 definition of "dispossession" can nonetheless result in defendants' liability for trespass.

A plaintiff can sustain an action for trespass to chattels, as opposed to an action for conversion, without showing a substantial interference with its right to possession of that chattel. Harm to the personal property or diminution of its quality, condition, or value as a result of defendants' use can also be the predicate for liability. RESTATEMENT § 218(b).

In the present case, any value CompuServe realizes from its computer equipment is wholly derived from the extent to which that equipment can serve its subscriber base. Michael Mangino, a software developer for CompuServe who monitors its mail processing computer equipment, states by affidavit that handling the enormous volume of mass mailings that CompuServe receives places a tremendous burden on its equipment. Defendants' more recent practice of evading CompuServe's filters by disguising the origin of their messages commandeers even more computer resources because CompuServe's computers are forced to store undeliverable e-mail messages and labor in vain to return the messages to an address that does not exist. To the extent that defendants' multitudinous electronic mailings demand the disk space and drain the processing power of plaintiff's computer equipment, those resources are not available to serve CompuServe subscribers. Therefore, the value of that equipment to CompuServe is diminished even though it is not physically damaged by defendants' conduct.

Next, plaintiff asserts that it has suffered injury aside from the physical impact of defendants' messages on its equipment. Restatement § 218(d) also indicates that recovery may be had for a trespass that causes harm to something in which the possessor has a legally protected interest. Plaintiff asserts that defendants' messages are largely unwanted by its subscribers, who pay incrementally to access their e-mail, read it, and discard it. Also, the receipt of a bundle of unsolicited messages at once can require the subscriber to sift through, at his expense, all of the messages in order to find the ones he wanted or expected to receive. These inconveniences decrease the utility of CompuServe's e-mail service and are the foremost subject in recent complaints from CompuServe subscribers.

Many subscribers have terminated their accounts specifically because of the unwanted receipt of bulk e-mail messages. Defendants' intrusions into CompuServe's computer systems, insofar as they harm plaintiff's business reputation and goodwill with its customers, are actionable under Restatement § 218(d).

Plaintiff CompuServe has attempted to exercise this privilege to protect its computer systems. However, defendants' persistent affirmative efforts to evade plaintiff's security measures have circumvented any protection those self-help measures might have provided. In this case CompuServe has alleged and supported by affidavit that it has suffered several types of injury as a result of defendants' conduct. The foregoing discussion simply underscores that the damage sustained by plaintiff is sufficient to sustain an action for trespass to chattels. However, this Court also notes that the implementation of technological means of self-help, to the extent that reasonable measures are effective, is particularly appropriate in this type of situation and should be exhausted before legal action is proper.

[The court then turned to a discussion of the appropriate remedy.] Normally, a preliminary injunction is not appropriate where an ultimate award of monetary damages will suffice. However, money damages are only adequate if they can be reasonably computed and collected. Plaintiff has demonstrated that defendants' intrusions into their computer systems harm plaintiff's business reputation and goodwill. This is the sort of injury that warrants the issuance of a preliminary injunction because the actual loss is impossible to compute.

Plaintiff has shown that it will suffer irreparable harm without the grant of the preliminary injunction.

It is improbable that granting the injunction will cause substantial harm to defendant. Even with the grant of this injunction, defendants are free to disseminate their advertisements in other ways not constituting trespass to plaintiff's computer equipment. Further, defendants may continue to send electronic mail messages to the tens of millions of Internet users who are not connected through CompuServe's computer systems.

Having considered the relevant factors, this Court concludes that the preliminary injunction that plaintiff requests is appropriate.

NOTES

1. Intent remains an element of trespass to chattels. Therefore, a plaintiff still must prove that the defendant had a purpose to invade her possessory interest in the property, or that the defendant was substantially certain that her conduct would do so. However, as we saw with trespass to land, a defendant's conduct will still be treated as intentional, even if he interferes with property without knowledge that it is owned by the plaintiff. *See* RESTATEMENT (SECOND) OF TORTS § 217 comment c (1965).

2. One way in which trespass to chattels differs from trespass to land is that courts have consistently refused to permit plaintiffs to maintain actions unless the defendant actually caused harm to the plaintiff's chattel. The defendant in *CompuServe* argued that it caused no actual harm. Do you understand why the court in *CompuServe* rejected the defendant's argument? Prosser suggests that the distinction between trespass to land and trespass to chattels concerning damages reflects the fact that the law historically has placed a greater interest on the inviolability of land as compared to personal property. PROSSER & KEETON ON TORTS § 14 at 87.

3. Despite the rule discussed in the previous note, some courts do recognize that harm to a chattel might include deprivation of use. *See* RESTATEMENT (SECOND) OF TORTS § 218(c) (1965). As a practical matter, this often makes it difficult to distinguish trespass to chattels from conversion — the other tort that protects interests in personal property. In fact, when a defendant *completely* dispossesses another of her interests in personal property (perhaps by destroying the property), the two torts might overlap. In the next section, we consider the tort of conversion in more detail.

PROBLEMS

1. Emily is a college student who rides her bicycle from class to class. One day, Emily left class and accidentally took a similar-looking bike belonging to Jennifer from the bike rack. Fifteen minutes later, Emily crashed the bike into a wall, causing $100 in damage to one of the bike's wheels. Can Jennifer recover the $100 in a trespass to chattels action against Emily?

2. Assume the same facts as above, but suppose that Emily realized the mistake five minutes after leaving class and returned the bike unharmed to the rack. Trespass to chattels?

3. Assume the same facts as above, but suppose that Emily used the bicycle for two full weeks before returning it unharmed to the same rack outside the Economics classroom. Before answering this problem, consider the next case on the tort of conversion.

F. CONVERSION

Conversion is used when a defendant completely dispossesses the plaintiff of an interest in personal property. However, one should understand two important wrinkles to this rule. First, a defendant need not physically damage a plaintiff's property to convert it. In other words, asserting dominion over a plaintiff's property can suffice. Second, courts historically have allowed a plaintiff to recover the full value of converted property, even if the defendant has not damaged the property. Thus, it is sometimes said that the primary distinctions between conversion and trespass to chattels are the degree of the invasion and the "forced sale" remedy. The following case demonstrates an application of both principles.

WISEMAN v. SCHAFFER
768 P.2d 800 (Idaho 1989)

SWANSTROM, JUDGE.

Larry and Freda Wiseman sued David Schaffer, alleging that he committed a tort when, without authorization, he towed their pickup to a location where it ultimately was stolen. A jury in the magistrate division found for Schaffer and a judgment dismissing the Wisemans' action was entered. The judgment was affirmed on the Wisemans' appeal to the district court. Appealing further, the Wisemans [argue] that the jury verdict was not supported by the evidence. We vacate [and] remand for a new trial.

The Wisemans left their Ford pickup parked at the Ross Point Husky Truck Stop in Post Falls, Idaho, while they were doing some long haul trucking. During their absence an imposter, identifying himself as Larry Wiseman, telephoned Schaffer and asked him to tow the Ford pickup at the Husky Truck Stop to the yard of a local welding shop. The imposter told Schaffer that $30 for the towing charge had been left on top of the sunvisor in the pickup. Schaffer located the pickup and the cash. He then towed the pickup to the welding shop as directed. Sometime later, the pickup was stolen. The Wisemans filed this action alleging [conversion] on the part of Schaffer.

Conversion traditionally has been defined as "any distinct act of dominion wrongfully exerted over another's personal property in denial or inconsistent with his rights therein, such as a tortious taking of another's chattels, or any wrongful exercise . . . over another's goods, depriving him of the possession, permanently or for an indefinite time." More recently, conversion has been described as an intentional exercise of dominion or control over a chattel which so seriously interferes with the right of another to control it that the actor may justly be required to pay the other the full value of the chattel. RESTATEMENT (SECOND) OF TORTS § 222A (1965) (hereinafter Restatement).

The instruction on conversion used here was patterned after Idaho Jury Instruction (IDJI) 450. Under this instruction, the jury was required to determine, first, whether Schaffer exercised dominion over the Wisemans' pickup without a right to do so, and second, whether the Wisemans had been "consequently deprived of possession" of their pickup. Finally, if the foregoing two elements were found to exist, the jury had to find the "nature and extent of the damages."

The evidence shows that Schaffer exercised dominion or control over the Wisemans' pickup inconsistent in fact with the Wisemans' right of ownership. This satisfied the first element of conversion. The jury could have found otherwise only if they postulated a "right" to exercise dominion upon the consent given by the imposter. No such "right" was embodied in the jury's instructions. Indeed, the law of conversion does not relieve an actor of liability due to his belief, because of a mistake of law or fact not induced by the other, that he has the consent of the other. RESTATEMENT § 244. Furthermore, to create liability for conversion it is not necessary that the actor intends to commit a trespass or a conversion; and the actor may be liable where he has in fact exercised dominion or control, although he may be quite unaware of the existence of the rights with which he interferes. *See* RESTATEMENT §§ 222, 223 and 224.

The evidence shows the second element of conversion was also satisfied. Schaffer's interference with the Wisemans' right of control ultimately resulted in the loss of the Wisemans' pickup. The jury could have found otherwise only if they postulated that the deprivation of possession did not follow "consequently" from Schaffer's actions because the pickup apparently was stolen by an unknown third party. The judge's instruction on conversion did not excuse liability if property were lost due to theft by a third party after the defendant wrongfully exercised dominion. Consequently, the jury's verdict is not supported by the evidence. The judgment must be vacated on the issue of Schaffer's liability for conversion.

On remand, [i]f the jury affirmatively answers that question, "the measure of damages is the full value of the chattel[s], at the time and place of the tort." RESTATEMENT § 222 A, comment c.

The case is remanded for a new trial on the issue of conversion.

NOTES

1. Why is this a "conversion" case instead of a "trespass to chattels" case? The Restatement of Torts distinguishes the two actions by defining conversion as an act that "so seriously interferes with the right of another to control [the property] that the actor may justly be required to pay the other the full value of the chattel." RESTATEMENT (SECOND) OF TORTS § 222A(1) (1965). The Restatement then sets forth factors that courts can use in determining the seriousness of the interference:

(a) the extent and duration of the actor's exercise of dominion or control;

(b) the actor's intent to assert a right in fact inconsistent with the other's right of control;

(c) the actor's good faith;

(d) the extent and duration of the resulting interference with the other's right of control;

(e) the harm done to the chattel;

(f) the inconvenience and expense caused to the other.

Did the *Wiseman* court do a good job of considering these factors in ruling that the Wisemans could maintain a conversion action?

2. Focus particularly on factor (c) from the previous note ("the actor's good faith"), and then recall that the *Wiseman* court found Schaffer potentially liable for conversion even though he did not know that the "real" Wisemans owned the truck. Is that fair?

3. At the end of the opinion, the *Wiseman* court states that a finding of liability should lead to recovery of "the full value of the chattel[s], at the time and place of the tort." This statement is consistent with the "forced sale" remedy described in the introductory note preceding the case, as well as with the language in section 222 of the Restatement. If taken literally, such a rule might mean that a plaintiff could refuse even a prompt offer to return a completely undamaged good. However, as Professor Epstein states, it is "virtually impossible to find any case where a court has declined to allow the return of goods under these circumstances." EPSTEIN, TORTS at § 1.12 at 37. Professor Epstein argues that "it would be better to *require*, instead of merely allow, the return of goods in these cases, should such a matter ever arise." *Id*. (Emphasis added). Do you agree?

PROBLEMS

1. Return to Problem 3 after the *CompuServe* case. Has Emily converted Jennifer's bicycle? How about in Problem 2 after the *CompuServe* case?

2. Collection Agency repossesses Plaintiff's car on behalf of Bank. Plaintiff claims that the car contained personal items not subject to Bank's security interest. Plaintiff then sues Collection Agency for converting those goods. Does Plaintiff have a good conversion claim? If so, what can Collection Agency and Bank do to protect themselves against conversion claims in similar cases? *See Larranaga v. Mile High Collection & Recovery Bureau, Inc.*, 807 F. Supp. 111 (D.N.M. 1992).

3. Several former and current staffers of a United States Senator entered the Senator's office at night and removed documents from his files. The staffers copied the documents and then returned the originals to the files. The staffers later gave the copies to a reporter for the Washington Post, who used information contained in the documents to write columns about the Senator. The Senator argued that the staffers had "converted" the information in his documents. Do you agree? *See Pearson v. Dodd*, 410 F.2d 701 (D.C. Cir. 1969). Would it matter that defendants had taken copies of documents that contained a company's unique formula for a food product? Or suppose the defendants had taken a business' customer list? Would the defendants be able to defend by arguing that they did not take the original documents?

4. Plaintiff underwent treatment for leukemia at State University Medical Center. During the course of treatment, Defendants (including Plaintiff's physician and a University researcher) performed tests on Plaintiff's blood and bone marrow. Through these tests, Defendants learned that Plaintiff's blood components had certain properties that would be extremely valuable for ongoing projects seeking to develop new medical treatments for blood disorders. Plaintiff's doctor subsequently recommended surgery to remove Plaintiff's spleen to slow the spread of disease. Before the operation, Defendants made an agreement to obtain portions of Plaintiff's spleen and take them to a separate research unit. Activities at the research unit were not intended to have any relation to Plaintiff's medical care. Defendants, however, did not inform Plaintiff of their plans to conduct this research, nor did they request his permission. Plaintiff consented to the operation, which was successfully performed. Subsequently, Defendants developed a valuable cell line from Plaintiff's blood components. They applied for (and received) a patent worth an estimated $500,000. Upon learning of this, Plaintiff sued Defendants for converting his blood components. If you were a judge, would let the claim proceed? *See Moore v. Regents of the University of California*, 793 P.2d 479 (Cal. 1990).

G. INTENTIONAL INFLICTION OF EMOTIONAL DISTRESS

So far, we have studied torts that protect personal integrity and property interests. At least with regard to the former, a plaintiff's damages easily could contain an emotional component. For example, a plaintiff in an assault action might base her damages on the degree of apprehension that she suffered due to the defendant's conduct. The law, however, has been hesitant to allow recovery for emotional distress *apart* from any invasion of a personal or property interest. In fact, it was not until about 100 years ago that courts began to allow recovery in such situations. The classic case is *Wilkinson v. Downton*, 2 Q.B.D 57 (1897), in which the defendant played a "practical joke" on the plaintiff by telling her that her husband had broken both of his legs in an accident and that she should go pick him up immediately. The "joke" severely distressed the plaintiff, and she suffered permanent physical consequences as a result. The court allowed the plaintiff to recover damages despite the fact that the case did not fit into any of the traditional trespassory actions.

In the early part of the twentieth century, American courts slowly began to follow the lead of *Wilkinson*. In 1948, the American Law Institute recognized an action for intentional infliction of emotional distress in the First Restatement of Torts. Today, the Restatement defines the action as follows: "One who by extreme and outrageous conduct intentionally or recklessly causes severe emotional distress to another is subject to liability for such emotional distress, and if bodily harm to the other results from it, for such bodily harm." RESTATEMENT (SECOND) OF TORTS § 46(1) (1965). Despite widespread recognition of this "new" cause of action for intentional infliction of emotional distress, the hurdles for a plaintiff remain high. The defendant's conduct must be "extreme and outrageous," and the plaintiff's distress must be "severe." The following two cases from the Maryland Court of Appeals are representative of how hard it is for a plaintiff to satisfy the standards.

FIGUEIREDO-TORRES v. NICKEL
584 A.2d 69 (Md. 1991)

CHASANOW, JUDGE.

Appellant Silvio Figueiredo-Torres (Torres) filed a complaint on March 2, 1989, in the Circuit Court for Montgomery County, against Appellee Herbert J. Nickel (Nickel) seeking damages for negligence [and] intentional infliction of emotional distress. The complaint alleged the following facts: In July 1985, Torres and his wife sought the counsel of Nickel, a licensed psychologist, for the purpose of preserving and improving their marital relationship. Most of the therapy sessions with Nickel were joint sessions attended by both Torres and his wife; however, Torres also attended some individual sessions with Nickel. Apparently, Nickel conducted individual sessions with Mrs. Torres as well, for the complaint maintains that, during the course of Nickel's treatment of Torres and his wife, Nickel commenced a romantic relationship with Mrs. Torres, engaging in "improper affectionate conduct" and "repeated sexual intercourse" with her, which culminated in the dissolution of the Torres' marriage. In therapy sessions with Torres, Nickel "consistently advised [him] to be distant from his wife, not to engage in intimate and/or sexual contact with her, and ultimately to separate from her." The complaint further alleged that, as a result of his psychologist-patient relationship with Torres, Nickel knew that Torres was particularly sensitive emotionally. Torres also set forth numerous injuries, both emotional and physical, and damages allegedly sustained as a result of Nickel's conduct.

Nickel [moved] to dismiss the complaint for failure to state a claim upon which relief can be granted. [The trial court granted the motion on the intentional infliction of emotional distress count.]

We recognized the tort of intentional infliction of emotional distress in *Harris v. Jones*, 281 Md. 560, 380 A.2d (1977). In that case, we set forth four elements essential to establish that cause of action:

(1) The conduct must be intentional or reckless;

(2) The conduct must be extreme and outrageous;

(3) There must be a causal connection between the wrongful conduct and the emotional distress;

(4) The emotional distress must be severe.

We emphasized that close adherence to these four elements would assure that "two problems which are inherent in recognizing a tort of this character can be minimized: (1) distinguishing the true from the false claim, and (2) distinguishing the trifling annoyance from the serious wrong." These inherent problems are of no less concern to us today; and we acknowledge the view expressed by Judge Bloom in *Hamilton v. Ford Motor Credit Co.*, 66 Md. App. 46, 61, 502 A.2d 1057, 1065, *cert. denied*, 306 Md. 118, 507 A.2d 631 (1986), that "[i]n developing the tort of intentional infliction of emotional distress, whatever the relationship between the parties, recovery will be meted out sparingly, its balm reserved for those wounds that are truly severe and incapable of healing themselves." With these qualifications firmly in mind, we consider Nickel's argument that Torres' complaint has not sufficiently plead the elements of extreme and outrageous conduct and severe emotional distress.

Torres avers that Nickel was a psychologist engaged to treat him for the purpose of bettering his mental and emotional health and to assist in resolving marital problems he was having with his wife. Despite the goals of this therapy and Nickel's knowledge that Torres was "particularly susceptible to emotional upset, anxiety and distress," Torres maintains that Nickel "developed a romantic relationship with [Torres'] wife, [and] engaged in improper affectionate conduct and repeated sexual intercourse with her." Nickel contends that, because Torres' wife was a consenting adult and sexual relations between consenting adults in modern society is not extreme and outrageous conduct, the intentional infliction of emotional distress count was properly dismissed. Nickel's analysis neglects one important detail. Nickel was not "the milkman, the mailman, or the guy next door"; he was Torres' psychologist and marriage counselor.

As we recognized in *Harris*, "the extreme and outrageous character of the defendant's conduct may arise from his abuse of a position, or relation with another person, which gives him actual or apparent authority over him, or power to affect his interests." 281 Md. at 569, 380 A.2d at 616 (citing RESTATE- MENT (SECOND) OF TORTS § 46 comment e (1965)). Furthermore, "[i]n cases where the defendant is in a peculiar position to harass the plaintiff, and cause emo- tional distress, his conduct will be carefully scrutinized by the courts." 281 Md. at 569, 380 A.2d at 615 (citing 1 F. HARPER & F. JAMES, JR., THE LAW OF TORTS § 9.1 at 666-67 (1956); W. PROSSER, HANDBOOK OF THE LAW OF TORTS § 12 at 56 (4th ed. 1971)). A psychologist-patient relationship, by its nature, focuses on the psyche of the patient; and a psychologist is in a unique position to influence the patient's emotional well-being. For this reason, a psychologist-patient rela- tionship falls squarely into the category of relationships which are carefully scrutinized by the courts. That is not to say that any patient who is unhappy with the results of psychotherapy has a cause of action against the therapist for intentional infliction of emotional distress; however, a jury may find extreme and outrageous conduct where a psychologist who is retained to improve a marital relationship implements a course of extreme conduct which is injurious to the patient and designed to facilitate a romantic, sexual relationship between the therapist and the patient's spouse.

In addition to the allegations of sexual misconduct, Torres further alleges that, despite his knowledge that Torres "was particularly susceptible to emotional upset, anxiety and distress" and "emotionally and mentally unstable," Nickel "demoralized [Torres] by making statements, and engaging in conduct that was destructive to [Torres'] ego development and self-respect," and "caused further and greater feelings of helplessness, discouragement, shame, guilt, fear and confusion by telling him he was a 'codfish' and that his wife deserved a 'fillet'; by telling him he had bad breath and should not go near his wife, and by falsely and systematically telling [Torres] that the deterioration of [Torres'] relationship with his wife was exclusively the result of [Torres'] conduct." As we stated in Harris, "'mere insults, indignities, threats, annoyances, petty oppressions, or other trivialities'" are insufficient to support a claim for intentional infliction of emotional distress, *Harris*, 281 Md. at 567, 380 A.2d at 614 (quoting RESTATE- MENT (SECOND) OF TORTS § 46 comment d). Nevertheless, we repeat our convic- tion that "[i]n determining whether conduct is extreme and outrageous, it should not be considered in a sterile setting, detached from the surroundings in which it occurred." Coming from a stranger, or even a friend, this conduct may not be outrageous; but we are not prepared to state as a matter of law that such behavior by a psychologist which takes advantage of the patient's known emo- tional problems is not extreme and outrageous conduct sufficient to support an intentional infliction of emotional distress claim.

As to the question of severity, Nickel argues that Torres "has not alleged that he has been unable to attend to his daily activities or that no person would be expected to endure such a situation." That degree of severity was found in *Moniodis v. Cook*, 64 Md. App. 1, 494 A.2d 212, *cert. denied*, 304 Md. 631, 500 A.2d 649 (1985), where the Court of Special Appeals upheld a verdict for inten- tional infliction of emotional distress. This Court has since discussed the degree of severity of emotional distress required to sustain a claim for intentional infliction of emotional distress in *B.N. v. K.K.*, 312 Md. 135, 538 A.2d 1175 (1988), a case posing the certified question "Does Maryland Recognize A Cause of Action for . . . Intentional Infliction of Emotional Distress, . . . Resulting From the Sexual Transmission Of A Dangerous, Contagious, and Incurable Disease, Such As Genital Herpes?" We stated,

> "We do not believe, however, that a showing like that in *Moniodis* is essential to recovery. While the emotional distress must be severe, it need not produce total emotional or physical disablement. . . . And severity must be measured in light of the outrageousness of the conduct and the other elements of the tort." (Citations omitted.)

Id. at 148, 538 A.2d at 1181-82 (quoting *Reagan v. Rider*, 70 Md. App. 503, 513, 521 A.2d 1246, 1251 (1987)).

The complaint in this case alleges that Torres suffered

> "systemic hypertension and loss of visual acuity in his left eye, required hospitalization for severe emotional distress, shock and fright to his nervous system; he suffered depression, anxiety, obsession . . . and impairment of his ability to form intimate relationships with women, all said injuries requiring psychological therapy and counseling; he lost the benefit received from prior psychological counseling. . . ."

While we are mindful that Torres must prove both that he suffered severe injury and that the injury was proximately caused by Nickel's tortious conduct, we believe that the complaint is sufficient to survive a [motion to dismiss for failure to state a claim upon which relief can be granted].

CALDOR, INC. v. BOWDEN
625 A.2d 959 (Md. 1993)

CHASANOW, JUDGE.

In March 1988, the respondent Samuel Bowden was sixteen years old when he applied for a position with Caldor, Inc., a national retail store. Caldor hired Bowden as a customer service representative and assigned him to its hardware department. In the early evening of June 15, 1988, Bowden arrived at Caldor to report for his 5:45 p.m. shift. Bowden went to punch in his time card and discovered that his time card was missing. He went to the acting store manager, Ms. Baldwin, to inquire about its absence. Baldwin, without further explanation, simply instructed Bowden to report to his normal post in the hardware department.

At approximately 6:45 p.m., Baldwin paged Bowden and instructed him to meet her at the upstairs customer service desk. Bowden ascended the escalator and met Baldwin at the customer service desk as instructed. Baldwin told Bowden that she needed his assistance and then led Bowden to a 10' x 10' window-less office on the upper level of the store.

Once inside, Bowden found Mr. Hedrick and Mr. Hodum, two of Caldor's loss prevention personnel, standing in the room. Bowden had not met either man before. The small office contained only a desk, two chairs, and a telephone. Hedrick greeted Bowden, instructed Bowden to sit down, and then closed the door, leaving Bowden alone with the two strangers.

Bowden was unaware why he was summoned to the upper-office. He asked Hedrick how long he would be there. According to Bowden, Hedrick replied "I don't think you'll be leaving anytime soon." Hedrick then sat down behind the desk and Hodum stood behind Bowden, blocking Bowden's potential egress from the small room. Hedrick asked Bowden a few casual questions about his personal life. Growing tired of the small talk and feeling the pressure of his sur-roundings, Bowden "bluntly" asked "what was my purpose for being in this room?" Hedrick replied that there had been some missing money and mer-chandise which had been traced back to Bowden.

Bowden denied this accusation and attempted to leave, but found Hodum blocking the door. Hedrick then stated "sit down or we'll help you sit down." Fearing reprisal, Bowden sat back down. When Bowden attempted to use the phone to contact his parents, his attempt was met by a similar, more emphatic, warning — Hedrick ordered Bowden "to put the damn phone down or [I'll] help [you] do it." On several occasions, Bowden could hear himself paged over the store's PA system. Bowden explained that his mother might be trying to contact him at the store and would be worried if she could not find him. Hedrick did not permit Bowden to respond and told Bowden that, if his mother called, they would tell her that Bowden was not in the store. This further disturbed Bowden.

Hedrick began interrogating Bowden. According to Bowden, Hedrick "kept drilling" him about the missing money. The series of accusations and denials went back and forth. The men forced Bowden to empty his pockets and reveal the contents of his wallet. Hedrick told Bowden that they had videotapes show-ing him stealing money from the registers and that he would not be permitted to leave until he cooperated.

The interrogation continued until approximately 8:00 p.m., when Hedrick placed a blank "voluntary statement" form in front of Bowden. Hedrick then told Bowden that he wanted a written statement from him admitting that he had taken amounts of money on a number of occasions. He told Bowden that if he signed the form, made restitution, and did not involve his parents that Caldor would not contact the police. Out of fear, Bowden gave in to Hedrick's demand. On the first side of the form, Hedrick dictated the terms of Bowden's "admis-sion," specifying the dates and amounts of money. Bowden finally signed the first side at 9:35 p.m. After Bowden completed the first side of the page, Hedrick left the room for thirty or forty minutes. Upon Hedrick's return, Bowden realized that the store was closed and all of the store lights were off. Hedrick then dictated the terms of the second side of the form, which Bowden signed. Hedrick told Bowden to return the next day and repay the money. Around 11:00 p.m., over four hours after Bowden was first summoned to the upstairs office, Hedrick allowed Bowden to leave the store.

Bowden arrived home at 11:30 p.m., an hour later than usual. Bowden's mother met him at the door and demanded an explanation for his tardiness. Bowden told his mother what had happened and denied stealing any money.

Bowden and his mother returned to Caldor the next afternoon. They went to the upstairs manager's office and asked to talk with Hedrick. Mrs. Bowden was informed that Hedrick had left the store. Instead, Mrs. Bowden spoke with Mr. Mehan, the store's security manager, and Mr. Forrester, another store manager, to inquire about the prior night's activities and to attempt "to get to the bottom of things." An argument ensued and, according to Bowden, Forrester barked "You people — you n_____ boys make me sick, but you're going to burn for this, you sucker." Bowden further testified that Mehan's only response to the exchange was "sort of a smirk" indicating his agreement with the remark.

Bowden and his mother left the store and returned to their car. Mehan followed them into the parking lot, approached them, and told Bowden that he could not leave. Mehan then seized Bowden's arm and forced him to return to the store through the rear employee entrance. Mehan led Bowden back to his office on the ground floor.

Mrs. Bowden followed Mehan and her son back to Mehan's office, where she called her husband, Reverend Horace Bowden. Rev. Bowden and Mehan discussed the events on the telephone, and Mehan demanded restitution. When Rev. Bowden asked to see the videotapes before making restitution, Mehan refused and stated that he had no other choice but to arrest Bowden and then hung up. Mehan handcuffed Bowden and called the Baltimore County Police. Mehan then escorted the handcuffed Bowden across the lower level of the store, up the escalators, and led him from the back of the upper level to the front door. Bowden remained in handcuffs in public view until the police arrived.

Bowden then filed a civil suit in the Circuit Court for Baltimore City, naming Caldor, Hedrick, Hodum, and Mehan as defendants. The complaint alleged [several counts, including one for] intentional infliction of emotional distress. The case was tried before a jury, and on August 20, 1991, the jury rendered a decision in favor of Bowden. The jury awarded [him] $25,000 for intentional infliction of emotional distress.

The defendants filed a motion for judgment not withstanding the verdict/remittitur and/or for a new trial. The circuit court granted the motion for J.N.W.V. on [plaintiff's] intentional infliction of emotional distress count. Bowden and the defendants appealed and we granted certiorari prior to the appeal being argued in the intermediate appellate court.

In 1977, this Court recognized the tort of intentional infliction of emotional distress in *Harris v. Jones*, 281 Md. 560, 380 A.2d 611 (1977). [The court then set out the elements of the claim.] *Harris* cautioned that courts must assure that each of the four elements of the tort are established by legally adequate proof. *Harris* and our subsequent cases have also noted "two problems which are inherent in recognizing a tort of this character . . . (1) distinguishing the true from the false claim, and (2) distinguishing the trifling annoyance from the serious wrong." In addition, we have made it clear that liability for the tort of intentional infliction of emotional distress should be imposed sparingly, and "'its balm reserved for those wounds that are truly severe and incapable of healing themselves.'" *Figueiredo-Torres*, 321 Md. at 653, 584 A.2d at 75 (quoting *Hamilton v. Ford Motor Credit Co.*, 66 Md. App. 46, 61, 502 A.2d 1057, 1065, *cert. denied*, 306 Md. 118, 507 A.2d 631 (1986)).

At the trial, Bowden testified about the mental and psychological effects he experienced after the incident. According to Bowden's testimony, he was distraught and worried; he "was hurt a lot" and felt ashamed because his peers saw him being removed from Caldor in handcuffs. Bowden also testified that he tended not to socialize as much as before, kept to himself, and did not trust others very readily. He stated that he was able, however, to continue his normal activities. He further testified that the incident did not affect his schoolwork; he continued playing baseball for his high school team and obtained other employment soon thereafter. In short, Bowden continued doing the same things that he did prior to the incident but just had "a different outlook." Bowden's "sadness" and insecurity continued for more than a year and as a result he paid one visit to a psychologist in the winter of 1990. At trial Bowden only introduced the psychologist's intake form and did not call the psychologist as a witness. In the intake form Bowden complained of weight loss over the past four months and reported that he felt "sad," "confused," and "bad about himself." The intake form did not contain any of the psychologist's conclusions; it only reported Bowden's own complaints. Bowden testified that he visited the psychologist only once because of his time commitments to both school and extracurricular activities. Bowden presented no expert testimony about his emotional distress.

At the hearing on the defendants' motion for J.N.W.V., the defendants argued that Bowden failed to establish the four elements of the intentional infliction of emotional distress cause of action. Specifically, the defendants focused on the severity of distress element and asserted that "the Plaintiff failed to establish the type of severe emotional distress necessary to establish a prima facie case of intentional infliction. . . ." Bowden's only response was that "I can't think of anything that [could be] as severe as the basic personality of a person being changed." The circuit court disagreed with Bowden and granted the defendants' motion for J.N.W.V. on this count. The circuit court found that "from the circumstances here [the emotional distress that was suffered,] was not the kind that the Court of Appeals contemplates to meet the standards of this tort." We agree.

The severity of the emotional distress is not only relevant to the amount of recovery, but is a necessary element to any recovery. *Harris*, 281 Md. at 570, 380 A.2d at 616. For emotional distress to be severe, it must be so acute that "'no reasonable man could be expected to endure it.'" *Id.* at 571, 380 A.2d at 616 (quoting RESTATEMENT (SECOND) OF TORTS § 46 cmt. j (1965)). We measure such severity by the intensity of the response as well as its duration. *Id.*

Although there is no clearly defined bright-line test for severe emotional distress, the trial judge did not err in concluding that there was legally insufficient evidence at trial from which a jury could properly have concluded that Bowden suffered the sort of emotional harm required in Harris and our subsequent line of cases. Bowden may have been "upset," "embarrassed," and "confused," and may have "felt bad about himself"; and this type of emotional distress may have been uncomfortable. None of these effects, however, indicate that Bowden had the severely disabling emotional response that hindered his ability to carry out his daily activities or the severe emotional distress this cause of action requires. [Rather,] [t]he evidence may have shown that Bowden was distressed, but it failed to establish the level of severe or extreme emotional injury that is needed to trigger liability for this tort. Not only did Bowden continue his normal activities, but he did not seek psychological assistance until his single visit on the eve of litigation. Bowden presented no expert testimony as to any emotional distress and his own description of his discomfort was insufficient to establish severe emotional distress. As a result, we affirm the circuit court's grant of J.N.W.V. on the count of intentional infliction of emotional distress.

NOTES

1. Do you agree with the decision in *Caldor*? Consider the following passage from Judge Eldridge's dissenting opinion:

> The majority opinion characterizes Samuel's emotional distress as "uncomfortable." I suggest that if the same thing had happened to most people, the resulting distress would have been considered more than "uncomfortable." The testimony disclosed that Caldor's conduct produced in Samuel very strong and debilitating negative emotions: shame, humiliation, embarrassment, nervousness, worry, distress, sadness, insecurity, distrust, confusion, and inferiority. Samuel suffered from these debilitating emotions for over a year, and is still affected to some degree. Under the evidence, the jury was entitled to draw the inference that Samuel's emotional distress was much more severe than "uncomfortable."

625 A.2d at 977 (Eldridge, J., dissenting). Does Judge Eldridge convince you that the majority was wrong? Can you distinguish the majority opinion in *Caldor* from *Figueiredo-Torres*?

2. Might the plaintiff in *Caldor* succeed on any other intentional tort claims? How about false imprisonment?

3. Both *Caldor* and *Figueiredo-Torres* focus on whether the plaintiff suffered from sufficiently severe emotional distress, instead of on whether the defendant's conduct was sufficiently outrageous. The emphasis in these cases, however, should not lead you to believe that the outrageous conduct element of a plaintiff's case is insignificant. In general, a defendant's conduct must be "so outrageous in character, and so extreme in degree, as to go beyond all possible bounds of decency, and to be regarded as atrocious, and utterly intolerable in a civilized community." RESTATEMENT (SECOND) OF TORTS § 46 comment c (1965). This means that mere insults, cursing, or even making sexist comments generally will not support an intentional infliction case. Instead, courts require a higher degree of misconduct — and one that frequently relates to the relationship of the parties. *See* DOBBS, THE LAW OF TORTS § 304 at 826-27. For example, courts are more willing to find a defendant's conduct outrageous where the defendant is taking advantage of a plaintiff's vulnerabilities (as in *Figueiredo-Torres*) or where the defendant is in a position of power over the plaintiff (as in *Caldor*). A recent (and high profile) example of a case that came out the other way is *Jones v. Clinton*, 990 F. Supp. 657 (E.D. Ark. 1998). In *Jones*, Paula Jones claimed that President Clinton, while governor of Arkansas, made flagrant sexual advances toward her while she was an Arkansas state employee. Jones filed a lawsuit against Clinton, claiming that he violated federal sexual harassment laws. She also sued Clinton for intentional infliction of emotional distress. Despite Clinton's powerful position, the court found that Jones did not plead outrageous conduct.

> The tort is clearly not intended to provide legal redress for every slight insult or indignity that one must endure. The Arkansas courts take a strict approach and give a narrow view to claims of outrage, and merely describing conduct as outrageous does not make it so.
>
> * * *
>
> While the Court will certainly agree that plaintiff's allegations describe offensive conduct, . . . [it] describes a mere sexual proposition or encounter, albeit an odious one, that was relatively brief in duration, did not involve any coercion or threats of reprisal, and was abandoned as soon as plaintiff made clear that the advance was not welcome. The Court is not aware of any authority holding that such a sexual encounter or proposition of the type alleged in this case, without more, gives rise to a claim of outrage.

990 F. Supp. at 677. How much "more" would be enough? What if Clinton had been Jones' direct supervisor? What if he offered to promote her if she complied? Or demote her if she did not? Would the conduct then be outrageous?

4. An interesting part of the Restatement's definition of intentional infliction of emotional distress is its apparent loosening of the intent requirement. Re-read

section 46 in the introductory note to this section carefully: A defendant who engages in extreme and outrageous conduct is liable if the conduct "intentionally *or recklessly* causes severe emotional distress to another. . . ." (Emphasis added.) The comments to the Restatement elaborate on the point:

> The rule stated in this Section applies where the actor desires to inflict severe emotional distress, and also where he knows that such distress is certain or substantially certain, to result from his conduct. *It applies also where he acts recklessly . . . in complete disregard of a high degree of probability that the emotional distress will follow.*

RESTATEMENT (SECOND) OF TORTS § 46 comment i (1965) (emphasis added). Why would the Restatement suggest loosening the intent requirement in the newest intentional tort, and the one that would appear to pose the greatest threat of abuse in the judicial system?

5. Does the concept of transferred intent apply in an intentional infliction of emotional distress case? Almost every court that has considered a fact pattern in which the rule might be applied has declined to do so. *See, e.g., Taylor v. Vallelunga*, 339 P.2d 910 (Cal. Ct. App. 1959) (daughter cannot recover emotional distress damages after witnessing defendants beat her father because there was "no allegation that defendants knew that [daughter] was present and witnessed the beating that was administered for the purpose of causing her to suffer emotional distress. . . ."). Prosser and Keeton suggest that the reason behind courts' refusals to extend transferred intent to intentional infliction cases is "that emotional distress did not fall within the framework of the old action of trespass where 'transferred intent' arose. . . ." PROSSER AND KEETON ON TORTS § 12 at 65. Is this alone a sufficient reason to refuse to extend the doctrine? What arguments might be made for and against the application of transferred intent to an intentional infliction claim?

6. Because intentional infliction of emotional distress cases frequently involve harm caused by what a defendant says to a plaintiff, the cases sometimes implicate freedom of speech issues. The constitutional protection of speech is covered later in the book. *See* Chapter 17. It is worth noting here, however, that when the target of offensive speech is a public figure, the United States Supreme Court has been willing to apply constitutional protections in intentional infliction of emotional distress cases. For example, in *Hustler Magazine v. Falwell*, 485 U.S. 46 (1988), the Reverend Jerry Falwell sued Hustler Magazine for intentional infliction of emotional distress after the magazine published an ad parody portraying Falwell as engaging in an incestuous relationship with his mother. A jury found in Falwell's favor, but the Court overturned the verdict on grounds that the offensive speech was constitutionally protected under the First Amendment.

PROBLEMS

1. Mere insults between normal adults do not normally constitute outrageous conduct for purposes of intentional infliction of emotional distress. Should the rule change if an adult insults a young child? How about an adult insulting an emotionally-fragile elderly person?

2. To what extent is the relationship between the parties important in establishing a cause of action? Suppose that Alex has a stuttering problem. One of Alex's professors teases her about the problem in class. Is the professor's conduct outrageous? What if a teaching assistant teases Alex? How about a classmate?

3. As mentioned in Note 3, a plaintiff can succeed in an intentional infliction action by showing that the defendant was reckless with regard to his emotional well-being. How much does this liberalize the normal intent standard? Suppose that Carla plays a prank on Brad by placing a realistic-looking plastic spider on his desk while Brad is away. Brad has a morbid fear of spiders and suffers severe distress after returning to his desk and viewing the plastic spider. Setting aside the issue of whether Carla's conduct was outrageous, can we say that she intended to cause Brad's severe distress? Was Carla "reckless" in this regard?

4. Same facts as above, except Shari stops at Brad's desk before Brad returns, and Shari is the person who suffers severe emotional distress. Does Shari have a stronger or weaker intentional infliction case than Brad had in the previous problem? Why?

Chapter 3
DEFENSES TO INTENTIONAL TORTS

A. INTRODUCTION

In the last chapter, we focused on the elements for each intentional tort. But, even those plaintiffs who establish a prima facie case are not automatically entitled to compensation. Defendants may try to justify their conduct through the use of various defenses. This means that even if a plaintiff proves all of the elements of her claim, a defendant can avoid liability by proving a different set of facts to support the defense. In this chapter, we will study the major defenses to intentional torts: Consent, self defense, defense of others, defense of property, and necessity.

B. CONSENT

Consent is a defense to an intentional tort claim. The defense derives from the common law principle *volenti non fit injuria* — to one who is willing, no wrong is done. PROSSER AND KEETON ON TORTS § 18 at 112. Consent poses few complications when a plaintiff verbally expresses assent to an otherwise tortious invasion. For example, if you point to your nose and tell your classmate to "go ahead and hit me," you will not be able to maintain a battery action if he accepts your invitation.

But consent extends beyond verbal expressions. For example, a plaintiff may communicate consent by actions as well as words. The famous case of *O'Brien v. Cunard Steamship Co.*, 28 N.E. 266 (Mass. 1891), demonstrates this principle. In *O'Brien*, the plaintiff silently extended her arm toward a doctor to receive a smallpox vaccination that was required for her entry into the United States. The plaintiff later claimed that she did not want the shot, and she sued the doctor for battery. The trial court directed a verdict in favor of the doctor, and the Supreme Judicial Court of Massachusetts affirmed:

> In determining whether the act was lawful or unlawful, the surgeon's conduct must be considered in connection with the surrounding circumstances. If the plaintiff's behavior was such as to indicate consent on her part, he was justified in his act, whatever her unexpressed feelings.
>
> * * *
>
> There was nothing in the conduct of the plaintiff to indicate to the surgeon that she did not wish to obtain a card which would save her from detention at quarantine, and to be vaccinated, if necessary for that purpose. Viewing his conduct in the light of the surrounding circumstances,

it was lawful; and there was not evidence tending to show that it was not.

28 N.E at 273-74. *O'Brien* is a relatively simple example of how one may demonstrate consent in a non-verbal fashion. Not all cases, however, are so easy. Consider the following case in thinking about the types of complications that can arise when a defendant raises the consent defense.

PETERSON v. SORLIEN
299 N.W.2d 123 (Minn. 1980)

SHERAN, CHIEF JUSTICE.

This action by plaintiff Susan Jungclaus Peterson for false imprisonment arises from an effort by her parents, in conjunction with other [named] defendants, to prompt her disaffiliation from an organization known as The Way Ministry. [The jury returned a verdict in favor of Susan's parents and the other defendants. The trial court denied Susan's motion for judgment notwithstanding the verdict.] [W]e affirm the determination of the district court.

Viewing the evidence in the light most favorable to the prevailing defendants, this case marks the emergence of a new cultural phenomenon: youth-oriented religious or psuedo-religious groups which utilize the techniques of what has been termed "coercive persuasion" or "mind control" to cultivate an uncritical and devoted following.

At the time of the events in question, Susan Jungclaus Peterson was 21 years old. For most of her life, she lived with her family on a farm near Bird Island, Minnesota. In 1973, she graduated with honors from high school, ranking second in her class. She matriculated that fall at Moorhead State College. A dean's list student during her first year, her academic performance declined and her interests narrowed after she joined the local chapter of a group organized internationally and identified locally as The Way of Minnesota, Inc.

The operation of The Way is predicated on the fund-raising activities of its members. The Way's fund-raising strategy centers upon the sale of pre-recorded learning programs. Members are instructed to elicit the interest of a group of ten or twelve people and then play for them, at a charge of $85 per participant, a taped introductory course produced by The Way International. Advanced tape courses are then offered to the participants at additional cost, and training sessions are conducted to more fully acquaint recruits with the orientation of the group and the obligations of membership. Recruits must contribute a minimum of 10 percent of their earnings to the organization; to meet the tithe, student members are expected to obtain part-time employment. Members are also required to purchase books and other materials published by the ministry, and are encouraged to make larger financial contributions and to engage in more sustained efforts at solicitation.

By the end of her freshman year, Susan was devoting many hours to The Way, listening to instructional tapes, soliciting new members and assisting in training sessions. As her sophomore year began, Susan committed herself significantly, selling the car her father had given her and working part-time as a waitress to finance her contributions to The Way. Susan spent the following summer in South Dakota, living in conditions described as appalling and overcrowded, while recruiting, raising money and conducting training sessions for The Way.

As her junior year in college drew to a close, the Jungclauses grew increasingly alarmed by the personality changes they witnessed in their daughter; overly tired, unusually pale, distraught and irritable, she exhibited an increasing alienation from family, diminished interest in education and decline in academic performance. The Jungclauses, versed in the literature of youth cults and based on conversations with former members of The Way, concluded that through a calculated process of manipulation and exploitation Susan had been reduced to a condition of psychological bondage.

On May 24, 1976, defendant Norman Jungclaus, father of plaintiff, arrived at Moorhead to pick up Susan following the end of the third college quarter. Instead of returning to their family home, defendant drove with Susan to Minneapolis to the home of Veronica Morgel. Entering the home of Mrs. Morgel, Susan was greeted by Kathy Mills and several young people who wished to discuss Susan's involvement in the ministry. Each of those present had been in some way touched by the cult phenomenon. Kathy Mills, the leader of the group, had treated a number of former cult members, including Veronica Morgel's son. It was Kathy Mills, a self-styled professional deprogrammer, to whom the Jungclauses turned, and intermittently for the next sixteen days, it was in the home of Veronica Morgel that Susan stayed.

The avowed purpose of deprogramming is to break the hold of the cult over the individual through reason and confrontation. Initially, Susan was unwilling to discuss her involvement; she lay curled in a fetal position, in the downstairs bedroom where she first stayed, plugging her ears and crying while her father pleaded with her to listen to what was being said. This behavior persisted for two days during which she intermittently engaged in conversation, at one point screaming hysterically and flailing at her father. But by Wednesday Susan's demeanor had changed completely; she was friendly and vivacious and that night slept in an upstairs bedroom. Susan spent all day Thursday reading and conversing with her father and on Saturday night went roller-skating. On Sunday she played softball at a nearby park, afterwards enjoying a picnic lunch. The next week Susan spent in Columbus, Ohio, flying there with a former cult member who had shared with her the experiences of the previous week. While in Columbus, she spoke every day by telephone to her fiancé who, playing tapes and songs from the ministry's headquarters in Minneapolis, begged that she return to the fold. Susan expressed the desire to extricate her fiancé from the dominion of the cult.

Susan returned to Minneapolis on June 9. Unable to arrange a controlled meeting so that Susan could see her fiancé outside the presence of other members of the ministry, her parents asked that she sign an agreement releasing them from liability for their past weeks' actions. Refusing to do so, Susan [left the Morgel's residence,] motioned to a passing police car and shortly thereafter was reunited with her fiancé in the Minneapolis headquarters of The Way. Following her return to the ministry, she was directed to counsel and initiated the present action.

Plaintiff seeks a judgment notwithstanding the verdict on the issue of false imprisonment, alleging that defendants unlawfully interfered with her personal liberty by words or acts which induced a reasonable apprehension that force would be used against her if she did not otherwise comply. The jury, instructed that an informed and reasoned consent is a defense to an allegation of false imprisonment and that a nonconsensual detention could be deemed consensual if one's behavior so indicated, exonerated defendants with respect to the false imprisonment claim.

The period in question began on Monday, May 24, 1976, and ceased on Wednesday, June 9, 1976, a period of 16 days. The record clearly demonstrates that Susan willingly remained in the company of defendants for at least 13 of those days. During that time she took many excursions into the public sphere, playing softball and picnicking in a city park, roller-skating at a public rink, flying aboard public aircraft and shopping and swimming while relaxing in Ohio. Had Susan desired, manifold opportunities existed for her to alert the authorities of her allegedly unlawful detention; in Minneapolis, two police officers observed at close range the softball game in which she engaged; en route to Ohio, she passed through the security areas of the Twin Cities and Columbus airports in the presence of security guards and uniformed police; in Columbus she transacted business at a bank, went for walks in solitude and was interviewed by an F.B.I. agent who sought assurances of her safety. At no time during the 13-day period did she complain of her treatment or suggest that defendants were holding her against her will. Damages may not be assessed for any period of detention to which one freely consents.

In his summation to the jury, the trial judge instructed that to deem consent a defense to the charge of false imprisonment for the entire period or for any part therein, a preponderance of the evidence must demonstrate that such plaintiff voluntarily consented. The central issue for the jury, then, was whether Susan voluntarily participated in the activities of the first three days. The jury concluded that her behavior constituted a waiver.

We believe the determination to have been consistent with the evidence. Were the relationship other than that of parent and child, the consent would have less significance.

To determine whether the findings of the jury can be supported upon review, the behavior Susan manifested during the initial three days at issue must be considered in light of her actions in the remainder of the period. Because, it is argued, the cult conditioning process induces dramatic and non-consensual change giving rise to a new temporary identity on the part of the individuals whose consent is under examination, Susan's volitional capacity prior to treatment may well have been impaired. Following her readjustment, the evidence suggests that Susan was a different person, "like her old self." As such, the question of Susan's consent becomes a function of time. We therefore deem Susan's subsequent affirmation of defendants' actions dispositive.

In light of our examination of the record and rules of construction providing that upon review the evidence must be viewed in a manner most favorable to the prevailing party, we find that a reasonable basis existed for the verdict exonerating defendants of the charge of false imprisonment. Although carried out under colorably religious auspices, the method of cult indoctrination, viewed in a light most favorable to the prevailing party, is predicated on a strategy of coercive persuasion that undermines the capacity for informed consent. While we acknowledge that other social institutions may utilize a degree of coercion in promoting their objectives, none do so to the same extent or intend the same consequences. Society, therefore, has a compelling interest favoring intervention. The facts in this case support the conclusion that plaintiff only regained her volitional capacity to consent after engaging in the first three days of the deprogramming process. As such, we hold that when parents, or their agents, acting under the conviction that the judgmental capacity of their adult child is impaired, seek to extricate that child from what they reasonably believe to be a religious or psuedo-religious cult, and the child at some juncture assents to the actions in question, limitations upon the child's mobility do not constitute meaningful deprivations of personal liberty sufficient to support a judgment for false imprisonment.

WAHL, JUSTICE (dissenting in part).

I must respectfully dissent. In every generation, parents have viewed their children's religious and political beliefs with alarm and dismay if those beliefs were different from their own. [H]owever, adults in our society enjoy freedoms of association and belief. In my view, it is unwise to tamper with those freedoms and with longstanding principles of tort law out of sympathy for parents seeking to help their "misguided" offspring, however well-intentioned and loving their acts may be. Whether or not, as the majority opinion asserts, The Way of Minnesota, Inc. is a "youth-oriented," "pseudo-religious group" which pursues its "fundraising strategy" in such a way as to inflict physical and psychological harm on its members, emphasis on this characterization beclouds the purely legal issues which are presented by this appeal.

The first of those legal issues is whether, as a matter of law, any of the defendants in this case are guilty of false imprisonment of the plaintiff. The elements of the tort of false imprisonment are (1) words or acts by defendant intended to confine plaintiff, (2) actual confinement, and (3) awareness by plaintiff that she is being confined. [T]he fact that the tortfeasor acted in good faith is no defense to a charge of false imprisonment. Thus, although the majority opinion correctly concludes that evidence concerning the activities of The Way and the impact of those activities upon plaintiff may have been relevant to the question of whether defendants acted so willfully and maliciously as to justify an award of punitive damages, such evidence has little bearing on the issue of defendants' liability for false imprisonment.

The unrebutted evidence shows that defendant Norman Jungclaus, the father of the 21-year-old plaintiff in this case, took his adult daughter, kicking and screaming, to a small bedroom in the basement of the Morgel home on Monday, May 23. Norman Jungclaus admitted that she did not go with him willingly. Plaintiff curled up on the bed, plugged her ears, and cried. Defendant Perkins testified that plaintiff screamed and cried and pleaded with several people to let her go, but her pleas were ignored. This situation continued until 3 a.m. Tuesday. At one point that morning, plaintiff flew at her father, and he held her arms around her from the back, in his words, "for maybe a half an hour, until she calmed down again." Plaintiff testified that defendant Mills told her papers had been drafted to commit her to Anoka State Hospital if she continued to refuse to cooperate with the "deprogramming."

The majority opinion finds, in plaintiff's behavior during the remainder of the 16-day period of "deprogramming," a reasonable basis for acquitting defendant Jungclaus of the false imprisonment charge for the initial three days, during which time he admittedly held plaintiff against her will. Under this theory, plaintiff's "acquiescence" in the later stages of deprogramming operates as consent which "relates back" to the events of the earlier three days, and constitutes a "waiver" of her claims for those days.

Certainly, parents who disapprove of or disagree with the religious beliefs of their adult offspring are free to exercise their own First Amendment rights in an attempt, by speech and persuasion without physical restraints, to change their adult children's minds. But parents who engage in tortious conduct in their "deprogramming" attempts do so at the risk that the deprogramming will be unsuccessful and the adult children will pursue tort remedies against their parents. To allow parents' "conviction that the judgmental capacity of their (adult) child is impaired (by her religious indoctrination)" to excuse their tortious conduct sets a dangerous precedent.

Here, the evidence clearly supported a verdict against Norman Jungclaus on the false imprisonment claim, and no reasonable basis existed for denying judgment notwithstanding the verdict. The trial court's holding in this regard should be reversed.

NOTES

1. Does the court's holding reflect a decision by the majority that Susan could not effectively consent to confinement during the initial three-day period?

Courts have held that plaintiffs must have sufficient mental capacity to consent to a tortious invasion of interests. For example, minors, intoxicated persons, and those with mental disabilities cannot effectively consent to an intentional tort. *See* DOBBS, THE LAW OF TORTS § 98 at 224; RESTATEMENT (SECOND) OF TORTS § 892 (1979). But was Susan really mentally incapacitated? If so, should that incapacity negate a *lack* of consent? Justice Wahl, in his dissent, thought not on both counts. Do you agree with Justice Wahl? Or do you agree with the majority opinion?

2. The issue of consent often arises in cases involving medical treatment. Traditionally, doctors who performed operations without fully informing patients of the risks associated with the procedure were liable for battery. Today, however, most courts deal with such "informed consent" cases under negligence theory. *See Spinosa v. Weinstein*, 571 N.Y.S.2d 747, 753 (N.Y. App. Div. 1991). Nevertheless, courts may still recognize a battery claim in "nonexigent situations involving no consent at all." *Id.* (citing *Rigie v. Goldman*, 543 N.Y.S.2d 983 (N.Y. App. Div. 1989); *Oates v. New York Hospital*, 517 N.Y.S.2d 6 (N.Y. App. Div. 1987)). As a practical matter, most patients today sign consent forms before undergoing medical procedures. Even so, disputes may arise over the sufficiency of such forms. For example, in *Distefano v. Bell*, 544 So. 2d 567 (La. Ct. App. 1989), a patient sued her doctor for complications that arose after the doctor performed surgery on her nose. The doctor raised consent as a defense, arguing that the patient had signed the necessary surgical consent forms. The court, however, found the forms insufficient: "Although the forms state that the plaintiff was given sufficient information concerning the surgery, the forms do not contain any information concerning possible complications of surgery. As such, the written consent forms fail . . . and accordingly no presumption of validity of consent arises." *Id.* at 570.

PROBLEMS

1. What if the defendant misleads the plaintiff or tricks her into consent? In *Doe v. Johnson*, 817 F. Supp. 1382 (W.D. Mich. 1993), "Jane Doe" engaged in consensual sex with Earvin Johnson, Jr. Doe later learned that Johnson was infected with HIV at the time, and she alleged that Johnson had transmitted the virus to her. Doe sued Johnson under a variety of theories, including battery. Johnson moved to dismiss, arguing that Doe had consented to the contact. How would you rule on the motion? What policies support your decision?

2. What if the defendant in a case like *Doe* did not have a sexually-transmissible disease, but instead impregnated the plaintiff after falsely telling her that he was sterile? Should the plaintiff have a viable cause of action? *See Barbara A. v. John G.*, 193 Cal. Rptr. 422 (Cal. Ct. App. 1983).

3. Should the existence of criminal laws impact a court's decision on intent in a tort action? Suppose that Paula is a mature-looking 15-year-old who has obtained a phony driver's license that identifies her as 21 years old. Paula used

the phony license to obtain entrance to a nightclub, where she met 21-year-old Daniel. Paula and Daniel later engaged in consensual sexual relations. Subsequently, Paula sued Daniel for battery. The jurisdiction in which Paula and Daniel live has a "statutory rape" law, making it a crime for a man to have sexual intercourse with a girl below the age of 16. Can Daniel effectively use the defense of consent?

4. Note 2 described the rule of "informed consent" in cases involving medical treatment. This rule, however, would not prevent a doctor from treating a patient when it would be impractical to obtain consent. For example, a doctor can treat a person under emergency circumstances where neither the patient nor an appropriate guardian or agent can make the decision for the patient. DOBBS, THE LAW OF TORTS § 106 at 247. But how far should this go? Suppose plaintiff consented to have a doctor perform an appendectomy. While doing the operation, the doctor noticed, and then punctured, enlarged cysts on one of the plaintiff's ovaries. Plaintiff later alleged that, while puncturing the cysts, the doctor cut a blood vessel and caused her to suffer from further medical complications. Plaintiff then sued for battery, arguing that she had not consented to the puncturing of the cysts. Was this an "emergency" situation that permitted the doctor to perform the procedure without obtaining consent from the patient? *See Kennedy v. Parrott*, 90 S.E.2d 754 (N.C. 1956).

5. What if a patient consents to have one doctor perform surgery on her, but another doctor is substituted after the patient is under anesthesia? Assuming the surgery is well-performed, does the patient have a battery action?

6. Should a doctor be able to treat a patient without her consent if doing so would benefit others who depend on her? In *In re Dubreuil*, 629 So. 2d 819 (Fla. 1994), a doctor determined that a pregnant woman needed a blood transfusion as part of a Caesarean section procedure. The mother refused, based on her beliefs as a Jehovah's Witness. Hospital officials obtained the consent of the mother's estranged husband (and father of her three children), and the doctor gave the mother the transfusion. The hospital later obtained an order from a trial court to continue transfusions over the mother's objections, based on the state's interest in having her care for her minor children. Was the trial court right in issuing the order? Would you allow the mother to make the same decision for a child if the child needed a blood transfusion?

7. To what extent do participants in athletic events consent to contact? According to the Restatement of Torts:

> Taking part in a game manifests a willingness to submit to such bodily contacts or restrictions of liberty as are permitted by its rules or usages. Participating in such a game does not manifest consent to contacts which are prohibited by rules and usages of the game if such rules and usages are designed to protect the participants and not merely to secure the better playing of the game as a test of skill. This is true although the

player knows that those with or against whom he is playing are habitual violators of such rules.

RESTATEMENT (SECOND) OF TORTS § 50, comment b (1965). Does this mean that when a competitor in an athletic event violates a rule and harms another player, the player can maintain a tort action? Consider the following case.

HACKBART v. CINCINNATI BENGALS, INC.
601 F.2d 516 (10th Cir. 1979)

DOYLE, CIRCUIT JUDGE.

The question in this case is whether in a regular season professional football game an injury which is inflicted by one professional football player on an opposing player can give rise to liability in tort where the injury was inflicted by the intentional striking of a blow during the game.

The injury occurred in the course of a game between the Denver Broncos and the Cincinnati Bengals, which game was being played in Denver in 1973. The Broncos' defensive back, Dale Hackbart, was the recipient of the injury and the Bengals' offensive back, Charles "Booby" Clark, inflicted the blow which produced it.

Clark was an offensive back and just before the injury he had run a pass pattern to the right side of the Denver Broncos' end zone. The injury flowed indirectly from this play. The pass was intercepted by Billy Thompson, a Denver free safety, who returned it to mid-field. The subject injury occurred as an aftermath of the pass play.

As a consequence of the interception, the roles of Hackbart and Clark suddenly changed. Hackbart, who had been defending, instantaneously became an offensive player. Clark, on the other hand, became a defensive player. Acting as an offensive player, Hackbart attempted to block Clark by throwing his body in front of him. He thereafter remained on the ground. He turned, and with one knee on the ground, watched the play following the interception.

The trial [court found] that Charles Clark, "acting out of anger and frustration, but without a specific intent to injure [stepped] forward and struck a blow with his right forearm to the back of the kneeling plaintiff's head and neck with sufficient force to cause both players to fall forward to the ground." Both players, without complaining to the officials or to one another, returned to their respective sidelines since the ball had changed hands and the offensive and defensive teams of each had been substituted. Clark testified at trial that his frustration was brought about by the fact that his team was losing the game.

Due to the failure of the officials to view the incident, a foul was not called. However, the game film showed very clearly what had occurred. Plaintiff did not at the time report the happening to his coaches or to anyone else during the game. However, because of the pain which he experienced he was unable to play golf the next day. He did not seek medical attention, but the continued pain caused him to report this fact and the incident to the Bronco trainer who gave him treatment. Apparently he played on the specialty teams for two successive Sundays, but after that the Broncos released him on waivers. (He was in his thirteenth year as a player.) He sought medical help and it was then that it was discovered by the physician that he had a serious neck fracture injury.

Despite the fact that the defendant Charles Clark admitted that the blow which had been struck was not accidental, that it was intentionally administered, the trial court ruled as a matter of law that the game of professional football is basically a business which is violent in nature, and that the available sanctions are imposition of penalties and expulsion from the game. Notice was taken of the fact that many fouls are overlooked; that the game is played in an emotional and noisy environment; and that incidents such as that here complained of are not unusual.

Contrary to the position of the court[,] there are no principles of law which allow a court to rule out certain tortious conduct by reason of general roughness of the game or difficulty of administering it.

Indeed, the evidence shows that there are rules of the game which prohibit the intentional striking of blows. Thus, Article 1, Item 1, Subsection C, provides that:

> All players are prohibited from striking on the head, face or neck with the heel, back or side of the hand, wrist, forearm, elbow or clasped hands.

[T]he very conduct which was present here is expressly prohibited by the rule which is quoted above.

The general customs of football do not approve the intentional punching or striking of others. That this is prohibited was supported by the testimony of all of the witnesses. They testified that the intentional striking of a player in the face or from the rear is prohibited by the playing rules as well as the general customs of the game. Punching or hitting with the arms is prohibited. Undoubtedly these restraints are intended to establish reasonable boundaries so that one football player cannot intentionally inflict a serious injury on another. Therefore, the notion is not correct that all reason has been abandoned, whereby the only possible remedy for the person who has been the victim of an unlawful blow is retaliation.

In sum, having concluded that the trial court did not limit the case to a trial of the evidence bearing on defendant's liability but rather determined that as a matter of social policy the game was so violent and unlawful that valid lines could not be drawn, we take the view that this was not a proper issue for determination and that plaintiff was entitled to have the case tried on an assessment of his rights and whether they had been violated.

The cause is reversed and remanded for a new trial in accordance with the foregoing views.

NOTE

Most courts require a plaintiff who seeks damages against a fellow participant in an athletic event to prove that the defendant acted at least recklessly. Proof of mere negligence will not suffice. *See Nabozny v. Barnhill*, 334 N.E.2d 258 (Ill. App. Ct. 1975) ("a player is liable for injury in a tort action if his conduct is such that it is either deliberate, willful or with reckless disregard for the safety of the other player so as to cause injury to that player").

PROBLEM

Plaintiff is a professional boxer who was injured by an opponent in a state where prize fighting was illegal. In a battery action, may plaintiff successfully argue that the court should deem his consent to participate in the illegal bout ineffective? What policies support preventing a participant in an illegal activity from recovering in tort? What policies might support an opposite approach? Would your answer change if the plaintiff, an untrained amateur, was injured in an illegal bout at a flea market, where a professional boxer would fight a round with anyone who would pay a ten dollar entrance fee? *Cf.* RESTATEMENT (SECOND) OF TORTS, § 60 (1965).

C. SELF DEFENSE

According to the Restatement of Torts:

> An actor is privileged to use reasonable force, not intended or likely to cause death or serious bodily harm, to defend himself against unprivileged harmful or offensive contact or other bodily harm which he reasonably believes that another is about to inflict intentionally upon him.

RESTATEMENT (SECOND) OF TORTS § 63(1) (1965). Self defense cases often turn on the meaning of the term "reasonable." Reasonableness is relevant in two respects. When is someone's belief that another is about to inflict bodily harm upon him reasonable? And how much force may a person reasonably use against an attacker? The following case considers these issues.

ROBERTS v. AMERICAN EMPLOYERS
INSURANCE COMPANY
221 So. 2d 550 (La. Ct. App. 1969)

CULPEPPER, JUDGE.

Plaintiff seeks damages for unlawful arrest and for personal injuries resulting from being shot by the arresting officer. From an adverse judgment, plaintiff appealed.

The issues on appeal are: (1) the lawfulness of the arrest, which was made without a warrant for violation of a city ordinance relative to disturbing the peace; (2) was the arresting officer justified in shooting plaintiff in self-defense?

The facts show that on December 28, 1966 at about 8:00 p.m. plaintiff went to Haven's Lounge, a bar [in] Jennings, Louisiana. A social organization, Club 21, was holding a private Christmas party in the bar room section. The bartender advised plaintiff it was a private party and refused to serve him a drink. Plaintiff refused to leave and ate some of the potato chips, which the members of the club had brought to the bar room. The members of the club objected and a disturbance ensued.

The bartender then telephoned the city police to complain that plaintiff was causing a disturbance at the lounge. However, before the police arrived plaintiff left Haven's Lounge and walked across the street to Shirley's Pool Hall, where he purchased a beer.

City Police Officer Horace J. Randolph arrived at Haven's Lounge at about 8:30 p.m. and was told that plaintiff had created a disturbance. The officer went in search of plaintiff and found him at Shirley's Pool Hall. He allowed plaintiff to finish drinking his beer and asked if he would go back to Haven's Lounge to discuss the complaint which had been made against him. Plaintiff went voluntarily.

After discussing the nature of the complaint with the bartender and the members of Club 21, Officer Randolph placed plaintiff under arrest for violation of the city ordinance against disturbing the peace. He did not have an arrest warrant.

The officer then ordered plaintiff to walk out of the lounge to the police car. There is a conflict in the testimony as to when the officer pulled his pistol from his belt holster. Plaintiff testified the officer pulled his gun before they left the lounge and held it in his back as they walked toward the police car. The officer says he did not pull his pistol until the instant before he fired it. In any event, plaintiff raised his hands above his head and was walking 5 or 6 feet ahead of the officer toward the police car when the incident in question occurred.

While walking toward the police vehicle, plaintiff stopped at least twice, cursing and stating "I ain't going to no G_ _ d_ _ jail. Kill me — shoot me in the back." Finally, as they neared the car, plaintiff turned around, lowered his hands and grabbed for the officer. The policeman stepped back and fired one shot from the hip, the bullet entering the lower left jaw and exiting the left rear portion of plaintiff's neck. Plaintiff recovered but suffered some permanent impairment of the use of his jaw.

[After concluding that the officer lawfully arrested the plaintiff, the court addressed the officer's self-defense claim.] The privilege of self-defense in tort actions is now well recognized by our jurisprudence. Where a person reasonably believes he is threatened with bodily harm, he may use whatever force appears to be reasonably necessary to protect against the threatened injury. Of course, each case depends on its own facts, such as, for instance, the relative size, age and strength of the parties, their reputations for violence, who was the aggressor, the degree of physical harm reasonably feared and the presence or absence of weapons.

Dr. Edward Simon described plaintiff as 'very well developed[,] 24 years of age and weigh[ing] between 150 and 155 pounds. Officer Randolph weighed 165 pounds. His age is not shown in the record, but from the fact that he had served 17 years as a peace officer, it can be inferred he was substantially older than plaintiff.

The record also shows that plaintiff had a long criminal record, including acts of violence, of which Officer Randolph was aware. Plaintiff's record in the City Court of Jennings reveals that from 1961 through 1966 he had 14 convictions for disorderly conduct, 2 for assault and battery, 1 for resisting arrest, 1 for fighting and 2 for escape. Officer Randolph testified that he knew plaintiff had 15 to 20 prior convictions, including escape and resisting arrest. Randolph himself had actually arrested plaintiff on several previous occasions. Plaintiff admitted that at the time of the incident in question he was on probation from the City Court of Jennings for a period of 5 years.

On the night of the arrest, plaintiff had been drinking. He admits having had 4 beers. After the arrest in Haven's Lounge, and while plaintiff was walking out to the police car, with his hands above his head and Officer Randolph 5 or 6 feet behind him, plaintiff cursed and made statements to the effect that he was not going to jail, that he was on probation and the judge would 'throw the book at him' and that he would as soon die as go to jail. Finally, plaintiff turned around, lowered his hands and grabbed for Officer Randolph. As stated above, the officer stepped back and fired 1 shot from the hip.

Officer Randolph testified that because of his knowledge of plaintiff's past record for violence and law violation, his drinking at the time, his cursing and stated determination not to go to jail, he thought plaintiff was going to resist arrest by physical force. The officer admits he did not see a weapon on plaintiff's person, but said he didn't know whether he was armed or not. Of course, the officer had a pistol in his belt holster and if a physical fight had ensued there was always the possibility that plaintiff could have obtained possession of the gun.

Plaintiff's counsel makes much of the fact that the officer had a 'slap-stick' in his pocket, which he could have used. This was a small leather device weighted with lead. Officer Randolph explained that since the slap-stick was in his pocket he did not have time to reach for it.

Of course, one of the factors to be considered in a tort action for battery is who was the aggressor. In this case plaintiff was the aggressor. He was in the officer's custody under a lawful arrest, which he attempted to resist by physical force. The mere fact that plaintiff was the aggressor does not alone require a denial of recovery, but it is a factor to be considered along with all of the other circumstances.

After carefully considering all of the circumstances, we think Officer Randolph reasonably believed he was in danger of substantial physical harm and that the force which he used to resist was not unreasonably excessive. Hence, the officer's privilege of self-defense is recognized and recovery in tort is rejected.

For the reasons assigned, the judgment appealed is affirmed.

NOTES

1. As explained in the introductory note, a defendant who raises self defense must demonstrate the reasonableness of his belief that he was under attack. This requirement poses little trouble if an attack has begun. But what if (as in *Roberts*) it has not? Surely a defendant need not "wait until a blow is struck, for, as was quaintly observed in the earliest case 'perhaps it will come too late afterwards.'" PROSSER AND KEETON ON TORTS § 19 at 125. *See Courvoisier v. Raymond*, 47 P. 284 (Colo. 1896) (self defense is a jury question where store owner shot police officer during a late night riot under a mistaken belief that the officer was a rioter). Was the defendant's belief reasonable in *Roberts*? Should the defendant's knowledge about the plaintiff's history of violence and lawbreaking make a difference?

2. A defendant also must demonstrate that the amount of force used in self defense was reasonable. Professor Epstein explains that if "two methods can repel a given attack equally well, the [defendant] must choose the one calculated to cause the least damage to the [plaintiff]." EPSTEIN, TORTS § 2.11 at 53. *See* RESTATEMENT (SECOND) OF TORTS § 70(1) (1965) ("The actor is not privileged to use any means of self defense which is intended or likely to cause a bodily harm or confinement in excess of that which the actor correctly or reasonably believes to be necessary for his protection.") In *Roberts*, the officer responded to the plaintiff's movements by stepping back and shooting his gun, despite the fact that he could have used his "slap-stick." The court brushed off the plaintiff's criticism of the officer's decision by accepting the officer's explanation that "since the slap-stick was in his pocket he did not have time to reach for it." Could reaching for the slap-stick have taken more time than stepping back and shoot-

ing a gun? Is the court too deferential to the officer? Or is the court simply deferring to the lower court's fact findings?

3. A person also may defend against an intentional tort claim by asserting a defense of others. In general, a person may defend a third person in the same manner, and under the same conditions, as the person being defended would be able to do in self defense. *See* Restatement (Second) of Torts § 76 (1965).

PROBLEMS

1. How immediate must the threat be for a defendant to raise self defense? Suppose Alice is a woman whose spouse has subjected her to long-term physical abuse. If Alice kills her spouse while he sleeps, can she raise self defense in a tort action?

2. The use of potentially deadly force in self defense poses special problems. As a general matter, one cannot use deadly force unless the threat against her was equally grave. But what about a defendant who has an opportunity to avoid a confrontation rather than using deadly force? Consider the following fact patterns.

   a. Alan threatens Bob with a knife in the middle of a crowded street. Bob has a clear opportunity to flee into the crowd, but instead pulls a gun and shoots Alan. Alan survives and sues Bob for battery. Can Bob successfully assert self defense?

   b. Alan threatens Bob with a knife in a dark alley and backs Bob against a wall. Bob pulls a gun and shoots Alan. Alan survives and sues Bob for battery. Can Bob successfully assert self defense?

   c. Alan threatens Bob with a knife after breaking into Bob's home. Bob has an opportunity to flee through an open door, but instead pulls a gun and shoots Alan. Alan survives and sues Bob for battery. Can Bob successfully assert self defense?

   d. Same facts as above, except that *Alan* flees the house as soon as he sees Bob pull his gun. Bob shoots Alan in the back as he is running away. Alan survives and sues Bob for battery. Can Bob successfully assert self defense?

3. Recall from Note 3 that the law generally provides a privilege to defend others in the same manner, and under the same conditions, as the person being defended would be able to defend herself. What if the defender is wrong about the legitimacy of the threat to the third person? For example, suppose that an undercover police officer is making a lawful arrest of Arthur on a street corner. Bernice, a pedestrian, attacks the officer in a mistaken belief that the officer is engaged in a mugging. If the officer sues Bernice for battery, can Bernice successfully raise the defense of others?

D. DEFENSE OF PROPERTY

The question of when an individual can engage in otherwise tortious activity to protect property is similar to the question of when an individual can do so in self defense. In general, a person may use reasonable force to protect property when she reasonably believes that force is necessary to prevent the intrusion. *See* RESTATEMENT (SECOND) OF TORTS § 77 (1965).

The issue of what constitutes reasonable force sometimes poses problems. As with self defense, the use of force must be proportional to the threatened interest. Proportionality generally does not exist, however, when a person uses deadly force to protect property alone. For example, in the famous English case of *Bird v. Holbrook*, 4 Bing. 628, 130 Eng. Rep. 911 (C.P. 1828), the defendant set a spring gun in his garden to prevent the theft of his tulips. Subsequently, the plaintiff climbed a wall to enter the garden in search of his neighbor's peahen, triggered the gun, and was seriously injured. The court found the defendant liable for the plaintiff's injuries.

Bird v. Holbrook, however, was not entirely clear about whether a defendant who used deadly force to protect property might avoid liability if he injured an actual thief. The following is a famous American decision that addresses this question.

KATKO v. BRINEY
183 N.W.2d 657 (Iowa 1971)

MOORE, CHIEF JUSTICE.

The primary issue presented here is whether an owner may protect personal property in an unoccupied boarded-up farm house against trespassers and thieves by a spring gun capable of inflicting death or serious injury.

We are not here concerned with a man's right to protect his home and members of his family. Defendants' home was several miles from the scene of the incident.

Plaintiff's action is for damages resulting from serious injury caused by a shot from a 20-gauge spring shotgun set by defendants in a bedroom of an old farm house which had been uninhabited for several years. Plaintiff and his companion, Marvin McDonough, had broken and entered the house to find and steal old bottles and dated fruit jars which they considered antiques.

The jury returned a verdict for plaintiff and against defendants for $20,000 actual and $10,000 punitive damages.

After careful consideration of defendants' motions for judgment notwithstanding the verdict and for new trial, the experienced and capable trial judge overruled them and entered judgment on the verdict. Thus we have this appeal by defendants.

Most of the facts are not disputed. In 1957 defendant Bertha L. Briney inherited her parents' farm land in Mahaska and Monroe Counties. Included was an 80-acre tract in southwest Mahaska County where her grandparents and parents had lived. No one occupied the house thereafter. Her husband, Edward, attempted to care for the land. He kept no farm machinery thereon. The outbuildings became dilapidated.

For about 10 years, 1957 to 1967, there occurred a series of trespassing and housebreaking events with loss of some household items, the breaking of windows and "messing up of the property in general." The latest occurred June 8, 1967, prior to the event on July 16, 1967 herein involved.

Defendants through the years boarded up the windows and doors in an attempt to stop the intrusions. They had posted "no trespass" signs on the land several years before 1967. The nearest one was 35 feet from the house. On June 11, 1967 defendants set "a shotgun trap" in the north bedroom. After Mr. Briney cleaned and oiled his 20-gauge shotgun, the power of which he was well aware, defendants took it to the old house where they secured it to an iron bed with the barrel pointed at the bedroom door. It was rigged with wire from the doorknob to the gun's trigger so it would fire when the door was opened. Briney first pointed the gun so an intruder would be hit in the stomach but at Mrs Briney's suggestion it was lowered to hit the legs. He admitted he did so "because I was mad and tired of being tormented' but 'he did not intend to injure anyone." He gave no explanation of why he used a loaded shell and set it to hit a person already in the house. Tin was nailed over the bedroom window. The spring gun could not be seen from the outside. No warning of its presence was posted.

Prior to July 16, 1967 plaintiff and McDonough had been to the premises [which they knew to be uninhabited,] and found several old bottles and fruit jars which they took and added to their collection of antiques. On the latter date about 9:30 p.m. they made a second trip to the Briney property. They entered the old house by removing a board from a porch window which was without glass. While McDonough was looking around the kitchen area plaintiff went to another part of the house. As he started to open the north bedroom door the shotgun went off striking him in the right leg above the ankle bone. Much of his leg, including part of the tibia, was blown away. Only by McDonough's assistance was plaintiff able to get out of the house and after crawling some distance was put in his vehicle and rushed to a doctor and then to a hospital. He remained in the hospital 40 days.

The main thrust of defendants' defense in the trial court and on this appeal is that "the law permits use of a spring gun in a dwelling or warehouse for the purpose of preventing the unlawful entry of a burglar or thief." They repeated this contention in their exceptions to the trial court's instructions [5 and 6].

Instruction 5 stated: "You are hereby instructed that one may use reasonable force in the protection of his property, but such right is subject to the qualification that one may not use such means of force as will take human life or inflict great bodily injury. Such is the rule even though the injured party is a trespasser and is in violation of the law himself."

Instruction 6 stated: "An owner of premises is prohibited from willfully or intentionally injuring a trespasser by means of force that either takes life or inflicts great bodily injury; and therefore a person owning a premise is prohibited from setting out 'spring guns' and like dangerous devices which will likely take life or inflict great bodily injury, for the purpose of harming trespassers. The fact that the trespasser may be acting in violation of the law does not change the rule. The only time when such conduct of setting a 'spring gun' or a like dangerous device is justified would be when the trespasser was committing a felony of violence or a felony punishable by death, or where the trespasser was endangering human life by his act."

The overwhelming weight of authority, both textbook and case law, supports the trial court's statement of the applicable principles of law.

[For example,] Prosser on Torts, Third Edition, pages 116-118, states:

> '[the] law has always placed a higher value upon human safety than upon mere rights in property, it is the accepted rule that there is no privilege to use any force calculated to cause death or serious bodily injury to repel the threat to land or chattels, unless there is also such a threat to the defendant's personal safety as to justify a self-defense. [S]pring guns and other mankilling devices are not justifiable against a mere trespasser, or even a petty thief. They are privileged only against those upon whom the landowner, if he were present in person would be free to inflict injury of the same kind.'

The legal principles stated by the trial court in [its instructions] are well established and supported by the authorities cited and quoted supra. There is no merit in defendants' objections and exceptions thereto. Defendants' various motions based on the same reasons stated in exceptions to instructions were properly overruled.

Affirmed.

LARSON, JUSTICE.

I respectfully dissent, first, because the majority wrongfully assumes that by installing a spring gun in the bedroom of their unoccupied house the defendants intended to shoot any intruder who attempted to enter the room. Under the record presented here, that was a fact question. Unless it is held that the property owners are liable for any injury to a intruder from such a device regardless of the intent with which it is installed, liability under these pleadings must rest upon two definite issues of fact, *i.e.*, did the defendants intend to shoot the invader, and if so, did they employ unnecessary and unreasonable force against him?

Although the court told the jury the plaintiff had the burden to prove "That the force used by defendants was in excess of that force reasonably necessary and which persons are entitled to use in the protection of their property," it utterly failed to tell the jury it could find the installation was not made with the intent or purpose of striking or injuring the plaintiff. There was considerable evidence to that effect. [D]efendants stated the installation was made for the purpose of scaring or frightening away any intruder, not to seriously injure him. It may be that the evidence would support a finding of an intent to injure the intruder, but obviously that important issue was never adequately or clearly submitted to the jury.

Unless, then, we hold for the first time that liability for death or injury in such cases is absolute, the matter should be remanded for a jury determination of defendant's intent in installing the device under instructions usually given to a jury on the issue of intent.

I feel the better rule is that an owner of buildings housing valuable property may employ the use of spring guns or other devices intended to repel but not seriously injure an intruder who enters his secured premises with or without a criminal intent, but I do not advocate its general use, for there may also be liability for negligent installation of such a device. What I mean to say is that under such circumstances as we have here the issue as to whether the [spring gun was set] with an intent to seriously injure or kill an intruder is a question of fact that should be left to the jury under proper instructions, [so] that the mere setting of such a device with a resultant serious injury should not as a matter of law establish liability.

If this is not a desirable expression of policy in this jurisdiction, I suggest the body selected and best fitted to establish a different public policy would be the State Legislature.

NOTES

1. Katko pled guilty to a criminal larceny charge as a result of his actions. A judge suspended a 30-day sentence and fined him $50. The Brineys later lost an appeal to block enforcement of Katko's judgment and had to sell 80 acres of their 120-acre farm to satisfy the judgment. Is this a fair conclusion to the saga?

2. In addition to limiting the amount of force that defendants can use, courts also limit the time during which defendants can take advantage of the defense of property. In general, defendants maintain a privilege only when their property is threatened or while in "fresh pursuit" of the property. If the property is already gone, the owner must sue to recover his loss, rather than attempt to recover it through self-help. There are, however, several exceptions to this rule. First, a defendant may peaceably enter another person's land in an attempt to

take possession of personal property to which he or she is entitled. This issue frequently arises when a buyer purchases goods on credit and fails to make her payments. In such cases, the Uniform Commercial Code permits the seller to repossess the property so long as he does so "without breach of the peace." UCC § 9-503 (3d ed. 1999). Similarly, landowners who are entitled to possession of property can peaceably retake possession against a wrongful occupant without liability for a trespass action. In some states, a landlord also may use reasonable force to evict a tenant. Many states, however, have forcible entry and detainer statutes that protect tenants against "self help" remedies involving force.

3. The defense of property may be raised by store owners who detain suspected shoplifters and later face a false imprisonment action. The common law privilege permits storeowners to detain others for a reasonable period of time to investigate reasonable suspicions of wrongdoing. *See Collyer v. S.H. Kress Co.*, 54 P.2d 20 (Cal. 1936); RESTATEMENT (SECOND) OF TORTS § 120A (1965). Today, most states have codified the common law privilege, and most decisions interpret state statutes rather than the common law on which they are based. *See Stienbaugh v. Payless Drug Store, Inc.*, 401 P.2d 104 (N.M. 1965); DOBBS, THE LAW OF TORTS § 84 at 196-98.

4. For an entertaining discussion of a law professor's experience in teaching *Katko v. Briney*, see Andrew J. McClurg, *Poetry in Commotion:* Katko v. Briney *and the Bards of First-Year Torts*, 74 OR. L. REV. 823 (1995).

PROBLEMS

1. Consider the following newspaper account of a case with facts very similar to *Katko v. Briney*.

Shotgun Booby Trap Lands Cabin's Owner in Jail

Turtle Lake, Wis. — What was he supposed to do?

It's not a question so much as a challenge. A challenge to anyone who thinks Lenny Miller was wrong to booby-trap his cabin with a shotgun.

Three times in eight months, the cabin had been burglarized.

His hunting rifles had been stolen. His fishing gear, too. And his tackle box. His new chain saw and his leaf blower and his Christmas present, a fillet knife in its box. Clothes. A BB gun. His boat had been vandalized. His outhouse trashed. His all-terrain vehicle had been torn apart.

'It had to be stopped,' Miller said.

His locks didn't help. Neither did the sheriff.

'Enough is enough,' Miller said.

So he loaded his 12-gauge shotgun. He bought some string, a pulley and some hooks. And he rigged up a booby trap to catch a burglar.

Miller figured he had no choice. Authorities, however, say he just made the wrong one.

Oh, Miller caught himself a burglar, all right. But he also landed himself a six-month jail sentence.

The case has raised an alarm in the remote woods of northwest Wisconsin.

Many residents express outrage that a man could go to jail for guarding what's his. Authorities are equally riled — at the idea that anyone would value property above life, [and] would set a potentially lethal trap to keep a burglar away from his stuff.

* * *

[The judge who sentenced Miller] warned that the booby trap could have been lethal. It could have severed an artery. It could have caught a crouching intruder in the chest.

Miller was also lucky that his gun nailed a bad guy. What if the firefighters had broken into the shed to save it? What if a child, desperate to find his lost puppy, had pried open the doors to peek inside?

. . . If Miller encountered an intruder in his cabin, he could shoot to defend himself. But he can't rig a gun to save his fishing tackle.

Stephanie Simon, *"Shotgun Booby Trap Lands Cabin's Owner in Jail,"* INDI-ANAPOLIS STAR A13 (December 27, 1999). Do you agree that the property owner should be punished criminally, as well as held liable in a tort action?

2. In Dave's backyard there is a particularly sunny and pleasant spot with a nice view. Dave's neighbor Bob likes to take a folding chair into this spot and sit, smoke cigars, and read. Dave wants to get Bob off his property. What may he do? If Bob refuses to leave, may Dave use force? How much? Suppose Dave tries to use force. May Bob resist?

3. Marla is a manager of a department store. One day, just before closing time, Marla called Sally, a salesperson, to her office for a closed-door meeting. With a security guard in the room, Marla told Sally that another employee had accused her of shoplifting. Sally denied the allegation. Marla, however, pressed Sally for a confession. Finally, after an hour in the office, Marla relented and told Sally that she was free to leave. Sally has sued Marla for false imprisonment. Can Marla successfully raise the defense of property?

4. Paul owns a small home near a local elementary school. Children frequently walk through his backyard as a shortcut to school. Last year, the chil-

dren were less than careful in avoiding Paul's vegetable garden as they walked on his property. Paul tried shouting at the children. He also tried placing small stakes around the garden as a barrier. But these warnings did not work, and Paul lost much of his vegetable crop due to the childrens' carelessness. Before the current school year, Paul built a four-foot steel fence around his property. At the top of the fence were extremely sharp metal "spikes." On the first day of classes, three children came to Paul's yard and noticed the fence. Instead of going around, they tried to jump it. One of the children slipped, and fell on a fence spike. The spike went into his abdomen and caused severe physical injuries. The child has filed an intentional tort claim against Paul. Paul has raised the defense of property. Evaluate Paul's defense.

5. Recall the Problems following the *Compuserve* case in Chapter 2. Emily took a bicycle belonging to Jennifer. If Jennifer sees her take her bicycle, what may she do? Can she grab Emily to stop her from leaving with the bicycle? Can she run after her and grab her? Can she forcibly remove Emily from the bicycle if Emily refuses to get off? Suppose Emily "defends" herself and pushes Jennifer away. Is Emily privileged to resist?

6. In the previous problem, suppose Jennifer does not see Emily take her bicycle. Two weeks later, however, she sees Emily riding a bicycle which she is sure is hers. What can she do to recover her property? Suppose Emily resists?

E. NECESSITY

1. Private Necessity

The law permits interference with another's property in certain emergency situations. Courts and commentators divide this "necessity" privilege into two categories — public necessity and private necessity. Public necessity (which is discussed in a separate section below) provides defendants with an absolute privilege to interfere with the property of others to avoid a "public disaster." *See* RESTATEMENT (SECOND) OF TORTS §§ 196, 262 (1965). Private necessity, on the other hand, provides defendants with a qualified privilege to interfere with property to protect their own interests, or those of a small group of others. Private necessity is a qualified privilege because it still requires the defendant to compensate the property owner for any damage caused. The Restatement of Torts explains:

> (1) One is privileged to commit an act which would otherwise be a trespass to the chattel of another or a conversion of it, if it is or is reasonably believed to be reasonable and necessary to protect the person or property of the actor, the other or a third person from serious harm, unless the actor knows that the person for whose benefit he acts is unwilling that he shall do so.

(2) Where the act is for the benefit of the actor or a third person, he is
subject to liability for any harm caused by the exercise of the privilege.

RESTATEMENT (SECOND) OF TORTS § 263 (1965); *see* RESTATEMENT (SECOND) OF
TORTS § 197 (1965) (stating similar privilege to trespass on land).

Necessity cases are difficult to resolve because they often do not involve an
inherently wrongful act by either party. This, of course, is unlike previous cases
we have studied where defendants have asserted a defense in response to a
plaintiff's wrongdoing (*i.e.*, the Brineys responded with force because Katko
was stealing their property; the police officer in *Roberts* shot the plaintiff
because the officer perceived him as threatening harm, etc.). In necessity cases,
however, the defendant often invades the plaintiff's interests due to circumstances beyond the control of either party. The two famous cases that follow represent the classic situation. As you read the opinions, think about the
justifications that might support a ruling for either party.

PLOOF v. PUTNAM
71 A. 188 (Vt. 1908)

MUNSON, J.

It is alleged [that] on the 13th day of November 1904, the defendant was the
owner of a certain island in Lake Champlain, and of a certain dock attached
thereto, which island and dock were then in charge of the defendant's servant;
that the plaintiff was then possessed of and sailing upon said lake a certain
loaded sloop, on which were the plaintiff and his wife and two minor children;
that there then arose a sudden and violent tempest, whereby the sloop and the
property and persons therein were placed in great danger of destruction; that,
to save these from destruction or injury, the plaintiff was compelled to, and
did, moor the sloop to defendant's dock; that the defendant, by his servant,
unmoored the sloop, whereupon it was driven upon the shore by the tempest,
without the plaintiff's fault; and that the sloop and its contents were thereby
destroyed, and the plaintiff and his wife and children cast into the lake and upon
the shore, receiving injuries. This claim is set forth in two counts — one in
trespass, charging that the defendant by his servant with force and arms willfully and designedly unmoored the sloop; the other in case, alleging that it was
the duty of the defendant by his servant to permit the plaintiff to moor his
sloop to the dock, and to permit it to remain so moored during the continuance
of the tempest, but that the defendant by his servant, in disregard of this duty,
negligently, carelessly, and wrongfully unmoored the sloop. Both counts are
demurred to generally. [The trial court overruled the demurrers.]

There are many cases in the books which hold that necessity, and an inability to control movements inaugurated in the proper exercise of a strict right, will

justify entries upon land and interferences with personal property that would otherwise have been trespasses.

This doctrine of necessity applies with special force to the preservation of human life. One assaulted and in peril of his life may run through the close of another to escape from his assailant.

It is clear [, therefore,] that an entry upon the land of another may be justified by necessity, and that the declaration before us discloses a necessity for mooring the sloop. But the defendant questions the sufficiency of the counts because they do not negative the existence of natural objects to which the plaintiff could have moored with equal safety. The allegations are, in substance, that the stress of a sudden and violent tempest compelled the plaintiff to moor to defendant's dock to save his sloop and the people in it. The averment of necessity is complete, for it covers not only the necessity of mooring to the dock; and the details of the situation which created this necessity, whatever the legal requirements regarding them, are matters of proof, and need not be alleged. It is certain that the rule suggested cannot be held applicable irrespective of circumstance, and the question must be left for adjudication upon proceedings had with reference to the evidence or the charge.

Judgment affirmed and cause remanded.

VINCENT v. LAKE ERIE TRANSP. CO.
124 N.W. 221 (Minn. 1910)

O'BRIEN, J.

The steamship Reynolds, owned by the defendant, was for the purpose of discharging her cargo on November 27, 1905, moored to plaintiff's dock in Duluth. While the unloading of the boat was taking place a storm from the northeast developed, which at about 10 o'clock p.m., when the unloading was completed, had so grown in violence that the wind was then moving at 50 miles per hour and continued to increase during the night. There is some evidence that one, and perhaps two, boats were able to enter the harbor that night, but it is plain that navigation was practically suspended from the hour mentioned until the morning of the 29th, when the storm abated, and during that time no master would have been justified in attempting to navigate his vessel, if he could avoid doing so. After the discharge of the cargo the Reynolds signaled for a tug to tow her from the dock, but none could be obtained because of the severity of the storm. If the lines holding the ship to the dock had been cast off, she would doubtless have drifted away; but, instead, the lines were kept fast, and as soon as one parted or chafed it was replaced, sometimes with a larger one. The vessel lay upon the outside of the dock, her bow to the east, the wind and waves striking her starboard quarter with such force that she was constantly being lifted and thrown against the dock, resulting in its damage, as found by the jury, to the amount of $500.

We are satisfied that the character of the storm was such that it would have been highly imprudent for the master of the Reynolds to have attempted to leave the dock or to have permitted his vessel to drift a way from it. One witness testified upon the trial that the vessel could have been warped into a slip, and that, if the attempt to bring the ship into the slip had failed, the worst that could have happened would be that the vessel would have been blown ashore upon a soft and muddy bank. The witness was not present in Duluth at the time of the storm, and, while he may have been right in his conclusions, those in charge of the dock and the vessel at the time of the storm were not required to use the highest human intelligence, nor were they required to resort to every possible experiment which could be suggested for the preservation of their property. Nothing more was demanded of them than ordinary prudence and care, and the record in this case fully sustains the contention of the appellant that, in holding the vessel fast to the dock, those in charge of her exercised good judgment and prudent seamanship.

The appellant contends by ample assignments of error that, because its conduct during the storm was rendered necessary by prudence and good seamanship under conditions over which it had no control, it cannot be held liable for any injury resulting to the property of others, and claims that the jury should have been so instructed. An analysis of the charge given by the trial court is not necessary, as in our opinion the only question for the jury was the amount of damages which the plaintiffs were entitled to recover, and no complaint is made upon that score.

The situation was one in which the ordinary rules regulating property rights were suspended by forces beyond human control, and if, without the direct intervention of some act by the one sought to be held liable, the property of another was injured, such injury must be attributed to the act of God, and not to the wrongful act of the person sought to be charged. If during the storm the Reynolds had entered the harbor, and while there had become disabled and been thrown against the plaintiffs' dock, the plaintiffs could not have recovered. Again, if [while] attempting to hold fast to the dock the lines had parted, without any negligence, and the vessel carried against some other boat or dock in the harbor, there would be no liability upon her owner. But here those in charge of the vessel deliberately and by their direct efforts held her in such a position that the damage to the dock resulted, and, having thus preserved the ship at the expense of the dock, it seems to us that her owners are responsible to the dock owners to the extent of the injury inflicted.

In *Ploof v. Putnam*, 71 Atl. 188, the Supreme Court of Vermont held that where, under stress of weather, a vessel was without permission moored to a private dock at an island in Lake Champlain owned by the defendant, the plaintiff was not guilty of trespass, and that the defendant was responsible in damages because his representative upon the island unmoored the vessel, permitting it to drift upon the shore, with resultant injuries to it. If, in that case, the vessel had been permitted to remain, and the dock had suffered an injury, we believe the shipowner would have been held liable for the injury done.

Theologians hold that a starving man may, without moral guilt, take what is necessary to sustain life; but it could hardly be said that the obligation would not be upon such person to pay the value of the property so taken when he became able to do so. And so public necessity, in times of war or peace, may require the taking of private property for public purposes; but under our system of jurisprudence compensation must be made.

Let us imagine in this case that for the better mooring of the vessel those in charge of her had appropriated a valuable cable lying upon the dock. No matter how justifiable such appropriation might have been, it would not be claimed that, because of the overwhelming necessity of the situation, the owner of the cable could not recover its value.

This is not a case where life or property was menaced by any object or thing belonging to the plaintiff, the destruction of which became necessary to prevent the threatened disaster. Nor is it a case where, because of the act of God, or unavoidable accident, the infliction of the injury was beyond the control of the defendant, but is one where the defendant prudently and advisedly availed itself of the plaintiffs' property for the purpose of preserving its own more valuable property, and the plaintiffs are entitled to compensation for the injury done.

Order affirmed.

NOTES

1. Cases like *Ploof* and *Vincent* touch on issues at the very heart of tort law. In general terms, the outcome of these cases might turn on whether you believe that the law of torts should be guided by principles of "corrective justice" or principles of "deterrence." These are nuanced and difficult concepts, but they are well worth thinking about, even at the beginning of your legal studies.

2. *Corrective Justice:* Generally speaking, the corrective justice view advocates that courts should decide tort cases by reference to moral principles of fairness — that is, a defendant should compensate a plaintiff whenever the defendant has invaded the plaintiff's personal or property rights. As one leading corrective justice scholar, wrote: "[Corrective justice] considers the position of the parties anterior to the transaction as equal, and it restores this antecedent equality by transferring resources from defendant to plaintiff so that the gain realized by the former is used to make up the loss suffered by the latter." Ernest J. Weinrib, *Toward a Moral Theory of Negligence Law*, 2 LAW & PHIL. 37, 38 (1982). From a corrective justice standpoint, the answer to the *Ploof/Vincent* fact pattern might seem easy — the shipowners should pay for the damage to the docks because they caused the damage. Professor Kenneth S. Abraham, however, asserts that the answer is not that easy:

The trouble with this answer is that if both parties are innocent — *i.e.*, neither was negligent — then the conditional privilege rule looks more like a way to break the moral tie between the parties than a method of achieving corrective justice. It will not do to argue that the shipowner made a choice to risk the dock, but that the dockowner made no such choice, since the dockowner chose to have a dock where ships might tie up when the storms arose. Until we know what legal rule governs the rights of ship and dockowners, we cannot make assertions about what they did and did not 'choose' to risk. This is an important point, for it reflects the fact that legal rules not only honor expectations of safety; sometimes expectations of safety are derived from legal rules. In such situations the decision about what legal rule to have is in essence a decision about what expectations of safety to create.

KENNETH S. ABRAHAM, THE FORMS AND FUNCTIONS OF TORT LAW 40 (Foundation Press 1997). Does Professor Abraham convince you that corrective justice principles might not lead to a rule that imposes liability on the shipowner?

3. *Deterrence:* Unlike corrective justice, the deterrence view focuses on creating tort law rules that maximize society's wealth. Under this view, the outcome of a particular case often should be based on which party is better situated to have prevented damage or injury in the first place. By "threatening" that party with liability, the law encourages efficiency by providing an incentive to that party to consider less costly alternatives. *See* GUIDO CALIBRESI, THE COST OF ACCIDENTS (1970). At first blush, it seems that the deterrence perspective would lead to a conclusion that the dockowner should bear the loss in a *Ploof/Vincent* situation. Certainly, the dockowner is in a better position than shipowners to determine how one might prevent damage to docks. The dockowner, for example, might fortify the structure, insure the dock for more money, or even charge shipowners more money for using his facilities to cover potential loss. Again, Professor Abraham calls this conclusion into question:

> But this is only half the story. . . . Denying dockowners the right to recover from shipowners in such situations will increase the tendency of shipowners to risk damaging docks, because shipowners will not have to pay for damage to docks. Shipowners will tend not to venture out into a storm, risking damage to the ship, if they can stay moored at the dock without having to pay for damage to the dock. In contrast, under the rule in *Vincent* the shipowner always has an incentive to compare the risk to the dock if the ship stays moored, against the risk to the ship if the ship does not stay moored, because under *Vincent* the shipowner must pay for whatever damage occurs; he is liable to the dockowner for damage, and as the owner of the ship he must bear the cost of any damage that occurs if the ship ventures out into the storm.

ABRAHAM, FORMS AND FUNCTIONS at 42. What do you think? Which theory do you find more persuasive in the *Ploof/Vincent* type of situation?

PROBLEMS

1. Should courts consider parties' wealth in deciding who should bear the loss in cases like *Vincent* and *Ploof*? Consider the following problems using the ship-dock paradigm:

    a. Suppose that the shipowner is a multi-millionaire named Rockefeller. Rockefeller's ship is worth $50,000. Suppose that the dock-owner is an impoverished individual named Jones. The dock (which has sustained $5000 worth of damage) is Jones' only asset. In deciding who is liable, should we consider the fact that Rockefeller can more easily absorb the $5000 loss? If so, why? If not, why not?

    b. Suppose that the shipowner is the impoverished individual named Jones. He makes monthly loan payments on the $50,000 ship, and incurring a $5000 debt would cause him to default on the loan. Suppose that Rockefeller owns the dock. Once again, should we consider the relative wealth of the parties in establishing our liability rule? Why or why not?

2. Should private necessity extend to the infliction of personal injury? Suppose that Jeff is driving alone on a two-lane road. As he rounds a curve, Jeff suddenly sees a truck in the wrong lane, heading straight toward him. Jeff's options are to swerve left into heavy oncoming traffic, or to swerve right toward a single pedestrian on the sidewalk. Jeff chooses the latter option, and he severely injures the pedestrian. If the pedestrian sues Jeff for battery, can Jeff successfully raise the defense of private necessity?

3. What if Jeff in the previous problem was a school bus driver with 50 children aboard. Would this change the result? Before answering, consider the materials in the following section.

2. Public Necessity

The Restatement (Second) of Torts § 262 provides:

> One is privileged to commit an act which would otherwise be a trespass to a chattel or a conversion if the act is or is reasonably believed to be necessary for the purpose of avoiding a public disaster.

See also RESTATEMENT (SECOND) OF TORTS §196 (1965) (stating same privilege for trespass to land). As noted in the introduction to this section, the most important distinction between public necessity and private necessity is that public necessity is an absolute privilege — in other words, a defendant who successfully raises the privilege need not compensate the plaintiff for his loss. For example, in a famous nineteenth century case, the mayor of San Francisco ordered the destruction of the plaintiff's house in order to prevent a fire from spreading. The plaintiff sought recovery for the value of property inside the house that he did not have time to recover. A jury ruled for the plaintiff, but the Supreme Court of California reversed.

> The right to destroy property, to prevent the spread of a conflagration, has been traced to the highest law of necessity, and the natural rights of man, independent of society or civil government.

* * *

> A house on fire, or those in its immediate vicinity, which serve to communicate the flames, becomes a nuisance, which it is lawful to abate, and the private rights of the individual yield to the considerations of general convenience, and the interests of society. Were it otherwise, one stubborn person might involve a whole city in ruin, by refusing to allow the progress of the fire, and that, too, when it was perfectly evident that his building must be consumed.

Surocco v. Geary, 3 Cal. 69, 73 (1853). More modern cases involving governmental actors focus less on the existence of the privilege and more on the question of whether the federal constitution (or state constitution) requires the government to compensate the owner for loss of his property. The following case shows that such compensation is not always a given.

UNITED STATES v. CALTEX (PHILIPPINES), INC.
344 U.S. 149 (1952)

MR. CHIEF JUSTICE VINSON delivered the opinion of the Court.

Each of the respondent oil companies owned terminal facilities in the Pandacan district of Manila at the time of the Japanese attack upon Pearl Harbor. These were used to receive, handle and store petroleum products from incoming ships and to release them for further distribution throughout the Philippine Islands. Wharves, rail and automotive equipment, pumps, pipe lines, storage tanks, and warehouses were included in the property on hand at the outbreak of the war, as well as a normal supply of petroleum products.

News of the Pearl Harbor attack reached Manila early in the morning of December 8, 1941. On the same day, enemy air attacks were mounted against our forces in the Philippines, and thereafter the enemy launched his amphibious assault.

On December 12, 1941, the United States Army, through its Chief Quartermaster, stationed a control officer at the terminals. Operations continued at respondents' plants, but distribution of the petroleum products for civilian use was severely restricted. A major share of the existing supplies was requisitioned by the Army.

The military situation in the Philippines grew worse. In the face of the Japanese advance, the Commanding General on December 23, 1941, ordered the withdrawal of all troops on Luzon to the Bataan Peninsula. On December 25, 1941, he declared Manila to be an open city. On that same day, the Chief Engineer on the staff of the Commanding General addressed to each of the oil companies letters stating that the Pandacan oil depots "are requisitioned by the U.S. Army." The letters further stated: "Any action deemed necessary for the destruction of this property will be handled by the U.S. Army." An engineer in the employ of one of the companies was commissioned a first lieutenant in the Army Corps of Engineers to facilitate this design.

On December 26, he received orders to prepare the facilities for demolition. On December 27, 1941, while enemy planes were bombing the area, this officer met with representatives of the companies. The orders of the Chief Engineer had been transmitted to the companies. Letters from the Deputy Chief of Staff, by command of General MacArthur, also had been sent to each of the oil companies, directing the destruction of all remaining petroleum products and the vital parts of the plants. Plans were laid to carry out these instructions, to expedite the removal of products which might still be of use to the troops in the field, and to lay a demolition network about the terminals. The representatives of Caltex were given, at their insistence, a penciled receipt for all the terminal facilities and stocks of Caltex.

At 5:40 p.m., December 31, 1941, while Japanese troops were entering Manila, Army personnel completed a successful demolition. All unused petroleum products were destroyed, and the facilities were rendered useless to the enemy. The enemy was deprived of a valuable logistic weapon.

After the war, respondents demanded compensation for all of the property which had been used or destroyed by the Army. The Government paid for the petroleum stocks and transportation equipment which were either used or destroyed by the Army, but it refused to compensate respondents for the destruction of the Pandacan terminal facilities. Claiming a constitutional right under the Fifth Amendment to just compensation for these terminal facilities, respondents sued in the Court of Claims. Recovery was allowed. We granted certiorari to review this judgment.

The [companies'] argument draws heavily from statements by this Court in *Mitchell v. Harmony*, 1852, 13 How. 115, and *United States v. Russell*, 1871, 13 Wall. 623. We agree that the opinions lend some support to [their] view. But the language in those two cases is far broader than the holdings. Both cases involved equipment which had been impressed by the Army for subsequent use by the Army. In neither was the Army's purpose limited, as it was in this case, to the sole objective of destroying property of strategic value to prevent the enemy from using it to wage war the more successfully.

A close reading of the *Mitchell* and *Russell* cases shows that they are not precedent to establish a compensable taking in this case. Nor do those cases exhaust all that has been said by this Court on the subject. In *United States v. Pacific R. Co.*, 1887, 120 U.S. 227, Justice Field, speaking for a unanimous

Court, discussed the question at length. That case involved bridges which had been destroyed during the war between the states by a retreating Northern Army to impede the advance of the Confederate Army. Though the point was not directly involved, the Court raised the question of whether this act constituted a compensable taking by the United States and answered it in the negative:

> 'The destruction or injury of private property in battle, or in the bombardment of cities and towns, and in many other ways in the war, had to be borne by the sufferers alone, as one of its consequences. Whatever would embarrass or impede the advance of the enemy, as the breaking up of roads, or the burning of bridges, or would cripple and defeat him, as destroying his means of subsistence, were lawfully ordered by the commanding general. Indeed, it was his imperative duty to direct their destruction. The necessities of the war called for and justified this. The safety of the state in such cases overrides all considerations of private loss.'

[120 U.S. at 234]

[W]hether or not the principle laid down by Justice Field was dictum when he enunciated it, we hold that it is law today. In our view, it must govern in this case. Respondents and the majority of the Court of Claims, arguing to the contrary, have placed great emphasis on the fact that the Army exercised "deliberation" in singling out this property, in "requisitioning" it from its owners, and in exercising "control" over it before devastating it. We need not labor over these labels; it may be that they describe adequately what was done, but they do not show the legal consequences of what was done. The "requisition" involved in this case was no more than an order to evacuate the premises which were slated for demolition. The "deliberation" behind the order was no more than a design to prevent the enemy from realizing any strategic value from an area which he was soon to capture.

Had the Army hesitated, had the facilities only been destroyed after retreat, respondents would certainly have no claims to compensation. The Army did not hesitate. It is doubtful that any concern over the legal niceties of the situation entered into the decision to destroy the plants promptly while there was yet time to destroy them thoroughly. [Footnote omitted.] Nor do we think it legally significant that the destruction was effected prior to withdrawal. The short of the matter is that this property, due to the fortunes of war, had become a potential weapon of great significance to the invader. It was destroyed, not appropriated for subsequent use. It was destroyed [so] that the United States might better and sooner destroy the enemy.

[W]e conclude that the court below erred in holding that respondents have a constitutional right to compensation on the claims presented to this Court.

Reversed.

MR. JUSTICE DOUGLAS, with whom MR. JUSTICE BLACK concurs, dissenting.

I have no doubt that the military had authority to select this particular property for destruction. But whatever the weight of authority may be, I believe that the Fifth Amendment requires compensation for the taking. The property was destroyed, not because it was in the nature of a public nuisance, but because its destruction was deemed necessary to help win the war. It was as clearly appropriated to that end as animals, food, and supplies requisitioned for the defense effort. As the Court says, the destruction of this property deprived the enemy of a valuable logistic weapon.

It seems to me that the guiding principle should be this: Whenever the government determines that one person's property — whatever it may be — is essential to the war effort and appropriates it for the common good, the public purse rather than the individual, should bear the loss.

NOTES

1. *Wegner v. Milwaukee Mutual Ins. Co.*, 479 N.W.2d 38 (Minn. 1991), provides an example of a case that came out the other way. In *Wegner*, members of the Minneapolis police department damaged the plaintiff's house while apprehending a narcotics suspect who was hiding inside. The plaintiff sought compensation from the city of Minneapolis in light of the Minnesota constitution which provided that "[p]rivate property shall not be taken, destroyed, or damaged for public use without just compensation, first paid or secured." The Minnesota Supreme Court agreed:

> We are not inclined to allow the city to defend its actions on grounds of public necessity under the facts of this case. We believe the better rule, in situations where an innocent third party's property is taken, damaged or destroyed by the police in the course of apprehending a suspect, is for the municipality to compensate the innocent party for the resulting damages. The policy considerations in this case center around the basic notions of fairness and justice. At its most basic level, the issue is whether it is fair to allocate the entire risk to an innocent homeowner for the good of the public. We do not believe the imposition of such a burden on the innocent citizens of this state would square with the underlying principles of our system of justice.

Wegner, 479 N.W.2d at 43. Do you agree with the court's decision?

2. The public necessity privilege extends to private citizens as well as governmental actors. The following problems raise the issue in that context.

PROBLEMS

1. Suppose that Florence lives on the edge of a river in a Weaversville, a village of 10,000 people. One spring day, weather forecasters predict a rainstorm later in the week, with the potential to cause a flood that threatens the entire village. A group of Weaversville men work feverishly placing sandbags along the edge of the river in an effort to protect the village. In the course of doing so, the men enter Florence's property and destroy her garden which sat near the river. The rainstorm comes and the sandbags save Weaversville from a tremendous amount of damage. Nonetheless, Florence sues the men who destroyed her garden for trespass to land. Can the men successfully assert the defense of public necessity?

2. Same facts as above, except the sandbagging effort was unsuccessful in preventing a devastating flood. Should this change the outcome in Florence's lawsuit?

3. Same facts as above, except the weather report turned out to be inaccurate and the storm never arrived. Should this change the outcome in Florence's lawsuit?

F. SUMMARY PROBLEM

We have now concluded our materials on intentional torts. The following problem will provide you with an opportunity to apply the principles that you have studied.

Thurston, Spud, and Jumbo live in a small community located 200 miles outside of Cumberland, a city of one million residents. Spud is a diminutive 35-year-old accountant. Jumbo is a 28-year professional wrestler who stands six feet, five inches tall and weighs 280 pounds. Thurston is a 45-year-old millionaire who owns a small airplane that he flies to Cumberland several times a year.

Last October, Thurston agreed to fly Jumbo to Cumberland for the Fall Fracas, an annual weekend wrestling tournament. Spud decided to join Thurston and Jumbo for the trip. The three men left for Cumberland on a clear day. About half-way to the city, an emergency light lit up on the plane's control panel, indicating that the plane had lost all of its hydraulic fluid. Thurston realized that, without hydraulic fluid, he could not safely land the plane at the small Cumberland Airport, which is surrounded by one of the city's most densely populated areas. Thurston felt that he could avoid disaster only by landing the plane on one of the large farms outside of the city. Several minutes later, Thurston saw farmland below him. He successfully landed the plane there, tearing a wide swath through a cornfield owned by Farmer Jones.

Relieved, Thurston fainted in the pilot's seat. In the passenger area, Spud became terrified and stood with his arms folded in front of the plane's only exit door. Spud screamed to Jumbo: "We're not leaving until Thurston tells us it's

O.K.!" Jumbo stood facing Spud for five minutes. Jumbo desperately wanted to leave the plane, but said nothing, as he was near paralyzed with fear. Finally, Jumbo hollered: "You're crazy, Spud! This plane could blow!" At that moment, Thurston woke up and yelled: "Let's get out of here!" Led by Spud, the three men left the plane through the exit door and ran across the cornfield toward Farmer Jones' home.

Fortunately, Thurston's plane never exploded, and none of the men on the plane were physically injured. Farmer Jones, however, has estimated that the emergency landing caused $10,000 worth of damage to his land. Consider the intentional torts and defenses involved in (a) Farmer Jones' lawsuit against Thurston and (b) Jumbo's lawsuit against Spud.

Chapter 4
NEGLIGENCE

A. INTRODUCTION

In this chapter, we begin our study of negligence. To succeed in a negligence action, a plaintiff must prove the following elements:

1. A Duty of Reasonable Care. In most cases, a person must behave as a reasonably prudent person under the same or similar circumstances.

2. Breach of Duty. The plaintiff must prove that the defendant failed to use reasonable care to avoid causing harm. Many people refer to this element alone as "negligence," although the entire cause of action also goes by that name.

3. Causation. The causation element has two parts. Plaintiff first must prove "cause in fact": that the defendant's breach of duty (the negligent conduct) in some way brought about the plaintiff's injury. Plaintiff also must prove "proximate cause": that the causal connection between the negligent conduct of the defendant and the plaintiff's injury was sufficiently close to hold the defendant liable.

4. Damages. The plaintiff must prove that actual injury resulted from the defendant's conduct. Nominal damages are not awarded for negligence that does not cause injury.

The concept of "negligence" is difficult to define. There is a certain vagueness, yet common sense understanding, to the term. Society recognizes this by placing the power to determine negligence primarily with the jury. In general, negligence is behavior that requires less than intent, but is deemed blameworthy because a jury finds that the defendant's behavior falls below a defined standard of care. We describe this standard as the "duty" that one person owes to another.

B. THE DUTY STANDARD

1. The Reasonably Prudent Person Standard of Care

As noted above, most courts evaluate people based on their duty to act as a reasonably prudent person under the same or similar circumstances. Therefore, our first point of emphasis is to look at the reasonably prudent person standard. What is the nature of this hypothetical "person"? Is the standard objective or is it subjective? And how does a jury determine whether a person's behavior meets or fails to meet this hypothetical person's level of care? Our first case is the classic opinion that helps answer these questions.

VAUGHAN v. MENLOVE
132 Eng. Rep. 490 (C.P. 1837)

[Picture a rural English setting. The plaintiff owned two cottages, which he rented out to two lessees. The defendant was a neighbor who had placed certain buildings and a hay stack, or rick, on his own property near the plaintiff's cottages.] At trial it appeared that the rick in question had been made by the Defendant near the boundary of his own premises: that the hay was in such a state when put together, as to give rise to discussion on the probability of fire; that though there were conflicting opinions on the subject, yet during a period of five weeks, the Defendant was repeatedly warned of his peril; that his stock was insured; and that upon one occasion, being advised to take the rick down to avoid all danger, he said "[I will] would chance it." He made an aperture or chimney through the rick; but in spite, or perhaps in consequence of this precaution, the rick at length burst into flames from the spontaneous heating of its materials; the flames communicated to the Defendant's barn and stables, and thence to the Plaintiff's cottages, which were entirely destroyed.

PATTESON, J. before whom the cause was tried, told the jury that the question [was] whether the fire had been occasioned by gross negligence on the part of the Defendant; adding, that he was bound to proceed with such reasonable caution as a prudent man would have exercised under such circumstances.

A verdict having been found for the Plaintiff, a rule nisi for a new trial was obtained, on the ground that the jury should have been directed to consider, not, whether the Defendant had been guilty of gross negligence with reference to the standard of ordinary prudence, a standard too uncertain to afford any criterion; but whether he had acted bona fide to the best of his judgment; if he had, he ought not to be responsible for the misfortune of not possessing the highest order of intelligence. The action under such circumstances, was of the first impression.

TINDAL, C.J. [T]here is a rule of law which says you must so enjoy your own property as not to injure that of another; and according to the rule the Defendant is liable for the consequence of his own neglect: and though the Defendant did not himself light the fire, yet mediately, he is as much the cause of it as if he had himself put the candle to the rick; for it is well known that hay will ferment and take fire if it be not carefully stacked. It has been decided that if an occupier burns weeds so near the boundary of his own land that damage ensues to the property of his neighbour, he is liable to an action for the amount of injury done, unless the accident were occasioned by a sudden blast which he could not foresee: *Tuberville v. Stamp* (1 Salk.13). But put the case of a chemist making experiments with ingredients, singly innocent, but when combined, liable to ignite if he leaves them together, and injury is thereby occasioned to the property of his neighbour, can any one doubt that an action on the case would lie?

[Defendant contends] that such a rule would be too uncertain to act upon; and that the question ought to have been whether the Defendant had acted honestly and bona fide to the best of his own judgment. That, however, would leave so vague a line as to afford no rule at all, the degree of judgment belonging to each individual being infinitely various: and though it has been urged that the care which a prudent man would take, is not an intelligible proposition as a rule of law, yet such has always been the rule adopted in cases of bailment, as laid down in *Coggs v. Bernard* (2 Ld. Raym. 909). Though in some cases a greater degree of care is exacted than in others, yet in "the second sort of bailment, viz. commodatum or lending gratis, the borrower is bound to the strictest care and diligence to keep the goods so as to restore them back again to the lender; because the bailee has a benefit by the use of them, so as if the bailee be guilty of the least neglect he will be answerable; as if a man should lend another a horse to go westward, or for a month; if the bailee put this horse in his stable, and he were stolen from thence, the bailee shall not be answerable for him: but if he or his servant leave the house or stable doors open and the thieves take the opportunity of that, and steal the horse, he will be chargeable, because the neglect gave the thieves the occasion to steal the horse." The care taken by a prudent man has always been the rule laid down; and as to the supposed difficulty of applying it, a jury has always been able to say, whether, taking that rule as their guide, there has been negligence on the occasion in question.

Instead, therefore, of saying that the liability for negligence should be co-extensive with the judgement of each individual, which would be as variable as the length of the foot of each individual, we ought rather to adhere to the rule which requires in all cases a regard to caution such as a man of ordinary prudence would observe. That was in substance the criterion presented to the jury in this case, and therefore the present rule must be discharged.

PARK, J. [As] to the direction of the learned judge, it was perfectly correct. Under the circumstances [to] leave it to the jury whether with reference to the caution which would have been observed by a man of ordinary prudence, the Defendant had not been guilty of gross negligence. After he had been warned repeatedly during the five weeks as to the consequences likely to happen, there is no colour for altering the verdict, unless it were to increase the damages.

VAUGHAN, J. The principle on which this action proceeds, is by no means new. It has been urged that the Defendant in such a case takes no duty on himself; but I do not agree in that position: every one takes upon himself the duty of so dealing with his own property as not to injure the property of others. It was, if any thing, too favourable to the Defendant to leave it to the jury whether he had been guilty of gross negligence; for when the Defendant upon being warned as to the consequences likely to ensue from the condition of the rick, said, "he would chance it," it was manifest he adverted to his interest in the insurance office. The conduct of a prudent man has always been the criterion for the jury in such cases: but it is by no means confined to them. . . . Here, there was not a single witness whose testimony did not go to establish gross negligence in the Defendant. He had repeated warnings of what was likely to occur, and the whole calamity was occasioned by his procrastination.

NOTES

1. *Objective Standard*: As *Vaughan* makes clear, the reasonably prudent person standard is objective. Justice Oliver Wendell Holmes explained why in his famous book, *The Common Law*:

> The standards of the law are standards of general application. The law takes no account of the infinite varieties of temperament, intellect, and education which make the internal character of a given act so different in different men. It does not attempt to see men as God sees them, for more than one sufficient reason. In the first place, the impossibility of nicely measuring a man's powers and limitations is far clearer than that of ascertaining his knowledge of law, which has been thought to account for what is called the presumption that every man knows the law. But a more satisfactory explanation is, that, when men live in society, a certain average of conduct, a sacrifice of individual peculiarities going beyond a certain point, is necessary to the general welfare. If, for instance, a man is born hasty and awkward, is always having accidents and hurting himself or his neighbors, no doubt his congenital defects will be allowed for in the courts of Heaven, but his slips are no less troublesome to his neighbors than if they sprang from guilty neglect. His neighbors accordingly require him, at his proper peril, to come up to the standard, and the courts which they establish decline to take his personal equation into account.

OLIVER WENDELL HOLMES, JR., THE COMMON LAW [108] (1881).

2. *Superior Skills or Knowledge*: Despite the fact that the reasonable person standard is normally objective, subjectivity occasionally does creep into the evaluation process. For example, where an individual has superior skill or knowledge in a particular area, the law expects that person to use her skill or knowledge to benefit others. *See LaVine v. Clear Creek Skiing Corp.*, 557 F.2d 730, 734 (10th Cir. 1977) (holding expert skier to a higher standard "by reason of his special training, knowledge and experience as a ski instructor"). With regard to professionals, such as doctors, the standard of care also is different. We will discuss the medical standard of care in section D.2. of this chapter.

3. *Physical Characteristics*: Courts also consider exceptional physical attributes in evaluating conduct under the reasonable person standard. Once again, Justice Holmes explains the rule:

> There are exceptions to the principle that every man is presumed to possess ordinary capacity to avoid harm to his neighbors, which illustrate

the rule, and also the moral basis of liability in general. When a man has a distinct defect of such a nature that all can recognize it as making certain precautions impossible, he will not be held answerable for not taking them. A blind man is not required to see at his peril; and although he is, no doubt, bound to consider his infirmity in regulating his actions, yet if he properly finds himself in a certain situation, the neglect of precautions requiring eyesight would not prevent his recovering for an injury to himself, and, it may be presumed, would not make him liable for injuring another.

OLIVER WENDELL HOLMES, JR., THE COMMON LAW [109] (1881).

Of course, defining a physical characteristic is not always easy. Does a person's age play into the equation? What about mental illness? We will consider these questions in the next several cases.

2. Minors

The law has long dealt differently with minors when defining the duty standard in negligence. The following two cases help explain when this might be the case and why.

CHARBONNEAU v. MacRURY
153 A. 457 (N.H. 1931)

SNOW, J.

The Plaintiff concedes that the infancy of a person is of material importance in determining whether he has been guilty of contributory negligence, but contends that a minor charged with actionable negligence is to be held to the standard of care of an adult without regard to his nonage and want of experience. [T]here is a dearth of judicial authority directly in point. . . .

[An] *obiter dictum* to like effect is to be found in *Roberts v. Ring*, 173 N.W. 437, 438 (Minn. 1919), where, after stating the rule that, in considering the contributory negligence of a seven-year-old boy plaintiff the standard is the degree of care commonly exercised by the ordinary boy of his age and maturity, the court remarked, "It would be different if he had caused injury to another. In such a case he could not take advantage of his age or infirmities."

Briese v. Maechtle [146 Wis. 89 (1911)] was an action in behalf of a boy nine years of age charging a defendant of ten years with negligent injury inflicted in a collision while playing games with their schoolmates — the plaintiff at marbles and the defendant at tag. The court there said: "[There is a] marked difference between the tests of negligence as applied to the act of an adult and the same act when committed by a child. The rule is that a child is only required to exercise that degree of care which the great mass of children of the same age ordinarily exercise under the same circumstances, taking into account the experience, capacity, and understanding of the child. This was the measure of the defendant's duty, no greater and no less."

On the other hand, Prof. Bohlen, in his Studies in the Law of Torts [59 Am. L. Rev. 864 (1926)], says: "[The] reports are full of cases in which infants have been held incapable of contributory negligence. . . . If our law recognizes infants and insane persons as incapable of exercising that care for their own protection which is required of normal persons as a condition to their right to redress for injuries caused by the wrongful acts of others and relieves them from the penalty which such lack of care would, but for their incapacity, impose, it would be inconsistent and arbitrary to penalize them by requiring them to compensate others whom they injure by conduct, which, though guilty in others, is, by reason of their incapacity, innocent in them. . . . It would therefore seem . . . that where a liability, like that for the impairment of the physical condition of another's body or property, is imposed upon persons capable of fault only if they have been guilty of fault, immaturity of age or mental deficiency which destroys the capacity for fault, should preclude the possibility of liability." . . .

The American Law Institute (Am. L. Inst. Restatement Torts, Tent.) § 167, in commenting upon the adopted standard of conduct which it defines as "that of a reasonable man under like circumstances," says (e) "A child of tender years is not required to conform to the standard of behavior which it is reasonable to expect of an adult, but his conduct is to be judged by the standard of behavior to be expected from a child of like age, intelligence and experience. A child may be so young as to be manifestly incapable of exercising any of those qualities of attention, intelligence and judgment which are necessary to enable him to perceive a risk and to realize its unreasonable character. On the other hand, it is obvious that a child who has not yet attained his majority may be as capable as an adult of exercising the qualities necessary to the perception of a risk and the realization of its unreasonable character. Between these two extremes there are children whose capacities are infinitely various. The standard of conduct required of such a child is that which it is reasonable to expect of children of like age, intelligence and experience. In so far as concerns the child's capacity to realize existence of a risk, the individual qualities of the child are taken into account. If the child is of sufficient age, intelligence and experience to realize the harmful potentialities of a given situation, he is required to exercise such prudence in caring for himself and such consideration for the safety of others as is common to children of like age, intelligence and experience." By way of "Special Note" it is further said "[O]n the whole, however, the contributory negligence cases do not seem to show an undue regard for the inevitable inferiorities of children and therefore it is probably safe to accept the standard to which a child must conform to avoid liability for harm caused to innocent outsiders as substantially the same as that to which he must conform to be free from contributory negligence."

Such are the opposing authorities and divergent views where the question has been directly considered. . . . [A] "plethora of authority" is to be found in the analogous field of contributory negligence. The reasons there expressed, or impliedly assigned, for limiting the measure of care required of infants in their own protection would, for the most part, support a like limitation in the case of their actionable fault. . . .

[The court then discussed a number of contributory negligence cases that used a different standard for children.] There is nothing in the language of these cases which suggests any distinction between the care required of an infant in his own protection and that exacted of him in his conduct toward others. On the contrary it tends to refute such a distinction. If the law requires a minor for his own protection "to exercise the degree of care and caution of which he is capable" or which he "would naturally be expected to use" to use "the reason he did possess" to conduct himself "free from fault" to do what one of his age, experience, opportunity, and capacity would have done, it is plain that to exact of him a higher standard of care for the protection of others would be to require him to exceed his capabilities, to transcend the natural expectation, to possess a reason which he did not have and to do what one of his age experience, opportunity, and capacity would not have done. The law makes no such unreasonable demand. . . .

Unless infants are to be denied the environment and association of their elders until they have acquired maturity, there must be a living relationship between them on terms which permit the child to act as a child in his stage of development. As well expect a boy to learn to swim without experience in the water as to expect him to learn to function as an adult without contact with his superiors. For the law to hold children to the exercise of the care of adults "would be to shut its eyes, ostrich-like to the facts of life and burden unduly the child's growth to majority." 37 Yale L.J. 618.

It is error, however, to assume that the law requires reasonable care of adults and not of minors, or applies different measures to the primary and contributory faults of the latter. The law of negligence has for its foundation the rule of reasonable conduct. The general rule is more fully stated as reasonable care under all the circumstances of the particular case. This is the true test or measure in all cases. In applying this rule to the conduct of adults recourse is had to a mythical person called the "standard man" with whose conduct that of the actor is to be compared, namely, the average prudent person placed in his position. . . . How and why does the rule, or its application, differ if the actor is a minor? And is there anything in the basis for such difference that calls for any distinction between the minor's primary and his contributory fault?

We are told that "the personification of a standard person helps us realize that the actor's conduct is to be compared with that of a human being with all the human failings." 41 Harv. L. Rev. 9. But such standard person is the average prudent adult. In striking this average the laws takes into account the failings only of those who have come to maturity. A minor, in the absence of evidence to the contrary, is universally considered to be lacking in judgment. His normal condition is one of recognized incompetency. He is a "human being" subject not only to the ordinary "human failings" but also to those normally incident to immaturity. It is a matter of common knowledge that the normal minor not only lacks the adult's knowledge of the probable consequences of his acts or omissions, but is wanting in capacity to make effective use of such knowledge as he has. His age is a factor in so far as it is a mark of capacity. 37 Yale L.J. 618. But other qualities which are ordinarily the product of experience, using the term in its broader sense as inclusive of education and of the understanding that comes from practice and opportunity for observation, are important considerations in determining his ability both to appreciate the dangerous character of his conduct and to avoid its consequences. A danger may be concealed by the obscurity of intelligence due to immaturity as well as by its own inherent obscurity.

It is for these reasons that the law recognizes that indulgence must be shown the minor in appraising the character of his conduct. This is accomplished however through no arbitrary exception to the general rule of reasonable care under all the circumstances. As we have said this is always the test. But what is reasonable when the actor is a minor? Manifestly the adult test of the standard man cannot be applied in disregard of the actor's youth and inexperience. Either a new standard denoting the average person of the minor's age and development must be taken as the yardstick, or else allowance must be made for the minor's stage of development as one of the circumstances incident to the application of the general rule of reasonable care. As a practical matter it is not important which course is pursued. This court, however, is inclined to approve the latter both as being in harmony with the universal rule that reasonable conduct under all the circumstances is the true test of due care, and the interest of simplicity in applying the law to the facts. The latter course merely requires the jury to apply the accepted rule of reasonable conduct under the circumstances, of which the stage of development of the minor is one, while the former imposes upon the jury the duty first to set up a standard youth for each particular case from the composite factors of age and experience as disclosed in the evidence, and then to apply that standard to the remaining circumstances in proof.

This is consonant with our treatment of the physical infirmities of adults. Ordinarily we do not take into consideration their mental incapacity short of insanity. But their physical defects are circumstances to be considered in the application of the rule. This is because their physical impairments, unlike their mental defects, are susceptible of ascertainment and not because the latter are logically irrelevant. An exception is made in favor of infants because their normal condition is one of incapacity and the state of their progress toward maturity is reasonably capable of determination. So far as defects, whether of adult or minor, can be reasonably ascertained and judged the law recognizes them. As in the case of the physical defect of the blind or one-legged adult, so the mental incapacity imputable to the minor, being deemed capable of proof, is recognized as a factor to be weighed in appraising the character of his conduct. 37 Yale L.J. 621. Reasonable conduct is alike demanded of both. The rule of reasonable conduct is constant but the reasonably ascertainable defects of the actor, whether adult or minor, are circumstances to be considered in its application. In neither case does the law make any distinction between the conduct of an actor when charged with actionable fault and when charged with contributory negligence.

The supplementary instruction here, following a statement of the general rule of care, by which the jury were told that "in judging of the conduct of the defendant his conduct should be judged according to the average conduct of persons of his age and experience" was a plain statement that they were to consider these factors in applying the rule already stated. The fact that in repeating the thought the application of these factors was spoken of as "the standard" could not have misled or confused the jury.

If, however, the jury could have understood the direction as to the application of the rule as setting up a special standard as to infants, it could not have affected their conclusion. The last sentence of the instruction at most purports to read into the rule of reasonable conduct the material circumstances of nonage and want of experience, leaving the rule, as thus modified, to be applied to the further material circumstances in evidence. It merely transferred from one side of the equation to the other an evidential fact; that is, it adds to the rule one of the items in evidence and subtracts it from the items properly to be considered in its application. The fact that such an instruction disregards the process of reasoning by which we arrive at the distinction between the rule and the factors to be considered in its application is of no controlling importance to the jury. It makes no difference to them whether the reason why they are to consider the factors of age and experience in judging the conduct of a minor is because such requirement is of the substance of a rule of law or is one incident to its application. As important as such distinction is to the court here in fixing the singleness and universality of the legal standard of care, any statement to the jury of the course of reasoning by which it is reached would have been of doubtful helpfulness to them.

Judgment for the defendant Elwood F. MacRury.

On Motion for Rehearing.

Attention is called [to] plaintiff's claim [that] all operators licensed under Pub. Laws 1926, c. 101, §§ 1, 2, 3, are held to the same degree of care. . . . [P]laintiff's contention is based upon a misconception [of] these provisions. The purpose [is to protect] the traveling public. This is accomplished by imposing certain positive limitations of the right to operate cars upon the public highways. Section 3 is a legislative declaration that minors under 16 years of age are incompetent to operate such vehicles. . . . Section 2 [denies] the right to all eligible applicants who do not pass the test, whether adults or minors above the prohibited age. [The] license is not a certificate of the physical perfection of the adult or of the mental maturity of the eligible minor. Had the intention been to modify the rule of reasonable conduct in the vital respect claimed by the plaintiff, more appropriate words would have been used. Former result affirmed.

NOTE

Note the different types of authority the court uses in justifying its rule of law in cases of first impression. What authorities are primary? Secondary? Is there a ranking of secondary authority? Why isn't the case law regarding children and contributory negligence sufficient to determine the rule of law where the child is a defendant? Note also how the court uses the lack of limitation placed by earlier courts in stating the rule regarding a child's contributory negligence — what would otherwise be dicta — into secondary authority for extension of the rule. Finally, note the plaintiff's use of the statute in the Motion for Rehearing, and compare the court's holding to the following case.

DANIELS v. EVANS
224 A.2d 63 (N.H. 1966)

LAMPRON, JUSTICE.

[Decedent, Robert E. Daniels, died at 19 years of age when the motorcycle he was riding collided with the defendant's car. The administrator of Daniels' estate brought an action to recover damages for his death. The defendant raised contributory negligence as a defense. A jury found the defendant liable and awarded the administrator $6,986. The defendant appealed, arguing that the trial court gave an improper instruction on the standard of care required of Daniels.]

As to the standard of care to be applied to the conduct of [Daniels], the Trial Court charged the jury in part as follows:

> "Now, he is considered a minor, being under the age of twenty-one, and a minor child must exercise the care of the average child of his or her age, experience and stage of mental development. In other words, he is not held to the same degree of care as an adult."

Concededly these instructions substantially reflect the rule by which the care of a minor has been judged heretofore in the courts of our State. *Charbonneau v. MacRury*, 153 A. 457 (N.H. 1931). However an examination of the cases will reveal that in most the minors therein were engaged in activities appropriate to their age, experience and wisdom. These included being a pedestrian, riding a bicycle, riding a horse, and coasting.

[M]inors are entitled to be judged by standards commensurate with their age, experience, and wisdom when engaged in activities appropriate to their age, experience, and wisdom. Hence when children are walking, running, playing with toys, throwing balls, operating bicycles, sliding or engaged in other childhood activities their conduct should be judged by the rule of what is reasonable conduct under the circumstances among which are the age, experience, and stage of mental development of the minor involved.

[Defendant raises the issue] whether the standard of care applied to minors in such cases should prevail when the minor is engaged in activities normally undertaken by adults. In other words, when a minor undertakes an adult activity which can result in grave danger to others and to the minor himself if the care used in the course of the activity drops below that care which the reasonable and prudent adult would use, the defendant maintains that the minor's conduct in that instance, should meet the same standards as that of an adult.

Many recent cases have held that "when a minor assumes responsibility for the operation of so potentially dangerous an instrument as an automobile, he should . . . assume responsibility for its careful and safe operation in the light of adult standards."

One of the reasons for such a rule has been stated thusly in *Dellwo v. Pearson*, 107 N.W.2d 859, 863 (Minn. 1961): "To give legal sanction to the operation of automobiles by teen-agers with less than ordinary care for the safety of others is impractical today, to say the least. We may take judicial notice of the hazards of automobile traffic, the frequency of accidents, the often catastrophic results of accidents, and the fact that immature individuals are no less prone to accidents than adults. . . . [I]t would be unfair to the public to permit a minor in the operation of a motor vehicle to observe any other standards of care and conduct than those expected of all others. A person observing children at play [may] anticipate conduct that does not reach an adult standard of care or prudence. However, one cannot know whether the operator of an approaching automobile [is] a minor or an adult, and usually cannot protect himself against youthful imprudence even if warned."

[The] Supreme Court of Delaware in *Wagner v. Shanks*, 194 A.2d 701, 708 (1963), [rendered a similar holding[:]

> [In] the circumstances of today's modern life, where vehicles moved by powerful motors are readily available and used by many minors, we question the propriety of a rule which would allow such vehicles to be operated to the hazard of the public, and to the driver himself, with less than the degree of care required of an adult. . . . We are of the opinion that to apply to minors a more lenient standard in the operation of motor vehicles, whether an automobile or a motorcycle, than that applied to adults is unrealistic, contrary to the expressed legislative policy, and inimical to public safety. Furthermore when a minor is operating a motor vehicle there is no reason for making a distinction based on whether he is charged with primary negligence, contributory negligence, or a causal violation of a statute and we so hold. . . .

We hold therefore that a minor operating a motor vehicle, whether an automobile or a motorcycle, must be judged by the same standard of care as an adult and the defendant's objection to the Trial Court's charge applying a different standard to the conduct of plaintiff's intestate was valid.

Exception sustained.

PROBLEMS

1. A ski resort's beginners' slope makes an abrupt left turn at the end. The accident occurred 60 feet beyond the end of the slope in a flat area where plaintiff happened to be standing taking pictures. Defendant, then 17 years of age, was a beginning skier who had limited cross country skiing experience but had never attempted a downhill run. Defendant went to the beginners' slope and confined his first run to the lower portion of the slope. He walked a quarter of the way up the hill and started to ski down, successfully completing the short run of 30 feet or so until he came to the abrupt left turn. In attempting to negotiate the turn, defendant lost control over his momentum and direction. He saw the two girls ahead of him but because of the short distance remaining, his efforts to regain control, and his lack of experience, he did not call out until he was almost upon them. Plaintiff attempted to get out of the way but was unable to do so and was struck and knocked down by defendant. How should the trial judge charge the jury regarding defendant's standard of care? Should it tell the jury that "The law imposes on a 17-year-old that standard of care that a 17-year-old with the experience and background that this 17-year-old had"? Or should the court hold that "skiing is an adult activity and that where a child engages in an activity which is normally undertaken by adults, such as skiing, he should be held to the standard of adult skill, knowledge, and competence, without allowance for his immaturity"?

2. What standard of care should apply when a minor uses:

    a. A snow board?

    b. A motor boat?

    c. A motor scooter?

    d. An airplane?

3. Imagine that you are the attorney for defendants, a family, whose thirteen-year-old ran over an adult plaintiff, who was standing in line waiting for a ski lift. The plaintiff is now a paraplegic. She demands two million dollars, though a jury might find her damages run more than that. The family has an insurance policy that protects the family members from lawsuits based on their negligence. The policy will cover damages up to two million dollars. You represent the family and the liability insurer. How would you counsel your client about what they should do? Suppose they are inclined to pay the full two million. What would you say to persuade them that they should not settle? Who controls the ultimate decision?

4. Although we are still discussing only the duty element of negligence, it is hard to avoid contemplating whether a person has *breached* the relevant standard. In doing so, should your feelings toward the injured individual affect your understanding of the "reasonableness" of his behavior? Suppose that John, a 16-year-old, only child, is sent by his mother to the grocery store, located over a mile

away, to pick up a gallon of milk. He decides to take his mountain bike. It is a cold November day, and by the time he reaches the store, it is snowing heavily. When he walks out of the store with the milk, snow is accumulating. As he rides home, he signals a right hand turn onto the street where he lives. As he starts to make the turn, his back wheel skids on a patch of icy snow, and he falls into the path of the following car. The car is unable to stop in time and proceeds to run into John. John dies from the collision. Did John breach the relevant standard of care (*i.e.*, is he negligent)?

3. The Elderly

As we have seen, courts often hold children to a more subjective standard in negligence to account for their developing capabilities. Should the law treat elderly persons in a similar fashion to account for diminishing capabilities? Normally, senior citizens are held to the ordinary adult standard of care. When senior citizens are *plaintiffs*, however, some courts appear to alter the standard, although this is often affected more by physical disability than age.

In determining the "contributory negligence" of an elderly plaintiff, a court may measure his conduct against the standard of conduct of the ordinary person suffering from the same or similar infirmities of old age. According to the Restatement (Second) of Torts, the weakness of age is treated merely as part of the "circumstances" under which a reasonable person must act. There is not a different standard from that of the reasonable person, but an application of it to the special circumstances of each case. RESTATEMENT (SECOND) OF TORTS § 283C cmt. a (1965).

In *Estate of Burgess v. Peterson*, 537 N.W.2d 115 (Wis. 1995), the court examined the reasoning behind the principle that in assessing the negligence of an adult, age may be considered only in the limited circumstances where old age was the cause of a physical infirmity. The logic of this position is that, while it is impossible to quantify or measure the degree to which age slows thought processes, physical infirmities (*e.g.*, arthritis, osteoporosis, etc.) have physical manifestations than can be objectively observed and measured. This allows for positive proof that a person is suffering from a certain condition. It assures that elderly persons who are negligent will not be shielded from liability for their acts by claiming that they "aren't as sharp as they used to be." Absent evidence that an individual suffered from an age-related disability affecting his cognitive abilities, the individual's age should not be considered when assessing his negligence.

PROBLEMS

1. Plaintiff, Bill, an elderly man, fell and broke his hip when he missed the step-down from defendant's store to the sidewalk. There was some dispute as to whether the defendant was in violation of a building code provision regarding

the direction in which the door swung open and the number of steps to the sidewalk. Should a court consider the affect of Bill's age on his ability to observe the condition, or his ability to exercise the level of care expected of a younger person? *See O'Connor & Raque Co. v. Bill*, 474 S.W.2d 344 (Ky. 1971).

2. A seventy-year-old plaintiff was injured when he fell over a raised break in the sidewalk. He sued the City of New Orleans charging it with negligence for permitting the dangerous condition. The city defended on the grounds that plaintiff's own negligence contributed to his injuries. What would plaintiff have to show to recover? Was age really a factor in the fall? *See LaCava v. New Orleans*, 159 So. 2d 362 (La. Ct. App. 1964).

3. An elderly woman suffered a fractured hip when she fell after the lights went out in her hotel room. Defendant argued that the plaintiff was guilty of contributory negligence because she did not stand still and await the assistance of her husband before attempting to move about the darkened room. What standard should a court apply to determine whether the elderly woman was contributorily negligent? *See Mutterperl v. Lake Spofford Hotel, Inc.*, 216 A.2d 35 (N.H. 1965).

4. Mental Disabilities

The line between age, physical deficiency, and mental deficiency is not always easy to draw. Therefore, courts struggle in defining the duty standard when dealing with people who suffer true mental disabilities. Should such persons simply be compared to a reasonably prudent person, like the defendant in *Vaughan*? Or should such persons receive the benefit of a more subjective standard, like persons with physical disabilities or children? Consider the following opinion.

BREUNIG v. AMERICAN FAMILY INSURANCE CO.
173 N.W.2d 619 (Wis. 1970)

HALLOWS, C.J.

There is no question that Erma Veith was subject at the time of the accident to an insane delusion which directly affected her ability to operate her car in an ordinarily prudent manner and caused the accident. The specific question considered by the jury under the negligence inquiry was whether she had such foreknowledge of her susceptibility to such a mental aberration, delusion or hallucination as to make her negligent in driving a car at all under such conditions.

At trial, Erma Veith testified she could not remember all the circumstances of the accident and this was confirmed by her psychiatrist who testified this loss of memory was due to his treatment of Erma Veith for her mental illness. This expert also testified to what Erma Veith had told him but could no longer recall. The evidence established that Mrs. Veith, while returning home after taking her husband to work, saw a white light on the back of a car ahead of her. She followed this light for three or four blocks. Mrs. Veith did not remember anything else except landing in a field, lying on the side of the road and people talking. She recalled awaking in the hospital.

The psychiatrist testified Mrs. Veith told him she was driving on a road when she believed that God was taking a hold of the steering wheel and was directing her car. She saw the truck coming and stepped on the gas in order to become airborne because she knew she could fly because Batman does it. To her surprise she was not airborne before striking the truck but after the impact she was flying.

Actually, Mrs. Veith's car continued west on highway 19 for about a mile. The road was straight for this distance and then made a gradual turn to the right. At this turn her car left the road in a straight line, negotiated a deep ditch and came to rest in a cornfield. When a traffic officer came to the car to investigate the accident, he found Mrs. Veith sitting behind the wheel looking off into space. He could not get a statement of any kind from her. She was taken to the Methodist Hospital and later transferred to the psychiatric ward of the Madison General Hospital.

The psychiatrist testified Erma Veith was suffering from "schizophrenic reaction, paranoid type, acute." He stated that from the time Mrs. Veith commenced following the car with the white light and ending with the stopping of her vehicle in the cornfield, she was not able to operate the vehicle with her conscious mind and that she had no knowledge or forewarning that such illness or disability would likely occur.

The insurance company argues Erma Veith was not negligent as a matter of law because there is no evidence upon which the jury could find that she had knowledge or warning or should have reasonably foreseen that she might be subject to a mental delusion which would suddenly cause her to lose control of the car. Plaintiff argues there was such evidence of forewarning and also suggests Erma Veith should be liable because insanity should not be a defense in negligence cases.

The case was tried on the theory that some forms of insanity are a defense to and preclude liability for negligence under the doctrine of *Theisen v. Milwaukee Automobile Mut. Ins. Co.*, . . . (Wis. 1962). We agree. Not all types of insanity vitiate responsibility for a negligent tort. The question of liability in every case must depend upon the kind and nature of the insanity. The effect of the mental illness or mental hallucinations or disorder must be such as to affect the person's ability to understand and appreciate the duty which rests upon him to drive his car with ordinary care, or if the insanity does not affect such understanding and appreciation, it must affect his ability to control his car in an ordinarily prudent manner. And in addition, there must be an absence of notice of forewarning to the person that he may be suddenly subject to such a type of insanity or mental illness.

In *Theisen* we recognized one was not negligent if he was unable to conform his conduct through no fault of his own but held a sleeping driver negligent as a matter of law because one is always given conscious warnings of drowsiness and if a person does not heed such warnings and continues to drive his car, he is negligent for continuing to drive under such conditions. But we distinguished those exceptional cases of loss of consciousness resulting from injury inflicted by an outside force, or fainting, or heart attack, or epileptic seizure, or other illness which suddenly incapacitates the driver of an automobile when the occurrence of such disability is not attended with sufficient warning or should not have been reasonably foreseen.

The policy basis of holding a permanently insane person liable for his tort is: (1) Where one of two innocent persons must suffer a loss it should be borne by the one who occasioned it; (2) to induce those interested in the estate of the insane person (if he has one) to restrain and control him; and (3) the fear an insanity defense would lead to false claims of insanity to avoid liability. These three grounds were mentioned in *In re Guardianship of Meyer*, 261 N.W. 211 (Wis. 1935), where a farm hand who was insane set fire to his employer's barn. The insurance company paid the loss and filed a claim against the estate of the insane person, and was allowed to recover.

In an earlier Wisconsin case involving arson, the same view was taken. *Karow v. Continental Ins. Co.*, 15 N.W. 27 (Wis. 1883). But it was said in *Karow* that an insane person cannot be said to be negligent. The cases holding an insane person liable for his torts have generally dealt with pre-existing insanity of a permanent nature and the question presented here was neither discussed nor decided. The plaintiff cites [*Johnson v. Lambotte,* 147 Colo. 203, 363 P.2d 165 (1961)] for holding insanity is not a defense in negligence cases. [However,] [i]n *Johnson*, the defendant was under observation by order of the county court and was being treated in a hospital for "chronic schizophrenic state of paranoid type." On the day in question, she wanted to leave the hospital and escaped therefrom and found an automobile standing on a street with its motor running a few blocks from the hospital. She got into the car and drove off, having little or no control over the car. She soon collided with the plaintiff. Later she was adjudged mentally incompetent and committed to a state hospital. *Johnson* is not a case of sudden mental seizure with no forewarning. The defendant knew she was being treated for a mental disorder and hence would not have come under the nonliability rule herein stated.

We think the statement that insanity is no defense is too broad when it is applied to a negligence case where the driver is suddenly overcome without forewarning by a mental disability or disorder which incapacitates him from conforming his conduct to the standards of a reasonable man under like circumstances. These are rare cases indeed, but their rarity is no reason for overlooking their existence and the justification which is the basis of the whole doctrine of liability for negligence, *i.e.*, that it is unjust to hold a man responsible for his conduct which he is incapable of avoiding and which incapability was unknown to him prior to the accident.

We need not reach the question of contributory negligence of an insane person or the question of comparative negligence as those problems are not now presented. All we hold is that a sudden mental incapacity equivalent in its effect to such physical causes as a sudden heart attack, epileptic seizure, stroke, or fainting should be treated alike and not under the general rule of insanity.

The insurance company argues that since the psychiatrist was the only expert witness who testified concerning the mental disability of Mrs. Veith and the lack of forewarning that as a matter of law there was no forewarning and she could not be held negligent; and the trial court should have so held. While there was testimony of friends indicating she was normal for some months prior to the accident, the psychiatrist testifies the origin of her mental illness appeared in August, 1965, prior to the accident. In that month Mrs. Veith visited the Necedah Shrine where she was told the Blessed Virgin had sent her to the shrine. She was told to pray for survival. Since that time she felt it had been revealed to her the end of the world was coming and that she was picked by God to survive. Later she had visions of God judging people and sentencing them to Heaven or Hell; she thought Batman was good and was trying to help save the world and her husband was possessed of the devil. Mrs. Veith told her daughter about her visions.

The question is whether she had warning or knowledge which would reasonably lead her to believe that hallucinations would occur and be such as to affect her driving an automobile. Even though the doctor's testimony is uncontradicted, it need not be accepted by the jury. It is an expert's opinion but it is not conclusive. It is for the jury to decide whether the facts underpinning an expert opinion are true. The jury could find that a woman, who believed she had a special relationship to God and was the chosen one to survive the end of the world, could believe that God would take over the direction of her life to the extent of driving her car. Since these mental aberrations were not constant, the jury could infer she had knowledge of her condition and the likelihood of a hallucination just as one who has knowledge of a heart condition knows the possibility of an attack. While the evidence may not be strong upon which to base an inference, especially in view of the fact that two jurors dissented on this verdict and expressly stated they could find no evidence of forewarning, nevertheless, the evidence to sustain the verdict of the jury need not constitute the great weight and clear preponderance.

It is argued the jury was aware of the effect of its answer to the negligence question because the jury after it started to deliberate asked the court the following question: "If Mrs. Veith is found not negligent, will it mean Mr. Breunig will receive no compensation?" The jury was not instructed on the effect of its answer. It has not been held that because a jury knew the effect of its answer that its verdict was perverse. Lawyers and judges are not so naive as to believe that most juries do not know the effect of their answers. The error is in instructing or telling the jury the effect of their answer with the exception which was made by this court on the basis of public policy in *State v. Shoffner*, 31 Wis. 2d

412, 143 N.W.2d 458 (1966), wherein we stated that it was proper for the court when the issue of insanity is litigated in a criminal case to tell the jury that the defendant will not go free if he is found not guilty by reason of insanity.

Judgment affirmed.

NOTES

1. The *Breunig* case is instructive in showing the role that the judge may play in influencing the outcome of the trial. It is the advocate's duty to "make a record" of the judge's expressions that may suggest his displeasure toward one side of the case. The *Breunig* court discussed the trial judge's conduct as follows:

> The defendant insurance company argues it did not receive a fair trial because: (1) The court engaged in extensive questioning of witnesses which amounted to interference; and (2) the court's manner during the trial indicated to the jury his disapproval of the defense. It is true the court interjected itself into the questioning of witnesses. In some instances the court was trying to clarify medical testimony but in other instances the court interjected itself more than was necessary under the circumstances. However, this is not necessarily a basis for reversal. A trial judge is not a mere moderator or a referee; but conversely, his duty is not to try the case but to hear it. He must control the conduct of the trial but he is not responsible for the proof. [L]itigants are entitled to a fair trial but the judge does not have to enjoy giving it.

> That seems to be the situation in the instant case. At the initial conference in chambers outside the presence of the jury, the trial judge made it clear he had no sympathy with the defendant's position and criticized the company for letting the case go to trial rather than paying the claim. On other occasions, outside the hearing of the jury, the court evidenced his displeasure with the defense and expressed his opinion that the Insurance Company should have paid the claim. However, he stated he was going to try not to say a word before the jury which would hint that the insurance company was "chincy." The trial judge may have been upset in chambers but he was careful not to go back on the bench until he had regained his composure.

> The responsibility for an atmosphere of impartiality during the course of a trial rests upon the trial judge. His conduct in hearing the case must be fair to both sides and he should refrain from remarks which might injure either of the parties to the litigation. Since a trial is and should be an adversary proceeding, the trial judge should take care not to be thrown off balance by his own emotions or by provocations of counsel. Because of the tremendous influence which the trial judge has on the jury by his conduct, his facial expressions, his [inflection] in the pro-

nouncement of words, and his asking questions of a witness, it is most important for a judge to be sensitive to his conduct.

Most judges do their utmost to maintain a poker face, an unperturbable mind and a noncommittal attitude during a contested trial, but judges are human and their emotions are influenced by the same human feelings as other people. Perhaps no judge during a hard-fought trial can remain completely indifferent, especially if the case is one which he thinks ought not to be tried.

In respect to the excessive examination by the court of the witnesses we think there is no ground for reversal although we do not approve of the procedure. In respect to remarks of the judge, these were out of hearing of the jury and, consequently, to prejudice the jury there must be some evidence in the record that the jury "got the word."

The insurance company seems to argue the judge admitted on motions after verdict that the jury got the word when he said, "You will have to find it in the record, you will have to put my facial expressions into the record some way." This statement is not an admission by the judge that he did by facial expressions indicate to the jury his feelings of the case. He expressly stated he thought he did not reveal his convictions during the trial. The judge's statement went to the type of proof necessary to be in the record on appeal.

Misconduct of a trial judge must find its proof in the record. The cold record on appeal fails to record the impressions received by those present in the courtroom. Facial expression, tonal quality, stares, smiles, sneers, raised eyebrows, which convey meaning and perhaps have more power than words to transmit a general attitude of mind are lost when testimony is put in writing. Facial expressions and gestures of a judge cannot appear in a record on appeal unless the trial lawyer makes them part of the record in some way. Like alleged errors, counsel should, when objectionable expressions and gestures occur, ask to make a record thereof and take exception to the tone, facial expression and gesture, give a proper description thereof, and perhaps move if serious for a mistrial. This court would be speculating if it were to say that this jury was prejudiced when we do not know what they saw or what they felt about the conduct of the trial by the trial judge.

173 N.W.2d at 625-28.

2. Like sudden mental illness, blackouts and seizures often present difficult issues for fact finders trying to make determinations about negligence. *Compare Storjohn v. Fay*, 519 N.W.2d 521, 530 (Neb. 1994) (appellate court reversed the trial court's entry of judgment on a jury verdict for defendant and remanded for a new trial, holding that defendant's past history of blackouts made it foreseeable that he would lose consciousness while driving) *with McCall v. Wilder*, 913 S.W.2d 150, 156 (Tenn. 1995) (court reversed and remanded the trial court's

grant of summary judgment to defendant, holding that fact issues existed as to whether decedent driver took an unreasonable risk by driving, knowing that he suffered from a seizure disorder that could cause loss of consciousness).

PROBLEMS

1. Rebecca is driving her car on a city street when she has an epileptic seizure, runs off the road, and smashes into plaintiff's home. How would you evaluate Rebecca's conduct? Would it matter that Rebecca had always been a careful driver and had never been involved in an accident? Would it matter that she had never suffered an epileptic seizure? What if she had sometimes suffered seizures (once a year or so), but had not suffered a seizure for some time? What if she had suffered a seizure last week?

2. Defendant shot and killed plaintiff's decedent. The evidence shows that, at the time of the shooting, defendant was acting under the insane delusion that plaintiff's decedent was a bear and that it was hunting season. What questions would you like answered before considering whether the defendant was negligent?

3. Defendant was diagnosed with Alzheimer's disease after displaying bizarre and irrational behavior. As a result of his deteriorating condition, his family was later forced to admit him to a health care center. The head nurse of the center's dementia unit took care of him on several occasions. Defendant was often disoriented, resistant to care, and occasionally combative. When not physically restrained, he often went into other patients' rooms and sometimes resisted being removed by staff. On one such occasion, Plaintiff, the head nurse, attempted to redirect the Defendant to his own room by touching him on the elbow. She sustained personal injuries when Defendant responded by knocking her to the floor. Should Defendant's motion for summary judgment be granted because Defendant is incapable of being shown to be negligent? Should Plaintiff's motion for a directed verdict be granted because the defendant is negligent as a matter of law? *See Gould v. American Mutual Family Insurance Co.*, 543 N.W.2d 282 (Wis. 1996). The *Gould* court provided an exception to the general rule of finding negligence when a person was mentally incompetent where it found that the rationales for the rule failed to apply:

> One recognized public policy reason for not imposing liability despite a finding of negligence is that allowance of recovery would place an unreasonable burden on the negligent tortfeasor. As explained in detail below, this court concludes that the circumstances of this case totally negate the rationale behind the *Meyer* rule imposing liability on the mentally disabled, and therefore application of the rule would place an unreasonable burden on the institutionalized mentally disabled tortfeasor.

The first rationale set forth in *Meyer* is that "where a loss must be borne by one of two innocent persons, it shall be borne by him who occasioned it." The record reveals that Gould was not an innocent member of the public unable to anticipate or safeguard against the harm when encountered. Rather, she was employed as a caretaker specifically for dementia patients and knowingly encountered the dangers associated with such employment. It is undisputed that Gould, as head nurse of the dementia unit, knew Monicken was diagnosed with Alzheimer's disease and was aware of his disorientation and his potential for violent outbursts. Her own notes indicate that Monicken was angry and resisted being removed from another patient's room on the day of her injury.

Holding Monicken negligent under these circumstances places too great a burden on him because his disorientation and potential for violence is the very reason he was institutionalized and needed the aid of employed caretakers. Accordingly, we conclude that the first Meyer rationale does not apply in this case.

The second rationale used to justify the rule is that "those interested in the estate of the insane person, as relatives or otherwise, may be under inducement to restrain him. . . ." This rationale also has little application to the present case. Monicken's relatives did everything they could to restrain him when they placed him in a secured dementia unit of a restricted health care center. When a mentally disabled person is placed in a nursing home, long-term care facility, health care center, or similar restrictive institution for the mentally disabled, those "interested in the estate" of that person are not likely in need of such further inducement.

The third reason for the common law rule set forth in Meyer is to prevent tortfeasors from "simulat[ing] or pretend[ing] insanity to defend their wrongful acts. . . ." This rationale is likewise inapplicable under the facts of this case. To suggest that Mr. Monicken would "simulate or pretend" the symptoms of Alzheimer's disease over a period of years in order to avoid a future tort liability is incredible. It is likewise difficult to imagine circumstances under which persons would feign the symptoms of a mental disability and subject themselves to commitment in an institution in order to avoid some future civil liability.

In sum, we agree with the Goulds that ordinarily a mentally disabled person is responsible for his or her torts. However, we conclude that this rule does not apply in this case because the circumstances totally negate the rationale behind the rule and would place an unreasonable burden on the negligent institutionalized mentally disabled. When a mentally disabled person injures an employed caretaker, the injured party can reasonably foresee the danger and is not "innocent" of the risk involved. By placing a mentally disabled person in an institution or similar restrictive setting, "those interested in the estate" of that person are not likely to be in need of an inducement for greater restraint. It is incredible to assert that a tortfeasor would "simulate or pretend insanity" over a prolonged period of time and even be institutionalized in order to avoid being held liable for damages for some future civil act. Therefore, we hold that a person institutionalized, as here, with a mental disability, and who does not have the capacity to control or appreciate his or her conduct cannot be liable for injuries caused to caretakers who are employed for financial compensation.

[We] reverse that part of the decision of the court of appeals remanding the case to the trial court for a determination on the issue of Monicken's mental capacity. We remand to the trial court with directions to enter judgment for American Family in accordance with this decision.

The decision of the court of appeals is affirmed in part and reversed in part; the cause is remanded to the circuit court with directions to enter judgment in accordance with this decision.

C. BREACH OF DUTY: CALCULUS OF RISK

The first section of this chapter has helped us understand the standard that judges and juries use to evaluate conduct in a negligence action. Our next chore is to determine whether a person has breached that standard of care. When using the normal "reasonably prudent person" standard, many courts apply some form of a risk-utility balancing test. *See* Restatement (Second) of Torts § 291 ("Where an act is one which a reasonable man would recognize as involving a risk of harm to another, the risk is unreasonable and the act is negligent if the risk is of such magnitude as to outweigh what the law regards as the utility of the act or of the particular manner in which it is done."). The following case contains what is perhaps the most famous formulation of this rule.

UNITED STATES v. CARROLL TOWING CO.
159 F.2d 169 (2d Cir. 1947)

L. HAND, J.

These appeals concern the sinking of the barge, "Anna C," on January 4, 1944, off Pier 51, North River. [The Anna C was tied to a pier. Five barges were moored outside her, but the Anna C's lines to the pier were not strengthened. Later, the Anna C broke loose in combination with the other barges and hit a tanker. The tanker's propellor broke a hole in the Anna C, which dumped her cargo and sank. A tug came to help the flotilla after it broke loose, but the Anna C's bargee had left the vessel the evening before and was not on board to observe the leak or guide the tug. The owner of the lost cargo, and others, sought to impose liability on the Anna C's owner, arguing that the presence of the bargee would have prevented the losses.]

As to the consequences of a bargee's absence from his barge there have been a number of decisions; and we cannot agree that it is never ground for liability even to other vessels who may be injured.

[It appears] that there is no general rule to determine when the absence of a bargee or other attendant will make the owner of the barge liable for injuries to other vessels if she breaks away from her moorings. However, in any cases where he would be so liable for injuries to others obviously he must reduce his damages proportionately, if the injury is to his own barge. It becomes apparent why there can be no such general rule, when we consider the grounds for such a liability. Since there are occasions when every vessel will break from her moorings, and since, if she does, she becomes a menace to those about her; the owner's duty, as in other similar situations, to provide against resulting injuries is a function of three variables: (1) The probability that she will break away; (2) the gravity of the resulting injury, if she does; (3) the burden of adequate precautions. Possibly it serves to bring this notion into relief to state it in algebraic terms: if the probability be called P; the injury, L; and the burden, B; liability depends upon whether B is less than L multiplied by P: i.e., whether B [is] less than PL. Applied to the situation at bar, the likelihood that a barge will break from her fasts and the damage she will do, vary with the place and time; for example, if a storm threatens, the danger is greater; so it is, if she is in a crowded harbor where moored barges are constantly being shifted about. On the other hand, the barge must not be the bargee's prison, even though he lives aboard; he must go ashore at times. We need not say whether, even in such crowded waters as New York Harbor a bargee must be aboard at night at all; it may be that the custom is otherwise, as Ward, J., supposed in *The Kathryn B. Guinan*, 176 F. 301 [2d Cir. 1910]; and that, if so, the situation is one where custom should control. We leave that question open; but we hold that it is not in all cases a sufficient answer to a bargee's absence without excuse, during working hours, that he has properly made fast his barge to a pier, when he leaves her. In the case at bar the bargee left at five o'clock in the afternoon of January 3rd, and the flotilla broke away at about two o'clock in the afternoon of the following day, twenty-one hours afterwards. The bargee had been away all the time, and we hold that his fabricated story was affirmative evidence that he had no excuse for his absence. At the locus in quo — especially during the short January days and in the full tide of war activity — barges were being constantly "drilled" in and out. Certainly it was not beyond reasonable expectation that, with the inevitable haste and bustle, the work might not be done with adequate care. In such circumstances we hold — and it is all that we do hold — that it was a fair requirement that the Conners Company should have a bargee aboard (unless he had some excuse for his absence), during the working hours of daylight.

NOTES

1. The Restatement (Third) of Torts essentially incorporates the Hand test in its basic section on breach of duty: "A person acts with negligence if the person

does not exercise reasonable care under all the circumstances. Primary factors to consider in ascertaining whether the person's conduct lacks reasonable care are the foreseeable likelihood that it will result in harm, the foreseeable severity of the harm that may ensue, and the burden that would be borne by the person and others if the person takes precautions that eliminate or reduce the possibility of harm." RESTATEMENT (THIRD) OF TORTS: LIABILITY FOR PHYSICAL HARM (BASIC PRINCIPLES) § 3 (Tentative Draft 2001).

2. Some prominent scholars believe that the Hand formula provides a perspective from which to view all of tort law. United States Court of Appeals Judge Richard Posner, for example, writes: "The Hand formula shows that it is possible to think about tort law in economic terms — that, in fact, a famous judge thought about it so. [I believe] that the Hand formula — more broadly economic analysis — provides a unifying perspective in which to view all of tort law. . . ." Posner himself, however, notes a number of immediate questions that an economic analysis poses: Does the Hand formula provide a good description of what judges and juries do in tort cases in general or negligence cases in particular? Do courts have enough information to apply the formula intelligently? *Should* the courts use either an explicit or implicit economic approach to questions of tort liability, or should noneconomic factors weigh as or more heavily in their decisions? POSNER, TORT LAW, CASES AND ECONOMIC ANALYSIS 2 (1982).

3. In a recent law review article, Professor Richard W. Wright challenges the conventional wisdom that "risk-utility" dominates the negligence landscape:

> [T]he common assumption that negligence is defined by an aggregate-risk-utility test is an academic myth. If one turns from the academic discussions of negligence law to the actual cases, it immediately becomes clear that the aggregate-risk-utility test of negligence that is set forth in Learned Hand's formula, in the various editions of the Restatement, and in Richard Posner's academic writings is almost never referred to in jury instructions, is seldom referred to in judicial opinions, and is inconsistent with the actual criteria applied by the courts in various types of situations. If one then follows the legal realists' advice and looks carefully, in those cases in which the aggregate-risk-utility test is mentioned, at what the courts are actually doing rather than (merely) at what they are saying, one finds that the courts almost never attempt to apply the test; instead, the test is merely trotted out as dicta or boilerplate separate from the real analysis. The very few judges who actually try to apply the test either fail in the attempt to do so or end up using the test as window-dressing for results reached on other (justice-based) grounds.

Richard W. Wright, "Hand, Posner, and the Myth of the 'Hand Formula,'" 4 THEORETICAL INQUIRIES IN LAW 145, 273 (2003). *See Wal-Mart Stores, Inc. v. Wright*, 754 N.E.2d 1013 (Ind. App. 2001) (approving the following negligence instruction, which contains no reference to the risk-utility test: "Negligence either on the part of the Plaintiff or on the part of the Defendant is the failure to do what a reasonably careful and prudent person would do under the same or similar circumstances or the doing of something that a reasonably careful and prudent person would not do under the same or similar circumstances. In other words, negligence is the failure to exercise reasonable or ordinary care.").

4. Consider Professor Wright's criticisms, along with the questions raised about the Hand test at the end of note 2, in responding to the following problems. After that we will consider two opinions that *do* attempt to apply the Hand test.

PROBLEMS

1. Suppose Contractor was repairing a water main buried beneath a busy highway. Contractor digs an excavation in one lane of the north-bound side of the highway in order to perform the repair, leaving the other lane open for traffic. What precautions should Contractor take against accidents in order to meet the standard of care? Be sure to consider dangers to motorists, workers, and anyone else who might be near the excavation. Can you think of precautions that would reduce accidents but would be too extravagant and costly to be worthwhile?

2. In the situation given in Problem 1, you will notice that many different safety precautions are possible. Some will guard against one type of harm, others may guard against different risks. Under the Hand formula, must Contractor adopt all possible safety precautions? If an additional safety precaution is possible, should the Hand formula be applied to that precaution in isolation, or should we consider whether it provides an additional margin of safety over and above that provided by the precautions already in place?

3. Consider how the Hand test can shape the approach that counsel takes to proving (or disputing) negligent conduct. In Problem 1, for example, suppose a car drove into the unlighted excavation at night. Under the Hand formula, would it be better to argue that defendant Contractor was negligent for failing to light the excavation, or for failing to fill in the excavation after work was completed each day (which would, of course, require that Contractor dig out the excavation before beginning work the next morning)?

4. An automobile company is considering whether to put rubber sleeves around the gas tanks of eleven million of its hatchback cars to help prevent fires that may harm drivers and passengers involved in rear and side impact collisions. Its safety experts estimate that spending eleven dollars per vehicle ($121,000,000) would prevent 200 cases of death or severe bodily injury. Its wrongful death estimates run at $250,000 per death, or $50,000,000, if all result in death. Using the Hand formula, will the car company be negligent if it does not install the eleven-dollar sleeve?

GRIMES v. NORFOLK RAILWAY CO.
116 F. Supp. 2d 995 (N.D. Ind. 2000)

SHARP, DISTRICT JUDGE.

The Plaintiff, Grimes, was employed as a brakeman/conductor for the Defendant Railroad since 1967. On August 15, 1997, he was working as a conductor on NSRC Number 195L6 which was running from Fort Wayne, Indiana to Detroit, Michigan. Early on the morning of August 15, 1997, at approximately 2:15 a.m., the crew became aware of a vehicle sitting on the tracks at the intersection of Parent Road and NSRC's mainline tracks northeast of New Haven, not far from Fort Wayne, Indiana. Despite the sounding of the locomotive whistle, the car did not move off the tracks and was struck by the NSRC train. Although efforts to stop the train began as soon as the car was spotted, the train did not come to complete halt until about ten railroad car lengths beyond the crossing. Both the Plaintiff and the Defendant NSRC allege that the driver of the car, Drewery, was intoxicated at the time his car was parked on the railroad tracks, and that it had been there for some time, but Drewery denies these allegations.

Pursuant to company policy, Grimes and a student conductor, DeWayne DeHart, exited the train and began walking back towards the crossing to inspect the train for damage or derailed cars, and to provide whatever assistance possible to the motorist. Grimes found himself in the position of having to find a safe place to walk along the edge of the railroad track while at the same time inspecting the train, with only the use of a railroad lantern to illuminate both his path and the train. He couldn't walk on the area directly adjacent to the track because the grade was too steep and the large stones used in the ballast rolled under his feet. Therefore, Grimes decided that the edge of the ballast, about ten to twelve feet from the ends of the ties, was the safest place to walk to conduct his inspection. The footing in this area was still problematic as it contained a mixture of grass, weeds, dirt and stray ballast stones. In addition, according to Grimes, it contained a hole about the size of a basketball that he accidentally stepped into as he was inspecting the train, resulting in his injuries. [Pursuant to federal law, Grimes filed an action against his employer, NSRC, alleging its negligent failure to maintain a safe walkway. NSRC moved for summary judgment.]

The Plaintiff alleges that NSRC's primary negligence was in failing to provide a safe walkway for employees when company policy requires them on specified occasions to walk along the tracks to inspect NSRC trains. The Plaintiff alleges that, on the stretch of track where he was injured, the grade was too steep and the ballast rocks too large to safely walk next to the ties. As a result, he found that the safest place to walk was at the base of the ballast where it joins the mowed grass. This area was still hazardous because of weeds, dead mowed grass, scattered ballast stones, and woodchuck holes. In addition, the Plaintiff alleges that NSRC has standards for track beds that include an area that is safe to walk on next to the ties, but for some reason on this section of track, failed to follow its own standards.

NSRC has invoked Judge Learned Hand's famous negligence formula from *Carroll Towing* in an effort to prove that it was not negligent. Judge Hand stated the formula algebraically, with liability depending on whether the burden of adequate precautions is less than the gravity of injury times the probability of an injury. *United States v. Carroll Towing Co.,* 159 F.2d 169 (2d Cir.1947). The Seventh Circuit has applied Judge Hand's formula . . . Under the formula, "a conclusion that the burden of precautions would substantially exceed the loss such precautions could prevent forecloses the possibility of recovery." The railroad argues that the burden of providing safe walkways on its almost 22,000 miles of railroads far exceeds the probability of injury times the severity of injury to employees walking along the right-of-way.

NSRC's Trainmaster William Banta, testified in his deposition that it was "very rare" for a conductor or other crewmen to have to walk along or near the tracks in the vicinity of the accident. He stated that in the past five years, he could recall no crew member having to walk the area in question. In direct contradiction, the Plaintiff has produced affidavits from two conductors and an engineer stating that they regularly work this route and estimate that incidents requiring them to stop occur in this area on as many as twenty to twenty-five percent of their runs. The affiants testified to a number of reasons for the stops, the primary one being a wayside detector called a "hot box" located in the area that detects overheating and other problems with the cars. When the "hot box" detects a problem, the train must stop and a conductor must get off and walk the train to make sure the parts are in proper working order.

Whether the railroad could provide safe walkways adjacent to the ties, how often they are needed, how much they would cost, and application of the cost benefit analysis implied in Judge Hand's formula are all factual issues that are particularly inappropriate for summary judgment. Therefore, NSRC's Motion for Summary Judgment is DENIED on the issue of safe walkways.

BROTHERHOOD SHIPPING CO.
v. ST. PAUL FIRE & MARINE INSURANCE CO.
985 F.2d 323 (7th Cir. 1993)

POSNER, J.

The *M/V Capetan Yiannis,* a freighter, was damaged and temporarily put out of service in an accident in the Port of Milwaukee on Lake Michigan. The owner of the ship, Brotherhood Shipping Company, brought suit against the charterer (i.e., lessee) of the ship, Afram Lines, and also against the City of Milwaukee, which owns the port, and the city's insurer, seeking damages for the damage to the ship and for the loss of revenues from the ship's being out of service because of the accident. The plaintiff designated the suit as one in admiralty, in accordance with Rule 9(h) of the Federal Rules of Civil Procedure. The city counter-claimed for the damage that the accident had caused to the slip in which the ship was berthed at the time of the accident. Both the claim against the char-terer and the counterclaim against the shipowner remain pending in the district court. The shipowner's principal claim against the city (and its insurer — for Wisconsin is a direct-action state — but we can ignore the insurer), and the only one we need discuss, is that the city was negligent and its negligence con-tributed to the accident. The district judge granted the city's motion for sum-mary judgment and dismissed the shipowner's claims against it. Since other claims remain pending in the district court, this was a partial dismissal only, making the shipowner's appeal interlocutory.

The only issue for us is whether, viewing the evidence obtained through pre-trial discovery as favorably to the shipowner as reason allows, we can say that no reasonable trier of fact could conclude that the city [was] negligent.

In answering that question, we apply the standard of negligence laid down by Judge Hand in [United States v. Carroll Towing Co.]. Under that standard, a defendant is negligent if the burden (cost) of the precautions that he could have taken to avoid the accident (B in Hand's formula) is less than the loss that the accident could reasonably be anticipated to cause (L), discounted (i.e., multi-plied) by the probability that the accident would occur unless the precautions were taken. So: B is less than PL. The cost-justified level of precaution (B) — the level that the defendant must come up to on penalty of being found to have vio-lated his duty of due care if he does not — is thus higher, the likelier the acci-dent that the precaution would have prevented was to occur (P) and the greater the loss that the accident was likely to inflict if it did occur (L). Looked at from a different direction, the formula shows that the cheaper it is to prevent the acci-dent (low B), the more likely prevention is to be cost-justified and the failure to prevent therefore negligent. Negligence is especially likely to be found if B is low and both P and L (and therefore PL, the expected accident cost) are high.

We now have a framework for analyzing the facts. The Port of Milwaukee has a breakwater, with, of course, a gap in it to allow ships to go in and out of the harbor. Two of the slips in the harbor, where ships berth, are directly opposite the gap in the breakwater. As a result of this geometry, and the occasional vio-lence of Lake Michigan storms, surprising to strangers to the Great Lakes, a northeast gale — and such gales are common on Lake Michigan — can afflict these slips with two severe patterns of wave action, which the parties refer to as "cross-slapping" and "over-topping." Waves from the open water surge through the gap in the breakwater, strike the wall on the other side, recoil, and collide with the next surge, creating a wave twice as high as the other waves stirred up in the harbor by the gale. This is cross-slapping. Overtopping occurs when waves in this area of the harbor become so violent that they spill over the wall of the slip at which a ship is berthed. The concern with these unusual conditions is not an academic one. Between 1964 and 1979, nine ships were damaged while berthed in the outer harbor (that is, in the area of the breakwater — there are safer births in an inner harbor). One of them sank. That disaster occurred in 1979, and the ship that sank had been berthed in the slip next to that in which the *Capetan Yiannis* became the tenth victim of cross-slapping and over-topping, in 1987. As early as 1951 the city had commissioned a study of wave conditions in the outer harbor that found those conditions to be unsafe. A series of additional studies, the last shortly before the accident that damaged the *Capetan Yiannis,* confirmed the hazard and recommended measures, such as the construction of a baffle device, that would reduce the violence of the waves in the outer harbor. The city did nothing.

Well, not quite nothing. After the *E.M. Ford* sank in 1979 (precipitating the lawsuit that produced our decision in the *Cement Division* case, cited earlier), the city had the following notice inserted in the *U.S. Coastal Pilot,* the manual that mariners use in unfamiliar ports: "vessels moored in the outer harbor [of the Port of Milwaukee] may be subject to severe surging when there are strong NNE to ENE winds." The city continued to promote the Port as a "harbor of refuge," adding that the Port provides "everything you'd expect a major world port to have," though in fact tugs and pilots are not available around the clock, as they are, at least according to some of the evidence, at other major ports. This evidence suggests, as we are about to see, that the master of the plaintiff's ship may have been induced to rely on nonexistent safety features of the Port of Milwaukee.

In December 1987, the *Capetan Yiannis,* a 590-foot ocean-going freighter owned by a Greek company and captained by a Greek mariner named Konstadinos, was ordered to the Port of Milwaukee to pick up a cargo for South Africa. Konstadinos berthed the ship, pursuant to directions by a lessee that a trier of fact might find was the city's agent, in one of the two slips opposite the gap in the breakwater. At noon the following day, while the ship was being loaded, Konstadinos heard (or was told about) a report on the radio that a gusty northeaster was brewing. He made some inquiries — not as yet from the city, however — and was reassured that he could ride out the storm. At 4 p.m., an hour after hearing a weather report similar to the one at noon, the city's harbor master received a Coast Guard report predicting waves five to twelve feet high and winds of 35 to 40 knots out of the northeast. He wrote this information, together with the expected duration of the storm (36 hours), at the bottom of a "weather notice." This is a printed form that states in its entirety:

> The Weather Bureau has warned the Milwaukee area that a North and/or Northeast storm is imminent.
>
> The resultant wave action can be very severe, causing your vessel to pitch, roll and yaw. These actions may be separate or simultaneous. This may result in damage to your vessel and/or the dock structure.
>
> This is not an order to vacate the berth. This is information to assist you in determining your course of action.

The harbor master waited till he left for home at 5 p.m. to deliver the weather notice to Konstadinos, who, receiving it at 5:30 and becoming alarmed, sent for a pilot to direct the ship to a safer berth. The pilot, however, had — despite the stormy weather, which might have been expected to alert him to a possible emergency need for his services — already left for the day and was en route to his home in Chicago. Even if Konstadinos had wanted to take his chances on leaving the berth without a pilot, he couldn't have done so, because there were no tugs or linesmen available at that hour. By the time the pilot arrived, at 11:30 p.m., the storm was too severe for the ship to leave the berth. Conditions continued to worsen and at 6:15 a.m. the stern ropes broke and the stern of the ship was dashed against the wall of the slip. The plaintiff estimates its total damages — the cost of repairs plus lost revenue while the ship was out of commission — at $4.5 to $5 million. The owner of the cargo, whose claim has yet to be adjudicated by the district court, also sustained a loss.

Evaluating these facts with the aid of the Hand formula, we note first that L in the formula — the magnitude or gravity of the loss that an accident that the precautions the defendant failed to take would have averted could be expected to inflict — was substantial. The ships that dock at the Port of Milwaukee are expensive machines carrying expensive goods. Moreover, an accident to such a ship, even while the ship is berthed, could endanger human life. The loss to the shipowner in this case has merely been alleged, not as yet determined, but there is nothing implausible in the claim that it is in the millions. The ship could have sunk, like the *E.M. Ford,* in which event the loss might easily have exceeded $ 5 million. (The damages sought for that sinking were $ 6.5 million. *Cement Division v. City of Milwaukee, supra,* 915 F.2d at 1156.) As for the likelihood of such an accident (P), it could not be reckoned small, given the history of accidents to ships at the two exposed slips in the outer harbor. So PL, the expected accident cost, was substantial and therefore imposed on the defendant a duty of taking substantial precautions.

At least three types of precaution were possible. One was a structural alteration to the harbor that would have eliminated the problem once and for all, or, more realistically, have greatly reduced the risk of accident. The second possible precaution was to have pilots, tugs, and linesmen available round the clock in the winter to remove endangered ships from the slips at short notice. The third was to give the masters of the ships berthed at the "bad" slips (a characterization offered by one of the city's own employees) sufficient early warning to enable them to obtain a pilot, tugs, and linesmen before the close of business on the day of a storm. The city did none of these things. It did not build a baffle or other device that would have prevented cross-slapping and over-topping. It did not arrange for pilots, tugs, and linesmen to stand by after 5 p.m. during the winter in case there was a storm. It did not include an explicit warning in the U.S. Coastal Pilot — the note on weather conditions makes no reference to the bad slips. It did not direct the *Capetan Yiannis* to an empty slip (if there was one) in a less exposed position. And it made no effort to communicate a clear and effective warning to Captain Konstadinos as soon as the harbor master found out that a dangerous northeaster was approaching.

Maybe every one of these precautions would have cost more than the benefit in averting the accident. But on that subject all that the city says is that it doesn't employ any pilots — they are independent contractors who deal directly with the ship's crew. This is hardly responsive. It is not beyond the city's power to make an arrangement with the pilots' association under which the association would undertake to have a pilot on stand-by status after 5 p.m. But this is not an issue worth pursuing here. Clearly the cheapest precaution was to include a candid, comprehensive explanation in *U.S. Coastal Pilot*. Second cheapest was to give a prompt warning if and when a storm was expected. In some cases the warning would come too late. But here the city's harbor master knew by 3 p.m. and probably earlier that a northeaster was approaching, and when he received the Coast Guard report at 4 p.m. he knew everything a reasonable person would have had to know to have a duty to warn the master of the *Capetan Yiannis* immediately that he must make arrangements to clear the slip at short notice. The printed weather notice was inexplicit but in any event was delivered too late.

Given the unpredictability of Lake Michigan storms and the vagaries of a notice system, sole reliance on such a system to protect mariners, many of whom like Captain Konstadinos are foreigners unfamiliar with Lake Michigan, might not suffice to fulfill the city's duty of care, provided one of the alternatives — a structural alteration to the harbor or the provision of stand-by rescue services — would be less costly than the expected accident cost that would remain once the notice system was in place. The *U.S. Coastal Pilot* warning, even if far more explicit than it was, might have been deemed inadequate if, in conjunction with the city's promotional literature, it left the impression that adequate rescue services were available on a stand-by basis, which they were not. But we need not get into any of these issues. They may or may not become important on remand. For purposes of this appeal it is enough that the plaintiff has raised a genuine issue of material fact concerning the adequacy of the precautions that the City of Milwaukee took to prevent the type of serious, and by no means remotely unlikely, accident that occurred. There is evidence from which a reasonable trier of fact could infer that the city was negligent and that the accident would not have occurred had it not been. No more need be decided to require that the judgment of the district court be REVERSED.

PROBLEMS

1. Think back to the very first case in this chapter — *Vaughan v. Menlove*. Suppose that a suburbanite, similar to Menlove, built up a pile of grass and weeds in his back yard. He knows little about the specific dangers of piling grass, but he does know that "spontaneous combustion" is caused by a chemical reaction and trapped heat. The suburbanite built a chimney into his clip-

pings pile to release heat. Some hours after he built the chimney, the pile caught on fire and burned down his neighbor's house.

   a. How should the judge charge the jury in this case? Should she make reference to the "reasonable person" standard? Should she recite the Hand test?

   b. If you were hired to represent the neighbor, how would you argue that defendant was negligent?

   c. If you were instead hired to represent the defendant, how would you argue that he was not negligent?

   d. On behalf of the plaintiff and the defendant, which facts and knowledge (or lack of knowledge) will you use to make your argument?

   2. On a cold snowy day, Jane finds that her car is covered with snow. In a hurry to get to work, she brushes the snow off of a small (5" x 5") area on her windshield. She does not have time to scrape snow off of her side windows or her back window, and she does not allow the car to warm up. As a result, as Jane starts on her journey, she is battling fog and moisture build-up on her front window. On the way to work, Jane has an accident because she fails to see a car that has right of way. Jane claims that she tried as hard as she could to see other cars, but just "didn't see" plaintiff's car. Has she breached a duty of care?

   3. Driver, in a moment of inattention, runs down Pedestrian. Is Driver negligent? Does the Hand formula help at all in deciding this question, since Driver did not make a conscious decision not to employ a safety precaution, but simply had the sort of unfortunate lapse of concentration that anyone (even the Reasonable Prudent Person) might suffer? How should the law respond to this type of accident?

   4. In a common law system, what messages are sent to the community by the jury's finding of liability? Are these the "right" messages? Might there be unintended consequences of a jury decision to impose liability?

D. THE ROLE OF CUSTOM

1. Introduction

In arguing about the reasonableness of an actor's conduct, parties sometimes point to the "custom" of those similarly situated. In effect, these parties try to equate typicality with reasonableness. If it is typically done, the argument goes, it is reasonable to do it. If it is typically not done, the argument goes, it is reasonable not to do it. Despite the appeal of such arguments, courts have struggled with the question of how much weight to give to custom evidence in negligence. Should custom be determinative? Should it be a factor? How does a jury determine what is "the custom"? By testimony of the parties? By expert witnesses? Consider the following cases in thinking through these questions.

TITUS v. BRADFORD, B & K. R. CO.
20 A. 517 (Pa. 1890)

MITCHELL, J.

Defendant, the Bradford, Bordell & Kinzua Railroad Company, operates a line of narrow-gauge railroad. In the operation of this road it has been customary, as with other narrow-gauge roads, to transfer broad-gauge cars, both loaded and unloaded, to narrow-gauge trucks for transportation to the different points on the line of defendant's road. These cars are transferred by means of a mechanical appliance, technically known as a hoist. ["Gauge" is the measure between the inside edges of the running rails. Narrow-gauge railways have tracks three feet, two inches apart. The American standard broad-gauge railway has tracks four feet, eight and one-half inches apart. The "trucks" are the sets of railroad wheels on which the body of the freight car rides. The problem in this case involved some broad gauge cars with rounded bottoms which did not sit flat on the narrow gauge trucks. To stabilize these cars, blocks of wood were wired to the trucks.]

James Titus, the person for whose death compensation is sought [in] this action, entered the employ of the defendant company some time [in 1887]. He was then employed on the "hoist," transferring these cars, and continued, excepting for a short time, in that employment, until some time in the spring of 1888, when he went upon the road as a brakeman. About June 1, 1888, while engaged as a brakeman, he was assisting in conducting a train of freight-cars on the defendant's road [when] the blocking under this box-car in some manner became loose, and the car, at the same time striking a curve in the road, tipped over. The body of the car rolled over, leaving the trucks upon the track. Titus, who was sitting on top of the brake, which was elevated several feet above the car, ran down across (the side of) the body of the car as it tipped over, and jumped upon the track just ahead of the rear trucks, which had been under the car. The rear portion of the train remaining on the track, by its momentum pushed these trucks upon Titus before he could escape, thereby causing the injuries which resulted in his death. At the time of his death he was 20 years and 3 months old, unmarried, and this action was brought by his mother, his father being dead, to recover compensation for the loss of his services.

[We] fail to find any evidence of defendant's negligence. The negligence declared upon is the placing of a broad-gauge car upon a narrow-gauge truck, and the use of "an unsafe, and not the best, appliance, to-wit, the flat center plate," or, as expressed by the learned judge in his charge, in using on the narrow-gauge road the standard car bodies, and particularly the New York, Pennsylvania & Ohio car body described by the witnesses. But the whole evidence, of plaintiff's witnesses as well as of defendant's, shows that the shifting of broad-gauge or standard car bodies onto narrow-gauge trucks for transportation is a regular part of the business of narrow-gauge railroads, and the plaintiff's evidence makes no attempt to show that the way in which it was done here was either dangerous or unusual.

Haleman says the majority of the bearings fit, and those that do not have hard-wood blocks put under them, and the blocks are fastened with telegraph wire, and he was not positive but that some were bolted on. The particular car complained of was blocked and wired. Cazely and Richmond say it was the custom to haul these broad-gauge cars on the narrow-gauge trucks, though most of the broad-gauge were Erie cars, of a somewhat different construction, and Morris says the car in question was put on a Hayes truck, fitted for carrying standard-gauge cars on a narrow-gauge road, and that this particular kind of "Nypans" car was so hauled quite often. These are plaintiff's own witnesses, and none of them say the practice was dangerous. The nearest approach to such testimony is by Morris, who says he "had his doubts."

[Even though] the practice had been shown to be dangerous, that would not show it to be negligent. Some employments are essentially hazardous, as [in] *Railway Co. v. Husson*, 101 Pa. St. 1, of coupling railway cars; and it by no means follows that an employer is liable "because a particular accident might have been prevented by some special device or precaution not in common use." [T]he master is not bound to use the newest and best appliances. He performs his duty when he furnishes those of ordinary character and reasonable safety, and the former is the test of the latter, for, in regard to the style of implement, or nature of the mode of performance of any work, "reasonably safe" means safe according to the usages, habits, and ordinary risks of the business. Absolute safety is unattainable, and employers are not insurers. They are liable for the consequences not of danger but of negligence, and the unbending test of negligence in methods, machinery, and appliances is the ordinary usage of the business. No man is held by law to a higher degree of skill than the fair average of his profession or trade, and the standard of due care is the conduct of the average prudent man. The test of negligence in employers is the same, and however strongly they may be convinced that there is a better or less dangerous way, no jury can be permitted to say that the usual and ordinary way, commonly adopted by those in the same business, is a negligent way for which liability shall be imposed. Juries must necessarily determine the responsibility of individual conduct, but they cannot be allowed to set up a standard which shall, in effect, dictate the customs, or control the business, of the community. . . . There was no countervailing evidence on part of plaintiff, though, as was said in the closely analogous case of *Railway Co. v. Husson*, 101 Pa. St. 1: "It was certainly a part of the duty of the plaintiff to affirmatively establish that the loading of cars in the manner complained of was an unusual occurrence." The deceased had been a brakeman on this train for five or six months, during which this mode of carrying broad-gauge cars had been used — cars similar to the one on which the accident occurred had been frequently carried — and that very car at least once, about 10 days before. He not only thus had ample opportunity to know the risks of such trains, but he had his attention specially called to the alleged source of the accident, by having worked, just before becoming a brakeman, on the hoist by which the car bodies were transferred to the trucks. It was a perfectly plain case of acceptance of an employment, with full knowledge of the risks.

Judgment reversed.

MAYHEW v. SULLIVAN MINING CO.
76 Me. 100 (1884)

BARROWS, J.

[The plaintiff, Mayhew, was an independent contractor hired by the defendant to trace veins of new ore. During the course of his duties Mayhew worked on a platform that was more than 250 feet above the bottom of a mine shaft. Near one corner of the platform was an unguarded "bucket-hole" which the plaintiff used in his work. Mayhew claimed that, on the day of the accident, the defendant negligently caused a hole three feet in length by twenty-six inches in breadth to be cut for a ladder-hole near the center of the platform, twenty inches behind the bucket-hole. According to Mayhew, the defendant provided no warning, barrier, or light to alert him to the ladder-hole's presence. Later, through no fault of his own, Mayhew fell through the ladder-hole and suffered serious injuries. The ladder-hole was made by a man named Stanley under the direction of the defendant's superintendent. The defendant sought to ask Stanley at trial whether he had "ever known ladder holes at a low level to be railed or fenced around," whether "as a miner" he thought it was "feasible" to use a ladder-hole with a railing around it, or whether he had "ever seen a ladder-hole in a mine, below the surface, with a railing around it." The court refused to allow the questions to be asked. Thereafter the jury found negligence and returned a verdict for Mayhew of $2,500.]

Defendants' counsel claim[s] that the favorable answers to these questions which they had a right to expect would have tended to show that there was no want of "average ordinary care" on the part of the defendants. We think the questions were properly excluded. The nature of the act in which the defendant's negligence was asserted to consist, with all the circumstances of time and place, whether of commission or omission, and its connection with the plaintiff's injury, presented a case as to which the jury were as well qualified to judge as any expert could be. It was not a case where the opinion of experts could be necessary or useful. . . . If the defendants had proved that in every mining establishment that has existed since the days of Tubal-Cain, it has been the practice to cut ladder-holes in their platforms, situated as this was while in daily use for mining operations, without guarding or lighting them, and without notice to contractors or workmen, it would have no tendency to show that the act was consistent with ordinary prudence or a due regard for the safety of those who were using their premises by their invitation. The gross carelessness of the act appears conclusively upon its recital. Defendants' counsel argue that "if it should appear that they rarely had railings, then it tends to show no want of ordinary care in that respect." The argument proceeds upon an erroneous idea of what constitutes ordinary care. "Custom" and "average" have no proper place in its definition.

It would be no excuse for a want of ordinary care that carelessness was universal about the matter involved, or at the place of the accident, or in the business generally.

THE T.J. HOOPER
60 F.2d 737 (2d Cir. 1932)

[Paraphrased Facts from the trial court opinion, *The T.J. Hooper*, 53 F.2d 107 (S.D.N.Y. 1931).]

These cases grow out of the foundering of coal barges in a storm off the New Jersey coast in March, 1928. The owner of the tugs T.J. Hooper and Montrose . . . instituted limitation proceedings, in which it seeks to be relieved from liability, and, at the same time, denies fault.

On March 7, 1928, the tug T.J. Hooper, with barges Carroll, A. H. Olwine, and Northern 30, and the tug Montrose, with barges Eastern, Joseph J. Hock, and Northern 17, left Hampton Roads, bound for New York and New England ports. The barges [under the charge of the T.J. Hooper and Montrose] were heavily laden with coal. The T.J. Hooper and tow proceeded by the inside course, and the Montrose by the outside course, it being optional with each tug which course it would follow.

There were no storm warnings at Hampton Roads, or at any of the stations along the coast, until after the tows had proceeded some distance beyond Delaware breakwater; the only order for such warnings issued by the United States Weather Bureau being at Delaware breakwater at 9:30 a.m., March 9th. [The T.J. Hooper and Montrose encountered good weather, and experienced no difficulties, until The Montrose at 10:20 a.m. and The T.J. Hooper at 12 o'clock noon encountered strong head winds and heavy seas.] The tows were then in the vicinity of Atlantic City, or about 50 miles north of Delaware breakwater.

Up to this point the tows had been making good progress, but, at the respective times stated, as tugs hauled head to the sea, and continued only with sufficient headway to keep the barges in line. . . . At 1:15 p.m. on March 10th, the Northern 30 sank as a result of a leak, [and later that night the Northern 17 also sank].

It is the contention of the cargo owners (1) that the Northern 17 and the Northern 30 were unseaworthy when they left Hampton Roads; (2) that the two tugs, T.J. Hooper and Montrose, were negligent in not anticipating the storm which broke on March 9th, and in not taking refuge at Delaware breakwater;

and (3) that the two tugs were unseaworthy in not having an effective radio set, capable of receiving the forecasts of unfavorable weather broadcast along the coast on March 8th. The owner of the tugs insists, on the other hand, that the weather conditions and glass readings were not unfavorable until the tows had proceeded far beyond Delaware breakwater; and that, when the storm broke suddenly on March 9th, it would have accomplished nothing, and have been extremely hazardous, to have turned back to Delaware breakwater. It is denied, therefore, that the tugs were in any way at fault; and it is insisted that the loss of the barges was due to their own unseaworthy condition. The owner of the tugs insists, also, that neither tug was under a duty, statutory or otherwise, to carry a radio receiving set, and it is denied that weather reports of any kind were received by the tugs on March 8th. The owner of the two barges disputes that the barges were unseaworthy, and contends that the loss of the barges and their cargoes was due to the fault of the tugs.

It is insisted, however, that the strongest argument against the tugs is to be found in the action of the other tugs, which put out from the Capes with the Hooper and Montrose tows, and went into Delaware breakwater on the evening of March 8th.

[The court then noted that of the 6 tugs that left with barges, 4 put in at the break water, and 3 of these 4 testified to having heard weather reports on their radios, which influenced their decisions to put in.]

[On appeal from the decision below. The court first noted that the evidence supported the claim that The T.J. Hooper would have taken shelter if its captain had received the naval broadcasts.]

L. HAND, J.

They did not, because their private radio receiving sets, which were on board, were not in working order. These belonged to them personally, and were partly a toy, partly a part of the equipment, but neither furnished by the owner, nor supervised by it. It is not fair to say that there was a general custom among coastwise carriers so to equip their tugs. One line alone did it; as for the rest, they relied upon their crews, so far as they can be said to have relied at all. An adequate receiving set suitable for a coastwise tug can now be got at small cost and is reasonably reliable if kept up; obviously it is a source of great protection to their tows. Twice every day they can receive these predictions, based upon the widest possible information, available to every vessel within two or three hundred miles and more. Such a set is the ears of the tug to catch the spoken word, just as the master's binoculars are her eyes to see a storm signal ashore. Whatever may be said as to other vessels, tugs towing heavy coal laden barges, strung out for half a mile, have little power to maneuver, and do not, as this case proves, expose themselves to weather which would not turn back stauncher craft. They can have at hand protection against dangers of which they can learn in no other way.

Is it then a final answer that the business had not yet generally adopted receiving sets? There are, no doubt, cases where courts seem to make the general practice of the calling the standard of proper diligence; we have indeed given some currency to the notion ourselves. Indeed in most cases reasonable prudence is in fact common prudence; but strictly it is never its measure; a whole calling may have unduly lagged in the adoption of new and available devices. It never may set its own tests, however persuasive be its usages. Courts must in the end say what is required; there are precautions so imperative that even their universal disregard will not excuse their omission. But here there was no custom at all as to receiving sets; some had them, some did not; the most that can be urged is that they had not yet become general. Certainly in such a case we need not pause; when some have thought a device necessary, at least we may say that they were right, and the others too slack. The statute does not bear on this situation at all. It prescribes not a receiving, but a transmitting set, and for a very different purpose; to call for help, not to get news. We hold the tugs therefore because had they been properly equipped, they would have got the Arlington reports. The injury was a direct consequence of this unseaworthiness.

Decree affirmed.

NOTE

One way to look at the relationship between calculus of risk and custom is to see custom as the market's way of verifying the overall calculus of risk. If individual actors are "rational" they should take that degree of care that lowers their overall costs. The market custom would indicate how the individual actors calculated the risks. Of course, the market would not be rational if it had poor, bad, or less than perfect information about the value of the activity or costs of the activity. It would also fail in times of change, or where there are new actors, new technology, and/or new risks. But is there a cart-before-the-horse problem here? Does the "custom" define the level of care, or does the court set the level of care, which determines the cost and affects behavior?

PROBLEMS

1. Defendant car manufacturer has provided seat belts in his automobiles for years. Recently the competition has provided automatic buckling designs that encourage driver use. Automatic buckling designs will add $100 to the cost of cars and are expected to save hundreds of lives. Should the defendant change its manufacturing process to institute the new designs?

2. Plaintiff and her family live out in the country, a long way from stores and shopping. Plaintiff customarily loads her 3-year-old child into the rear seat of her hatchback automobile. Every mom she knows does the same thing. Today she needs to use the hatchback to carry groceries home from the store. She loads the

child into the front seat, in a car seat. She gets involved in an accident, where defendant is speeding and runs a red light. If the child had been in the back seat, the child would not have been injured. Is the plaintiff contributorily negligent as a matter of law?

3. Plaintiff and her husband push a grocery cart filled with cans and bottles that they have collected during the course of the day. They usually make their way to the recycling store by way of walking against traffic on Highway 1. There are no sidewalks on Highway 1. Most pedestrians in the area walk against traffic so that the oncoming traffic can see them to avoid them. The day Plaintiff was hit and killed, she was walking with traffic, because the oncoming traffic was much heavier than traffic going in the same direction Plaintiff was traveling. How should the court instruct the jury on the existence of the custom regarding the question of the Plaintiff's contributory negligence?

2. Custom as Applied in Medical Malpractice

BRUNE v. BELINKOFF
235 N.E.2d 793 (Mass. 1968)

SPALDING, J.

[The] plaintiff [delivered] a baby on October 4, 1958, at St. Luke's Hospital in New Bedford. During the delivery, the defendant, a specialist in anesthesiology practicing in New Bedford, administered a spinal anesthetic to the plaintiff containing eight milligrams of pontocaine in one cubic centimeter of ten per cent solution of glucose. When the plaintiff attempted to get out of bed eleven hours later, she slipped and fell on the floor. The plaintiff subsequently complained of numbness and weakness in her left leg, an affliction which appears to have persisted to the time of trial.

Testimony was given by eight physicians. Much of it related to the plaintiff's condition. There was ample evidence that her condition resulted from an excessive dosage of pontocaine. There was medical evidence that the dosage of eight milligrams of pontocaine was excessive and that good medical practice required a dosage of five milligrams or less. There was also medical evidence, including testimony of the defendant, to the effect that a dosage of eight milligrams in one cubic centimeter of ten per cent dextrose was proper. There was evidence that this dosage was customary in New Bedford in a case, as here, of a vaginal delivery.

Plaintiffs assert: "As a specialist, the defendant owed the plaintiff the duty to have and use the care and skill commonly possessed and used by similar specialist(s) in like circumstances." The relevant portion of the charge excepted to was as follows: "(The defendant) must measure up to the standard of professional care and skill ordinarily possessed by others in his profession in the community, which is New Bedford, and its environs, of course, where he practices, having regard to the current state of advance of the profession. If, in a given case, it were determined by a jury that the ability and skill of the physician in New Bedford were fifty percent inferior to that which existed in Boston, a defendant in New Bedford would be required to measure up to the standard of skill and competence and ability that is ordinarily found by physicians in New Bedford."

The basic issue raised by the exceptions to the charge and to the refused request is whether the defendant was to be judged by the standard of doctors practicing in New Bedford.

The instruction given to the jury was based on the rule, often called the "community" or "locality" rule first enunciated in *Small v. Howard*, 128 Mass. 131 (1880). There the defendant, a general practitioner in a country town with a population of 2,500, was consulted by the plaintiff to treat a severe wound which required a considerable degree of surgical skill. In an action against the defendant for malpractice this court defined his duty as follows: "It is a matter of common knowledge that a physician in a small country village does not usually make a specialty of surgery, and, however well informed he may be in the theory of all parts of his profession, he would, generally speaking, be but seldom called upon as a surgeon to perform difficult operations. He would have but few opportunities of observation and practice in that line such as public hospitals or large cities would afford. The defendant was applied to, being the practitioner in a small village, and we think it was correct to rule that 'he was bound to possess that skill only which physicians and surgeons of ordinary ability and skill, practicing in similar localities, with opportunities for no larger experience, ordinarily possess; and he was not bound to possess that high degree of art and skill possessed by eminent surgeons practicing in large cities, and making a specialty of the practice of surgery'." The rule in *Small* has been followed and applied in a long line of cases, some of which are quite recent. Although in some of the later decisions the court has said that the doctor must exercise the care prevailing in "the locality where he practiced" it is doubtful if the court intended to narrow the rule in *Small* where the expression "similar localities" was used.

The rationale of the rule of *Small* is that a physician in a small or rural community will lack opportunities to keep abreast with the advances in the profession and that he will not have the most modern facilities for treating his patients. Thus, it is unfair to hold the country doctor to the standard of doctors practicing in large cities. The plaintiffs earnestly contend that distinctions based on geography are no longer valid in view of modern developments in transportation, communication and medical education, all of which tend to promote a certain degree of standardization within the profession. Hence, the plaintiffs urge that the rule laid down in *Small* almost ninety years ago now be re-examined in the light of contemporary conditions. The "community" or "locality" rule has been modified in several jurisdictions and has been subject to critical comment in legal periodicals.

One approach, in jurisdictions where the "same community rule" obtains, has been to extend the geographical area which constitutes the community. The question arises not only in situations involving the standard of care and skill to be exercised by the doctor who is being sued for malpractice, but also in the somewhat analogous situations concerning the qualifications of a medical expert to testify. *See Sampson v. Veenboer*, 234 N.W. 170 (Mich.) (expert from another State permitted to testify as to standards in Grand Rapids, in view of evidence that he was familiar with standards in similar localities). In Connecticut, which has the "same locality rule," it was said by the Supreme Court of Errors, "Our rule does not restrict the territorial limitation to the confines of the town or city in which the treatment was rendered, and under modern conditions there is perhaps less reason than formerly for such restriction. There is now no lack of opportunity for the physician or surgeon in smaller communities to keep abreast of the advances made in his profession, and to be familiar with the latest methods and practices adopted. It is not unreasonable to require that he have and exercise the skill of physicians and surgeons in similar localities in the same general neighborhood. It may not be sufficient if he exercise only that degree of skill possessed by other practitioners in the community in which he lives."

Other courts have emphasized such factors as accessibility to medical facilities and experience. *See Tvedt v. Haugen*, 297 N.W. 183 (N.D. 1940), where the defendant doctor recognized that the plaintiff's injury required the care of a specialist but failed to call this to the attention of the plaintiff. "The duty of a doctor to his patient is measured by conditions as they exist, and not by what they have been in the past or may be in the future. Today, with the rapid methods of transportation and easy means of communication, the horizons have been widened, and the duty of a doctor is not fulfilled merely by utilizing the means at hand in the particular village where he is practicing. So far as medical treatment is concerned, the borders of the locality and community have, in effect, been extended so as to include those centers readily accessible where appropriate treatment may be had which the local physician, because of limited facilities or training, is unable to give." And in *Cavallaro v. Sharp*, 121 A.2d 669 (R.I. 1956), a medical expert formerly of Philadelphia was allowed to testify as to required degree of care in Providence. "The two localities cannot be deemed so dissimilar as to preclude an assumption that mastoidectomies are performed by otologists in Providence with the same average degree of careful and skillful technique as in Philadelphia. It is to be remembered in this connection that Providence is not a small city but is the metropolitan center of upwards of a million people, and moreover is in reasonable proximity to Boston, one of the principal medical centers of the country."

Recently the Supreme Court of Washington (sitting en banc) virtually abandoned the "locality" rule in *Pederson v. Dumouchel*, 431 P.2d 973, 978 (Wash. 1967). There the trial judge charged that the defendant doctor was required to exercise the care and skill of others in the same or similar localities. This instruction, on appeal, was held to be erroneous. In the course of its well reasoned opinion the court said, "the 'locality rule' has no present-day vitality except that it may be considered as one of the elements to determine the degree of care and skill which is to be expected of the average practitioner of the class to which he belongs. The degree of care which must be observed is, of course, that of an average, competent practitioner acting in the same or similar circumstances. In other words, local practice within geographic proximity is one, but not the only factor to be considered. No longer is it proper to limit the definition of the standard of care which a medical doctor or dentist must meet solely to the practice or custom of a particular locality, a similar locality, or a geographic area." In another recent case the Supreme Court of Appeals of West Virginia criticized the "locality" rule and appears to have abandoned it in the case of specialists. *Hundley v. Martinez*, 158 S.E.2d 159 (W. Va. 1967).

In cases involving specialists the Supreme Court of New Jersey has abandoned the "locality" rule. *See Carbone v. Warburton*, 94 A.2d 680, 683 (N.J. 1953), "(O)ne who holds himself out as a specialist must employ not merely the skill of a general practitioner, but also the special degree of skill normally possessed by the average physician who devotes special study and attention to the particular organ or disease or injury involved, having regard to the present state of scientific knowledge."

Because of the importance of the subject, and the fact that we have been asked to abandon the "locality" rule, we have reviewed the relevant decisions at some length. We are of opinion that the "locality" rule of *Small* which measures a physician's conduct by the standards of other doctors in similar communities is unsuited to present day conditions. The time has come when the medical profession should no longer be Balkanized by the application of varying geographic standards in malpractice cases. Accordingly, *Small v. Howard* is hereby overruled. The present case affords a good illustration of the inappropriateness of the "locality" rule to existing conditions. The defendant was a specialist practicing in New Bedford, a city of 100,000, which is slightly more than fifty miles from Boston, one of the medical centers of the nation, if not the world. This is a far cry from the country doctor in *Small*, who ninety years ago was called upon to perform difficult surgery. Yet the trial judge told the jury that if the skill and ability of New Bedford physicians were "fifty percent inferior" to those obtaining in Boston the defendant should be judged by New Bedford standards, "having regard to the current state of advance of the profession." This may well be carrying the rule of *Small* to its logical conclusion, but it is, we submit, a reductio ad absurdum of the rule.

The proper standard is whether the physician, if a general practitioner, has exercised the degree of care and skill of the average qualified practitioner, taking into account the advances in the profession. In applying this standard it is permissible to consider the medical resources available to the physician as one circumstance in determining the skill and care required. Under this standard some allowance is thus made for the type of community in which the physician carries on his practice. *See* Prosser, Torts (3d ed.) § 32 (pp. 166–167); *but see* Restatement (Second) Torts, § 299A, cmt. g.

One holding himself out as a specialist should be held to the standard of care and skill of the average member of the profession practicing the specialty, taking into account the advances in the profession. And, as in the case of the general practitioner, it is permissible to consider the medical resources available to him.

Because the instructions permitted the jury to judge the defendant's conduct against a standard that has now been determined to be incorrect, the plaintiffs' exceptions to the charge and to the refusal of his request must be sustained.

PROBLEMS

1. General Psychiatric Hospital (GPH) is contemplating renovating its facility. It believes that modern psychiatry and design bring about the need to remove the bars from the third floor windows of the hospital to give a more humane look for the patients who live on the floor. The windows will be designed with one-quarter inch laminated safety glass, and won't be able to be opened. As their lawyer, would you recommend they make these changes? Would you institute any rules to insure the safety of patients on the third floor? *See Lucy Webb Haynes National Training School v. Perotti*, 419 F.2d 704, 712 (D.C. Cir. 1969).

2. Armed with your legal advice, GPH makes the changes. Two years after the changes have been made, a patient, P, was admitted, and was diagnosed with "paranoid depression." As was customary with new patients generally, P was admitted to the closed portion of the psychiatric wing, which is separated from the front or open section, reserved for less-disturbed patients, by a solid door that was kept locked. P spent a quiet afternoon talking with his wife when she visited. Early the next morning P asked a technician whether he could go to the open side. The technician told him that the hospital regulations required him to stay in the closed section. Shortly thereafter, a nurse observed P standing in the corridor in the open section. Although no one knew how he got there, the most obvious possibility was that he had slipped through while the normally locked door was open to permit the food cart carrying breakfast to enter the closed section. The nurse asked a psychiatric technician to return P to the proper section. When the technician reached the patient, P cooperated and began walking back to the closed section. After the two had walked some ten paces, P wheeled and ran back toward the solarium. Before the technician could catch up, he dived through the window.

The window in the solarium, the main portion of which was four and one-half by five feet, was one-quarter inch laminated safety glass. Like the bedroom windows in both sections of the psychiatric wing, which were also safety glass, it was unbarred.

Was GPH negligent in its decision to change its hospital design? Is it relevant that most modern psychiatric hospitals have taken the bars off of their windows? Is it relevant that overall, most psychiatric hospitals still have bars on the windows? Does it matter why most psychiatric hospitals have bars on the windows in order to determine the relevance of the custom? *See Lucy Webb Hayes National Training School v. Perotti*, 419 F.2d 704 (D.C. Cir. 1969).

3. Same facts as above. Does GPH's internal safety rule about not allowing patients to be in an atrium unattended set a new "custom" of safety for the hospital?

HELLING v. CARY
519 P.2d 981 (Wash. 1974)

HUNTER, A. J.

This case arises from a malpractice action instituted by the plaintiff (petitioner), Barbara Helling. The plaintiff suffers from primary open angle glaucoma. Primary open angle glaucoma is essentially a condition of the eye in which there is an interference in the ease with which the nourishing fluids can flow out of the eye. Such a condition results in pressure gradually rising above the normal level to such an extent that damage is produced to the optic nerve and its fibers with resultant loss in vision. The first loss usually occurs in the periphery of the field of vision. The disease usually has few symptoms and, in the absence of a pressure test, is often undetected until the damage has become extensive and irreversible.

The defendants (respondents) are partners who practice the medical specialty of ophthalmology. Ophthalmology involves the diagnosis and treatment of defects and diseases of the eye. The plaintiff first consulted the defendants for myopia, nearsightedness, in 1959. At that time she was fitted with contact lenses. She next consulted the defendants in September, 1963, concerning irritation caused by the contact lenses. Additional consultations occurred in October, 1963; February, 1967; September, 1967; October, 1967; May, 1968; July, 1968; August, 1968; September, 1968; and October, 1968. Until the October 1968 consultation, the defendants considered the plaintiff's visual problems to be related solely to complications associated with her contact lenses. On that occasion, the defendant, Dr. Carey, tested the plaintiff's eye pressure and field of vision for the first time. This test indicated that the plaintiff had glaucoma. The plaintiff, who was then 32 years of age, had essentially lost her peripheral vision and her central vision was reduced to approximately 5 degrees vertical by 10 degrees horizontal. Thereafter, in August of 1969, after consulting other physicians, the plaintiff filed a complaint against the defendants alleging, among other things, that she sustained severe and permanent damage to her eyes as a proximate result of the defendants' negligence. During trial, the testimony of the medical experts for both the plaintiff and the defendants established that the standards of the profession for that specialty in the same or similar circumstances do not require routine pressure tests for glaucoma upon patients under 40 years of age. The reason the pressure test for glaucoma is not given as a regular practice to patients under the age of 40 is that the disease rarely occurs in this age group. Testimony indicated, however, that the standards of the profession do require pressure tests if the patient's complaints and symptoms reveal to the physician that glaucoma should be suspected.

The trial court entered judgment for the defendants following a defense verdict. The plaintiff thereupon appealed to the Court of Appeals, which affirmed the judgment of the trial court. The plaintiff then petitioned this Court for review, which we granted.

In her petition for review, the plaintiff's primary contention is that under the facts of this case the trial judge erred in giving certain instructions to the jury and refusing her proposed instructions defining the standard of care which the law imposes upon an ophthalmologist. As a result, the plaintiff contends, in effect, that she was unable to argue her theory of the case to the jury that the standard of care for the specialty of ophthalmology was inadequate to protect the plaintiff from the incidence of glaucoma, and that the defendants, by reason of their special ability, knowledge and information, were negligent in failing to give the pressure test to the plaintiff at an earlier point in time which, if given, would have detected her condition and enabled the defendants to have averted the resulting substantial loss in her vision.

We find this to be a unique case. The testimony of the medical experts is undisputed concerning the standards of the profession for the specialty of ophthalmology. It is not a question in this case of the defendants having any greater special ability, knowledge and information than other ophthalmologists which would require the defendants to comply with a higher duty of care than that "degree of care and skill which is expected of the average practitioner in the class to which he belongs, acting in the same or similar circumstances." The issue is whether the defendants' compliance with the standard of the profession of ophthalmology, which does not require the giving of a routine pressure test to persons under 40 years of age, should insulate them from liability under the facts in this case where the plaintiff has lost a substantial amount of her vision due to the failure of the defendants to timely give the pressure test to the plaintiff.

The defendants argue that the standard of the profession, which does not require the giving of a routine pressure test to persons under the age of 40, is adequate to insulate the defendants from liability for negligence because the risk of glaucoma is so rare in this age group. . . .

[T]he incidence of glaucoma in one out of 25,000 persons under the age of 40 may appear quite minimal. However, that one person, the plaintiff in this instance, is entitled to the same protection, as afforded persons over 40, essential for timely detection of the evidence of glaucoma where it can be arrested to avoid the grave and devastating result of this disease. The test is a simple pressure test, relatively inexpensive. There is no judgment factor involved, and there is no doubt that by giving the test the evidence of glaucoma can be detected. The giving of the test is harmless if the physical condition of the eye permits. The testimony indicates that although the condition of the plaintiff's eyes might have at times prevented the defendants from administering the pressure test, there is an absence of evidence in the record that the test could not have been timely given.

In *The T.J. Hooper*, 60 F.2d 737, 740 (2d Cir. 1932), Justice Hand stated:

> (I)n most cases reasonable prudence is in fact common prudence; but strictly it is never its measure; a whole calling may have unduly lagged in the adoption of new and available devices. It never may set its own tests, however persuasive be its usages. Courts must in the end say what is required; *there are precautions so imperative that even their universal disregard will not excuse their omission*. (Emphasis added).

Under the facts of this case reasonable prudence required the timely giving of the pressure test to this plaintiff. The precaution of giving this test to detect the incidence of glaucoma to patients under 40 years of age is so imperative that irrespective of its disregard by the standards of the ophthalmology profession, it is the duty of the courts to say what is required to protect patients under 40 from the damaging results of glaucoma.

We therefore hold, as a matter of law, that the reasonable standard that should have been followed under the undisputed facts of this case was the timely giving of this simple, harmless pressure test to this plaintiff and that, in failing to do so, the defendants were negligent, which proximately resulted in the blindness sustained by the plaintiff for which the defendants are liable.

There are no disputed facts to submit to the jury on the issue of the defendants' liability. Hence, a discussion of the plaintiff's proposed instructions would be inconsequential in view of our disposition of the case. The judgment of the trial court and the decision of the Court of Appeals is reversed, and the case is remanded for a new trial on the issue of damages only.

UTTER, A. J. (concurring).

I concur in the result reached by the majority. I believe a greater duty of care could be imposed on the defendants than was established by their profession. The duty could be imposed when a disease, such as glaucoma, can be detected by a simple, well-known harmless test whose results are definitive and the disease can be successfully arrested by early detection, but where the effects of the disease are irreversible if undetected over a substantial period of time.

The difficulty with this approach is that we as judges, by using a negligence analysis, seem to be imposing a stigma of moral blame upon the doctors who, in this case, used all the precautions commonly prescribed by their profession in diagnosis and treatment. Lacking their training in this highly sophisticated profession, it seems illogical for this court to say they failed to exercise a reasonable standard of care. It seems to me we are, in reality, imposing liability, because, in choosing between an innocent plaintiff and a doctor, who acted reasonably according to his specialty but who could have prevented the full effects of this disease by administering a simple, harmless test and treatment, the plaintiff should not have to bear the risk of loss. As such, imposition of liability approaches that of strict liability.

Strict liability or liability without fault is not new to the law. Historically, it predates our concepts of fault or moral responsibility as a basis of the remedy. Wigmore, *Responsibility for Tortious Acts: Its History*, 7 HARV. L. REV. 315, 383, 441 (1894). As noted in W. PROSSER, THE LAW OF TORTS § 74, 507-08 (3d cd. 1964):

There are many situations in which a careful person is held liable for an entirely reasonable mistake. . . . In some cases the defendant may be held liable, although he is not only charged with no moral wrongdoing, but has not even departed in any way from a reasonable standard of intent or care. . . . There is "a strong and growing tendency, where there is blame on neither side, to ask, in view of the exigencies of social justice, who can best bear the loss and hence to shift the loss by creating liability where there has been no fault."

Tort law has continually been in a state of flux. It is "not always neat and orderly. But this is not to say it is illogical. Its central logic is the logic that moves from premises — its objectives — that are only partly consistent, to conclusions — its rules — that serve each objective as well as may be while serving others too. It is the logic of maximizing service and minimizing disservice to multiple objectives." Keeton, *Is There a Place for Negligence in Modern Tort Law?*, 53 VA. L. REV. 886, 897 (1967). When types of problems rather than numbers of cases are examined, strict liability is applied more often than negligence as a principle which determines liability. Peck, *Negligence and Liability Without Fault in Tort Law*, 46 WASH. L. REV. 225, 239 (1971). There are many similarities in this case to other cases of strict liability. Problems of proof have been a common feature in situations where strict liability is applied. Where events are not matters of common experience, a juror's ability to comprehend whether reasonable care has been followed diminishes. There are few areas as difficult for jurors to intelligently comprehend as the intricate questions of proof and standards in medical malpractice cases.

The failure of plaintiff to raise this theory at the trial and to propose instructions consistent with it should not deprive her of the right to resolve the case on this theory on appeal. Where this court has authoritatively stated the law, the parties are bound by those principles until they have been overruled.

PROBLEMS

1. How would this case come out if the court applied the Hand formula to the problem? Consider carefully what costs would factor into each element of the

test. Why should the courts not routinely submit medical decisions to this standard test for negligence?

2. D, an HMO, directed its participating physicians not to blood test for "auto immune inner ear disease" (AIIED) in patients under the age of 50, who presented with the symptom of "full ear," *i.e.,* the feeling that you are under water. (AIIED, if left untreated, can cause severe hearing loss.) The incidence of AIIED in patients under 50 is less than one in a million. The blood test at issue also tests for other conditions. It costs $100 to administer. If a patient under 50 has AIIED that leads to deafness and that would have been prevented by the blood test, is his physician protected by the "custom" in the market place of not doing blood tests? Is the HMO liable for its role in preventing the timely diagnosis of the patient?

One of the most interesting modern issues for negligence law is the level of protection, if any, that should be given to HMOs against negligence suits. HMOs are set up for the benefit of employers in order to pool employee health risks and control costs. HMOs contract with hospitals and physicians and restrict costs by setting up payment caps and restrictions on various services that are to be performed. Some HMOs also serve as gatekeepers to health care, in order to control costs by denying unnecessarily expensive treatments. HMOs have the power in the market place to set the custom with regard to the care taken in individual cases.

The problem is that HMOs can act negligently in denying coverage, or in restricting the medical care that can be given to care that may be cost effective to the population as a whole, but not to a particular patient with a particular problem. In addition, the HMO standard can become substandard through the passage of time and the ever-changing nature of the practice of medicine. The issue for state legislatures, and Congress is whether HMOs should be immune from lawsuits because of the greater good that comes from controlling health costs and restricting access to some more expensive kinds of treatment.

Protective legislation might be attacked on equal protection grounds, as was done with guest statutes (see p. 193 *infra*). Of course, the problem is whether plaintiffs injured as a result of a physician's decision to restrict care according to the terms of the HMO contract and/or HMO decision makers should have fewer remedies than plaintiffs injured in some other way, for example by a driver on the highway. Why should one group of defendants be given more protection against their acts of negligence than other defendants whose decisions affect the health and safety of the public? One distinguishing point is that the plaintiff can still sue the doctor for the doctor's negligence, unless the doctor and the HMO are seen as one by the legislation.

If the HMO and the doctor are not viewed as one and the same, then legislation that provided immunity to the HMO would put great pressure on the doctor to disclose alternative treatments not covered by the HMO in order for the patient to choose whether to pay for the alternative treatment. HMO liability cases raise important informed consent issues that have intentional tort ramifications. In fact, the Supreme Court put the focus back on physician informed consent by providing immunity to HMOs under a federal preemption analysis. *See Pegram v. Herdrich*, 530 U.S. 211 (2000) (The beneficiary of a health insurance plan brought a state court action against an HMO and a physician, alleging medical malpractice and fraud. Defendants removed the action to federal court. Following amendment of the complaint to add a count for breach of fiduciary duty in violation of the Employee Retirement Income Security Act (ERISA), the United States District Court for the Central District of Illinois, Michael M. Mihm, C.J., dismissed such count. After entry of judgment in favor of the beneficiary on the malpractice count, the beneficiary appealed the dismissal of the ERISA count. The Court of Appeals for the Seventh Circuit, 154 F.3d 362, reversed and remanded. Upon granting certiorari, the Supreme Court, Souter, J., held that mixed eligibility and treatment decisions made by the HMO, acting through its physicians, were not fiduciary acts within meaning of ERISA, and reversed the Court of Appeals.). Another point of attack, where HMO coverage is denied on the basis of the type of disease, is to argue that the HMO has violated equal protection rights under the Americans with Disabilities Act.

CANTERBURY v. SPENCE
464 F.2d 772 (D.C. Cir. 1972)

ROBINSON, CIRCUIT JUDGE.

[At the time of the events in question], appellant was nineteen years of age, a clerk-typist employed by the Federal Bureau of Investigation. In December, 1958, he began to experience severe pain between his shoulder blades. He consulted two general practitioners, but the medications they prescribed failed to eliminate the pain. Thereafter, appellant secured an appointment with Dr. Spence, who is a neurosurgeon.

Dr. Spence examined appellant in his office at some length but found nothing amiss. On Dr. Spence's advice appellant was x-rayed, but the films did not identify any abnormality. Dr. Spence then recommended that appellant undergo a myelogram — a procedure in which dye is injected into the spinal column and traced to find evidence of disease or other disorder — at the Washington Hospital Center.

Appellant entered the hospital on February 4, 1959. The myelogram revealed a "filling defect" in the region of the fourth thoracic vertebra. Since a myelogram often does no more than pinpoint the location of an aberration, surgery may be necessary to discover the cause. Dr. Spence told appellant that he would have to undergo a laminectomy — the excision of the posterior arch of the vertebra — to correct what he suspected was a ruptured disc. Appellant did not raise any objection to the proposed operation nor did he probe into its exact nature.

Appellant explained to Dr. Spence that his mother was a widow of slender financial means [and] that she could be reached through a neighbor's telephone. Appellant [left] Dr. Spence's telephone number with the neighbor. When Mrs. Canterbury returned the call, Dr. Spence told her that the surgery was occasioned by a suspected ruptured disc. Mrs. Canterbury then asked if the recommended operation was serious and Dr. Spence replied "not anymore than any other operation." [The] testimony is contradictory as to whether during the course of the conversation Mrs. Canterbury expressed her consent to the operation. Appellant himself apparently did not converse again with Dr. Spence prior to the operation.

Dr. Spence performed the laminectomy on February 11 at the Washington Hospital Center. Mrs. Canterbury traveled to Washington, arriving on that date but after the operation was over, and signed a consent form at the hospital. The laminectomy revealed several anomalies: a spinal cord that was swollen and unable to pulsate, an accumulation of large tortuous and dilated veins, and a complete absence of epidural fat which normally surrounds the spine. A thin hypodermic needle was inserted into the spinal cord to aspirate any cysts which might have been present, but no fluid emerged. In suturing the wound, Dr. Spence attempted to relieve the pressure on the spinal cord by enlarging the dura — the outer protective wall of the spinal cord — at the area of swelling.

For approximately the first day after the operation appellant recuperated normally, but then suffered a fall and an almost immediate setback. . . . Dr. Spence left orders that appellant was to remain in bed during the process of voiding. These orders were changed to direct that voiding be done out of bed, and the jury could find that the change was made by hospital personnel. Just prior to the fall, appellant summoned a nurse and was given a receptacle for use in voiding, but was then left unattended. Appellant testified that during the course of the endeavor he slipped off the side of the bed, and that there was no one to assist him, or side rail to prevent the fall.

Several hours later, appellant began to complain that he could not move his legs and that he was having trouble breathing; paralysis seems to have been virtually total from the waist down. Dr. Spence was notified on the night of February 12, and he rushed to the hospital. Mrs. Canterbury signed another consent form and appellant was again taken into the operating room. The surgical wound was reopened and Dr. Spence created a gusset to allow the spinal cord greater room in which to pulsate.

At the time of the trial in April, 1968, appellant required crutches to walk, still suffered from urinal incontinence and paralysis of the bowels, and wore a penile clamp. In November, 1959 on Dr. Spence's recommendation, appellant was transferred by the F.B.I. to Miami where he could get more swimming and exercise. Appellant worked three years for the F.B.I. in Miami, Los Angeles and Houston, resigning finally in June, 1962. From then until the time of the trial, he held a number of jobs, but had constant trouble finding work because he needed to remain seated and close to a bathroom. The damages appellant claims include extensive pain and suffering, medical expenses, and loss of earnings.

[The] complaint stated several causes of action against each defendant. Against Dr. Spence it alleged, among other things, negligence in the performance of the laminectomy and failure to inform him beforehand of the risk involved. Against the hospital the complaint charged negligent post-operative care in permitting appellant to remain unattended after the laminectomy, in failing to provide a nurse or orderly to assist him at the time of his fall, and in failing to maintain a side rail on his bed. The answers denied the allegations of negligence and defended on the ground that the suit was barred by the statute of limitations.

[A]t trial, disposition of the threshold question whether the statute of limitations had run was held in abeyance until the relevant facts developed. Appellant introduced no evidence to show medical and hospital practices, if any, customarily pursued in regard to the critical aspects of the case, and only Dr. Spence, called as an adverse witness, testified on the issue of causality. Dr. Spence described the surgical procedures he utilized in the two operations and expressed his opinion that appellant's disabilities stemmed from his pre-operative condition as symptomized by the swollen, non-pulsating spinal cord. He stated, however, that neither he nor any of the other physicians with whom he consulted was certain as to what that condition was, and he admitted that trauma can be a cause of paralysis. Dr. Spence further testified that even without trauma paralysis can be anticipated "somewhere in the nature of one percent" of the laminectomies performed, a risk he termed "a very slight possibility." He felt that communication of that risk to the patient is not good medical practice because it might deter patients from undergoing needed surgery and might produce adverse psychological reactions which could preclude the success of the operation.

At the close of appellant's case in chief, each defendant moved for a directed verdict and the trial judge granted both motions. The basis of the ruling, he explained, was that appellant had failed to produce any medical evidence indicating negligence on Dr. Spence's part in diagnosing appellant's malady or in performing the laminectomy; that there was no proof that Dr. Spence's treatment was responsible for appellant's disabilities; and that notwithstanding some evidence to show negligent post-operative care, an absence of medical testimony to show causality precluded submission of the case against the hospital to the jury. The judge did not allude specifically to the alleged breach of duty by Dr. Spence to divulge the possible consequences of the laminectomy.

We reverse. The testimony of appellant and his mother that Dr. Spence did not reveal the risk of paralysis from the laminectomy made out a prima facie case of violation of the physician's duty to disclose which Dr. Spence's explanation did not negate as a matter of law. There was also testimony from which the jury could have found that the laminectomy was negligently performed by Dr. Spence, and that appellant's fall was the consequence of negligence on the part of the hospital. The record, moreover, contains evidence of sufficient quantity and quality to tender jury issues as to whether and to what extent any such negligence was causally related to appellant's post-laminectomy condition. These considerations entitled appellant to a new trial.

[S]uits charging failure by a physician adequately to disclose the risks and alternatives of proposed treatment are not innovations in American law. They date back a good half-century, and in the last decade they have multiplied rapidly. There is, nonetheless, disagreement among the courts and the commentators on many major questions, and there is no precedent of our own directly in point. For the tools enabling resolution of the issues on this appeal, we are forced to begin at first principles.

[The court found that a physician's duty to inform the patient of risks is rooted in principles of individual autonomy and control over one's own body.]

We hold that the standard measuring performance of that duty by physicians, as by others, is conduct which is reasonable under the circumstances.

Once the circumstances give rise to a duty on the physician's part to inform his patient, the next inquiry is the scope of the disclosure the physician is legally obliged to make. The courts have frequently confronted this problem but no uniform standard defining the adequacy of the divulgence emerges from the decisions. Some have said "full" disclosure, a norm we are unwilling to adopt literally. It seems obviously prohibitive and unrealistic to expect physicians to discuss with their patients every risk of proposed treatment — no matter how small or remote — and generally unnecessary from the patient's viewpoint as well. Indeed, the cases speaking in terms of "full" disclosure appear to envision something less than total disclosure, leaving unanswered the question of just how much. . . .

In our view, the patient's right of self-decision shapes the boundaries of the duty to reveal. That right can be effectively exercised only if the patient possesses enough information to enable an intelligent choice. The scope of the physician's communications to the patient, then, must be measured by the patient's need, and that need is the information material to the decision. Thus the test for determining whether a particular peril must be divulged is its materiality to the patient's decision: all risks potentially affecting the decision must be unmasked. And to safeguard the patient's interest in achieving his own determination on treatment, the law must itself set the standard for adequate disclosure. . . .

The scope of the standard is not subjective as to either the physician or the patient; it remains objective with due regard for the patient's informational needs and with suitable leeway for the physician's situation. In broad outline, we agree that "[a] risk is thus material when a reasonable person, in what the physician knows or should know to be the patient's position, would be likely to attach significance to the risk or cluster of risks in deciding whether or not to forego the proposed therapy."

The topics importantly demanding a communication of information are the inherent and potential hazards of the proposed treatment, the alternatives to that treatment, if any, and the results likely if the patient remains untreated. The factors contributing significance to the dangerousness of a medical technique are, of course, the incidence of injury and the degree of the harm threatened. A very small chance of death or serious disablement may well be significant; a potential disability which dramatically outweighs the potential benefit of the therapy or the detriments of the existing malady may summons discussion with the patient.

Two exceptions to the general rule of disclosure have been noted by the courts. Each is in the nature of a physician's privilege not to disclose, and the reasoning underlying them is appealing. Each, indeed, is but a recognition that, as important as is the patient's right to know, it is greatly outweighed by the magnitudinous circumstances giving rise to the privilege. The first comes into play when the patient is unconscious or otherwise incapable of consenting, and harm from a failure to treat is imminent and outweighs any harm threatened by the proposed treatment. When a genuine emergency of that sort arises, it is settled that the impracticality of conferring with the patient dispenses with need for it. Even in situations of that character the physician should, as current law requires, attempt to secure a relative's consent if possible. But if time is too short to accommodate discussion, obviously the physician should proceed with the treatment.

The second exception obtains when risk-disclosure poses such a threat of detriment to the patient as to become unfeasible or contraindicated from a medical point of view. It is recognized that patients occasionally become so ill or emotionally distraught on disclosure as to foreclose a rational decision, or complicate or hinder the treatment, or perhaps even pose psychological damage to the patient. Where that is so, the cases have generally held that the physician is armed with a privilege to keep the information from the patient, and we think it clear that portents of that type may justify the physician in action he deems medically warranted. The critical inquiry is whether the physician responded to a sound medical judgment that communication of the risk information would present a threat to the patient's well-being.

No more than breach of any other legal duty does nonfulfillment of the physician's obligation to disclose alone establish liability to the patient. An unrevealed risk that should have been made known must materialize, for otherwise the omission, however unpardonable, is legally without consequence. Occurrence of the risk must be harmful to the patient, for negligence unrelated to injury is nonactionable. And, as in malpractice actions generally, there must be a causal relationship between the physician's failure to adequately divulge and damage to the patient.

A causal connection exists when, but only when, disclosure of significant risks incidental to treatment would have resulted in a decision against it. The patient obviously has no complaint if he would have submitted to the therapy notwithstanding awareness that the risk was one of its perils. On the other hand, the very purpose of the disclosure rule is to protect the patient against consequences which, if known, he would have avoided by foregoing the treatment. The more difficult question is whether the factual issue on causality calls for an objective or a subjective determination.

It has been assumed that the issue is to be resolved according to whether the factfinder believes the patient's testimony that he would not have agreed to the treatment if he had known of the danger which later ripened into injury. We think a technique which ties the factual conclusion on causation simply to the assessment of the patient's credibility is unsatisfactory. To be sure, the objective of risk-disclosure is preservation of the patient's interest in intelligent self-choice on proposed treatment, a matter the patient is free to decide for any reason that appeals to him. When, prior to commencement of therapy, the patient is sufficiently informed on risks and he exercises his choice, it may truly be said that he did exactly what he wanted to do. But when causality is explored at a post injury trial with a professedly uninformed patient, the question whether he actually would have turned the treatment down if he had known the risks is purely hypothetical: "Viewed from the point at which he had to decide, would the patient have decided differently had he known something he did not know?" And the answer which the patient supplies hardly represents more than a guess, perhaps tinged by the circumstance that the uncommunicated hazard has in fact materialized.

In our view, this method of dealing with the issue on causation comes in second-best. It places the physician in jeopardy of the patient's hindsight and bitterness. It places the factfinder in the position of deciding whether a speculative answer to a hypothetical question is to be credited. It calls for a subjective determination solely on testimony of a patient-witness shadowed by the occurrence of the undisclosed risk. Better it is, we believe, to resolve the causality issue on an objective basis: in terms of what a prudent person in the patient's position would have decided if suitably informed of all perils bearing significance. If adequate disclosure could reasonably be expected to have caused that person to decline the treatment because of the revelation of the kind of risk or danger that resulted in harm, causation is shown, but otherwise not. The patient's testimony is relevant on that score of course but it would not threaten to dominate the findings. And since that testimony would probably be appraised congruently with the factfinder's belief in its reasonableness, the case for a wholly objective standard for passing on causation is strengthened. Such a standard would in any event ease the fact-finding process and better assure the truth as its product.

In the context of trial of a suit claiming inadequate disclosure of risk information by a physician, the patient has the burden of going forward with evidence tending to establish prima facie the essential elements of the cause of action, and ultimately the burden of proof — the risk of nonpersuasion — on those elements. These are normal impositions upon moving litigants, and no reason why they should not attach in nondisclosure cases is apparent. The burden of going forward with evidence pertaining to a privilege not to disclose, however, rests properly upon the physician. This is not only because the patient has made out a prima facie case before an issue on privilege is reached, but also because any evidence bearing on the privilege is usually in the hands of the physician alone. Requiring him to open the proof on privilege is consistent with judicial policy laying such a burden on the party who seeks shelter from an exception to a general rule and who is more likely to have possession of the facts.

As in much malpractice litigation, recovery in nondisclosure lawsuits has hinged upon the patient's ability to prove through expert testimony that the physician's performance departed from medical custom. . . . We now delineate our view on the need for expert testimony in nondisclosure cases.

[T]he guiding consideration our decisions distill . . . is that medical facts are for medical experts and other facts are for any witnesses — expert or not — having sufficient knowledge and capacity to testify to them. It is evident that many of the issues typically involved in nondisclosure cases do not reside peculiarly within the medical domain. Lay witness testimony can competently establish a physician's failure to disclose particular risk information, the patient's lack of knowledge of the risk, and the adverse consequences following the treatment. Experts are unnecessary to a showing of the materiality of a risk to a patient's decision on treatment, or to the reasonably, expectable effect of risk disclosure on the decision. . . .

We now confront the question whether appellant's suit was barred, wholly or partly, by the statute of limitations. The statutory periods relevant to this inquiry are one year for battery actions and three years for those charging negligence. . . . Appellant has asserted and litigated a violation of . . . duty throughout the case. That claim, like the others, was governed by the three-year period of limitation applicable to negligence actions and was unaffected by the fact that its alternative was barred by the one-year period pertaining to batteries.

This brings us to the remaining question, common to all three causes of action: whether appellant's evidence was of such caliber as to require a submission to the jury. On the first, the evidence was clearly sufficient to raise an issue as to whether Dr. Spence's obligation to disclose information on risks was reasonably met or was excused by the surrounding circumstances. . . .

Reversed and remanded for a new trial.

NOTES

1. What the court gives with one hand — a "right" to information necessary to make an informed decision — it severely limits with the other — the need to show that the reasonable patient in the plaintiff's circumstance would not have submitted to the procedure if he or she knew of the undisclosed risks. In the end,

the doctor may need to disclose only risks that would keep a reasonable patient from going forward with the procedure.

2. Even this amount of disclosure is too much for the British. In a case remarkably similar to *Canterbury*, the Court of Appeals affirmed a dismissal of plaintiff's suit for non-disclosure of a paralysis risk associated with an operation,

> [A] contrary result would be damaging to the relationship of trust and confidence between doctor and patient, and might well have an adverse effect on the practice of medicine. It is doubtful whether it would be of any significant benefit to patients, most of whom prefer to put themselves unreservedly in the hands of their doctors. This is not . . . A paternalism[.] It is simply an acceptance of the doctor/patient relationship as it has developed in this country. The principal effect of [plaintiff's proposition] would be likely [an] increase in the number of claims for professional negligence against doctors. This would [have] an adverse effect on the general standard of medical care, since doctors would inevitably [try] to safeguard themselves against such claims, rather than [concentrating] on their primary duty of treating their patients.

Sidaway v. Bethlem Royal Hospital, All Eng. Rep. 1018, 1030–31 (1984). Perhaps the existence of a nationalized medical system affected the court's reasoning.

3. *Expert Testimony in Informed Consent Cases.* In a medical malpractice case, when plaintiff is required to produce an expert on negligent treatment and causation of injury in medical malpractice, must plaintiff also produce an expert on whether the risk not disclosed is material? Contrary to *Canterbury,* which suggests that materiality is a question to be determined by reference to the reasonable patient, one court said the plaintiff must produce a medical expert on disclosure: "[a]fter all, in the usual case, the patient unquestionably will have obtained experts to establish the negligent treatment phase of his malpractice action." *Bly v. Rhoads*, 222 S.E.2d 783, 787-88 (Va. 1976). In other words, the expert must add an opinion on materiality of the risk, and if the expert cannot, then the case will fail.

4. *Contract Remedy to Informed Consent Cases.* At least one prominent legal commentator, Professor Richard Epstein, has proposed to allow physicians and patients to alter the doctor's duty regarding informed consent by private contract. *See* Epstein, *Medical Malpractice, The Case for Contract*, 1 AM. B. FOUND. RES. J. 87, 119–28 (1976). *Cf.* Schuck, *Rethinking Informed Consent*, 103 YALE L.J. 899, 957–58 (1994) (where the author notes that, while *Canterbury* can hardly allow a knowing waiver by contract that cannot be provided in person, the existing doctrine has an "endemic vice: it deprives patients of choice in the name of choice").

E. CRIMINAL STATUTES, CIVIL STATUTES, AND NEGLIGENCE PER SE

1. Overview

In addition to custom, another tool to help judges and juries decide whether a party has breached the reasonable person standard of care is the existence of criminal or civil statutes that address the blameworthiness of similar conduct. Surely, a reasonable person follows the law. If a person is violating a statute and causes injury to another, shouldn't the jury be instructed to find civil liability?

OSBORNE v. McMASTERS
41 N.W. 543 (Minn. 1889)

MITCHELL, J.

[D]efendant's drug-store clerk, in the course of his employment,] sold to plaintiff's intestate a deadly poison without labeling it "Poison," as required by statute; that she, in ignorance of its deadly qualities, partook of the poison which caused her death. . . . It is immaterial for present purposes whether section 329 of the Penal Code or section 14, c. 147, Laws 1885, or both, are still in force, and constitute the law governing this case. The requirements of both statutes are substantially the same, and the sole object of both is to protect the public against the dangerous qualities of poison. It is now well settled [that] where a statute or municipal ordinance imposes upon any person a specific duty for the protection or benefit of others, if he neglects to perform that duty he is liable to those for whose protection or benefit it was imposed for any injuries of the character which the statute or ordinance was designed to prevent, and which were proximately produced by such neglect. *Bott v. Pratt*, 33 Minn. 323, 23 N.W. 237. Defendant contends that this is only true where a right of action for the alleged negligent act existed at common law; that no liability existed at common law for selling poison without labeling it, and therefore none exists under this statute, no right of civil action being given by it. [It] is sufficient to say [that] defendant's contention proceeds upon an entire misapprehension of the nature and gist of a cause of action of this kind. The common law gives a right of action to every one sustaining injuries caused proximately by the negligence of another. The present is a common-law action, the gist of which is defendant's negligence, resulting in the death of plaintiff's intestate. Negligence is the breach of legal duty. It is immaterial whether the duty is one imposed by the rule of common law requiring the exercise of ordinary care not to injure another, or is imposed by a statute designed for the protection of others. In either case the failure to perform the duty constitutes negligence, and renders the party liable for injuries resulting from it. The only difference is that in the one case the measure of legal duty is to be determined upon common-law principles, while in the other the statute fixes it, so that the violation of the statute constitutes conclusive evidence of negligence, or, in other words, negligence per se. The action in the latter case is not a statutory one, nor does the statute give the right of action in any other sense, except that it makes an act negligent which otherwise might not be such, or at least only evidence of negligence. All that the statute does is to establish a fixed standard by which the fact of negligence may be determined. The gist of the action is still negligence, or the non-performance of a legal duty to the person injured.

What has been already said suggests the answer to the further contention that if any civil liability exists it is only against the clerk who sold the poison, and who alone is criminally liable. Whether the act constituting the actionable negligence was such on common-law principles, or is made such by statute, the doctrine of agency applies, to-wit, that the master is civilly liable for the negligence of his servant committed in the course of his employment, and resulting in injuries to third persons.

Judgment affirmed.

PROBLEM

How would this case come out under the Hand formula?

2. Is the Statute Designed to Protect this Particular Plaintiff from this Risk of Injury?

Many courts use a two-part test in deciding whether a statute is relevant to a determination of negligence: (1) Whether the statute is designed to protect a person similar to the plaintiff in the case from (2) a risk of injury that is similar to that suffered by this plaintiff. Consider, for example, *Gorris v. Scott*, L.R. Ex. 125 (1874), in which the plaintiff had shipped a number of sheep with the defendant ship owner. The ship owner failed to pen them and the animals were washed overboard in the storm. The Contagious Disease (Animals) Act of 1869 required ship owners to pen. Even though there was a causal connection between the defendant's failure to pen the animals and the plaintiff's harm, the court denied recovery:

> [I]f we could see that it was the object, or among the objects of this Act, that the owners of sheep and cattle coming from a foreign port should be protected by the means described against the danger of their property being washed overboard, or last by the perils of the sea, the present action would be within the principle.

> But, looking at the Act, it is perfectly clear that its provisions were all enacted with a totally different view; there was no purpose, direct or indirect to protect against such damage; but as is recited in the preamble, the Act is directed against the possibility of sheep or cattle being

exposed to disease on their way to this country. . . . That being so, if by reason of the default in question the plaintiffs' sheep had been over-crowded, or had been caused unnecessary suffering, and so had arrived in this country in a state of disease, I do not say that they might not have maintained this action. But the damage complained of here is something totally apart from the object of the Act Parliament, and it is in accordance with all the authorities to say that the action is not main-tainable.

Id. at 129. *Cf. Stimpson v. Wellington*, 246 N.E.2d 801 (Mass. 1969) (recogniz-ing that statutes can have multiple purposes).

PROBLEMS

1.   Plaintiff is driving in Virginia on Interstate 95. Virginia is one of six juris-dictions that makes contributory negligence by a plaintiff a complete bar to recovery in a negligence cause of action. In the 1970s, in response to a gasoline shortage, Virginia enacted a 55 mph speed limit on Interstate 95 between Rich-mond and Washington, D.C. Plaintiff is driving 75 mph when Defendant's car makes a sudden and un-signaled lane change. Had Plaintiff been going 55 he would have been able to avoid an accident with Defendant. The average speed of cars on that stretch of I-95 is between 75 and 80 mph. Plaintiff was going the speed of traffic. Is Virginia's 55 mph speed limit relevant to the question of Plaintiff's contributory negligence?

2.   Defendant is driving in D.C., another jurisdiction where contributory neg-ligence bars recovery. Defendant misses a turn and decides to do a U-turn across a "safety lane" (a 5th lane down the middle of 4 lanes of traffic, 2 each running in opposite directions) and hits a delivery person on a bicycle, who was also traveling in the safety zone. D.C. statutes provide that the safety zone is to kept free of "all traffic." For whose safety is the safety zone provided? Does it apply to Defendant's U-turn? Does it apply to bicyclists?

3.   Defendant owns a store in the city shopping center, with a sidewalk that runs in front of all the stores on the street. At about 6:00 p.m., Plaintiff, who was shopping in Defendant's store, was asked to leave through the front door, as all other doors had been closed and locked for the night. Plaintiff slipped and fell on the front sidewalk and broke his hip. At the time of Plaintiff's fall, there existed a municipal ordinance providing that shop owners should keep sidewalks clear of accumulations of snow and ice. Should the statute determine the liability of the shop owner?

4.   One day, Bob sets out for work. The roads are very icy. Bob, who usually exceeds the speed limit when driving, decides to drive cautiously. While in a 35 mph speed zone, he proceeds at a rate of 34 mph. In addition, although Bob nor-mally tailgates the cars in front of him, he decides to leave two car lengths today. The car in front of Bob stops suddenly. Bob slams on his brakes, but is

unable to stop, and he slides into the car. Bob will argue that the speed limit defines the appropriate standard of care, with regard to car speed, and that he cannot be held negligent since he was proceeding at a rate below the limit. Did Bob breach a duty of care?

5. Federal statutes can create private rights of action and thereby set standards of conduct that affect the rights of private parties. In fact, federal law can pre-empt state law in certain areas. And even when federal law does not pre-empt state law, the usual difficulties of tort actions for breach of a statute may be compounded because the right in question involves both federal and state law. In the corporate securities area, in *J.I. Case Co. v. Borak*, 377 U.S. 426 (1964), the Supreme Court held that a securities holder had a private right of action where his proxy rights were violated. Eleven years later the makeup of the Supreme Court had changed, and a state's right to set its own standard started to be given more weight. In the watershed case of *Cort v. Ash*, 422 U.S. 66, 78 (1975), the Court cut back on the reach of implied federal causes of action, holding that there was no private right of action under federal law for damages, in favor of a corporate shareholder against the corporate directors for violation of federal statutes prohibiting certain political contribution to presidential candidates. The Court set out a four part test:

> In determining whether a private remedy is implicit in a statute not expressly providing one, several factors are relevant. First, is the plaintiff "one of the class for whose especial benefit the statute was enacted"? . . . Second, is there any indication of legislative intent, explicit or implicit, either to create such a remedy or to deny one? . . . Third, is it consistent with the underlying nature of the legislative scheme to imply such a remedy for the plaintiff? . . . [A]nd finally, is the cause of action one traditionally relegated to state law, in an area basically the concern of the States, so that it would be inappropriate to infer a cause of action based solely on federal law?

What if the statute is a federal statute concerning the environment, or employee health and safety, or automobile recall, or securities trading, or banking? In *Virginia Bankshares v. Sandberg*, 501 U.S. 1083 (1991), the Court restricted the plaintiff's ability to use federal law to derive a substantive tort right holding that the Court must ultimately ground the recognition of a private right of action on congressional intent. Does this mean that existence of a federal statute — one especially designed to protect the public, but which doesn't express or imply intent for a private right of action — is irrelevant? Or might it constitute some evidence of negligence, or even negligence per se in state court? *Cf., Lowe v. General Motors*, 654 F.2d 1373 (5th Cir. 1980) (the court found a state cause of action in Alabama for a plaintiff who alleged a violation of a federal recall statute by General Motors. In Alabama the violation of federal law could even amount to negligence per se.)

3. How Are Relevant Statutes Applied? What is the Jury's Role?

Assuming that the court decides the statute is relevant, the court still needs to tell the jury what effect the statute should have on its deliberations. Should the statute raise a conclusive presumption of negligence? Should it raise a conclusive presumption of negligence, but allow for certain exceptions? Should the statute raise a rebuttable presumption of negligence? Or should the statute only raise prima facie negligence? With this myriad of possibilities in mind, consider the following case.

MARTIN v. HERZOG
126 N.E. 814 (N.Y. 1920)

CARDOZO, J.

[Decedent was killed in a collision between the buggy he was driving and defendant's automobile. The accident occurred after dark, and decedent was driving the buggy without any lights, in violation of a statute. The defendant requested a ruling that the absence of a light on the plaintiff's vehicle was "prima facie evidence of contributory negligence." This request was refused, and the jury was instructed that it might consider the absence of lights as some evidence of negligence. The plaintiff then requested a charge that "the fact that the plaintiff's intestate was driving without a light is not negligence in itself," and to this the court acceded. The jury found defendant liable and decedent free from contributory negligence and the plaintiff had judgement. The appellate division reversed for error in the instructions.]

We think the unexcused omission of the statutory signals is more than some evidence of negligence. It *is* negligence in itself. Lights are intended for the guidance and protection of other travelers on the highway (Highway Law, sec. 329a). By the very terms of the hypothesis, to omit, willfully or heedlessly, the safeguards prescribed by law for the benefit of another that he may be preserved in life or limb, is to fall short of the standard of diligence to which those who live in organized society are under a duty to conform.

In the case at hand, we have [an] admitted violation of a statute intended for the protection of travelers on the highway, of whom the defendant at the time was one. Yet the jurors were instructed in effect that they were at liberty in their discretion to treat the omission of lights either as innocent or as culpable. They were allowed to "consider the default as lightly or gravely" as they would. They might as well have been told that they could use a like discretion in holding a master at fault for the omission of a safety appliance prescribed by positive law for the protection of a workman. Jurors have no dispensing power, by which they may relax the duty that one traveler on the highway owes under the statute to another. It is error to tell them that they have. The omission of these lights was a wrong, and being wholly unexcused, was also a negligent wrong. No license should have been conceded to the triers of the facts to find it anything else.

We must be on our guard, however, against confusing the question of negligence with that of the causal connection between the negligence and the injury. A defendant who travels without lights is not to pay damages for his fault, unless the absence of lights is the cause of the disaster. A plaintiff who travels without them is not to forfeit the right to damages, unless the absence of lights is at least a contributing cause of the disaster. To say that conduct is negligence is not to say that it is always contributory negligence. "Proof of negligence in the air, so to speak, will not do." Pollack Torts (10th Ed.) p.472

[A] statute designed for the protection of human life is not to be brushed aside as a form of words, its commands reduced to the level of cautions, and the duty to obey attenuated into an option to conform.

NOTE

Other efforts to escape the doctrine of negligence per se have proved more successful. In *Tedla v. Ellman*, 19 N.E.2d 987, 989 (N.Y. 1939), the plaintiff and her brother, a deaf mute, were walking along a divided highway shortly after dark, pushing baby carriages filled with junk that they had collected for sale as part of their regular business. Instead of walking on the far left-hand side of the double highway, as required by statute, so that they would be facing oncoming traffic, they walked on the far right-hand side, so that the traffic going in their direction approached them from behind. Defendant struck them with his car, hurting the plaintiff and killing her brother. The defendant's negligence was clearly established at trial and judgement was entered for plaintiff. The only issue on appeal was "whether, as a matter of law, disregard of the statutory rule that pedestrians shall keep to the left of the center line of a highway constitutes contributory negligence which bars any recovery by the plaintiff." To answer that question, the judge noted that prior to the enactment of the statute, the common-law custom usually required pedestrians to walk against traffic in order to be alert to dangers from oncoming traffic. The general customary rule, however, also contained a customary exception that required pedestrians to walk with the traffic when the traffic coming from behind was much lighter than the oncoming traffic. The case thus presented a knotty issue of statutory construction: should the court read into the legislation the customary exception when the statute embodied the customary rule? If the statute had defined "specified safeguards against recognized dangers," the judge would have been prepared to apply the *Martin v. Herzog* rule. But since this statute was designed to "codify, supplement or even change common-law rules" themselves designed to prevent accidents, the judge thought it proper to imply the exception to the statute for the benefit of the plaintiff. The argument appears to turn on legislative intent, as the judge dismissed the defendant's contentions as follows:

Disregard of the statutory rule of the road and observance of a rule based on immemorial custom, it is said, is negligence which as matter of law is a proximate cause of the accident, though observance of the statutory rule might, under the circumstances of the particular case, expose a pedestrian to serious danger from which he would be free if he followed the rule that had been established by custom. If that be true, then the Legislature has decreed that pedestrians must observe the general rule of conduct which it has prescribed for their safety even under circumstances where observance would subject them to unusual risk; that pedestrians are to be charged with negligence as a matter of law for acting as prudence dictates. It is unreasonable to ascribe to the Legislature an intention that the statute should have so extraordinary a result, and the courts may not give to a statute an effect not intended by the Legislature.

The one-sentence dissent argued that the plaintiff's action should have been dismissed on the authority of *Martin v. Herzog.*

The Restatement (Second) of Torts § 288A, comment I, illustration 6, supports the court's position in *Tedla.* The Restatement also notes that violations of a statute may be excused by necessity or emergency, or by reason of incapacity, just as is the case with various forms of common law negligence.

PROBLEMS

1. P, a 15-year-old girl, was struck by D's car while jaywalking. D was drunk and driving in excess of the posted 25 mph speed limit for residential streets. P contends that it is customary for local citizens to violate the jaywalking statute. Should the court regard the showing of a custom or practice of violating the law as a legal excuse not to follow the law? Does it excuse her violation of the statute to say that she is only 15? *See Alley v. Siepman,* 214 N.W.2d 7 (S.D. 1974).

2. D drives his car a short distance straight ahead although the pavement markings required him to make a left-hand turn. P and D get in an accident. Both automobiles were traveling in an easterly direction before the collision, and both drivers intended to make left turns so as to proceed north on 48th Street. South of Thomas Road there are two separate 48th Streets, paralleling each other and divided by a canal. The westernmost 48th Street abuts into Thomas Road to form a "T" intersection ending at that point. Immediately to the north of the stem of this "T" is a driveway leading from Thomas Road into a restaurant parking lot. The easternmost 48th Street continues north and forms a normal intersection with Thomas Road. D entered the left-turn lane at its inception approximately 100 feet west of the "T" intersection. P did not enter the left-turn lane until she arrived at the point where the westernmost portion of 48th Street going south formed the "T" intersection with Thomas Road. After stopping at a crosswalk at this location, P pulled into the left-turn lane in front

of D's vehicle, and there was a collision involving D's vehicle and the left-side of P's vehicle. A City ordinance provides as follows:

> When authorized signs, *pavement markings,* or other traffic control devices are placed *within or on the approach to an intersection* directing the course to be traveled by vehicles traveling thereat, *no driver of a vehicle shall disobey* the direction of such signs, *pavement markings*, or other traffic control devices." (Emphasis added).

Code of the City of Phoenix, Arizona, Vehicles and Traffic, Art. IV, §§ 36-45 (1969).

It is P's contention that certain pavement markings at these intersections required that a person entering the left-turn lane at a point west of the "T" intersection (where D entered it) must turn left into the restaurant parking lot, and that D's action in proceeding past the entrance to the restaurant parking lot was a violation of the ordinance as implemented by the pavement markings and thus constituted negligence per se.

In return, D shows it is customary for close to 95% of the drivers in D's position to proceed in violation of the pavement markings. Even if the custom did not excuse D's negligence, should the court hold it admissible on the question of P's contributory negligence and sustain a jury verdict for D because P knows about such custom? *Johnson v. Garnand*, 501 P.2d 32 (Ariz. Ct. App. 1972).

3. Should the effect of a statute vary, depending on the particular public policy reasons behind it? P drives his motorcycle without a helmet. He is involved in a collision with D, who was served too much alcohol by O. D had gotten into K's car, thinking it was his. When he reached for the ignition, he found K's keys left in it, in violation of a statute prohibiting the leaving of keys in unattended vehicles. How should each statutory violation affect the jury's determination of the parties' negligence?

4. Assume that plaintiff is driving his car on a very foggy evening. The fog is so thick that he can only see a few feet in front of him. Plaintiff stops on a two lane highway to make a left hand turn across traffic when he is hit from behind by a truck and badly injured. Following the accident, the truck driver notices that plaintiff's tail lights were not working properly. This equipment failure violates the Highway and Traffic Safety Code that requires automobiles' tail lights to be in working order at all times. Will the plaintiff lose? Not necessarily. Courts might not impose liability even in jurisdictions that treat the plaintiff's absence of working tail lights as negligence per se, and therefore as conclusive evidence of negligence. If the plaintiff argues and the jury finds that the defendant was negligent in driving too quickly for the weather conditions, and if the jury finds that it was so foggy the defendant would have hit the plaintiff even if the tail lights had been working, then there is no cause-in-fact and no resulting contributory negligence that would bar recovery.

4. Negligence Per Se Applied

VESELEY v. SAGER
486 P.2d 151 (Cal. 1971)

WRIGHT, Chief Justice.

In this case we are called upon to decide whether civil liability may be imposed upon a vendor of alcoholic beverages for providing alcoholic drinks to a customer who, as a result of intoxication, injures a third person. The traditional common law rule would deny recovery on the ground that the furnishing of alcoholic beverages is not the proximate cause of the injuries suffered by the third person. We have determined that this rule is patently unsound and that civil liability results when a vendor furnishes alcoholic beverages to a customer in violation of Business and Professions Code section 25602 and each of the conditions set forth in Evidence Code section 669, subdivision (a) is established.

Plaintiff Miles Vesely brought this action to recover for personal injuries and property damage sustained in an automobile accident. The only defendant involved on this appeal is William A. Sager, individually and doing business as the Buckhorn Lodge. Other defendants are James G. O'Connell, the driver of the vehicle which collided with plaintiff's automobile, and Earl Dirks, the owner of the car driven by O'Connell. The facts which are alleged in the complaint and which we must accept for the purposes of this appeal are as follows:

Defendant [William] Sager owned and operated the Buckhorn Lodge, a roadhouse located near the top of Mount Baldy in San Bernardino County, and was engaged in the business of selling alcoholic beverages to the general public. Beginning about 10 p.m. on April 8, 1968, Sager served or permitted defendant [James] O'Connell to be served large quantities of alcoholic beverages. . . . Sager knew that O'Connell was becoming excessively intoxicated and that O'Connell was "incapable of exercising the same degree of volitional control over his consumption of intoxicants as the average reasonable person." Sager also knew that the only route leaving the Buckhorn Lodge was a very steep, winding, and narrow mountain road and that O'Connell was going to drive down that road. Nevertheless, Sager continued to serve O'Connell alcoholic drinks past the normal closing time of 2 a.m. until 5:15 a.m. . . . After leaving the lodge, O'Connell drove down the road, veered into the opposite lane, and struck plaintiff's vehicle. The complaint also alleges that O'Connell drove the automobile with the consent, permission, and knowledge of the remaining defendants, that each defendant was the employee and agent of the other defendants, and that each of the defendants "was at all times acting within the purpose and scope of said agency and employment."

Defendant Sager demurred to the complaint on the ground that a "seller of intoxicating liquors is not liable for injuries resulting from intoxication" of a buyer thereof, and he moved to strike [allegations] that O'Connell drove the automobile with the permission of the other defendants and that each defendant was the employee and agent of the remaining defendants. . . . Sager [declared] that O'Connell and Dirk "were not in (his) employment on the date of the accident" and that he never had any ownership interest or any other interest in the automobile driven by O'Connell.

The trial court sustained the demurrer without leave to amend, granted the motion to strike, and dismissed the complaint as to defendant Sager. Plaintiff appeals.

Until fairly recently, it was uniformly held that an action could not be maintained at common law against the vendor of alcoholic beverages for furnishing such beverages to a customer who, as a result of being intoxicated, injured himself or a third person. The rationale for the common law rule was that the consumption and not the sale of liquor was the proximate cause of injuries sustained as a result of intoxication. "The rule was based on the obvious fact that one cannot be intoxicated by reason of liquor furnished him if he does not drink it." The common law rule has been substantially abrogated in many states by statutes which specifically impose civil liability upon a furnisher of intoxicating liquor under specified circumstances. California, however, has not enacted similar legislation.

The common law doctrine that the furnishing of alcoholic beverages is not the proximate cause of injuries resulting from intoxication was first mentioned in this state in *Lammers v. Pacific Electric Railway Company* (1921) 186 Cal. 379, 199 P. 523. In that case the defendant railroad ejected the plaintiff, a passenger who was unable to find his fare, from one of its trains while the plaintiff was quite helpless from intoxication and mental deficiency. The plaintiff, who apparently had been struck by a train, was discovered more than six hours later, lying badly maimed on another set of railroad tracks some three quarters of a mile from the point where he had been ejected from the defendant's train. The court held that the defendant's action in ejecting the plaintiff from its train was not the proximate cause of the injuries sustained thereafter. In dictum the court stated that "The sale of whiskey to the plaintiff would come nearer being a proximate cause of the injury than the ejection from the railway train. [Y]et it has been uniformly held, in the absence of statute to the contrary, that the sale of intoxicating liquor is not the proximate cause of injuries subsequently received by the purchaser because of his intoxication."

To the extent that the common law rule of nonliability is based on concepts of proximate cause, we are persuaded by the reasoning of the cases that have abandoned that rule. The decisions in those jurisdictions which have abandoned the common law rule invoke principles of proximate cause similar to those established in this state by cases dealing with matters other than the furnishing of alcoholic beverages. Prosser, *Proximate Cause in California* (1950) 38 CAL. L. REV. 369. Under these principles an actor may be liable if his negligence is a substantial factor in causing an injury, and he is not relieved of liability because of the intervening act of a third person if such act was reasonably foreseeable at the time of his negligent conduct. Moreover, "If the likelihood that a third person may act in a particular manner is the hazard or one of the hazards which makes the actor negligent, such an act whether innocent, negligent, intentionally tortious or criminal does not prevent the actor from being liable for harm caused thereby."

Insofar as proximate cause is concerned, we find no basis for a distinction founded solely on the fact that the consumption of an alcoholic beverage is a voluntary act of the consumer and is a link in the chain of causation from the furnishing of the beverage to the injury resulting from intoxication. Under the above principles of proximate cause, it is clear that the furnishing of an alcoholic beverage to an intoxicated person may be a proximate cause of injuries inflicted by that individual upon a third person. If such furnishing is a proximate cause, it is so because the consumption, resulting intoxication, and injury-producing conduct are foreseeable intervening causes, or at least the injury-producing conduct is one of the hazards which makes such furnishing negligent.

The central question in this case, therefore, is not one of proximate cause, but rather one of duty: Did defendant Sager owe a duty of care to plaintiff or to a class of persons of which he is a member?

A duty of care, and the attendant standard of conduct required of a reasonable man, may of course be found in a legislative enactment which does not provide for civil liability. In this state a presumption of negligence arises from the violation of a statute which was enacted to protect a class of persons of which the plaintiff is a member against the type of harm which the plaintiff suffered as a result of the violation of the statute.

In the instant case a duty of care is imposed upon defendant Sager by Business and Professions Code section 25602, which provides: "Every person who sells, furnishes, gives, or causes to be sold, furnished, or given away, any alcoholic beverage to any habitual or common drunkard or to any obviously intoxicated person is guilty of a misdemeanor." This provision was enacted as part of the Alcoholic Beverage Control Act of 1935 (Stats.1935, ch. 330, § 62, at p. 1151) and was adopted for the purpose of protecting members of the general public from injuries to person and damage to property resulting from the excessive use of intoxicating liquor.

Our conclusion concerning the legislative purpose in adopting section 25602 is compelled by Business and Professions Code section 23001, which states that one of the purposes of the Alcoholic Beverage Control Act is to protect the safety of the people of this state. Moreover, our interpretation of section 25602 finds support in the decisions of those jurisdictions in which similar statutes, and statutes prohibiting the sale of alcoholic beverages to minors, have been found to have been enacted for the purpose of protecting members of the general public against injuries resulting from intoxication.

From the facts alleged in the complaint it appears that plaintiff is within the class of persons for whose protection section 25602 was enacted and that the injuries he suffered resulted from an occurrence that the statute was designed to prevent. Accordingly, if these two elements are proved at trial, and if it is established that Sager violated section 25602 and that the violation proximately caused plaintiff's injuries, a presumption will arise that Sager was negligent in furnishing alcoholic beverages to O'Connell. (*See* Evid.Code, § 669.)

Defendant Sager maintains, however, that a change in the common law rule governing the liability of a tavern keeper to an injured third person is unwarranted and that if there is to be a change in the rule, it should be made by the Legislature, not by the courts. [D]efendant contends that imposition of civil liability upon tavern keepers would not alter the extent to which the consumption of intoxicants contributes to automobile accidents and that such liability would not be an adequate deterrent to the unlawful sale of alcoholic beverages. Moreover, defendant asserts that the injured third person is already assured of compensation for his injuries by Vehicle Code sections 16000–16053 and Insurance Code section 11580.2. [Defendant also] maintains the Legislature is better equipped to determine whether civil liability should be imposed for furnishing alcoholic beverages to an individual who injures himself or third persons. Defendant contends that the decision to impose liability presents various questions as to the scope of such liability, *e.g.*, whether an intoxicated patron ought to recover for injuries sustained as a result of his intoxication and whether liability should be imposed upon a package liquor store or a noncommercial furnisher of intoxicating liquor. . . .

Defendant's argument[s are] faulty in two respects. [L]iability has been denied in cases such as the one before us solely because of the judicially created rule that the furnishing of alcoholic beverages is not the proximate cause of injuries resulting from intoxication. . . . [T]here is no sound reason for retaining the common law rule presented in this case. [Also,] the Legislature has expressed an intention [consistent with our decision].

The judgment of dismissal is reversed. . . .

NOTES

1. Although there may be clear "cause-in-fact," negligence per se does not always mean victory for the injured party. In *Ross v. Hartman*, 139 F.2d 14 (D.C. Cir. 1943), appellee's agent violated a traffic ordinance by leaving his truck unattended in a public alley, with the ignition unlocked and the key in the switch. A statute provided that, "[no] person shall allow any motor vehicle operated [to] stand or remain unattended on any street or in any public place without first having locked the lever, throttle, or switch by which said motor vehicle may be set in motion." Appellee left the truck outside a garage "so that it might be taken inside the garage by the garage attendant for the night storage," but he did not notify anyone that he had left it. Within two hours, an unknown person drove the truck away and negligently ran over the appellant. Case law at the time provided that there was no *proximate* cause between a car owner and

the person injured by the car's thief. The *Ross* court held that the statute required a different result, so that the intervening act of the thief was immaterial and the injury was foreseeable.

2. In an earlier problem involving GPH (General Psychiatric Hospital) we discussed the problem of an internal company safety rule that required no "dangerous patient" to be left unattended in the third floor atrium of the hospital. P had thrown himself through an unbarred window of the atrium. What is the effect of the violation of an internal company rule, especially one that makes no mention of the mental state of the actor? Does it raise a strict liability standard in the guise of a negligence case? And what if GPH resides in a jurisdiction with the following regulation?

> No person, being the owner or superintendent or employee of any private hospital or asylum, shall permit any delirious or maniacal patient or any patient who may reasonably be expected soon to become delirious or maniacal to remain in any room that is not properly barred or closed so as to prevent the escape of such patient or accident or injury to him unless such patient is in the actual physical presence of an attendant capable of controlling and restraining him.

See *Lucy Webb Haynes National Training School v. Perotti*, 419 F.2d 704, 712 (D.C. Cir. 1969) (where the court determined the statute did not apply, not because it was enacted in 1909, and not because the licensing board had not addressed the lack of bars on the windows when it inspected the hospital, but because the court did not find that P was delirious or maniacal, according to the plain meaning of those words).

BROWN v. SHYNE
151 N.E. 197 (N.Y. 1926)

LEHMAN, J.

The plaintiff employed the defendant to give chiropractic treatment to her for a disease or physical condition. The defendant had no license to practice medicine, yet he held himself out as being able to diagnose and treat disease, and under the provisions of the Public Health Law (Cons. Laws, ch. 45) he was guilty of a misdemeanor. The plaintiff became paralyzed after she had received nine treatments by the defendant. She claims, and upon this appeal we must assume, that the paralysis was caused by the treatment she received. She has recovered judgement in the sum of $10,000 for the damages caused by said injury.

[Plaintiff alleged] "that in so treating the plaintiff the defendant was engaged in the practice of medicine contrary to and in violation of the provisions of the Public Health Law of the State of New York in [that he was not] a duly licensed physician or surgeon of the State of New York." [The] trial judge charged the jury that they might bring in a verdict in favor of the plaintiff if they found that the evidence established that the treatment given to the plaintiff was not in accordance with the standards of skill and care which prevail among those treating disease. [He] continued: "[You can], if you think proper under the evidence in the case to predicate negligence [upon the] public health laws of this state, prescribe that no person shall practice medicine unless he is licensed so to do by the board of regents of this state and registered pursuant to statute. . . . This Statute [is] a general police regulation. Its violation, and it has been violated by the defendant, is some evidence [of] negligence which you may consider for what it is worth, along with all the other evidence in the case. If the defendant attempted to treat the plaintiff and to adjust the vertebrae in her spine when he did not possess the requisite knowledge and skill as prescribed by the statute to know what was proper and necessary to do under the circumstances, or how to do it, even if he did know what to do, you can find him negligent." In so charging the jury that from the violation of the statue the jury might infer negligence which produced injury to the plaintiff, the trial justice in my opinion erred.

The provisions of the Public Health Law prohibiting the practice of medicine without a license granted upon proof of preliminary training, and after examination intended to show adequate knowledge, are of course intended for the protection of the general public against injury which unskilled and unlearned practitioners might cause. If violation of the statute by the defendant was the proximate cause of the plaintiff's injury, then the plaintiff may recover upon proof of violation. If violation of the statute has no direct bearing on the injury, proof of the violation becomes irrelevant. For injury caused by neglect of duty imposed by the penal law there is civil remedy; but of course the injury must follow from the neglect.

Proper formulation of general standards of preliminary education and proper examination of the particular applicant should serve to raise the standards of skill and care generally possessed by members of the profession in this state; but the license to practice medicine confers no additional skill upon the practitioner, nor does it confer immunity from physical injury upon a patient if the practitioner fails to exercise care. Here, injury may have been caused by lack of skill or care; it would not have been obviated if the defendant had possessed a license yet failed to exercise the skill and care required of one practicing medicine. True, if the defendant had not practiced medicine in this state, he could not have injured the plaintiff, but the protection which the statute was intended to provide was against risk of injury by the unskilled or careless practitioner, and unless the plaintiff's injury was caused by carelessness or lack of skill, the defendant's failure to obtain a license was not connected with the injury. The plaintiff's cause of action is for negligence or malpractice. The defendant undertook to treat the plaintiff for a physical condition which seemed to require remedy. Under our law such treatment may be given only by a duly qualified practitioner who has obtained a license.

The defendant in offering to treat the plaintiff held himself out as qualified to give treatment. He must meet the professional standards of skill and care prevailing among those who do offer treatment lawfully. If injury follows through failure to meet those standards, the plaintiff may recover. The provisions of the Public Health Law may result in the exclusion from practice of some who are unqualified. Even a skilled and learned practitioner who is not licensed commits an offense against the state; but against such practitioners the statute was not intended to protect, for no protection was needed, and neglect to obtain a license results in no injury to the patient and, therefore, no private wrong. The purpose of the statute is to protect the public against unfounded assumption of skill by one who undertakes to prescribe or treat for disease. In order to show that the plaintiff has been injured by defendant's breach of the statutory duty, proof must be given that defendant in such treatment did not exercise the care and skill which would have been exercised by qualified practitioners within the state, and that such lack of skill and care caused the injury. Failure to obtain a license as required by law gives rise to no remedy if it has caused no injury. No case has been cited where neglect of a statutory duty has given rise to private cause of action where it has not appeared that private injury has been caused by danger against which the statute was intended to afford protection, and which obedience to the statute would have obviated. . . .

It is said that the trial justice did not charge that plaintiff might recover for defendant's failure to obtain a license, but only that failure to obtain a license might be considered "some evidence" of defendant's negligence. Argument is made that, even if neglect of the statutory duty does not itself create liability, it tends to prove that injury was caused by lack of skill or care. That can be true only if logical inference may be drawn from defendant's failure to obtain or perhaps seek a license that he not only lacks the skill and learning which would enable him to diagnose and treat disease generally, but also that he lacks even the skill and learning necessary for the physical manipulation he gave to this plaintiff. Evidence of defendant's training, learning, and skill and the method he used in giving the treatment was produced at the trial, and upon such evidence the jury could base a finding either of care or negligence, but the absence of a license does not seem to strengthen inference that might be drawn from such evidence, and a fortiori would not alone be a basis for such inference. Breach or neglect of duty imposed by statute or ordinance may be evidence of negligence only if there is logical connection between the proven neglect of statutory duty and the alleged negligence.

CRANE, J., dissenting.

[I] think this rule all too liberal to the defendant. What he did was prohibited by law. He could not practice medicine without violating the law. The law did not recognize him as a physician. How can the courts treat him as such? Provided his act, in violation of the law, is the direct and proximate cause of injury, in my judgement he is liable, irrespective of negligence. It seems somewhat strange that the courts, one branch of the law, can hold up for such a man the standards of the licensed physician, while the Legislature, another branch of the law, declares that he cannot practice at all as a physician. The courts thus afford the protection which the Legislature denies.

What is the rule which is to guide us in determining whether a violation of a statute or ordinance is evidence of negligence? It is no answer to say that the statute provides a penalty, and, therefore, no other consequences can follow. Such is not the law. We are to determine it [from] the purpose and object of the law, and also from the fact whether a violation of the law may be the direct and proximate cause of an injury to an individual. . . .

The prohibition against practicing medicine without a license was for the very purpose of protecting the public from just what happened in this case. The violation of this statute has been the direct and proximate cause of the injury. The courts will not determine in face of this statute whether a faith healer, a patent medicine man, a chiropractor, or any other class of practitioner acted according to the standards of his own school, or according to the standards of a duly licensed physician. The law, to insure against ignorance and carelessness, has laid down a rule to be followed; namely, examinations to test qualifications, and a license to practice. If a man, in violation of this statute, takes his chances in trying to cure disease, and his acts result directly in injury, he should not complain if the law, in a suit for damages, says that his violation of the statute is some evidence of his incapacity.

PROBLEMS

1. Your state has enacted the following legislation: "Every person who sells, furnishes, gives, or causes to be sold, furnished, or given away, any alcoholic beverage to [any] obviously intoxicated person is guilty of a misdemeanor." If an apartment complex holds a picnic and serves alcohol, and its manager serves alcohol to an obviously intoxicated individual who thereafter injures himself when he runs into a road abutment, will it be liable? *See Coulter v. Schwartz & Co. & Reynolds*, 577 P.2d 669 (Cal. 1978). Not all jurisdictions agree on this issue. *See Edgat v. Kajet*, 375 N.Y.S.2d 548 (N.Y. Sup. Ct. 1975). *Cf. Klein v. Raysinger*, 470 A.2d 507 (Pa. 1983). *See* RESTATEMENT (SECOND) OF TORTS, § 876. Indeed, *Coulter* was superseded by a later statute.

2. What result if the provider of alcohol is a fraternity?

3. What result if the provider of alcohol is a neighborhood association at a block party?

F. PROOF OF NEGLIGENCE

1. Overview

Some cases are said to be "easy" cases that should not consume too much of the court's time. In these "easy" cases, a court will conclude, on the particular facts of the case, that the plaintiff (or sometimes the defendant) was negligent "as a matter of law." In other words, the court concludes on the facts that reasonable persons could not find otherwise and accordingly directs a verdict for the opposing party on this issue. There are other cases, fewer in number, in which the court, having reached such a conclusion on the facts of the case, generalizes its conclusion and states it as a legal rule for all cases. Sometimes these cases are "easy" cases and provide rules for the future. For example, a court decides that there will not be liability to the defendant if the plaintiff did *not* do something to protect his own safety.

As you are learning in your Civil Procedure class, defendants can move for summary judgment in a case where there is no dispute on the facts as pleaded. Similarly, the court can dismiss the plaintiff's case at the close of the plaintiff's case if the court finds that no jury could reasonably conclude for the plaintiff. On the issue of negligence, either the plaintiff has submitted no evidence of the defendant's negligence, or submitted no evidence upon which a jury could reasonably conclude that the defendant was negligent. Similarly, the judge can grant the plaintiff a summary judgment or grant the plaintiff a judgment notwithstanding the verdict at the close of the case if the judge feels that the defendant was negligent and for a jury to conclude otherwise would be unreasonable. In other words, in "easy yes" cases and in "easy no" cases, the judge can save everybody a lot of time and direct a verdict.

Yet what about a developing area of law? Isn't there a role that a judge should play in providing consistency and certainty where society could go either way on whether there is negligence? On the other hand, what if the judge is a law and economics judge who believes that calculus of risk dictates resolution of the question of negligence? For the "Judge Posners" of the world, isn't every negligence question one for the judge because the judge must ultimately do the calculus of risk? But then, what does it mean that the parties have a Seventh Amendment right to a trial by jury? Shouldn't the judge be bound not to decide any question of negligence for fear of restricting the parties' right to have a jury decide all questions of fact?

BALTIMORE & OHIO R.R. v. GOODMAN
275 U.S. 66 (1927)

Mr. Justice HOLMES delivered the opinion of the Court.

This is a suit brought by the widow and administratrix of Nathan Goodman against the petitioner for causing his death by running him down at a grade crossing. The defence is that Goodman's own negligence caused the death. At the trial, the defendant asked the Court to direct a verdict for it, but the request, and others looking to the same direction, were refused, and the plaintiff got a verdict and a judgment which was affirmed by the Circuit Court of Appeals.

Goodman was driving an automobile truck in an easterly direction and was killed by a train running southwesterly across the road at a rate of not less than 60 miles an hour. The line was straight, but it is said by the respondent that Goodman "had no practical view" beyond a section house 243 feet north of the crossing until he was about 20 feet from the first rail, or, as the respondent argues, 12 feet from danger, and that then the engine was still obscured by the section house. He had been driving at the rate of 10 or 12 miles an hour, but had cut down his rate to 5 or 6 miles at about 40 feet from the crossing. It is thought that there was an emergency in which, so far as appears, Goodman did all that he could.

We do not go into further details as to Goodman's precise situation, beyond mentioning that it was daylight and that he was familiar with the crossing, for it appears to us plain that nothing is suggested by the evidence to relieve Goodman from responsibility for his own death. When a man goes upon a railroad track he knows that he goes to a place where he will be killed if a train comes upon him before he is clear of the track. He knows that he must stop for the train, not the train stop for him. In such circumstances it seems to us that if a driver cannot be sure otherwise whether a train is dangerously near he must stop and get out of his vehicle, although obviously he will not often be required to do more than to stop and look. It seems to us that if he relies upon not hearing the train or any signal and takes no further precaution he does so at his own risk. If at the last moment Goodman found himself in an emergency it was his own fault that he did not reduce his speed earlier or come to a stop. It is true as said in *Flannelly v. Delaware & Hudson Co.*, 225 U.S. 597, 603 (1912), that the question of due care very generally is left to the jury. But we are dealing with a standard of conduct, and when the standard is clear it should be laid down once for all by the Courts. *See Southern Pacific Co. v. Berkshire*, 254 U.S. 415, 417, 419 (1921).

Judgment reversed.

POKORA v. WABASH RY.
292 U.S. 98 (1934)

Mr. Justice CARDOZO delivered the opinion of the Court.

John Pokora, driving his truck across a railway grade crossing in the city of Springfield, Ill., was struck by a train and injured. Upon the trial of his suit for damages, the District Court held that he had been guilty of contributory negligence, and directed a verdict for the defendant. The Circuit Court of Appeals affirmed, resting its judgment on the opinion of this court in *Baltimore & O.R. Co. v. Goodman*, 275 U.S. 66 (1927). A writ of certiorari brings the case here.

Pokora was an ice dealer, and had come to the crossing to load his truck with ice. The tracks of the Wabash Railway are laid along Tenth street, which runs north and south. There is a crossing at Edwards street running east and west. Two ice depots are on opposite corners of Tenth and Edward streets; one at the northeast corner, the other at the southwest. Pokora, driving west along Edwards street, stopped at the first of these corners to get his load of ice, but found so many trucks ahead of him that he decided to try the depot on the other side of the way. In this crossing of the railway, the accident occurred.

The defendant has four tracks on Tenth street; a switch track on the east, then the main track, and then two switches. Pokora, as he left the northeast corner where his truck had been stopped, looked to the north for approaching trains. He did this at a point about ten or fifteen feet east of the switch ahead of him. A string of box cars standing on the switch, about five to ten feet from the north line of Edwards street, cut off his view of the tracks beyond him to the north. At the same time he listened. There was neither bell nor whistle. Still listening, he crossed the switch, and reaching the main track was struck by a passenger train coming from the north at a speed of twenty-five to thirty miles an hour.

The burden of proof was on the defendant to make out the defense of contributory negligence. The record does not show in any conclusive way that the train was visible to Pokora while there was still time to stop. A space of eight feet lay between the west rail of the switch and the east rail of the main track, but there was an overhang of the locomotive (perhaps two and a half or three feet), as well as an overhang of the box cars, which brought the zone of danger even nearer. When the front of the truck had come within this zone, Pokora was on his seat, and so was farther back (perhaps five feet or even more), just how far we do not know, for the defendant has omitted to make proof of the dimensions. Nice calculations are submitted in an effort to make out that there was a glimpse of the main track before the switch was fully cleared. Two feet farther back the track was visible, it is said, for about 130 or 140 feet. But the view from that position does not tell us anything of significance unless we know also the position of the train. Pokora was not protected by his glimpse of 130 feet if the train at the same moment was 150 feet away or farther. For all that appears he had no view of the main track northward, or none for a substantial distance, till the train was so near that escape had been cut off.

In such circumstances the question, we think, was for the jury whether reasonable caution forbade his going forward in reliance on the sense of hearing, unaided by that of sight. No doubt it was his duty to look along the track from his seat, if looking would avail to warn him of the danger. This does not mean, however, that if vision was cut off by obstacles, there was negligence in going on, any more than there would have been in trusting to his ears if vision had been cut off by the darkness of the night. *Cf. Norfolk & W. Ry. v. Holbrook*, 27 F.2d 326 (6th Cir. 1928). Pokora made his crossing in the daytime, but like the traveler by night he used the faculties available to one in his position. A jury, but not the court, might say that with faculties thus limited he should have found some other means of assuring himself of safety before venturing to cross. The crossing was a frequented highway in a populous city. Behind him was a line of other cars, making ready to follow him. To some extent, at least, there was assurance in the thought that the defendant would not run its train at such a time and place without sounding bell or whistle. Indeed, the statutory signals did not exhaust the defendant's duty when to its knowledge there was special danger to the traveler through obstructions on the roadbed narrowing the field of vision. All this the plaintiff, like any other reasonable traveler, might fairly take into account. All this must be taken into account by us in comparing what he did with the conduct reasonably to be expected of reasonable men.

The argument is made, however, that our decision in *Baltimore & O.R. Co.* is a barrier in the plaintiff's path, irrespective of the conclusion that might commend itself if the question were at large. There is no doubt that the opinion in that case is correct in its result. Goodman, the driver, traveling only five or six miles an hour, had, before reaching the track, a clear space of eighteen feet within which the train was plainly visible. With that opportunity, he fell short of the legal standard of duty established for a traveler when he failed to look and see. This was decisive of the case. But the court did not stop there. It added a remark, unnecessary upon the facts before it, which has been a fertile source of controversy. "In such circumstances it seems to us that if a driver cannot be sure otherwise whether a train is dangerously near he must stop and get out of his vehicle, although obviously he will not often be required to do more than to stop and look."

There is need at this stage to clear the ground of brushwood that may obscure the point at issue. We do not now inquire into the existence of a duty to stop, disconnected from a duty to get out and reconnoiter. The inquiry, if pursued, would lead us into the thickets of conflicting judgments. Some courts apply what is often spoken of as the Pennsylvania rule, and impose an unyielding duty to stop, as well as to look and listen, no matter how clear the crossing or the tracks on either side. *See, e.g., Benner v. Philadelphia & Reading R. Co.*, 105 A. 283 (Pa. 1918). Other courts, the majority, adopt the rule that the traveler must look and listen, but that the existence of a duty to stop depends upon the circumstances, and hence generally, even if not invariably, upon the judgment of the jury. *See, e.g., Judson v. Central Vermont R. Co.*, 53 N.E. 514 (N.Y. 1899); *Love v. Fort Dodge R. Co.*, 224 N.W. 815 (Iowa 1929). The subject has been less considered in this court, but in none of its opinions is there a suggestion that at any and every crossing the duty to stop is absolute, irrespective of the danger. Not even in *Baltimore & O.R. Co.*, which goes farther than the earlier cases, is there support for such a rule. To the contrary, the opinion makes it clear that the duty is conditioned upon the presence of impediments whereby sight and hearing become inadequate for the traveler's protection.

Choice between these diversities of doctrine is unnecessary for the decision of the case at hand. Here the fact is not disputed that the plaintiff did stop before he started to cross the tracks. If we assume that by reason of the box cars, there was a duty to stop again when the obstructions had been cleared, that duty did not arise unless a stop could be made safely after the point of clearance had been reached. *See, e.g., Dobson, supra.* For reasons already stated, the testimony permits the inference that the truck was in the zone of danger by the time the field of vision was enlarged. No stop would then have helped the plaintiff if he remained seated on his truck, or so the triers of the facts might find. His case was for the jury, unless as a matter of law he was subject to a duty to get out of the vehicle before it crossed the switch, walk forward to the front, and then, afoot, survey the scene. We must say whether his failure to do this was negligence so obvious and certain that one conclusion and one only is permissible for rational and candid minds. *Grand Trunk Ry. Co., supra.*

Standards of prudent conduct are declared at times by courts, but they are taken over from the facts of life. To get out of a vehicle and reconnoiter is an uncommon precaution, as everyday experience informs us. Besides being uncommon, it is very likely to be futile, and sometimes even dangerous. If the driver leaves his vehicle when he nears a cut or curve, he will learn nothing by getting out about the perils that lurk beyond. By the time he regains his seat and sets his car in motion, the hidden train may be upon him. Often the added safeguard will be dubious though the track happens to be straight, as it seems that this one was, at all events as far as the station, about five blocks to the north. A train traveling at a speed of thirty miles an hour will cover a quarter of a mile in the space of thirty seconds. It may thus emerge out of obscurity as the driver turns his back to regain the waiting car, and may then descend upon him suddenly when his car is on the track. Instead of helping himself by getting out, he might do better to press forward with all his faculties alert. So a train at a neighboring station, apparently at rest and harmless, may be transformed in a few seconds into an instrument of destruction. At times the course of safety may be different. One can figure to oneself a roadbed so level and unbroken that getting out will be a gain. Even then the balance of advantage depends on many circumstances and can be easily disturbed. Where was Pokora to leave his truck after getting out to reconnoiter? If he was to leave it on the switch, there was the possibility that the box cars would be shunted down upon him before he could regain his seat. The defendant did not show whether there was a locomotive at the forward end, or whether the cars were so few that a locomotive could be seen. If he was to leave his vehicle near the curb, there was even stronger reason to believe that the space to be covered in going back and forth would make his observations worthless. One must remember that while the traveler turns his eyes in one direction, a train or a loose engine may be approaching from the other.

Illustrations such as these bear witness to the need for caution in framing standards of behavior that amount to rules of law. The need is the more urgent when there is no background of experience out of which the standards have emerged. They are then, not the natural flowerings of behavior in its customary forms, but rules artificially developed, and imposed from without. Extraordinary situations may not wisely or fairly be subjected to tests or regulations that are fitting for the commonplace or normal. In default of the guide of customary conduct, what is suitable for the traveler caught in a mesh where the ordinary safeguards fail him is for the judgment of a jury. The opinion in Goodman's Case has been a source of confusion in the federal courts to the extent that it imposes a standard for application by the judge, and has had only wavering support in the courts of the states. We limit it accordingly.

The judgment should be reversed, and the cause remanded for further proceedings in accordance with this opinion.

It is so ordered.

WILKERSON v. McCARTHY
336 U.S. 53 (1949)

Mr. Justice BLACK delivered the opinion of the Court.

The petitioner, a railroad switchman, was injured while performing duties as an employee of respondents in their railroad coach yard at Denver, Colorado. He brought this action for damages under the Federal Employers' Liability Act. The complaint alleged that in the performance of his duties in the railroad yard it became necessary for him to walk over a wheel-pit on a narrow boardway, and that due to negligence of respondents, petitioner fell into the pit and suffered grievous personal injuries. The complaint further alleged that respondents had failed to furnish him a safe place to work in several detailed particulars, namely, that the pit boardway (1) was not firmly set, (2) was not securely attached, and (3) although only about 20 inches wide, the boardway had been permitted to become greasy, oily, and slippery, thereby causing petitioner to lose his balance, slip, and fall into the pit.

The respondents in their answer to this complaint admitted the existence of the pit and petitioner's injuries as a result of falling into it. They denied, however, that the injury resulted from the railroad's negligence, charging that plaintiff's own negligence was the sole proximate cause of his injuries. On motion of the railroad the trial judge directed the jury to return a verdict in its favor. The Supreme Court of Utah affirmed, one judge dissenting.

The opinion of the Utah Supreme Court strongly indicated, as the dissenting judge pointed out, that its finding of an absence of negligence on the part of the railroad rested on that court's independent resolution of conflicting testimony. This Court has previously held in many cases that where jury trials are required, courts must submit the issues of negligence to a jury if evidence might justify a finding either way on those issues. It was because of the importance of preserving for litigants in FELA cases their right to a jury trial that we granted certiorari in this case.

The evidence showed the following facts without dispute:

Petitioner fell into the pit July 26, 1945. The pit, constructed in 1942, ran approximately forty feet east and west underneath three or more parallel tracks which crossed the pit from north to south. The pit was 11 feet deep and 4 feet 2½ inches wide, with cement walls and floor. Car wheels in need of repair were brought to the pit, lowered into it, there repaired, and then lifted from the pit for return to use. When not in use the pit was kept solidly covered with heavy boards. These boards were used as a walkway by all employees. When the pit was in use the cover boards were removed except one 75 pound "permanent board" 22 inches wide and 4 feet 2½ inches long. While the solid covering was off, this "permanent board," built to fit snugly and firmly, was unquestionably used as a walkway by all employees up to about May 1, 1945.

On this latter date, the railroad put up "safety chains" fastened to guard posts, inclosing 16½ feet of the pit, on its north, south and west sides. The posts, 42 inches high, fitted into tubes imbedded in the ground, the tubes being larger than the posts — enough larger to allow the posts to work freely. The chains, attached two inches from the top of the posts, were to be kept up while the pit was in use and taken down when the pit was not in use. They were up when plaintiff slipped from the "permanent board" into the pit. At that time a tourist car was standing over the pit on track "23½." This track "23½" was east of the two east chain posts, its west rail being about 36 inches, and the tourist car overhand about 7 inches from the two east chain supporting posts. The floor of the "overhang" was about 51 inches above the ground, or 9 inches above the top of the posts, thus allowing an unobstructed clearance of 51 inches under the overhand. The "permanent board" was inside the chain enclosure, the board's east side being about 9½ inches from the two eastern chain posts. Despite the proximity of the tourist car to the posts there was sufficient space east of each chain post so that pit workers had access to and used the board as a walkway. One of the defendant's witnesses, a very large man weighing 250 pounds, passed through it, though according to his testimony, with "very bad discomfort." Petitioner was a much smaller man, weighing 145 pounds, and it was by passing between one of these posts and the tourist car that petitioner reached the "permanent board" which bridged the pit. Oil from wheels would sometimes accumulate at the bottom of the pit, and as stated by the Utah Supreme Court the "permanent board" was "almost certain to become greasy or oily" from use by the pit-men.

Neither before nor after the chains were put up, had the railroad ever forbidden pit workers or any other workers to walk across the pit on the "permanent board." Neither written rules nor spoken instructions had forbidden any employees to use the board. And witnesses for both sides testified that pit workers were supposed to, and did, continue to use the board as a walkway after the chains and posts were installed. The Utah Supreme Court nevertheless held that erection of the chain and post enclosure was itself the equivalent of company orders that no employees other than pit workers should walk across the permanent board when the chains were up. And the Utah Supreme Court also concluded that there was insufficient evidence to authorize a jury finding that employees generally, as well as pit workers, had continued their long standing and open practice of crossing the pit on the permanent board between the time the chains were put up and the time petitioner was injured.

It is the established rule that in passing upon whether there is sufficient evidence to submit an issue to the jury we need look only to the evidence and reasonable inferences which tend to support the case of a litigant against whom a peremptory instruction has been given. Viewing the evidence here in that way it was sufficient to show the following:

Switchmen and other employees, just as pit workers, continued to use the permanent board to walk across the pit after the chains were put up as they had used it before. Petitioner and another witness employed on work around the pit, testified positively that such practice continued. It is true that witnesses for the respondents testified that after the chains were put up only the car men, in removing and applying wheels, used the board 'to walk from one side of the pit to another. . . . Thus the conflict as to continued use of the board as a walkway after erection of the chains was whether the pit workers alone continued to use it as a walkway, or whether employees generally so used it. While this left only a very narrow conflict in the evidence, it was for the jury, not the court, to resolve the conflict.

It was only as a result of its inappropriate resolution of this conflicting evidence that the State Supreme Court affirmed the action of the trial court in directing the verdict. Following its determination of fact the Utah Supreme Court acted on the assumption that the respondents "had no knowledge, actual or constructive, that switchmen were using the plank to carry out their tasks," and the railroad had "no reason to suspect" that employees generally would so use the walkway. From this, the Court went on to say that respondents "were only required to keep the board safe for the purposes of the pit crewmen . . . and not for all the employees in the yard." But the court emphasized that under different facts maintenance of "a 22-inch board for a walkway, which is almost certain to become greasy or oily, constitutes negligence." And under the evidence in this case as to the board, grease and oil, the court added: "It must be conceded that if defendants knew or were charged with knowledge that switchmen and other workmen generally in the yard were habitually using the plank as a walkway in the manner claimed by plaintiff, then the safety enclosure might be entirely inadequate, and a jury question would have been presented on the condition of the board and the adequacy of the enclosure."

We agree with this last quoted statement of the Utah court, and since there was evidence to support a jury finding that employees generally had habitually used the board as a walkway, it was error for the trial judge to direct a verdict in favor of respondent.

There was, as the state court pointed out, evidence to show that petitioner could have taken a slightly longer route and walked around the pit, thus avoiding the use of the board. This fact, however, under the terms of the Federal Employers' Liability Act, would not completely immunize the respondents from liability if the injury was "in part" the result of respondents' negligence. For while petitioner's failure to use a safer method of crossing might be found by the jury to be contributory negligence, the Act provides that "contributory negligence shall not bar a recovery, but the damages shall be diminished by the jury in proportion to the amount of negligence attributable to such employee . . . ."

Much of respondents' argument here is devoted to the proposition that the Federal Act does not make the railroad an absolute insurer against personal injury damages suffered by its employees. That proposition is correct, since the Act imposes liability only for negligent injuries. *Cf. Coray v. Southern Pac. Co.*, 335 U.S. 520 (1949). But the issue of negligence is one for juries to determine according to their finding of whether an employer's conduct measures up to what a reasonable and prudent person would have done under the same circumstances. And a jury should hold a master "liable for injuries attributable to conditions under his control when they are not such as a reasonable man ought to maintain in the circumstances," bearing in mind that "the standard of care must be commensurate to the dangers of the business." *Tiller v. Atlantic Coast Linc R. Co.*, 318 U.S. 54, 67 (1943).

There are some who think that recent decisions of this Court which have required submission of negligence questions to a jury make, "for all practical purposes, a railroad an insurer of its employees." *See Griswold v. Gardner*, 155 F.2d 333, 334 (7th Cir. 1946), Major, J. *But see Griswold*, at 337 (Kerner, J., dissenting); *Griswold*, at 337-38 (Lindley, J., dissenting). This assumption, that railroads are made insurers where the issue of negligence is left to the jury, is inadmissible. It rests on another assumption, this one unarticulated, that juries will invariably decide negligence questions against railroads. This is contrary to fact, as shown for illustration by other Federal Employers Liability cases. Moreover, this Court stated some sixty years ago when considering the proper tribunal for determining questions of negligence: "We see no reason, so long as the jury system is the law of the land and the jury is made the tribunal to decide disputed questions of fact, why it should not decide such questions as these as well as others." And peremptory instructions should not be given in negligence cases "where the facts are in dispute, and the evidence in relation to them is that from which fair-minded men may draw different inferences." Such has ever since been the established rule for trial and appellate courts. Courts should not assume that in determining these questions of negligence juries will fall short of a fair performance of their constitutional function. In rejecting a contention that juries could be expected to determine certain disputed questions on whim, this Court, speaking through Mr. Justice Holmes, said: "But it must be assumed that the constitutional tribunal does its duty, and finds facts only because they are proved."

In reaching its conclusion as to negligence, a jury is frequently called upon to consider many separate strands of circumstances, and from these circumstances to draw its ultimate conclusion on the issue of negligence. Here there are many arguments that could have been presented to the jury in an effort to persuade it that the railroad's conduct was not negligent, and many counter arguments which might have persuaded the jury that the railroad was negligent. The same thing is true as to whether petitioner was guilty of contributory negligence. Many of such arguments were advanced by the Utah Supreme Court to support its finding that the petitioner was negligent and that the railroad was not. But the arguments made by the State Supreme Court are relevant and appropriate only for consideration by the jury, the tribunal selected to pass on the issues. For these reasons, the trial court should have submitted the case to the jury, and it was error for the Utah Supreme Court to affirm its action in taking the case from the jury.

It is urged by petitioner that other fact issues should have been submitted to the jury in addition to those we have specifically pointed out. We need not consider these contentions now, since they may not arise on another trial of the case.

The judgment of the Supreme Court of Utah is reversed and the cause is remanded for further action not inconsistent with this opinion. It is so ordered.

Reversed and remanded.

2. Res Ipsa Loquitur

Res ipsa loquitur is a doctrine in negligence law that allows a plaintiff to survive the defendant's motion to dismiss at the close of the plaintiff's case. It means the court feels that the jury, having heard these facts, could reasonably conclude that there is negligence on the part of the defendant. The facts are said to speak for themselves.

BYRNE v. BOADLE
159 Eng. Rep. 299 (Ex. 1863)

[Plaintiff was passing along the highway in front of defendant's premises when he was struck by a barrel of flour that was apparently being lowered from a window above the premises of Defendant, a dealer in flour. Defendant claimed "that there was no evidence of negligence for the jury." The trial court, agreeing and nonsuited plaintiff after the jury had awarded damages of £50. The court, however, granted Plaintiff leave to move the Court of Exchequer to enter a verdict for him in that amount. Plaintiff then obtain a rule nisi from the Court of Exchequer to enter the verdict.

Defendant now seeks to show cause for a reversal. Defendant's attorney argued that there was no evidence to connect Defendant or his servants to the occurrence: "Surmise ought not to be substituted for strict proof when it is thought to fix a defendant with serious liability. The plaintiff should establish his case by affirmative evidence. . . . The plaintiff was bound to give affirmative proof of negligence. But there was not a scintilla of evidence, unless the occurrence is of itself evidence of negligence."

In discussion with counsel, the court then commented: "There are certain cases of which it may be said *res ipsa loquitur* and this seems one of them. In some cases the Court had held that the mere fact of the accident having occurred is evidence of negligence. . . ."]

POLLOCK, C.B. We are all of opinion that the rule must be absolute to enter the verdict for the plaintiff. The learned counsel was quite right in saying that there are many accidents form which no presumption of negligence can arise, but I think it would be wrong to lay down as a rule that in no case can presumption of negligence arise from the fact of an accident. Suppose in this case the barrel had rolled out of the warehouse and fallen on the plaintiff, how could he possibly ascertain from what cause it occurred? It is the duty of persons who keep barrels in a warehouse to take care that they do not roll out, and I think that such a case would, beyond all doubt, afford prima facie evidence of negligence. A barrel could not roll out of a warehouse without some negligence, and to say that a plaintiff who is injured by it must call witnesses from the warehouse to prove negligence seems to me preposterous. So in the building or repairing a house, or putting pots on the chimneys, if a person passing along the road is injured by something falling upon him, I think the accident alone would be prima facie evidence of negligence. Or if an article calculated to cause damage is put in a wrong place and does mischief, I think that those whose duty it was to put it in the right place are prima facie responsible, and if there is any state of facts to rebut the presumption of negligence, they must prove them. The present case upon the evidence comes to this, a man is passing in front of the premises of a dealer in flour, and there falls down upon him a barrel of flour. I think it apparent that the barrel was in the custody of the defendant who occupied the premises, and who is responsible for the acts of his servants who had the control of it; and in my opinion the fact of its falling is prima facie evidence of negligence, and the plaintiff who was injured by it is not bound to show that it could not fall without negligence, but if there are any facts inconsistent with negligence it is for the defendant to prove them.

NOTE

The following provide comparisons in various treatises of when the doctrine of *res ipsa loquitur* applies:

WIGMORE ON EVIDENCE § 2509 (1905) [Prosser & Keeton at 244.]

(1) The event must be of a kind which ordinarily does not occur in the absence of someone's negligence;

(2) It must be caused by an agency or instrumentality within the exclusive control of the defendant; and

(3) It must not have been due to any voluntary action or contribution of the part of the plaintiff.

RESTATEMENT (SECOND) TORTS § 328D [More expansive view.]

(1) It may be inferred that harm suffered by the plaintiff is caused by negligence of the defendant when

(a) the event is of a kind which ordinarily does not occur in the absence of negligence;

(b) other responsible causes, including the conduct of the plaintiff and third persons, are sufficiently eliminated by the evidence; and

(c) the indicated negligence is within the scope of the defendant's duty to the plaintiff.

(2) It is the function of the court to determine whether the inference may be reasonably drawn by the jury, or whether it must be necessarily drawn.

(3) It is the function of the jury to determine whether the inference is to be drawn in any case where different conclusions may be reasonably reached.

LARSON v. ST. FRANCIS HOTEL
188 P.2d 513 (Cal. Ct. App. 1948)

BRAY, J.

The accident out of which this action arose was apparently the result of the effervescence and ebullition of San Franciscans in their exuberance of joy on V-J Day, August 14, 1945. Plaintiff (who is not included in the above description), while walking on the sidewalk on Post Street adjoining the St. Francis Hotel, just after stepping out from under the marquee, was struck on the head by a heavy, overstuffed arm chair, knocked unconscious, and received injuries for which she is asking damages from the owners of the hotel. Although there were a number of persons in the immediate vicinity, no one appears to have seen from whence the chair came nor to have seen it before it was within a few feet of plaintiff's head, nor was there any identification of the chair as belonging to the hotel. However, it is a reasonable inference that the chair came from some portion of the hotel. For the purposes of this opinion, we will so assume, in view of the rule on nonsuit cases that every favorable inference fairly deducible from the evidence must be drawn in favor of plaintiff, and that all the evidence must be construed most strongly against the defendants.

At the trial, plaintiff, after proving the foregoing facts and the extent of her injuries, rested, relying upon the doctrine of res ipsa loquitur. On motion of defendant the court granted a nonsuit. The main question to be determined is whether under the circumstances shown, the doctrine applies. The trial court correctly held that it did not.

In *Gerhart v. Southern California Gas Co.*, 132 P.2d 874, 877 (Cal. App. 1942), cited by plaintiff, the court sets forth the test for the applicability of the doctrine. "[F]or a plaintiff to make out a case entitling him to the benefit of the doctrine, *he must prove* (1) that there was an accident; (2) that the thing or instrumentality which caused the accident was at the time of and prior thereto under the *exclusive* control and management of the defendant; (3) *that the accident was such that in the ordinary course of events, the defendant using ordinary care, the accident would not have happened.* . . . The doctrine of res ipsa loquitur applies only where the cause of the injury is shown to be under the exclusive control and management of the defendant and can have no application . . . to a case having a divided responsibility where an unexplained accident may have been attributable to one of several causes, for some of which the defendant is not responsible, and when it appears that the injury was caused by one of two causes for one of which defendant is responsible but not for the other, plaintiff must fail, if the evidence does not show that the injury was the result of the former cause, or leaves it as probable that it was caused by one or the other."

Applying the rule to the facts of this case, it is obvious that the doctrine does not apply. While, as pointed out by plaintiff, the rule of exclusive control "is not limited to the actual physical control but applies to the right of control of the instrumentality which causes the injury" it is not clear to us how this helps plaintiff's case. A hotel does not have exclusive control, either actual or potential, of its furniture. Guests have, at least, partial control. Moreover, it cannot be said that with the hotel using ordinary care "the accident was such that in the ordinary course of events . . . would not have happened." On the contrary, the mishap would quite as likely be due to the fault of a guest or other person as to that of defendants. The most logical inference from the circumstances shown is that the chair was thrown by some such person from a window. It thus appears that this occurrence is not such as ordinarily does not happen without the negligence of the party charged, but, rather, one in which the accident ordinarily might happened despite the fact that the defendants used reasonable care and were totally free from negligence. To keep guests and visitors from throwing furniture out windows would require a guard to be placed in every room in the hotel, and no one would contend that there is any rule of law requiring a hotel to do that.

The cases cited by plaintiff as authority for the application of the doctrine of res ipsa loquitur are easily distinguishable from this case. In *Gerhart*, which involved an explosion from leaking gas, the court found that defendant was in the exclusive ownership, control and management of the supply, flow and existence of the gas which exploded. *Gerhart*, at 874. In *Helms v. Pacific Gas & Elec-*

tric Co., 70 P.2d 247 (Cal. App. 1937), a glass portion of an electrolier fell and injured the plaintiff, who was standing on the sidewalk beneath it. The parties stipulated that the electrolier was owned and maintained by the defendant. There, not only was the instrumentality which caused the accident in the *exclusive* control and management of the defendant, but the falling of the glass portion was something that in the ordinary course of events would not occur if the defendant used ordinary care in maintaining it.

In *Michener v. Hutton*, 265 P. 238 (Cal. 1928), the length of pipe which fell and caused the injury was "unquestionably under the management of the appellants at the time of the accident." While the court holds that, "The doctrine has also found frequent application in actions for damages for injuries incurred by reason of being struck by falling objects," it is limited to situations in which the thing is shown to be under the exclusive management or control of the defendant or his servants, or in which it must necessarily follow that the injury would not have occurred had the defendant used ordinary care.

In *Mintzer v. Wilson*, 68 P.2d 370 (Cal. Ct. App. 1937), a paid guest in defendant's hotel was injured while in bed by the falling of a huge piece of plaster from the ceiling. It was held by the court that the ceiling was in the exclusive control of the hotel, and that plaster does not ordinarily fall from properly constructed ceilings.

"The mere fact that an accident has occurred does not of itself result in any inference of negligence as against a defendant. . . . To justify the invocation of the rule res ipsa loquitur the instrumentality which caused the injury must have been under the exclusive management of the defendant." *Hubbert v. Aztec Brewing Co.*, 80 P.2d 185, 197 (Cal. Ct. App. 1938). "Neither does it apply where the cause of the accident is unexplained and might have been due to one of several causes for some of which the defendant is not responsible." *Biddlecomb v. Haydon*, 40 P.2d 873 (Cal. Ct. App. 1935). *See also Hilson v. Pacific Gas & Electric Co.*, 21 P.2d 662, 665 (Cal. Ct. App. 1933), which held that in a situation as last above quoted, the doctrine "can in no event apply."

Plaintiff quotes 9 Cal. Jur. 548 to the effect "that a motion for a nonsuit must point the attention of the court and counsel to the precise grounds upon which it is made" and contends that the motion for nonsuit in the trial court did not do this. The motion was made on the ground that "there is no evidence from which it might be inferred that the hotel was guilty of any negligence which caused the chair" to hit plaintiff. It further points out that the only evidence attempting to connect the hotel with the accident is the fact that it occurred in the proximity of the hotel, and that such proof is not sufficient to establish liability. The motion was sufficient.

In her complaint plaintiff alleged in paragraph III that the defendant was engaged in the hotel business on all the premises described therein and had the right of control and management thereof. In its answer defendants denied all of the allegations of paragraph III and then stated: "Further answering paragraph III, these defendants admit that they operated the St. Francis Hotel at said time as copartners." Plaintiff contends that in some way this is an admission that defendants had exclusive control and management of the furniture of the hotel so as to warrant the application of the doctrine of res ipsa loquitur. It is obvious that such contention is without merit.

The judgment appealed from is affirmed.

NOTE

Cf. Connolly v. Nicollet Hotel, 95 N.W.2d 657, 669 (Minn. 1959) (the appellate court reversed the trial court and ordered the plaintiff be allowed to get to the jury, where the defendant hotel was taken over by a party that led to plaintiff's injury. The court never used the words *res ipsa loquitur*, yet distinguished *Larson* because in *Larson* the celebration was a surprise).

MILES v. ST. REGIS PAPER CO.
467 P.2d 307 (Wash. 1970)

FINLEY, A.J.

This lawsuit was brought by Dorothy Miles individually as the surviving wife and as the administratrix of the estate of Claud Miles, Sr., the deceased. Negligence was alleged on the part of the St. Regis Paper Company, Inc., the Northern Pacific Railroad Company, Inc., and certain employees of both entities.

A motion by St. Regis challenging the sufficiency of the evidence at the end of the plaintiff's case was granted and St. Regis is not involved in this appeal. Similar motions by Northern Pacific Railroad at the end of plaintiff's case and at the end of all of the evidence were denied. The jury returned a verdict of $35,000 for the plaintiff. A motion for a judgment n.o.v. or for a new trial was denied and this appeal followed.

Claud Miles, Sr., was crushed and instantly killed by one of three logs which rolled from the top of a flatcar loaded with logs. The flatcar and its load of logs were in a logging train in the process of being unloaded at the premises of the 'D' Street Rafting Company, Inc., of Tacoma, Washington.

The logging train was loaded with logs by employees of St. Regis at Lake Kapowsin. Much testimony was introduced tending to show that due care was exercised by St. Regis employees in loading the logs on the flatcars at Lake Kapowsin; furthermore, that subsequent repetitive inspections of the log loads were made both by St. Regis and Northern Pacific to insure safe transportation and safe unloading. After arrival of the log train at the railroad yards in Tacoma, a Northern Pacific switch engine was coupled to it and moved the train from the railroad yards to the premises of the 'D' Street Rafting Company. There is a conflict in the evidence as to what happened there. The employees of the railroad testified that the train did not move after the last car in the string was positioned under the crane of the 'D' Street Rafting Company in preparation for unloading. They stated that no logs had been unloaded prior to the accident. But, in direct conflict there is the testimony of the operator of the crane at the time of the accident, a Mr. Keblbek, who was an employee of 'D' Street Rafting Company. He testified that some logs had been unloaded and that the train was moved just 15 or 20 seconds prior to the time he heard the locomotive whistle blow, indicating an accident had occurred.

The testimony of witnesses for the railroad indicated that movement of the train in positioning the cars for unloading was under the control of members of the unloading crew of the 'D' Street Rafting Company who relayed signals to the train crew. In conflict, other testimony indicated that movement of the train was subject to control and authority of the train crew, principally the engineer or fireman on duty in the locomotive engine. As will be seen later, this question of control has become the primary issue in this appeal.

Two cables with fasteners or "binders" were placed around each end of each load of logs on the railroad flatcars. Apparently the cables and binders were used at the behest of the railroad as a safety measure and had the capacity to provide some stability for the log loads. The cables were not of sufficient strength to hold if an entire log load shifted significantly. They would resist and contain some shifting as to a load or as to one log, depending upon the size and weight of logs and the shifting involved. Normally the cables would hang somewhat loosely at the bottom of each log load. One method of ascertaining stability and safety of the log loads at the time of unloading was to inspect and determine whether each of the cables and the binders were intact and whether the cables were hanging somewhat loosely beneath each log load. On the day of the accident, Mr. Miles, the deceased, was a member of the unloading crew of the 'D' Street Rafting Company. He was assigned the duty of releasing the binders encircling the loads of logs on the flatcars. After releasing the binders, it was part of his work to return to the crane and to assist in handling two slings which were attached to the crane and utilized in unloading logs. These were passed under and around the loads of logs, then attached to the crane. When each end was secured, the crane was then used to pull the slings tight, and then to lift and unload the logs. At the time of the accident Mr. Miles had not returned to the crane to work with the slings. After the accident it was ascertained that except for the flatcar immediately in front of the switch engine, the binders had been released. One of the binders on the fatal load of logs had been released by hand, ostensibly by Mr. Miles. The other binder had not been released but the cable was broken.

The engineer, Mr. Casey, had changed places in the cab of the switch engine with the fireman and was eating his lunch, sitting with his back to the log load on the flatcar immediately in front of the switch engine. He did not see the three logs roll off the top of the load and did not see Mr. Miles until after the accident when he looked and saw him under one of the logs. The fireman seated by the throttle on the opposite side of the engine cab could not see Mr. Miles. He did see the top or "peaker" log and the other two logs begin to roll from the railroad flat-car. The foreman of the railroad switching crew, Mr. Harper, was on a platform adjacent to the crane, several car lengths distance from the switch engine, and on the side of the train opposite from where Mr. Miles was killed. From his location at the time of the accident, Mr. Harper could not see Mr. Miles. Two other members of the railroad switching crew had temporarily left the log train and had gone to have coffee after the train was initially positioned on the premises of the 'D' Street Rafting Company. Obviously they could not see and evaluate the situation of Mr. Miles just prior to the accident. Mr. Keblbek testified that from his position operating the crane he could not see Mr. Miles alongside the fatal load of logs.

There was very positive testimony on the part of members of the railroad switching crew that the train had not been handled roughly in its movement from the railroad yard to the 'D' Street Rafting Company premises; furthermore, that two of these employees had walked the train observing the condition of the binders and carefully inspecting each of the log loads on the several flatcars of the train. There was positive testimony that if an inspection of the binders and the logs showed a possibility that any load of logs was unstable, the suspect loads would be tagged with a white card and the binders and cables would not be released by hand. Such loads would be moved to the crane site and the slings placed around the logs as a safety precaution before the binders would be released.

The appellant assigns error: (1) to the denial of motions attacking the sufficiency of the evidence, (2) to the failure of the trial court to give several jury instructions offered by the appellant, and (3) to the giving of an instruction submitting the doctrine res ipsa loquitur to the jury. We are convinced there was sufficient evidence that the trial court did not err in denying appellant's motions in this regard. We agree with the trial court that it was not error to refuse to give the instructions offered by appellant. The essence of these was adequately covered in other instructions given to the jury. This appeal focuses essentially on whether it was error for the trial court to instruct the jury on the doctrine of res ipsa loquitur.

A common statement of the doctrine of res ipsa loquitur appears in *Kind v. Seattle*, 312 P.2d 811 (Wash. 1957): "Where a plaintiff's evidence establishes that an instrumentality under the exclusive control of the defendants caused an injurious occurrence, which ordinarily does not happen if those in control of the instrumentality use ordinary care, there is an inference, permissible from the occurrence itself, that it was caused by the defendant's want of care."

The three prerequisites to application of the doctrine are: (1) an event which ordinarily does not occur unless someone is negligent; (2) the agency or instrumentality causing the event must be within the exclusive control of the defendant; and (3) there must be no voluntary action or contribution to the event on the part of the plaintiff. It is a well-known fact that great quantities of logs are loaded, transported, and unloaded every day throughout the state by truck and rail facilities. It is also well known that in most substantial part logs are loaded, transported, and unloaded properly, safely, and without accidents. So, despite the occurrence of some accidents, as in the instant case, we are convinced it can be said that they do not happen unless there has been some negligence on the part of someone involved in loading, transporting, or unloading the logs.

The question of control poses a close and difficult problem. Appellant makes a strong argument that employees of 'D' Street Rafting Company had exclusive control of not only the unloading of the logs involving the use of the crane, but also other operations, including positioning of the cars and movement of the train. There is conflicting testimony, and the hand on the throttle of the switch engine was obviously the hand of the engineer or the fireman (employees of the railroad). Furthermore, any movement of the train ultimately was the responsibility and within the exclusive control of such employees. It is not denied that movement of the train and positioning of the railroad flatcars loaded with logs occurred in accordance with the unloading plans and desires of employees of 'D' Street Rafting Company, communicated by hand signal or otherwise to the foreman of the railroad switching crew and relayed by him to the engine crew. We believe that the ultimate decision to move the train was made by employees of the railroad. Thus, In terms of the requisites for application of res ipsa loquitur in this case, we are convinced that at the time of the accident the train of flatcars loaded with logs was in the "exclusive control" of the railroad.

It is not of crucial consequence that Mr. Miles apparently released the binder at one end of the load of logs shortly before the accident. There was evidence that a load of logs could be stable at one end and not at the other end. The jury could have inferred from this evidence that the fatal log load was unstable at the end where the cable had snapped, but stable at the end where the binder had been released. There was evidence that a binder could not be released by hand when the weight of a log put tension on a cable and binder. In this respect there was evidence tending to show that a load of logs could be made unstable by rough or jerky movement of the train either before or after a binder had been released. In addition, this lack of stability apparently would not always be shown by a taut or snapped binder until it was too late. We are convinced that the evidence supports the conclusion that Mr. Miles did not contribute to the log's fall.

Without Mr. Keblbek's testimony that the train was moved 15 to 20 seconds prior to the time that the three logs spilled or rolled off the flatcar, there would indeed be a more difficult question as to any possible inference of negligence on the part of the railroad. However, on the basis of the evidence brought out at the trial, we cannot say that the instruction on res ipsa loquitur was error.

Indeed this case seems to us to have a classic similarity to *Byrne v. Boadle*, 159 Eng. Rep. 299 (1863), which originated application of the Doctrine of res ipsa loquitur. There it was a barrel of flour which mysteriously fell on plaintiff; here it was a log. In that case the learned judge stated "the plaintiff who was injured by (the falling barrel) is not bound to shew that it could not fall without negligence, but if there are any facts inconsistent with negligence it is for the defendant to prove them."

The judgment of the trial court should be affirmed. It is so ordered.

NEILL, A.J. (dissenting).

I am in disagreement with the majority on its conclusion that the res ipsa loquitur instruction (No. 5) was properly given. There was insufficient evidence to support the instruction and the instruction was not a correct statement of the doctrine. It is uncontested that, absent res ipsa loquitur, the plaintiff's evidence is insufficient to establish a prima facie case. One of the prerequisites to application of the doctrine of res ipsa loquitur is that the instrumentality causing the event must be within the exclusive control of the defendant. The majority finds sufficient evidence of exclusive control to justify application of the doctrine. I disagree.

Three members of the train crew, the 'D' Street crew foreman and the resident manager of 'D' Street Rafting Company all substantially agreed in their testimony on the normal practices followed in these unloading operations. The switch engine would spot the first car under the unloading crane. No further movement of the train would occur until directed by employees of the rafting company. Instructions to move the cars would be given to the switchman standing at the end of the train near the unloading platform, who would relay them by hand signals to the engineer at the other end of the train.

The three railroad company employees who were present at the time of the accident all testified that the train was originally positioned so that the car farthest from the engine was under the crane. The train was not moved and none of the cars were unloaded until after the accident, which occurred 5 to 10 minutes after they had positioned the first car. However, Mr. Keblbek, a boom man for the rafting company, testified that one car had been unloaded and that the train had been moved immediately prior to the accident. He also testified, contrary to the later testimony of his manager, Mr. Reid, that sometimes the railroad crew was aware of the sequence in which the cars were to be unloaded and that each movement of the train might not be in direct response to individual commands given by rafting company employees. In this specific instance, Mr. Keblbek could not say who gave the instructions to move the train.

"Control" does not necessarily mean actual physical control, but can include the present ability to exercise a right of control. All the witnesses agree that once the train arrived at 'D' Street Rafting Company, the unloading process was essentially directed by employees of that company. While it is true that the hand on the throttle of the switch engine remained that of a railroad employee, and while it may also be true that the engineer had a legal right to refuse to follow any instructions from employees of the rafting company, it does not follow that the railroad so controlled the unloading process that any negligence occurring therein may be automatically attributable to it. Even Mr. Keblbek, who testified that the engine moved immediately before the accident, cannot say who ordered this movement; and he specifically admitted that the engine may have moved under instructions from him or Mr. Reid, both employees of the rafting company. Under these circumstances, I see no basis for the majority's conclusion that the train was in the "exclusive control" of the railroad at the time of the accident.

As we noted in *Vogreg v. Shepard Ambulance Service, Inc.*, no special witchcraft is invoked by murmuring the Latin phrase, "res ipsa loquitur." The doctrine is nothing more than a legal formulation of the common sense conclusion that if an instrumentality for which defendant is responsible injures somebody, and this injury would not normally occur without negligence, then defendant is responsible for the injury. But when, as here, the evidence does not establish exclusive control in the defendant, and the possible causes include negligence by others as well as the defendant, or causes involving no negligence at all, then the doctrine does not apply. Therefore, it was error to instruct the jury on the doctrine of res ipsa loquitur. The case should have been dismissed upon defendant's motion at the close of the evidence.

Instruction No. 5, to which defendant took exception, reads in relevant part:

> (Y)ou are instructed that it is for you to determine whether the manner of the occurrence of the death of Claud Miles and the attendant circumstances connected therewith are of such character as would, in your judgment, warrant an inference that the injury would not have occurred had due diligence and care been exercised by the defendant's employees. The rule is that when an agency or instrumentality which produces injury is under the control of a defendant or its employees, and the injury which occurred would ordinarily not have resulted if those in control had used proper care, then, in the absence of satisfactory explanation, you are at liberty to infer though you are not required to infer that the defendant, or its employees, were at some point negligent, and that such negligence produced the death of Claud Miles.

My concern is with the words "under the control of a defendant or its employees." These words do not specify for the jury the degree of control (exclusive) that is necessary before *res ipsa* can be applied. As instructed, the jury could have subjected defendant to the effects of the doctrine upon a finding that defendant had partial control, potential partial control, or any of the other myriad degrees of control ranging from the almost exclusive to the almost nil. If such an instruction is to be given at all, it should be given accurately. Here, the instruction is deficient in that it allows the jury to apply the doctrine upon a finding that defendant had *any* degree of control over the instrumentality. The instruction is plainly erroneous.

I would reverse and dismiss.

PROBLEM

In the hands of a conservative court, *res ipsa* almost never applies. Consider the following facts, and see if you can justify not applying the doctrine of *res ipsa loquitur*:

The plaintiff's evidence showed that near 5:00 p.m., she was operating an automobile southbound on a Highway, and stopped at the intersection with Hopkins Road in obedience to a red traffic signal. The plaintiff's vehicle was in the left of three southbound lanes.

At the same time, D's employee, Prince E. Rich, III, was operating D's truck southbound on the Highway, and stopped in the center lane at the intersection. Both vehicles were "first in line" at the signal.

According to the plaintiff, both vehicles moved forward when the light changed to green. Before the plaintiff's automobile "cleared Hopkins Road," she heard "a loud thump and a warning screamed at her" by a passenger. "She immediately looked over her right shoulder and saw D's tractor proceeding but it had become separated from the trailer which was also moving forward barely to her right." Believing the trailer "was angling toward her" and fearing it would strike her vehicle, the plaintiff, "in a panic move," steered hard to her left and accelerated. "In so doing, she testified, she struck the concrete median that was on her left with much force," causing her injuries. There was no contact between the plaintiff's vehicle and defendant's tractor or trailer.

The plaintiff's evidence about the maintenance of D's truck was presented solely through defendant's employee Rich, called by the plaintiff as an adverse witness. He testified that early on the day in question he had driven the tractor-trailer unit from D's place of business on the Highway to Baltimore, Maryland, making four deliveries of freight within a 25-mile radius of Baltimore before returning to his home city in the late afternoon.

Rich described the manner in which he had connected the tractor to the loaded trailer at the D's premises before he left. The employee, with six years' experience in joining tractors and trailers, said the tractor has a part called a "fifth wheel," mounted on the tractor's frame behind the cab. The fifth wheel is a round, flat device containing a "slot" opening to the rear. Built into the fifth wheel is a "locking pin," a heavy steel bar. Mounted on the trailer's leading edge is a vertical "pole" about three inches in diameter.

In order to connect the two pieces of equipment, the tractor was backed against the stationary trailer, which was standing on a "landing gear," causing the trailer pole to fit into the slot of the fifth wheel. The fifth wheel's locking pin, which is "spring triggered," came "across" with an audible "click" and enclosed the trailer pole "like a cage," securing the trailer to the tractor. After the locking occurred, Rich performed a "series of checks." Air lines were connected and a visual inspection was made to verify that the locking device was properly seated. The trailer's landing gear was "cranked up," the brakes on the tractor were released, and the trailer brakes were left "charged." The tractor was put "in gear" and an effort was made to pull away from the trailer. If the locking "has not been done right," the tractor "will pull right away" from the trailer; if the locking has been properly done, "you can't pull away from it." On the day in question, the tractor would not pull away.

Rich further testified that he experienced no difficulty or trouble with the "rig" at any time during the trip to Baltimore and return. He permitted no one to operate the rig, he carried no passengers, and allowed no one to "do anything with the rig or the connection or the hookup."

Describing the incident in question, Rich testified he traveled about 200 feet southbound from his stopped position at the intersection and heard a noise. In an "almost panicked reaction," he immediately "shut the tractor down, popped the brakes on it, and jumped straight out the door" because he could see the trailer had "come loose." The tractor was stopped in the center lane. He ran back to the trailer, which had stopped "dead" in the center lane about 30 feet behind the tractor. Rich stated he was "positive" that at the moment he noticed in his rear-view mirror that the trailer was loose, there was no automobile in the lane to his left and no car on or near the median strip.

When Rich reached the stopped trailer, the tractor's fifth wheel mechanism was still locked. The "stout metal bar" was still in proper locking position and was unbroken. The employee testified he did not know "how the tractor and the trailer got loose from each other with the [locking pin] still being locked."

See Joann E. Lewis v. Carpenter Company, 252 Va. 296 (1996). *Cf. McDougald v. Perry*, 716 So. 2d 783 (Fla. 1998) (plaintiff was driving behind a tractor-trailer when a 130-pound spare tire suddenly dropped from the cradle underneath the truck and bounced into his windshield). *Res ipsa* held particularly applicable in wayward wheel cases. *Cf. Ex parte Cabtree Indus. Waste, Inc.*, 728 So. 2d 155 (Ala. 1998) (the facts were the same except that three days earlier a third party had repaired the tire and *res ipsa* held inapplicable).

3. Res Ipsa in Medical Malpractice

Res ipsa has been particularly helpful to plaintiff patients in medical malpractice cases where they submit themselves to what is usually a routine operation, and they wake up with some unexpected condition or symptom. Where the patient is unconscious, the sympathies are with the patient. The doctor seems to be in control, and if the operation usually goes well, and unusual symptoms show up after the operation, do these facts alone give rise to a reasonable inference of negligence? Is circumstantial evidence sufficient to get to the jury without more?

YBARRA v. SPANGARD
154 P.2d 687 (Cal.1944)

GIBSON, C.J.

This is an action for damages for personal injuries alleged to have been inflicted on plaintiff by defendants during the course of a surgical operation. The trial court entered judgments of nonsuit as to all defendants and plaintiff appealed.

On October 28, 1939, plaintiff consulted defendant Dr. Tilley, who diagnosed his ailment as appendicitis, and made arrangements for an appendectomy to be performed by defendant Dr. Spangard at a hospital owned and managed by defendant Dr. Swift. Plaintiff entered the hospital, was given a hypodermic injection, slept, and later was awakened by Drs. Tilley and Spangard and wheeled into the operating room by a nurse whom he believed to be defendant Gisler, an employee of Dr. Swift. Defendant Dr. Reser, the anesthetist, also an employee of Dr. Swift, adjusted plaintiff for the operation, pulling his body to the head of the operating table and, according to plaintiff's testimony, laying him back against two hard objects at the top of his shoulders, about an inch below his neck. Dr. Reser then administered the anesthetic and plaintiff lost consciousness. When he awoke early the following morning, he was in his hospital room attended by defendant Thompson, the special nurse, and another nurse who was not made a defendant.

Plaintiff testified that prior to the operation he had never had any pain in, or injury to, his right arm or shoulder, but that when he awakened he felt a sharp pain about half way between the neck and the point of the right shoulder. He complained to the nurse, and then to Dr. Tilley, who gave him diathermy treatments while he remained in the hospital. The pain did not cease but spread down to the lower part of his arm, and after his release from the hospital the condition grew worse. He was unable to rotate or lift his arm, and developed paralysis and atrophy of the muscles around the shoulder. He received further treatments from Dr. Tilley until March, 1940, and then returned to work, wearing his arm in a splint on the advice of Dr. Spangard.

Plaintiff also consulted Dr. Wilfred Sterling Clark, who had X-ray pictures taken which showed an area of diminished sensation below the shoulder and atrophy and wasting away of the muscles around the shoulder. In the opinion of Dr. Clark, plaintiff's condition was due to trauma or injury by pressure or strain applied between his right shoulder and neck.

Plaintiff was also examined by Dr. Fernando Garduno, who expressed the opinion that plaintiff's injury was a paralysis of traumatic origin, not arising from pathological causes, and not systemic, and that the injury resulted in atrophy, loss of use and restriction of motion of the right arm and shoulder.

Plaintiff's theory is that the foregoing evidence presents a proper case for the application of the doctrine of res ipsa loquitur, and that the inference of negligence arising therefrom makes the granting of as nonsuit improper. Defendants take the position that, assuming that plaintiff's condition was in fact the result of an injury, there is no showing that the act of any particular defendant, nor any particular instrumentality, was the cause thereof. They attack plaintiff's action as an attempt to fix liability "en masse" on various defendants, some of whom were not responsible for the acts of others; and they further point to the failure to show which defendants had control of the instrumentalities that may have been involved. Their main defense may be briefly stated in two propositions: (1) that where there are several defendants, and there is a division of responsibility in the use of an instrumentality causing the injury, and the injury might have resulted from the separate act of either one of two or more persons, the rule of res ipsa loquitur cannot be invoked against any one of them; and (2) that where there are several instrumentalities, and no showing is made as to which caused the injury or as to the particular defendant in control of it, the doctrine cannot apply. We are satisfied, however, that these objections are not well taken in the circumstances of this case.

The doctrine of res ipsa loquitur has three conditions: "(1) the accident must be of a kind which ordinarily does not occur in the absence of someone's negligence; (2) it must be caused by an agency or instrumentality within the exclusive control of the defendant; (3) it must not have been due to any voluntary action or contribution on the part of the plaintiff." Prosser, Torts, p. 295. It is applied in a wide variety of situations, including cases of medical or dental treatment and hospital care.

There is, however, some uncertainty as to the extent to which res ipsa loquitur may be invoked in cases of injury from medical treatment. This is in part due to the tendency, in some decisions, to lay undue emphasis on the limitations of the doctrine, and to give too little attention to its basic underlying purpose. The result has been that a simple, understandable rule of circumstantial evidence, with a sound background of common sense and human experience, has occasionally been transformed into a rigid legal formula, which arbitrarily precludes its application in many cases where it is most important that it should be applied. If the doctrine is to continue to serve a useful purpose, we should not forget that "the particular force and justice of the rule, regarded as a presumption throwing upon the party charged the duty of producing evidence, consists in the circumstance that the chief evidence of the true cause, whether culpable or innocent, is practically accessible to him but inaccessible to the injured person." In [*Maki v. Murray Hospital*, 91 Mont. 251], where an unconscious patient in a hospital received injuries from a fall, the court declared that without the doctrine the maxim that for every wrong there is a remedy would be rendered nugatory, "by denying one, patently entitled to damages, satisfaction merely because he is ignorant of facts peculiarly within the knowledge of the party who should, in all justice, pay them."

The present case is of a type which comes within the reason and spirit of the doctrine more fully perhaps than any other. The passenger sitting awake in a railroad car at the time of a collision, [or] the pedestrian walking along the street [who was] struck by a falling object or the debris of an explosion, are surely not more entitled to an explanation than the unconscious patient on the operating table. Viewed from this aspect, it is difficult to see how the doctrine can, with any justification, be so restricted in its statement as to become inapplicable to a patient who submits himself to the care and custody of doctors and nurses, is rendered unconscious, and receives some injury from instrumentalities used in his treatment. Without the aid of the doctrine a patient who received permanent injuries of a serious character, obviously the result of someone's negligence, would be entirely unable to recover unless the doctors and nurses in attendance voluntarily chose to disclose the identity of the negligent person and the facts establishing liability. If this were the state of the law of negligence, the courts, to avoid gross injustice, would be forced to invoke the principles of absolute liability, irrespective of negligence, in actions by persons suffering injuries during the course of treatment under anesthesia. But we think this juncture has not yet been reached, and that the doctrine of res ipsa loquitur is properly applicable to the case before us.

The condition that the injury must not have been due to the plaintiff's voluntary action is of course fully satisfied under the evidence produced herein; and the same is true of the condition that the accident must be one which ordinarily does not occur unless someone was negligent. We have here no problem of negligence in treatment, but of distinct injury to a healthy part of the body not the subject of treatment, nor within the area covered by the operation. The decisions in this state make it clear that such circumstances raise the inference of negligence and call upon the defendant to explain the unusual result.

The argument of defendants is simply that plaintiff has not shown an injury caused by an instrumentality under a defendant's control, because he has not shown which of the several instrumentalities that he came in contact with while in the hospital caused the injury; and he has not shown that any one defendant or his servants had exclusive control over any particular instrumentality. Defendants assert that some of them were not the employees of other defendants, that some did not stand in any permanent relationship from which liability in tort would follow, and that in view of the nature of the injury, the number of defendants and the different functions performed by each, they could not all be liable for the wrong, if any.

We have no doubt that in a modern hospital a patient is quite likely to come under the care of a number of persons in different types of contractual and other relationships with each other. For example, in the present case it appears that Drs. Smith, Spangard and Tilley were physicians or surgeons commonly placed in the legal category of independent contractors; and Dr. Reser, the anesthetist, and defendant Thompson, the special nurse, were employees of Dr. Swift and not of the other doctors. But we do not believe that either the number or relationship of the defendants alone determines whether the doctrine of res ipsa loquitur applies. Every defendant in whose custody the plaintiff was placed for any period was bound to exercise ordinary care to see that no unnecessary harm came to him and each would be liable for failure in this regard. Any defendant who negligently injured him, and any defendant charged with his care who so neglected him as to allow injury to occur, would be liable. The defendant employers would be liable for the neglect of their employees; and the doctor in charge of the operation would be liable for the negligence of those who became his temporary servants for the purpose of assisting in the operation.

In this connection, it should be noted that while the assisting physicians and nurses may be employed by the hospital, or engaged by the patient, they normally become the temporary servants or agents of the surgeon in charge while the operation is in progress, and liability may be imposed upon him for their negligent acts under the doctrine of *respondeat superior*. Thus a surgeon has been held liable for the negligence of an assisting nurse who leaves a sponge or other object inside a patient, and the fact that the duty of seeing that such mistakes do not occur is delegated to others does not absolve the doctor from responsibility for their negligence.

It may appear at the trial that, consistent with the principles outlined above, one or more defendants will be found liable and others absolved, but this should not preclude the application of the rule of res ipsa loquitur. The control at one time or another, of one or more of the various agencies or instrumentalities which might have harmed the plaintiff was in the hands of every defendant or of his employees or temporary servants. This, we think, places upon them the burden of initial explanation. Plaintiff was rendered unconscious for the purpose of undergoing surgical treatment by the defendants; it is manifestly unreasonable for them to insist that he identify any one of them as the person who did the alleged negligent act.

The other aspect of the case which defendants so strongly emphasize is that plaintiff has not identified the instrumentality any more than he has the particular guilty defendant. Here, again, there is a misconception which, if carried to the extreme for which defendants contend, would unreasonably limit the application of the res ipsa loquitur rule. It should be enough that the plaintiff can show an injury resulting from an external force applied while he lay unconscious in the hospital; this is as clear a case of identification of the instrumentality as the plaintiff may ever be able to make.

An examination of the recent cases, particularly in this state, discloses that the test of actual exclusive control of an instrumentality has not been strictly followed, but exceptions have been recognized where the purpose of the doctrine of res ipsa loquitur would otherwise be defeated. Thus, the test has become one of right of control rather than actual control. In the bursting bottle cases where the bottler has delivered the instrumentality to a retailer and thus has given up actual control, he will nevertheless be subject to the doctrine where it is shown that no change in the condition of the bottle occurred after it left the bottler's possession, and it can accordingly be said that he was in constructive control. *Escola v. Coca Bottling Co.,* 150 P.2d 436 (Cal. 1944). Moreover, this court departed from the single instrumentality theory in the colliding vehicle cases, where two defendants were involved, each in control of a separate vehicle. Finally, it has been suggested that the hospital cases may properly be considered exceptional, and that the doctrine of res ipsa loquitur "should apply with equal force in cases wherein medical and nursing staffs take the place of machinery and may, through carelessness or lack of skill, inflict, or permit the infliction of injury upon a patient who is thereafter in no position to say how he received his injuries." *[S]ee also, Whetstine v. Moravec,* 228 Iowa 352, 291 N.W. 425, 435, where the court refers to the "instrumentalities" as including "the unconscious body of the plaintiff."

In the face of these examples of liberalization of the tests for res ipsa loquitur, there can be no justification for the rejection of the doctrine in the instant case. As pointed out above, if we accept the contention of defendants herein, there will rarely be any compensation for patients injured while unconscious. A hospital today conducts a highly integrated system of activities, with many persons contributing their efforts. There may be, *e.g.*, preparation for surgery by nurses and interns who are employees of the hospital; administering of an anesthetic by a doctor who may be an employee of the hospital, an employee of the operating surgeon, or an independent contractor; performance of an operation by a surgeon and assistants who may be his employees, employees of the hospital, or independent contractors; and post surgical care by the surgeon, a hospital physician, and nurses. The number of those in whose care the patient is placed is not a good reason for denying him all reasonable opportunity to recover for negligent harm. It is rather a good reason for re-examination of the statement of legal theories which supposedly compel such a shocking result.

We do not at this time undertake to state the extent to which the reasoning of this case may be applied to other situations in which the doctrine of res ipsa loquitur is invoked. We merely hold that where a plaintiff receives unusual injuries while unconscious and in the course of medical treatment, all those defendants who had any control over his body or the instrumentalities which might have caused the injuries may properly be called upon to meet the inference of negligence by giving an explanation of their conduct.

The judgment is reversed.

PROBLEMS

1. Mr. F has a chest cold, which turns into heart disease that requires a heart transplant. Dr. M, a world-renowned heart transplant surgeon, is to perform the operation. The night before the operation, Dr. M's wife of 17 years throws him out of the house and he spends the night on the couch of his first surgical assistant, a Dr. Phyllis T. The next morning Dr. M performs a 4-hour quadruple bi-pass surgery. The donor heart becomes available that afternoon. The operation takes two hours longer that expected, because Mr. F is a "bleeder." Other than the length of the operation, everything appears to go smoothly. Just four hours after the transplant, Mr. F's blood pressure drops rapidly and he is brain dead shortly thereafter. When an autopsy was performed, the suture that was to tie the new heart to the aorta was discovered to have separated. F's widow sues Dr. M, the suture manufacturer, and the hospital. Must one of the defendant's be responsible? Is this a case of "conditional *res ipsa*"? *Cf. Anderson v. Somberg*, 338 A.2d 1, 5, 9-10 (N.J. 1975) (where the New Jersey Supreme Court reversed a verdict in favor of each defendant and remanded for a determination of which defendant was liable on a theory of *res ipsa*.) *See also*, *Quin v. George Washington University*, 407 A.2d 580 (D.C. 1979) (where the source of unexplained bleeding from a spleen operation couldn't be determined and so *res ipsa* between the surgeon and the suture manufacturer was inappropriate. Should the jury have been given a "conditional" *res ipsa* instruction, that: "If you find that source was most likely at the suture line, then you must return a verdict in favor of the plaintiff, unless each defendant proves that they were not negligent."?

2. Same facts as in Problem 1. What should be the effect of finding that *res ipsa* applies? Does it just mean the plaintiff's cause of action survives the defendant's motion to dismiss? Does it raise a rebuttable presumption of negligence? Does it raise a conclusive presumption of negligence?

3. What is the difference between *res ipsa loquitur* and strict liability?

Chapter 5
CAUSE IN FACT

Causation is the concept that focuses on the necessary link between the defendant's conduct and the plaintiff's injury. Causation expresses the common sense notion that the defendant does not have to pay for the plaintiff's injuries unless the defendant, in some way, brought them about. In the analysis of a negligence cause of action, the element of causation is divided into two distinctive inquiries. The plaintiff first must prove that the negligence of the defendant was a "cause in fact" or "actual cause" of the injuries. Once cause in fact is established, the plaintiff must then demonstrate that the conduct was also sufficiently important in bringing about the harm that the defendant should be legally responsible for paying compensation. The second part of the causation element is usually referred to as "proximate cause."

This chapter will study the "cause in fact" inquiry. It will begin by examining how courts approach the issue using the "but-for" test of causation, which asks whether the accident would have occurred "but for" the defendant's negligent conduct. The question requires us to imagine what would have occurred if we remove only the element of the defendant's negligent conduct while holding all other facts of the situation constant.

A. "BUT-FOR" CAUSATION

LYONS v. MIDNIGHT SUN
TRANSPORTATION SERVICES
928 P.2d 1202 (Alaska 1996)

PER CURIAM.

Esther Hunter-Lyons was killed when her Volkswagen van was struck broadside by a truck driven by David Jette and owned by Midnight Sun Transportation Services, Inc. When the accident occurred, Jette was driving south in the right-hand lane of Arctic Boulevard in Anchorage. Hunter-Lyons pulled out of a parking lot in front of him. Jette braked and steered to the left, but Hunter-Lyons continued to pull out further into the traffic lane. Jette's truck collided with Hunter-Lyons's vehicle. David Lyons, the deceased's husband, filed suit, asserting that Jette had been speeding and driving negligently.

At trial, conflicting testimony was introduced regarding Jette's speed before the collision. Lyons's expert witness testified that Jette may have been driving as fast as 53 miles per hour. Midnight Sun's expert testified that Jette probably had been driving significantly slower and that the collision could have occurred even if Jette had been driving at the speed limit, 35 miles per hour. Lyons's expert later testified that if Jette had stayed in his own lane, and had not steered to the left, there would have been no collision. Midnight Sun's expert contended that steering to the left when a vehicle pulls out onto the roadway from the right is a normal response and is generally the safest course of action to follow. . . .

[T]he jury found that Jette, in fact, had been negligent, but his negligence was not a legal cause of the accident. . . . The jury finding of negligence indicates that the jury concluded David Jette was driving negligently or responded inappropriately when Ms. Hunter- Lyons entered the traffic lane and, thus, did not exercise the care and prudence a reasonable person would have exercised under the circumstances. [Although] the jury found Jette to have been negligent, it also found that this negligence was not the legal cause of the accident. Duty, breach of duty, causation, and harm are the separate and distinct elements of a negligence claim, all of which must be proven before a defendant can be held liable for the plaintiff's injuries. . . .

[W]e cannot say that the jury's finding of lack of causation was unreasonable. There was evidence presented at trial from which the jury could reasonably have drawn the conclusion that even though Jette was driving negligently, his negligence was not the proximate cause of the accident. Midnight Sun introduced expert testimony to the effect that the primary cause of the accident was Ms. Hunter-Lyons's action in pulling out of the parking lot in front of an oncoming truck. Terry Day, an accident reconstruction specialist testified that, depending on how fast Ms. Hunter- Lyons was moving, the accident could have happened even if Jette had been driving within the speed limit. Midnight Sun also introduced expert testimony to the effect that Jette responded properly to the unexpected introduction of an automobile in his traffic lane. Although all of this testimony was disputed by Lyons, a reasonable jury could have concluded that Ms. Hunter-Lyons caused the accident by abruptly pulling out in front of an oncoming truck, and that David Jette's negligence was not a contributing factor. With the element of causation lacking, even the most egregious negligence cannot result in liability.

AFFIRMED.

NOTE

The "but-for" test is applied by considering only the negligent aspect of the defendant's conduct. In the *Lyons* case, for example, it is clear that the conduct of driving the truck caused the accident, in the sense that had the defendant not driven at all, the accident would not have occurred. This is not the issue, however. Instead, the court focuses on whether the accident would have occurred but for the defendant's *negligent* conduct. How could the jury be allowed to conclude that the defendant's negligence did not cause the accident?

PROBLEMS

1. Plaintiff's decedent died in a hotel fire. The deceased was discovered still in his bed, and an autopsy showed that death resulted from smoke inhalation. Subsequent investigation revealed that the defendant hotel operator negligently allowed the door leading to the fire escape on the decedent's floor to become stuck so that it could not be used. Was the defendant's negligence a cause in fact of the decedent's death? What must the Plaintiff prove? *Cf. Smith v. The Texan*, 180 S.W.2d 1010 (Tex. Civ. App. 1944).

2. Plaintiff's decedent drowned after falling off a boat owned by the defendant. The defendant had negligently failed to provide the boat with proper life-saving equipment such as life rings and throwing lines. However, the testimony of the other people on the boat is that the deceased disappeared under the water at once and never came up again. Did the defendant's negligent failure to provide life-saving equipment cause the death? *See New York Central R.R. Co. v. Grimstad*, 264 F. 334 (2d Cir. 1920). Suppose the decedent struggled on the surface for some time before going under for good. Cause in fact? *See Kirincich v. Standard Dredging Co.*, 112 F.2d 163 (3d Cir. 1940).

3. Plaintiff's decedent was walking home from work when defendant fired a gun at him. In an effort to evade defendant, decedent darted down an alley and took a route home — different than the one he normally takes. About a mile away from the point where the firing occurred, decedent carelessly stepped off a curb without looking both ways and was struck by a truck. He died from the resulting injuries. Was defendant a "cause in fact" of the death?

B. PROVING BUT-FOR CAUSE: THE SLIP AND FALL CASE

Proving "but-for" causation can be a challenge even in fairly ordinary fact situations. Consider, for example, that staple of tort litigation known as the "slip and fall." Even if the plaintiff can prove that the defendant negligently created a dangerous situation — a pool of spilled liquid or a banana peel left on the floor, a slippery or poorly lighted staircase — the plaintiff must still prove that the dangerous condition caused the fall. In many cases that has proved suprisingly difficult to do. Consider in the following cases just how much evidence the plaintiff should be required to present on the issue of causation.

DAPP v. LARSON
659 N.Y.S.2d 130 (N.Y. App. Div. 1997)

CARDONA, Presiding Justice.

Appeal from an order of the Supreme Court (Ellison, J.), entered July 24, 1996 in Chemung County, which granted defendant's motion for summary judgment dismissing the complaint.

On April 30, 1992, while visiting defendant in her capacity as a home health aide, plaintiff sustained injuries when she fell down the front steps of defendant's residence. It was raining at the time of the accident. The steps and the porch of defendant's residence were covered in green all-weather carpeting and a brown plastic doormat lay near the doorway. As plaintiff was leaving the residence, she claims that she took a few steps across the porch and started to descend the stairs when she fell. Upon landing at the bottom of the stairs, she noticed that the brown plastic doormat that had been on the porch was laying on the bottom step and the sidewalk.

We affirm. Initially, we note that in order to establish a prima facie case of negligence against defendant, plaintiff was required to "establish that defendant either created the allegedly dangerous or defective condition or had actual or constructive notice thereof". . . .

[P]laintiff alleges that the plastic mat in front of defendant's house constituted a dangerous condition that defendant created or had notice thereof. Regardless of the merit of this assertion, however, plaintiff failed to submit proof establishing that her accident was caused by this condition. Significantly, failure to prove what actually caused a plaintiff to fall in a situation where there could be other causes is fatal to a plaintiff's cause of action. . . . Here, plaintiff specifically testified at her examination before trial that she could not remember the location of the plastic mat when she arrived at defendant's home on the date of the accident. Furthermore, she also stated that when she left work that day, she did not notice the location of the doormat immediately preceding her fall. Only after her fall did plaintiff see the mat at the bottom of the stairs on the sidewalk. Although plaintiff presumes that the doormat caused her to fall, "conclusions based upon surmise, conjecture, speculation or assertions are without probative value." . . . From this proof, it is just as possible that the mat was already at the bottom of the stairs when she fell and her accident could be attributed to the wet condition of the stairway caused by the rainy weather. Since plaintiff failed to raise a triable issue as to causation, we conclude that defendant's summary judgment motion was properly granted.

WILLIAMS v. EMRO MARKETING COMPANY
494 S.E.2d 218 (Ga. Ct. App. 1997)

BEASLEY, Judge.

Nathaniel Williams and his wife sued EMRO Marketing Company for injuries suffered when Williams allegedly slipped and fell on ice on the pavement at premises of a store owned by EMRO. EMRO moved for and was granted summary judgment on [its argument] that Nathaniel Williams failed to present any evidence that ice was the cause in fact of his fall. The trial court [did] not explain its ruling. . . .

"To recover damages in a tort action, a plaintiff must prove that the defendant's negligence was both the 'cause in fact' and the 'proximate cause' of [the] injury." . . . To avoid summary judgment, a plaintiff who alleges he slipped on a foreign substance must offer some evidence of a foreign substance on the ground where he slipped. . . .

Viewed in favor of the non-movant plaintiffs, the evidence is that Williams was on his way to work on February 19, 1993, when he stopped for gas at a store operated by EMRO. He first paid in the store and then returned along the same route to pump gas. On his return, he slipped and fell, injuring his knee and other parts of his body. He never saw what he slipped on and he never saw any ice, and his clothes were not wet from ice or water. He stated in an affidavit, "I didn't personally witness on February 19, 1993 exactly what substance caused me to fall. . . ." No other person directly witnessed Williams' fall.

It had rained the day before, the temperature overnight had reached about 20 degrees, and water from the canopy over the gas pumps had flowed out of the down spout onto the pavement near the gas pump at which Williams had parked his car. When it rains, water drips from that down spout and collects on the ground. At the time of the fall, the temperature was still at or below freezing.

Although EMRO contends that no evidence showed Williams slipped on ice, another customer, Gregory Perkins, swore by affidavit that after he offered to help Williams, "I then took his arm and assisted him from the iced area." He also stated that he picked up a large piece of ice, which he believed was part of the ice Williams slipped on. Perkins was a regular customer and had previously seen water dripping from a down spout near the pump where Williams fell. After the fall he noticed "[t]he water had drained from a down spout and collected on the ground below and frozen." Perkins also noted "ice cubes hanging down, directly over where [Williams] had fallen." Williams recalls the sensation of a slick surface beneath his feet as his feet flew out from under him.

Circumstantial evidence which raises a reasonable inference of the cause of the fall, unrebutted by positive evidence, is sufficient to survive summary judgment. In *Kenny v. M & M Supermarket*, 183 Ga. App. 225, 358 S.E.2d 641 (1987), there was no evidence of any foreign substance, even after inspection, unlike here where Williams was lying in the "iced area." Further, Williams' own testimony is not positive evidence of no ice which therefore rebuts the circumstantial evidence of ice as a cause. He testified only that he never saw ice, not that he inspected and found no ice as in *Kenny*. Indeed, he was somewhat disoriented by the fall.

Giving the non-movant the benefit of all inferences, this evidence would tend to support a finding of fact that Williams slipped on the ice upon which he lay. Although Williams may have slipped on something else and landed on the ice, his location on ice after the fall, together with the fact that a witness saw ice where Williams fell, is some evidence of what caused his fall. Williams' own lack of knowledge of the substance on which he slipped is not dispositive. A person who is injured may become unconscious or disoriented by the fall and be unable or unconcerned then to investigate what he slipped on. That does not prevent other evidence on the issue.

Judgment reversed.

RUFFIN, Judge, concurring specially.

[We] must view the foregoing facts and inferences in a light most favorable to Williams. Clearly, as pointed out by the dissent, there are numerous other substances on which Williams might have slipped. But by speculating that Williams did in fact slip on some other substance, the dissent does not view the evidence and the reasonable inferences in Williams' favor, as required on a motion for summary judgment. . . .

HAROLD R. BANKE, Senior Appellate Judge, dissenting.

[Notwithstanding] the majority's contention to the contrary, inferring that Williams slipped on ice is not warranted in light of Williams' positive and unrebutted testimony that he did not know what caused his fall. *Kenny v. M & M Supermarket*, 183 Ga. App. 225, 226, 358 S.E.2d 641 (1987). . . . As in *Kenny*, Williams did not see any substance, feel any substance, experience any substance on his clothing, and did not inspect the ground after his fall, all of which "leads inescapably to the conclusion that only a fall [of unknown origin] was involved." . . . Thus, the circumstantial evidence, in view of Williams' unrefuted testimony, does not demand a conclusion that ice caused the slip and fall.

NOTES

1. To recover in a slip and fall case, the plaintiff must first show that the defendant was negligent. This usually requires proof that a dangerous condition existed on the premises, that the defendant knew or should have known of the condition, and that the defendant failed to use reasonable care to correct it. The plaintiff must then show that the dangerous condition created by the defendant's negligence caused the fall.

2. Proof of causation is often made difficult precisely because the plaintiff, as the court in the *Williams* case notes, "may become unconscious or disoriented by

the fall and be unable or unconcerned then to investigate what he slipped on." Some evidence must be produced to link the dangerous condition with the plaintiff's fall.

PROBLEMS

1. Plaintiff, who weighed 250 pounds, was waiting for her train in a well-lighted waiting room late at night. When her train arrived, the railroad employees tried to hurry the passengers on board. Plaintiff was hustled out of the waiting room and down an unlighted stairway with no handrails. She missed her footing and fell, suffering severe injury. What evidence might be available to provide the causal link between the dangerous condition of the stair and the Plaintiff's fall? *Cf. Reynolds v. Texas & Pacific Ry.*, 37 La. Ann. 694 (1895).

2. Plaintiff, a child of eleven, was injured when she fell from a three-meter diving board and struck the concrete edge of the pool. Plaintiff's testimony is that she remembers climbing the ladder up to the board and preparing for her dive. The next thing she remembers is waking up in the hospital. Several witnesses saw her while she was falling and saw her hit the ground, but none can testify as to how the Plaintiff came to fall. On the other hand, evidence is available to show that the side-rails of the diving board were lower than those required by the National Spa & Pool Institute for diving boards of this type. If suit is brought against the operator of the pool, will this be enough to establish causation? *Cf. Fleming v. Kings Ridge Recreation Park, Inc.*, 525 N.Y.S.2d 866 (N.Y. App. Div. 1988).

3. Plaintiff was attending a wedding at a restored plantation owned by the Garden Club, which rents it out for such functions. Plaintiff was upstairs when she was told that the ceremony was about to begin. She hurried down the back staircase so she would be in her place on time. The back staircase was extremely steep, lacked a handrail, and the steps were worn, uncarpeted, and slippery. The Plaintiff fell and was injured. When asked at her deposition why she fell, the Plaintiff testified that she had no idea. What arguments can be made in favor of a finding of causation? What arguments could be made against such a finding? *Cf. Boyd v. Garden Center, Inc.*, 397 S.E.2d 626 (Ga. 1990).

4. Verl injured his knee and back when he slipped on a grape in the produce section of the Supermarket. The grape had apparently fallen from a display in which grapes, watermelon, pineapple and other fresh fruit were offered to customers as free samples to convince them of the quality and freshness of the store's produce. The sample display provided toothpicks for picking up the fruit and a small wastebasket on the floor for discarding the toothpicks and unwanted samples. If you represented plaintiff, what evidence would you seek in order to prove the negligence of Supermarket? How will you obtain that evidence? Now assume you represent Supermarket. What evidence could you use to rebut the charge of negligence? How would you obtain this evidence?

5. On a freezing February day, the plaintiff slipped and fell in the parking lot of the Defendant's shopping center. She believes that the fall must have been caused by an accumulation of ice that Defendant had allowed to build up. You file a complaint on her behalf. At her deposition, the Plaintiff responds to defense counsel's questions about the accident as follows:

Q. Was there any snow in the parking lot?

A. Yes. Well, it was all piled up on one side.

Q. What did you do after you parked your car?

A. I got out of my car, closed the door and walked straight ahead.

Q. And what happened?

A. And — I don't even know. I don't know whether I was in between the next two cars, but — I mean, I only took about three, four, five steps and I just went.

Q. What do you mean when you say you went?

A. I went right on down, slipped right down, yes.

Q. What did you slip on?

A. I don't know.

Q. Where were you looking when you fell down?

A. Straight down to the ground. I walk with my eyes on the ground. I always look at the ground when I'm walking.

Q. What did you see immediately before you fell on the ground?

A. Nothing, just it was wet, but I knew that when I went there.

Q. Did you see any snow in your path?

A. No, there was no snow. I didn't see any snow.

Q. Did you see any ice in your path?

A. No, I didn't see any ice.

Q. Now, in your complaint I believe there's an allegation that you slipped on ice. What is the basis of that statement?

A. I just figured it must have been. I mean, I just couldn't think of — I mean, I know — I mean — well, I don't know, but I didn't see a thing on the ground except — you know, it was wet and I know there was nothing in my path to trip over or to fall on.

Based on this deposition testimony, can the defendant obtain a summary judgment based on the lack of cause in fact? What, if anything, could counsel for the plaintiff have done to avoid having the client give such damaging testimony? The next three problems suggest some of the issues that counsel must face in deciding whether to accept the representation of a client in situations such as this.

6. Clarence Client has made an appointment to consult you about filing a personal injury suit on his behalf. All you know from his telephone call making the appointment is that it involves a possible slip and fall claim against Giganto-Mart, a company with a reputation for fighting such claims tooth and nail. In preparing for the interview, consider what information you will need. What questions should be asked? How much of the law of slip-and-fall should you explain? Should you explain the elements of the cause of action before letting Clarence describe the incident? What problems should you anticipate with the approach you decide to adopt?

7. At the interview, Clarence tells you that he fell in front of a Giganto-Mart Store on a clear, dry day. He saw nothing on the ground that might have caused the fall. He did not report the fall, but instead hobbled back to his car by leaning on a shopping cart. His roommate was waiting in the car and drove him to the doctor, where it was determined that he had suffered a broken ankle. You explain the law of slip and fall to Clarence and suggest that the case has little chance of succeeding since he did not see any foreign substance that might have caused the fall and did not even report it to Giganto-Mart. Clarence departs but returns the next day. He tells you that he has "refreshed his recollection" of the events. It turns out that the fall did not happen at Giganto-Mart, but rather at his apartment. Clarence and his roommate are prepared to testify that Clarence slipped on a puddle of floor wax that was spilled in the common entry-way to the apartment. What are your obligations at this point? Consider the following sections from the Model Rules of Professional Conduct:

Rule 1.2. . . .

(d) A lawyer shall not counsel a client to engage, or assist a client, in conduct that the lawyer knows is criminal or fraudulent, but a lawyer may discuss the legal consequences of any proposed course of conduct with a client and may counsel or assist a client to make a good faith effort to determine the validity, scope, meaning or application of the law.

Rule 3.3

(a) A lawyer shall not knowingly:

(1) make a false statement of material fact or law to a tribunal;

(2) fail to disclose a material fact to a tribunal when disclosure is necessary to avoid assisting a criminal or fraudulent act by the client;

. . . .

(4) offer evidence that the lawyer knows to be false. If a lawyer has offered material evidence and comes to know of its falsity, the lawyer shall take reasonable remedial measures.

(b) The duties stated in paragraph (a) continue to the conclusion of the proceeding, and apply even if compliance requires disclosure of information otherwise protected by Rule 1.6.

Rule 4.1

In the course of representing a client a lawyer shall not knowingly:

(a) make a false statement of material fact or law to a third person; or

(b) fail to disclose a material fact to a third person when disclosure is necessary to avoid assisting a criminal or fraudulent act by a client, unless disclosure is prohibited by Rule 1.6.

Consider also Federal Rule of Civil Procedure 11, a version of which is in force in many jurisdictions:

Rule 11. Signing of Pleadings, Motions, and Other Papers; Representations to Court; Sanctions

. . . .

(b) Representations to Court.

By presenting to the court (whether by signing, filing, submitting, or later advocating) a pleading, written motion, or other paper, an attorney or unrepresented party is certifying that to the best of the person's knowledge, information, and belief, formed after an inquiry reasonable under the circumstances, —

. . . .

(3) the allegations and other factual contentions have evidentiary support or, if specifically so identified, are likely to have evidentiary support after a reasonable opportunity for further investigation or discovery . . .

Violation of Rule 11 subjects both the individual attorney and her firm to sanctions. You will study Rule 11 in greater detail in your course in Civil Procedure.

8. After the meeting Clarence, perhaps detecting a lack of enthusiasm on your part, retains a different attorney. This attorney contacts you and asks for any information you have about the landlord slip and fall. You are certain that the new attorney has never heard about the Giganto-Mart slip and fall. How much may you disclose? Before answering, consider another section of the Model Rules of Professional Conduct:

Rule 1.6

(a) A lawyer shall not reveal information relating to representation of a client unless the client consents after consultation, except for disclosures that are impliedly authorized in order to carry out the representation, and except as stated in paragraph (b).

(b) A lawyer may reveal such information to the extent the lawyer reasonably believes necessary:

(1) to prevent the client from committing a criminal act that the lawyer believes is likely to result in imminent death or substantial bodily harm;. . . .

C. MULTIPLE CAUSES AND THE "SUBSTANTIAL FACTOR" TEST

ANDERSON v. MINNEAPOLIS, ST. PAUL & SAULT STE. MARIE RY. CO.
179 N.W. 45 (Minn. 1920)

LEES, C.

This is a fire case, brought against the defendant railway company and the Director General of Railroads. . . . Plaintiff had a verdict. The appeal is from an order denying a motion in the alternative for judgment notwithstanding the verdict or for a new trial. . . .

Plaintiff's case in chief was directed to proving that in August, 1918, one of defendant's engines started a fire in a bog near the west side of plaintiff's land; that it smoldered there until October 12, 1918, when it flared up and burned his property, shortly before it was reached by one of the great fires which swept through Northeastern Minnesota at the close of that day. Defendant introduced evidence to show that on and prior to October 12th fires were burning west and northwest of, and were swept by the wind towards, plaintiff's premises. It did not show how such fires originated, neither did it clearly and certainly trace the destruction of plaintiff's property to them. By cross-examination of defendant's witnesses and by his rebuttal evidence plaintiff made a showing which would have justified the jury in finding that the fires proved by defendant were started by its locomotive on or near its right of way in the vicinity of Kettle River.

[I]n instructing the jury, the court said in part:. . . .

'If plaintiff's property was damaged by fire originally set by one of defendant's locomotives, then defendant became liable for such damages, and was not released from such liability by anything that happened thereafter. . . .

'If the plaintiff was burned out by some fire other than the bog fire, which other fire was not set by one of defendant's engines, then, of course, defendant is not liable. If plaintiff was burned out by fire set by one of defendant's engines in combination with some other fire not set by one of its engines, then it is liable. . . .

'If you find that other fires not set by one of defendant's engines mingled with one that was set by one of defendant's engines, there may be difficulty in determining whether you should find that the fire set by the engine was a material or substantial element in causing plaintiff's damage. If it was, the defendant is liable; otherwise, it is not. . . .

'If you find that bog fire was set by defendant's engine, and that some greater fire swept over it before it reached plaintiff's land, then it will be for you to determine whether the bog fire [was] a material or substantial factor in causing plaintiff's damage. If it was, defendant was liable. If it was not, defendant was not liable. . . .)'

The following proposition is stated in defendant's brief and relied on for a reversal:

'If plaintiff's property was damaged by a number of fires combining, one being the fire pleaded, and the others being of no responsible origin, but of such sufficient or superior force that they would have produced the damage to plaintiff's property, regardless of the fire pleaded, then defendant was not liable.'

This proposition is based upon *Cook v. M., St. P. & S. S. M. Ry. Co.*, 98 Wis. 624, 74 N.W. 561. . . . If the *Cook* case merely decides that one who negligently sets a fire is not liable if another's property is damaged, unless it is made to appear that the fire was a material element in the destruction of the property, there can be no question about the soundness of the decision. But if it decides that if such fire combines with another of no responsible origin, and after the union of the two fires they destroy the property and either fire independently of the other would have destroyed it, then, irrespective of whether the first fire was or was not a material factor in the destruction of the property, there is no liability, we are not prepared to adopt the doctrine as the law of this state. If a fire set by the engine of one railroad company unites with a fire set by the engine of another company, there is joint and several liability, even though either fire would have destroyed plaintiff's property. But if the doctrine of the *Cook* case is applied, and one of the fires is of unknown origin, there is no liability. G.S. 1913, § 4426, leaves no room for the application of a rule which would relieve a railroad company from liability under such circumstances. . . .We therefore hold that the trial court did not err in refusing to instruct the jury in accordance with the rule laid down in the *Cook* case. In the foregoing discussion we have assumed, although it is doubtful, that the evidence was such that a foundation was laid for the application of the rule, if it was otherwise applicable. . . .

We find no error requiring a reversal, and hence the order appealed from is affirmed.

DILLON v. TWIN STATE GAS & ELECTRIC CO.
163 A. 111 (N.H. 1932)

Action for negligently causing the death of the plaintiff's intestate, a boy of 14. A jury trial resulted in a disagreement.

The defendant maintained wires to carry electric current over a public bridge in Berlin. In the construction of the bridge there were two spans of girders on each side between the roadway and footway. In each span the girders at each end sloped upwards towards each other from the floor of the bridge until connected by horizontal girders about nineteen feet above the floor.

The wires were carried above the framework of the bridge between the two rows of girders. To light the footway of the bridge at its center a lamp was hung from a bracket just outside of one of the horizontal girders and crossing over the end of the girder near its connection with a sloping girder. Wires ran from a post obliquely downward to the lamp and crossed the horizontal girder a foot or more above it. The construction of the wire lines over and upon the bridge is termed aerial. The wires were insulated for weather protection but not against contact.

The decedent and other boys had been accustomed for a number of years to play on the bridge in the daytime, habitually climbing the sloping girders to the horizontal ones, on which they walked and sat and from which they sometimes dived into the river. No current passed through the wires in the daytime except by chance.

The decedent, while sitting on a horizontal girder at a point where the wires from the post to the lamp were in front of him or at his side, and while facing outwards from the side of the bridge, leaned over, lost his balance, instinctively threw out his arm, and took hold of one of the wires with his right hand to save himself from falling. The wires happened to be charged with a high voltage current at the time and he was electrocuted.

Transferred by Oakes, J., on the defendant's exception to the denial of its motion for a directed verdict.

ALLEN, J.

[T]he circumstances of the decedent's death give rise to an unusual issue of its cause. In leaning over from the girder and losing his balance, he was entitled to no protection from the defendant to keep from falling. Its only liability was in exposing him to the danger of charged wires. If but for the current in the wires he would have fallen down on the floor of the bridge or into the river, he would without doubt have been either killed or seriously injured. Although he died from electrocution, yet, if by reason of his preceding loss of balance he was bound to fall except for the intervention of the current, he either did not have long to live or was to be maimed. In such an outcome of his loss of balance, the defendant deprived him, not of a life of normal expectancy, but of one too short to be given pecuniary allowance, in one alternative, and not of normal, but of limited, earning capacity, in the other.

If it were found that he would have thus fallen with death probably resulting, the defendant would not be liable, unless for conscious suffering found to have been sustained from the shock. In that situation his life or earning capacity had no value. To constitute actionable negligence there must be damage, and damage is limited to those elements the statute prescribes.

If it should be found that but for the current he would have fallen with serious injury, then the loss of life or earning capacity resulting from the electrocution would be measured by its value in such injured condition. Evidence that he would be crippled would be taken into account in the same manner as though he had already been crippled.

His probable future but for the current thus bears on liability as well as damages. Whether the shock from the current threw him back on the girder or whether he would have recovered his balance, with or without the aid of the wire he took hold of, if it had not been charged, are issues of fact, as to which the evidence as it stands may lead to different conclusions.

Exception overruled.

NOTES

1. The dilemma posed by cases such as the foregoing can be understood when one attempts to apply the but-for test of causation to the defendants' negligent conduct. What would have happened to the plaintiff's premises in *Anderson* if the defendant railroad had not negligently started the bog fire? How can the railroad's negligence be a "substantial factor" in bringing about the harm if the harm would have occurred anyway? Similarly, what would have happened to the plaintiff's son in *Dillon* if the defendant had not negligently placed an uninsulated wire near where boys were known to play and climb? Since the boy died of electrocution, why did the court not rule that the electric company's negligence was a substantial factor in bringing about the harm?

2. In *Anderson*, should the court have ruled that the railroad only deprived the plaintiff of property of reduced value, since it would soon have been burned by the other fire in any event? Why should the plaintiff recover the full amount of his damages?

3. In *Dillon*, should the court have ruled that the electric company's negligence combined with the conduct of the operators of the bridge in allowing children to climb on the girders to cause the death, and that the electric company

should therefore be liable for the entire harm? Why is the plaintiff's recovery limited?

PROBLEMS

1. Agro owned a commercial catfish farming operation. His business was located in Texas near the Gulf of Mexico. The operation required that Agro maintain large ponds of fresh water. Not far from Agro's catfish ponds two oil companies, Conoil and Boylan Oil, were engaged in oil drilling operations. As a byproduct of these operations, each oil company maintained large ponds in which they deposited waste salt water. Both Conoil and Boylan Oil were negligent in maintaining these salt water ponds. As a result, these ponds both began to leak within a few hours of each other. The salt water discharged from each pond separately entered Agro's catfish pond, killing all the fish. *Cf. Landers v. East Texas Salt Water Disposal Co.*, 248 S.W.2d 731 (Tex. 1952).

    a. If the salt water from the two oil companies arrived at Agro's catfish pond at virtually the same time, who is the cause of Agro's injury?

    b. If it appears that the salt water from Boylan Oil's pond arrived several hours before that from Conoil, and that the fish were already dead before the salt water from Conoil entered the catfish pond, who is the cause of Agro's injury? Is this more like *Anderson* or *Dillon*?

    c. If Agro's catfish were killed by the salt water leaking from Conoil, should it matter that the next day a major hurricane struck the Gulf coast nearby, bringing with it a fifteen foot storm surge of ocean water that flooded Agro's pond, and which would have killed all his fish anyway? Is this more like *Anderson* or *Dillon*?

    d. If Agro cannot establish whose salt water arrived first, has Agro failed to prove causation? Should Agro's suit be dismissed?

2. Would the result in *Dillon* change if the plaintiff had also sued the operator of the bridge and had succeeded in establishing that this defendant was negligent in failing to prevent the boys from climbing on the girders? Would this make the case more like *Anderson*, or should the original ruling in *Dillon* still prevail?

3. Bunny drove his car to Otto's repair shop to have the brakes checked. Otto's repairs were so poorly performed that the brakes now no longer worked at all. Bunny picked up his car and drove it off the lot. Before Bunny had gone a block from the shop he ran over Walker, a pedestrian. Bunny never saw Walker because he was fiddling with his cellular phone. Bunny therefore never even tried to use the inoperative brakes. Who was the cause of the injuries to Walker? What test should be used? *Cf. Saunders System Birmingham Co. v. Adams*, 117 So. 72 (Ala. 1928).

4. A dangerous industrial fire occurred at a chemical plant operated by Chlor-Chem, Inc. Because the fire produced toxic fumes, emergency personnel had to evacuate nearby residents from their homes. One of those evacuated was Paula, who was wheelchair-bound due to complications of arteriosclerosis and diabetes. Paula suffered breathing problems as a result of inhaling the toxic fumes from the fire. She was taken from her home to a nearby emergency shelter operated by the County, which was set up in an unused school building. The school building was an older structure which was not wheelchair-accessible. In attempting to carry Paula up a flight of stairs into the building, one of the emergency personnel tripped and fell, causing Paula to fall as well. The fall caused severe bruising to Paula's left arm and hand. After the emergency was over, Paula was returned to her home without further incident. Six weeks later, Paula was admitted to the hospital for a variety of complaints, including severe chest pains and the failure of her bruised hand to heal. Her hand eventually had to be amputated, and her chest pains proved to result from a further advance of her artery disease.

Medical testimony indicated that the inhalation of toxic fumes may have compromised Paula's breathing somewhat, which may have combined with her pre-existing arteriosclerosis to further damage her heart. Paula's arterial disease and diabetes may also have compromised her circulation, resulting in the failure of her bruises to heal, which may have resulted in the need for the amputation. However, experts agreed that Paula may well have faced much the same problems even if she had not been injured.

What damages were caused by Chem-Chlor and the County? *Cf. Litera v. East Chicago Fire Dept.*, 692 N.E.2d 898 (Ind. Ct. App. 1998).

D. CAUSE IN FACT AND PROOF OF MATHEMATICAL PROBABILITIES

WEYMERS v. KHERA
563 N.W.2d 647 (Mich. 1997)

RILEY, Justice.

In this appeal, we address [whether] Michigan recognizes a cause of action for the loss of an opportunity to avoid physical harm less than death. . . .We hold that Michigan does not recognize a cause of action for the loss of an opportunity to avoid physical harm less than death. . . . Accordingly, we reverse the Court of Appeals decision. . . .

FACTS AND PROCEEDINGS

In early October 1990, plaintiff Kimberly Weymers, who was twenty years old, became ill with coughing, fever, nausea, aching, and chest congestion. After her condition did not improve for more than a week, she went to defendant

Walled Lake Medical Center where she was initially examined by a physician's assistant. The physician's assistant concluded from plaintiff's symptoms that she suffered from a respiratory infection and gave her antibiotics. After another week, plaintiff returned to the medical center because her symptoms intensified. The physician's assistant diagnosed plaintiff with pneumonia and sent her home with a stronger prescription of antibiotics. On October 23, 1990, plaintiff visited the medical center a third time because her condition had not improved. A blood sample indicated that plaintiff suffered from severe anemia. Defendant Dr. Frank Fenton, the owner of the medical center, arranged for plaintiff to be admitted to defendant St. Joseph's Hospital in Pontiac.

On the evening of October 23, 1990, plaintiff was admitted to St. Joseph's intensive care unit and was given blood transfusions to combat the anemia. On October 24, 1990, defendant Dr. Rheka Khera examined plaintiff and suspected the possibility of a kidney problem and asked defendant Dr. Gregorio Ferrer, a nephrologist, to examine her. Dr. Ferrer examined her that day and concluded that she could have a rare disease, Goodpasture's syndrome. He began an immunosuppressive therapy immediately, and scheduled a kidney biopsy for October 25, 1990. Plaintiff initially responded to the treatment, but soon after her condition began to deteriorate. . . . On October 26, 1990, plaintiff was transferred to William Beaumont Hospital in Royal Oak and placed under the care of Dr. Isam Salah. At the time, plaintiff had only ten to fifteen percent of her kidney functions. . . . The hospital performed a plasma exchange, but it failed to save plaintiff's kidney functioning. Plaintiff was placed on dialysis after her kidneys totally failed and eventually underwent a kidney transplant.

On August 16, 1991, plaintiff filed this medical malpractice suit against defendants Drs. Khera, Ferrer, and Fenton, and against Walled Lake Medical Center and St. Joseph Mercy Hospital. During discovery, plaintiff presented an affidavit by expert witness Dr. Eric Neilson, Chief of the Renal Division of the University of Pennsylvania Hospital, who testified that if defendants had given plaintiff proper care she would have had a thirty to forty percent chance of retaining the functioning of her kidneys. Dr. Neilson noted that plaintiff's life expectancy had been "significantly shortened" as a consequence of the loss of her kidneys, and that she would ultimately suffer a premature death. After discovery was closed, St. Joseph's Hospital moved for summary disposition pursuant to MCR 2.116(C)(10), arguing that plaintiff had failed to demonstrate that the alleged negligence caused the loss of her kidneys. The other defendants joined the motion. In response to defendants' motion, plaintiff asserted that she could recover for her kidney damage even though there was less than a fifty percent chance that defendants' negligence caused the damage on the basis of the lost opportunity doctrine recognized in *Falcon v. Memorial Hosp.*, 436 Mich. 443, 462 N.W.2d 44 (1990).

The trial court agreed with defendants and granted their motion for summary disposition. The trial court noted that plaintiff had failed to show that it was more probable than not that her kidney failure was caused by defendants' alleged negligence, and refused to extend the lost opportunity doctrine recognized in *Falcon*, a wrongful death case, to situations in which the injury did not result in death. . . . Plaintiff appealed in the Court of Appeals, which reversed the decision of the trial court, holding that the lost opportunity doctrine applied to physical injury less than death. . . . Defendant Drs. Khera and Ferrer appealed. . . .

I. LOST OPPORTUNITY DOCTRINE

[Under] Michigan medical malpractice law, as part of its prima facie case, a plaintiff must prove that the defendant's negligence proximately caused the plaintiff's injuries. . . . To establish cause in fact, . . . "the plaintiff must present substantial evidence from which a jury may conclude that more likely than not, but for the defendant's conduct, the plaintiff's injuries would not have occurred. . . .

> "The plaintiff must introduce evidence which affords a reasonable basis for the conclusion that it is more likely than not that the conduct of the defendant was a cause in fact of the result. A mere possibility of such causation is not enough; and when the matter remains one of pure speculation or conjecture, or the probabilities are at best evenly balanced, it becomes the duty of the court to direct a verdict for the defendant."

[*Skinner v. Square D Co.* at 164-65, 516 N.W.2d 475, *quoting* Prosser & Keeton, Torts (5th ed.), § 41, p. 269]. . . .

The antithesis of proximate cause is the doctrine of lost opportunity. The lost opportunity doctrine allows a plaintiff to recover when the defendant's negligence possibly, *i.e.*, a probability of fifty percent or less, caused the plaintiff's injury. . . .

There are three alternative approaches to the lost opportunity doctrine: (1) the pure lost chance approach, (2) the proportional approach, and (3) the substantial possibility approach. Each approach lowers the standard of causation, with the effect that a plaintiff is allowed to recover without establishing cause in fact.

The pure lost chance approach allows a plaintiff to recover for his injury even though it was more likely than not that he would have suffered the injury if the defendant had not been negligent. . . . The plaintiff only has to show that the defendant's negligence decreased the plaintiff's chance, no matter how slight, of avoiding the injury. *Id*. If the plaintiff makes such a showing, he receives full damages.

The proportional approach is identical to the pure lost chance approach; however, the plaintiff's recovery is limited to the percent of chance lost multiplied by the total amount of damages that would ordinarily be recovered in that action. [F]or example,

> if a patient had forty percent chance of recovering from breast cancer and a negligent physician's misdiagnosis results in her chances dropping

to ten percent, then the plaintiff can recover thirty percent of her total death-related injuries. Thus, if her damages totaled $100,000, the plaintiff could recover $30,000.

[Moore, *South Carolina Rejects the Lost Chance Doctrine*, 48 S.C. L. R. 201, 202 (1996).]

The last approach, the substantial possibility approach, was adopted by this Court in *Falcon* for wrongful death cases. It also is a variation of the pure lost chance approach. Under this approach, the plaintiff must show that there is a substantial possibility that the defendant's negligence caused his injury. . . . It is unclear what constitutes a "substantial possibility." . . . It is clear, however, that it does not have to be more than fifty percent. Thus, the substantial possibility approach is identical to the other approaches to the extent that each approach allows a plaintiff to recover for his injury even though it was more likely than not that he would have suffered the injury if the defendant had not been negligent.

Turning to the case now before this Court, the Court of Appeals, relying on the substantial possibility approach, extended the lost opportunity doctrine to the loss of a substantial opportunity to avoid any physical harm. The Court justified its decision on the often proffered reason of deterrence:

> If the lost opportunity doctrine is limited to cases only involving death, potentially flagrant examples of malpractice could go uncompensated in cases in which the same negligent failure to diagnose or treat results in a lost opportunity to avoid egregious harm, *i.e.*, paralysis or coma. Thus, the deterrent and loss-allocation functions of tort law would be undermined if defendants could escape liability for the effects of negligent conduct that cause demonstrable losses.

We acknowledge that the deterrent and loss-allocation functions of tort law are important. However, we reject scrapping causation (the bedrock of our tort law) in negligence cases where the injury alleged by the plaintiff is something less than death, for the lost opportunity doctrine's deterrent effect. As the Texas Supreme Court succinctly stated:

> [W]e reject the notion that the enhanced deterrence of the loss of chance approach might be so valuable as to justify scrapping our traditional concepts of causation. If deterrence were the sole value to be served by tort law, we could dispense with the notion of causation altogether and award damages on the basis of negligence alone.

[*Kramer v. Lewisville Mem. Hosp.*, 858 S.W.2d 397, 406 (Tex. 1993).] . . .

Accordingly, because we refuse to discard causation in negligence actions of this kind, we do not recognize a cause of action for the loss of an opportunity to avoid physical harm less than death. Therefore, the Court of Appeals' recognition of such a cause of action was in error and is reversed.

KELLY, Justice (concurring in part and dissenting in part).

[I] would recognize a cause of action for the loss of an opportunity to avoid physical harm less than death. . . .

The lost opportunity doctrine, adopted by this Court for wrongful death cases in *Falcon v. Memorial Hospital* provides an exception to the general rule of proving causation in medical malpractice actions. According to the doctrine, damages are recoverable for the lost opportunity to survive, even though the opportunity was less than fifty percent. A plaintiff must show only that there is a substantial possibility that the defendant's negligence caused the injury.

Several reasons have been advanced for adoption of the doctrine. First, because medicine is an inexact science, questions regarding causation are not easily answered, especially where a physician's failure to act is alleged to be responsible for the harm. Fundamental fairness dictates that the uncertainty be imposed on the tortfeasor, not on the patient. . . .

Second, the doctor-patient relationship should be taken into account. Patients retain physicians not only to cure disease or heal injury, but also to maximize their chance of recovery and to assuage their pain and suffering. The lost opportunity doctrine helps ensure that physicians are liable for negligence or gross negligence that deprives their patients of less than an even chance of obtaining a better result.

Third, as the Court of Appeals stated, where the chance of recovery is fifty percent or less, the traditional rule undermines the loss allocations and deterrent functions of tort law. . . .

The majority acknowledges the importance of the deterrent and loss-allocation functions of tort law. However, it refuses to jettison the element of causation in order to gain the lost opportunity's deterrent effect. In *Falcon*, Justice Levin remarked that causation principles are not discarded where the injury is viewed as the lost chance rather than the ultimate harm. A plaintiff must still establish more-probable-than-not causation. It must be proven that, more probably than not, the defendant reduced the opportunity of avoiding harm.

The policy reasons behind the lost opportunity doctrine apply equally to fatal and nonfatal cases. Patients seek treatment from doctors for maladies other than potentially fatal diseases. In both fatal and nonfatal cases, the patient seeks to improve the opportunity of "avoiding, ameliorating, or reducing physical harm and pain and suffering."

The majority fails to explain why the doctrine is proper if death occurs, but not if a lesser injury is involved. . . . Other jurisdictions have adopted a cause of action for the loss of an opportunity to avoid physical harm less than death. . . . In *Delaney v. Cade*, 255 Kan. 199, 873 P.2d 175 (1994), the Kansas Supreme Court considered recognizing a cause of action for the loss of a chance of a better recovery as contrasted with the lost chance to survive. After reviewing the policy arguments relating to the lost chance doctrine, the court found that the lost chance of a better recovery stated a legitimate cause of action. It stated:

We have found no authority or rational argument which would apply the loss of chance theory solely to survival actions or to loss of a better recovery actions and not to both. As noted by plaintiff in her brief: "There is certainly nothing in that rationale to justify leaving the season open on persons who suffer paralysis, organ loss, or other serious injury short of death while protecting only those who do not survive the negligence."

We acknowledge that the vast majority of cases we have reviewed involved death of the patient and a loss of chance of survival. We also recognize that the apportionment of damages may be more difficult in a loss of a better recovery case than in the cases resulting in death. However, the fact that most cases have involved death of the patient and that damages may be difficult to resolve in a loss of a better recovery case should not be grounds to refuse to recognize the doctrine when medical malpractice has substantially reduced a person's chance of a better recovery.

[*Id.* at 210, 873 P.2d 175.]

The court acknowledged that several jurisdictions have refused to recognize the loss of chance doctrine in either type of case. However, it found no jurisdiction which applied the theory in one type of case and denied it in the other. The court found that most jurisdictions, like Kansas, had simply not had occasion to address the doctrine in both situations. . . .

[The other dissenting opinion is omitted.]

NOTES

1. In *Falcon v. Memorial Hosp.*, 462 N.W.2d 44 (Mich. 1990), the Michigan Supreme Court adopted the lost opportunity doctrine in wrongful death cases. The Michigan Legislature immediately rejected *Falcon* and the lost opportunity doctrine. M.C.L. § 600.2912a(2); M.S.A. § 2912(1)(2). However, the legislation did not apply to causes of action that arose before the statute's effective date. Accordingly, *Falcon* only applies to causes of action, such as that involved in the above appeal, that arose before October 1, 1993.

2. Does the lost opportunity doctrine redefine causation, or redefine what counts as a legally recognized injury?

PROBLEMS

1. Patience visited her physician complaining of a persistent cough. The doctor diagnosed bronchitis and prescribed cough syrup. In fact, Patience had lung cancer, which was not diagnosed until some months later when Patience returned for a second visit. Patience started immediate chemotherapy, but the

cancer was too far advanced and she died. Her survivors sued the doctor for mal-practice for failing to diagnose the disease during the first visit. At trial, the doc-tor conceded that the failure to diagnose lung cancer was negligent. In addition, it was established that if the doctor had diagnosed the disease at the first visit and begun immediate treatment, Patience would have had a 39% chance of surviving for at least five years. Because of the delay in diagnosing the cancer and beginning the treatment, however, Patience in fact had only a 25% chance of surviving five years. What would be the measure of damages under each of the approaches set forth in the case above?

2. In a jurisdiction that allows a plaintiff in a situation such as that in Prob-lem 1 to recover a proportionate share of the damages based on the percentage chance of survival that was lost, what should the court do if the facts show that the victim of the malpractice had a 51% chance of survival, which was lost by the physician's negligence? Should the plaintiffs suing to recover for the death of the victim recover only 51% of the damages? Or should they recover in full on the ground that they have shown that the defendant "more likely than not" caused the death?

3. Suppose, in a situation such as that in the *Weymers* case, that the victim of the malpractice does die prematurely, perhaps ten years after the malprac-tice. Would the case now be actionable since death, attributable to the mal-practice, has finally occurred? Would her survivors be able to sue at that time for wrongful death? What arguments would you anticipate that the defendants would raise? How might you respond?

4. Due to the negligence of the operator, a small amount of radiation leaked from the Happy Valley nuclear power plant. As a result of this leak, approxi-mately 5,000 people living in the vicinity were exposed to sufficient radiation to cause a 1% increase in their future chances of getting cancer. Should these peo-ple be able to recover for the increased risk of illness due to the exposure? How would their damages be calculated? If one of these individuals does develop cancer, would they be able to demonstrate that the exposure to the radiation caused the cancer, as opposed to some other cause? If not, should they be allowed to recover on an "increased risk" theory analogous to the "lost chance" theory?

5. In the case set forth in Problem 4, how should we value the fear of future harm suffered by those who were exposed to the radiation? Should the defendant be liable for the costs of tests necessary to monitor those who have an increased risk of cancer?

6. Suppose Clarence Client, the slip and fall victim of the previous section, approached Adlai Hock, a plaintiff's personal injury attorney, to file suit against Giganto-Mart. Hock explains to Client that the chances of prevailing are not good, but that he thinks he could get about $5,000 "just for the nuisance value of the suit." Although Hock normally runs a careful practice, this claim slips through the cracks and no complaint is filed before the statute of limitations expires. Client then files suit against Hock for legal malpractice. Hock defends

on the ground that the suit had only about a 10% chance of success if it had gone to trial. Should Client be allowed to recover if he can show that the damages resulting from the fall were $100,000, although the chances of actually prevailing at trial were only 10%? Should Client be allowed to recover if he can show that Giganto-Mart routinely settled these cases if the demand was $5,000 or less? Or based on Hock's own evaluation of the case's "nuisance value"? *Cf. Daugert v. Pappas*, 704 P.2d 600 (Wash. 1985).

DAUBERT v. MERRELL DOW PHARMACEUTICALS, INC.
43 F.3d 1311 (9th Cir. 1995)

KOZINSKI, Circuit Judge.

On remand from the United States Supreme Court, we undertake "the task of ensuring that an expert's testimony both rests on a reliable foundation and is relevant to the task at hand." *Daubert v. Merrell Dow Pharmaceuticals, Inc.*, 509 U.S. 579 (1993).

I

Two minors brought suit against Merrell Dow Pharmaceuticals, claiming they suffered limb reduction birth defects because their mothers had taken Bendectin, a drug prescribed for morning sickness to about 17.5 million pregnant women in the United States between 1957 and 1982. . . . This appeal deals with an evidentiary question: whether certain expert scientific testimony is admissible to prove that Bendectin caused the plaintiffs' birth defects.

For the most part, we don't know how birth defects come about. We do know they occur in 2-3% of births, whether or not the expectant mother has taken Bendectin. . . . Limb defects are even rarer, occurring in fewer than one birth out of every 1000. But scientists simply do not know how teratogens (chemicals known to cause limb reduction defects) do their damage: They cannot reconstruct the biological chain of events that leads from an expectant mother's ingestion of a teratogenic substance to the stunted development of a baby's limbs. Nor do they know what it is about teratogens that causes them to have this effect. No doubt, someday we will have this knowledge, and then we will be able to tell precisely whether and how Bendectin (or any other suspected teratogen) interferes with limb development; in the current state of scientific knowledge, however, we are ignorant.

Not knowing the mechanism whereby a particular agent causes a particular effect is not always fatal to a plaintiff's claim. Causation can be proved even when we don't know precisely how the damage occurred, if there is sufficiently compelling proof that the agent must have caused the damage somehow. One method of proving causation in these circumstances is to use statistical evidence. If 50 people who eat at a restaurant one evening come down with food poisoning during the night, we can infer that the restaurant's food probably contained something unwholesome, even if none of the dishes is available for analysis. This inference is based on the fact that, in our health-conscious society, it is highly unlikely that 50 people who have nothing in common except that they ate at the same restaurant would get food poisoning from independent sources.

It is by such means that plaintiffs here seek to establish that Bendectin is responsible for their injuries. They rely on the testimony of three groups of scientific experts. One group proposes to testify that there is a statistical link between the ingestion of Bendectin during pregnancy and limb reduction defects. These experts have not themselves conducted epidemiological (human statistical) studies on the effects of Bendectin; rather, they have reanalyzed studies published by other scientists, none of whom reported a statistical association between Bendectin and birth defects. Other experts proffered by plaintiffs propose to testify that Bendectin causes limb reduction defects in humans because it causes such defects in laboratory animals. A third group of experts sees a link between Bendectin and birth defects because Bendectin has a chemical structure that is similar to other drugs suspected of causing birth defects.

The opinions proffered by plaintiffs' experts do not, to understate the point, reflect the consensus within the scientific community. The FDA — an agency not known for its promiscuity in approving drugs — continues to approve Bendectin for use by pregnant women because "available data do not demonstrate an association between birth defects and Bendectin." U.S. Department of Health and Human Services News, No. P80-45 (Oct. 7, 1980). Every published study here and abroad—and there have been many—concludes that Bendectin is not a teratogen. In fact, apart from the small but determined group of scientists testifying on behalf of the Bendectin plaintiffs in this and many other cases, there doesn't appear to be a single scientist who has concluded that Bendectin causes limb reduction defects.

It is largely because the opinions proffered by plaintiffs' experts run counter to the substantial consensus in the scientific community that we affirmed the district court's grant of summary judgment the last time the case appeared before us. . . . The standard for admissibility of expert testimony in this circuit at the time was the so-called *Frye* test: Scientific evidence was admissible if it was based on a scientific technique generally accepted as reliable within the scientific community. . . . We found that the district court properly applied this standard, and affirmed. The Supreme Court reversed, holding that *Frye* was superseded by Federal Rule of Evidence 702, . . . and remanded for us to consider the admissibility of plaintiffs' expert testimony under this new standard.

II

A. Brave New World

Federal judges ruling on the admissibility of expert scientific testimony face a far more complex and daunting task in a post-*Daubert* world than before. The judge's task under *Frye* is relatively simple: to determine whether the method employed by the experts is generally accepted in the scientific community. . . . Under *Daubert*, we must engage in a difficult, two-part analysis. First, we must determine nothing less than whether the experts' testimony reflects "scientific knowledge," whether their findings are "derived by the scientific method," and whether their work product amounts to "good science." . . . Second, we must ensure that the proposed expert testimony is "relevant to the task at hand," . . . *i.e.*, that it logically advances a material aspect of the proposing party's case. The Supreme Court referred to this second prong of the analysis as the "fit" requirement. . . .

The first prong of *Daubert* puts federal judges in an uncomfortable position. The question of admissibility only arises if it is first established that the individuals whose testimony is being proffered are experts in a particular scientific field; here, for example, the Supreme Court waxed eloquent on the impressive qualifications of plaintiffs' experts. . . . Yet something doesn't become "scientific knowledge" just because it's uttered by a scientist; nor can an expert's self-serving assertion that his conclusions were "derived by the scientific method" be deemed conclusive. . . . As we read the Supreme Court's teaching in *Daubert*, therefore, though we are largely untrained in science and certainly no match for any of the witnesses whose testimony we are reviewing, it is our responsibility to determine whether those experts' proposed testimony amounts to "scientific knowledge," constitutes "good science," and was "derived by the scientific method."

[In discussing the first part of the *Daubert* test, the court noted that the plaintiff's experts had had not conducted independent research and had never published their findings in a peer reviewed scienctific journal. The court also found that the experts' depositions and affidavits did not themselves contain sufficient information about the methodology used to enable the court to find that it constituted "good science." With regard to one of the plaintiff's experts, the court concluded as follows:]

This is especially true of Dr. Palmer — the only expert willing to testify "that Bendectin did cause the limb defects in each of the children." . . . In support of this conclusion, Dr. Palmer asserts only that Bendectin is a teratogen and that he has examined the plaintiffs' medical records, which apparently reveal the timing of their mothers' ingestion of the drug. Dr. Palmer offers no tested or testable theory to explain how, from this limited information, he was able to eliminate all other potential causes of birth defects, nor does he explain how he alone can state as a fact that Bendectin caused plaintiffs' injuries. We therefore agree with the Sixth Circuit's observation that "Dr. Palmer does not testify on the basis of the collective view of his scientific discipline, nor does he take issue with his peers and explain the grounds for his differences. Indeed, no understandable scientific basis is stated. Personal opinion, not science, is testifying here." . . . For this reason, Dr. Palmer's testimony is inadmissible as a matter of law under Rule 702.

The failure to make any objective showing as to admissibility under the first prong of Rule 702 would also fatally undermine the testimony of plaintiffs' other experts, but for the peculiar posture of this case. Plaintiffs submitted their experts' affidavits while *Frye* was the law of the circuit and, although they've not requested an opportunity to augment their experts' affidavits in light of *Daubert*, the interests of justice would be disserved by precluding plaintiffs from doing so. Given the opportunity to augment their original showing of admissibility, plaintiffs might be able to show that the methodology adopted by some of their experts is based on sound scientific principles. For instance, plaintiffs' epidemiologists might validate their reanalyses by explaining why they chose only certain of the data that was available, or the experts relying on animal studies might point to some authority for extrapolating human causation from teratogenicity in animals.

Were this the only question before us, we would be inclined to remand to give plaintiffs an opportunity to submit additional proof that the scientific testimony they proffer was "derived by the scientific method." *Daubert*, however, establishes two prongs to the Rule 702 admissibility inquiry. We therefore consider whether the testimony satisfies the second prong of Rule 702: Would plaintiffs' proffered scientific evidence "assist the trier of fact to . . . determine a fact in issue"? Fed. R. Evid. 702.

C. No Visible Means of Support

In elucidating the second requirement of Rule 702, *Daubert* stressed the importance of the "fit" between the testimony and an issue in the case: "Rule 702's 'helpfulness' standard requires a valid scientific connection to the pertinent inquiry as a precondition to admissibility." . . . Here, the pertinent inquiry is causation. In assessing whether the proffered expert testimony "will assist the trier of fact" in resolving this issue, we must look to the governing substantive standard, which in this case is supplied by California tort law.

Plaintiffs do not attempt to show causation directly; instead, they rely on experts who present circumstantial proof of causation. Plaintiffs' experts testify that Bendectin is a teratogen because it causes birth defects when it is tested on animals, because it is similar in chemical structure to other suspected teratogens, and because statistical studies show that Bendectin use increases the risk of birth defects. Modern tort law permits such proof, but plaintiffs must nevertheless carry their traditional burden; they must prove that their injuries were the result of the accused cause and not some independent factor. In the case of birth defects, carrying this burden is made more difficult because we know that some defects — including limb reduction defects — occur even when expectant mothers do not take Bendectin, and that most birth defects occur for no known reason.

California tort law requires plaintiffs to show not merely that Bendectin increased the likelihood of injury, but that it more likely than not caused their injuries. . . . In terms of statistical proof, this means that plaintiffs must establish not just that their mothers' ingestion of Bendectin increased somewhat the likelihood of birth defects, but that it more than doubled it — only then can it be said that Bendectin is more likely than not the source of their injury.

Because the background rate of limb reduction defects is one per thousand births, plaintiffs must show that among children of mothers who took Bendectin the incidence of such defects was more than two per thousand.

None of plaintiffs' epidemiological experts claims that ingestion of Bendectin during pregnancy more than doubles the risk of birth defects. To evaluate the relationship between Bendectin and limb reduction defects, an epidemiologist would take a sample of the population and compare the frequency of birth defects in children whose mothers took Bendectin with the frequency of defects in children whose mothers did not. . . . The ratio derived from this comparison would be an estimate of the "relative risk" associated with Bendectin. . . . For an epidemiological study to show causation under a preponderance standard, "the relative risk of limb reduction defects arising from the epidemiological data . . . will, at a minimum, have to exceed '2'." . . . That is, the study must show that children whose mothers took Bendectin are more than twice as likely to develop limb reduction birth defects as children whose mothers did not. While plaintiffs' epidemiologists make vague assertions that there is a statistically significant relationship between Bendectin and birth defects, none states that the relative risk is greater than two. These studies thus would not be helpful, and indeed would only serve to confuse the jury, if offered to prove rather than refute causation. A relative risk of less than two may suggest teratogenicity, but it actually tends to disprove legal causation, as it shows that Bendectin does not double the likelihood of birth defects.

With the exception of Dr. Palmer, whose testimony is inadmissible under the first prong of the Rule 702 analysis, the remaining experts proffered by plaintiffs were equally unprepared to testify that Bendectin caused plaintiffs' injuries; they were willing to testify only that Bendectin is "capable of causing" birth defects. Plaintiffs argue "these scientists use the words 'capable of causing' meaning that it does cause. This is an ambiguity of language. . . . If something is capable of causing damage in humans, it does." But what plaintiffs must prove is not that Bendectin causes some birth defects, but that it caused their birth defects. To show this, plaintiffs' experts would have had to testify either that Bendectin actually caused plaintiffs' injuries (which they could not say) or that Bendectin more than doubled the likelihood of limb reduction birth defects (which they did not say).

As the district court properly found below, "the strongest inference to be drawn for plaintiffs based on the epidemiological evidence is that Bendectin could possibly have caused plaintiffs' injuries." . . . The same is true of the other testimony derived from animal studies and chemical structure analyses — these experts "testify to a possibility rather than a probability." . . . Plaintiffs do not quantify this possibility, or otherwise indicate how their conclusions about causation should be weighted, even though the substantive legal standard has always required proof of causation by a preponderance of the evidence. Unlike these experts' explanation of their methodology, this is not a shortcoming that could be corrected on remand; plaintiffs' experts could augment their affidavits with independent proof that their methods were sound, but to augment the substantive testimony as to causation would require the experts to change their conclusions altogether. Any such tailoring of the experts' conclusions would, at this stage of the proceedings, fatally undermine any attempt to show that these findings were "derived by the scientific method." Plaintiffs' experts must, therefore, stand by the conclusions they originally proffered, rendering their testimony inadmissible under the second prong of Fed. R. Evid. 702.

The district court's grant of summary judgment is AFFIRMED.

QUESTIONS

Because California adheres to the "more likely than not" test of causation, the plaintiffs in this case had to establish that Bendectin doubled the risk of limb reduction defects, so that it could be argued that any such injury was "more likely than not" caused by the drug. In a jurisdiction that accepts "loss of chance" causation, should the result differ? If a drug increased the risk of limb reduction defects, but did not double them, should the plaintiff be allowed to recover? If so, how should damages be calculated?

PROBLEMS

Even if the relative risk is less than 2, there might be other evidence of causation that will serve to bolster the plaintiff's proof and avoid dismissal. Consider the probative value of the evidence offered in the following problems:

1. Yukko Chemical Corp. has discharged chemical waste into holding ponds on its property. Some of the chemicals have leached into the ground water, and traces of the chemicals have appeared in the well water consumed by nearby residents. Those drinking the water have suffered a higher incidence of cancer cases than experienced by the overall population of the area, but the increase is nowhere near the magic relative risk of 2. Yukko denies that the chemicals cause cancer in the concentrations found in the well water. However, a careful study reveals the following information: the relative cancer risk of those drinking water from wells within one-quarter mile of the Yukko plant is 1.9, and this risk decreases gradually as the distance of the wells from the plant increases. What is the significance of these data? Is it enough to allow the case to go to the jury on the causation issue, given that even the highest relative risk is less than 2?

2. On the same facts, what is the significance of evidence that a similar increase in cancer rates occurred in other places where the ground water was polluted with the same chemicals?

3. On the same facts, what is the significance of evidence that the increase in the cancer rates occurred only after the chemicals began to contaminate the well water?

4. On the same facts, what is the significance of evidence that laboratory tests have established that the chemicals in question are carcinogenic?

5. On the same facts, what is the significance of evidence that the chemicals in question have been shown to cause the particular type of cancer suffered by one of the individual plaintiffs?

EXERCISE

Research the standard jury instruction used in your jurisdiction (or a jurisdiction designated by your instructor) for cause in fact in a slip and fall case. Examine the cases on which this instruction is supposed to be based, and look for any more recent cases addressing the cause in fact issue. Write a memorandum explaining how the jurisdiction allocates the burden of proof on causation in fact in such cases. Analyze whether the instruction correctly sets forth the law as it appears in the cases, and propose an improved instruction that will more accurately and more clearly embody the law on this topic.

Chapter 6

PROXIMATE CAUSE

After establishing that the defendant's negligent conduct was the cause in fact of the plaintiff's injury, the next step in the negligence analysis is determining whether the negligence was the "proximate cause" as well. The term "proximate cause" is as mysterious as any in law, and many have criticized the very use of the term to describe this next stage of the analysis, proposing such alternative descriptions as "legal cause" (itself hardly illuminating) or "scope of liability." The key is that this inquiry asks different questions than the preceding cause in fact analysis. Granting that the negligent conduct of the defendant was in some way the cause of the harm, we now ask whether the defendant should in fact be held liable for it.

A. INTRODUCTORY PROBLEM: JURY INSTRUCTIONS ON PROXIMATE CAUSE

As noted, proximate cause in theory is a distinct step in the analysis, which is reached if and only if actual cause is established. In practice, unfortunately, the two issues are not always kept cleanly separated. Consider, for example, the following jury instructions, which will serve to introduce the type of issues presented in proximate cause analysis, as well as to present the two dominant approaches used in resolving them:

Jury Instruction: Direct Cause

The "proximate cause" is that which produces an injury directly, or in the natural and normal sequence of events without the intervention of any independent, intervening cause. It is the direct and immediate cause, the predominant cause which, acting directly or in the natural sequence of events, produces the accident and resulting injury, and without which the injury would not have occurred.

Jury Instruction: Foreseeability of Injury

The "proximate cause" of an injury is a cause which in its natural and continuous sequence produces an event, and without which the event would not have occurred. In order to warrant a finding that the defendant's negligence is the proximate cause of an injury, it must appear from a preponderance of the evidence that facts and circumstances existed that were such that a person of ordinary prudence would have reasonably foreseen that the injury would be the natural and probable consequence of the negligence.

Examine these jury instructions. Both contain a "but-for" cause element ("and without which the event would not have occurred"). But they also contain an additional requirement, and it is those additional elements that will be the focus of study in this chapter. In the "Direct Cause" instruction, the emphasis, as the name suggests, is on the directness of the causation and the lack of any "independent, intervening causes." The second instruction also speaks to the sequence of events, but adds the requirement that the defendant be able to foresee that the injury would be the result of the negligence. In considering the meaning of these two instructions, it may be helpful to try to apply them to the type of factual problem they were supposedly designed to address. Consider the following fact situation, which is taken from *Allen v. Shiroma*, 514 P.2d 545 (Or. 1973):

> The circumstances leading up to plaintiff's injury are unusual. Vehicles driven by the two defendants, Shiroma and Leathers, collided. The collision was not horrendous and the cars remained operable; however, some glass and debris did fall on the pavement. A jury could find the defendant Mrs. Leathers negligently caused the collision.

> Plaintiff [Allen] was in his car, waiting at a stop sign, when the collision occurred on the cross street in front of him. He stopped in his lane, got out and instructed Mrs. Leathers to move her car, which she did. Plaintiff put out flares and directed traffic. Plaintiff noticed his car was impeding traffic. He asked a young man, White, to move his car out of the way. White was too young to be licensed as a vehicle operator. He got in the car, lurched forward, struck another vehicle, veered across the street and struck plaintiff. Plaintiff was struck about 15 minutes after the initial collision.

Should defendants Leathers and Shiroma be held liable to plaintiff Allen? First identify the negligent conduct of the defendants and why that conduct was a cause in fact of the plaintiff's injury. Now try to apply each of the jury instructions to this fact situation. With regard to the "direct cause" instruction, you will of course want to consider what is meant by the notion of causing an injury "directly" and what a "normal sequence of events" might be. What is an "independent, intervening cause?" Were any such causes acting in this fact situation? If you discern any such causes, consider why you might classify them as "independent" and "intervening."

With regard to the "foreseeability of injury" instruction, consider just what it is that defendant must foresee: the possibility of injury, or the exact sequence of events, or something else? Since the foreseeability of injury is already considered in deciding whether the defendant's conduct was negligent, why is foreseeability again considered in this element of the cause of action? Does this approach lead to a different result from the direct cause test?

Finally, why are we even asking these questions, if it is granted that the defendants were negligent and their negligence was a cause in fact of the harm?

What purpose or goal of tort law is served by limiting liability in this way? As the remainder of the chapter will suggest, some sort of limitation on the scope of liability often seems necessary, but stating the rule for drawing that line is difficult. Both approaches suggested by the two jury instructions are used to accomplish this purpose, and we will first consider the meaning and application of the direct cause test.

B. THE DIRECT CAUSE TEST

IN RE AN ARBITRATION BETWEEN POLEMIS AND FURNESS, WITHY & CO., LTD.
3 K.B. 560 (C.A. 1921)

APPEAL from the judgment of Sankey J. on an award in the form of a special case.

The Owners of the Greek steamship *Thrasyvoulos* claimed to recover damages for the total loss of the steamship by fire.

By a charterparty, dated February 21, 1917, Messrs. Polemis and Boyazides, the owners of the Greek steamship *Thrasyvoulos* (hereinafter called the owners), chartered the steamship to Furness, Withy & Co., Ltd. (hereinafter called the charterers), for the period of the duration of the war and at charterers' option up to six months afterwards from the day she was placed at the charterers' disposal ready to load in the port of Cardiff, she being then tight, staunch, strong and every way fitted for ordinary cargo service. . . .

The vessel by the directions of the charterers or their agents in or about the months of June and July, 1917, loaded at Nantes a part cargo of cement and general cargo for Casablanca, Morocco. She then proceeded to Lisbon and was loaded with further cargo, consisting of cases of benzine and/or petrol and iron for Casablanca and other ports on the Morocco coast. She arrived at Casablanca on July 17, and there discharged a portion of her cargo. The cargo was discharged by Arab workmen and winchmen from the shore supplied and sent on board by the charterers' agents. The cargo in No. 1 hold included a considerable quantity of cases of benzine or petrol which had suffered somewhat by handling and/or by rough weather on the voyage, so that there had been some leakage from the tins in the cases into the hold. . . . In consequence of the breakage of the cases there was a considerable amount of petrol vapour in the hold. In the course of heaving a sling of the cases from the hold the rope by which the sling was being raised or the sling itself came into contact with the boards placed across the forward end of the hatch, causing one of the boards to fall into the lower hold, and the fall was instantaneously followed by a rush of flames from the lower hold, and this resulted eventually in the total destruction of the ship.

The owners contended (so far as material) that the charterers were liable for the loss of the ship; that fire caused by negligence was not an excepted peril; and that the ship was in fact lost by the negligence of the stevedores, who were the charterers' servants, in letting the sling strike the board, knocking it into the hold, and thereby causing a spark which set fire to the petrol vapour and destroyed the ship.

The charterers contended that fire however caused was an excepted peril; that there was no negligence for which the charterers were responsible, inasmuch as to let a board fall into the hold of the ship could do no harm to the ship and therefore was not negligence towards the owners; and that the danger and/or damage were too remote — *i.e.*, no reasonable man would have foreseen danger and/or damage of this kind resulting from the fall of the board.

The three arbitrators made the following findings of fact:

"(a) That the ship was lost by fire.

"(b) That the fire arose from a spark igniting petrol vapour in the hold.

"(c) That the spark was caused by the falling board coming into contact with some substance in the hold.

"(d) That the fall of the board was caused by the negligence of the Arabs (other than the winchman) engaged in the work of discharging.

"(e) That the said Arabs were employed by the charterers or their agents the Cie. Transatlantique on behalf of the charterers, and that the said Arabs were the servants of the charterers.

"(f) That the causing of the spark could not reasonably have been anticipated from the falling of the board, though some damage to the ship might reasonably have been anticipated.

"(g) There was no evidence before us that the Arabs chosen were known or likely to be negligent.

"(h) That the damages sustained by the owners through the said accident amount to the sum of 196165*l*. 1*s*. 11*d*. as shown in the second column of the schedule hereto."

Subject to the opinion of the Court on any questions of law arising the arbitrators awarded that the owners were entitled to recover from the charterers the before-mentioned sum.

If the Court should be of opinion that the above award was wrong, then the arbitrators awarded that the owners should recover nothing from the charterers.

Sankey J. affirmed the award. The charterers appealed.

. . . .

BANKES, L.J.

By a time charterparty dated February 21, 1917, the respondents chartered their vessel to the appellants. . . . The vessel was employed by the charterers to carry a cargo to Casablanca in Morocco. The cargo included a quantity of benzine or petrol in cases. While discharging at Casablanca a heavy plank fell into the hold in which the petrol was stowed, and caused an explosion, which set fire to the vessel and completely destroyed her. The owners claimed the value of the vessel from the charterers, alleging that the loss of the vessel was due to the negligence of the charterers' servants. The charterers contended that they were protected by the exception of fire contained in clause 21 of the charterparty, and they also contended that the damages claimed were too remote. . . . These findings are no doubt intended to raise the question whether the view taken, or said to have been taken, by Pollock C.B. in *Bigby* v. *Hewitt* [5 Ex. 243.] and *Greenland* v. *Chaplin* [5 Ex. 248.] or the view taken by Channell B. and Blackburn J. in *Smith* v. *London and South Western By. Co.*, [L.B. 6 C.P. 21.] is the correct one. . . . [T]he difference between the two views is this: According to the one view, the consequences which may reasonably be expected to result from a particular act are material only in reference to the question whether the act is or is not a negligent act; according to the other view, those consequences are the test whether the damages resulting from the act, assuming it to be negligent, are or are not too remote to be recoverable. . . . In two recent judgments dealing with the question, the view taken by the Court in *Smith* v. *London and South Western By. Co.* [L. B. 6 C.P. 21.] has been adopted — namely, by the late President (Sir Samuel Evans) in *H.M.S. London*, [(1914) P. 72,76.] and by Lord Sumner in *Weld-Blundell* v. *Stephens.* [(1920) A.C. 983, 984.] In the former case the President said: "The court is not concerned in the present case with any inquiry as to the chain of causes resulting in the creation of a legal liability from which such damages as the law allows would flow. The tortious act — *i.e.*, the negligence of the defendants, which imposes upon them a liability in law for damages — is admitted. This gets rid at once of an element which requires consideration in a chain of causation in testing the question of legal liability — namely, the foresight or anticipation of the reasonable man. In *Smith* v. *London and South Western By. Co.* [L.B. 6 C.P. 21.] Channell B. said: 'Where there is no direct evidence of negligence, the question what a reasonable man might foresee is of importance in considering the question whether there is evidence for the jury of negligence or not. . . . but when it has been once determined that there is evidence of negligence, the person guilty of it is equally liable for its consequences, whether he could have foreseen them or not.' And Blackburn J. in the same case said: 'What the defendants might reasonably anticipate is only material with reference to the question, whether the defendants were negligent or not, and cannot alter their liability if they were guilty of negligence'"; and after referring to the various phrases used in connection with remoteness of damages he said: "But it must be remembered, to use the words of a well-known American author (Sedgwick), that 'the legal' distinction between what is proximate and what is remote is not a logical one, nor does it depend upon relations of time and space;

it is purely practical, the reason for distinguishing between the proximate and remote causes and consequences being a purely practical one'; and again, to use the words of an eminent English jurist (Sir F. Pollock [11th ed., pp. 35, 36.] 'In whatever form we state the rule of "natural and probable consequences," we must remember that it is not a logical definition, but only a guide to the exercise of common sense. The lawyer cannot afford to adventure himself with philosophers in the logical and metaphysical controversies that beset the idea of cause.'" In the latter case Lord Sumner said: "What are 'natural, probable and necessary' consequences? Everything that happens, happens in the order of nature and is therefore 'natural.' Nothing that happens by the free choice of a thinking man is 'necessary,' except in the sense of predestination. To speak of 'probable' consequence is to throw everything upon the jury. It is tautologous to speak of 'effective' cause or to say that damages too remote from the cause are irrecoverable, for an effective cause is simply that which causes, and in law what is ineffective or too remote is not a cause at all. I still venture to think that direct cause is the best expression. Proximate cause has acquired a special connotation through its use in reference to contracts of insurance. Direct cause excludes what is indirect, conveys the essential distinction, which causa causans and causa sine qua non rather cumbrously indicate, and is consistent with the possibility of the concurrence of more direct causes than one, operating at the same time and leading to a common result. . . ."

In the present case the arbitrators have found as a fact that the falling of the plank was due to the negligence of the defendants' servants. The fire appears to me to have been directly caused by the falling of the plank. Under these circumstances I consider that it is immaterial that the causing of the spark by the falling of the plank could not have been reasonably anticipated. The appellant's junior counsel sought to draw a distinction between the anticipation of the extent of damage resulting from a negligent act, and the anticipation of the type of damage resulting from such an act. He admitted that it could not lie in the mouth of a person whose negligent act had caused damage to say that he could not reasonably have foreseen the extent of the damage, but he contended that the negligent person was entitled to rely upon the fact that he could not reasonably have anticipated the type of damage which resulted from his negligent act. I do not think that the distinction can be admitted. Given the breach of duty which constitutes the negligence, and given the damage as a direct result of that negligence, the anticipations of the person whose negligent act has produced the damage appear to me to be irrelevant. I consider that the damages claimed are not too remote. . . .

For these reasons I think that the appeal fails, and must be dismissed with costs.

WARRINGTON L.J.

[The] result may be summarised as follows: The presence or absence of reasonable anticipation of damage determines the legal quality of the act as negligent or innocent. If it be thus determined to be negligent, then the question whether particular damages are recoverable depends only on the answer to the question whether they are the direct consequence of the act. . . .

In the present case it is clear that the act causing the plank to fall was in law a negligent act, because some damage to the ship might reasonably be anticipated. If this is so then the appellants are liable for the actual loss, that being on the findings of the arbitrators the direct result of the falling board. . . .

On the whole in my opinion the appeal fails and must be dismissed with costs.

SCRUTTON L.J.

[The] second defence is that the damage is too remote from the negligence, as it could not be reasonable foreseen as a consequence. On this head we were referred to a number of well known cases in which vague language, which I cannot think to be really helpful, has been used in an attempt to define the point at which damage becomes too remote from, or not sufficiently directly caused by, the breach of duty, which is the original cause of action, to be recoverable. For instance, I cannot think it useful to say the damage must be the natural and probable result. This suggests that there are results which are natural but not probable, and other results which are probable but not natural. I am not sure what either adjective means in this connection; if they mean the same thing, two need not be used; if they mean different things, the difference between them should be defined. And as to many cases of fact in which the distinction has been drawn, it is difficult to see why one case should be decided one way and one another. Perhaps the House of Lords will some day explain why, if a cheque is negligently filled up, it is a direct effect of the negligence that some one finding the cheque should commit forgery; . . . while if some one negligently leaves a libellous letter about, it is not a direct effect of the negligence that the finder should show the letter to the person libelled. . . . In this case, however, the problem is simpler. To determine whether an act is negligent, it is relevant to determine whether any reasonable person would foresee that the act would cause damage; if he would not, the act is not negligent. But if the act would or might probably cause damage, the fact that the damage it in fact causes is not the exact kind of damage one would expect is immaterial, so long as the damage is in fact directly traceable to the negligent act, and not due to the operation of independent causes having no connection with the negligent act, except that they could not avoid its results. Once the act is negligent, the fact that its exact operation was not foreseen is immaterial. . . . In the present case it was negligent in discharging cargo to knock down the planks of the temporary staging, for they might easily cause some damage either to workmen, or cargo, or the ship. The fact that they did directly produce an unexpected result, a spark in an atmosphere of petrol vapour which caused a fire, does not relieve the person who was negligent from the damage which his negligent act directly caused.

For these reasons the experienced arbitrators and the judge appealed from came, in my opinion, to a correct decision, and the appeal must be dismissed with costs.

Appeal dismissed.

NOTES

1. As a foundation for the proximate cause analysis, be sure to identify what was the negligent conduct of the defendant, why it was negligent, and whether it was the cause in fact of the harm.

2. *Polemis* is the first of the great "proximate cause" cases to be studied here. Be sure to study not only the rule it adopts, but also the alternative rule argued by the appellants. How do they differ? What justifications might be asserted for each rule?

PROBLEMS

To test the meaning of the direct cause test, consider how it would treat the following fact situations:

1. One dark night, Mrs. Leary left her lighted kerosene lantern in the shed where she kept her cow. The cow kicked the lantern over, which caused a fire that quickly consumed the shed. Sparks from the fire ignited her neighbor's house, which also burned down. From there, the fire continued to spread until, by morning, most of the city of Chicago had burned down. Consider: a) Was Mrs. Leary's conduct negligent? Why? b) Was her conduct the cause in fact of the loss of the city of Chicago? c) Was it the proximate cause of the loss of the entire city, under the direct cause test of *Polemis*?

2. Chemco was performing some outdoor blasting tests in an abandoned gravel quarry using a highly unstable liquid explosive. Chemco employees left behind a container of this explosive when they ended their tests. The explosive was contained in a metal can clearly labeled "Danger — High Explosive."

   a. The next day two young children came to play at the quarry. Unaware of the presence of the explosive, the two played happily until the heat of the sun caused the can of explosive to detonate, injuring the children. Was the conduct of Chemco and its employees a direct cause of the children's injury? Would it make any difference if one of the children accidentally dislodged a rock that struck the can, triggering the explosion? What if one of the children discovered the can but was too young to read the warning and began throwing rocks at it, thereby causing the explosion that injured the two children?

b. The same explosion blows out the windows of a house over a mile away. Was the conduct of Chemco and its employees a direct cause of the broken windows? Does it matter how the explosion was triggered?

c. Suppose that before the children begin throwing rocks at the can, one of the children tells her older brother. The brother warns the children to stay away from the can and tries to move it away from the edge of the quarry. Unfortunately, the can is heavier than it looks and the brother drops it, causing an explosion which injures both the brother and the other children. Was the conduct of Chemco the direct cause of any of these injuries?

d. Suppose that before the children begin throwing rocks at the can, one of them decides to tell a grown-up and goes to get her father. Father, arriving on the scene, carefully examines the material in the can and determines that it is, in fact, nitroglycerin. "I'll take care of this," says father, who then places the can in the back of his pick-up and heads for town. Father, however, neglected to secure the can carefully to the truck. When he rounds a corner in town at high speed, the can slides across the bed of the truck, hits the side, and explodes. Father is injured, and so are many bystanders on the sidewalk. Is Chemco's conduct the direct cause of these injuries? Is anyone's conduct a direct cause of these injuries?

3. After doing some home repairs in his family room, Carver left behind his electric saw, plugged in, even though he knew that his children frequently played in the room and often invited their friends in to play as well. The Carver children and their friends did come into the family room to play, but they ignored the saw. Later, Mr. Smith, a neighbor, came into the room looking for his child. (He entered the room without permission through a sliding glass door to the Carver's back yard.) He did not notice the saw on the floor and tripped over it, injuring his ankle. Was Carver negligent, and if so, was his conduct the direct cause of the injury? Should it matter that the risk which seems to make his conduct negligent (the risk of a child turning on the saw and getting severely cut) is different from the risk that actually resulted in injury?

C. FORESEEABILITY AS A DUTY LIMITATION

As the problems above may suggest, the direct cause test seems to produce questionable results in two types of situations. First, it would impose liability in cases where the results seem remote and surprising, so long as no intervening causes interrupt the flow of events between the negligent conduct and the harm. Second, it would deny liability in any case where an "independent cause" intervened, even if the resulting harm seems to be exactly the type of injury that a reasonably prudent person would have foreseen. This problem is especially acute in situations such as the explosives problem above, where some type of force has to operate in order to trigger the harmful potential created by the defendant's negligent conduct. The proper resolution of the difficulties in determining proximate cause was the subject of the famous debate between the majority and dissent in the following case.

PALSGRAF v. LONG ISLAND R. CO.
162 N.E. 99 (N.Y. 1928)

CARDOZO, C. J.

Plaintiff was standing on a platform of defendant's railroad after buying a ticket to go to Rockaway Beach. A train stopped at the station, bound for another place. Two men ran forward to catch it. One of the men reached the platform of the car without mishap, though the train was already moving. The other man, carrying a package, jumped aboard the car, but seemed unsteady as if about to fall. A guard on the car, who had held the door open, reached forward to help him in, and another guard on the platform pushed him from behind. In this act, the package was dislodged, and fell upon the rails. It was a package of small size, about fifteen inches long, and was covered by a newspaper. In fact it contained fireworks, but there was nothing in its appearance to give notice of its contents. The fireworks when they fell exploded. The shock of the explosion threw down some scales at the other end of the platform many feet away. The scales struck the plaintiff, causing injuries for which she sues.

The conduct of the defendant's guard, if a wrong in its relation to the holder of the package, was not a wrong in its relation to the plaintiff, standing far away. Relatively to her it was not negligence at all. Nothing in the situation gave notice that the falling package had in it the potency of peril to persons thus removed. Negligence is not actionable unless it involves the invasion of a legally protected interest, the violation of a right. "Proof of negligence in the air, so to speak, will not do." Pollock, Torts (11th Ed.) p. 455. . . . The plaintiff, as she stood upon the platform of the station, might claim to be protected against intentional invasion of her bodily security. Such invasion is not charged. She might claim to be protected against unintentional invasion by conduct involving in the thought of reasonable men an unreasonable hazard that such invasion would ensue. These, from the point of view of the law, were the bounds of her immunity, with perhaps some rare exceptions, survivals for the most part of ancient forms of liability, where conduct is held to be at the peril of the actor. . . . If no hazard was apparent to the eye of ordinary vigilance, an act innocent and harmless, at least to outward seeming, with reference to her, did not take to itself the quality of a tort because it happened to be a wrong, though apparently not one involving the risk of bodily insecurity, with reference to someone else. . . . The plaintiff sues in her own right for a wrong personal to her, and not as the vicarious beneficiary of a breach of duty to another.

A different conclusion will involve us, and swiftly too, in a maze of contradictions. A guard stumbles over a package which has been left upon a platform. It seems to be a bundle of newspapers. It turns out to be a can of dynamite.

To the eye of ordinary vigilance, the bundle is abandoned waste, which may be kicked or trod on with impunity. Is a passenger at the other end of the platform protected by the law against the unsuspected hazard concealed beneath the waste? If not, is the result to be any different, so far as the distant passenger is concerned, when the guard stumbles over a valise which a truckman or a porter has left upon the walk? The passenger far away, if the victim of a wrong at all, has a cause of action, not derivative, but original and primary. His claim to be protected against invasion of his bodily security is neither greater nor less because the act resulting in the invasion is a wrong to another far removed. In this case, the rights that are said to have been violated, are not even of the same order. The man was not injured in his person nor even put in danger. The purpose of the act, as well as its effect, was to make his person safe. It there was a wrong to him at all, which may very well be doubted it was a wrong to a property interest only, the safety of his package. Out of this wrong to property, which threatened injury to nothing else, there has passed, we are told, to the plaintiff by derivation or succession a right of action for the invasion of an interest of another order, the right to bodily security. The diversity of interests emphasizes the futility of the effort to build the plaintiff's right upon the basis of a wrong to someone else. The gain is one of emphasis, for a like result would follow if the interests were the same. Even then, the orbit of the danger as disclosed to the eye of reasonable vigilance would be the orbit of the duty. One who jostles one's neighbor in a crowd does not invade the rights of others standing at the outer fringe when the unintended contact casts a bomb upon the ground. The wrongdoer as to them is the man who carries the bomb, not the one who explodes it without suspicion of the danger. Life will have to be made over, and human nature transformed, before prevision so extravagant can be accepted as the norm of conduct, the customary standard to which behavior must conform.

The argument for the plaintiff is built upon the shifting meanings of such words as "wrong" and "wrongful," and shares their instability. What the plaintiff must show is "a wrong" to herself; *i.e.*, a violation of her own right, and not merely a wrong to someone else, nor conduct "wrongful" because unsocial, but not "a wrong" to anyone. We are told that one who drives at reckless speed through a crowded city street is guilty of a negligent act and therefore of a wrongful one, irrespective of the consequences. Negligent the act is, and wrongful in the sense that it is unsocial, but wrongful and unsocial in relation to other travelers, only because the eye of vigilance perceives the risk of damage. If the same act were to be committed on a speedway or a race course, it would lose its wrongful quality. The risk reasonably to be perceived defines the duty to be obeyed, and risk imports relation; it is risk to another or to others within the range of apprehension. . . . This does not mean, of course, that one who launches a destructive force is always relieved of liability, if the force, though known to be destructive, pursues an unexpected path. "It was not necessary that the defendant should have had notice of the particular method in which an accident would occur, if the possibility of an accident was clear to the ordinarily prudent eye." *Munsey v. Webb*, 231 U.S. 150, 156. . . . Some acts, such as shooting, are so imminently dangerous to any one who may come within reach of the missile however unexpectedly, as to impose a duty of prevision not far from that of an insurer. Even today, and much oftener in earlier stages of the law, one acts sometimes at one's peril. . . . Under this head, it may be, fall certain cases of what is known as transferred intent, an act willfully dangerous to A resulting by misadventure in injury to B. . . . These cases aside, wrong is defined in terms of the natural or probable, at least when unintentional. . . . The range of reasonable apprehension is at times a question for the court, and at times, if varying inferences are possible, a question for the jury. Here, by concession, there was nothing in the situation to suggest to the most cautious mind that the parcel wrapped in newspaper would spread wreckage through the station. If the guard had thrown it down knowingly and willfully, he would not have threatened the plaintiff's safety, so far as appearances could warn him. His conduct would not have involved, even then, an unreasonable probability of invasion of her bodily security. Liability can be no greater where the act is inadvertent.

Negligence, like risk, is thus a term of relation. Negligence in the abstract, apart from things related, is surely not a tort, if indeed it is understandable at all. . . . Negligence is not a tort unless it results in the commission of a wrong, and the commission of a wrong imports the violation of a right, in this case, we are told, the right to be protected against interference with one's bodily security. But bodily security is protected, not against all forms of interference or aggression, but only against some. One who seeks redress at law does not make out a cause of action by showing without more that there has been damage to his person. If the harm was not willful, he must show that the act as to him had possibilities of danger so many and apparent as to entitle him to be protected against the doing of it though the harm was unintended. Affront to personality is still the keynote of the wrong. . . . The victim does not sue derivatively, or by right of subrogation, to vindicate an interest invaded in the person of another. Thus to view his cause of action is to ignore the fundamental difference between tort and crime. Holland, Jurisprudence (12th Ed.) p. 328. He sues for breach of a duty owing to himself.

The law of causation, remote or proximate, is thus foreign to the case before us. The question of liability is always anterior to the question of the measure of the consequences that go with liability. If there is no tort to be redressed, there is no occasion to consider what damage might be recovered if there were a finding of a tort. We may assume, without deciding, that negligence, not at large or in the abstract, but in relation to the plaintiff, would entail liability for any and all consequences, however novel or extraordinary. . . . *[C]f. Matter of Polemis*, L.R. 1921, 3 K.B. 560. . . . There is room for argument that a distinction is to be drawn according to the diversity of interests invaded by the act, as where conduct negligent in that it threatens an insignificant invasion of an interest in property results in an unforeseeable invasion of an interest of another order, as, *e.g.*, one of bodily security. Perhaps other distinctions may be necessary. We do not go into the question now. The consequences to be followed must first be rooted in a wrong.

The judgment of the Appellate Division and that of the Trial Term should be reversed, and the complaint dismissed, with costs in all courts.

ANDREWS, J. (dissenting).

Assisting a passenger to board a train, the defendant's servant negligently knocked a package from his arms. It fell between the platform and the cars. Of its contents the servant knew and could know nothing. A violent explosion followed. The concussion broke some scales standing a considerable distance away. In falling, they injured the plaintiff, an intending passenger.

Upon these facts, may she recover the damages she has suffered in an action brought against the master? The result we shall reach depends upon our theory as to the nature of negligence. Is it a relative concept — the breach of some duty owing to a particular person or to particular persons? Or, where there is an act which unreasonably threatens the safety of others, is the doer liable for all its proximate consequences, even where they result in injury to one who would generally be thought to be outside the radius of danger? This is not a mere dispute as to words. We might not believe that to the average mind the dropping of the bundle would seem to involve the probability of harm to the plaintiff standing many feet away whatever might be the case as to the owner or to one so near as to be likely to be struck by its fall. If, however, we adopt the second hypothesis, we have to inquire only as to the relation between cause and effect. We deal in terms of proximate cause, not of negligence.

Negligence may be defined roughly as an act or omission which unreasonably does or may affect the rights of others, or which unreasonably fails to protect one's self from the dangers resulting from such acts. Here I confine myself to the first branch of the definition. Nor do I comment on the word "unreasonable." For present purposes it sufficiently describes that average of conduct that society requires of its members.

There must be both the act or the omission, and the right. It is the act itself, not the intent of the actor, that is important. . . . In criminal law both the intent and the result are to be considered. Intent again is material in tort actions, where punitive damages are sought, dependent on actual malice — not one merely reckless conduct. But here neither insanity nor infancy lessens responsibility. . . .

As has been said, except in cases of contributory negligence, there must be rights which are or may be affected. Often though injury has occurred, no rights of him who suffers have been touched. A licensee or trespasser upon my land has no claim to affirmative care on my part that the land be made safe. . . . Where a railroad is required to fence its tracks against cattle, no man's rights are injured should he wander upon the road because such fence is absent. . . . An unborn child may not demand immunity from personal harm. . . .

But we are told that "there is no negligence unless there is in the particular case a legal duty to take care, and this duty must be one which is owed to the plaintiff himself and not merely to others." Salmond Torts (6th Ed.) 24. This I think too narrow a conception. Where there is the unreasonable act, and some right that may be affected there is negligence whether damage does or does not result. That is immaterial. Should we drive down Broadway at a reckless speed, we are negligent whether we strike an approaching car or miss it by an inch. The act itself is wrongful. If is a wrong not only to those who happen to be within the radius of danger, but to all who might have been there — a wrong to the public at large. Such is the language of the street. Such [is] the language of the courts when speaking of contributory negligence. Such again and again [is] their language in speaking of the duty of some defendant and discussing proximate cause in cases where such a discussion is wholly irrelevant on any other theory. . . . As was said by Mr. Justice Holmes many years ago:

> "The measure of the defendant's duty in determining whether a wrong has been committed is one thing, the measure of liability when a wrong has been committed is another."

Spade v. Lynn & B. R. Co., 172 Mass. 488, 491, 52 N. E. 747. . . . Due care is a duty imposed on each one of us to protect society from unnecessary danger, not to protect A, B, or C alone.

It may well be that there is no such thing as negligence in the abstract. "Proof of negligence in the air, so to speak, will not do." In an empty world negligence would not exist. It does involve a relationship between man and his fellows, but not merely a relationship between man and those whom he might reasonably expect his act would injure; rather, a relationship between him and those whom he does in fact injure. If his act has a tendency to harm some one, it harms him a mile away as surely as it does those on the scene. We now permit children to recover for the negligent killing of the father. It was never prevented on the theory that no duty was owing to them. A husband may be compensated for the loss of his wife's services. To say that the wrongdoer was negligent as to the husband as well as to the wife is merely an attempt to fit facts to theory. An insurance company paying a fire loss recovers its payment of the negligent incendiary. We speak of subrogation — of suing in the right of the insured. Behind the cloud of words is the fact they hide, that the act, wrongful as to the insured, has also injured the company. Even if it be true that the fault of father, wife, or insured will prevent recovery, it is because we consider the original negligence, not the proximate cause of the injury. Pollock, Torts (12th Ed.) 463.

In the well-known *Polemis* case, [1921] 3 K.B. 560, Scrutton, L.J., said that the dropping of a plank was negligent, for it might injure "workman or cargo or ship." Because of either possibility, the owner of the vessel was to be made good for his loss. The act being wrongful, the doer was liable for its proximate results. Criticized and explained as this statement may have been, I think it states the law as it should be and as it is. . . .

The proposition is this: Everyone owes to the world at large the duty of refraining from those acts that may unreasonably threaten the safety of others. Such an act occurs. Not only is he wronged to whom harm might reasonably be expected to result, but he also who is in fact injured, even if he be outside what would generally be thought the danger zone. There needs be duty due the one complaining, but this is not a duty to a particular individual because as to him harm might be expected. Harm to someone being the natural result of the act, not only that one alone, but all those in fact injured may complain. We have never, I think, held otherwise. . . . Unreasonable risk being taken, its consequences are not confined to those who might probably be hurt.

If this be so, we do not have a plaintiff suing by "derivation or succession." Her action is original and primary. Her claim is for a breach of duty to herself — not that she is subrogated to any right of action of the owner of the parcel or of a passenger standing at the scene of the explosion.

The right to recover damages rests on additional considerations. The plaintiff's rights must be injured, and this injury must be caused by the negligence. We build a dam, but are negligent as to its foundations. Breaking, it injures property down stream. We are not liable if all this happened because of some reason other than the insecure foundation. But, when injuries do result from out unlawful act, we are liable for the consequences. It does not matter that they are unusual, unexpected, unforeseen, and unforeseeable. But there is one limitation. The damages must be so connected with the negligence that the latter may be said to be the proximate cause of the former.

These two words have never been given an inclusive definition. What is a cause in a legal sense, still more what is a proximate cause, depends in each case upon many considerations, as does the existence of negligence itself. Any philosophical doctrine of causation does not help us. A boy throws a stone into a pond. The ripples spread. The water level rises. The history of that pond is altered to all eternity. It will be altered by other causes also. Yet it will be forever the resultant of all causes combined. Each one will have an influence. How great only omniscience can say. You may speak of a chain, or, if you please, a net. An analogy is of little aid. Each cause brings about future events. Without each the future would not be the same. Each is proximate in the sense it is essential. But that is not what we mean by the word. Nor on the other hand do we mean sole cause. There is no such thing.

Should analogy be though helpful, however, I prefer that of a stream. The spring, starting on its journey, is joined by tributary after tributary. The river, reaching the ocean, comes from a hundred sources. No man may say whence any drop of water is derived. Yet for a time distinction may be possible. Into the clear creek, brown swamp water flows from the left. Later, from the right comes water stained by its clay bed. The three may remain for a space, sharply divided. But at last inevitably no trace of separation remains. They are so commingled that all distinction is lost.

As we have said, we cannot trace the effect of an act to the end, if end there is. Again, however, we may trace it part of the way. A murder at Serajevo may be the necessary antecedent to an assassination in London twenty years hence. An overturned lantern may burn all Chicago. We may follow the fire from the shed to the last building. We rightly say the fire started by the lantern caused its destruction.

A cause, but not the proximate cause. What we do mean by the word "proximate" is that, because of convenience, of public policy, of a rough sense of justice, the law arbitrarily declines to trace a series of events beyond a certain point. This is not logic. It is practical politics. Take our rule as to fires. Sparks from my burning haystack set on fire my house and my neighbor's. I may recover from a negligent railroad. He may not. Yet the wrongful act as directly harmed the one as the other. We may regret that the line was drawn just where it was, but drawn somewhere it had to be. We said the act of the railroad was not the proximate cause of our neighbor's fire. Cause it surely was. The words we used were simply indicative of our notions of public policy. Other courts think differently. But somewhere they reach the point where they cannot say the stream comes from any one source.

Take the illustration given in an unpublished manuscript by a distinguished and helpful writer on the law of torts. A chauffeur negligently collides with another car which is filled with dynamite, although he could not know it. An explosion follows. A, walking on the sidewalk nearby, is killed. B, sitting in a window of a building opposite, is cut by flying glass. C, likewise sitting in a window a block away, is similarly injured. And a further illustration: A nursemaid, ten blocks away, startled by the noise, involuntarily drops a baby from her arms to the walk. We are told that C may not recover while A may. As to B it is a question for court or jury. We will all agree that the baby might not. Because, we are again told, the chauffeur had no reason to believe his conduct involved any risk of injuring either C or the baby. As to them he was not negligent.

But the chauffeur, being negligent in risking the collision, his belief that the scope of the harm he might do would be limited is immaterial. His act unreasonably jeopardized the safety of any one who might be affected by it. C's injury and that of the baby were directly traceable to the collision. Without that, the injury would not have happened. C had the right to sit in his office, secure from such dangers. The baby was entitled to use the sidewalk with reasonable safety.

The true theory is, it seems to me, that the injury to C, if in truth he is to be denied recovery, and the injury to the baby, is that their several injuries were not the proximate result of the negligence. And here not what the chauffeur had reason to believe would be the result of his conduct, but what the prudent would foresee, may have a bearing — may have some bearing, for the problem of proximate cause is not to be solved by any one consideration. It is all a question of expediency. There are no fixed rules to govern our judgment. There are simply matters of which we may take account. We have in a somewhat different connection spoken of "the stream of events." We have asked whether that stream was deflected — whether it was forced into new and unexpected channels. . . . This is rather rhetoric than law. There is in truth little to guide us other than common sense.

There are some hints that may help us. The proximate cause, involved as it may be with many other causes, must be, at the least, something without which the event would not happen. The court must ask itself whether there was a natural and continuous sequence between cause and effect. Was the one a substantial factor in producing the other? Was there a direct connection between them, without too many intervening causes? Is the effect of cause on result not too attenuated? Is the cause likely, in the usual judgment of mankind, to produce the result? Or, by the exercise of prudent foresight, could the result be foreseen? Is the result too remote from the cause, and here we consider remoteness in time and space? . . . Clearly we must so consider, for the greater the distance either in time or space, the more surely do other causes intervene to affect the result. When a lantern is overturned, the firing of a shed is a fairly direct consequence. Many things contribute to the spread of the conflagration — the force of the wind, the direction and width of streets, the character of intervening structures, other factors. We draw an uncertain and wavering line, but draw it we must as best we can.

Once again, it is all a question of fair judgment, always keeping in mind the fact that we endeavor to make a rule in each case that will be practical and in keeping with the general understanding of mankind.

Here another question must be answered. In the case supposed, it is said, and said correctly, that the chauffeur is liable for the direct effect of the explosion, although he had no reason to suppose it would follow a collision. "The fact that the injury occurred in a different manner than that which might have been expected does not prevent the chauffeur's negligence from being in law the cause of the injury." But the natural results of a negligent act — the results which a prudent man would or should foresee — do have a bearing upon the decision as to proximate cause. We have said so repeatedly. What should be foreseen? No human foresight would suggest that a collision itself might injure one a block away. On the contrary, given an explosion, such a possibility might be reasonably expected. I think the direct connection, the foresight of which the courts speak, assumes prevision of the explosion, for the immediate results of which, at least, the chauffeur is responsible.

If may be said this is unjust. Why? In fairness he should make good every injury flowing from his negligence. Not because of tenderness toward him we say he need not answer for all that follows his wrong. We look back to the catastrophe, the fire kindled by the spark, or the explosion. We trace the consequences, not indefinitely, but to a certain point. And to aid us in fixing that point we ask what might ordinarily be expected to follow the fire or the explosion.

This last suggestion is the factor which must determine the case before us. The act upon which defendant's liability rests is knocking an apparently harmless package onto the platform. The act was negligent. For its proximate consequences the defendant is liable. If its contents were broken, to the owner; if it fell upon and crushed a passenger's foot, then to him; if it exploded and injured one in the immediate vicinity, to him also as to A in the illustration. Mrs. Palsgraf was standing some distance away. How far cannot be told from the record — apparently 25 or 30 feet, perhaps less. Except for the explosion, she would not have been injured. We are told by the appellant in his brief, "It cannot be denied that the explosion was the direct cause of the plaintiff's injuries." So it was a substantial factor in producing the result — there was here a natural and continuous sequence — direct connection. The only intervening cause was that, instead of blowing her to the ground, the concussion smashed the weighing machine which in turn fell upon her. There was no remoteness in time, little in space. And surely, given such an explosion as here, it needed no great foresight to predict that the natural result would be to injure one on the platform at no greater distance from its scene than was the plaintiff. Just how no one might be able to predict. Whether by flying fragments, by broken glass, by wreckage of machines or structures no one could say. But injury in some form was most probable.

Under these circumstances I cannot say as a matter of law that the plaintiff's injuries were not the proximate result of the negligence. That is all we have before us. The court refused to so charge. No request was made to submit the matter to the jury as a question of fact, even would that have been proper upon the record before us.

The judgment appealed from should be affirmed, with costs.

NOTES

1. Try to articulate the limitation on the scope of liability that the majority constructs here. Consider:

   a. What was the negligent conduct of the railroad employees, and why was it negligent?

   b. Was the negligent conduct of the railroad employees the direct cause of the harm to Mrs. Palsgraf?

   c. On what basis might you argue that the railroad owed a duty to Mrs. Palsgraf? Why does the majority conclude that no duty was owed?

2. Does this new limitation, when used with the direct cause test, solve the problems of the direct cause test? Consider how the new limitation would apply in the problems that follow the *Polemis* case, above.

3. Does the dissent by Judge Andrews help to resolve the problems of the direct cause test? What is Judge Andrews' approach and how would it resolve the problems that follow the *Polemis* case?

4. How would the analysis of the *Palsgraf* case work if the plaintiff had asserted that the railroad was negligent for failing to secure the scale properly? Does the railroad owe a duty to Mrs. Palsgraf?

PROBLEMS

1. Driver approached an intersection at an excessive speed. The intersection was controlled by a traffic light, which turned red as Driver approached. Driver attempted to stop, but could not because of the excessive speed. Driver lost control of the car, which skidded off the road and smashed into a public utility box located near the intersection. The box was the master controller for the traffic lights in the area, and by smashing it Driver knocked out of operation all the traffic lights within a three-mile radius.

    a. The loss of the traffic lights causes confusion at the intersection where Driver lost control. Passenger is hurt in a collision that occurs when two cars try to go through the uncontrolled intersection at the same time. Assume that both cars involved in this second collision were in the vicinity when Driver lost control and smashed the signal controller. How would the analysis of the *Palsgraf* majority apply to these facts? The dissent?

    b. Suppose that Passenger was injured in a collision that occurred hours (or days) later, although still attributable to the confusion caused by the loss of the traffic signals. How does the *Palsgraf* analysis apply now? Suppose the collision occurs at an intersection three miles away from the point where driver hit the controller, though still attributable, as before, to the loss of the traffic signals? *Cf. Ferroggiaro v. Bowline*, 153 Cal. App. 2d 759 (1957).

2. Consider a variation on the facts of the *Palsgraf* case. It is the summer following the Court of Appeals' ruling in the case. Mrs. Palsgraf and her daughters again decide to travel to Long Island. They are standing on the same platform, waiting for the same train (although keeping a safe distance from the scale). With an eerie sense of deja vu, they see two men running to catch a train that has begun to pull out of the station. One of the men is carrying a package wrapped in newspaper. The first man gets on the train safely. The other, carrying the package, is holding on to the moving train with one hand and struggling to get a footing on the entry platform of the train car. The conductor, having learned from the prior experience what to do, grabs the package from the man and goes inside to lay it carefully down. This causes its owner to lose his footing, and he is now in danger of falling from the train, which is rapidly gaining speed. Seeing the danger, one of Mrs. Palsgraf's daughters sprints to the res-

cue. She is able to catch up to the train and push the passenger inside to safety, but in so doing she falls and injures her leg.

    a. The Palsgrafs ask you to represent them in another action against the Long Island Railroad. You can see that the conductor probably exposed the passenger to an unreasonable risk of injury by rescuing only the package and not making sure that the passenger got safely aboard. The problem, again, will be duty. The conductor's negligence did not appear to create any risks to the Palsgrafs standing "many feet away." However, your research uncovers an earlier New York Court of Appeals decision, also, curiously enough, written by Judge Cardozo. In *Wagner v. International Railway Co.*, 133 N.E. 437 (N.Y. 1921), the plaintiff was injured while trying to find and rescue his cousin who had fallen from a passenger train while it was passing over a trestle or bridge. The cousin fell off as the result of the negligence of the railroad's employees in not closing the door of the train. The plaintiff looked for his cousin on the bridge and was injured when he, too, fell. "The trial judge held that negligence toward the cousin would not charge the defendant with liability for injuries suffered by the plaintiff unless two other facts were found: First, that the plaintiff had been invited by the conductor to go upon the bridge; and, second, that the conductor had followed with a light." (Conflicting evidence had been presented on whether or not the conductor had done so.) So instructed, the jury returned a verdict for the railroad. The New York Court of Appeals, per Judge Cardozo, found that the instructions were incorrect, and stated:

> Danger invites rescue. The cry of distress is the summons to relief. The law does not ignore these reactions of the mind in tracing conduct to its consequences. It recognizes them as normal. It places their effects within the range of the natural and probable. The wrong that imperils life is a wrong to the imperiled victim; it is a wrong also to his rescuer. The state that leaves an opening in a bridge is liable to the child that falls into the stream, but liable also to the parent who plunges to its aid. . . . The railroad company whose train approaches without signal is a wrongdoer toward the traveler surprised between the rails, but a wrongdoer also to the bystander who drags him from the path. . . . The risk of rescue, if only it be not wanton, is born of the occasion. The emergency begets the man. The wrongdoer may not have foreseen the coming of a deliverer. He is accountable as if he had.

Does *Wagner* survive the decision in *Palsgraf*? It was not even cited in either of the *Palsgraf* opinions. Or, has the duty analysis of *Palsgraf*, with its emphasis on the relational aspects of negligence, effectively overruled the earlier case? Would you accept this representation?

b. Before deciding whether to accept the representation of the Pals-
grafs, consider another aspect of the situation: Given the ruling in the
earlier *Palsgraf* case, would it be an ethical violation to bring the new
lawsuit? The ABA Model Rules provide as follows:

Rule 3.1: Meritorious Claims and Contentions

A lawyer shall not bring or defend a proceeding, or assert or con-
trovert an issue therein, unless there is a basis for doing so
that is not frivolous, which includes a good faith argument for
an extension, modification or reversal of existing law. A lawyer
for the defendant in a criminal proceeding, or the respondent in
a proceeding that could result in incarceration, may nevertheless so defend the proceedings as to require that every element
of the case be established.

Could you persuasively argue that the new *Palsgraf* suit was not frivolous?
How would you do so? Would you be arguing for a reversal of the position taken
in *Palsgraf*? Is there any way to reconcile the *Wagner* and *Palsgraf* cases?

3. If *Wagner* and *Palsgraf* are somehow reconciled, how should the following
problems be resolved?

a. Defendant Driver negligently struck Victim with her automobile,
breaking his leg. Victim had to wear a large, heavy cast on the leg
while it healed. Shortly thereafter, torrential rains caused a dangerous flood in the area where Victim lived. Victim was trapped in his
house, since he could neither swim nor walk through the raging
floodwaters with the cast on his leg. Neighbor tried to carry Victim
to safety, but the flood swept them both away and they drowned.
Should Driver be liable for the deaths of either Victim or Neighbor?

b. Defendant Driver negligently struck Pedestrian with his automobile. The collision severely damaged both of Pedestrian's kidneys,
which had to be removed. As a result, Pedestrian required a kidney
transplant. Plaintiff, a cousin of Pedestrian, was found to be a potential kidney donor and agreed to donate a kidney. The transplant
operation was performed successfully. Of course, Driver is liable for
Pedestrian's injuries, but is he also liable for the injuries to Plaintiff,
who now has suffered the pain of a major surgery and the loss of one
kidney? Is Plaintiff a "rescuer" under *Wagner*, or an unforeseeable
plaintiff as in *Palsgraf*?

D. FORESEEABILITY AND THE RISK RULE

OVERSEAS TANKSHIP (U.K.), LTD. v. MORTS DOCK & ENGINEERING CO., LTD. (THE WAGON MOUND)
Privy Council, 1961
[1961] A.C. 388, 1 All ER 404, 2 WLR 126

[Appeal] from an order of the Full Court of the Supreme Court of New South Wales . . . dismissing an appeal by the appellants, Overseas Tankship (U.K.), Ltd., from a judgment of Kinsella, J. . . . [I]n the action, the respondents sought to recover from the appellants compensation for the damage which its property, known as the Sheerlegs Wharf in Sydney Harbour and the equipment thereon, had suffered by reason of fire which broke out on Nov. 1, 1951. For this damage they claimed that the appellants were, in law, responsible. . . .

The respondents at the relevant time carried on the business of ship-building, ship-repairing and general engineering at Morts Bay, Balmain, in the Port of Sydney. They owned and used for their business the Sheerlegs Wharf, a timber wharf about four hundred feet in length and forty feet wide, where there was a quantity of tools and equipment. In October and November, 1951, a vessel known as the *Corrimal* was moored alongside the wharf and was being refitted by the respondents. Her mast was lying on the wharf and a number of the respondents' employees were working both on it and on the vessel itself, using for this purpose electric and oxy-acetylene welding equipment.

At the same time, the appellants were charterers by demise of the *s.s. Wagon Mound*, an oil-burning vessel which was moored at the Caltex Wharf on the northern shore of the harbour at a distance of about six hundred feet from the Sheerlegs Wharf. She was there from about 9 a.m. on Oct. 29, until 11 a.m. on Oct. 30, 1951, for the purpose of discharging gasolene products and taking in bunkering oil.

During the early hours of Oct. 30, 1951, a large quantity of bunkering oil was, through the carelessness of the appellants' servants, allowed to spill into the bay, and, by 10.30 on the morning of that day, it had spread over a considerable part of the bay, being thickly concentrated in some places and particularly along the foreshore near the respondents' property. The appellants made no attempt to disperse the oil. The *Wagon Mound* unberthed and set sail very shortly after.

When the respondents' works manager became aware of the condition of things in the vicinity of the wharf, he instructed their workmen that no welding or burning was to be carried on until further orders. He inquired of the manager of the Caltex Oil Co., at whose wharf the *Wagon Mound* was then still berthed, whether they could safely continue their operations on the wharf or on the *Corrimal*. The results of this inquiry, coupled with his own belief as to the inflammability of furnace oil in the open, led him to think that the respondents could safely carry on their operations. He gave instructions accordingly, but directed that all safety precautions should be taken to prevent inflammable material falling off the wharf into the oil.

For the remainder of Oct. 30 and until about 2 p.m. on Nov. 1, work was carried on as usual, the condition and congestion of the oil remaining substantially unaltered. But at about that time the oil under or near the wharf was ignited and a fire, fed initially by the oil, spread rapidly and burned with great intensity. The wharf and the *Corrimal* caught fire and considerable damage was done to the wharf and the equipment on it.

The outbreak of fire was due, as the learned judge found, to the fact that there was floating in the oil underneath the wharf a piece of debris on which lay some smouldering cotton waste or rag which had been set on fire by molten metal falling from the wharf; that the cotton waste or rag burst into flames; that the flames from the cotton waste set the floating oil afire either directly or by first setting fire to a wooden pile coated with oil and that, after the floating oil became ignited, the flames spread rapidly over the surface of the oil and quickly developed into a conflagration which severely damaged the wharf.

1961. January 18. The judgment of their Lordships was delivered by Viscount Simonds, who stated the facts set out above and continued: The trial judge also made the all-important finding, which must be set out in his own words: "The raison d'etre of furnace oil is, of course, that it shall burn, but I find the [appellants] did not know and could not reasonably be expected to have known that it was capable of being set afire when spread on water." This finding was reached after a wealth of evidence which included that of a distinguished scientist, Professor Hunter. It receives strong confirmation from the fact that, at the trial, the respondents strenuously maintained that the appellants had discharged petrol into the bay on no other ground than that, as the spillage was set alight, it could not be furnace oil. An attempt was made before their Lordships' Board to limit in some way the finding of fact, but it is clear that it was intended to cover precisely the event that happened.

One other finding must be mentioned. The learned judge held that, apart from damage by fire, the respondents had suffered some damage from the spillage of oil in that it had got on their slipways and congealed on them and interfered with their use of the slips. He said: "The evidence of this damage is slight and no claim for compensation is made in respect of it. Nevertheless it does establish some damage, which may be insignificant in comparison with the magnitude of the damage by fire, but which nevertheless is damage which beyond question was a direct result of the escape of the oil." It is on this footing that their Lordships will consider the question whether the appellants are liable for the fire damage. . . .

It is inevitable that first consideration should be given to *Re Polemis and Furness, Withy & Co., Ltd.* which will henceforward be referred to as *Polemis*. For it was avowedly in deference to that decision and to decisions of the Court of

Appeal that followed it that the full court was constrained to decide the present case in favour of the respondents. . . .

What, then, did *Polemis* decide? . . . [I]t is clear . . . that, before Sankey, J., and the Court of Appeal, the case proceeded as one in which, independently of contractual obligations, the claim was for damages for negligence. It was on this footing that the Court of Appeal held that the charterers were responsible for all the consequences of their negligent act, even though those consequences could not reasonably have been anticipated. The negligent act was nothing more than the carelessness of stevedores (for whom the charterers were assumed to be responsible) in allowing a sling or rope by which it was hoisted to come into contact with certain boards, causing one of them to fall into the hold. The falling board hit some substances in the hold and caused a spark; the spark ignited petrol vapour in the hold; there was a rush of flames and the ship was destroyed. The Special Case submitted by the arbitrators found that the causing of the spark could not reasonably have been anticipated from the falling of the board, though some damage to the ship might reasonably have been anticipated. They did not indicate what damage might have been so anticipated.

There can be no doubt that the decision of the Court of Appeal in *Polemis* plainly asserts that, if the defendant is guilty of negligence, he is responsible for all the consequences, whether reasonably foreseeable or not. The generality of the proposition is, perhaps, qualified by the fact that each of the lords justices refers to the outbreak of fire as the direct result of the negligent act. There is thus introduced the conception that the negligent actor is not responsible for consequences which are not "direct", whatever that may mean. It has to be asked, then, why this conclusion should have been reached. The answer appears to be that it was reached on a consideration of certain authorities, comparatively few in number, that were cited to the court. . . . [Discussion of the precedents relied upon in *Polemis* is omitted.]

Before turning to the cases that succeeded it, it is right to glance at yet another aspect of the decision in *Polemis*. Their Lordships, as they have said, assume that the court purported to propound the law in regard to tort. But up to that date it had been universally accepted that the law in regard to damages for breach of contract and for tort was, generally speaking, and particularly in regard to the tort of negligence, the same. Yet *Hadley v. Baxendale* was not cited in argument nor referred to in the judgments in *Polemis*. This is the more surprising when it is remembered that, in that case, as in many another case, the claim was laid alternatively in breach of contract and in negligence. If the claim for breach of contract had been pursued, the charterers could not have been held liable for consequences not reasonably foreseeable. It is not strange that Sir Frederick Pollock said that Blackburn and Willes, JJ., would have been shocked beyond measure by the decision that the charterers were liable in tort: see Pollock On Torts, 15th Ed., p. 29. Their Lordships refer to this aspect of the matter not because they wish to assert that in all respects today the measure of damages is in all cases the same in tort and in breach of contract, but because it emphasises how far *Polemis* was out of the current of contemporary thought. The acceptance of the rule in *Polemis* as applicable to all cases of tort would directly conflict with the view theretofore generally held.

Enough has been said to show that the authority of *Polemis* has been severely shaken, though lip-service has from time to time been paid to it. In their Lordships' opinion, it should no longer be regarded as good law. It is not probable that many cases will for that reason have a different result, though it is hoped that the law will be thereby simplified, and that, in some cases at least, palpable injustice will be avoided. For it does not seem consonant with current ideas of justice or morality that, for an act of negligence, however slight or venial, which results in some trivial foreseeable damage, the actor should be liable for all consequences, however unforeseeable and however grave, so long as they can be said to be "direct". It is a principle of civil liability, subject only to qualifications which have no present relevance, that a man must be considered to be responsible for the probable consequences of his act. To demand more of him is too harsh a rule, to demand less is to ignore that civilised order requires the observance of a minimum standard of behaviour.

This concept, applied to the slowly developing law of negligence has led to a great variety of expressions which can, as it appears to their Lordships, be harmonised with little difficulty with the single exception of the so-called rule in *Polemis*. For, if it is asked why a man should be responsible for the natural or necessary or probable consequences of his act (or any other similar description of them), the answer is that it is not because they are natural or necessary or probable, but because, since they have this quality, it is judged, by the standard of the reasonable man, that he ought to have foreseen them. Thus it is that, over and over again, it has happened that, in different judgments in the same case and sometimes in a single judgment, liability for a consequence has been imposed on the ground that it was reasonably foreseeable, or alternatively on the ground that it was natural or necessary or probable. The two grounds have been treated as conterminous, and so they largely are. But, where they are not, the question arises to which the wrong answer was given in *Polemis*. For, if some limitation must be imposed on the consequences for which the negligent actor is to be held responsible — and all are agreed that some limitation there must be — why should that test (reasonable foreseeability) be rejected which, since he is judged by what the reasonable man ought to foresee, corresponds with the common conscience of mankind, and a test (the "direct" consequence) be substituted which leads to nowhere but the never ending and insoluble problems of causation. "The lawyer" said Sir Frederick Pollock "cannot afford to adventure himself with philosophers in the logical and metaphysical controversies that beset the idea of cause." Yet this is just what he has most unfortunately done and must continue to do if the rule in *Polemis* is to prevail. . . .

In the same connection may be mentioned the conclusion to which the full court finally came in the present case. Applying the rule in *Polemis* and holding, therefore, that the unforeseeability of the damage by fire afforded no defence, they went on to consider the remaining question. Was it a "direct" consequence? On this, Manning, J., said: "Notwithstanding that, if regard is had separately to each individual occurrence in the chain of events that led to this fire, each occurrence was improbable and, in one sense, improbability was heaped upon improbability, I cannot escape from the conclusion that if the ordinary man in the street had been asked, as a matter of common sense, without any detailed analysis of the circumstances, to state the cause of the fire at Morts Dock, he would unhesitatingly have assigned such cause to spillage of oil by the appellants' employees." Perhaps he would, and probably he would have added "I never should have thought it possible." But, with great respect to the full court, this is surely irrelevant, or, if it is relevant, only serves to show that the *Polemis* rule works in a very strange way. After the event even a fool is wise. Yet it is not the hindsight of a fool, but it is the foresight of the reasonable man which alone can determine responsibility. The *Polemis* rule, by substituting "direct" for "reasonably foreseeable" consequence, leads to a conclusion equally illogical and unjust. . . .

It is, no doubt, proper when considering tortious liability for negligence to analyse its elements and to say that the plaintiff must prove a duty owed to him by the defendant, a breach of that duty by the defendant, and consequent damage. But there can be no liability until the damage has been done. It is not the act but the consequences on which tortious liability is founded. Just as (as it has been said) there is no such thing as negligence in the air, so there is no such thing as liability in the air. Suppose an action brought by A for damage caused by the carelessness (a neutral word) of B, for example a fire caused by the careless spillage of oil. It may, of course, become relevant to know what duty B owed to A, but the only liability that is in question is the liability for damage by fire. It is vain to isolate the liability from its context and to say that B is or is not liable, and then to ask for what damage he is liable. For his liability is in respect of that damage and no other. If, as admittedly it is, B's liability (culpability) depends on the reasonable foreseeability of the consequent damage, how is that to be determined except by the foreseeability of the damage which in fact happened — the damage in suit? And, if that damage is unforeseeable so as to displace liability at large, how can the liability be restored so as to make compensation payable?

But, it is said, a different position arises if B's careless act has been shown to be negligent and has caused some foreseeable damage to A. Their Lordships have already observed that to hold B liable for consequences, however unforeseeable, of a careless act, if, but only if, he is at the same time liable for some other damage, however trivial, appears to be neither logical nor just. This becomes more clear if it is supposed that similar unforeseeable damage is suffered by A and C, but other foreseeable damage, for which B is liable, by A only. A system of law which would hold B liable to A but not to C for the similar damage suffered by each of them could not easily be defended. Fortunately, the attempt is not necessary. For the same fallacy is at the root of the proposition. It is irrelevant to the question whether B is liable for unforeseeable damage that he is liable for foreseeable damage, as irrelevant as would the fact that he had trespassed on Whiteacre be to the question whether he had trespassed on Blackacre. Again, suppose a claim by A for damage by fire by the careless act of B. Of what relevance is it to that claim that he has another claim arising out of the same careless act? It would surely not prejudice his claim if that other claim failed; it cannot assist it if it succeeds. Each of them rests on its own bottom and will fail if it can be established that the damage could not reasonably be foreseen. . . .

Their Lordships will humbly advise Her Majesty that this appeal should be allowed and the respondents' action so far as it related to damage caused by the negligence of the appellants be dismissed with costs but that the action so far as it related to damage caused by nuisance should be remitted to the full court to be dealt with as that court may think fit. The respondents must pay the costs of the appellants of this appeal and in the courts below.

NOTES AND QUESTIONS

1. What was wrong, according to this opinion, with the rule of the *Polemis* case? What is the new rule and how does it correct the problems created by *Polemis*?

2. The opinion makes reference to the famous case of *Hadley v. Baxendale*, 9 Exch. 341 (1854), which involved the damages recoverable for breach of a contract. In that case the owner of a mill contracted with a carrier to transport the broken mill shaft of the mill to London so that a replacement could be made. The carrier promised to transport the broken shaft within one day but failed to perform. As a result, the mill was shut down for several days and the operator sustained losses as a result. The mill operator attempted to recover this loss as damage for the breach of the contract. The court refused to allow such damages, limiting recovery in contract to those damages that would usually be anticipated in the normal course of things, as well as those additional losses that were contemplated by the parties at the time of contracting. Is this in fact the same type of foreseeability limitation that was adopted in *Wagon Mound*? While this type of damage limitation is often thought applicable primarily to contract damages, it has also shown up in some recent tort cases as well, especially those dealing with economic losses. *Cf. Evra Corp. v. Swiss Bank Corp.*, 673 F.2d 951 (7th Cir. 1982).

3. The risk rule makes all the elements of the negligence cause of action interrelate closely. We have already seen that the test of cause in fact requires us to examine the negligent aspect of the defendant's conduct — that is, the conduct that constitutes the breach of duty. When proximate cause is addressed in terms of the risk rule we again go back to the duty and breach and try to determine the type of unreasonable risk of harm that the defendant has imposed on the plaintiff, in order to determine whether the harm the plaintiff has suffered is "within the risk." As will be seen, the application of the test will vary depend-

ing upon what conduct is focused upon as negligent, and the type of risks that negligent conduct creates.

4. An example of how the test is supposed to work is suggested by an illustration adapted from the Second Restatement of Torts, section 281: Suppose Defendant gives a large, heavy, loaded handgun to a small child. (Negligent? Why?) The child, as expected, handles the gun clumsily and drops it. The gun crushes the toe of D, and the impact causes it to go off. The bullet strikes and wounds C. According to the Restatement, Defendant would be liable for the wounding of C but not the crushed toe of D.

5. Under the risk rule, it is important to characterize the risks imposed by the defendant's negligent conduct. Note how this issue appears in the *Wagon Mound* opinion above: "The trial judge also made the all-important finding, which must be set out in his own words: 'The raison d'etre of furnace oil is, of course, that it shall burn, but I find the [appellants] did not know and could not reasonably be expected to have known that it was capable of being set afire when spread on water.'" Apparently the claimants did not dispute the basic correctness of this finding of fact. Consider why they may not have done so. Consider also why, if no foreseeable risk of fire existed, the conduct was negligent at all. What unreasonable risk of harm was created?

6. If the fact finding on the foreseeable risks is changed, the result of the risk rule analysis may change as well. That is what happened in another case arising out of the same fire as the *Wagon Mound* case, above. In *Overseas Tankship (U.K.), Ltd. v. Miller Steamship Co. (Wagon Mound No. 2)*, [1967] 1 A.C. 617, the owners of the Corrimal, the ship that was under repair at Mort's Dock, also sought compensation for the damage caused by the oil fire. In contrast to the finding of the first case, the trial court here seemed to find that the foreseeable risk of fire from furnace oil floating on the water was slight, but not non-existent. And once the risk of fire becomes foreseeable, the result (fire) is by definition within the risk. Of course if the risk was in fact so slight, it might not have represented an *unreasonable* risk by itself. To find the defendants negligent in pouring the bunkering oil into the harbor, the court noted that the defendants could offer no justification for dumping the oil in the harbor, since the loss of the fuel oil was a loss and not a benefit to the ship. Therefore the defendants were negligent in disregarding even this small risk of harm.

7. There is a close correspondence between the risk rule and the rule of negligence per se, which limits the use of statutes to establish the standard of care to situations in which the plaintiff was a member of the class that the statute was intended to protect, and suffered the type of harm that the statute was intended to prevent.

PROBLEMS

1. Defendant, who operated a coffee shop, stored a container of rat poison, containing strychnine, next to a coffee burner. This conduct violated a statute that made it a misdemeanor to store strychnine or other poisons except in a safe place. The poison, unknown to defendant, also contained phosphorous. The heat of the coffee burner caused the poison to explode, injuring the plaintiff. Under the rule of negligence per se, would the defendant be liable for the plaintiff's injuries? *Cf. Larrimore v. American National Insurance Co.*, 89 P.2d 340 (Okla. 1939).

2. Assume the same facts given in Problem 1, above, except that no statute in force prohibits the storage of poison next to the coffee burner. How would your analysis proceed? Would your conclusions change?

3. Defendant Utility employees were repairing an underground telephone cable. When they took a dinner break, they left the access hole open, but covered it with a small tent and set four kerosene lamps around the area as a warning. Plaintiffs, aged eight and ten, decided to explore the access hole while the workers were away. They took one of the lamps down with them as they explored. Upon returning to the street level, one of the Plaintiffs tripped over the lamp, which fell into the hole. There followed an explosion from the hole with flames reaching over thirty feet high. With the explosion, one of the Plaintiffs fell into the hole and sustained severe burns. Evidence indicated that kerosene lamps are relatively safe, although some danger obviously exists if one touches the burning wick while handling it. Normally, kerosene would not explode. The explosion following the fall of the lamp down the hole was termed a low probability event caused by the kerosene escaping from the tank, turning into vapor, and the vapor exploding upon contact with the burning wick.

   a. As counsel for the Plaintiffs, how would you attempt to describe the following issues to the court:

     • Were the Defendants negligent, and if so, what unreasonable risks of harm did the Defendants' conduct create?

     • Was the harm that occurred foreseeable? Was it within the risk created by the Defendants' negligent conduct?

   b. As counsel for the Defendants, how would you attempt to describe the same issues? You might, of course, attempt to argue that the Defendants committed no negligence at all. But even if negligence must be conceded, could you describe the negligence and the resulting injury in such a way that the harm would not be within the risk? *Cf. Hughes v. Lord Advocate*, [1963] A.C. 837 (H.L.).

4. Defendant Manufacturing Company, as part of its processes, maintained a facility called the heat treatment room. In this room special containers held liquid sodium cyanide at a temperature of 800° F. Asbestos cement covers were

used to help retain the heat in these containers. One day while Plaintiff was standing near one of the containers, a worker accidentally bumped the cover, which fell into the liquid cyanide. Fortunately, as it seemed, the cover slipped into the 800° F liquid without splashing on the Plaintiff or other workers standing nearby. About one minute later, however, the liquid erupted from the container, splashing the Plaintiff and causing severe burns. Experiments later proved that the reason for the eruption was that the asbestos cement used in the cover contained hydrogen and oxygen. When heated to 800° F, the hydrogen and oxygen combined to form water, which turned into steam, which then caused the eruption of the cyanide from the container. Before the incident, no one had known that such an accident was possible.

    a. As counsel for the Plaintiff, how would you attempt to describe the following issues to the court:

- Were the Defendant's employees negligent, and if so, what unreasonable risks of harm did their conduct create?

- Was the harm that occurred foreseeable? Was it within the risk created by the employees' negligent conduct?

    b. As counsel for the Defendant, how would you attempt to describe the same issues? You might, of course, attempt to argue that the Defendant committed no negligence at all. But even if negligence must be conceded, could you describe the negligence and the resulting injury in such a way that the harm would not be within the risk? *Cf. Doughty v. Turner Manufacturing Co., Ltd.,* [1964] 1 Q.B. 518 (C.A. 1963).

    5. Defendant's ship was moored to a dock on the bank of a swiftly flowing river. Defendant negligently failed to secure the ship properly to the dock and it eventually became unmoored and began to drift out of control down the river. Many other docks and maritime businesses lined the river, and the Defendant's ship struck another moored vessel, causing it to become dislodged as well. Together, the two ships drifted into a drawbridge, which City employees had negligently failed to raise in time. The two ships wedged into the wreckage of the bridge and formed a kind of dam, which caused the river to back up and flood many of the riverside businesses.

    a. As above, consider how you would characterize the risks and results of the Defendant's negligence, as both counsel for the Defendant and as counsel for the victims of the flooding. *Cf. Petition of Kinsman Transit Co.,* 338 F.2d 708 (2d Cir. 1964) ("*Kinsman No. 1*").

    b. How would you characterize the case if the Plaintiffs were flood victims whose property was located *upstream* of the position where the Defendant's ship was moored? Do you see why it might make a difference whether the Plaintiffs' property were upstream or downstream of the position where the ship was moored?

    c. Would the thousands of individuals and businesses inconvenienced by the accident have any claim for damages? Consider the claims of shippers whose cargoes are delayed by the wreckage blocking the river, or the local residents put to greater expense for commuting because the bridge is out. *Cf. Petition of Kinsman Transit Co.*, 388 F.2d 821 (2d Cir. 1968) (*"Kinsman No. 2"*).

E. FORESEEABILITY AND THE EXTENT OF HARM

Should the risk rule limitation also apply to the extent of harm suffered by the plaintiff? If the plaintiff suffers greater harm than would have been foreseeable as resulting from the defendant's negligent conduct, should that additional harm be recoverable? This issue is known as the thin-skulled (or eggshell skulled) plaintiff problem, after the usual hypothetical of a plaintiff who suffers a blow to the head that would only foreseeably inflict a minor lump on the average person. The plaintiff's skull, which is eggshell thin, is fractured, resulting in much higher damages. Should the plaintiff's recovery be limited to the amount of harm that would be foreseeable?

STOLESON v. UNITED STATES
708 F.2d 1217 (7th Cir. 1983)

POSNER, Circuit Judge.

This appeal brings before us for the second time the celebrated case of Helen Stoleson and her "dynamite heart." *See, e.g.*, Time, July 12, 1971, at 41. The issues on appeal this time concern the causal relationship, if any, between the defendant's now conceded negligence and the symptoms that Mrs. Stoleson has continued to experience long after the elimination of their organic cause.

Mrs. Stoleson, now 64 years old, began working in a federal munitions plant in Wisconsin in 1967 as an employee of the contractor operating the plant. Within a few months she began experiencing the characteristic chest pains of coronary artery disease — but, oddly, only on weekends. One weekend in February 1968 the chest pains were so severe that she was hospitalized. She was diagnosed as having suffered either an actual heart attack (myocardial infarction) or an episode of coronary insufficiency (meaning that the coronary arteries were not supplying the heart with an adequate supply of blood). She returned to work shortly after this incident but continued having weekend chest pains with increasing frequency till she left the plant in 1971.

Her work at the plant required her to handle nitroglycerin and she became convinced that this was causing her heart problem. But the doctors she consulted rejected her theory until she came under the care of a Dr. Lange in 1971. He was convinced by her experience and that of several of her coworkers, who had similar symptoms, that excessive exposure to nitroglycerin had caused their coronary arteries to expand — much as nitroglycerin tablets given for the treatment of coronary artery disease do — and that the sudden withdrawal of nitroglycerin on the weekends had caused the arteries to contract violently. . . .

Mrs. Stoleson brought suit under the Federal Tort Claims Act . . . alleging that the government had been negligent in failing to protect the workers at the plant from excessive exposure to nitroglycerin. [T]he district judge found that the government had been negligent and that its negligence had caused Mrs. Stoleson's heart disease, and he awarded her $53,000 in damages. But he declined to award any damages for her psychosomatic illness after she left the plant, and she appeals.

Although Mrs. Stoleson's heart disease should have abated completely soon after she left the plant, her health at the time of the second trial was poor. She had chest pains, though not so acute as when she was working at the plant and not more frequent on weekends than at other times; she was often dizzy and short of breath, and easily fatigued; she had bouts of high blood pressure, and coughing spells leading to vomiting; she was extremely obese, having gained 100 pounds in 10 years; and she was unshakably convinced that her health was ruined and that she could no longer work full time. These complaints have no organic basis, unless it is her obesity. Her heart disease from nitroglycerin exposure did no medically significant lasting damage. Dr. Goldbloom, the psychiatrist who testified for her, diagnosed her condition as "hypochondriacal neurosis — what is more commonly referred to just as hypochondria — that had been induced by her heart disease at the plant, particularly the possible heart attack in February 1968, and that had been aggravated both by Dr. Lange's having incorrectly advised her that she had serious, permanent heart damage and by this lawsuit. (Lange did not testify; he died before the first trial.) Dr. Roberts, the psychiatrist who testified for the government, testified that Mrs. Stoleson was indeed a hypochondriac but had probably been one all her adult life.

The district judge found that "the matter of the hypochondriacal neurosis, the presence of which today is agreed upon by both experts, is difficult to resolve. Dr. Roberts seemed to me to be on shaky ground when, based upon his 1981 observations and the other information available to him, he undertook to testify that this neurosis existed prior to February, 1968. On the other hand, while intending no disrespect, Dr. Goldbloom seemed to me to be scrambling when he undertook to elevate the 1968 heart episode itself to the level of a substantial factor in causing the neurosis. I do not believe plaintiff met the burden of proof in this latter respect." The judge found that if Mrs. Stoleson had proved a causal linkage between the defendant's negligence and her neurotic symptoms, she would have been entitled to additional damages for lost earnings and for pain and suffering (physical and emotional) of $238,000. A predicate for this finding was the judge's view that these symptoms had begun no earlier than November 1975, when the first trial had ended. Mrs. Stoleson disagrees with this predicate but does not challenge the adequacy of the $238,000 damage figure.

The district judge's finding on causation presents an interpretive problem. It can be read to mean that he thought the important thing was whether Mrs. Stoleson's possible heart attack in February 1968, which was due to the government's negligence in failing to protect her from excessive exposure to nitroglycerin, had caused her hypochondria, and that if it had not she could not recover damages for her hypochondriacal illness. So read, the finding would be inconsistent with the "thin skull" or "eggshell skull" or "you take your victim as you find him" rule of the common law. The substantive law of Wisconsin is conceded to govern this case, . . . and, by an odd coincidence, what has come to be the leading case announcing the eggshell skull rule is a Wisconsin case, *Vosburg v. Putney*, 80 Wis. 523, 50 N.W. 403 (1891). . . . In *Vosburg*, one school boy kicked another in the shin, in circumstances that made the kicking a battery. The kick would not have seriously injured a normal person, but the victim had an infection in his tibia and the kick aggravated the infection, causing serious injury. The court held the defendant liable for the entire damages. Although we cannot find any modern eggshell skull cases from Wisconsin, the rule is so well established in tort . . . that the government would have a heavy burden of persuading us that Wisconsin has abandoned it, and as a matter of fact has made no effort to persuade us of this.

It would therefore make no difference to the extent of the government's liability that a normal person in Mrs. Stoleson's situation would have recovered her health completely once she found out that her heart disease had been caused by an environmental factor that had been eliminated before it could do any permanent damage. . . .

Even if the February 1968 episode did not trigger Mrs. Stoleson's hypochondriacal symptoms, the government might still be liable if the symptoms were triggered by Dr. Lange's having alarmed her, whether or not he committed professional malpractice in exaggerating the extent of her organic impairment. A principle distinct from that of Vosburg but equally the law in Wisconsin makes a tortfeasor liable for aggravation of the injury he inflicted, even aggravation brought about by the treatment — even the negligent treatment — of the injury by a third party. . . . If a pedestrian who has been run down by a car is taken to a hospital and because of the hospital's negligence incurs greater medical expenses or suffers more pain and suffering than he would have if the hospital had not been negligent, he can collect his incremental as well as his original damages from the person who ran him down, since they would have been avoided if that person had used due care. So here, if the government had been careful Mrs. Stoleson would have had no occasion to consult Dr. Lange and might therefore not have become a hypochondriac.

If we were persuaded that the district judge had misapplied any of these principles the logical course would be to remand the case for new findings, but we think an alternative reading of his findings on causation is not only possible but more plausible in light of the evidence: that he was unpersuaded that Mrs. Stoleson had established causation as a matter not of law but of fact. On this reading, when he referred to Mrs. Stoleson's "hypochondriacal neurosis" he meant her symptoms, not the underlying psychological condition on which a traumatic event might act to produce symptoms of ill health. This usage would not be surprising. Hypochondria is usually defined in terms of its symptoms rather than its underlying psychological structure, which anyway is not well understood. "Hypochondriasis is a term used to refer to a psychoneurotic pattern of overconcern and focusing of interest on sickness or bodily symptoms. . . ."

Mrs. Stoleson's counsel acknowledged at oral argument that it would be appropriate to require a plaintiff to prove by clear and convincing evidence that the defendant's negligence had caused hypochondriacal symptoms. We treat this acknowledgment not as a binding concession upon which to base decision of this appeal but as a recognition of the dangers of allowing proof of hypochondria to magnify the damages in personal injury suits. Since the physical symptoms of hypochondria have by definition no organic basis, and since so "little is known about the cause, nature, or effective treatment of hypochondria," the condition is impossible to diagnose with confidence. There is no way of verifying Mrs. Stoleson's claim that she has chest pains, or of confidently attributing them to hypochondria rather than to an undiagnosed physical condition. The claim invites the trier of fact to speculate. . . .

Without going so far as to hold that liability for hypochondria must be proved by clear and convincing evidence, we advise our district judges to approach such claims with the healthy skepticism necessary to prevent excessive and unfounded damage awards, bearing in mind that there is not much difficulty in finding a medical expert witness to testify to virtually any theory of medical causation short of the fantastic. . . .

Evaluated in light of these general considerations, the finding by the able and experienced district judge that Mrs. Stoleson failed to prove a causal linkage between the government's negligence and her present ill health must be affirmed. The testimony of both experts was speculative, neither having examined her before 1980 — nine years after she left the munitions plant. Dr. Goldbloom's testimony was also inconsistent. He began by saying, "I think that the whole thing started with a heart attack that she suffered in 1968," but then he said that the onset of her hypochondriacal symptoms "probably began sometime after Dr. Lange's death" in 1972. Dr. Goldbloom's uncertainty about the date of the onset allowed the district court to conclude that Mrs. Stoleson had not proved that it preceded the end of the first trial in November 1975. Hypochondria had not been so much as mentioned at the first trial, though the trial had taken place four years after she left the plant and she had put in her entire case on damages as well as liability before the suit was dismissed.

With the date of onset pushed forward to November 1975 or later it became a matter of conjecture whether Mrs. Stoleson's hypochondriacal illness really was the delayed consequence of a "dynamite heart" problem that ended in 1971 or whether it was the result of other stress factors, including the litigation itself, which Dr. Goldbloom testified had contributed to her continuing ill health.

It would be strange if stress induced by litigation could be attributed in law to the tortfeasor. An alleged tortfeasor should have the right to defend himself in court without thereby multiplying his damages more than five-fold — the damage multiple if Mrs. Stoleson prevails on this appeal.

There are other grounds for doubting whether the causal connection between the government's negligence and Mrs. Stoleson's present condition was proved. . . .

There is another reason for concluding that Mrs. Stoleson failed to carry her burden of proof. A companion principle to the eggshell skull rule, discussed in our recent decision in *Abernathy v. Superior Hardwoods, Inc.*, 704 F.2d 963 at 973 (7th Cir.1983), is that in calculating damages in an eggshell skull case the trier of fact must make an adjustment for the possibility that the preexisting condition would have resulted in harm to the plaintiff even if there had been no tort. The necessity for such an adjustment was argued in *Vosburg* although rejected on the facts. But in *Abernathy*, where the victim of a tortious back injury already had a back disease that might eventually have produced symptoms similar to those produced by the tortious injury, we held that this possibility had to be considered in calculating the victim's damages from the tort. We were interpreting Indiana law in that case but Wisconsin law is to the same effect. *See Helleckson v. Loiselle*, 37 Wis. 2d 423, 430, 155 N.W.2d 45, 49 (1967). If we assume, as the judge and both medical witnesses did, that Mrs. Stoleson has long been prone to exaggerate her health problems, it is likely that sooner or later some symptom unrelated to the defendant's misconduct would have triggered the neurosis and led to psychosomatic symptoms similar to those she is suffering from. Few people go through middle age without some health problems and a good deal of other stress. If Mrs. Stoleson was so vulnerable that a heart ailment from which she recovered completely, in circumstances that gave no rational basis for thinking it would recur, nevertheless caused the permanent and complete disability of which she complains, the chances are that some lesser trauma, highly likely for a woman of her age, would have caused some lesser disability; and the expected costs of this nontortious injury would have to be subtracted from the damages that she claims. She made no attempt to make this calculation. We do not question the district court's finding that the damages from her neurotic condition amount to $238,000, but not all of this amount can be attributed to the defendant's misconduct, and it was her burden to show what part could be. . . .

AFFIRMED.

NOTES AND QUESTIONS

1. The eggshell skull rule is well established. It eliminates the argument that the defendant need not pay for the full damage caused on the ground that it is unexpectedly severe. It does not, as the case above illustrates, eliminate all other causation-based arguments.

2. Does the "companion principle" that "in calculating damages in an eggshell skull case the trier of fact must make an adjustment for the possibility that the preexisting condition would have resulted in harm to the plaintiff even if there had been no tort" effectively take away what the eggshell skull rule purports to give?

3. The third principle introduced in this opinion is the rule that the original defendant will be liable for aggravation of the harm caused, for example, by medical malpractice in the course of treating the injury. This problem will be taken up more fully in the next section.

PROBLEMS

1. Driver negligently struck plaintiff's decedent, a cancer patient, with her car. Because of his weakened condition, the decedent did not survive the collision, although most persons in ordinary health would have been expected to do so. In calculating damages for the wrongful death, should any of the following facts make a difference in calculating the amount awarded?

    a. That the decedent was terminally ill and had less than one month to live.

    b. That the decedent was weakened by chemotherapy and his prognosis was uncertain, but patients with the type of cancer he had contracted had less than a 20% chance of surviving for five years.

    c. That the decedent was weakened by chemotherapy but was in remission from the cancer and had a good prospect for survival.

2. Defendant Driver negligently sideswiped the car in which Plaintiff was riding. Although Plaintiff suffered no physical injury from the collision, she was badly frightened and disturbed by the incident. This emotional upset worsened, until Plaintiff developed schizophrenia, paranoid type, and is now mentally disabled. Before the accident Plaintiff had been considered a bit odd in some ways, but certainly not mentally ill. It appears that the collision triggered the development of schizophrenia. Should the eggshell skull plaintiff rule apply to strictly mental injuries of this type? If so, how should the damages be calculated in this situation? Should the court consider evidence that the Plaintiff was predisposed to develop mental illness? *Cf. Steinhauser v. Hertz Corp.*, 421 F.2d 1169 (2d Cir. 1970); *Bartolone v. Jeckovich*, 481 N.Y.S.2d 545 (N.Y. App. Div. 1984).

F. FORESEEABILITY AND INTERVENING CAUSES

The final issue to be considered in this chapter concerns the proper treatment of what are called "intervening causes." The cases presenting this problem usually present the same general fact pattern. First, the defendant will act negligently. This negligent conduct may not immediately cause the plaintiff any harm at all. Instead, the negligence creates a dangerous situation or, more broadly, places the plaintiff in a position of vulnerability. Some other actor or force then comes into play to trigger the potential danger created by the defendant and to thereby cause injury to the plaintiff. This other actor or force is the intervening cause. The difficulty is to decide whether this intervening force is so extraordinary or so independent of the original negligent conduct that the defendant should be excused from liability. (If the intervening cause is deemed to be so significant that it excuses the defendant, it is referred to as a "superseding cause.")

HERMAN v. MARKHAM AIR RIFLE CO.
258 F. 475 (E.D. Mich 1918)

Tuttle, District Judge.

This matter comes before the court on a demurrer to the declaration in an action of trespass on the case. The declaration, which contains three counts, alleges in substance that the defendant, a resident of Michigan, is a manufacturer, dealer, and vendor of a certain air rifle known as the "King air rifle," and advertised by the defendant as a harmless instrument for the amusement of young persons and others; that the defendant so advertised, manufactured, and sold such air rifle in large quantities to the public, and thereby induced a belief in the minds of the public generally, and in the mind of the plaintiff, a resident of Illinois, that the same was harmless to handle and without danger to life or limb; that defendant sold a quantity of such rifles to a wholesale dealer in St. Louis, Mo., for the purpose, as was well known to the defendant, of resale to other dealers, and for the purpose of ultimately being handled in retail stocks and sold to individual customers; that it then and there became and was the duty of the defendant to use reasonable care to ship such air rifles not loaded and without any shot therein, but the defendant disregarded such duty, and negligently shipped to such wholesale dealer for such resale a certain air rifle loaded with shot; that such dealer, being unaware of the presence of such shot, resold the rifle to a certain retail dealer, who, being likewise ignorant of the fact that the rifle contained shot, placed the same in his stock and in charge of the plaintiff, who was employed as a stockkeeper and saleswoman in his store; that while this air rifle was so in charge of the plaintiff in such store it was handled by a certain prospective customer or visitor, who, believing that it was not loaded and was harmless, and being ignorant of the fact that it contained shot, proceeded to handle it and pulled the trigger, discharging said shot, which violently struck plaintiff, while she was exercising due care, and destroyed the sight of her right eye and endangered the sight of the other eye, so that it will probably be also lost, whereby plaintiff has suffered certain damages specifically claimed.

The three counts are identical, except that in the first count the negligence alleged consists in the careless shipment of the air rifle with the shot therein; in the second count the negligence charged is the failure to use reasonable care not to permit any shot to be placed and left in such air rifle, and the consequent negligent causing and permitting such shot to be so placed and left in the air rifle while it was being shipped; and in the third count the negligence counted on is the alleged failure to make proper examination and inspection of the air rifle, to ascertain that no shot had been placed or left therein before its shipment.

The demurrer sets forth several objections to the sufficiency, in law, of the declaration, which may be conveniently grouped . . . as follows: First, that such declaration does not allege any actionable negligence on the part of the defendant; second, that the facts therein stated fail to show that any negligence of the defendant was the proximate cause of the injury complained of. . . . These grounds will be considered in the order named.

1. It seems to me plain that the averments in the declaration just referred to sufficiently allege actionable negligence on the part of the defendant. . . . It seems to me too plain for argument that if the allegations in this declaration are true, and the defendant, after advertising this air rifle as a harmless instrument, loaded it with shot, or failed to use ordinary care to find and remove such shot, and then sold the rifle in this dangerous condition to a purchaser, who was without knowledge of the danger and believed, as the defendant must have known he would believe, that it was unloaded, and would naturally pass it on to some other person in that condition, the defendant did not exercise the care which an ordinarily prudent person would have exercised under such circumstances. . . . I have no doubt that the declaration alleges actionable negligence on the part of the defendant, and the contention to the contrary must be overruled.

2. It is urged by the defendant that, conceding that it was guilty of negligence as alleged, such negligence was not the proximate cause of the injury sustained by plaintiff. It is insisted that the act of the person who handled the air rifle, in causing it to be discharged at the plaintiff, was such an independent and intervening cause as to be the proximate cause of the injury, so that the original negligence, if any, of the defendant, became the remote cause of such injury.

I cannot agree with this contention. I think it clear that the circumstances surrounding the discharge of this weapon, and the consequent injury to the plaintiff, were what an ordinarily prudent person would and should expect to follow as a consequence of the act of placing upon the market this loaded gun. I am satisfied that the inflicting of this injury upon the plaintiff by the person mentioned, under the circumstances shown, was the natural and probable result of the negligence of the defendant, assuming that its acts in the premises constituted negligence. The mere fact that the act of the defendant did not directly and immediately cause this injury does not, of course, render such act any the less the proximate cause of such injury. It has been well settled, . . . that one who by his negligent act puts into operation a train of events which is likely to lead, in a continuous sequence, to an injury which is the natural and probable result of his original act, so that there is a natural causal connection between the two, is responsible for such injury, notwithstanding the fact that the latter may have been directly and immediately caused by the last link in this natural chain of events. . . . If, therefore, the defendant was guilty of negligence in shipping this loaded air rifle under the circumstances alleged, the act of this person in discharging the rifle at the plaintiff was only incidental to, and the natural and probable result of, such negligence, which was the proximate cause of the injury resulting.

Nor is the situation affected by the fact, if, as strenuously insisted by defendant, it be a fact, that the person actually discharging the rifle in question was also guilty of negligence in pulling the trigger without ascertaining whether the rifle was loaded, or in pointing it toward the plaintiff. [A]t most, such negligence would be merely a concurring cause of the injury, co-operating with the negligence of the defendant to produce it, and would not relieve defendant from liability therefor. . . .

For the reasons stated, an order will be entered overruling the demurrer and requiring the defendant to plead to the declaration within the usual time.

DERDIARIAN v. FELIX CONTRACTING CORP.
414 N.E.2d 666 (N.Y. 1980)

COOKE, Chief Judge.

[D]uring the fall of 1973 defendant Felix Contracting Corporation was performing a contract to install an underground gas main in the City of Mount Vernon for defendant Con Edison. Bayside Pipe Coaters, plaintiff Harold Derdiarian's employer, was engaged as a subcontractor to seal the gas main.

On the afternoon of November 21, 1973, defendant James Dickens suffered an epileptic seizure and lost consciousness, allowing his vehicle to careen into the work site and strike plaintiff with such force as to throw him into the air. When plaintiff landed, he was splattered over his face, head and body with 400 degree boiling hot liquid enamel from a kettle struck by the automobile. The enamel was used in connection with sealing the gas main. Although plaintiff's body ignited into a fire ball, he miraculously survived the incident.

At trial, plaintiff's theory was that defendant Felix had negligently failed to take adequate measures to insure the safety of workers on the excavation site. Plaintiff's evidence indicates that the accident occurred on Oak Street, a two-lane, east-west roadway. The excavation was located in the eastbound lane, and ran from approximately one foot south of the center line to within 2 or 3 feet of the curb. When plaintiff arrived on the site, he was instructed by Felix' foreman to park his truck on the west side of the excavation, parallel to the curb. As a result, there was a gap of some 7 1/2 feet between the side of the truck and the curb line. Derdiarian testified that he made a request to park his truck on the east side of the hole, so he could set up the kettle away from the oncoming eastbound traffic. The Felix foreman instructed him to leave his truck where it was, and plaintiff then put the kettle near the curb, on the west side of the excavation.

James Dickens was driving eastbound on Oak Street when he suffered a seizure and lost consciousness. Dickens was under treatment for epilepsy and had neglected to take his medication at the proper time. His car crashed through a single wooden horse-type barricade that was set up on the west side of the excavation site. As it passed through the site, the vehicle struck the kettle containing the enamel, as well as the plaintiff, resulting in plaintiff's injuries.

To support his claim of an unsafe work site, plaintiff called as a witness Lawrence Lawton, an expert in traffic safety. According to Lawton, the usual and accepted method of safeguarding the workers is to erect a barrier around the excavation. Such a barrier, consisting of a truck, a piece of heavy equipment or a pile of dirt, would keep a car out of the excavation and protect workers from oncoming traffic. The expert testified that the barrier should cover the entire width of the excavation. He also stated that there should have been two flagmen present, rather than one, and that warning signs should have been posted advising motorists that there was only one lane of traffic and that there was a flagman ahead.

Following receipt of the evidence, the trial court charged the jury, among other things, that it could consider, as some evidence of negligence, the violation of a Mount Vernon ordinance. The ordinance imposed upon a construction "permittee" certain safety duties. . . . The jury found for plaintiff, apportioning liability at 55% for Felix, 35% for Dickens and 10% for Con Ed. Defendant Felix now argues that plaintiff was injured in a freakish accident, brought about solely by defendant Dickens' negligence, and therefore there was no causal link, as a matter of law, between Felix' breach of duty and plaintiff's injuries. [The intermediate court of appeals affirmed.]

The concept of proximate cause, or more appropriately legal cause, has proven to be an elusive one, incapable of being precisely defined to cover all situations. . . . This is, in part, because the concept stems from policy considerations that serve to place manageable limits upon the liability that flows from negligent conduct. . . . Depending upon the nature of the case, a variety of factors may be relevant in assessing legal cause. Given the unique nature of the inquiry in each case, it is for the finder of fact to determine legal cause, once the court has been satisfied that a prima facie case has been established. . . . To carry the burden of proving a prima facie case, the plaintiff must generally show that the defendant's negligence was a substantial cause of the events which produced the injury. . . . Plaintiff need not demonstrate, however, that the precise manner in which the accident happened, or the extent of injuries, was foreseeable. . . .

Where the acts of a third person intervene between the defendant's conduct and the plaintiff's injury, the causal connection is not automatically severed. In such a case, liability turns upon whether the intervening act is a normal or foreseeable consequence of the situation created by the defendant's negligence. . . . If the intervening act is extraordinary under the circumstances, not foreseeable in the normal course of events, or independent of or far removed from the defendant's conduct, it may well be a superseding act which breaks the causal nexus. . . . Because questions concerning what is foreseeable and what is normal may be the subject of varying inferences, as is the question of negligence itself, these issues generally are for the fact finder to resolve.

There are certain instances, to be sure, where only one conclusion may be drawn from the established facts and where the question of legal cause may be decided as a matter of law. Those cases generally involve independent intervening acts which operate upon but do not flow from the original negligence. Thus, for instance, we have held that where an automobile lessor negligently supplies a car with a defective trunk lid, it is not liable to the lessee who, while stopped to repair the trunk, was injured by the negligent driving of a third party (*Ventricelli v. Kinney System Rent A Car*, [383 N.E.2d 1149 (N.Y. 1978)]). Although the renter's negligence undoubtedly served to place the injured party at the site of the accident, the intervening act was divorced from and not the foreseeable risk associated with the original negligence. And the injuries were different in kind than those which would have normally been expected from a defective trunk. In short, the negligence of the renter merely furnished the occasion for an unrelated act to cause injuries not ordinarily anticipated.

By contrast, in the present case, we cannot say as a matter of law that defendant Dickens' negligence was a superseding cause which interrupted the link between Felix' negligence and plaintiff's injuries. From the evidence in the record, the jury could have found that Felix negligently failed to safeguard the excavation site. A prime hazard associated with such dereliction is the possibility that a driver will negligently enter the work site and cause injury to a worker. That the driver was negligent, or even reckless, does not insulate Felix from liability. . . . Nor is it decisive that the driver lost control of the vehicle through a negligent failure to take medication, rather than a driving mistake. The precise manner of the event need not be anticipated. The finder of fact could have concluded that the foreseeable, normal and natural result of the risk created by Felix was the injury of a worker by a car entering the improperly protected work area. An intervening act may not serve as a superseding cause, and relieve an actor of responsibility, where the risk of the intervening act occurring is the very same risk which renders the actor negligent. . . .

[Affirmed.]

NOTES AND QUESTIONS

1. In each case above, what was the negligent conduct of the defendant? Why was it negligent; that is, what unreasonable risks of harm did it create? What injuries in fact occurred?

2. In each case above, who (or what) was the intervening force? How did that force contribute to causing the plaintiff's injury? Why was the defendant held liable in spite of the intervention?

3. How would the direct cause test work in each of the cases above?

PROBLEMS

1. In violation of the usual custom and practice, a municipal bus stops and lets off passengers without pulling over to the curb, stopping instead in the second lane from the right. Is this negligent? If so, why — what unreasonable risk of harm does this create? In each of the circumstances below, consider whether this conduct would be the proximate cause of an injury to a passenger who got off the bus while it was stopped in this fashion:

    a. Passenger is struck by a meteorite while still walking in the street between the bus and the curb.

    b. Passenger slips on a banana peel lying in the street.

    c. Passenger slips on a slippery patch of oil in the street.

    d. Passenger is hit by an automobile that is proceeding along the right hand side of the bus, between the bus and the curb.

    e. Suppose instead that while the bus is stopped in the second lane from the curb, and after the passengers who wish to have safely exited the bus, the bus is rear-ended by a truck whose brakes had failed. A passenger who remained on the bus suffers whiplash in the collision. Was the negligence of the bus driver a proximate cause of this injury? *Cf. Sheehan v. City of New York*, 40 N.Y.2d 496 (N.Y. 1976).

2. Defendant Mechanic negligently repaired Motorist's automobile. Because of this negligence, the car stalled shortly after Motorist picked it up from Mechanic's shop. Unfortunately, it stalled right in the middle of a narrow bridge over a deep, swiftly flowing river. The bridge was poorly lit, night was falling, and it was raining.

    a. Shortly after the car stalled, while Motorist was still trying to get it re-started, a truck driven at 20 miles an hour over the speed limit rear-ended Motorist, causing Motorist severe injuries. Had the truck been driven within the speed limit, no collision would have occurred.

Was the negligence of Mechanic the proximate cause of the injuries to Motorist?

b. Suppose instead that Motorist, after failing to restart the car, walks back into town and checks into a motel for the night, leaving the car on the bridge and without turning on the emergency flasher. A car driven by Victim runs into the stopped car in the dark. Would defendant's negligence be the proximate cause of the injuries Victim suffers in this collision?

c. Suppose, finally, that shortly after the car stalls, the bridge is washed out by floods caused by the heavy rain. Motorist is swept away in her car and drowns. Would defendant's conduct be a proximate cause of Motorist's death?

3. A pop music radio station announced one Saturday morning that Belle Star, the biggest pop singer of the moment, was at its studio and would autograph her latest CD for the next thirty minutes. "After that, she's gone, so get here fast," said the announcer. Racing to get to the station in their cars, two young fans reached speeds of ninety miles an hour and forced another car off the road, resulting in the death of the driver. The decedent's survivors bring a wrongful death action against the station. Was the station negligent? If so, was that negligence the proximate cause of the driver's death? *Cf. Weirum v. RKO General, Inc.*, 539 P.2d 36 (Cal. 1975).

MARSHALL v. NUGENT
222 F.2d 604 (1st Cir. 1955)

[Marshall was a passenger in a car driven by his son-in-law, Harriman. The car was proceeding southbound along an icy highway in New Hampshire when it approached a blind curve at the top of a hill. A northbound oil truck owned by defendant Socony Oil Co. and driven by Prince cut the corner of the curve as the Harriman car approached from the other direction. To avoid a collision with the truck, Harriman tried to maneuver his car off the road, but it skidded on the icy highway and came to a stop in the snow on the side of the road. Prince stopped his truck in the northbound travel lane and offered to help Harriman get his car back onto the road. At this point the two stopped vehicles were in a dangerous situation, since a northbound vehicle might suddenly come around the same curve and be unable to maneuver safely between them. Prince suggested that Marshall go to the top of the hill to warn oncoming drivers of the danger. As Marshall was walking in that direction, a car driven by defendant Nugent came over the top of the hill. Seeing the obstruction created by the oil truck, Nugent tried to maneuver around it by pulling his car to the left. He lost control on the icy road and ran into Marshall, who was unable to get out of the way. Marshall suffered severe injuries from the collision.

[Marshall sued Nugent and Socony. The jury returned a verdict in favor of Nugent, but held Socony liable to Marshall for $25,000. Socony appeals, claiming that the conduct of its employee, Prince, was not a proximate cause of the injury Marshall suffered.]

MAGRUDER, Chief Judge.

. . . [C]oming then to contention (2) above mentioned, this has to do with the doctrine of proximate causation, a doctrine which appellant's arguments tend to make out to be more complex and esoteric than it really is. To say that the situation created by the defendant's culpable acts constituted "merely a condition", not a cause of plaintiff's harm, is to indulge in mere verbiage, which does not solve the question at issue, but is simply a way of stating the conclusion, arrived at from other considerations, that the causal relation between the defendant's act and the plaintiff's injury is not strong enough to warrant holding the defendant legally responsible for the injury.

The adjective "proximate", as commonly used in this connection, is perhaps misleading, since to establish liability it is not necessarily true that the defendant's culpable act must be shown to have been the next or immediate cause of the plaintiff's injury. In many familiar instances, the defendant's act may be more remote in the chain of events; and the plaintiff's injury may more immediately have been caused by an intervening force of nature, or an intervening act of a third person whether culpable or not, or even an act by the plaintiff bringing himself in contact with the dangerous situation resulting from the defendant's negligence. . . . Therefore, perhaps, the phrase "legal cause", as used in Am. L. Inst., Rest. of Torts § 431, is preferable to "proximate cause"; but the courts continue generally to use "proximate cause", and it is pretty well understood what is meant.

Back of the requirement that the defendant's culpable act must have been a proximate cause of the plaintiff's harm is no doubt the widespread conviction that it would be disproportionately burdensome to hold a culpable actor potentially liable for all the injurious consequences that may flow from his act, i.e., that would not have been inflicted "but for" the occurrence of the act. This is especially so where the injurious consequence was the result of negligence merely. And so, speaking in general terms, the effort of the courts has been, in the development of this doctrine of proximate causation, to confine the liability of a negligent actor to those harmful consequences which result from the operation of the risk, or of a risk, the foreseeability of which rendered the defendant's conduct negligent.

Of course, putting the inquiry in these terms does not furnish a formula which automatically decides each of an infinite variety of cases. Flexibility is still preserved by the further need of defining the risk, or risks, either narrowly, or more broadly, as seems appropriate and just in the special type of case.

Regarding motor vehicle accidents in particular, one should contemplate a variety of risks which are created by negligent driving. There may be injuries resulting from a direct collision between the carelessly driven car and another vehicle. But such direct collision may be avoided, yet the plaintiff may fall and injure himself in frantically racing out of the way of the errant car. . . . Or the plaintiff may be knocked down and injured by a human stampede as the car rushes toward a crowded safety zone. . . . Or the plaintiff may faint from intense excitement stimulated by the near collision, and in falling sustain a fractured skull. . . . Or the plaintiff may suffer a miscarriage or other physical illness as a result of intense nervous shock incident to a hair-raising escape. . . . This bundle of risks could be enlarged indefinitely with a little imagination. In a traffic mix-up due to negligence, before the disturbed waters have become placid and normal again, the unfolding of events between the culpable act and the plaintiff's eventual injury may be bizarre indeed; yet the defendant may be liable for the result. . . . In such a situation, it would be impossible for a person in the defendant's position to predict in advance just how his negligent act would work out to another's injury. Yet this in itself is no bar to recovery. . . .

When an issue of proximate cause arises in a borderline case, as not infrequently happens, we leave it to the jury with appropriate instructions. We do this because it is deemed wise to obtain the judgment of the jury, reflecting as it does the earthy viewpoint of the common man — the prevalent sense of the community — as to whether the causal relation between the negligent act and the plaintiff's harm which in fact was a consequence of the tortious act is sufficiently close to make it just and expedient to hold the defendant answerable in damages. That is what the courts have in mind when they say the question of proximate causation is one of fact for the jury. . . . It is similar to the issue of negligence, which is left to the jury as an issue of fact. Even where on the evidence the facts are undisputed, if fair-minded men might honestly and reasonably draw contrary inferences as to whether the facts do or do not establish negligence, the court leaves such issue to the determination of the jury, who are required to decide, as a matter of common-sense judgment, whether the defendant's course of conduct subjected others to a reasonable or unreasonable risk, *i.e.*, whether under all the circumstances the defendant ought to be recognized as privileged to do the act in question or to pursue his course of conduct with immunity from liability for harm to others which might result. . . .

Exercising that judgment on the facts in the case at bar, we have to conclude that the district court committed no error in refusing to direct a verdict for the defendant Socony on the issue of proximate cause. . . .

[P]laintiff Marshall was a passenger in the oncoming Chevrolet car, and thus was one of the persons whose bodily safety was primarily endangered by the negligence of Prince, as might have been found by the jury, in "cutting the corner" with the Socony truck in the circumstances above related. In that view, Prince's negligence constituted an irretrievable breach of duty to the plaintiff. Though this particular act of negligence was over and done with when the truck pulled up alongside of the stalled Chevrolet without having actually collides with it, still the consequences of such past negligence were in the bosom of time, as yet unrevealed.

If the Chevrolet had been pulled back onto the highway, and Harriman and Marshall, having got in it again, had resumed their journey and had had a collision with another car five miles down the road, in which Marshall suffered bodily injuries, it could truly be said that such subsequent injury to Marshall was a consequence in fact of the earlier delay caused by the defendant's negligence, in the sense that but for such delay the Chevrolet car would not have been at the fatal intersection at the moment the other car ran into it. But on such assumed state of facts, the courts would no doubt conclude, "as a matter of law", that Prince's earlier negligence in cutting the corner was not the "proximate cause" of this later injury received by the plaintiff. That would be because the extra risks to which such negligence by Prince had subjected the passengers in the Chevrolet car were obviously entirely over; the situation had been stabilized and become normal, and, so far as one could foresee, whatever subsequent risks the Chevrolet might have to encounter in its resumed journey were simply the inseparable risks, no more and no less, that were incident to the Chevrolet's being out on the highway at all. But in the case at bar, the circumstances under which Marshall received the personal injuries complained of presented no such clear-cut situation.

As we have indicated, the extra risks created by Prince's negligence were not all over at the moment the primary risk of collision between the truck and the Chevrolet was successfully surmounted. Many cases have held a defendant, whose negligence caused a traffic tie-up, legally liable for subsequent property damage or personal injuries more immediately caused by an oncoming motorist. . . . This would particularly be so where, as in the present case, the negligent traffic tie-up and delay occurred in a dangerous blind spot, and where the occupants of the stalled Chevrolet, having got out onto the highway to assist in the operation of getting the Chevrolet going again, were necessarily subject to risks of injury from cars in the stream of northbound traffic coming over the crest of the hill. It is true, the Chevrolet car was not owned by the plaintiff Marshall, and no doubt, without violating any legal duty to Harriman, Marshall could have crawled up onto the snowbank at the side of the road out of harm's way and awaited there, passive and inert, until his journey was resumed. But the plaintiff, who as a passenger in the Chevrolet car had already been subjected to a collision risk by the negligent operation of the Socony truck, could reasonably be expected to get out onto the highway and lend a hand to his host in getting the Chevrolet started again, especially as Marshall himself had an interest in facilitating the resumption of the journey in order to keep his business appointment in North Stratford. Marshall was therefore certainly not an "officious intermeddler", and whether or not he was barred by contributory negligence in what he did was a question for the jury, as we have already held. The injury Marshall received by being struck by the Nugent car was not remote, either in time or place, from the negligent conduct of defendant Socony's servant, and it occurred while the traffic mix-up occasioned by defendant's negligence was still persisting, not after the traffic flow had become normal again. In the circumstances presented we conclude that the district court committed no error in leaving the issue of proximate cause to the jury for determination. . . .

NOTES AND QUESTIONS

1. What is the negligent conduct of Socony's employee? What risks did it create? What actions or forces intervened between the negligence of Defendant and Plaintiff's injuries?

2. How would the direct cause test apply in this situation?

3. What is an "officious intermeddler," and why would it make any difference if Marshall were such a creature?

4. At what point does the responsibility of Socony come to an end?

PROBLEMS

1. Defendant Town maintains a narrow, unrailed foot bridge over a gully that cuts through downtown. One day a group of children decided to race across the footbridge on rollerblades. One of the children lost control and skated off the bridge, suffering injuries in the fall from the bridge. Is Town liable for the injuries to the child?

2. On the facts of Problem 1, suppose one of the children ran into Pedestrian who was attempting to walk across the footbridge, knocking him into the gully. Would Town be liable for the injuries to Pedestrian?

3. Defendant's employees were working on a scaffold, repairing the side of a building in the downtown business district. Because of the careless way in which the scaffold was erected, it began to collapse. As it tilted, tools and equipment began to slide off it and fall to the street below. Before beginning work, defendant's employees had roped off the area beneath the scaffold, but the debris was falling outside this barrier. The pedestrians walking past the scaffold panicked as the objects from the scaffold began to fall around them. In the ensuing rush to get away from the danger, several of those fleeing ran into Plaintiff and knocked her down. Plaintiff broke her arm in the fall. At the time, Plaintiff was outside of any zone of danger from the falling objects from the scaffold, and indeed would have been safe if the entire scaffold had collapsed. Will defendant be liable for Plaintiff's broken arm?

McLAUGHLIN v. MINE SAFETY APPLIANCES COMPANY
181 N.E.2d 430 (N.Y. 1962)

FOSTER, Judge.

Frances Ann McLaughlin, an infant six years of age, was visiting her uncle and aunt in West Deering, New Hampshire, during the Summer of 1952. While bathing in Whittemore Lake, she almost drowned and was carried from the lake in an unconscious condition. The local lifeguard administered first aid, and the

Bennington Volunteer Fire Department was summoned. A fire department truck arrived shortly thereafter, and two men removed a resuscitator and some blankets from the truck. The resuscitator was placed over the infant's mouth, and she was wrapped in blankets by a woman who identified herself as a nurse.

More heat was needed to revive the child, so the firemen returned to the truck and obtained some boxes containing "heat blocks". The blocks were removed from their containers by the firemen who activated them and turned them over to the nurse. The nurse proceeded to apply several of them directly to the child's body under the blankets. Subsequently, the child began to heave about and moan. At this point, the infant was taken, still wrapped in the blankets, to a doctor's car and placed on the back seat. The heat blocks had fallen out from under the blankets. After a short stay at the doctor's office, the infant was taken home, and that evening blisters were observed about her body. It was soon ascertained that she was suffering from third degree burns, and she was taken to the Peterborough Hospital where she underwent extensive treatment.

The "M–S–A Redi-Heat Blocks", which were applied to the infant's body and caused the burns, were manufactured by Catalyst Research Corporation for defendant and packaged in defendant's cardboard container at defendant's plant and were sold and distributed by defendant to industrial houses, government agencies and departments for use in emergency. The "heat blocks" actually were small magnesium blocks which were activated by raising the spring lever on the block, inserting a loaded cartridge therein, then permitting the spring lever to close and strike the cap of the cartridge, causing the firing pin to ignite the chemical enclosed in the cartridge and to create the heat. The block was covered in its entirety by a red woolen insulating material called "flocking" which appeared and felt like a "blanket" or "flannel" covering or just ordinary "wool". Tests made upon the device indicated that the block attained a high surface temperature of 204 degrees Fahrenheit within two minutes after triggering in one case and a high of 195 degrees Fahrenheit within three minutes after triggering in another case. In both cases, after 39 minutes, the blocks retained a temperature of 138 degrees.

Affixed to each block on top of the "flocking" was an oval-like label containing the trade name of the block, and the name and design of the defendant. The blocks and two cartridges were sold in cardboard containers which contained these words in bold capital letters on the face thereof:

'ALWAYS READY FOR USE'

'ENTIRELY SELF CONTAINED'

'ONE HOUR'S HEAT PER CHARGE'

'TOP HEAT IN ONE MINUTE'

'NO LIQUIDS USED TO OPERATE'

'IMPERVIOUS TO HEAT, COLD AND MOISTURE KEEPS INDEFINITELY'

On both ends of the container, instructions were given as to how to order further charges or cartridges, thus revealing that the blocks could be reused over and over again. On the opposite face of the container, three small diagrams were printed, demonstrating how to activate the blocks, and alongside the diagrams in small print were the "Instructions for use" which read as follows:

'When fast emergency heat is needed for victims of accident, exposure, or sudden illness, the M.S.A. Redi-Heat Block is always ready for service. Fully raise the activating lever. . . .

'Insert the Redi-Heat Charge into the Block's receptacle plain end first and release the lever.

'Note: The activating lever must be raised to maximum stroke before releasing, or the charge will not activate. . . .

'The lever indents the head of the Redi-Heat Charge, creating top heat within one minute. Retain Charge in Block for at least one-half hour.

'Wrap in insulating medium, such as pouch, towel, blanket or folded cloth.'

The particular heat blocks involved were sold by defendant for use by the Bennington Fire Department in 1947 or 1948. At the time of the sale, defendant's representative demonstrated the proper mode of use in the Town Hall. Several firemen were present. The representative warned everyone that the heat block was to be covered with a towel or some other material to keep the block from coming into contact with the skin.

Among the firemen who were present at the scene of the accident herein was Paul Traxler. He testified that he had been present when defendant's representative demonstrated the blocks; that he recalled being told not to use the blocks without further insulating them; that, furthermore, instructional classes had been held as to proper use of the blocks prior to the accident; that he was fully aware that the blocks were to be wrapped in a towel or blanket before they were used; and that he had told the "nurse" at the scene to wrap up the blocks before using. Nevertheless, the blocks were applied directly to the infant's person under the blankets, while the fireman, Traxler, who had activated the blocks, stood next to her and watched. The infant's aunt could recall no warning given by the firemen to the nurse as to the danger in applying the unwrapped blocks to the infant's body.

This action was commenced by the infant and her father for loss of services against the defendant, the exclusive distributor of the heat blocks, upon the theory that it had failed adequately to warn the public of the danger involved in the use of the blocks and to properly "instruct" ultimate users as to the "proper application of the said blocks".

After a jury trial in Supreme Court, Nassau County, a verdict was returned in favor of the infant plaintiff in the sum of $17,500, and in favor of her father in the sum of $2,500, and judgment was entered thereupon. The Appellate Division unanimously reversed and ordered a new trial, unless the infant plaintiff stipulated to reduce the verdict in her favor to $10,000, and her father stipulated to reduce the verdict in his favor to $1,000, in which event the judgment was to be affirmed as modified. Plaintiffs so stipulated, and final judgment was entered.

Defendant appeals, as of right, contending . . . that the trial court committed reversible error in its charge. . . .

The court instructed the jury that, if they found that the heating block was an inherently dangerous article, then the defendant distributor was under a duty to give reasonable warning of latent dangers in the use thereof, if any were known to it. This was correct under the common law of New Hampshire which governs this case. . . .

The jury, under the court's instructions could have found that a hidden or latent danger existed in the use of the product, or at least that the form and design of the product itself, together with the printing on the container, could mislead ultimate users as to the need for further insulation. . . . The blocks were dressed in "flocking" and appeared to be insulated, and the bold lettering on the containers revealed that the blocks were "ALWAYS READY FOR USE" and "ENTIRELY SELF CONTAINED", all of which seemed to indicate that nothing extrinsic to the contents of the package was needed. And inasmuch as the blocks were designed for use on the human body, and if improperly used could cause severe injuries, the jury was justified in finding that the final sentence of the instructions, found in small print on the back side of the containers, advising use of a further insulating medium, was totally inadequate as a warning commensurate with the risk. . . .

But the true problem presented in this case is one of proximate causation, and not one concerning the general duty to warn or negligence of the distributor. In this regard the trial court instructed the jury that the defendant would not be liable if "an actual warning was conveyed to the person or persons applying the blocks that they should be wrapped in insulation of some kind before being placed against the body" for in that event the "failure to heed that warning would be a new cause which intervened." Subsequently, and after the jury retired, they returned and asked this question: "Your Honor, if we, the jury, find that the M.S.A. Company was negligent in not making any warning of danger on the heat block itself, but has given proper instructions in its use up to the point of an intervening circumstance (the nurse who was not properly instructed), is the M.S.A. Company liable?"

The trial court answered as follows: "Ladies and gentlemen of the jury, if you find from the evidence that the defendant, as a reasonably prudent person under all of the circumstances should have expected use of the block by some person other than those to whom instruction as to its use had been given, either by the wording on the container or otherwise, and that under those circumstances a reasonably prudent person would have placed warning words on the heat block itself, and if you find in addition to that that the nurse was not warned at the scene and that a reasonably prudent person in the position of the nurse, absent any warning on the block itself, would have proceeded to use it without inquiry as to the proper method of use, then the defendant would be liable." Counsel for the defendant excepted to that statement. The jury then returned its verdict for the plaintiffs.

From the jury's question, it is obvious that they were concerned with the effect of the fireman's knowledge that the blocks should have been wrapped, and his apparent failure to so advise the nurse who applied the blocks in his presence. The court in answering the jury's question instructed, in essence, that the defendant could still be liable, even though the fireman had knowledge of the need for further insulation, if it was reasonably foreseeable that the blocks, absent the containers, would find their way from the firemen to unwarned third persons.

We think that the instruction, as applied to the facts of this case, was erroneous. In the cases discussed above, the manufacturer or distributor failed to warn the original vendee of the latent danger, and there were no additional acts of negligence intervening between the failure to warn and the resulting injury or damage. This was not such a case, or at least the jury could find that it was not. Nor was this simply a case involving the negligent failure of the vendee to inspect and discover the danger; in such a case the intervening negligence of the immediate vendee does not necessarily insulate the manufacturer from liability to third persons, nor supersede the negligence of the manufacturer in failing to warn of the danger. . . .

In the case before us, the jury obviously believed that the fireman, Traxler, had actual knowledge of the need for further insulation, and the jury was preoccupied with the effect of his failure to warn the nurse as she applied the blocks to the plaintiff's person. The jury also could have believed that Traxler removed the blocks from the containers, thereby depriving the nurse of any opportunity she might have had to read the instructions printed on the containers, and that Traxler actually activated the blocks, turned them over, uninsulated, to the nurse for her use, and stood idly by as they were placed directly on the plaintiff's wet skin.

Under the circumstances, we think the court should have charged that if the fireman did so conduct himself, without warning the nurse, his negligence was so gross as to supersede the negligence of the defendant and to insulate it from liability. This is the rule that prevails when knowledge of the latent danger or defect is actually possessed by the original vendee, who then deliberately passes on the product to a third person without warning. . . .

In short, whether or not the distributor furnished ample warning on his product to third persons in general was not important here, if the jury believed that Traxler had actual notice of the danger by virtue of his presence at demonstration classes or otherwise, and that he deprived the nurse of her opportunity to read the instructions prior to applying the blocks. While the distributor might have been liable if the blocks had found their way into the hands of the nurse in a more innocent fashion, the distributor could not be expected to foresee that its demonstrations to the firemen would callously be disregarded by a member of the department. We have indicated that knowledge of the danger possessed by the original purchaser, knowledge actually brought home to him, might protect the manufacturer or distributor from liability to third persons harmed by the failure of the purchaser to warn, where the purchaser had the means and opportunity to do so. . . .

Here, the jury might have found that the fireman not only had the means to warn the nurse, but further that, by his actions, he prevented any warning from reaching her, and, indeed, that he actually had some part in the improper application of the blocks. Such conduct could not have been foreseen by the defendant.

The judgment should be reversed and a new trial granted, with costs to abide the event.

VAN VOORHIS, Judge (dissenting).

The recovery by plaintiff should not, as it seems to us, be reversed on account of lack of foreseeability or a break in the chain of causation due to any intervening act of negligence on the part of a volunteer fireman. These heat blocks were dangerous instrumentalities unless wrapped in "insulating" media, "such as pouch, towel, blanket or folded cloth" as the instructions on the container directed. What happened here was that the container, with the instructions on it, was thrown away, and the nurse who applied the heat block was unaware of this safety requirement. In our minds the circumstance that the fireman who knew of the danger failed to warn the nurse, even if negligent, did not affect the fact, as the jury found it, that this was a risk which the manufacturer of the heat block ought to have anticipated in the exercise of reasonable care, nor intercept the chain of causation. . . .

The rule is not absolute that it is not necessary to anticipate the negligence or even the crime of another. It has been said in the Restatement of Torts (§ 449): "If the realizable likelihood that a third person may act in a particular manner is the hazard or one of the hazards which makes the actor negligent, such an act whether innocent, negligent, intentionally tortious or criminal does not prevent the actor from being liable for harm caused thereby." It is further provided by section 447: "The fact that an intervening act of a third person is negligent in itself or is done in a negligent manner does not make it a superseding cause of harm to another which the actor's negligent conduct is a substantial factor in bringing about, if (a) the actor at the time of his negligent conduct should have realized that a third person might so act". . . .

The judgment appealed from should be affirmed.

NOTES AND QUESTIONS

1. Read carefully the trial judge's answer to the jury's question. What exactly was wrong with it?

2. Formulate your own answer to the jury's question that properly states the law as set forth in the majority opinion.

3. What exactly is the disagreement between the majority and the dissent? On what issue are they in disagreement? On the scope of duty? On whether the defendant breached its duty of care? On whether defendant's conduct was the proximate cause of the harm? All of the above?

4. Why isn't this a simple joint causation case similar to those studied in the chapter on cause in fact, where the combined negligence of the manufacturer and the fireman joined to cause injury to the plaintiff? What is it about the conduct of the fireman that exonerates the manufacturer?

PROBLEMS

The defendant drove in a negligent fashion and hit plaintiff while he was crossing the street. Defendant is of course liable for this initial injury. Should the defendant also be liable for the following additional injuries?

a. The plaintiff's injuries are aggravated by the malpractice of the doctor who treated him in the hospital emergency room. As a result, plaintiff took longer to heal than would have been expected, and ended up with some permanent disabilities that would not have occurred if the doctor had not been negligent.

b. The plaintiff's injuries are aggravated when the ambulance transporting him to the emergency room is struck by another automobile, and plaintiff receives additional injuries in this second collision. In considering this problem, would it matter whether the accident was caused by:

   • The negligence of the ambulance driver?

   • The negligence of the driver of the other vehicle?

   • The recklessness of the driver of the other vehicle? Suppose the driver of the other vehicle was fleeing from the police at speeds in excess of 100 m.p.h.

c. The plaintiff's injuries are aggravated when the hospital employees treating him get his identity tag switched with that of another patient who requires open heart surgery. The plaintiff's chest is opened before the physician realizes that a mistake has been made.

WATSON v. KENTUCKY & INDIANA BRIDGE & R. CO.
126 S.W. 146 (Ky. 1910)

[Plaintiff John Watson brought this action against defendant Bridge & Railroad Company to recover for injuries suffered in a gasoline explosion. A railroad tanker car filled with gasoline derailed due to the negligence of the defendant, damaging the valve on the bottom of the car. The gasoline leaked out and filled the area nearby with flammable liquid and explosive vapor. A bystander named Charles Duerr ignited the gasoline when he threw away a lighted match. Plaintiff suffered severe injuries in the subsequent explosion. Duerr stated that he threw the match away after lighting a cigar, not knowing of the dangerous condition created by the gasoline. On the other hand, the defendant Bridge & Railroad Company showed that it had that day discharged Duerr from employment. Further, witnesses testified that they overheard Duerr say to a companion, some 20 minutes before the explosion, "Let us go and set the damn thing on fire." Another witness testified that he saw Duerr light the match and throw it in the fire, and that Duerr had no cigar at that time. At the close of all the evidence, the trial judge directed the jury to find for the defendant. Plaintiff appeals, asserting that the trial court erred in giving a directed verdict.]

SETTLE, J.

. . . The lighting of the match by Duerr having resulted in the explosion, the question is, was that act merely a contributing cause, or the efficient and, therefore, proximate cause of appellant's injuries? The question of proximate cause is a question for the jury. In holding that Duerr in lighting or throwing the match acted maliciously or with intent to cause the explosion, the trial court invaded the province of the jury. There was, it is true, evidence tending to prove that the act was wanton or malicious, but also evidence conducing to prove that it was inadvertently or negligently done by Duerr. It was therefore for the jury and not the court to determine from all the evidence whether the lighting of the match was done by Duerr inadvertently or negligently, or whether it was a wanton and malicious act. . . .

If the presence on Madison street in the city of Louisville of the great volume of loose gas that arose from the escaping gasoline was caused by the negligence of the appellee Bridge & Railroad Company, it seems to us that the probable consequences of its coming in contact with fire and causing an explosion was too plain a proposition to admit of doubt. Indeed, it was most probable that some one would strike a match to light a cigar or for other purposes in the midst of the gas. In our opinion, therefore, the act of one lighting and throwing a match under such circumstances cannot be said to be the efficient cause of the explosion. It did not of itself produce the explosion, nor could it have done so without the assistance and contribution resulting from the primary negligence, if there was such negligence, on the part of the appellee Bridge & Railroad Company in furnishing the presence of the gas in the street. This conclusion, however, rests upon the theory that Duerr inadvertently or negligently lighted and threw the match in the gas. . . .

If, however, the act of Duerr in lighting the match and throwing it into the vapor or gas arising from the gasoline was malicious, and done for the purpose of causing the explosion, we do not think appellees would be responsible, for while the appellee Bridge & Railroad Company's negligence may have been the efficient cause of the presence of the gas in the street, and it should have understood enough of the consequences thereof to have foreseen that an explosion was likely to result from the inadvertent or negligent lighting of a match by some person who was ignorant of the presence of the gas or of the effect of lighting or throwing a match in it, it could not have foreseen or deemed it probable that one would maliciously or wantonly do such an act for the evil purpose of producing the explosion. Therefore, if the act of Duerr was malicious, we quite agree with the trial court that it was one which the appellees could not reasonably have anticipated or guarded against, and in such case the act of Duerr, and not the primary negligence of the appellee Bridge & Railroad Company, in any of the particulars charged, was the efficient or proximate cause of appellant's injuries. The mere fact that the concurrent cause or intervening act was unforeseen will not relieve the defendant guilty of the primary negligence from liability, but if the intervening agency is something so unexpected or extraordinary as that he could not or ought not to have anticipated it, he will not be liable, and certainly he is not bound to anticipate the criminal acts of others by which damage is inflicted and hence is not liable therefor. . . .

BRAUER v. NEW YORK CENTRAL & H. R.R. CO.
103 A. 166 (N.J. 1918)

SWAYZE, J.

This is a case of a grade crossing collision. We are clear that the questions of negligence and contributory negligence were for the jury. If there were nothing else, the testimony of the plaintiff as to signals of the flagman would carry the case to the jury. The only question that has caused us difficulty is that of the extent of the defendant's liability. The complaint avers that the horse was killed, and the wagon and harness and the cider and barrels with which the wagon was loaded were destroyed. What happened was that as a result of the collision, aside from the death of the horse and the destruction of the wagon, the contents of the wagon, consisting of empty barrels and a keg of cider, were scattered, and probably stolen by people at the scene of the accident. The driver, who was alone in charge for the plaintiff, was so stunned that one of the railroad detectives found him immediately after the collision in a fit. There were two railroad detectives on the freight train to protect the property it was carrying against thieves, but they did nothing to protect the plaintiff's property. The controversy on the question of damages is as to the right of the plaintiff to recover the value of the barrels, cider, and blanket. An objection was based solely on the ground that the complaint alleged that they were destroyed; counsel said "there is no use proving value unless they were destroyed." We think that, if they were taken by thieves, they were destroyed as far as was important to the case; at least the averment was sufficient to justify the evidence and the charge, since the case was fully tried. It is now argued that the defendant's negligence was not in any event the proximate cause of the loss of this property, since the act of the thieves intervened. The rule of law exempting the one guilty of the original negligence from damage due to an intervening cause is well settled. The difficulty lies in the application. Like the question of proximate cause, this is ordinarily a jury question. . . .

We think these authorities justified the trial judge in his rulings as to the recovery of the value of the barrels, cider, and blanket. The negligence which caused the collision resulted immediately in such a condition of the driver of the wagon that he was no longer able to protect his employer's property; the natural and probable result of his enforced abandonment of it in the street of a large city was its disappearance; and the wrongdoer cannot escape making reparation for the loss caused by depriving the plaintiff of the protection which the presence of the driver in his right senses would have afforded.

"The act of a third person," said the Supreme Court of Massachusetts, "intervening and contributing a condition necessary to the injurious effect of the original negligence, will not excuse the first wrongdoer, if such act ought to have been foreseen." *Lane v. Atlantic Works*, 111 Mass. 136.

A railroad company which found it necessary or desirable to have its freight train guarded by two detectives against thieves is surely chargeable with knowledge that portable property left without a guard was likely to be made off with. Again, strictly speaking, the act of the thieves did not intervene between defendant's negligence and the plaintiff's loss; the two causes were to all practical intent simultaneous and concurrent; it is rather a case of a joint tort than an intervening cause. . . . An illustration will perhaps clarify the case. Suppose a fruit vendor at his stand along the street is rendered unconscious by the negligence of the defendant, who disappears, and boys in the street appropriate the unfortunate vendor's stock in trade; could the defendant escape liability for their value? We can hardly imagine a court answering in the affirmative. Yet the case is but little more extreme than the jury might have found the present case.

The judgment is affirmed, with costs.

GARRISON, J. (dissenting).

The collision afforded an opportunity for theft of which a thief took advantage, but I cannot agree that the collision was therefore the proximate cause of loss of the stolen articles. Proximate cause imports unbroken continuity between cause and effect, which, both in law and in logic, is broken by the active intervention of an independent criminal actor. This established rule of law is defeated if proximate cause is confounded with mere opportunity for crime. A maladjusted switch may be the proximate cause of the death of a passenger who was killed by the derailment of the train or by the fire or collision that ensued, but it is not the proximate cause of the death of a passenger who was murdered by a bandit who boarded the train because of the opportunity afforded by its derailment. This clear distinction is not met by saying that criminal intervention should be foreseen, for this implies that crime is to be presumed, and the law is directly otherwise. . . .

NOTES AND QUESTIONS

1. How does the risk rule apply in the *Watson* case? Why does it not result in the conclusion that the Bridge Company is liable? Can these two cases be distinguished?

2. What is the relationship between these cases and the *McLaughlin* case, above?

PROBLEMS

1. Plaintiff's decedent died in an apartment building fire. She was unable to escape from the burning building because the defendant landlord failed to have proper fire escapes available. However, fire investigators have conclusively demonstrated that the fire was deliberately set by Pyro, a deranged individual who liked to start fires. Does the deliberate conduct of Pyro supercede the negligence of landlord in failing to provide proper fire escapes?

2. State law forbids selling alcoholic beverages to anyone under the age of 21, or to any person who is obviously intoxicated. As part of a gang initiation, two teenagers succeed in buying several cases of beer from a convenience store, whose clerks are well known for not carding. They share the beer with other members of the gang, who become intoxicated. Later, two members of the gang have a head-on collision with Plaintiff motorist while attempting to drive home while legally intoxicated. Several other members of the gang severely beat up another teenager who inadvertently encountered them while walking home. Both the motorist and the beating victim sue the convenience store for selling beer to the underage patrons, claiming that this conduct was the actual and proximate cause of their injuries. What result in each suit?

3. City passed an ordinance requiring that the owners of vacant buildings secure them so that they cannot be entered or used by unauthorized persons. In adopting the ordinance, the City Council held hearings and made findings, set forth in the ordinance, that vacant buildings were often the focus of criminal activity, and that the purpose of the ordinance was to reduce crime by denying access to the buildings. In violation of the ordinance, Landlord failed to secure a vacant apartment building, which he was intending to renovate later in the year. Plaintiff, a young woman walking past the apartment building, was

attacked and dragged back into the building, where she was raped in one of the vacant apartments. Plaintiff sues Landlord for her injuries. What result?

4. What result in Problem 3 if no statute requires Landlord to secure the vacant building?

EXERCISE

Wallis was walking quickly through downtown Metropolis to meet her brother Baldwin for lunch. She stopped for a red light and then hurried across the street, without looking, as soon as the light turned green. A car driven by Racer ran the red light and bore down upon Wallis as she hurried across the street. Racer applied the brakes hard, swerved, and managed to avoid hitting Wallis head-on. He did, however, sideswipe her and knock her down. Wallis hit the pavement hard, and lay there in a dazed condition. Bystanders called the police, and soon an ambulance was on its way. The police set up traffic control, but did not attempt to move Wallis before the ambulance arrived.

Baldwin was working in a copy center in downtown Metropolis. It was nearly noon and Baldwin was expecting Wallis any moment. He heard the squeal of brakes and the commotion following the accident, but did not connect them to Wallis' failure to appear for several moments. When Wallis, who was usually punctual, did not arrive, Baldwin began to worry. He got permission to leave for lunch, ran outside, and headed in the direction of the flashing lights he could see about a block away. As he approached, he worked his way through a crowd of onlookers to a spot where he could see his sister being put on stretcher in preparation for being placed into a waiting ambulance. "Wallis!" yelled Baldwin, as he pushed his way forward to get to her side. A police officer who was keeping the crowd at bay yelled at Baldwin to stop and grabbed him by the arm when Baldwin continued to push forward. "Wallis!" yelled Baldwin again, frantic with worry as he tried to push the officer aside. The officer grabbed Baldwin again and tried to throw him down. Baldwin pulled free but tripped over the curb and fell, hitting his head against the sharp corner of a coin operated newsrack. Baldwin suffered a serious head injury and soon joined his sister in the ambulance.

Baldwin has now brought suit for his injuries against Racer. An important issue that must be addressed, to both the court and the jury, is whether the negligent driving of Racer was the proximate cause of Baldwin's head injury.

You will be assigned to represent either Baldwin or Racer. You will also be assigned a jurisdiction whose law will govern the dispute.

Part 1: Research the law in your assigned jurisdiction governing proximate cause. Based on this research, prepare a short memorandum of points and authorities either supporting or opposing, as the case may be, a motion for directed verdict by Racer asserting lack of proximate cause as a matter of law. You may assume that all the facts given above have been placed into evidence at the trial.

Part 2: Research the jury instruction used in your assigned jurisdiction for proximate or legal cause. Based on this jury instruction, prepare in written form an argument to the jury explaining why proximate cause has or has not been proved.

Chapter 7
MULTIPLE TORTFEASORS

In previous chapters, most of our study revolved around the potential liability of individual defendants. In this chapter, we will focus on cases involving multiple tortfeasors. Such cases often involve issues of causation where a plaintiff cannot easily identify the source of her harm. They also involve questions of how to distribute loss among jointly responsible parties. We will begin by considering a case that describes the traditional approach to these problems.

A. JOINT AND SEVERAL LIABILITY

CAROLINA, C. & O. RY. v. HILL
89 S.E. 902 (Va. 1916)

HARRISON, J.

This action was brought by the plaintiff, Elkanah Hill, against Carolina, Clinchfield & Ohio Railway and certain contractors, the defendants, to recover damages for injuries alleged to have been done to the plaintiff's real estate.

[P]laintiff owned a farm in Dickenson county, on the bank of Russell Fork river, a nonnavigable stream, where he had resided for many years, containing 103 acres, upon which he had a mill which had for many years done the grinding for the people of the mountainous section in which it was located. In 1912 the defendants commenced the construction of a railroad down Russell Fork river on the opposite bank from the plaintiff, which resulted in the injuries to the plaintiff which are herein complained of.

The evidence [shows that] the defendants, while constructing the railroad along Russell Fork river opposite the plaintiff's land, by blasting, excavating, and the use of explosives, hurled rocks, dirt, stumps, trees and other material upon his land, destroying his vegetation, timber, brush, shrubbery, grass and orchards; tore down and destroyed his fences, walls, and barns, damaged his fields, bottom lands, milldam and water power, filled up his milldam, choked his water wheel, millrace, mill appendages, and destroyed his mill site. The declaration further alleges that in constructing the railroad down the right bank, said embankment was so carelessly constructed out of loose material, and so impinged upon the bed of the river, that it diverted rainwater, natural floods and freshets towards the left bank, so that a portion of plaintiff's bottom land was washed away and the loose material, gravel, and stones from the embankment and banks and bottom land were washed in around the mill, and below the waterfall, so as to fill up the millrace, choke up the mill wheel, destroy the water power at that place, and divert the natural flow of the water away from the mill. By virtue of all which the plaintiff alleges that he is greatly damaged. [At the same time,] the Yellow Poplar Lumber Company was engaged in removing from this section large quantities of lumber, which was done by floating or splashing the same down the river. This was accomplished by building in the river large splash dams which floated the logs out and down the river; that in March, 1913, an unusual freshet occurred in which great numbers of logs floated by the plaintiff's mill, thereby, as contended, contributing to the injuries complained of. [The trial resulted in a verdict and judgment in favor of the plaintiff for $2,000.]

[Defendants contend] that the splashes of the Yellow Poplar Lumber Company largely contributed to the damage sustained by the plaintiff, and that there could be no recovery in this action for that part of the damage properly chargeable to the Yellow Poplar Lumber Company; that where there are several concurrent causes due to independent authors, neither being sufficient to produce the entire loss, then each of the several parties concerned is liable only for the injuries due to his negligence.

In support of this contention the defendants rely upon the case of *Pulaski Coal Co. v. Gibboney Sand Bar Co.*, 110 Va. 444, 66 S.E. 73. In the case cited the plaintiff owned a bar of valuable marketable sand and gravel, and a number of independent mine owners, each engaged in operating his separate mine, deposited their slack, slate, culm, and mine refuse in and along the banks of New river, where it was carried down and thrown upon the sand bar of the plaintiff, thereby causing the damage complained of. The plaintiff sued one of the mine owners to recover the entire damage sustained from all of them. There was a verdict and judgment in favor of the plaintiff, which this court reversed, holding that[: "Where there are several concurrent negligent causes, the effects of which are separable, due to independent authors, neither being sufficient to produce the entire loss, then each of the several parties concerned is liable only for the injuries due to his negligence."]

In the case at bar the facts are wholly different from those in the case cited and relied on by the defendants. There is here no question of the pollution of the stream, and the doctrine in such cases is not applicable to the facts involved in the case under consideration. It does not satisfactorily appear from the evidence what, if any, part the Yellow Poplar Lumber Company had in bringing about the injuries sustained by the plaintiff. If the lumber company caused any part of the damage, it is manifest from the evidence that it would be impossible to separate the effects and ascertain what part of the injury was attributable to its negligence. It is further clear from the evidence in the present case that the acts of the defendants alone were sufficient to have produced the entire damage complained of. Under the circumstances disclosed by the record, it is immaterial how many others may have been in fault, if the defendants' act was an efficient cause of the injury.

The doctrine is thoroughly established that where there are several concurrent negligent causes, the effects of which are not separable, though due to independent authors, either of which is sufficient to produce the entire loss, all are jointly or severally liable for the entire loss. . . .

We are of opinion that, under the evidence of record, and in the light of the authorities cited, the plaintiff had the right to sue for and recover from the defendants alone the entire damages sustained by him, and therefore the action of the circuit court in giving, refusing, and modifying instructions was without to their prejudice rights.

For these reasons the judgment complained of must be affirmed.

NOTES

1. *Hill* describes the long-established rule of joint and several liability. Under this rule, each negligent defendant is fully responsible for a plaintiff's damages, assuming that the defendants caused an indivisible harm. As *Hill* suggests, however, liability is several only where defendants cause distinct or separable components of a plaintiff's harm. *See* Restatement (Third) of Torts: Apportionment of Liability § 50 (1999).

2. Should comparative fault states continue to apply joint and several liability? No consensus has emerged. In fact, jurisdictions are so splintered that the Restatement refused to endorse a position. Instead, the Restatement sets out five separate "tracks" to describe the competing approaches. The first track reflects approximately eleven jurisdictions that have retained joint and several liability even after adopting comparative fault. *See id.* § 27A. The second track describes the opposite approach (adopted by approximately 14 states) of applying only several liability to multiple defendants who have caused indivisible harm. *See id.* § 27B. The remaining tracks reflect jurisdictions that have come down somewhere in the middle. One of the remaining tracks suggests the imposition of joint and several liability, subject to a reallocation of unenforceable shares to all parties in proportion to their share of comparative responsibility. *See id.* §§ 27C, 30C. Another track suggests the imposition of joint and several liability for a plaintiff's economic damages, but only several liability for noneconomic damages, such as pain and suffering. *See id.* § 27E. A fifth track suggests the imposition of joint and several liability only against defendants who are assigned "a percentage of comparative responsibility equal to or in excess of the legal threshold." *See id.* § 27D. Among states that follow this approach, the "threshold" runs from 10% to 60%. Below the threshold, defendants are only severally liable for a plaintiff's harm.

3. Where a defendant commits an intentional tort, the Restatement suggests joint and several liability for indivisible harm regardless of which "track" a jurisdiction follows in cases involving negligent tortfeasors. *See id.* § 22.

4. Not all commentators are pleased with the Restatement's approach to the issue of joint and several liability. Professor Frank Vandall, for example, argues that the Restatement should not have considered *legislative* changes to the rule of joint and several liability and, instead, should have restated the predominant approach of those jurisdictions that have addressed the problem *judicially*. According to Professor Vandall, that would have provided a clear majority in favor of retaining the traditional rule of joint and several liability:

> The track system contained in the Restatement (Third), Apportionment is a presentation [of] defense and insurance policy. . . . A popular approach for limiting consumer suits was the modification of the rules of apportionment by means of state legislation. The [Restatement sections] label these insurance-driven legislative intrusions into the common law as tracks.

* * *

> The solution is for the ALI to return to a Restatement of common law and to ignore the state statutes. This would result in a Restatement resembling joint and several liability. . . . The tracks could be treated in one short comment, as interesting variations among the states.

Frank J. Vandall, *A Critique of the Restatement (Third), Apportionment as it Affects Joint and Several Liability,* 49 EMORY L.J. 565, 620-21 (2000). Do you agree with Professor Vandall's critique? Does it make a difference that some courts expressly defer to legislatures in making decisions regarding joint and several liability?

5. The concept of joint and several liability is important in environmental law. In 1980, Congress passed the Comprehensive Environmental Response, Compensation and Liability Act (CERCLA). CERCLA permits the imposition of strict liability on a wide range of entities that produce, transport, or store hazardous waste. Although Congress deleted specific references to joint and several liability from the final version of CERCLA, courts have uniformly interpreted the statute as permitting the imposition of joint and several liability on responsible parties. *See United States v. Monsanto*, 858 F.2d 160 (4th Cir. 1988), *cert. denied*, 490 U.S. 1106 (1989).

PROBLEMS

1. Frank and George each negligently run a stop sign at a four-way intersection and hit Charlie at the same time. Charlie breaks his collarbone and incurs $2,000 in damages. Charlie sues Frank. Under the traditional rule of joint and several liability, can Charlie recover the full $2,000?

2. Same facts as Problem 1, but suppose the jury concluded that that George *intended* to hit Charlie by running the stop sign. Will this finding change your answer?

3. Frank and George each negligently run a stop sign at a four-way intersection. Frank hits Charlie and breaks his leg. A moment later George runs over Charlie's arm, fracturing his forearm. Charlie suffers $1,000 in damages relating to the leg and $1,000 in damages relating to the arm. Will either Frank or George be jointly and severally liable for all of Charlie's damages?

4. Suppose the facts in Problem 1 took place in a comparative fault jurisdiction. Suppose further that the jury found Frank to be 30% at fault for the accident, and George to be 70% at fault. Is Frank jointly and severally liable for Charlie's damages? What approaches might a court use to apportion liability?

5. Plaintiff and her fiancé were driving bumper cars at DisneyWorld. The fiancé's car collided with the plaintiff's car, causing her to suffer $75,000 in damages. At trial, a jury applied Florida's pure comparative fault principles and found the plaintiff 14% at fault for her own injuries, the fiancé (by then, the plaintiff's husband) 85% at fault, and Disney 1% at fault. Spousal immunity, however, shielded the fiancé/husband from liability. Should joint and several liability require Disney to pay 86% of the damage award? If not, how would you allocate damages? *See Walt Disney World Co. v. Wood*, 515 So. 2d 198 (Fla. 1987).

B.   THEORIES OF JOINT LIABILITY

Cases involving multiple tortfeasors frequently raise questions of causation. These questions become particularly difficult when a plaintiff has trouble identifying which defendant actually caused her harm. In the following section, we consider three theories that courts have used to help plaintiffs overcome this difficulty — concert of action, enterprise liability, and market share liability.

1.   Concert of Action

BIERCZYNSKI v. ROGERS
239 A.2d 218 (Del. 1968)

HERRMANN, J.

This appeal involves an automobile accident in which the plaintiffs claim that the defendant motorists were racing on the public highway, as the result of which the accident occurred. [The] plaintiffs Cecil B. Rogers and Susan D. Rogers brought this action against Robert C. Race and Ronald Bierczynski, ages 18 and 17 respectively, alleging concurrent negligences in that they violated various speed statutes and various other statutory rules of the road, and in that they failed to keep a proper lookout and failed to keep their vehicles under proper control. The jury, by answer to interrogatories in its special verdict, expressly found that Race and Bierczynski were each negligent and that the negligence of each was a proximate cause of the accident. Substantial verdicts were entered in favor of the plaintiffs against both defendants jointly. The defendant Bierczynski appeals therefrom. The defendant Race does not appeal; rather, he joins with the plaintiffs in upholding the judgment below.

Bierczynski puts his appeal upon [the ground] that it was error for the Trial Court to submit the issue of proximate cause to the jury, insofar as he was concerned, because the plaintiffs failed to prove that any negligence of Bierczynski was a proximate cause of the accident. . . . There was sufficient evidence of proximate causation as to Bierczynski, in our opinion, to warrant the submission of that issue to the jury. The trial court had before it the following evidence.

Bierczynski and Race worked at the same place, located a short distance east of Governor Printz Boulevard near Lore Avenue. They lived near each other in the southerly part of Wilmington. On the day before the accident, Bierczynski drove Race to work. On the day of the accident, Bierczynski intended to pick Race up again; but, upon meeting, Race told Bierczynski he would take his own automobile too, because he intended to leave work early. Thereupon, one following the other, they drove toward their place of employment northerly across Wilmington to Lore Avenue in a suburban area of Brandywine Hundred. The accident occurred on Lore Avenue about 300 feet east of its intersection with River Road. Lore Avenue runs east and west and River Road north and south. Lore Avenue was 18 feet wide, macadam surfaces, without a marked center line, and was lined by guard rails at various places. For a distance of about 1,000 feet west of its intersection with River Road, Lore Avenue is a moderately steep hill; after crossing River Road, it levels off. The speed limit at the scene was 25 m.p.h.

Cecil Rogers testified as follows: He was returning from a Girl Scout trip with his daughter, headed for their home located about three blocks from the scene of the accident. He entered Lore Avenue from Governor Printz Boulevard, thus driving in a westerly direction on Lore Avenue. At a point about 300 feet east of River Road, Rogers' car was struck by Race's car which approached him sideways, moving in an easterly direction on the westbound lane. Rogers saw Race's car coming at him; he stopped in the westbound lane; but he was unable to move out of the way because there was a guard rail along that part of the road and no shoulder. Rogers first saw the Race vehicle when it was about 550 feet up Lore Avenue — or about 250 feet west of River Road. At that point, the Race car was being driven easterly on Lore Avenue in the westbound lane, almost along-side the Bierczynski car which was moving easterly in the eastbound lane. The front bumper of the Race car was opposite the back bumper of the Bierczynski car. Both cars were moving at about 55 or 60 m.p.h. down the hill. Before reaching River Road, Race swerved back into the eastbound lane behind Bierczynski, who was about a car length in front. As it crossed River Road, the Race automobile "bottomed on the road"; and it "careened down against the pavement and gave an impression of an explosion"; dust "flew everywhere" sufficiently to obscure the Race car momentarily from Rogers' view. At that point, the Race and Bierczynski automobiles were only "inches apart". The

Race car then emerged from behind the Bierczynski car and careened sideways, at about 70 m.p.h., a distance of about 300 feet to the Rogers car standing in the westbound lane. The left side of the Race car struck the front of the Rogers car. Meanwhile, the Bierczynski car was brought to a stop in the eastbound lane, about 35 feet from the area of impact. The Bierczynski car did not come into contact with the Rogers vehicle.

Bierczynski's contention as to lack of proximate cause is based mainly upon the facts that his automobile remained in the proper lane at all times and was stopped about 35 feet before reaching the area of impact, without coming into contact with the Rogers car. These facts notwithstanding, [there was] sufficient evidence of proximate cause, in our opinion, to warrant the submission of that issue to the jury as to both drivers.

In many States, automobile racing on a public highway is prohibited by statute, the violation of which is negligence per se. Delaware has no such statute. Nevertheless, speed competition in automobiles on the public highway is negligence in this State, for the reason that a reasonably prudent person would not engage in such conduct. This conclusion is in accord with the general rule, prevailing in other jurisdictions which lack statutes on the subject, that racing motor vehicles on a public highway is negligence.

It is also generally held that all who engage in a race on the highway do so at their peril, and are liable for injury or damage sustained by a third person as a result thereof, regardless of which of the racing cars directly inflicted the injury or damage. The authorities reflect generally accepted rules of causation that all parties engaged in a motor vehicle race on the highway are wrongdoers acting in concert, and that each participant is liable for harm to a third person arising from the tortious conduct of the other, because he has induced and encouraged the tort. *See* RESTATEMENT OF THE LAW OF TORTS § 876.

We subscribe to those rules; and hold that, as a general rule, participation in a motor vehicle race on a public highway is an act of concurrent negligence imposing liability on each participant for any injury to a non-participant resulting from the race. If, therefore, Race and Bierczynski were engaged in a speed competition, each was liable for the damages and injuries to the plaintiffs herein, even though Bierczynski was not directly involved in the collision itself. Bierczynski apparently concedes liability if a race had, in fact, been in progress. Clearly there was ample evidence to carry to the jury the issue of a race — and with it, implicit therein, the issue of proximate cause as to Bierczynski.

The foregoing disposes of the appellant's contention that there was no evidence upon which it was proper for plaintiffs' counsel to argue to the jury that the defendants were racing. [W]e see no merit in the appellant's contention that the Trial Court should have permitted a showing that Rogers brought criminal charges against Race but not against Bierczynski after the accident. . . .

We find no error as asserted by the appellant. The judgments below are affirmed.

NOTES

1. The plaintiff's injury in *Bierczynski* occurred after Race's car hit him. Why doesn't the court describe this as a "separable" injury and assign liability solely to Race?

2. Does the *Bierczynski* case represent a departure from the traditional rule of "but for" causation? Consider Roscoe Pound's statement: "What is peculiar to American legal thinking, is an ultra-individualism, an uncompromising insistence upon individual interests and individual property as the focal point of jurisprudence." ROSCOE POUND, THE SPIRIT OF THE COMMON LAW 37 (1921). In tort law, this insistence upon individualism manifests itself in the principle that a defendant is only responsible for what he has done. Doesn't the court really hold defendant Bierczynski responsible for something that he *did not* do?

3. What if a case like *Bierczynski* involved more than two defendants? Or what if a similar situation arose where the agreement among tortfeasors was less clear? Consider these questions in the case that follows.

2. Enterprise Liability

HALL v. E. I. DU PONT DE NEMOURS & CO.
345 F. Supp. 353 (E.D.N.Y. 1972)

WEINSTEIN, DISTRICT JUDGE.

Thirteen children were allegedly injured by blasting caps in twelve unrelated accidents between 1955 and 1959. The injuries occurred in the states of Alabama, California, Maryland, Montana, Nevada, North Carolina, Tennessee, Texas, Washington and West Virginia. Plaintiffs are citizens of the states in which their injuries occurred. They are now claiming damages against six manufacturers of blasting caps and the I.M.E. on the grounds of negligence, common law conspiracy, assault and strict liability in tort.

While plaintiffs' injuries occurred at widely varied times and places, the complaint alleges certain features common to them all. Each plaintiff, according to the complaint, "came into possession" of a dynamite blasting cap which was not labeled or marked with a warning of danger, and which could be easily detonated by a child. In each instance, an injurious explosion occurred.

The complaint does not identify a particular manufacturer of the cap which caused a particular injury. It alleges that each cap in question was designed and manufactured jointly or severally by the six corporate defendants or by other named manufacturers, and by their trade association, the I.M.E.

Plaintiffs' central contention is that injuries were caused by the defendants' failure to place a warning on the blasting caps and to manufacture caps which would have been less easily detonated. This failure, according to the plaintiffs, was not the result of defendants' ignorance of the dangerousness of their product to children. The complaint states that the defendants had actual knowledge that children were frequently injured by blasting caps and, through the trade association, kept statistics and other information regarding these accidents. Recognizing the dangerousness of their product to children, the defendants, through the trade association, used various means, such as placards and printed notices, to warn users of the caps and the general public. These matters were allegedly inadequate in light of the known risks of injury. Moreover, defendants are said to have jointly explicitly considered the possibility of labeling the caps, to have rejected this possibility, and to have engaged in lobbying activities against legislation which would have required such labeling. The long-standing industry practice of not placing a warning message on individual blasting caps was, it is urged, the result of a conscious agreement among the defendants, in the light of known dangers, with regard to this aspect of their product.

Defendants move to dismiss on the grounds that the plaintiff-children do not state claims upon which relief can be granted.

Joint Liability

The central question raised by defendants' motion is whether the defendants can be held responsible as a group under any theory of joint liability for injuries arising out of their individual manufacture of blasting caps [due to the defendants' parallel safety practices]. The reasoning underlying current policy justifies the extension of established doctrines of joint tort liability to the area of industry-wide cooperation in product manufacture and design.

Joint liability has historically been imposed in four distinguishable kinds of situations: (1) the actors knowingly join in the performance of the tortious act or acts; (2) the actors fail to perform a common duty owed to the plaintiff; (3) there is a special relationship between the parties (*e.g.*, master and servant or joint entrepreneurs); (4) although there is no concerted action, nevertheless the independent acts of several actors concur to produce indivisible, harmful consequences.

These categories reflect three overlapping but distinguishable problems with which the law of joint liability has been concerned. The first is the problem of joint or group control of risk: the need to deter hazardous behavior by groups or multiple defendants, as well as by individuals. The second is the problem of enterprise liability: the policy of assigning the foreseeable costs of an activity to those in the most strategic position to reduce them. The third is the problem of fairness with respect to burden of proof: the desire to avoid denying recovery to an innocent injured plaintiff because proof of causation may be within defendants' control or entirely unavailable. The complaint and defendants' motion to dismiss raise all the problems for consideration.

American courts have imposed joint liability for concerted action. . . . "Cooperation" or "concert" has been found in various business and property relationships, group activities, such as automobile racing, cooperative efforts in medical care or railroad work and concurrent water pollution. "Express agreement is not necessary; all that is required is that there shall be a common design or understanding." Prosser, *Joint Torts and Several Liability*, 25 CAL. L. REV. 413, 429-30 (1937).

Defendants argue that their participation in the I.M.E. safety program, and their cooperative or parallel activities regarding the safety features of blasting caps do not give them joint control over the risks of injury for purposes of tort liability. Joint control of risk and consequent joint responsibility arises, in their view, only when manufacturers enter into a conspiracy to commit intentional harm, or into a partnership or joint venture. The key to a joint venture, they assert, is an agreement to share profits and to pursue a limited number of business objectives over a short period of time. Since the defendants' membership in their trade association involves neither profit-sharing nor a limited time-span, they contend that no joint responsibility arises from the association and its members' activities.

The lesson [however] is clear that joint control of risk can exist among actors who are not bound in a profit-sharing joint venture. This point is thoroughly confirmed by cases imposing joint liability on "joint enterprises," which are distinguished from "joint ventures" as being "non-profit undertaking[s] for the mutual benefit or pleasure of parties" and on which joint liability is imposed because of the parties' effective joint control of the risk.

[Here,] plaintiffs can submit evidence that defendants, acting independently, adhered to an industry-wide standard or custom with regard to the safety features of blasting caps. [T]he existence of industry-wide standards or practices alone will not support, in all circumstances, the imposition of joint liability. But where, [as in this case] individual defendant-manufacturers cannot be identified, the existence of industry-wide standards or practices could support a finding of joint control of risk and a shift of the burden of proving causation to the defendants.

The allegations in this case suggest that the entire blasting-cap industry and its trade association provide the logical locus at which precautions should be taken and liability imposed. It is unlikely that individual manufacturers would collect information about the nationwide incidence and circumstances of blasting-cap accidents involving children, and it is entirely reasonable that the manufacturers should delegate this function to a jointly-sponsored and jointly-financed association.

In the event that the evidence warrants it, the imposition of joint liability on the trade association and its members should in no way be interpreted as "punishment" for the establishment of industry-wide institutions. Such liability would represent rather the law's traditional function of reviewing the risk and cost decisions inherent in industry-wide safety practices, whether organized or unorganized. *See, e.g., The T.J. Hooper*, 60 F.2d 737 (2d Cir. 1932).

To establish that the explosives industry should be held jointly liable on enterprise liability grounds, plaintiffs, pursuant to their pleading, will have to demonstrate defendants' joint awareness of the risk at issue in this case and their joint capacity to reduce or affect those risks. By noting these requirements, we wish to emphasize their special applicability to industries composed of a small number of units. What would be fair and feasible with regard to an industry of five or ten producers might be manifestly unreasonable if applied to a decentralized industry composed of thousands of small producers.

Plaintiffs contend that they should be relieved of the usual burden of proving a causal connection between each of their injuries and a particular manufacturer. Their problem is that a blasting cap found and exploded by a child often destroys what will be the only reliable evidence of its manufacturer-markings on the casing. As a solution, they invoke Section 433B of the Second Restatement of Torts.

Subsection (3) of Section 433B shifts the burden of proving causation to independently-acting defendants. It arises not from the problem of combined causation but rather from alternative causation of injury. The best known example is *Summers v. Tice*, 33 Cal. 2d 80, 199 P.2d 1 (1948), in which a hunter's injury could have been caused by only one of his two independently negligent companions. [*Summers v. Tice* is the next case in this unit. — Eds.]

Plaintiffs must show by a preponderance of the evidence, *i.e.*, that it is more probable than not that the caps involved in the accidents were the products of the named defendant-manufacturers. Plaintiffs do not have to identify which one of the defendant-manufacturers made each injury-causing cap. To impose such a requirement would obviate the entire rule of shifting the burden of proving causation to three defendants. It must be more probable than not that an injury was caused by a cap made by some one of the named defendant-manufacturers, though which one is unknown.

[P]laintiffs cannot identify the particular manufacturers of the injury-causing caps. They have joined substantially the entire blasting-cap industry and its trade association as defendants, and their recovery turns on theories of joint liability. [Defendants' motion to dismiss is denied.]

NOTES

1. How does "enterprise" liability (or "industry-wide" liability) in *Hall* differ from concert of action in *Bierczynski*?

2. In *Hall*, Judge Weinstein suggests that enterprise liability should be limited to industries with a small number of companies. How can courts determine a point at which the theory is no longer applicable? Should it matter if industry members are no longer solvent or otherwise unavailable as defendants? For example, which of the following situations would be more appropriate for an application of enterprise liability — a situation with 100 solvent manufacturers,

all of whom are before the court, or a situation where only two of six manufacturers are viable defendants?

3. Should enterprise liability apply in a case where the plaintiff *is* able to
identify the manufacturer of the product that caused his injury? Why or why
not?

3. Alternative Liability

SUMMERS v. TICE
199 P.2d 1 (Cal. 1948)

CARTER, J.

Each of the two defendants appeals from a judgment against them in an
action for personal injuries. . . . Plaintiff's action was against both defendants
for an injury to his right eye and face as the result of being struck by bird shot
discharged from a shotgun. The case was tried by the court without a jury and
the court found that on November 20, 1945, plaintiff and the two defendants
were hunting quail on the open range. Each of the defendants was armed with
a 12 gauge shotgun loaded with shells containing 7½ size shot. Prior to going
hunting plaintiff discussed the hunting procedure with defendants, indicating
that they were to exercise care when shooting and to "keep in line." In the
course of hunting plaintiff proceeded up a hill, thus placing the hunters at the
points of a triangle. The view of defendants with reference to plaintiff was
unobstructed and they knew his location. Defendant Tice flushed a quail which
rose in flight to a ten foot elevation and flew between plaintiff and defendants.
Both defendants shot at the quail, shooting in plaintiff's direction. At that time
defendants were 75 yards from plaintiff. One shot struck plaintiff in his eye and
another in his upper lip. Finally it was found by the court that as the direct
result of the shooting by defendants the shots struck plaintiff as above mentioned and that defendants were negligent in so shooting and plaintiff was not
contributorily negligent.

The problem presented in this case is whether the judgment against both
defendants may stand. It is argued by defendants that they are not joint tortfeasors, and thus jointly and severally liable, as they were not acting in concert,
and that there is not sufficient evidence to show which defendant was guilty of
the negligence which caused the injuries the shooting by Tice or that by Simon-
son.

[W]e believe it is clear that the court sufficiently found on the issue that
defendants were jointly liable and that thus the negligence of both was the
cause of the injury or to that legal effect. It found that both defendants were negligent and "That as a direct and proximate result of the shots fired by defendants, and each of them, a birdshot pellet was caused to and did lodge in

plaintiff's right eye and that another birdshot pellet was caused to and did lodge in plaintiff's upper lip." It thus determined that the negligence of both defendants was the legal cause of the injury or that both were responsible. Implicit in such finding is the assumption that the court was unable to ascertain whether the shots were from the gun of one defendant or the other or one shot from each of them. The one shot that entered plaintiff's eye was the major factor in assessing damages and that shot could not have come from the gun of both defendants. It was from one or the other only.

It has been held that where a group of persons are on a hunting party, or otherwise engaged in the use of firearms, and two of them are negligent in firing in the direction of a third person who is injured thereby, both of those so firing are liable for the injury suffered by the third person, although the negligence of only one of them could have caused the injury[. Also,] both drivers have been held liable for the negligence of one where they engaged in a racing contest causing an injury to a third person. These cases speak of the action of defendants as being in concert as the ground of decision, yet it would seem they are straining that concept and the more reasonable basis appears in *Oliver v. Miles*. There two persons were hunting together. Both shot at some partridges and in so doing shot across the highway injuring plaintiff who was traveling on it. The court stated they were acting in concert and thus both were liable. The court then stated (110 So. 668): "We think that [each] is liable for the resulting injury to the boy, although no one can say definitely who actually shot him. *To hold otherwise would be to exonerate both from liability, although each was negligent, and the injury resulted from such negligence.*" (Emphasis added.) It is said in the Restatement: "For harm resulting to a third person from the tortious conduct of another, a person is liable if [he] (b) knows that the other's conduct constitutes a breach of duty and gives substantial assistance or encouragement to the other so to conduct himself, or (c) gives substantial assistance to the other in accomplishing a tortious result and his own conduct, separately considered, constitutes a breach of duty to the third person." (REST., TORTS, § 876(b)(c).) Under subsection (b) the example is given: "A and B are members of a hunting party. Each of them in the presence of the other shoots across a public road at an animal this being negligent as to persons on the road. A hits the animal. B's bullet strikes C, a traveler on the road. A is liable to C." (REST., TORTS, § 876(b), Com., Illus. 3.) An illustration given under subsection (c) is the same as above except the factor of both defendants shooting is missing and joint liability is not imposed. It is further said that: "If two forces are actively operating, one because of the actor's negligence, the other not because of any misconduct on his part, and each of itself sufficient to bring about harm to another, the actor's negligence may be held by the jury to be a substantial factor in bringing it about." (REST., TORTS, § 432.) Dean Wigmore has this to say: "When two or more persons by their acts are possibly the sole cause of a harm, or when two or more acts of the same person are possibly the sole cause, and the plaintiff has introduced evidence that the one of the two persons, or the one of the same person's two acts, is culpable, then the defendant has the burden of proving that the other person, or his other act, was the sole cause of the harm. (b) [The] real reason for the rule that each joint tortfeasor is responsible for the whole damage is the practical unfairness of denying the injured person redress simply because he cannot prove how much damage each did, when it is certain that between them they did all; let them be the ones to apportion it among themselves. Since, then, the difficulty of proof is the reason, the rule should apply whenever the harm has plural causes, and not merely when they acted in conscious concert. . . .” (WIGMORE, SELECT CASES ON THE LAW OF TORTS, § 153.) Similarly Professor Carpenter has said: “(Suppose) the case where A and B independently shoot at C and but one bullet touches C’s body. In such case, such proof as is ordinarily required that either A or B shot C, of course fails. It is suggested that there should be a relaxation of the proof required of the plaintiff [where] the injury occurs as the result of one where more than one independent force is operating, and it is impossible to determine that the force set in operation by defendant did not in fact constitute a cause of the damage, and where it may have caused the damage, but the plaintiff is unable to establish that it was a cause.” (20 CAL. L. REV. 406.)

When we consider the relative position of the parties and the results that would flow if plaintiff was required to pin the injury on one of the defendants only, a requirement that the burden of proof on that subject be shifted to defendants becomes manifest. They are both wrongdoers both negligent toward plaintiff. They brought about a situation where the negligence of one of them injured the plaintiff, hence it should rest with them each to absolve himself if he can. The injured party has been placed by defendants in the unfair position of pointing to which defendant caused the harm. If one can escape the other may also and plaintiff is remediless. Ordinarily defendants are in a far better position to offer evidence to determine which one caused the injury. This reasoning has recently found favor in this Court. In a quite analogous situation this Court held that a patient injured while unconscious on an operating table in a hospital could hold all or any of the persons who had any connection with the operation even though he could not select the particular acts by the particular person which led to his disability. *Ybarra v. Spangard*, 25 Cal.2d 486, 154 P.2d 687.

[I]t should be pointed out that the same reasons of policy and justice [that] shift the burden to each of [the] defendants to absolve himself if he can relieving the wronged person of the duty of apportioning the injury to a particular defendant, apply here where we are concerned with whether plaintiff is required to supply evidence for the apportionment of damages. If defendants are independent tortfeasors and thus each liable for the damage caused by him alone, and, at least, where the matter of apportionment is incapable of proof, the innocent wronged party should not be deprived of his right to redress. The wrongdoers should be left to work out between themselves any apportionment. Some of the cited cases refer to the difficulty of apportioning the burden of damages between the independent tortfeasors, and say that where factually a correct division cannot be made, the trier of fact may make it the best it can, which would be more or less a guess, stressing the factor that the wrongdoers are not [in] a position to complain of uncertainty.

It is urged that plaintiff now has changed the theory of his case in claiming a concert of action; that he did not plead or prove such concert. From what has been said it is clear that there has been no change in theory. The joint liability, as well as the lack of knowledge as to which defendant was liable, was pleaded and the proof developed the case under either theory. We have seen that for the reasons of policy discussed herein, the case is based upon the legal proposition that, under the circumstances here presented, each defendant is liable for the whole damage whether they are deemed to be acting in concert or independently.

The judgment is affirmed.

NOTES

1. Dean Prosser called the *Summers* burden shifting rule "double fault and alternative liability." *See* PROSSER & KEETON, § 41, at 270-71. Today, most courts and commentators simply refer to the theory as "alternative liability." *See* RESTATEMENT (SECOND) OF TORTS § 433B (1965)

2. Could the court in *Summers* have achieved the same result by applying a different theory? For example, what is the relationship between alternative liability and *res ipsa loquitur*? Why not concert of action?

3. Note that the court envisions the defendants as jointly and severally liable for the plaintiff's harm. Is this fair? Would your answer change if the number of defendants involved were greater?

4. Market Share Liability

SINDELL v. ABBOTT LABORATORIES
607 P.2d 924 (Cal. 1980)

MOSK, JUSTICE.

This case involves a complex problem both timely and significant: may a plaintiff, injured as the result of a drug administered to her mother during pregnancy, who knows the type of drug involved but cannot identify the manufacturer of the precise product, hold liable for her injuries a maker of a drug produced from an identical formula?

Plaintiff Judith Sindell brought an action against eleven drug companies and Does 1 through 100, on behalf of herself and other women similarly situated. The complaint alleges as follows:

Between 1941 and 1971, defendants were engaged in the business of manufacturing, promoting, and marketing diethylstilbesterol (DES), a drug which is a synthetic compound of the female hormone estrogen. The drug was administered to plaintiff's mother and the mothers of the class she represents, for the purpose of preventing miscarriage. In 1947, the Food and Drug Administration authorized the marketing of DES as a miscarriage preventative, but only on an experimental basis, with a requirement that the drug contain a warning label to that effect.

DES may cause cancerous vaginal and cervical growths in the daughters exposed to it before birth, because their mothers took the drug during pregnancy. The form of cancer from which these daughters suffer is known as adenocarcinoma, and it manifests itself after a minimum latent period of 10 or 12 years. It is a fast-spreading and deadly disease, and radical surgery is required to prevent it from spreading. DES also causes adenosis, precancerous vaginal and cervical growths which may spread to other areas of the body. Women who suffer from this condition must be monitored by biopsy or colposcopic examination twice a year, a painful and expensive procedure. Thousands of women whose mothers received DES during pregnancy are unaware of the effects of the drug.

In 1971, the Food and Drug Administration ordered defendants to cease marketing and promoting DES for the purpose of preventing miscarriages, and to warn physicians and the public that the drug should not be used by pregnant women because of the danger to their unborn children.

During the period defendants marketed DES, they knew or should have known that it was a carcinogenic substance, that there was a grave danger after varying periods of latency it would cause cancerous and precancerous growths in the daughters of the mothers who took it, and that it was ineffective to prevent miscarriage. Nevertheless, defendants continued to advertise and market the drug as a miscarriage preventative. They failed to test DES for efficacy and safety; the tests performed by others, upon which they relied, indicated that it was not safe or effective. In violation of the authorization of the Food and Drug Administration, defendants marketed DES on an unlimited basis rather than as an experimental drug, and they failed to warn of its potential danger.

Because of defendants' advertised assurances that DES was safe and effective to prevent miscarriage, plaintiff was exposed to the drug prior to her birth. She became aware of the danger from such exposure within one year of the time she filed her complaint. As a result of the DES ingested by her mother, plaintiff developed a malignant bladder tumor which was removed by surgery. She suffers from adenosis and must constantly be monitored by biopsy or colposcopy to insure early warning of further malignancy.

[In her complaint, plaintiff] alleges that defendants are jointly liable because they acted in concert, on the basis of express and implied agreements, and in reliance upon and ratification and exploitation of each other's testing and marketing methods.

Defendants demurred to the complaint. While the complaint did not expressly allege that plaintiff could not identify the manufacturer of the precise drug ingested by her mother, she stated in her points and authorities in opposition to the demurrers filed by some of the defendants that she was unable to make the identification, and the trial court sustained the demurrers of these defendants without leave to amend on the ground that plaintiff did not and stated she could not identify which defendant had manufactured the drug responsible for her injuries. Thereupon, the court dismissed the action. This appeal involves only five of ten defendants named in the complaint.

We begin with the proposition that, as a general rule, the imposition of liability depends upon a showing by the plaintiff that his or her injuries were caused by the act of the defendant or by an instrumentality under the defendant's control. The rule applies whether the injury resulted from an accidental event or from the use of a defective product.

There are, however, exceptions to this rule. Plaintiff's complaint suggests several bases upon which defendants may be held liable for her injuries even though she cannot demonstrate the name of the manufacturer which produced the DES actually taken by her mother. The first of these theories, classically illustrated by *Summers v. Tice* (1948) 33 Cal. 2d 80, 199 P.2d 1, places the burden of proof of causation upon tortious defendants in certain circumstances. The second basis of liability emerging from the complaint is that defendants acted in concert to cause injury to plaintiff. There is a third and novel approach to the problem, sometimes called the theory of "enterprise liability," but which we prefer to designate by the more accurate term of "industry-wide" liability, which might obviate the necessity for identifying the manufacturer of the injury-causing drug. We shall conclude that these doctrines, as previously interpreted, may not be applied to hold defendants liable under the allegations of this complaint. However, we shall propose and adopt a fourth basis for permitting the action to be tried, grounded upon an extension of the *Summers* doctrine.

Plaintiff places primary reliance upon cases which hold that if a party cannot identify which of two or more defendants caused an injury, the burden of proof may shift to the defendants to show that they were not responsible for the harm. This principle is sometimes referred to as the "alternative liability" theory. [The court then described the decision in *Summers v. Tice, supra*.] [P]laintiff may not prevail in her claim that the *Summers* rationale should be employed to fix the whole liability for her injuries upon defendants, at least as those principles have previously been applied. There is an important difference between the situation involved in *Summers* and the present case. There, all the parties who were or could have been responsible for the harm to the plaintiff were joined as defendants. Here, by contrast, there are approximately 200 drug companies which made DES, any of which might have manufactured the injury-producing drug.

The second principle upon which plaintiff relies is the so-called "concert of action" theory. [Plaintiff] alleges that defendants' wrongful conduct "is the result of planned and concerted action, express and implied agreements, collaboration in, reliance upon, acquiescence in and ratification, exploitation and adoption of each other's testing, marketing methods, lack of warnings [and] other acts or omissions . . ." and that "acting individually and in concert, (defendants) promoted, approved, authorized, acquiesced in, and reaped profits from sales" of DES. These allegations, plaintiff claims, state a "tacit understanding" among defendants to commit a tortious act against her.

In our view, this litany of charges is insufficient to allege a cause of action. The gravamen of the charge of concert is that defendants failed to adequately test the drug or to give sufficient warning of its dangers and that they relied upon the tests performed by one another and took advantage of each others' promotional and marketing techniques. These allegations do not amount to a charge that there was a tacit understanding or a common plan among defendants to fail to conduct adequate tests or give sufficient warnings, and that they substantially aided and encouraged one another in these omissions.

A third theory upon which plaintiff relies is the concept of industry-wide liability, or according to the terminology of the parties, "enterprise liability." This theory was suggested in *Hall v. E. I. Du Pont De Nemours & Co., Inc.* (E.D.N.Y. 1972) 345 F. Supp. 353. [The court then described the decision in *Hall*.] We decline to apply this theory in the present case. At least 200 manufacturers produced DES; *Hall*, which involved 6 manufacturers representing the entire blasting cap industry in the United States, cautioned against application of the doctrine espoused therein to a large number of producers. Moreover, in *Hall*, the conclusion that the defendants jointly controlled the risk was based upon allegations that they had delegated some functions relating to safety to a trade association. There are no such allegations here, and we have concluded above that plaintiff has failed to allege liability on a concert of action theory.

Equally important, the drug industry is closely regulated by the Food and Drug Administration, which actively controls the testing and manufacture of drugs and the method by which they are marketed, including the contents of warning labels. To a considerable degree, therefore, the standards followed by drug manufacturers are suggested or compelled by the government. Adherence to those standards cannot, of course, absolve a manufacturer of liability to which it would otherwise be subject. But since the government plays such a pervasive role in formulating the criteria for the testing and marketing of drugs, it would be unfair to impose upon a manufacturer liability for injuries resulting from the use of a drug which it did not supply simply because it followed the standards of the industry.

If we were confined to the theories of *Summers* and *Hall*, we would be constrained to hold that the judgment must be sustained. Should we require that plaintiff identify the manufacturer which supplied the DES used by her mother or that all DES manufacturers be joined in the action, she would effectively be precluded from any recovery. As defendants candidly admit, there is little likelihood that all the manufacturers who made DES at the time in question are still in business or that they are subject to the jurisdiction of the California courts. There are, however, forceful arguments in favor of holding that plaintiff has a cause of action.

In our contemporary complex industrialized society, advances in science and technology create fungible goods which may harm consumers and which cannot be traced to any specific producer. The response of the courts can be either to adhere rigidly to prior doctrine, denying recovery to those injured by such products, or to fashion remedies to meet these changing needs. Just as Justice Traynor in his landmark concurring opinion in *Escola v. Coca Cola Bottling Company* (1944) 24 Cal. 2d 453, 467-468, 150 P.2d 436, recognized that in an era of mass production and complex marketing methods the traditional standard of negligence was insufficient to govern the obligations of manufacturer to consumer, so should we acknowledge that some adaptation of the rules of causation and liability may be appropriate in these recurring circumstances.

The most persuasive reason for finding plaintiff states a cause of action is that advanced in *Summers*: as between an innocent plaintiff and negligent defendants, the latter should bear the cost of the injury. Here, as in *Summers*, plaintiff is not at fault in failing to provide evidence of causation, and although the absence of such evidence is not attributable to the defendants either, their conduct in marketing a drug the effects of which are delayed for many years played a significant role in creating the unavailability of proof.

From a broader policy standpoint, defendants are better able to bear the cost of injury resulting from the manufacture of a defective product. As was said by Justice Traynor in *Escola*, "(t)he cost of an injury and the loss of time or health may be an overwhelming misfortune to the person injured, and a needless one, for the risk of injury can be insured by the manufacturer and distributed among the public as a cost of doing business." The manufacturer is in the best position to discover and guard against defects in its products and to warn of harmful effects; thus, holding it liable for defects and failure to warn of harmful effects will provide an incentive to product safety. These considerations are particularly significant where medication is involved, for the consumer is virtually helpless to protect himself from serious, sometimes permanent, sometimes fatal, injuries caused by deleterious drugs.

Where, as here, all defendants produced a drug from an identical formula and the manufacturer of the DES which caused plaintiff's injuries cannot be identified through no fault of plaintiff, a modification of the rule of *Summers* is warranted. As we have seen, an undiluted *Summers* rationale is inappropriate to shift the burden of proof of causation to defendants because if we measure the chance that any particular manufacturer supplied the injury-causing product by the number of producers of DES, there is a possibility that none of the five defendants in this case produced the offending substance and that the responsible manufacturer, not named in the action, will escape liability.

But we approach the issue of causation from a different perspective: we hold it to be reasonable in the present context to measure the likelihood that any of the defendants supplied the product which allegedly injured plaintiff by the percentage which the DES sold by each of them for the purpose of preventing miscarriage bears to the entire production of the drug sold by all for that purpose.

If plaintiff joins in the action the manufacturers of a substantial share of the DES which her mother might have taken, the injustice of shifting the burden of proof to defendants to demonstrate that they could not have made the substance which injured plaintiff is significantly diminished.

The presence in the action of a substantial share of the appropriate market also provides a ready means to apportion damages among the defendants. Each defendant will be held liable for the proportion of the judgment represented by its share of that market unless it demonstrates that it could not have made the product which caused plaintiff's injuries. In the present case, as we have see, one DES manufacturer was dismissed from the action upon filing a declaration that it had not manufactured DES until after plaintiff was born. Once plaintiff has met her burden of joining the required defendants, they in turn may cross-complaint against other DES manufacturers, not joined in the action, which they can allege might have supplied the injury-causing product.

Under this approach, each manufacturer's liability would approximate its responsibility for the injuries caused by its own products.

We are not unmindful of the practical problems involved in defining the market and determining market share, but these are largely matters of proof which properly cannot be determined at the pleading stage of these proceedings. Defendants urge that it would be both unfair and contrary to public policy to hold them liable for plaintiff's injuries in the absence of proof that one of them supplied the drug responsible for the damage. Most of their arguments, however, are based upon the assumption that one manufacturer would be held responsible for the products of another or for those of all other manufacturers if plaintiff ultimately prevails. But under the rule we adopt, each manufacturer's liability for an injury would be approximately equivalent to the damages caused by the DES it manufactured.

The judgments are reversed.

NOTES

1. By allowing the plaintiff to recover without identifying the actual cause of her injury — and by allowing the plaintiff to go forward without naming each potential cause in the lawsuit — *Sindell* represented a significant step away from the traditional rule of individualized causation. *Sindell*, however, was only the first of several important market share decisions during the 1980s. The following article excerpt traces the development of the theory in DES cases:

> Four years after the California Supreme Court decided *Sindell*, the supreme courts of Washington and Wisconsin adopted new versions of market share liability. Both courts expanded *Sindell* by eliminating its requirement that a plaintiff sue the manufacturers of a "substantial share" of the DES taken by her mother. . . .

In *Martin v. Abbott Laboratories*, the Washington Supreme Court labeled its version of market share liability "Market-Share Alternate Liability." Expanding the *Sindell* rule, the *Martin* court ruled that a DES "plaintiff need commence suit against only one" manufacturer to maintain a market-share-liability action. The *Martin* court remained consistent with *Sindell*, however, by premising its ruling on a defendant's ability to exculpate itself and on the unique nature of DES: Individual defendants are entitled to exculpate themselves from liability by establishing, by a preponderance of the evidence, that they did not produce or market the particular type of DES taken by the plaintiff's mother; that they did not market the DES in the geographic market area of plaintiff's mother's obtaining the drug; or that they did not distribute DES in the time period of plaintiff's mother's ingestion of the drug.

In *Collins v. Eli Lilly Co.*, the Wisconsin Supreme Court also adopted a version of market share liability, basing its variant on the assumption that each DES manufacturer created a risk to the public as a whole. Like *Martin*, the *Collins* court did not require plaintiffs to join a "substantial share" of DES manufacturers as defendants. Instead, plaintiffs needed to sue only one defendant and allege the following elements: that the plaintiff's mother took DES; that DES caused the plaintiff's subsequent injuries; that the defendant produced or marketed the type of DES taken by the plaintiff's mother; and that the defendant's conduct in producing or marketing the DES constituted a breach of a legally recognized duty to the plaintiff.

Also like *Martin*, the *Collins* court explicitly permitted defendants to exculpate themselves if they could prove that they did not manufacture or market any DES that reached the plaintiff's mother.

Throughout the 1980s, courts and commentators lined up on both sides of the market-share-liability dispute. Some rejected market share liability as an unwarranted destruction of the traditional cause-in-fact requirement. Others accepted the theory as the only equitable way to resolve DES litigation. In 1989, however, the New York Court of Appeals decided *Hymowitz v. Eli Lilly & Co.*[, 539 N.E.2d 1069 (N.Y. 1989),] and authored an important new chapter in the development of market share liability.

In *Hymowitz,* the New York Court of Appeals completely eliminated the first two [important limitations on the rule of] *Summers v. Tice* . . . : the need to bring all possible culpable defendants before the court and the ability of a defendant to exculpate itself. . . .

With respect to the [first limitation], the *Hymowitz* court agreed with the *Collins* and *Martin* courts that a plaintiff need not join the manufacturers of a substantial share of the DES market. However, the

Hymowitz court very broadly defined "the DES market" for purposes of apportioning liability. Rather than defining the relevant market as a narrow geographic area where the plaintiff's mother used DES, the *Hymowitz* court defined the relevant market as national in every DES case. The court conceded that use of a national market would not connect liability to the likelihood of culpability in any individual case. "Instead," the court stated, "we choose to apportion liability so as to correspond to the overall culpability of each defendant, measured by the amount of risk of injury each defendant created to the public-at-large." . . .

Even more dramatically, the *Hymowitz* court eliminated the second [limitation]: the requirement that a defendant be able to exculpate itself by proving that it did not cause the plaintiff's harm. The court stated that, because its decision was based on overall risk creation, exculpation would create a fortuitous "windfall" for certain manufacturers. . . . *Hymowitz*, therefore, created a situation in which a plaintiff could successfully recover damages from a DES manufacturer despite proof that the plaintiff's mother never used that manufacturer's product.

Only one link remained between *Hymowitz* and the principles on which the *Summers* court first relaxed the requirement of individualized causation: the uniform nature of the instrumentality causing the plaintiff's harm. The *Hymowitz* court recognized this link at the outset of its market share discussion:

We stress, however, that the DES situation is a singular case, with manufacturers acting in a parallel manner to produce an identical, generically marketed product, which causes injury many years later. . . . Given this unusual scenario, it is more appropriate that the loss be borne by those that produced the drug for use during pregnancy, rather than by those who were injured by the use, even where the precise manufacturer of the drug cannot be identified in a particular action.

Andrew R. Klein, *Beyond DES: Rejecting the Application of Market Share Liability in Blood Products Litigation*, 68 Tul. L. Rev. 883, 901-05 (1994).

2. Do you agree with the decision in *Hymowitz*? Should a court really impose liability on a defendant that can prove it *did not* cause the plaintiff's harm? Professor Aaron Twerski defended *Hymowitz* in this way:

Closely related to the market size question is whether a defendant can free itself from paying its market share if it can establish that it was not responsible for the harm to the particular plaintiff. Until *Hymowitz*, the courts have answered the question in the affirmative. With all due respect to the courts, I believe that this position is arrant nonsense. Market share posits the view that causation will be viewed writ large over a broad market. Of what importance is it that a defendant establishes that it did not sell a particular pill to a particular patient? Not only is it irrelevant to market share theory, it cuts against the fair administration of it. A defendant who exits a particular case because by chance it can establish that it did not sell to a particular pharmacy, dumps its percentage of the harm upon other defendants who cannot prove the negative. Those defendants end up paying a disproportionate share of the costs of DES harm. Furthermore, the costs of litigating individual causation are very high. Defendants who have the defense available to them, expend large sums of money for the detective work necessary to establish the defense. And courts must decide whether they have met their burden of establishing no causation. And all this for what?

Ultimately, the court's fumblings of this issue is explainable only because it made them feel better that in they were paying their dues to the "nineteenth century causation club.'" It is as if they were saying "Now we really aren't that radical after all. If you can prove that you did not cause harm to this particular plaintiff, we will let you walk.'" Old doctrine really does die hard. That *Hymowitz* has refused to play this charade is to its credit. It has honestly faced the fact that market share cannot be reconciled with traditional causation theory.

Aaron D. Twerski, *Market Share — A Tale of Two Centuries*, 55 BROOK. L. REV. 869 (1989). Does Professor Twerski's argument convince you of *Hymowitz*'s correctness? If so, should the theory be limited to the unique situation of DES?

3. Several courts have rejected the application of market share liability in the DES setting. For one example, see *Smith v. Eli Lilly & Co.*, 560 N.E.2d 324, 344-45 (Ill. 1990).

4. In 1991, the Hawaii Supreme Court adopted market share liability in a case involving Factor VIII concentrate, a plasma-based derivative used by hemophiliacs to replace the missing clotting protein in their blood. *Smith v. Cutter Biological, Inc.*, 823 P.2d 717 (Haw. 1991). The court defended the extension by stating:

> No longer can we apply traditional rules of negligence, such as those used in individual and low level negligence to mass tort cases, especially here, where we are dealing with a pharmaceutical industry that dispenses drugs on a wide scale that could cause massive injuries to the public, and where fungibility makes the strict requirements difficult to meet. The problem calls for adopting new rules of causation, for otherwise innocent plaintiffs would be left without a remedy.

Id. at 724. A dissenting justice disagreed, arguing that Factor VIII concentrate was not sufficiently similar to DES to merit extending the doctrine:

> Unlike DES, Factor VIII is not a generic, fungible drug. Each processor prepares its Factor VIII concentrate by its own proprietary processes, using plasma collected from its own sources. Each firm's Factor VIII concentrate is clearly distinguishable by brand name, package color, lot

number and number of units of Factor VIII per vial; each firm's Factor VIII concentrate is separately licensed by the Food and Drug Administration. There is no evidence that all Factor VIII products caused or were equally capable of causing HIV infection. Thus, the risk posed by the different brands of Factor VIII is not identical.

Id. at 733 (Moon, J., dissenting). Do you agree with the majority or with Justice Moon? Why might it be important that the "risk posed by different brands of Factor VIII is not identical?" *See generally* Andrew R. Klein, *Beyond DES: Rejecting the Application of Market Share Liability in Blood Products Litigation,* 68 Tul. L. Rev. 883 (1994).

5. In 1993, a federal district court judge in Chicago certified a class action lawsuit on behalf of HIV-infected hemophiliacs against the companies that manufactured Factor VIII concentrate. Two years later, a federal appellate court issued a writ of mandamus that effectively de-certified the class. *See In re Rhone-Poulenc Rorer Inc.,* 51 F.3d 1293 (7th Cir. 1995). The class, however, was subsequently re-certified for settlement purposes, and a federal district court approved an agreement under which the defendants agreed to pay each class member $100,000. *See In re Factor VIII or IX Concentrate Blood Products Litigation,* 159 F.3d 1016 (7th Cir. 1998). Recently, Congress passed legislation to provide additional monetary assistance to victims of contaminated blood products. *See* Ricky Ray Hemophilia Relief Fund Act of 1998 (Pub. L. 105-369, Nov. 12, 1998, 112 Stat. 3368). For an earlier proposal of assistance, see Andrew R. Klein, *A Legislative Alternative to "No Cause" Liability in Blood Products Litigation,* 12 Yale J. on Reg. 107 (1995).

PROBLEMS

1. Plaintiff received a breast implant during surgery performed by her doctor. The implant later ruptured, causing the plaintiff to suffer harm. Plaintiff sued one of three companies that sold breast implants to the doctor who performed the operation. Unfortunately, the doctor retained no records to indicate which company made the plaintiff's implant. Can the plaintiff proceed on a market share theory? If you were the plaintiff's lawyer, what evidence would you seek in discovery? *See Lee v. Baxter Healthcare Corp.,* 721 F. Supp. 89, 93-94 (D. Md. 1989).

2. Plaintiff was injured when a car battery exploded in a nearby Mercedes Benz automobile. Plaintiff could not identify the manufacturer of the battery that exploded, so he sued all manufacturers that made batteries that would fit the Mercedes Benz. Is market share liability a viable theory? Again, what evidence would be helpful for the plaintiff's attorney? *See York v. Lunkes,* 545 N.E.2d 478, 480-81 (Ill. App. Ct. 1989).

3. Plaintiff was injured in a car accident involving a multi-piece wheel assembly. The wheel was subsequently lost. Plaintiff, who could not identify the man-

ufacturer of the wheel assembly that led to the accident, sued numerous manufacturers of similar multi-piece wheel assemblies. Can the plaintiff succeed on a market share theory? *See Bradley v. Firestone,* 590 F. Supp. 1177 (D.S.D. 1984).

4. Plaintiff spent his career as an industrial welder at several different companies. In these jobs, he installed and removed numerous asbestos-containing products, some of which were manufactured by Defendant. Plaintiff now suffers from mesothelioma, a deadly form of cancer caused by exposure to asbestos. Plaintiff, however, cannot identify any specific asbestos exposure as having caused his illness. Can he use market share liability against the manufacturers of the products that contained asbestos? *See Leng v. Celotex Corp.*, 554 N.E.2d 468, 470 (Ill. App. Ct. 1990).

5. Plaintiff asserts injury based on prolonged exposure to lead-based paint in a 100-year old house. He sued various companies that marketed lead used in such paint over a 50-year period. Plaintiff asserts that these companies should have warned consumers of the risks of exposure to their products. But he cannot connect his own illness to the exposure of any single company's paint. Will market share liability be available to help the plaintiff overcome this problem? *See Santiago v. Sherwin-Williams Co.*, 782 F. Supp. 186, 193-95 (D. Mass. 1992), *aff'd*, 3 F.3d 546 (1st Cir. 1993).

HAMILTON v. ACCU-TEK
62 F. Supp. 2d 802 (E.D.N.Y. 1999)

WEINSTEIN, SENIOR DISTRICT JUDGE.

Relatives of six people killed by handguns, as well as one injured survivor and his mother, have sued twenty-five handgun manufacturers for negligence. They claim that the manufacturers' indiscriminate marketing and distribution practices generated an underground market in handguns, providing youths and violent criminals like the shooters in these cases with easy access to the instruments they have used with lethal effect.

Plaintiffs' claims raise novel issues of duty and of collective liability under governing New York state law. For this reason, it is respectfully recommended that the Court of Appeals for the Second Circuit certify these substantive law questions to the New York Court of Appeals for definitive resolution.

After a four-week trial, the jury found negligent fifteen of the defendants; nine of them were found to have proximately caused injury to one or more plaintiffs. Damages were found only in favor of plaintiff Steven Fox and his mother, Gail Fox, against American Arms, Inc. (.23% liability), Beretta U.S.A. Corp. (6.03% liability), and Taurus International Manufacturing, Inc. (6.8% liability).

FACTS

Stephen Fox was shot in Queens, New York on November 14, 1994. He was sixteen years old at the time, as was his friend, the shooter, Alfred Adkins, Jr. Mr. Fox survived, but a bullet remains lodged in his brain, causing severe permanent disability. There was evidence that the handgun Mr. Adkins used had been bought by him a short time before the shooting from a seller — unlikely to have been licensed — who declared it came from "the south" when he dispensed it from the trunk of a car.

Charged initially with attempted murder, Mr. Adkins later pled guilty to reckless endangerment in Queens County Family Court. A .25 caliber spent cartridge case was recovered from the crime scene. The gun used to shoot Mr. Fox was never found. Mr. Adkins testified at his deposition that he did not recall how he came to possess it.

Suit was initially brought by Gail Fox, Mr. Fox's mother and guardian. When Mr. Fox attained his majority, he was substituted as plaintiff. Ms. Fox remained in the case, suing on her own behalf for loss of her son's services and for her own nursing care of him.

[T]he jury calculated total damages of $3,950,000 and $50,000, respectively, to be assessed against the three defendants found liable in the percentages indicated above — .23, 6.03, and 6.8. [The defendants moved for judgment as a matter of law pursuant to Federal Rule of Civil Procedure 50(b).]

LAW AND ITS APPLICATION

To prevail on a negligence claim, a plaintiff must establish the following elements under New York law: (1) that the defendant owed him or her a duty of care, (2) that the defendant breached this duty by engaging in conduct posing an unreasonable risk of harm and (3) that defendant's breach proximately resulted in damage to the plaintiff. Each element will be discussed separately. [The court concluded that New York law would support the existence of a duty, as well as a jury finding of breach.]

The third element of a negligence claim under New York law is "proximate cause." To satisfy this element, a plaintiff must establish that defendant's negligence was a substantial foreseeable factor in bringing about his or her injury. As used in this memorandum and in the jury charge, the term "proximate cause" includes both the concept of "actual," or "in-fact", causation and the requirement that a defendant's liability be limited to injuries which foreseeably flow from its conduct. *See* PROSSER & KEETON § 30, at 165 ("legal" or "proximate" cause includes notion of "in-fact" causation).

Where circumstances have made it impossible for plaintiffs to determine which one of a number of manufacturers made the particular unit of the product which caused their injury, some states have fashioned alternative theories of [collective] liability which eliminate this identification requirement.

Predicting whether the New York Court of Appeals would impose collective liability in this case requires analysis of existing precedent as well as policy considerations on which that and other courts have relied in relaxing the traditional requirements of specific causation by defendants to avoid unjust results.

Four theories of collective liability are recognized under New York law: alternative, enterprise, concerted action, and market share. In each of these theories, liability of a single causative defendant in the traditional case is replaced with liability of a group of defendants. [The court then described each of these theories.]

Decisions to impose collective liability have been grounded in both moral and pragmatic considerations. A primary motivating factor has been the injustice of barring innocent plaintiffs' recovery solely because of their inability to identify which of a number of wrongdoing defendants caused their injuries.

Courts adopting collective liability have pointed to defendants' superior ability both to absorb and to minimize the costs associated with their activities.

Also relied upon in imposing market share liability have been the potentially deterrent effect of imposing collective liability, the helplessness of plaintiffs, and the magnitude of the harm inflicted.

An important theme running through all of the market share cases is the expanding nature of tort law and the need for courts to adapt traditional theories of recovery to keep pace with the evolving requirements of contemporary society.

Expansion of both substantive and procedural law in mass torts to permit appropriate compensation to those injured by negligent manufacturers is a necessary aspect of the law's role as protector of the public against massive delicts.

The New York Court of Appeals has, as already pointed out, been particularly responsive to the needs of today's plaintiffs struggling against doctrinal barriers erected to accommodate litigants of an earlier era. In *Hymowitz*, the Court of Appeals noted its multiple prior modifications of the rules of personal injury "in order to achieve the ends of justice in a more modern context" and declared that, "here judicial action is again required to overcome the inordinately difficult problems of proof caused by contemporary products and marketing techniques." *Hymowitz*, 73 N.Y.2d at 507, 539 N.E.2d at 1074, 541 N.Y.S.2d at 946 (citations and internal quotation marks omitted).

New York's approach to market share liability is in some sense more radical than that of other courts which have adopted the theory. In contrast to other versions of market share, under the rule laid down in *Hymowitz*, defendants who are able to prove that they could not have made the particular DES pills which caused a given plaintiff's injury — *e.g.*, because they sold only to certain pharmacies or because their pills were more easily identifiable — are not permitted to exculpate themselves. *Hymowitz*, 73 N.Y.2d at 512, 539 N.E.2d at 1078, 541

N.Y.S.2d at 950. Such "fortuities," the court reasoned, should not inure to the benefit of these equally culpable defendants.

Alternative, enterprise and concerted action theories of collective liability need not be applied to these handgun cases. Alternative liability is inappropriate for largely the same reasons the *Hymowitz* court deemed it inapplicable to DES: a large but fluctuating number of potential wrongdoers, equivalency of defendants' and plaintiffs' positions in terms of the ability to identify the manufacturer whose product caused the injury, and the unfairness of imposing joint and several liability where the probability that any one defendant's product actually injured the plaintiff is small.

The heart of enterprise liability, as already pointed out, is joint control of risk. Concerted action liability requires proof of an express or tacit agreement to engage in tortious conduct. Plaintiffs in the instant cases have presented insufficient evidence of both.

Many of the same factors which have previously led the New York Court of Appeals and other courts to relax the traditional rules of causation militate heavily in favor of the imposition of market share liability in the instant case. First, as in the case of DES, handgun plaintiffs are faced with intractable problems of proof. A large proportion of crime guns are never recovered. Expert evidence at trial supported the conclusion that the ability to determine the precise make of a gun through analysis of expended bullets and shell casings is limited. Thus, even though ballistics may help to eliminate possible manufacturers from consideration, plaintiffs usually are still faced with a group of wrongdoers none of whose conduct can definitively be established as an "actual" cause of damages.

Contemporary developments are relevant in deciding legal policy in favor of market share liability. The proliferation of illegal handguns in urban areas, the resultant epidemic of handgun violence among urban youth, and the gun industry's design and sale of increasingly lethal readily concealed and cheap handguns have created a crisis in today's cities. Many have now filed suits against handgun manufacturers.

The same factors compelling recognition of a duty [also] support the imposition of market share liability: (1) the superior ability of defendants to bear the costs foreseeably associated with the manufacture and widespread distribution of handguns; (2) the fairness of requiring them to do so since they can reduce the risks by their ability to choose merchandising techniques; (3) the deterrent potential of placing the burden on manufacturers careless of their responsibilities to the public; and (4) the fact that injured plaintiffs, unlike the users of products which later turn out to be defective, did not choose their connection with handguns. Under such circumstances the law will not leave the injured unrequited.

Defendants maintain that a market share instruction was not warranted here because handgun market share is not an accurate gauge of the degree of unreasonable risk produced by each negligent manufacturer. This is so, defendants contend, because each defendant's market share includes all sales, and the ratio of negligent to non-negligent sales may vary from manufacturer to manufacturer. Where the sale of DES was concerned, in contrast, each sale of a pill was tortious. This argument must be rejected. First, those defendants who placed restrictions on sales were found non-negligent by the jury. The precise breach alleged and proved against the others was their overall policy and practice of indiscriminate marketing and distribution of handguns. Given the nature of the breach, as found by the jury, any variations in the ratio of tortious to non-tortious sales among the negligent defendants must be regarded as accidental and irrelevant rather than a reflection of differing degrees of culpability. Under these circumstances, defendants' national market share — whether of total guns produced or by class of gun — is "an equitable way to provide plaintiffs with the relief they deserve, while also rationally distributing the responsibility for plaintiffs' injuries among defendants." *Hymowitz*, 73 N.Y.2d at 512, 539 N.E.2d at 1078, 541 N.Y.S.2d at 950.

Finally, defendants take issue with plaintiffs' failure to produce either a breakdown of defendants' market shares by caliber of handgun or evidence of the year of sale of the Fox gun. The absence of such direct evidence is not fatal to the verdict since evidence in the case supported the inference drawn by the jury as to market share for .25 caliber guns for relevant periods.

Defendants' motion for judgment as a matter of law is denied.

It is respectfully recommended that the panel for the court of appeals reviewing this decision certify state law issues to the New York Court of Appeals, whose interpretations, under Erie, control.

NOTES

1. The Second Circuit accepted Judge Weinstein's suggestion to certify the issues to the New York Court of Appeals. *Hamilton v. Beretta U.S.A. Corp.*, 222 F.3d 36 (2d Cir. 2000). The New York Court of Appeals later ruled that market share liability did not apply. *Hamilton v. Beretta U.S.A. Corp.*, 750 N.E.2d 1055 (N.Y. 2001). Did the court get it right? Are handguns similar to DES? To blood products?

2. For a critique of Judge Weinstein's opinion in *Accu-Tek*, see Aaron Twerski and Anthony J. Sebok, *Liability Without Cause? Further Ruminations on Cause-in-Fact as Applied to Handgun Liability*, 32 CONN. L. REV. 1379 (2000).

PROBLEM

The Cumberland Military Institute ("CMI") is a private military college. CMI enrolls 50 cadets each year. Upon matriculation, each cadet is issued an identical steel "brotherhood tag" (inscribed "CMI Brothers Forever") connected to a thin steel chain. Each cadet is required to wear the brotherhood tag around his neck until he graduates from CMI. Last spring, five class officers gathered to plan events for the annual CMI graduation ceremony. At this ceremony, the graduating cadets stand in a semicircle facing a seated audience 15 yards away. This year, the officers organized a celebratory gesture whereby each graduate would simultaneously remove his brotherhood tag and throw it into the crowd. On graduation day, each of the 50 cadets followed the plan and simultaneously threw his brotherhood tag into the audience of approximately 300 people. One of the tags struck Peter, an audience member, in his right eye. The tag scratched Peter's cornea and caused him to suffer from permanently blurred vision. Peter has come to your law office for advice. He does not know which cadet threw the tag that struck his eye. Nevertheless, he has asked you to evaluate a possible negligence action against some or all of the 50 graduates. Evaluate Peter's possible lawsuit.

C. INDEMNITY AND CONTRIBUTION

NATIONAL HEALTH LABORATORIES, INC. v. AHMADI
596 A.2d 555 (D.C. App. 1991)

STEADMAN, ASSOCIATE JUDGE:

The plaintiff in this litigation suffered permanent paralysis as a result of misdiagnosis of her ailment. She brought a malpractice action against the two appellants, one the medical group that was treating the plaintiff and the other a laboratory which improperly conducted a blood test. A jury found both appellants negligent. The principal issue in these consolidated appeals is whether the trial court erred in refusing to hold either appellant solely responsible for the judgment [under the theory of indemnification,] and instead imposing on each appellant an equal, fifty percent contribution to the judgment. We affirm.

I.

On June 30, 1986, Pari Ahmadi, the plaintiff below and appellee in the instant appeals, came to the Neurology Center (the "NC") with a history of numbness in her lower extremities and other symptoms. She was about thirty years old. Her first NC physician, Dr. Elliott Wilner, performed an examination which led him tentatively to conclude that Ahmadi suffered from a spinal cord lesion caused either by (1) vitamin B-12 deficiency; (2) multiple sclerosis ("MS"); or (3) mass lesion from a tumor or ruptured disk.

To narrow the diagnosis, Wilner ordered various tests, including a vitamin B-12 level test to rule out B-12 deficiency. Although Wilner was quickly able to exclude the tumor or ruptured disk alternatives, he could not so easily exclude either MS or B-12 deficiency by the other tests that the NC administered. Since the NC did not have the capability to perform the vitamin B-12 level test on Ahmadi, blood was drawn on July 7 and sent to the National Health Laboratories (the "NHL") for such a test. The NHL conducted the B-12 test on July 8. Because of an admitted error in the testing methodology, the NHL technicians incorrectly reached a normal-range finding, which was accordingly reported to Dr. Wilner and the NC on July 11.

On July 8, Ahmadi had been admitted to George Washington University Hospital ("GW") by another NC physician, Dr. Phillip Pulaski, for further workups due to increased symptomatology. On admission, a GW resident ordered a second vitamin B-12 level test, unaware of the first apparently normal result which had not yet been reported to Wilner and the NC. The hospital staff never carried out the new test, and Pulaski testified that he relied on the normal-range result of the NHL's test to rule out B-12 deficiency; he thereby made the probable diagnosis of MS. Pulaski did admit, however, that her symptoms were consistent not only with MS but also with B-12 deficiency.

Ahmadi marginally improved with outpatient treatment by the NC's Dr. Richard Edelson from the end of July to November, when she worsened again. The NC again ruled out vitamin B-12 deficiency without conducting a new B-12 level test, instead suggesting risky drug treatment for MS. Finally, in February, while on a trip to see her sister in California, Ahmadi suffered a serious bladder infection for which she went to see Dr. Bruce Spertell at Stanford University Medical Center. Over the next few days, she became much weaker, and, on the verge of paralysis, went to Stanford on an emergency basis, again seeing Dr. Spertell. Spertell diagnosed B-12 deficiency even before the results of a new B-12 test came back at a dangerously low level. Ahmadi has remained paralyzed from the waist down ever since.

Ahmadi brought suit against the NC for negligence and medical malpractice; against the NHL, for negligent failure to perform the B-12 test properly and for falsely reporting a normal result; and against GW for negligence in failing to complete a second B-12 test and failure to diagnose. The jury exonerated GW, but found for Ahmadi as against the NC and NHL, rendering a $10 million verdict against both. Previously filed cross-claims for contribution and indemnity by each liable defendant against the other were argued in a bench hearing. The trial court ruled that while each was entitled to contribution of 50% from the other, neither was entitled to indemnification under District law. The NC has since settled its share of the judgment with Ahmadi.

II.

In its appeal, the NC challenges the trial court's refusal to order the NHL to indemnify it for its half share of liability for Ahmadi's injuries. The NC argues that indemnification by the NHL is required as a matter of law.

At common law, there existed no right of contribution between joint tortfeasors who contributed to a single injury, and until the passage of specific statutes about twenty years ago, the great majority of American courts followed this rule.

The District of Columbia, however, was one of nine American jurisdictions to come to the contrary conclusion without legislation.

Thus, ordinarily, when two tortfeasors jointly contribute to harm to a plaintiff, both are potentially liable to the injured party for the entire harm. As between themselves, however, through the principle of contribution, they share equally in satisfaction of the judgment. Such equal contribution by the NHL and NC was what the trial court ordered here, from which they both appeal.

Under certain circumstances, however, a trial court may require that one of the two tortfeasors bear, as against the other, sole responsibility for satisfaction of the judgment. One of the common bases for such a right of indemnity is the existence of an express contractual duty to indemnify. Another is where one is held responsible solely by operation of law because of a relation to the original wrongdoer, such as the liability of an employer for acts of his employee or an owner of an automobile for acts of the driver. Likewise, one who is wrongfully directed or induced by another to do the negligent act may be entitled to indemnity from the other.

It may be seen from these examples that the right to indemnity depends essentially upon the relationship between the parties, which may be expressly contractual or may be such that an obligation to indemnify, in a sense quasi-contractual in nature, [footnote omitted] may be fairly imposed. So it is that while indeed a right to indemnity may extend to those personally at fault, it is granted in such circumstances normally only where "a duty to indemnify may . . . be implied 'out of a relationship between the parties,' to prevent a result 'which is regarded as unjust or unsatisfactory.'"

We have recently upheld an award of implied indemnity flowing from a relationship between the parties involving justified reliance where the joint tortfeasors stood in a manufacturer-retailer relationship. *See* [*East Penn Mfg. Co. v. Pineda*, 578 A.2d 1113 (D.C. 1990)]. There, we found an implied duty on the manufacturer of a battery to indemnify the retailer where the retailer's "only fault" was to rely on the manufacturer's skill and experience in its duplication of the wording of the manufacturer's warning label.

The NC contends that the same principle entitles it to indemnification. It argues that the NHL "had a critical relationship with the [NC] which pre-existed its negligence, and which gave rise to a duty . . . to render accurate, complete information regarding Pari Ahmadi's blood test results" to the NC. The NC then argues that the NHL breached this duty to it by failing both to provide a correct test result and to warn it that the test result was unreliable where its employees knowingly failed to follow proper testing protocols.

We think the trial court was correct in rejecting these arguments and concluding that whatever the duty or relationship of the NHL to the NC may have been initially, over time the NC could no longer rely reasonably on the test result. As the trial court found, the NC pursued a "misdiagnosis that initially perhaps was a difficult one . . . but which over the passage of time, perhaps soon after the report of the test from the [NHL], should have . . . caused [it] to doubt the accuracy of the laboratory result in favor of the clinical symptoms which were consistent with vitamin B-12 deficiency . . . " and "the [NC] doctors [were] independently negligent and actively negligent in failing to reopen the whole question of what the correct diagnosis was and to pursue that new inquiry . . . by ordering another . . . B-12 test." Certainly the different NC neurologists could at least collectively be expected to rely on their own clinical impressions as much as on the expertise of the testers where the B-12 test result itself represented only one piece of the diagnostic mosaic according to the standard of care of the profession.

[The *East Penn* decision does not entitle NC to indemnity.] *East Penn* does involve a situation in which a subsequent tortfeasor sought indemnity but is clearly distinguishable. The sole involvement of the retailer there was to rely upon the manufacturer's warning label. It had no independent reason to suspect error or impetus to investigate further. Here, the NC was an active and ongoing participant, indeed the chief participant, in the effort to diagnose a mysterious ailment. The NHL's negligent test was only a part of the overall mosaic of the NC's activity. As the trial court reasoned, while the NC may have initially relied on the NHL's duty to provide it with accurate test results, the NC could not properly have relied on these results over the entire seven-month period. Any "independent duty" that the NHL may have had to the NC was thus dissipated for purposes of seeking indemnity.

The trial court quite properly denied the NC's indemnification claim against the NHL. We now turn to the arguments made by the NHL on appeal.

III.

Any indemnity claim by the NHL against the NC must be judged by the same principles applicable to the NC's like claim against the NHL and found wanting for substantially the same reasons. The NHL as a prior tortfeasor can establish no duty imposed on the NC arising out of the relationship. The NC's responsibility ran to the plaintiff to render her competent medical service. There can be no legitimate claim that the NC had a separate duty to the NHL to discover that the NHL had made an error in its blood test. As we said in [*Myco v. Super Concrete*, 565 A.2d 293, 300 (D.C. 1989)], "imposition of such a duty would stand 'indemnity on its head.'" [footnote omitted] Moreover, given that indemnification is founded in principles of equity, we can find no difference in the relative fault of the NHL and the NC of such a "kind" or "quality" as to have required the trial court to make the NC bear the entire cost of their dual negligence.

Perhaps realizing that it would not be able to succeed on an indemnification argument, the NHL instead stresses an argument that the damages should be "apportioned" as between itself and the NC favorably to it. On the facts here, this is essentially an argument for adopting comparative negligence, which as already mentioned has never been the law in the District.

In sum, we find no ground for reversal in the trial court's ultimate conclusion that "based on the necessary facts decided by the jury by which . . . I am bound," this was a "classic case for contribution between joint tortfeasors." We uphold the trial court's award of 50% contribution by each appellant, and in all other respects affirm the judgment appealed from.

Affirmed.

BERVOETS v. HARDE RALLS PONTIAC-OLDS, INC.
891 S.W.2d 905 (Tenn. 1994)

DROWOTA, JUSTICE

Adanac, Inc. (d/b/a Cactus Jack's) appeals from the holding of the Court of Appeals denying its motion to dismiss and requiring the contribution action brought against it by Safeco Insurance Company to be tried under the principles of the Uniform Contribution Among Tortfeasors Act (UCATA) — Tenn. Code Ann. § 29-11-101 – 29-11-106 — instead of the principles of comparative fault as announced in *McIntyre v. Balentine*, 833 S.W.2d 52 (Tenn. 1992). [In *McIntyre*, the Tennessee Supreme Court adopted a system of comparative negligence and abolished the doctrine of joint and several liability. — Eds.] After carefully considering the arguments of the parties, we modify the decision of the Court of Appeals and hold that this contribution action shall be tried pursuant to the principles of comparative fault.

FACTS AND PROCEDURAL HISTORY

The underlying lawsuit upon which this action for contribution is predicated arose on July 5, 1980 when Lee Jackson, after consuming alcoholic beverages at Cactus Jack's restaurant, wrecked his car in which Michael Bervoets was a passenger, causing Bervoets to suffer severe and permanent injuries. After the accident, Bervoets brought a negligence action against Jackson and his parents. Thereafter, the Jacksons and their insuror, Safeco, filed a third party complaint against Adanac, alleging that because Lee Jackson was a minor for the purpose of purchasing alcoholic beverages at the time of the accident, Adanac was guilty of negligence per se for serving the alcoholic beverages to him, and that this negligence proximately caused the plaintiff Bervoets' injuries.

On May 11, 1983, Jackson and Safeco entered into a settlement with Bervoets in the amount of $1,250,000; this settlement served to release all Bervoets' claims against all defendants. Safeco then pursued its third party complaint in contribution under the UCATA against Adanac. The first trial in the matter resulted in a verdict for Adanac; this verdict was, however, set aside by the trial court. The second trial resulted in a verdict for Safeco; but this judgment was reversed by the Court of Appeals.

After the matter had been continued several times, this Court released its decision in *McIntyre v. Balentine*, 833 S.W.2d 52 (Tenn.1992) on May 4, 1992.

Thereafter Safeco filed an amended third party complaint, alleging that Adanac was liable to it on theories of contribution and common law indemnity. Adanac filed a motion to dismiss the complaint; and the trial court granted the motion as to the common law indemnity claim but denied it as to the contribution claim.

Adanac appealed. The Court of Appeals affirmed the judgment of the trial court, denying the motion to dismiss and holding that the contribution claim was to be determined with reference to the principles of the Uniform Contribution Among Tortfeasors Act despite our decision in McIntyre. We granted Adanac's [appeal] in order to clarify this situation.

ANALYSIS

Adanac's basic argument is that because this Court abolished the doctrine of joint and several liability in *McIntyre*, and because contribution can be had under the UCATA only if the parties are jointly and severally liable for a judgment, the Court effectively abolished the remedy of contribution in Tennessee. Moreover, Adanac points out that we unequivocally stated in *McIntyre* that the principles of comparative fault adopted in that case are to apply to "all cases tried or retried after the date of this opinion." Therefore, Adanac concludes, Safeco cannot now maintain an action against it for contribution, and the third party complaint, which has been pending for several years, is without foundation and should be dismissed.

We must reject this sweeping argument because it extends our *McIntyre* decision beyond its permissible and intended bounds. Although we stated in *McIntyre* that "today's holding renders the doctrine of joint and several liability obsolete," and thus did abolish the doctrine of joint and several liability to the extent that it allows a plaintiff to sue and obtain a full recovery against any one or more of several parties against whom liability could be established, it does not follow that we abolished the remedy of contribution. In fact we did not, and could not, completely abolish the remedy of contribution in *McIntyre* because that remedy was granted to the parties by the legislature. Moreover, our statements in *McIntyre* with regard to the effect of our adoption of a scheme of comparative fault on the remedy of contribution make it clear that we did not intend to deprive litigants of the right to pursue a claim for contribution in an appropriate case:

> [B]ecause a particular defendant will henceforth be liable only for the percentage of a plaintiff's damages occasioned by that defendant's negligence, situations where a defendant has paid more than his "share" of a judgment will no longer arise, and therefore the Uniform Contribution Among Tortfeasors Act, T.C.A. § 29-11-101 – 106 (1980) *will no longer determine the apportionment of liability between co-defendants.*

833 S.W.2d at 58 (emphasis added).

Although we certainly did not intend in *McIntyre* to totally abolish the remedy of contribution, it is obvious from the above-quoted passage that we did intend that the "pro rata share of damages" approach of the UCATA, which provides that the fault of the parties is not to be considered in determining each party's share of damages, should not continue to be utilized after the *McIntyre* decision was released. Because we intended to adopt a comprehensive scheme of comparative fault in *McIntyre*, and because the "pro rata share" approach set forth in the UCATA is in direct conflict with such a scheme, we felt it necessary to explicitly provide such guidance to the trial courts charged with the duty of trying tort cases in this state.

Although Safeco readily admits that the "pro rata share" approach to contribution is inconsistent with the principles of comparative fault, it contends that our substantial dictum regarding contribution in *McIntyre* should not apply to the retrial in this case for two basic reasons. First, Safeco contends that it had an expectation that it would be able to pursue a UCATA-type contribution claim against Adanac at the time it entered into the settlement agreement, that this expectation constituted an accrued or vested right, and that it is therefore impermissible to retroactively apply the principles of *McIntyre* so as to deprive it of that vested right. We are not convinced, however, that the retroactive application of *McIntyre* in fact serves to deprive Safeco of any "right," vested or otherwise. In fact, it is entirely possible that Safeco could actually obtain a better result under the principles of comparative fault than it could under the UCATA approach. Nor do we find persuasive Safeco's second argument — that our holding in *McIntyre*, while not totally abolishing the remedy of contribution, nevertheless constitutes an impermissible nullification of constitutionally valid legislation because it changed the method by which contribution is determined. Other jurisdictions that have both the UCATA and comparative fault schemes have interpreted the UCATA to require contribution to be made on the basis of the relative fault of the parties.

Therefore, we today reaffirm *McIntyre* and hold that actions for contribution that are to be tried or retried after May 4, 1992, are to be tried in accordance with the principles of comparative fault. Because this case unquestionably fits in this category, on retrial the jury will determine the percentage of fault attributable to each of the defendants, and contribution will be ordered accordingly.

The judgment of the Court of Appeals is modified and the case remanded for proceedings consistent with this opinion.

NOTES

1. The two cases above describe contribution and indemnity — the primary methods by which jointly-responsible tortfeasors seek reimbursement from one another. Indemnity is a rule that compels one tortfeasor to *completely* reimburse another who has paid a judgment to a plaintiff. Often, the rule applies where one party has contractually agreed to reimburse another. However, indemnity also

applies in several other circumstances. For example, a defendant whose liability was premised on vicarious liability can seek indemnity from the "active" tortfeasor who actually harmed the plaintiff. In addition, indemnity can apply where tortfeasors have committed wrongs of a different "magnitude" against the plaintiff. *See* EPSTEIN, TORTS § 9.8 at 236 (noting that a comment to Restatement (Second) of Torts § 866B allows for indemnity by a negligent actor against intentional, reckless, or even grossly negligent actors). Finally, product retailers or wholesalers sometimes can seek indemnity against manufacturers in a products liability action. *See East Penn Mfg. Co. v. Pineda*, 578 A.2d 1113 (D.C. 1990) (permitting retailer to seek indemnity against manufacturer where retailer's liability was based on duplication of manufacturer's warning label). *See generally* RESTATEMENT (THIRD) OF TORTS: APPORTIONMENT OF LIABILITY § 31 (1999).

2. As an "all or nothing" rule, indemnity is consistent with traditional tort principles such as contributory negligence and joint and several liability. This is not true of contribution, which envisions joint tortfeasors sharing responsibility for a plaintiff's harm. As recently as the 1970s, only a handful of American jurisdictions permitted contribution absent legislative action. *See* PROSSER & KEETON ON TORTS § 50 at 337. The District of Columbia, which still retains the rule of contributory negligence, was one of those jurisdictions, and the *Ahmadi* decision from that jurisdiction reflects the basic contribution rule whereby jointly-liable tortfeasors can seek "pro rata" contribution from one another. *See* UNIFORM CONTRIBUTION AMONG TORTFEASORS ACT § 2 (1955). Today, however, a majority of states have enacted statutes that permit contribution on a comparative basis. Such statutes are consistent with states' adoption of comparative fault. *See* RESTATEMENT OF TORTS (THIRD): APPORTIONMENT OF LIABILITY § 32, cmt. e (1999) (citing statutes and cases).

3. Is contribution an inherently good thing? Professor Epstein points out that, "[f]or risk-averse wrongdoers, the level of deterrence achieved may be greater once the level of compensation is fixed, so that accident deterrence is arguably superior under the traditional no-contribution rule than under any of its modern, and more complex, rivals." EPSTEIN, TORTS § 9.5 at 231. Do you agree? Does Professor Epstein's point about deterrence outweigh fairness considerations that might support the ability of one tortfeasor to seek contribution against others?

4. Is the availability of contribution a reason for a jurisdiction to retain a plaintiff's ability to seek joint and several liability against any single tortfeasor? Why or why not?

5. As with joint and several liability, contribution only applies among tortfeasors who have caused an *indivisible* harm to the plaintiff. For example, suppose that Darren was driving an automobile when he ran over Paul and broke his arm. Five minutes later, David hit Paul and broke his leg. Each defendant is responsible for the separate injury that he caused, and neither could seek contribution against the other. *See* RESTATEMENT (THIRD) OF TORTS: APPORTIONMENT OF LIABILITY § 32, cmt. c (1999).

PROBLEMS

1. What about settlements? Suppose Defendant #1 settles for $300 with Plaintiff, who suffered $1,000 in damages. If Plaintiff continues her action against Defendant #2, should we view the $300 as a "credit" on the claim that would limit the Plaintiff's recovery against Defendant #2 to $700? Or should we view the settlement as a pro rata "claim reduction," so that the Plaintiff can seek only $500 from Defendant #2?

2. Suppose Defendant #1 in the problem above settled for $700 before Plaintiff resolved her claim against Defendant #2. Can Defendant #1 seek contribution from Defendant #2?

3. Andy broke his arm in a multi-car accident. He sues Ed, Russ, and John, alleging that the negligence of each caused his injury. A jury awards Andy a $10,000 judgment against the three defendants, assigning Ed 50% responsibility, Russ 30% responsibility, and John 20% responsibility.

    a. Suppose Ed pays Andy the full $10,000. How much might Ed recover in contribution from Russ and John?

    b. Suppose Ed pays Andy $8,000. How might this impact his recovery in the contribution action?

    c. Suppose Andy settles with Ed for $5,000. Can Ed recover anything in contribution from Russ and John?

Chapter 8
DAMAGES FOR PERSONAL INJURIES

Damages are a separate element of the causes of action in negligence and strict liability. With the trepassory intentional torts, general damages will be awarded once the jury finds that the intentional tort has been committed. In other words, damages are not a separate required element.

The amount of damages is a question of fact for the jury, (or judge, when the judge is the fact finder.) Jurors are told that they are to compensate the injured to the extent possible, so as to place the person injured by the defendant into a position he or she would have been in had the defendant not injured him or her. To the common law, though money may never be a sufficient compensation, it is better than nothing at all, and theoretically substitutes for violence and provides for the peaceful resolution of disputes.

Under an economic theory of tort law, damages provide the deterrence necessary to provide for efficient safety. The damages factor provides the incentive for the rational defendant to calculate the care they should provide in the making of their product or doing of their activity. What if they calculate the risk incorrectly? What if they calculate the risk correctly and determine it is inefficient to provide more protection? Should they then pay for the damages their activity causes?

Many of the personal injury cases that we will examine in this chapter involve tragic situations in which an individual has suffered very severe injuries (being turned into a quadraplegic). In such a case, plaintiff might seek to recover for economic loss; lost wages (past, present and future), medical expenses (both past, present and future), as well as noneconomic loss; damages for pain and suffering, and mental anguish. In addition, plaintiff's spouse and children might seek to recover for loss of consortium.

A. ECONOMIC LOSSES CAUSED BY PHYSICAL INJURY

Economic losses from personal injury generally include awards for medical expenses to treat the injury and for lost wages. The first category, medical expenses, of course includes all charges for treatment of the injury up to the date of the trial. In addition, however, the plaintiff is also entitled to recover the cost of all future medical treatments or nursing care that may be needed. Although inevitably somewhat uncertain in amount, these expenses are often reasonably certain to be incurred. For example, if the accident left the plaintiff totally disabled, the plaintiff will certainly need nursing care in the future. The need for surgery in the future may also be predictable. The cost of this care is recoverable. Thus, figuring past medical expenses is fairly easy, but determining future medical expenses requires predicting the future. Will continuing care be more or less expensive? What if a miracle cure is found? What incentives are there for the patient to try to get better, compensate for their injury and move on with life? How do you factor in all these uncertainties and come up with any reasonably accurate figure for future medical expenses?

The second important element of economic loss is an award of lost wages. Again, this award will include the wages lost before trial, as well as all wages that will be lost in the future as a result of inability to work resulting from the injury. In general, the calculation of lost wages relies on the following variables; the person's present wages and benefits, expected wage growth due to expected increases in job responsibility and promotion, years of work expectancy, a subtraction for other employment in mitigation, a discounting to present value, and a determination of the tax effect on the award, if any.

A person's wage can be difficult to determine. For example, if a ball player is injured just when he is about to sign a pro contract, past wages are not relevant to his reasonably expected wage. And how is the law to deal with children, who are permanently disabled or killed before they ever worked? One way is to use average wages of others similarly situated. Here, damages experts can consult national labor statistics for information about average wages, average wage growth, and average work expectancies. There may be personal characteristics of the injured person that may reasonably affect these averages.

Whether to discount awards for future losses to present value is also a matter of debate. Some jurisdictions determine that wage growth and inflation will balance out any need to discount total wages to its present value. Others recognize that paying a lump sum up front for all the wages a person would have lost over a number of years doesn't account for the fact that investing the unused portion of that money during that work expectancy of the injured person will produce an income stream well in excess of the lost wages. And so damages experts try to calculated a figure which will pay the expected wage of the individual, invest the excess, and thereby produce a stream of income equal to the exact amount of money a person would have been paid over their work expectancy. One way of looking at what the damages expert is doing is to ask yourself how much life insurance you would need to buy to pay your family what you would have made for them over the years you would be working. You would buy too much insurance if you just multiplied the number of years you would work times your expected wages, because of the investment factor. This issue will be explored in more detail in Part B of this Chapter.

SEFFERT v. LOS ANGELES TRANSIT LINES
364 P.2d 337 (Cal. 1961)

JUSTICE PETERS.

Defendants appeal from a judgment for plaintiff for $187,903.75 entered on a jury verdict. Their motion for a new trial for errors of law and excessiveness of damages was denied.

At the trial plaintiff contended that she was properly entering defendants' bus when the doors closed suddenly catching her right hand and left foot. The bus started, dragged her some distance, and then threw her to the pavement. Defendants contended that the injury resulted from plaintiff's own negligence, that she was late for work and either ran into the side of the bus after the doors had closed or ran after the bus and attempted to enter after the doors had nearly closed. . . .

The evidence most favorable to the plaintiff shows that prior to the accident plaintiff was in good health, and had suffered no prior serious injuries. She was single, and had been self-supporting for 20 of her 42 years. The accident happened on October 11, 1957. The trial took place in July and August of 1959.

The record is uncontradicted that her injuries were serious, painful, disabling and permanent. The major injuries were to plaintiff's left foot. The main arteries and nerves leading to that foot, and the posterior tibial vessels and nerve of that foot, were completely severed at the ankle. The main blood vessel which supplies blood to that foot had to be tied off, with the result that there is a permanent stoppage of the main blood source. The heel and shin bones were fractured. There were deep lacerations and an avulsion which involved the skin and soft tissue of the entire foot.

These injuries were extremely painful. They have resulted in a permanently raised left heel, which is two inches above the floor level, caused by the contraction of the ankle joint capsule. Plaintiff is crippled and will suffer pain for life. Although this pain could, perhaps, be alleviated by an operative fusion of the ankle, the doctors considered and rejected this procedure because the area has been deprived of its normal blood supply. The foot is not only permanently deformed but has a persistent open ulcer on the heel, there being a continuous drainage from the entire area. Medical care of this foot and ankle is to be reasonably expected for the remainder of plaintiff's life.

Since the accident, and because of it, plaintiff has undergone nine operations and has spent eight months in various hospitals and rehabilitation centers. These operations involved painful skin grafting and other painful procedures. One involved the surgical removal of gangrenous skin leaving painful raw and open flesh exposed from the heel to the toe. Another involved a left lumbar sympathectomy in which plaintiff's abdomen was entered to sever the nerves affecting the remaining blood vessels of the left leg in order to force those blood vessels to remain open at all times to the maximum extent. Still another operation involved a cross leg flap graft of skin and tissue from plaintiff's thigh which required that her left foot be brought up to her right thigh and held at this painful angle, motionless, and in a cast for a month until the flap of skin and fat, partially removed from her thigh, but still nourished there by a skin connection, could be grafted to the bottom of her foot, and until the host site could develop enough blood vessels to support it. Several future operations of this nature may be necessary. One result of this operation was to leave a defective area of the thigh where the normal fat is missing and the muscles exposed, and the local nerves are missing. This condition is permanent and disfiguring.

Another operation called a debridement, was required. This involved removal of many small muscles of the foot, much of the fat beneath the skin, cleaning the end of the severed nerve, and tying off the severed vein and artery.

The ulcer on the heel is probably permanent, and there is the constant and real danger that osteomyelitis may develop if the infection extends into the bone. If this happens the heel bone would have to be removed surgically and perhaps the entire foot amputated.

Although plaintiff has gone back to work, she testified that she has difficulty standing, walking or even sitting, and must lie down frequently; that the leg is still very painful; that she can, even on her best days, walk not over three blocks and that very slowly; that her back hurts from walking; that she is tired and weak; that her sleep is disturbed; that she has frequent spasms in which the leg shakes uncontrollably; that she feels depressed and unhappy, and suffers humiliation and embarrassment.

Plaintiff claims that there is evidence that her total pecuniary loss, past and future, amounts to $53,903.75. This was the figure used by plaintiff's counsel [in] which he also claimed $134,000 for pain and suffering, past and future. Since the verdict was exactly the total of these two estimates, it is reasonable to assume that the jury accepted the amount proposed by counsel for each item.

The summary of plaintiff as to pecuniary loss, past and future, is as follows:

Doctor and Hospital Bills	$10,330.50	
Drugs and other medical expenses stipulated to in the amount of	2,273.25	
Loss of earnings from time of accident to time of trial	5,500.00	$18,103.75
Future Medical Expenses:		
$2,000 per year for next 10 years	20,000.00	
$200 per year for the 24 years thereafter	4,800.00	
Drugs for 34 years	1,000.00	25,800.00
		43,903.75

Possible future loss of earnings   10,000.00

Total Pecuniary Loss $53,903.75

There is substantial evidence to support these estimates. The amounts for past doctor and hospital bills, for the cost of drugs, and for a past loss of earnings, were either stipulated to, evidence was offered on, or is a simple matter of calculation. These items totaled $18,103.75. While the amount of $25,800 estimated as the cost of future medical expenses, for loss of future earnings and for the future cost of drugs, may seem high, there was substantial evidence that future medical expense is certain to be high. There is also substantial evidence that plaintiff's future earning capacity may be substantially impaired by reason of the injury. The amounts estimated for those various items are not out of line, and find support in the evidence.

This leaves the amount of $134,000 presumably allowed for the nonpecuniary items of damage, including pain and suffering, past and future. It is this allowance that defendants seriously attack as being excessive as a matter of law. [The court's discussion of this point can be found in Part C of this chapter, in Note 3 following *McDougald v. Garber*.]

The judgment appealed from is affirmed.

PROBLEMS: LOST WAGES

1. Plaintiff, a 30-year-old clerical worker, suffered a severely broken leg and arm in an automobile accident. At the time of the accident, she was making $27,000 a year. She was off work for four weeks, but was fully recovered by the time of trial. How much should she recover in lost wages?

2. A law student was severely injured in an automobile accident. Her brain and cognitive abilities were unimpaired, but she was confined to a wheelchair. The average law graduate earns $35,000 a year upon graduation. A student high in her class earns as much as $70,000 per year. Can the wheelchair-bound student recover lost wages?

PROBLEMS: MEDICAL EXPENSES

1. Plaintiff, a 30-year-old clerical worker, suffered a severely broken leg and arm in an automobile accident. She was off work for four weeks undergoing a medical operation to set the arm and the leg. The operation cost $10,000. Post-surgery rehabilitation was initially done on an in-patient basis at a cost of $5,000. Additional rehabilitation was done on an out-patient basis at a cost of $3,000. Plaintiff also spent $200 for crutches, and another $200 for wheelchair rental. How much can she recover in medical expenses?

2. A student suffered facial disfiguration in an automobile accident. She underwent surgery at a cost of $30,000. Doctors have recommended that she have two follow-up operations, designed to make her look better, at a cost of $10,000 each. How much can she recover in medical expenses?

B. FUTURE DAMAGES AND DISCOUNTING TO PRESENT VALUE

Many personal injury cases involve a claim for future earnings and future medical expenses. One issue is whether awards for these types of damages should be reduced to present value.

To understand what this means, begin by considering future earnings. Suppose that, absent a debilitating accident, plaintiff might have expected to work for 20 more years at a wage of $40,000 per year. In other words, he might have expected to receive $800,000. If plaintiff is given the entire $800,000 at the conclusion of the law suit, and can invest it in a safe security, for example, at 5% per annum, he will earn, on interest alone, before taxes, $40,000 a year. Won't the plaintiff be overcompensated? Plaintiff will receive the expected $40,000 per year at the end of each of the twenty years, for twenty years, but will have the entire $800,000 left at the end of the 20 years. Some argue that such an award represents overcompensation because the award should only compensate plaintiff for his actual loss ($40,000 per year for 20 years) and not provide him with a windfall (the remaining $800,000). As a result, some argue that the award should be reduced to present value — giving plaintiff the amount needed to generate $40,000 a year for 20 years, but exhausting the principal at the end of that time. Some might disagree with the "windfall" analysis. After all, inflation is a fact of life. So is expected wage growth, as responsibility rises, and a person becomes more efficient and experienced, and so can take on more work. A plaintiff who expects to earn $40,000 this year would expect to be earning far more than $40,000 a year, 10 to 20 years later. How then should these competing forces on future economic losses be factored into the damages awarded by a jury? This next case examines the problems presented by future awards.

JONES & LAUGHLIN STEEL CORP. v. PFEIFER
462 U.S. 523 (1983)

JUSTICE STEVENS delivered the opinion of the Court.

Respondent was injured in the course of his employment as a loading helper on a coal barge. As his employer, petitioner was required to compensate him for his injury under § 4 of the Longshoremen's and Harbor Workers' Compensation Act (Act). 33 U.S.C. § 904. As the owner pro hac vice of the barge, petitioner may also be liable for negligence under § 5 of the Act. We granted certiorari [to] consider whether the Court of Appeals correctly upheld the trial court's computation of respondent's damages.

Petitioner owns a fleet of barges that it regularly operates on three navigable rivers in the vicinity of Pittsburgh, Pa. Respondent was employed for 19 years to aid in loading and unloading those barges at one of petitioner's plants located on the shore of the Monongahela River. On January 13, 1978, while carrying a heavy pump, respondent slipped and fell on snow and ice that petitioner had negligently failed to remove from the gunnels of a barge. His injury made him permanently unable to return to his job with the petitioner, or to perform anything other than light work after July 1, 1979.

In November 1979, respondent brought this action against petitioner, alleging that his injury had been "caused by the negligence of the vessel" within the meaning of § 5(b) of the Act. The District Court found in favor of respondent and awarded damages of $275,881.36. The court held that receipt of compensation payments from petitioner under § 4 of the Act did not bar a separate recovery of damages for negligence.

The District Court's calculation of damages was predicated on a few undisputed facts. At the time of his injury respondent was earning an annual wage of $26,025. He had a remaining work expectancy of 12½ years. On the date of trial (October 1, 1980), respondent had received compensation payments of $33,079.14. If he had obtained light work and earned the legal minimum hourly wage from July 1, 1979, until his 65th birthday, he would have earned $66,352.

The District Court arrived at its final award by taking 12½ years of earnings at respondent's wage at the time of injury ($325,312.50), subtracting his projected hypothetical earnings at the minimum wage ($66,352) and the compensation payments he had received under § 4 ($33,079.14), and adding $50,000 for pain and suffering. The court did not increase the award to take inflation into account, and it did not discount the award to reflect the present value of the future stream of income. The court instead decided to follow a decision of the Supreme Court of Pennsylvania, which had held "as a matter of law that future inflation shall be presumed equal to future interest rates with these factors offsetting." *Kaczkowski v. Bolubasz*, 491 Pa. 561, 583. Thus, although the District Court did not dispute that respondent could be expected to receive regular cost-of-living wage increases from the date of his injury until his presumed date of retirement, the court refused to include such increases in its calculation, explaining that they would provide respondent "a double consideration for inflation." For comparable reasons, the court disregarded changes in the legal minimum wage in computing the amount of mitigation attributable to respondent's ability to perform light work.

It does not appear that either party offered any expert testimony concerning predicted future rates of inflation, the interest rate that could be appropriately used to discount future earnings to present value, or the possible connection between inflation rates and interest rates. Respondent did, however, offer an estimate of how his own wages would have increased over time, based upon recent increases in the company's hourly wage scale.

The Court of Appeals affirmed. It held that a longshoreman may bring a negligence action against the owner of a vessel who acts as its own stevedore. . . . On the damages issue, the Court of Appeals [held that] inflation must be taken into account:

> "Full compensation for lost prospective earnings is most difficult, if not impossible, to attain if the court is blind to the realities of the consumer price index and the recent historical decline of purchasing power. Thus if we recognize, as we must, that the injured worker is entitled to reimbursement for his loss of future earnings, an honest and accurate calculation must consider the stark reality of inflationary conditions."

The court understood, however, that the task of predicting future rates of inflation is quite speculative. It concluded that such speculation could properly be avoided in the manner chosen by the District Court — by adopting Pennsylvania's "total offset method" of computing damages. The Court of Appeals approved of the way the total offset method respects the twin goals of considering future inflation and discounting to present value, while eliminating the need to make any calculations about either, "because the inflation and discount rates are legally presumed to be equal and cancel one another." Accordingly, it affirmed the District Court's judgment. . . .

The Damages Issue

[T]o summarize, the first stage in calculating an appropriate award for lost earnings involves an estimate of what the lost stream of income would have been. The stream may be approximated as a series of after-tax payments, one in each year of the worker's expected remaining career. In estimating what those payments would have been in an inflation-free economy, the trier of fact may begin with the worker's annual wage at the time of injury. If sufficient proof is offered, the trier of fact may increase that figure to reflect the appropriate influence of individualized factors (such as foreseeable promotions) and societal factors (such as foreseeable productivity growth within the worker's industry).

Of course, even in an inflation-free economy the award of damages to replace the lost stream of income cannot be computed simply by totaling up the sum of the periodic payments. For the damages award is paid in a lump sum at the conclusion of the litigation, and when it — or even a part of it — is invested, it will earn additional money. It has been settled since our decision in *Chesapeake & Ohio R. Co. v. Kelly*, 241 U.S. 485 (1916), that "in all cases where it is reasonable to suppose that interest may safely be earned upon the amount that is awarded, the ascertained future benefits ought to be discounted in the making up of the award." *Id.* at 490.

The discount rate should be based on the rate of interest that would be earned on "the best and safest investments." Once it is assumed that the injured worker would definitely have worked for a specific term of years, he is entitled to a risk-free stream of future income to replace his lost wages; therefore, the discount rate should not reflect the market's premium for investors who are willing to accept some risk of default. Moreover, since under *Norfolk & Western R. Co. v. Liepelt*, 444 U.S. 490 (1980), the lost stream of income should be estimated in after-tax terms, the discount rate should also represent the after-tax rate of return to the injured worker.

Thus, although the notion of a damages award representing the present value of a lost stream of earnings in an inflation-free economy rests on some fairly sophisticated economic concepts, the two elements that determine its calculation can be stated fairly easily. They are: (1) the amount that the employee would have earned during each year that he could have been expected to work after the injury; and (2) the appropriate discount rate, reflecting the safest available investment. The trier of fact should apply the discount rate to each of the estimated installments in the lost stream of income, and then add up the discounted installments to determine the total award.

II

Unfortunately for triers of fact, ours is not an inflation-free economy. Inflation has been a permanent fixture in our economy for many decades, and there can be no doubt that it ideally should affect both stages of the calculation described in the previous section. The difficult problem is how it can do so in the practical context of civil litigation under § 5(b) of the Act.

The first stage of the calculation required an estimate of the shape of the lost stream of future income. For many workers, including respondent, a contractual "cost-of-living adjustment" automatically increases wages each year by the percentage change during the previous year in the consumer price index calculated by the Bureau of Labor Statistics. Such a contract provides a basis for taking into account an additional societal factor — price inflation — in estimating the worker's lost future earnings.

The second stage of the calculation requires the selection of an appropriate discount rate. Price inflation — or more precisely, anticipated price inflation — certainly affects market rates of return. If a lender knows that his loan is to be repaid a year later with dollars that are less valuable than those he has advanced, he will charge an interest rate that is high enough both to compensate him for the temporary use of the loan proceeds and also to make up for their shrinkage in value.

At one time many courts incorporated inflation into only one stage of the calculation of the award for lost earnings. In estimating the lost stream of future earnings, they accepted evidence of both individual and societal factors that would tend to lead to wage increases even in an inflation-free economy, but required the plaintiff to prove that those factors were not influenced by predictions of future price inflation. No increase was allowed for price inflation, on the theory that such predictions were unreliably speculative. In discounting the estimated lost stream of future income to present value, however, they applied the market interest rate. *See Blue v. Western R. of Alabama*, 469 F.2d 487, 496-97 (5th Cir. 1972).

The effect of these holdings was to deny the plaintiff the benefit of the impact of inflation on his future earnings, while giving the defendant the benefit of inflation's impact on the interest rate that is used to discount those earnings to present value. Although the plaintiff in such a situation could invest the proceeds of the litigation at an "inflated" rate of interest, the stream of income that he received provided him with only enough dollars to maintain his existing nominal income; it did not provide him with a stream comparable to what his lost wages would have been in an inflationary economy. This inequity was assumed to have been minimal because of the relatively low rates of inflation.

In recent years, of course, inflation rates have not remained low. There is now a consensus among courts that the prior inequity can no longer be tolerated. *See, e.g., United States v. English*, 521 F.2d 63, 75 (9th Cir. 1975) ("While the administrative convenience of ignoring inflation has some appeal when inflation rates are low, to ignore inflation when the rates are high is to ignore economic reality"). There is no consensus at all, however, regarding what form an appropriate response should take.

[The Court then reviewed a number of different approaches.] Common-law nations generally continue to adhere to the position that inflation is too speculative to be considered in estimating the lost stream of future earnings; they have sought to counteract the danger of systematically undercompensating plaintiffs by applying a discount rate that is below the current market rate. Nevertheless, they have each chosen different rates, applying slightly different economic theories. In England, [it has been] sugggested that it would be appropriate to allow for future inflation "in a rough and ready way" by discounting at a rate of 4¾%. The Supreme Court of Canada has recommended discounting at a rate of 7%, a rate equal to market rates on long-term investments minus a government expert's prediction of the long-term rate of price inflation. And in Australia, the High Court has adopted a 2% rate, on the theory that it represents a good approximation of the long-term "real interest rate."

In this country, some courts have taken the same "real interest rate" approach as Australia. They have endorsed the economic theory suggesting that market interest rates include two components — an estimate of anticipated inflation, and a desired "real" rate of return on investment — and that the latter component is essentially constant over time. They have concluded that the inflationary increase in the estimated lost stream of future earnings will therefore be perfectly "offset" by all but the "real" component of market interest rate.

Still other courts have preferred to continue relying on market interest rates. To avoid undercompensation, they have shown at least tentative willingness to permit evidence of what future price inflation will be in estimating the lost stream of future income.

[W]ithin the past year, two Federal Courts of Appeals have decided to allow litigants a choice of methods.

Finally, some courts have applied a number of techniques that have loosely been termed "total offset" methods. What these methods have in common is that they presume that the ideal discount rate — the after-tax market interest rate on a safe investment — is (to a legally tolerable degree of precision) completely offset by certain elements in the ideal computation of the estimated lost stream of future income. They all assume that the effects of future price inflation on wages are part of what offsets the market interest rate. The methods differ, however, in their assumptions regarding which if any other elements in the first stage of the damages calculation contribute to the offset.

The litigants and the amici in this case urge us to select one of the many rules that have been proposed and establish it for all time as the exclusive method in all federal trials for calculating an award for lost earnings in an inflationary economy. We are not persuaded, however, that such an approach is warranted. For our review of the foregoing cases leads us to draw three conclusions. First, by its very nature the calculation of an award for lost earnings must be a rough approximation. Because the lost stream can never be predicted with complete confidence, any lump sum represents only a "rough and ready" effort to put the plaintiff in the position he would have been in had he not been injured. Second, sustained price inflation can make the award substantially less precise. Inflation's current magnitude and unpredictability create a substantial risk that the damages award will prove to have little relation to the lost wages it purports to replace. Third, the question of lost earnings can arise in many different contexts. In some sectors of the economy, it is far easier to assemble evidence of an individual's most likely career path than in others.

These conclusions all counsel hesitation. Having surveyed the multitude of options available, we will do no more than is necessary to resolve the case before us. We limit our attention to suits under § 5(b) of the Act, noting that Congress has provided generally for an award of damages but has not given specific guidance regarding how they are to be calculated. Within that narrow context, we shall define the general boundaries within which a particular award will be considered legally acceptable.

[I]n calculating an award for a longshoreman's lost earnings caused by the negligence of a vessel, the discount rate should be chosen on the basis of the factors that are used to estimate the lost stream of future earnings. If the trier of fact relies on a specific forecast of the future rate of price inflation, and if the estimated lost stream of future earnings is calculated to include price inflation along with individual factors and other societal factors, then the proper discount rate would be the after-tax market interest rate. But since specific forecasts of future price inflation remain too unreliable to be useful in many cases, it will normally be a costly and ultimately unproductive waste of longshoremen's resources to make such forecasts the centerpiece of litigation under § 5(b). As Judge Newman has warned: "The average accident trial should not be converted into a graduate seminar on economic forecasting." *Doca v. Marina Mercante Nicaraguense, S. A.*, 634 F.2d at 39. For that reason, both plaintiffs and trial courts should be discouraged from pursuing that approach.

On the other hand, if forecasts of future price inflation are not used, it is necessary to choose an appropriate below-market discount rate. As long as inflation continues, one must ask how much should be "offset" against the market rate. Once again, that amount should be chosen on the basis of the same factors that are used to estimate the lost stream of future earnings. If full account is taken of the individual and societal factors (excepting price inflation) that can be expected to have resulted in wage increases, then all that should be set off against the market interest rate is an estimate of future price inflation. This would result in one of the "real interest rate" approaches described above. Although we find the economic evidence distinctly inconclusive regarding an essential premise of those approaches, we do not believe a trial court adopting such an approach in a suit under § 5(b) should be reversed if it adopts a rate between 1 and 3% and explains its choice.

[A]s a result, the judgment below must be set aside. In performing its damages calculation, the trial court applied the theory of *Kaczkowski v. Bolubasz*, 491 Pa. 561, 421 A.2d 1027 (1980), as a mandatory federal rule of decision, even though the petitioner had insisted that if compensation was to be awarded, it "must be reduced to its present worth." Moreover, this approach seems to have colored the trial court's evaluation of the relevant evidence. At one point, the court noted that respondent had offered a computation of his estimated wages from the date of the accident until his presumed date of retirement, including projected cost-of-living adjustments. It stated: "We do not disagree with these projections, but feel they are inappropriate in view of the holding in *Kaczkowski*." Later in its opinion, however, the court declared: "We do not believe that there was sufficient evidence to establish a basis for estimating increased future productivity for the plaintiff, and therefore we will not inject such a factor in this award."

[T]he present record already gives reason to believe a fair award may be more confidently expected in this case than in many. The employment practices in the longshoring industry appear relatively stable and predictable. The parties seem to have had no difficulty in arriving at the period of respondent's future work expectancy, or in predicting the character of the work that he would have been performing during that entire period if he had not been injured. Moreover, the record discloses that respondent's wages were determined by a collective-bargaining agreement that explicitly provided for "cost of living" increases, and that recent company history also included a "general" increase and a "job class increment increase." Although the trial court deemed the latter increases irrelevant during its first review because it felt legally compelled to assume they would offset any real interest rate, further study of them on remand will allow the court to determine whether that assumption should be made in this case.

We do not suggest that the trial judge should embark on a search for "delusive exactness." It is perfectly obvious that the most detailed inquiry can at best produce an approximate result. And one cannot ignore the fact that in many instances the award for impaired earning capacity may be overshadowed by a highly impressionistic award for pain and suffering. But we are satisfied that whatever rate the District Court may choose to discount the estimated stream of future earnings, it must make a deliberate choice, rather than assuming that it is bound by a rule of state law.

The judgment of the Court of Appeals is vacated, and the case is remanded for further proceedings consistent with this opinion.

It is so ordered.

NOTE

In 1983, inflation was running high compared to the late 90s and early 2000s. More recently, the "real interest" rate may have been less than a percent during this time, or even a negative, for a while. Why does the court want to set up a range? Doesn't it still force the use of an expert economist?

PROBLEMS: FUTURE LOST WAGES

1. Plaintiff, a 25-year-old construction worker, was paralyzed in an automobile accident. At the time of the accident, he was making $30,000 a year. Because of the accident, he was no longer able to work. Before the accident, he expected to live until age 72. After the accident, he expected to live only until age 50. A normal, healthy, construction worker usually retires at age 60. How much should he recover in lost wages?

2. Joshua Johnson suffered severe brain injuries at birth due to medical malpractice. Both of Joshua's parents are physicians who earn an average of $200,000 each per year. Because of his injuries, it is unlikely that Joshua will ever be able to work, much less become a physician. Prior to the accident, Joshua would have expected to live until age 72. Afterwards, his life expectancy was reduced to 43 years. How much should he recover in lost wages?

PROBLEMS: FUTURE MEDICAL EXPENSES

1. Plaintiff, a 25-year-old construction worker, was paralyzed in an automobile accident. Before the accident, he expected to live until age 72. After the accident, he expected to live only until age 50. He was forced to spend $20,000 on a special van to transport himself. He was also forced to spend $500 on a wheelchair that has a useful life of 7 years. He also expects to undergo regular medical treatments at a cost of $3,000 per year. How much should he recover in medical expenses?

2. Joshua Johnson suffered severe brain injuries at birth due to medical malpractice. Because of his injuries, Joshua will require constant nursing attention for the remainder of his life. Such attention costs an average of $80,000 a year on an out-patient basis, and $40,000 a year on an in-patient basis. Prior to the accident, Joshua would have expected to live until age 72. Afterwards, his life expectancy was reduced to 43 years. How much should he recover in medical expenses?

PROBLEMS: FUTURE LOST WAGES AND MEDICAL EXPENSES

There are not only uncertainties with future wages, but even more uncertainties regarding future medical expenses. Sometimes the two elements work off each other, and are related to each other.

1. B lied to his girlfriend, A, when she asked him if he has been sleeping with other women. He also knew that he was HIV positive, but insisted on having unprotected sex. A contracts AIDS as a result of having sex with B. In a lawsuit against B, in a jurisdiction allowing such suits, what will A's damages for future medical expenses be?

Depending on current drugs, A's work may need to be curtailed at various times. New drugs are on the way. How do these future medical developments affect the payment for future lost wages and future medical expenses?

2. A negligently crashes into B on the ski slopes, severing B's anterior cruciate ligament in his right knee. B is a 21-year-old first round draft pick of the NBA. He had contracted to play next year for the Dallas Mavericks for 5 million dollars a year for 5 years. Knee surgery will cost $2,500 to "repair" the ligament. What damages will B get for future lost wages and future medical expenses?

NOTE ON STRUCTURED SETTLEMENTS

One way to handle the uncertainty of future damages is for the parties to enter into structured settlements. These agreements are annuity contracts that provide regular payment over time for future damages. Rather than giving plaintiff a single lump sum to invest, these settlements provide a regular yearly (or more frequent) payout of compensation. Structure settlements provide certain tax advantages, and protect the plaintiff from squandering the lump sum damage payment. Some oppose these settlements, however, on the grounds that, if there is a fair way to determine the total sum of the future damages, there is no economic reason to favor the defendant keeping the unpaid sum for reinvestment, over the plaintiff getting the sum and investing. Each will take risks in investing the money that may or may not pan out. Yet despite these difficulties, structured, or "periodic," payments is the method of payment provided by worker's compensation statutes, because the conduct and health of the plaintiff can be effectively monitored by the worker's compensation system of providing health benefits.

C. NON-ECONOMIC LOSSES: PAIN AND SUFFERING

One type of damage that is recoverable in a personal injury case is for "pain and suffering." Pain is the physical pain that plaintiff suffers from his injuries (*i.e.*, the loss of a leg). Suffering is the psychological pain that plaintiff feels because of his condition.

The difficulty is that, unlike lost wages or medical expenses, few "pain and suffering" cases can truly be measured in dollar terms. Consider the prior problems in which one plaintiff suffered paralysis, another suffered facial disfiguration and a third suffered brain injury. All of these injuries may involve a great deal of pain. They may also impose psychological suffering on the plaintiff subjected to them. Consider the following case.

McDOUGALD v. GARBER
536 N.E.2d 372 (N.Y. 1989)

WACHTLER, Chief Judge.

This appeal raises fundamental questions about the nature and role of nonpecuniary damages in personal injury litigation. By nonpecuniary damages, we mean those damages awarded to compensate an injured person for the physical and emotional consequences of the injury, such as pain and suffering and the loss of the ability to engage in certain activities. Pecuniary damages, on the other hand, compensate the victim for the economic consequences of the injury, such as medical expenses, lost earnings and the cost of custodial care.

The specific questions raised here deal with the assessment of nonpecuniary damages and are (1) whether some degree of cognitive awareness is a prerequisite to recovery for loss of enjoyment of life and (2) whether a jury should be instructed to consider and award damages for loss of enjoyment of life separately from damages for pain and suffering. We answer the first question in the affirmative and the second question in the negative.

I.

On September 7, 1978, plaintiff Emma McDougald, then 31 years old, underwent a Caesarean section and tubal ligation at New York Infirmary. Defendant Garber performed the surgery; defendants Armengol and Kulkarni provided anesthesia. During the surgery, Mrs. McDougald suffered oxygen deprivation which resulted in severe brain damage and left her in a permanent comatose condition. This action was brought by Mrs. McDougald and her husband, suing derivatively, alleging that the injuries were caused by the defendants' acts of malpractice.

A jury found all defendants liable and awarded Emma McDougald a total of $9,650,102 in damages, including $1,000,000 for conscious pain and suffering and a separate award of $3,500,000 for loss of the pleasures and pursuits of life. The balance of the damages awarded to her were for pecuniary damages — lost earnings and the cost of custodial and nursing care. Her husband was awarded $1,500,000 on his derivative claim for the loss of his wife's services. On defendants' post-trial motions, the Trial Judge reduced the total award to Emma McDougald to $4,796,728 by striking the entire award for future nursing care ($2,353,374) and by reducing the separate awards for conscious pain and suffering and loss of the pleasures and pursuits of life to a single award of $2,000,000. Her husband's award was left intact. On cross appeals, the Appellate Division affirmed and later granted defendants leave to appeal to this court.

[What] remains in dispute, primarily, is the award to Emma McDougald for nonpecuniary damages. At trial, defendants sought to show that Mrs. McDougald's injuries were so severe that she was incapable of either experiencing pain or appreciating her condition. Plaintiffs, on the other hand, introduced proof that Mrs. McDougald responded to certain stimuli to a sufficient extent to indicate that she was aware of her circumstances. Thus, the extent of Mrs. McDougald's cognitive abilities, if any, was sharply disputed.

The parties and the trial court agreed that Mrs. McDougald could not recover for pain and suffering unless she were conscious of the pain. Defendants maintained that such consciousness was also required to support an award for loss of enjoyment of life. The court, however, accepted plaintiffs' view that loss of enjoyment of life was compensable without regard to whether the plaintiff was aware of the loss. Accordingly, because the level of Mrs. McDougald's cognitive abilities was in dispute, the court instructed the jury to consider loss of enjoyment of life as an element of nonpecuniary damages separate from pain and suffering. [The court's charge to the jury on these points was that while Mrs. McDougald needed to be conscious in order to be compensated for pain and suffering, she didn't need to be conscious to be awarded damages for loss of enjoyment of life.]

We conclude that the court erred, both in instructing the jury that Mrs. McDougald's awareness was irrelevant to their consideration of damages for loss of enjoyment of life and in directing the jury to consider that aspect of damages separately from pain and suffering.

We begin with the familiar proposition that an award of damages to a person injured by the negligence of another is to compensate the victim, not to punish the wrongdoer. The goal is to restore the injured party, to the extent possible, to the position that would have been occupied had the wrong not occurred. To be sure, placing the burden of compensation on the negligent party also serves as a deterrent, but purely punitive damages — that is, those which have no compensatory purpose — are prohibited unless the harmful conduct is intentional, malicious, outrageous, or otherwise aggravated beyond mere negligence.

Damages for nonpecuniary losses are, of course, among those that can be awarded as compensation to the victim. This aspect of damages, however, stands on less certain ground than does an award for pecuniary damages. An economic loss can be compensated in kind by an economic gain; but recovery for noneconomic losses such as pain and suffering and loss of enjoyment of life rests on "the legal fiction that money damages can compensate for a victim's injury" (*Howard v. Lecher*, 42 N.Y.2d 109, 111). We accept this fiction, knowing that although money will neither ease the pain nor restore the victim's abilities, this device is as close as the law can come in its effort to right the wrong. We have no hope of evaluating what has been lost, but a monetary award may provide a measure of solace for the condition created.

Our willingness to indulge this fiction comes to an end, however, when it ceases to serve the compensatory goals of tort recovery. When that limit is met, further indulgence can only result in assessing damages that are punitive. The question posed by this case, then, is whether an award of damages for loss of enjoyment of life to a person whose injuries preclude any awareness of the loss serves a compensatory purpose. We conclude that it does not.

Simply put, an award of money damages in such circumstances has no meaning or utility to the injured person. An award for the loss of enjoyment of life "cannot provide [such a victim] with any consolation or ease any burden resting on him. . . . He cannot spend it upon necessities or pleasures. He cannot experience the pleasure of giving it away."

We recognize that, as the trial court noted, requiring some cognitive awareness as a prerequisite to recovery for loss of enjoyment of life will result in some cases "in the paradoxical situation that the greater the degree of brain injury inflicted by a negligent defendant, the smaller the award the plaintiff can recover in general damages." The force of this argument, however — the temptation to achieve a balance between injury and damages — has nothing to do with meaningful compensation for the victim. Instead, the temptation is rooted in a desire to punish the defendant in proportion to the harm inflicted. However relevant such retributive symmetry may be in the criminal law, it has no place in the law of civil damages, at least in the absence of culpability beyond mere negligence.

Accordingly, we conclude that cognitive awareness is a prerequisite to recovery for loss of enjoyment of life. We do not go so far, however, as to require the fact finder to sort out varying degrees of cognition and determine at what level a particular deprivation can be fully appreciated. With respect to pain and suffering, the trial court charged simply that there must be "some level of awareness" in order for plaintiff to recover. We think that this is an appropriate standard for all aspects of nonpecuniary loss. No doubt the standard ignores analytically relevant levels of cognition, but we resist the desire for analytical purity in favor of simplicity. A more complex instruction might give the appearance of greater precision but, given the limits of our understanding of the human mind, it would in reality lead only to greater speculation.

We turn next to the question whether loss of enjoyment of life should be considered a category of damages separate from pain and suffering. There is no dispute here that the fact finder may, in assessing nonpecuniary damages, consider the effect of the injuries on the plaintiff's capacity to lead a normal life. Traditionally, in this State and elsewhere, this aspect of suffering has not been treated as a separate category of damages; instead, the plaintiff's inability to enjoy life to its fullest has been considered one type of suffering to be factored into a general award for nonpecuniary damages, commonly known as pain and suffering.

Recently, however, there has been an attempt to segregate the suffering associated with physical pain from the mental anguish that stems from the inability to engage in certain activities, and to have juries provide a separate award for each.

Some courts have resisted the effort, primarily on the ground that duplicative and therefore excessive awards would result. Other courts have allowed separate awards, noting that the types of suffering involved are analytically distinguishable. Still other courts have questioned the propriety of the practice but held that, in the particular case, separate awards did not constitute reversible error.

[We] do not dispute that distinctions can be found or created between the concepts of pain and suffering and loss of enjoyment of life. If the term "suffering" is limited to the emotional response to the sensation of pain, then the emotional response caused by the limitation of life's activities may be considered qualitatively different. But suffering need not be so limited — it can easily encompass the frustration and anguish caused by the inability to participate in activities that once brought pleasure. Traditionally, by treating loss of enjoyment of life as a permissible factor in assessing pain and suffering, courts have given the term this broad meaning.

If we are to depart from this traditional approach and approve a separate award for loss of enjoyment of life, it must be on the basis that such an approach will yield a more accurate evaluation of the compensation due to the plaintiff. We have no doubt that, in general, the total award for nonpecuniary damages would increase if we adopted the rule. That separate awards are advocated by plaintiffs and resisted by defendants is sufficient evidence that larger awards are at stake here. But a larger award does not by itself indicate that the goal of compensation has been better served.

The advocates of separate awards contend that because pain and suffering and loss of enjoyment of life can be distinguished, they must be treated separately if the plaintiff is to be compensated fully for each distinct injury suffered. We disagree. Such an analytical approach may have its place when the subject is pecuniary damages, which can be calculated with some precision. But the estimation of nonpecuniary damages is not amenable to such analytical precision and may, in fact, suffer from its application. Translating human suffering into dollars and cents involves no mathematical formula; it rests, as we have said, on a legal fiction. The figure that emerges is unavoidably distorted by the translation. Application of this murky process to the component parts of nonpecuniary injuries (however analytically distinguishable they may be) cannot make it more accurate. If anything, the distortion will be amplified by repetition.

Thus, we are not persuaded that any salutary purpose would be served by having the jury make separate awards for pain and suffering and loss of enjoyment of life. We are confident, furthermore, that the trial advocate's art is a sufficient guarantee that none of the plaintiff's losses will be ignored by the jury.

The errors in the instructions given to the jury require a new trial on the issue of nonpecuniary damages to be awarded to plaintiff Emma McDougald. Defendants' remaining contentions are either without merit, beyond the scope of our review or are rendered academic by our disposition of the case.

Accordingly, the order of the Appellate Division, insofar as appealed from, should be modified, with costs to defendants, by granting a new trial on the issue of nonpecuniary damages of plaintiff Emma McDougald, and as so modified, affirmed.

TITONE, J. (dissenting).

The majority's holding represents a compromise position that neither comports with the fundamental principles of tort compensation nor furnishes a satisfactory, logically consistent framework for compensating nonpecuniary loss. Because I conclude that loss of enjoyment of life is an objective damage item, conceptually distinct from conscious pain and suffering, I can find no fault with the trial court's instruction authorizing separate awards and permitting an award for "loss of enjoyment of life" even in the absence of any awareness of that loss on the part of the injured plaintiff. Accordingly, I dissent.

[T]he compensatory nature of a monetary award for loss of enjoyment of life is not altered or rendered punitive by the fact that the unaware injured plaintiff cannot experience the pleasure of having it. The fundamental distinction between punitive and compensatory damages is that the former exceed the amount necessary to replace what the plaintiff lost. As the Court of Appeals for the Second Circuit has observed, "[the] fact that the compensation [for loss of enjoyment of life] may inure as a practical matter to third parties in a given case does not transform the nature of the damages." (*Rufino v. United States*, 829 F.2d 354, 362).

[In] the final analysis, the rule that the majority has chosen is an arbitrary one, in that it denies or allows recovery on the basis of a criterion that is not truly related to its stated goal. In my view, it is fundamentally unsound, as well as grossly unfair, to deny recovery to those who are completely without cognitive capacity while permitting it for those with a mere spark of awareness, regardless of the latter's ability to appreciate either the loss sustained or the benefits of the monetary award offered in compensation. In both instances, the injured plaintiff is in essentially the same position, and an award that is punitive as to one is equally punitive as to the other. Of course, since I do not subscribe to the majority's conclusion that an award to an unaware plaintiff is punitive, I would have no difficulty permitting recovery to both classes of plaintiffs.

Having concluded that the injured plaintiff's awareness should not be a necessary precondition to recovery for loss of enjoyment of life, I also have no difficulty going on to conclude that loss of enjoyment of life is a distinct damage item which is recoverable separate and apart from the award for conscious pain and suffering. The majority has rejected separate recovery, in part because it apparently perceives some overlap between the two damage categories and in part because it believes that the goal of enhancing the precision of jury awards for nonpecuniary loss would not be advanced. However, the overlap the majority perceives exists only if one assumes, as the majority evidently has, that the "loss of enjoyment" category of damages is designed to compensate only for "*the emotional response* caused by the limitation of life's activities" and "*the frustration and anguish caused by* the inability to participate in activities that once brought pleasure" (emphasis added), both of which are highly subjective concepts.

In fact, while "pain and suffering compensates the victim for the physical and mental discomfort caused by the injury; [loss] of enjoyment of life compensates the victim for the limitations on the person's life created by the injury", a distinctly objective loss. In other words, while the victim's "emotional response" and "frustration and anguish" are elements of the award for pain and suffering, the "limitation of life's activities" and the "inability to participate in activities" that the majority identifies are recoverable under the "loss of enjoyment of life" rubric. Thus, there is no real overlap, and no real basis for concern about potentially duplicative awards where, as here, there is a properly instructed jury.

[For] all of these reasons, I approve of the approach that the trial court adopted in its charge to the jury. Accordingly, I would affirm the order below affirming the judgment.

NOTES

1. The principal case struggles with the basis for awarding non-economic damages. The rationale for non-economic damages has not always been apparent to the courts. Earl of Halsbury L.C. in *The Mediana* [1900] A.C. 113, 116-17 (H.L.) said:

> Nobody can suggest that you can by any arithmetical calculation establish what is the exact amount of money which would represent such a

thing as the pain and suffering which a person has undergone by reason of an accident. In truth, I think it would be very arguable to say that a person would be entitled to no damages for such things. What manly mind cares about pain and suffering that is past? But nevertheless the law recognizes that as a topic upon which damages may be given.

The mind of the common law has been empathetic to the need for non-economic damages. Michael Koenig & Michael Rustad, *His and Her Tort Reform: Gender Injustice in Disguise*, 70 WASH. L. REV. 1 (1995), argue that to curb or abolish non-economic damages would disproportionately hurt women.

2. Almost a century after the Lord Chancellor uttered his words, skeptical of the juridical basis of non-economic damages, the justification of non-economic damages has again been called in question. The arguments turn on the foundation of tort liability. The first category views liability as mimicking the bargain that the parties would have reached in the absence of transaction costs. Here the plaintiff would have bargained for insurance to cover economic losses. One commentator argues that non-economic losses introduce moral hazards that cause insurance coverage to be infeasible. Alan Schwartz, *Proposals for Products Liability Reform: A Theoretical Synthesis*, 97 YALE L.J. 353, 262-67 (1988). But Professors Croley and Hanson, *The Nonpecuniary Costs of Accidents: Pain and Suffering in Tort Law*, 108 HARV. L. REV. 1785 (1995), argue that consumers may demand insurance of this kind and tort law is a superior institution to provide it. The second, and politically polar, category is founded on the notion that the pool of funds to compensate injuries is limited and more coverage, albeit less generous, could be obtained by restricting damages to economic loss alone: J. O'CONNELL & R. SIMON, PAYMENT FOR PAIN AND SUFFERING: WHO WANTS WHAT, WHEN AND WHY? (1972). Yet others from diverse theoretical viewpoints argue that non-economic damages should be recoverable as representing a real loss, the failure to measure in damages would underdeter tortfeasors, or as a loss which is not rectifiable in money terms but should be compensable redressing the disrespect of the plaintiff's rights wrought by the defendant's wrong. Professor Margaret Radin elaborates on this in her article, *Compensation and Commensurability*, 43 DUKE L.J. 56 (1993), but compare Bruce Chapman, *Wrongdoing, Welfare, and Damages: Recovery for Non-Pecuniary Loss in Corrective Justice*, in DAVID G. OWEN, PHILOSOPHICAL FOUNDATIONS OF TORT LAW (1995), 409 (taking corrective justice as not justifying non-economic damages). This debate concerns the desirability of non-economic damages.

But equal analysis is focused upon the measurability of those damages, Mark Geistfeld, *Placing a Price on Pain and Suffering: A Method for Helping Juries Determine Tort Damages for Nonmonetary Injuries*, 83 CAL. L. REV. 773 (1995) (who also critiques Radin, *id.* at 815).

3. In *Seffert v. Los Angeles Transit Lines, supra*, the court also awarded damages for pain and suffering:

This leaves the amount of $134,000 presumably allowed for the non-pecuniary items of damage, including pain and suffering, past and future. It is this allowance that defendants seriously attack as being excessive as a matter of law.

It must be remembered that the jury fixed these damages, and that the trial judge denied a motion for new trial, one ground of which was excessiveness of the award. These determinations are entitled to great weight. The amount of damages is a fact question, first committed to the discretion of the jury and next to the discretion of the trial judge on a motion for new trial. . . . An appellate court can interfere on the ground that the judgment is excessive only on the ground that the verdict is so large that, at first blush, it shocks the conscience and suggests passion, prejudice or corruption on the part of the jury. . . . While the appellate court should consider the amounts awarded in prior cases for similar injuries, obviously, each case must be decided on its own facts and circumstances. Such examination demonstrates that such awards vary greatly. Injuries are seldom identical and the amount of pain and suffering involved in similar physical injuries varies widely. . . .

In the instant case, the nonpecuniary items of damage include allowances for pain and suffering, past and future, humiliation as a result of being disfigured and being permanently crippled, and constant anxiety and fear that the leg will have to be amputated. While the amount of the award is high, and may be more than we would have awarded were we the trier of the facts, considering the nature of the injury, the great pain and suffering, past and future, and the other items of damage, we cannot say, as a matter of law, that it is so high that it shocks the conscience and gives rise to the presumption that it was the result of passion or prejudice on the part of the jurors.

Defendants next complain that it was prejudicial error for plaintiff's counsel to argue to the jury that damages for pain and suffering could be fixed by means of a mathematical formula predicated upon a per diem allowance for this item of damages. The propriety of such an argument seems never to have been passed upon in this state. In other jurisdictions there is a sharp divergence of opinion on the subject. It is not necessary to pass on the propriety of such argument in the instant case because, when plaintiff's counsel made the argument in question, defendants' counsel did not object, assign it as misconduct or ask that the jury be admonished to disregard it. Moreover, in his argument to the jury, the defendants' counsel also adopted a mathematical formula type of argument. This being so, even if such argument were error (a point we do not pass upon), the point must be deemed to have been waived, and cannot be raised, properly, on appeal.

PROBLEMS

1. Plaintiff, a 30-year-old clerical worker, suffered a severely broken leg and arm in an automobile accident. She was off work for four weeks, but was fully recovered by the time of trial. How much should she recover for pain and suffering?

2. Plaintiff, a 25-year-old construction worker, was paralyzed in an automobile accident. Prior to the accident, he enjoyed playing basketball and hiking in the woods. After the accident, he was unable to do either. Because of the accident, he was no longer able to work. Before the accident, he expected to live until age 72. After the accident, he expected to live only until age 50. A normal, healthy, construction worker usually retires at age 60. How much should he recover for pain and suffering?

3. If you were going to argue the prior case to a jury, how would you do it? Would you try to make a per diem argument (that plaintiff should be given so much per day as compensation for his injuries)? Could you ask jurors how much they would require to switch places with plaintiff?

4. Joshua Johnson suffered severe brain injuries at birth due to medical malpractice. Because of his injuries, it is unlikely that Joshua will ever be able to work, much less become a physician. Prior to the accident, Joshua would have expected to live until age 72. Afterwards, his life expectancy was reduced to 43 years. How much can he recover for pain and suffering?

5. A law student was severely injured in an automobile accident. Her brain and cognitive abilities were unimpaired, but she was confined to a wheelchair. How much can she recover for pain and suffering?

6. Recall the prior problem in which a woman suffered disfiguring facial injuries in an automobile accident and was forced to undergo reconstructive surgery. In addition, doctors recommended two additional reconstructive surgeries. If you were hired to represent her, how would you argue for higher pain and suffering damages?

D. MITIGATION

Once injured, plaintiffs must take reasonable steps to mitigate their injuries. They must seek appropriate medical care. They must work, if they are able to. But again, what does "reasonable" mean? Must a Jehovah's Witness have a blood transfusion? Must an injured person submit to back surgery? What must be shown and by whom (is the burden of proof of reasonableness on the plaintiff or defendant), to force an operation on someone, or subtract subsequent pain and suffering and disability for failure to mitigate?

COLTON v. BENES
176 Neb. 483 (1963)

[The Plaintiff injured his back in auto accident where the defendant ran a stop sign and hit his car.]

[The] instruction as given by the trial court is here set out.

"If you find from a preponderance of the evidence that plaintiff sustained injuries arising out of the motor vehicle accident, it was plaintiff's duty to take all reasonable care of such injuries, and if he failed to take such care, and conducted himself in a manner to aggravate and enhance the alleged injuries, and on account of his failure the injuries were increased or enhanced, he is not entitled to such damages as resulted from his failure to take proper and reasonable care. However, the mere fact that a competent physician may have advised plaintiff to submit to a serious operation does not justify an inference that plaintiff was negligent or unreasonable in failing to have the operation performed. Other factors as they confronted plaintiff must be considered in determining whether or not he exercised reasonable diligence in caring for himself and his injuries. Such other factors are plaintiff's condition in relation to the risks of the proposed operation; the degree of seriousness and danger, if any, involved in the operation; whether or not it would or might permanently maim or otherwise disable him; whether or not possible benefits from the operation are almost certain or are only probable or doubtful; whether or not any alternative method of treatment is available, and, if so, what the comparative possibilities and probabilities are between it and the operation; and whether or not physicians and surgeons agree among themselves as to the advisability of the operation. After considering all or any such factors as are shown by the evidence the jury must decide whether or not the failure of plaintiff to undergo an operation constituted a failure to exercise reasonable diligence in the care of his injuries."

[The court then determined the better rule found in a great majority of cases is to submit questions of mitigation to the jury, rather than for the court to make this determination as a matter of law. The court then reviewed the medical evidence in the case before it as follows:]

The testimony concerning the contemplated operation was related by Dr. House, an orthopedic surgeon and medical witness for the plaintiff. He testified that in his opinion the plaintiff had a nerve root irritation the result of a bony impingement or encroachment between the fifth and sixth cervical vertebrae, causing a narrowing of the joint space, particularly on the right side; and that the plaintiff would require a fusion operation on his neck. The fee therefor according to a certain Nebraska fee schedule would be $300. Such an operation would require future hospitalization of 10 days to 2 weeks and would not be 100 percent effective. This would have a reasonable chance of success based on percentages but he did not state what those percentages were; and that there was a reasonable chance that upon a recovery therefrom he could go back to work and all of his complaints would be taken care of. The doctor said a fusion operation involved the stabilization or growing together of two vertebrae. It would consist of taking a portion of bone, preparing the area of the neck in which to place it, and allowing bone taken from the hip to grow in the neck, where so placed, making this area all one piece. He had recommended such an operation to the plaintiff as early as 1960. Plaintiff testified at the trial in February 1962, that he had been so advised and intended to have the operation but had not because he could not afford it.

Plaintiff contends there was no evidence upon which the court might have submitted several of the matters for consideration of the jury designated in this instruction as "factors." He asserts there was no evidence as to the risks of the proposed operation; the seriousness and danger involved; or the possibility of the plaintiff being permanently maimed or disabled.

In the cited annotation, many of the different decisions are arranged with respect to the various hazards that arose in the particular cases under paragraphs which have headings corresponding to the propositions set out as "factors" in this instruction. The trial court submitted most of these factors as set out in the headings to those paragraphs without relating the particular hazards to the evidence before it. An instruction should be given in the present case only if there is evidence showing the extent of the hazards to the plaintiff growing out of the operation contemplated. It should then be related only to the risks shown to be involved and which are covered in the evidence without undue repetition.

In the record before us there appears no evidence in the testimony from which the jury might determine the risks and hazards to the plaintiff incident to the proposed operation. The substantive law applicable does not require the injured person to undergo such an operation where the hazards to him are great. In an action in tort for personal injuries the question of whether or not the injured party should have mitigated his damages by submitting to an operation should not be submitted to the jury in the absence of evidence showing the extent of the hazards of death or injury and of the pain or suffering involved.

Further objection by the plaintiff to instruction No. 10 is made because he asserts the evidence does not show the chances or prospects of the plaintiff being benefited if the operation is performed. Though his doctor does not equate the chances in percentages he does indicate they were reasonable and the plaintiff himself must have deemed them sufficient because he intends to take them. We do not regard the instruction defective in this regard.

In the evidence before us there is no medical testimony in disagreement with that of Dr. House with respect to the contemplated operation. The plaintiff's condition and the other treatment given him however are testified to at length.

It appears from *Simmerman v. Felthauser*, that mitigation of damages being defensive in nature the burden of proving the plaintiff should submit to an operation to lessen his damage is upon the defendant.

The plaintiff further objects to the instruction in that the trial court did not include as an element for the jury to consider the inability of the plaintiff to pay for the same. This is based on his testimony that he could not afford it. There was no further factual evidence in the record. The annotation cites cases holding that where an unreasonable expenditure would be required to undergo the treatment, the injured person is justified in refusing to undergo it. The plaintiff's pecuniary situation is within his own peculiar knowledge and could not be shown by the defendants in the first instance. Under such circumstances the plaintiff's financial condition should be shown if he asserts it as a reason for avoidance of surgery and such testimony should be subject to cross-examination.

Because of the submission of the issue of contributory negligence to the jury herein, the judgment must be reversed and the cause remanded for new trial. The issue of liability having been determined the cause should be tried only as to the damages involved.

The judgment is reversed and the cause remanded for new trial in accordance with this opinion.

REVERSED AND REMANDED.

NOTE

Comparative negligence is now the rule in the vast majority of states. Depending on the wording of the comparative negligence statute, comparative fault may obviate the need to employ a mitigation theory. Do you see why?

PROBLEM

Religious beliefs are a legitimate reason for refusing treatment in some wrongful death cases. Are religious beliefs "reasons" that are sufficiently reasonable to hold the defendant responsible for the wrongful death? Many cases involve Jehovah's Witness accident victims who refuse blood transfusions. In *Williams v. Bright*, 632 N.Y.S.2d 760 (N.Y. Sup. Ct. 1995), Greenfield J. stated the issues thus:

> The context in which the issue is raised in this case, is the extent of the duty to mitigate damages when a proposed course of treatment would violate a plaintiff's deeply held religious beliefs. The law is clear that with respect to damages, a plaintiff has a duty to mitigate so as not to unduly penalize a defendant. Normally, that obligation is to do what a reasonable person would have done to alleviate or cure the condition. Ordinarily that involves a weighing of the costs, benefits and medical

risks involved. However, when a person declines a particular course of medical treatment, not because of the risk or the cost, but because it violates his or her deeply held religious scruples, can damages be denied because alleviation or cure has been declined? Plaintiff contends that to permit a jury to pass upon the soundness of religious beliefs would constitute discrimination, imposing a possible penalty on the free exercise of religion. Defendant, on the other hand, contends that it should not be penalized by having to pay higher damages, since then the court would be giving a preference to a party who is excused from a duty to mitigate as a result of her religion.

How should these issues be resolved?

E. LOSS OF CONSORTIUM

"Consortium" refers to the benefits that one party is entitled to receive from another. Originally applied to the benefits of companionship and service that a husband could expect from his wife, the common law recognized a cause of action on behalf of the husband against a third party who injured his wife and thus deprived him of these benefits. Loss of consortium claims are wrapped in the sexism of early (and not so early) English common law. As late as 1952, in England, while a husband was allowed compensation for loss of society and sexual services of his wife, a wife was not allowed compensation for the loss of her husband. *Best v. Samuel Fox and Co. Ltd.* [1052] A.C. 716. The wife was treated like the man's property or as a servant. The American cases, however, since the 1950s, universally vest the action for loss of consortium in the wife as well as the husband. *See Hitaffer v. Argonne Co.*, 183 F.2d 811 (D.C. Cir. 1950); RESTATEMENT (SECOND) OF TORTS § 693(1).

The debate over the loss of consortium has now shifted to suits by children whose parents have been injured or killed. The leading case against providing for the loss of a parent by a minor child is *Borer v. American Airlines, Inc.*, 563 P.2d 858, 860-61 (Cal. 1977), where Justice Torbiner rejected the damage claims of the injured party's nine children. Michigan is mixed, allowing recovery to parents for loss of their children *Berger v. Weber*, 303 N.W.2d 424 (Mich. 1981) but not to children for loss of their parents. *Sizemore v. Smock*, 422 N.W.2d 666 (Mich. 1988).

More recently, a different perspective emerged in *Villareal v. Arizona*, 774 P.2d 213 (Ariz. 1989). The Arizona rule allows parents to recover for the loss of companionship of their adult children, even though the parents were not dependent upon those adult children for financial support. To the Arizona courts, the nature of the loss — companionship, love and support — required recovery without regard to the archaic pecuniary theory of parental rights.

Following the reasoning of Arizona, should loss of consortium rights be provided to unmarried couples? And if the loss is companionship, should the defendant be able to cross-examine the claiming spouse on the fights as well as the good times; or in wrongful death cases, what if there is a new love interest? Should remarriage be required to mitigate damages?

F. COLLATERAL BENEFITS

We live in an age of liability insurance, medical insurance, property insurance, disability insurance, and workers' compensation insurance. The government also provides various social services including veteran benefits, social security, medicaid and medicare. Should the fact that an injured individual has these kinds of collateral benefits change the amount of damages the injured person can recover? Does it matter whether the defendant is a private party, or is the government, where taxpayer money also contributes collateral benefits to the injured plaintiff?

HELFEND v. SOUTHERN CALIFORNIA RAPID TRANSIT DISTRICT
465 P.2d 61 (Cal. 1970)

TOBRINER, Acting Chief Justice.

Defendants appeal from a judgment of the Los Angeles Superior Court entered on a verdict in favor of plaintiff, Julius J. Helfend, for $16,400 in general and special damages for injuries sustained in a bus-auto collision that occurred on July 19, 1965, in the City of Los Angeles. [After] the jury verdict in favor of plaintiff in the sum of $16,400, defendants appealed, raising only two contentions: (1) The trial court committed prejudicial error in refusing to allow the introduction of evidence to the effect that a portion of the plaintiff's medical bills had been paid from a collateral source. (2) The trial court erred in denying defendant the opportunity to determine if plaintiff had been compensated from more than one collateral source for damages sustained in the accident.

We must decide whether the collateral source rule applies to tort actions involving public entities and public employees in which the plaintiff has received benefits from his medical insurance coverage.

[The] collateral source rule as applied here embodies the venerable concept that a person who has invested years of insurance premiums to assure his medical care should receive the benefits of his thrift. The tortfeasor should not garner the benefits of his victim's providence.

The collateral source rule expresses a policy judgment in favor of encouraging citizens to purchase and maintain insurance for personal injuries and for other eventualities. Courts consider insurance a form of investment, the benefits of which become payable without respect to any other possible source of funds. If we were to permit a tortfeasor to mitigate damages with payments from plaintiff's insurance, plaintiff would be in a position inferior to that of having bought no insurance, because his payment of premiums would have earned no benefit. Defendant should not be able to avoid payment of full compensation for the injury inflicted merely because the victim has had the foresight to provide himself with insurance.

Some commentators object that the above approach to the collateral source rule provides plaintiff with a "double recovery," rewards him for the injury, and defeats the principle that damages should compensate the victim but not punish the tortfeasor. We agree with Professor Fleming's observation, however, that "double recovery is justified only in the face of some exceptional, supervening reason, as in the case of accident or life insurance, where it is felt unjust that the tortfeasor should take advantage of the thrift and prescience of the victim in having paid the premium." (FLEMING, INTRODUCTION TO THE LAW OF TORTS (1967) p. 131.) [R]ecovery in a wrongful death action is not defeated by the payment of the benefit on a life insurance policy.

Furthermore, insurance policies increasingly provide for either subrogation or refund of benefits upon a tort recovery, and such refund is indeed called for in the present case. (*See* Fleming, *The Collateral Source Rule and Loss Allocation in Tort Law, supra*, 54 CAL.L.REV. 1478, 1479.) Hence, the plaintiff receives no double recovery; the collateral source rule simply serves as a means of bypassing the antiquated doctrine of non-assignment of tortious actions and permits a proper transfer of risk from the plaintiff's insurer to the tortfeasor by way of the victim's tort recovery. The double shift from the tortfeasor to the victim and then from the victim to his insurance carrier can normally occur with little cost in that the insurance carrier is often intimately involved in the initial litigation and quite automatically receives its part of the tort settlement or verdict.

Even in cases in which the contract or the law precludes subrogation or refund of benefits, or in situations in which the collateral source waives such subrogation or refund, the rule performs entirely necessary functions in the computation of damages. For example, the cost of medical care often provides both attorneys and juries in tort cases with an important measure for assessing the plaintiff's general damages. To permit the defendant to tell the jury that the plaintiff has been recompensed by a collateral source for his medical costs might irretrievably upset the complex, delicate, and somewhat indefinable calculations which result in the normal jury verdict.

We also note that generally the jury is not informed that plaintiff's attorney will receive a large portion of the plaintiff's recovery in contingent fees or that personal injury damages are not taxable to the plaintiff and are normally deductible by the defendant. Hence, the plaintiff rarely actually receives full compensation for his injuries as computed by the jury. The collateral source rule partially serves to compensate for the attorney's share and does not actually render "double recovery" for the plaintiff. Indeed, many jurisdictions that have abolished or limited the collateral source rule have also established a means for assessing the plaintiff's costs for counsel directly against the defendant rather than imposing the contingent fee system. In sum, the plaintiff's recovery for his medical expenses from both the tortfeasor and his medical insurance program will not usually give him "double recovery," but partially provides a somewhat closer approximation to full compensation for his injuries.

If we consider the collateral source rule as applied here in the context of the entire American approach to the law of torts and damages, we find that the rule presently performs a number of legitimate and even indispensable functions. Without a thorough revolution in the American approach to torts and the consequent damages, the rule at least with respect to medical insurance benefits has become so integrated within our present system that its precipitous judicial nullification would work hardship. In this case the collateral source rule lies between two systems for the compensation of accident victims: the traditional tort recovery based on fault and the increasingly prevalent coverage based on non-fault insurance. Neither system possesses such universality of coverage or completeness of compensation that we can easily dispense with the collateral source rule's approach to meshing the two systems. The reforms which many academicians propose cannot easily be achieved through piecemeal common law development; the proposed changes, if desirable, would be more effectively accomplished through legislative reform. In any case, we cannot believe that the judicial repeal of the collateral source rule, as applied in the present case, would be the place to begin the needed changes.

[We] therefore reaffirm our adherence to the collateral source rule in tort cases in which the plaintiff has been compensated by an independent collateral source — such as insurance, pension, continued wages, or disability payments — for which he had actually or constructively paid or in cases in which the collateral source would be recompensed from the tort recovery through subrogation, refund of benefits, or some other arrangement. Hence, we conclude that in a case in which a tort victim has received partial compensation from medical insurance coverage entirely independent of the tortfeasor the trial court properly followed the collateral source rule and foreclosed defendant from mitigating damages by means of the collateral payments. [The court held that the collateral source rule applied to governmental entities as defendants.]

Defense counsel did not even attempt to inquire, out of the hearing of the jury, as to the nature and extent of plaintiff's insurance coverage, the cost of such coverage, the benefits plaintiff received, the arrangements for refund of benefits, or subrogation. Nor did he develop any of the other considerations which would be relevant to assessing the prejudicial effect of the introduction of the evidence of insurance coverage against any proper relationship, however limited, to the issues of the case. [Lacking] any proper offer of proof as to these issues we must conclude that the trial court correctly refused to permit defendant to inquire within the hearing of the jury as to the nature and extent of plaintiff's insurance coverage.

The judgment is affirmed.

NOTES

1. Often family members provide care for injured or disabled plaintiffs. The prevailing rule is that plaintiffs may recover the reasonable value of these services. The services are provided as a gift and the wrongdoer should not benefit from the provision of gratuitous services. *Selleck v. Janesville*, 80 N.W. 944 (Wis. 1899). What if the services are provided by a third party? Numbers of cases have raised the question of recovery of medical services costs where the services are provided by the United States government where the United States is the defendant. In *United States v. Brooks*, 176 F.2d 482 (4th Cir. 1949), the court found that the benefits should be set off the damages. Disability payments, pensions, and social security benefits are distinguishable and are collateral because they are contributed to by the victim, in a manner similar to an insurance policy. *United States v. Price*, 288 F.2d 448 (4th Cir. 1961). The application of the *Brooks* case to future medical care has been controversial since it would oblige the victim to seek care from the governmental agency, rather than a private provider. But the prospect of a "double recovery" in *Burke v. United States*, 605 F. Supp. 981 (D. Md. 1985), a United States Torts Claims Act case, sufficed to persuade the court to take account of the benefit the plaintiff would receive for future medical care. The court reasoned that the plaintiff had not contributed to the fund which supplied her with future medical benefits. (She was the spouse of a retired serviceman.) Is it true that military health benefits are properly classified as "non-contributory"? Are there other arguments for the treating of public benefits as not collateral benefits?

2. The collateral benefits rule has been criticized and reformed in about half the states. For example, see AMERICAN LAW INSTITUTE REPORTERS' STUDY, "ENTERPRISE RESPONSIBILITY FOR PERSONAL INJURY," Vol. II pp. 161-82 (1991) (recommending abolition of the collateral benefits rule except for life insurance).

G. PUNITIVE DAMAGES

In recent years there has been a proliferation of claims for punitive damages in tort cases, and to some, the awards of punitive damages have grown too high. Accompanying this increase in punitive damages claims is renewed criticism of the concept of punitive damages in a tort system that is designed primarily to compensate injured parties for harm. The result has been for states to examine characterizations of a defendant's conduct in the light of the historic objectives of punitive damages, try to more precisely define the nature of the conduct potentially subject to a punitive damages award, and heighten the standard of proof required of someone seeking an award of punitive damages. Moreover, some argue that if the punishment in a given case is too great, it may be arbitrary, may violate due process, and may violate both state and the federal constitutions.

STURM, RUGER & CO., INC. v. DAY
594 P.2d 38 (Alaska 1979)

CONNOR, Justice.

This is a products liability case. Appellee Michael James Day bought a .41 magnum single action revolver on June 1, 1972. The gun had been manufactured two years before by appellant Sturm, Ruger and Company, in August of 1970, but was purchased new by Day. On July 30, 1972, Day was sitting in the cab of his small pickup truck with two young friends when he decided to unload his gun. As he was unloading the revolver, the gun slipped out of his hands. When he grabbed for the gun it fired, the bullet striking his leg and causing serious injuries.

The Sturm, Ruger .41 magnum single action revolver had four hammer positions which were described [in] the instruction booklet provided by the manufacturer: [Four positions were described.] The safety and loading notches are designed so that the hammer cannot be released from either of these positions by normally pulling the trigger.

The third page of the instruction booklet accompanying the revolver warned that the gun could be fired from the loading notch position by exerting "excessive pull on the trigger." This warning was set off from the rest of the instructions in a separate box:

> WARNING: This revolver can be fired by excessive pull on the trigger from either the safety notch position, indicated by No. 2 in Figure 1, or the loading notch position indicated by No. 3 in Figure 1.

> The loading notch and the safety notch provide only partial security. If these notches are damaged, as they may be by "fanning," they offer no security. Never depend on this or any other mechanical safety device to justify pointing the firearm at any person.

> Fanning is unsafe for you and abusive to your revolver.

Day filed suit against Sturm, Ruger and Company. His second amended complaint was based on a theory of strict tort liability, and included a claim for punitive damages. It was Day's contention that the hammer had been on the loading notch and that the gun fired after he accidentally pulled the hammer off that notch, presumably by pulling the trigger as he caught the falling gun.

The jury returned a verdict for the plaintiff, finding specifically that the revolver was designed defectively and that it had a manufacturing defect as well. The jury awarded $137,750.00 in compensatory damages and $2,895,000.00 in punitive damages to the plaintiff.

Sturm, Ruger filed a timely motion for new trial and for judgment notwithstanding the verdict. This motion included a request that the trial judge consider reducing the punitive damages award. The trial judge declined to order any remittitur. This appeal followed.

[Sturm,] Ruger urges us to repudiate the doctrine of punitive damages in Alaska on the ground that imposition of punitive damages violates the state and federal constitutions. Appellant also contends that punitive damages should not be awarded as a matter of public policy. In addition, Sturm, Ruger argues that punitive damages have no place in the "fault-free" context of strict products liability.

[In] the event that we should decline to rule in appellant's favor on the above questions, Sturm, Ruger maintains that the evidence introduced in the instant case was not sufficient to support an award of punitive damages. Appellant also challenges certain evidentiary rulings relevant to the area of punitive damages, and claims that the amount of damages awarded was excessive.

Sturm, Ruger's constitutional arguments, summarized briefly, are that imposition of punitive damages violates due process guarantees because the jury had no standards by which to determine the extent of a defendant's culpability and the amount of damages to be assessed. Appellant further argues that the punitive damages doctrine lends itself to arbitrary application and does not provide fair warning of what conduct will subject a person to punishment.

In *Bridges v. Alaska Housing Authority*, 375 P.2d 696, 702 (Alaska 1962), this court noted that in order to recover punitive or exemplary damages, the plaintiff must prove that the wrongdoer's conduct was "outrageous, such as acts done with malice or bad motives or a reckless indifference to the interests of another." Actual malice need not be proved. Rather, "reckless indifference to the rights of others, and conscious action in deliberate disregard of them [may] provide the necessary state of mind to justify punitive damages." RESTATEMENT (SECOND) OF TORTS, § 908 (Tent. Draft No. 19, 1973).

In the instant case, the jury was instructed to consider whether the defendant knew its design was defective and had caused injuries or death. The jury was then told that if the defendant "acted with reckless indifference toward the safety of its customers, or that its acts were maliciously or wantonly done," punitive damages could be awarded in addition to compensatory damages. The trial judge cautioned the jury to exercise discretion and reason and not to be motivated by sympathy, bias, or prejudice with regard to the punitive damages question.

We find these standards to be sufficient in order to meet a void-for-vagueness [challenge].

We also reject the argument that punitive damages have no place in a strict liability case, although we do agree with appellant that punitive damages ought not be awarded in every products liability case. Where, however, as in the instant case, plaintiff is able to plead and prove that the manufacturer knew that its product was defectively designed and that injuries and deaths had resulted from the design defect, but continued to market the product in reckless disregard of the public's safety, punitive damages may be awarded.

Punitive damages are designed not only to punish the wrongdoer, but also to deter him and others like him from similar wrongdoing in the future. RESTATE-MENT (SECOND) OF TORTS, § 908(1) (Tent. Draft No. 19, 1973). We believe that as a matter of public policy, punitive damages can serve several useful functions in the products liability area. For example, the threat of punitive damages serves a deterrence function in cases in which a product may cause numerous minor injuries for which potential plaintiffs might decline to sue, or in cases in which it would be cheaper for the manufacturer to pay compensatory damages to those who did present claims than it would be to remedy the product's defect. In addition, if punitive damages could not be awarded in the products liability context, a reckless manufacturer might gain an unfair advantage over its more socially responsible competitors. On balance, we find the arguments advanced by appellant in favor of its position to be outweighed by the sound public policy considerations supporting the imposition of punitive damages in appropriate cases. We therefore decline to jettison the doctrine of punitive damages in this area of the law.

We turn next to Sturm, Ruger's claim that there was insufficient evidence to sustain the jury's award of punitive damages. The evidence presented at trial indicated that top officials at Sturm, Ruger knew that the safety and loading notches of their single action revolver presented a danger of accidental discharge because of the propensity of the engaging middle parts to fail or break. The evidence also reflects knowledge on the part of Sturm, Ruger management that serious injuries had resulted from this deficiency, coupled with procrastination in changing the basic design, at an increased cost of $1.93 per gun. Because we find that fair-minded jurors in the exercise of reasonable judgment could differ as to whether Sturm, Ruger's actions amounted to reckless indifference to the rights of others, and conscious action in deliberate disregard of them, thereby evidencing a state of mind which could justify the imposition of punitive damages, we will not upset the jury's conclusions that punitive damages were warranted.

. . . .

Appellant's final contention regarding punitive damages is that the amount awarded was excessive. We have previously held that the decision to order a remittitur or a new trial rests within the sound discretion of the trial [court].

One means of determining if an award of punitive damages is excessive is to compare it with the amount of actual damages. Professor McCormick observes:

> "The punitive damages given, it is said, must bear some reasonable proportion to the actual damages. As a rough working scale, this is better than nothing."

McCORMICK, LAW OF DAMAGES, Sec. 85, 298 (1935). Exemplary damages may exceed the actual damages, however, and no definite ratio between them is prescribed. *Taylor v. Williamson*, 197 Iowa 88, 196 N.W. 713 (Iowa 1924). Other important factors which bear on the question include "the magnitude and flagrancy of the offense, the importance of the policy violated, and the wealth of the defendant." *Zhadan v. Downtown L.S. Motors*, 66 Cal. App. 3d 481, 136 Cal. Rptr. 132, 143 (Cal. App. 1976).

In his comprehensive law review article, *Punitive Damages in Products Liability Litigation*, 74 MICH. L. REV. 1258 (1976), Professor Owen argues cogently that while punitive damages should be awarded in appropriate cases, the awards should be subjected to greater scrutiny than in many cases in the past. Indeed, he finds a recent trend toward tightened judicial control over punitive damages. Moreover, judicial scrutiny over the awards provides a partial justification for allowing such awards in the first place. The spectre of bankruptcy and excessive punishment can be in part dispelled to the extent that trial and appellate courts exercise their powers of review.

The compensatory damages awarded to Michael Day and against Sturm, Ruger amounted to $137,750, exclusive of costs, prejudgment interest, and attorney's fees. The punitive damage award of $2,895,000 appears to be so out of proportion to the amount of actual damages as to suggest that the jury's award was the result of passion or prejudice. The jurors apparently responded to an invitation to punish Sturm, Ruger for all wrongs committed against all purchasers and users of its products, rather than for the wrong done to this particular plaintiff. *See Egan v. Mutual of Omaha Inc. Co.*, 63 Cal. App. 3d 659, 133 Cal. Rptr. 899, 919-20 (Cal. App. 1976). Under the circumstances, it was a mistake and an abuse of discretion for the trial judge not to have reduced the punitive damages or to have ordered a new trial.

[In] summary, we reverse the award of compensatory damages, and remand for a new trial as to both compensatory and punitive damages. We need not address the question of attorney's fees raised by appellee on cross-appeal.

BURKE, Justice, Dissenting in part.

The evidence showed that Sturm, Ruger manufactured over 1,501,000 revolvers of the type causing Day's injury. Sturm, Ruger's profit from the manufacture and sale of those firearms alone was enormous, totaling many millions of dollars. At trial, William Ruger, the president and founder of Sturm, Ruger, testified that redesign of the revolver to cure the defect cost approximately $199,000 and that the increased manufacturing cost per revolver was $1.93. The figure agreed upon by the jury as an appropriate award for punitive damages equaled the amount of the increased manufacturing cost per item multiplied by the approximate number of revolvers sold: $1.93 x 1,500,000 = $2,895,000. Thus, the amount of the award is roughly equal to the profit directly attributable to Sturm, Ruger's callous disregard for the safety of its customers. Such being the case, I think there is no merit to the contention that the figure was the result of improper passion or prejudice. Certainly, the amount of the punitive damage award far exceeded Day's actual damages. However, given the purpose of punitive damages, the award was not excessive.

NOTE

Professor David Owen's influential article, cited by the court, lists these factors in establishing punitive damages:

(1) the amount of the plaintiff's litigation expenses;

(2) the seriousness of the hazard to the public;

(3) the profitability of the marketing misconduct (increased by an appropriate multiple);

(4) the attitude and conduct of the enterprise upon discovery of the misconduct;

(5) the degree of the manufacturer's awareness of the hazard and of its excessiveness;

(6) the number and level of employees involved in causing or covering up the marketing misconduct;

(7) the duration of both the improper marketing behavior and its cover-up;

(8) the financial condition of the enterprise and the probable effect thereon of a particular judgment; and

(9) the total punishment the enterprise will probably receive from other sources.

74 Mich. L. Rev. 1258, (1976). *Cf.* Zwier, *Due Process and Punitive Damages,* 1991 Utah L. Rev. 407 (arguing that jurors should have broad discretion because they are our system's embodiment of the reasonable person, and are just as capable and expert in making their decisions as the judges who might review them. While jurors are influenced by nonrational factors, they are not acting arbitrarily in awarding large punitive damages because real deterrence may require some unpredictability. Otherwise the rational business would be able to factor in the cost of fraud as a cost of doing business. As to whether this non-rationality is constitutional, see Scalia and Thomas's dissent in *BMW of North America v. Gore,* 517 U.S. 559 (1996)).

PROBLEMS

1. Advise your client Alice in the following circumstances. Alice, while crossing the street, was run over by Barbara who was working for Passion Pizza delivering pizzas to homes. Passion Pizza had a policy guaranteeing thirty

minute delivery. If the pizza is not delivered within the 30-minute period, it is given free to the customer. Barbara was racing at 65 m.p.h. in a 35 m.p.h. zone in an attempt to make timely delivery. There is no doubt about culpability, nor does the evidence suggest any contributory negligence on Alice's part. Can Alice obtain more than compensatory damages? What evidence needs to be adduced? *Wauchop v. Domino's Pizza*, 832 F. Supp. 1577 (N.D. Ind. 1993).

2. What if the plaintiffs discover a memo written to Passion's CEO by a safety expert, that said, "While the 30 minute guarantee could increase profits to Passion in the amount of $1,000,000 a year, this policy makes it virtually certain that in the next six months someone (driver or others on the road) will die or be severely injured as a result of the pressure placed on the drivers to hurry up the delivery." Does the memo prove that punitive damages should be awarded? If the plaintiff is awarded compensatory damages of $50,000.00 for Passion's driver's negligence, how much should the plaintiff be awarded in punitive damages?

3. Same facts as Problem 2, but what if profits were expected to be $500,000? What if the profits were expected to be only $50.00 a year? How do expected profits reflect on reprehensibility? Or if there are low profits, but higher risk of personal injury — say five deaths — should the punitive damages awarded be even greater than where there is only one expected death, and greater profit?

4. Same facts as Problem 2, but what if no study had been done on the increased risk factor to the drivers and others? Should safety studies be required any time someone acts in a way that might cause injury to others? Should their absence give rise to punitive damages?

5. What if the risk of injury is merely financial injury from fraud? A sells liability insurance contracts without any intent to cover for any losses. A is not risking personal injury in the selling of the policy, but damages the economic safety net the person might have had if liability arises and plaintiff had had protection. What is the appropriate measure of deterrence in this situation? Is it related to the cost of the one policy sold, or the amount of liability any one policy holder might experience? Is it related to the profits gained from all policies sold?

6. Company X makes a "dalkon shield," designed and sold as a safe and effective birth control device. The product was not adequately tested. It risks infection causing bad health effects in women who use the product. What if paying punitive damages in one suit affects the ability of the defendant to pay compensatory damages in other suits? Does bankruptcy provide adequate protection to the defendant? Does bankruptcy adequately deter against willful misconduct?

STATE FARM MUTUAL AUTOMOBILE INSURANCE COMPANY v. CAMPBELL
123 S. Ct. 1513 (2003)

Justice KENNEDY delivered the opinion of the Court.

We address once again the measure of punishment, by means of punitive damages, a State may impose upon a defendant in a civil case. The question is whether, in the circumstances we shall recount, an award of $145 million in punitive damages, where full compensatory damages are $1 million, is excessive and in violation of the Due Process Clause of the Fourteenth Amendment to the Constitution of the United States.

I

In 1981, Curtis Campbell (Campbell) was driving with his wife, Inez Preece Campbell, in Cache County, Utah. He decided to pass six vans traveling ahead of them on a two-lane highway. Todd Ospital was driving a small car approaching from the opposite direction. To avoid a head-on collision with Campbell, who by then was driving on the wrong side of the highway and toward oncoming traffic, Ospital swerved onto the shoulder, lost control of his automobile, and collided with a vehicle driven by Robert G. Slusher. Ospital was killed, and Slusher was rendered permanently disabled. The Campbells escaped unscathed.

In the ensuing wrongful death and tort action, Campbell insisted he was not at fault. Early investigations did support differing conclusions as to who caused the accident, but "a consensus was reached early on by the investigators and witnesses that Mr. Campbell's unsafe pass had indeed caused the crash." Campbell's insurance company, petitioner State Farm Mutual Automobile Insurance Company (State Farm), nonetheless decided to contest liability and declined offers by Slusher and Ospital's estate (Ospital) to settle the claims for the policy limit of $50,000 ($25,000 per claimant). State Farm also ignored the advice of one of its own investigators and took the case to trial, assuring the Campbells that "their assets were safe, that they had no liability for the accident, that [State Farm] would represent their interests, and that they did not need to procure separate counsel." To the contrary, a jury determined that Campbell was 100 percent at fault, and a judgment was returned for $185,849, far more than the amount offered in settlement.

At first State Farm refused to cover the $135,849 in excess liability. Its counsel made this clear to the Campbells: " 'You may want to put for sale signs on your property to get things moving.' " Nor was State Farm willing to post a supersedeas bond to allow Campbell to appeal the judgment against him. Campbell obtained his own counsel to appeal the verdict. During the pendency of the appeal, in late 1984, Slusher, Ospital, and the Campbells reached an agreement whereby Slusher and Ospital agreed not to seek satisfaction of their claims against the Campbells. In exchange the Campbells agreed to pursue a bad faith action against State Farm and to be represented by Slusher's and

Ospital's attorneys. The Campbells also agreed that Slusher and Ospital would have a right to play a part in all major decisions concerning the bad faith action. No settlement could be concluded without Slusher's and Ospital's approval, and Slusher and Ospital would receive 90 percent of any verdict against State Farm.

In 1989, the Utah Supreme Court denied Campbell's appeal in the wrongful death and tort actions. *Slusher v. Ospital*, 777 P.2d 437 (Utah 1989). State Farm then paid the entire judgment, including the amounts in excess of the policy limits. The Campbells nonetheless filed a complaint against State Farm alleging bad faith, fraud, and intentional infliction of emotional distress. The trial court initially granted State Farm's motion for summary judgment because State Farm had paid the excess verdict, but that ruling was reversed on appeal. On remand State Farm moved in limine to exclude evidence of alleged conduct that occurred in unrelated cases outside of Utah, but the trial court denied the motion. At State Farm's request the trial court bifurcated the trial into two phases conducted before different juries. In the first phase the jury determined that State Farm's decision not to settle was unreasonable because there was a substantial likelihood of an excess verdict. Before the second phase of the action against State Farm we decided *BMW of North America, Inc. v. Gore*, 517 U.S. 559, 116 S. Ct. 1589, 134 L. Ed. 2d 809 (1996), and refused to sustain a $2 million punitive damages award which accompanied a verdict of only $4,000 in compensatory damages. Based on that decision, State Farm again moved for the exclusion of evidence of dissimilar out-of-state conduct. The trial court denied State Farm's motion.

The second phase addressed State Farm's liability for fraud and intentional infliction of emotional distress, as well as compensatory and punitive damages. The Utah Supreme Court aptly characterized this phase of the trial: "State Farm argued during phase II that its decision to take the case to trial was an 'honest mistake' that did not warrant punitive damages. In contrast, the Campbells introduced evidence that State Farm's decision to take the case to trial was a result of a national scheme to meet corporate fiscal goals by capping payouts on claims company wide. This scheme was referred to as State Farm's 'Performance, Planning and Review,' or PP & R, policy. To prove the existence of this scheme, the trial court allowed the Campbells to introduce extensive expert testimony regarding fraudulent practices by State Farm in its nation-wide operations. Although State Farm moved prior to phase II of the trial for the exclusion of such evidence and continued to object to it at trial, the trial court ruled that such evidence was admissible to determine whether State Farm's conduct in the Campbell case was indeed intentional and sufficiently egregious to warrant punitive damages." Evidence pertaining to the PP & R policy concerned State Farm's business practices for over 20 years in numerous States. Most of these practices bore no relation to third-party automobile insurance claims, the type of claim underlying the Campbells' complaint against the company. The jury awarded the Campbells $2.6 million in compensatory damages and $145 million in punitive damages, which the trial court reduced to $1 million and $25 million respectively. Both parties appealed.

The Utah Supreme Court sought to apply the three guideposts we identified in *Gore*, supra, and it reinstated the $145 million punitive damages award. Relying in large part on the extensive evidence concerning the PP & R policy, the court concluded State Farm's conduct was reprehensible. The court also relied upon State Farm's "massive wealth" and on testimony indicating that "State Farm's actions, because of their clandestine nature, will be punished at most in one out of every 50,000 cases as a matter of statistical probability," and concluded that the ratio between punitive and compensatory damages was not unwarranted. Finally, the court noted that the punitive damages award was not excessive when compared to various civil and criminal penalties State Farm could have faced, including $10,000 for each act of fraud, the suspension of its license to conduct business in Utah, the disgorgement of profits, and imprisonment. We granted certiorari.

II

[W]hile States possess discretion over the imposition of punitive damages, it is well established that there are procedural and substantive constitutional limitations on these awards. The Due Process Clause of the Fourteenth Amendment prohibits the imposition of grossly excessive or arbitrary punishments on a tortfeasor. . . . The reason is that "[e]lementary notions of fairness enshrined in our constitutional jurisprudence dictate that a person receive fair notice not only of the conduct that will subject him to punishment, but also of the severity of the penalty that a State may impose." . . . To the extent an award is grossly excessive, it furthers no legitimate purpose and constitutes an arbitrary deprivation of property. . . . We have admonished that "[p]unitive damages pose an acute danger of arbitrary deprivation of property. Jury instructions typically leave the jury with wide discretion in choosing amounts, and the presentation of evidence of a defendant's net worth creates the potential that juries will use their verdicts to express biases against big businesses, particularly those without strong local presences." Our concerns are heightened when the decisionmaker is presented, as we shall discuss, with evidence that has little bearing as to the amount of punitive damages that should be awarded. Vague instructions, or those that merely inform the jury to avoid "passion or prejudice," do little to aid the decisionmaker in its task of assigning appropriate weight to evidence that is relevant and evidence that is tangential or only inflammatory.

In light of these concerns, in *Gore*, supra, we instructed courts reviewing punitive damages to consider three guideposts: (1) the degree of reprehensibility of the defendant's misconduct; (2) the disparity between the actual or potential harm suffered by the plaintiff and the punitive damages award; and (3) the difference between the punitive damages awarded by the jury and the civil penalties authorized or imposed in comparable cases. We reiterated the importance of these three guideposts in *Cooper Industries* and mandated appellate courts to conduct de novo review of a trial court's application of them to the jury's award. Exacting appellate review ensures that an award of punitive damages is based upon an " 'application of law, rather than a decisionmaker's caprice.' "

III

Under the principles outlined in *BMW of North America, Inc. v. Gore*, this case is neither close nor difficult. It was error to reinstate the jury's $145 million punitive damages award. We address each guidepost of *Gore* in some detail.

A

"[T]he most important indicium of the reasonableness of a punitive damages award is the degree of reprehensibility of the defendant's conduct." We have instructed courts to determine the reprehensibility of a defendant by considering whether: the harm caused was physical as opposed to economic; the tortious conduct evinced an indifference to or a reckless disregard of the health or safety of others; the target of the conduct had financial vulnerability; the conduct involved repeated actions or was an isolated incident; and the harm was the result of intentional malice, trickery, or deceit, or mere accident. The existence of any one of these factors weighing in favor of a plaintiff may not be sufficient to sustain a punitive damages award; and the absence of all of them renders any award suspect. It should be presumed a plaintiff has been made whole for his injuries by compensatory damages, so punitive damages should only be awarded if the defendant's culpability, after having paid compensatory damages, is so reprehensible as to warrant the imposition of further sanctions to achieve punishment or deterrence.

Applying these factors in the instant case, we must acknowledge that State Farm's handling of the claims against the Campbells merits no praise. The trial court found that State Farm's employees altered the company's records to make Campbell appear less culpable. State Farm disregarded the overwhelming likelihood of liability and the near-certain probability that, by taking the case to trial, a judgment in excess of the policy limits would be awarded. State Farm amplified the harm by at first assuring the Campbells their assets would be safe from any verdict and by later telling them, postjudgment, to put a for-sale sign on their house. While we do not suggest there was error in awarding punitive damages based upon State Farm's conduct toward the Campbells, a more modest punishment for this reprehensible conduct could have satisfied the State's legitimate objectives, and the Utah courts should have gone no further. This case, instead, was used as a platform to expose, and punish, the perceived deficiencies of State Farm's operations throughout the country. The Utah Supreme Court's opinion makes explicit that State Farm was being condemned for its nationwide policies rather than for the conduct direct toward the Campbells. . . . This was, as well, an explicit rationale of the trial court's decision in approving the award, though reduced from $145 million to $25 million. . . .

The Campbells contend that State Farm has only itself to blame for the reliance upon dissimilar and out-of-state conduct evidence. The record does not support this contention. From their opening statements onward the Campbells

framed this case as a chance to rebuke State Farm for its nationwide activities.
. . . This was a position maintained throughout the litigation. In opposing State
Farm's motion to exclude such evidence under *Gore*, the Campbells' counsel
convinced the trial court that there was no limitation on the scope of evidence
that could be considered under our precedents. ("As I read the case [Gore], I was
struck with the fact that a clear message in the case . . . seems to be that courts
in punitive damages cases should receive more evidence, not less. And that the
court seems to be inviting an even broader area of evidence than the current rulings of the court would indicate").

A State cannot punish a defendant for conduct that may have been lawful
where it occurred. *Gore*, supra. . . . Nor, as a general rule, does a State have a
legitimate concern in imposing punitive damages to punish a defendant for
unlawful acts committed outside of the State's jurisdiction. Any proper adjudication of conduct that occurred outside Utah to other persons would require
their inclusion, and, to those parties, the Utah courts, in the usual case, would
need to apply the laws of their relevant jurisdiction. . . . Lawful out-of-state conduct may be probative when it demonstrates the deliberateness and culpability
of the defendant's action in the State where it is tortious, but that conduct
must have a nexus to the specific harm suffered by the plaintiff. . . .

For a more fundamental reason, however, the Utah courts erred in relying
upon this and other evidence: The courts awarded punitive damages to punish
and deter conduct that bore no relation to the Campbells' harm. A defendant's
dissimilar acts, independent from the acts upon which liability was premised,
may not serve as the basis for punitive damages. A defendant should be punished for the conduct that harmed the plaintiff, not for being an unsavory individual or business. Due process does not permit courts, in the calculation of
punitive damages, to adjudicate the merits of other parties' hypothetical claims
against a defendant under the guise of the reprehensibility analysis, but we
have no doubt the Utah Supreme Court did that here. . . . Punishment on these
bases creates the possibility of multiple punitive damages awards for the same
conduct; for in the usual case nonparties are not bound by the judgment some
other plaintiff obtains. . . .

The Campbells have identified scant evidence of repeated misconduct of the
sort that injured them. Nor does our review of the Utah courts' decisions convince us that State Farm was only punished for its actions toward the Campbells. . . . The reprehensibility guidepost does not permit courts to expand the
scope of the case so that a defendant may be punished for any malfeasance,
which in this case extended for a 20-year period. In this case, because the
Campbells have shown no conduct by State Farm similar to that which harmed
them, the conduct that harmed them is the only conduct relevant to the reprehensibility analysis.

B

Turning to the second *Gore* guidepost, we have been reluctant to identify
concrete constitutional limits on the ratio between harm, or potential harm, to

the plaintiff and the punitive damages award. *Gore*, supra. . . . We decline again to impose a bright-line ratio which a punitive damages award cannot exceed. Our jurisprudence and the principles it has now established demonstrate, however, that, in practice, few awards exceeding a single-digit ratio between punitive and compensatory damages, to a significant degree, will satisfy due process. . . . Single-digit multipliers are more likely to comport with due process, while still achieving the State's goals of deterrence and retribution, than awards with ratios in range of 500 to 1, or, in this case, of 145 to 1.

Nonetheless, because there are no rigid benchmarks that a punitive damages award may not surpass, ratios greater than those we have previously upheld may comport with due process where "a particularly egregious act has resulted in only a small amount of economic damages.". . . The converse is also true, however. When compensatory damages are substantial, then a lesser ratio, perhaps only equal to compensatory damages, can reach the outermost limit of the due process guarantee. The precise award in any case, of course, must be based upon the facts and circumstances of the defendant's conduct and the harm to the plaintiff.

In sum, courts must ensure that the measure of punishment is both reasonable and proportionate to the amount of harm to the plaintiff and to the general damages recovered. In the context of this case, we have no doubt that there is a presumption against an award that has a 145-to-1 ratio. The compensatory award in this case was substantial; the Campbells were awarded $1 million for a year and a half of emotional distress. This was complete compensation. The harm arose from a transaction in the economic realm, not from some physical assault or trauma; there were no physical injuries; and State Farm paid the excess verdict before the complaint was filed, so the Campbells suffered only minor economic injuries for the 18-month period in which State Farm refused to resolve the claim against them. The compensatory damages for the injury suffered here, moreover, likely were based on a component which was duplicated in the punitive award. Much of the distress was caused by the outrage and humiliation the Campbells suffered at the actions of their insurer; and it is a major role of punitive damages to condemn such conduct. Compensatory damages, however, already contain this punitive element. See Restatement (Second) of Torts§ 908, Comment c, p. 466 (1977) ("In many cases in which compensatory damages include an amount for emotional distress, such as humiliation or indignation aroused by the defendant's act, there is no clear line of demarcation between punishment and compensation and a verdict for a specified amount frequently includes elements of both"). . . .

C

The third guidepost in Gore is the disparity between the punitive damages award and the "civil penalties authorized or imposed in comparable cases." We note that, in the past, we have also looked to criminal penalties that could be imposed. The existence of a criminal penalty does have bearing on the seriousness with which a State views the wrongful action. When used to determine the dollar amount of the award, however, the criminal penalty has less utility. Great care must be taken to avoid use of the civil process to assess criminal penalties that can be imposed only after the heightened protections of a criminal trial have been observed, including, of course, its higher standards of proof. Punitive damages are not a substitute for the criminal process, and the remote possibility of a criminal sanction does not automatically sustain a punitive damages award.

Here, we need not dwell long on this guidepost. The most relevant civil sanction under Utah state law for the wrong done to the Campbells appears to be a $10,000 fine for an act of fraud, an amount dwarfed by the $145 million punitive damages award. The Supreme Court of Utah speculated about the loss of State Farm's business license, the disgorgement of profits, and possible imprisonment, but here again its references were to the broad fraudulent scheme drawn from evidence of out-of-state and dissimilar conduct. This analysis was insufficient to justify the award.

IV

An application of the *Gore* guideposts to the facts of this case, especially in light of the substantial compensatory damages awarded (a portion of which contained a punitive element), likely would justify a punitive damages award at or near the amount of compensatory damages. The punitive award of $145 million, therefore, was neither reasonable nor proportionate to the wrong committed, and it was an irrational and arbitrary deprivation of the property of the defendant. The proper calculation of punitive damages under the principles we have discussed should be resolved, in the first instance, by the Utah courts.

The judgment of the Utah Supreme Court is reversed, and the case is remanded for proceedings not inconsistent with this opinion.

It is so ordered.

[Justices Scalia and Thomas dissented on the ground that the Constitution does not put a limit on "excessive punitive damage awards.}

Justice GINSBURG, dissenting.

I

The large size of the award upheld by the Utah Supreme Court in this case indicates why damage-capping legislation may be altogether fitting and proper. Neither the amount of the award nor the trial record, however, justifies this Court's substitution of its judgment for that of Utah's competent decisionmakers. In this regard, I count it significant that, on the key criterion "reprehensibility," there is a good deal more to the story than the Court's abbreviated account tells.

Ample evidence allowed the jury to find that State Farm's treatment of the Campbells typified its "Performance, Planning and Review" (PP & R) program; implemented by top management in 1979, the program had "the explicit objective of using the claims-adjustment process as a profit center." "[T]he Campbells presented considerable evidence," the trial court noted, documenting "that the PP & R program . . . has functioned, and continues to function, as an unlawful scheme . . . to deny benefits owed consumers by paying out less than fair value in order to meet preset, arbitrary payout targets designed to enhance corporate profits." That policy, the trial court observed, was encompassing in scope; it "applied equally to the handling of both third-party and first-party claims." . . .

Evidence the jury could credit demonstrated that the PP & R program regularly and adversely affected Utah residents. Ray Summers, "the adjuster who handled the Campbell case and who was a State Farm employee in Utah for almost twenty years," described several methods used by State Farm to deny claimants fair benefits, for example, "falsifying or withholding of evidence in claim files." A common tactic, Summers recounted, was to "unjustly attac[k] the character, reputation and credibility of a claimant and mak[e] notations to that effect in the claim file to create prejudice in the event the claim ever came before a jury." State Farm manager Bob Noxon, Summers testified, resorted to a tactic of this order in the Campbell case when he "instruct[ed] Summers to write in the file that Todd Ospital (who was killed in the accident) was speeding because he was on his way to see a pregnant girlfriend." In truth, "[t]here was no pregnant girlfriend." Expert testimony noted by the trial court described these tactics as "completely improper."

The trial court also noted the testimony of two Utah State Farm employees, Felix Jensen and Samantha Bird, both of whom recalled "intolerable" and "recurrent" pressure to reduce payouts below fair value. . . . Eventually, Bird quit. Utah managers superior to Bird, the evidence indicated, were improperly influenced by the PP & R program to encourage insurance underpayments. For example, several documents evaluating the performance of managers Noxon and Brown "contained explicit preset average payout goals."

Regarding liability for verdicts in excess of policy limits, the trial court referred to a State Farm document titled the "Excess Liability Handbook"; written before the Campbell accident, the handbook instructed adjusters to pad files with "self-serving" documents, and to leave critical items out of files, for example, evaluations of the insured's exposure. Divisional superintendent Bill Brown used the handbook to train Utah employees. Id., at 134a. While overseeing the Campbell case, Brown ordered adjuster Summers to change the portions of his report indicating that Mr. Campbell was likely at fault and that the settlement cost was correspondingly high.. . . .

The trial court further determined that the jury could find State Farm's policy "deliberately crafted" to prey on consumers who would be unlikely to defend themselves. In this regard, the trial court noted the testimony of several former State Farm employees affirming that they were trained to target "the weakest of the herd" — "the elderly, the poor, and other consumers who are least knowledgeable about their rights and thus most vulnerable to trickery or deceit, or who have little money and hence have no real alternative but to accept an inadequate offer to settle a claim at much less than fair value.". . .

To further insulate itself from liability, trial evidence indicated, State Farm made "systematic" efforts to destroy internal company documents that might reveal its scheme, efforts that directly affected the Campbells. For example, State Farm had "a special historical department that contained a copy of all past manuals on claim-handling practices and the dates on which each section of each manual was changed." Yet in discovery proceedings, State Farm failed to produce any claim-handling practice manuals for the years relevant to the Campbells' bad-faith case.

State Farm's inability to produce the manuals, it appeared from the evidence, was not accidental. Documents retained by former State Farm employee Samantha Bird, as well as Bird's testimony, showed that while the Campbells' case was pending, Janet Cammack, "an in-house attorney sent by top State Farm management, conducted a meeting . . . in Utah during which she instructed Utah claims management to search their offices and destroy a wide range of material of the sort that had proved damaging in bad-faith litigation in the past — in particular, old claim-handling manuals, memos, claim school notes, procedure guides and other similar documents." "These orders were followed even though at least one meeting participant, Paul Short, was personally aware that these kinds of materials had been requested by the Campbells in this very case."

Consistent with Bird's testimony, State Farm admitted that it destroyed every single copy of claim-handling manuals on file in its historical department as of 1988, even though these documents could have been preserved at minimal expense. Fortuitously, the Campbells obtained a copy of the 1979 PP & R manual by subpoena from a former employee. Although that manual has been requested in other cases, State Farm has never itself produced the document.

"As a final, related tactic," the trial court stated, the jury could reasonably find that "in recent years State Farm has gone to extraordinary lengths to stop damaging documents from being created in the first place.". . .

State Farm's "wrongful profit and evasion schemes," the trial court underscored, were directly relevant to the Campbells' case: "The record fully supports the conclusion that the bad-faith claim handling that exposed the Campbells to an excess verdict in 1983, and resulted in severe damages to them, was a product of the unlawful profit scheme that had been put in place by top management at State Farm years earlier. . . . In particular, when Brown declined to pay the excess verdict against Curtis Campbell, or even post a bond, he had a special need to keep his year-end numbers down, since the State Farm incentive scheme meant that keeping those numbers down was important to helping Brown get a much-desired transfer to Colorado. . . . There was ample evidence that the concepts taught in the Excess Liability Handbook, including the dishonest alteration and manipulation of claim files and the policy against posting any supersedeas bond for the full amount of an excess verdict, were dutifully carried out in this case. . . . There was ample basis for the jury to find that everything that had happened to the Campbells — when State Farm repeatedly refused in bad-faith to settle for the $50,000 policy limits and went to trial, and then failed to pay the 'excess' verdict, or at least post a bond, after trial — was a direct application of State Farm's overall profit scheme, operating through Brown and others." State Farm's "policies and practices," the trial evidence thus bore out, were "responsible for the injuries suffered by the Campbells," and the means used to implement those policies could be found "callous, clandestine, fraudulent, and dishonest." . . . The Utah Supreme Court, relying on the trial court's record-based recitations, understandably characterized State Farm's behavior as "egregious and malicious."

II

The Court dismisses the evidence describing and documenting State Farm's PP & R policy and practices as essentially irrelevant, bearing "no relation to the Campbells' harm.". . . It is hardly apparent why that should be so. What is infirm about the Campbells' theory that their experience with State Farm exemplifies and reflects an overarching underpayment scheme, one that caused "repeated misconduct of the sort that injured them,"? The Court's silence on that score is revealing: Once one recognizes that the Campbells did show "conduct by State Farm similar to that which harmed them," it becomes impossible to shrink the reprehensibility analysis to this sole case. . . .

Evidence of out-of-state conduct, the Court acknowledges, may be "probative [even if the conduct is lawful in the state where it occurred] when it demonstrates the deliberateness and culpability of the defendant's action in the State where it is tortious. . . ." "Other acts" evidence concerning practices both in and out of State was introduced in this case to show just such "deliberateness" and "culpability.". . .

[I] remain of the view that this Court has no warrant to reform state law governing awards of punitive damages. . . . Even if I were prepared to accept the flexible guides prescribed in *Gore*, I would not join the Court's swift conversion of those guides into instructions that begin to resemble marching orders. For the reasons stated, I would leave the judgment of the Utah Supreme Court undisturbed.

NOTES

1. In *BMW of North America, Inc. v. Gore*, 517 U.S. 559, 116 S. Ct. 1589, 134 L. Ed. 2d 809 (1996), the Supreme Court overturned a punitive damage award against BMW for failing to disclose that a car sold as new was actually repainted because of damage to the finish after the car left the factory. In that case as well, the plaintiff had submitted evidence to the jury about cars sold in other states

with the same problem, even though the conduct may not have been illegal in those other states.

2. These two cases raise one of the most important questions regarding the award of punitive damages. There is no "double jeopardy" protection that prevents another jury, in another case, from awarding $145 million dollars to another State Farm policyholder for the same set of corporate misdeeds. This may in part explain some of the concern the majority has if the jury can consider conduct too far removed from the injury to the particular plaintiff in the case.

3. Some states provide that some of the punitive damages awarded be paid into a state's general revenue fund. *E.g.*, COLO. REV. STAT. ANN. § 13-21-102(3)(B) (one-third to state fund); OR. REV. STAT. § 18.540 (one-half to compensation fund for crime victims).

4. As part of "tort reform," some states enacted punitive damage award caps. Colorado provides for both contribution to a state fund (*see* above) and provides that punitive damages are limited to the amount of actual damages. COLO. REV. STAT. § 13-21-102. Texas limits punitive damages to four times actual damages or $200,000, whichever is greater. TEX. CIV. PRAC. AND REM. CODE § 41.007. Virginia's cap is $350,000. VA. CODE § 8.01-38.1 (1992). Other legislatures have enacted caps on damages generally and their courts have reacted differently to the caps. *Compare Smith v. Department of Insurance*, 507 So. 2d 1080 (Fla. 1987) ($450,000 cap on non-economic damages violates state constitution) *with Fein v. Permanete Medical Group,* 695 P.2d 665 (Cal. 1985) (where California court held the state may expand or limit recoverable damages so long as its actions are rationally related to a legitimate state interest).

Chapter 9

LIMITED DUTY: SPECIAL LIMITATIONS ON THE SCOPE OF DUTY

A. INTRODUCTION

As we have seen, there can be no negligence unless the plaintiff establishes that the defendant has breached some legally-recognized duty of care. In most cases that we have studied thus far, the alleged negligence has been based upon some type of affirmative misconduct (*i.e.*, misfeasance) between the parties. In this Chapter we examine a variety of situations where the defendant has done nothing at all (*i.e.*, non-feasance) under circumstances where the law imposes an affirmative duty to act in a certain manner, as well as in situations when the law simply does not recognize that any legal harm has occurred.

YANIA v. BIGAN
155 A.2d 343 (Pa. 1959)

JONES, J.

[On] September 25, 1957, John E. Bigan was engaged in a coal strip-mining operation [in] Somerset County. On the property being stripped were large cuts or trenches created by Bigan when he removed the earthen overburden for the purpose of removing the coal underneath. One cut contained water 8 to 10 feet in depth with side walls or embankments 16 to 18 feet in height; at this cut Bigan had installed a pump to remove the water.

At approximately 4 p.m. on that date, Joseph F. Yania, the operator of another coal strip-mining operation, [and] Boyd M. Ross went upon Bigan's property for the purpose of discussing a business matter with Bigan, and, while there, were asked by Bigan to aid him in starting the pump. Ross and Bigan entered the cut and stood at the point where the pump was located. Yania stood at the top of one of the cut's side walls and then jumped from the side wall — a height of 16 to 18 feet — into the water and was drowned.

Yania's widow, in her own right and on behalf of her three children, instituted wrongful death and survival actions against Bigan contending Bigan was responsible for Yania's death. Preliminary objections, in the nature of demurrers, to the complaint were filed on behalf of Bigan. The court below sustained the preliminary objections. . . .

The complaint avers negligence in the following manner: (1) "The death by drowning of [Yania] was caused entirely by the acts of [Bigan] in *urging, enticing taunting and inveigling* [Yania] to jump into the water, which [Bigan] knew or ought to have known was of a depth of 8 to 10 feet and dangerous to the life of anyone who would jump therein" (Emphasis supplied); (2) [Bigan] violated his obligations to a business invitee in not having his premises reasonably safe, and not warning his business invitee of a dangerous condition and to the contrary urged, induced and inveigled [Yania] into a dangerous position and a dangerous act, whereby [Yania] came to his death"; (3) "After [Yania] was in the water, a highly dangerous position, having been induced and inveigled therein by [Bigan], [Bigan] failed and neglected to take reasonable steps and action to protect or assist [Yania], or extradite [Yania] from the dangerous position in which [Bigan] had placed him". Summarized, Bigan stands charged with three-fold negligence: (1) by urging, enticing, taunting and inveigling Yania to jump into the water; (2) by failing to warn Yania of a dangerous condition on the land, *i.e.*, the cut wherein lay 8 to 10 feet of water; (3) by failing to go to Yania's rescue after he had jumped into the water. . . .

Appellant initially contends that Yania's descent from the high embankment into the water and the resulting death were caused "entirely" by the spoken words and blandishments of Bigan delivered at a distance from Yania. The complaint does not allege that Yania slipped or that he was pushed or that Bigan made any *physical* impact upon Yania. On the contrary, the only inference deducible from the facts alleged in the complaint is that Bigan, by the employment of cajolery and inveiglement, caused such a *mental* impact on Yania that the latter was deprived of his volition and freedom of choice and placed under a compulsion to jump into the water. Had Yania been a child of tender years or a person mentally deficient then it is conceivable that taunting and enticement could constitute actionable negligence if it resulted in harm. However to contend that such conduct directed to an adult in full possession of all his mental faculties constitutes actionable negligence is not only without precedent but completely without merit.

Appellant next urges that Bigan, as the possessor of the land, violated a duty owed to Yania in that his land contained a dangerous condition, *i.e.*, the waterfilled cut or trench, and he failed to warn Yania of such condition. Yania was a business visitor in that he entered upon the land for a common business purpose for the mutual benefit of Bigan and himself (RESTATEMENT, TORTS § 332). As possessor of the land, Bigan would become subject to liability to Yania for any physical harm caused by any artificial or natural condition upon the land (1) if, but only if, Bigan knew or could have discovered the condition which, if known to him he should have realized involved an unreasonable risk of harm to Yania, (2) if Bigan had no reason to believe Yania would discover the condition or realize the risk of harm and (3) if he invited or permitted Yania to enter upon the land without exercising reasonable care to make the condition reasonably safe or give adequate warning to enable him to avoid the harm. *Schon, Admx. v. Scranton-Springbrook Water Service Co.*, 381 Pa. 148, 152, 112 A.2d 89. The inapplicability of this rule of liability to the instant facts is readily apparent.

The *only* condition on Bigan's land which could possibly have contributed in any manner to Yania's death was the water-filled cut with its high embankment. Of this condition there was neither concealment nor failure to warn, but, on the contrary, the complaint specifically avers that Bigan not only requested Yania and Boyd to assist him in starting the pump to remove the water from the cut but "led" them to the cut itself. If this cut possessed any potentiality of danger, such a condition was as obvious and apparent to Yania as to Bigan, both coal strip-mine operators. Under the circumstances herein depicted Bigan could not be held liable in this respect.

Lastly, it is urged that Bigan failed to take the necessary steps to rescue Yania from the water. The mere fact that Bigan saw Yania in a position of peril in the water imposed upon him no legal, although a moral, obligation or duty to go to his rescue unless Bigan was legally responsible, in whole or in part, for placing Yania in the perilous position: RESTATEMENT, TORTS § 314. *Cf.* RESTATEMENT, TORTS § 322. The language of this Court in *Brown v. French*, 104 Pa. 604, 607, 608, is apt: "If it appeared that the deceased, by his own carelessness, contributed in any degree to the accident which caused the loss of his life, the defendants ought not to have been held to answer for the consequences resulting from that accident. [He] voluntarily placed himself in the way of danger, and his death was the result of his own act. . . . That his undertaking was an exceedingly reckless and dangerous one, the event proves, but there was no one to blame for it but himself. He had the right to try the experiment, obviously dangerous as it was, but then also upon him rested the consequences of that experiment, and upon no one else; he may have been, and probably was, ignorant of the risk which he was taking upon himself, or knowing it, and trusting to his own skill, he may have regarded it as easily superable. But in either case, the result of his ignorance, or of his mistake, must rest with himself — and cannot be charged to the defendants". The complaint does not aver any facts which impose upon Bigan legal responsibility for placing Yania in the dangerous position in the water and, absent such legal responsibility, the law imposes on Bigan no duty of rescue.

Recognizing that the deceased Yania is entitled to the benefit of the presumption that he was exercising due care and extending to appellant the benefit of every well pleaded fact in this complaint and the fair inferences arising therefrom, yet we can reach but one conclusion: that Yania, a reasonable and prudent adult in full possession of all his mental faculties, undertook to perform an act which he knew or should have known was attended with more or less peril and it was the performance of that act and not any conduct upon Bigan's part which caused his unfortunate death.

NOTES

1. According to the plaintiff, exactly *what* did the defendant do wrong in *Yania*? The plaintiff alleged that the defendant "failed to take the necessary

steps to rescue Yania from the water." Does this mean that the defendant failed to (successfully) rescue Yania from the water, or that he failed to even *attempt* such a rescue? Does it matter?

2. Upon what legal basis did the court decline to impose an affirmative duty in *Yania*?

B. "MISFEASANCE" vs. "NON-FEASANCE"

The traditional common law "no duty" to rescue rule seems particularly harsh because it offends commonly accepted notions of morality. Most people in a civilized society are morally outraged by any person's refusal, as in *Yania,* to render aid or assistance to someone who is in life-threatening peril, especially when to do so does not subject the rescuer to any personal danger. Nevertheless, as one commentator has observed: "[t]he law has persistently refused to recognize the moral obligation of common decency and common humanity, to come to the aid of another human being who is in danger. . . ." W. PROSSER, HANDBOOK ON THE LAW OF TORTS § 56, p. 340 (West Publ. Co. 4th ed. 1971).

At the opposite end of the moral spectrum, however, the imposition of an *affirmative* legal duty to render aid may be just as offensive to society's notions of individual autonomy and the freedom to act (or *not* to act) in a certain way. Historically, courts have sometimes attempted to balance these competing interests by characterizing the actor's conduct as one involving either "misfeasance" or "nonfeasance." However, the distinctions between these concepts are not easily understood, as illustrated by the following case.

WEIRUM v. RKO GENERAL, INC.
539 P.2d 36 (Cal. 1975)

MOSK, J.

A rock radio station with an extensive teenage audience conducted a contest which rewarded the first contestant to locate a peripatetic disc jockey. Two minors driving in separate automobiles attempted to follow the disc jockey's automobile. . . . In the course of their pursuit, one of the minors negligently forced a car off the highway, killing its sole occupant. In a suit filed by the surviving wife and children of the decedent, the jury rendered a verdict against the radio station. We now must determine whether the station owed decedent a duty of due care.

The facts are not disputed. Radio station KHJ is a successful Los Angeles broadcaster with a large teenage following. At the time of the accident, KHJ commanded a 48 percent plurality of the teenage audience in the Los Angeles area. In contrast, its nearest rival during the same period was able to capture only 13 percent of the teenage listeners. In order to attract an even larger portion of the available audience and thus increase advertising revenue, KHJ inaugurated in July of 1970 a promotion entitled "The Super Summer Spectacular." The "spectacular," with a budget of approximately $40,000 for the month, was specifically designed to make the radio station "more exciting." Among the programs included in the "spectacular" was a contest broadcast on July 16, 1970, the date of the accident.

On that day, Donald Steele Revert, known professionally as "The Real Don Steele," a KHJ disc jockey and television personality, traveled in a conspicuous red automobile to a number of locations in the Los Angeles metropolitan area. Periodically, he apprised KHJ of his whereabouts and his intended destination, and the station broadcast the information to its listeners. The first person to physically locate Steele and fulfill a specified condition received a cash prize. In addition, the winning contestant participated in a brief interview on the air with "The Real Don Steele." The following excerpts from the July 16 broadcast illustrate the tenor of the contest announcements:

> "9:30 and The Real Don Steele is back on his feet again with some money and he is headed for the Valley. Thought I would give you a warning so that you can get your kids out of the street."

> "The Real Don Steele is out driving on — could be in your neighborhood at any time and he's got bread to spread, so be on the lookout for him."

> "The Real Don Steele is moving into Canoga Park — so be on the lookout for him. I'll tell you what will happen if you get to The Real Don Steele. He's got twenty-five dollars to give away if you can get it . . . and baby, all signed and sealed and delivered and wrapped up."

> "10:54 — The Real Don Steele is in the Valley near the intersection of Topanga and Roscoe Boulevard, right by the Loew's Holiday Theater — you know where that is at, and he's standing there with a little money he would like to give away to the first person to arrive and tell him what type car I helped Robert W. Morgan give away yesterday morning at KHJ. What was the make of the car? If you know that, split. Intersection of Topanga and Roscoe Boulevard — right nearby the Loew's Holiday Theater — you will find The Real Don Steele. Tell him and pick up the bread."

In Van Nuys, 17-year-old Robert Sentner was listening to KHJ in his car while searching for "The Real Don Steele." Upon hearing that "The Real Don Steele" was proceeding to Canoga Park, he immediately drove to that vicinity. Meanwhile, in Northridge, 19-year-old Marsha Baime heard and responded to the same information. Both of them arrived at the Holiday Theater in Canoga Park to find that someone had already claimed the prize. Without knowledge of the other, each decided to follow the Steele vehicle to its next stop and thus be the first to arrive when the next contest question or condition was announced.

For the next few miles the Sentner and Baime cars jockeyed for position closest to the Steele vehicle, reaching speeds up to 80 miles an hour. About a mile and a half from the Westlake offramp the two teenagers heard the following broadcast: "11:13 — The Real Don Steele with bread is heading for Thousand Oaks to give it away. Keep listening to KHJ. . . . The Real Don Steele out on the highway — with bread to give away — be on the lookout, he may stop in Thousand Oaks and may stop along the way. . . . Looks like it may be a good stop Steele — drop some bread to those folks."

The Steele vehicle left the freeway at the Westlake offramp. Either Baime or Sentner, in attempting to follow, forced decedent's car onto the center divider, where it overturned. Baime stopped to report the accident. Sentner, after pausing momentarily to relate the tragedy to a passing peace officer, continued to pursue Steele, successfully located him and collected a cash prize. . . .

The primary question for our determination is whether defendant owed a duty to decedent arising out of its broadcast of the giveaway contest. The determination of duty is primarily a question of law. It is the court's "expression of the sum total of those considerations of policy which lead the law to say that the particular plaintiff is entitled to protection." Any number of considerations may justify the imposition of duty in particular circumstances, including the guidance of history, our continually refined concepts of morals and justice, the convenience of the rule, and social judgment as to where the loss should fall. (Prosser, *Palsgraf Revisited* (1953) 52 MICH. L. REV. 1, 15.) While the question whether one owes a duty to another must be decided on a case-by-case basis, every case is governed by the rule of general application that all persons are required to use ordinary care to prevent others from being injured as the result of their conduct. However, foreseeability of the risk is a primary consideration in establishing the element of duty. Defendant asserts that the record here does not support a conclusion that a risk of harm to decedent was foreseeable.

While duty is a question of law, foreseeability is a question of fact for the jury. The verdict in plaintiffs' favor here necessarily embraced a finding that decedent was exposed to a foreseeable risk of harm. It is elementary that our review of this finding is limited to the determination whether there is any substantial evidence, contradicted or uncontradicted, which will support the conclusion reached by the jury.

We conclude that the record amply supports the finding of foreseeability. These tragic events unfolded in the middle of a Los Angeles summer, a time when young people were free from the constraints of school and responsive to relief from vacation tedium. Seeking to attract new listeners, KHJ devised an "exciting" promotion. Money and a small measure of momentary notoriety awaited the swiftest response. It was foreseeable that defendant's youthful listeners, finding the prize had eluded them at one location, would race to arrive first at the next site and in their haste would disregard the demands of highway safety.

Indeed, "The Real Don Steele" testified that he had in the past noticed vehicles following him from location to location. He was further aware that the same contestants sometimes appeared at consecutive stops. This knowledge is not rendered irrelevant [by] the absence of any prior injury. Such an argument confuses foreseeability with hindsight, and amounts to a contention that the injuries of the first victim are not compensable. "The mere fact that a particular kind of an accident has not happened before does [not] show that such accident is one which might not reasonably have been anticipated." (*Ridley v. Grifall Trucking Co.* (1955) 136 Cal. App. 2d 682, 686 [289 P.2d 31].) Thus, the fortuitous absence of prior injury does not justify relieving defendant from responsibility for the foreseeable consequences of its acts.

It is of no consequence that the harm to decedent was inflicted by third parties acting negligently. Defendant invokes the maxim that an actor is entitled to assume that others will not act negligently. This concept is valid, however, only to the extent the intervening conduct was not to be anticipated. If the likelihood that a third person may react in a particular manner is a hazard which makes the actor negligent, such reaction whether innocent or negligent does not prevent the actor from being liable for the harm caused thereby. Here, reckless conduct by youthful contestants, stimulated by defendant's broadcast, constituted the hazard to which decedent was exposed.

It is true, of course, that virtually every act involves some conceivable danger. Liability is imposed only if the risk of harm resulting from the act is deemed unreasonable — *i.e.*, if the gravity and likelihood of the danger outweigh the utility of the conduct involved. (*See* Prosser, Law of Torts (4th ed. 1971) pp. 146-49.)

We need not belabor the grave danger inherent in the contest broadcast by defendant. The risk of a high speed automobile chase is the risk of death or serious injury. Obviously, neither the entertainment afforded by the contest nor its commercial rewards can justify the creation of such a grave risk. Defendant could have accomplished its objectives of entertaining its listeners and increasing advertising revenues by adopting a contest format which would have avoided danger to the motoring public.

Defendant's contention that the giveaway contest must be afforded the deference due society's interest in the First Amendment is clearly without merit. The issue here is civil accountability for the foreseeable results of a broadcast which created an undue risk of harm to decedent. The First Amendment does not sanction the infliction of physical injury merely because achieved by word, rather than act.

We are not persuaded that the imposition of a duty here will lead to unwarranted extensions of liability. Defendant is fearful that entrepreneurs will henceforth be burdened with an avalanche of obligations: an athletic department will owe a duty to an ardent sports fan injured while hastening to purchase one of a limited number of tickets; a department store will be liable for injuries incurred in response to a "while-they-last" sale. This argument, however, suffers from a myopic view of the facts presented here. The giveaway contest was no commonplace invitation to an attraction available on a limited basis. It was a competitive scramble in which the thrill of the chase to be the one and only victor was intensified by the live broadcasts which accompanied the pursuit. In the assertedly analogous situations described by defendant, any haste involved in the purchase of the commodity is an incidental and unavoidable result of the scarcity of the commodity itself. In such situations there is no attempt, as here, to generate a competitive pursuit on public streets, accelerated by repeated importuning by radio to be the very first to arrive at a particular destination. Manifestly the "spectacular" bears little resemblance to daily commercial activities.

Defendant, relying upon the rule stated in section 315 of the RESTATEMENT SECOND OF TORTS, urges that it owed no duty of care to decedent. The section provides that, absent a special relationship, an actor is under no duty to control the conduct of third parties. [T]his rule has no application if the plaintiff's complaint, as here, is grounded upon an affirmative act of defendant which created an undue risk of harm.

The rule stated in section 315 is merely a refinement of the general principle embodied in section 314 that one is not obligated to act as a "good samaritan." (REST. 2D TORTS, § 314, com. (a); James, *Scope of Duty in Negligence Cases* (1953) 47 Nw. U. L. REV. 778, 803.) This doctrine is rooted in the common law distinction between action and inaction, or misfeasance and nonfeasance. Misfeasance exists when the defendant is responsible for making the plaintiff's position worse, *i.e.*, defendant has created a risk. Conversely, nonfeasance is found when the defendant has failed to aid plaintiff through beneficial intervention. As section 315 illustrates, liability for nonfeasance is largely limited to those circumstances in which some special relationship can be established. If, on the other hand, the act complained of is one of misfeasance, the question of duty is governed by the standards of ordinary care discussed above.

Here, there can be little doubt that we review an act of misfeasance to which section 315 is inapplicable. Liability is not predicated upon defendant's failure to intervene for the benefit of decedent but rather upon its creation of an unreasonable risk of harm to him. [*See Shafer v. Keeley Ice Cream Co.*, 234 P. 300 (Utah 1925).] Defendant's reliance upon cases which involve the failure to prevent harm to another is therefore misplaced, *e.g.*, *Wright v. Arcade School Dist.*, *supra*, 230 Cal. App. 2d 272 (school district held free of a duty of care to children injured on their way to and from school). . . .

The judgment and the orders appealed from are affirmed. Plaintiffs shall recover their costs on appeal. The parties shall bear their own costs on the cross-appeal.

NOTES

1. Did *Weirum* conclude that the defendant's conduct constituted misfeasance or nonfeasance? What difference does it make, anyway? Would the outcome have been any different, regardless of how the court characterized the defendant's conduct?

2. "Misfeasance" and "non-feasance" represent two distinctly different legal concepts, but these differences are not always easy to articulate with any degree of particularity. Commenting on the distinction between acts of commission (*i.e.*, misfeasance) and acts of omission (*i.e.*, non-feasance), Justice Cardozo had this to say:

> It is ancient learning that one who assumes to act, even though gratuitously, may thereby become subject to the duty of acting carefully, if he acts at all. (*Glanzer v. Shepard*, 233 N.Y. 236, 239; *Marks v. Nambil Realty Co., Inc.*, 245 N.Y. 256, 258). The plaintiff would bring its case within the orbit of that principle. The hand once set to a task may not always be withdrawn with impunity though liability would fail if it had never been applied at all. A time-honored formula often phrases the distinction as one between misfeasance and non-feasance. Incomplete the formula is, and so at times misleading. Given a relation involving in its existence a duty of care irrespective of a contract, a tort may result as well from acts of omission as of commission in the fulfillment of the duty thus recognized by law (POLLOCK, TORTS [12th ed.], p. 555; *Kelley v. Met. Ry. Co.*, 1895, 1 Q. B. 944). *What we need to know is not so much the conduct to be avoided when the relation and its attendant duty are established as existing. What we need to know is the conduct that engenders the relation. It is here that the formula, however incomplete, has its value and significance. If conduct has gone forward to such a stage that inaction would commonly result, not negatively merely in withholding a benefit, but positively or actively in working an injury, there exists a relation out of which arises a duty to go forward.* So the surgeon who operates without pay is liable though his negligence is in the omission to sterilize his instruments[;] as is the maker of automobiles, at the suit of someone other than the buyer, though his negligence is merely in inadequate inspection. . . . The query always is whether the putative wrongdoer has advanced to such a point as to have launched a force or instrument of harm, or has stopped where inaction is at most a refusal to become an instrument for good. . . .

H.R. Moch Co., Inc. v. Rensselaer Water Co., 159 N.E. 896, 898 (N.Y. 1928). (Emphasis supplied.)

C. EXCEPTIONS TO THE "NO-DUTY" RULE

Judicial attempts to define precise boundaries between these two competing social concerns have produced a significant number of now well-recognized "exceptions" to the traditional "no-duty" rule applied in cases like *Yania*. The remaining cases in this Section illustrate the scope and extent of these various exceptions with respect to some of the most commonly recognized "limited duty" situations.

1. Defendant's Negligence Places the Plaintiff in a Position of Peril

DAY v. WAFFLE HOUSE, INC.
743 P.2d 1111 (Okla. Ct. Civ. App. 1987)

BAILEY, J.

Appellant Susan Day and her friend, Freddie Farris, went to Appellee Waffle House restaurant (Appellee or Restaurant) for a meal. Freddie went into the restaurant and ordered his meal, while Appellant went across the street to a convenience store to make a telephone call. While eating, Freddie discovered broken glass in his food, and began spitting out food, broken glass and blood.

At this time, Appellant entered the restaurant, discovered Freddie in distress, and observed a bloody napkin with food and broken glass. She then requested that restaurant employees summon an ambulance. Apparently, the only outgoing telephone line was behind locked doors, and, professing their inability to telephone for assistance, the restaurant demanded payment for Freddie's meal. Payment was made, and Appellant placed Freddie in her automobile with the intention to take Freddie to the nearest hospital.

En route to the hospital and as Appellant entered an intersection adjacent to the restaurant on a green light, another automobile collided with Appellant, causing Appellant and Freddie injury. Appellant and Freddie then filed suit against Appellee for their injuries under a negligence theory. On Appellee's motion for summary judgment, Appellant asserted [that] Waffle House was negligent as to Freddie as evidenced by the presence of the broken glass in his food, and that Appellee was liable to Appellant for her injuries from the auto accident under the "rescue doctrine." The Trial Court found that Appellee was not negligent as to Appellant, and granted summary judgment. . . . From that ruling, Appellant seeks review.

[I]t is clear under Oklahoma law that an injured person may recover from a food supplier in negligence for injuries sustained by virtue of consumption of tainted or adulterated foods sold by that supplier. *Linker v. Quaker Oats Co.*, 11 F. Supp. 794 (D. Okla. 1935). Under a negligence theory, the injured consumer must establish the traditional elements of the existence of a duty to the injured party, a breach of that duty, and damages proximately flowing therefrom.

The law of this state also recognizes that one who rescues or attempts to rescue a person from a dangerous situation and incurs injury by virtue of the rescue or attempt, may recover from the party whose negligence caused the party or another to be in a dangerous situation. *Fulton v. St. Louis-San Francisco Ry. Co.*, 675 F.2d 1130 (10th Cir.1982); *Carter v. U.S.*, 248 F. Supp. 105 (E.D. Okla. 1965). Under the "rescue doctrine," negligence as to the victim constitutes negligence as to the rescuer, and there exists an independent duty of care as between the negligent party and the rescuer:

> "[Under] the 'rescue doctrine,' efforts to protect the personal safety of another have been held not to supercede the liability for the original negligence which has endangered it. Whether or not the rescuer is to be recognized as 'foreseeable,' it has been recognized since the early case of the crowd rushing to assist the descending balloonist that [a rescuer] is nothing abnormal. 'The risk of rescue if only it be not wanton, is born of the occasion. The emergency begets the man.' THERE IS THUS AN INDEPENDENT DUTY OF CARE OWED TO THE RESCUER HIMSELF, which arises even when the defendant endangers no one's safety but his own."

PROSSER, HANDBOOK OF THE LAW OF TORTS, § 44, p. 277, (1971 Ed.) (Emphasis added).

The Honorable Justice Cardozo, on whose statement of the law the Oklahoma Supreme Court relied in *Merritt v. Okla. Nat. Gas. Co.*, [165 P.2d 342 (Okla. 1946),] established the rule thusly:

> "Danger invites rescue. The cry of distress is the summons to relief. The law does not ignore these reactions of the mind in tracing conduct to its consequences. It recognizes them as normal. It places their effects within the range of the natural and probable. THE WRONG THAT IMPERILS LIFE IS A WRONG TO THE IMPERILED VICTIM; IT IS A WRONG ALSO TO HIS RESCUER."

Wagner v. International Railway Co., 232 N.Y. 176, 133 N.E. 437 (1921).

Thus, in actions based on the rescue doctrine under Oklahoma law, an injured party may recover damages for injury sustained in a rescue or attempt from the original tortfeasor if it can be shown that it was the original tortfeasor's negligence that placed the rescued person in peril, and that the rescuer suffered injuries in the rescue or attempt.

[W]e find the trial court erred in granting Appellee judgment. The facts show, although reasonable men might differ, that Appellee arguably breached its duty of reasonable care in serving glass-laced food to Freddie, and that Freddie suffered injuries caused thereby. Appellee owed a commensurate duty to others, such as Appellant, to use ordinary care not to place Appellee's customers in peril, especially since a rescue attempt is a foreseeable consequence of the restaurant's breach of duty. That Appellant's injuries were sustained in the course of a rescue attempt is undisputed, and an attempt to obtain medical treatment or assistance is such an act as to come within the purview of compensability under the rescue doctrine. There remained substantial fact questions as to the reasonableness of or negligence in Appellant's and Appellee's respective actions, whether the acts of Appellee were the cause of Appellant's injuries and the application of Oklahoma Law to these facts. As there remained substantial fact questions to be determined, the grant of summary judgment was error. The motion for summary judgment should have been denied since reasonable men, in the exercise of fair and impartial judgment, and indulging all inferences in favor of Appellant, might reach different conclusions under the facts of this case.

The order of the Trial Court granting summary judgment for Appellee is therefore REVERSED, and this cause REMANDED for further proceedings not inconsistent with this opinion.

REVERSED AND REMANDED.

NOTES

1. As *Day* points out, the defendant restaurant owed a duty to all of its customers to exercise reasonable care not to serve them tainted or adulterated food. However, since the defendant never actually served any food to the plaintiff, what is the basis for imposing a duty upon the defendant with respect to the plaintiff? If she had been a complete stranger who, after witnessing this incident, had merely offered to drive the victim to the hospital and was then herself injured in this same accident, would the defendant restaurant have owed the same duty to her as to the plaintiff under these circumstances?

2. Why didn't the obvious negligence of the driver of the other vehicle that subsequently collided with the plaintiff's automobile constitute an intervening cause that superceded any duty owed by the defendant restaurant to the plaintiff?

3. In *Yazoo & M.V.R. Co. v. Leflar*, 150 So. 220 (Miss. 1933), the court held that the defendant railroad, although not negligent initially in causing injury to a person on its train tracks, nevertheless was subsequently liable for negligence by failing to promptly obtain medical aid for the injured victim.

2. Voluntarily Assumed Duties

Even when there is otherwise no legal duty to act in a given situation, a duty may arise where the defendant *voluntarily* undertakes to render some type of aid or assistance and does so negligently.

FLORENCE v. GOLDBERG
375 N.E.2d 763 (N.Y. 1978)

JASEN, J.

This appeal raises the issue whether a municipality may be held liable for injuries suffered by an infant struck by an automobile while attempting to negotiate a school crossing where the municipality's police department, having voluntarily assumed a duty to supervise school crossings — an assumption upon which the infant's parent relied — negligently omitted to station a guard at one of the designated crossings.

On November 14, 1967, Darryle Davis, a 6½-year-old infant, was struck by a taxicab, the impact of which resulted in the infliction of severe brain damage to the infant. At the time of the injury, the infant plaintiff was a first-grade student at Public School 191, located on Park Place between Ralph and Buffalo Avenues in Brooklyn. Although he resided on Park Place, only one block away from the school, the infant plaintiff was required to cross Ralph Avenue to attend school.

Prior to the occurrence of the accident resulting in the infant's injury, a civilian school crossing guard had been assigned regularly to cover the intersection of Park Place and Ralph Avenue, a busy two-way street. For the first two weeks of class, a period throughout which the infant's mother accompanied her son to and from school, a crossing guard had been stationed at the intersection of Park Place and Ralph Avenue. Having witnessed the daily presence of a crossing guard at this intersection, the infant's mother, who accepted employment two weeks after her son started class, felt confident that she need not arrange for someone to provide a similar service for her child.

Tragically, however, on the day in question no crossing guard was stationed at the intersection of Park Place and Ralph Avenue. The regularly assigned crossing guard, having felt ill that day, notified the 77th precinct at 7:30 a.m that she would not be able to report for duty. . . . Upon receiving notification of the crossing guard's unavailability for duty, the police department neither assigned a patrolman to substitute for the crossing guard nor notified the school principal of the absence of a crossing guard at the Park Place and Ralph Avenue intersection. It was shortly after 11:45 a.m., while the infant plaintiff was returning home from school, that he was struck by a taxicab while attempting to cross this intersection.

The infant's mother, as natural guardian, commenced this action against New York City, Lilly Transportation Corp., the owner of the taxicab, and Meyer Goldberg, the operator of the vehicle, seeking damages for the personal injuries suffered by the infant. She also sought, in a derivative cause of action, damages for loss of the infant's services and medical expenses. At trial, the action was discontinued against Goldberg.

The jury returned a verdict against Lilly and New York City, apportioning the liability between them in the ratio of 25% against Lilly and 75% against the city.

On appeal, the Appellate Division affirmed the judgment of liability, but ordered a new trial on the issue of damages. . . .

On retrial of the issue of damages, the jury awarded the infant $500,000 and his mother $270,000. On appeal, the Appellate Division, holding the award to the infant's mother excessive, ordered a new trial on the issue of damages unless plaintiff agreed to accept a reduction to $125,000. Plaintiff having so stipulated, the Appellate Division affirmed the judgment of the trial court.

On appeal to this court, the City of New York contends that a municipality acting in its governmental capacity to protect the public from external hazards cannot be held liable in damages for its failure to furnish adequate protection. We hold that a municipality whose police department voluntarily assumes a duty to supervise school crossings — the assumption of that duty having been relied upon by parents of school children — may be held liable for its negligent omission to provide a guard at a designated crossing or to notify the school principal or take other appropriate action to safeguard the children. . . .

[T]o sustain liability against a municipality, the duty breached must be more than a duty owing to the general public. There must exist a special relationship between the municipality and the plaintiff, resulting in the creation of "a duty to use due care for the benefit of particular persons or classes of persons" (*Motyka v. City of Amsterdam*, 15 N.Y.2d 134 at 139).

For example, as a general rule, a municipality's duty to furnish water to protect its residents against damage caused by fire is a duty inuring to the benefit of the public at large, rather than to the individual members of the community. (*Steitz v. City of Beacon*, 295 N.Y. 51, 57.) Similarly, a municipality cannot be held liable for failure to furnish adequate police protection. This duty, like the duty to provide protection against fire, flows only to the general public.

Where, however, a special relationship exists between a municipality and a plaintiff creating a duty, albeit one normally inuring only to the benefit of the public at large, a municipality may be held liable for damages suffered as a consequence of its negligence. For example, a municipality possesses a special duty to provide police protection to an informer who collaborates with the police in the arrest and prosecution of a criminal. Moreover, where a municipality assumes a duty to a particular person or class of persons, it must perform that duty in a nonnegligent manner, notwithstanding that absent its voluntary assumption of that duty, none would have otherwise existed. As Chief Judge Cardozo succinctly stated: "The hand once set to a task may not always be withdrawn with impunity though liability would fail if it had never been applied at all." (*Moch Co. v. Rensselaer Water Co.*, 247 N.Y. 160 at 167.)

It is within this analytical framework that the issue posed on this appeal must be resolved: that is whether the City of New York, through its police department, assumed a particular duty to a special class of persons, not generally true of police control of pedestrian or vehicle traffic, and whether having assumed that duty, the city negligently omitted its performance, resulting in the infliction of physical injury to a member of the benefitted class. In this regard, there is little question that the police department voluntarily assumed [a] duty to supervise school crossings. Its departmental rules and regulations expressly provided that a crossing guard unable to report for duty advise the precinct sufficiently in advance to permit the police to make other arrangements to cover the crossing. (Rules and Regulations of New York City Police Dept, ch. 23, § 12.1.) Upon notification by a patrolman or superior officer of the absence of a crossing guard from his or her position, the precinct's desk officer was required by departmental regulations to assign a patrolman to cover the crossing. (*Id*. ch. 23, § 12.3.) Where more urgent police duty necessitated a patrolman's presence elsewhere, he was required to notify the precinct and the school principal so that the latter could make arrangements to safeguard the children's welfare. (*Id*. ch. 15, § 35.0.)

Significantly, the duty assumed by the police department was a limited one: a duty intended to benefit a special class of persons — *viz.*, children crossing designated intersections while traveling to and from school at scheduled times. Thus, the duty assumed constituted more than a general duty to provide police protection to the public at large. Having witnessed the regular performance of this special duty for a two-week period, the plaintiff infant's mother relied upon its continued performance. To borrow once more from Chief Judge Cardozo, "[if] conduct has gone forward to such a stage that in action would commonly result, not negatively merely in withholding a benefit, but positively or actively in working an injury, there exists a relation out of which arises a duty to go forward" (*Moch Co. v. Rensselaer Water Co.*, 247 N.Y. at 167, *supra*). Application of this principle to the present case leads unmistakably to the conclusion that the police department, having assumed a duty to a special class of persons, and having gone forward with performance of that duty in the past, had an obligation to continue its performance. (*Cf. Bloom v. City of New York*, 78 Misc. 2d 1077, 1078-79.) Had the police department not assumed a duty to supervise school crossings, plaintiff infant's mother would not have permitted her child to travel to and from school alone. The department's failure to perform this duty placed the infant plaintiff in greater danger than he would have been had the duty not been assumed, since the infant's mother would not have had reason to rely on the protection afforded her child and would have been required, in her absence, to arrange for someone to accompany her child to and from school.

As to whether the police department, having assumed this duty, negligently omitted its performance, the city contended [that] sufficient patrolmen were not available to permit assignment of a patrolman to cover the intersection. . . . The city placed great weight upon a departmental regulation mandating that "[when] all school crossings cannot be covered, those considered most dangerous shall be covered." (Rules and Regulations of New York City Police Dept, ch. 15, § 34.1.) It was the city's contention that the intersection of Park Place and Ralph Avenue was not considered one of the most hazardous school crossings. Whether or not the police department negligently performed its duty to supervise school crossings is a question of fact properly left for determination by the jury. In returning a verdict against defendants, the jury resolved this question against the city.

In passing, we caution [that] a municipality cannot be held liable solely for its failure to provide adequate public services. The extent of public services afforded by a municipality is, as a practical matter, limited by the resources of the community. Deployment of these resources remains, as it must, a legislative-executive decision which must be made without the benefit of hindsight. (*Riss v. City of New York*, 22 N.Y.2d at 581-82.) Had the city established that a shortage of personnel precluded assignment of a patrolman to cover the intersection of Park Place and Ralph Avenue, notification of this contingency to the school principal or other appropriate action would have been sufficient to relieve the police department and New York City from liability for the failure to supervise the designated school crossing. To place a greater burden upon the police department would be unwarranted.

The order of the Appellate Division should be affirmed, with costs.

PROBLEMS

1. Suppose that a group of concerned parents had gone to the police department under facts similar to those in *Florence* and formally requested that an officer be assigned to patrol the school crossing in question, but the police department had simply refused such a request, citing no particular reason at all. Does the police department have an affirmative duty to post a guard at the school crossing under these circumstances?

2. If an affirmative duty is owed by the police department to keep a school crossing guard at the intersection of Park Place and Ralph Avenue as a result of the decision in *Florence*, does this mean that the crossing guard at this particular intersection can *never* be discontinued? What if the police department must cut back its uniformed personnel because of a shortage of funding? Must it always continue to maintain the crossing guard even if the guard could be used more effectively to patrol another, even more dangerous, intersection?

3. There are numerous examples of cases in which, although the defendant initially owed no duty to the plaintiff, nevertheless, by voluntarily undertaking to render some type of aid or assistance to an imperiled plaintiff and then failing to exercise reasonable care, the defendant was held to have subsequently assumed a duty. For example, in *DeLong v. County of Erie*, 457 N.E.2d 717 (N.Y. 1983), the plaintiff's decedent was killed by a burglar who broke into her home and attacked her with a knife. As the burglar was breaking in, the decedent called the emergency 911 number and requested help. The defendant's 911 operator apparently wrote down the wrong street address, and after police were unable to locate that address when they were sent to investigate the emergency call, they discontinued any further rescue efforts. The court upheld a verdict in favor of the decedent based upon the negligence of the defendant's 911

operator. Relying upon the defendant's voluntarily assumed duty to respond to the decedent's emergency 911 call, the court explained that:

> [I]n this case the decision had been made by the [defendant] munici-palities to provide a special emergency service which was intended and proclaimed to be more efficient than normal police services. Those seek-ing emergency assistance were advised not to attempt to call the general number for the local police, which ironically might have avoided the tragedy encountered in this case, but were encouraged to dial the 911 number to obtain a quicker response. In addition, and most signifi-cantly, the victim's plea for assistance was not refused. Indeed, she was affirmatively assured that help would be there 'right away.' Considering the fact that she was merely a block and a half from the local police sta-tion, and was not yet at the mercy of the intruder, it cannot be said as a matter of law that this assurance played no part in her decision to remain in her home and not seek other assurance.

Id. at 720. Was the duty assumed in *DeLong* based upon the defendant munic-ipalities' decision to provide 911 emergency service, or upon the dispatcher's decision to respond (versus not to respond at all) to the decedent's emergency call for assistance? What if the dispatcher in *DeLong* had agreed to send emer-gency assistance to an address that was in fact located beyond the jurisdiction of the defendants' emergency service district so that the defendants' police offi-cers were unable to respond to the call? Has any duty been voluntarily assumed under these circumstances?

3. Special Relationships

One of the most frequently asserted justifications for imposing an affirmative duty to render aid to persons in peril is based upon the existence of some type of "special relationship" between the affected parties. Such relationships are often said to give rise to an initial duty to provide aid, even in situations where the victim may not otherwise have even detrimentally relied upon any action by the defendant. For example, RESTATEMENT (SECOND) OF TORTS § 315 (1965) pro-vides specifically that:

> There is no duty so to control the conduct of a third person as to prevent him from causing physical harm to another unless
>
> (a) a *special relation* exists between the actor and the third person which imposes a duty upon the actor to control the third person's conduct, or
>
> (b) a *special relation* exists between the actor and the other which gives to the other a right to protection. (Emphasis supplied).

Although the courts have been somewhat reluctant to articulate a precise def-inition for the term "special relationship," they have recognized certain general categories of "relationships" that do give rise to a duty to aid in a variety of different factual settings. Among the traditional examples are common-carrier-passenger relationships; business invitor-invitee relationships; custodial relationships; landlord-tenant relationships; and employer-employee relationships. *See, e.g.*, RESTATEMENT (SECOND) OF TORTS § 314A (1965). The following case illustrates just how far a court can go in recognizing a "special relationship" upon which to impose a duty of care.

FARWELL v. KEATON
240 N.W.2d 217 (Mich. 1976)

LEVIN, J.

On the evening of August 26, 1966, Siegrist and Farwell drove to a trailer rental lot to return an automobile which Siegrist had borrowed from a friend who worked there. While waiting for the friend to finish work, Siegrist and Farwell consumed some beer.

Two girls walked by the entrance to the lot. Siegrist and Farwell attempted to engage them in conversation; they left Farwell's car and followed the girls to a drive-in restaurant down the street.

The girls complained to their friends in the restaurant that they were being followed. Six boys chased Siegrist and Farwell back to the lot. Siegrist escaped unharmed, but Farwell was severely beaten. Siegrist found Farwell underneath his automobile in the lot. Ice was applied to Farwell's head. Siegrist then drove Farwell around for approximately two hours, stopping at a number of drive-in restaurants. Farwell went to sleep in the back seat of his car. Around midnight Siegrist drove the car to the home of Farwell's grandparents, parked it in the driveway, unsuccessfully attempted to rouse Farwell, and left. Farwell's grandparents discovered him in the car the next morning and took him to the hospital. He died three days later of an epidural hematoma.

At trial, plaintiff contended that had Siegrist taken Farwell to the hospital, or had he notified someone of Farwell's condition and whereabouts, Farwell would not have died. A neurosurgeon testified that if a person in Farwell's condition is taken to a doctor before, or within half an hour after, consciousness is lost, there is an 85 to 88 per cent chance of survival. Plaintiff testified that Siegrist told him that he knew Farwell was badly injured and that he should have done something.

The jury returned a verdict for plaintiff and awarded $15,000 in damages. The Court of Appeals reversed, finding that Siegrist had not assumed the duty of obtaining aid for Farwell and that he neither knew nor should have known of the need for medical treatment. . . .

Without regard to whether there is a general duty to aid a person in distress, there is a clearly recognized legal duty of every person to avoid any affirmative acts which may make a situation worse. "[I]f the defendant does attempt to aid him, and takes charge and control of the situation, he is regarded as entering voluntarily into a relation which is attended with responsibility. [Such] a defendant will then be liable for a failure to use reasonable care for the protection of the plaintiff's interests." Prosser, *supra*, § 56, pp. 343-44. "Where performance clearly has been begun, there is no doubt that there is a duty of care."

There was ample evidence to show that Siegrist breached a legal duty owed Farwell. Siegrist knew that Farwell had been in a fight, and he attempted to relieve Farwell's pain by applying an ice pack to his head. While Farwell and Siegrist were riding around, Farwell crawled into the back seat and laid down. The testimony showed that Siegrist attempted to rouse Farwell after driving him home but was unable to do so. . . . Siegrist contends that he is not liable for failure to obtain medical assistance for Farwell because he had no duty to do so.

Courts have been slow to recognize a duty to render aid to a person in peril. Where such a duty has been found, it has been predicated upon the existence of a special relationship between the parties; in such a case, if defendant knew or should have known of the other person's peril, he is required to render reasonable care under all the circumstances.

Farwell and Siegrist were companions on a social venture. Implicit in such a common undertaking is the understanding that one will render assistance to the other when he is in peril if he can do so without endangering himself. Siegrist knew or should have known when he left Farwell, who was badly beaten and unconscious, in the back seat of his car that no one would find him before morning. Under these circumstances, to say that Siegrist had no duty to obtain medical assistance or at least to notify someone of Farwell's condition and whereabouts would be "shocking to humanitarian considerations" and fly in the face of "the commonly accepted code of social conduct." "[C]ourts will find a duty where, in general, reasonable men would recognize it and agree that it exists."

Farwell and Siegrist were companions engaged in a common undertaking; there was a special relationship between the parties. Because Siegrist knew or should have known of the peril Farwell was in and could render assistance without endangering himself he had an affirmative duty to come to Farwell's aid.

The Court of Appeals is reversed and the verdict of the jury reinstated.

NOTE

What is the actual legal basis upon which the court imposes a duty to render aid in *Farwell*? Does it really matter what legal reason(s) the court gives, so long as it recognizes a duty owed by the defendant to the plaintiff in any given circumstance?

TARASOFF v. REGENTS OF UNIVERSITY OF CALIFORNIA
551 P.2d 334 (Cal. 1976)

TOBRINER, J.

On Octobr 27, 1969, Prosenjit Poddar killed Tatiana Tarasoff. Plaintiffs, Tatiana's parents, allege that two months earlier Poddar confided his intention to kill Tatiana to Dr. Lawrence Moore, a psychologist employed by the Cowell Memorial Hospital at the University of California at Berkeley. They allege that on Moore's request, the campus police briefly detained Poddar, but released him when he appeared rational. They further claim that Dr. Harvey Powelson, Moore's superior, then directed that no further action be taken to detain Poddar. No one warned plaintiffs of Tatiana's peril.

Concluding that these facts set forth causes of action against neither therapists and policemen involved, nor against the Regents of the University of California as their employer, the superior court sustained defendants' demurrers to plaintiffs' second amended complaints without leave to amend. This appeal ensued.

Plaintiffs' complaints predicate liability on two grounds: defendants' failure to warn plaintiffs of the impending danger and their failure to bring about Poddar's confinement. . . . Defendants, in turn, assert that they owed no duty of reasonable care to Tatiana and that they are immune from suit under the California Tort Claims Act of 1963.

[D]efendant therapists cannot escape liability merely because Tatiana herself was not their patient. When a therapist determines, or pursuant to the standards of his profession should determine, that his patient presents a serious danger of violence to another, he incurs an obligation to use reasonable care to protect the intended victim against such danger. The discharge of this duty may require the therapist to take one or more of various steps, depending upon the nature of the case. Thus it may call for him to warn the intended victim or others likely to apprise the victim of the danger, to notify the police, or to take whatever other steps are reasonably necessary under the circumstances.

In the case at bar, plaintiffs admit that defendant therapists notified the police, but argue [that] the therapists failed to exercise reasonable care to protect Tatiana in that they did not confine Poddar and did not warn Tatiana or others likely to apprise her of the danger. Defendant therapists, however, are public employees. Consequently, to the extent that plaintiffs seek to predicate liability upon the therapists' failure to bring about Poddar's confinement, the therapists can claim immunity under Government Code section 856. No specific statutory provision, however, shields them from liability based upon failure to warn Tatiana or others likely to apprise her of the danger. . . .

Plaintiffs therefore can amend their complaints to allege that, regardless of the therapists' unsuccessful attempt to confine Poddar, since they knew that Poddar was at large and dangerous, their failure to warn Tatiana or others likely to apprise her of the danger constituted a breach of the therapists' duty to exercise reasonable care to protect Tatiana.

Plaintiffs, however, plead no relationship between Poddar and the police defendants which would impose upon them any duty to Tatiana, and plaintiffs suggest no other basis for such a duty. Plaintiffs have, therefore, failed to show that the trial court erred in sustaining the demurrer of the police defendants without leave to amend.

[Although] under the common law, as a general rule, one person owed no duty to control the conduct of another, nor to warn those endangered by such conduct, the courts have carved out an exception to this rule in cases in which the defendant stands in some special relationship to either the person whose conduct needs to be controlled or in a relationship to the foreseeable victim of that conduct. Applying this exception to the present case, we note that a relationship of defendant therapists to either Tatiana or Poddar will suffice to establish a duty of care; as explained in section 315 of the Restatement Second of Torts, a duty of care may arise from either "(a) a special relation [between] the actor and the third person which imposes a duty upon the actor to control the third person's conduct, or (b) a special relation . . . between the actor and the other which gives to the other a right of protection."

Although plaintiffs' pleadings assert no special relation between Tatiana and defendant therapists, they establish as between Poddar and defendant therapists the special relation that arises between a patient and his doctor or psychotherapist. Such a relationship may support affirmative duties for the benefit of third persons. Thus, for example, a hospital must exercise reasonable care to control the behavior of a patient which may endanger other persons. A doctor must also warn a patient if the patient's condition or medication renders certain conduct, such as driving a car, dangerous to others.

Although the California decisions that recognize this duty have involved cases in which the defendant stood in a special relationship *both* to the victim and to the person whose conduct created the danger, we do not think that the duty should logically be constricted to such situations. Decisions of other jurisdictions hold that the single relationship of a doctor to his patient is sufficient to support the duty to exercise reasonable care to protect others against dangers emanating from the patient's illness. The courts hold that a doctor is liable to persons infected by his patient if he negligently fails to diagnose a contagious disease, or, having diagnosed the illness, fails to warn members of the patient's family.

Since it involved a dangerous mental patient, the decision in *Merchants Nat. Bank & Trust Co. of Fargo v. United States* (D.N.D. 1967) 272 F. Supp. 409 comes closer to the issue. The Veterans Administration arranged for the patient to work on a local farm, but did not inform the farmer of the man's background. The farmer consequently permitted the patient to come and go freely during nonworking hours; the patient borrowed a car, drove to his wife's residence and killed her. Notwithstanding the lack of any "special relationship" between the Veterans Administration and the wife, the court found the Veterans Administration liable for the wrongful death of the wife.

Defendants contend [that] imposition of a duty to exercise reasonable care to protect third persons is unworkable because therapists cannot accurately predict whether or not a patient will resort to violence. In support of this argument amicus representing the American Psychiatric Association and other professional societies cites numerous articles which indicate that therapists, in the present state of the art, are unable reliably to predict violent acts; their forecasts, amicus claims, tend consistently to overpredict violence, and indeed are more often wrong than right. Since predictions of violence are often erroneous, amicus concludes, the courts should not render rulings that predicate the liability of therapists upon the validity of such predictions. . . .

We recognize the difficulty that a therapist encounters in attempting to forecast whether a patient presents a serious danger of violence. Obviously, we do not require that the therapist, in making that determination, render a perfect performance; the therapist need only exercise "that reasonable degree of skill, knowledge, and care ordinarily possessed and exercised by members of [that professional specialty] under similar circumstances." Within the broad range of reasonable practice and treatment in which professional opinion and judgment may differ, the therapist is free to exercise his or her own best judgment without liability; proof, aided by hindsight, that he or she judged wrongly is insufficient to establish negligence.

In the instant case, however, the pleadings do not raise any question as to failure of defendant therapists to predict that Poddar presented a serious danger of violence. On the contrary, the present complaints allege that defendant therapists did in fact predict that Poddar would kill, but were negligent in failing to warn.

Amicus contends [that] even when a therapist does in fact predict that a patient poses a serious danger of violence to others, the therapist should be absolved of any responsibility for failing to act to protect the potential victim. In our view, however, once a therapist does in fact determine, or under applicable professional standards reasonably should have determined, that a patient poses a serious danger of violence to others, he bears a duty to exercise reasonable care to protect the foreseeable victim of that danger. While the discharge of this duty of due care will necessarily vary with the facts of each case, in each instance the adequacy of the therapist's conduct must be measured against the traditional negligence standard of the rendition of reasonable care under the circumstances. . . .

The risk that unnecessary warnings may be given is a reasonable price to pay for the lives of possible victims that may be saved. We would hesitate to hold that the therapist who is aware that his patient expects to attempt to assassinate the President of the United States would not be obligated to warn the authorities because the therapist cannot predict with accuracy that his patient will commit the crime.

Defendants further argue that free and open communication is essential to psychotherapy. . . . The giving of a warning, defendants contend, constitutes a breach of trust which entails the revelation of confidential communications.

We recognize the public interest in supporting effective treatment of mental illness and in protecting the rights of patients to privacy, and the consequent public importance of safeguarding the confidential character of psychotherapeutic communication. Against this interest, however, we must weigh the public interest in safety from violent assault. The Legislature has undertaken the difficult task of balancing the countervailing concerns. In Evidence Code section 1014, it established a broad rule of privilege to protect confidential communications between patient and psychotherapist. In Evidence Code section 1024, the Legislature created a specific and limited exception to the psychotherapist-patient privilege: "There is no privilege [if] the psychotherapist has reasonable cause to believe that the patient is in such mental or emotional condition as to be dangerous to himself or to the person or property of another and that disclosure of the communication is necessary to prevent the threatened danger." . . .

The revelation of a communication under the above circumstances is not a breach of trust or a violation of professional ethics; as stated in the Principles of Medical Ethics of the American Medical Association (1957), section 9: "A physician may not reveal the confidence entrusted to him in the course of medical attendance . . . *unless he is required to do so by law or unless it becomes necessary in order to protect the welfare of the individual or of the community.*" (Italics added.) We conclude that the public policy favoring protection of the confidential character of patient-psychotherapist communications must yield to the extent to which disclosure is essential to avert danger to others. The protective privilege ends where the public peril begins. . . .

Turning now to the police defendants, we conclude that they do not have any such special relationship to either Tatiana or to Poddar sufficient to impose upon such defendants a duty to warn respecting Poddar's violent intentions. Plaintiffs suggest no theory, and plead no facts that give rise to any duty to warn on the part of the police defendants absent such a special relationship. They have thus failed to demonstrate that the trial court erred in denying leave to amend as to the police defendants. . . .

MOSK, J., (concurring and dissenting)

I concur in the result in this instance only because the complaints allege that defendant therapists did in fact predict that Poddar would kill and were therefore negligent in failing to warn of that danger. Thus the issue here is very narrow: we are not concerned with whether the therapists, pursuant to the standards of their profession, "should have" predicted potential violence; they allegedly did so in actuality. Under these limited circumstances I agree that a cause of action can be stated.

Whether plaintiffs can ultimately prevail is problematical at best. As the complaints admit, the therapists *did* notify the police that Poddar was planning to kill a girl identifiable as Tatiana. While I doubt that more should be required, this issue may be raised in defense and its determination is a question of fact.

I cannot concur, however, in the majority's rule that a therapist may be held liable for failing to predict his patient's tendency to violence if other practitioners, pursuant to the "standards of the profession," would have done so. The question is, what standards? Defendants and a responsible amicus curiae . . . demonstrate that psychiatric predictions of violence are inherently unreliable. . . .

I would restructure the rule designed by the majority to eliminate all reference to conformity to standards of the profession in predicting violence. If a psychiatrist does in fact predict violence, then a duty to warn arises. The majority's expansion of that rule will take us from the world of reality into the wonderland of clairvoyance.

PROBLEM

Sally was one of several invited guests who attended Ted's party. After drinking several beers, Sally went out onto the balcony of Ted's third-story apartment. There, she spotted Ted in the patio area below, after he had gone downstairs to greet another guest who had just arrived. Sally climbed onto the narrow metal railing that surrounded Ted's balcony and, balancing precariously atop the railing, she shouted out to Ted that she wanted to come down to join him. Before anyone could say or do anything, Sally jumped (or fell) off the balcony and landed on the concrete patio below. Ted rushed to her, but she was unconscious, although apparently still breathing. Leaning over her, he waited several minutes to see if she might "come to." Finally, he called an ambulance, but that is all. He did nothing else. He didn't move her, or render any sort of first aid. Within ten minutes paramedics arrived at the scene and transported Sally to a nearby hospital where she was pronounced dead by the ER physician, apparently due to a massive head trauma.

In effect in the jurisdiction at the time of this incident was the following statute (Section 2-1-101) that provides:

(a) A person who knows that another is exposed to grave physical harm shall, to the extent that the same can be rendered without danger or peril to himself or without interference with important duties owed to others, give reasonable assistance to the exposed person unless that assistance or care is being provided by others.

(b) A person who provides reasonable assistance in compliance with subsection (a) of this section shall not be liable in civil damages unless his acts constitute gross negligence or unless he will receive or expects to receive remuneration. Nothing contained in this subsection shall alter existing law with respect to tort liability of a practitioner of the healing arts for acts committed in the ordinary course of his practice.

(c) A person who willfully violates subsection (a) of this section shall be fined not more than $100.00.

In a subsequent action brought on behalf of Sally's estate against Ted for wrongful death, both parties have filed motions in reliance upon Section 2-1-101 (quoted *supra*). As to Sally's estate, does this statute create an affirmative legal duty to rescue persons in peril? If so, in what specific situations? As for Ted, is he entitled to immunity under this statute? How should the court resolve this question? *See Lindsey v. Miami Development Corp.*, 689 S.W.2d 856 (Tenn. 1985).

D. PUBLIC VERSUS PRIVATE DUTIES

It is one thing for the court to impose an affirmative duty to act upon a *private* individual; it is quite a different matter to impose such a duty upon a *public* entity. The potential economic implications of requiring public entities to take affirmative action in various potential negligence situations have led many courts to refrain from imposing affirmative duties to act, at least absent some special circumstance. As we have seen already, if the public entity (even though under no duty to take action) nevertheless *voluntarily* acts so as to induce reliance by the plaintiff, a duty may be imposed. Likewise, if some "special relationship" can be shown to exist between the plaintiff and the public entity, an affirmative duty to act may be recognized. However, in order to create a "special relationship" between a private citizen and a public entity, something more is usually required, as illustrated by the following case.

THOMPSON v. COUNTY OF ALAMEDA
614 P.2d 728 (Cal. 1980)

RICHARDSON, J.

[Plaintiffs,] husband and wife, and their minor son lived in the City of Piedmont, a few doors from the residence of the mother of James F. (James), a juvenile offender. . . . James had been in the custody and under the control of County and had been confined in a county institution under court order. County knew that James had "latent, extremely dangerous and violent propensities regarding young children and that sexual assaults upon young children and violence connected therewith were a likely result of releasing [him] into the community." County also knew that James had "indicated that he would, if released, take the life of a young child residing in the neighborhood." (James gave no indication of which, if any, young child he intended as his victim.) County released James on temporary leave into his mother's custody at her home, and "[at] no time did [County] advise and/or warn [James' mother], the local police and/or parents of young children within the immediate vicinity of [James' mother's] house of the known facts. . . ." Within 24 hours of his release on temporary leave, James murdered plaintiffs' son in the garage of James' mother's home.

The complaint [alleges] that the death was caused by County's "reckless, wanton and grossly negligent" actions in releasing James into the community[;] failing to advise and/or warn James' mother, the local police, or "parents of young children within the immediate vicinity" of the residence of James' mother[;] failing to exercise due care in maintaining custody and control over James through his mother in her capacity as County's agent[;] and failing to exercise reasonable care in selecting James' mother to serve as County's agent in maintaining custody and control over James[.]

County demurred on the ground that the complaint failed to state a cause of action. [The court first considered allegations that the County was negligent in its decision to release James from custody, and in its selection of his mother as James' custodian and in the supervision of her activities as custodian. The court concluded that as to these alleged negligent acts, the County was immune from liability by virtue of its governmental immunity under California Government Code sections 818.2, 845, and 846.]

We now examine the principal and most troublesome contention [that] County is liable for its failure to warn the local police and the parents of neighborhood children that James was being released or, alternatively, to warn James' mother of his expressed threat. We first inquire whether there would be liability in the absence of immunity and determine initially whether in any event County had a duty to warn for the protection of plaintiffs. . . .

The existence of "duty" is a question of law. "[Legal] duties are not discoverable facts of nature, but merely conclusory expressions that, in cases of a particular type, liability should be imposed for damage done." It is a fundamental proposition of tort law that one is liable for injuries caused by a failure to exercise reasonable care. We have said, however, that in considering the existence of "duty" in a given case several factors require consideration including "the foreseeability of harm to the plaintiff, the degree of certainty that the plaintiff suffered injury, the closeness of the connection between the defendant's conduct and the injury suffered, the moral blame attached to the defendant's conduct, the policy of preventing future harm, the extent of the burden to the defendant and consequences to the community of imposing a duty to exercise care with resulting liability for breach, and the availability, cost, and prevalence of insurance for the risk involved." (*Rowland v. Christian* (1968) 69 Cal. 2d 108, 113 [70 Cal. Rptr. 97, 443 P.2d 561]).When public agencies are involved, additional elements include "the extent of [the agency's] powers, the role imposed upon it by law and the limitations imposed upon it by budget; . . ." (*Raymond v. Paradise Unified School Dist.* (1963) 218 Cal. App. 2d 1, 8 [31 Cal. Rptr. 847]).

Bearing in mind the foregoing controlling considerations, we examine the propriety of imposing on those responsible for releasing or confining criminal offenders a duty to warn of the release of a potentially dangerous offender who, as here, has made a generalized threat to a segment of the population. Our earlier rulings in *Johnson v. State of California, supra,* 69 Cal. 2d 782, and *Tarasoff v. Regents of University of California* [(1976) 17 Cal. 3d 425, 435-37, 131 Cal. Rptr. 14, 551 P.2d 334], furnish considerable guidance in our inquiry and plaintiffs rely heavily on both cases in support of their view that County had an affirmative duty to warn someone (the police, the offender's parent, or neighborhood parents) of the dangers arising from James' release.

In *Johnson*, the state, acting through a Youth Authority placement officer, placed a minor with "homicidal tendencies and a background of violence and cruelty" in the plaintiff's home. Following his attack on the plaintiff, she sued the state. In sustaining plaintiff's cause of action, we held "[we] can dispose summarily of the contention [that] that the judgment should be affirmed because the state owed no duty of care to plaintiff. As the party placing the youth with Mrs. Johnson, the state's relationship to plaintiff was such that its duty extended to warning of latent, dangerous qualities suggested by the parolee's history or character. These cases impose a duty upon those who create a *foreseeable peril*, not readily discoverable by endangered persons, to warn them of such potential peril. Accordingly, the state owed a duty to inform Mrs. Johnson of any matter that its agents knew or should have known that might endanger the Johnson family. . . ." [W]e emphasized the *relationship* between the state and plaintiff-victim, and the fact that the state by its conduct placed the specific plaintiff in a position of clearly foreseeable danger. In contrast with the situation in *Johnson*, in which the risk of danger focused precisely on plaintiff, here County bore no special and continuous relationship with the specific plaintiffs nor did County knowingly place the specific plaintiffs' decedent into a foreseeably dangerous position. Thus the reasoning of our holding in *Johnson* would not sustain the complaint in this action.

Likewise in *Tarasoff* we were concerned with the duty of therapists, after determining that a patient posed a serious threat of violence, to protect the "foreseeable victim of that danger." In reaching the conclusion that the therapists had a duty to warn either "the endangered party or those who can reasonably be expected to notify him[,]" we relied on an exception to the general rule that one owes no duty to control the conduct of another. As declared in section 315 of the Restatement, such a duty may arise if "(a) a special relation exists between the actor and the third person which imposes a duty upon the actor to control the third person's conduct, or (b) a special relation exists between the actor and the other which gives the other a right to protection."

We noted in *Tarasoff* that a special relationship existed between the defendant therapists and the patient which "*may* support affirmative duties for the benefit of third persons." The *Tarasoff* decedent was the known and specifically foreseeable and identifiable victim of the patient's threats. We concluded that under such circumstances it was appropriate to impose liability on those defendants for failing to take reasonable steps to protect her.

In *Tarasoff*, in reference to the police defendants who had been requested by defendant therapists to detain the patient, we further held that the police had no duty of care to the decedent because there was no "special relationship" between them and either the victim or the patient. We also rejected any application of the principle enunciated in the Restatement to the effect that "[i]f the actor does an act, and subsequently realizes or should realize that it has created an unreasonable risk of causing physical harm to another, he is under a duty to exercise reasonable care to prevent the risk from taking effect." (REST. 2D TORTS, *supra*, § 321.) We reasoned that "[t]he assertion of a cause of action against the police defendants under this theory would raise difficult problems of causation and of public policy, . . ."

We recognized in *Tarasoff* that "the open and confidential character of psychotherapeutic dialogue encourages patients to express threats of violence, few of which are ever executed. Certainly a therapist should not be encouraged routinely to reveal such threats; such disclosures could seriously disrupt the patient's relationship with his therapist and with the persons threatened." We further concluded that "the therapist's obligations to his patient require that he not disclose a confidence unless such disclosure is necessary to avert danger to others, and even then that he do so discreetly, and in a fashion that would preserve the privacy of his patient to the fullest extent compatible with the prevention of the threatened danger." Thus, we made clear that the therapist has no *general* duty to warn of each threat. Only if he "does in fact determine, or under applicable professional standards reasonably should have determined, that a patient poses a serious danger of violence to others, [does he bear] a duty to exercise reasonable care to protect the *foreseeable victim* of that danger." Although the intended victim as a precondition to liability need not be specifically named, he must be "readily identifiable."

Unlike *Johnson* and *Tarasoff*, plaintiffs here have alleged neither that a direct or continuing relationship between them and County existed through which County placed plaintiffs' decedent in danger, nor that their decedent was a foreseeable or readily identifiable target of the juvenile offender's threats. Under such circumstances, while recognizing the continuing obligation of County, as with all public entities, to exercise reasonable care to protect *all* of its citizens, we decline to impose a blanket liability on County for failing to warn plaintiffs, the parents of other neighborhood children, the police or James' mother of James' threat. As will appear, our conclusion is based in part on policy considerations and in part upon an analysis of "foreseeability" within the context of this case.

By their very nature parole and probation decisions are inherently imprecise. According to a recent study by the California Probation Parole and Correction

Association, during 1977 in California a total of 315,143 persons (225,331 adults and 89,912 juveniles) were supervised on probation. (The Future of Probation, A Report of the CPPCA Committee on the Future of Probation (July 1979) p. 15.) During the same year, cases removed from probation because of violations totaled 13.4 percent in the superior courts, 14.8 percent in the lower courts, and 11.5 percent in the juvenile courts. Additionally, a large number of parole violations occur. National parole violation rates reflect that 18-20 percent of parolees fail on one-year follow-up, 25 percent on two-year follow-up, and 26 percent on three-year follow-up. Although we fully recognize that not all violations involve new or violent offenses, a significant proportion do.

Notwithstanding the danger illustrated by the foregoing statistics, parole and probation release nonetheless comprise an integral and continuing part in our correctional system authorized by the Legislature, serving the public by rehabilitating substantial numbers of offenders and returning them to a productive position in society. The result, as we observed in *Johnson*, is that "each member of the general public who chances to come into contact with a parolee [bears] the risk that the rehabilitative effort will fail. . . ." The United States Supreme Court very recently reached a similar conclusion in *Martinez v. California* (1980) 444 U.S. 277. In *Martinez*, the high court rejected a contention that the California governmental immunity statutes (Gov. Code, § 845.8 in particular) deprived plaintiffs' decedent of her life without due process of law because of a parole decision that led indirectly to her death. The Supreme Court observed that "the basic risk that repeat offenses may occur is always present in any parole system."

Bearing in mind the ever present danger of parole violations, we nonetheless conclude that public entities and employees have no affirmative duty to warn of the release of an inmate with a violent history who has made *nonspecific threats of harm directed at nonspecific victims*. Obviously aware of the risk of failure of probation and parole programs the Legislature has nonetheless as a matter of public policy elected to continue those programs even though such risks must be borne by the public. (*See Beauchene v. Synanon Foundation, Inc.* (1979) 88 Cal. App. 3d 342, 347 [151 Cal. Rptr. 796].)

Similar general public policy considerations were described in a recent analysis of the *Tarasoff* issue. The author reasoned: "Assume that one person out of a thousand will kill. Assume also that an exceptionally accurate test is created which differentiates with 95% effectiveness those who will kill from those who will not. If 100,000 people were tested, out of the 100 who would kill 95 would be isolated. Unfortunately, of the 99,900 who would not kill, 4,995 people would also be isolated as potential killers. In these circumstances, it is clear that we could not justify incarcerating all 5,090 people. If, in the criminal law, it is better that ten guilty men go free than that one innocent man suffer, how can we say in the civil commitment area that it is better that fifty-four harmless people be incarcerated lest one dangerous man be free?" (Comment, *Tarasoff and the Psychotherapist's Duty to Warn* (1975) 12 SAN DIEGO L. REV. 932, 942-43, fn.75.)

Furthermore, we foresee significant practical obstacles in the imposition of a duty in the form that plaintiffs seek, concluding that it would be unwieldy and of little practical value. As previously indicated a large number of persons are released and supervised on probation and parole each year in this state. Notification to the public at large of the release of each offender who has a history of violence and who has made a generalized threat at some time during incarceration or while under supervision would, in our view, produce a cacaphony of warnings that by reason of their sheer volume would add little to the effective protection of the public. . . .

We are skeptical of any net benefit which might flow from a duty to issue a generalized warning of the probationary release of offenders. In our view, the generalized warnings sought to be required here would do little to increase the precautions of any particular members of the public who already may have become conditioned to locking their doors, avoiding dark and deserted streets, instructing their children to beware of strangers and taking other precautions. By their very numbers the force of the multiple warnings required to accompany the release of all probationers with a potential for violence would be diluted as to each member of the public who by such release thereby becomes a potential victim. Such a warning may also negate the rehabilitative purposes of the parole and probation system by stigmatizing the released offender in the public's eye.

Unlike members of the general public, in *Tarasoff* and *Johnson* the potential victims were specifically known and designated individuals. The warnings which we therein required were directed at making those individuals aware of the danger to which they were uniquely exposed. The threatened targets were precise. In such cases, it is fair to conclude that warnings given discreetly and to a limited number of persons would have a greater effect because they would alert those particular targeted individuals of the possibility of a specific threat pointed at them. In contrast, the warnings sought by plaintiffs would of necessity have to be made to a broad segment of the population and would be only general in nature. In addition to the likelihood that such generalized warnings when frequently repeated would do little as a practical matter to stimulate increased safety measures, as we develop below, such extensive warnings would be difficult to give.

Warning the Police. In our view, warnings to the police as urged by plaintiffs ordinarily would be of little benefit in preventing assaults upon members of the public by dangerous persons unless we were simultaneously and additionally to impose a concurrent duty on the police to act upon such warnings. As we noted in *Tarasoff, supra,* no such duty to act exists.

In *Tarasoff* we required that warnings be given directly to the *identifiable* potential victim or to those who, in turn, would advise such individuals of potential danger. In contrast, the requirement that local police be warned would not, in our view, guarantee effective notice to potential victims unless the police also, upon receipt of the warning, were thereupon required to knock on individual doors in the community and give warning, or to provide a 24-hour police escort either for the offender or for all possible victims. Requiring such police action to attend every release of every person who had expressed a generalized intent to commit a violent act against society at large would necessitate the diversion of an inordinate expenditure of time and manpower.

In a somewhat parallel situation, we note that the Legislature has expressly spoken in requiring those who have been convicted of certain sex crimes to inform the police of their presence in the community. (*See* Pen. Code § 290.) No similar requirement exists for other kinds of offenders or for persons temporarily released on probation or parole. Furthermore, even section 290 does not require the police to take any specific action to warn the community of the offender's presence, or to supervise the offender's movements. All that is required under the section is recordkeeping by the police which, at the discretion of the police, may be utilized when appropriate. Similar recordkeeping which would be required if regular and numerous warnings such as are requested here were given to the police would create a mass of paper, the upkeep and review of which might well divert police personnel from more effective activities.

Thus, unlike the situation in *Tarasoff*, requiring warning to the police ordinarily would result in no benefit to any potential victims of possible violence.

Warnings to Parents of Neighborhood Children. In similar fashion, requiring the releasing agent to warn all neighborhood parents of small children that a potentially dangerous offender had been released in the area would require an expenditure of time and limited resources that parole and probation agencies cannot spare and would be of questionable value. The magnitude of the problem may be understood in the light of statistics contained in the above cited CPPCA report. In 1978 California probation departments employed a total of 18,331 persons, including professional probation officers, group counselors, clerical staff, business management professionals, psychiatrists, psychologists, medical specialists, other treatment personnel, and 5,156 part-time or volunteer staff members. As previously noted, these personnel exercised supervision over 315,000 probationers "on the streets" during that year. (CPPCA Rep., at p. 16.)

Furthermore, such notice might substantially jeopardize rehabilitative efforts both by stigmatizing released offenders and by inhibiting their release. It is also possible that, in addition, parole or probation authorities would be far less likely to authorize release given the substantial drain on their resources which such warnings might require. A stated public policy favoring innovative release programs would be thwarted. (*See Whitcombe v. County of Yolo, supra*, 73 Cal. App. 3d 698, 716.)

Warning to the Juvenile's Mother. Finally, notification to the offender's mother of James' threat in our opinion would not have the desired effect of warning potential victims, at least in a case such as that herein presented. In the usual instance we doubt that the mother of the juvenile offender would be likely voluntarily to inform other neighborhood parents or children that her son posed a general threat to their welfare, thereby perhaps thwarting any rehabilitative effort, and also effectively stigmatizing both the mother and son in the community. The imposition of an affirmative duty on the County to warn a parent of generalized threats without additionally requiring, in turn, some affirmative action by the parent would prove ineffective.

The dissent speculates that the mother "might" have taken special care to control her son had she been warned of James' threats, inferring thereby that she would have maintained such constant surveillance over her son as to prevent any possible harm. Such attenuated conjecture, however, cannot alone support the imposition of civil liability. This is particularly true inasmuch as the County's original decision to release James from close confinement into the obviously less restrictive custody of his mother is a decision we already hold is immunized from liability.

In *Johnson*, [we] required notification to those placed in imminent danger by the state's action. There the county had placed a *stranger* into the home and we noted that the failure "to warn the foster parents of latent dangers facing *them* . . ." presented a "classic case for the imposition of tort liability." In contrast, the duty sought to be imposed here is that of warning a mother, aware of her son's incarceration for the previous 18 months and not herself endangered, for the remote benefit of a third party, an unidentifiable potential victim. Furthermore, it is contrary to the very purpose of such a release to speculate that a mother in whose care a nearly 18-year-old offender has been temporarily placed would thereby assume the constant minute-to-minute supervision that would have been required to prevent the tragedy.

In summary, whenever a potentially dangerous offender is released and thereafter commits a crime, the possibility of the commission of that crime is statistically foreseeable. Yet the Legislature has concluded that the benefits to society from rehabilitative release programs mandate their continuance. Within this context and for policy reasons the duty to warn depends upon and arises from the existence of a prior threat to a specific identifiable victim. In those instances in which the released offender poses a predictable threat of harm to a named or readily identifiable victim or group of victims who can be effectively warned of the danger, a releasing agent may well be liable for failure to warn such persons. Despite the tragic events underlying the present complaint, plaintiffs' decedent was not a known, identifiable victim, but rather a member of a large amorphous public group of potential targets. Under these circumstances we hold that County had no affirmative duty to warn plaintiffs, the police, the mother of the juvenile offender, or other local parents.

Because we have concluded that County was either statutorily immunized from liability or, alternatively, bore no affirmative duty that it failed to perform, we need not reach the other contentions raised by County.

The judgment of dismissal is affirmed.

TOBRINER, J.

I dissent from the conclusion of the majority opinion that plaintiffs' complaint states no cause of action arising from Alameda County's negligence in failing to warn James' mother that he might harm neighborhood children. In holding that the county is not legally responsible for its negligence, the majority in effect amend the Government Code, creating an immunity from liability which the Legislature has not enacted. . . .

The issue before us is whether the foregoing allegations state a cause of action for wrongful death against the county. The basis for upholding the complaint is clear and straightforward. The county, having custody of James, stood in a "special relationship" to James that imports a duty to control his conduct and to warn of danger. The county placed James in the temporary custody of his mother without informing her that James had threatened to kill a neighborhood child. Whether that failure to warn was negligent and proximately caused Jonathan's death are questions of fact which cannot be resolved on demurrer. Since under the alleged facts the county can claim no statutory immunity from liability arising from its failure to warn, the complaint states a cause of action.

The majority opinion in reaching a contrary result misreads controlling precedent. Although both *Johnson v. State of California* and *Tarasoff v. Regents of University of California*, involved a failure to warn an identifiable victim, the reasoning of those decisions cannot be confined to that narrow scope. Instead, the cases stand for the principle that a special relationship, such as that between the state and a person in its custody, establishes a duty to use reasonable care to avert danger to foreseeable victims. If the victim can be identified in advance, a warning to him may discharge that duty; if he cannot be identified, reasonable care may require other action. But the absence of an identifiable victim does not postulate the absence of a duty of reasonable care.

Our opinion in *Tarasoff* makes clear that failure to warn a victim who is identifiable does not constitute an essential element of the cause of action. We noted that the duty of care requires the defendant "to take one or more of various steps, depending upon the nature of the case. Thus it may call for him to warn the intended victim or others likely to apprise the victim of the danger, to notify the police, or to take whatever other steps are reasonably necessary under the circumstances."

The principles underlying the *Tarasoff* decision indicate that even the existence of an identifiable victim is not essential to the cause of action. Our decision rested upon the basic tenet of tort law that a "'defendant owes a duty of care to all persons who are *foreseeably* endangered by his conduct.'" The "avoidance of foreseeable harm," we explained, "requires a defendant to control the conduct of another person, or [to] warn of such conduct . . . if the defendant bears some special relationship to the dangerous person or to the potential victim." The relationship between therapist and patient fulfilled this requirement in *Tarasoff*; the relationship between the county and a juvenile under its custody suffices in the present case.

At no point did we hold that such duty of care runs only to identifiable victims. We cited numerous examples to the contrary. One example makes the point particularly clear: "[a] doctor must . . . warn a patient if the patient's condition or medication renders certain conduct, such as driving a car, dangerous to others." It would be absurd to confine that duty to motorists or pedestrians whom the doctor could identify in advance.

Thus under the reasoning of *Tarasoff* and the principles of tort law endorsed in the case, the proper inquiry turns on whether Jonathan Thompson was a foreseeable victim. The complaint alleges that James had threatened to "take the life of a young child residing in the neighborhood"; since Jonathan falls within that description his killing was clearly a foreseeable consequence of James' release and subsequent lack of supervision. Whether Jonathan was also an identifiable victim is relevant not to the existence of a duty of care, but only to whether a warning to Jonathan personally was a reasonable means of discharging that duty. If, as the majority claim, a warning to the neighborhood families was not a reasonable way to reduce the danger, that fact cannot absolve the state of the duty to employ other methods. In particular, it cannot absolve the state from its failure to warn James' mother so that she could exercise proper care in observing and supervising James and thereby preventing the harm that ensued.

Thus no precedent supports the majority's unique attempt to limit the imposition upon defendant of a duty of due care to warn only to a situation in which a person commits a tort upon a victim who can be identified in advance of the wrongful conduct. Even the reading of precedent most favorable to the majority will reveal only that most, but not all, prior cases did involve identifiable victims. Thus the majority position must stand, if it can stand at all, upon the policy considerations it advances.

As to policy considerations, the majority first state that although parole and probation decisions are imprecise, and necessarily present an element of danger to the public, "the Legislature has nonetheless as a matter of public policy elected to continue those programs even though such risks must be borne by the public." We appreciate the majority's fear that imposition of liability might interfere with the discretion of agencies who must decide whether to grant parole or probation. The Legislature, however, has considered that subject and determined that providing immunity to the state for basic policy decisions is a sufficient safeguard, and that it is unnecessary further to shield the state from liability for implementation of those decisions. As we explained in *Johnson*: "once the proper authorities have made the basic policy decision — to place a youth with foster parents, for example — the role [of] immunity ends; subsequent negligent actions, such as the failure to give reasonable warnings to the foster parents actually selected, are subject to legal redress."

Twelve years have passed since we filed the decision in *Johnson*. The Legislature has not amended the Government Code to enlarge governmental immunity beyond that described in *Johnson*. We have heard no outcry that *Johnson* imperils the state's parole and probation programs, no claim that the liability for failure to warn imposed by that case has interfered with legislative policy. We thus perceive no need for judicial creation of an expanded immunity.

In sum, whatever policy considerations impelled the Legislature to establish parole and probation programs, the Legislature did not believe those considerations preclude liability for negligent failure to warn. The majority cannot rely on legislative policy to grant a larger immunity than the Legislature has elected to provide. In rejecting the Legislature's judgment, the majority protect the government from liability for its own negligence when the Legislature finds such protection unnecessary.

The policy considerations favoring plaintiffs' cause of action in the present setting — considerations not taken into account by the majority — are weighty and substantial. The principle of compensating victims of negligence in order to recompense their injury and to deter future negligence is fundamental in our judicial system. Thus as a general principle, a plaintiff injured as a proximate result of a defendant's negligence is entitled to compensation. (*See* Civ. Code § 1714, subd. (a).) Even if the government is the tortfeasor, "when there is negligence, the rule is liability, immunity is the exception." (*Muskopf v. Corning Hospital Dist.* (1961) 55 Cal. 2d 211, 219 [11 Cal. Rptr. 89, 359 P.2d 457]). Consequently "[unless] the Legislature has clearly provided for immunity, the important societal goal of compensating injured parties for damages caused by willful or negligent acts must prevail." (*Ramos v. Madera* (1971) 4 Cal. 3d 685, 692 [94 Cal. Rptr. 421, 484 P.2d 93].) In the balance, I believe these basic precepts outweigh the majority's anxiety that the Legislature did not go far enough in immunizing implementation of parole and probation programs.

[T]he majority note the practical problems of warning the public at large. When it comes to warning James' mother, however, the majority say only that she would be unlikely to relay that warning to others in the neighborhood. They do not consider that a mother, when warned that her son is a serious danger to young children, might take special care to watch him, to control his activities, to know his whereabouts, and to make sure he is not alone with small children. Neither do they consider that James' mother as his legal custodian would, given proper warnings, have a legal duty to so control James' behavior. Confined by their narrow concept of warning identifiable victims, the majority do not consider the obvious.

In sum, the policy considerations discussed by the majority relate to the discretionary decision whether to grant parole or probation, the wisdom of civil commitment of dangerous persons, and the practical problems of warning large classes of possible victims. It is striking how little relevance these considerations have to the present case. None bear significantly on the question whether the county should have warned James' mother.

I believe that as a matter of law and common sense the county, before it released James to his mother's custody, had a duty to tell her of his homicidal threats and inclinations. The complaint alleges that the county's failure to warn her was negligent, and proximately caused Jonathan's death. Thus under settled principles of tort law as explained in our prior opinion in *Tarasoff*, the complaint states a cause of action. I would therefore reverse the judgment dismissing plaintiffs' complaint and remand the cause to the superior court for further proceedings.

NOTES

1. According to the plaintiff in *Thompson*, to whom did the defendant County owe an affirmative duty to warn?

2. The California Supreme Court in *Thompson* discussed two of its own earlier decisions, *Johnson* and *Tarasoff*, both of which imposed an affirmative duty upon the defendants to warn foreseeable third party victims with whom the defendants had "special relationships" regarding the threat of potential violence from persons in their custody or care. According to the majority opinion in *Thompson*, how did the County's "relationship" with the victim differ from the "special relationships" previously found in both *Johnson* and *Tarasoff*?

3. How does Justice Tobriner in his dissent in *Thompson* construe the meaning of the "special relationship" necessary to impose an affirmative duty to warn third party victims in cases like these? Which interpretation (the majority opinion or the dissent) is more consistent with the actual holdings in *Johnson* and *Tarasoff*?

4. The majority opinion in *Thompson* presents several "public policy" reasons for declining to impose an affirmative duty to warn the plaintiff under the circumstances presented by the case, to which the dissent strongly disagreed. Who should decide such important policy questions: the court or the Legislature?

E. CONTRACTUAL DUTIES

Most of the cases presented throughout this Section have dealt with the general question of whether courts should impose a common law duty to affirmatively act under circumstances where the law does not otherwise recognize any such duty. One other situation that deserves attention is when the defendant, by contract, has expressly agreed to assume some duty that would otherwise not have been imposed by the common law. For the most part, contractual duty cases are fairly straightforward insofar as the parties have expressly agreed to assume specific duties with respect to one another. The general rule is quite clear: absent some public policy reason that would prevent the enforcement of the parties' contractual undertakings, most courts will not interfere with the parties' contractual allocation of their respective duties regarding one another. A problem arises when some third party, in reliance upon the contractual undertakings of the defendant, seeks to assert an affirmative duty owed to the third party, despite any contractual privity between them.

The majority position is expressed by Judge Cardozo, writing for the New York Court of Appeals in *H.R. Moch Co., Inc. v. Rensselaer Water Co.*, 159 N.E. 896 (N.Y. 1928):

> "No legal duty rests upon a city to supply its inhabitants with protection against fire. That being so, a member of the public may not maintain an action [against one] contracting with the city to furnish water at the hydrants, unless an intention appears that the promisor is to be answerable to individual members of the public as well as to the city for any loss ensuing from the failure to fulfill the promise. No such intention is discernible here. On the contrary, the contract is significantly divided into two branches: one a promise to the city for the benefit of the city in its corporate capacity, in which [is] included the service at the hydrants; and the other a promise to the city for the benefit of private takers, in which [is] included the service at their homes and factories. In a broad sense it is true that every city contract, not improvident or wasteful, is for the benefit of the public. More than this, however, must be shown to give a right of action to a member of the public not formally a party. The benefit [must] be one that is not merely incidental and secondary. It must be primary and immediate in such a sense and to such a degree as to bespeak the assumption of a duty to make reparation directly to the individual members of the public if the benefit is lost. The field of obligation would be expanded beyond reasonable limits if less than this were to be demanded as a condition of liability. A promisor undertakes to supply fuel for heating a public building. He is not liable for breach of contract to a visitor who finds the building without fuel, and thus contracts a cold. The list of illustrations can be indefinitely extended. The carrier of the mails under contract with the government is not answerable to the merchant who has lost the benefit of a bargain through negligent delay. The householder is without a remedy against manufacturers of hose and engines, though prompt performance of their contracts would have stayed the ravages of fire. The law does not spread its protection so far."

Nevertheless, in a case that was factually quite similar to *H.R. Moch Co., Inc.*, the Kentucky Court of Appeals reached the opposite conclusion, relying upon established Kentucky case precedent to the effect that, "where a water company has contracted with a city to furnish a supply of water sufficient for the protection of property within the city against fire, a citizen may sue to recover damages sustained by him on account of the failure of the water company to perform its contract." *See Harlan Water Co. v. Carter*, 295 S.W. 426, 427 (Ky. 1927). The distinction between these two very different results is probably more reflective of basic differences in public policy considerations deemed important by the two respective courts.

PROBLEM

Grouch was an elderly tenant who lived on the top floor of a multi-level apartment building with many other senior citizens. PowerCo was an electric utility company that had contracted with the owner of the apartment building to supply electric service to all common areas of the apartment premises, including the elevators, entrance-ways, and common stairways. During the second day of a city-wide power outage (caused by bad weather that knocked down utility poles throughout a several-state area), Grouch was injured when he fell in a darkened stairway while attempting to descend the stairs in search of groceries. If Grouch sues PowerCo for negligence based upon its alleged breach of a contractual duty to supply electricity to the apartment building, what is the likely outcome of Grouch's suit? What specific policy arguments can be asserted in favor of each party? Should the outcome in this case be any different if Grouch was one of PowerCo's customers?

The cases that have been presented throughout this Section illustrate a diversity of legal rationales that have been offered to justify imposing an *affirmative* duty to act in what might otherwise appear to be classic "no duty" situations. As the courts struggle to balance the various competing policy concerns that permeate this complex area of Tort law, the traditional "no duty" rule continues to be eroded. Consider the following case.

SOLDANO v. O'DANIELS
190 Cal. Rptr. 310 (Cal. Ct. App. 1983)

ANDREEN, J.

This action arises out of a shooting death occurring on August 9, 1977. Plaintiff's father [Darrell Soldano] was shot and killed by one Rudolph Villanueva [at the . . .] defendant's Happy Jack's Saloon. This defendant owns and operates the Circle Inn which is an eating establishment located across the street from Happy Jack's. Plaintiff's second cause of action [is] for negligence.

Plaintiff alleges "that on the date of the shooting, a patron of Happy Jack's Saloon came into the Circle Inn and informed a Circle Inn employee that a man had been threatened at Happy Jack's. He requested the employee either call the police or allow him to use the Circle Inn phone to call the police. That employee allegedly refused to call the police and allegedly refused to allow the patron to use the phone to make his own call. Plaintiff alleges that the actions of the Circle Inn employee were a breach of the legal duty that the Circle Inn owed to the decedent." [T]he employee was the defendant's bartender. [W]e assume the telephone was not in a private office but in a position where it could be used by a patron without inconvenience to the defendant or his guests. We also assume the call was a local one and would not result in expense to defendant.

There is a distinction, well rooted in the common law, between action and nonaction. It has found its way into the prestigious Restatement Second of Torts which provides in section 314: "The fact that the actor realizes or should realize that action on his part is necessary for another's aid or protection does not of itself impose upon him a duty to take such action." Comment c of section 314 is instructive on the basis and limits of the rule and is set forth in the footnote. The distinction between malfeasance and nonfeasance, between active misconduct working positive injury and failure to act to prevent mischief not brought on by the defendant, is founded on "that attitude of extreme individualism so typical of anglo-saxon legal thought." (Bohlen, *The Moral Duty to Aid Others as a Basis of Tort Liability*, pt. I, (1908) 56 U. PA. L. REV. 217, 219-20.)

Defendant argues that the request that its employee call the police is a request that it *do* something. He points to the established rule that one who has not created a peril ordinarily does not have a duty to take affirmative action to assist an imperiled person. It is urged that the alternative request of the patron from Happy Jack's Saloon that he be allowed to use defendant's telephone so that he personally could make the call is again a request that the defendant do something — assist another to give aid. Defendant points out that the Restatement sections which impose liability for negligent interference with a third person giving aid to another do not impose the additional duty to *aid* the good samaritan.

The refusal of the law to recognize the moral obligation of one to aid another when he is in peril and when such aid may be given without danger and at little cost in effort has been roundly criticized. Prosser describes the case law sanctioning such inaction as a "[refusal] to recognize the moral obligation of common decency and common humanity" and characterizes some of these decisions as "shocking in the extreme. . . . Such decisions are revolting to any moral sense. They have been denounced with vigor by legal writers." (PROSSER, LAW OF TORTS (4th ed. 1971) § 56, pp. 340-41). A similar rule has been termed "morally questionable" by our Supreme Court. (*Tarasoff v. Regents of University of California* (1976) 17 Cal. 3d 425, 435, fn.5[, 131 Cal. Rptr. 14, 551 P.2d 334].)

Francis H. Bohlen, in his article *The Moral Duty to Aid Others as a Basis of Tort Liability*, commented:

"Nor does it follow that because the law has not as yet recognized the duty to repair harm innocently wrought, that it will continue indefinitely to refuse it recognition. While it is true that the common law does not attempt to enforce all moral, ethical, or humanitarian duties, it is, it is submitted, equally true that all ethical and moral conceptions, which are not the mere temporary manifestations of a passing wave of sentimentalism or puritanism, but on the contrary, find a real and permanent place in the settled convictions of a race and become part of the normal habit of thought thereof, of necessity do in time color the judicial conception of legal obligation. . . ."

"While courts of law should not yield to every passing current of popular thought, nonetheless, it appears inevitable that unless they adopt as legal those popular standards which they themselves, as men, regard as just and socially practicable, but which, as judges, they refuse to recognize solely because they are not the standards of the past of Brian, of Rolle, of Fineux, and of Coke; they will more and more lose their distinctive common law character as part of the machinery whereby free men do justice among themselves."

(Bohlen, *The Moral Duty to Aid Others as a Basis of Tort Liability,* pt. 1, 56 U. PA. L. REV. 217, 334-37.) . . .

Here there was no special relationship between the defendant and the deceased. It would be stretching the concept beyond recognition to assert there was a relationship between the defendant and the patron from Happy Jack's Saloon who wished to summon aid. But this does not end the matter.

It is time to reexamine the common law rule of nonliability for nonfeasance in the special circumstances of the instant case.

Besides well-publicized actions taken to increase the severity of punishments for criminal offenses, the Legislature has expressed a societal imperative to diminish criminal activity. Thus, in 1965, it enacted a provision for indemnification of citizens for injuries or damages sustained in crime suppression efforts. (Former Pen. Code, § 13600, added by Stats. 1965, ch. 1395, § 1, p. 3315.) In that section the Legislature declared that "[direct] action on the part of private citizens in preventing the commission of crimes against the person or property of others, or in apprehending criminals, benefits the entire public." The section does not require direct action by a private citizen; it merely recognizes the societal benefit if one does so. It was designed to stimulate active public involvement in crime control. (Note, *California Enacts Legislation To Aid Victims of Criminal Violence* (1965) 18 STAN. L. REV. 266.)

Crime is a blight on our society and a matter of great citizen concern. The President's Commission on Law Enforcement and the Administration of Justice, Task Force Report: The Police (1967) recognized the importance of citizen involvement in crime prevention: "[Crime] is not the business of the police alone. . . . The police need help from citizens, . . ." (The Community's Role in Law Enforcement, ch. 9, p. 221.) The commission identified citizen crime reporting programs in some cities. These have proliferated in recent years.

The National Advisory Commission on Criminal Justice Standards and Goals, Report on Community Crime Prevention (1973) stated: "Criminal justice professionals readily and repeatedly admit that, in the absence of citizen assistance, neither more manpower, nor improved technology, nor additional money will enable law enforcement to shoulder the monumental burden of combating crime in America." (Crime Prevention and The Citizen, ch. 1, Citizen Action, pp. 7-8.)

The Legislature has recognized the importance of the telephone system in reporting crime and in summoning emergency aid. Penal Code section 384 makes it a misdemeanor to refuse to relinquish a party line when informed that it is needed to call a police department or obtain other specified emergency services. This requirement, which the Legislature has mandated to be printed in virtually every telephone book in this state, may have wider printed distribution in this state than even the Ten Commandments. It creates an affirmative duty to do something — to clear the line for another user of the party line — in certain circumstances.

In 1972 the Legislature enacted the Warren-911-Emergency Assistance Act. This act expressly recognizes the importance of the telephone system in procuring emergency aid. "The Legislature further finds and declares that the establishment of a uniform, statewide emergency [telephone] number is a matter of statewide concern and interest to all inhabitants and citizens of this state." (Gov. Code, § 53100, subd. (b).) The act also impliedly recognizes that "police, fire, medical, rescue, and other emergency services" are frequently sought by use of the telephone. Further acknowledgment of the importance of the telephone system for summoning emergency aid is found in the act's provision that, by a specified date, all pay telephones "shall . . . enable a caller to dial '911' for emergency services, and to reach an operator by dialing 'O', without the necessity of inserting a coin." (Gov. Code, § 53112.) Moreover, Pacific Telephone, the largest telephone company in California, recognizing that the telephone can at times be a lifeline, has provided since 1968 a basic minimum rate "designed for the customer needing inexpensive low-usage residential telephone service for essential calls (Lifeline Service)." (Cal. P.U.C. Tariff 4-T (Rate Practice 4-T, 1st Revised Sheet 12).)

The above statutes are cited without the suggestion that the defendant violated a statute which would result in a presumption of a failure to use due care under Evidence Code section 669. Instead, they, and the quotations from the prestigious national commissions, demonstrate that "that attitude of extreme individualism so typical of anglo-saxon legal thought" may need limited reexamination in the light of current societal conditions and the facts of this case to determine whether the defendant owed a duty to the deceased to permit the use of the telephone.

We turn now to the concept of duty in a tort case. The Supreme Court has identified certain factors to be considered in determining whether a duty is owed to third persons. These factors include: "the foreseeability of harm to the plaintiff, the degree of certainty that the plaintiff suffered injury, the closeness of the connection between the defendant's conduct and the injury suffered, the moral blame attached to the defendant's conduct, the policy of preventing future harm, the extent of the burden to the defendant and consequences to the community of imposing a duty to exercise care with resulting liability for breach, and the availability, cost, and prevalence of insurance for the risk involved." (*Rowland v. Christian* (1968) 69 Cal. 2d 108, 113 [70 Cal. Rptr. 97, 443 P.2d 561]).

We examine those factors in reference to this case. (1) The harm to the decedent was abundantly foreseeable; it was imminent. The employee was expressly told that a man had been threatened. The employee was a bartender. As such he knew it is foreseeable that some people who drink alcohol in the milieu of a bar setting are prone to violence. (2) The certainty of decedent's injury is undisputed. (3) There is arguably a close connection between the employee's conduct and the injury: the patron wanted to use the phone to summon the police to intervene. The employee's refusal to allow the use of the phone prevented this anticipated intervention. If permitted to go to trial, the plaintiff may be able to show that the probable response time of the police would have been shorter than the time between the prohibited telephone call and the fatal shot. (4) The employee's conduct displayed a disregard for human life that can be characterized as morally wrong: he was callously indifferent to the possibility that Darrell Soldano would die as the result of his refusal to allow a person to use the telephone. Under the circumstances before us the bartender's burden was minimal and exposed him to no risk: all he had to do was allow the use of the telephone. It would have cost him or his employer nothing. It could have saved a life. (5) Finding a duty in these circumstances would promote a policy of preventing future harm. A citizen would not be required to summon the police but would be required, in circumstances such as those before us, not to impede another who has chosen to summon aid. (6) We have no information on the question of the availability, cost, and prevalence of insurance for the risk, but note that the liability which is sought to be imposed here is that of employee negligence, which is covered by many insurance policies. (7) The extent of the burden on the defendant was minimal, as noted.

The consequences to the community of imposing a duty, the remaining factor mentioned in *Rowland v. Christian, supra,* is termed "the administrative factor" by Professor Green in his analysis of determining whether a duty exists in a given case. (Green, *The Duty Problem in Negligence Cases,* I (1929) 28 COLUM. L. REV. 1014, 1035-45.) The administrative factor is simply the pragmatic concern of fashioning a workable rule and the impact of such a rule on the judicial machinery. It is the policy of major concern in this case.

As the Supreme Court has noted, the reluctance of the law to impose liability for nonfeasance, as distinguished from misfeasance, is in part due to the difficulties in setting standards and of making rules workable. (*Tarasoff v. Regents of University of California, supra,* 17 Cal. 3d at 435, fn.5.)

Many citizens simply "don't want to get involved." No rule should be adopted which would require a citizen to open up his or her house to a stranger so that the latter may use the telephone to call for emergency assistance. As Mrs. Alexander in Anthony Burgess' *A Clockwork Orange* learned to her horror, such an action may be fraught with danger. It does not follow, however, that use of a telephone in a public portion of a business should be refused for a legitimate emergency call. Imposing liability for such a refusal would not subject innocent citizens to possible attack by the "good samaritan," for it would be limited to an establishment open to the public during times when it is open to business, and to places within the establishment ordinarily accessible to the public. Nor would a stranger's mere assertion that an "emergency" situation is occurring create the duty to utilize an accessible telephone because the duty would arise if and only if it were clearly conveyed that there exists an imminent danger of physical harm. (*See* REST. 2D TORTS, *supra*, § 327.)

Such a holding would not involve difficulties in proof, overburden the courts or unduly hamper self-determination or enterprise.

A business establishment such as the Circle Inn is open for profit. The owner encourages the public to enter, for his earnings depend on it. A telephone is a necessary adjunct to such a place. It is not unusual in such circumstances for patrons to use the telephone to call a taxicab or family member.

We acknowledge that defendant contracted for the use of his telephone, and its use is a species of property. But if it exists in a public place as defined above, there is no privacy or ownership interest in it such that the owner should be permitted to interfere with a good faith attempt to use it by a third person to come to the aid of another.

The facts of this case come very nearly within section 327 of the Restatement (*see* fn. 5, *ante*) which provides that if one knows that a third person is ready to give aid to another and negligently prevents the third person from doing so, he is subject to liability for harm caused by the absence of the aid. Section 327 is contained in topic 8 of the Restatement, "Prevention of Assistance by Third Persons." The scope note for this topic provides that the "actor can prevent a third person from rendering aid to another in many ways including the following: . . . second, by interfering with his efforts to give aid; third, by injuring or destroying the usefulness of a thing which the third person is using to give aid *or by otherwise preventing him from using it*. . . ." (REST. 2D TORTS, *supra*, scope note, p. 145, italics added.)

We conclude that the bartender owed a duty to the plaintiff's decedent to permit the patron from Happy Jack's to place a call to the police or to place the call himself.

It bears emphasizing that the duty in this case does not require that one must go to the aid of another. That is not the issue here. The employee was not the good samaritan intent on aiding another. The patron was.

It would not be appropriate to await legislative action in this area. The rule was fashioned in the common law tradition, as were the exceptions to the rule.

To the extent this opinion expands the reach of section 327 of the Restatement, it represents logical and needed growth, the hallmark of the common law. It does not involve the sacrifice of other respectable interests.

The courts have a special responsibility to reshape, refine and guide legal doctrine they have created. As our Supreme Court summarized in *People v. Pierce* (1964) 61 Cal. 2d 879, 882 [40 Cal. Rptr. 845, 395 P.2d 893], in response to an argument that any departure from common law precedent should be left to legislative action, "In effect the contention is a request that courts abdicate their responsibility for the upkeep of the common law. That upkeep it needs continuously, as this case demonstrates."

The words of the Supreme Court on the role of the courts in a common law system are well suited to our obligation here: " 'The inherent capacity of the common law for growth and change is its most significant feature. Its development has been determined by the social needs of the community which it serves. It is constantly expanding and developing in keeping with advancing civilization and the new conditions and progress of society, and adapting itself to the gradual change of trade, commerce, arts, inventions, and the needs of the country.' . . ."

In short, as the United States Supreme Court has aptly said, 'This flexibility and capacity for growth and adaptation is the peculiar boast and excellence of the common law.' (*Hurtado v. California* (1884) 110 U.S. 516, 530) But that vitality can flourish only so long as the courts remain alert to their obligation and opportunity to change the common law when reason and equity demand it: 'The nature of the common law requires that each time a rule of law is applied, it be carefully scrutinized to make sure that the conditions and needs of the times have not so changed as to make further application of it the instrument of injustice. Whenever an old rule is found unsuited to present conditions or unsound, it should be set aside and a rule declared which is in harmony with those conditions and meets the demands of justice.' (15 Am.Jur.2d, Common Law, § 2, p. 797.) Although the Legislature may of course speak to the subject, in the common law system the primary instruments of this evolution are the courts, adjudicating on a regular basis the rich variety of individual cases brought before them." (*Rodriguez v. Bethlehem Steel Corp.* (1974) 12 Cal. 3d 382, 394[, 115 Cal. Rptr. 765, 525 P.2d 669].)

The creative and regenerative power of the law has been strong enough to break chains imposed by outmoded former decisions. What the courts have power to create, they also have power to modify, reject and re-create in response to the needs of a dynamic society. The exercise of this power is an imperative function of the courts and is the strength of the common law. It cannot be surrendered to legislative inaction.

Prosser puts it this way: "New and nameless torts are being recognized constantly, and the progress of the common law is marked by many cases of first impression, in which the court has struck out boldly to create a new cause of action, where none had been recognized before. . . . The law of torts is anything but static, and the limits of its development are never set. When it becomes clear that the plaintiff's interests are entitled to legal protection against the conduct of the defendant, the mere fact that the claim is novel will not of itself operate as a bar to the remedy." (Prosser, *supra*, at pp. 3-4.)

The possible imposition of liability on the defendant in this case is not a global change in the law. It is but a slight departure from the "morally questionable" rule of nonliability for inaction absent a special relationship. It is one of the predicted "inroads upon the older rule." (REST. 2D TORTS, *supra*, § 314, com. c.) It is a logical extension of Restatement section 327 which imposes liability for negligent interference with a third person who the defendant knows is attempting to render necessary aid. However small it may be, it is a step which should be taken.

We conclude there are sufficient justiciable issues to permit the case to go to trial and therefore reverse.

NOTE

As the cases throughout this Section clearly illustrate, creating an affirmative duty to act by recognizing the existence of some exception to the traditional "no duty" rule is not a particularly difficult task. However, the real conflict in many of these cases, as suggested by *Soldano*, is much more controversial. This involves questions of policy, such as *whether* a duty should even be recognized in the first instance, and, if so, whether the courts or the legislatures should bear the ultimate responsibility for doing so. For example, in *Riss v. City of New York*, 240 N.E.2d 860 (N.Y. 1968), the plaintiff, a young woman, went to the defendant's police department and asked to receive special protection from a rejected suitor who had been terrorizing her for more than six months. The defendant declined to provide such protection, and subsequently the suitor hired a thug who threw lye in the plaintiff's face, permanently disfiguring her. Rejecting the plaintiff's claim that the defendant police owed her an affirmative duty to provide protection for her against a specific threat from a known, specific individual, the court explained that "there is no warrant in judicial tradition or in the proper allocation of the powers of government for the courts, in the absence of legislation, to carve out an area of tort liability for police protection to members of the public." 240 N.E.2d at 861. Do you agree with this statement? Are there any areas in which such a duty should be left to the courts as opposed to the legislature?

PROBLEM

Tourist was killed after being shot by an unknown assailant in the parking lot of a "Motel 5" in which the decedent had been staying as a paying guest. The neighborhood in which the motel was situated had been in decline for years, and this was not the first serious criminal episode to occur in the vicinity of the Motel 5 within the past several months. Tourist had previously booked his reservation in the Motel 5 in reliance upon a "satisfactory" rating that had been assigned to that particular motel in the defendant Motorclub's Tourbook. In a suit for negligence against Motorclub on behalf of the deceased Tourist, how should the court respond to the plaintiff's argument that the defendant automobile club had a "special relationship" with each of its members who relied on information furnished in Motorclub's Tourbook when selecting their travel accommodations whereby the defendant had voluntarily assumed to provide accurate information about various travel accommodations? Does Motorclub even initially owe any duty to its members as to the accuracy of the information contained within its Tourbook ratings? Once the Tourbook has been published, does Motorclub subsequently owe any duty to its members to review and update the accuracy of the information in its Tourbook ratings? If so, for how long, and under what circumstances? Has Motorclub breached any contractual duty owed to Tourist? *See Yanase v. Automobile Club of Southern California*, 260 Cal. Rptr. 513 (Cal. Ct. App. 1989).

F. NEGLIGENT INFLICTION OF (SOLELY) EMOTIONAL INJURIES

One of the most controversial areas of negligence law is duty as it relates to emotional distress injuries sustained by "bystanders" and caused (either directly or indirectly) to a third-party victim. The tort cause of action is generally referred to as "negligent infliction of emotional distress" (*i.e.*, NIED). In this tort, however, the plaintiff has suffered no actual physical harm that can be directly attributed to the defendant's alleged negligence. Instead, the plaintiff seeks to recover for purely emotional distress injuries (which may or may not be accompanied by some physical symptoms or manifestations) that are allegedly caused by the actor's original negligence toward some other person with whom the plaintiff claims some type of close or other special relationship.

At the outset, it must be noted that "negligent infliction of emotional distress" cases can be analyzed from either a "no duty" or a "no proximate cause" perspective. Although considerable debate among courts continues to surround this basic question, the legal distinction between these two very different analytical approaches was nicely explained in *Ballard v. Uribe*, 715 P.2d 624 (Cal. 1986):

> "[A] court's task — in determining 'duty' — is not to decide whether a particular plaintiff's injury was reasonably foreseeable in light of a particular defendant's conduct, but rather to evaluate more generally whether the category of negligent conduct at issue is sufficiently likely to result in the kind of harm experienced that liability may appropriately be imposed on the negligent party.

The jury, by contrast, considers 'foreseeability' in two more focused, fact-specific settings. First, the jury may consider the likelihood or foreseeability of injury in determining whether, in fact, the particular defendant's conduct was negligent in the first place. Second, foreseeability may be relevant to the jury's determination of whether the defendant's negligence was a proximate or legal cause of the plaintiff's injury."

715 P.2d at 628 n.6.

DZIOKONSKI v. BABINEAU
380 N.E.2d 1295 (Mass. 1978)

WILKINS, J.

These appeals require us to reexamine the question whether a person who negligently causes emotional distress which leads to physical injuries may be liable for those injuries even if the injured person neither was threatened with nor sustained any direct physical injury. At the heart of the plaintiffs' claims is the argument that this court should abandon the so called "impact" rule of *Spade v. Lynn & Boston R.R.*, 168 Mass. 285, 290 (1897), which denies recovery for physical injuries arising solely from negligently caused mental distress. We agree that the rule of the *Spade* case should be abandoned. Our inquiry does not cease at that point, however, because we must determine what new limits of liability are appropriate and how those limits affect the plaintiffs' decedents, parents of a child alleged to have been injured by the defendants' negligence.

On October 24, 1973, Norma Dziokonski, a minor, alighted from a motor vehicle, used as a school bus, on Route 117 in Lancaster. That motor vehicle was owned by the defendant Pelletier and operated by the defendant Kroll. A motor vehicle owned and operated by the defendant Babineau struck Norma as she was crossing the road. The complaints allege the negligence of each defendant on various grounds.

The complaint filed by the administratrix of the estate of Lorraine Dziokonski (Mrs. Dziokonski) alleges that Mrs. Dziokonski was the mother of Norma and that she "lived in the immediate vicinity of the accident, went to the scene of the accident and witnessed her daughter lying injured on the ground." Mrs. Dziokonski "suffered physical and emotional shock, distress and anguish as a result of the injury to her daughter and died while she was a passenger in the ambulance that was driving her daughter to the hospital." This complaint alleges one count for wrongful death and one count for conscious suffering against each of the three defendants.

The complaint filed by the administratrix of the estate of Anthony Dziokonski (Mr. Dziokonski) alleged the facts previously set forth and added that he was the father of Norma and the husband of Mrs. Dziokonski. Mr. Dziokonski "suffered an aggravated gastric ulcer, a coronary occlusion, physical and emotional shock, distress and anguish as a result of the injury to his daughter and the death of his wife and his death was caused thereby." This complaint similarly alleged a count for wrongful death and one count for conscious suffering against each of the three defendants.

The Spade Case.

We start with an analysis of *Spade* which announced a principle of tort law that has been limited and refined by our subsequent decisions but not heretofore abandoned. Margaret Spade had been a passenger on a crowded car of the Lynn & Boston Railroad Company late one Saturday night in February, 1895. She was so frightened by the negligent conduct of an employee of the defendant in removing an unruly passenger from the car that she sustained emotional shock and consequent physical injury. The trial judge instructed the jury that, when physical injury results from fear or nervous shock, "there may be a recovery for that bodily injury, and for all the pain, mental or otherwise, which may arise out of that bodily injury." The jury returned a verdict for Mrs. Spade, but this court held that the judge's charge misstated the law.

We acknowledged that fright might cause physical injury and that "it is hard on principle" to say why there should not be recovery even for the mental suffering caused by a defendant's negligence. The court concluded, however, that "in practice it is impossible satisfactorily to administer any other rule." We noted that recovery for fright or distress of mind alone is barred and, that being so, there can be no recovery for physical injuries caused solely by mental disturbance. It was said to be unreasonable to hold persons bound to anticipate and guard against fright and its consequences and thought that a contrary rule would "open a wide door for unjust claims."

Subsequent Treatment of the Spade Rule in Massachusetts.

In *Smith v. Postal Tel. Cable Co.*, 174 Mass. 576, 577-78 (1899), which applied the *Spade* rule to a case involving a claim of gross negligence, Chief Justice Holmes, speaking for the court, said that the point decided in the *Spade* case "is not put as a logical deduction from the general principles of liability in tort, but as a limitation of those principles upon purely practical grounds." Later, he described the *Spade* rule as "an arbitrary exception, based upon a notion of what is practicable." *Homans v. Boston Elevated Ry.*, 180 Mass. 456, 457 (1902).

Consistently and from its inception, the Spade rule has not been applied to deny recovery where immediate physical injuries result from negligently induced fright or emotional shock. Thus, recovery has been allowed "[w]hen the fright reasonably induces action which results in external injury." *Cameron v. New England Tel. & Tel. Co.*, 182 Mass. 310, 312 (1902) (defendant's negligent blasting caused the plaintiff to faint and sustain physical harm). *Freedman v. Eastern Mass. St. Ry.*, 299 Mass. 246, 250 (1938) (plaintiff's shoulder injured when she jumped to escape impending danger). *Gannon v. New York, N.H. & H.R.R.*, 173 Mass. 40 (1899) (physical injuries sustained when plaintiff moved in fright to avoid injury).

Moreover, recovery for emotionally based physical injuries, sometimes described as "parasitic claims," has been allowed in tort cases founded on traditional negligent impact. *Driscoll v. Gaffey*, 207 Mass. 102, 105, 107 (1910). Thus, where the plaintiff sustained direct physical injuries as a result of the defendant's negligence and the plaintiff also sustained paralysis, perhaps resulting solely from nervous shock, we did not require the plaintiff to prove that the nervous shock or paralysis was a consequence of the direct physical injuries. *Homans v. Boston Elevated Ry.*, 180 Mass. 456, 458 (1902). We note that allowing recovery for emotionally based physical injuries unrelated to the physical consequences of the negligently caused impact also presents the threat of "unjust claims" or, perhaps more exactly, the threat of exaggerated claims.

We have never applied the *Spade* rule to bar recovery for intentionally caused emotional distress. The *Spade* opinion itself recognized that the result might be different if the defendant's conduct had been intentional and not negligent. We left that question open in *Smith v. Postal Tel. Cable Co.*, 174 Mass. 576, 578 (1899), and it so remained until 1971, when we decided *George v. Jordan Marsh Co.*, 359 Mass. 244 (1971).

The *George* case involved allegations that, in their debt collection practices, the defendants intentionally caused emotional distress to the plaintiff and, as a result, her health deteriorated and she suffered two heart attacks. We held that "one who, without a privilege to do so, by extreme and outrageous conduct intentionally causes severe emotional distress to another, with bodily harm resulting from such distress, is subject to liability for such emotional distress and bodily harm." We expressly left open the question now before us, whether there could be liability for negligent conduct causing emotional distress resulting in bodily injury.

The question of liability for intentionally or recklessly caused severe emotional distress in the absence of bodily harm came before us in *Agis v. Howard Johnson Co.*, 371 Mass. 140 (1976). There, we held that a complaint alleging extreme, outrageous, and unprivileged conduct by the defendant stated a cause of action in favor of both the female plaintiff who sustained emotional distress but no bodily harm and her husband for loss of consortium. We rejected arguments that we should deny recovery for emotional distress where there is no physical injury because of the insurmountable difficulties of proof and the danger of fraudulent or frivolous claims. Although we recognized these problems, we rejected them as an absolute bar in all such cases and concluded that these were proper matters for consideration by the trier of fact in the adversary, trial process.

Although many industrial States initially required some impact as a basis for liability for physical harm resulting from fright, that rule has been abandoned in more recent times to the point where it has been said that "the courts which deny all remedy in such cases are fighting a rearguard action." W. PROSSER, TORTS § 54, at 333 (4th ed. 1971). As we have already indicated, we think the *Spade* rule should be abandoned. The threat of fraudulent claims cannot alone justify the denial of recovery in all cases. Whether a plaintiff's injuries were a reasonably foreseeable consequence of the defendant's negligence and whether the defendant caused those injuries are best left to determination in the normal manner before the trier of fact.

Recovery for Injuries Arising from Concern over Harm to Another.

The abandonment of the *Spade* rule is only the beginning in the process of determining whether the complaints in these cases state valid claims for relief. The typical case involving physical harm resulting from emotional distress concerns a person who was put in fear for his own safety as a result of alleged negligence of the defendant. Here, neither Mr. nor Mrs. Dziokonski was threatened with direct, contemporaneous injury as a result of the negligence of any defendant. Thus, we must consider the extent to which any defendant in this case may be held liable to the father or the mother, each of whom sustained physical injuries as a result of emotional distress over injuries incurred by their child.

The weight of authority in this country would deny recovery in these cases. W. PROSSER, TORTS § 54, at 333 (4th ed. 1971). Thus, as we fall back from the *Spade* rule, we could find comfort in numbers in denying recovery in these cases. We conclude, however, that we should not adopt a rule which absolutely denies recovery to every parent for whatever negligently caused, emotionally based physical injuries result from his concern over the safety of or injury to his injured child.

The arguments against imposing liability for a parent's injuries from shock and fear for his child have been stated clearly and forcefully in numerous opinions. *See, e.g., Tobin v. Grossman*, 24 N.Y.2d 609, 615-19 (1969); *Amaya v. Home Ice, Fuel & Supply Co.*, 59 Cal. 2d 295 (1963). The reasons advanced for not permitting recovery are principally that (1) there is still a difficulty of proof of causation which has not been mitigated by any change in technology or medical science, (2) no logical justification exists for limiting recovery solely to parents who are affected physically by fear for the safety of an injured child, and (3) the extension of liability will impose an inordinate burden on defendants. In short, under this view, liability should be denied for injuries from shock and fear for another's safety regardless of (a) the relationship of the plaintiff to the accident victim, (b) the plaintiff's proximity to the accident, or (c) whether the plaintiff observed either the accident or its immediate consequences.

Until 1968, the nearly unanimous weight of authority in this country denied recovery for emotionally based physical injuries resulting from concern for the safety of another where the plaintiff was not himself threatened with contemporaneous injury. W. PROSSER, TORTS § 54, at 334 (4th ed. 1971). There was support for recovery where the plaintiff was himself threatened with direct bodily harm because of the defendant's conduct. This rule, known as the zone of danger test, is expressed in RESTATEMENT (SECOND) OF TORTS § 313(2) (1965). It denies recovery for bodily harm "caused by emotional distress arising solely from harm or peril to a third person, unless the negligence of the actor has otherwise created an unreasonable risk of bodily harm to the [plaintiff]." This Restatement rule was recommended with reluctance by the Reporter (Dean Prosser) and the advisers (RESTATEMENT [SECOND] OF TORTS 9-11 [Tent. Draft No. 5, 1960]), but the recommendation was thought to be compelled by the absence of then recent authority in support of a contrary view. As a result of adding § 313 (2), a caveat appearing in the first Restatement of Torts was deleted. That caveat had left open the question whether a person might be liable "to the parent or spouse who witnesses the peril or harm of the child or spouse and thereby suffers anxiety or shock" causing bodily harm to the parent or spouse. RESTATEMENT OF TORTS § 313, at 851 (1934).

The "zone of danger" rule has something to commend it as a measure of the limits of liability. It permits a relatively easy determination of the persons who might recover for emotionally caused bodily injury by including only those to whom contemporaneous bodily harm of some sort might reasonably have been foreseen. It is arguably reasonable to impose liability for the physical consequences of emotional distress where the defendant's negligent conduct might have caused physical injury by direct impact but did not. The problem with the zone of danger rule, however, is that it is an inadequate measure of the reasonable foreseeability of the possibility of physical injury resulting from a parent's anxiety arising from harm to his child. The reasonable foreseeability of such a physical injury to a parent does not turn on whether that parent was or was not a reasonable prospect for a contemporaneous injury because of the defendant's negligent conduct. Although the zone of danger rule tends to produce more reasonable results than the *Spade* rule and provides a means of limiting the scope of a defendant's liability, it lacks strong logical support.

In 1968, the Supreme Court of California, by a divided court (four to three), broke the solid ranks, overruled its decision in *Amaya v. Home Ice, Fuel & Supply Co.*, 59 Cal. 2d 295 (1963), and held that a cause of action was properly stated on behalf of a mother, in no danger herself, who witnessed her minor daughter's death in a motor vehicle accident allegedly caused by the defendant's negligence, and who sustained emotional disturbance and shock to her nervous system which caused her physical and mental pain and suffering. *Dillon v. Legg*, 68 Cal. 2d 728 (1968). An intermediate appellate court in California has since applied the reasoning of *Dillon v. Legg* to permit recovery by a mother who came on the scene of the accident but did not witness it. *Archibald v. Braverman*, 275 Cal. App. 2d 253 (1969). That court said, "Manifestly, the shock of seeing a child severely injured immediately after the tortious event may be just as profound as that experienced in witnessing the accident itself."

Some tendency toward allowing recovery seems to be developing. The Supreme Court of Rhode Island has reached the same conclusion as the California Supreme Court in *Dillon v. Legg*, on substantially similar facts. *D'Ambra v. United States*, 114 R.I. 643 (1975). The results in these cases have the general support of commentators. *See* 2 F. HARPER & F. JAMES, TORTS § 18.4, at 1035-39

(1956). In *Leong v. Takasaki*, 55 Haw. 398, 399 (1974), the Supreme Court of Hawaii held that a complaint stated a cause of action "for nervous shock and psychic injuries suffered without accompanying physical impact or resulting physical consequences" when the plaintiff, a ten-year old boy, witnessed from a distance of several feet the death of his stepfather's mother who was struck by a motor vehicle driven by the defendant. In *Toms v. McConnell*, 45 Mich. App. 647 (1973), the Michigan Court of Appeals held that a mother alleged a cause of action where, from outside the zone of danger, she saw her daughter struck by the defendant's vehicle after her daughter alighted from a school bus and, as a result, the mother sustained significant depression. The Supreme Court of Washington has construed a statute as authorizing recovery by a parent for mental anguish in cases involving the wrongful death of or injury to a child. *Wilson v. Lund*, 80 Wash. 2d 91 (1971).

It is not argued seriously here, nor has it been regularly a basis for decisions denying liability, that the threat of fraudulent claims requires the adoption of a rule denying recovery to a parent who sustains physical harm from distress over peril to his child. The facts of cases of this character involve tortious injury to the child and substantial physical consequences to the parent. The tortfeasor is not confronted with the results of a fleeting instance of fear or excitement of which he might be unaware and against which he would be unable to present a defense. The fact that some claims might be manufactured or improperly expanded cannot justify the wholesale rejection of all claims. Of course, there is no suggestion that the physical injuries to Mr. and Mrs. Dziokonski were contrived. We have rejected the idea that tort liability in particular classes of cases must be denied because of the threat of fraud. We have chosen to leave the detection of fraud and collusion to the adversary process.

The fact that the causal connection between a parent's emotional response to peril to his child and the parent's resulting physical injuries is difficult to prove or disprove cannot justify denying all recovery. No one asserts, and we have never claimed, that physical reactions to emotional responses do not occur. We have recognized liability for exclusively emotional reactions to tortious conduct in particular circumstances (*see, e.g., Agis v. Howard Johnson Co.*, 371 Mass. 140 [1976]), and, in other instances, we have recognized liability for bodily harm resulting from emotional distress (*George v. Jordan Marsh Co.*, 359 Mass. 244 [1971]). We have upheld claims of the character involved here, as so called "parasitic" claims, where they are accompanied by a traditional form of tortious injury. *See Homans v. Boston Elevated Ry.*, 180 Mass. 456, 457-58 (1902). Indeed, certain elements of pain and suffering, recoverable in almost all personal injury actions, may be as tenuous causally as the harm for which recovery is sought in these cases.

The scope of duty in tort is often defined in terms of the reasonable foreseeability of the harm to the plaintiff resulting from the defendant's negligent conduct. Sometimes, liability is predicated on a judicial characterization that the defendant owed a duty to the plaintiff, or that the defendant's negligence was the proximate cause of the plaintiff's injury, or that the defendant is liable for the natural and probable consequences of his conduct. Each of these characterizations is actually a conclusion and is not a helpful guide to arriving at the proper answer in a given set of circumstances. We think reasonable foreseeability is a proper starting point in determining whether an actor is to be liable for the consequences of his negligence. Measured by this standard, it is clear that it is reasonably foreseeable that, if one negligently operates a motor vehicle so as to injure a person, there will be one or more persons sufficiently attached emotionally to the injured person that he or they will be affected. [The] problem, however, is that the class of persons vicariously affected by the tortfeasor's conduct may be large. This concern has prompted many courts to deny all liability. They perceive no logical place at which to impose reasonable limits on the scope of a defendant's liability without going to the full extent of reasonable foreseeability, which would produce, as they see it, a risk of liability disproportionate to the defendant's culpability. The result has been that, as a matter of policy, courts have decided not to give full effect to reasonable foreseeability and have adopted limitations on liability, such as the impact rule or the zone of danger rule.

Every effort must be made to avoid arbitrary lines which "unnecessarily produce incongruous and indefensible results." The focus should be on underlying principles. In cases of this character, there must be both a substantial physical injury and proof that the injury was caused by the defendant's negligence. Beyond this, the determination whether there should be liability for the injury sustained depends on a number of factors, such as where, when, and how the injury, to the third person entered into the consciousness of the claimant, and what degree there was of familial or other relationship between the claimant and the third person. It does not matter in practice whether these factors are regarded as policy considerations imposing limitations on the scope of reasonable foreseeability, or as factors bearing on the determination of reasonable foreseeability itself. The fact is that, in cases of this character, such factors are relevant in measuring the limits of liability for emotionally based injuries resulting from a defendant's negligence. In some instances, it will be clear that the question is properly one for the trier of fact, while in others the claim will fall outside the range of circumstances within which there may be liability.

With these considerations in mind, we conclude that the allegations concerning a parent who sustains substantial physical harm as a result of severe mental distress over some peril or harm to his minor child caused by the defendant's negligence state a claim for which relief might be granted, where the parent either witnesses the accident or soon comes on the scene while the child is still there. . . .

On this premise, we think it clear that the complaint concerning Mrs. Dziokonski states a claim which withstands a motion to dismiss. The allegations of the complaint concerning Mr. Dziokonski, however, are far more indefinite. We do not know where, when, or how Mr. Dziokonski came to know of the injury to his daughter and the death of his wife. We do not have a clear indication of the relationship of his discovery of this information to any mental distress and physical injury he sustained. We cannot say, as matter of law, that, within the scope of the allegations of the complaint concerning Mr. Dziokonski, there are no circumstances which could conceivably justify recovery. Consequently, we conclude that neither of the complaints should be dismissed for failure to state a claim.

Judgments reversed.

QUIRICO, J. (dissenting).

Although I am in full agreement with the court in its conclusion that *Spade* should be overruled, I do not believe that liability should be extended to the degree described by the court in its opinion here. Therefore, I dissent from the reversal of the dismissal of the complaints of the two plaintiffs.

It is my view that liability for negligently causing emotional distress that results in physical injury should be extended as far as would be allowed by the rule of the RESTATEMENT (SECOND) OF TORTS § 313 (1965). That section, while allowing recovery under some circumstances, provides that no recovery may be had for "illness or bodily harm of another which is caused by emotional distress arising solely from harm or peril to a third person, unless the negligence of the actor has otherwise created an unreasonable risk of bodily harm to the other." I would agree also that if, contrary to the facts in the present cases, a parent had been present at the time of the alleged negligent conduct which caused the injury, and such parent had suffered emotional distress and resulting physical injury, then he or she should recover regardless of whether they were within the zone of risk of bodily harm created by the negligent act. *Dillon v. Legg*, 68 Cal. 2d 728, 730-31 (1968); *D'Ambra v. United States*, 114 R.I. 643, 657-58 (1975); W. PROSSER, TORTS § 54, at 334-35 (4th ed. 1971). I do not believe, however, that liability should be extended further to allow recovery by a parent who comes on the scene of an accident after an injury has occurred to the child but before the child is removed. It is my opinion that we should not prescribe rules that allow or deny recovery by the parent on the basis of the speed and efficiency of an ambulance team in responding to an accident call, or on the haste with which a parent can be notified and rushed to the accident scene.

NOTES

1. The "Impact Rule." As discussed in *Dziokonski*, the "impact rule" (referred to as the "*Spade*" rule in Massachusetts, after its namesake, *Spade v. Lynn & Boston R.R.*, 168 Mass. 285 (1897)), denies recovery for *all* emotional distress injuries received by *anyone* who was not also *physically impacted* by the actor's original negligence. The reasons most often given for this rule are set forth in the main opinion in *Dziokonski*. The legal effect of the "impact rule" is to deny recovery by even the closest relatives of the victim of a negligently inflicted

injury in any case where they merely witnessed or (as in *Dziokonski*) where they learned nearly contemporaneously of the victim's injury, but were not themselves physically harmed by the actor's negligence. As indicated by *Dziokonski*, most (although not all) courts have abandoned the "impact rule." *See, e.g., Tobin v. Grossman*, 24 N.Y.2d 609 (1969).

2. Under the "impact rule," the typical inquiry involves whether a particular "impact" was sufficient to support the imposition of a duty owed to the victim of the impact. For example, does the "impact rule" require some actual physical injury to the plaintiff, or is a mere "touching" that causes no actual physical harm sufficient?

3. The "Zone of Impact Rule." *Dziokonski* also discusses the "zone of impact" rule that permits recovery for purely emotional distress injuries to persons who, although *not* themselves *physically impacted* by the actor's negligent conduct toward a third-person, are so closely situated to the accident scene (*i.e.,* within the "zone of impact") that they *could* have been physically impacted. The rationale is that such persons are just as foreseeable victims of the actor's negligence as those who are, in fact, actually impacted . Thus, under this rule there is no legal justification for denying recovery to such closely-situated (*i.e.,* foreseeable) bystanders.

The "zone of impact" rule expands the scope of potential liability, but it still does not permit recovery for emotional distress injuries sustained by those persons (even though close relatives as in *Dziokonski*) who are not physically situated within close proximity to the actual scene of the victim's injury. Courts often become occupied with trying to delineate the precise limits of the permissible "zone" of impact.

Does it make any sense to permit recovery under the "zone of impact" rule to a close relative who happened to be situated physically close enough to the defendant's victim to fall within the "zone of impact," but who did not contemporaneously learn of the injury to the victim until after the accident? How is this person's emotional distress any greater than the distress experienced by the parents in *Dziokonski*?

4. The "*Dillon* Rule." Dissatisfied with the inconsistent results produced under the "impact" rule and the "zone of impact" rule, the California Supreme Court in *Dillon v. Legg*, 441 P. 2d 912 (Cal. 1968), articulated a new "rule" relative to the recovery of emotional distress injuries by bystanders in negligent infliction cases. Instead of relying solely upon the occurrence of a physical impact (*i.e.,* the "impact" rule) or the physical location of the bystander relative to the location of the injured victim (*i.e.,* the "zone of impact" rule), the court in *Dillon* adopted a test for the imposition of duty that was determined simply by the foreseeability of the bystander's emotional distress injury under the circumstances. To aid courts in identifying the types of situations most likely to produce foreseeable emotional distress injuries, *Dillon* identified three distinct "factors" to be taken into consideration in determining whether a duty was owed in a given case. Specifically, these factors included:

(1) whether plaintiff [the bystander] was located near the scene of the accident (as contrasted with one who was a distance away from it);

(2) whether the shock resulted from a direct emotional impact upon plaintiff from the sensory and contemporaneous observance of the accident (as contrasted with learning of the accident from others after its occurrence); and

(3) whether plaintiff and the victim were closely related (as contrasted with the absence of any relationship or the presence of only a distant relationship).

Although the *Dillon* factors were merely intended as guidelines to be used in determining the ultimate issue: foreseeability of emotional distress under the specific circumstances involved, the so-called *Dillon* test, by which it is now often referred to, has taken on a "life" of its own. Some courts have ignored the *Dillon* factors altogether, or applied them only occasionally, as needed to justify a particular desired result. Other courts have treated them as a rigid set of requirements for the imposition of a duty in bystander negligent infliction of emotional distress cases. In any event, the flexibility that was intended by *Dillon* has produced no less certainty and predictability than its predecessor rules as the following case illustrates.

THING v. La CHUSA
771 P.2d 814 (Cal. 1989)

EAGLESON, J.

The narrow issue presented by the parties in this case is whether the Court of Appeals correctly held that a mother who did not witness an accident in which an automobile struck and injured her child may recover damages from the negligent driver for the emotional distress she suffered when she arrived at the accident scene. The more important question this issue poses for the court, however, is whether the "guidelines" enunciated by this court in *Dillon v. Legg* (1968) 68 Cal. 2d 728[, 69 Cal. Rptr. 72, 441 P.2d 912] are adequate, or if they should be refined to create greater certainty in this area of the law.

Although terms of convenience identify the cause of action here as one for negligent infliction of emotional distress (NIED) and the plaintiff as a "bystander" rather than a "direct victim," the common law tort giving rise to plaintiff's claim is negligence. *(Dillon v. Legg, supra.)* It is in that context that we consider the appropriate application of the concept of "duty" in an area that has long divided this court — recognition of the right of persons, whose only injury is emotional distress, to recover damages when that distress is caused by knowledge of the injury to a third person caused by the defendant's negligence. Although we again find ourselves divided, we shall resolve some of the uncertainty over the parameters of the NIED action, uncertainty that has troubled lower courts, litigants, and, of course, insurers.

Upon doing so, we shall conclude that the societal benefits of certainty in the law, as well as traditional concepts of tort law, dictate limitation of bystander recovery of damages for emotional distress. In the absence of physical injury or impact to the plaintiff himself, damages for emotional distress should be recoverable only if the plaintiff: (1) is closely related to the injury victim, (2) is present at the scene of the injury-producing event at the time it occurs and is then aware that it is causing injury to the victim and, (3) as a result suffers emotional distress beyond that which would be anticipated in a disinterested witness.

Background

On December 8, 1980, John Thing, a minor, was injured when struck by an automobile operated by defendant James V. La Chusa. His mother, plaintiff Maria Thing, was nearby, but neither saw nor heard the accident. She became aware of the injury to her son when told by a daughter that John had been struck by a car. She rushed to the scene where she saw her bloody and unconscious child, who she believed was dead, lying in the roadway. Maria sued defendants, alleging that she suffered great emotional disturbance, shock, and injury to her nervous system as a result of these events, and that the injury to John and emotional distress she suffered were proximately caused by defendants' negligence.

The trial court granted defendants' motion for summary judgment, ruling that, as a matter of law, Maria could not establish a claim for negligent infliction of emotional distress because she did not contemporaneously and sensorily perceive the accident. Although prior decisions applying the guidelines suggested by this court in *Dillon* compelled the ruling of the trial court, the Court of Appeal reversed the judgment dismissing Maria's claim after considering the decision of this court in *Ochoa v. Superior Court* (1985) 39 Cal. 3d 159[, 216 Cal. Rptr. 661, 703 P.2d 1]. The Court of Appeals reasoned that while Maria's argument, premised on *Molien v. Kaiser Foundation Hospitals* (1980) 27 Cal. 3d 916[, 167 Cal. Rptr. 831, 616 P.2d 813], that she was a direct victim of La Chusa's negligence, did not afford a basis for recovery, contemporaneous awareness of a sudden occurrence causing injury to her child was not a prerequisite to recovery under *Dillon*. . . .

We granted review to consider whether *Ochoa* supports the holding of the Court of Appeal. We here also further define and circumscribe the circumstances in which the right to such recovery exists. To do so it is once again necessary to return to basic principles of tort law. . . .

In [*Dillon v. Legg*], the issue was limited. The mother and sister of a deceased infant each sought damages for "great emotional disturbance and shock and injury to her nervous system" which had caused them great mental pain and suffering. Allegedly these injuries were caused by witnessing the defendant's negligently operated vehicle collide with and roll over the infant as she lawfully crossed a street. The mother was not herself endangered by the defendant's conduct. The sister may have been. The trial court had therefore granted the defendant's motion for judgment on the pleadings as to the mother, but had denied it with respect to the sister of the decedent. Faced with the incongruous result demanded by the "zone of danger" rule which denied recovery for emotional distress and consequent physical injury unless the plaintiff himself had been threatened with injury, the court overruled *Amaya v. Home Ice, Fuel & Supply Co.*, 59 Cal. 2d 295, 29 Cal. Rptr. 33, 379 P.2d 513 (1963).

Reexamining the concept of "duty" as applicable to the *Dillon* facts, the court now rejected the argument that the possibility of fraudulent claims justified denial of recovery, at least insofar as a mother who sees her child killed is concerned, as "no one can seriously question that fear or grief for one's child is as likely to cause physical injury as concern over one's own well-being." The court held instead that the right to recover should be determined by application of "the neutral principles of foreseeability, proximate cause and consequential injury that generally govern tort law."

The difficulty in defining the limits on recovery anticipated by the *Amaya* court was rejected as a basis for denying recovery, but the court did recognize that "to limit the otherwise potentially infinite liability which would follow every negligent act, the law of torts holds defendant amenable only for injuries to others which to defendant at the time were reasonably foreseeable." Thus, while the court indicated that foreseeability of the injury was to be the primary consideration in finding duty, it simultaneously recognized that policy considerations mandated that infinite liability be avoided by restrictions that would somehow narrow the class of potential plaintiffs. But the test limiting liability was itself amorphous.

In adopting foreseeability of the injury as the basis of a negligent actor's duty, the *Dillon* court identified the risks that could give rise to that duty as both physical impact and emotional disturbance brought on by the conduct. Having done so, the *Dillon* court conceded: "We cannot now predetermine defendant's obligation in every situation by a fixed category; no immutable rule can establish the extent of that obligation for every circumstance of the future." In an effort to give some initial definition to this newly approved expansion of the cause of action for NIED the court enunciated "guidelines" that suggested a limitation on the action to circumstances like those in the case before it.

We note, first, that we deal here with a case in which plaintiff suffered a shock which resulted in physical injury and we confine our ruling to that case. In determining, in such a case, whether defendant should reasonably foresee the injury to plaintiff [mother], or in other terminology, whether defendant owes plaintiff a duty of due care, the courts will take into account such factors as the following: (1) Whether plaintiff was located near the scene of the accident as contrasted with one who was a distance away from it. (2) Whether the shock resulted from a direct emotional impact upon plaintiff from the sensory and contemporaneous observance of the accident, as contrasted with learning of the accident from others after its occurrence. (3) Whether plaintiff and the victim were closely related, as contrasted with an absence of any relationship or the presence of only a distant relationship.

The evaluation of these factors will indicate the *degree* of the defendant's foreseeability; obviously defendant is more likely to foresee that a mother who observes an accident affecting her child will suffer harm than to foretell that a stranger witness will do so. Similarly, the degree of foreseeability of the third person's injury is far greater in the case of his contemporaneous observance of the accident than that in which he subsequently learns of it. The defendant is more likely to foresee that shock to the nearby, witnessing mother will cause physical harm than to anticipate that someone distant from the accident will suffer more than a temporary emotional reaction. All of these elements, of course, shade into each other; the fixing of the obligation, intimately tied into the facts, depends upon each case.

In light of these factors the court will determine whether the accident and harm was *reasonably* foreseeable. Such reasonable foreseeability does not turn on whether the particular [defendant] as an individual would have in actuality foreseen the exact accident and loss; it contemplates that *courts, on a case-to-case basis, analyzing all the circumstances, will decide what the ordinary man under such circumstances should reasonably have foreseen*. The courts thus mark out the areas of liability, excluding the remote and unexpected.

The *Dillon* court anticipated and accepted uncertainty in the short term in application of its holding, but was confident that the boundaries of this NIED action could be drawn in future cases. In sum, as former Justice Potter Stewart once suggested with reference to that undefinable category of materials that are obscene, the *Dillon* court was satisfied that trial and appellate courts would be able to determine the existence of a duty because the court would know it when it saw it. Underscoring the questionable validity of that assumption, however, was the obvious and unaddressed problem that the injured party, the negligent tortfeasor, their insurers, and their attorneys had no means short of suit by which to determine if a duty such as to impose liability for damages would be found in cases other than those that were "on all fours" with *Dillon*. Thus, the only thing that was foreseeable from the *Dillon* decision was the uncertainty that continues to this time as to the parameters of the third party NIED action.

Post-Dillon Extension

The expectation of the *Dillon* majority that the parameters of the tort would be further defined in future cases has not been fulfilled. Instead, subsequent decisions of the Courts of Appeal and this court, have created more uncertainty. And, just as the "zone of danger" limitation was abandoned in *Dillon* as an arbitrary restriction on recovery, the *Dillon* guidelines have been relaxed on grounds that they, too, created arbitrary limitations on recovery. Little consideration has been given in post-*Dillon* decisions to the importance of avoiding the limitless exposure to liability that the pure foreseeability test of "duty" would create and towards which these decisions have moved. . . .

[For example,] [b]oth the physical harm and accident or sudden occurrence elements were eliminated, however, in *Molien v. Kaiser Foundation Hospitals, supra,* 27 Cal. 3d 916, at least as to those plaintiffs who could claim to be "direct victims" of the defendant's negligence. The court held in *Molien* that a defendant hospital and doctor owed a duty directly to the husband of a patient who had been diagnosed erroneously as having syphilis, and had been told to so advise the husband in order that he could receive testing and, if necessary, treatment.

In finding the existence of a duty to the husband of the patient, the court reasoned that the risk of harm to the husband was reasonably foreseeable, and that the tortious conduct was directed to him as well as the patient. (*Molien v. Kaiser Foundation Hospitals, supra,* 27 Cal. 3d 916, 922.) The status of the plaintiff mother in *Dillon* was distinguished as she suffered her injury solely as a "percipient witness" to the infliction of injury on another. She was therefore a "bystander" rather than a "direct victim." . . .

Molien neither established criteria for characterizing a plaintiff as a "direct" victim, nor explained the justification for permitting "direct" victims to recover when "bystander" plaintiffs could not. The immediate effect of the decision, however, was to permit some persons who had no prior relationship with the defendant that gave rise to a duty, who did not suffer physical injury as a result of emotional distress, who did not observe the negligent conduct, and who had not been at or near the scene of the negligent act to recover for emotional distress on a pure foreseeability-of-the-injury basis. The limitations on recovery for emotional distress that had been suggested in the *Dillon* "guidelines" were not applicable to "direct" victims of a defendant's negligence. . . .

Clarification of the Right to Recover for NIED

Not surprisingly, this "case-to-case" or ad hoc approach to development of the law that misled the Court of Appeal in this case has not only produced inconsistent rulings in the lower courts, but has provoked considerable critical comment by scholars who attempt to reconcile the cases.

Proposals to eliminate the arbitrary results of the proliferating, inconsistent and often conflicting *Dillon* progeny include the suggestion that recovery be allowed in any case in which recovery for physical injury is permitted. Another would limit recovery to the close-relatives class contemplated by *Dillon*, but allow recovery whenever mental distress to the plaintiff was foreseeable. At the other extreme, respondent here and amicus curiae Association for California Tort Reform argue, in essence, that the *Dillon* "guidelines" should be recognized as substantive limitations or elements of the tort.

[In our view, no] policy supports extension of the right to recover for NIED to a larger class of plaintiffs. Emotional distress is an intangible condition experienced by most persons, even absent negligence, at some time during their lives. Close relatives suffer serious, even debilitating, emotional reactions to the injury, death, serious illness, and evident suffering of loved ones. These reactions occur regardless of the cause of the loved one's illness, injury, or death. That relatives will have severe emotional distress is an unavoidable aspect of the "human condition." The emotional distress for which monetary damages may be recovered, however, ought not to be that form of acute emotional distress or the transient emotional reaction to the occasional gruesome or horrible incident to which every person may potentially be exposed in an industrial and sometimes violent society. Regardless of the depth of feeling or the resultant physical or mental illness that results from witnessing violent events, persons unrelated to those injured or killed may not now recover for such emotional upheaval even if negligently caused. Close relatives who witness the accidental injury or death of a loved one and suffer emotional trauma may not recover when the loved one's conduct was the cause of that emotional trauma. The overwhelming majority of "emotional distress" which we endure, therefore, is not compensable.

Unlike an award of damages for intentionally caused emotional distress which is punitive, the award for NIED simply reflects society's belief that a negligent actor bears some responsibility for the effect of his conduct on persons other than those who suffer physical injury. In identifying those persons and the circumstances in which the defendant will be held to redress the injury, it is appropriate to restrict recovery to those persons who will suffer an emotional impact beyond the impact that can be anticipated whenever one learns that a relative is injured, or dies, or the emotion felt by a "disinterested" witness. The class of potential plaintiffs should be limited to those who because of their relationship suffer the greatest emotional distress. When the right to recover is limited in this manner, the liability bears a reasonable relationship to the culpability of the negligent defendant.

The elements which justify and simultaneously limit an award of damages for emotional distress caused by awareness of the negligent infliction of injury to a close relative are those noted in *Ochoa* — the traumatic emotional effect on the plaintiff who contemporaneously observes both the event or conduct that causes serious injury to a close relative and the injury itself. Even if it is "foreseeable" that persons other than closely related percipient witnesses may suffer emotional distress, this fact does not justify the imposition of what threatens to become unlimited liability for emotional distress on a defendant whose conduct is simply negligent. Nor does such abstract "foreseeability" warrant continued reliance on the assumption that the limits of liability will become any clearer if lower courts are permitted to continue approaching the issue on a "case-to-case" basis some 20 years after *Dillon*.

We conclude, therefore, that a plaintiff may recover damages for emotional distress caused by observing the negligently inflicted injury of a third person if, but only if, said plaintiff: (1) is closely related to the injury victim; (2) is present at the scene of the injury-producing event at the time it occurs and is then aware that it is causing injury to the victim; and (3) as a result suffers serious emotional distress — a reaction beyond that which would be anticipated in a disinterested witness and which is not an abnormal response to the circumstances.

These factors were present in *Ochoa* and each of this court's prior decisions upholding recovery for NIED.

The dictum in *Ochoa* suggesting that the factors noted in the *Dillon* guidelines are not essential in determining whether a plaintiff is a foreseeable victim of defendant's negligence should not be relied on. The merely negligent actor does not owe a duty the law will recognize to make monetary amends to all persons who may have suffered emotional distress on viewing or learning about the injurious consequences of his conduct. To the extent they are inconsistent with this conclusion, *Nazaroff v. Superior Court, supra,* 80 Cal. App. 3d 553, and *Archibald v. Braverman, supra,* 275 Cal. App. 2d 253, are disapproved. Experience has shown that, contrary to the expectation of the *Dillon* majority, and with apology to Bernard Witkin, there are clear judicial days on which a court can foresee forever and thus determine liability but none on which that foresight alone provides a socially and judicially acceptable limit on recovery of damages for that injury.

The undisputed facts establish that plaintiff was not present at the scene of the accident in which her son was injured. She did not observe defendant's conduct and was not aware that her son was being injured. She could not, therefore, establish a right to recover for the emotional distress she suffered when she subsequently learned of the accident and observed its consequences. The order granting summary judgment was proper.

The judgment of the Court of Appeal is reversed.

Each party shall bear its own costs on appeal.

BROUSSARD, J.

I dissent.

"[The] problem [of negligent infliction of emotional distress] should be solved by the application of the principles of tort, not by the creation of exceptions to them. Legal history shows that artificial islands of exceptions, created from the fear that the legal process will not work, usually do not withstand the waves of reality and, in time, descend into oblivion."

The majority grope for a "bright line" rule for negligent infliction of emotional distress actions, only to grasp an admittedly arbitrary line which will deny recovery to victims whose injuries from the negligent acts of others are very real. In so doing, the majority reveal a myopic reading of *Dillon*. They impose a strict requirement that plaintiff be present at the scene of the injury-producing event at the time it occurs and is aware that it is causing injury to the victim. This strict requirement rigidifies what *Dillon* forcefully told us should be a flexible rule, and will lead to arbitrary results. I would follow the mandate of *Dillon* and maintain that forseeability and duty determine liability, with a view toward a policy favoring reasonable limitations on liability. There is no reason why these general rules of tort law should not apply to negligent infliction of emotional distress actions. . . .

NOTES

1. What happened to the *Dillon* rule as a result of the decision in *Thing*? How was it changed, if at all? Does either of these approaches provide a greater degree of predictability and consistency in result?

2. Do you agree or disagree with the dissent by Justice Broussard which argues that the *Dillon* approach can never be applied as a "bright line" rule for determining whether a duty exists? Why or why not?

3. Many of the criticisms of the traditional *Dillon* rule are discussed in the opinions presented in *Thing*, along with a summary of how the rule itself has been received by various different jurisdictions. What effect is the new interpretation of the *Dillon* rule that was adopted by the court in *Thing* likely to have upon these other jurisdictions? *See, e.g., Cameron v. Pepin*, 610 A.2d 279 (Me. 1992).

4. What is "serious" emotional distress? In *Rodriguez v. State*, 173 P.2d 509, 519-20 (Haw. 1970), the Hawaii Supreme Court explained that "serious mental distress may be found where a reasonable [person] normally constituted, would be unable to adequately cope with the mental distress engendered by the circumstances of the case."

5. Just how far away from the accident scene can the plaintiff physically be situated and still recover for emotional distress damages under the *Dillon* rule? In *Kelley v. Kokua Sales & Supply, Ltd.,* 56 Haw. 204 (1975), the Supreme Court of Hawaii denied recovery of emotional distress injuries to a person who died in California after learning of the deaths of their daughter and granddaughter which occurred in Hawaii. The court explained that no duty of care was owed to one who was not located within a *reasonable distance* from the scene of the accident.

PROBLEM

Mary went shopping one day with her Mother. As the two women were walking along a public sidewalk in the downtown shopping district, Ralph, who had just left a nearby tavern in which he had consumed a large quantity of beer, sped his car recklessly down the adjacent street. Due to his intoxication, Ralph lost control of his car and crashed onto the nearby sidewalk, striking and instantly killing Mary's Mother. The two women had been talking just prior to the accident and neither of them saw the car as it approached from behind them. Ralph's car narrowly missed Mary who sustained no physical injury whatsoever, although she experienced severe emotional distress as a result of witnessing this tragic incident. Mary wishes to file an action for negligent infliction of emotional distress against Ralph as a result of this incident. Discuss the probable outcome of Mary's suit in each of the following situations.

a. Mary brings her action in a jurisdiction that applies the "impact rule."

b. Mary brings her action in a jurisdiction that applies the "zone of impact rule."

c. Mary brings her action in a jurisdiction that applies the "*Dillon* test."

d. Mary brings her action in a jurisdiction that applies the approach taken by *Thing*.

How would the outcome change, if at all, in each of the previous jurisdictions if Mary had been walking with her best friend, Sue, instead of her Mother?

How would the outcome change, if at all, in each of the previous jurisdictions if the plaintiff is Bob, a total stranger (instead of Mary), who experienced severe emotional distress after witnessing this entire incident from his second-story office across the street from the accident scene?

Chapter 10

PREMISES LIABILITY: DUTIES OF OWNERS AND OCCUPIERS OF LAND

As we have seen, the political, social, and economic influences of early English feudal society played an important role in shaping tort law. At that time, England was a rural, essentially agrarian society, in which not only land, but wealth and power were directly associated with the ownership of real property. Not surprisingly, the newly-developing English common law rules reflected this feudal heritage by creating various "status" categories which often favored the landowner in claims brought by injured entrants. These categories involved simplistic classifications based solely upon the legal "status" of the injured entrant — *trespasser*, *licensee*, and *invitee*.

When the American colonies became states, formed their own governments and created their own judicial systems, they adopted legal precedents from the existing body of English common law. Since the early American society was also largely rural and agrarian, American courts gave a warm reception to the English common law "status" categories. Just like their English counterparts, American courts strictly enforced and rigidly applied the categories. The results were often harsh and uncompromising, frequently favoring the landowner.

As both English and American societies evolved, becoming more urban and industrialized, the legal rules that had once favored the feudal landowners began to change. Courts recognized new subcategories of entrants such as "discovered trespassers" and "child trespassers." Desirous of achieving more just and fair results, courts began to blur the once clear distinctions between the original status categories. By the middle of the twentieth century, virtually every American jurisdiction had developed an impressive array of legal rules, exceptions, limitations and even "fictions," each patterned around the traditional tri-partite common law "status" categories. The resulting body of law has persisted largely intact today in most American jurisdictions, despite continued and often severe criticisms from both courts and legal commentators. For example, in a 1959 decision that rejected the traditional common law distinctions between "licensees" and "invitees" in admiralty law, the United States Supreme Court characterized this myriad of common law rules as a "semantic morass." *See Kermac v. Compagnie Generale Translantique*, 358 U.S. 625, 630-31 (1959).

Most of these traditional doctrines continue to be recognized and applied, in at least some form, in virtually every American jurisdiction. To understand why, it is necessary to examine the historical doctrines, as well as the modern pressures for change. The resulting body of case law, often referred to as "premises liability" law, represents one of the most litigious and diverse areas in all of torts today. Concerned primarily with the myriad of tort liabilities that arise

443

out of conditions existing on real property, as well as the various activities which are conducted thereon, the law of premises liability encompasses far more than the ubiquitous "slip and fall" case. Indeed, there may be no single area of modern tort litigation that involves so diverse and complex an array of legal issues as that of "premises liability."

A. COMMON LAW "STATUS" CATEGORIES OF ENTRANTS

Common law negligence is the most frequently asserted cause of action in premises liability cases. However, sometimes plaintiffs also rely on other tort theories, such as those involving various intentional torts, nuisance, or even strict liability. Moreover, there are an ever-increasing number of statutes and ordinances that regulate individual aspects of the law governing the tort liability of owners and occupiers of real property.

The duty of care owed by a landowner or occupant of real property to persons injured on the premises is dependent, in whole or in part, upon the legal "status" of the entrant as either a *trespasser*, a *licensee*, or an *invitee*. Absent a statute or some other special circumstance to the contrary, the landowner ordinarily owes no duty with respect to a mere trespasser, and only a limited duty with respect to licensees. In fact, the only category of entrants to whom the landowner owes a traditional duty of *reasonable care* is the *invitee*. Of course, as will become evident, there are numerous exceptions to these general rules for determining the landowner's duty of care in common law negligence actions. The following case illustrates the traditional approach that is typically applied in premises liability cases based upon negligence.

HOLZHEIMER v. JOHANNESEN
871 P.2d 814 (Idaho 1994)

Trout, Justice.

The parties are both fruit orchard owners in Emmett, Idaho. This appeal arises from a suit filed by Holzheimer for personal injuries he suffered after he fell from a stack of boxes in Johannesen's warehouse. Holzheimer contends that he was injured in the warehouse while retrieving fruit packing boxes which he was purchasing from Johannesen. He maintains that he was a business invitee entitled to a higher standard of care than a licensee.

On July 2, 1990, Holzheimer went to Johannesen's fruit farm to purchase or borrow "L.A. lug" (lid attached) fruit packing boxes. Testimony at trial demonstrated that the farmers in the Emmett area routinely sold at cost or loaned packing boxes to each other, as needed, as a favor to one another. Four days prior to the accident, William McConnell, the foreman at Johannesen's fruit farm, took Holzheimer into the warehouse and pointed out where the boxes were stored. He showed Holzheimer how he could retrieve them in the future by himself. McConnell informed Holzheimer that if he needed additional boxes in the future he could retrieve them on his own.

On the day of the accident, July 4, 1990, Holzheimer entered the Johannesen warehouse to obtain more boxes. The pallets of boxes were arranged in rows with gaps between the stacks of pallets. In addition, some of the boxes were "chimney stacked" on the pallets in such a way that there was an eight to ten inch hole in the center of the pallets. There was also an inventory area left open in the middle of the rows in the warehouse. In order to retrieve the boxes, Holzheimer apparently climbed on top of the pallets and in the process fell into the center of them, suffering head and shoulders injuries.

Holzheimer filed a complaint for personal injuries. Johannesen answered and asserted that Holzheimer was a licensee when he entered the warehouse and was only entitled to a lower standard of care. Johannesen filed a summary judgment motion asking the court to rule, as a matter of law, that Holzheimer was a licensee and that Johannesen did not violate the standard of care owed to a licensee. The court denied the motion and ruled that Holzheimer's status while in the warehouse was a question of fact for the jury. At trial, . . . [t]he court . . . excluded evidence of past fruit sales, but allowed the invoices to be modified so that they still showed past box sales, in order to establish a past business relationship between the parties regarding fruit boxes.

The court instructed the jury that there was a question of fact as to whether Holzheimer was an invitee or licensee and then gave the jury an instruction defining both and setting forth the appropriate standards of care. Holzheimer objected to the jury instruction regarding licensee status on the ground that it was not supported by the evidence. The jury found for Johannesen, although there is nothing in the verdict form from which it can be determined on which definition they relied.

On appeal, Holzheimer asserts that he was an invitee as a matter of law and that the jury should not have been instructed on licensee status or the standard of care owed to a licensee. In addition, he asserts that the district court committed reversible error by excluding as irrelevant evidence of past fruit sales contained in the invoices.

Holzheimer argues that any visitor on another's property for a business purpose is an invitee as a matter of law. He argues that he was an invitee because he was visiting the Johannesen fruit farm for the purpose of acquiring boxes, which is a business purpose connected with the Johannesen's fruit farm business, and that his visit to the Johannesen farm rendered a benefit to Johannesen.

Idaho courts have maintained that the duty of owners and possessors of land is determined by the status of the person injured on the land (*i.e.*, whether the person is an invitee, licensee or trespasser). An invitee is one who enters upon the premises of another for a purpose connected with the business conducted on the land, or where it can reasonably be said that the visit may confer a business, commercial, monetary or other tangible benefit to the landowner. *Wilson v. Bogert*, 81 Idaho 535, 347 P.2d 341 (1959). A landowner owes an invitee the duty to keep the premises in a reasonably safe condition, or to warn of hidden or concealed dangers. A licensee is a visitor who goes upon the premises of another with the consent of the landowner in pursuit of the visitor's purpose. *See Pincock v. McCoy*, 48 Idaho 227, 281 P. 371 (1929); *Evans v. Park*, 112 Idaho 400, 732 P.2d 369 (Ct. App. 1987). Likewise, a social guest is also a licensee. The duty owed to a licensee is narrow. A landowner is only required to share with the licensee knowledge of dangerous conditions or activities on the land. Additionally, this Court has held that "[t]he fact that a guest may be rendering a minor, incidental service to the host does not change the relationship [between them as a landowner and a licensee]." *Wilson*, 81 Idaho at 545, 347 P.2d at 851.

Holzheimer's argument that he was an invitee simply because he was purchasing or borrowing fruit boxes, which is arguably connected with the Johannesen fruit farm business, is not conclusive as to his status on the property. The standard of review of whether a jury instruction should or should not have been given, is whether there is evidence at trial to support the instruction. There is no question that the district court was correct in instructing the jury as to invitee status. The only question is whether the jury should also have been instructed on the definition of and standard of care owed to a licensee. We agree with the district court's decision to instruct the jury on both licensees and invitees.

Evidence was adduced at trial that was sufficient to warrant the district court instructing the jury on licensee status and the standard of care owed to a licensee. Both Johannesen and Holzheimer, as well as two other witnesses engaged in the fruit business, testified that loaning or selling boxes at cost to neighboring fruit farmers in the Emmett area was customary. The farmers loaned boxes to one another in the spirit of cooperation, and in hopes that favors would be returned when needed. Johannesen testified that he expected Holzheimer to either purchase the boxes at cost or replace them. Johannesen testified that he made no profit on the sale of boxes and in fact the sale may have cost him money once the cost of labor unloading the boxes and breaking up a pallet of boxes was included. The testimony reflected that this was in actuality more of a benefit to Holzheimer since he would have either had to buy an entire pallet, which he didn't need, or pay more than Johannesen's cost to buy a partial pallet. Arguably there was a business transaction between Johannesen and Holzheimer. Equally supportable is the assertion that the transaction between Johannesen and Holzheimer was the minimal type of service between a landowner and visitor referred to in Wilson, which does not alter their relationship as landowner and licensee.

There was sufficient evidence adduced at trial from which the jury could reasonably conclude that Holzheimer was a licensee. Thus we find no error in the court's decision to instruct the jury both as to the status of licensee and invitee. [W]e hold that the district court was correct in instructing the jury on Holzheimer's status both as an invitee and as a licensee. . . . The decision of the district court is affirmed. Respondent is awarded costs on appeal. No attorney fees on appeal.

NOTES

1. *Landowner's Duty of Care to Entrants.* As illustrated by *Holzheimer*, the landowner's common law duty of care with respect to entrants who are injured on the premises is based solely on the classification of the plaintiff as a trespasser, a licensee, or an invitee. Therefore, much of the court's discussion in *Holzheimer*, as in any premises liability case, focuses upon the formal classification of the entrant into one of these three traditional "status" categories. For a discussion of each of these categories, *see generally* N. LANDAU & E. MARTIN, PREMISES LIABILITY: LAW AND PRACTICE §§ 1.05[2]-[4] (Matthew Bender Co. 2001). [Hereinafter cited as PREMISES LIABILITY.]

Duty Owed to Trespassers. A trespasser is a person who enters or remains upon the land of another without any permission or an invitation to do so. Traditionally, the only duty imposed upon the owner or occupant of land with respect to trespassers is to refrain from inflicting *willful or wanton injury* upon them. Though subject to a number of exceptions, this common law rule is typically referred to as simply imposing "no duty" with respect to trespassers.

Duty Owed to Licensees. A licensee enters or remains upon land with the permission or consent of the owner, either express or implied, but not under such circumstances as would otherwise justify classifying the entrant as an invitee. Under this common law classification scheme, a licensee is entitled to some slightly greater protection than a mere trespasser, but not much more. The landowner or occupant still owes no affirmative duty to prepare the premises for entry by a licensee. However, if the landowner has *knowledge* of a *hidden or concealed danger* existing on the premises, there is a *duty to warn* the licensee of such dangers.

Duty Owed to Invitees. The most favored category of entrants under the common law tri-partite system of classification is the invitee. An invitee is a person who enters or remains on the premises at the express or implied invitation of the landowner or occupant, for some purpose either directly or indirectly associated with the business of the owner, or for some other public purpose. The landowner or occupant owes to an invitee a duty to exercise *reasonable care* in maintaining the premises. Typically, this duty involves not only a duty to warn of known, concealed dangers, but also to make reasonable, periodic inspections of the premises for the purpose of *discovering* such hazards. Moreover, once a hazard is discovered, the landowner's duty of reasonable care may require more than simply a warning of the danger. Depending upon the circumstances, the landowner may be required to take further steps to actually remove or repair the hazard, thereby making the premises safe for entry by invitees.

2. *Differences in Terminology.* The common law duties are fairly standard in all jurisdictions which continue to apply the traditional tri-partite scheme for classifying entrants. However, occasional variations in terminology with respect to the precise articulation of these duties do occur. For example, some courts may refer to the fact that "no duty" is owed to a *mere licensee* or to a *bare licensee. See, e.g., Hundt v. LaCroisse Grain Co.*, 425 N.E.2d 687 (Ind. Ct. App. 1981) (defining a "mere licensee"); *Baltimore Gas & Elec. Co. v. Flippo*, 705 A.2d 1144, 1148 (Md. 1998) (defining a "bare licensee"). Ordinarily, however, such a statement does not mean that the bare licensee is being treated the same as a trespasser. Even though phrased as a "no duty" rule with respect to the licensee, the landowner will typically still be subject to the qualifications discussed in Note 1, *supra,* which require at least a warning to be given as to any known, concealed dangerous artificial conditions existing on the premises. Likewise, even though the landowner is typically regarded as owing "no duty" with respect to trespassers, this rule remains subject to the traditional limitation that the landowner has refrained from inflicting a willful or wanton injury upon the entrant. *See, e.g., Hoots v. Pryor*, 417 S.E.2d 269 (N.C. Ct. App. 1992).

Once a specific duty of care has been established, the landowner's liability for negligence in a premises liability case is determined just as in any traditional negligence action. The defendant's breach of the applicable duty of care must be found to have been both the cause in fact and the proximate cause of the entrant's legally-recognized damages. Moreover, traditional common law defenses based upon the plaintiff's own conduct, such as contributory/comparative negligence and assumption of the risk, are fully applicable to either bar or reduce any potential recovery.

PALMTAG v. GARTNER CONSTRUCTION CO.
513 N.W.2d 495 (Neb. 1994)

CAPORALE, Justice.

Plaintiff [Janet Palmtag] and her husband, John Palmtag, hired defendant [Gartner Construction Co.] to remodel their newly purchased home under an oral arrangement whereunder defendant was to be paid for time and materials. Defendant was given the keys to the house, and plaintiff and her husband visited the structure to monitor the progress of the work; the husband visited on a daily basis and plaintiff once or twice a week.

Defendant's employees were usually present during the husband's visits on workdays, and the house was open. Even during those times when the employees were not around, the house was usually left open, and the husband would be able to "just go in." According to the husband, defendant's employees never limited or restricted where he could go. Plaintiff had once met a Caroline Gartner at the house to look at tile and possibly paint colors.

The remodeling included the removal of a spiral staircase which was located in the main floor entry area and descended therefrom to the basement through a 5-foot-square opening. The staircase was made up of pie-shaped treads. Attached to the narrow end of each tread was a round disk which when stacked one on top of another formed a center post with the treads fanned around it. The top disk fit up under the main floor landing. Working without reference to any plans, David Njus, an employee of defendant, disassembled the staircase by beginning with the top tread and working his way down. As he took out each tread and disk, the center post was whittled down.

A handrailing located around the staircase was taken out after the treads and center post were removed, leaving an empty opening in the floor. Njus also removed the plywood aprons and angle irons which were located along the underside of the landing, thus leaving the plywood floor around the opening jutting "something like a diving board out in the air."

After Njus removed the treads, aprons, and angle irons, he wondered how springy the outer edge of the flooring would be and checked it before leaving that evening by reaching up from the basement and hanging his full weight, 165 pounds, on it; nothing gave way. He then hung a wire and plywood barricade across the handrailing and walked on top of the landing area; he felt no sensation of weakness in it. In Njus' opinion, the landing felt solid, and he was "not anymore" concerned about the landing "not holding anybody's weight." Njus believed the landing would stay in place because he thought it was a contiguous part of the rest of the floor of the house. The landing, however, was a separate piece of wood which had been toenailed into the rest of the floor.

The barricade Njus hung was suspended diagonally across the landing from handrail to handrail on the main floor. It consisted of a wire, in the middle of which was hung a piece of plywood approximately 18 inches by 6 to 8 inches in size. It did not cover the hole and left half of the landing unguarded. No warning signs were attached to the barricade.

Plaintiff and her husband had arranged to meet at the house to review the remodeling work. Plaintiff, who was then 8 months pregnant and weighed 200 pounds, arrived at the house at about 5 p.m., accompanied by her 3-year-old son. She met and spoke briefly with Njus and an unidentified employee of defendant, who were leaving for the day.

As she walked through the entry area, she did not know the staircase had been removed, but noticed "a wire with something hanging on it" and paused approximately 8 to 9 inches from the wire. She then saw that the staircase was gone, at which time she was probably about a foot from the opening. Plaintiff warned her son not to get close to the stairwell. As she paused long enough for her son to pass by, the landing collapsed. As a consequence, she fell to the basement floor and landed on her seat and hands, after which her back and head hit the floor. Her face hit something on the way down.

When the husband found plaintiff, she was in extreme pain and somewhat delirious. Plaintiff could not feel the fetus move, and both she and her husband thought she had ruptured her uterus. Plaintiff was hospitalized for 3 days following the accident and was diagnosed as having a 20-percent compression fracture of her 12th thoracic vertebra, a torus fracture of her right wrist, a sprained left ankle, and a very painful tailbone area. As a result of the compression fracture in her back, plaintiff suffered a 20- to 25-percent permanent disability. Her pregnancy successfully came to term approximately a month after she fell.

The husband remembered that the staircase had been removed for a couple of days before the accident, and he had seen the barricade in place across the stairwell handrailing. He also stated that he had walked across the landing without any problems, although he weighed 250 pounds at the time of the accident.

Jesse Sutton, a semiretired general contractor knowledgeable about the installation and removal of spiral staircases, was of the opinion that the spiral staircase provided the support for the landing area and that when it was removed, the whole structure of the landing area was weakened. Sutton testified that removing the plywood aprons and angle irons, coupled with the earlier removal of the center post, left nothing to support the landing other than the nails toenailing the landing to the rest of the flooring and the approximate 1-percent stability given by the tile which covered the entire area.

Sutton further testified that the better way to support the landing when it was originally installed would have been to scab some joists from the surrounding floor so that they ran under the landing. While the subfloor rested on top of a joist, its edges flush with the joist underneath it, the landing butted against the edges of the subfloor but did not rest on a joist. That this was not done when the house was originally built should have been apparent to Njus.

Moreover, in Sutton's opinion, the barricade Njus made did not comply with industry standards. He indicated that the proper barricade would have been either metal framing or a 2-by-4 stud wall with signs and flagging on it. Njus agreed with Sutton's opinion regarding the support for the landing area, admitting that the center post had supported the landing and that the angle irons and plywood aprons provided "maybe some support."

[D]efendant complains that the district court determined as a matter of law that plaintiff was an invitee. Defendant urges that had the jury been permitted to consider the matter, it might well have found that plaintiff was but a licensee. We note at this point that the parties raise no issue as to whether the fact that plaintiff is an owner of the premises renders the invitee-licensee analysis inappropriate. However, because no such issue has been raised and because the case was tried on that theory, we, without passing any judgment on the matter, dispose of the case upon the theory on which it was tried. *See Ingerslew v. Bartholomew*, 216 Neb. 836, 346 N.W.2d 258 (1984).

Under that circumstance, the determination as to whether plaintiff is an invitee or a licensee is indeed important, for the law imposes a duty of greater care for the protection of an invitee than it does for a licensee. *Presho v. J.M. McDonald Co.*, 181 Neb. 840, 151 N.W.2d 451 (1967).

Under our law, a licensee is defined as one who is privileged to enter or remain upon land by virtue of the possessor's consent. *Wiles v. Metzger*, 238 Neb. 943, 473 N.W.2d 113 (1991). A licensee is on the premises of another for the licensee's own interest or gratification. Such person is exercising the privilege solely for that person's own convenience or benefit and does not stand in any contractual relation with the owner or occupant of the premises.

In general, an invitee is a person who goes on the premises of another in answer to the express or implied invitation of the owner or occupant on the business of the owner or occupant for the mutual advantage of both parties. *Kliewer v. Wall Constr. Co.*, 229 Neb. 867, 429 N.W.2d 373 (1988).

A business visitor or invitee, on the other hand, is one who is expressly or impliedly invited or permitted to enter or remain on the premises in the possession of another for a purpose directly or indirectly connected with the business of the possessor or with business dealings between them. Similar definitions are found in *Schild v. Schild*, 176 Neb. 282, 125 N.W.2d 900 (1964), and *Lindelow v. Peter Kiewit Sons', Inc.*, 174 Neb. 1, 115 N.W.2d 776 (1962).

The distinction between invitees and licensees rests on the purpose for which the invitation was extended. If it is an invitation for the personal pleasure, convenience, or benefit of the person enjoying the privilege, the person receiving it is a licensee. But if the invitation relates to the business of the one who gives it or for the mutual advantage of a business nature for both parties, the party receiving the invitation is an invitee.

Under this "economic benefit" test of invitee status, one who enters upon land of another is not entitled to the status of invitee unless the visit is directly or indirectly connected with business dealings between them.

In *Presho v. J.M. McDonald Co., supra*, we relied on the elements of the economic benefit test to determine whether the injured party, who went into the backroom of a retail store for an empty packing box to mail an article she had purchased elsewhere and for which no charge would be made, was an invitee or a licensee. Concluding that the injured party was not an invitee, we distinguished that part of the store in which merchandise was displayed and sold from that part in which the party was injured.

In similar fashion, the *Lindelow* court concluded that where the employees' use of the employer's recreational facilities conferred no immediate business benefit to the employer and the employees' attendance at the facilities had nothing to do with their work, the injured employee had been granted the privilege to make use of the facilities as a licensee and not as an invitee.

While the facts in *Von Dollen v. Stulgies*, 177 Neb. 5, 128 N.W.2d 115 (1964), are not identical to those now at hand, *Von Dollen* is nonetheless instructive. Therein, Von Dollen's sister was having a new house built. One afternoon when Von Dollen visited the premises to view the progress of the construction and to measure a window for a traverse rod, wallboard that had been stacked against a wall fell, scraping Von Dollen's right leg and pinning her right foot to the floor. Von Dollen argued that she was an invitee entitled to the affirmative duty of reasonable care to keep the premises safe and to anticipate her presence. We, however, concluded that Von Dollen was a mere licensee. Determinative was the fact that as Von Dollen had no contract with the builder, the builder was not responsible to Von Dollen for its work, and, thus, Von Dollen's visits had no relationship to any business or matter of mutual advantage to her and the builder. . . .

The facts essential to the determination of plaintiff's status here are likewise not in dispute. Defendant was doing work for plaintiff, and she thus had a right to control what was done under her arrangement with defendant. It is this circumstance which distinguishes the case at hand from *Von Dollen v. Stulgies, supra.*

Although there was no direct testimony that defendant expressly invited the Palmtags,

> [a]n invitation is inferred where there is a common interest or mutual advantage, or where an owner or occupant of premises, by acts or conduct, leads another to believe the premises, or something thereon, were intended to be used by such other person; that such use is not only acquiesced in by the owner or occupant, but is in accordance with the intention or design for which the way, place or thing was adapted or prepared or allowed to be used. . . .

Kruntorad v. Chicago, R.I. & P.R. Co., 111 Neb. 753, 755-56, 197 N.W. 611, 612 (1924). The only permissible inference from the undisputed facts is that plaintiff was at the jobsite for the mutual benefit of herself and defendant and that her visit served defendant's economic interest. Thus, she was, as a matter of law, an invitee. . . .

[T]he judgment of the district court must be, and hereby is, reversed and the cause remanded for further proceedings consistent with this opinion.

REVERSED AND REMANDED FOR FURTHER PROCEEDINGS.

NOTES

1. Court vs. Jury. *Holzheimer* and *Palmtag* are fairly typical premises liability cases. As indicated in both of these opinions, the classification of an individual entrant within one of the common law status categories may be made by either the court or the jury, depending upon the particular jurisdiction and the cir-

cumstances involved. Generally, where the status of the plaintiff can be determined from facts which are undisputed as in *Palmtag, supra*, the court will determine the appropriate category as a matter of law. However, where reasonable minds might differ as to some specific fact or facts that could affect the classification of the plaintiff entrant, most jurisdictions will permit the jury to determine the applicable facts that, in turn, also resolve the plaintiff's legal status. *See Holzheimer, supra*. The procedural importance of this distinction cannot be overstated, since the classification of an entrant into one of the common law status categories in most jurisdictions will determine the specific duty of care owed to that person by the defendant landowner.

2. Changing Categories. Even where the facts are undisputed, it may not always be a simple matter to classify the entrant into one of the three common law status categories. *Holzheimer, supra*, illustrates some of the potential problems inherent in making any such classification. Often a person will be placed into one category immediately upon their entry onto the defendant's premises, only to be later re-classified into another category based upon subsequent changes in the circumstances or the parties' relationship relative to one another. For example, an invited social guest might enter the host's premises as a licensee and subsequently lose that status to become a trespasser by entering into some portion of the host's premises to which the original invitation did not reasonably extend. Similarly, a trespasser, after being discovered on the defendant's property, might become elevated in status to a licensee. *See* PREMISES LIABILITY § 1.05[5].

PROBLEMS

1. Ten-year-old Sally walked door-to-door throughout her neighborhood selling Girl Scout cookies. As she stepped onto Elmer's front porch and pressed the doorbell, she received a slight electrical shock due to a short circuit in the doorbell switch. Startled, she jumped backwards quickly, lost her balance, and fell off the porch, seriously injuring her back. Elmer knew about the switch, and had been meaning to fix it, but he just hadn't gotten around to making the repairs. What is Sally's legal "status" at the time of her injury?

Would your answer to this question change in any of the following situations? Explain.

    a. Elmer had a sign clearly posted in his front yard that read "ABSOLUTELY NO SOLICITORS ALLOWED!" Sally did not read the sign.

    b. Elmer had a sign clearly posted in his front yard that read "ABSOLUTELY NO SOLICITORS ALLOWED!" Sally could not read the sign, or she read the sign and did not understand what it meant.

    c. Elmer had a sign clearly posted in his front yard that read "ABSOLUTELY NO SOLICITORS ALLOWED!" Sally read the sign, understood it, but completely disregarded it and proceeded to Elmer's front door anyway, because she was anxious to try and sell her cookies.

d. Elmer had a sign clearly posted in his front yard that read "ABSOLUTELY NO SOLICITORS ALLOWED!" Sally read the sign, understood it, but completely disregarded it and proceeded to Elmer's front door anyway, because Elmer had been her best cookie customer last year and she didn't think that the sign applied to her.

e. Elmer, intending to purchase some cookies, invited Sally inside his house when she came to his front door. While he was writing her a check for the cookies, Sally fell down an unlighted, open stairwell just inside his front door.

2. Alice, in preparation for her move to a new apartment, entered Supermarket in search of some empty boxes that she could use in packing her dishes. She had no intention of purchasing anything. After looking down several aisles for an empty box and finding none, she asked Manager for help. He pointed toward the rear of the store and told her that all empty boxes were kept in the storeroom. Alice walked to the rear of the store where she then proceeded through a doorway, completely disregarding a clearly marked sign that read: "EMPLOYEES ONLY. NO ADMITTANCE." Once inside the darkened storeroom, Alice immediately located a pile of empty boxes and began sorting through them. She selected a couple of boxes that suited her and then turned to leave, whereupon she slipped and fell on a banana peel that had been inadvertently left on the floor by some unidentified Supermarket employee. If Alice sues Supermarket for negligence to recover damages for the injuries sustained in her fall in a jurisdiction that determines duty on the basis of the traditional tri-partite status categories, how should she be classified at the time of her injury? What is the most probable outcome of her claim against Supermarket?

B. SPECIAL CATEGORIES OF ENTRANTS

Even under the traditional tri-partite system of classifying entrants according to their status as trespassers, licensees, or invitees, the common law has long recognized certain unique categories of entrants that require special treatment. Generally, the landowner's duty of care to persons falling into one of these special categories will *not* be determined solely on the basis of the entrant's legal status, but according to exceptions created just for these situations. Depending upon the special category, the landowner's duty of care in these situations may be either greater or less than that which would ordinarily have been owed to the entrant under one of the traditional status categories.

1. Trespassing Children

Young children who are injured after trespassing onto the land of another have always created special problems under the traditional common law scheme for determining the landowner's duty of care. Because of their tender age and lack of experience in recognizing potential dangers which might be encountered, young children, even though technically classified as trespassers, have generally been treated less harshly than other types of trespassers. Known variously as the "turntable doctrine," "the playground theory," the "dangerous instrumentality doctrine" or most commonly as the doctrine of "attractive nuisance," these rules represent an attempt to avoid the harsh effects of the traditional "no duty" rule applied to ordinary trespassers in those special situations where the injured entrant is a young child. *See* PREMISES LIABILITY § 19A.03 for a thorough discussion of the historical development of the "attractive nuisance" doctrine.

Under the "attractive nuisance" doctrine, the child's legal status as a trespasser is not conclusive with respect to the landowner's duty of care. Instead, it represents merely one of many factors that must be considered by the trier of fact. Thus, a duty of reasonable care may still be imposed upon a landowner who has *reason to anticipate* the presence of trespassing young children on the premises and the danger created by some *dangerous condition* existing on the property is of such a nature that the injured child, because of his/her young age, inexperience, or other circumstances is not otherwise likely to have appreciated it. Historically, the name of this doctrine derives from the fact that the injury-causing condition or activity must have actually "lured" or "enticed" the child to commit the trespass. However, this requirement is no longer necessary in the majority of jurisdictions which continue to apply the doctrine today.

MOZIER v. PARSONS
887 P.2d 692 (Kan. 1995)

HOLMES, Chief Justice:

[On] April 21, 1991, the Moziers were social guests at the home of defendants Charles and Brenda Parsons. The Parsons had completed installation of a swimming pool on their property just two weeks earlier. Those present had been swimming in the pool during the afternoon and then returned to the house for supper. Some time after supper Emily left the house. She was later found floating in the pool. She was not breathing and had no heart beat. Resuscitation efforts at the pool side and the hospital served only to restore breathing with the aid of a respirator. Heart beat was restored after emergency treatment at the hospital. Emily never regained consciousness, but did blink her eyes and make some slight movement. She died two days later.

Emily was a generally well-behaved 3½-year-old girl who listened to her parents and other adults. On the day of the accident, Emily was told by her parents and Brenda Parsons not to go near the pool without an adult. Emily was old enough to understand what that meant. Emily's parents were present at the Parsons' home at all times that day with Emily, and had not specifically entrusted the supervision of Emily to the Parsons. At the same time, both families informally shared responsibility for supervising each other's children.

The Parsons' home is located on a 60-acre tract in rural Bourbon County, just outside of Fort Scott, Kansas. The nearest house is approximately a quarter of a mile away, and their pool is shielded from public view by the house. The Parsons did not install a fence or any other safety devices at the time their pool was completed. The doors leading from the house to the pool area had latches that were out of Emily's reach, but they were not locked or latched at the time of the accident. There had been no injuries at the pool prior to this accident.

Prior to installing the pool, the Parsons discussed the desirability of a fence as a safety measure with Kendall Baumann, the pool salesman and installer. The Parsons ultimately decided against installing a fence because of the cost, the fact that there were no neighbors nearby, and information that they had received indicating that a fence was not required by their insurer. Baumann supplied the pool, but Charles Parsons acted as owner-contractor. Baumann also described other safety devices such as door locks and alarms which would alert residents when someone left the house. Baumann furnished the Parsons with safety pamphlets which contained information regarding the propensity of children to be attracted to pools. The Parsons finally did install a fence in 1993 after the birth of their youngest child, at a cost of $800.00.

The plaintiffs filed both a wrongful death and a survival action against defendants, seeking recovery for the injury and death suffered by their three-and-one-half-year-old daughter. . . . The defendants moved for summary judgment, arguing in part that plaintiffs could not establish willful or wanton negligence on their part as required in cases involving negligent injury to licensees. The plaintiffs responded, asserting the evidence was sufficient to require that the "attractive nuisance doctrine" question be submitted to the jury, thus raising the standard of care owed by the defendants to one of reasonable care. The district court denied defendants' motion for summary judgment and certified the question of law before us for consideration.

[T]he district court concluded that sufficient evidence was present to submit the case to a jury on the theory of attractive nuisance. In asserting that the attractive nuisance theory did not apply, the defendants proposed two principal arguments. First, they maintained that the theory was limited to trespassers only, and as the decedent was an invited guest or licensee and not a trespasser, the theory was not applicable. Next, defendants contended that Kansas courts have held that a residential swimming pool is never an attractive nuisance. [D]efendants relied upon this court's ruling in *McCormick v. Williams*, 194 Kan. 81, 397 P.2d 392 (1964), where the court determined that a residential swimming pool was not an attractive nuisance. . . . In dismissing defendant's first argument, the district court cited to one case where this court held that the attractive nuisance theory was applicable when the injured child was a licensee and not a trespasser. *See Gerchberg v. Loney*, 223 Kan. 446, 576 P.2d 593. The district court also concluded that the language in *McCormick* regarding swimming pools was "dicta" and "would not be followed by Kansas courts today."

In *Gerchberg*, we stated the elements of the attractive nuisance theory as follows:

A possessor of land is subject to liability for bodily harm to children intruding thereon caused by some condition that he maintains on the premises if:

(1) the possessor knows, or in the exercise of ordinary care should know, that young children are likely to trespass upon the premises, and

(2) the possessor knows, or in the exercise of ordinary care should know, that the condition exists and that it involves an unreasonable risk of bodily harm to young children, and

(3) the children because of their youth either do not discover the condition or understand the danger involved in coming into the dangerous area, and

(4) one using ordinary care would not have maintained the condition when taking into consideration the usefulness of the condition and whether or not the expense or inconvenience to the defendant in remedying the condition would be slight in comparison to the risk of harm to children. [576 P.2d at 592.]

In *Gerchberg*, a five-year-old boy was severely burned when he went upon a neighbor's property and started playing with and around the neighbor's trash burner. Earlier in the day the neighbor's 10-year-old son had been burning trash, and there was still smoke coming from the trash burner when the plaintiff entered upon defendant's premises, tried to throw papers into the trash burner, and somehow set himself on fire. Although this court viewed the plaintiff as a licensee, the facts would have supported a determination that the young boy was in fact a trespasser. However, based upon the question now before us, we do not consider the status of the Mozier child, as a trespasser or licensee, to be controlling.

What is now known as the attractive nuisance doctrine or theory of liability was first recognized in Kansas in *K.C. Rly. Co. v. Fitzsimmons*, 22 Kan. 686 (1879). In *Fitzsimmons*, a 12-year-old boy was injured while playing upon a railroad turntable located in an open pasture. On appeal by the railroad the court stated:

No person has a right to leave, even on his own land, dangerous machinery calculated to attract and entice boys to it, there to be injured, unless he first takes proper steps to guard against all danger; and any person

who thus does leave dangerous machinery exposed, without first providing against all danger, is guilty of negligence. It is a violation of that
beneficent maxim, *sic utere tuo ut alienum non laedas*. It is true that the
boys in such cases are technically trespassers. But even trespassers
have rights which cannot be ignored. . . .

In later years the theory of liability recognized in the "turntable" cases came to
be known as the attractive nuisance exception to the willful, wanton, or reckless
conduct required for recovery by a child trespasser. While the strict requirement
that the injured child be at least a technical trespasser has been relaxed somewhat, other elements of the attractive nuisance theory remain viable.

   The first Kansas case to consider whether a swimming pool fell within the
attractive nuisance theory was *Gilliland v. City of Topeka*, 124 Kan. 726, 262
Pac. 493 (1928). In *Gilliland*, a six-year-old boy drowned in a swimming pool in
a public park in Topeka. The plaintiff asserted liability on the part of the City,
alleging "the swimming pool with its equipment and appurtenances was a nuisance attractive to children." The court discussed the turntable cases and held:

   The swimming pool was doubtless attractive to children, but it was not
   a nuisance. . . .

   A swimming pool forming one of the public attractions in a city park
   does not belong in the same class with the places regarded as attractive
   nuisances within the rule of the turntable cases, as that rule is applied
   by this court. [124 Kan. at 727.]

McCormick v. Williams, 194 Kan. 81, 397 P.2d 392, is the only Kansas case we
have located which applies directly to a residential swimming pool. In
McCormick, a six-and-one-half-year-old boy drowned in a residential swimming pool. The pool was located in defendant's backyard which was surrounded
by a two and one-half- to three-foot high picket fence. The pool itself was
enclosed by a six-foot high fence; however, the gate was open at the time of the
accident. Snow tracks leading to the pool established that the child had entered
defendant's backyard through the gate of the picket fence. At the time of the accident, the pool contained six feet of water which was covered by a layer of both
ice and snow. Apparently, the child broke through the ice underneath the diving board; his body was found at the bottom of the pool.

   In determining whether the evidence was sufficient to establish liability
under the attractive nuisance theory, this court stated in pertinent part:

   [It] may be suggested that this court has squarely held that a swimming pool does not belong in the same class with instrumentalities
   regarded as attractive nuisances, and that the question of attractive nuisance is entirely eliminated in this state from cases where the injury or
   death occurs at or in a modern swimming pool. . . .

      It is necessary that the instrumentality alleged to be an attractive
   nuisance should have been so situated as to entice the child onto the

premises before liability could be imposed. It is not sufficient that it attract him after he had already become a trespasser. It was established by the evidence in this case that the swimming pool could not be seen from the street or sidewalk where the gate to the back yard was located.

Unfortunate as the accident to the child may be, a case must not be determined on sympathy rather than sound principles of law. A higher degree of care for the protection of a trespassing child should not be imposed on a property owner than is expected of a parent or custodian. Rules should not be adopted which, if carried to their logical conclusion, would make a property owner an insurer of a trespassing child against all injury. Such rules would make the ownership of property and modern conveniences well-nigh intolerable. [194 Kan. at 84.]

Following our decision in *McCormick*, there was a lull of nearly 30 years before this court was again called upon to consider the relationship of the attractive nuisance doctrine to swimming pool injuries. In *Kerns v. G.A.C., Inc.*, 255 Kan. 264, 875 P.2d 949 (1994), a six-year-old child sustained serious injuries after falling into a closed swimming pool and nearly drowning. The pool was a public accommodation for residents of a mobile home park and was open during the summer months. At the time of the accident the pool had been closed for the season; however, three to four feet of murky water, algae, and leaves had collected in the pool, making both the bottom and sides of the pool slippery. The pool was surrounded by a five-foot high chain link fence. The injured child had climbed over the fence and entered the pool to retrieve his baseball cap which had been thrown into the pool by his friend. . . . In concluding that the attractive nuisance doctrine was not applicable, the *Kerns* court reaffirmed our prior holding in *McCormick*. . . .

Although recent decisions by this court may have relaxed the rule that the injured child must be an actual, if technical, trespasser, we take notice that under our recent decision in *Jones v. Hansen*, 254 Kan. 499, 867 P.2d 303, the attractive nuisance doctrine or theory of recovery is now limited exclusively to trespassing children. This element, as well as the others set forth in *Gerchberg*, including that the child must be attracted or enticed onto the property by the alleged nuisance, remain as prescribed requirements under the attractive nuisance theory.

In *Kerns*, this court noted that it has "refused to categorically exclude swimming pools from application of the attractive nuisance doctrine." [255 Kan. at 283.] However, this court has never extended the doctrine to swimming pools, whether public or private. Similarly, most courts which have examined this issue have refused to extend the attractive nuisance doctrine to swimming pools. *See e.g., Earnest v. Regent Pool, Inc.*, 288 Ala. 63, 257 So. 2d 313 (1972); *Carlson v. Tucson Racquet and Swim Club, Inc.*, 127 Ariz. 247, 619 P.2d 756 (Ct. App. 1980); *Wilford v. Little*, 144 Cal. App. 2d 477, 301 P.2d 282 (1956). . . . All of our cases to date, beginning with *Gilliland v. City of Topeka* in 1928, have consistently held that a swimming pool does not constitute an attractive nuisance and that the doctrine does not apply. We adhere to our prior cases. A swimming pool, public or private, does not belong in the same class with instrumentalities and places regarded as attractive nuisances.

While we do not rule out the remote possibility that there could be a highly unusual and aggravated factual situation that might support consideration of the attractive nuisance doctrine, we hold that, generally, swimming pools, whether public or private, do not constitute an attractive nuisance and are not subject to the attractive nuisance doctrine. . . .

NOTES

1. *Dangerous Conditions vs. Activities.* Currently, the RESTATEMENT (SECOND) OF TORTS § 339 formulation of the "attractive nuisance" doctrine requires that the injury must be caused by an *artificial condition* on the landowner's property. As a consequence of this limitation, there has been significant litigation in many jurisdictions to determine whether particular hazards constitute "artificial" or "natural" conditions. The results of such litigation are not always consistent from one jurisdiction to another, or even within the same jurisdiction from one case to another. *Compare Clarke v. Edging*, 512 P.2d 30 (Ariz. Ct. App. 1973) (holding that a natural gully caused by the defendant's improper irrigation techniques was an "artificial condition" for purposes of applying the doctrine of "attractive nuisance," *with Weber v. Springville City*, 725 P.2d 1360 (Utah 1986) (holding that a manmade and unfenced irrigation ditch was not an "artificial condition" for purposes of applying the "attractive nuisance" doctrine). Moreover, not all "attractive nuisance" jurisdictions have even attempted to limit the doctrine solely to *artificial* conditions. *See* PREMISES LIABILITY § 19A.03[3].

2. *Requirement of "Attraction."* Historically, before the "attractive nuisance" doctrine could be applied to alter the landowner's duty of care owed to a trespassing minor child, the child must have been "attracted," lured, or otherwise enticed to commit the trespass by the instrumentality actually responsible for causing the child's injury. For example, if a trespassing child was injured after falling into a swimming pool on the defendant's property, the child's original entry onto the property must have actually been "enticed" because of the presence of that same swimming pool. Some jurisdictions continue to require an "attraction" as a predicate to any duty owed by the landowner to an injured trespassing child. *See, e.g., Ambrose v. Buhl Joint School Dist. # 412*, 887 P.2d 1088 (Idaho 1994). However, many American jurisdictions no longer require that the injury result from the same activity or condition that originally "attracted" the child onto the property. *See, e.g., Brown v. Arizona Pub. Serv. Co.*, 790 P.2d 290 (Ariz. 1990). Nevertheless, the allurement or enticement of the child by the injury-causing danger may still be considered by the trier of fact in determining whether the child's trespass was foreseeable.

PROBLEMS

1. Early one morning after a big snowfall, Homer went outside and shoveled snow off his driveway. He pushed the excess snow into a large pile several feet high in his front yard and then returned inside for some hot chocolate. Later that same morning seven-year-old Billy, Homer's neighbor, went outside to play in the snow. Spotting the huge pile of snow in Homer's yard, Billy ran over, climbed to the top of the pile, and jumped off. When he landed in what appeared to be a soft mound of snow at the foot of the large snow pile, Billy severely cut his arm on the edge of a rusty metal snow shovel that Homer had inadvertently left buried in the snow. If Billy's parents sue Homer for negligence, what duty will be owed by Homer to Billy?

2. Norma, an elderly widow, owned a home in an older residential neighborhood where she had lived for her entire adult life. Like most of her neighbors, Norma's children had all grown up and moved away. In the backyard of Norma's house was an old tire swing that still hung from the tree where her deceased husband had attached it years ago when her children played at home. The swing had not been used in many years and, in fact, the rope from which it was suspended was visibly frayed. Junior, a ten-year-old boy, recently moved into the neighborhood with his parents who purchased a house just down the street, One day, while Junior was walking through his new neighborhood, he spotted the tire swing in Norma's backyard and immediately ran to try it out. As he did so, the rope broke and the swing fell, injuring Junior. Assuming that this incident occurred in a jurisdiction that still adheres to the traditional common law status categories, how should Junior be classified, and what is the most probable outcome in any negligence action brought on behalf of Junior against Norma?

2. Firefighters, Police Officers, and Other Public Officials: The "Firefighter's Rule"

Another category of entrants that deserves special attention is that of firefighters, police officers, and other public officials who enter onto the premises while performing their official duties. Under the traditional status classifications, these entrants would naturally fall into the "invitee" category, to whom the landowner owes a duty of reasonable care under the circumstances since the presence of such entrants on the premises is due solely to their performance of some official duty or an employment-related function from which the landowner typically derives a distinct benefit. Thus, it is not surprising that various types of public officials and employees, including postal workers, trash collectors and numerous government inspectors, who enter on premises have been classified as "invitees" for purposes of defining the landowner's duty of care. *See, e.g., Atchley v. Berlen*, 408 N.E.2d 1177 (Ill. App. Ct. 1980) (state meat inspector); *Suhr v. Sears, Roebuck & Co.*, 450 P.2d 87 (Mont. 1969) (trash collector); *Schwartz v. Selvage*, 277 N.W.2d 681 (Neb. 1979) (mail carrier). This is the approach that has been taken by the RESTATEMENT (SECOND) OF TORTS § 345, in comment c.

Despite the classification of various types of government and public officials as invitees, there is one particular subgroup within this general category of entrants (consisting solely of firefighters and police officers) that traditionally has been denied invitee status by many jurisdictions, and treated, instead, as mere "licensees." *See generally* PREMISES LIABILITY § 1.05[3][c]. Typically referred to as the "firefighter's rule," this special treatment has been justified by the argument that it would be unfair to impose a duty of reasonable care upon landowners to protect such entrants from injuries due to the unusual circumstances which often necessitate their entry. *See, e.g., Sherman v. Suburban Trust Co.*, 384 A.2d 76 (Md. 1978). Other courts continue to support the "firefighter's rule" on the basis that firefighters and police officers have been specially trained to confront dangerous situations as a necessary part of their occupations, and should be denied the favored "invitee" status by virtue of their assumption of the risk with respect to such dangers. *See, e.g., Rosa v. Dunkin' Donuts of Passaic*, 583 A.2d 1129 (N.J. 1991). Some courts have justified their continued adherence to this rule on the basis that firefighters and police officers are specially compensated for their high-risk occupations. *See, e.g., Malo v. Willis*, 178 Cal. Rptr. 774 (Cal. Ct. App. 1981).

Whatever the justification, the application of the "firefighter's rule" typically bars recovery by an injured firefighter or police officer for those injuries which have been caused by the same conduct or activity that was responsible for the entrant's original presence at the scene, just as any true "licensee" would be barred. It is only when the injury to a public safety officer results from some cause that is truly separate and distinct from those circumstances which necessitated the original entry that the landowner or occupant will normally be held liable. Of course, when a firefighter or police officer has been classified as a "licensee" under the "firefighter's rule," the landowner still remains subject to the same limitations which are applicable to any other "licensee." Thus, the landowner may still have a duty to warn firefighters and police officers who enter the premises as to the presence of certain hazards which are known to exist, as well as to refrain from inflicting any willful or wanton injury.

While a few jurisdictions have abolished the "firefighter's rule" in favor of a standard based upon reasonable care under the circumstances, the majority of jurisdictions continue to recognize the landowner's limited liability relative to this special category of public safety officers. The opinion in *Chapman v. Craig* is fairly typical.

CHAPMAN v. CRAIG
431 N.W.2d 770 (Iowa 1988)

SCHUKTZ, Justice.

We are asked to reconsider our adoption of the fireman's rule and to abolish it. We recently adopted the rule in a dramshop action denying a policeman a recovery in those cases in which the action is grounded on the same conduct that created the need to call for the officer's assistance. *Pottebaum v. Hinds*, 347 N.W.2d 642, 647 (Iowa 1984). We later limited the rule by refusing to apply it to situations in which the officer is performing a law enforcement activity unrelated to the violation that required the officer's presence. *Gail v. Clark*, 410 N.W.2d 662, 666 (Iowa 1987). The district court applied the fireman's rule in granting partial summary judgment. We affirm.

During the evening of November 21, 1985, Randall Burkhead was served alcoholic beverages at the Main Street Tap in Lorimor. This tavern is operated by William Craig, who is also the licensee under Iowa Code chapter 123 (1985).

After leaving the Main Street Tap, Burkhead went to Winterset and was served at the Southfork Restaurant & Lounge. The Southfork is operated by Gary and Glenda Rogers (Rogers), who similarly are licensees.

When Burkhead refused to leave the Southfork, an employee summoned the police. Officer Timothy Chapman of the Winterset Police Department responded to the call. Chapman found it necessary to arrest Burkhead, and in the process, Chapman was injured.

Chapman brought a dramshop action under Iowa Code section 123.92 (1985) against Craig and the Rogers. The defendants filed motions for summary judgment. The trial court granted the Rogers' motion for summary judgment, based on the fireman's rule, and that is the only issue before this court.

Chapman first urges the Court to abolish the fireman's rule because a growing number of courts have refused to apply it or have restricted its scope. Minnesota has legislatively abolished the rule. Minn.Stat. § 604.06. Oregon also had abolished the rule. *Christensen v. Murphy*, 296 Or. 610, 678 P.2d 1210, 1216-18 (1984), based in part on the legislative abolition of implied assumption of risk. Prior to our adoption of comparative fault, we in contrast, have abolished only secondary assumption of risk where contributory negligence was a defense. *Rosenau v. City of Esterville*, 199 N.W.2d 125, 132-33 (Iowa 1972). Primary assumption of risk has been retained as an affirmative defense. Since our adoption of comparative negligence, we have not changed this position.

We cannot view the change of position of two states as a growing trend in this area of law when the majority of states have either adopted or affirmed the application of the fireman's rule. *See, e.g., Walters v. Sloan*, 20 Cal.3d 199, 142 Cal.Rpt. 152, 571 P.2d 609 (1977); *Grable v. Varela*, 115 Ariz. 222, 564 P.2d 911, 912 (App. 1977); *see generally* N. Landau, E. Martin, M. Thomas, 2 Premises Liability § 14.03 [2][a][iii] (1987). Regardless, in the short span of time since we have adopted the rule, we see no new policy reasons to abandon our position.

We similarly find no merit in Chapman's assertion that officers' losses would be more fairly compensated through liability insurance. As we stated in *Pottebaum*, "we believe these risks are more effectively and fairly spread by passing them on to the public through the government entities that employ firefighters and police officers."

Chapman next contends that the fireman's rule violates the Equal Protection clauses of the United States and Iowa Constitutions. He asserts that members of the class of public safety officers are treated differently. He cites *Gail v. Clark*, 410 N.W.2d 662 (Iowa 1987) (where the officer was allowed to recover under the dramshop act for injuries sustained in an auto accident caused by an intoxicated driver when it was a high speed chase that created the need for the officer's presence) and Pottebaum (the officer was denied recovery for being assaulted by a drunk patron after being called to quell a disturbance at a tavern) as authority. Chapman correctly states that laws must apply equally to all members within a class, however he wrongly defines the class as all public safety officers.

Under *Pottebaum*, we held that recovery is denied for the firefighter or policeman only when the cause of action is based on the same conduct that initially created the need for the officer's presence in an official capacity. The class is therefore very narrowly defined and our rule treats all members of the class equally.

Because this classification involves no fundamental right or suspect class as defined by the United States Supreme Court, we must determine if a rational basis exists for the denial of recovery for class members. The test is whether the classification is reasonably related to the promotion of one or more legitimate state interests. As we stated in *Pottebaum*, citizens should be encouraged and not in any way discouraged from relying on those public employees who have been specially trained and paid to deal with these hazards. The government also employs and trains its personnel specifically to deal with those hazards that may result from an uncircumspect citizenry, and it offends public policy to have citizens invite private liability merely because they create a need for those public services. Finally, we are aware of the wide-spread existence of liability insurance, however, we believe these risks are more effectively and fairly spread by passing them on to the public through the government entities that employ firefighters and police officers. The classification is amply supported by reasons which promote legitimate state interests.

Other courts considering this issue have similarly held the classification denied no equal protection rights. *England v. Tasker*, 129 N.H. 467, 529 A.2d 938, 941 (1987); *Flowers v. Rock Creek Terrace Ltd. Partnership*, 308 Md. 432, 452 n.12, 520 A.2d 361, 371 n.12 (1987).

Finally, Chapman asserts that the Rogers waived their rights under the fireman's rule by significantly enhancing the dangerous condition. He contends that by serving an allegedly already intoxicated patron even more alcoholic beverages, they relinquished any protection that the fireman's rule may have provided. Chapman also misconstrues this exception to the rule. The exception is limited to allowing recovery "if the individual responsible for their presence engaged in subsequent acts of negligence or misconduct once the officer was on the scene." *Pottebaum*, 347 N.W.2d at 646. Plaintiff's deposition indicates that after plaintiff responded to the call, Burkhead left the tavern. The assault on plaintiff occurred outside the tavern after plaintiff arrested and attempted to handcuff Burkhead. If [the] Rogers unlawfully served an intoxicated patron, they did so prior to plaintiff's arrival, thereby making this exception inapplicable.

In conclusion, we hold that the fireman's rule, as set forth in *Pottebaum* and further refined in *Gail*, is amply supported by sound reasoning and is not violative of the Equal Protection clause. The conduct of [the] Rogers also did not constitute a waiver of its protection under the facts of this case. Accordingly, the trial court's ruling on the summary judgment motion is affirmed.

AFFIRMED.

LARSON, Justice (dissenting).

The fireman's rule is founded largely on public policy, a concern that, if a fireman (or similar public employee), is allowed to sue for injuries arising out of a call for assistance, it might discourage citizens from calling for help. *See Pottebaum v. Hinds*, 347 N.W.2d 642, 645 (Iowa 1984). There is, however, no empirical data presented in this case, or in *Pottebaum*, to support that conclusion. In fact, I believe there is considerable doubt that the thought of possible tort liability would even enter the mind of a citizen contemplating a call for help. That is especially true now, it seems to me, when virtually all property owners are covered by insurance against premises injuries.

On the other hand, there can be no doubt that in every case where the fireman's rule is invoked, another public policy is frustrated. That is the public policy favoring a party's right to seek reimbursement for injuries caused by the negligence of another. That right should not be denied a broad class of persons on the basis of a public policy as speculative as that supposedly underlying the fireman's rule.

I would reverse.

PROBLEM

Wilbur was a full-time employee of the State Health Department whose regular duties included making periodic "surprise" health inspections of all public restaurants situated within a three-county area of the State. One day while conducting a health inspection of Wanda's Eatery, he parked his car in the alley behind the restaurant and proceeded toward the back door of the premises, an area normally used only by Wanda's employees and various delivery persons. As he stepped onto a small wooden porch to enter the premises, his foot suddenly crashed through a step that had become rotten with age. Wilbur fell and was injured. If Wilbur sues Wanda's Eatery for negligence in causing his injuries, how should the court classify him for purposes of determining the appropriate duty of care owed by Wanda's?

3. Social Guests

Another category of entrants in premises cases which requires special consideration is that of social guests. A social guest is one who has been expressly invited onto the premises for some social, non-business purpose. Despite the fact that such persons have been *invited* to enter the premises, the majority of American jurisdictions treat them as mere *licensees*, to whom the landowner's only duty is to provide a warning of known, hidden dangers. This is true, even where the social guest also provides some service or other incidental benefit to the landowner while on the premises. *See* PREMISES LIABILITY § 1.05[3][b].

The rationale most frequently offered in support of this reduced duty of care owed to invited social guests on the premises is that such persons should be entitled to no greater protection from hazards on the host's premises than would any other member of the host's own family. Since the host is not required to inspect the premises to discover and remove hazards which might injure members of his own family, such an inspection (ordinarily required to prepare the premises for an invitee) should also not be required for the visit of a mere social guest. Not surprisingly, however, this harsh treatment of social guests has been the subject of much criticism and debate among courts and legal commentators. As the following case illustrates, the "social guest" category is not always limited in its scope to those persons who enter the premises for purely "social" purposes.

HAMBRIGHT v. FIRST BAPTIST CHURCH-EASTWOOD
638 So. 2d 865 (Ala. 1994)

INGRAM, Justice.

Minnie Hambright was injured when she slipped and fell while attending services at First Baptist Church-Eastwood in Jacksonville, Alabama. She and her husband, Frank Hambright, sued the church, alleging negligence, wantonness, and loss of consortium. The trial court entered a summary judgment for the church on all claims.

The dispositive issue is whether Mrs. Hambright held the legal status of a licensee while visiting the church. Mrs. Hambright was a member of the Ebenezer Baptist Church choir; she and other members of the Ebenezer church were asked to participate in the First Baptist Church's anniversary celebration church service on November 10, 1991. Upon arrival at First Baptist, Mrs. Hambright used the church restroom. She then went to the buffet table that had been set up by the church in its fellowship hall for its members and for visitors attending the service. Mrs. Hambright almost slipped near the table, but caught herself. She then obtained plates of food for herself and others. After eating her lunch, Mrs. Hambright started to leave the fellowship hall to visit relatives. As she was leaving, she slipped and fell on the floor of the fellowship hall and was injured. Mrs. Hambright did not sing at the anniversary service, either before or after the accident.

[T]he church produced deposition testimony from persons present on the date of the accident, including Mrs. Hambright; that evidence indicated that the deponents did not notice any foreign substance on the floor where Mrs. Hambright fell. The church also produced an affidavit from Walter Herman Goggins, the church member who had waxed the floor before the service. In the affidavit Goggins testified that he used the routine waxing and buffing methods that he had previously used on the floor.

[T]he Hambrights produced various items of evidence, including testimony from a witness who stated that the area where Mrs. Hambright fell was "oily like." They also produced deposition testimony from Goggins in which he said that he was unaware of whether the wax applied to the floor was recommended for use on tile floors, such as the floor on which Mrs. Hambright fell. The Hambrights presented an unsworn report from a product testing firm that indicated that the floor where Mrs. Hambright fell had an abnormally low friction coefficient when tested with her vinyl-soled shoe and that wax was found on the skirt she was wearing when she fell.

[T]he Hambrights ask this Court to adopt the business and public invitee tests as set forth in § 332, RESTATEMENT (SECOND) OF TORTS (1965); to do so would modify our caselaw so as to classify visitors as those who enter land for the purpose for which the land is held open ("public invitees") and those who enter for a purpose connected with the landowner's business ("business visitors"). However, we decline their invitation to depart from our existing caselaw classifying visitors as invitees, licensees, or trespassers for determining what duty the landowner may owe in a particular circumstance.

The Hambrights then assert that, under our existing classification for visitors listed above, Mrs. Hambright held the legal status of an invitee during her visit to the church because she was invited, along with the rest of the Ebenezer choir, to sing at the anniversary service to raise funds for the church. Therefore, the thrust of their argument is that the church breached a duty to Mrs. Hambright by failing to keep the premises reasonably safe or by failing to warn her of a slippery floor.

The church maintains that it breached no duty to Mrs. Hambright because, it argues, she was a licensee, not an invitee, during her visit. The church argues that the Hambrights produced no evidence of wantonness on the church's part and no evidence that the church allowed Mrs. Hambright to be negligently injured after becoming aware of her peril.

This Court looks to the status of the injured party in relation to the defendant's land or premises in deciding whether the defendant should be held liable for an injury to a visitor upon the land or premises. *Tolbert v. Gulsby*, 333 So. 2d 129 (Ala. 1976); *Copeland v. Pike Liberal Arts School*, 553 So. 2d 100 (Ala. 1989).

A person who enters the land with the landowner's consent to bestow some material or commercial benefit upon the landowner is deemed an invitee. *Lloyd v. Joseph*, 496 So. 2d 771 (Ala. 1986). A landowner owes an invitee the duty to keep the premises in a reasonably safe condition and, if the premises are unsafe, to warn of hidden defects and dangers that are known to the landowner but that are hidden or unknown to the invitee.

In contrast, a person who visits a landowner's property with the landowner's consent or as the landowner's guest but with no business purpose occupies the status of a licensee. *Bryant v. Morley*, 406 So. 2d 394 (Ala. 1981). The duty owed by a landowner to a licensee is to abstain from willfully or wantonly injuring the licensee and to avoid negligently injuring the licensee after the landowner discovers a danger to the licensee. *Graveman v. Wind Drift Owners' Ass'n, Inc.*, 607 So. 2d 199 (Ala. 1992). This duty is not an active one to safely maintain the premises; instead, the landowner has the duty not to set traps or pitfalls and not to willfully or wantonly injure the licensee. A "trap" is a danger that a person who does not know the premises could not avoid by the use of reasonable care. Wantonness has been defined as the conscious doing of some act or conscious omission of some duty by one who has knowledge of the existing conditions and who is conscious that doing, or failing to do, some act will probably result in injury.

We have held that a person attending a church service is a licensee on the church premises. *Autry v. Roebuck Park Baptist Church*, 285 Ala. 76, 229 So. 2d 469 (1969). In *Cagle v. Johnson*, 612 So. 2d 1158 (Ala. 1992), this Court expressly declined to overrule *Autry*.

The record reveals that Mrs. Hambright visited the church as a member of the Ebenezer choir to attend the church's anniversary service. We do not consider her attendance at the church's anniversary service as providing a material benefit to the church under the facts presented in this case. Church affairs such as this anniversary service are very common. Such services benefit both the communities in which the churches are located and the visitors to the services, by providing spiritual direction and social fellowship. The facts of this case indicate that Mrs. Hambright and the other persons present at First Baptist were in much the same position as social guests "enjoying unrecompensed hospitality in a private home by invitation." Therefore, we hold that Mrs. Hambright was a licensee during her visit to the church.

After carefully reviewing the record, we conclude that on its motion for summary judgment the church made a prima facie showing that it did not breach a duty owed to Mrs. Hambright as a licensee, and we conclude that the Hambrights did not rebut that prima facie showing. The Hambrights did not produce substantial evidence that the church willfully or wantonly injured Mrs. Hambright. They did not produce substantial evidence that the church was conscious that the condition of the floor would cause Mrs. Hambright's injury. Further, they did not produce substantial evidence that the church acted negligently after learning of Mrs. Hambright's peril. As noted above, substantial evidence creating a genuine issue of material fact is required to rebut a properly supported motion for summary judgment.

The trial court properly concluded that there was no genuine issue of material fact regarding the Hambrights' claims against the church. Therefore, the judgment is affirmed.

AFFIRMED.

NOTES

1. *Avoiding the Harsh Rule Limiting Landowners' Liability to Social Guests within the Traditional Tri-Partite Classifications.* Some courts have managed to avoid the harsh effects of the "social guest" rule by simply re-classifying all *invited* social guests as true "invitees," thereby elevating the landowner's duty of care. *See, e.g., Beresford v. Starsky*, 571 N.E.2d 1257 (Ind. 1991). Other courts have achieved the same result within the traditional tri-partite system of classification by simply finding some "economic benefit" to the host as a result of the social guest's presence on the premises, thereby elevating the guest's status to that of an "invitee." *See, e.g., LeBranche v. Johnson*, 193 S.E.2d 228 (Ga. Ct. App. 1972) (guest invited to defendant's home to assist in making a quilt was "invitee"); *Madrazo v. Michaels*, 274 N.E.2d 635 (Ill. App. Ct. 1971) (guest invited to help host move to new house and care for her children was "invitee").

2. *Abolition of "Licensee" Category.* In those jurisdictions where the traditional common law distinctions between the "licensee" and "invitee" categories have been abolished, either by judicial action (*see, e.g., Hudson v. Gaitan*, 675 S.W.2d 699 (Tenn. 1984)) or by statute (*see, e.g.,* CONN. GEN. STAT. § 52-557a; ILL. REV. STAT. ch. 80, & 302; ME. REV. STAT. ANN. tit. 14, § 159), the "social guest" category has effectively been eliminated altogether for purposes of determining the landowner's duty of care.

C. RECREATIONAL PREMISES

The application of the common law tri-partite scheme for classifying entrants to land has been particularly troublesome in situations involving persons who are injured after having been gratuitously permitted to enter land for recreational purposes. Under the traditional scheme such persons could possibly be classified as "invitees," to whom a duty might be owed by the landowner either to warn or remove known dangers from the premises. However, such duties have been perceived as particularly burdensome on recreational landowners. As a result, the legislatures in almost every state have enacted statutes (referred to as "recreational use" statutes) that expressly articulate a lesser duty of care in certain recreational settings. Basically, these statutes treat recreational entrants as "licensees" rather than "invitees," and impose only a duty to refrain from intentionally inflicting an injury to the recreational entrant.

REED v. EMPLOYERS MUTUAL CASUALTY CO.
741 So. 2d 1285 (La. Ct. App. 1999)

NORRIS, Chief Judge.

Reed and Gimber were members of the San Patricio Bayou Hunting Club (Club), an unincorporated association of persons who, for purposes of sport hunting, leased a tract of land in DeSoto Parish owned by International Paper Company. Gimber was the Club treasurer and signed the lease on behalf of the Club.

On October 30, 1994, Reed climbed into a movable tree stand near a game trail on the leased premises. The tree stand had been installed by Gimber. As Reed prepared to fasten his safety belt, the tree stand collapsed beneath him and caused him to fall to the ground. Reed sued Gimber and his insurer, Employer's Mutual, for his personal injuries resulting from Gimber's alleged negligent installation of the tree stand.

The defendants answered, asserting immunity under La. R.S. 9:2791, a Recreational Use Statute. Defendants then moved for summary judgment on the question of their liability under this statute. The trial court granted the motions and dismissed Reed's lawsuit. Reed now appeals.

A landowner may be held liable for injuries which occurred on his property when in the management of his property he acted unreasonably in view of the probability of injuries to others. La. C.C. art. 2315, 2316; *Shipley v. Shipley*, 30,283 (La. App. 2d Cir. 2/25/98), 709 So. 2d 901. However, the Recreational Use Statutes provide immunity in that an

> "owner, lessee, or occupant owes no duty of care to keep such premises safe for entry or use by others for hunting . . . or to give warning of any hazardous conditions . . . on such premises to persons entering for such purposes. If such an owner, lessee or occupant give permission to another to enter the premises for such recreational purposes he does not thereby extend any assurance that the premises are safe."

La. R.S. 9:2791, 9:2795. To qualify for the immunity, the defendant must be an owner, lessee, or occupant; the land upon which the injury occurred must be undeveloped, nonresidential, and rural or semi-rural land; the injury must have been the result of a recreational activity enumerated in the statute; and the injury-causing instrumentality must be of the type normally encountered in the "true outdoors." *Ward v. Hermitage Ins. Co.*, 28,236 (La. App. 2d Cir. 4/3/96), 671 So. 2d 1229, *writ denied* 94-1141 (La. 9/3/96), 678 So. 2d 554. This immunity is also extended to hunting clubs who have leased land for recreational hunting. La. R.S. 9:2791D. Owners of land used for commercial recreational purposes have similar immunities. Under La. R.S. 9:2795D, this immunity is not extended to fellow hunters.

The purpose of the Recreational Use Statutes is "to encourage owners of land to make land and water areas available to the public for recreational purposes by limiting their liability toward persons entering thereon for such purposes." *Monteville v. Terrebonne Parish Consolidated Government*, 567 So. 2d 1097 (La. 1990). When a "suitable tract is properly dedicated to one or more of the specified recreational purposes, the landowner or occupier's exposure to liability to a person who enters or uses the premises for such a recreational purpose is drastically limited. In such cases, the owner owes no duty of care to keep the premises safe or to give warnings of hazards, use, structure or activity on the premises." The Recreational Use Statutes are designed "to induce the owners or occupiers of 'large acreages of private land' to open them up 'for one or more public recreational' purposes, as defined in the acts, 'without compensation or other favor in return', by 'limiting the liability' of such owners to recreational users to situations in which 'injury results from malicious or willful acts of the owner.'"

Immunity statutes are strictly construed against the party claiming the immunity. Statutes are interpreted in light of each other when they are laws on the same subject. La. C.C. art. 13. An unincorporated association possesses legal personality and has full capacity. *Ermert v. Hartford Ins*. Co, 559 So. 2d 467 (La. 1990). The most commonly regulated form of unincorporated association has been partnerships, and [they] are thus bound by the rules and regulations governing partnerships. La. C.C. art. 2801. A partnership is a juridical person, distinct from its members. Among other things, a partnership has its own patrimony and has the right to sue or be sued in its own behalf. A partner is a mandatary of the partnership.

The parties concede that the land on which Reed was injured is undeveloped, non-residential, rural or semi-rural land, and as such is covered by R.S. 9:2791. Additionally, hunting is a recreational activity which is specifically enumerated in the statute. Reed argues that Gimber is not an owner, lessee, or occupant of the land, and in the alternative that a movable deer stand is not an instrumentality normally encountered in the "true outdoors." Gimber concedes that he is not an owner, but argues that as an officer and the signer of the lease, he is a lessee and an occupant.

The trial court found that Gimber, as a hunting club officer and member, is an "occupant" of the property and as such he did not owe Reed a duty of care to keep the leased premises safe for hunting, or to give a warning for the condition of any structure. The trial court held that without a duty of care or to warn, that Gimber is not liable for injuries which Reed incurred.

The term "occupant" is susceptible of different meanings, so we interpret it to have the meaning that best conforms to the purpose of the law. Further, we consider the meaning of the term by examining the context in which it occurs and the text of the Recreational Use Statutes as a whole. Although the revised statutes themselves do not define the term "occupant," they are ancillaries to the Louisiana Civil Code which does define occupancy. La. C.C. art. 3412 provides that "occupancy is the taking of possession of a corporeal movable that does not belong to anyone. The occupant acquires ownership the moment he takes possession." This article governs the ownership of corporeal movables. As defined in La. R.S. 9:2791(C), the term "premises" will seldom if ever include corporeal movables; the list provided in the definition generally describes corporeal immovables. Accordingly, the legislature could not have intended for the term "occupant" in the Recreational Use Statute to carry the meaning given in La. C.C. art. 3412. Because the legislature did not intend for the term to carry its technical meaning, the term should be given its generally prevailing meaning.

Black's Law Dictionary, Deluxe Sixth Edition, defines occupant as a "person in possession. Person having possessory rights, who can control what goes on on premises. One who has actual use, possession or control of a thing." We believe that this definition conforms with the generally understood meaning of the term "occupant." An occupant is a person who, in his own name, has the right to control the premises, *i.e.*, to make land and water areas available to the public for recreational purposes. *See Monteville v. Terrebonne Parish Consolidated Government, supra.* This interpretation excludes James Gimber as a person who may be considered an "occupant" of the leased premises for purposes of the Recreational Use Statutes. Additionally, although Gimber signed the lease for the property, he did so as a mandatary of the hunting club and not in his own name or in his capacity as an individual.

In sum, as a member of the hunting club, Gimber has the right to hunt on the land, but he is not a person who has the right "to make land and water areas available to the public for recreational purposes" as contemplated by the statutes. Including a member of a hunting club within the definition of "occupant" would not comport with the purpose of the immunity statutes and would unnecessarily broaden the scope of immunity. Considering the purpose of the Recreational Use Statutes and mindful that the statutes are to be strictly construed, we disagree with the trial court's conclusion that Gimber, merely because he is a hunting club officer and member, is entitled to immunity as an "occupant" of the land. Accordingly, the district court should have denied defendants' motion for summary judgment based upon immunity from the Recreational Use Statutes. We hereby reverse the decision of the district court and remand this matter for further proceedings. Costs of this proceeding are assessed to appellees.

REVERSED AND REMANDED.

NOTES

1. *Recreational Use Statutes.* The Louisiana statute quoted in the *Reed* case is fairly typical of most recreational use statutes. Virtually every state has enacted some version of such a statute. *See generally* PREMISES LIABILITY ch. 5. *See also* Barrett, *Good Sports and Bad Lands: The Application of Washington's Recreational Use Statute Limiting Landowner Liability*, 53 WASH. L. REV. 1 (1977).

2. *Key Elements of Most Recreational Use Statutes.* Although individual statutes vary from one jurisdiction to another, most recreational use statutes do have certain common features. They all either list various specific recreational purposes for which the landowner's limited immunity applies (*See, e.g.,* CAL. CIV. CODE § 846 (2000)), or they provide such immunity for more broadly construed "recreational purposes." They all restrict application of the limited statutory immunity in situations where the landowner charges a fee for the use of the premises or otherwise receives some valuable consideration from the entrant. (*See, e.g.,* WASH. REV. CODE § 4.24.210 (2000)). Most of these statutes pertain only to outdoor recreational activities (*see, e.g.,* FLA. STAT. ANN. § 375.251 (2000)), and many further restrict the scope of the landowner's immunity to rural (*see, e.g.,* COLO. REV. STAT. ANN. § 33-41-101 (2000)) as opposed to urban land.

PROBLEM

Gentleman Farmer lived in the city but owned a large tract of undeveloped land in a rural part of the county where he occasionally went to hunt and fish. Felix, a friend and office co-worker, asked Gentleman Farmer if he and some friends could use his land to hunt quail during the upcoming hunting season. Gentleman Farmer agreed (asking only that they bring him back a couple of quail for his dinner). On opening day of the hunting season, Felix and his friends proceeded on their hunting expedition to Gentleman Farmer's property. While walking through a partially overgrown field, Felix tripped over a barbed wire fence that was obscured by weeds. As he fell, cutting himself on the rusty wire fence, his finger accidentally bumped the trigger of his shotgun, causing the gun to discharge and injure Oscar, one of his hunting companions. Can either Felix or Oscar recover for negligence against Gentleman Farmer in a jurisdiction that has enacted a typical "recreational use" statute?

D. CRIMINAL ASSAILANTS

Traditionally, the common law declined to impose any liability for negligence against the owners or possessors of property for injuries inflicted upon entrants by the criminal actions of unknown third parties. *See* RESTATEMENT (SECOND) OF TORTS § 315 (1965). The reason most often given by courts for such a no-duty rule relates to the absence of foreseeability by the landowner or occupant with respect to criminal attacks by third party assailants. For example, in *Doe v. Manheimer*, 563 A.2d 699 (Conn. 1989), the plaintiff pedestrian was abducted from a public sidewalk and subsequently sexually assaulted by an unknown assailant as she walked adjacent to the defendant landowner's vacant lot that was overgrown with brush and tall grass. The court held that even if the defendant had been negligent in allowing the lot to become overgrown with weeds, such negligence was not the proximate cause of the plaintiff's assault injuries. Instead, applying the traditional rationale based upon the absence of foreseeability, the court concluded that the intentional misconduct of the assailant constituted an independent cause that superceded any such negligence by the defendant.

Despite the traditional rationale for this no-duty rule, certain specific types of criminal activity by third parties are not always unforeseeable. How should a court respond to this "absence of foreseeability" argument when the criminal assault is foreseeable?

McCLUNG v. DELTA SQUARE LTD. PARTNERSHIP
937 S.W.2d 891 (Tenn. 1996)

WHITE, J.

On September 7, 1990, thirty-seven-year-old Dorothy McClung, plaintiff's wife, went shopping at Wal-Mart in the Delta Square Shopping Center in Memphis. As she was returning to her parked car around noon, Mrs. McClung was abducted at gunpoint and forced into her car by Joseph Harper, a fugitive from Chattanooga. Later, Harper raped Mrs. McClung and forced her into the trunk of her car where she suffocated. Her body was found by hunters in a field in Arkansas the day after the abduction. Harper confessed, and was convicted of kidnapping, rape, and murder. He committed suicide after being sentenced to life in prison.

Plaintiff filed suit against defendants on his own behalf and on behalf of his and Mrs. McClung's three minor children. In his suit, he alleged that defendant Wal-Mart, the anchor tenant at the Delta Square Shopping Center, and defendant Delta Square, the owner and operator of the center, were negligent in failing to provide security measures for the parking lot and that their negligence was the proximate cause of Mrs. McClung's death. . . .

The trial court and the Court of Appeals based the award of summary judgment in this case on *Cornpropst v. Sloan*, 528 S.W.2d 188 (Tenn. 1975), in which this Court held that shop owners do not owe to customers a duty to protect them against criminal acts of third parties unless the owner knew or should have know the acts were occurring or about to occur. In that case, decided more than two decades ago, a female shopper, while walking to her car in a shopping center's parking lot, was assaulted and narrowly escaped being kidnapped. She sued the shopping center's owners, operators, and tenants for negligence in failing to provide adequate security measures to protect customers from reasonably foreseeable criminal conduct. She alleged that there were no security guards in the parking lot and that no other protective measures were used or installed. She claimed that, prior to her attack, other acts of violence had occurred either on the premises or in the immediate area of the shopping center. Thus, plaintiff contended that defendants were negligent in that they "knew, or in the exercise of reasonable care and ordinary care should have known . . .

that the Plaintiff invitee would be exposed to potential danger and personal harm, and unprotected against criminal acts. . . ."

Choosing to follow the then-prevailing rule, the *Cornpropst* Court refused to impose a duty in the case which it characterized as involving "vague allegation[s] that various crimes, assaults and other acts of violence had been committed either on the premises or in the immediate area." The Court deemed it unfair to impose a duty upon the shopping center owner because the attacker "gave no notice by word, act, dress or deed prior to the commission of the attack that would have indicated to anyone an intention of purpose to commit an assault." In affirming the dismissal of the complaint, the Court adopted the following rule, which has become the analytical focal point in these types of cases:

> There is no duty upon the owners or operators of a shopping center, individually or collectively, or upon merchants and shopkeepers generally, whose mode of operation of their premises does not attract or provide a climate for crime, to guard against the criminal acts of a third party, unless they know or have reason to know that acts are occurring or about to occur on the premises that pose imminent probability of harm to an invitee: whereupon a duty of reasonable care to protect against such act arises. [528 S.W.2d at 198.]

Thus, *Cornpropst* established the principle in Tennessee that businesses not attracting or providing a favorable environment for crime have no duty to protect customers, unless (1) the business knows or has reason to know that criminal acts are occurring or about to occur on the premises, which (2) pose an imminent probability of harm to a customer. In determining whether the business had reason to know, the Court concluded that "conditions in the area [of the defendant business] are irrelevant."

The *Cornpropst* Court had little case law to guide its decision. Since *Cornpropst*, however, numerous courts and commentators have considered a business owner's duty to protect its customers from injuries caused by criminal acts of unknown third persons. Not only has the subject received considerable attention in the legal literature, courts, as a result of the prevalence of violent crimes at commercial establishments, have reexamined the law. *See* Comment, *Business Owners' Duty to Protect Invitees from Third-Party Criminal Attacks*, 54 Mo. L. Rev. 443, 455 (1989). Parking lots in particular have provided fertile ground for crime because customers usually possess money or recently purchased merchandise. Thus, the criminal "in search of valuables need not take a chance on the unknown assets of some passerby." Even so, while courts agree that businesses have a duty to exercise reasonable care in maintaining their premises in a reasonably safe condition, disagreement still exists on whether that duty encompasses taking any measures to protect customers from injuries caused by the criminal acts of unknown third persons.

In the early cases, courts generally denied recovery to customer victims under the theory that the business had no duty to protect its patrons from criminal attacks. The initial reluctance to impose a duty was attributed to several reasons, including general principles of fairness given the unpredictable nature of criminal conduct; fear of creating an undue economic burden upon commercial enterprise and the consuming public; belief that protecting citizens is a function of the government that should not be shifted to the private sector; desire that merchants not become insurers of customer safety; and the notion that the criminal's act constituted a superseding, intervening cause sufficient to break the causational chain of liability. These justifications for not imposing a duty relied upon in *Cornpropst*, form the basis of defendants' argument here.

Notwithstanding the reluctance to impose a duty on business owners, the majority of courts that have considered the issue have been unwilling to hold that a business never has a duty to protect customers from criminal acts. Instead, most have held that, while not insurers of their customers' safety, businesses do have a duty to take reasonable precautions to protect customers from foreseeable criminal acts. This is the position taken in section 344 of the RESTATEMENT (SECOND), comment f, and followed by several states.

Based on this analysis of the decisions of other jurisdictions, we must disavow the observation made in *Cornpropst* that "conditions in the area [of the defendant business] are irrelevant" in assessing the foreseeability of a criminal act. It makes little sense to ignore the frequency and nature of criminal activity in the immediate vicinity of the business, such as an adjacent parking lot, if the crucial inquiry is the foreseeability of a criminal act occurring on defendant's premises. Conditions in the immediate vicinity of defendant's premises are relevant in making this determination. We also find that foreseeability of harm on which liability may be imposed is not limited to criminal acts of third parties that are known or should be known to pose an imminent probability of harm to customers. Conditions other than those which pose an imminent threat to persons on the premises are relevant to the foreseeability of harm.

We, therefore, join those courts which generally impose a duty upon businesses to take reasonable measures to protect their customers from foreseeable criminal attacks. Because those courts do not universally agree on the meaning of "foreseeability," further consideration is required. In determining foreseeability, some courts have utilized the so-called "prior incidents rule." Under this rule, plaintiff must introduce evidence of prior incidents of crime on or near defendant's premises in order to establish foreseeability. Courts vary, however, on whether the prior crimes must be of the same general type and nature as the present offense. The modern trend, however, does not deem foreseeability as necessarily dependent upon evidence of the same type of prior crimes occurring on or near defendant's premises, but requires "inquiry [into] the location, nature and extent of previous criminal activities and their similarity, proximity or other relationship to the crime in question." *Polomie v. Golub Corp.*, 640 N.Y.S.2d at 701.

The prior incidents approach to foreseeability has been lauded as preventing businesses from effectively becoming insurers of public safety since "it is difficult, if not impossible, to envision any locale open to the public where the occurrence of violent crime seems improbable." At the same time, the rule has been labeled "fatally flawed" in several respects:

First, the rule leads to results which are contrary to public policy. The rule has the effect of discouraging landowners from taking adequate measures to protect premises which they know are dangerous. This result contravenes the policy of preventing future harm. Moreover, under the rule, the first victim always loses, while subsequent victims are permitted recovery. Such a result is not only unfair, but it is inimical to the important policy of compensating injured parties. Surely, a landowner should not get one free assault before he can be held liable for criminal acts which occur on his property.

Second, a rule which limits evidence of foreseeability to prior similar criminal acts leads to arbitrary results and distinctions. Under this rule, there is uncertainty as to how "similar" the prior incidents must be to satisfy the rule. The rule raises a number of other troubling questions. For example, how close in time do the prior incidents have to be? How near in location must they be? The rule invites different courts to enunciate different standards of foreseeability based on their resolution of these questions.

Third, the rule erroneously equates foreseeability of a particular act with previous occurrences of similar acts. . . . "The fortuitous absence of prior injury does not justify relieving defendant from responsibility for the foreseeable consequences of its acts."

Finally, the "prior similar incidents rule" improperly removes too many cases from the jury's consideration. It is well-established that foreseeability is ordinarily a question of fact. *Isaacs v. Huntington Memorial Hosp.*, 38 Cal. 3d 112, 695 P.2d 653, 658-59, 211 Cal. Rptr. 356 (Cal. 1985).

Because of these criticisms, several courts have rejected the prior incidents rule in favor of a "totality of the circumstances" approach, in which the foreseeability of criminal conduct may be determined by considering all of the circumstances including the nature or character of the business, its location, and prior incidents of crime, if any. *See, e.g., Doud v. Las Vegas Hilton Corp.*, 109 Nev. 1096, 864 P.2d 796; *Seibert v. Vic Regnier Builder's Inc.*, 856 P.2d at 1332; *Reitz v. May*, 66 Ohio App. 3d 188, 583 N.E.2d 1071 (Ohio App. 1990). The totality approach seeks to avoid determining foreseeability by the "rigid application of a mechanical" prior incidents rule, which requires "finite distinctions between how similar prior incidents must be," *Reitz v. May*, 583 N.E.2d at 1075.

Nonetheless, the totality of the circumstances approach has been criticized as well, as being too broad a standard, effectively imposing an unqualified duty to protect customers in areas experiencing any significant level of criminal activity. The approach might deem criminal attacks on customers foreseeable as a result of circumstances such as the level of crime in the neighborhood, inadequate lighting, or architectural designs, even if no prior instances of crime had occurred. As a practical matter, the totality approach arguably requires businesses to implement expensive security measures (with the costs passed on to consumers) and makes them the insurers of customer safety, two results which courts seek to avoid. Businesses may react by moving from poorer areas where crime rates are often the highest. Not surprisingly then, the totality of the circumstances test has been described as "imprecise," "unfair," and "troublesome" because it makes liability for merchants even less predictable than under the prior incidents rule. . . .

After careful consideration of the jurisprudence of other jurisdictions and our own, we adopt the following principles to be used in determining the duty of care owed by the owners and occupiers of business premises to customers to protect them against the criminal acts of third parties: A business ordinarily has no duty to protect customers from the criminal acts of third parties which occur on its premises. The business is not to be regarded as the insurer of the safety of its customers, and it has no absolute duty to implement security measures for the protection of its customers. However, a duty to take reasonable steps to protect customers arises if the business knows, or has reason to know, either from what has been or should have been observed or from past experience, that criminal acts against its customers on its premises are reasonably foreseeable, either generally or at some particular time.

As a practical matter, the requisite degree of foreseeability essential to establish a duty to protect against criminal acts will almost always require that prior instances of crime have occurred on or in the immediate vicinity of defendant's premises. Courts must consider the location, nature, and extent of previous criminal activities and their similarity, proximity, or other relationship to the crime giving rise to the case of action. To hold otherwise would impose an undue burden upon merchants.

The balancing approach we adopt appropriately addresses both the economic concerns of businesses and the safety concerns of customers who are harmed due to the negligence of one seeking their business. The interpretation of the notice requirement of *Cornpropst*, virtually eliminated these causes of action. The criminal who intends to strike in defendant's parking lot will not enter defendant's store to announce his intentions and thereby provide defendant actual notice of the impending attack. In short, this new rule provides the fairest and most equitable results. It creates a duty in limited circumstances, giving merchants neither absolute immunity nor imposing absolute liability. It recognizes the national trend that businesses must justifiably expect to share in the cost of crime attracted to the business. It encourages a reasonable response to the crime phenomenon without making unreasonable demands.

The standard we adopt is the product of attempts by many jurisdictions to deal with this admittedly difficult issue. While embracing neither the totality of the circumstances nor the prior incidents tests in toto, we have retained the desirable features of both approaches, while avoiding the inherent problems associated with each. For example, we have preserved the primary advantage of the prior incidents rule by not creating an environment where businesses are essentially held strictly liable for customer safety. At the same time, our approach should enable meritorious cases to proceed to the jury which is typical of deserving cases tried under the totality of the circumstances approach. Moreover, rather than having an incentive to do nothing (out of fear of having assumed a duty), businesses will be encouraged to take reasonable security precautions, another characteristic of the totality of the circumstances test. The merchant is in the best position to know the extent of crime on the premises and is better equipped than customers to take measures to thwart it and to distribute the costs.

Here, plaintiff's wife was returning to her car in defendants' parking lot when she was accosted. Plaintiff argues that because of past crimes committed on or near defendants' parking lot, a requisite degree of foreseeability to impose a duty to take reasonable precautions was established. To support this contention, plaintiff relies upon records from the Memphis Police Department, which indicate that from May, 1989 through September, 1990, when plaintiff's wife was abducted, approximately 164 criminal incidents had occurred on or near defendants' parking lot. He also relies on the fact that defendants' nearby competitors provide outdoor security measures and that Wal-Mart uses heightened security measures at other locations.

In response, defendants argue that no duty of reasonable care should be imposed because the attack on plaintiff's wife was neither foreseeable nor preventible. Defendants claim they had no notice that Harper was likely to abduct plaintiff's wife, no reason to have anticipated the attack when it occurred, and no reasonable way to have prevented it. They also assert that providing security is prohibitively expensive, and that security has little impact on preventing crime.

We reject defendants' argument that it owed plaintiff's wife no duty because the attack was not reasonably foreseeable. In the seventeen months prior to the abduction, the numerous reports of crime to police on or near defendants' premises included a bomb threat, fourteen burglaries, twelve reports of malicious mischief, ten robberies, thirty-six auto thefts, ninety larcenies, and one attempted kidnapping on a parking lot adjacent to defendants' parking lot. All of these crimes occurred on or in the immediate vicinity of defendants' parking lot, took place within a relatively short period of time prior to the abduction of plaintiff's wife, and involved a significant threat of personal harm. The record also establishes that defendants' premises was located in a high crime area, and that other nearby major retail centers utilized security measures to protect customers. The manager of the Wal-Mart store at the time of the abduction testified that he would not hold "sidewalk sales" or place merchandise outside the store, except for "dirt," out of fear it would be stolen.

Considering the number, frequency, and nature of the crimes reported to police, management's acknowledgement of security problems, and other evidence in the record, we conclude that the proof would support a finding that the risk of injury to plaintiff's wife was reasonably foreseeable. Of course, foreseeability alone does not establish the existence of a duty. On remand, the magnitude of the potential harm and the burden imposed upon defendants must also be weighed to determine the existence of a duty. While we know little from this record about the extent of injury to customers as a result of criminal acts on or near defendants' premises, we are persuaded that whatever the extent of the injuries, the magnitude of the potential harm was substantial given the nature of the crimes reported to police.

On remand, the court must also consider the burden which the duty would impose upon defendants. We note, for example, that defendants contend that they have no reasonable means of foreseeing the possibility of crime on their premises; that security measures are not effective in reducing crime; and that providing security is cost prohibitive. These arguments must be considered on remand in light of conflicting information supplied by one of Wal-Mart's senior security and loss prevention executives.

In weighing the magnitude of harm and the burden imposed upon defendant, the court must consider whether imposing a duty to take reasonable measures to protect patrons from the consequences of criminal acts of third persons would place an onerous burden — economic or otherwise — upon defendants. If it does not, then the court must consider whether the burden outweighs the foreseeability and gravity of the possible harm, so as to preclude the finding of a duty to take reasonable steps to protect patrons. We hasten to point out, however, that the question of duty and of whether defendants have breached that duty by taking or not taking certain actions is one for the jury to determine based upon proof presented at trial. Additionally, if properly raised as a defense, under our doctrine of comparative fault, a plaintiff's duty to exercise reasonable care for her own safety would be weighed in the balance. *Perez v. McConkey*, 872 S.W.2d 897 (Tenn. 1994).

Finally, we must address defendants' argument that random criminal acts of unknown third persons amount to superseding, intervening causes for which defendants cannot be held liable as a matter of law. It is true, as pointed out by defendants, that a superseding, intervening cause can break the chain of causation. In this regard, we have stated that there is no requirement that a cause, to be regarded as the proximate cause of an injury, be the sole cause, the last act, or the one nearest to the injury, provided it is a substantial factor in producing the end result. An intervening act, which is a normal response created by negligence, is not a superseding, intervening cause so as to relieve the original wrongdoer of liability, provided the intervening act could have reasonably been foreseen and the conduct was a substantial factor in bringing about the harm.

Proximate cause, as well as the existence of a superseding, intervening cause, are jury questions unless the uncontroverted facts and inferences to be drawn from the facts make it so clear that all reasonable persons must agree on the proper outcome.

In conclusion, this record, viewed in light of the principles set forth in this opinion, precludes an award of summary judgment. Assuming for purposes of this analysis that defendants were negligent, we are unable to conclude that all reasonable persons must agree, as a matter of law, that defendants' negligence in failing to provide any security measures did not create a favorable environment for criminal activity. Considering the number, nature, and frequency of crimes committed on or near defendants' premises, it is not beyond the realm of reasonable anticipation that a jury could conclude that defendants' negligence created a foreseeable risk of harm to plaintiff's wife, and that defendants' negligence was a substantial factor in bringing about that harm. Such questions are "peculiarly for the jury" given the present state of this record.

For the reasons stated above, the judgments of the lower courts are reversed. The case is remanded to the trial court for further proceedings consistent with this opinion. The principles set forth today apply to all cases tried or retried after the date of this opinion and all cases on appeal in which the issue in this case has been raised. Costs shall be taxed to defendants.

NOTE

The *McClung* opinion provides an excellent overview of the history and development of the current law regarding the liability in negligence of landowners and occupiers of land for injuries criminally inflicted upon their patrons and customers by third parties. Most of the major cases, as well as the different analytical approaches, pertaining to this area of the law from all jurisdictions are summarized and discussed in *McClung*.

E. ABOLITION/MODIFICATION OF COMMON LAW "STATUS" CATEGORIES

ROWLAND v. CHRISTIAN
443 P.2d 561 (Cal. 1968)

PETERS, Justice.

Plaintiff appeals from a summary judgment for defendant Nancy Christian in this personal injury action. [Plaintiff alleged that he] was a social guest and that he suffered injury when the faucet handle broke; they do not show that the faucet handle crack was obvious or even nonconcealed. Without in any way contradicting her affidavit or his own admissions, plaintiff at trial could establish that [defendant] was aware of the condition and realized or should have realized that it involved an unreasonable risk of harm to him, that defendant should have expected that he would not discover the danger, that she did not exercise reasonable care to eliminate the danger or warn him of it, and that he did not know or have reason to know of the danger. Plaintiff also could establish, without contradicting Miss Christian's affidavit or his admissions, that the crack was not obvious and was concealed. Under the circumstances, a summary judgment is proper in this case only if, after proof of such facts, a judgment would be required as a matter of law for Miss Christian. The record supports no such conclusion.

Section 1714 of the Civil Code provides: 'Every one is responsible, not only for the result of his willful acts, but also for an injury occasioned to another by his want of ordinary care or skill in the management of his property or person, except so far as the latter has, willfully or by want of ordinary care, brought the injury upon himself. . . .' This code section, which has been unchanged in our law since 1872, states a civil law and not a common law principle.

California cases have occasionally stated a similar view. . . . Although it is true that some exceptions have been made to the general principle that a person is liable for injuries caused by his failure to exercise reasonable care in the circumstances, it is clear that in the absence of statutory provision declaring an exception to the fundamental principle enunciated by section 1714 of the Civil Code, no such exception should be made unless clearly supported by public policy.

A departure from this fundamental principle involves the balancing of a number of considerations; the major ones are the foreseeability of harm to the plaintiff, the degree of certainty that the plaintiff suffered injury, the closeness of the connection between the defendant's conduct and the injury suffered, the moral blame attached to the defendant's conduct, the policy of preventing future harm, the extent of the burden to the defendant and consequences to the community of imposing a duty to exercise care with resulting liability for breach, and the availability, cost, and prevalence of insurance for the risk involved

One of the areas where this court and other courts have departed from the fundamental concept that a man is liable for injuries caused by his carelessness is with regard to the liability of a possessor of land for injuries to persons who have entered upon that land. It has been suggested that the special rules regarding liability of the possessor of land are due to historical considerations stemming from the high place which land has traditionally held in English and American thought, the dominance and prestige of the landowning class in England during the formative period of the rules governing the possessor's liability, and the heritage of feudalism.

The departure from the fundamental rule of liability for negligence has been accomplished by classifying the plaintiff either as a trespasser, licensee, or invitee and then adopting special rules as to the duty owed by the possessor to each of the classifications. Generally speaking a trespasser is a person who enters or remains upon land of another without a privilege to do so; a licensee is a person like a social guest who is not an invitee and who is privileged to enter or remain upon land by virtue of the possessor's consent, and an invitee is a business visitor who is invited or permitted to enter or remain on the land for a purpose directly or indirectly connected with business dealings between them. (*Oettinger v. Stewart*, 24 Cal. 2d 133, 136, 148 P.2d 19) Although the invitor owes the invitee a duty to exercise ordinary care to avoid injuring him, the general rule is that a trespasser and licensee or social guest are obliged to take the premises as they find them insofar as any alleged defective condition thereon may exist, and that the possessor of the land owes them only the duty of refraining from wanton or willful injury. (*Palmquist v. Mercer*, 43 Cal. 2d 92, 102, 272 P.2d 26.) The ordinary justification for the general rule severely restricting the occupier's liability to social guests is based on the theory that the guest should not expect special precautions to be made on his account and that if the host does not inspect and maintain his property the guest should not expect this to be done on his account.

An increasing regard for human safety has led to a retreat from this position, and an exception to the general rule limiting liability has been made as to active operations where an obligation to exercise reasonable care for the protection of the licensee has been imposed on the occupier of land. (*Oettinger v. Stewart, supra*) In an apparent attempt to avoid the general rule limiting liability, courts have broadly defined active operations, sometimes giving the term a strained construction in cases involving dangers known to the occupier. . . .

Another exception to the general rule limiting liability has been recognized for cases where the occupier is aware of the dangerous condition, the condition amounts to a concealed trap, and the guest is unaware of the trap. In none of these cases, however, did the court impose liability on the basis of a concealed trap; in some liability was found on another theory, and in others the court concluded that there was no trap. A trap has been defined as a 'concealed' danger, a danger with a deceptive appearance of safety. (*E.g., Hansen v. Richey, supra*, 237 Cal. App. 2d 475, 480, 46 Cal. Rptr. 909.) It has also been defined as something akin to a spring gun or steel trap. In the latter case it is pointed out that the lack of definiteness in the application of the term 'trap' to any other situation makes its use argumentative and unsatisfactory.

The cases dealing with the active negligence and the trap exceptions are indicative of the subtleties and confusion which have resulted from application of the common law principles governing the liability of the possessor of land. Similar confusion and complexity exist as to the definitions of trespasser, licensee, and invitee.

In refusing to adopt the rules relating to the liability of a possessor of land for the law of admiralty, the United States Supreme Court stated: "The distinctions which the common law draws between licensee and invitee were inherited from a culture deeply rooted to the land, a culture which traced many of its standards to a heritage of feudalism. In an effort to do justice in an industrialized urban society, with its complex economic and individual relationships, modern common-law courts have found it necessary to formulate increasingly subtle verbal refinements, to create subclassifications among traditional common-law categories, and to delineate fine gradations in the standards of care which the landowner owes to each. Yet even within a single jurisdiction, the classifications and subclassifications bred by the common law have produced confusion and conflict. As new distinctions have been spawned, older ones have become obscured. Through this semantic morass the common law has moved, unevenly and with hesitation, towards 'imposing on owners and occupiers a single duty of reasonable care in all circumstances." (*Kermarec v. Compagnie Generale*, 358 U.S. 625, 630-31, 79 S. Ct. 406, 410, 3 L. Ed. 2d 550.)

The courts of this state have also recognized the failings of the common law rules relating to the liability of the owner and occupier of land. In refusing to apply the law of invitees, licensees, and trespassers to determine the liability of an independent contractor hired by the occupier, we pointed out that application of those rules was difficult and often arbitrary. In refusing to apply the common law rules to a known trespasser on an automobile, the common law rules were characterized as 'unrealistic, arbitrary, and inelastic,' and it was pointed out that exceedingly fine distinctions had been developed resulting in confusion and that many recent cases have in fact applied the general doctrine of negligence embodied in section 1714 of the Civil Code rather than the rigid common law categories test.

There is another fundamental objection to the approach to the question of the possessor's liability on the basis of the common law distinctions based upon the status of the injured party as a trespasser, licensee, or invitee. Complexity can be borne and confusion remedied where the underlying principles governing liability are based upon proper considerations. Whatever may have been the historical justifications for the common law distinctions, it is clear that those distinctions are not justified in the light of our modern society and that the complexity and confusion which has arisen is not due to difficulty in applying the original common law rules — they are all too easy to apply in their original formulation — but is due to the attempts to apply just rules in our modern society within the ancient terminology. Without attempting to labor all of the rules relating to the possessor's liability, it is apparent that the classifications of trespasser, licensee, and invitee, the immunities from liability predicated upon those classifications, and the exceptions to those immunities, often do not reflect the major factors which should determine whether immunity should be conferred upon the possessor of land. Some of those factors, including the closeness of the connection between the injury and the defendant's conduct, the moral blame attached to the defendant's conduct, the policy of preventing future harm, and the prevalence and availability of insurance, bear little, if any, relationship to the classifications of trespasser, licensee and invitee and the existing rules conferring immunity.

Although in general there may be a relationship between the remaining factors and the classifications of trespasser, licensee, and invitee, there are many cases in which no such relationship may exist. Thus, although the foreseeability of harm to an invitee would ordinarily seem greater than the foreseeability of harm to a trespasser, in a particular case the opposite may be true. The same may be said of the issue of certainty of injury. The burden to the defendant and consequences to the community of imposing a duty to exercise care with resulting liability for breach may often be greater with respect to trespassers than with respect to invitees, but it by no means follows that this is true in every case. In many situations, the burden will be the same, *i.e.*, the conduct necessary upon the defendant's part to meet the burden of exercising due care as to invitees will also meet his burden with respect to licensees and trespassers. The last of the major factors, the cost of insurance, will, of course, vary depending upon the rules of liability adopted, but there is no persuasive evidence that applying ordinary principles of negligence law to the land occupier's liability will materially reduce the prevalence of insurance due to increased cost or even substantially increase the cost.

Considerations such as these have led some courts in particular situations to reject the rigid common law classifications and to approach the issue of the duty of the occupier on the basis of ordinary principles of negligence. And the common law distinctions after thorough study have been repudiated by the jurisdiction of their birth. (Occupiers' Liability Act, 1957, 5 and 6 Eliz. 2, ch. 31.)

A man's life or limb does not become less worthy of protection by the law nor a loss less worthy of compensation under the law because he has come upon the land of another without permission or with permission but without a business purpose. Reasonable people do not ordinarily vary their conduct depending upon such matters, and to focus upon the status of the injured party as a trespasser, licensee, or invitee in order to determine the question whether the landowner has a duty of care, is contrary to our modern social mores and humanitarian values. The common law rules obscure rather than illuminate the proper considerations which should govern determination of the question of duty.

It bears repetition that the basic policy of this state set forth by the Legislature in section 1714 of the Civil Code is that everyone is responsible for an injury caused to another by his want of ordinary care or skill in the management of his property. The factors which may in particular cases warrant departure from this fundamental principle do not warrant the wholesale immunities resulting from the common law classifications, and we are satisfied that continued adherence to the common law distinctions can only lead to injustice or, if we are to avoid injustice, further fictions with the resulting complexity and confusion. We decline to follow and perpetuate such rigid classifications. The proper test to be applied to the liability of the possessor of land in accordance with section 1714 of the Civil Code is whether in the management of his property he has acted as a reasonable man in view of the probability of injury to others, and, although the plaintiff's status as a trespasser, licensee, or invitee may in the light of the facts giving rise to such status have some bearing on the question of liability, the status is not determinative.

Once the ancient concepts as to the liability of the occupier of land are stripped away, the status of the plaintiff relegated to its proper place in determining such liability, and ordinary principles of negligence applied, the result in the instant case presents no substantial difficulties. As we have seen, when we view the matters presented on the motion for summary judgment as we must, we must assume defendant Miss Christian was aware that the faucet handle was defective and dangerous, that the defect was not obvious, and that plaintiff was about to come in contact with the defective condition, and under the undisputed facts she neither remedied the condition nor warned plaintiff of it. Where the occupier of land is aware of a concealed condition involving in the absence of precautions an unreasonable risk of harm to those coming in contact with it and is aware that a person on the premises is about to come in contact with it, the trier of fact can reasonably conclude that a failure to warn or to repair the condition constitutes negligence. Whether or not a guest has a right to expect that his host will remedy dangerous conditions on his account, he should reasonably be entitled to rely upon a warning of the dangerous condition so that he, like the host, will be in a position to take special precautions when he comes in contact with it.

It may be noted that by carving further exceptions out of the traditional rules relating to the liability to licensees or social guests, other jurisdictions reach the same result, that by continuing to adhere to the strained construction of active negligence or possibly, by applying the trap doctrine the result would be reached on the basis of some California precedents (*e.g., Hansen v. Richey, supra*, 237 Cal. App. 2d 475, 481, 46 Cal. Rptr. 909), and that the result might even be reached by a continued expansion of the definition of the term 'invitee' to include all persons invited upon the land who may thereby be led to believe that the host will exercise for their protection the ordinary care of a reasonable man. However, to approach the problem in these manners would only add to the confusion, complexity, and fictions which have resulted from the common law distinctions. The judgment is reversed.

BURKE, Justice (dissenting).

I dissent. In determining the liability of the occupier or owner of land for injuries, the distinctions between trespassers, licensees and invitees have been developed and applied by the courts over a period of many years. They supply a reasonable and workable approach to the problems involved, and one which provides the degree of stability and predictability so highly prized in the law. The unfortunate alternative, it appears to me, is the route taken by the majority in their opinion in this case; that such issues are to be decided on a case by case basis under the application of the basic law of negligence, bereft of the guiding principles and precedent which the law has heretofore attached by virtue of the relationship of the parties to one another. . . . Surely a homeowner should not be obliged to hover over his guests with warnings of possible dangers to be found in the condition of the home (*e.g.*, waxed floors, slipping rugs, toys in unexpected places, etc., etc.). Yet today's decision appears to open the door to potentially unlimited liability despite the purpose and circumstances motivating the plaintiff in entering the premises of another, and despite the caveat of the majority that the status of the parties may 'have some bearing on the question of liability,' whatever the future may show that language to mean.

In my view, it is not a proper function of this court to overturn the learning, wisdom and experience of the past in this field. Sweeping modifications of tort liability law fall more suitably within the domain of the Legislature, before which all affected interests can be heard and which can enact statutes providing uniform standards and guidelines for the future.

I would affirm the judgment for defendant.

NOTES

1. *Rejection" of the Common Law Status Categories. Rowland* was the first American decision to completely abandon dependence upon the tri-partite status categories as a means of determining the landowner's duty of care with respect to an entrant injured on the premises. In place of the status categories, *Rowland* adopted the traditional negligence standard based upon "reasonable" or "ordinary care" under the circumstances. Under *Rowland*, does the entrant's former legal status as an "invitee," "licensee," or "trespasser" have any bearing at all upon the landowner's duty of "reasonable care"?

2. *Popularity of Rowland.* Initially, *Rowland* was quite well-received by legal commentators and courts. During the first few years after the decision, several other jurisdictions followed its newly-established precedent by fully abandoning their reliance upon the tri-partite status categories as a sole means for determining the landowner's duty of care. *See* PREMISES LIABILITY § 1.06[1]. However, after 1985, the "trend" toward total abrogation of the tri-partite status categories that had been started by *Rowland* stopped just as suddenly as it had begun. An increasing number of jurisdictions chose, instead, to only *partially* discard the common law status categories. Moreover, a significant number of jurisdictions have rejected the *Rowland* approach altogether, in favor of retaining the tri-partite common law system.

3. *Judge vs. Jury.* One of the most significant aspects of the *Rowland* decision is its effect upon the traditional roles of the judge and the jury in premises liability litigation. Traditionally, under the common law tri-partite system, once the legal status of the entrant was determined (either by the court as a matter of law when the circumstances were not in dispute, or otherwise by the jury), the landowner's duty of care became fixed. Thus, the court in many instances could control the ultimate outcome in a case simply by determining which status category to apply, and then instruct the jury as to the duty of care appropriate for that particular category. However, under *Rowland,* regardless of the entrant's status, the jury will still be permitted to determine the reasonableness of the defendant's conduct. Under *Rowland*, it is the jury and not the court which may ultimately determine the outcome in most cases. *See generally* Hawkins, *Premises Liability After Repudiation of the Status Categories: Allocation of Judge and Jury Functions*, 15 UTAH L. REV. 15 (1981).

JONES v. HANSEN
867 P.2d 303 (Kan. 1994)

DAVIS, Justice:

This is a premises liability action. Plaintiff, while a social guest in the home of the defendants, fell down a flight of stairs, severely injuring herself. She appeals from a summary judgment entered in favor of the defendants. Summary judgment was based upon the undisputed facts and the court's conclusion that defendants did not breach the duty to refrain from wilfully, wantonly, or recklessly injuring plaintiff.

The question presented is whether this court should change Kansas law regarding the duty owed by an occupier of land to a social guest licensee by adopting a standard of reasonable care under all the circumstances. Under present Kansas law, the duty owed to an entrant upon property is dependent upon the status of the entrant. A majority of this court believes that a partial change in our premises liability law is warranted as more reflective of modern social mores and as a more reasonable method of fault determination in our society.

The facts in this case are not in dispute. Plaintiff was invited to play bridge in the defendants' home. When plaintiff had the dummy hand, she began looking at defendants' art work. Mrs. Hansen told her that there were more paintings in another room. That room was adjacent to the one in which bridge was being played, and it was dimly lit. Plaintiff testified she had to be within a foot of the paintings to see them. She did not ask the defendants where the light switch was located. There were two table lamps, one floor lamp, and eight ceiling floodlights available in the room. Only the floor lamp was lit. It was the first time plaintiff had been in the defendants' home. As plaintiff walked sideways around the room looking at the paintings, she fell down a flight of stairs and was severely injured.

The stairwell was blocked off on two sides with a 33-inch-high bookcase, which defendants placed there to prevent people from just walking into the stairwell. There were three paintings hung on the wall above the stairwell. The paintings had hung at that location since 1977, and no one other than the plaintiff has been injured on the stairway.

Under Kansas law, the common-law classifications of trespassers, licensees, and invitees are used to determine the duty owed by an occupier of land to the entrants on the land. The duty owed is dependent upon the status of the entrant. This classification system has deep roots in Anglo-American jurisprudence as well as in Kansas law. In *Gerchberg v. Loney*, 223 Kan. 446, 448-49, 576 P.2d 593 (1978), this court summarized the duty of care owed to the classes of injured parties coming upon property:

> Under the law in this jurisdiction a social guest has the status of a licensee and his [or her] host owes him [or her] only the duty to refrain from wilfully, intentionally, or recklessly injuring him [or her].

Plaintiff was a social guest in defendants' home. Based on the law existing at the time of plaintiff's injury, defendants owed plaintiff only a duty to refrain from wilfully, intentionally, wantonly, or recklessly injuring her. Under existing Kansas law, the trial court properly granted defendants' motion for summary judgment based upon its finding that the "discovery record . . . in no way suggests total indifference to the consequences and reckless disregard for the rights of others."

Despite several invitations since *Gerchberg*, the majority of this court has elected to maintain the common-law classification of tort plaintiffs as trespassers, licensees, and invitees. *Bowers v. Ottenad*, 240 Kan. 208, 729 P.2d 1103 (1986). This case is the first time in seven years that we have been asked to reevaluate whether our premises liability law should continue to base the occupier's duty of care upon the status of the entrant. Advocates for change argue that a standard of reasonable care under all the circumstances is a more realistic standard in modern society; one that is easily understood and applied because it is used in almost all other tort actions. They argue that a reason may have existed in feudal times and even beyond for the protection of vested property interests, but that modern times demand a recognition that requiring all to exercise reasonable care for the safety of others is the more humane approach. Finally, they argue that the present common-law classifications are rigid and mechanical in application and overly protective of property interests at the expense of human safety.

However, both before and after our decision in *Bowers v. Ottenad*, several jurisdictions elected to modify the duty owed by occupiers of land to persons coming on the property. A majority of jurisdictions still retain the common-law classifications and duties arising from those classifications. Some of those that have changed abolished altogether the classifications and adopted negligence standards calling for the occupier of the lands to exercise reasonable care for the safety of persons coming on their property. Other jurisdictions have elected to retain the classification of trespasser with concomitant duties, but have abandoned the distinction between invitees and licensees. These jurisdictions require an occupier of land to exercise reasonable care under the circumstances for any person entering upon the premises with the express or implied permission of the occupier of the property.

Those jurisdictions that reject altogether the common-law status classifications and require an occupier of land to exercise reasonable care under all the circumstances accept the principle that the foreseeability of the injury rather than the injured party's status is the controlling factor in determining liability. Those jurisdictions that have adopted an intermediate position by abolishing the common-law distinctions between the duties owed to licensees and invitees, while retaining the common-law rules regarding trespassers generally agree that the foreseeability of the injury ought to be the foundation of liability. We believe that this intermediate position is sound.

The majority of jurisdictions considering this issue have retained the common-law classifications, reasoning that the interest in judicial certainty advanced by the maintenance of well-established and predictable allocations of liability under the common law is best for society. Some courts rejecting change have reasoned that replacement of a stable and established system of loss allocation results in the establishment of a system devoid of standards for liability. It also has been suggested that the harshness of the common-law rules has been ameliorated by the judicial grafting of exceptions and that the creation of subclassifications ameliorated the distinctions between active and passive negligence.

We note that the common-law status distinctions between licensees and invitees have not been adopted by the United States Supreme Court in admiralty law. *Kermarec v. Compagnie Generale*, 358 U.S. 625, 630 (1959). Moreover, England, by passage of the Occupiers' Liability Act of 1957, 5 & 6 Eliz. II, c. 31, abrogated the distinction between licensees and invitees, imposing upon occupiers of land a common duty of care towards all visitors except trespassers.

Fifteen years ago, in *Gerchberg v. Loney*, 223 Kan. 446, 576 P.2d 593, this court refused to adopt the standard of reasonable care under all the circumstances for licensees. Not unlike other jurisdictions that have rejected change, we said that such a standard "would have to be applied by the jury to the specific facts of each case. Can a lay jury be expected to consider the proper relative effect of natural and artificial conditions on the premises which are or may be dangerous, the degree of danger inherent in such conditions, the extent of the burden which should be placed on the possessor of the premises to alleviate the danger, the nature, use, and location of the condition or force involved, the foreseeability of the presence of the plaintiff on the premises, the obviousness of such dangerous condition or the plaintiff's actual knowledge of the condition or force which resulted in injury? It would appear these considerations should be imparted to the jury if it is to be placed in a position to decide whether reasonable care was exercised by the possessor of the premises. Otherwise the jury will have a free hand to impose or withhold liability."

Based upon the same reasoning, we again rejected change in *Britt v. Allen County Community Jr. College*, 230 Kan. 502, 638 P.2d 914. Quoting at length from Hawkins, *Premises Liability After Repudiation of the Status Categories: Allocation of Judge and Jury Functions*, UTAH L. REV. 15 (1981), the majority in *Britt* reasoned that it seemed apparent from 80 cases surveyed in that article that courts would still find it necessary to fix the limits of premises liability even after they had repudiated the status categories of entrants on land.

However, even the majority in *Britt* notes that [Hawkins] concludes: " 'In a majority of the cases surveyed the outcome would probably be the same as if the status rules had been applied.' . . ."

In *Britt*, Justice Prager highlights one of the main criticisms of basing liability on the status of the entrant rather than upon the assessment of the duty of due care of the occupier of the premises. He states:

The manifest injustice of the distinction between invitees and licensees is well illustrated by the present case. If the plaintiff, Ella May Britt, had been on the premises attending a lecture sponsored by the junior college on another evening and had been injured as the result of the negligence of its employee, she could have recovered for those personal injuries. Her trouble is that she went to the auditorium on the wrong night. Although she may have been injured in the same way by the negligence of an employee of the junior college, the majority have held that she is completely without remedy because she did not have the status of an invitee, since the program was not being sponsored by the junior college. The inherent injustice of the invitee-licensee differentiation becomes quite obvious in this case. [638 P.2d at 951.]

Our most recent case dealing with this question highlights another criticism leveled by courts rejecting or partially rejecting the common-law status classification. Adoption of a true negligence standard eliminates the complex, confusing, and unpredictable state of law created by courts' attempts to avoid the harshness resulting from rigid application of the traditional rule by increasing the number of classifications. In *Bowers v. Ottenad*, 240 Kan. 208, 729 P.2d 1103, plaintiff, a social guest at a dinner party hosted by one of the defendants, was severely burned when the host prepared a flaming Irish coffee. A bottle of alcohol used in preparation for the Irish coffee ignited and fire burst forth in the form of a "fireball." Justice Holmes wrote the majority opinion and traced the development of the doctrine of "active" negligence in the Kansas law of premises liability. He noted in this case that "appellant's injuries were not the result of any defective or dangerous property conditions existing at the Ottenad residence. Rather, the injuries were the result of the activity of appellant and appellees mixing the flaming drinks." In arriving at the conclusion that the "active" negligence doctrine was the law of Kansas based upon a historical analysis, Justice Holmes notes:

. . . when a licensee, whose presence is known or should be known, is injured or damaged by activity conducted upon the property by the occupier of the property, the duty owed to such person is one of reasonable care under the circumstances. When the injury or damage results from the condition of the premises as opposed to the activity thereon, the duty of the occupier to the licensee is only to refrain from willfully or wantonly injuring the licensee.

240 Kan. 208, Syl. P 4, 729 P.2d 1103. Justice Holmes concludes:

We recognize that there will be instances when it will be difficult to determine whether the alleged negligence falls within the area of an activity carried on by the occupier of the property or is due to the condition of the premises. However, the fact that some cases may be difficult for determination is no justification for refusing to recognize a proper rule of law. Our prior cases are overruled to the extent that they are inconsistent with the views expressed in this opinion. [729 P.2d at 1114.]

The same may now be said in this case: "[T]he fact that some cases may be difficult for determination is no justification for refusing to recognize a proper rule of law." That rule does away with the artificial classifications and distinctions arising therefrom between licensee and invitees, classifications that we have recognized no longer fit contemporary society. Adoption of this rule places the focus where it should be rather than upon allowing the duty in a particular case to be determined by the status of the person who enters upon property. We invest judges and juries with the ultimate authority to resolve disputes in our society. We trust the system, and over the years that system has proven admirable in resolving complex problems in tort cases entrusted to its care. Both judges and juries are familiar with and able to apply ordinary negligence standards. Studies suggest that abolition of the distinctions between the duty owed to an invitee and that owed to a licensee has not altered greatly the results reached, has not left the juries without direction or standards by which to judge the action of the occupier of lands, and has resulted in outcomes that would probably be the same as if the status rules had been applied. We believe that the occupier of land owes a duty of reasonable care under the circumstances to all entrants on the property who are present with the occupier's consent.

We hold that in Kansas, the duty owed by an occupier of land to licensees shall no longer be dependent upon the status of the entrant on the land; the common-law classification and duty arising from the classification of licensees shall no longer be applied. The duty owed by an occupier of land to invitees and licensees alike is one of reasonable care under all the circumstances. Included in the factors that are to be considered in determining whether, in the maintenance of his or her property, the land occupier exercises reasonable care under all circumstances are the foreseeability of harm to the entrant, the magnitude of the risk of injury to others in maintaining such a condition of the premises, the individual and social benefit of maintaining such a condition, and the burden upon the land occupier and/or community, in terms of inconvenience or cost, in providing adequate protection.

At the same time, the effect of the common-law classification of a tort plaintiff as a trespasser is to remain unchanged. A trespasser is defined under Kansas law as one who enters the premises of another without any right, lawful authority, or an express or implied invitation of license. A possessor of the premises upon which a trespasser intrudes owes a trespasser a duty to refrain from wilfully, wantonly, or recklessly injuring him or her. We have determined that the status of a trespasser retains significance in our contemporary society.
. . .

Perhaps the rationale of our decision may be best expressed through the words of Justice Cardozo:

I think that when a rule, after it has been duly tested by experience, has been found to be inconsistent with the sense of justice or with the social welfare, there should be less hesitation in frank avowal and full abandonment. . . . There should be greater readiness to abandon an untenable position when the rule to be discarded may not reasonably be supposed to have determined the conduct of the litigants, and particularly when in its origin it was the product of institutions or conditions which have gained a new significance or development with the progress of the years. . . . If judges have woefully misinterpreted the mores of their day, or if the mores of their day are no longer those of ours, they ought not to tie, in helpless submission, the hands of their successors.

CARDOZO, THE NATURE OF THE JUDICIAL PROCESS, pp. 150-52 (1921).

Having adopted a new rule by adopting a standard of reasonable care under all the circumstances for licensees and invitees in premises liability cases, we conclude that this new rule is to be applied prospectively from the date of this decision. Prior to this decision, all citizens were on notice of premises liability law in the State of Kansas. We deem it, therefore, fair to apply this new rule prospectively, with the exception of the parties to this action.

Upon remand, it remains an open question whether the facts of this particular case would warrant a summary judgment under the new rule adopted by this court. Defendants note in their brief before the trial court: "It is questionable whether plaintiff's evidence is sufficient to present a question of negligence of the defendants." The trial court in its decision noted: "It may be ordinary negligence, it may not be." Because of the law in existence at the time this matter was argued on motion for summary judgment, the only question was whether the defendants' actions were wanton. The parties did not present or argue whether the defendants' actions under all the circumstances were negligent. It remains for determination by the trial court whether, under the new rule adopted by this court, the defendants are entitled to summary judgment.

Reversed and remanded for further proceedings consistent with this opinion.

MCFARLAND, Justice, dissenting:

The traditional classifications relative to premises liability constitute a cornerstone of tort law in Kansas which has been reaffirmed on multiple occasions in recent years. For no legally supportable reason, the majority abandons our prior decisions. This result is wholly contrary to the important doctrine of stare decisis. . . .

An excellent summary of Kansas case law relative to the doctrine of stare decisis is contained in Chief Justice Schroeder's dissent in *Bowers v. Ottenad* . . . wherein he stated:

"Addressing the doctrine of stare decisis, Justice Alex Fromme, writing for the court in *Guffy v. Guffy*, 230 Kan. 89, 96-97, 631 P.2d 646 (1981), said:

'It is not always easy to determine the proper ambit of the court's authority on an issue of the present kind. We must not discard the time-tested advantages of consistency and uniformity in the fabric of the law to do that which we might conceive to be justice in a particular instance. . . . We as judges may have the power, though not the right, to ignore the ultimate effects of legislative pronouncements. History teaches us that departures from clear principles of law lead to more and more departures, many of which for the moment may seem in the highest public interest; but, when that happens, the day will soon come when personal preferences of judges overcome long established principles, and the law instead of being rules governing action becomes vacillating judgments dependent upon the particular membership of the court at any given time.

"'The judge, even when he is free, is still not wholly free. He is not to innovate at pleasure. He is not a knight-errant roaming at will in pursuit of his own ideal of beauty or of goodness. He is to draw his inspiration from consecrated principles. He is not to yield a spasmodic sentiment, to vague and unregulated benevolence. He is to exercise a discretion informed by tradition, methodized by analogy, disciplined by system, and subordinated to 'the primordial necessity of order in the social life.'" CARDOZO, THE NATURE OF THE JUDICIAL PROCESS, at 141 (1921).'

"That doctrine [stare decisis], its literal Latin meaning being 'let the decision stand,' is essential to maintaining certainty and stability in the legal community. By this doctrine, attorneys are able to advise their clients and their clients, in turn, are able to behave accordingly.

"In the early case of *Beamish v. Beamish*, 9 H.L.Cas. (1861), it was said that an appellate court's decision is binding authority upon itself as well as upon inferior courts. The function of the judiciary is not to make the law, but to ascertain and apply existing law to the facts before it. The fact the composition of the court may have changed since an earlier decision is not sufficient reason to overrule established precedent set by that earlier decision. This court has stated the doctrine of stare decisis is not inflexible, and that if an earlier decision is clearly erroneous or conditions have changed materially, the earlier rule should be set aside."

In the case before us, the rationale for departure from the rule of stare decisis is stated as follows:

A majority of this court believes that a partial change in our premises liability law is warranted as more reflective of modern social mores and as a more reasonable method of fault determination in our society.

This is obviously not a determination that our prior decisions were erroneous. The majority finds it is adopting "a more reasonable method." Inherent in this statement is that the existing method is reasonable. If we were deciding a case of first impression, and choosing between two alternatives, such a rationale could be asserted. That is not the situation herein. This leaves us with the determination that the change is "warranted as more reflective of modern social mores." Presumably, this is intended to be the equivalent of the alternative justification for not following the doctrine of stare decisis — conditions having changed materially. . . .

Stare decisis would have little meaning if, no matter how frequently the same issue arises, the court compares historical English social conditions with those of the current year. The issue is whether to change the existing law of Kansas. Under the doctrine of stare decisis, only significant material changes occurring since 1986 should be considered, or, at the earliest, the date should be 1978. The majority identifies no such changes as none exist. The rationale of our decision in the 1970s and 1980s is just as valid now as then and, arguably, more so.

The classifications have been developed over many years and are grounded in reality. In the real world there are enormous differences between businesses and residences. Businesses extend invitations to prospective customers, clients, etc., to come to their places of business for commercial purposes. Persons so coming are, for the most part, personally unknown to those extending the invitation. It is anticipated these invitees will roam freely about the public areas of businesses, and a part of the cost of doing business is providing reasonably safe premises. These establishments are, ordinarily, professionally designed, built, and equipped. Safety and convenience account for much of their sterile uniformity.

Residences are designed to please the homeowners and meet their needs and wants. A residence reflects the homeowners' individuality and is equipped and operated by the homeowners according to how they want to live. We live in the age of the do-it-yourselfer. Few homes would meet OSHA's standards, and few individuals would desire to live in such a home. Modern businesses do not have polished hardwood floors, throw rugs, extension cords, rough flagstone paths, stairways without handrails, unsupervised small children, toys on the floor, pets, and all the clutter of living — homes do. There are good reasons behind the old adage that most accidents occur in the home.

Here, we are specifically concerned with the business invitee and social guest in the home. The argument is made: Why should liability rest on the injured party's status as a business invitee or social guest (licensee)? As any homeowner knows, the business invitee is in the residence on a much different basis than is the social guest. The invitee is there for a limited specific purpose. For example, when the Maytag man is called to repair the washing machine, he is shown where the machine is and advised of the machine's problem. The repairperson will be in the laundry room or wherever the machine is located. If he or she wants to go to the basement to check the plumbing, or use the bathroom or the telephone, permission and location are asked. The homeowner shows the repairperson where the basement, phone, bathroom, etc. is. The repairperson does not have free run of the premises. The homeowner knows just where the repairperson is. If there is a known hazard with which the repairperson will be in contact, such as a frayed electrical cord on the washing machine, it is logical to require that a warning be given. Likewise, if an insurance agent comes in to discuss insurance, he or she will be escorted to a particular place and seated. If the homeowner goes to the kitchen to get coffee, he or she has every reason to expect the agent to be exactly where the agent was seated. The social guest, on the other hand, is there on a much more informal basis and can be anywhere in the residence. Commonly, guests are told to leave their coats on the bed upstairs while the homeowner returns to the kitchen to finish meal preparations. Relatives and close friends wander at will, making themselves at home, as the saying goes. The homeowner simply does not have the awareness of all guests' locations in mind at all times or even know where they might be. Social guests and hosts take each other as they are, in a relaxed informal situation.

The idea that one's home is one's castle has even greater meaning today. The increasing crime rate makes many people afraid to be away from home at night. Their safe sanctuary is their home. The cares, concerns, and pressures of their lives make the home this sanctuary. Over and over again, one hears victims of residential burglaries describe their feelings as being those of violation or of psychological rape. Their one safe place is not safe any more. This is an area where people have an expectation of privacy — a carefully guarded term in criminal law. Our times produce high frustration levels — not only from crime but also from increasing job and economic pressures, governmental restrictions on activities, etc.

One's home is where one can be oneself. Neighbors, relatives, and friends stop by to visit. Our highly mobile society makes social visits more common than ever. To place the same standard on an individual in his or her home relative to a social guest as in a business relationship entails an unreasonable intrusion.

How can a homeowner protect himself or herself from liability? Must the homeowner close out the world, padlock off-limit areas, make the home a safe sterile place devoid of individuality, post warning signs, lock up children and pets, regiment all guests, forbid the children to invite friends over, or eliminate all elderly or handicapped persons as persons who may enter the home socially?

Even if the homeowner is not negligent, it will take a jury trial, in most instances, to determine that fact. Interestingly, the jury, in determining whether or not the defendant homeowner has exercised reasonable care, will be considering, inter alia, the status of the injured guest. The circumstances of the visit are an integral part of a foreseeability determination.

There is another serious effect from the majority's decision. Present day homeowners and renters insurance rates in Kansas reflect our present law on premises liability. The potential for increased liability and defense costs, whether in real or exaggerated terms, will be used to justify increased premiums for such insurance.

Kansas has, in the past, created exceptions to the present standards where justified and can continue to do so in the future (active negligence, attractive nuisance, etc.). In this manner, undue hardship can be ameliorated while adhering to the basic principles.

As used in this dissent, "homeowner" includes individuals who rent or lease the premises in which they reside. The majority decision is not just adding a burden to the landed estate owner; the homeowner of even the most modest residence or apartment will be subject to far greater liability than exists at present.

The case before us is a sleeper in every sense of the word. It raises an issue that has been put to rest. No new argument is made in support of the proposed change. [O]ne of the basic tenets of well-established Kansas law is being dramatically altered with no sound or sufficient reason being stated in the majority opinion to justify such a change. Stare decisis is grounded on very important principles. A body of law is established on precedent in order that people will know what the law is and can depend on it. Lawyers can hardly advise their clients as to the law if precedent means nothing.

Our established law is neither clearly erroneous, nor has there been a material change in circumstances justifying a change. This court is, accordingly, bound by our prior decisions. If a change is to be considered on a public policy basis, it should be addressed to the legislature, where the public policy may be determined after the receipt of input from all parties potentially affected thereby.

I would adhere to our existing law and affirm the district court.

NOTES

1. *The role of "stare decisis."* As indicated by the separate majority and the dissenting opinions in *Hansen, supra*, the role of the doctrine of *stare decisis* among modern-day judges continues to represent a point of strong disagreement. Notice how BOTH the majority and the dissenting opinions in *Hansen* rely upon quotes from Justice Cardozo to support their respective arguments.

2. *Rowland Standard of Care.* Consistent with the majority opinion in *Jones*, a number of other jurisdictions have likewise adopted modified versions of the *Rowland* rule by eliminating only the distinction between licensee and invitee categories. *See, e.g., Poulin v. Colby College,* 402 A.2d 846 (Me. 1979); *Mounsey v. Ellard*, 297 N.E.2d 43 (Mass. 1979); *see generally* PREMISES LIABILITY § 1.06[2][a].

3. *Retention of Common Law "Status" Categories and Stare Decisis.* Despite the influence of *Rowland* on the development of modern American premises liability law, the majority of jurisdictions continue to adhere to the traditional common law approach by defining the landowner's duty of care in relation to the classification of the injured entrant into one of the tri-partite status categories. As illustrated by Justice McFarland's dissenting opinion in *Jones*, the most

frequently asserted rationale for retaining the traditional common law rule has been based upon the doctrine of *stare decisis* and the stability and predictability which is provided by the continued adherence to the traditional rules. *See* PREMISES LIABILITY § 1.06[3] for a thorough discussion of these cases.

F. LESSORS OF REAL PROPERTY

Unlike the traditional rules regarding liability for ordinary landowners with respect to premises-related injuries, lessors of real property enjoyed a much greater common law immunity. Even though the tenant/lessee might be classified as an "invitee" on the leased premises, most courts refused to impose any common law duty of care whatsoever upon the lessor with respect to injured tenants, or even their injured guests (licensees). By analogy to the common law sales doctrine of *caveat emptor* ("let the buyer beware"), this traditional rule of non-liability of lessors has sometimes been referred to as *caveat lessee* ("let the lessee beware.") *See generally* Love, *Landlord's Liability for Defective Premises: Caveat Lessee, Negligence, or Strict Liability?* 1975 WIS. L. REV. 19. Over the years, the harshness of this rule of non-liability has given rise to the creation of numerous "exceptions" whereby a duty of reasonable care has been imposed against lessors of real property in a wide variety of special situations. The following case is fairly typical of the manner in which many courts have attempted to avoid the harshness of the traditional common law rule of non-liability with respect to lessors.

COGGIN v. STARKE BROTHERS REALTY CO., INC.
391 So. 2d 111 (Ala. 1980)

JONES, J.

Appellant appeals from the trial court's granting of summary judgment for Defendants-Appellees on the issue of a landlord's duty to maintain common areas and passageways of residential premises. We reverse and remand.

Appellant Marguerite G. Coggin is a 68-year-old widow who executed a residential lease for an apartment at 101-A Carey Drive in Montgomery, Alabama, in June of 1978. Upon taking possession of the premises, she noticed that the back steps leading up to her dwelling were "steep and narrow" and lacked a handrail. These steps were a portion of the common area of the rental property used by Ms. Coggin and the other tenants.

A short time thereafter, Ms. Coggin noticed two long iron railings leaning against the exterior walls of her apartment building. Later, in the fall of 1978, she observed a third railing leaning against the southern exterior wall of the building in which her apartment was located. Prior to September of 1978, she primarily used the front steps to her apartment for ingress and egress, using the back steps on occasion for carrying out the garbage to containers located behind her building. After her automobile battery was stolen from her car parked in front of her residence, she began substantial use of the back steps to her apartment. On February 8, 1979, Ms. Coggin slipped and fell down the back steps. As a result of her fall, she sustained a broken arm as well as numerous bruises and abrasions, hospitalizing her from February 8 until February 14, 1979.

Generally, landlords have the same responsibilities to exercise due care with regard to common areas over which they retain control as ordinary owners of land would have. In this regard, tenants are considered to be the invitees of the landlord while utilizing the common areas of the landlord's property. *Hancock, supra*; *Mudd v. Gray*, 200 Ala. 92, 75 So. 468 (1917). *See* Comment, *Liability of an Alabama Landlord for Defects in the Premises*, 3 ALA. L. REV. 335, 349 (1951).

RESTATEMENT (SECOND) OF TORTS, § 360 (1965), adopted by this Court in *Hancock*, reads as follows:

> "Parts of Land Retained in Lessor's Control Which Lessee is Entitled to Use.
>
> A possessor of land who leases a part thereof and retains in his own control any other part which the lessee is entitled to use as appurtenant to the part leased to him, is subject to liability to his lessee and others lawfully upon the land with the consent of the lessee or a sublessee for physical harm caused by a dangerous condition upon that part of the land retained in the lessor's control, *if the lessor by the exercise of reasonable care could have discovered the condition and the unreasonable risk involved therein and could have made the condition safe*." (Emphasis added.)

In *Chambers v. Buettner*, 295 Ala. 8, 321 So.2d 650 (1975), this Court stated that the "rule . . . embodied in . . . RESTATEMENT (SECOND) OF TORTS, § 361 (1965)," which we now reaffirm, reads as follows:

> "Parts of Land Retained in Lessor's Control but Necessary to Safe Use of Part Leased.
>
> A possessor of land who leases a part thereof and retains in his control any other part which is necessary to the safe use of the leased part, is subject to liability to his lessee and others lawfully upon the land with the consent of the lessee or a sublessee for physical harm caused by a dangerous condition upon that part of the land retained in the lessor's control, if the lessor by the exercise of reasonable care
>
> (a) *could have discovered the condition and risk involved, and*
>
> (b) *could have made the condition safe*." (Emphasis added.)

Appellees [direct] our attention to relatively recent invitee cases in which we affirmed summary judgments adverse to the claimants: *Sledge v. Carmichael*, 366 So. 2d 1117 (Ala. 1979); and *Tice v. Tice*, 361 So. 2d 1051 (Ala. 1978).

The former of these two cases is so clearly distinguishable as to require little discussion. There, the plaintiff Sledge "missed the [porch] steps entirely, causing her to fall approximately two feet and resulting in injury to her leg." No defect in the steps, or the lighting conditions in the vicinity of the steps, was claimed or shown. Thus, no genuine issue of material fact was presented.

Although not as extreme in its contrast, *Tice*, likewise, is readily distinguishable. There, the yard in which the plaintiff fell was not, of itself, defective, nor was there shown any "instrumentality located on the premises as a result of the defendants' negligence of which the defendants had or should have had notice at the time of the accident."

Appellees lay great stress on the similarity of *Tice* and the instant case in that the plaintiff in each case was unable to testify as to "what caused you to fall." The mere similarity of plaintiffs' testimony on causation, however, does not mandate identical holdings. Under the circumstances of *Tice*, lack of evidence of causation went to the very heart of the requisite elements of plaintiff's claim — primarily, the breach of any duty owed to her. In the instant case, on the other hand, the Plaintiff's testimony that she did not know what caused her to fall relates more narrowly to the precise mechanics of her accident. When the evidence is viewed most favorably to the Plaintiff, it is clear that she fell while descending a steep stairway with narrow steps and without a handrail. All of the elements of her claim could reasonably be inferred by the factfinder from the totality of the circumstances as shown by the evidence.

We hold, therefore, that the evidence, including evidence bearing on the defense of "open and obvious danger," viewed in light of the applicable substantive law, presents genuine issues of material fact which Plaintiff is entitled to have submitted, pursuant to appropriate instructions, for a jury's determination.

Thus, the trial court erred in granting Defendants' motion for summary judgment.

REVERSED AND REMANDED.

NOTES

1. *"Common areas" retained in the landlord's exclusive control.* The *Coggin* court applied the "common area" exception to impose a duty of reasonable care upon the landlord. Essentially, this exception elevates the duty of care owed by the lessor to persons injured on various "common areas" of the leased premises to the same duty that is owed by other owners and occupiers of land. Exactly what portion of the leased premises may be classified as a "common area" is subject to interpretation by the courts. Certainly those areas such as entryways, hallways, and parking lots which are used in common by all tenants would be classified as part of the common area of the leased premises. However, where an entryway leads only to an individual apartment, some courts have refused to

classify such areas as "common." *See Golds v. Del Aguila*, 686 N.Y.S.2d 908 (App. Div. 1999). Other areas which may not be commonly accessible by tenants but which remain within the exclusive control of the landlord may also be classified as a "common area." Thus, in *Griffin v. West RS, Inc.*, 984 P.2d 1070 (Wash. Ct. App. 1999), the court held that the overhead attic space that connected two adjoining apartment units in the defendant landlord's apartment complex was a "common area" of the leased premises over which the defendant owed a duty to exercise reasonable care to prevent the unauthorized access by one tenant who had crawled through the attic opening into another tenant's apartment.

2. *Other Exceptions to the Lessor's Common Law Rule of Non-liability: Voluntary repairs (negligently) performed.* Even where the landlord, under no legal obligation to make repairs to the leased premises, voluntarily does so anyway, the common law immunity may be lost if such repairs are negligently made. *See* RESTATEMENT (SECOND) TORTS § 362 (1965). For example, in *Minoletti v. Sabini*, 103 Cal. Rptr. 528 (Cal. Ct. App. 1972), the plaintiff tenant was injured when a double-hung window that had been installed by the landlord in her apartment fell down and amputated her finger. The court held that although the landlord may have had no duty initially to repair the window, liability could still be imposed where such repairs were voluntary undertaken and performed in a negligent manner. The majority of courts have been willing to apply this exception regardless of whether the landlord has made the repair pursuant to an express covenant in the parties' lease agreement or merely gratuitously, *See, e.g., Towers Tenant Ass'n, Inc. v. Towers Ltd. Partnership*, 563 F. Supp. 566 (D.D.C. 1983) (gratuitous renovations); *Southern Apartments, Inc. v. Emmett*, 114 So. 2d 453 (Ala. 1959) (gratuitous repairs). However, some courts have refused to apply this exception for purely gratuitous repairs unless the landlord has been grossly negligent in making them. *See Haga v. Childress*, 258 S.E.2d 836 (N.C. Ct. App. 1979).

3. *Undisclosed latent defects existing at the time of leasing.* When the landlord knows (or has reason to know) of the existence of some defect in the leased premises that is hidden and not otherwise discoverable by the tenant at the time of leasing, courts have recognized a duty on behalf of the landlord to at least disclose the existence of the defect to the tenant. *See, e.g., Francis v. Pic*, 226 N.W.2d 654 (N.D. 1975); *Barrett v. Lusk*, 695 N.Y.S.2d 776 (App. Div. 1999). Questions whether any given defect in the premises is latent or patent are ordinarily for the trier of fact. *See, e.g., Richards v. Dahl*, 618 P.2d 418 (Or. 1980). *Cf. Marsh v. Bliss Realty, Inc.*, 195 A.2d 331 (R.I. 1963) (defect was *not* latent within the meaning of this exception where it was equally known by both the landlord and the tenant).

4. *Premises leased for public use.* When the lessor knows or has reason to know at the time of leasing that the premises will be used for some purpose for which members of the general public will be admitted, the lessor may be liable for negligence with respect to injuries caused by latent defects in the leased

premises. *See* RESTATEMENT (SECOND) TORTS § 359 (1965). *See, e.g., Graves v. United States Coast Guard*, 692 F.2d 71 (9th Cir. 1982) (applying California law). This exception is only applicable where the defect actually exists at the time of the leasing. *See, e.g., Reicheneker v. Seward*, 277 N.W.2d 539 (Neb. 1979). Cases applying this exception have not always agreed as to precisely what types of use constitute a "public use." A few courts still apply the traditional common law interpretation of this exception that requires the leased premises to be held open to large numbers of the public rather than to merely occasional entrants onto the premises by members of the public. *See, e.g., Roth v. Zukowski*, 757 S.W.2d 581 (Mo. 1988). The modern trend is to permit the exception in any situation where it is known by the lessor at the time of leasing that the premises will be held open for use by any members of the public. *See* PREMISES LIABILITY § 9A.03[2].

5. Although many courts today continue to apply the traditional rule of non-liability as modified by the various common law exceptions to lessors of real property with respect to injuries to persons situated on or in the vicinity of the leased property, a number of courts have taken an entirely different approach, as indicated by the following case.

PAGELSDORF v. SAFECO INS. CO. OF AMERICA
284 N.W.2d 55 (Wis. 1979)

CALLOW, J.

The defendant Richard J. Mahnke owned a two-story, two-family duplex. There were four balcony porches: one in front and one in back of each flat. Mahnke rented the upper unit to John and Mary Katherine Blattner who lived there with their three children until Mr. Blattner left the family. Mahnke and his wife lived in the lower unit. The Blattners held the flat under an oral lease which included an agreement that Mahnke would make all necessary repairs on the premises. Mahnke worked as a mechanic for Wisconsin Electric Power Company and considered himself a good handyman.

All the railings on the porches were originally wooden, but Mahnke had begun to replace them with wrought iron as the wooden railings began to deteriorate. By May 10, 1974, wrought iron railings had been placed on the lower back porch, but the wooden railing on the upper back porch had not been replaced. The wooden railing consisted of 2 x 4's running parallel to the floor of the porch connected by 2 x 2 spacers running perpendicular to the floor. The railing sections were approximately 3 feet from top to bottom and were between 4 and 6 feet long. They were attached to upright 4 x 4's by means of nails driven at approximately a 45 degrees angle; none of them were held in place by screws, bolts, or braces.

Mr. Blattner left the family, and in April, 1974, Mrs. Blattner left the apartment and moved with her children to Kansas. She left her furniture in the apartment and paid her rent for the month of May, having arranged with the

Mahnkes to have her brothers move the furniture on May 11. On May 10, 1974, Mrs. Blattner's two brothers arrived to move her belongings to Kansas. They rented a truck and parked it behind the duplex. While moving the furniture out of the duplex, they felt they would need help with the heavier items. They asked Carol Pagelsdorf, a next-door neighbor who had been packing Mrs. Blattner's belongings, to ask her husband James to help them. He agreed to help.

While moving the bedroom furniture, Pagelsdorf and one of Mrs. Blattner's brothers felt that the box spring was too cumbersome to be taken down the back stairway. The Blattner brother decided that the best way to remove it from the apartment would be to lower it from the rear balcony to the ground. Pagelsdorf and a Blattner brother went out on the porch and visually inspected it for safety, but Pagelsdorf did not touch or shake the railings before taking the box spring out. The railings, which had been painted by Mahnke within the past two years, appeared safe. The Blattner brother and Pagelsdorf took the box spring out onto the balcony and leaned it on a railing section. They picked up the spring and leaned over the railing while passing it down to the other brother. While letting the spring down, Pagelsdorf applied pressure straight down on the railing with his body. After both men released the box spring, Pagelsdorf began to straighten up, placing his hands on the railing, and bending his knees slightly. His knees then touched the 2 x 2 spokes in the railing, and the bottom swung out as if on a hinge. The entire railing section came loose, and Pagelsdorf fell to the ground below, suffering injuries.

Mahnke testified that after the incident he examined the 4 x 4 posts and the railing section which gave way and found that the railing ends had dry rot in them. He stated that wood with dry rot would retain its form but not its strength and that this condition would not be readily visible if the wood had been painted over.

Mrs. Blattner testified that Mahnke had warned her of the railing's rotting condition prior to painting the railing. She also testified that several times she had asked Mahnke to repair the railing because it was rotting; she stated that each time Mahnke responded by telling her that he was busy and would make the repair when he had time to do so. Mahnke testified that prior to the accident he had no knowledge of the rotting condition in the railing and that neither Mrs. Blattner nor her husband ever complained to him about the condition of the railing on the back porch. However, on June 7, 1974, Mahnke gave a statement to an investigator in which he related that several times he had warned Mrs. Blattner to be careful of the upstairs porch railing because he did not trust its strength. Mahnke also testified in a deposition taken April 29, 1976, that he had warned Mrs. Blattner to keep her children off the porch because of his concerns that they would crawl over the railing and that the railing would give way. At trial, Mahnke testified that these warnings merely reflected his distrust of railings in general. . . .

[The trial court instructed the jury that] "[a] possessor has no duty to discover dangers of which he is himself unaware. His duty only is to give proper and timely warning of those dangers which are known to him, and then only as to those dangers which he realizes or, in the exercise of ordinary care, should realize, involve an unreasonable risk of causing bodily harm to the licensee."

[T]he jury found that Mahnke had no knowledge of the railing's defective condition and, hence, apportioned no negligence to Mahnke. Following motions after verdict, the trial court entered judgment on the verdict, dismissing the Pagelsdorfs' complaint. The plaintiffs appeal.

The question on which the appeal turns is whether the trial court erred in failing to instruct the jury that Mahnke owed Pagelsdorf a duty to exercise ordinary care in maintaining the premises.

Prior to December 10, 1975, the duty of an occupier of land toward visitors on the premises was determined in Wisconsin law on a sliding scale according to the status of the visitor. To trespassers, land occupiers owed only the duty of refraining from willful and intentional injury. *Copeland v. Larson*, 46 Wis. 2d 337, 341,174 N.W.2d 745 (1970). A person who had permission to enter the land, but who went upon it for his own purposes rather than to further an interest of the possessor, was labeled a licensee. Toward a licensee, the occupier owed the limited duty of keeping the property safe from traps and avoiding active negligence. There was no obligation regarding dangers unknown to the possessor. The highest duty — that of ordinary care — was owed to an invitee, one who entered the land upon business concerning the possessor and at his invitation. In *Antoniewicz v. Reszczynski*, 70 Wis. 2d 836, 854-55, 236 N.W.2d 1 (1975), we abolished, prospectively, the distinction between the different duties owed by an occupier to licensees and to invitees. . . .

The facts of the instant case arose before the *Antoniewicz* decision; the parties agree that the extent of Mahnke's duty toward Pagelsdorf turns on whether Pagelsdorf was an invitee or a licensee with respect to Mahnke. Pagelsdorf maintains he was Mahnke's invitee; if he was, the jury should have been instructed that Mahnke owed him a duty of ordinary care. The defendants contend that the trial court properly determined that Pagelsdorf was Mahnke's licensee and, therefore, properly instructed the jury that he owed Pagelsdorf only a duty to warn of known hazards.

These arguments overlook the effect on a landowner's common law duty upon transfer of the premises from the owner to a lessee. The classification of visitors identified the degree of duty of the possessor or occupier of the premises. When the property is leased, the duty of the landlord was controlled by a different rule: That, with certain exceptions, a landlord is not liable for injuries to his tenants and their visitors resulting from defects in the premises. *See, e.g., Skrzypczak v. Konieczka*, 224 Wis. 455, 458, 272 N.W. 659 (1937). The general rule of nonliability was based on the concept of a lease as a conveyance of property and the consequent transfer of possession and control of the premises to the tenant.

There are exceptions to this general rule of nonliability. The landlord is liable for injuries to the tenant or his visitor caused by a dangerous condition if he contracts to repair defects, or if, knowing of a defect existing at the time the tenant took possession, he conceals it from a tenant who could not reasonably be expected to discover it. *Skrzypczak v. Konieczka, supra; Kurtz v. Pauly,* 158 Wis. 534, 538-39, 149 N.W. 143 (1914); *Flood v. Pabst Brewing Co.*, 158 Wis. 626, 631-32, 149 N.W. 489 (1914). Additionally, the general rule is not applicable where the premises are leased for public use, or are retained in the landlord's control, or where the landlord negligently makes repairs. RESTATEMENT (SECOND) OF TORTS, secs. 359-62 (1965). The rule of nonliability persists despite a decided trend away from application of the general rule and toward expansion of its exceptions. RESTATEMENT (SECOND) OF PROPERTY, (Tentative Draft No. 4), Ch. 16 (1976); RESTATEMENT (SECOND) OF TORTS, secs. 35-56 (1965).

None of the exceptions to the general rule are applicable to the facts of this case. The premises were not leased for public use, nor was the porch within Mahnke's control, nor did he negligently repair the railing. The plaintiffs argue that Mahnke contracted to repair defects; but according to Mrs. Blattner's testimony, Mahnke's promise extended only to items the Blattners reported as being in disrepair. Therefore, error cannot be predicated on the trial court's failure to give an instruction concerning Mahnke's constructive knowledge where the asserted contract was to repair defects of which Mahnke actually knew. Finally, the concealed-defect exception does not apply because there was no evidence that the dry rot existed in 1969 when the Blattners moved in and because Mrs. Blattner testified that she knew of the rot in the railing.

Therefore, if we were to follow the traditional rule, Pagelsdorf was not entitled to an instruction that Mahnke owed him a duty of ordinary care. We believe, however, that the better public policy lies in the abandonment of the general rule of nonliability and the adoption of a rule that a landlord is under a duty to exercise ordinary care in the maintenance of the premises.

Such a rule was adopted by the New Hampshire court in *Sargent v. Ross*, 113 N.H. 388, 308 A.2d 528 (1973). The plaintiff's four-year-old child fell to her death from an outdoor stairway of a residential building owned by the defendant. In a wrongful death action against the landlord, the plaintiff claimed the stairs were too steep and the railing inadequate. The jury awarded the plaintiff damages, and the landlord appealed from a judgment entered on the verdict. After eliminating the established exceptions to the rule of nonliability, the court concluded that the rule had nothing to recommend itself in a contemporary, urban society and ought to be abandoned. Instead, general principles of negligence should apply. The court stated that the "'quasisovereignty of the landowner'" had its genesis in "agrarian England of the dark ages." Whatever justification the rule might once have had, there no longer seemed to be any reason to except landlords from a general duty of exercising ordinary care to prevent foreseeable harm. The court reasoned that the modern trend away from special immunities in tort law and the recognition of an implied warranty of habitability in an apartment lease transaction argued in favor of abolishing the common law rule of nonliability. Accordingly, a landlord's conduct should be appraised according to negligence principles. Questions of control, hidden defects, and common use would be relevant only as bearing on the general determination of negligence, including foreseeability and unreasonableness of the risk of harm.

In *Antoniewicz*, we cited *Sargent* as one of many cases whose reasoning supported the abolition of the common law distinctions between licensees and invitees. The policies supporting our decision to abandon these distinctions concerning a land occupier's duty toward his visitors compel us, in the instant case, to abrogate the landlord's general cloak of immunity toward his tenants and their visitors. . . .

It would be anomalous indeed to require a landlord to keep his premises in good repair as an implied condition of the lease, yet immunize him from liability for injuries resulting from his failure to do so. We conclude that there is no remaining justification for the landlord's general cloak of common law immunity and hereby abolish the general common law principle of nonliability of landlords toward persons injured as a result of their defective premises. . . .

We have considered whether the rule we adopt today was so strongly implied in *Antoniewicz* that it might be unfair, in light of the prospective operation of that holding, to apply it to these facts which occurred before that decision. While the instant holding is a natural outgrowth of *Antoniewicz*, we believe the rule abrogated herein is distinguishable from *Antoniewicz* because the rule governing landlord liability was predicated on lack of control over the premises. Accordingly, the application of the new standard to landlord liability is not governed by the prospective operation of *Antoniewicz*. Nor are we persuaded that the rule adopted herein should operate prospectively only. Generally, a decision overruling or repudiating other cases is given retrospective operation. *Fitzgerald v. Meissner & Hicks, Inc.*, 38 Wis. 2d 571, 575, 157 N.W.2d 595 (1968). The rule of landlords' nonliability was riddled with many exceptions; thus reliance on the rule could not have been great. *See*, Love, *Landlord's Liability for Defective Premises: Caveat Lessee, Negligence, or Strict Liability?*, 1975 WIS. L. REV. 19, 116-17. We find no reason to depart from the general rule of retrospective operation of the mandate herein.

In conclusion, a landlord owes his tenant or anyone on the premises with the tenant's consent a duty to exercise ordinary care. If a person lawfully on the premises is injured as a result of the landlord's negligence in maintaining the premises, he is entitled to recover from the landlord under general negligence principles. Issues of notice of the defect, its obviousness, control of the premises, and so forth are all relevant only insofar as they bear on the ultimate question: Did the landlord exercise ordinary care in the maintenance of the premises under all the circumstances?

Judgment reversed and cause remanded for proceedings consistent with this opinion.

NOTE

Residential vs. Commercial Lessors. The court in *Pagelsdorf* abolished the lessor's traditional common law non-liability with respect to both residential and commercial property. Only a few other courts have been willing to do this. *See, e.g., Brennan v. Cockrell Invs., Inc.,* 111 Cal. Rptr. 122 (Cal. Ct. App. 1973); *Young v. Garwacki,* 402 N.E.2d 1045 (Mass. 1981); *Corrigan v. Janney,* 626 P.2d 838 (Mont. 1981). Most other courts that have formally abolished the non-liability rule of landlords have done so only with respect to *residential* landlords. *See, e.g., Presson v. Mountain States Properties,* 501 P.2d 17 (Ariz. Ct. App. 1972); *Mansur v. Eubanks,* 401 So. 2d 1328 (Fla. 1981). Despite the reasoning offered by cases like *Pagelsdorf* for abandoning the common law non-liability rule, a significant number of jurisdictions, as in *Coggins,* continue to adhere to the traditional rule, modifying it as necessary in individual cases by the various common law exceptions that have been developed. *See generally* PREMISES LIABILITY § 9A.02[2].

PROBLEM

Johnson owns a duplex (*i.e.*, two-unit) apartment. The front door of each unit opens onto a common front porch, however, each individual unit has its own separate back door that opens onto a small rear stoop surrounded by a wrought iron railing. Johnson rented one unit to tenant Abbott and the second unit to tenant Baker. Aware that the iron railing around Baker's back porch was loose and in need of repair, Johnson pointed out the defect to Baker at the time of leasing and agreed to charge $25.00 per month less than the regular rental for the apartment unit. Two weeks later, after visiting inside Baker's apartment, Abbott was injured while exiting through the back door and onto Baker's rear porch stoop, when the iron railing collapsed as he leaned against it. Is Johnson liable to Abbott based upon a claim for common law negligence? Is Baker liable to Abbott based upon a common law negligence claim?

Chapter 11
WRONGFUL DEATH

In prior chapters, we examined how courts handle cases involving personal injury. But what happens when death results? At common law, a tortfeasor's liability was cut-off by the death of the victim. The tort action died with the victim.

MORAGNE v. STATES MARINE LINES, INC.
398 U.S. 375 (1970)

Mr. Justice HARLAN delivered the opinion of the Court.

[In *The Harrisburg*, the Court held in 1886 that maritime law does not afford a cause of action for wrongful death. The decision] acknowledged that the result reached had little justification except in primitive English legal history — a history far removed from the American law of remedies for maritime deaths. . . . Legal historians have concluded that the sole substantial basis for the rule at common law is a feature of the early English law that did not survive into this century — the felony-merger doctrine. According to this doctrine, the common law did not allow civil recovery for an act that constituted both a tort and a felony. The tort was treated as less important than the offense against the Crown, and was merged into, or pre-empted by, the felony. The doctrine found practical justification in the fact that the punishment for the felony was the death of the felon and the forfeiture of his property to the Crown; thus, after the crime had been punished, nothing remained of the felon or his property on which to base a civil action. Since all intentional or negligent homicide was felonious, there could be no civil suit for wrongful death.

[The] historical justification marshaled for the rule in England never existed in this country. . . . American law did adopt a vestige of the felony-merger doctrine, to the effect that a civil action was delayed until after the criminal trial. However, in this country the felony punishment did not include forfeiture of property; therefore, there was nothing [to] bar a subsequent civil suit. Nevertheless, despite some early cases in which the rule was rejected as "incapable of vindication," American courts generally adopted the English rule as the common law of this country. . . . [The] courts failed to produce any satisfactory justification for applying the rule in this country.

Some courts explained that their holdings were prompted by an asserted difficulty in computation of damages for wrongful death or by a "repugnance [to] setting a price upon human life." [S]ome courts and commentators [suggested] that the prohibition of nonstatutory wrongful-death actions derived support from the ancient common-law rule that a personal cause of action in tort did not survive the death of its possessor. [The] most likely reason that the English rule was adopted in this country [is] simply that it had the blessing of age. . . .

[We hold that the] rule against recovery for wrongful death is sharply out of keeping with the policies of modern American maritime law. . . . The English House of Lords in 1937 emasculated the rule without expressly overruling it. *Rose v. Ford*, (1937) A.C. 826. . . . The first statute partially abrogating the rule was Lord Campbell's Act, 9 & 10 Vict., c. 93 (1846), which granted recovery to the families of persons killed by tortious conduct, "although the Death shall have been caused under such Circumstances as amount in Law to Felony."

In the United States, every State today has enacted a wrongful-death statute. The Congress has created actions for wrongful deaths of railroad employees, of merchant seamen, Jones Act, and of persons on the high seas. Congress has also, in the Federal Tort Claims Act, made the United States subject to liability in certain circumstances for negligently caused wrongful death to the same extent as a private person.

These numerous and broadly applicable statutes, taken as a whole, make it clear that there is no present public policy against allowing recovery for wrongful death. [The] policy thus established has become itself a part of our law, to be given its appropriate weight not only in matters of statutory construction but also in those of decisional law. . . .

[We] accordingly overrule *The Harrisburg*, and hold that an action does lie under general maritime law for death caused by violation of maritime duties. . . .

Reversed and remanded.

NOTES

Today, every jurisdiction permits recovery for wrongful death. The following statutory provisions are illustrative:

California

§ 377.20. Cause of action survives; limitations; loss or damage simultaneous with death

(a) Except as otherwise provided by statute, a cause of action for or against a person is not lost by reason of the person's death, but survives subject to the applicable limitations period.

(b) This section applies even though a loss or damage occurs simultaneously with or after the death of a person who would have been liable if the person's death had not preceded or occurred simultaneously with the loss or damage.

§ 377.21. Pending actions

A pending action or proceeding does not abate by the death of a party if the cause of action survives.

§ 377.60. Persons with standing

A cause of action for the death of a person caused by the wrongful act or neglect of another may be asserted by any of the following persons or by the decedent's personal representative on their behalf:

(a) The decedent's surviving spouse, children, and issue of deceased children, or, if there is no surviving issue of the decedent, the persons, including the surviving spouse, who would be entitled to the property of the decedent by intestate succession.

(b) Whether or not qualified under subdivision (a), if they were dependent on the decedent, the putative spouse, children of the putative spouse, stepchildren, or parents. As used in this subdivision, "putative spouse" means the surviving spouse of a void or voidable marriage who is found by the court to have believed in good faith that the marriage to the decedent was valid.

(c) A minor, whether or not qualified under subdivision (a) or (b), if, at the time of the decedent's death, the minor resided for the previous 180 days in the decedent's household and was dependent on the decedent for one-half or more of the minor's support.

. . . .

§ 377.61. Damages recoverable

In an action under this article, damages may be awarded that, under all the circumstances of the case, may be just, but may not include damages recoverable under Section 377.34. The court shall determine the respective rights in an award of the persons entitled to assert the cause of action.

§ 377.62. Joinder with decedent's cause of action

(a) An action under Section 377.30 may be joined with an action under Section 377.60 arising out of the same wrongful act or neglect.

(b) An action under Section 377.60 and an action under Section 377.31 arising out of the same wrongful act or neglect may be consolidated for trial as provided in Section 1048.

O'GRADY v. BROWN
654 S.W.2d 904 (Mo. 1983)

PUDLOWSKI, Special Judge.

In January of 1979, appellant Terri O'Grady was nine months pregnant with an expected delivery date of January 25, 1979. During her pregnancy she had been under the care of respondent doctors Robert Brown and Robert Slickman; her prenatal course was uneventful. On January 15, 1979, appellant began experiencing severe back pains. She spoke with one of her physicians by telephone and then proceeded to St. Joseph Hospital where she was admitted shortly after midnight. During the course of the 24 hours following Terri O'Grady's admission, her uterus ruptured and the fetus was delivered stillborn.

Appellants contend that Terri O'Grady was not properly monitored, observed, or treated by respondents and that her injuries and the death of the fetus were the direct result of respondents' negligence. [The] trial court sustained respondents' motions to dismiss Count III of the petition on the authority of *State ex rel. Hardin v. Sanders*, 538 S.W.2d 336 (Mo. 1976), which denied recovery for the death of a viable but unborn child. . . .

Appellants urge us to reconsider our ruling in *Hardin*. . . . In *Hardin* we held that a fetus was not a "person" within the meaning of the statute, observing that "if there had been an intention to create such an action it would have been specifically so stated." In support of this conclusion, we noted in *Hardin* that the United States Supreme Court in *Roe v. Wade*, 410 U.S. 113 (1973), has stated that a fetus is not a "person" within the protection of the Fourteenth Amendment. We interpreted § 537.080 as requiring the deceased "person" to "be entitled to maintain an action at the time the injury was sustained and not at some later time," and then concluded it was "obvious" that a fetus could not meet this standard.

Appellants argue that the rule announced in *Hardin* should be reconsidered because it is unduly harsh and not in accord with the result reached in the majority of jurisdictions which have recently considered the issue. [The] manifest purpose of our statute is clearly to provide, for a limited class of plaintiffs, compensation for the loss of the "companionship, comfort, instruction, guidance, counsel, [and] support" of one who would have been alive but for the defendants' wrong. Appellants point out that the loss suffered by parents of an unborn child is in every respect a substantial and genuine loss, which is not distinguishable from the loss suffered when the child dies shortly after birth. To deny recovery based on the arbitrary requirement of live birth would work an injustice, in appellants' view. Furthermore, the wrongful death statute evidences a legislative intent to place the cost of "unsafe" activities upon the actors who engage in them, and thereby provide a deterrent to tortious conduct. The timing of the tortious conduct does not affect either the extent of the child's injuries or the desirability of the defendant's conduct. Appellant suggests that there is no substantial reason why a tortfeasor who causes prenatal death should be treated more favorably than one who causes prenatal injury, with the death of the child following its birth. This would simply perpetuate the much-criticized rule of the common law which made it "more profitable for the defendant to kill the plaintiff than to scratch him." . . .

Permitting appellant to maintain a wrongful death action for the death of a viable fetus would, therefore, be consistent with the broad purpose for which the statute was passed. Nothing in the language of the statute prevents this conclusion.

Respondents maintain that a fetus cannot be viewed as a "person" within the meaning of § 537.080. We do not agree. We note that the term "person" is used in many disparate senses in common speech, in philosophy, psychology, and in the law; it has no "plain and ordinary meaning" which we can apply. The term must therefore be construed in light of purpose for which this statute was passed. The relevant inquiry is whether the death of a human fetus is the type of loss for which the legislature intended to establish a remedy. We can discern three basic objectives behind the statute: to provide compensation to bereaved plaintiffs for their loss, to ensure that tortfeasors pay for the consequences of their actions, and generally to deter harmful conduct which might lead to death. It should be clear that these reasons apply with equal force whether the deceased is born or unborn. Parents clearly have an interest in being protected against or compensated for the loss of a child they wish to have. The fetus itself has an interest in being protected from injury before birth. It follows logically that it should be protected against fatal injuries as well.

The United States Supreme Court in *Roe v. Wade*, 410 U.S. 113, 150 (1973), recognized a legitimate societal interest in providing legal protection to the fetus. . . . Fetal interests are presently recognized in several areas of the law. Missouri criminal law, for instance, provides that "[t]he willful killing of an unborn quick child, by any injury to the mother of such child, which would be murder if it resulted in the death of such mother, shall be deemed manslaughter." The Missouri abortion statute recognizes a state interest in protecting the life and health of a viable fetus. Some state courts have held that the fetus is a "child" for purposes of child neglect statutes. A guardian ad litem may be appointed to protect the interests of an unborn child. And it is widely recognized that an unborn child has property rights which are entitled to legal protection. *Roe v. Wade*, while holding that the fetus is not a "person" for purposes of the 14th Amendment, does not mandate the conclusion that the fetus is a legal nonentity. . . .

We conclude that the term "person" as used in 537.080 includes the human fetus *en ventre sa mere*. To hold otherwise would frustrate the remedial purpose for which the statute was intended. This conclusion is supported by a strong positive trend among other jurisdictions holding that the fetus is a "person," "minor," or "minor child" within the meaning of their particular wrongful death statutes.

[We] hold, therefore, that § 537.080 does provide a cause of action for the wrongful death of a viable fetus. *Hardin* is hereby overruled. We limit our holding in this case to the facts presented and do not decide whether the same action would lie for the death of a nonviable fetus. . . . Reversed and remanded.

NOTES

1. *Recovery by illegitimate children. Armijo v. Wesselius*, 440 P.2d 471 (Wash. 1968), presented the question of whether an illegitimate child could claim as a beneficiary under a state wrongful death statute. The court answered the question in the affirmative:

> [O]ur decision [is] clearly in accord with a decisive current trend in legislative and decisional law which ignores legitimacy when creating or applying statutes designed to benefit children. [The] reason for this trend is clear. Society is becoming progressively more aware that children deserve proper care, comfort, and protection even if they are illegitimate. The burden of illegitimacy in purely social relationships should be enough, without society adding unnecessarily to the burden with legal implications having to do with the care, health, and welfare of children. . . .

In *Levy v. Louisiana*, 391 U.S. 68 (1968), on equal protection grounds, the Court struck down a Louisiana statute which construed that state's wrongful death law to exclude illegitimate children:

> [The] rights asserted here involve the intimate, familial relationship between a child and his own mother. When the child's claim [is] of damage for loss of his mother, [why should] the tortfeasors go free merely because the child is illegitimate? Why should the illegitimate child be denied rights merely because of his birth out of wedlock? [How] under our constitutional regime can he be denied correlative rights which other citizens enjoy?

> Legitimacy or illegitimacy of birth has no relation to the nature of the wrong allegedly inflicted on the mother. These children, though illegitimate, were dependent on her; she cared for them and nurtured them; they were indeed hers in the biological and in the spiritual sense; in her death they suffered wrong in the sense that any dependent would.

We conclude that it is invidious to discriminate against them when no action, conduct, or demeanor of theirs is possibly relevant to the harm that was done the mother.

2. *Action by mother of illegitimate child.* In a companion case to *Levy, Glona v. American Guarantee & Liability Insurance Co.*, 391 U.S. 73 (1968), the Court struck down a Louisiana law which precluded the mother of an illegitimate child from suing for his wrongful death:

[W]e see no possible rational basis for assuming that if the natural mother is allowed recovery for the wrongful death of her illegitimate child, the cause of illegitimacy will be served. It would, indeed, be far-fetched to assume that women have illegitimate children so that they can be compensated in damages for their death. A law which creates an open season on illegitimates in the area of automobile accidents gives a windfall to tortfeasors. But it hardly has a causal connection with the "sin," which is, we are told, the historic reason for the creation of the disability. . . . Opening the courts to suits of this kind may conceivably be a temptation to some to assert motherhood fraudulently. That problem, however, concerns burden of proof. Where the claimant is plainly the mother, the State denies equal protection of the laws to withhold relief merely because the child, wrongfully killed, was born to her out of wedlock.

3. *Suit by the father of an illegitimate child.* Under Georgia law, the mother of an illegitimate child could recover for his death, but the father could not recover unless he had legitimated the child prior to death. In *Parham v. Hughes*, 441 U.S. 347 (1979), the Court upheld the law:

[The] appellant, as the natural father, was responsible for conceiving an illegitimate child and had the opportunity to legitimate the child but failed to do so. Legitimation would have removed the stigma of bastardy and allowed the child to inherit from the father in the same manner as if born in lawful wedlock. Unlike the illegitimate child for whom the status of illegitimacy is involuntary and immutable, [appellant] was responsible for fostering an illegitimate child and for failing to change its status. It is thus neither illogical nor unjust for society to express its "condemnation of irresponsible liaisons beyond the bonds of marriage" by not conferring upon a biological father the statutory right to sue for the wrongful death of his illegitimate child. The justifications for judicial sensitivity to the constitutionality of differing legislative treatment of legitimate and illegitimate children are simply absent when a classification affects only the fathers of deceased illegitimate children.

[T]he Georgia statute does not invidiously discriminate against the appellant simply because he is of the male sex. The fact is that mothers and fathers of illegitimate children are not similarly situated. Under Georgia law, only a father can by voluntary unilateral action make an illegitimate child legitimate. Unlike the mother of an illegitimate child whose identity will rarely be in doubt, the identity of the father will frequently be unknown. [C]onferral of the right of a natural father to sue for the wrongful death of his child only if he has previously acted to identify himself, undertake his paternal responsibilities, and make his child legitimate, does not reflect any overbroad generalizations about men as a class, but rather the reality that in Georgia only a father can by unilateral action legitimate an illegitimate child. . . .

MURPHY v. MARTIN OIL CO.
308 N.E.2d 583 (Ill. 1974)

WARD, Justice:

[P]laintiff, Charryl Murphy, as administratrix of her late husband, Jack Raymond Murphy, and individually, and as next friend of Debbie Ann Murphy, Jack Kenneth Murphy and Carrie Lynn Murphy, their children, filed a complaint in the circuit court of Cook County against the defendants, Martin Oil Company and James Hocker. [C]ount II sought damages for conscious pain and suffering, loss of wages and property damage. The circuit court allowed the defendants' motion to strike the second count of the complaint on the ground that it failed to state a cause of action. . . .

[The] second count of the complaint asked for damages for the decedent's physical and mental suffering, for loss of wages for the nine-day period following his injury and for the loss of his clothing worn at the time of injury. These damages were claimed under the common law and under our survival statute, which provides that certain rights of action survive the death of the person with the right of action. . . .

On this appeal we shall consider: (1) whether the plaintiff can recover for the loss of wages which her decedent would have earned during the interval between his injury and death; (2) whether the plaintiff can recover for the destruction of the decedent's personal property (clothing) at the time of the injury; (3) whether the plaintiff can recover damages for conscious pain and suffering of the decedent from the time of his injuries to the time of death.

This State in 1853 enacted the Wrongful Death Act and in 1872 enacted the so-called Survival Act. This court first had occasion to consider the statutes in combination in 1882 in *Holton v. Daly*, 106 Ill. 131. The court declared that the effect of the Wrongful Death Act was that a cause of action for personal injuries, which would have abated under the common law upon the death of the injured party from those injuries, would continue on behalf of the spouse or the next of kin and would be "enlarged to embrace the injury resulting from the death." In other words, it was held that the Wrongful Death Act provided the exclusive remedy available when death came as a result of given tortious conduct. In considering the Survival Act the court stated that it was intended to allow for the survival of a cause of action only when the injured party died from a cause other than that which caused the injuries which created the cause of action. Thus, the court said, an action for personal injury would not survive death if death resulted from the tortious conduct which caused the injury.

This construction of the two statutes persisted for over 70 years. Damages, therefore, under the Wrongful Death Act were limited to pecuniary losses, as from loss of support, to the surviving spouse and next of kin as a result of the death. Under the survival statute damages recoverable in a personal injury action, as for conscious pain and suffering, loss of earnings, medical expenses and physical disability, could be had only if death resulted from a cause other than the one which gave rise to the personal injury action.

[In] PROSSER, HANDBOOK OF THE LAW OF TORTS (4th ed. 1971), at page 901, it is said: "[T]he modern trend is definitely toward the view that tort causes of action and liabilities are as fairly a part of the estate of either plaintiff or defendant as contract debts, and that the question is rather one of why a fortuitous event such as death should extinguish a valid action. Accordingly, survival statutes gradually are being extended; and it may be expected that ultimately all tort actions will survive to the same extent as those founded on contract." And at page 906 Prosser observes that where there have been wrongful death and survival statutes the usual holding has been that actions may be concurrently maintained under those statutes. The usual method of dealing with the two causes of action, he notes, is to allocate conscious pain and suffering, expenses and loss of earnings of the decedent up to the date of death to the survival statute, and to allocate the loss of benefits of the survivors to the action for wrongful death.

[T]he majority of jurisdictions which have considered the question allow an action for personal injuries in addition to an action under the wrongful death statute, though death is attributable to the injuries. Recovery for conscious pain and suffering is permitted in most of these jurisdictions.

Too, recovery is allowed under the Federal Employers' Liability Act for a decedent's conscious pain and suffering provided it was not substantially contemporaneous with his death.

We consider that those decisions which allow an action for fatal injuries as well as for wrongful death are to be preferred to this court's holding in *Holton*. [The] remedy available under *Holton* will often be grievously incomplete. There may be a substantial loss of earnings, medical expenses, prolonged pain and suffering, as well as property damage sustained, before an injured person may succumb to his injuries. To say that there can be recovery only for his wrongful death is to provide an obviously inadequate justice. . . .

Affirmed in part; reversed in part.

BULLARD v. BARNES
468 N.E.2d 1228 (Ill. 1984)

UNDERWOOD, Justice.

Robert G. Bullard, as administrator of the estate of his deceased son, Scott Bullard, and Robert and Sharon Bullard, in their individual capacities as Scott's parents, filed an action in Livingston County circuit court seeking recovery against Bruce Barnes and Livingston County Ready-Mix, Inc., under the Wrongful Death Act, the Survival Act, and for funeral expenses for which parents are liable under section 15 of "An Act to revise the law in relation to husband and wife" (hereinafter referred to as the Family Expense Act). The complaint also sought punitive as well as compensatory damages for injury to property, a recovery for the emotional distress the parents suffered due to the death of their son, and damages for negligent entrustment.

The cause of action arose out of a motor vehicle accident [in] which 17-year-old Scott Bullard was fatally injured. Sometime between 7:30 and 8 a.m., Scott was driving south on a paved, two-lane road, known in Livingston County as the Katydid Road, in order to get to his parttime cooperative education job in Cornell. Northbound defendant Bruce Barnes, who was driving a semitrailer truck for his employer and codefendant, Livingston County Ready-Mix, Inc., despite fog and poor visibility, moved into the southbound lane and proceeded to pass two vehicles. He passed the vehicle directly in front of him, a station wagon driven by Robert Graves, and then continued traveling in the southbound lane past a truck loaded with road-building materials driven by Harold Bohm. Bohm and Graves both testified that the approaching Bullard car swerved onto the west shoulder of the road to avoid a collision with the Ready-Mix truck. Graves further noted that Scott appeared to lose control of his car when he suddenly swung back on the road to avoid hitting a culvert. The Bullard car then crossed the road in front of the truck Bohm was driving, and the front of the Bohm truck struck the passenger side of the Bullard car.

Both Bohm and Graves stopped at the accident scene, although Barnes did not. Bohm went up to the Bullard car, where decedent was lying on his right side on the seat, and asked him whether he was "okay." Scott did not respond, except to shake his shoulders. Graves went to [a nearby home] to phone the police. Sharon Bullard, Scott's mother, and her youngest son, Todd, came upon the scene on their way to school shortly after 8 a.m. Mrs. Bullard spoke to Scott, and observed that he was rubbing his left shoulder although he did not respond. While Mrs. Bullard did not notice it at the time, her oldest son, who arrived later, observed that Scott's neck was swollen and that blood was dripping from his mouth. Later, upon retrieving Scott's personal effects from the car, he found teeth on the car floor, which were apparently knocked out by the force of the collision. By approximately 8:15 a.m., Eldon Finkenbinder, a Livingston County deputy sheriff, had arrived. Finkenbinder took decedent's pulse and determined that he was still alive, although unconscious. Approximately 10 minutes after Finkenbinder's arrival, an ambulance came and Scott was taken to [a hospital where he died] without regaining consciousness.

[The] verdicts were $285,000 in the wrongful death action and $40,000 in the survival action. In the second part of the trial, the parties stipulated to compensatory property damages of $750 and the jury returned a verdict of $500 in punitive property damages against defendant Barnes only. Judgments were entered accordingly.

The appellate court held that the jurors had been improperly instructed that they could consider the parents' loss of their son's society as an element of the presumption prevailing under the Wrongful Death Act that the parents suffered a pecuniary loss due to his death. . . .

Section 2 of our Wrongful Death Act governs all recoveries under the Act, and it provides in relevant part:

> "[I]n every such action the jury may give such damages as they shall deem a fair and just compensation with reference to the *pecuniary injuries* resulting from such death, to the surviving spouse and next of kin of such deceased person." (Emphasis added.)

Of the 23 jurisdictions with statutes or decisional law limiting wrongful death recoveries to pecuniary loss, 14 now allow parental recovery in a wrongful death action for the loss of society of a child. [In Illinois,] the trend in our more recent decisions under the Wrongful Death Act has been to expand the scope of pecuniary injury to encompass nonmonetary losses. [Defendant] urges that we await further indication from the General Assembly as to whether its intent was or is to permit parents to recover for loss of their children's society in a wrongful death action. We have concluded, however, in view of our earlier decisions indicating similar recoveries would have been allowed in cases involving loss of a parent and spouse, that it would be anomalous to now deny parents this form of recovery.

Our consideration of this question has provided us with an opportunity to thoroughly review a closely connected issue — the presumption of pecuniary loss as it is applied in actions to recover for the wrongful death of children. The legal basis for this presumption is traceable to an era far removed in time and values from the 1980's. The Illinois Wrongful Death Act, first enacted in 1853 was patterned after what is commonly referred to as Lord Campbell's Act. Although the British statute did not contain a pecuniary-loss limitation, as the Illinois act does, early cases interpreting the British act established the narrow rule that parents could recover only for actual loss of the child's income, and it was this common law rule that drafters of the Illinois act incorporated. Such a rule accurately reflected the social conditions of the nineteenth century, when children were valued largely for their capacity to contribute to the family income.

[A] presumption is an inference which common sense draws from the known course of events. In its current form the presumption of pecuniary loss no longer conforms to this definition. We therefore hold [that] there can be no presumption of loss of earnings upon the death of a child since such a presumption represents an aberration from, rather than a reflection of, the typical family experience. However, we have concluded that parents are entitled to a presumption of pecuniary injury in the loss of a child's society, based on the holding [that] the pecuniary injury for which parents may recover under the wrongful death statute includes this form of loss. Defendants may rebut the presumption by presenting evidence that a parent and child were estranged. Although the presumption of a loss of earnings no longer applies, in the rare case where the child earned income that was used to support the family these facts may [be] proved and a recovery had. This case does not present, and we therefore need not decide, the question of whether the loss-of-society presumption applies to children who have reached the age of majority.

Although we have considered our decisions in wrongful death cases involving the loss of a spouse or parent to be persuasive precedent on the issue of whether loss of a child's society is compensable under the pecuniary-injury standard in our statute, the fact remains that the loss of a child is distinguishable from these other forms of loss in one important respect, which must be considered in computing damages. As a general rule, neither children nor spouses bear the same heavy financial responsibility for either their parents or spouse that a parent automatically assumes upon the birth of a child. This court acknowledged in *Cockrum* [*v. Baumgartner*, 95 Ill.2d 193, 198-202, 69 Ill. Dec. 168, 447 N.E.2d 385 (1983),] the very substantial expenses associated with child-rearing. We have concluded [that] for a wrongful death verdict to accurately reflect the parents' pecuniary injury, juries must be instructed not only to assign a dollar value to the loss of the child's society, but also to arrive at a figure, based on the evidence presented to them, which represents expenditures the parents would have been likely to incur had the child lived. Jurors should be directed to deduct these projected child-rearing expenses from any award for loss of society and any proved loss of income.

Since [the] trial judge [did] not direct that anticipated child-rearing expenses be deducted from the loss, we agree with the appellate court that this wrongful death verdict must be reversed and the cause remanded for a new trial on this claim. . . .

Affirmed and remanded, with directions.

CLARK, Justice, specially concurring:

I am pleased that the majority has decided to join the modern trend and allow parents to recover damages for the loss of society in wrongful death actions involving their children. [I] do not agree with the majority's application of a setoff for child-rearing expenses. . . . In the case at bar, damages were awarded for the loss-of-society count of the complaint. Since plaintiff's decedent was 17 years old at the time of his death, a setoff for college tuition and living expenses could substantially reduce the loss-of-society award.

NOTE

Contributory Negligence of the Beneficiary. In *Mitchell v. Akers*, 401 S.W.2d 907 (Tex. Civ. App. 1966), plaintiff's three-year-old son drowned in a swimming pool. The boy's mother was deemed to be contributorily negligent for failing to supervise him, and the court held that the mother's negligence barred recovery under the wrongful death statute. As to the survival statute, the court noted that the child was contributorily negligent. However, because of his age, the negligence was not chargeable against him. The court held that the mother could recover: "The cases hold that a negligent parent, spouse, child, etc. cannot recover under a death statute if his negligence caused or contributed to cause the death; but that he can recover as heir under a survival statute."

PROBLEMS

1. John Huff was 51 years old when he died and had a life expectancy of 23 years and a worklife expectancy of 14.1 years. His annual earnings were between $50,000 and $60,000. He was also entitled to fringe benefits. His employer contributed the equivalent of 10% of Huff's salary to his pension plan, gave him $100,000 worth of life insurance (worth $500), disability insurance ($100 value), and medical insurance ($4,000 value).

The evidence on intangible elements of damages was as follows: The Huffs were high school sweethearts. He was the only man she had ever dated. They had been married for 30 years and had raised four children. The family had moved only once during the marriage. Huff had changed jobs only once. The Huffs loved each other, and she relied on him for advice in making all decisions of consequence.

Suppose that you are hired to bring wrongful death and survival actions on decedent's behalf. How would you calculate damages in a case like this? Would the compensation differ under your state's wrongful death statute? *See Huff v. White Motor Corp.*, 609 F.2d 286 (7th Cir. 1979).

2. Jane Madison died instantly in a work place explosion. The estate incurred a funeral expense of $1,505.00. Mrs. Madison was 43 years old at her death and had a work life expectancy of 9.7 years. She was earning $20 per hour. She was also receiving fringe benefits worth $3 per hour. There was little likelihood of promotion.

In addition to her job, Mrs. Madison provided household services to her family. At the time of her death, her life expectancy was 31.3 years. The estate presented testimony that Mrs. Madison performed 38.7 hours per week of household services. About a year after her death, her husband remarried. Her husband also claims for mental anguish and loss of consortium seeking $100,000. Under the California statute set forth above, how much should the husband be allowed to recover? *See Lowe v. United States*, 662 F. Supp. 1089 (W.D. Ark. 1987).

3. Decedent was employed by defendant from 1990 to 1998 with periodic intervals of unemployment due to psychiatric problems. At one point, decedent reported difficulty sleeping and delusions. During 1992 and 1997, he was treated institutionally in Staten Island, New York, and Fort Worth, Texas, for "psychotic depressive reaction" and "schizoid personality." In 1998, he resumed employment with defendant and he was employed as second mate on a vessel. At the time of his death, decedent was 43 with a life expectancy of 31.3 years and

was earning $33,000 a year. However, in addition to his psychiatric problems, he had a history of alcoholism and of suicidal tendencies. In addition, there were difficulties in the marriage between decedent and plaintiff which created doubt about the amount the plaintiff wife would have received from decedent's earnings. How would you calculate damages in a case like this? Would the compensation differ under your state's wrongful death statute? *See Bednar v. United States Lines, Inc.*, 360 F. Supp. 1313 (N.D. Ohio 1973).

4. Decedent was a nun, a member of the Sisters of Charity, who had taken the simple but perpetual vow of poverty upon entering the Order. She died some fifteen days after receiving injuries in an automobile accident. Following her death, decedent's brother brought a wrongful death action. The applicable wrongful death statute provides as follows:

> Every wrongful death action shall be brought by and in the name or names of the personal representative or representatives of such deceased person, and the jury in every such action may give such damages, compensatory and exemplary, as they shall deem fair and just, taking into consideration the pecuniary injury or injuries resulting from such death to the surviving party or parties entitled to the judgment, or any interest therein, recovered in such action, and also having regard to the mitigating or aggravating circumstances attending such wrongful act, neglect or default. . . .

How much can the brother recover? *See Stang v. Hertz Corp.*, 467 P.2d 14 (N.M. 1970).

5. *Damages for death of minor children.* Plaintiffs' three minor children were killed in an automobile accident. The negligent defendant agreed to pay the children's medical expenses ($43,000) and ultimately their funeral expenses ($18,000). However, the parents also seek recovery for loss of "society, comfort and companionship." In addition, they seek recovery for expenses incurred in raising the children prior to their death, as well as for lost future earnings. How would you calculate damages in a case like this? Would the compensation differ under your state's wrongful death statute?

6. In the prior problem, assume that the parents are entitled to recover for their children's lost future earnings. If you are plaintiff's attorney, how would you prove such earnings? Assume that the children were 3, 5 and 7 at the time of their deaths. What facts might help you establish "lost future earnings" for children so young? *See Selders v. Armentrout*, 207 N.W.2d 686 (Neb. 1973).

7. Robert, a sixteen-year-old boy, was struck by a car and killed. The evidence showed that he was a highly intelligent, industrious and talented individual, a senior in high school, headed for pre-medical college and a dental career thereafter. He was short in height, his health was excellent, he participated in wrestling activities in school and loved all sports. According to the testimony adduced at the trial, he had passed his Driver Education course in high school and, had he lived, would have received his driver's license but two months after

the fatal bicycle accident. He was a quiet, conservative lad who neither drank nor smoked, who dressed neatly, obeyed his parents, went to summer school to obtain better grades (although he had never failed any of his courses) and who did odd jobs in local shops and neighbors' homes since he was 13 years old in order to raise pin money with which he bought gifts for the family (a toaster, for example, as well as pearl earrings for mother, bathrobe for father), depositing the balance of any such monies in the bank for college and other expenses. Robert was cautious when using tools; he did minor repair work and performed gardening tasks for his own family as well as for neighbors. One such neighbor, in fact, testified that Robert did the gardening work around her home twice a week, that he worked hard and did a beautiful job, that he was a fine boy and that she "would have been proud to have had him as her grandson." Similarly, one of Robert's teachers who had known the boy for over five years testified that he would have been proud to have had Robert "as a son." What damages might the parents recover for his death? *See Gary v. Schwartz*, 72 Misc. 2d 332, 339 N.Y.S.2d 39 (1972); *Hart v. Forchelli*, 445 F.2d 1018 (2d Cir. 1971); *Haumersen v. Ford Motor Co.*, 257 N.W.2d 7 (Iowa 1977); *Prather v. Lockwood*, 310 N.E.2d 815 (Ill. App. Ct. 1974); and *Anderson v. Lale*, 216 N.W.2d 152 (S.D. 1974).

Chapter 12
DEFENSES

In this chapter we examine a number of defenses available in negligence (and some strict liability) actions. These defenses are similar to the "privileges" that apply to intentional torts, in that they have the effect of defeating (or at least reducing) the plaintiff's recovery even though the plaintiff has established a prima facie case of liability on defendant's part. The most important of these defenses are based upon plaintiff's own conduct, and include contributory negligence, assumption of the risk, the blending of these two doctrines into comparative negligence, and the seat belt defense. In addition, the chapter will also examine statutes of limitation and repose and immunities.

A. DEFENSES BASED ON THE PLAINTIFF'S CONDUCT

Courts have long recognized the importance of considering the plaintiff's own conduct in determining whether the plaintiff is entitled to recover compensation. At one time the basis for such decisions may have been the moral notion that the plaintiff's own misconduct somehow cancelled out the defendant's negligence or otherwise rendered the plaintiff undeserving. In more recent times law and economics scholars have justified such policies on the basis of efficiency and incentives. The plaintiff may be the party who can most easily and cheaply take precautions to avoid an accident, and denying or reducing recovery when the plaintiff fails to do so will provide an important incentive to take appropriate precautions.

1. Contributory Negligence

Contributory negligence is the plaintiff's failure to use due care for his or her own safety, which is an actual and proximate cause of the plaintiff's injuries. As will be seen, this defense originally was a complete bar to all recovery by the plaintiff.

BUTTERFIELD v. FORRESTER
103 Eng. Rep 926 (K.B. 1809)

This was an action on the case for obstructing a highway, by means of which obstruction the plaintiff, who was riding along the road, was thrown down with his horse, and injured, &c. At the trial, . . . it appeared that the defendant, for the purpose of making some repairs to his house, which was close by the road side at one end of the town, had put up a pole across this part of the road, a free passage being left by another branch or street in the same direction. That the plaintiff left a public house not far distant from the place in question at 8 o'clock in the evening in August, when they were just beginning to light candles, but while there was light enough left to discern the obstruction at 100 yards distance: and the witness, who proved this, said that if the plaintiff had not been riding very hard he might have observed and avoided it: the plaintiff however, who was riding violently, did not observe it, but rode against it, and fell with his horse and was much hurt in consequence of the accident; and there was no evidence of his being intoxicated at the time. On this evidence Bayley J. directed the jury, that if a person riding with reasonable and ordinary care could have seen and avoided the obstruction; and if they were satisfied that the plaintiff was riding along the street extremely hard, and without ordinary care, they should find a verdict for the defendant: which they accordingly did. [Plaintiff] objected to this direction, on moving for a new trial; and referred to Buller's Ni. Pri. 26 (a) where the rule is laid down, that "if a man lay logs of wood across a highway; though a person may with care ride safely by, yet if by means thereof my horse stumble and fling me, I may bring an action."

BAYLEY J. The plaintiff was proved to be riding as fast as his horse could go, and this was through the streets of Derby. If he had used ordinary care he must have seen the obstruction; so that the accident appeared to happen entirely from his own fault.

LORD ELLENBOROUGH C.J. A party is not to cast himself upon an obstruction which has been made by the fault of another, and avail himself of it, if he do not himself use common and ordinary caution to be in the right. In cases of persons riding upon what is considered to be the wrong side of the road, that would not authorise another purposely to ride up against them. One person being in fault will not dispense with another's using ordinary care for himself. Two things must concur to support this action, an obstruction in the road by the fault of the defendant, and no want of ordinary care to avoid it on the part of the plaintiff.

Per Curiam. Rule refused.

NOTES

1. Like many early cases that supposedly establish great principles of law, *Butterfield v. Forrester* is not clear about the reasons for its holding. Note that the two judges whose opinions are reported gave different justifications for the rule. What did Bayley, J. mean when he said that "the accident appeared to happen entirely from his own fault"? Did he mean that the defendant was not at fault (that is, not negligent) in creating the obstruction? Or did he mean that, in some way, the plaintiff's own conduct was a superseding cause? Lord Ellenborough, on the other hand, seems to concede the fault of the defendant, but to require no want of care by the plaintiff as a prerequisite to recovery. Why should

that be so? Are important policies served by denying recovery to a careless plaintiff?

2. The rule that the plaintiff must have acted with due care in order to recover for negligent injury received widespread acceptance. In *Brown v. Kendall*, 60 Mass. (6 Cush.) 292 (1850), often cited as an early American expression of the negligence doctrine, Chief Justice Shaw articulated the rule as follows:

> . . . if both the plaintiff and defendant at the time of the blow were using ordinary care, or if at that time the defendant was using ordinary care, and the plaintiff was not, or if at that time, both the plaintiff and defendant were not using ordinary care, then the plaintiff could not recover.

As both this quotation and the principle case suggest, the plaintiff's contributory negligence was a total bar to recovery.

3. Although the opinion of Lord Ellenborough could be read to suggest otherwise, the general rule is that contributory negligence is an affirmative defense for the defendant to plead and prove. In other words, the plaintiff is not required to show due care as part of a prima facie case.

4. In general, contributory negligence principles applied whether the plaintiff's negligence involved a simple failure to exercise due care for his or her own safety or also involved an unreasonable risks to others. Thus, an inattentive plaintiff driving a car who collides with another negligently driven vehicle would be barred, but so would the inattentive pedestrian who crosses the street against a red light, even though the pedestrian's conduct appeared to create risks only to herself. To understand these results, consider what would happen if a rescuer pushed the pedestrian in the above example to safety but was herself struck by the negligent motorist's car. Could the rescuer sue the *pedestrian* for her injuries? Did the pedestrian's failure to use due care for her own safety also create unreasonable risks of harm to third parties? It is also important to note that, before the plaintiff can be barred from recovery, the defendant must demonstrate not only that the plaintiff was negligent, but also that the plaintiff's negligence was the actual and proximate cause of the plaintiff's injuries.

5. The question of the plaintiff's contributory negligence, like that of the defendant's negligence, is usually one for the trier of fact unless the evidence is so clear that only one conclusion is possible.

6. Consider whether the following scenario calls for a different approach to the problem of the plaintiff's contributory negligence. Suppose Plaintiff was driving on a two lane highway on a clear, sunny day. Feeling drowsy, Plaintiff pulled to the side of the road to take a nap. However, Plaintiff did not take care to pull entirely off the road, and his car remained partially in the travel lane. Plaintiff quickly fell asleep in the front seat. Defendant soon approached, traveling in the same direction. Defendant saw the Plaintiff's car and realized it was partially blocking the road. Defendant tried to steer around the Plaintiff's

car (no traffic was approaching in the other direction), but failed to move over enough because he was trying to change channels on the radio at the same time. Defendant's car rear-ended Plaintiff's, causing Plaintiff severe whiplash injuries, for which Plaintiff now sues. Defendant concedes that he was negligent, but defends by asserting that the Plaintiff was contributorily negligent for failing to pull completely off the road.

Notice the features of this hypothetical. The Plaintiff was probably negligent in failing to get all the way off the highway, but at the time of the accident the Plaintiff was helpless and unable to do anything to correct the situation. The Defendant, on the other hand, recognized that the Plaintiff was in a bad spot, had every opportunity to avoid the accident by using ordinary care, but failed to do so and caused the accident. Should Plaintiff be allowed to recover in spite of his contributory negligence? What reasons and policies might support or undermine such a result?

This sort of fact situation gave rise to the doctrine of "last clear chance," which was a significant exception to the rule of contributory negligence. First appearing in *Davies v. Mann*, 152 Eng. Rep. 588 (1842), this doctrine allowed the plaintiff to recover in full in spite of even admitted contributory negligence. As the name of the doctrine suggests, last clear chance was justified on the ground that the defendant's negligence, coming as it did at the end of the chain of causation and in a situation where the defendant could have avoided the accident, ought to be viewed as the responsible cause of the harm.

7. The Plaintiff in the previous note was asleep and therefore "helpless"; that is, unable at the moment of crisis to do anything to protect himself. In this sort of fact situation, the "helpless" plaintiff could invoke the doctrine of last clear chance so long as the defendant either knew or should have known of the plaintiff's danger in time to take protective action. A variation of this fact pattern involved the plaintiff who was "inattentive" rather than "helpless". Suppose, for example, that the Plaintiff in the previous note was not asleep but only looking at a map while pulled partially off the highway. The Plaintiff could at any time look up, take notice of the dangerous position he was in, and pull the car farther off the road into a safer position. Plaintiff does not and his car is struck as before. Most courts in this type of situation would apply last clear chance only if the Defendant actually knew (as opposed to "should have known") of the Plaintiff's danger in time to avoid the accident.

8. Contributory negligence is not a defense to intentional torts. In most jurisdictions it is also not a defense to reckless or "willful and wanton" conduct. The extent to which it is a defense to strict liability claims (including product liability) is considered in the chapters dealing with those torts.

PROBLEMS

1. Plaintiff was confined to a mental hospital after a court determined that he was a danger to himself and others because of his mental illness. By court decision in the jurisdiction, the mental hospital owes its patients a duty of care, including a duty to protect them from injuring themselves. Plaintiff did not appreciate being confined "for his own good" and was anxious to escape. He discovered that an exit leading to an outside fire escape ladder was unlocked and one day attempted to escape via the ladder. In his haste to get away, he slipped while descending the ladder and fell, sustaining severe injuries. Plaintiff sues the mental hospital, arguing that the hospital was negligent in failing to supervise him and in leaving the fire escape unlocked. The Hospital asserts as a defense the Plaintiff's contributory negligence in trying to escape and in failing to use due care while on the fire escape ladder. Should this defense succeed? If it did, what effect would it have on the Hospital's duty?

2. A statute forbids the sale of alcoholic beverages to persons under 21 years of age. Pop's Grocery and Liquor sold two cases of beer to a group of seventeen year olds, making no attempt to verify their ages by asking for a driver's license. The teenagers drove to a secluded spot and drank the beer. On the way home, the driver, who was legally and actually intoxicated, lost control of the car and ran into a tree. Both the driver and the passengers sustained severe injuries. All sue Pop's Grocery and Liquor, alleging negligence per se in the violation of the liquor control statute. Pop's defends by claiming that all the plaintiffs were contributorily negligent. Should this defense succeed? Is there any basis for arguing that it should succeed against the driver but not the passengers (or vice versa)?

3. Parent was driving Child home from a soccer game one evening, rushing so that Child would have time for homework. At a four way stop, Parent slowed down, looked quickly, and proceeded into the intersection without stopping. Parent did not see Defendant approaching rapidly from the left at a high rate of speed. Defendant ran the stop sign and broadsided the car occupied by Parent and Child. Parent was killed in the crash and Child sustained severe injuries. Child now sues Defendant, bringing two causes of action: 1) a wrongful death action for the death of Parent; and 2) a negligence action for Child's own physical injuries. Defendant asserts the contributory negligence of Parent as a defense to both actions. Should the defense succeed in either case? Is there a difference between the two actions that would be relevant to this question?

2. Comparative Negligence

The "all or nothing" aspect of contributory negligence provoked increasing criticism through the first half of the twentieth century. Many argued that the defense produced unfair results since it often let a negligent defendant escape without liability. The justification for the doctrine — that the plaintiff's negligence disqualified him from recovery — could be used against the defendant: if the plaintiff's fault made it unjustified to throw the entire loss on the defendant, so the defendant's fault made it unjustified to leave the entire loss with the plaintiff. Others were concerned that efforts to escape the doctrine, such as last clear chance, unnecessarily confused and complicated the law. There was also a concern that the doctrine encouraged unprincipled behavior by the jury, which might decide in the plaintiff's favor on contributory negligence, in spite of the evidence, but then surreptitiously reduce the damages. Better, it was felt, to handle this explicitly by adopting a rule that would mitigate the all or nothing aspect of contributory negligence, while retaining its effect of penalizing the plaintiff whose lack of care contributed to her own injury. This was the background to the adoption of what is generally referred to as comparative negligence. As the materials below illustrate, comparative negligence (or some variation thereof) has been adopted by statute in many jurisdictions, and by judicial decision in a few others. However the doctrine is adopted, there are certain basic choices that must be made.

BRADLEY v. APPALACHIAN POWER COMPANY
256 S.E.2d 879 (W. Va. 1979)

MILLER, Justice:

In these two cases, which have been consolidated on appeal, we are asked to re-examine and ameliorate the common law doctrine of contributory negligence.

In each case the plaintiff sought by way of an instruction to utilize the doctrine of comparative negligence to avoid the defense of contributory negligence. The tendered instruction was rejected and the usual contributory negligence instruction was given, with the jury returning a verdict for the defendant in each case.

I

[T]here is an almost universal dissatisfaction among leading scholars of tort law with the harshness of the doctrine of contributory negligence. Neither intensive scholarship nor complex legal arguments need be advanced to demonstrate its strictness. A plaintiff can, if the jury is faithful to the contributory negligence instruction it receives, be barred from recovery if his negligence "contributed in the slightest degree" to the accident. . . . Thus, our system of jurisprudence, while based on concepts of justice and fair play, contains an anomaly in which the slightest negligence of a plaintiff precludes any recovery and thereby excuses the defendant from the consequences of all of his negligence, however great it may be. . . .

[L]egislatures in a number of states have enacted comparative negligence statutes of one variety or another. The basic framework of these statutes is to permit a negligent plaintiff to recover so long as his negligence does not exceed some established percentage, usually 50 percent. Such statutes require that his recovery be reduced by the percentage of contributory negligence found to exist.

Four states — Alaska, California, Florida, and Michigan — have by judicial decision abolished the doctrine of contributory negligence and substituted in its place a "pure" comparative negligence concept. Under this principle, a plaintiff may recover regardless of the degree of his contributory negligence, but the jury is required to reduce his award in proportion to his contributory negligence.

Most commentators and the four courts which have adopted the pure comparative negligence position are critical of the 50 percent approach, primarily on the basis that it involves the drawing of an arbitrary line beyond which contributory negligence can still be asserted as a bar to the plaintiff's action. . . . [T]he difficulty with the pure comparative negligence rule, however, is that it focuses solely on the hypothetical "plaintiff" without recognizing that once pure comparative negligence is embraced, all parties whose negligence or fault combined to contribute to the accident are automatically potential plaintiffs unless a particular party is found to be 100 percent at fault.

The fundamental justification for the pure comparative negligence rule is its fairness in permitting everyone to recover to the extent he is not at fault. Thus, the eye of the needle is "no fault," and we are asked not to think about the larger aspect—the camel representing "fault." It is difficult, on theoretical grounds alone, to rationalize a system which permits a party who is 95 percent at fault to have his day in court as a plaintiff because he is 5 percent fault-free.

The practical result of such a system is that it favors the party who has incurred the most damages regardless of his amount of fault or negligence. To illustrate, a plaintiff who has sustained a moderate injury with a potential jury verdict of $20,000, and who is 90 percent fault-free, may be reluctant to file suit against a defendant who is 90 percent at fault, but who has received severe injuries and whose case carries a potential of $800,000 in damages from a jury verdict. In this situation, even though the defendant's verdict is reduced by his 90 percent fault to $80,000, it is still far in excess of the plaintiff's potential recovery of $18,000.

While it can be conceded that there is an obvious injustice in the current contributory negligence rule which bars recovery no matter how slight the plaintiff's negligence, nevertheless the pure comparative negligence rule seems equally extreme at the other end of the spectrum. . . . The history of the common law is one of gradual judicial development and adjustment of the case law to fit the changing conditions of society. We see no practical benefit to be gained by the radical break from the common law's tort-fault methodology that the pure comparative negligence rule requires. There are basic inequities inherent in the pure comparative negligence rule and its resulting singular emphasis on the amount of damages and insurance coverage as the ultimate touchstone of the viability of instituting a suit.

We do not accept the major premise of pure comparative negligence that a party should recover his damages regardless of his fault, so long as his fault is not 100 percent. [O]ur present judicial rule of contributory negligence is therefore modified to provide that a party is not barred from recovering damages in a tort action so long as his negligence or fault does not equal or exceed the combined negligence or fault of the other parties involved in the accident. To the extent that our prior contributory negligence cases are inconsistent with this rule, they are overruled.

[S]ome explanation is warranted as to how this new rule operates. We do not intend to consider exhaustively all the particular ramifications of the new rule, since they are best resolved within the particular factual framework of the individual case.

We do state what may be the obvious, that the sum of the negligence of all the parties to a given accident cannot exceed 100 percent. Furthermore, it will be the jury's obligation to assign the proportion or degree of this total negligence among the various parties, beginning with the plaintiff.

The requirements of proximate cause have not been altered by the new rule. Consequently, before any party is entitled to recover, it must be shown that the negligence of the defendant was the proximate cause of the accident and subsequent injuries. The same is true of contributory fault or negligence. Before it can be counted against a plaintiff, it must be found to be the proximate cause of his injuries.

The jury should be required by general verdict to state the total or gross amount of damages of each party whom they find entitled to a recovery, and by special interrogatory the percentage of fault or contributory negligence, if any, attributable to each party. After the verdicts have been accepted, the trial court will calculate the net amount by deducting the party's percentage of fault from his gross award. To this extent, we follow the mechanics of the jury verdict award employed by the courts which have adopted pure comparative negligence, which is compatible with most of the statutory approaches.

Our comparative negligence rule has no effect on the plaintiff's right to sue only one of several joint tortfeasors. However[,] the joint tortfeasor so sued may implead the other joint tortfeasors as third-party defendants. . . . Thus, while the original defendant may have to respond only to the plaintiff for the latter's damages, the defendant in the third-party action can have these damages apportioned among the third-party defendants. . . .

[O]ur comparative negligence rule is [not] designed to alter our basic law which provides for joint and several liability among joint tortfeasors after judgment. . . . Most courts which have considered the question after either a statutory or judicial adoption of some form of comparative negligence have held that the plaintiff can sue one or more joint tortfeasors, and if more than one is sued and a joint judgment is obtained, he may collect the entire amount from any one of the defendants. . . .

Our comparative negligence rule does not change the right of a joint tortfeasor to obtain a Pro tanto credit on the plaintiff's judgment for monies obtained by the plaintiff in a settlement with another joint tortfeasor. . . .

Since we have not completely abolished the doctrine of contributory negligence, we recognize that in appropriate circumstances the doctrine of last clear chance is still available. In the case of an intentional tort, contributory negligence is not a defense. Therefore, comparative negligence would not come into play, and the plaintiff would recover his damages undiminished by any contributory negligence.

By way of summary, we believe that moderating the harshness of our contributory negligence rule achieves a more satisfactory balance in the allocation of fault as it relates to recovery in our tort system. Our comparative negligence rule still bars the substantially negligent plaintiff from obtaining a recovery, but it does permit the plaintiff who is more than slightly at fault to recover his injuries diminished by his percentage of contributory negligence. The rule is an intermediate position between the absolute bar of the present contributory negligence rule and the almost total permissiveness of the pure comparative negligence rule. It represents a considerable improvement over the present rule without undertaking a radical change in our present fault-based tort system, as would be the case with pure comparative negligence. . . .

For the foregoing reasons, the judgment in each case is reversed and the cases are remanded for further proceedings not inconsistent with this opinion.

Reversed and remanded.

NOTES AND QUESTIONS

1. Consider the following statutory provisions adopting comparative negligence in New York and Texas:

New York Civil Practice Law § 1411

In any action to recover damages for personal injury, injury to property, or wrongful death, the culpable conduct attributable to the claimant or to the decedent, including contributory negligence or assumption of risk, shall not bar recovery, but the amount of damages otherwise recoverable shall be diminished in the proportion which the culpable conduct attributable to the claimant or decedent bears to the culpable conduct which caused the damages.

Texas Civil Practice and Remedies Code § 33.001

Proportionate Responsibility:

In an action to which this chapter applies, a claimant may not recover damages if his percentage of responsibility is greater than 50 percent.

2. Once a court or legislature decides to adopt comparative negligence, it must choose between so-called "pure" and "modified" forms of comparative negligence. As *Bradley* indicates, the courts that adopted comparative negligence by judicial decision at first tended to choose the "pure" form, which the court accurately describes as allowing a party some recovery unless that party is assigned 100% of the fault. The New York statute also adopts this rule. Under the "modified" scheme, by contrast, a party whose percentage of negligence reaches some specified level is at that point totally barred from recovery, just as with traditional contributory negligence. The point at which recovery is barred is obviously of some importance. What happens under the rule of the *Bradley* case if the jury finds both plaintiff and defendant are 50% negligent? Compare the result under the Texas statute.

3. A second important issue in adopting a comparative scheme is deciding exactly what is to be compared. How does one compare "fault" (the term used in the *Bradley* opinion), "culpable conduct" (the New York statute) or "responsibility" (the Texas statute)? The question becomes more complicated if comparative "negligence" or "responsibility" is applied to strict liability and strict products liability cases, since in theory the defendant in such a case is not at fault. How then can the fault of the plaintiff (contributory negligence) be compared with the liability producing but not faulty conduct of the defendant? Nevertheless, it is common to see the comparative negligence rules applied in strict liability cases as well. *See, e.g., Daly v. General Motors Corp.*, 575 P.2d 1162 (Cal. 1978). This issue will be explored in more detail in the chapter on products liability, below.

4. Note how the issue of comparative negligence is presented to the jury. Rather than performing the calculation itself and simply returning a verdict for a particular amount of damages, juries are typically given specific interrogatories or special verdicts. These ask the jury to separately assign percentages of negligence to each party and then to calculate the total amount of damages suffered by each claimant. It is then the judge's responsibility to calculate the judgment.

5. How should multiple party cases be handled? Should the jury decide the percentage of negligence of plaintiffs and defendants as a group, or individually, party by party? What rule does the *Bradley* court adopt?

6. The *Bradley* court states that the adoption of comparative negligence does not affect the rule of joint and several liability. Why not? What would happen if a defendant's liability were limited to its percentage of fault? This issue is of particular concern to "deep pocket" defendants who may be only marginally responsible for the harm. Consider the most extreme case: A wealthy defendant and an insolvent defendant are sued by the plaintiff. The jury returns a million dollar verdict for the plaintiff, finds the defendants jointly and severally liable, and apportions 99% of the negligence to the insolvent defendant and 1% to the wealthy defendant. Under a rule of joint and several liability, the wealthy defendant can be required to pay the entire judgment. On the other hand, if joint and

several liability is abolished, much of the judgment will be uncollectable and the plaintiff will go largely uncompensated. Should the interest in compensating the injured and innocent plaintiff prevail here? Or is the disproportion between the seriousness of the defendant's fault and the magnitude of the liability too great to justify imposing liability? Some statutory schemes abolish joint and several liability in extreme situations such as this, while retaining it for cases in which the fault of the defendant is more significant.

7. In a comparative negligence regime, what should happen to doctrines such as last clear chance, which softened the harshness of the all or nothing rule of contributory negligence? Most courts have decided that the last clear chance should no longer survive as a separate doctrine allowing recovery. The West Virginia court changed its mind and abolished last clear chance a few years after the *Bradley* decision. *Ratlief v. Yokum*, 280 S.E.2d 584 (W. Va. 1981). Under this view, the factors that make up last clear chance should now be part of the jury's calculus in assigning percentages of negligence to the various parties. For example, a jury might decide to charge the defendant with a higher percentage of negligence in a situation in which the defendant had a clear opportunity to avoid the accident, but failed to take advantage of it.

8. Assumption of the risk is another doctrine that may be affected by the move to comparative negligence. This topic will be examined in more detail in the next section.

PROBLEMS

1. Plaintiff was waiting at an intersection controlled by a traffic light. She was looking to her left at the signal controlling the cross-traffic, which was green. When the light for the cross-traffic turned yellow, she began to cross the street without looking to her right. She therefore failed to see a car driven by defendant at a high rate of speed, which was trying to beat the red light. Defendant saw Plaintiff begin to cross the intersection in front of him, but thought he could pass in front of her. By the time Defendant realized he could not and began to apply his brakes, it was too late. Defendant's car struck Plaintiff, causing injuries. Plaintiff sues for negligence and Defendant asserts the defense of comparative negligence. Based on these facts, what percentage of negligence would you assign to each party? If Plaintiff's damages were found to be $500,000, how much would she recover based on your allocation of negligence? (Would it make a difference which form of comparative negligence — "pure," modified 50%, or modified 51% — applied in the jurisdiction?) Finally, consider how you would argue the case for each side. What arguments would you make to the jury concerning how the percentages of fault should be allocated? Would your arguments vary depending on the type of comparative negligence that applied?

2. Alpha and Omega both drove negligently, resulting in a collision in which both were injured. Each files a claim against the other, and each defends based

on the contributory fault of the other. If the jury agrees that both were at fault, what would happen to the claims of Alpha and Omega under the all or nothing rule of contributory negligence? Under comparative negligence rules, suppose the jury allocates 50% of the negligence to each. Suppose also that the jury finds that Alpha suffered $100,000 in damages, and Omega $70,000. How should judgment be entered in the case? Does it matter which type of comparative negligence applies? Can each party obtain a judgment against the other, or should the recoveries be offset? Does it make any difference if both parties are insured? Suppose only one party has liability insurance? Suppose only one party is solvent?

3. Complications increase if multiple parties are involved. Consider the following hypothetical as the basis for the questions below: Plaintiff sues two defendants for a joint tort in a comparative negligence jurisdiction. The jury returns special verdicts finding the Plaintiff to be 40% negligent, Defendant 1 to be 35% negligent, and Defendant 2 to be 25% negligent, and the Plaintiff's damages to be $100,000.

    a. Should it make any difference that the Plaintiff is more at fault than either of the two defendants? What do the *Bradley* opinion and the two statutes quoted above say about this issue?

    b. Should the defendants be jointly and severally liable, or individually liable only for the percentage share of the judgment represented by their shares of negligence? In each case, how would judgement be entered on this hypothetical verdict?

    c. Suppose that Defendant 1 settles with Plaintiff before trial for $10,000. How should the case proceed? Assume that the jurisdiction retains joint and several liability and uses a dollar-for-dollar ("pro tanto") credit for settlements. How should the court enter judgment against Defendant 2?

    d. Suppose that Defendant 1 settles with Plaintiff before trial for $10,000. How should the case proceed if the jurisdiction uses a prorata credit for settlements? Should the court use the percentage of negligence of Defendant 1 to establish the percentage of the case that Plaintiff settled? If so, do you foresee any problems that might arise in submitting to the jury the question of the percentage of fault belonging to a person who is no longer an actual party to the suit? Assuming that the court does submit the issue of the percentage of the settling defendant's negligence and uses that number to establish Defendant 1's proportionate share, how should the court enter judgment against Defendant 2?

LAW v. SUPERIOR COURT
755 P.2d 1135 (Ariz. 1988)

FELDMAN, Vice Chief Justice.

On the evening of November 8, 1985, Cindy Law was driving her parents' car in Tempe, Arizona. She apparently pulled in front of an automobile operated by James Harder, who swerved violently to avoid a collision. Unfortunately, his evasive maneuver overturned the Harder vehicle. Harder and his wife were not wearing their seat belts and were thrown from their car — James through a closed sunroof. The Harders suffered severe orthopedic injuries as a result of the accident.

The Harders (plaintiffs) brought a negligence action against Cindy Law and her parents (defendants). During the course of discovery, defendants sought information concerning plaintiffs' use and experience with seat belts and shoulder restraints. Plaintiffs objected to these discovery requests on the grounds that the subject was irrelevant under the holding of *Nash v. Kamrath*, 21 Ariz. App. 530, 521 P.2d 161 (1974). In that case, division two of our court of appeals held that evidence of a passenger's failure to wear a seat belt was inadmissible either to show breach of a duty to minimize damages or to prove contributory negligence.

Defendants moved to compel discovery. In June 1986, the trial judge denied the motion and issued a protective order, concluding that under *Nash* motorists have no duty to wear seat belts. [T]he court of appeals vacated the trial judge's protective order and held that evidence of seat belt nonuse was admissible so long as defendants could demonstrate a causal relationship between the nonuse and the injuries. . . . The court concluded that under the interrelated doctrines of avoidable consequences and mitigation of damages, motorists were responsible to take reasonable pre-accident measures to prevent or reduce damages from foreseeable injury. Failure to avoid or mitigate foreseeable damages would result in a corresponding reduction in the damages awardable. The court found that the absence of a mandatory state seat belt law did not negate the duty to mitigate damages. Nor did the comparative negligence statute . . . limit the jury's power to reduce damages solely to cases of contributory negligence or assumption of the risk.

In their petition for review, plaintiffs ask us to resolve the conflict between this case and *Nash*. . . .

I. AN OVERVIEW OF THE SEAT BELT PROBLEM

In 1968, Federal Motor Vehicle Safety Standard No. 208 required automakers to install a lap belt for each occupant as well as a shoulder harness for the outboard front occupants on all automobiles made after January 1968. State and federal requirements for seat belt installation were a response to increasingly authoritative evidence that seat belts could prevent many deaths and injuries arising from automobile accidents.

As seat belts became a standard automotive fixture, defendants increasingly raised the "seat belt defense." At first, defense attorneys attempted to use the defense as a complete bar to recovery by showing that plaintiff was contributorily negligent. These efforts were generally unsuccessful. Courts were unwilling to totally deny recovery based on a finding of contributory negligence when it was almost certain in every case that nonuse of the seat belt was not a cause of the primary accident.

The focus of defense efforts rapidly shifted to asserting that the victim had failed to properly mitigate damages by not wearing a seat belt. The mitigation theory sharply split the courts. Some jurisdictions accepted the idea that a plaintiff was responsible to take reasonable pre-accident safety measures. Most courts refused to bend traditional mitigation concepts to cover the victim's pre-accident conduct. Arizona followed this majority rule in *Nash*, decided in 1974. . . . *Nash* was based upon a three-prong rationale. The first was that evidence of seat belt nonuse was irrelevant because it ran "counter to the traditional notion that, unless put on notice to the contrary, one has a right to assume that other persons upon the highway will not be negligent." . . . The next basis for the *Nash* analysis was the concept that use of a seat belt might in itself present dangers to motorists. If that were true, the law could hardly hold nonuse to be a violation of reasonable standards. As a corollary to the last mentioned principle, the court finally held there was no duty to fasten a seat belt, and failure to do so could not be considered a breach of any duty to minimize damages. . . .

[I]n our view, the technological and legal changes that have occurred in the twelve years that passed between *Nash* and the decision in the present case must determine which view of the law represents better policy. One of the most dramatic changes that has occurred in this period is the general acceptance of comparative negligence principles.

[T]raditional contributory negligence theory, of course, militates for rejection of the seat belt defense. Contributory negligence is conceptualized in terms of conduct by plaintiff which contributed to the occurrence of the accident. . . . Because seat belt nonuse seldom contributes to the occurrence of the accident, it does not easily fit into the theory of contributory negligence. . . .

Further, if the seat belt defense is considered a form of contributory negligence, it would totally bar recovery. Theoretically, that was the situation under the former Arizona law. . . . However, nonuse of a seat belt rarely causes all of plaintiff's injuries. In the typical accident, nonuse simply increases the number or severity of injuries beyond those which would have occurred had the plaintiff used a seat belt. Thus, under traditional contributory negligence principles, the seat belt defense would have constituted a harsh and untenable policy denying all recovery to nonusers, despite the lack of any causal nexus between seat belt nonuse and some of the injuries.

Comparative negligence theories eliminate most of those problems because an adverse finding on nonuse does not bar recovery but merely reduces the damages in proportion to the contributing factor of seat belt nonuse. . . . [T]he rise of comparative negligence undermined much of the theoretical basis for rejection of the defense. . . .

[The court then reviewed state and federal laws mandating seat belt use, but noted that the Arizona legislature has not passed such a law.]

II. THE SEAT BELT DEFENSE IN ARIZONA

With the foregoing in mind, we must now decide whether Arizona will adopt some version of the so-called seat belt defense. To do so, we first examine the current validity of the principles underlying the *Nash* decision.

Because *Nash* held that motorists could assume that all who use the highways will drive with care, the decision imposed no duty to anticipate injury. Over a lifetime, however, it is almost certain that a motor vehicle accident will injure the average motorist. The clear foreseeability of automobile accidents is the reason most courts now hold automobile manufacturers responsible to make vehicles capable of providing a reasonable level of protection to automobile occupants. . . . [W]e conclude as a matter of public policy that the law must recognize the responsibility of every person to anticipate and take reasonable measures to guard against the danger of motor vehicle accidents that are not only foreseeable but virtually certain to occur sooner or later. . . .

In *Nash*, the court noted that seat belts may actually create or enhance injuries instead of preventing them. . . . There are reports of tragic situations when wearing a seat belt may trap a vehicle occupant in a burning, sinking, or disabled automobile. Such cases are noteworthy precisely because they are so rare. It is statistically far safer for motorists to remain in their vehicles than to suffer the vagaries of a violent ejection from the automobile. There are also claims that properly worn seat belts can cause direct and serious harm to users [including] abdominal and spinal injuries that may be attributable to seat belt use. However, [in] almost every instance seat belt-induced injuries are far less drastic than those that would have been incurred without the seat belt use. As a general rule, a motorist is simply better off wearing a seat belt. We conclude from the technological data that continued nonrecognition of the seat belt defense cannot be based on the general concept that seat belts cause harm. The opposite is generally true.

Nash held there was no duty to wear seat belts. We acknowledge that "duty" to use restraints is generally considered the prime question in cases such as this. . . . Whatever its relevance to the *Nash* analysis, however, we do not believe that duty in its usual formulation remains a relevant component of the seat belt defense analysis. "Duty" is normally defined in terms of the obligation of care owed to one's neighbors. . . . Because in all but the rarest situation nonuse of a seat belt presents no foreseeable danger to others, it is probably incorrect to conceptualize the seat belt defense in terms of duty.

More importantly, evaluating seat belt nonuse under the rubric of duty fundamentally confuses that concept with the evaluation of the conduct that may or may not fulfill it. . . . Everyone has a "duty" to use due care to prevent injury to others. Nonuse of a seat belt is not a question of duty but rather a matter of conduct which only occasionally impinges on others. Thus, we believe that injuries sustained by the plaintiff as a result of his nonuse of an available seat belt are not so much a failure to use care to avoid endangering others but part of the related obligation to conduct oneself reasonably to minimize damages and avoid foreseeable harm to oneself. . . .

Thus, the seat belt defense would ordinarily raise issues concerning the doctrine of avoidable consequences — a theory that denies recovery for those injuries plaintiff could reasonably have avoided. . . . Plaintiffs argue that this doctrine is applied only to post-accident conduct and is inapplicable to events preceding the accident — a time when plaintiffs supposedly had a right to assume that others would not act negligently. Assuming this is ordinarily true, we believe the common law conceptualization of the doctrine of avoidable consequences has been modified by our comparative negligence statute, which applies that doctrine to pre-accident conduct.

When the Arizona legislature enacted the Uniform Contribution Among Tortfeasors Act in 1984, it added several important provisions to the model law. . . . These new sections constituted the statutory adoption of comparative negligence for our state. . . . If the jury does apply comparative negligence standards, the plaintiff's action is not barred, "but the full damages shall be reduced in proportion to the relative degree of *fault which is a proximate cause of the injury or death,* if any." A.R.S. § 12-2505(A) (emphasis added).

The essential question is whether a plaintiff who does not wear an automobile seat belt is at "fault" for injuries enhanced or caused by the failure to use the seat belt. Neither the Arizona comparative negligence statute nor its progenitor uniform law contains any definition of "fault." We do note the instructive definition of this term given in § 1(b) of the Uniform Comparative Fault Act (UCFA), 12 U.L.A. 39-40 (Cum. Supp. 1987).

> "Fault" includes acts or omissions that are in any measure negligent or reckless toward the person or property of the actor or others, or that subject a person to strict tort liability. *The term also includes . . . unreasonable failure to avoid an injury or to mitigate damages.* Legal requirements of causal relation apply both to fault as the basis for liability and to contributory fault.

(Emphasis added.) As stated in the official comment to the UCFA, negligent failure to use a seat belt would reduce damages solely for those injuries directly attributable to the lack of seat belt restraint. . . . Thus, as far as the calculation of damages is concerned, the comparative negligence statutes apply the doctrine of avoidable consequences to pre-accident conduct. . . . [T]hus, if a person chooses not to use an available, simple safety device, that person may be at "fault."

Plaintiffs claim that recognition of the seat belt defense is a matter we should leave to the legislature. . . . Some courts hold that creation of a "seat belt defense" is solely a matter for legislative action. . . . We believe, however, that this court has an obligation to participate in the evolution of tort law so that it may reflect societal and technological changes. . . . In some cases, this responsibility has compelled us to recognize duties that further public policy and legislative objectives, even though the specifics have not been enacted by the legislature. . . .

Acceptance of the seat belt defense does not require us to violate the proper deference owed the legislature. We neither carry a legislative enactment past the intent which existed at the time of its passage nor recognize an obligation not already reflected in the lives of our citizens. We only acknowledge reality: the use or nonuse of a seat belt is an everyday matter of conduct which plays a significant role in determining the extent of injuries. . . .

Plaintiffs claim that by recognizing the seat belt defense, we would confer a windfall on tortfeasors. [T]he crux of comparative negligence is a proper apportionment of damages based upon the fault of the respective parties. If a victim unreasonably failed to use an available, simple prophylactic device, then he will not be able to recover for damages created or enhanced by the nonuse. Thus, although some tortfeasors may pay less than they otherwise *would*, they will not pay less than they *should*. We do not believe this rule creates a windfall to the tortfeasor; it is an unavoidable consequence of our comparative negligence system.

Petitioners maintain that allowing apportionment of damages based on failure to use seat belts will unnecessarily complicate and protract litigation. . . . [D]efendant may utilize qualified experts in the medical, scientific, and accident reconstruction fields. It is then up to the factfinder to evaluate the evidence and quantify the results under comparative negligence principles. . . . There is no doubt that the seat belt defense will complicate and lengthen litigation in some cases. While this certainly does not militate in favor of its acceptance, we believe the problem is no different in principle from that posed by any legal, technological or scientific advance. Neither law nor society can ignore technological change simply because it makes decision more complex.

As the final argument, plaintiffs assert that introducing evidence of seat belt nonuse would propel our courts into a morass of unforeseen consequences. If seat belt nonuse is relevant, why not introduce evidence of failure to install air bags? Why not hold the plaintiff responsible for failure to buy a large car which is normally much safer in a crash than a small car? [We] deal in this case only with a plaintiff's use or nonuse of a common, simple safety device available in his or her car. In making use of an available seat belt, a motorist need not possess engineering expertise, suffer significant inconvenience, install special equipment or purchase a different vehicle. . . . The exact bounds of fault in other fact situations is a matter for the common law to address in its customary evolutionary fashion. . . .

We conclude that irrespective of a duty to avoid injuring others, under the theory of comparative "fault," nonuse of a seat belt is a factor that the jury may consider and use to reduce damages. . . .

The burden of establishing these matters, as with other matters of comparative negligence, is upon the defendant. [T]he jury must be clearly instructed that nonuse of a seat belt is an issue bearing upon the extent of damages that may be recovered and not on any other issue. . . .

HOLOHAN, Justice, dissenting.

The court adopts an analytical approach based on principles of comparative negligence. . . . It is not necessary or correct to use a comparative negligence formula to arrive at the ruling by the court. . . . Using an expansion of the avoidable consequences theory makes more sense than attempting to wedge a solution under so-called comparative negligence principles. The seat belt defense deals with diminution of damages and not with the existence of a cause of action. Diminution of damages is appropriate when the injured party could have avoided some of the injury by the use of reasonable efforts. Full recovery is denied because part of the harm is due to the injured person's lack of care, and public policy requires that persons should be discouraged from wasting their resources, both physical or economic. *See* RESTATEMENT (SECOND) OF TORTS § 918 comment a (1977).

Whether the court's comparative negligence principles or the theory of avoidable consequences is employed, we are ultimately faced with the vital issue in this case — Public Policy. Despite the court's claim that nonuse of a seat belt is not a question of duty, [this] decision imposes upon all motorists and passengers of this state the duty to wear seat belts, and it fixes the penalty for nonuse as reduction of the amount of damages to be recovered by an injured motorist or passenger. . . . Implicit in the court's decision is the rationale that seat belts should be used, and it is time that all of us used them. Although we held no hearings on the subject, the technical literature and opinions of experts seems to support the utility of using seat belts. The important consideration is who should make the decision to impose the duty (or non duty)? What branch of government under our constitutional system should make such a public policy decision?

Some courts such as our colleagues in our neighboring state of New Mexico faced with a similar problem, held that the creation of a "seat belt defense" is a matter for the legislature, not for the judiciary. . . . There are sound reasons for such a position, none of which have apparently been considered by this court in its rush to "participate in the evolution of tort law." . . . [T]here is more involved in this matter than the development of tort law. We are urged to adopt a rule which may reduce the recovery of the plaintiff in this case, but the rule may also result in lessening the extent of personal injuries in future automobile accidents. The latter is certainly a good objective, but in this area of public safety the courts, with the case-by-case method, are powerless to provide a comprehensive program of policy, enforcement and education. The legislative branch is the proper one to deal with this complex problem if there is to be an effective and unified solution. . . .

NOTES AND QUESTIONS

1. Jurisdictions vary widely on how to treat the seatbelt defense. Some jurisdictions statutorily require that occupants of automobiles use seatbelts, but also make evidence of the violation of the statute inadmissible in civil actions. In some jurisdictions, the defense is allowed but the percentage of damage reduction is limited. Where courts have decided the issue, some have allowed the defense to fully reduce damages while others have refused to allow the defense at all.

2. As the case above illustrates, courts have been uncertain how to classify the defense, because it does not seem to fit the traditional requirements for either contributory negligence, assumption of the risk, or avoidable consequences. Which of these doctrines, if any, seems to provide the best approach to the issue of the enhancement of injury due to the failure to wear seatbelts?

3. The same issues, with some of the same divisions, arise with regard to the failure to wear a helmet when riding motorcycles, bicycles and ATV's.

4. The doctrine of avoidable consequences states that a plaintiff cannot recover for losses that could have been avoided by reasonable precautions taken after the accident. For example, suppose the defendant negligently drives into the front window of plaintiff's store. Plaintiff does nothing to secure the store, and during the night the store is looted. The plaintiff cannot recover from defendant for the loss of merchandise if simple and reasonable precautions, such as boarding up the damaged window, would have prevented the loss. It would be the defendant's burden to demonstrate that the precautions were feasible and would in fact have likely prevented the loss.

5. One application of the avoidable consequences rule that can arise in personal injury actions concerns whether the plaintiff has a duty to obtain medical care to treat the injury and correct any disabling condition caused by the accident. For example, if an operation can correct a disability and allow an individual to return to work, should the plaintiff who refuses to undergo the operation be barred from recovering damages, such as future lost wages, attributable to the disability? In general, the answer is that a duty does require that plaintiff obtain basic medical treatment and rehabilitation. More problematic is whether there is a duty to undergo major operations to correct disabilities. Courts usually give deference to the victim's assessment of the risks and benefits, and ultimately the decision whether to undergo, a major operation.

PROBLEMS

1. In cases like *Law*, what evidence might defendant present to meet its burden of proof? How can defendant show the amount of damage attributable to the failure to wear a seatbelt? What evidence might plaintiff present to rebut the defendant's showing?

2. Plaintiff, who was not wearing a seatbelt, was driving 60 miles per hour in a 40 mile per hour zone approaching an intersection controlled by a traffic light. The light was green for Plaintiff. Defendant was approaching the same intersection on the cross street. Defendant was trying to adjust the air conditioner vents and did not see the red light in his direction. Defendant entered the intersection against the red light, directly in Plaintiff's path. Plaintiff swerved to avoid Defendant, but lost control of the car because of his excessive speed. Plaintiff's car overturned and spun around, throwing Plaintiff through the driver's side window. Because Plaintiff was ejected from the car, Plaintiff suffered severe spinal injuries that left her paralyzed. Although Plaintiff's car overturned, the accident did not crush the passenger compartment, and Plaintiff would probably not have suffered severe injuries had she been wearing a seatbelt. In a jurisdiction that applies both comparative negligence and the seatbelt defense, how should the court submit the case to the jury? Do these facts call for a double reduction, once for the negligence in driving at an excessive speed and a second for the failure to use the seatbelt? What arguments would you make for each side regarding the proper method of reducing the Plaintiff's damages in this situation?

3. Suppose, in the prior problem, that Defendant ran the red light because he was extremely intoxicated. Does the analysis change?

4. Defendant ran a stop sign and struck Plaintiff's wife while she was walking across the street. An ambulance took her to a local emergency room, where the doctors determined that she was suffering from internal bleeding. The doctors advised immediate surgery to stop the bleeding, but she refused to consent to a blood transfusion during the surgery because of religious scruples. Without the transfusion the operation was impossible, and the Plaintiff's wife died from her injuries. Plaintiff brought a wrongful death action against defendant. Defendant asserted the avoidable consequences rule, claiming that the refusal of medical treatment was unreasonable, and that proper care would have saved the decedent's life. Plaintiff moves to exclude this evidence, arguing that the court and jury cannot second-guess a decision that was religiously motivated. How should the court rule on Defendant's defense? Cf. *Munn v. Algee*, 924 F.2d 568 (5th Cir. 1991).

3. Assumption of the Risk

The common law took the position that there was no legal injury to one who consented to bear a risk. In tort law, this maxim became the doctrine of assumption of the risk. One aspect of this doctrine involves the explicit release of liability by contract. The more difficult problem is whether one can imply such an "agreement" to bear the risk from the plaintiff's conduct.

a. Express Assumption of the Risk

A party may agree by contract to bear a risk. But courts are wary lest such agreements undermine the safety and compensation policies of tort law. When such a release is challenged, courts must decide whether or not to enforce the release of liability.

WOLF v. FORD
644 A.2d 522 (Md. 1994)

KARWACKI, Judge.

[T]he eighteen-year-old appellant received $145,700 in settlement of a lawsuit [for] injuries arising out of a 1983 automobile accident. On April 2, 1986, Wolf and her mother visited the home of the appellee, Harry M. Ford, who [was] employed as a stockbroker at the investment firm of the appellee, Legg Mason Wood Walker, Inc. ("Legg Mason"). The purpose of the meeting was to discuss Wolf's options for investing the money she had received from the settlement. At the meeting, Wolf told Ford that her goals were to get a college education and to preserve the bulk of her money. She [told] Ford, "I don't want it to flitter away, it was something I wanted to hold on to."

The following day, Ford sent Wolf a letter stating that he was looking forward to working with Wolf in her investments. The letter contained three enclosures that Wolf was to sign and return to Ford; among the enclosures was a Discretionary Account Agreement. The Agreement provided in pertinent part:

> You are hereby authorized to buy, sell and generally trade in securities, on margin, in cash or otherwise in accordance with your terms and conditions for my account and risk. . . .
>
> . . . I hereby exonerate you from any and all liability for losses which may occur while you are acting on my behalf except for such as may result from your gross negligence or willful misconduct. . . .
>
> I hereby reserve the power to direct and terminate at any and all times the selection of securities for purchase or sale, but the exercise of such power shall not be deemed a revocation of this agreement, the same to remain in full force and effect until revoked by me by written notice addressed to you . . . but such revocation shall not affect any liability in any way resulting from transactions initiated prior to such revocation.

Wolf signed this Agreement on April 7, 1986 and returned it to Legg Mason. . . . Legg Mason received $135,000.00 from Wolf. Ford used this money to purchase 22 different stocks for Wolf's portfolio.

Later that same year, Wolf began to withdraw large sums of cash from her account with Legg Mason. In August, 1986, Wolf withdrew $8,000.00. In October and November, 1986, she withdrew a total of $4,500.00. In December, 1986, she withdrew $500.00. In January, 1987, she withdrew $6,000.00.

In July, 1987, Wolf received a letter from C.A. Bacigalupo, a senior vice president of Legg Mason, which stated:

> As a service to our clients, we periodically review discretionary authorizations at Legg Mason Wood Walker, Inc. This enables us to verify that the authority is to continue.
>
> It is requested that you sign and return this letter indicating whether or not you wish to continue the discretionary authority which you conferred upon your investment broker. . . . If we do not hear from you by August 7, 1987, the discretionary authority will be terminated.

Wolf signed the letter on September 4, 1987, indicating on the letter that she wished to continue the discretionary authorization. In November and December, 1988, Wolf withdrew $5398.44. In January, 1989, she withdrew over $5,200.00. During the time her account was handled by Ford, she withdrew a total of $64,650.00 from her account. Each withdrawal required the prompt sale of one or more of the stocks from her portfolio.

Apparently upset with the performance of some of the stocks in her portfolio, Wolf called Legg Mason in June, 1990 and terminated the discretionary authority she had given Ford. In August, 1990, she instructed Legg Mason to transfer her account from Ford to John Seifert, another stockbroker at Legg Mason. Wolf closed her account with Legg Mason in March, 1991.

Wolf filed suit in the Circuit Court [against] Ford, Seifert, and Legg Mason in May, 1992. [A]fter the close of Wolf's case at a jury trial, the court (Bollinger, J.) granted the defendants' motion for judgment [ruling] that the exculpatory clause [in] the Discretionary Account Agreement limited defendants' potential liability to those losses resulting from gross negligence or intentional misconduct. He further ruled that there was no evidence of either gross negligence or willful misconduct. . . .

Wolf [noted] an appeal. . . . We issued a writ of certiorari on our own motion before consideration of the case [to] consider the effect of the exculpatory clause in the Discretionary Account Agreement.

I

[Wolf] argues that the exculpatory clause contained in the Discretionary Account Agreement is void as against public policy and that the case should therefore be remanded for a determination of the existence of simple negligence on the part of Ford or Legg Mason. We disagree.

[*Winterstein v. Wilcom*, 16 Md. App. 130, 293 A.2d 821, *cert. denied*, 266 Md. 744 (1972), held that in] the absence of legislation to the contrary, exculpatory clauses are generally valid, and the public policy of freedom of contract is best served by enforcing the provisions of the clause. . . . There are circumstances, however, under which the public interest will not permit an exculpatory clause in a contract; these have often been grouped into three general exceptions to the rule. First, a party will not be permitted to excuse its liability for intentional harms or for the more extreme forms of negligence, *i.e.*, reckless, wanton, or gross. . . . Second, "[w]hen one party is at such an obvious disadvantage in bargaining power that the effect of the contract is to put him at the mercy of the other's negligence, the agreement is void as against public policy." *Winterstein*, 16 Md. App. at 135-36. . . . Third, public policy will not permit exculpatory agreements in transactions affecting the public interest. . . . This last category includes the performance of a public service obligation, *e.g.*, public utilities, common carriers, innkeepers, and public warehousemen. It also includes those transactions, not readily susceptible to definition or broad categorization, that are so important to the public good that an exculpatory clause would be "patently offensive," such that " 'the common sense of the entire community would . . . pronounce it' invalid." . . . This standard is a strict one, in keeping with our general reluctance to invoke the nebulous public interest to disturb private contracts. . . .

Because the concept of the "public interest" is amorphous, it is difficult to apply. Courts, therefore, have struggled to refine and narrow the definition in an attempt to make the concept more concrete. *Winterstein* referred to a six-factor test developed by the Supreme Court of California in *Tunkl v. Regents of the Univ. of Calif.*, 60 Cal. 2d 92, 383 P.2d 441, 32 Cal. Rptr. 33 (1963), that was intended to determine which exculpatory agreements affect the "public interest" and which do not. *Winterstein* quoted the following passage from *Tunkl*, noting that it is to be used as a rough outline of that type of transaction in which exculpatory provisions will be held invalid:

> [T]he attempted but invalid exemption involves a transaction which exhibits some or all of the following characteristics. It concerns a business of a type generally thought suitable for public regulation. The party seeking exculpation is engaged in performing a service of great importance to the public, which is often a matter of practical necessity for some members of the public. The party holds himself out as willing to perform this service for any member of the public who seeks it, or at least for any member coming within certain established standards. As a result of the essential nature of the service, in the economic setting of the transaction, the party invoking exculpation possesses a decisive advantage of bargaining strength against any member of the public who seeks his services. In exercising a superior bargaining power the

party confronts the public with a standardized adhesion contract of exculpation, and makes no provision whereby a purchaser may pay additional reasonable fees and obtain protection against negligence. Finally, as a result of the transaction, the person or property of the purchaser is placed under the control of the seller, subject to the risk of carelessness by the seller or his agents.

[S]ince *Winterstein* was decided [t]he Court of Special Appeals [has] considered exculpatory clauses in several matters. [In] *Boucher v. Riner*, 68 Md. App. 539, 514 A.2d 485 (1986), the court held enforceable an exculpatory clause signed by a parachute student shortly before he jumped and suffered injuries in his descent. [*See also*] *Schrier v. Beltway Alarm Co.*, 73 Md. App. 281, 533 A.2d 1316 (1987). [E]ven though these cases have not found an activity that is sufficiently connected to the "public interest" so as to invalidate the exculpatory clause, we are concerned that the six-factor test of *Tunkl*, originally intended to be a rough outline in guiding a court's determination as to whether a given transaction affects the public interest, may become too rigid a measuring stick. . . . No definition of the concept of public interest can be contained within the four corners of a formula." [W]e expressly decline, therefore, to adopt the six-factor test set forth in *Tunkl*. This is not to say that the factors listed cannot be considered by a court in determining whether a given transaction involves the public interest, but the six factors are not conclusive. The ultimate determination of what constitutes the public interest must be made considering the totality of the circumstances of any given case against the backdrop of current societal expectations.

II

Turning to the merits of the case sub judice, we perceive no reason why the exculpatory clause should not be enforced. None of the three exceptions to the general rule permitting exculpatory clauses is applicable here.

First, there has been no allegation of fraud or willful misconduct, and Wolf concedes that there is no evidence of gross negligence. To the contrary, Wolf testified [that] Ford never lied to her or made any misrepresentations to her. Second, contrary to Wolf's assertion, we do not believe that there was any disparate bargaining advantage. Wolf claims that the very fact that she was eighteen years old and an unsophisticated investor renders the relationship so lopsided as to impose an extraordinary duty upon Ford. . . . Although young, she had attained her legal majority at the time. She was not solicited by Legg Mason; rather, she initiated contact with Ford. Wolf was under no compulsion, economic or otherwise, to invest her money in the stock market with Legg Mason or any other securities investment firm. She had numerous options available to her, including placing her money in an interest-bearing bank account or long-term certificates of deposit. Moreover, even within Legg Mason, she was under no compulsion to give Ford discretionary authority over her account. Had she wished to retain control over each transaction, she could have received the benefit of Ford's knowledge, experience, and advice, yet still have made every decision on the sale and purchase of individual securities. She, however, signed the Discretionary Account Agreement, including the exculpatory clause, five days after her initial discussion with Ford, and she reiterated her desire to have her account handled on a discretionary basis in September of the following year. Furthermore, even with the Discretionary Account Agreement in place, Wolf did not cede control over her account. According to the terms of the agreement, she retained at all times the right to make investment decisions, to withdraw funds, and to terminate the stockbroker's discretionary authority. Wolf invoked all of these rights during the course of her relationship with Legg Mason.

Third, a stockbroker-client relationship is not one that so affects the public interest that we should disturb the parties' ability to contractually exempt a party from liability for negligence. Wolf argues that we should adopt the six-factor *Tunkl* test for defining the public interest, and that under that test, a stockbroker-client relationship is affected with public interest. We have stated [that] we do not adopt the six-factor test as conclusive, and we will not invalidate a private contract on grounds of public policy unless the clause at issue is patently offensive. This clause does not meet that test. Individuals who choose freely to invest their money in the stock market understand that there is some risk involved; such is the nature of the securities industry. If the parties to a contract determine that one party will bear the burden of the other party's simple negligence, they are entitled to do just that. This is particularly important where an account is accepted on a discretionary basis, as in the instant case, and the investor asks the broker to purchase stocks using the broker's best judgment. This is not a case in which an investment is made based upon a broker's misrepresentation. . . . Rather, the possibility of poor performance of the securities chosen is precisely the sort of harm that is within the contemplation of the parties at the time they entered the agreement. Because of the volatile nature of financial markets, what may appear to be negligence in the purchase of securities one year may eventually turn out to be a stroke of genius in following years, and vice versa. Thus, the allocation of risk of negligence between parties to a private contract is not patently offensive; rather, it is part and parcel of the freedom to contract in private matters.

We hold, therefore, that the exculpatory clause in the Discretionary Account Agreement between Wolf and Ford is valid and enforceable.

PROBLEMS

1. *Winterstein*, referred to in the opinion above, involved a release that the plaintiff signed as a condition of being allowed to participate in a drag race at the defendant's race track. The court found no public policy violation and enforced the release. *Tunkl*, on the other hand, involved a release required as a condition of admission to a university hospital, a requirement that the Califor-

nia Supreme Court found violated public policy. How would the *Tunkl* factors have applied to the contract with the stockbroker at issue in *Wolf v. Ford*?

2. Examine the exculpatory clause in the case above. What liabilities are being released? What sort of conduct does it cover? What sort of liabilities are not released?

3. Should express assumption of the risk be a complete bar to recovery if the jurisdiction has adopted some form of comparative negligence?

4. Suppose the release in the *Wolf* case did not contain the language creating an exception for gross negligence and willful misconduct. Would the release be effective to protect the defendant for losses caused by gross negligence or fraud? If public policy would prohibit enforcement of the release for such misconduct, would the clause still be effective to protect against liability for negligence?

5. Mr. and Mrs. Parent signed their Child up for the local soccer league. As part of the application to play, Mr. and Mrs. Parent and Child were required to sign a "Release of All Claims," which contained the following language: "Parents and Child hereby release and hold harmless the league, all other participants, players, coaches, trainers, referees, spectators and total strangers, from any and all liability from any claims for injury, death, property damage, or any other loss whatsoever, resulting from any act, whether negligent or willful, or from any event of any kind, including acts of God and acts of war." At the first game of the season, a player on the opposing team deliberately tripped Child while the latter was running. Child fell awkwardly and hard, resulting in a broken arm. Mr. and Mrs. Parent both rushed onto the field to help Child. Mrs. Parent began yelling at the player who had tripped Child, which prompted the referee to rush over to keep order. The referee pushed Mrs. Parent toward the sideline and told her to stay off the field. Mr. Parent, upset at Child's injury, demanded that the referee throw the other player out of the game. When the referee told Mr. Parent it was just part of the game, the latter began shouting obscenities. The referee got mad and punched Mr. Parent in the nose. The other bystanders had to separate the two, and the game was suspended until medical treatment was provided for Child. Unfortunately, the doctor who set Child's broken arm did so in such an incompetent fashion that the arm was permanently weakened. What claims do Mr. and Mrs. Parent and Child have, based upon the foregoing facts? Which of these claims are covered by the release? Of the covered claims, are there public policy arguments that would prevent enforcement of the release?

b. Implied Assumption of the Risk

Implied assumption of the risk involves situations where the plaintiff has voluntarily encountered a known risk. Should this be construed as an implied agreement to release from liability the party that created the risk? The courts must decide what the consequences of such an implied agreement should be.

One of the problems with this doctrine is deciding whether it is really something distinct from ordinary contributory negligence.

MURPHY v. STEEPLECHASE AMUSEMENT CO., INC.
166 N.E. 173 (N.Y. 1929)

CARDOZO, C. J.

The defendant, Steeplechase Amusement Company, maintains an amusement park at Coney Island, N.Y. One of the supposed attractions is known as 'the Flopper.' It is a moving belt, running upward on an inclined plane, on which passengers sit or stand. Many of them are unable to keep their feet because of the movement of the belt, and are thrown backward or aside. The belt runs in a groove, with padded walls on either side to a height of four feet, and with padded flooring beyond the walls at the same angle as the belt. An electric motor, driven by current furnished by the Brooklyn Edison Company, supplies the needed power.

Plaintiff, a vigorous young man, visited the park with friends. One of them, a young woman, now his wife, stepped upon the moving belt. Plaintiff followed and stepped behind her. As he did so, he felt what he describes as a sudden jerk, and was thrown to the floor. His wife in front and also friends behind him were thrown at the same time. Something more was here, as every one understood, than the slowly moving escalator that is common is shops and public places. A fall was foreseen as one of the risks of the adventure. There would have been no point to the whole thing, no adventure about it, if the risk had not been there. The very name, above the gate, 'the Flopper,' was warning to the timid. If the name was not enough, there was warning more distinct in the experience of others. We are told by the plaintiff's wife that the members of her party stood looking at the sport before joining in it themselves. Some aboard the belt were able, as she viewed them, to sit down with decorum or even to stand and keep their footing; others jumped or fell. The tumbling bodies and the screams and laughter supplied the merriment and fun. 'I took a chance,' she said when asked whether she thought that a fall might be expected.

Plaintiff took the chance with her, but, less lucky than his companions, suffered a fracture of a knee cap. He states in his complaint that the belt was dangerous to life and limb, in that it stopped and started violently and suddenly and was not properly equipped to prevent injuries to persons who were using it without knowledge of its dangers, and in a bill of particulars he adds that it was operated at a fast and dangerous rate of speed and was not supplied with a proper railing, guard, or other device to prevent a fall therefrom. No other negligence is charged.

We see no adequate basis for a finding that the belt was out of order. It was already in motion when the plaintiff put his foot on it. He cannot help himself to a verdict in such circumstances by the addition of the facile comment that it threw him with a jerk. One who steps upon a moving belt and finds his heels above his head is in no position to discriminate with nicety between the successive stages of the shock, between the jerk which is a cause and the jerk, accompanying the fall, as an instantaneous effect. There is evidence for the defendant that power was transmitted smoothly, and could not be transmitted otherwise. If the movement was spasmodic, it was an unexplained and, it seems, an inexplicable departure from the normal workings of the mechanism. An aberration so extraordinary, if it is to lay the basis for a verdict, should rest on something firmer than a mere descriptive epithet, a summary of the sensations of a tense and crowded moment. . . . But the jerk, if it were established, would add little to the case. Whether the movement of the belt was uniform or irregular, the risk at greatest was a fall. This was the very hazard that was invited and foreseen. . . .

Volenti non fit injuria. One who takes part in such a sport accepts the dangers that inhere in it so far as they are obvious and necessary, just as a fencer accepts the risk of a thrust by his antagonist or a spectator at a ball game the chance of contact with the ball. . . . The antics of the clown are not the paces of the cloistered cleric. The rough and boisterous joke, the horseplay of the crowd, evokes its own guffaws, but they are not the pleasures of tranquillity. The plaintiff was not seeking a retreat for meditation. Visitors were tumbling about the belt to the merriment of onlookers when he made his choice to join them. He took the chance of a like fate, with whatever damage to his body might ensue from such a fall. The timorous may stay at home.

A different case would be here if the dangers inherent in the sport were obscure or unobserved, [or] so serious as to justify the belief that precautions of some kind must have been taken to avert them. Nothing happened to the plaintiff except what common experience tells us may happen at any time as the consequence of a sudden fall. Many a skater or a horseman can rehearse a tale of equal woe. A different case there would also be if the accidents had been so many as to show that the game in its inherent nature was too dangerous to be continued without change. The president of the amusement company says that there had never been such an accident before. A nurse employed at an emergency hospital maintained in connection with the park contradicts him to some extent. She says that on other occasions she had attended patrons of the park who had been injured at the Flopper, how many she could not say. None, however, had been badly injured or had suffered broken bones. Such testimony is not enough to show that the game was a trap for the unwary, too perilous to be endured. According to the defendant's estimate, 250,000 visitors were at the Flopper in a year. Some quota of accidents was to be looked for in so great a mass. One might as well say that a skating rink should be abandoned because skaters sometimes fall.

There is testimony by the plaintiff that he fell upon wood, and not upon a canvas padding. He is strongly contradicted by the photographs and by the witnesses for the defendant, and is without corroboration in the testimony of his companions who were witnesses in his behalf. If his observation was correct, there was a defect in the equipment, and one not obvious or known. The padding should have been kept in repair to break the force of any fall. The case did not go to the jury, however, upon any such theory of the defendant's liability, nor is the defect fairly suggested by the plaintiff's bill of particulars, which limits his complaint. The case went to the jury upon the theory that negligence was dependent upon a sharp and sudden jerk.

The judgment of the Appellate Division and that of the Trial Term should be reversed, and a new trial granted, with costs to abide the event.

NOTES AND QUESTIONS

1. The *Murphy* case is one of the best known "assumption of the risk" cases and well illustrates the fundamental uncertainties of the doctrine. Try to define the precise holding of the case and the rule or standard that the court applies. Consider which of the following statements best describes the basis of the ruling in *Murphy*:

a. The defendant owed no duty of care to plaintiff and therefore was not negligent.

b. The defendant owed a duty of care to plaintiff but did not breach it (did nothing to create an unreasonable risk of harm) and therefore was not negligent.

c. The defendant owed a duty of care and breached it (did create an unreasonable risk of harm) but the plaintiff is barred from recovery because the plaintiff recognized the unreasonable nature of the risk and voluntarily agreed to encounter it, and this conduct is evidence of an implied agreement on the part of the plaintiff to release the defendant from liability for the negligent conduct.

d. The defendant owed a duty of care and breached it (did create an unreasonable risk of harm) but the plaintiff is barred from recovery because the plaintiff recognized the unreasonable nature of the risk and voluntarily agreed to encounter it, and this conduct constitutes contributory negligence on the part of the plaintiff.

2. The uncertainty in assumption of the risk doctrine concerned whether or not assumption of the risk was really something distinct from contributory negligence. When both doctrines resulted in a total bar to recovery, the confusion may not have mattered a great deal as a practical matter. With the adoption of comparative negligence, however, the question arose whether assumption of the risk should survive as a separate doctrine that resulted in a total bar to recovery, or whether it was simply another variety of fault that should be folded into the process of comparing negligence. The following case illustrates one court's attempt to resolve this debate.

KNIGHT v. JEWETT
834 P.2d 696 (Cal. 1992)

GEORGE, Justice.

[On] January 25, 1987, the day of the 1987 Super Bowl football game, plaintiff Kendra Knight and defendant Michael Jewett, together with a number of other social acquaintances, attended a Super Bowl party at the home of a mutual friend. During half time of the Super Bowl, several guests decided to play an informal game of touch football on an adjoining dirt lot, using a "peewee" football. Each team had four or five players and included both women and men; plaintiff and defendant were on opposing teams. No rules were explicitly discussed before the game.

Five to ten minutes into the game, defendant ran into plaintiff during a play. According to plaintiff, at that point she told defendant "not to play so rough or I was going to have to stop playing." Her declaration stated that "[defendant] seemed to acknowledge my statement and left me with the impression that he would play less rough prospectively." In his deposition, defendant recalled that plaintiff had asked him to "be careful," but did not remember plaintiff saying that she would stop playing.

On the very next play, plaintiff sustained the injuries that gave rise to the present lawsuit. As defendant recalled the incident, his team was on defense on that play, and he jumped up in an attempt to intercept a pass. He touched the ball but did not catch it, and in coming down he collided with plaintiff, knocking her over. When he landed, he stepped backward onto plaintiff's right hand, injuring her hand and little finger.

Both plaintiff and Andrea Starr, another participant in the game who was on the same team as plaintiff, recalled the incident differently from defendant. According to their declarations, at the time plaintiff was injured, Starr already had caught the pass. Defendant was running toward Starr, when he ran into plaintiff from behind, knocked her down, and stepped on her hand. Starr also stated that, after knocking plaintiff down, defendant continued running until he tagged Starr, "which tag was hard enough to cause me to lose my balance, resulting in a twisting or spraining of my ankle."

The game ended with plaintiff's injury, and plaintiff sought treatment shortly thereafter. After three operations failed to restore the movement in her little finger or to relieve the ongoing pain of the injury, plaintiff's finger was amputated. Plaintiff then instituted the present proceeding, seeking damages from defendant on theories of negligence and assault and battery.

After filing an answer, defendant moved for summary judgment. . . . [D]efendant maintained that "reasonable implied assumption of risk" continues to operate as a complete defense after *Li v. Yellow Cab Co*, [(1975) 13 Cal. 3d 804, 119 Cal. Rptr. 858, 532 P.2d 1226,] and that plaintiff's action was barred under that doctrine. In this regard, defendant asserted that "[b]y participating in [the touch football game that resulted in her injury], plaintiff . . . impliedly agreed to reduce the duty of care owed to her by defendant . . . to only a duty to avoid reckless or intentionally harmful conduct," and that the undisputed facts established both that he did not intend to injure plaintiff and that the acts of defendant which resulted in plaintiff's injury were not reckless. In support of his motion, defendant submitted his own declaration setting forth his version of the incident [and] specifically stating that he did not intend to step on plaintiff's hand or to injure her. Defendant also attached a copy of plaintiff's deposition in which plaintiff acknowledged that she frequently watched professional football on television and thus was generally familiar with the risks associated with the sport of football, and in which she conceded that she had no reason to believe defendant had any intention of stepping on her hand or injuring her.

In opposing the summary judgment motion, plaintiff first [argued that the] doctrine of "reasonable implied assumption of risk" had been eliminated by the adoption of comparative fault principles, and thus . . . the basic premise of defendant's summary judgment motion was untenable and plaintiff was entitled to have the lawsuit proceed under comparative fault principles. . . .

Second, plaintiff vigorously disputed defendant's claim that, by participating in the game in question, she impliedly had agreed to reduce the duty of care, owed to her by defendant, to only a duty to avoid reckless or intentionally harmful conduct. Plaintiff maintained in her declaration that in view of the casual, social setting, the circumstance that women and men were joint participants in the game, and the rough dirt surface on which the game was played, she anticipated from the outset that it was the kind of "mock" football game in which there would be no forceful pushing or hard hitting or shoving. Plaintiff also asserted that the declarations and depositions of other players in the game, included in her opposition papers, demonstrated that the other participants, including defendant, shared her expectations and assumptions that the game was to be a "mellow" one and not a serious, competitive athletic event. Plaintiff claimed that there had been no injuries during touch football games in which she had participated on previous occasions, and that in view of the circumstances under which the game was played, "[t]he only type of injury which I reasonably anticipated would have been something in the nature of a bruise or bump." [P]laintiff maintained that her statement during the game established that a disputed factual issue existed as to whether she voluntarily had chosen to assume the risks of the type of conduct allegedly engaged in by defendant. . . .

After considering the parties' submissions, the trial court granted defendant's motion for summary judgment. . . .

II

As every leading tort treatise has explained, the assumption of risk doctrine long has caused confusion both in definition and application, because the phrase "assumption of risk" traditionally has been used in a number of very different factual settings involving analytically distinct legal concepts. . . . In some settings — for example, most cases involving sports-related injuries — past assumption of risk decisions largely have been concerned with defining the contours of the legal duty that a given class of defendants — for example, owners of baseball stadiums or ice hockey rinks — owed to an injured plaintiff. . . . In other settings, the assumption of risk terminology historically was applied to situations in which it was clear that the defendant had breached a legal duty of care to the plaintiff, and the inquiry focused on whether the plaintiff knowingly and voluntarily had chosen to encounter the specific risk of harm posed by the defendant's breach of duty. . . .

Prior to the adoption of comparative fault principles of liability, there often was no need to distinguish between the different categories of assumption of risk cases, because if a case fell into either category, the plaintiff's recovery was totally barred. With the adoption of comparative fault, however, it became essential to differentiate between the distinct categories of cases that traditionally had been lumped together under the rubric of assumption of risk. This court's seminal comparative fault decision in *Li* explicitly recognized the need for such differentiation, and attempted to explain which category of assumption of risk cases should be merged into the comparative fault system and which category should not. Accordingly, in considering the current viability of the assumption of risk doctrine in California, our analysis necessarily begins with the *Li* decision.

In *Li*, our court undertook a basic reexamination of the common law doctrine of contributory negligence. . . . After determining that the "all-or-nothing" contributory negligence doctrine should be replaced by a system of comparative negligence, the *Li* court went on to undertake a rather extensive discussion of the effect that the adoption of comparative negligence would have on a number of related tort doctrines, including the doctrines of last clear chance and assumption of risk. . . .

[W]ith respect to the effect of the adoption of comparative negligence on the assumption of risk doctrine[,] the *Li* decision [stated] as follows: "As for assumption of risk, we have recognized in this state that this defense overlaps that of contributory negligence to some extent and in fact is made up of at least two distinct defenses. 'To simplify greatly, it has been observed . . . that in one kind of situation, to wit, where a plaintiff *unreasonably* undertakes to encounter a specific known risk imposed by a defendant's negligence, plaintiff's conduct, although he may encounter that risk in a prudent manner, is in reality a form of contributory negligence. . . . Other kinds of situations within the doctrine of assumption of risk are those, for example, where plaintiff is held to agree to relieve defendant of an obligation of reasonable conduct toward him. Such a situation would not involve contributory negligence, but rather a reduction of defendant's duty of care.' . . . We think it clear that the adoption of a system of comparative negligence should entail the merger of the defense of assumption of risk into the general scheme of assessment of liability in proportion to fault in those particular cases in which the form of assumption of risk involved is no more than a variant of contributory negligence. . . ."

As this passage indicates, the *Li* decision [clearly] contemplated that the assumption of risk doctrine was to be *partially* merged or subsumed into the comparative negligence scheme. Subsequent Court of Appeal decisions have disagreed, however, in interpreting *Li*, as to what category of assumption of risk cases would be merged into the comparative negligence scheme.

A number of appellate decisions, focusing on the language in *Li* indicating that assumption of risk is in reality a form of contributory negligence "where a plaintiff *unreasonably* undertakes to encounter a specific known risk imposed by a defendant's negligence" . . . have concluded that *Li* properly should be interpreted as drawing a distinction between those assumption of risk cases in which a plaintiff "unreasonably" encounters a known risk imposed by a defendant's negligence and those assumption of risk cases in which a plaintiff "reasonably" encounters a known risk imposed by a defendant's negligence. . . . These decisions interpret *Li* as subsuming into the comparative fault scheme those cases in which the plaintiff acts *unreasonably* in encountering a specific known risk, but retaining the assumption of risk doctrine as a complete bar to recovery in those cases in which the plaintiff acts *reasonably* in encountering such a risk. Although aware of the apparent anomaly of a rule under which a plaintiff who acts *reasonably* is *completely barred* from recovery while a plaintiff who acts *unreasonably* only has his or her recovery reduced, these decisions nonetheless have concluded that this distinction and consequence were intended by the *Li* court.

In our view, these decisions — regardless whether they reached the correct result on the facts at issue — have misinterpreted *Li* by suggesting that our decision contemplated less favorable legal treatment for a plaintiff who reasonably encounters a known risk than for a plaintiff who unreasonably encounters such a risk. Although the relevant passage in Li indicates that the assumption of risk doctrine would be merged into the comparative fault scheme in instances in which a plaintiff " '*unreasonably* undertakes to encounter a specific known risk imposed by a defendant's negligence,' " . . . nothing in this passage suggests that the assumption of risk doctrine should survive as a total bar to the plaintiff's recovery whenever a plaintiff acts *reasonably* in encountering such a risk. Instead, this portion of our opinion expressly contrasts the category of assumption of risk cases which " 'involve contributory negligence' " (and which therefore should be merged into the comparative fault scheme) with those assumption of risk cases which involve " 'a reduction of defendant's duty of care.' " . . .

[T]he distinction in assumption of risk cases to which the *Li* court referred in this passage was not a distinction between instances in which a plaintiff unreasonably encounters a known risk imposed by a defendant's negligence and instances in which a plaintiff reasonably encounters such a risk. Rather, the distinction to which the *Li* court referred was between (1) those instances in which the assumption of risk doctrine embodies a legal conclusion that there is "no duty" on the part of the defendant to protect the plaintiff from a particular risk

— the category of assumption of risk that the legal commentators generally refer to as "primary assumption of risk" — and (2) those instances in which the defendant does owe a duty of care to the plaintiff but the plaintiff knowingly encounters a risk of injury caused by the defendant's breach of that duty — what most commentators have termed "secondary assumption of risk." Properly interpreted, the relevant passage in *Li* provides that the category of assumption of risk cases that is not merged into the comparative negligence system and in which the plaintiff's recovery continues to be completely barred involves those cases in which the defendant's conduct did not breach a legal duty of care to the plaintiff, *i.e.*, "primary assumption of risk" cases, whereas cases involving "secondary assumption of risk" properly are merged into the comprehensive comparative fault system adopted in *Li*.

Although the difference between the "primary assumption of risk"/"secondary assumption of risk" nomenclature and the "reasonable implied assumption of risk"/"unreasonable implied assumption of risk" terminology embraced in many of the recent Court of Appeal decisions may appear at first blush to be only semantic, the significance extends beyond mere rhetoric. First, in "primary assumption of risk" cases — where the defendant owes no duty to protect the plaintiff from a particular risk of harm — a plaintiff who has suffered such harm is not entitled to recover from the defendant, whether the plaintiff's conduct in undertaking the activity was reasonable or unreasonable. Second, in "secondary assumption of risk" cases — involving instances in which the defendant has breached the duty of care owed to the plaintiff — the defendant is not entitled to be entirely relieved of liability for an injury proximately caused by such breach, simply because the plaintiff's conduct in encountering the risk of such an injury was reasonable rather than unreasonable. Third and finally, the question whether the defendant owed a legal duty to protect the plaintiff from a particular risk of harm does not turn on the reasonableness or unreasonableness of the plaintiff's conduct, but rather on the nature of the activity or sport in which the defendant is engaged and the relationship of the defendant and the plaintiff to that activity or sport. For these reasons, use of the "reasonable implied assumption of risk"/"unreasonable implied assumption of risk" terminology, as a means of differentiating between the cases in which a plaintiff is barred from bringing an action and those in which he or she is not barred, is more misleading than helpful.

The dissenting opinion suggests, however, that, even when a defendant has breached its duty of care to the plaintiff, a plaintiff who reasonably has chosen to encounter a known risk of harm imposed by such a breach may be totally precluded from recovering any damages, without doing violence to comparative fault principles, on the theory that the plaintiff, by proceeding in the face of a known risk, has "impliedly consented" to any harm. . . . For a number of reasons, we conclude this contention does not withstand analysis.

First, the argument that a plaintiff who proceeds to encounter a known risk has "impliedly consented" to absolve a negligent defendant of liability for any ensuing harm logically would apply as much to a plaintiff who unreasonably has chosen to encounter a known risk, as to a plaintiff who reasonably has chosen to encounter such a risk. . . .

Second, the implied consent rationale rests on a legal fiction that is untenable, at least as applied to conduct that represents a breach of the defendant's duty of care to the plaintiff. [I]t is thoroughly unrealistic to suggest that, by engaging in a potentially dangerous activity or sport, an individual consents to (or agrees to excuse) a breach of duty by others that increases the risks inevitably posed by the activity or sport itself, even where the participating individual is aware of the possibility that such misconduct may occur. . . . [T]hird, the dissenting opinion's claim that the category of cases in which the assumption of risk doctrine operates to bar a plaintiff's cause of action after *Li* properly should be gauged on the basis of an implied consent analysis, rather than on the duty analysis [is] untenable for another reason. In support of its implied consent theory, the dissenting opinion relies on a number of pre-*Li* cases, which arose in the "secondary assumption of risk" context, and which held that, in such a context, application of the assumption of risk doctrine was dependent on proof that the particular plaintiff subjectively knew, rather than simply should have known, of both the existence and magnitude of the specific risk of harm imposed by the defendant's negligence. . . . Consequently, [were the] implied consent theory to govern application of the assumption of risk doctrine in the sports setting, the basic liability of a defendant who engages in a sport would depend on variable factors that the defendant frequently would have no way of ascertaining (for example, the particular plaintiff's subjective knowledge and expectations), rather than on the nature of the sport itself. As a result, there would be drastic disparities in the manner in which the law would treat defendants who engaged in precisely the same conduct, based on the often unknown, subjective expectations of the particular plaintiff who happened to be injured by the defendant's conduct. . . .

It may be helpful at this point to summarize our general conclusions as to the current state of the doctrine of assumption of risk in light of the adoption of comparative fault principles in *Li*. . . . In cases involving "primary assumption of risk" — where, by virtue of the nature of the activity and the parties' relationship to the activity, the defendant owes no legal duty to protect the plaintiff from the particular risk of harm that caused the injury — the doctrine continues to operate as a complete bar to the plaintiff's recovery. In cases involving "secondary assumption of risk" — where the defendant does owe a duty of care to the plaintiff, but the plaintiff proceeds to encounter a known risk imposed by the defendant's breach of duty — the doctrine is merged into the comparative fault scheme, and the trier of fact, in apportioning the loss resulting from the injury, may consider the relative responsibility of the parties.

Accordingly, in determining the propriety of the trial court's grant of summary judgment in favor of the defendant in this case, . . . our resolution of this issue turns on whether, in light of the nature of the sporting activity in which defendant and plaintiff were engaged, defendant's conduct breached a legal duty of care to plaintiff. We now turn to that question.

III

As a general rule, persons have a duty to use due care to avoid injury to others, and may be held liable if their careless conduct injures another person. . . . Thus, for example, a property owner ordinarily is required to use due care to eliminate dangerous conditions on his or her property. . . . In the sports setting, however, conditions or conduct that otherwise might be viewed as dangerous often are an integral part of the sport itself. Thus, although moguls on a ski run pose a risk of harm to skiers that might not exist were these configurations removed, the challenge and risks posed by the moguls are part of the sport of skiing, and a ski resort has no duty to eliminate them. . . . In this respect, the nature of a sport is highly relevant in defining the duty of care owed by the particular defendant.

Although defendants generally have no legal duty to eliminate (or protect a plaintiff against) risks inherent in the sport itself, it is well established that defendants generally do have a duty to use due care not to increase the risks to a participant over and above those inherent in the sport. Thus, although a ski resort has no duty to remove moguls from a ski run, it clearly does have a duty to use due care to maintain its towropes in a safe, working condition so as not to expose skiers to an increased risk of harm. The cases establish that the latter type of risk, posed by a ski resort's negligence, clearly is not a risk (inherent in the sport) that is assumed by a participant. . . .

In some situations, however, the careless conduct of others is treated as an "inherent risk" of a sport, thus barring recovery by the plaintiff. For example, numerous cases recognize that in a game of baseball, a player generally cannot recover if he or she is hit and injured by a carelessly thrown ball, . . . and that in a game of basketball, recovery is not permitted for an injury caused by a carelessly extended elbow. . . . The divergent results of the foregoing cases lead naturally to the question how courts are to determine when careless conduct of another properly should be considered an "inherent risk" of the sport that (as a matter of law) is assumed by the injured participant.

Contrary to the implied consent approach to the doctrine of assumption of risk, discussed above, the duty approach provides an answer which does not depend on the particular plaintiff's subjective knowledge or appreciation of the potential risk. Even where the plaintiff, who falls while skiing over a mogul, is a total novice and lacks any knowledge of skiing whatsoever, the ski resort would not be liable for his or her injuries. . . . And, on the other hand, even where the plaintiff actually is aware that a particular ski resort on occasion has been negligent in maintaining its towropes, that knowledge would not preclude the skier from recovering if he or she were injured as a result of the resort's repetition of such deficient conduct. In the latter context, although the plaintiff may have acted with knowledge of the potential negligence, he or she did not consent to such negligent conduct or agree to excuse the resort from liability in the event of such negligence. . . .

In the present case, defendant was a participant in the touch football game in which plaintiff was engaged at the time of her injury, and thus the question before us involves the circumstances under which a participant in such a sport may be held liable for an injury sustained by another participant.

The overwhelming majority of the cases, both within and outside California, that have addressed the issue of coparticipant liability in such a sport, have concluded that it is improper to hold a sports participant liable to a coparticipant for ordinary careless conduct committed during the sport — for example, for an injury resulting from a carelessly thrown ball or bat during a baseball game — and that liability properly may be imposed on a participant only when he or she intentionally injures another player or engages in reckless conduct that is totally outside the range of the ordinary activity involved in the sport. . . .

In reaching the conclusion that a coparticipant's duty of care should be limited in this fashion, the cases have explained that, in the heat of an active sporting event like baseball or football, a participant's normal energetic conduct often includes accidentally careless behavior. . . .

[A]ccordingly, we conclude that a participant in an active sport breaches a legal duty of care to other participants — *i.e.*, engages in conduct that properly may subject him or her to financial liability — only if the participant intentionally injures another player or engages in conduct that is so reckless as to be totally outside the range of the ordinary activity involved in the sport.

As applied to the present case, the foregoing legal principle clearly supports the trial court's entry of summary judgment in favor of defendant. The declarations filed in support of and in opposition to the summary judgment motion establish that defendant was, at most, careless or negligent in knocking over plaintiff, stepping on her hand, and injuring her finger. Although plaintiff maintains that defendant's rough play as described in her declaration and the declaration of Andrea Starr properly can be characterized as "reckless," the conduct alleged in those declarations is not even closely comparable to the kind of conduct — conduct so reckless as to be totally outside the range of the ordinary activity involved in the sport — that is a prerequisite to the imposition of legal liability upon a participant in such a sport.

Therefore, we conclude that defendant's conduct in the course of the touch football game did not breach any legal duty of care owed to plaintiff. Accordingly, this case falls within the primary assumption of risk doctrine, and thus the trial court properly granted summary judgment in favor of defendant. Because plaintiff's action is barred under the primary assumption of risk doctrine, comparative fault principles do not come into play.

The judgment of the Court of Appeal, upholding the summary judgment entered by the trial court, is affirmed.

[Justice Mosk concurred "generally" with the reasoning in Part II of Justice George's opinion, thus providing a majority for that approach, although Justice Mosk went on to advocate totally abolishing the defense of implied assumption of risk.]

KENNARD, Justice, dissenting.

[T]he plurality opinion uses this case as a forum to advocate a radical transformation of tort law. The plurality proposes to recast the analysis of implied assumption of risk from a subjective evaluation of what a particular plaintiff knew and appreciated about the encountered risk into a determination of the presence or absence of duty legally imposed on the defendant. By thus transforming an affirmative defense into an element of the plaintiff's negligence action, the plurality would abolish the defense without acknowledging that it is doing so.

The plurality opinion also announces a rule that those who engage in active sports do not owe coparticipants the usual duty of care — measured by the standard of a reasonable person in like or similar circumstances — to avoid inflicting physical injury. According to the plurality, a sports participant has no duty to avoid conduct inherent in a particular sport. Although I agree that in organized sports contests played under well-established rules participants have no duty to avoid the very conduct that constitutes the sport, I cannot accept the plurality's nearly boundless expansion of this general principle to eliminate altogether the "reasonable person" standard as the measure of duty actually owed between sports participants. . . .

[The dissent concluded that the evidence presented in support of the motion for summary judgment did not conclusively establish that the plaintiff had consented to the kind of rough play engaged in by defendant, and that the trial court should therefore have denied defendant's motion.]

NOTES

Should spectators be treated differently from participants? One common assumption of risk fact pattern involves a spectator at a hockey or baseball game who is struck by a flying object, such as a puck, a batted or thrown ball, or even a bat or hockey stick. Is the operator of the stadium liable for such an injury? The cases present a good framework for examining the practical differences of the various approaches to assumption of risk. If, for example, the subjective awareness of the risk is most significant, it makes a difference whether the victim was familiar with the game and the risks it poses, or on the other hand was encountering the sport for the first time. Consider, for example, the position of a southern Californian who had never seen or attended a hockey game. Should such a person be held to have assumed the risk of being struck by a puck? *Cf. Thurman v. Ice Palace*, 97 P.2d 999 (Cal. Ct. App. 1939). On the other hand, if the issue is the scope of duty, such subjective awareness is irrelevant.

The question will be what the proprietor of the baseball field was required to do and whether it was done. The duty is often described something like this: The proprietor must provide a screen behind home plate, where the danger of injury is greatest, that is sufficient to provide screened seating for as many spectators as might be expected to request it. *Cf. Friedman v. Houston Sports Association*, 731 S.W.2d 572 (Tex. App. 1987). Once that duty is satisfied, those sitting elsewhere do so at their own risk.

PROBLEMS

1. In light of the debate in *Knight v. Jewett*, reconsider your characterization of the holding in *Murphy*: Which of the following best describes the court's position in *Murphy*? In *Knight*?

    a. The defendant owed no duty of care to plaintiff and therefore was not negligent.

    b. The defendant owed a duty of care to plaintiff but did not breach it (did nothing to create an unreasonable risk of harm) and therefore was not negligent.

    c. The defendant owed a duty of care and breached it (did create an unreasonable risk of harm) but the plaintiff is barred from recovery because the plaintiff recognized the unreasonable nature of the risk and voluntarily agreed to encounter it, and this conduct is evidence of an implied agreement on the part of the plaintiff to release the defendant from liability for the negligent conduct.

    d. The defendant owed a duty of care and breached it (did create an unreasonable risk of harm) but the plaintiff is barred from recovery because the plaintiff recognized the unreasonable nature of the risk and voluntarily agreed to encounter it, and this conduct constitutes contributory negligence on the part of the plaintiff.

2. Under a comparative negligence regime, what is the proper way to deal with a plaintiff who knowingly and voluntarily but reasonably confronts the unreasonable risk created by the defendant? The opinions in *Knight* suggest two possible approaches; are there others?

3. Plaintiff attends the opening day game at one of the new "intimate" baseball stadiums, in which the foul territory has been reduced in order to place the spectators close to the action. Plaintiff has a seat close to the field near first base. In the second inning one of the batters hits a hard foul ball directly at Plaintiff. Although Plaintiff was not inattentive, he did not react quickly enough to protect himself and was struck in the right eye by the ball, destroying the eye socket. If the jurisdiction has adopted the definition of the owner's duty given above, and the owner did provide a screen behind home plate, does the plaintiff have any arguments in favor of liability against the stadium operator? What

counter-arguments would you expect the defendant to make? Would it make any difference that the game was sold out and the plaintiff could not obtain a seat in the screened section? Would it make any difference if the entire screened section was pre-sold to season ticket holders?

4. Skier and Driver hitched up Driver's boat and went to the lake to water-ski. At the lake they launched the boat and began to set up for their day of fun. They both remarked about Driver's badly frayed tow rope, and joked about how they did not have a third person available to act as a spotter while Driver steered the boat. They noted how much boat traffic was out on the lake that day, and congratulated each other on how skillful and daring they were. Then they started skiing, with Driver steering the boat and occasionally glancing over his shoulder to see how Skier was doing. Once they were well offshore, Driver suddenly increased the speed of the boat. The sudden increase in speed caused the frayed tow rope to break. The broken end of the rope recoiled toward Skier, striking him in the head and stunning him before he fell into the water. Skier fell face down in the water and began to drown. Driver, however, had not noticed anything. He finally looked around and was surprised to find that Skier was no longer behind the boat. Driver put the boat into a sharp left hand turn. Unfortunately, he did not look where he was going and his boat ran into the side of another boat that was also pulling a skier in the same area. The collision injured Driver and the two occupants of the other ski-boat, the Bystanders. Because of the delay in rescuing him, Skier nearly drowned and suffered a significant brain injury. Under the rule of the *Knight* case, how should the claims of Skier and the Bystanders against Driver be handled? Did Driver owe any duty to Skier? To the Bystanders? Was either duty breached? Should primary assumption of the risk apply to the Bystanders as "co-participants" in the sport of water skiing? Does comparative fault apply to either claim? How would the approach advocated by Justice Kennard resolve these questions?

B. OTHER DEFENSES: LIMITATIONS AND IMMUNITIES

This section deals with other types of defenses that do not involve the issue of the plaintiff's conduct. Statutes of limitation and repose are designed to prevent the litigation of claims after the passage of a sufficient period of time. Immunities, on the other hand, are bars to litigation based on the status of the defendant.

1. Statutes of Limitation and Repose

Statutes of limitation and statutes of repose both operate to bar claims after a specified period of time has elapsed since the claims "accrued." These statutes express the decision of the legislature that after a certain period of time, such claims have become too old or, as they are often described, "stale." The reasons for barring stale claims are many, but the most important usually put forward are, first, the loss of evidence over time and, second, the need eventually to put disputes to rest. The first reason recognizes that the passage of time creates unfairness as evidence disappears, memories fade, and witnesses die or disappear. The defendant who did not preserve, or cannot now find, exculpatory evidence may therefore be prejudiced if a claim can be pursued many years after the events that gave rise to it. It is worth noting, however, that in theory a statute of limitations bars the claim simply by the passage of time. The defendant asserting the statute does not need to prove that prejudice would in fact occur in order to make use of the defense. The second reason is founded on the problems that can occur when settled expectations are overturned after many years. There is a value placed on prompt assertion of rights and in the security of knowing that a dispute cannot be pursued after the passage of a certain number of years. Here again, however, the defendant is not obligated to prove that any settled expectations will in fact be upset. The passage of the prescribed time period without filing suit is sufficient to allow the defense.

Statutes of limitation must begin to run at some identifiable point in time. Usually this is said to be at the moment the cause of action "accrues." Accrual occurs at the moment the cause of action is complete, in that all the events necessary to satisfy the elements of the cause of action have occurred so that the case is now ripe for the plaintiff to file suit. Because negligence cases, for example, require actual damages in order to be actionable, the statute of limitations in most personal injury cases begins to run at the moment the plaintiff is injured. While this moment is readily identifiable in accident cases, it may be much harder to pinpoint in toxic exposure cases, in which exposure may have occurred over a period of many years, and symptoms of illness only gradually manifested themselves. To start the statute running at the first exposure would likely mean that the cause of action was barred before the plaintiff ever knew that a problem existed. The same problem can occur in medical malpractice cases in which the existence of a problem, such as a misdiagnosis, is not discovered until several years after the doctor's act.

Statutes of repose also impose a time limit, but it is calculated in a wholly different fashion. Statutes of repose are designed to place an outer limit on the responsibility of a party for a particular act, without regard for the timing of the injury to the plaintiff. An example is the construction statute of repose, which bars suits against the architects and builders of an improvement to real property a specified number of years after the substantial completion of construction. For example, if the statute of repose barred suits after ten years, the plaintiff who was injured because of a defect in design or construction of the building eleven years after substantial completion would be barred from suing, no matter how quickly the suit was filed after the injury occurred. In other words, the suit would be effectively barred even before the injury occurred. Similar statutes are on the books in some jurisdictions to protect manufacturers of durable products against product liability suits. Such product liability statutes of repose would typically begin to run on the date the defendant sold the defective product that caused the injury.

The operation of both types of limit can be harsh and arbitrary, and tend to cut against the preference of courts to decide cases on the merits. As might be predicted, some courts have developed doctrines to allow a certain amount of flexibility in the application of the statutes, although usually at some expense to clarity and ease of administration. Some of these doctrines are illustrated below.

As a final note of caution, it should be kept in mind that the failure to meet the statute of limitations is one of the most common complaints in legal malpractice suits. This may be in part because the determination of the proper statute of limitations can be difficult, as surprising as that may sound. The first step is to look the statutes up and determine which statute applies to a particular case. That is not quite the statement of the obvious that it may appear. First, it may not be clear from the text of the statute itself what categories of cases it applies to, and in some cases more than one statute can appear to govern. Research into the application of the statutes is often necessary to determine how the courts actually apply the statutes. Furthermore, different statutes may apply to the same claim depending on the legal theory used. For example, a personal injury caused by a defective product might be brought as a claim in tort for strict product liability or as claim for breach of implied warranty. Very different statutes of limitations are likely to apply depending upon the theory chosen, and it can happen that the claim is time barred under one theory but not the other. Sometimes a plaintiff can obtain a longer statute by suing the defendant in a different jurisdiction. Finally, many ameliorating doctrines exist that may toll the running of the statute for a period of time. Because many legislatures in recent years have altered or reformed these statutes and how they operate, there is no substitute for thorough understanding of a particular jurisdiction's current statutes and their application.

GARCIA v. TEXAS INSTRUMENTS, INC.
610 S.W.2d 456 (Tex. 1980)

STEAKLEY, Justice.

This is a products liability case involving personal injuries resulting from an alleged breach of implied warranty under the Uniform Commercial Code.

During the period of August 16, 1974, to January 31, 1975, Texas Instruments, Inc., the Respondent, sold and delivered various quantities of concentrated sulfuric acid to the Mostek Corporation, the employer of our Petitioner, Richard Y. Garcia. On February 18, 1975, Garcia was moving cartons of acid from one location to another. The cartons, constructed of fiberboard, each contained four one-gallon glass containers. While carrying one of the cartons, Garcia tripped and fell, breaking a container and suffered severe acid burns.

On October 18, 1978, approximately three years and eight months after the accident, Garcia instituted suit against Texas Instruments for damages for personal injuries alleging a breach of the implied warranty of merchantability under Section 2.314 of the Texas Uniform Commercial Code arising out of the sale of acid from Texas Instruments to Mostek Corporation. Garcia alleged that the acid was not merchantable in that it was not adequately contained, packaged and labeled and was not fit for the use for which it was intended. In the alternative, Garcia alleged that he was a third party beneficiary of the contract between Mostek and Texas Instruments. The pleadings cast the suit solely as a breach of implied warranty. No theory of recovery based on tort was alleged. Texas Instruments filed a general denial and a motion for summary judgment which alleged that Garcia's lawsuit was barred by TEX. REV. CIV. STAT. ANN. art. 5526(4) (Supp. 1980), the two year statute of limitations for personal injuries, and that Garcia was not entitled to maintain an action under the warranty provisions of the Code because he was not a party to the sales contract between Texas Instruments and Mostek Corporation. [The] trial court granted the motion for summary judgment and rendered judgment for Texas Instruments. [The] Court of Civil Appeals affirmed. . . .

On appeal to this Court, Garcia argues that the Code expressly authorizes a cause of action for personal injuries and therefore his action is governed by the statute of limitations contained in the Code. Further, Garcia contends that the thrust of the holding of the Court of Civil Appeals is that the adoption of strict liability in tort relegated persons suffering product caused injuries to tort remedies exclusively. Garcia argues that this Court in its adoption of [strict products liability] did not abrogate the statutory remedies given by the Code regardless of whether products liability law would be simplified by requiring personal injury claims to be pursued exclusively in negligence and strict liability in tort. . . .

Texas Instruments replies that the gravamen of the complaint determines the applicable statute of limitations. Accordingly, it concludes that the present case is governed by the tort statute of limitations because a personal injury action based on a breach of implied warranty was considered at common law to lie in tort. . . . Therefore, Texas Instruments concludes that a cause of action for personal injuries resulting from a breach of warranty does not exist under the Uniform Commercial Code even when the suit is between parties in direct privity of contract, but that such remedies lie solely in tort.

[T]he threshold question is whether a cause of action exists under the Uniform Commercial Code for personal injuries resulting from the breach of an implied warranty of merchantability. If this question is answered in the negative, then Garcia's remedies for his injuries lie solely in tort, and his cause of action is barred by Article 5526, the two year personal injury statute of limitations. If we determine that Garcia is entitled to maintain a personal injury claim under the implied warranty provisions of the Code, we must then decide to what extent, if any, privity operates as a defense to the maintenance of this action. If lack of privity prevents Garcia from maintaining an action based on the Code it would follow that the Code statute of limitations is inapplicable and his suit is barred by Article 5526(4).

[P]rior to the enactment of the Code, the majority of jurisdictions treated a personal injury action based on a breach of implied warranty as a tort action for purposes of the statute of limitations. . . . Under this approach, the Court, without concern for the form of the action, looked to the type of damage, *i.e.*, personal injury or property loss, and the nature of the duty breached, *i.e.*, one expressed in the agreement of the parties or one implied in law, in determining whether to apply the tort or contract statute of limitations. . . .

[We] reject the argument of Texas Instruments that a cause of action for personal injuries resulting from a breach of warranty does not exist under the Code. . . . Our adoption of [strict products liability] cannot be held to repeal the Code sections providing redress for personal injury based on a breach of implied warranty as such would be an invasion of the legislative field. . . .

Despite the explicit language of the Code, Texas Instruments additionally contends that the form of the pleadings, *i.e.*, the gravamen of the complaint, should determine whether a cause of action sounds in tort or contract and hence the applicable statute of limitations, citing *Huizar v. Four Seasons Nursing Centers*, 562 S.W.2d 264 (Tex. Civ. App. 1978, writ ref'd). *Huizar* does not govern the disposition of this appeal for two reasons. First, Garcia did not plead negligence or any facts which would constitute negligence. Second, *Huizar* involved a common law cause of action in which nature of the remedy and the governing statute of limitations was determined by the facts alleged. In contrast, this cause does not involve a common law remedy but involves a statutory cause of action.

We recognize that this Court has broadly stated when considering a common law remedy that an implied warranty arising from sales sounds in tort and not in contract. . . . These decisions, however, are not determinative of our holding here that a statutory cause of action exists under the Code for personal injuries suffered as result of a breach of implied warranty. The Code provides a statutory remedy, hence the traditional distinctions between tort and contract are not relevant. . . . [The court then examined whether privity of contract was required in order for plaintiff to sue for breach of the implied warranty of merchantability.]

[W]e hold that privity of contract is not a requirement for a Uniform Commercial Code implied warranty action for personal injuries. Therefore, the implied warranty action of Garcia, filed approximately three years and eight months after the sale of the sulfuric acid, is not barred by limitations; it is governed in its entirety by the Uniform Commercial Code, including the four year statute of limitations set forth in § 2.725(a).

Accordingly, the judgments of the courts below are reversed and the cause is remanded to the trial court.

PROBLEMS

1. If the case were filed as a negligence or strict liability case, what is the liability producing conduct of the defendant? When did the cause of action accrue? When did it expire?

2. Treating the case as breach of warranty, what is the liability producing conduct of the defendant? When did the cause of action accrue? The court does not quote subpart (b) of § 2.725, which bears on this issue, although it alludes to it in the penultimate paragraph of the opinion. That subpart reads as follows:

> (b) A cause of action accrues when the breach occurs, regardless of the aggrieved party's lack of knowledge of the breach. A breach of warranty occurs when tender of delivery is made, except that where a warranty explicitly extends to future performance of the goods and discovery of the breach must await the time of such performance the cause of action accrues when the breach is or should have been discovered.

3. Texas Instruments' argument about the "gravamen" of the complaint raises the problem of how much freedom the plaintiff should have to plead the case so as to avoid a statute of limitations problem or obtain some other perceived advantage. Suppose, for example, that a jurisdiction has a longer statute of limitations for negligently inflicted harm than for intentionally inflicted harm. Should the plaintiff be allowed to plead a battery as a negligence claim in order to take advantage of the longer statute? If you wonder how that could be done, consider again the facts of *Garratt v. Dailey*, *supra,* and the nature of intent. Is there some inherent core to a cause of action that should compel a court to treat it as necessarily one type of action or another? Or should the plaintiff, as in *Garcia*, be able to use any cause of action into which the facts will fit?

NELSON v. KRUSEN
678 S.W.2d 918 (Tex. 1984)

SPEARS, Justice.

[T]om and Gloria Nelson brought a wrongful birth suit in their own behalf and a wrongful life suit as next friends of Mark Nelson, their minor son, against Dr. Edward Krusen and Baylor University Medical Center. The Nelsons' suits alleged that Dr. Krusen negligently advised them that Mrs. Nelson was not a genetic carrier of Duchenne muscular dystrophy and was no more likely than any other woman to have a child afflicted by the disease. The Nelsons further alleged that, had they known of the risk that their child would be born with the disease, they would have terminated the pregnancy. The Nelsons alternatively claimed that Baylor negligently conducted or reported certain tests thereby causing Dr. Krusen to misinform them.

The trial court rendered summary judgment for Dr. Krusen and Baylor on the grounds that the statute of limitations had run on the wrongful birth claim and that no cause of action for wrongful life exists in Texas. The court of appeals affirmed. . . . We reverse the court of appeals insofar as it held the statute of limitations . . . barred the Nelsons' claims. We affirm the court of appeals holding that no cause of action for wrongful life exists in Texas.

[T]he summary judgment evidence showed that the Nelsons already had one child with Duchenne muscular dystrophy when they learned in 1976 that Mrs. Nelson was again pregnant. The Nelsons consulted Dr. Krusen to determine whether Mrs. Nelson was a genetic carrier of the disease. Dr. Krusen examined Mrs. Nelson on three separate occasions between April and June of 1976, and based on test results, assured Mrs. Nelson that she was not a carrier. In light of Dr. Krusen's opinion, the Nelsons chose not to terminate the pregnancy, and Mark Nelson was born November 24, 1976. On November 12, 1979, a nursery school examination revealed that Mark had tight heel cords bilaterally. As a result, Mark was referred to a pediatric neurologist, who determined from an examination on February 20, 1980, that Mark had Duchenne muscular dystrophy. Mark was three years and three months old at this time.

The neurologist based his diagnosis in part on Mark's "lordotic and clumsy gait." Although this clumsiness may have been evident during Mark's first two years, during that time these symptoms could be discounted as simply the result of being two years old and learning to walk. Only as the child grew older and continued to exhibit this clumsiness, however, did the possibility of a neuromuscular defect become detectable to the trained eye.

I. Statute of Limitations

Dr. Krusen and Baylor moved for summary judgment, claiming that the Nelsons' actions were barred because they were not brought within two years of the last examination by Dr. Krusen. The defendants relied on the limitations period prescribed by article 5.82, section 4 of the Insurance Code, which provides:

> Notwithstanding any other law, no claim . . . for compensation for a medical treatment or hospitalization may be commenced unless the action is filed within two years of the breach or the tort complained of or from the date the medical treatment that is the subject of the claim or the hospitalization for which the claim is made is completed. . . .

The limitations period of article 5.82, by its terms, arguably began running on the date of the last examination by Dr. Krusen or on the date of Mark's birth and barred the Nelsons' claims two years later. Under our holding in *Sax v. Votteler*, 648 S.W.2d 661 (Tex. 1983), the statute cannot cut off Mark's cause of action before he reaches the age of legal capacity. If applied literally, the statute would, however, operate to bar the parents' cause of action before they knew it existed, even though they did not discover, and could not reasonably have discovered, their injury within two years. The Nelsons contend that applying the statute in this manner is unconstitutional.

[T]he Nelsons challenge the statute on several constitutional grounds. They claim that the statute denies them equal protection and due process under the fourteenth amendment to the United States Constitution. Under the Texas Constitution, they claim that the statute violates . . . the section 13 "open courts" provision. Article I, section 13 provides in part:

> . . . All courts shall be open, and every person for an injury done him, in his lands, goods, person or reputation, shall have remedy by due course of law.

Tex. Const. art. I, § 13. The Nelsons argue that this guarantee of a remedy by due course of law makes any legislative attempt to bar their cause of action prior to its discovery unconstitutional. Our disposition of the Nelsons' open courts argument makes consideration of the other constitutional claims unnecessary.

[T]he common thread of this court's decisions construing the open courts provision is that the legislature has no power to make a remedy by due course of law contingent on an impossible condition. . . .

The reasoning of these decisions was reaffirmed in *Sax v. Votteler*, 648 S.W.2d 661 (Tex. 1983), a medical malpractice case specifically addressing the constitutionality of article 5.82, section 4 of the Insurance Code as applied to minors. We recognized that article I, section 13 of the Texas Constitution guarantees that Texas citizens bringing common law causes of action will not unreasonably be denied access to the courts. . . . [W]e held that "the right to bring a well-established common law cause of action cannot be effectively abrogated by the legislature absent a showing that the legislative basis for the statute outweighs the denial of the constitutionally-guaranteed right of redress."

[T]hese decisions lead to the conclusion that article 5.82 as applied here violates the open courts provision by cutting off a cause of action before the party knows, or reasonably should know, that he is injured. . . .

The limitation period of article 5.82, section 4, if applied as written, would require the Nelsons to do the impossible — to sue before they had any reason to know they should sue. Such a result is rightly described as "shocking" and is so absurd and so unjust that it ought not be possible. . . . Deferring to the legislative imposition of such an unreasonable condition would amount to an abdication of our judicial duty to protect the rights guaranteed by the Texas Constitution, the source and limit of legislative as well as judicial power. This, we cannot do. We hold that article 5.82, section 4 of the Insurance Code is unconstitutional, under the open courts provision, to the extent it purports to cut off an injured person's right to sue before the person has a reasonable opportunity to discover the wrong and bring suit.

We hold that article 5.82, section 4 of the Insurance Code as applied in this case violates the open courts provision of article I, section 13 of the Texas Constitution. Therefore, the parents' cause of action for "wrongful birth" is not barred by limitations. . . . [The majority then held that Texas would not recognize a cause of action on the child's behalf for "wrongful life."]

NOTE

Courts sometimes hold, as earlier Texas cases did, that the cause of action does not accrue until discovery is made. Other courts hold that the statute is tolled until discovery. Under both of these approaches, the statutory time limit does not begin to run until discovery is made, so at that point the plaintiff has the full two years (or whatever time period the statute provides) within which to file suit. Cases such as *Nelson v. Krusen*, which find the statute of limitations unconstitutional only to the extent it imposes an impossible condition, do not logically require that the plaintiff be given the full limitations period after making the discovery. Some cases following *Nelson* held that the plaintiff must file suit within a reasonable time after making the discovery.

PROBLEMS

1. Note that the statute of limitations at issue in *Nelson* was apparently passed to overrule the "no accrual until discovery" rule of the earlier Texas cases. Has the Texas Supreme Court gotten the last word?

2. Once the court decides to adopt the discovery rule many additional points need to be clarified. For example, just what is it that needs to be "discovered"? Is the fact that the plaintiff becomes aware that something is wrong enough? Should awareness that something is wrong at least impose on the plaintiff a duty to inquire, so that the statutory period should now begin to run? Or, on the other hand, must the plaintiff discover not only the fact of injury, but also the defendant's role in causing it before the clock starts running? Also, who must make the discovery? Is it enough that someone employed by the plaintiff (a doctor or lawyer, for example) becomes aware of facts suggesting that there is a problem? In other words, if the discovery rule is at issue in a case, "what did the plaintiff know, and when did the plaintiff know it" will be issues that must be litigated. Indeed, they are issues that could well absorb a substantial portion of discovery and trial time. The benefit to doing so, of course, is that it will preserve the right of plaintiff to a decision on the merits. If the policies underlying the statute of limitations are undermined to some extent by the discovery rule, are the benefits sufficient to outweigh these policies?

3. Vera Victim, a potential client, comes into your office to ask you to handle a personal injury suit for her. According to Victim, she was injured in an automobile accident at an intersection. She was driving a rented car at the time of the accident. She entered the intersection with the green light when she saw a car coming into the intersection from her left, against the red light. She hit the brakes, but the other car, driven by Doug Driver, hit the left front of the rental

car. The impact caused her to hit her head against the driver's side window, briefly knocking her unconscious. She spent one night at a local hospital for observation, but was then released. She thought she was fine. The rental car company settled with Doug's insurer for the damage to the car. Vera's medical insurance paid for the hospital stay. She had not thought the matter worth pursuing further. She thought that maybe the police had cited Doug for running the red light, but is not sure.

Vera came to you because she has begun suffering blackouts and has had a seizure. Her doctor thinks it might be related to the blow to the head she suffered in the accident. Your further questions to Vera lead to the information that in three days it will be exactly two years since the accident took place. This is significant because the statute of limitations for "injuries to the person" is two years in your jurisdiction. If the injuries were the result of "reckless and wanton" conduct, however, the statute of limitations is three years. Your jurisdiction also recently adopted the discovery rule. Your additional questions disclose that although Doug Driver ran the red light, he was not going at a high rate of speed and may simply have been inattentive. Vera recalls that a friend told her that a witness at the scene of the accident, whose name she does not know, mentioned that Doug Driver "smelled like a beer vat" and may have been drinking before the accident. This information, however, is highly uncertain. To complicate matters further, your obligations to existing clients will make it impossible for you to conduct a full investigation in the next three days.

a. What are your professional obligations to Vera at this point? Can you simply tell her that you are not interested in taking her case? Must you inform her of the statute of limitations problem? If you do inform her of the statute of limitations problem, does that legal advice create an attorney-client relationship? *Cf. Miller v. Metzinger*, 154 Cal. Rptr. 22 (Cal. Ct. App. 1979). It is not necessary for the attorney and client to sign a formal contract in order to create an attorney client relationship. On the other hand, would it be best to file a complaint immediately, without investigation of the facts, in order to protect the statute? Should you plead reckless conduct on the part of Doug Driver (based on intoxication) without further investigation? Consider here Federal Rules of Civil Procedure Rule 11, regarding the duty of the attorney in federal court in making representations of fact in pleadings. Does your jurisdiction impose similar duties on attorneys in state court?

b. Assume that no complaint can be filed until more than two years has lapsed since the accident. As counsel for Vera Victim, what arguments would you raise to try to invoke the discovery rule? If you were counsel for Doug Driver how would you respond in arguing for strict application of the statute of limitations?

2. Immunities

"Immunities" generally are protections against being sued based on the status of the defendant. For our purposes the most common immunities are the family immunities (based on the status of the defendant as a member of the plaintiff's family), charitable immunities (based on the defendant's status as a charitable organization) and the governmental immunities. Recent court decisions and legislative changes have tended to narrow or even eliminate the protection of the family and charitable immunities. Governmental immunities are still very much alive but are frequently subject to limited waivers by statute. This section will attempt to highlight the issues of the most general significance in these areas. The student should then be prepared to grapple with the particular problems presented by local variations.

a. Family Immunities

The origin of family immunities lies in the common law doctrine that husband and wife were a single legal person. For that reason one spouse could not sue the other for a tort, because it would be as if a person were suing herself — or himself. This was thought to be a logical impossibility. Logical or not, the strictness of this rule began to erode in the nineteenth century as legislatures began to pass legislation, called Married Women's Property Acts, that granted women the right to own property separately from their husbands and to sue to protect it if need be. Courts joined in this trend by allowing spouses to sue each other to recover for intentional torts. From that point on the spousal immunity continued to weaken to the point that, today, it is generally abrogated. The RESTATEMENT (SECOND) OF TORTS § 895F, for example, now takes the position that no immunity exists between spouses solely because of the marriage relationship.

A separate doctrine, traceable to the Mississippi case of *Hewlett v. George*, 9 So. 895 (Miss. 1891), recognized parental immunity from tort actions filed by their children. No legal fiction about the legal oneness of parent and child supported this immunity, which came to be justified by a variety of somewhat inconsistent arguments. One concern was that allowing such actions would potentially disrupt family harmony and interfere with the right of the parents to discipline their children. A separate concern, which likely became more acute as automobiles and automobile insurance became more common, was that such actions would encourage collusive lawsuits. For example, if Parent got into an accident while driving the family car with Child as a passenger, Child could sue Parent alleging negligent driving. If Parent had automobile insurance, there would be every incentive on Parent's part to tearfully confess to negligence and thereby collect on the automobile liability policy in Child's behalf. (You will note that family harmony seems to survive in this example.) If Parent were immune from suit, however, the insurer would be safe from such suits.

As with spousal immunity, parental immunity has gradually eroded. Courts began to allow suits when the child was injured while working in the parents' commercial endeavors. Some courts then began to allow suits for intentional torts. Others allowed suits in exactly the situations that most worried the insurers: for automobile accidents or, more generally, whenever insurance was available to pay the claim. The concern with collusion tended to get brushed aside as insufficient to justify the total ban on liability. Today, many jurisdictions have totally abolished the immunity. With abolition (or steps toward abolition) new problems began to arise under the general heading of "negligent supervision." As example of this type of issue, consider the parent who allows a five-year-old child to play in the front yard without supervision. If the child wanders into the street and it struck by an automobile, should the child have an action against the parent for negligent supervision? Is this careless parenting, or proper encouragement of the child's independence? The implications of this sort of liability on proper parental discretion are troubling to some courts that have otherwise abolished the immunity. In New York, for example, the Court of Appeals refused to allow an action for negligent supervision. *Holodook v. Spencer*, 324 N.E.2d 338 (N.Y. 1974). California and some other jurisdictions, by contrast, have abolished the immunity and replaced it with a "reasonable parent" standard of care that is supposed to allow sufficient leeway for the proper exercise of parental discretion and discipline. *Gibson v. Gibson,* 479 P.2d 648 (Cal. 1971). In the view of these courts, the proper limitation is not an absolute or even limited immunity but a sensibly drawn substantive rule of liability.

Even if the "correct" standard of liability is adopted once the parental immunity is abolished, some interesting new possibilities are opened up. Consider the proper resolution of the issues in the following cases.

BONTE v. BONTE
616 A.2d 464 (N.H. 1992)

THAYER, Justice.

[D]efendant, Sharon Bonte, when seven months pregnant, was struck by a car while crossing Elm Street in Manchester. She was taken to a local hospital emergency room where plaintiff Stephanie Bonte was delivered by emergency caesarean section the next day. Stephanie was born with catastrophic brain damage and has been diagnosed as having cerebral palsy. She is severely and permanently disabled and will require medical and supervisory care for the remainder of her life. Stephanie's father, Andre Bonte, brought this action individually, and as next friend of Stephanie, against the defendant, alleging that the defendant was negligent in failing to use reasonable care in crossing the street and failing to use a designated crosswalk. The defendant is represented by counsel provided by her insurance company, American Global.

[O]ur first inquiry is whether a child born alive may maintain a cause of action for injuries sustained while the child was in utero. We held in *Bennett v.*

Hymers, 101 N.H. 483, 486, 147 A.2d 108, 110 (1958), that "an infant born alive can maintain an action to recover for prenatal injuries inflicted upon it by the tort of another. . . ." We stated:

> In weighing the factors for and against allowing recovery we are impressed with the injustice of denying to a child born alive a right to recover for injuries which he might bear for the remainder of his life because of the tortious conduct of another. One cannot examine the cases in which a child, physically or mentally deformed for life as a result of prenatal injuries caused by the wrongful act of another, has been denied a right of recovery for such injuries, without being impressed by the harshness of such a result.

Id. In *Bennett* we did not limit those against whom the child may bring suit for injuries sustained while in utero, and, in fact, we recognized that the injuries suffered by the child while in the womb are "distinct and independent" from any injuries suffered by the mother. . . .

Having established that New Hampshire case law permits a child to maintain a cause of action for negligence resulting in prenatal injury, we must next determine whether that child may maintain an action against his or her mother. [The court then traced the origin and gradual abolition of the parental immunity doctrine in New Hampshire, and concluded that it] abolished the court-created parental immunity doctrine. . . . The issue presented . . . was whether unemancipated children could sue their father in tort for injuries sustained in an automobile accident. We examined arguments in favor of parental immunity including: preservation of parental authority and family harmony; depletion of the family exchequer; and the danger of fraud and collusion. . . . While those considerations were admittedly valid, we determined that none were truly unique to a lawsuit between parent and child, nor did "[t]hey furnish . . . sufficient grounds for denying unemancipated minors as a class a right commonly enjoyed by other individuals." . . . We stated that "as a practical matter, the prevalence of insurance cannot be ignored in determining whether a court should continue to discriminate against a class of individuals by depriving them of a right enjoyed by all other individuals." . . . In abolishing the parental immunity doctrine for tort actions, we noted the inconsistency in allowing suits between a minor and his parent based upon contract or for the protection of property rights, but disallowing an action in tort. . . .

Because our cases hold that a child born alive may maintain a cause of action against another for injuries sustained while in utero, and a child may sue his or her mother in tort for the mother's negligence, it follows that a child born alive has a cause of action against his or her mother for the mother's negligence that caused injury to the child when in utero.

The defendant urges us to immunize the mother from tort liability based upon public policy reasons grounded in the unique relationship of the pregnant woman to her fetus. While we recognize that the relationship between mother and fetus is unique, we are not persuaded that based upon this relationship, a mother's duty to her fetus should not be legally recognized. If a child has a cause of action against his or her mother for negligence that occurred after birth and that caused injury to the child, it is neither logical, nor in accord with our precedent, to disallow that child's claim against the mother for negligent conduct that caused injury to the child months, days, or mere hours before the child's birth.

The defendant further argues that public policy dictates against the plaintiff's cause of action because allowing this matter to proceed "deprives women of the right to control their lives during pregnancy and] unfairly subjects them to unlimited liability for unintended and often unforeseen consequences of every day living." We disagree that our decision today deprives a mother of her right to control her life during pregnancy; rather, she is required to act with the appropriate duty of care, as we have consistently held other persons are required to act, with respect to the fetus. The mother will be held to the same standard of care as that required of her once the child is born. Whether her actions are negligent is a determination for the finder of fact, considering the facts and circumstances of the particular case. Moreover, if a determination based upon public policy can be made denying a cause of action logically recognized by our case law, that determination should be made by the legislature.

Accordingly, we hold that a child born alive has a cause of action in tort against his or her mother for the mother's negligent conduct that results in prenatal injury.

Reversed and remanded.

BROCK, C.J., and BATCHELDER, J., dissenting:

The majority concludes that because parental immunity has been abrogated and we previously have recognized that a child born alive may maintain a cause of action against a third party for prenatal injuries, "it follows that a child born alive has a cause of action against his or her mother for the mother's negligence that caused injury to the child when in utero." In our view, the majority has failed to fully appreciate the extent of the intrusion into the privacy and physical autonomy rights of women — policy concerns which are central to this issue — and has ignored the profound implications that such a rule of law holds for all women in this state who are, or may, become pregnant.

[Holding] a third party liable for negligently inflicted prenatal injuries furthers the child's legal right to begin life free of injuries caused by the negligence of others, but does not significantly restrict the behavior or actions of the defendant beyond the limitations already imposed by the duty owed to the world at a large by long standing rules of tort law. Third parties, despite this recently imposed duty to the fetus, are able to continue to act much as they did before the cause of action was recognized. Imposing the same duty on the mother, however, will constrain her behavior and affirmatively mandate acts which have traditionally rested solely in the province of the individual free from judicial scrutiny, guided, until now, by the mother's sense of personal responsibility and moral, not legal, obligation to her fetus.

Although it is true that the law may impose liability based on the special relationship between certain parties, we can think of no existing legal duty analogous to this one, which could govern such details of a woman's life as her diet, sleep, exercise, sexual activity, work and living environment, and, of course, nearly every aspect of her health care. Imposing a legal duty upon a mother to her fetus creates a legal relationship which is irrefutably unique. "No other plaintiff depends exclusively on any other defendant for everything necessary for life itself. . . . As opposed to the third-party defendant, it is the mother's every waking and sleeping moment which, for better or worse, shapes the prenatal environment which forms the world for the developing fetus. That this is so is not a pregnant woman's fault: it is a fact of life." . . .

The majority discounts the problems associated with legally recognizing a mother's duty to her fetus and assures, that by subjecting the relationship to an "appropriate duty of care" and by allowing the factfinder to make a determination of negligence, no significant rights will be deprived. This conclusion begs the question: What will be the judicially defined standard of conduct for a pregnant woman? Indeed, is it possible to subject a women's judgment, action, and behavior as they relate to the well-being of her fetus to a judicial determination of reasonableness in a manner that is consistent and free from arbitrary results? We have serious doubts.

While we are less troubled with the role of the factfinder in assessing foreseeability, despite the myriad circumstances and complexities of the factors at play, we question whether the nature and scope of the duty can be articulated with consistency and predictability by the courts. Presumably, the determination would "vary according to whether a pregnancy was planned or unplanned, to whether a woman knew she was pregnant soon after conception or only knew after several months, to whether she had the financial resources with which to access the best possible medical care available or was unable to get any prenatal care." . . . In addition to these general circumstances, the court would have to consider the more specific day-to-day decisions of the mother and the detailed circumstances surrounding her pregnancy. Moreover, because "[t]he extent of duty can seldom, if ever, be determined until all the facts of a transaction in its environmental setting are known, and some appropriate rule of law is found available," the question of duty is, unfortunately, one of hindsight. . . . Such after-the-fact judicial scrutiny of the subtle and complicated factors affecting a woman's pregnancy may make life for women who are pregnant or who are merely contemplating pregnancy intolerable. For these reasons, we are convinced that the best course is to allow the duty of a mother to her fetus to remain a moral obligation which, for the vast majority of women, is already freely recognized and respected without compulsion by law.

This issue is difficult, and we have not reached our conclusion with ease or without doubts. The countervailing concerns for the child's right to be born free of negligently inflicted prenatal injuries and his or her right to recover for such harm are significant. We are also aware that a fetus may sustain injuries from the negligent acts of its mother that may not directly implicate the unique relationship between mother and fetus. We are concerned, however, that a rule of law attempting to distinguish between acts of the mother that involve privacy interests and those that may be considered common torts would result in arbitrary line-drawing resulting in inconsistent verdicts. On this point, we find the cases dealing with partial abrogation of parental immunity excepting for acts involving "the exercise of parental authority and discretion" to be closely analogous and instructive. . . .

We conclude that if a cause of action based upon public policy can be created with sufficient safeguards protecting the mother's privacy interests, it should be fashioned by the legislature. Until then, as a matter of both judicial and public policy, we would decline to recognize a cause of action by a child born alive against his or her mother for the mother's negligent acts resulting in prenatal injury.

NOTE

If homeowner's insurance provides liability coverage for the mother in cases such as this, the child, as a member of the household, is also technically an "insured" under the policy. Suppose the insurer inserts a clause in its policy stating that it will not cover claims by one insured against another. In other words, suppose the insurer refuses to provide coverage for claims such as this. Should such a clause be enforceable? If it is enforceable, then the liability may truly fall on the mother, which could be of great significance if she owns property or has other assets in her own name. The same issue arises with automobile liability policies, which now often contain "household exclusion" clauses that deny coverage for suits by members of the insured household against one another.

PROBLEMS

1. Suppose the child had been born alive but then died from the injuries sustained in utero. Would the father have a wrongful death action against the mother?

2. Could a child maintain an action against a mother who caused injury to the child due to drug or alcohol use during pregnancy? *Cf. Chenault v. Huie*, 989 S.W.2d 474 (Tex. App. 1999). How intrusive is this rule?

3. The court makes several references to insurance during the course of its opinion. What is the significance of insurance in a case like this? As a practical matter, what would the effect of the mother's liability be if there were no insurance coverage?

SHOEMAKE v. FOGEL, LTD., A.T.
826 S.W.2d 933 (Tex. 1992)

MAUZY, Justice.

In this cause, we consider whether a defendant in a survival action arising from the death of a child may seek contribution from a negligent parent of the deceased child. We hold that the doctrine of parental immunity bars such contribution when the parent's negligence involves only negligent supervision of the child.

One month before her second birthday, Miranda Gilley nearly drowned in the swimming pool at her apartment complex. The child was rescued and temporarily revived, but four months later died from the injuries she had suffered. Her mother, Janet Shoemake, then brought this suit against the apartment complex owners, Fogel, Ltd. A.T. and Federal Group I, and the apartment complex manager, International Property Management, Inc. (collectively "Fogel"). In addition to seeking damages in her own capacity for wrongful death, Shoemake brought a survival action in her capacity as representative of the child's estate. . . . The jury awarded $285,492.28 to Shoemake on her wrongful death claim, and $50,969 to the child's estate in the survival action. Considering the negligence that caused the near-drowning, the jury attributed a total of fifty-five percent to the Fogel defendants, and the remaining forty-five percent to Janet Shoemake.

As to the wrongful death action, the trial court reduced Shoemake's recovery by forty-five percent, in accordance with the findings on comparative negligence. . . . That aspect of the judgment was not appealed.

In connection with the survival action, Fogel argued that a similar result should obtain; *i.e.*, that it was entitled to a forty-five percent contribution from Shoemake, to be credited against the amount owed her on the wrongful death claim. The trial court rejected that argument and rendered judgment for the estate in the full amount of the jury verdict, along with pre-judgment interest. The court of appeals reversed, holding that the requested contribution was available. . . .

Shoemake now argues that Fogel is barred from contribution against Shoemake, because the doctrine of parental immunity bars Miranda Gilley's estate from recovering damages against Shoemake. We agree.

A defendant's claim of contribution is derivative of the plaintiff's right to recover from the joint defendant against whom contribution is sought. . . . Thus, Fogel's claim of contribution depends upon whether Miranda Gilley's estate has the right to recover damages from Shoemake.

The right of an unemancipated minor to bring a tort action against his or her parent is restricted by the doctrine of parental immunity. . . . The purpose of the doctrine is "to prevent the judicial system from being used to disrupt the wide sphere of reasonable discretion which is necessary in order for parents to properly exercise their responsibility to provide nurture, care, and discipline for their children." . . .

[T]his court [has] held that parental immunity does not extend to suits arising in the course of the parent's business activities. More recently, this court held that the doctrine is inapplicable to automobile tort actions. . . . In both cases, though, we adhered to the view that a parent retains immunity as to "alleged acts of ordinary negligence which involve a reasonable exercise of parental authority or the exercise of ordinary parental discretion with respect to provisions for the care and necessities of the child." . . .

In the present case, Fogel alleged that Shoemake was negligent in the "management, supervision and control" of Miranda Gilley, and that this negligence proximately caused Miranda's death. . . . Those responsibilities entail exactly the sort of parental authority that remains protected. . . . If Shoemake's negligence entailed some other sort of authority, such as business authority or driving responsibilities, Fogel has failed to sustain its burden of presenting a sufficient record to show the trial court's error. . . .

The court of appeals considered the policy concerns underlying parental immunity, but concluded that they were not implicated by the present facts. The usual rationale for retaining parental immunity, the court determined, is that "parental immunity is necessary for the protection of family peace and tranquility and any change in the rule would unduly interfere with the rights of parents to discipline, control, and care for their children." . . . Applying the first half of that rationale to the present case, the court decided that "the public policy consideration of family peace and tranquility disappeared upon Miranda's death and at the time that Shoemake's action accrued." . . . The court therefore held that parental immunity did not bar Fogel from seeking contribution against Shoemaker. . . .

The real objective of parental immunity [is] not to promote family harmony; rather, it is simply to avoid undue judicial interference with parental discretion. The discharge of parental responsibilities, such as the provision of a home, food and schooling, entails countless matters of personal, private choice. In the absence of culpability beyond ordinary negligence, those choices are not subject to review in court.

As the court of appeals observed, family harmony may not be a practical concern in cases like the present one, where the family unit no longer exists. Concerns about judicial interference with parental authority, though, do survive the death of a child. Though hindsight may be clear, a court should still be reluctant to "second-guess a parent's management of family affairs" beyond basic, statutory protections. . . . We hold, therefore, that a child's death does not, by itself, extinguish the parent's immunity from liability for negligent supervision.

Because the child's estate has no viable negligence claim against Shoemake, Fogel has no viable contribution claim against Shoemake. . . . Shoemake's negligence does affect her recovery under the wrongful death statute; but it does not affect the recovery of her child's estate under the survival statute. . . .

We conclude that the court of appeals erred in reforming the trial court's judgment to reflect a $29,851.52 credit in favor of Fogel. We reverse the judgment of the court of appeals and affirm the trial court's judgment in favor of the estate of Miranda Gilley.

PROBLEMS

1. Consider the way the suit would be structured if the child survived the accident and was suing the apartment owners on her own behalf (probably represented by a guardian ad litem). The apartment owners might try to bring a third party action against the mother for negligent supervision, claiming that if they are liable to the child, the mother should be liable to them for a portion of the damages by way of contribution. What issues does such a contribution claim raise? Should it be allowed?

2. Would your analysis of the foregoing question change if the mother had liability insurance coverage available? Should the availability of the parental immunity defense vary depending upon the existence of insurance coverage?

3. If a court decides to retain the parental immunity for "negligent supervision" claims, it becomes important to decide just what counts as "supervision." For example, suppose a parent decides not to secure a child in a car seat for a drive to pre-school. If an accident occurs and the child suffers injuries that would have been avoided had the child been properly secured, should the parent be held liable? Is this, as the Texas court put it, an improper interference with "parental discretion"? *Cf. Thurel v. Vargese*, 207 App. Div. 2d 220, 621 N.Y.S.2d 633 (1995).

b. Charitable Immunity

The immunity of charitable organizations from suit by those injured by their beneficent activities is also something of an historical curiosity whose time has largely passed. Courts put forward various explanations and justifications for the immunity, none of which were totally satisfactory and all of which the critics of the rule have attacked and debunked. In recent times courts and legislatures have tended to abrogate the immunity more or less completely, although it survives in some jurisdictions in limited forms thanks to legislative action. The rule applied in one's own jurisdiction must therefore be researched before any counsel is provided on this topic.

Courts seem to have originally embraced the immunity out of a sense that it would protect and encourage those who tried to provide charitable benefits to others. Perhaps there was a time when most charities were small, underfunded affairs in need of such protection, and perhaps courts were right to be concerned that the threat of liability would mean that, for example, there would be no health care at all for the poor. Today the charitable or non-profit hospital is apt to be a multi-million dollar concern that, at the very least, is able to purchase adequate liability insurance. As the perception of the nature of the charitable enterprise changed, the attitude of the courts towards the charitable immunity changed as well. As a result, the RESTATEMENT (SECOND) OF TORTS § 895E today takes the position that "One engaged in a charitable, educational, religious or benevolent enterprise or activity is not for that reason immune from tort liability." Most jurisdictions today agree. *Cf.* D. DOBBS, THE LAW OF TORTS § 282 (2000).

c. Governmental Immunity

The liability of governmental entities for torts committed by their agents and employees is a huge topic. Whole treatises have addressed the problems involved in suing governmental entities. Because governmental liability is subject to many specific local variations, no detailed examination of the topic is possible here. This section will attempt only to provide an overview of a few of the issues raised by this type of tort liability.

At the outset, it should be understood that governmental tort liability can potentially create separation of powers problems, as the courts attempt to assess liability for the actions of the executive and legislative branches. For example, a litigant disgruntled by the way that police protection is distributed in a municipality might sue, claiming that the decision creates unreasonable risks of harm to persons living in a particular neighborhood that receives less coverage than others. But these decisions are the executive's to make, not the court's. Allowing second guessing of such decisions via the courts would be a judicial usurpation of the executive function. On the other hand, many injuries inflicted by governmental agents raise no issue of governmental authority. If a city employee negligently drives a city vehicle on city business and injures a pedestrian, it is hard to see how imposing liability on the municipality is any different from imposing vicarious liability on a delivery company for the negligent driving of an employee. A third type of litigation involves governmental action that violates fundamental constitutional rights. This type of suit against government is explored in Chapter 19. The difficulty in defining governmental tort liability is constructing a system that allows recovery to injured victims in appropriate situations, without allowing improper interference with the lawful authority of the legislature and executive.

It is also important to understand that not all governmental entities are treated the same way. The federal government and the states are considered "sovereign" and therefore enjoy sovereign immunity. The doctrine of sovereign immunity began with the rule that the king, as the "sovereign," could not be sued. The immunity was then transferred from the person of the king to the abstract entity of the government itself. In the process, the rule was justified on the theory that the sovereign authority, which is the source of laws and rights and creates the courts and gives them their powers, cannot be made to answer in those same courts. The effect of this doctrine in its pure form was to bar totally all suits against the sovereign. This result solves the problem of improper interference by the courts in government affairs, but at the cost of leaving victims of injuries inflicted by government agents without a remedy against the government. One possibility for relief would be a suit against the government agent personally, since the doctrine of sovereign immunity did not protect the individual government official from suit. As a practical matter, however, this remedy was often unsatisfactory, since the individual official might not have sufficient assets to pay a judgment, or in some cases was protected by some form of official immunity. In the federal system, the doctrine of immunity meant that the only way to get redress from the federal government was to persuade Congress to pass a private bill authorizing compensation. The pressure of dealing with vast numbers of these private bills finally persuaded Congress in 1946 to pass the Federal Tort Claims Act (FTCA). The FTCA waived federal sovereign immunity in certain specified types of claims. It is considered below.

The sovereign immunity of the states underwent a similar development. In some states the legislature passed a limited waiver of immunity, allowing suit on certain types of claims such as automobile accidents. In some states the courts took the lead in abolishing sovereign immunity, *Cf. Muskopf v. Corning Hospital Dist.*, 359 P.2d 457 (Cal. 1961). When this occurred, the legislature was usually spurred to action to pass a statute defining the scope of governmental liability. These statutes vary greatly, but all are designed to try to answer, to some degree, the question of the proper scope of governmental liability. Both state and federal tort claims statutes require careful reading and research by the attorney in order to determine not only the scope of the waiver and what suits are permitted, but also to learn the required procedure for making a claim against the government.

d. Municipal Immunity

In contrast, municipal governments were not considered to be sovereigns, and therefore could not take advantage of sovereign immunity. Municipalities were creatures of state law, similar to corporations, and as such were amenable to suit. Municipalities, however, were authorized to discharge governmental functions, and to that extent the problem of the proper scope of municipal liability presented many of the same issues as did sovereign immunity. For that reason, courts developed the rule that municipalities were immune from suit for injuries caused by "governmental" activities, but could be sued if the activities were "proprietary," which meant the sort of activities that a private corporation might engage in. Unfortunately, the distinction between the two types of activities was uncertain, and as a result the decisions about when to allow or deny the right to sue were often arbitrary.

In many jurisdictions today the immunity for governmental decisions has either been abolished or more clearly defined by statute. The cases below, however, illustrate the enduring problem: even if the immunity is abolished and the municipality is liable to suit, there remains the issue of the scope of the duty owed to the individual citizen. This issue will now be examined in two contexts.

CUFFY v. CITY OF NEW YORK
505 N.E.2d 937 (N.Y. 1987)

Titone, Judge.

[We have] recognized a narrow right to recover from a municipality for its negligent failure to provide police protection where a promise of protection was made to a particular citizen and, as a consequence, a "special duty" to that citizen arose. . . . Essential to recovery is proof that the plaintiff relied on the promise and that his reliance was causally related to the harm he suffered. In this case, there was proof of a promise of protection made by an agent of the City, but, for a variety of reasons, the reliance element was not established by any of these three plaintiffs. Accordingly, we now reverse the order appealed from . . . and hold that the complaint against the City should have been dismissed.

The violence that led to plaintiffs' injuries originated in a landlord-tenant dispute between Joseph and Eleanor Cuffy, who occupied the upper apartment of their two-family house in The Bronx, and Joel and Barbara Aitkins, who had leased the ground-floor apartment from the Cuffys for approximately a year. Even before the incidents that are directly involved in this action, there had been episodes between the two couples which the police had been called to mediate. Eleanor Cuffy had previously filed a formal criminal complaint against the Aitkinses, and a prior effort at supervised informal dispute resolution had terminated in an arbitrator's order directing Ms. Cuffy and the Aitkinses to avoid further contact. This history of repeated confrontation and police intervention forms the backdrop for the events at issue in the trial of the Cuffys' claims against the City.

Viewed in the light most favorable to plaintiffs [the evidence] showed that on July 27, 1981, the night immediately preceding the incident, Joel Aitkins physically attacked Eleanor Cuffy, tearing her blouse and bruising her eye. Officer Pennington, who had responded to reports of skirmishes between the Aitkinses and the Cuffys on two or three prior occasions, came to the house once again to investigate, but declined to take any specific action because, in his judgment, the offense was merely a matter of "harassment" between landlord and tenant and an arrest was not warranted.

In frustration, Joseph Cuffy, who had been to see the police four or five times before, went to the local precinct with a neighbor at about 11:00 that night to ask for protection for his family. Cuffy spoke with Lieutenant Moretti, the desk officer, and told him that the Aitkinses had threatened his family's safety. . . . Cuffy specifically told Moretti that he intended to move his family out of its upper floor apartment immediately if an arrest was not made. In response, Moretti told Cuffy that he should not worry and that an arrest would be made or something else would be done about the situation "first thing in the morning." Cuffy then went back to his family and instructed his wife to unpack the family's valises, thereby signifying his intention to remain in the house. Despite Lieutenant Moretti's assurances, the police did not, in fact, undertake any further action in response to Cuffy's complaint.

At approximately 7:00 p.m. on the following evening, the Cuffys' son Ralston, who did not live with his parents, came to their house for a visit. Immediately after Ralston alit from his car, Joel Aitkins accosted him and the two men had an altercation, which culminated in Ralston's being struck with a baseball bat. Eleanor Cuffy, who observed the fight from her upstairs window, and another son, Cyril, rushed to Ralston's rescue. Barbara Aitkins then joined in the attack, slashing at both Eleanor and Cyril with a knife. Joseph Cuffy, who had come home from work at about 6:30 and then gone to his neighbor's house, arrived at the scene while the fight was in progress, but was not in time to avert the harm. By the time the fight was over, all three Cuffys had sustained severe injuries.

Eleanor, Cyril and Ralston Cuffy thereafter commenced this action against the City, alleging that the police had a "special duty" to protect them because of the promise that Lieutenant Moretti had made on the night preceding the incident. . . . The ensuing trial ended in a verdict awarding each of the plaintiffs substantial damages. [The Appellate Division] unanimously affirmed the judgment. . . . We conclude [that] the judgment should have been reversed.

As a general rule, a municipality may not be held liable for injuries resulting from a simple failure to provide police protection. . . . This rule is derived from the principle that a municipality's duty to provide police protection is ordinarily one owed to the public at large and not to any particular individual or class of individuals. . . . Additionally, a municipality's provision of police protection to its citizenry has long been regarded as a resource-allocating function that is better left to the discretion of the policy makers. . . . Consequently, we have generally declined to hold municipalities subject to tort liability for their failure to furnish police protection to individual citizens.

There exists, however, a narrow class of cases in which we have recognized an exception to this general rule and have upheld tort claims based upon a "special relationship" between the municipality and the claimant. . . . The elements of this "special relationship" are: (1) an assumption by the municipality, through promises or actions, of an affirmative duty to act on behalf of the party who was injured; (2) knowledge on the part of the municipality's agents that inaction could lead to harm; (3) some form of direct contact between the municipality's agents and the injured party; and (4) that party's justifiable reliance on the municipality's affirmative undertaking. . . .

[T]he injured party's reliance is as critical in establishing the existence of a "special relationship" as is the municipality's voluntary affirmative undertaking of a duty to act. That element provides the essential causative link between the "special duty" assumed by the municipality and the alleged injury. Indeed, at the heart of most of these "special duty" cases is the unfairness that the courts have perceived in precluding recovery when a municipality's voluntary undertaking has lulled the injured party into a false sense of security and has thereby induced him either to relax his own vigilance or to forego other available avenues of protection. . . . On the other hand, when the reliance element is either not present at all or, if present, is not causally related to the ultimate harm, this underlying concern is inapplicable, and the invocation of the "special duty" exception is then no longer justified.

Another element of the "special duty" exception is the requirement that there be "some direct contact between the agents of the municipality and the injured party" . . . . This element, which is conceptually related to the reliance element, exists first as a natural corollary of the need to show a "special relationship" between the claimant and the municipality, beyond the relationship with government that all citizens share in common. In addition, the "direct contact" requirement serves as a basis for rationally limiting the class of citizens to whom the municipality's "special duty" extends. . . .

[I]n this case, the requirement that there be some direct contact with an agent of the municipality is fatal to the cause of action asserted by plaintiff Ralston Cuffy, the older son who was not a member of Joseph and Eleanor Cuffy's household and did not himself have any direct contact with the police. The absence of direct contact is dispositive of Ralston's claim for two reasons. First, . . . none of the factors militating in favor of relaxing the "direct contact" requirement are present in his case. Since Ralston did not live in the Cuffy's home, his interests were not tied to those of the rest of his family, and it cannot be said that the assurances of protection his father had received directly from Lieutenant Moretti were obtained on his behalf. Accordingly, Ralston's connection to the official promises that form the basis of this action is simply too remote to support recovery.

Second, and perhaps more importantly, there was no indication Ralston even knew of the promise of protection that his father had received. His presence at the house on the day of the incident was thus merely an unfortunate coincidence and, in any event, was certainly not the result of his own reliance on any promise of protection that the police might have made. . . . In the absence of such reliance, his claim is insufficient as a matter of law.

The claims asserted against the City by Eleanor and Cyril Cuffy present a more complex problem. Although neither of those parties had "direct contact" with the public servant who had promised to provide the family with protection, the "special duty" undertaken by the City through its agent must be deemed to have run to them. It was their safety that prompted Joseph Cuffy to solicit the aid of the police, and it was their safety that all concerned had in mind when

Lieutenant Moretti promised police assistance. It would thus be wholly unrealistic to suggest that Eleanor and Cyril Cuffy were in no different position from any other citizen or that the City owed them no "special duty" simply because Joseph Cuffy, rather than they, had been the party who had "direct contact" with Lieutenant Moretti. . . .

Nonetheless, Eleanor and Cyril Cuffy's recovery is precluded for the entirely separate reason that, as a matter of law, their injuries cannot be deemed to have been the result of their justifiable reliance on the assurances of police protection that Joseph Cuffy had received. It is true that the evidence supported an inference that both of these plaintiffs remained in the house during the night of July 27, 1981 and throughout the following morning primarily because of their reliance on Lieutenant Moretti's promise to Joseph that Joel Aitkins would be arrested or something else would be done "first thing in the morning." However, Ms. Cuffy also testified that she had periodically looked out her front window throughout the day of the incident and had not seen any police cars pull up in front of her house and that she continued to be nervous about the situation. Thus, plaintiffs' own evidence established that by midday on July 28th Ms. Cuffy was aware that the police had not arrested or otherwise restrained Mr. Aitkins as had been promised.

This evidence was sufficient, as a matter of law to defeat any colorable claim that Eleanor and Cyril Cuffy's injuries were the result of any justifiable reliance on the lieutenant's assurances. . . .

[I]t may well be that the police were negligent in misjudging the seriousness of the threat to the Cuffys that the Aitkinses' continued presence posed and in not taking any serious steps to assure their safety. It may also be that the police had a "special duty" to Eleanor and Cyril Cuffy because of the promise that Lieutenant Moretti had made and those plaintiffs' overnight, justifiable reliance on that promise. It is clear, however, that those plaintiffs' justifiable reliance, which had dissipated by midday, was not causally related to their involvement in the imbroglio with the Aitkinses on the evening of July 28th. Thus, they too failed to meet the requirements of the doctrine allowing recovery for a municipality's failure to satisfy a "special duty," and their claims, like those of Ralston Cuffy, should have been dismissed.

For all of the foregoing reasons, the order of the Appellate Division should be reversed, with costs, and the complaint dismissed.

NOTES

While the administration of the police force is quintessentially governmental, other activities of municipalities do not seem to rise to the same level. Thus many courts impose a duty on municipalities to maintain roads in a safe condition. Even here, however, the courts recognize that some scope for governmental discretion must remain protected. The extent of that protection is debated in the following case.

PROBLEMS

1. In New York, decisions about the proper allocation of the police are considered both governmental and particularly inappropriate for judicial second guessing. This has been explicitly recognized at least since the notorious case of *Riss v. City of New York*, 240 N.E.2d 860 (N.Y. 1968). In that case a young woman, Linda Riss, complained about threats of harm from a man she had formerly dated. She requested police protection but was refused. She received further threats after she announced her engagement to another man, again sought police protection, and again was refused. The next day an assailant hired by the stalker threw lye in her face, causing scarring and partial blindness. Her suit against the City of New York for its failure to protect her was rejected, one judge dissenting, on the ground that no such duty to protect could be imposed on the city. The court found that imposing such a duty would improperly interfere with the proper discretion of the city in allocating limited police resources. Later cases developed the doctrine discussed in *Cuffy*. How do these rules address the problem of improper judicial interference with the allocation of police protection?

2. What is the relationship between the doctrine discussed in *Cuffy* and the rules regarding liability for nonfeasance?

3. Should similar rules apply to other municipal activities? For example, how should we treat the decision by an emergency room physician at a municipal hospital not to admit a patient? Should that be regarded as a purely medical decision subject to the professional standard of care, or as a governmental decision on the allocation of municipal health care resources?

4. Suppose the 911 operator, upon receiving information about a severe auto accident, directs the ambulance to the wrong location. If a victim dies because of the resulting delay in obtaining medical treatment, should the city be responsible? What duty should be imposed?

AGUEHOUNDE v. DISTRICT OF COLUMBIA
666 A.2d 443 (D.C. 1995)

KING, Associate Judge:

[At] approximately 5:00 p.m. on April 23, 1990, Aguehounde was struck by a car driven by Erica Davis ("Davis") after he stepped into the crosswalk on Fessenden Street as he walked north on the east side of Wisconsin Avenue (which runs in a north-northwest/south-southeast direction) in northwest Washington, D.C. The Davis vehicle, which was proceeding east on Fessenden St., (which runs in an east/west direction) struck Aguehounde in the crosswalk on the east side of Wisconsin Ave. Aguehounde testified that as he approached the Fessenden St./Wisconsin Ave. intersection, and when he was three or four steps from the southeast corner of that intersection, he looked to his left and did not see any vehicles approaching from the west on Fessenden Street. He further testified that when he reached the corner he saw that the light facing him was green and that cars, pointed in a westerly direction, were stopped to his right on Fessenden Street. He could not recall whether the "walk" or "don't walk" sign was on. Aguehounde acknowledged that he did not stop at the corner before stepping into the crosswalk. He also stated that he did not remember looking to his left or seeing Davis's car approach him from that direction as he stepped into the intersection.

Davis, the driver of the car which struck Aguehounde, testified that the light facing her turned from red to green when she was approximately one block from the Wisconsin Ave. intersection. She further testified that the traffic light was still green and she was traveling approximately 20 miles per hour as she proceeded through the intersection in her easterly course on Fessenden St. She first noticed Aguehounde standing on the curb as she passed through the intersection into the crosswalk. Aguehounde then took a big step out in front of her car while it was in the crosswalk. Davis testified that Aguehounde was looking away from her car and she never saw him look in her direction. She applied her brakes, but nonetheless struck Aguehounde who landed 3-5 feet in front of her car.

As a result of the injuries sustained in the collision, Aguehounde and his wife brought this negligence action against the District, alleging that: the District failed to follow the proper engineering standards in setting the length of the "clearance interval" at the intersection; this failure caused the District to set a clearance interval of too short a duration to allow cars to clear the intersection and the crosswalks; and consequently, Davis's car was still in the intersection when Aguehounde stepped into the crosswalk on a green light.

A jury trial was conducted in May, 1993 before Judge Burgess. The District's motion for judgment as a matter of law on the ground that it was immune from suit because the setting of the clearance interval was a discretionary act, was denied. The jury found that the District's setting of the timing of the clearance interval was the proximate cause of Aguehounde's paralyzing injuries, and awarded him $7,318,313.20 in damages, and his wife $602,913 on her claim for loss of consortium. In addition, the jury rejected the District's contention that Aguehounde had been contributorily negligent.

Thereafter, the District moved for judgment as a matter of law on the grounds that the timing of the light is a discretionary function immune from tort liability. . . . [J]udge Burgess granted the District's motion, concluding that the District was immune from liability because the decision to set the length of the clearance interval involved policy considerations. [On appeal,] Aguehounde contends the trial court erred in granting the District's Motion for judgment as a matter of law. . . .

Before turning to the merits, a brief discussion of practices relating to the timing of traffic lights will be helpful to understanding the issue presented. The clearance interval of a traffic light is the amount of time allocated to the yellow light which occurs between the green light for one street and the green light for the cross street at an intersection. At some intersections an "all-red" sequence is added, meaning there is a red light in each direction at the same time for the duration of that sequence, which is ordinarily no more than one or two seconds. The purpose of the clearance interval is: (1) to allow a driver sufficient time to either come to a complete stop before entering the intersection or to clear the intersection before the crossing light turns green; and (2) to keep opposing traffic and pedestrians from entering the intersection until the vehicles headed in the opposite direction have passed through the intersection.

It is undisputed that in 1985 the clearance interval at the Wisconsin Ave./Fessenden St. intersection for traffic coming from Davis's direction was 4.5 seconds, meaning the light facing traffic on Fessenden St. would turn from green to yellow for 4.5 seconds before the light facing traffic on Wisconsin Ave. would turn to green. In October 1989, the interval was changed to 4.0 seconds. [An explanation of a formula used to calculate the interval is omitted.]

A six-second clearance interval involving four seconds of yellow and two of all-red, which Aguehounde contends should have been set for the intersection, would have allowed vehicles to clear the intersection and the crosswalks before the green light for opposing traffic and pedestrians would permit entry to the intersection, thus maximizing pedestrian safety. A four or 4.5 second clearance interval, however, might not necessarily permit all traffic to fully clear the intersection before pedestrians were permitted to enter the intersection and, consequently, traffic flow, but not pedestrian safety, would be maximized.

[U]nder the common law, a municipality is immune from suit for decisions made pursuant to the exercise of discretion, but not for actions which are ministerial. . . . It is a determination to be made by the trial judge, not the jury, and this court conducts a de novo review of the trial court's determination of whether or not the action was discretionary. . . .

At the outset, the trial court must determine whether the act is a discretionary or ministerial function under the circumstances presented. . . . While "[c]haracterizing an act as discretionary or ministerial is not always an easy task," . . . discretionary acts are generally defined as those acts involving the formulation of policy while ministerial acts are defined as those relating to the execution of policy. . . . Administrative decisions which require the government to balance competing considerations are considered discretionary acts. . . . By barring suit for such actions, Congress "prevent[s] judicial 'second-guessing' of legislative and administrative decisions grounded in social, economic and political policy through the medium of an action in tort." . . .

To determine whether a given governmental action is discretionary or ministerial, we first determine whether it is the kind of action "that the discretionary function exception was designed to shield;" that is, whether the action involves "the permissible exercise of policy judgment." . . . If the answer to this first inquiry is yes, then the action is immune from suit, unless the government has adopted a "statute, regulation or policy [that] specifically prescribes a course of action for an employee to follow." . . . If such a specific directive exists which removes the otherwise unfettered discretion of the government employee, the action is ministerial, opening the government to suit if not performed correctly.

Aguehounde contends that the trial court erred in finding that the setting of the clearance intervals was a discretionary act because the decision did not involve policy considerations making it the type of action intended to be shielded by immunity. . . .

It was clear to the trial court that setting traffic signal intervals "is the type of function that the discretionary function rule is designed to shield." The trial court further observed that setting traffic signal intervals:

> involves considerations of safety not only for pedestrians but for travelers, and it involves a balancing of safety needs against the need to assure adequate traffic flow, which itself involves considerations of safety as well as commerce and convenience. Balancing these factors also requires the ascertainment of facts, such as numbers of vehicles and pedestrians, and ways in which drivers and pedestrians behave in the aggregate, which are peculiarly subject to study and expertise. Subjecting the decisions of traffic engineers to litigation and to second-guessing by jurors would deter effective government.

We fully agree, and therefore hold, for the reasons relied upon by the trial court, that the timing of signal intervals involves balancing various economic, political and social considerations and is therefore a discretionary function. . . .

[N]or do we find any support for our dissenting colleague's assertion that government conduct is insulated from liability only where the official "actually exercised discretion." . . . [A]n act is deemed discretionary where it is shown to involve policy judgment and decisions, but does not require proof that every myriad and intricate decision involved in the process required a specific balancing of policy decisions. . . .

[A]ffirmed.

SCHWELB, Associate Judge, dissenting:

[I] respectfully dissent. [T]he majority has outlined in some detail the distinction between discretionary and ministerial governmental functions. I have no quarrel with much of its discussion. I cannot agree, however, that because the determination of the duration of the clearance interval at Wisconsin and Fessenden was a de facto part of the District's overall traffic plan, the decision to set it at four seconds was necessarily a protected discretionary act. In my opinion, this proposition, followed to its logical conclusion, would insulate the District from liability for negligent conduct under circumstances which the discretionary function doctrine was never designed to reach. . . .

[T]he goal of the discretionary function exception is to "prevent judicial 'second-guessing' of legislative and administrative decisions grounded in social, economic and political policy through the medium of an action in tort." . . . "The discretionary function exception applies only to conduct that involves the permissible exercise of policy judgments." . . . Accordingly, when that exception is invoked, the court must make "a particularized and fact-specific inquiry to determine whether the acts or omissions in question flowed from a choice based on economic or social policy." . . . That inquiry is designed to determine not whether the government employee has a choice, but whether that choice is a policy judgment. . . .

Moreover, there is persuasive authority for the proposition that governmental conduct is insulated from liability only "where the official or employee actually exercised some discretion." . . . Although some decisions reflect a different focus, proof that an administrative decision was not based on economic or social considerations is surely probative on the question whether the "discretionary function" exception applies, especially where, as in this case, the testimony of the District's own representatives . . . demonstrates that the failure to weigh such factors was the norm rather than the exception. . . .

PROBLEMS

1. Should the discretionary function test require proof that discretion was actually exercised, or only that the decision was the type that would normally involve the exercise of discretion?

2. Can you formulate a test for which functions or decisions are discretionary and which are ministerial? Does the court in the case above come to the correct conclusion?

3. If the discretionary function test applies, should the municipality be liable if the plaintiff proves that the decision reached was negligent? Totally unreasonable? *Cf. Weiss v. Fote*, 167 N.E.2d 63 (N.Y. 1960).

4. What result if the municipality explicitly adopted as a rule a four second clearance interval for all intersections?

e. Federal Immunity

As noted above, the immunity of the federal government is subject to a limited waiver by the Federal Tort Claims Act:

The Federal Tort Claims Act

28 U.S.C. § 2674. Liability of United States

The United States shall be liable, respecting the provisions of this title relating to tort claims, in the same manner and to the same extent as a private individual under like circumstances, but shall not be liable for interest prior to judgment or for punitive damages.

If, however, in any case wherein death was caused, the law of the place where the act or omission complained of occurred provides, or has been construed to provide, for damages only punitive in nature, the United States shall be liable for actual or compensatory damages, measured by the pecuniary injuries resulting from such death to the persons respectively, for whose benefit the action was brought, in lieu thereof.

With respect to any claim under this chapter, the United States shall be entitled to assert any defense based upon judicial or legislative immunity which otherwise would have been available to the employee of the United States whose act or omission gave rise to the claim, as well as any other defenses to which the United States is entitled.

. . . .

28 U.S.C. § 2675. Disposition by federal agency as prerequisite; evidence

(a) An action shall not be instituted upon a claim against the United States for money damages for injury or loss of property or personal injury or death caused by the negligent or wrongful act or omission of any employee of the Government while acting within the scope of his office or employment, unless the claimant shall have first presented the claim to the appropriate Federal agency and his claim shall have been finally denied by the agency in writing and sent by certified or registered mail. The failure of an agency to make final disposition of a claim within six months after it is filed shall, at the option of the claimant any time thereafter, be deemed a final denial of the claim for purposes of this section. The provisions of this subsection shall not apply to such claims as may be asserted under the Federal Rules of Civil Procedure by third party complaint, cross-claim, or counterclaim. . . .

28 U.S.C. § 2678. Attorney fees; penalty

No attorney shall charge, demand, receive, or collect for services rendered, fees in excess of 25 per centum of any judgment rendered pursuant to section 1346(b) of this title or any settlement made pursuant to section 2677 of this title, or in excess of 20 per centum of any award, compromise, or settlement made pursuant to section 2672 of this title.

Any attorney who charges, demands, receives, or collects for services rendered in connection with such claim any amount in excess of that allowed under this section, if recovery be had, shall be fined not more than $2,000 or imprisoned not more than one year, or both.

28 U.S.C. § 2680. Exceptions

The provisions of this chapter and section 1346(b) of this title shall not apply to —

(a) Any claim based upon an act or omission of an employee of the Government, exercising due care, in the execution of a statute or regulation, whether or not such statute or regulation be valid, or based upon the exercise or performance or the failure to exercise or perform a discretionary function or duty on the part of a federal agency or an employee of the Government, whether or not the discretion involved be abused.

(b) Any claim arising out of the loss, miscarriage, or negligent transmission of letters or postal matter.

. . . .

(h) Any claim arising out of assault, battery, false imprisonment, false arrest, malicious prosecution, abuse of process, libel, slander, misrepresentation, deceit, or interference with contract rights: Provided, That, with regard to acts or omissions of investigative or law enforcement officers of the United States Government, the provisions of this chapter and section 1346(b) of this title shall apply to any claim arising, on or after the date of the enactment of this proviso, out of assault, battery, false imprisonment, false arrest, abuse of process, or malicious prosecution. For the purpose of this subsection, "investigative or law enforcement officer" means any officer of the United States who is empowered by law to execute searches, to seize evidence, or to make arrests for violations of Federal law.

(i) Any claim for damages caused by the fiscal operations of the Treasury or by the regulation of the monetary system.

(j) Any claim arising out of the combatant activities of the military or naval forces, or the Coast Guard, during time of war.

(k) Any claim arising in a foreign country.

NOTE

Identify the scope of the waiver accomplished by the provision above, and the scope of the exceptions. In particular, note that in § 2680 (a) the statute includes the "discretionary function" exception. The following case examines the scope of this exception, and can be compared with the approach of the court in the *Aguehounde* case.

BERKOVITZ v. UNITED STATES
486 U.S. 531 (1988)

MARSHALL, J., delivered the opinion for a unanimous Court.

The question in this case is whether the discretionary function exception of the Federal Tort Claims Act (FTCA or Act), 28 U.S.C. § 2680(a), bars a suit based on the Government's licensing of an oral polio vaccine and on its subsequent approval of the release of a specific lot of that vaccine to the public.

I

On May 10, 1979, Kevan Berkovitz, then a 2-month-old infant, ingested a dose of Orimune, an oral polio vaccine manufactured by Lederle Laboratories. Within one month, he contracted a severe case of polio. The disease left Berkovitz almost completely paralyzed and unable to breathe without the assistance of a respirator. The Communicable Disease Center, an agency of the Federal Government, determined that Berkovitz had contracted polio from the vaccine.

Berkovitz, joined by his parents as guardians, subsequently filed suit against the United States in Federal District Court. The complaint alleged that the United States was liable for his injuries under the FTCA, 28 U.S.C. §§ 1346(b), 2674, because the Division of Biologic Standards (DBS), then a part of the National Institutes of Health, had acted wrongfully in licensing Lederle Laboratories to produce Orimune and because the Bureau of Biologics of the Food and Drug Administration (FDA) had acted wrongfully in approving release to the public of the particular lot of vaccine containing Berkovitz's dose. According to petitioners, these actions violated federal law and policy regarding the inspection and approval of polio vaccines.

The Government moved to dismiss the suit for lack of subject-matter jurisdiction on the ground that the agency actions fell within the discretionary function exception of the FTCA. The District Court denied this motion, concluding that neither the licensing of Orimune nor the release of a specific lot of that vaccine to the public was a "discretionary function" within the meaning of the FTCA. . . . At the Government's request, the District Court certified its decision for immediate appeal to the Third Circuit. . . .

A divided panel of the Court of Appeals reversed. [T]he court concluded that the licensing and release of polio vaccines were wholly discretionary actions and, as such, could not form the basis for suit against the United States. . . .

We granted certiorari, . . . to resolve a conflict in the Circuits regarding the effect of the discretionary function exception on claims arising from the Government's regulation of polio vaccines. . . . We now reverse the Third Circuit's judgment.

The FTCA, 28 U.S.C. § 1346(b), generally authorizes suits against the United States for damages

> "for injury or loss of property, or personal injury or death caused by the negligent or wrongful act or omission of any employee of the Government while acting within the scope of his office or employment, under circumstances where the United States, if a private person, would be liable to the claimant in accordance with the law of the place where the act or omission occurred."

The Act includes a number of exceptions to this broad waiver of sovereign immunity. The exception relevant to this case provides that no liability shall lie for

> "[a]ny claim . . . based upon the exercise or performance or the failure to exercise or perform a discretionary function or duty on the part of a federal agency or an employee of the Government, whether or not the discretion involved be abused."

28 U.S.C. § 2680(a). This exception . . . "marks the boundary between Congress' willingness to impose tort liability upon the United States and its desire to protect certain governmental activities from exposure to suit by private individuals." *United States v. Varig Airlines*, 467 U.S. at 808, 104 S. Ct. at 2761-2762.

The determination of whether the discretionary function exception bars a suit against the Government is guided by several established principles. This Court stated in *Varig* that "it is the nature of the conduct, rather than the status of the actor, that governs whether the discretionary function exception applies in a given case." . . . In examining the nature of the challenged conduct, a court must first consider whether the action is a matter of choice for the acting employee. This inquiry is mandated by the language of the exception; conduct cannot be discretionary unless it involves an element of judgment or choice. . . . Thus, the discretionary function exception will not apply when a federal statute, regulation, or policy specifically prescribes a course of action for an employee to follow. In this event, the employee has no rightful option but to adhere to the directive. And if the employee's conduct cannot appropriately be the product of judgment or choice, then there is no discretion in the conduct for the discretionary function exception to protect. . . .

Moreover, assuming the challenged conduct involves an element of judgment, a court must determine whether that judgment is of the kind that the discretionary function exception was designed to shield. The basis for the discretionary function exception was Congress' desire to "prevent judicial 'second-guessing' of legislative and administrative decisions grounded in social, economic, and political policy through the medium of an action in tort." . . . The exception, properly construed, therefore protects only governmental actions and decisions based on considerations of public policy. . . . In sum, the discretionary function exception insulates the Government from liability if the action challenged in the case involves the permissible exercise of policy judgment. . . .

In restating and clarifying the scope of the discretionary function exception, we intend specifically to reject the Government's argument, pressed both in this Court and the Court of Appeals, that the exception precludes liability for any and all acts arising out of the regulatory programs of federal agencies. That argument is rebutted first by the language of the exception, which protects "discretionary" functions, rather than "regulatory" functions. The significance of Congress' choice of language is supported by the legislative history. As this Court previously has indicated, the relevant legislative materials demonstrate that the exception was designed to cover not all acts of regulatory agencies and their employees, but only such acts as are "discretionary" in nature. . . . This coverage accords with Congress' purpose in enacting the exception: to prevent "[j]udicial intervention in . . . the political, social, and economic judgments" of governmental — including regulatory — agencies. . . . [I]n *Varig*, we ignored the precise argument the Government makes in this case, focusing instead on the particular nature of the regulatory conduct at issue. To the extent we have not already put the Government's argument to rest, we do so now. The discretionary function exception applies only to conduct that involves the permissible exercise of policy judgment. The question in this case is whether the governmental activities challenged by petitioners are of this discretionary nature.

Petitioners' suit raises two broad claims. First, petitioners assert that the DBS violated a federal statute and accompanying regulations in issuing a license to Lederle Laboratories to produce Orimune. Second, petitioners argue that the Bureau of Biologics of the FDA violated federal regulations and policy in approving the release of the particular lot of Orimune that contained Kevan Berkovitz's dose. We examine each of these broad claims by reviewing the applicable regulatory scheme and petitioners' specific allegations of agency wrongdoing. Because the decision we review adjudicated a motion to dismiss, we accept all of the factual allegations in petitioners' complaint as true and ask whether, in these circumstances, dismissal of the complaint was appropriate.

Under federal law, a manufacturer must receive a product license prior to marketing a brand of live oral polio vaccine. . . . In order to become eligible for such a license, a manufacturer must first make a sample of the vaccine product. . . . This process begins with the selection of an original virus strain. The manufacturer grows a seed virus from this strain; the seed virus is then used to produce monopools, portions of which are combined to form the consumer-level product. Federal regulations set forth safety criteria for the original strain, [the seed virus,] and the vaccine monopools. . . . Under the regulations, the manufacturer must conduct a variety of tests to measure the safety of the product at each stage of the manufacturing process. . . . Upon completion of the manufacturing process and the required testing, the manufacturer is required to submit an application for a product license to the DBS. . . . In addition to this application, the manufacturer must submit data from the tests performed and a sample of the finished product. . . .

In deciding whether to issue a license, the DBS is required to comply with certain statutory and regulatory provisions. The Public Health Service Act provides:

> "Licenses for the maintenance of establishments for the propagation or manufacture and preparation of products [including polio vaccines] may be issued only upon a showing that the establishment and the products for which a license is desired meet standards, designed to insure the continued safety, purity, and potency of such products, prescribed in regulations, and licenses for new products may be issued only upon a showing that they meet such standards. All such licenses shall be issued, suspended, and revoked as prescribed by regulations. . . ."

A regulation similarly provides that "[a] product license shall be issued only upon examination of the product and upon a determination that the product complies with the standards prescribed in the regulations. . . ." . . . In addition, a regulation states that "[a]n application for license shall not be considered as filed" until the DBS receives the information and data regarding the product that the manufacturer is required to submit. . . . These statutory and regulatory provisions require the DBS, prior to issuing a product license, to receive all data the manufacturer is required to submit, to examine the product, and to make a determination that the product complies with safety standards.

Petitioners' first allegation with regard to the licensing of Orimune is that the DBS issued a product license without first receiving data that the manufacturer must submit showing how the product, at the various stages of the manufacturing process, matched up against regulatory safety standards. . . . The discretionary function exception does not bar a cause of action based on this allegation. The statute and regulations described above require, as a precondition to licensing, that the DBS receive certain test data from the manufacturer relating to the product's compliance with regulatory standards. . . . The DBS has no discretion to issue a license without first receiving the required test data; to do so would violate a specific statutory and regulatory directive. Accordingly, to the extent that petitioners' licensing claim is based on a decision of the DBS to issue a license without having received the required test data, the discretionary function exception imposes no bar.

Petitioners' other allegation regarding the licensing of Orimune is difficult to describe with precision. Petitioners contend that the DBS licensed Orimune even though the vaccine did not comply with certain regulatory safety standards. . . . This charge may be understood in any of three ways. First, petitioners may mean that the DBS licensed Orimune without first making a determination as to whether the vaccine complied with regulatory standards. Second, petitioners may intend to argue that the DBS specifically found that Orimune failed to comply with certain regulatory standards and nonetheless issued a license for the vaccine's manufacture. Third, petitioners may concede that the DBS made a determination of compliance, but allege that this determination was incorrect. Neither petitioners' complaint nor their briefs and argument before this Court make entirely clear their theory of the case.

If petitioners aver that the DBS licensed Orimune either without determining whether the vaccine complied with regulatory standards or after determining that the vaccine failed to comply, the discretionary function exception does not bar the claim. Under the scheme governing the DBS's regulation of polio vaccines, the DBS may not issue a license except upon an examination of the product and a determination that the product complies with all regulatory standards. . . . The agency has no discretion to deviate from this mandated procedure. Petitioners' claim, if interpreted as alleging that the DBS licensed Orimune in the absence of a determination that the vaccine complied with regulatory standards, therefore does not challenge a discretionary function. Rather, the claim charges a failure on the part of the agency to perform its clear duty under federal law. When a suit charges an agency with failing to act in accord with a specific mandatory directive, the discretionary function exception does not apply.

If petitioners' claim is that the DBS made a determination that Orimune complied with regulatory standards, but that the determination was incorrect, the question of the applicability of the discretionary function exception requires a somewhat different analysis. In that event, the question turns on whether the manner and method of determining compliance with the safety standards at issue involve agency judgment of the kind protected by the discretionary function exception. Petitioners contend that the determination involves the application of objective scientific standards, . . . whereas the Government asserts that the determination incorporates considerable "policy judgment" . . . . In making these assertions, the parties have framed the issue appropriately; application of the discretionary function exception to the claim that the determination of compliance was incorrect hinges on whether the agency officials making that determination permissibly exercise policy choice. The parties, however, have not addressed this question in detail, and they have given us no indication of the way in which the DBS interprets and applies the regulations setting forth the criteria for compliance. Given that these regulations are particularly abstruse, we hesitate to decide the question on the scanty record before us. We therefore leave it to the District Court to decide, if petitioners choose to press this claim, whether agency officials appropriately exercise policy judgment in determining that a vaccine product complies with the relevant safety standards.

The regulatory scheme governing release of vaccine lots is distinct from that governing the issuance of licenses. The former set of regulations places an obligation on manufacturers to examine all vaccine lots prior to distribution to ensure that they comply with regulatory standards. . . . These regulations, however, do not impose a corresponding duty on the Bureau of Biologics. Although the regulations empower the Bureau to examine any vaccine lot and prevent the distribution of a noncomplying lot, . . . they do not require the Bureau to take such action in all cases. The regulations generally allow the Bureau to determine the appropriate manner in which to regulate the release of vaccine lots, rather than mandating certain kinds of agency action. The regulatory scheme governing the release of vaccine lots is substantially similar in this respect to the scheme discussed in *United States v. Varig Airlines*. . . .

Given this regulatory context, the discretionary function exception bars any claims that challenge the Bureau's formulation of policy as to the appropriate way in which to regulate the release of vaccine lots. . . . In addition, if the policies and programs formulated by the Bureau allow room for implementing officials to make independent policy judgments, the discretionary function exception protects the acts taken by those officials in the exercise of this discretion. . . . The discretionary function exception, however, does not apply if the acts complained of do not involve the permissible exercise of policy discretion. Thus, if the Bureau's policy leaves no room for an official to exercise policy judgment in performing a given act, or if the act simply does not involve the exercise of such judgment, the discretionary function exception does not bar a claim that the act was negligent or wrongful. . . .

Viewed in light of these principles, petitioners' claim regarding the release of the vaccine lot from which Kevan Berkovitz received his dose survives the Government's motion to dismiss. Petitioners allege that, under the authority granted by the regulations, the Bureau of Biologics has adopted a policy of testing all vaccine lots for compliance with safety standards and preventing the distribution to the public of any lots that fail to comply. Petitioners further allege that notwithstanding this policy, which allegedly leaves no room for implementing officials to exercise independent policy judgment, employees of the Bureau knowingly approved the release of a lot that did not comply with safety standards. . . . Thus, petitioners' complaint is directed at a governmental action that allegedly involved no policy discretion. Petitioners, of course, have not proved their factual allegations, but they are not required to do so on a motion to dismiss. If those allegations are correct — that is, if the Bureau's policy did not allow the official who took the challenged action to release a noncomplying lot on the basis of policy considerations — the discretionary function exception does not bar the claim. Because petitioners may yet show, on the basis of materials obtained in discovery or otherwise, that the conduct challenged here did not involve the permissible exercise of policy discretion, the invocation of the discretionary function exception to dismiss petitioners' lot release claim was improper.

For the foregoing reasons, the Court of Appeals erred in holding that the discretionary function exception required the dismissal of petitioners' claims respecting the licensing of Orimune and the release of a particular vaccine lot. The judgment of the Court of Appeals is accordingly reversed, and the case is remanded for further proceedings consistent with this opinion.

It is so ordered.

602   DEFENSES   CH. 12

NOTES

1. The scope of the discretionary function exception has increased in significance with the increasing regulatory activity of the federal government. The greater the scope of discretion in setting policy that the Congress grants to the regulatory agency, the broader the scope of the exception will be. The limits on the power of Congress to delegate in this fashion are considered in courses on Administrative law.

2. Suits against federal officers for violation of constitutional rights are considered in Chapter 19, Civil Rights, *infra*.

3. An additional important exception to the liability created by the FTCA is the *Feres* doctrine, *Feres v. United States*, 340 U.S. 135 (1950), which holds that the government is not liable for injuries received incident to military service. The Supreme Court read this exception into the FTCA even though Congress had not explicitly created such a broad exception. Since the doctrine was first announced the Supreme Court has continued to uphold and indeed extend it, so that it covers even injuries inflicted by deliberate abuse of authority by military officials, *cf. United States v. Stanley*, 483 U.S. 669 (1987).

Chapter 13
VICARIOUS LIABILITY

In some situations tort liability is imposed against one party for a tort actually committed by another. In the eyes of the law, the liability of the party committing the tortious act is imputed to a different party who is held responsible for the harm to the plaintiff even though she did not directly effect that harm. The most commonly asserted legal justification for imputing tort liability is the existence of some type of "special relationship" between the tortfeasor and the party held legally responsible. Usually, this special relationship arises out of an employer-employee relation, but as we will see, there are many other bases for imputing vicarious liability.

Unlike the bases of liability we have studied thus far, the imposition of vicarious liability is not dependent upon any notion of fault or wrongdoing by that party. Instead, liability is imputed for reasons of policy or practicality. In this sense, vicarious liability is often said to relate more closely to strict liability than either negligence or intentional tort liability. In this Chapter we will also examine the specific policy arguments typically offered in support of vicarious liability.

At the outset, it should be noted that vicarious liability is not the only type of imputed or "secondary" liability. Another broad category of imputed liability, called *contributory* liability, is invoked when the defendant provides assistance to the tortfeasor in committing the tort. Such assistance can come in the form of encouraging the tortfeasor or providing the tortfeasor the tools used in commission of the tort. Thus, if seller sells a weapon to buyer, knowing that buyer will use the weapon to injure plaintiff, seller may be contributorily liable for the eventual tort. Unlike vicarious liability, where the person being held liable is completely innocent of any wrongdoing, a party held contributorily liable has committed an act that is considered in some way wrongful. Because of this difference, and because contributory liability tends to arise in certain narrow categories of cases (particularly the competitive torts discussed in Chapter 22), it is beyond the scope of this chapter.

A. RESPONDEAT SUPERIOR

Traditionally, courts imposed vicarious liability when some type of employer-employee relationship existed between the party held legally responsible and the party (also legally responsible) who actually inflicted the injury. Vicarious liability derives from the doctrine of *respondeat superior*, which, in Latin meant literally to "let the superior respond" (by paying for the damages), and was originally applied by English common law courts against "masters" for various injuries tortiously inflicted by their "servants" in pursuit of their masters' business purposes. Today, the term is still used to refer to the vicarious liability of employers for torts committed by their employees in the scope of their employment. However, the scope of the traditional "employer-employee" relationship is applied much more broadly to include situations where no formal employer-employee relationship exists at all.

FRUIT v. SCHREINER
502 P.2d 133 (Alaska 1972)

BOOCHEVER, J.

At the time of the accident, Fruit, a life insurance salesman, was attending a sales convention of his employer, Equitable Life Assurance Society (Equitable). [The] convention was being conducted at the resort location of Land's End. . . . Sales employees [were] required to attend the convention. [T]he agency manager decided that participants should [use] private transportation [and] be reimbursed a lump sum for their expenses. Clay Fruit chose to drive his own automobile. . . . Insurance experts from California and Washington were also invited as guests to the convention, and the Alaska salesmen were encouraged to mix freely with these guests to learn as much as possible about sales techniques during the three-day gathering. Scheduled events included business [and] evening dinners and at least two cocktail parties. . . . A desk clerk [testified] that loud and sometimes disorderly partying continued around the room of the agency manager [until] the early hours of the morning. . . . A business meeting on Friday morning proceeded on schedule followed by a cocktail party. . . . [B]y mid-afternoon Fruit was asleep on the floor. That evening, a scheduled cocktail party and seafood dinner on the beach proceeded without Fruit who was still asleep in a room. . . . At some time between 10:00 and 11:30 p.m., [Fruit drove to] the Waterfront Bar and Restaurant [, but] departed when he did not find any of his colleagues.

His return route to Land's End took him past the Salty Dawg Bar where Schreiner's automobile was disabled on or immediately off the side of the road opposite Fruit's lane. While the facts of the . . . accident which occurred at approximately 2:00 a.m. [are] unclear, it appears that Fruit applied his brakes and skidded across the dividing line of the highway, colliding with the front of Schreiner's car. The hood of Schreiner's automobile had been raised and Schreiner was standing in front of his car. The collision crushed his legs.

The subsequent amputation and crippling of Schreiner was exacerbated by a urinary disorder resulting from exploratory surgery necessitated by the accident. Schreiner sued Fruit and his employer, Equitable, for damages including pain and suffering, mental anguish, interference with normal activities, continuing medical expenses, loss of income and financial losses incurred from the forced sale of his home, a lot and securities. The jury found on special interrogatories that Fruit's negligence was the proximate cause of the accident; that he was acting within the course and scope of his employment for Equitable; that Equitable was directly negligent in planning and conducting the convention, which negligence was a proximate cause of the accident; and that Schreiner was not contributorily negligent. The jury awarded damages of $635,000 against both defendants. Both moved for a judgment notwithstanding the verdict and presently appeal from the respective denials of the motions.

Equitable contends that the evidence was insufficient to establish that Fruit was acting within the course and scope of his employment at the time of the accident; that Equitable cannot be held directly liable for the manner in which it conducted the summer conference; and that Equitable did not receive a fair trial because the facts adduced by the plaintiff in support of its direct negligence claim "tainted the jury's consideration of respondeat superior." In addition Equitable contends that the jury's verdict was excessive.

Fruit likewise questions the amount of damages and also contends that Schreiner was guilty of contributory negligence as a matter of law or in the alternative that the jury's verdict on this issue was clearly erroneous. . . .

II. EQUITABLE'S LIABILITY UNDER THE DOCTRINE OF RESPONDEAT SUPERIOR

[Equitable argues] that the evidence was insufficient to establish that Fruit was acting within the course and scope of his employment. Equitable contends that any business purpose was completed when Fruit left the Waterfront Bar and Restaurant. It cites cases holding that an employee traveling to his home or other personal destination cannot ordinarily be regarded as acting in the scope of his employment. But Fruit was not returning to his home. He was traveling to the convention headquarters where he was attending meetings as a part of his employment.

In addition, Equitable seeks to narrow the scope of respondeat superior to those situations where the master has exercised control over the activities of employees. Disposition of this issue requires an analysis of the doctrine of respondeat superior, one of the few anomalies to the general tort doctrine of no liability without fault.

The origins of the principle [of vicarious liability] are in dispute. . . . The doctrine emerged in English law in the 17th Century. Initially a master was held liable for those acts which he commanded or to which he expressly assented. This was expanded to include acts by implied command or authority and eventually to acts within the scope of employment. The modern theory evolved with the growth of England's industry and commerce.

A truly imaginative variety of rationale have been advanced by courts and glossators in justification of this imposition of liability on employers. Among the suggestions are the employer's duty to hire and maintain a responsible staff of employees, to "control" the activities of his employees and thus to insist upon appropriate safety measures; the belief that the employer should pay for the inherent risks which result from hiring others to carry on his business; the observation that the employer most often has easier access to evidence of the facts surrounding the injury; and the metaphysical identification of the employer and employee as a single "persona" jointly liable for the injury which occurred in the context of the business. [One commentator] more cynically states: "In hard fact, the reason for the employers' liability is the damages are taken from a deep pocket."

The two theories which carry the greatest weight in contemporary legal thought are respectively, the "control" theory which finds liability whenever the act of the employee was committed with the implied authority, acquiescence or subsequent ratification of the employer, and the "enterprise" theory which finds liability whenever the enterprise of the employer would have benefited by the context of the act of the employee but for the unfortunate injury.

Since we are dealing with vicarious liability, justification may not be found on theories involving the employer's personal fault such as his failure to exercise proper control over the activities of his employees or his failure to take proper precautions in firing or hiring them. Lack of care on the employer's part would subject him to direct liability without the necessity of involving respondeat superior.

The concept of vicarious liability is broad enough to include circumstances "where the master has been in no way at fault; where the work which the servant was employed to do was in no sense unlawful or violative of the plaintiff's rights; where there has been no delegation of a special duty; where the tortious conduct of the servant was neither commanded nor ratified; but nevertheless the master is made responsible." This liability arises from the relationship of the enterprise to society rather than from a misfeasance on the part of the employer.

The aspect of the relationship most commonly advanced to delimit the theory is the "scope of employment" of the employee-tortfeasor. While the factual determination generally is left to the jury, many cases lying in the penumbras of "scope of employment" have produced confusing and contradictory legal results in the development of an otherwise worthy doctrine of law. To assist in delineating the areas of tortious conduct imposing liability, it is helpful to consider what we believe to be the correct philosophical basis for the doctrine.

There was a time when the artisans, shopkeepers and master craftsmen could directly oversee the activities of their apprentices and journeymen. Small, isolated communities or feudal estates evinced a provincial sense of social interaction which ensured that many enterprises would conduct their businesses with a careful concern for the community of its patrons. But in the present day when hundreds of persons divide labors under the same corporate roof and produce a single product for market to an unidentified consumer, the communal spirit and shared commitment of enterprises from another age is sacrificed to other efficiencies. At the same time, the impersonal nature of such complex enterprises and their mechanization make third parties considerably more vulnerable to injury incidentally arising from the pursuit of the business. Business corporations are granted a personal identification in legal fiction to limit liability of the investors, but not to insulate the corporate entity itself from liability for the unfortunate consequences of its enterprise.

"Scope of employment" as a test for application of respondeat superior would be insufficient if it failed to encompass the duty of every enterprise to the social community which gives it life and contributes to its prosperity.

[The] basis of respondeat superior has been correctly stated as "the desire to include in the costs of operation inevitable losses to third persons incident to carrying on an enterprise, and thus distribute the burden among those benefited by the enterprise." The desirability of the result is readily discernible when an employee obviously engaged in his employer's business causes injury to a third party as a result of the employee's negligence. Thus, if an employee is engaged in trucking merchandise for an employer and through negligence in driving injuries a pedestrian, it appears more socially desirable for the employer, although faultless itself, to bear the loss than the individual harmed. Insurance is readily available for the employer so that the risk may be distributed among many like insureds paying premiums and the extra cost of doing business may be reflected in the price of the product.

The principle has been recognized by every state in the enactment of workmen's compensation laws whereby employees may recover compensation for injuries arising out of and in the course of their employment without reference to negligence on the part of employers. The costs to the employers are distributed to the public in the price of the product.

Indeed the concept whereby the enterprise bears the loss caused by it has been recently extended to cover any loss caused by a defect in a manufactured product even without fault of employees or employers. The rule of respondeat superior, however, has not been extended to that length and is limited to requiring an enterprise to bear the loss incurred as a result of the employee's negligence. The acts of the employee need be so connected to his employment as to justify requiring that the employer bear that loss.

Although not usually enunciated as a basis for liability, in essence the enterprise may be regarded as a unit for tort as opposed to contract liability purposes. Employees" acts sufficiently connected with the enterprise are in effect considered as deeds of the enterprise itself. Where through negligence such acts cause injury to others it is appropriate that the enterprise bear the loss incurred.

Consistent with these considerations, it is apparent that no categorical statement can delimit the meaning of "scope of employment" once and for all times. Applicability of respondeat superior will depend primarily on the findings of fact in each case. In this particular case, Clay Fruit's employment contract required that he attend the sales conference. Each employee was left to his own resources for transportation, and many of the agents, including Fruit, chose to drive their own automobiles. By the admission of Equitable's agency manager, the scope of the conference included informal socializing as well as formal meetings. Social contact with the out-of-state guests was encouraged, and there is undisputed evidence that such associations were not limited to the conference headquarters at Land's End. Some agents, including Fruit, gathered with the guests in Homer the evening before the accident, and groups of agents and their wives visited [local bars] on various occasions.

When Fruit left for the Waterfront Bar and Restaurant his principal purpose was to join the out-of-state guests. This testimony of his was further confirmed by the fact that once he discovered that they were not present at the Waterfront he departed immediately. Had he been engaged in a "frolic of his own" it would appear likely that he would have remained there. There was evidence from which the jury would find that he was at least motivated in part by his desire to meet with the out-of-state guests and thus to benefit from their experience so as to improve his abilities as a salesman.

Because we find that fair-minded men in the exercise of reasonable judgment could differ as to whether Fruit's activities in returning from Homer to the convention headquarters were within the scope of his employment, we are not disposed to upset the jury's conclusion that liability for damages may be vicariously imputed to Equitable.

III. EQUITABLE'S DIRECT LIABILITY

In addition to finding that Equitable was liable for the negligence of its employee, the jury by its answers to interrogatories held that Equitable itself was negligent in "its planning and conducting the summer conference, and that such negligence was a proximate cause of the accident."

To reach this conclusion the jury must have believed that the convention involved improper use of intoxicating beverages which proximately caused the collision. We have grave doubts as to whether the record would sustain a finding that the collision was due to intoxication. Although Fruit had apparently been drinking heavily prior to falling asleep[,] the evidence indicates that he went to bed and slept from 4:00 to 10:00 p.m. or later when he was awakened. He had little to drink between then and the time of the accident, approximately 2:00 a.m. . . . He walked to and from the Salty Dawg (one-half mile from Land's End) and appeared fresh and not to be intoxicated.

There is no indication that Fruit's presence on the highway was the direct result of affirmative action by Equitable placing him there or ordering him to undertake the fateful trip. Equitable may have created the environment in which one so inclined might behave as Fruit did, but we cannot go so far as to hold, as a matter of law, that the necessary degree of causation exists for direct negligence.

Even with the evidence viewed most favorably to the plaintiff, we find that it was insufficient to present a jury question on Equitable's direct liability.

[The] judgment below is affirmed.

WONG-LEONG v. HAWAIIAN
INDEPENDENT REFINERY, INC.
879 P.2d 538 (Haw. 1994)

KLEIN, J.

[On] June 11, 1989, Rellamas crashed into a vehicle carrying Christopher Chong, Elizabeth Lacaran, and Shasadee Lacaran-Chong. All four were killed in the two-car accident. The medical examiner determined that alcohol and marijuana consumed by Rellamas were contributing factors to the fatal accident.

Rellamas was employed by HIRI at its Campbell Industrial Park refinery. He was returning home after drinking beer at a party celebrating his recent promotion. The party consisted of about nine co-workers and was held at the picnic area on HIRI's premises. [I]n keeping with an apparent tradition of celebrating promotions at HIRI, Rellamas provided money and had a co-worker purchase beer for the party. The party started at about 6:00 p.m. and continued until about 7:30 p.m., when the evening shift supervisor directed the workers to leave the premises. Rellamas was on his way home from the party when the accident occurred at about 8:30 p.m. He did not make any stops between leaving work and the accident.

The affidavits and depositions before the court on HIRI's motion for summary judgment reveal the following facts: The consumption of beer at HIRI was extensive, taking place nearly every day. Specifically, three main events involving alcoholic consumption regularly occurred at the refinery: 1) pau hana (end-of-work) parties on the last Friday of every month; 2) playing horseshoes almost daily; and 3) "mini" parties for promotions, birthdays, babies, vacations, and other similar events. All of these events took place in the picnic area on HIRI's property, next to the parking lot but outside the fence enclosing the refinery's operations. HIRI placed picnic tables and a grill in the area. There was also an eighteen cubic foot "cooler" constructed by HIRI's maintenance department for the drinks.

[The] tradition of holding pau hana parties began sometime around late 1974. [HIRI] sponsored these parties, paying for the food and alcohol. . . . These parties continued as a regular event until after the Rellamas accident. . . . Parties are also held regularly for promotions, birthdays, and other events. These parties were not as extensive as the pau hana parties and were not paid for by the company or contractors. At promotion parties, the promoted workers provide the beer, much like Rellamas had done for his promotion party.

The horseshoe club gatherings consisted of various HIRI employees who got together after their shifts to throw horseshoes and drink beer. The club met practically every day. At most, if not all of these gatherings, the drinks were stored in the cooler provided by HIRI.

Deposition testimony revealed that the company and its managers obviously knew about the different parties and drinking get-togethers. In fact, supervisors often attended these parties. Kennard Vandergrift, the Refinery Administrative Manager, testified that around 1985 HIRI instituted a policy prohibiting consumption of alcoholic beverages in the refinery at any time. Vandergrift also noted, however, that this policy only governed the area inside the fenced-in portion of HIRI's property; consumption of alcohol was not prohibited in HIRI's picnic and parking lot area. After further questioning, Vandergrift admitted that "the company tolerated [the drinking, but] certainly didn't encourage it in any way."

Furthermore, Shift Supervisor Don Drogowski testified that a petition was circulated about a year before the accident requesting that the "current practice, which allows employees to consume alcohol during lunch or break hours [be] reviewed by the policy task force and discontinued due to its safety sensitive nature." [E]ighty-five employees signed this petition. Another company policy provided that no one could remain in the picnic area after 5:30 p.m. This policy was apparently not strictly enforced; on the night of the Rellamas accident, the group was in the picnic area drinking until after 7:30 p.m. In fact, the promotion party did not begin until after 5:30 p.m.

Finally, after the Rellamas accident, management discussed terminating the pau hana parties. Aldrich Kane, HIRI's Maintenance Manager, testified that alcohol was no longer served at the pau hana parties after the Rellamas accident, and that the parties themselves were discontinued about three to five months after the subject accident. . . .

Under the theory of respondeat superior, an employer may be liable for the negligent acts of its employees that occur within the scope of their employment. *Henderson v. Professional Coatings Corp.*, 72 Haw. 387, 391-92, 819 P.2d 84, 88 (1991). In *Henderson*, we cited the RESTATEMENT (SECOND) OF AGENCY § 228 (1958), for the definition of "scope of employment" . . . . [T]o recover under the respondeat superior theory, a plaintiff must establish: 1) a negligent act of the employee, in other words, breach of a duty that is the legal cause of plaintiff's injury; and 2) that the negligent act was within the employee's scope of employment.

The analysis of negligence under the theory of respondeat superior should focus completely on the actions of the employee, without consideration of the acts of the employer. A plaintiff need not show any act or fault of the employer when defining the allegedly negligent act in a respondeat superior claim.

[In] *Costa v. Able Distributors, Inc.*, 3 Haw. App. 486, 653 P.2d 101 (1982)[,] the court affirmed summary judgment in favor of the employer. [The] record indicated that the alcoholic consumption took place at a purely social event after work hours, with no evidence of any connection to the employer. [*Costa* does] not preclude an assertion of negligence prior to the actual accident. For reasons set forth below, we hold that a respondeat superior claim may be predicated upon the actor's allegedly negligent act of drinking while aware of the need to drive, provided that the act takes place within the scope of employment. Thus, respondeat superior liability may be imposed notwithstanding the fact that the foreseeable effects of the actor's negligent conduct occur outside the scope of employment. . . .

Arguably, Rellamas' act of drinking while aware of the need to drive home thereafter can be viewed as a negligent act that was a legal cause of the particular accident before us. . . . Rellamas was aware he had to drive home and yet, by becoming intoxicated, he impaired his ability to drive. Consequently, Rellamas' self-intoxication may have breached the general duty of due care he owed innocent members of the public and created a foreseeable risk of harm to them. Whether or not Rellamas breached this duty presents a question of fact for the jury.

There is sufficient evidence in the record to support a jury finding that Rellamas breached his duty of due care owed to the public based on the autopsy report, which indicates that Rellamas' blood alcohol content was .08 percent. Furthermore, testimony that Rellamas consumed two to three beers at the party, and a reasonable inference that he consumed marijuana at HIRI that day, provide additional support for a finding of negligence.

The second requirement for recovery under the doctrine of respondeat superior is that the employee's negligent act must have been "within the scope of the employment." Whether an employee is acting within the scope of his or her employment is ordinarily a question of fact to be determined in light of the evidence of the particular case.

In determining the scope of employment, the applicable test is whether the employee's conduct was related to the employment enterprise or if the enterprise derived any benefit from the activity. More specifically[,] two key factors must be considered: 1) whether "the enterprise of the employer would have benefitted by the context of the act of the employee but for the unfortunate injury"; and 2) "whether the employer's risks are incident to [the] enterprise." *Henderson*, 72 Haw. at 395, 819 P.2d at 89. Liability under the respondeat superior theory, however, does not require fault or knowledge on the part of the employer. . . .

Although the party in the instant case took place after work hours, the record reveals that it was held on HIRI's premises immediately thereafter. . . . Considering the facts in a light most favorable to Appellants, a reasonable trier of fact could infer that the promotion party was a custom incidental to the enterprise rather than a purely social function. Arguably, the party may have been "actuated, in part, by a purpose to serve" HIRI, or at least "was of some direct benefit" to HIRI. . . . HIRI's Maintenance Manager, Aldrich Kane, testified that the tradition of parties began shortly after his predecessor went "to the company asking for this pau hana thing as a morale builder for the employees." Shift Supervisor Joseph Drogowski testified that the horseshoe games and pau hana parties were not intended as family gatherings but were "for employees." He acknowledged further that these parties were "more for company purposes."

In his deposition, Kane noted that pau hana party attendance decreased significantly in the three-to-five months following Rellamas' accident. Alcohol was no longer served at the parties after the accident. Kane's testimony supports a reasonable inference that the presence of alcohol was a crucial ingredient of these parties, which were designed to boost employee morale and foster good will. According to Kane, during the many years of alcohol consumption at the pau hana parties, the horseshoe club gatherings, and the promotion parties, the HIRI administration discussed the propriety of these activities and possible efforts to control them, but "they never said stop it."

Drogowski testified that pau hana party attendance had already "died out substantially" (down from sixty or seventy people to just the contractors, who provided the beer, and a few HIRI employees) at least six months before the accident. . . . Drogowski also testified, however, that supervisors continued to get together with their crews to celebrate birthdays, promotions, and other events.

Based on this testimony, viewed in a light most favorable to Appellants, a reasonable trier of fact could find that HIRI benefitted either directly or indirectly from the promotion party. . . . A reasonable trier of fact could find a sufficient nexus in the instant circumstances between the employee's negligent act (drinking while aware of the need to drive) and the employer's interest (fostering employee good will). The record provides support for a finding that there was a history and tradition of drinking activities in HIRI's picnic area, and that this practice benefitted the enterprise. The trier of fact could reasonably find that Rellamas was acting within the scope of his employment when he negligently drank alcohol at this party; therefore, HIRI could be held vicariously liable for Rellamas' negligent act. . . .

Appellants raise an alternative argument that, even if Rellamas was not acting within the scope of his employment, HIRI may be held directly liable for failing to control Rellamas while he was on company premises. [After reviewing Hawaii case law in regard to the applicability of the RESTATEMENT (SECOND) OF TORTS § 317 standards for imposing direct liability against an employer for negligent failure to control an employee, the court concluded that there was no factual basis upon which a reasonable trier of fact could find that the defendant employer either knew or had reason to know of the need for and the opportunity to exercise control over its employee.]

HIRI cannot be held liable for its alleged independent negligence as a social host under our decision in KFC. Appellants have, however, presented a colorable claim of liability under the theory of respondeat superior because the pleadings, affidavits, and depositions filed by Appellants raise genuine issues of material fact. On remand, two questions related to Appellants' respondeat superior claim are presented for the jury's consideration. The first is whether Rellamas acted negligently by drinking while aware that he had to drive (including whether that act proximately caused the deaths of Christopher, Elizabeth and Shasadee). The second is whether the act of drinking at his promotion party was within the scope of Rellamas' employment, in other words, whether the party furthered a business purpose sufficient to impose respondeat superior liability. Of course, the issue of causation with respect to the accident is also a jury question. Finally, Appellants have also presented a viable claim for negligent failure to control an employee under Restatement § 317.

We affirm the lower court's decision in part, reverse in part, and remand for proceedings consistent with this opinion.

NOTES

1. *Fruit* is a typical example of traditional *respondeat superior* analysis imposing liability against an employer for the negligence of its employee. The opinion contains an excellent discussion of the historically varied legal justifications for the doctrine under English common law, tracing its historical development from the earliest cases through modern times. As pointed out in *Fruit*, the most commonly asserted reasons for continuing to apply the doctrine of *respondeat superior* are based upon either the "control" theory or the "enterprise" theory. Which of these two very different analytical approaches does the court in *Fruit* apply? Would the outcome in *Fruit* have been the same if the court had utilized the other approach?

2. *Wong-Leong* represents an entirely different analytical approach to a factually similar situation. Precisely how does the Hawaii court's legal analysis differ from that utilized by the Alaska court in *Fruit*? Does the decision in *Wong-Leong* apply the same legal justification (*i.e.*, a "control" theory or an "enterprise" theory) as that in *Fruit*? What were the specific negligent acts allegedly committed by the respective employees in *Fruit* and in *Wong-Leong*? Was the consumption of alcohol by the employees at social events, allegedly sanctioned by their employers in these two respective cases, a dispositive factor in either case? What real difference does any of this make in the first place, since the outcomes in both cases were the same?

3. In *Belanger v. Village Pub I, Inc.*, 603 A.2d 1173 (Conn. App. Ct. 1992), the plaintiff's decedent was killed when his vehicle was struck by another vehicle being operated by a heavily-intoxicated driver who had just consumed excessive amounts of alcohol served by the defendant café owner's employee. Upholding a jury verdict against the defendant café owner on the basis of *respondeat superior* for the negligence of the defendant's bartender who had continued to serve an obviously intoxicated patron, even though contrary to the defendant's express orders, the court explained that:

> [I]t has long been recognized that "[a] master is liable for the willful torts of his servant committed within the scope of the servant's employment and in furtherance of his master's business." *Pelletier v. Bilbiles*, 154 Conn. 544, 547, 227 A.2d 251 (1967). "The doctrine of *respondeat superior* focuses on the employee's conduct rather than on the employer's knowledge or approval of the acts. If the employee acted with apparent

authority in furtherance of employer business, the employer's consent or ratification of the misconduct is irrelevant . . . even an innocent employer must compensate an injured party." *Paine Webber Jackson & Curtis, Inc. v. Winters*, 22 Conn. App. 640, 646, 579 A.2d 545, *cert. denied*, 216 Conn. 820, 581 A.2d 1055 (1990). The doctrine of *respondeat superior*, which makes the employer liable for actions by an employee, is based on public policy considerations that the employer "shall be held responsible for the acts of those whom he employs, done in and about his business, *even though such acts are directly in conflict with the orders which he has given on the* subject." . . . § 603A.2d at 1179.

What was the legal justification for the court's imposition of *respondeat superior* liability against the employer in *Belanger*? Was it based upon an "enterprise" theory or a "control" theory?

4. In both the *Fruit* and *Wong-Leong* opinions, in addition to the plaintiffs' claims asserting indirect liability pursuant to the doctrine of *respondeat superior*, the courts also addressed the defendants' direct liability for negligence. This was based upon separate allegations by the respective plaintiffs that the defendant employers in both cases had been negligent in hiring, supervising, or otherwise controlling the after-work activities of their employees with respect to certain employer-sanctioned (or permitted) events. In both cases the courts concluded that there was no evidence upon which any such negligence could be imposed *directly* against the respective employers. Why did the plaintiffs in these cases even bother to pursue claims asserting direct liability for negligence against their respective employers? Assuming that the plaintiffs were confident in establishing their claims based upon vicarious liability against the respective defendant employers, what, if any, possible benefit would there be in also establishing these separate claims based upon the defendant employers' *direct* negligence? Can the plaintiffs recover their damages twice, once under each separate theory of recovery? What other practical advantage(s) might there be?

PROBLEM

Acme Trucking needed to hire a new driver. After interviewing three applicants for the position, Acme hired Tom, the least qualified for the position, because he was willing to work for less money than the other applicants. On Tom's very first day at work, one of Acme's regular drivers called in sick, so Acme's dispatcher assigned Tom to take his place, despite the fact that Tom had not received safety training as mandated by Acme's own rules for all new drivers. Tom started off on his first delivery, but soon he began to realize that Acme's large delivery truck was more difficult to maneuver in traffic than anything he had ever driven before. As he approached a busy intersection, the traffic light changed. He tried to stop, but he became flustered, stepping on the accelerator instead of the brake pedal. His truck slammed into a car driven by

Wilma as she proceeded lawfully into the intersection. If Wilma wishes to sue Acme Trucking to recover damages for her injuries caused by Tom's negligence in driving its truck, should she allege that Acme is vicariously liable for Tom's negligent driving, or should she sue Acme directly for its own negligence? Does it make any difference under these facts? Explain.

B. EMPLOYER-EMPLOYEE RELATIONSHIP

1. Who is an "Employee"?

In the majority of situations involving the doctrine of *respondeat superior* in work-related environments, the success or failure of plaintiff's claim depends upon the resolution of two basic questions. First, was the person who caused the plaintiff's injury properly classified as an "employee"? Only if an employer-employee relationship exists between the defendant and the tortfeasor does the analysis proceed to the second question: whether the employee was acting within the "scope of employment" at the time of the injury-causing event. If the tortfeasor is not found to be an "employee," he or she will likely be classified as an "independent contractor" and held accountable in a purely individual capacity, subject to the various limitations discussed in Section C, *infra*. Although many *respondeat superior* cases seem to focus almost entirely on the second of these questions (*i.e.*, whether the tortfeasor was acting within the "scope of employment" at the time of the injury-causing accident), if the requisite employer-employee relationship is not first established there can be no vicarious liability against the employer. In this section, we examine both of these important questions.

BUITRAGO v. ROHR
672 So. 2d 646 (Fla. Dist. Ct. App. 1996)

KLEIN, J.

[Chuck] Rohr caused a death and two severe injuries in an automobile accident. Rohr owns a company named Canary Enterprises, Inc., which is in the business of using hot air and cold air balloons to advertise other people's businesses.

Rohr [had] entered into an agreement with the owner of some Blockbuster franchises, Donovan Entertainment, for advertising with balloons during the weekend of a springtime festival in Tallahassee. Donovan agreed to pay Rohr $1,500 to cover everything.

Rohr participated in a hot air balloon ride in the festival on Saturday; installed a cold air balloon displaying Blockbuster's name over a Blockbuster store; and later that day installed the cold air balloon to be displayed at a college baseball game at the request of a Donovan employee. Following the game,

Rohr took the balloon down and drove back to his motel. As he was turning into the parking lot, he pulled into the path of an oncoming vehicle causing the accident.

In this suit, plaintiffs named Donovan Entertainment as a defendant on the theory that Rohr was acting as Donovan's agent at the time of the accident. The trial court granted Donovan's motion for summary judgment because Rohr was an independent contractor, and plaintiffs appeal.

In *Cantor v. Cochran*, 184 So. 2d 173 (Fla. 1966), the court adopted the 10-factor test contained in section 220 of the RESTATEMENT (2D) OF AGENCY, for determining whether a party is an independent contractor or an employee:

(a) the extent of control which, by the agreement, the master may exercise over the details of the work;

(b) whether or not the one employed is engaged in a distinct occupation or business;

(c) the kind of occupation, with reference to whether, in the locality, the work is usually done under the direction of the employer or by a specialist without supervision;

(d) the skill required in the particular occupation;

(e) whether the employer or the workman supplies the instrumentalities, tools, and the place of work for the person doing the work;

(f) the length of time for which the person is employed;

(g) the method of payment, whether by the time or by the job;

(h) whether the work is part of the regular business of the employer;

(i) whether or not the parties believe they are creating the relation of master and servant; and

(j) whether the principal is or is not in business.

The first factor, the extent of control over the details of the work, is the most significant. In the present case, the only control exercised by Donovan over Rohr was to tell him where the cold air balloons should be displayed and approximately when. The amount of control over the details of the work in the present case is less than the amount of control the furniture company had over the carpet installer in *Kane*, in which the second district [held] that the trial court should have granted the furniture store's motion for summary judgment.

The second factor, whether the businesses are distinct, also favors Donovan. Rohr's company was incorporated, had its own employees, had numerous other clients besides Donovan, and was engaged in a business which was entirely different from Donovan's business. Nor do any of the other factors assist plaintiffs.
. . .

A movant for summary judgment has the initial burden of demonstrating the nonexistence of any genuine issue of material fact. But once he tenders competent evidence to support his motion, the opposing party must come forward with counter-evidence sufficient to reveal a genuine issue. It is not enough for the opposing party merely to assert that an issue does exist.

The granting of Donovan's motion for summary judgment here not only saved Donovan the expense of going through a trial when it had no legal exposure, but also eliminated an unnecessary issue, agency, from the trial, and left the parties remaining in the case with a more accurate picture of financial responsibility which should facilitate settlement.

Affirmed.

NOTES

1. In *Keitz v. National Paving and Contracting Co.*, 134 A.2d 296, 301 (Md. 1957), the Maryland Court of Appeals set forth the following factors to be considered in determining the existence of an employer-employee relationship: (1) the selection and engagement of the employee; (2) the payment of wages; (3) the power to discharge; (4) the power to control the employee's conduct; and (5) whether the work is part of the regular business of the employer. Of these five factors, the court emphasized that the employer's right to control and direct the employee in the performance of his or her work was the most significant.

2. Also of interest in *Buitrago* is the manner by which the court procedurally disposed of the plaintiff's claim against the defendant employer. What reasons does the court give for granting a summary judgment in this case? Do they seem proper under these circumstances? Who should make the determination as to whether the tortfeasor in any given circumstance should be classified as an "employee" or an "independent contractor?"

ERMERT v. HARTFORD INSURANCE CO.
559 So. 2d 467 (La. 1990)

DENNIS, J.

[Plaintiff,] Karl F. Ermert III, was accidentally shot in the foot by Kenneth Decareaux while a guest at a hunting camp. The hunting camp was located on Bayou Bienvenue near Lake Borgne in the marshlands of St. Bernard Parish. It was built in 1975 on property leased from the owner by the defendant Russell Larrieu. Larrieu, Decareaux, Alkaney Cummings, Leon Brumfield, Joseph Caillouette and Robert Bourcq, all long-time friends or acquaintances, constructed the camp building. They had been involved in groups that had hunted together at two other camps, the first of which was destroyed [and] the second of which burned down. Only Larrieu contributed money toward the construction of the new camp. The rest of the men contributed various materials, furniture and/or labor. In a transaction separate from the ground lease, Larrieu negotiated an oral lease to hunt ducks on ponds owned by one Dubuchel. Each man paid approximately $52 per year to cover the annual $120 rental for the ponds, as well as supplies for weekends when the group hunted together. Larrieu held the remainder of the funds, and he used these funds for necessities such as butane, utensils, and pots and pans. The cost of groceries was divided equally. The other hunters always sought Larrieu's permission before visiting or bringing guests to the camp as they all considered Larrieu to be its owner; however, he did not deny permission so guests were there fairly frequently.

The group had no written constitution, by-laws or rules. Some basic written safety rules and regulations had been formulated for the earlier camps at monthly meetings held in the 1960s, but these rules were no longer followed by the new group. Although no one voted to abolish these rules, indeed no one voted on anything, the rules "went out of the window" because the group of hunters were friends and got along well together. There were no formal meetings. The men had informal discussions and were generally in agreement about hunting safety matters. The only "rules" the camp had regarding hunting safety were simply common sense guidelines to which all hunters, whether experienced or not, should adhere. Among the guidelines adhered to by the group was the rule that guns should always be empty while in the camp, loaded only while in the duck blinds, and unloaded prior to leaving the blinds for the camp. The men had also decided that they would attempt to tame wild animals near the camp, so they agreed not to shoot at animals near the camp.

Besides being a member of the hunting group, Decareaux was president of and majority stockholder in Nu-Arrow Fence Company. He allowed Larrieu to purchase materials for the construction of the camp at cost through Nu-Arrow's account and then reimburse Nu-Arrow, and he also donated scrap lumber from old fences to Larrieu for use at the camp. In addition, he used Nu-Arrow equipment to help with the camp's construction, and he often transported materials to the camp in Nu-Arrow trucks without compensation.

As the president of Nu-Arrow, Decareaux was expected to seize any opportunity to further the business regardless of time and place. Accordingly, once the camp was built, Decareaux used it to entertain his employees and to promote his business. He invited all of the Nu-Arrow employees to the camp either at the same time or a few at a time. Decareaux paid for their expenses out of the Nu-Arrow petty cash fund. He invited the company-sponsored softball team to the camp as well, because several employees were on the team. Decareaux also took advantage of the camp to develop customers and make sales. He had sold fences to the majority of his fellow hunters, and he derived other business through references given by the regular members of the hunting group. He invited people who had purchased fences from Nu-Arrow to the camp, and these customers also referred business to Nu-Arrow. [S]ome of the guests were invited because they were relatives or friends, but the relatives were employees and the friends were customers. Thus Nu-Arrow both derived economic benefit and provided economic assistance to the hunting camp.

At the time of the accident, plaintiff Ermert was spending the weekend as a guest of Russell Larrieu at the hunting camp. Ermert, Larrieu, Brumfield, Caillouette, Bourcq and Decareaux were at the hunting camp to build duck blinds for the upcoming duck season. . . . Alkaney Cummings [was] not there that weekend. The six men spent Saturday building the duck blinds. Saturday night they all ate, drank a little, talked for a while and went to bed.

[On] Sunday morning, someone told Decareaux that there was a nutria swimming across the canal. . . . Decareaux picked up a shotgun and some shells. In violation of the general agreement among the group, he began loading the shells into the shotgun as he was walking in the camphouse. The gun accidentally fired and struck Ermert's foot, severely injuring it. He was rushed to a hospital, where several surgeries were performed. As a result of this injury, Ermert, a welder, is permanently disabled. . . .

[The trial] judge found that the hunters constituted a "somewhat loose unincorporated association," but they were not a partnership because they were not organized for profit. [H]e concluded that there was no vicarious liability arising solely out of membership in such an organization. He applied "general agency principles" and concluded that the club members were not vicariously liable [because Decareaux's] tort because his actions were in direct contravention of the group's established policy. He also found that they had no duty to supervise the safety practices of Decareaux. . . . Finally, he stated that La. R.S. 9:2791, which grants tort immunity to landowners who open their land to the public for recreational purposes, further precluded any imposition of liability upon the hunting group. The trial court also held that Nu-Arrow, defendant's employer, benefited from the camp's existence and was therefore liable for its president's negligence while working at the camp, because Decareaux was within the scope of his employment at the time of the accident. The court entered judgment against Decareaux and Nu-Arrow for damages in the amount of $595,000. . . . The court of appeal [concluded] that on the weekend of the accident Decareaux was engaged in a purely personal recreational pursuit. The court reasoned that the risk of Decareaux shooting someone during such activity was not fairly attributable to Nu-Arrow. . . . [Due] to the novel legal issues raised, we granted the writs and consolidated the applications.

The issues of primary responsibility are easily resolved. Without a doubt Decareaux was guilty of negligent acts that caused severe injuries to the plaintiff, Ermert; the lower courts' findings that Decareaux was negligent are not challenged here. Decareaux and his homeowner's insurer are solidarily liable for those damages. On the other hand, the remaining members of the hunting group clearly were not guilty of any separate or joint negligence, imprudence or want of skill that caused the accident. . . . Due to the speed with which he grabbed, loaded, and accidentally fired the shotgun, none of the other members of the hunting party had a realistic opportunity to admonish or restrain

Decareaux. As a coequal member of the group, Decareaux was not the charge of anyone. He was an experienced hunter who apparently had not been known to act carelessly before. He was well aware of the group's firmly established, though unwritten, rules against loading guns in the camphouse and shooting animals near the building, but he ignored these prohibitions. Under these circumstances, none of the members of group could have anticipated or taken precautions against Decareaux's careless action. The evidence is also clear that none of the other hunters caused, assisted or encouraged Decareaux's negligent act of loading the shotgun inside the camphouse as he moved quickly toward the door. Although Caillouette approved the general idea of cooking a nutria, he did so while in the outhouse, and he was not in a position to either approve or influence the negligent method chosen by Decareaux to accomplish that end. Accordingly, Larrieu, Cummings, Brumfield, Caillouette and Bourcq cannot be held primarily liable for the injuries to Ermert. . . .

The second issue of vicarious liability concerns that of Decareaux's employer, Nu-Arrow. . . . Decareaux was not a rank and file employee but the founder, majority stockholder (60%), president and chief executive officer and primary business generator of a closely-held corporate business. . . . [W]e find that the court of appeal erred in reversing as to Nu-Arrow, because the trial court's conclusion that Decareaux was within the scope of his employment was not clearly wrong.

Masters and employers are answerable for the damage caused by their servants in the exercise of the functions in which they are employed. Both the civilian master-servant doctrine and its common law counterpart, vicarious or imputed liability or respondeat superior, are based on Roman law. . . . A servant is a person employed to perform services in the affairs of another and who with respect to the physical conduct in the performance of the services is subject to the other's control or right to control. RESTATEMENT (2D) OF AGENCY § 220(1) (1958). The word "servant" does not exclusively denote a person rendering manual labor; rather, it includes anyone who performs continuous service for another and whose physical movements are subject to the control or right to control of the other as to the manner of performing the service. Thus, ship captains and managers of great corporations are considered servants, albeit superior servants, differing only in the dignity and importance of their positions from those working under them. While the rules for determining liability of the employer for the conduct of both superior servants and the humblest employees are the same, the application of these rules may differ due to the dissimilarity of their duties and responsibilities. RESTATEMENT (2D) OF AGENCY § 220 comment (a).

The master's vicarious liability for the acts of its servant rests not so much on policy grounds consistent with the governing principles of tort law as in a deeply rooted sentiment that a business enterprise cannot justly disclaim responsibility for accidents which may fairly be said to be characteristic of its activities. In determining whether a particular accident may be associated with the employer's business enterprise, courts often attempt to determine whether, considering the authority given to the employee, the employee's tortious conduct was reasonably foreseeable. What is considered reasonably foreseeable in this context, however, is quite different from the "foreseeably unreasonable risk of harm" that spells negligence. Rather than looking for risks that can and should be avoided, as is the case with negligence, the court must essentially decide whether the particular accident is a part of "the more or less inevitable toll of a lawful enterprise." 5 F. HARPER, F. JAMES & O. GRAY, [THE LAW OF TORTS], § 26.7, at 28. The foresight that should impel the prudent man to take precautions is not the same measure as that by which he should perceive the harm likely to flow from his commercial activity in spite of all reasonable precautions on his own part. If the particular harm was reasonably foreseeable and the employer failed to take proper precautions to prevent it, he could be primarily liable for his own fault rather than secondarily liable for the fault of his employee. When considering which risks the employer must bear under vicarious liability, however, the proper test bears more resemblance to that which limits liability for workers' compensation than to the test for negligence, because the employer should be held to anticipate and allow for risks to the public that "arise out of and in the course of" his employment of labor.

Because vicarious liability is imposed based upon the attribution of business-related risks to the enterprise, specific conduct may be considered within the scope of employment even though it is done in part to serve the purposes of the servant or of a third person. The fact that the predominant motive of the servant is to benefit himself or a third person does not prevent the act from being within the scope of employment. *Miller v. Keating*, 349 So. 2d 265, 269 (La. 1977); RESTATEMENT (2D) OF AGENCY § 236. If the purpose of serving the master's business actuates the servant to any appreciable extent, the master is subject to liability if the act is otherwise within the service. So also, the act may be found to be in the service if not only the manner of acting but the act itself is done largely for the servant's purposes. RESTATEMENT (2D) OF AGENCY § 236 comment (b).

The scope of risks attributable to an employer increases with the amount of authority and freedom of action granted to the servant in performing his assigned tasks. This is the logical extrapolation of a rule that fixes liability based upon the course of employment: The greater potential course of employment expands the servant's potential opportunities to commit torts. These opportunities are maximized where the servant effectively determines the course of his own employment, as is the case when the servant is actually the owner of the enterprise. One of the advantages of creating a separate entity for the operation of the enterprise is that the business enterprise is not liable for all of the torts of its owner. Nevertheless, because of both the business owner's inherent incentives to pursue company interests whenever possible and the fact that the "servant" often controls the "master" rather than vice-versa, the line between "business" and "personal" activity is often a hazy one. . . .

In contrast [to] intentional tort cases, in which it must be determined whether the tortious act itself was within the scope of the servant's employment, the court in a negligence case need only determine whether the servant's general activities at the time of the tort were within the scope of his employment. Considering these principles of master-servant liability, we cannot say that the trial court was clearly wrong in determining that Decareaux was acting within the scope of his employment while he was at the camp. While Decareaux used the camp partially for his own personal enjoyment and recreation, the record also indicates that he repeatedly and consistently used it for business purposes. Developing new business was a major part of Decareaux's employment with Nu-Arrow. Decareaux testified that he had sold fences to almost every other member of the camp, and that the other members had all referred business to him. He had also taken a number of his preferred customers to the camp for entertainment, and these customers had likewise referred business to Nu-Arrow. Another important aspect of Decareaux's duties was dealing with employees. He testified that he had taken his employees to the camp on several occasions for picnics or entertainment, and he had also hosted his company-sponsored softball team at the camp. Considering this evidence, the finder of fact could reasonably conclude that one of Decareaux's motives for participating in the camp was to provide a place to entertain both customers and employees of Nu-Arrow.

Risks associated with waterfowling are not normally characteristic of the activities of fence companies, of course, but the trial court found that Nu-Arrow had made these risks a part of its business by having Decareaux promote and engage in the activities of the hunting camp in order to obtain direct and referral fence sales. Nor can we say that the trial court erred manifestly in finding that Decareaux was engaged in this facet of his company's business at the time of the accident and that the particular risk which led to the plaintiff's injury was reasonably foreseeable within the context of respondeat superior or master-servant vicarious liability. On the weekend of the accident, Decareaux had gone to the camp to help prepare the hunting blinds for the upcoming season and to fraternize with his hunting companions. We may assume that a major or even a predominant motive for Decareaux's presence was to benefit himself recreationally, but the evidence also supports a finding that the purpose of serving his business actuated him to an appreciable extent. His hunting companions were also his company's customers and referrers of business, and he had to join in preparing the duck blinds to continue to reap the potential benefits of entertaining his company's customers, referrers and employees at the camp during the coming duck season.

It is immaterial that Decareaux's precise action in loading a shotgun while bolting toward the camphouse door was not to be foreseen and was in violation of the usages of his group. In determining vicarious liability, the focus is on the employee's general activities at the time of the accident rather than on the specific tortious act, and the fact that an act is forbidden or is done in a forbidden manner does not remove that act from the scope of employment. RESTATEMENT

(2D) OF AGENCY § 230. The risk that duck hunters might cause damage to companions by mishandling shotguns is enough to make it fair that the loss be borne by the enterprise that made waterfowling activities a part of its business by having its chief executive officer foster and participate in the hunting group for profit. Consequently, the trial court's determination that Decareaux was acting in the scope of his employment when he accidentally injured Ermert was not manifestly erroneous or clearly wrong.

For the reasons set forth above, the decision of the court of appeal is reversed and the judgment of the trial court is reinstated.

REVERSED; TRIAL COURT JUDGMENT REINSTATED.

MARCUS, J. (concurring in part and dissenting in part).

[I] do not consider that the negligent hunter's conduct at the time of the accident was within the scope of his employment. . . .

NOTES

1. In *Ermert*, the employee was not a typical "employee." Instead, he was an *executive* employee. Do the same policy considerations apply with respect to the imposition of vicarious liability against employers regarding the tortious conduct of executive employees as distinguished from more "ordinary" employees? Should they? What other considerations might suggest a different approach to the problem of vicarious liability for the torts of executive employees? How would the courts go about distinguishing between which employees are "executive" employees and which are not for purposes of applying *respondeat superior*?

2. In *Ermert*, the plaintiff filed suit directly against the company that provided liability insurance coverage for the defendants. Upon what legal basis can any tort liability be imposed against the defendants' insurance company? Is this also a form of vicarious liability?

3. Louisiana is somewhat unique among most jurisdictions in that where the defendant has liability insurance coverage with respect to certain types of conduct alleged to have been tortious, the plaintiff is permitted to file the lawsuit directly against the defendant's insurance carrier. What advantages does such a statute provide to either the individual litigants or to the legal system in general? Are there any disadvantages? Why don't more jurisdictions permit suits to be filed directly against defendants' liability insurance carriers?

4. The RESTATEMENT (SECOND) OF AGENCY, § 227 (1958), recognizes a corollary doctrine called the "loaned servant" or "borrowed servant" doctrine. That section provides that a "servant directed or permitted by his master to perform services for another may become the servant of such other in performing the services. He may become the other's servant as to some acts and not as to others." The determination of whether an employer-employee relationship exists in the con-

text of a borrowed servant situation turns on the same factors as determine the existence of any employment relationship. *See* RESTATEMENT (SECOND) OF AGENCY, § 220 (1958); Jones v. Halvorsen-Berg, 847 P.2d 945 (Wash. App. 1993).

PROBLEM

Henry was the President and Chief Executive Officer of MegaCorp, Inc., a large, multi-national corporation. As part of his official duties, Henry was expected to be "available" to MegaCorp on a "24-7" basis (*i.e.*, 24 hours a day, 7 days a week) as needed. Henry received a six-figure salary as compensation, together with various "fringe" benefits that included stock options in Mega-Corp, Inc. and a profit-sharing arrangement. Additional "fringe" compensations included a brand new luxury automobile of his choice each year, and a pre-paid membership in Country Club, an exclusive private golf and tennis club. One day, while entertaining a group of visiting Japanese business delegates from a company interested in investing in MegaCorp's latest business venture, Henry became visibly intoxicated at Country Club's bar. Insisting on demonstrating his prowess and skill at golf to the visitors, Henry proceeded to the nearby golf course where he grabbed a golf club and swung it clumsily. As he did so, the club flew out of his hands, striking and injuring Marla just as she walked out of Country Club's lounge. Is MegaCorp vicariously liable under principles of *respondeat superior* for Marla's injuries?

2. Was the Employee Acting Within the "Scope of Employment"?

Even if an employer-employee relationship is found to exist between the tortfeasor and the party against whom vicarious liability is sought to be imposed, the employer may escape liability by establishing that the employee was not acting within the "scope of employment." The following materials address this question.

SKINNER v. BRAUM'S ICE CREAM STORE
890 P.2d 922 (Okla. 1995)

KAUGER, V.C.J.:

[A]ppellant, James D. Skinner (Skinner), was injured when his car was rear-ended by the defendant, Donna L. Razvizadeh (Razvizadeh/employee). Razvizadeh was employed by the appellee, Braum's Ice Cream Store (Braums/employer) at the Braums store located on North Western in Oklahoma City. When the accident occurred, Razvizadeh was en route to a Braums store on Rockwell. [She was] called at home and asked to pick up supplies from Braums Rockwell store on her way to her regular work station. . . . Razavizadeh's supervisor [testified] that she did not remember calling the employee to ask her to pick up supplies. [Skinner] filed suit alleging that the employee was acting within the scope of her employment at the time of the collision. . . . Braums [disputed] the employment issue, and mov[ed] for summary judgment on the employment claim. The trial judge sustained the Braums motion and awarded costs. . . . [The] Court of Appeals affirmed. It held that because the employee had not arrived at her assigned work place when the accident occurred, she was not acting within the scope of employment. We granted certiorari . . . to consider whether an employee, instructed to complete a task by an employer while traveling to work, is acting within the scope of employment during the commute. . . .

Skinner and the employer recognize the general rule that an employee, going to or coming from work, is not considered to be within the scope of employment. However, Skinner insists that Braums' direction to Razavizadeh to pick up supplies on her way to work is an exception to the "going and coming rule." Braums argues that because the employee's conduct had been of no benefit to it when the accident occurred, Razavizadeh was outside the scope of employment. We disagree.

This Court has recognized exceptions to the "going and coming rule." Liability is imposed upon the employer if the employee is rendering a service, either express or implied, to the employer with his/her consent. An exception also exists if the trip involves an incidental benefit to the employer not common to ordinary commuting trips of the work force.

Because the facts in *Haco Drilling Co v. Burchette*, 364 P.2d 674, 677 (Okla. 1961) are similar to those presented here, it is instructive. In *Haco*, it was the practice for members of a drilling crew to car pool. The person responsible for driving was also to provide water and ice at the drilling site. Early one morning, the employee-driver in *Haco* picked up two co-workers, obtained ice and water, and was on the way to work when an accident occurred. The car being driven was a private one; the wreck happened before the work shift began; and the employee was not being paid at the time of the accident.

We recognized the general rule that the employment relationship does not exist during a commute to and from work in *Haco*. Nevertheless, we held that the driver was acting within the scope of his employment when the accident occurred. The water and ice were necessary to the workforce of the drilling rig. The driver's pick up and delivery of the water was incidental to the business operation.

Braums attempts to distinguish *Haco* on the premise that because the supplies were not delivered, the employee did not confer a benefit on the employer. The distinction is unpersuasive where, as here, Razavizadeh alleges that she was under the express direction of her supervisor to drive to the Rockwell store to obtain and transport supplies to the North Western location. She would not have been in the location of the accident without instructions of her employer.

Presumably, the supplies were to be used for the employer's benefit once they were delivered. . . . [W]e find that an employee, instructed to complete a task by an employer while traveling to work, may be within the scope of employment during the commute. . . .

Summary judgment is proper only when the pleadings, affidavits, depositions, admissions or other evidentiary materials establish that there is no genuine issue as to any material fact, and that the moving party is entitled to judgment as a matter of law. We have determined that an employee, instructed to complete a task by an employer while traveling to work, may be within the scope of employment during the commute. However, the material fact in question is whether Razavizadeh was given instructions to obtain supplies on her way to work. We express no opinion on this issue.

REVERSED AND REMANDED.

COURTLESS v. JOULLIFE
507 S.E.2d 136 (W. Va. 1998)

PER CURIAM:

[On] May 16, 1995, Bobby Courtless, while riding his bicycle, was struck by a vehicle driven by David Clyde Jolliffe. Bobby was rendered permanently disabled due to the injuries sustained in that accident and is now a paraplegic. Mr. Jolliffe was employed by Princess and was en route to work at the time of the accident. While traveling from his home to the Princess mine site, Mr. Jolliffe had stopped to buy shocks for his vehicle.

[Appellants] filed a civil action against both Mr. Jolliffe and Princess, alleging that Princess was liable under the doctrine of respondeat superior. Discovery . . . confirmed that although Mr. Jolliffe owned the vehicle, Princess paid Mr. Jolliffe $400 monthly, the amount of the monthly payment on the truck. Princess also paid maintenance and repair costs on Mr. Jolliffe's truck, and Mr. Jolliffe had free use of gasoline from the Princess gas tanks. In exchange, Mr. Jolliffe used the vehicle at the Princess sites on a daily basis.

[Princess] filed a motion for summary judgment, alleging that Mr. Jolliffe was not acting within the scope of his employment at the time of the accident. . . . [The lower court ruled granted the motion finding that the evidence did not support an exception to the "coming and going" rule. Although Jolliffe stopped to get shock absorbers, which were ultimately paid for by his employer, and although he used his vehicle on the job, Jolliffe was not acting in the scope of his employment at the time of this accident.]

Appellant appeals the judgment [contending that there was sufficient evidence] to raise a jury question regarding whether Mr. Jolliffe was acting within the scope of his employment at the time of the accident. . . .

As we have recognized, "the fundamental rule in West Virginia is that if it can be shown that an individual is an agent and if he is acting within the scope of his employment when he commits a tort, then the principal is liable for the tort as well as the agent." *Barath v. Performance Trucking Co., Inc.*, 188 W. Va. 367, 370, 424 S.E.2d 602, 605 (1992). . . .

In *Griffith v. George Transfer & Rigging, Inc.*, 157 W. Va. 316, 201 S.E.2d 281 (1973), we explained:

> The universally recognized rule is that an employer is liable to a third person for any injury to his person or property which results proximately from tortious conduct of an employee acting within the scope of his employment. The negligent or tortious act may be imputed to the employer if the act of the employee was done in accordance with the expressed or implied authority of the employer. . . . [201 S.E.2d at 287.]

As we noted in *Griffith*, "'scope of employment' is a relative term and requires a consideration of surrounding circumstances including the character of the employment, the nature of the wrongful deed, the time and place of its commission and the purpose of the act." . . .

Princess contends that the lower court was accurate in basing its determination upon the "going and coming rule," which essentially declares that the doctrine of respondeat superior is not typically applicable while the employee is coming or going to work. The "going and coming rule" has its foundations in workers' compensation law [and] traditionally applies where the only evidence linking the employer to the accident was the fact that the employee was coming or going to work. Various nuances of the rule may serve to alter its application where additional evidence exists linking the employer to the accident. For instance, in *Harris v. State Workmen's Compensation Commissioner*, 158 W. Va. 66, 208 S.E.2d 291 (1974), we noted the general rule that injuries incurred through the ordinary use of streets and highways while going or coming to work are not considered within the scope of employment "unless such use is required of the employee in the performance of his duties for the employer." 158 W. Va. at 70, 208 S.E.2d at 293, quoting *Buckland v. State Compensation Commissioner*, 115 W. Va. 323, 326, 175 S.E. 785, 787 (1934). That exception was designated as the "special errand" exception to the "going and coming rule" and was held inapplicable in *Harris* due to the absence of any requirement that the employee return home to retrieve tools while en route between job sites.

Professor Larson, in LARSON'S WORKMEN'S COMPENSATION LAW, addresses the special errand rule, as follows:

> When an employee, having identifiable time and space limits on his employment, makes an off-premises journey which would normally not be covered under the usual going and coming rule, the journey may be brought within the course of employment by the fact that the trouble and time of making the journey, or the special inconvenience, hazard, or urgency of making it in the particular circumstances, is itself suffi-

ciently substantial to be viewed as an integral part of the service itself.
. . . [1 Larson's Workmen's Compensation Law § 16.10 (1972).]

The issue on the motion for summary judgment in the present case concerned the presence or absence of a genuine issue of material fact regarding whether Mr. Jolliffe was acting within the scope of his employment at the time of the collision that caused Bobbie Courtless' injuries. . . . To develop a complete and exhaustive determination of that application, all facts surrounding Princess' connection to the truck involved in the accident and the purposes for the travel undertaken by Mr. Jolliffe on the day of the accident must be discovered. The granting of summary judgment prematurely discontinued that gathering process.

We have not previously had occasion to wander extensively through the vicissitudes of the "going and coming rule," nor to delineate whether the rule as it has been interpreted in the workers' compensations context is equally applicable to the tort context. Without a more complete factual record, we decline to render any judgments on these issues at this juncture. . . . [A]dditional discovery regarding potential application of the "going and coming" rule within the scope of employment and respondeat superior should have been permitted prior to a determination on the motion for summary judgment. . . . [W]e find that the lower court erred in granting summary judgment and we remand for further proceedings. . . . We find only that a genuine issue of material fact exists and inquiry concerning the facts is desirable to clarify the application of the law.

Reversed and remanded.

NOTES

Exceptions to the "Going and Coming" Rule:

1. *Special Hazards. Courtless* refers to an exception to the common law "going and coming" rule where the travel to the place of employment subjects the employee to some "special hazard." In *Faul v. Jelco, Inc.*, 595 P.2d 1035 (Ariz. Ct. App. 1979), the defendant's employee, while returning in his own vehicle from his home one weekend to the defendant employer's remote construction site where he stayed during the work week, was involved in a collision with plaintiff's vehicle allegedly caused by the employee's negligent driving. The court discussed the special hazard exception to the "going and coming" rule which applies whenever the employee's travel to and from work subjects the employee to special hazards not common to other members of the traveling public. Concluding that distance alone did not constitute a "special hazard," the court upheld a summary judgment for the defendant employer. What if the employee in *Faul* had been required to transport explosives to the employer's remote construction site? What if the employee could only reach the employer's remote construction site via some particularly hazardous route?

2. *Employer Compensates Employee for Time and Travel.* In *Hinman v. Westinghouse Electric Co.*, 471 P.2d 988 (Cal. 1970), the plaintiff was struck and injured by a car negligently driven by the defendant's employee who was returning from the defendant's remote worksite where he was employed. In order to attract more qualified employees, the defendant paid its employees separate travel time to and from the worksite, together with travel expenses. Relying upon such evidence, the court concluded that the defendant's employee was acting within the scope of employment at the time of the accident, thereby holding the defendant employer vicariously liable for the plaintiff's injuries.

3. *Dual Purpose.* Where the employee, in addition to traveling to and from the employer's worksite, also performs some additional service for the employer not common to an ordinary commute to work, this secondary (or "dual") purpose may be sufficient in itself to justify a finding that the employee was acting within the scope of employment for purposes of applying the doctrine of *respondeat superior*. In *Skinner, supra*, the employee had been sent to another store to pick up supplies and bring them to her regular place of employment. Was this a "dual purpose?"

PROBLEMS

1. Karla, a personal secretary employed by Maurice, stopped on her own time to pick up Maurice's laundry on her way to work one morning in order to keep from making a separate return trip back to the laundry after she got to work, only to then be ordered by Maurice to "go pick up my laundry," as was his usual custom. As she hurried to get to work on time, she negligently ran a stop sign and injured Vern. Is Maurice vicariously liable for Vern's injuries? What if Karla had stopped and bought doughnuts (with her own money) on her way to work, intending to share the doughnuts with her co-workers when she arrived at the office?

2. Mario worked at Nancy's Nursery where he mowed grass and hauled dirt and fertilizer using his own truck. To assist in his work, he often carried some of Nancy's yard equipment with him. One morning on his way to work, Mario stopped by a drugstore to purchase some medicine for his wife who was home sick. Afterwards, he drove across the street to a gas station and purchased a gallon can of gasoline for use in the lawnmower at the nursery, because Nancy had instructed him to keep the lawn mowers filled with gasoline at all times. He then headed home again to deliver his wife's medicine before going to work. On his way, he decided to buy gas for his truck, so he pulled into a second service station and filled up his truck. Realizing that he was running late for work, he pulled out from the second station without looking and crashed into Wilson's car. Is Nancy's Nursery vicariously liable for Mario's negligence? *See Standley v. Johnson*, 276 So. 2d 77 (Fla. Dist. Ct. App. 1973).

3. Employer hosted a banquet for all of its employees to honor those workers who had fifteen years or more of service. Employer rented banquet facilities at

a private club, and paid for all food and beverages (including beer, wine and champagne). Employer deducted all expenses for the banquet as a business expense. Buster, one of Employer's newest employees also attended the banquet, where he consumed large quantities of alcohol. Thereafter, he left the banquet and proceeded to drive toward Employer's plant where he was scheduled to work the night shift. En route, Buster swerved his vehicle into the oncoming lane of traffic (because of his alcohol-impaired faculties), and struck Motorcyclist who was proceeding lawfully on his motorcycle from the opposite direction. Is Employer vicariously liable for Motorcyclist's injuries? *See Dickinson v. Edwards*, 716 P.2d 814 (Wash. 1986). Is Employer *directly* liable?

4. Mort was a traveling salesman who worked for Acme Products. To control his occasional attacks of "depression," Mort regularly took a prescription anti-depressant medication. One day, while Mort was driving to a new business appointment, he suddenly became very depressed. Fearing that his depressed state of mind might adversely affect his upcoming sales presentation, Mort decided to take a double dose of his medication. Unfortunately, the drugs caused Mort to hallucinate. While in that drug-impaired state of mind, Mort stopped at Customer's business address to give his sales presentation. However, Customer mistook Mort for a drug-crazed maniac and demanded that he leave the premises at once. When Mort refused to leave, an argument ensued, and Mort physically assaulted Customer. Is Mort's employer, Acme Products, vicariously liable for Customer's injuries? Would your answer be any different if Mort had stopped at the wrong address (because of his drug-impaired condition) and assaulted a total stranger? Explain.

3. "Frolics" and "Detours"

Even if an employee is very clearly engaged within the "scope of employ-ment" while traveling to or from the place of employment, or while otherwise traveling within the actual course of such employment, the inquiry does not always end here. Often, the question in such cases becomes whether an employer nevertheless should be held vicariously liable for injuries tortiously inflicted by a traveling employee who has somehow managed to depart from the scope of his or her employment, even if only temporarily, while in pursuit of some personal goal that is not directly related to the employment itself. Such tem-porary departures by employees from the duties of their employment are all too common in many vicarious liability situations. This, in turn, often gives rise to subsequent inquiries by the courts seeking to characterize the employee's par-ticular deviation as either a "detour" or a "frolic."

LAIRD v. BAXTER HEALTH CARE CORP.
650 N.E.2d 215 (Ill. App. Ct. 1994)

BUCKLEY, J.

Plaintiff brought this action against decedent's employer, Baxter, her coemployee, Hudson, and two third parties, Link and Payne, for damages decedent's next of kin sustained as a result of her death due to a motor vehicle accident on July 16, 1990. Counts I, II, and III are premised on common law negligence; the former two against Baxter and Hudson and the latter against Link and Payne. Count IV alleges in the alternative to counts I and II that at the time of the accident Hudson had departed from the scope of her employment and was engaged in a "frolic." . . .

On July 16, 1990, Hudson and decedent were employed by Baxter. Their duties consisted of calling on hospitals in Illinois and Wisconsin to sell Baxter's products. Hudson was a new employee who began work four weeks prior to the accident. Because Hudson was taking over decedent's accounts, decedent accompanied Hudson to introduce her to the accounts.

On the day of the accident, the two met at the Hinsdale Oasis at 6 a.m. They decided to drive Hudson's car to their appointments. Hudson believed they were to call on four or five hospitals that day. They proceeded to Kankakee for their first appointment at St. Mary's Hospital where they met with a blood bank supervisor for about 20 minutes. They next went to another hospital in Kankakee but Hudson could not remember which one. However, she testified that they left that hospital around 9 a.m. after which they went to McDonald's at the I-57 interchange where they had coffee and remained for 15 to 20 minutes. Prior to arriving at McDonald's, they had discussed the route they would take to Peoria. According to Hudson, decedent planned the route. However, Hudson could not recall the route nor could she recall if the two discussed that they had gone too far prior to the accident. As far as she could recall, Hudson believed they were on the proper route. She testified that while driving, the two had a general conversation and talked about having lunch with an "old friend" in Peoria.

According to Hudson, the last thing she remembers was leaving McDonald's, getting on I-57, and proceeding south on I-57. She did not remember seeing the semi-trailer, any flashing lights, or orange markers before the accident. The next thing she recalled was waking up at a hospital two days later.

Hudson did not recall speaking to a State trooper subsequent to the accident and telling him "that while traveling southbound on I-57 [I] was listening to the radio and must have driven off the roadway striking the disabled truck and trailer." In a conversation with plaintiff's investigator, Hudson answered that she was not lost at the time of the accident and that her intended route was to take I-57 from Kankakee south to Route 24, and Route 24 into Peoria. Hudson did not recall making this statement.

Subsequent to her deposition, Hudson executed an affidavit in which she stated that at the time of the accident, she and decedent were en route to meet a blood bank supervisor in Peoria. She indicated that the meeting was to begin at the hospital and then they planned to take the supervisor out to lunch. The affidavit avers:

> That the reference in my deposition of June 7, 1991 to having lunch with an old friend is a reference to the blood bank supervisor we were going to have lunch with in order to generate additional sales on behalf of Baxter Health Care Corporation.

The most direct route between Kankakee and Peoria is I-57 to Route 24, then Route 24 westbound into Peoria. In her answer, Hudson admits that the accident occurred at milepost 267, or 16 miles south of Route 24 and 45 miles south of Kankakee.

Decedent's appointment book for July 16, 1990, indicated that [she had] appointments at St. Francis Hospital and Proctor Hospital for that afternoon. Also appearing between the morning and afternoon appointments is the name "Methodist." However, there is no time, address, city or contact identified.

In the affidavit of Margaret Cranford, blood bank supervisor at St. Francis Hospital, the affidavit of Joyce Blank, blood bank supervisor at Proctor Hospital, and the affidavit of Deb Reichen, a blood bank technologist at Methodist Hospital, the respective affiants deny that the decedent was an "old friend," deny having any lunch plans with decedent or any other Baxter representative, and Deb Reichen stated that while she knew decedent in a business capacity, she was not scheduled to meet with her that day.

It is undisputed that a collision occurred between Hudson's Toyota and a semi-trailer that was parked on the shoulder of I-57. When State Trooper Tarro arrived at the scene, the driver of the Toyota was still in the vehicle and the passenger was lying on the highway. Tarro indicated that he had passed the area about an hour and a half prior and at that time three triangular road flares were set up behind the trailer. According to him, the abandoned truck was not a road hazard. The weather was clear and it was daylight.

Upon his arrival at the scene of the accident Trooper Tarro found evidence that the hazard warnings had been in place; he found their bases. However, now only bits and pieces of the markers were scattered behind the truck. He could not determine whether Hudson's vehicle was the one that had run over the markers. He did not measure the distance between the bases of the markers and the rear of the truck. However, he measured the distance between the left side of the trailer and the traveled portion of the highway as three feet, nine inches. Tarro did not observe any skid marks at the scene, and testified that if he had, he would have recorded them. The shoulder width is 10 feet wide and is divided from the traveled portions of the highway by a painted white line. Both surfaces are asphalt, although the shoulder may be a little darker. Payne, the truck's driver, testified in his deposition that he inspected the semi-trailer before he began driving it to Champaign on July 15, 1990. He left Elkhart, Indiana around 6 p.m., stopped at a truck stop on I-57 outside of Chicago around midnight, and left there about an hour later. Up to this point, Payne did not notice anything out of the ordinary about the truck. About 3 a.m. Payne pulled the truck over to the side of the road because he blew the engine. He set three plastic triangle reflectors behind the truck. He stated that he placed them based on Illinois Department of Transportation regulations: 10 feet, 100 feet, and 200 feet behind the truck angled toward the highway, "eyeballing the distance." He turned off the hazard lights because he did not want to run down the battery.

Payne returned to the truck at about 9:25 a.m. after the accident had occurred. When he arrived, he did not see the reflectors and had no knowledge of what happened to them. According to him, the truck was in the same position as when he left it and all four wheels of the trailer were on the shoulder. . . .

[The court first concluded that the exclusive remedy provision within the Illinois Workers' Compensation Act barred the plaintiff's common law negligence claim against the defendant employer and the defendant co-employee, and then proceeded to discuss whether a genuine issue of material fact was presented regarding whether Hudson was within the scope of her employment at the time of the accident or whether she had embarked upon a "frolic."]

The pivotal question in this case is whether plaintiff adequately supported allegations that Hudson was on a "frolic" at the time of the accident. Generally, when course of employment is at issue, summary judgment is inappropriate. (*Pyne v. Witmer* (1989), 129 Ill. 2d 351, 359, 543 N.E.2d 1304, 1308, 135 Ill. Dec. 557.) Only if no reasonable person could conclude from the evidence that an employee was acting within the course of employment should a court hold as a matter of law that the employee was not so acting. *Boehmer v. Norton* (1946), 328 Ill. App. 17, 24, 65 N.E.2d 212, 215.

Illinois courts have not precisely defined "scope of employment" but instead apply a broad range of criteria adopted from the RESTATEMENT (SECOND) OF AGENCY section 228. Illinois long ago recognized a distinction between "frolic," where the employee's personal business is seen as unrelated to employment and a (detour, where the employee's deviation for personal reasons is nonetheless seen as sufficiently related to the employment. (*Pyne*, 129 Ill. 2d at 361, 543 N.E.2d at 1309.) An employer will not necessarily be relieved of liability for an employee's negligence even if the employee was combining personal business with the employer's business:

> Where an employee's deviation from the course of employment is slight and not unusual, a court may find as a matter of law that the employee was still executing the employer's business. (*Boehmer v. Norton* (1946), 328 Ill. App. 17, 21, 24, 65 N.E.2d 212.) Conversely, when a deviation is exceedingly marked and unusual, as a matter of law the employee may be found to be outside the scope of employment. But in cases falling

between these extremes, where a deviation is uncertain in extent and degree, or where the surrounding facts and circumstances leave room for legitimate inferences as to whether, despite the deviation, the employee was still engaged in the employer's business, the question is for the jury. (*Pyne*, 129 Ill. 2d at 361, 543 N.E.2d at 1309.)

Where the employee is a traveling employee, the test for course of employment is "the reasonableness of the conduct in which the employee was engaged and whether it might normally be anticipated or foreseen by the employer." *Bailey v. Industrial Commission* (1993), 247 Ill. App. 3d 204, 208, 617 N.E.2d 305, 308, 187 Ill. Dec. 97. . . .

In this case we have only circumstantial evidence of the events prior to the accident. Circumstantial evidence must show a probability of the existence of the fact, and the circumstantial facts must be of such nature and so related as to make the conclusion reached the more probable. *Pyne*, 129 Ill. 2d at 369, 543 N.E.2d at 1313. The essential facts in this case are undisputed. The record shows that Hudson and decedent were traveling employees. They were visiting various hospital downstate and at the time of the accident were in between appointments. Plaintiff has the burden of showing facts which demonstrate that Hudson was on a frolic at the time. The only evidence offered was a statement in Hudson's deposition that the two were going to have lunch with an "old friend." Plaintiff infers from this that the two were on their way to Champaign for lunch. According to plaintiff, this is the only reason they would have passed Route 24. Plaintiff also provided three affidavits indicating that none of the affiants were "old friends" of either Hudson or decedent. Hudson rebutted her statement in an affidavit where she averred that the reference to an "old friend" was to a blood bank supervisor. While the blood bank supervisor indicated that she had no plans with Hudson and decedent for lunch, Hudson and decedent may have planned to ask her out once they arrived at the hospital.

As to the fact that Hudson and decedent were not on the most direct route to Peoria, *Pyne* implies that a traveling employee need not take the most direct route. Hudson and decedent were on a route which, although somewhat out of the way, led them to Peoria. The deviation, if any, was slight particularly given the fact that Hudson and decedent were traveling employees and were heading in the direction of their next appointment. Therefore, as a matter of law no genuine issue of material fact exists. . . .

For the foregoing reasons, the judgment of the circuit court of Cook County is affirmed.

Affirmed.

NOTES

1. What constitutes a "deviation" for purposes of applying the rule discussed in *Laird*?

2. What is the difference between a "frolic" and a "detour"?

3. Who determines whether the employee has been engaged in a "frolic" or a "detour" (*i.e.*, the court or the jury)?

4. If an employee has left the scope of employment (*i.e.*, entered into some personal "frolic"), can he or she then return to the scope of employment? How?

PROBLEM

Defendant's employee, Elrod, while engaged in the scope of his employment as a delivery truck driver for Hapless Furniture Company, decided to stop by the "drive-through" window at a local fast food restaurant. Hapless has a written (and strictly enforced) policy that specifically prohibits its truck drivers from engaging in "any personal errands whatsoever while using company vehicles during work hours." As he pulled away from the window after picking up his order, Elrod accidentally spilled a cup of steaming hot coffee on his leg, causing his foot to suddenly mash down on the accelerator. Elrod's truck lurched forward suddenly, striking Toddler, a three-year old child, as he darted across the drive-through lane just in front of Elrod's truck at that same instant. If suit is brought against Hapless Furniture Company on behalf of Toddler to recover for injuries caused by Elrod's negligent driving, specifically *what* will the plaintiff be required to prove? What is the most likely outcome in such a lawsuit?

4. Employer's Vicarious Liability for Intentional Torts

A surprising number of claims arising from employment situations involve willfully or intentionally inflicted injuries. However, unlike "negligence" analysis which treats most intentionally inflicted injuries as unforeseeable and, thus, not proximately caused by the tortfeasor's alleged negligent act(s), in many types of employment-related situations certain intentional torts may be entirely foreseeable as a part of the employment. For example, when a tavern owner hires a "bouncer" to remove drunken or disorderly patrons from the premises, it is certainly foreseeable, indeed even likely, that a patron will sustain injury from the intentional acts of an over-exuberant bouncer, even though the bouncer is acting entirely within the scope of employment. Other employment relationships present similar opportunities for the commission of intentional torts that are within the scope of employment and very foreseeable.

SUNSERI v. PUCCIA
422 N.E.2d 925 (Ill. App. Ct. 1981)

HARTMAN, J.,

Plaintiff Samuel J. Sunseri brought an action against defendant Patrick Puccia, owner of a restaurant and lounge, and defendant Larry Goeske, his bartender, for injuries received during an altercation on the restaurant premises. . . . Plaintiff [arrived] at the restaurant at approximately 10 p.m. . . . Goeske asked to see his identification verifying his legal age to purchase liquor. Plaintiff displayed some identification cards and Goeske walked away. Plaintiff complained to a friend that he was "tired of being carded." Goeske overheard this remark and told plaintiff that if he didn't like it, he should leave. Plaintiff apologized, but Goeske became increasingly angered. As plaintiff stood up to leave, he waved a universally understood obscene gesture at Goeske. Goeske threatened to "beat the hell" out of him. Plaintiff became frightened because Goeske was considerably taller and heavier, and quickly started towards the exit, but Goeske [grabbed] him. Plaintiff swung at Goeske to defend himself but missed. Goeske then threw plaintiff to the floor and kicked him repeatedly. Goeske allowed plaintiff to stand up, escorted him to the door and once outside, Goeske punched plaintiff in the face. He then threw plaintiff to the ground and jumped on top of him. While holding him there, Goeske began to "gnaw" on plaintiff's ear and he felt Goeske's teeth pierce his ear at least three times. Goeske commented "I hope you see this when I'm done," then stood up and walked away. Patrick Puccia, Richard Sikorski, and several others had been outside watching the entire occurrence, but no one had attempted to stop Goeske. Plaintiff was taken to a hospital where Dr. Allen McClean treated him. About one week later, the doctor amputated the damaged part of his ear. . . .

Turning to the directed verdict in Puccia's favor, the question [is] whether the evidence, when viewed most favorably to plaintiff, failed to establish the basis for applying the doctrine of respondeat superior or ordinary negligence against Puccia. Under traditional respondeat superior analysis, an employer is liable for an employee's torts committed within the scope of that employment. No precise definition has been accorded the term "scope of employment"; however, the focus is generally upon the issues of whether the employee's act was conducted substantially within the constraints of authorized time and location of the employment, and whether the conduct was actuated at least in part by a purpose to further the employer's business. If an employee commits an intentional tort with the dual purpose of furthering the employer's interest and venting personal anger, respondeat superior may lie; however, if the employee acts purely in his own interest, liability under respondeat superior is inappropriate. *Hoover v. University of Chicago Hospitals*; *Awe v. Striker*; RESTATEMENT (SECOND) OF AGENCY §§ 235, 245 (1958).

An employer is liable for intentional torts of an employee which are not unexpectable in view of the latter's duties. The fact that the employee has acted in an outrageous manner or inflicted a punishment out of proportion to the necessities of his employer's business is evidence that the employee departed from the scope of employment, and instead acted for purely personal reasons (RESTATEMENT (SECOND) OF AGENCY § 245, comment f (1958)); however, such an act alone is not conclusive because the employee may have been acting with a dual purpose, under which circumstances liability under respondeat superior may attach. Whether an employee has departed from the scope of employment by acting purely for his own interest, rather than at least in part for the employer, is normally a question for the jury. Other jurisdictions which have considered a dramshop keeper's respondeat superior liability for a bartender's or bouncer's assault on a patron have not precluded liability merely because the force used was unnecessary and excessive since under such circumstances, the use of even excessive force may be anticipated. (*See, e.g.,* *Davis v. DelRosso* (1977), 371 Mass. 768, 359 N.E.2d 313; *Monk v. Veillon* (La. App. 1975). *See also* RESTATEMENT (SECOND) OF AGENCY § 245, comment i (1958).) The jury here should have been allowed to determine whether Goeske's conduct was within the scope of his employment, based upon the occurrence within the time and location of the employment, the foreseeability of the assault in view of the nature of Puccia's business and Goeske's responsibilities, and Puccia's presence during the commission of the act without intervention.

Aside from respondeat superior, an employer may be liable under ordinary negligence principles for breach of a duty to prevent an employee or others from physically harming their patrons on the employer's premises, and the employer knows or should know that control over the employee is necessary and the ability to control exists. (*O'Roark v. Gergley* (Ky. 1973), 497 S.W.2d 931; RESTATEMENT (SECOND) OF TORTS § 317 (1965).) Viewing the evidence most favorably to plaintiff, Puccia's failure to act in any manner to terminate the fight, either by direction to Goeske or in cooperation with Sikorski, establishes a potential basis for negligence liability which the jury should have been allowed to consider.

From the foregoing, we conclude that the directed verdicts were improperly granted as to both defendants. The cause is therefore reversed and remanded for a new trial.

Reversed and remanded.

NOTES

1. *Sunseri* referred to the "dual purpose" doctrine as a means of justifying *respondeat superior*, even in situations where the employee has committed an intentional tort against the plaintiff while acting, at least in part, in furtherance of the employer's interest (hence, the "dual purpose"). Under this doctrine, an employee's intentional tort may be included within the "scope of employment" if it is committed with the dual purpose of venting the employee's personal feelings, while at the same time being intended to further the employer's inter-

est. What is the primary inquiry that must be made when applying this doctrine to determine whether an employer can be held vicariously liable for an intentional tort committed by an employee? In addition to the employee's *purpose* for committing the intentional tort, *Sunseri* also referred to those intentional torts committed by employees "which are not unexpectable" in view of the employee's duties. Does such a statement represent an attempt by the court to utilize "*foreseeability*" as an additional factor that is taken into consideration in making this determination? *See* RESTATEMENT (SECOND) AGENCY § 228(1)(d) (1958).

2. *Employee's Motive.* It is clear from cases such as *Sunseri* that an employee's intentional torts are not within the "scope of employment" when they are motivated by purely personal reasons, or when they are so willful or malicious as to signal a clear departure from the scope of employment, or where the amount of force actually exerted by the employee is clearly excessive under the circumstances, even though some degree of physical force may have been authorized by the employer. Obviously, it is difficult to draw the line with precision. What actual percentage of the employee's *personal* motives for engaging in misconduct should be permitted (*i.e.*, 80%; not greater than 50%; only 10%)? Who should make such decisions, and how? Should the employee's personal motives be considered when the employer's business interest is also being legitimately advanced?

PLUMMER v. CENTER PSYCHIATRISTS, LTD.
476 S.E.2d 172 (Va. 1996)

LEROY R. HASSELL, SR., J.

The sole issue we consider in this appeal is whether the trial court erred by holding, as a matter of law, that a psychologist who had sexual intercourse with a patient was acting outside the scope of his employment, thus rendering the doctrine of respondeat superior inapplicable.

Dr. Roque Gerald, a licensed clinical psychologist, was employed by the defendant, Center Psychiatrists, Ltd. Gerald provided therapy and counseling services to the plaintiff, Katrina Q. Plummer, who was suffering from depression. Gerald was cognizant of [the] plaintiff's psychological and emotional history, which included her prior attempts at suicide, and he knew "that she was suffering from suicide ideation, and depression."

On February 8, 1989, while the plaintiff was receiving counseling from Gerald at the defendant's place of business, Gerald committed "an act of sexual intercourse upon plaintiff [which] constituted an assault and battery upon her since, Dr. Roque Gerald, through his education, experience and knowledge of plaintiff overcame her will so that she was unable to act with volition."

The plaintiff filed her motion for judgment against the defendant seeking to recover, inter alia, damages caused by the assault and battery. The plaintiff alleged that Gerald was an employee, agent, and servant of the defendant and that he was acting within the scope of his employment when he engaged in sexual intercourse with her.

The defendant filed a demurrer to the plaintiff's motion for judgment asserting, among other things, that as a matter of law, it cannot be liable to the plaintiff because Gerald was not acting in the course of his employment when he committed the act of sexual intercourse and, therefore, the doctrine of respondeat superior is not applicable. The trial court granted the defendant's demurrer. [P]laintiff argues that the trial court erred by dismissing her claim for assault and battery against the defendant because she pled sufficient facts in her motion for judgment which, if proven at trial, would create a jury issue on the question whether Gerald was acting within the course of his employment when he committed an act of sexual intercourse upon her. The defendant argues that, as a matter of law, Gerald was not acting within the scope of his employment, but "solely for his own personal interests." We disagree with the defendant.

[P]ursuant to the doctrine of respondeat superior, an employer is liable for the tortious acts of its employee if the employee was performing his employer's business and acting within the scope of his employment when the tortious acts were committed. *Kensington Associates v. West*, 234 Va. 430, 432, 362 S.E.2d 900, 901 (1987). Additionally, "when an employer-employee relationship has been established, "the burden is on the [employer] to prove that the [employee] was not acting within the scope of his employment when he committed the act complained of, [and] if the evidence leaves the question in doubt it becomes an issue to be determined by the jury." *Kensington Associates*, 234 Va. at 432-33, 362 S.E.2d at 901.

We recently discussed the principles which are dispositive of this dispute in *Commercial Business Systems v. BellSouth*, 249 Va. 39, 453 S.E.2d 261 (1995). In *Commercial Business Systems*, we noted that "in determining whether an agent's tortious act is imputed to the principal, the doctrine's primary focus is on whether the activity that gave rise to the tortious act was within or without the agent's scope of employment." We also stated the test that we believe is applicable here:

> "The courts . . . have long since departed from the rule of non-liability of an employer for wilful or malicious acts of his employee. Under the modern view, the wilfulness or wrongful motive which moves an employee to commit an act which causes injury to a third person does not of itself excuse the employer's liability therefor. The test of liability is not the motive of the employee in committing the act complained of, but whether that act was within the scope of the duties of employment and in the execution of the service for which he was engaged." [453 S.E.2d at 266.]

[T]he facts alleged in the motion for judgment are sufficient to support the plaintiff's legal conclusion that Gerald acted within the scope of his employment when he committed the wrongful acts against the plaintiff. According to the plaintiff's allegations, Gerald's act was committed while he was performing his duties as a psychologist in the execution of the services for which he was employed, in this instance, counseling and therapy. Additionally, Gerald's education, experience, and knowledge of the plaintiff, who was depressed and had suicidal ideations, enabled him "[to overcome] her will so that she was unable to act with volition." Furthermore, at this stage of the proceedings, there simply are not sufficient facts which would permit us to hold, as a matter of law, that the defendant has met its burden of showing that its employee was not acting within the scope of his employment.

The defendant asserts that our recent decision in *Tomlin v. McKenzie*, 251 Va. 478, 468 S.E.2d 882 (1996), supports his contention that Gerald's acts, as a matter of law, were outside the scope of his employment. We disagree. In *Tomlin*, the plaintiffs filed their motion for judgment against Patsye D. McKenzie, a licensed clinical social worker, and her employer, a professional corporation owned solely by McKenzie. The motion for judgment alleged that McKenzie provided family therapy to the plaintiffs pursuant to an order of referral by the Juvenile & Domestic Relations District Court of the City of Chesapeake. The motion for judgment further alleged that in the course of providing that therapy, McKenzie and her employer intentionally and maliciously committed certain acts constituting malpractice and defamation.

The defendants filed a plea in bar, seeking dismissal of the action on the basis that McKenzie and her employer were entitled to common law and statutory immunity. McKenzie and her employer asserted that common law sovereign immunity protected them from civil suits for actions performed in McKenzie's capacity as a court-appointed officer. We reversed the judgment of the trial court which had sustained their motions because McKenzie's conduct was outside the scope of the court-ordered referral.

Tomlin is not implicated here. McKenzie's employer did not claim that she was acting outside the scope of her employment when she committed the allegedly tortious acts. Rather, we reviewed the facts pled in the plaintiffs' motion for judgment, considered her specific factual allegations, applied the principles relevant to the doctrine of sovereign immunity, and held that the intentional torts alleged were outside the scope of McKenzie's court-appointed role. Here, however, we do not concern ourselves with sovereign immunity, but with the doctrine of respondeat superior. Our review of the facts and reasonable inferences therefrom alleged in the plaintiff's motion for judgment compels us to conclude that she has pled sufficient facts which, if proven, would create a jury issue whether Gerald was acting within the scope of his employment.

Accordingly, we will reverse the judgment of the trial court and remand this case for further proceedings consistent with this opinion.

Reversed and remanded.

KOONTZ, J, with whom CHIEF JUSTICE CARRICO and JUSTICE COMPTON join, dissenting.

I respectfully dissent. [T]he trial court correctly determined that the facts alleged [are] insufficient, as a matter of law, to support her legal conclusion that Dr. Roque Gerald, her psychologist, acted within the scope of his employment with Center Psychiatrists, Ltd. when he "seduced [her] into an act of sexual intercourse." . . .

Surely it is undisputed that sexual intimacy between professional counselors and their clients is unethical, has no place in the therapy process, and is universally condemned. *See, e.g.*, American Psychological Association, Standard 4.05 (1992) ("Psychologists do not engage in sexual intimacies with current patients or clients"). . . .

In *Tri-State Coach Corp. v. Walsh*, 188 Va. 299, 49 S.E.2d 363 (1948), we noted that: "the exact line of demarcation between what acts are within the scope of employment and what are not is, at times, difficult of ascertainment. The inferences to be drawn from the facts proved are often within the province of the jury." Assuming that all the allegations in Plummer's motion for judgment are true, they clearly establish that Dr. Gerald's "seduction" of Plummer was not an act intended by him to advance or maintain his employer's business. It is equally clear that in undertaking that seduction, Dr. Gerald must have stepped aside from the business of Center Psychiatrists, Ltd. and that he engaged in an independent venture of his own. Under such circumstances, and as we held in *Kensington Associates*, a jury issue was not presented and the trial court correctly determined that Dr. Gerald's act was a "great and unusual" deviation from his employer's business and, thus, not committed within the scope of his employment as a matter of law.

Our decision in *Commercial Business Systems* does not dictate a contrary conclusion. There the tortious act of the employee was committed while the employee was performing the duties of his employment and in the execution of the services for which he was employed. Thus, we held that the facts presented a jury issue whether he acted within the scope of his employment when he committed the wrongful acts. In the present case, the deviation from the employer's business is so extreme that no jury issue is implicated.

In short, while the limits of the scope of employment in a given case may be sufficiently broad to include various willful and malicious acts of the employee, a sexual assault upon a client by a professional counselor or psychologist falls well beyond that scope as a matter of law.

Finally, I am compelled to relate that the majority of our sister jurisdictions are in accord with the view I would take of this appeal. *See, e.g., P.S. and R.S. v. Psychiatric Coverage, Ltd.*, 887 S.W.2d 622, 625 (Mo. Ct. App. 1994); *Sharples v. State*, 71 Haw. 404, 793 P.2d 175, 176-77 (Haw. 1990) (respondeat superior does not apply even though counselor maintained sexual intercourse "was part of his therapy"). . . .

For these reasons, I would affirm the judgment of the trial court.

NOTES

1. The majority opinion in *Plummer* applied a test (the "activity test") that focused upon the nature of the *particular activity* that gave rise to the intentionally tortious conduct by the employee, rather than one that focused upon the *employee's personal motive* in committing the tortious act (*i.e.*, the "motive test"). What test is applied by the dissenting opinion? Is each of these tests based upon "objective" or "subjective" criteria? Which of the two tests is more appropriate for a court to apply as a matter of law in determining whether an employee's intentionally tortious conduct should be included within the scope of employment for purposes of *respondeat superior*?

2. RESTATEMENT (SECOND) AGENCY § 228(2) (1958) provides that: "Conduct of a servant is not within the scope of employment if it is different in kind from that authorized, far beyond the authorized time or space limits, or too little actuated by a purpose to serve the master." Is the Restatement's approach to this question based upon a "motive test" or an "activity test"?

3. Upon what specific legal basis did the Virginia Supreme Court in *Plummer* distinguish its own arguably contrary precedent in *Tomlin v. McKenzie*, 468 S.E.2d 882 (Va. 1996)? Was this proper?

4. What is "horseplay"?

PROBLEMS

1. Lucky's Tavern hired Biff, an ex-wrestler, to work evenings in the bar as a "bouncer." Biff's duties were to keep order in the Tavern during business hours and to remove unruly patrons, by physical force if necessary. Lucky's Tavern had a strict policy that prohibited the use of all firearms inside the bar, even by Tavern employees. In addition to Biff's other duties, he was also expected to check all persons who entered the Tavern for firearms and to remove any weapons that he found. One evening while at work Biff noticed Customer flirting with Biff's girlfriend at the bar. As the evening progressed, Biff became more and more angry as he watched the flirtations continue. Finally, he walked up to Customer (who was not visibly intoxicated or otherwise behaving in an unruly manner) and demanded that he leave the premises immediately. Customer refused to leave and he stood up in a threatening manner. Biff, the larger of the two men, pulled out a handgun from inside his belt, and fired it at Customer. The bullet narrowly missed Customer, but struck Patron (who was seated across the room) in the back. What tort(s) has Biff committed? Is Lucky's Tavern vicariously liable for any of Biff's intentional torts? Explain.

2. Homer and Gus were both employees at the Midvale Manufacturing plant. Both men worked on the last station of the assembly line where they sealed large cardboard shipping containers using heavy-duty staples. One day, during a temporary lull in their assembly work, Gus pulled his staple gun out and

pointed it at Homer, teasingly challenging him to "make my day!" Homer kiddingly grabbed for his own staple gun as if to take up Gus' challenge, but when he did so, his finger accidently squeezed the trigger, causing the gun to "fire" a staple which hit Gus in the eye. Gus subsequently filed a worker's compensation claim against his employer Midvale Manufacturing. Midvale's insurer has denied coverage, claiming that Gus was not acting within the "scope of his employment" at the time of his injury, but was engaged in "horseplay" instead. Homer's only recourse, the insurer claims, is against Gus. How should the court respond?

5. Vicarious Liability for Punitive Damages

BRUECKNER v. NORWICH UNIVERSITY
730 A.2d 1086 (Vt. 1999)

AMESTOY, C.J.

Norwich University appeals from the denial of its post-trial motions for judgment as a matter of law, or in the alternative, for a new trial, following a jury verdict finding it liable and awarding compensatory and punitive damages on several tort claims arising from incidents of hazing suffered by plaintiff while a freshman. . . . We affirm the court's rulings on liability and lost earnings damages, but reverse the award of punitive damages because there was an insufficient showing of malice to support the award.

Viewing the evidence in the light most favorable to the plaintiff, as we must on the appeal of both a motion for judgment as a matter of law, and a motion for a new trial, . . . the facts are as follows. In August 1990, plaintiff William C. Brueckner, Jr. arrived as an incoming freshman, or "rook," at the Military College of Vermont of Norwich University (Norwich). At the time, he was a twenty-four-year-old, five-year veteran of the United States Navy, having been awarded a four-year naval ROTC scholarship in the amount of $80,000 to attend Norwich. Under the authority and training of Norwich and its leadership, certain upperclassmen were appointed by the university to indoctrinate and orient the incoming rooks, including plaintiff. These upperclassmen were known as the "cadre."

Plaintiff attended Norwich for only sixteen days as a result of his subjection to, and observation of, numerous incidents of hazing. In those sixteen days, plaintiff withstood a regular barrage of obscene, offensive and harassing language. He was interrogated at meals and thereby prevented from eating. He was ordered to disrobe in front of a female student, although he did not follow the order. He was prevented from studying during some of the assigned study periods and, on several occasions, cadre members destroyed his academic work with water. Members of the cadre also forced him to squat in the hall as they squirted him with water. He was forced to participate in unauthorized calisthenic sessions, despite an injured shoulder. He was slammed into a wall by a cadre member riding a skateboard in the hall. After cadre members vandalized his room by dumping water in it, plaintiff was ordered to clean up the mess. On two occasions, plaintiff was prevented from attending mandatory ROTC study hall on time, leading him to believe his scholarship status was endangered. One morning, [he] encountered two cadre members, one of whom asked plaintiff where plaintiff's name tag was. When plaintiff responded that he had forgotten it, one cadre member hit plaintiff hard in the shoulder, which was injured and in a sling. After the other cadre member told the hitter to stop, the hitter struck plaintiff again in the same shoulder, causing pain and bruises. After reporting the hazing problems to Norwich officials, plaintiff left the campus, believing that his situation would not improve. He returned briefly once more, then withdrew from Norwich, his scholarship terminated. Norwich investigated plaintiff's complaints and, as a result, several cadets were disciplined.

Plaintiff brought this action [for] assault and battery, negligent infliction of emotional distress, intentional infliction of emotional distress and negligent supervision. [T]he jury found Norwich liable on all counts and awarded plaintiff $100,000 for emotional distress, $8,600 for medical expenses, $80,000 for the lost four-year college scholarship and $300,000 to cover lost earnings (past and future). The jury also awarded $1.75 million in punitive damages. The court denied Norwich's post-trial motions for judgment as a matter of law and for a new trial. Norwich appeals. . . .

Norwich claims error in the court's entry of judgment on the claims of assault and battery, as well as negligent and intentional infliction of emotional distress, because those claims are premised on acts of the cadre members that were not authorized and did not occur within the scope of their employment. Norwich claims it should not be held vicariously liable for the cadre's hazing. Under the settled doctrine of respondeat superior, an employer or master is held vicariously liable for the tortious acts of an employee or servant committed during, or incidental to, the scope of employment. *See Anderson v. Toombs*, 119 Vt. 40, 44-45, 117 A.2d 250, 253 (1955). Norwich concedes that cadre members acted as its agents in "indoctrinating and orienting" rooks such as plaintiff. Norwich claims, however, that the tortious acts complained of were not committed within the cadre members' "scope of employment." Whether a given act is committed within the scope of employment is properly determined by the finder of fact after consideration of the attendant facts and circumstances of the particular case. . . .

Here, the cadre were authorized by Norwich to indoctrinate and orient rooks through activities performed at various times of the day and night. A jury could reasonably find members of the cadre were acting in furtherance of their general duties to indoctrinate and orient the rooks and thus within their "scope of employment" at the time of the hazing incidents of which plaintiff complains.

Norwich argues that, because it had adopted policies against hazing and had instructed the cadre to refrain from mistreating the rooks, the tortious conduct was outside the scope of employment. Norwich contends that *McHugh v. University of Vermont*, 966 F.2d 67 (2d Cir. 1992), supports this result. In

McHugh, the Second Circuit Court of Appeals, applying Vermont law, concluded that an employee who sexually and religiously harassed a fellow employee was not acting within the scope of employment. There, a major in the United States Army and an employee at the University of Vermont's Department of Military Studies told plaintiff, a female secretary, that his definition of a "secretary" was a "paid whore." The employee repeatedly joked about plaintiff contracting AIDS, stating that he hoped she would be able to avoid infection. The employee also told plaintiff that it was "a good day to watch Catholic babies burn." The court rejected the argument that the employee's conduct was within his scope of employment because it was within that scope for him to talk with the plaintiff, either to give instructions or to avoid the awkwardness of silence at work. It held: "It can hardly be contended that [the employee's] alleged conduct furthered the business" of his employer.

The same cannot be said of this case, where the actions involved in hazing rooks may fairly be seen as qualitatively similar to the indoctrination and orientation with which the cadre members were charged.

Indeed, Norwich described some of the acts[,] such as forced calisthenics and questioning at mealtime, as not far removed from the official system of military discipline and training which recruits are expected to endure. The evidence supported the jury's conclusion that the cadre members were acting within the scope of employment. *See Belanger v. Village Pub I, Inc.*, 26 Conn. App. 509, 603 A.2d 1173, 1179 (Conn. App. Ct. 1992). . . .

Norwich next claims that there was insufficient evidence to support plaintiff's claim for assault and battery and thus, that the court erred when it denied Norwich judgment as a matter of law. Norwich concedes that an assault and battery occurred, but claims that vicarious liability cannot be established because insufficient evidence exists to identify the assailant as a member of the cadre. At trial, plaintiff could not recall whether the person who had struck him in the shoulder was a member of the cadre, but testified that he knew the assailant was not a rook and thought he was a member of the senior class.

Plaintiff's counsel stressed [that], although plaintiff's memory failed him at trial, a report prepared in connection with plaintiff's case contained his earlier statement to his roommate that the hitter had been a cadre member. Norwich claims that the identification in the report is triple hearsay and amounts to "conjecture, surmise or suspicion," which is inadequate as a matter of law to support the jury's verdict.

There is no absolute prohibition against the use of admitted hearsay evidence to support a jury's verdict. Particularly in light of the fact that Norwich commissioned the report and moved for its introduction at trial, it cannot complain of the jury's consideration of a statement recorded therein.

Notwithstanding plaintiff's memory lapse at trial, the jury reasonably could have concluded that plaintiff's earlier statement accurately recorded the attacker's identity. The court correctly denied the motion for judgment as a matter of law. . . .

The purpose of punitive damages is to "punish conduct which is morally culpable [and] to deter a wrongdoer [from] repetitions of the same or similar actions." *Coty v. Ramsey Assocs.*, 149 Vt. 451, 467, 546 A.2d 196, 207 (1988). Punitive damages are permitted "where the defendant's wrongdoing has been intentional and deliberate, and has the character of outrage frequently associated with crime." W. KEETON, ET AL., PROSSER AND KEETON ON THE LAW OF TORTS § 2, at 9 (5th ed. 1984). It is not enough to show that defendant's acts are wrongful or unlawful "there must be proof of defendant's bad spirit and wrong intention." Consistent with the view that punitive damages are to be applied to deter and to punish "truly reprehensible conduct," Vermont has long required a plaintiff to demonstrate that a defendant acted with malice in order to recover punitive damages. *See Sparrow v. Vermont Savings Bank*, 95 Vt. 29, 33, 112 A. 205, 207 (1921). . . .

Here, plaintiff's theory of Norwich's liability for punitive damages was predicated not upon a showing of defendant's "bad motive" in engaging in intentional misconduct, but instead upon "Norwich's conscious choice to remain ignorant [of hazing] activities." In upholding the punitive damages award, the judge described the rationale for the punitive damages request: "The jury was asked to impose punitive damages in order to punish Norwich for its inaction and inattention to the issue of hazing on campus." A corporation may be held directly liable for punitive damages. . . .

While we have made clear our view that the board of trustees and management hierarchy of a corporation cannot insulate itself from the malice or its equivalent exhibited by staff, we are not prepared to hold that inaction or inattention of senior corporate officers constitutes malice sufficient to establish punitive damages liability. This is particularly true where, as here, the findings of fact [are] insufficient to support an inference that the defendant's inaction was infused with "a bad motive," giving rise to "outrage frequently associated with crime[.]"

Viewing the evidence in the light most favorable to plaintiff, as we must, the facts demonstrate that senior leadership at Norwich knew of numerous, often serious, hazings by the cadre that had taken place on campus during the years preceding plaintiff's arrival there, and that Norwich officials left the cadre in "virtually unsupervised control" of plaintiff as a rook.

A senior vice-president knew that rooks felt intimidated by the prospect of entering a complaint about hazing through the chain of command, and that no formal method of complaining about hazing outside of the chain of command existed while plaintiff was a rook. Furthermore, a security officer testified that he felt he was not encouraged to report hazing.

From 1987 to 1991, Norwich did not implement any changes to its training of student leaders related to hazing, and no changes were introduced to the training patterns that were aimed at avoiding or reducing hazing.

Significantly, however, the evidence indicates that Norwich considered hazing to be an inappropriate behavior and, when training the cadre, advised its members to stay within the rule and treat each other suitably.

Norwich had an honor code, sworn to by all students, which prohibited hazing. When specific incidents of hazing were reported to the senior vice-president, investigations were conducted. If reports were found to be valid, disciplinary action was taken, ranging from punishment within the corps or loss of a cadet's rank, to suspension or dismissal from Norwich.

Disciplines were announced to the students by publishing an order from the administrative officer of the commandant's office, posting it on all bulletin boards, and giving it to all members of the corps. It was also read in company formation.

On the basis of this record it may be fair to conclude, as indeed the court did, that the defendant was "indifferent to the health and safety of the rooks in its custody and control." But indifference attributable to negligence is not malice. "To sanction punitive damages solely upon the basis of conduct characterized as 'heedless disregard of the consequences' would be to allow virtually limitless imposition of punitive damages." *Tuttle*, 494 A.2d at 1361.

We conclude, then, with the view that Norwich's action or inaction, "however wrongful, did not evince the degree of malice required" under our cases. Punitive damages awarded on these facts would only "dull[ ] the potentially keen edge of the doctrine as an effective deterrent of truly reprehensible conduct."

The judgment of punitive damages is reversed. The judgment is affirmed in all other respects.

NOTES

1. According to *Brueckner*, does a showing of "malice" necessary to impose vicarious liability also require a *bad motive* by the party against whom those damages are actually imposed, or is a showing of mere "reckless disregard" sufficient?

2. Chief Judge Amestoy states that "plaintiff's theory of Norwich's liability for punitive damages was predicated not upon a showing of defendant's 'bad motive' in engaging in intentional misconduct, but instead upon Norwich's conscious choice to remain ignorant [of the hazing] activities." Would the outcome in this case have been different had the plaintiff alleged in his complaint that Norwich University had acted with a "bad motive" by consciously choosing to remain ignorant of the hazing activities by its student cadre, despite overwhelming evidence of such misconduct?

3. *The "Complicity Theory."* Under RESTATEMENT (SECOND) OF TORTS § 909 (1977), a principal may be held vicariously liable for punitive damages awarded on the basis of an agent's misconduct where the principal has either authorized or subsequently ratified such misconduct, or where the principal has recklessly hired an otherwise unfit agent. *See also* RESTATEMENT (SECOND) AGENCY § 217C (1958). Often referred to as the "complicity theory," the purpose of this rule is to strike some sort of balance between the protection of the public interests against malicious or reckless torts authorized by the principal, and the legitimate interests of those principals who take reasonable measures to protect members of the public against such harms. *See Cerminara v. California Hotel and Casino*, 760 P.2d 108 (Nev. 1988). *See generally* J. GHIARDI & J. KIRCHNER, PUNITIVE DAMAGES LAW AND PRACTICE, Ch. 24, 36-39 (1987), for a jurisdictional survey regarding an employer's vicarious liability for the payment of punitive damages under the "complicity theory."

PROBLEM

Rosalind, a twenty-two-year-old (legal) Haitian immigrant, was wrongfully accused of shoplifting a package of chewing gum from Murphy's Emporium. Rosalind was placed in handcuffs and detained by the store manager and another employee in a small windowless storeroom at the rear of the store for more than thirty minutes. While inside the room, the two men threatened to have her "deported" if she did not admit to their charges. They also seized her purse, dumped its contents onto a table and sprayed her with her own cannister of "pepper spray," inflicting serious injury to her eyes. Assuming that the two employees are found to have committed sufficiently egregious misconduct to justify the imposition of punitive damages for their tortious actions, can Murphy's Emporium be held vicariously liable for such punitive damages? What, if any, additional facts would be helpful in resolving this question? *See Smith Food & Drug Centers, Inc. v. Bellegarde*, 958 P.2d 1208 (Nev. 1998).

C. INDEPENDENT CONTRACTORS

The common law rule provides that a principal who hires an independent contractor to perform work will not be held vicariously liable to persons who may be tortiously injured in the course of such work. However, as with most rules, it is subject to a number of exceptions that can be used to overcome the principal's non-liability in various individual circumstances. The following case provides a typical example of just how this rule and its exceptions often interact.

BAGLEY v. INSIGHT COMMUNICATIONS CO., L.P.
658 N.E.2d 584 (Ind. 1995)

DICKSON, J.

[On] January 26, 1988, Richard Bagley suffered severe brain and head injuries while working as an employee of Sam Friend, a subcontractor for Steve Crawford, a television cable installer. Crawford, in turn, was functioning as a subcontractor for Insight Communications Co., L.P. (Insight), a central Indiana cable television company. A damages action based upon various theories of liability was brought on behalf of Bagley against Insight, Crawford, and Friend. The trial court entered summary judgment in favor of Insight and Crawford. The Court of Appeals affirmed in a divided opinion.

Plaintiff Bagley's appeal asserts that summary judgment was improperly granted because disputed factual issues existed as to: (a) whether Insight and Crawford were negligent in hiring a subcontractor; (b) whether Insight and Crawford breached a duty to provide proper safety procedures; and (c) whether Insight and Crawford had assumed a duty to provide insurance to cover Bagley's injuries. With respect to the latter two questions, we summarily affirm the opinion of the Court of Appeals, which rejected these claims of error. In order to address Bagley's contention that summary judgment was improper as to the remaining negligent hiring issue, we first consider the viability of his theory of liability, the question which divided the Court of Appeals.

In Indiana, the long-standing general rule has been that a principal is not liable for the negligence of an independent contractor. *Prest-O-Lite Co. v. Skeel* (1914), 182 Ind. 593, 597, 106 N.E. 365, 367. However, five exceptions have been recognized for more than half a century. The exceptions are: (1) where the contract requires the performance of intrinsically dangerous work; (2) where the principal is by law or contract charged with performing the specific duty; (3) where the act will create a nuisance; (4) where the act to be performed will probably cause injury to others unless due precaution is taken; and (5) where the act to be performed is illegal. *Perry v. Northern Ind. Pub. Serv. Co.* (1982), Ind. App., 433 N.E.2d 44, 47.

The plaintiff contends that Indiana courts will [also] impose liability for the negligent hiring of an independent contractor. He argues that summary judgment was improper because a genuine issue of fact exists as to whether Crawford was negligent in the hiring of subcontractor Friend. Defendant Crawford agrees that Indiana courts have recognized actions for negligent hiring but urges that the duty to use reasonable care in hiring does not extend to protect the employees of an incompetent contractor. Defendant Insight contends that Indiana has not recognized, and should not permit, a cause of action for the negligent hiring of an independent contractor.

The assertions [that] the doctrine of negligent hiring represents an additional exception to the rule of non-liability of independent contractors are primarily based upon two Indiana appellate decisions, *Board of Comm'rs of Wabash County v. Pearson* (1889), 120 Ind. 426, 22 N.E. 134, and *Detrick v. Midwest Pipe & Steel, Inc.* (1992), Ind. App., 598 N.E.2d 1074, and find further support in two cases from the United States Court of Appeals for the Seventh Circuit, *Stone v. Pinkerton Farms, Inc.* (7th Cir. 1984), 741 F.2d 941, and *Hixon v. Sherwin-Williams Co.* (7th Cir. 1982), 671 F.2d 1005. All three of the latter cases either rest directly upon, or can be traced back to, *Pearson*. From the facts set forth in the *Pearson* opinion, it appears that the plaintiff sought damages for injuries, alleging that the defendant, the Wabash County Board of Commissioners, "knew when it employed persons to make the repairs that they were incompetent" and "knew that the work was so unskillfully and negligently done as to leave the bridge in an unsafe condition." The *Pearson* court stated, "A corporation charged with the duty of keeping a bridge in repair must select the proper means and persons to do the work, if by the exercise of ordinary care such a selection can be made." *Pearson* did not create a new doctrine of tort liability for the negligent hiring of an independent contractor but rather permitted an action for the breach of a non-delegable duty imposed by law. To the extent that it may be considered as implicating the general principle of non-liability for torts of an independent contractor, the holding in *Pearson* does not create a new exception but merely reflects the second of the five established exceptions (where the principal is charged with the specific duty by law or contract).

Other early Indiana cases similarly noted a responsibility on the part of a county or municipality to exercise reasonable care in the selection of persons to repair bridges and streets, not as a separate and discrete common-law duty or as an exception to a general rule of non-liability for torts of independent contractors, but rather as an obligation arising from specific governmental duties with respect to public travel.

As correctly observed by Judge Staton's lead opinion in the present case, the theory of tort liability for the negligent hiring of an independent contractor has received acceptance in several states and is reflected in Section 411 of the RESTATEMENT (SECOND) OF TORTS. We are in agreement with the basic concepts embodied in Section 411, and we find that these are subsumed in the existing exceptions to the rule of non-liability for the conduct of independent contractors.

Both Indiana's non-liability rule exceptions and Section 411 identify circumstances in which sound legal policy requires the maintenance of personal responsibility through the recognition of certain duties of care. The duties associated with Indiana's five exceptions are considered non-delegable, and an employer will be liable for the negligence of the contractor, because the responsibilities are deemed "so important to the community" that the employer should not be permitted to transfer these duties to another. Similarly, Restatement Section 411 recognizes that an employer is responsible to exercise reasonable care in the hiring of a contractor under certain circumstances. We find the general policies of Section 411 to be already embodied in the existing exceptions to the non-liability rule, and we decline to recognize Section 411 as creating a new, independent cause of action. However, an employer of an independent contractor may be subject to liability for personal injuries caused by the employer's failure to exercise reasonable care to employ a competent and careful contractor when one of the five exceptions to the rule on non-liability for the torts of independent contractors is applicable.

The plaintiff's action confronts not only the requirement of falling within one of the five exceptions but also the defendants' contention that these exceptions apply only to claims brought by third parties, not the employees of independent contractors.

We acknowledge that several decisions of our Court of Appeals have restricted the application of the exceptions to benefit only "third persons and not servants actually involved in doing the work which results in the injuries." The Court of Appeals has based this restrictive application upon the presence of worker's compensation benefits, and the likelihood that workers are more aware than third persons of the dangers associated with the work. We disagree, however, and conclude that such restriction of the exceptions to exclude injured workers is contrary to the purpose of the exceptions and is not compelled by their underlying policy concerns.

As noted above, the five exceptions represent specific, limited situations in which the associated duties are considered non-delegable because public policy concerns militate against permitting an employer to absolve itself of all further responsibility by transferring its duties to an independent contractor. The exceptions encourage the employer of the contractor to participate in the control of work covered by the exceptions in order to minimize the risk of resulting injuries. Our objective is no less to protect workers who may be exposed to such risks than it is to protect non-employee third parties. The fact that partial remuneration through worker's compensation benefits may be available to an employee of an independent contractor does not diminish the policy rationale of providing an additional incentive to eliminate or minimize particular risks of injuries which arise from non-delegable duties. Where a contractor's employer is responsible for a non-delegable duty, the contractor's injured worker should not discriminately be deprived of access to full compensatory damages but should have recourse equal to that of an injured bystander. Likewise, to the extent that an injured worker's awareness of a job-related risk may be greater than that of a non-worker, substantial fairness and equal treatment are ensured because in a worker's action against the contractor's employer, any incurred risk on the part of a worker will be treated as "fault" and will be reflected in a proportionately reduced damages award under our comparative fault statute. We hold, therefore, that Richard Bagley's status when injured as an employee of an independent contractor does not deprive him of the right to seek application of one or more of the five exceptions to the rule of non-liability for the torts of an independent contractor.

The nature of the plaintiff's claim in the present case qualifies for possible consideration only under the fourth exception(where the act to be performed by the independent contractor will probably cause injury to others unless due precaution is taken. The essence of this exception is the foreseeability of the peculiar risk involved in the work and of the need for special precautions. The exception applies where, at the time of the making of the contract, a principal should have foreseen that the performance of the work or the conditions under which it was to be performed would, absent precautionary measures, probably cause injury.

Application of this fourth exception to the plaintiff's claim thus requires an examination of whether, at the time Friend was employed as an independent contractor, there existed a peculiar risk which was reasonably foreseeable and which recognizably called for precautionary measures. The undisputed facts of the accident are that Bagley was injured as he was hammering a rod into the ground near a ladder on which Friend was working. The ladder slipped on snow and ice, and Friend landed on Bagley, driving Bagley's head down onto the protruding rod.

The facts of the incident being undisputed, the issue is whether, as a matter of law, Insight or Crawford should have foreseen that the performance of the work for which Friend was ultimately hired would probably cause injury absent due precaution, so as to qualify for the fourth exception. We hold that the requirements of the fourth exception are not satisfied. At the time the contracts were made, the delegated work did not present the peculiar probability that an injury such as Bagley's would result unless precautionary measures were taken, and the employers could not have been expected to foresee the sort of injury which actually occurred. Because the fourth exception to the general rule of non-liability for the torts of independent contractors is inapplicable here, the general rule applies, and the plaintiff's claim must fail.

Transfer is granted, the opinion of the Court of Appeals is vacated, and the trial court's entry of summary judgment is affirmed.

NOTES

1. *What is a "peculiar risk"?* The mere fact that the work to be performed by an independent contractor involves some degree of special danger is generally not sufficient for the application of the "peculiar risk" exception. In *McDaniel v. Business Investment Group*, 709 N.E.2d 17 (Ind. Ct. App. 1999), the court explained how the uniqueness of the work represents only one of the relevant considerations:

> we find that cave-ins do not represent a peculiar risk of trenching. The relevant statistics demonstrate that cave-ins are a routine and predictable hazard of trenching, and even the construction industry has acknowledged that reality by devising and promoting safety measures to prevent such accidents. Had Wilson's employees utilized those safety measures, the cave-in and McDaniel's death could have been avoided.

There is no evidence that the Shepard job involved a risk of cave-in that was somehow unique or distinguishable from the general risk of cave-ins associated with trenching, nor is there evidence that extraordinary precautions were necessary and should have been taken. Under the circumstances, Acme cannot be held liable for the accident that caused McDaniel's death.

Id. at 22.

2. *Inherently (or intrinsically) dangerous work.* In some jurisdictions the "peculiar risk" exception is referred to as the "inherently 'or intrinsically' dangerous work" exception. Despite differences in terminology, the doctrines are essentially identical. *See* RESTATEMENT (SECOND) OF TORTS § 416 (1965), comment a.

3. *Non-delegable duties.* Certain legal responsibilities are imposed upon employers and contractees by law. These duties simply cannot be delegated to any other persons, even including an otherwise qualified independent contractor. Typical examples of such non-delegable duties involve safe workplace requirements that are imposed upon many employers by statute. *See Porter v. Nutter*, 913 F.2d 37 (1st Cir. 1990).

PROBLEMS

1. Rafael owned a very exclusive French restaurant. He hired world-famous Chef Fillippe, known for his eccentric kitchen behavior, as the head cook. Fillippe, although compensated just like any other employee at the restaurant, was given "total authority" over day-to-day kitchen operations, including the direction of all food-related activities with respect to the kitchen staff. Because of his eccentricities, Chef Fillippe did not permit anyone other than himself to physically "touch" food once *he* prepared and personally arranged it on plates. Fillippe considered his "presentation" of the food an art form that was as important as the artistry involved in actually preparing the food. One evening Chef Fillippe became enraged after witnessing Marvin, one of the waiters, re-arrange a garnish that had been artistically placed on his signature entrée creation. Fillippe grabbed one of his personal chef knives from his knife belt and threw it at Marvin. The knife narrowly missed and ricocheted off the wall, striking Patron who helplessly watched these events unfold in horror. If Patron sues Rafael to recover damages for the injuries that she sustained because of this incident, what specific theory or theories of liability should she assert? Against whom should she assert her claim's), and what is the most likely outcome with respect to each? What types of facts should Patron seek in discovery?

2. Farmer Fred allows the County Fair to be conducted in a vacant field that he owns near the outskirts of town. The Fair is operated by a number of individual concessionaires who own and manage their own amusement booths and fairway attractions along the "midway" of the Fair. Hotshot is one such con-

cessionaire who operates a shooting gallery that he has erected along the "midway." At the rear of Hotshot's booth, he set up targets against a flimsy, thin backstop. One of Hotshot's customers fired a bullet that missed the target and passed completely through the backstop, striking Visitor. Unaware that anything had happened, the customer left Hotshot's booth (and cannot be located, since his identity is unknown). Hotshot is insolvent. If Visitor sues Fred, how should the court respond to Fred's motion to dismiss on the basis that Hotshot was an independent contractor?

D. JOINT ENTERPRISES, JOINT VENTURES, AND PARTNERSHIPS

Apart from employer-employee relationships, the law also recognizes a variety of other situations in which vicarious liability may be imputed. As with most other situations in which the doctrine of *respondeat superior* is asserted, some type of "special relationship" is still required before such liability may be imputed from one person to another person or legal entity. One particular setting in which vicarious liability is frequently asserted involves situations when the defendant has agreed, either expressly or by implication, in advance of the tortious activity, to participate with other persons in some type of common enterprise or activity. The materials which follow discuss various legal distinctions that exist among the most common types of such agreements.

CULLIP v. DOMANN
972 P.2d 776 (Kan. 1999)

DAVIS, J.

The plaintiff, David Cullip, age 14, and two friends the same age, the defendants Johnny Jack Mercer (J.J.) and William Domann, went hunting on property not owned by them. A 12-gauge shotgun carried by William accidentally discharged, striking the plaintiff and causing permanent paralysis. After discovery and partial settlement with other named defendants, the trial court granted summary judgment to J.J. and his parents, Joe and LuElla Mercer, on all of the plaintiff's negligence claims. The plaintiff appeals and we affirm.

[The evidence] established that it was the plaintiff's idea for the boys to go hunting just outside of Eskridge. The plaintiff provided two .22 rifles and a 12-gauge shotgun for the hunting trip. The plaintiff's mother, Lula O'Hara, gave the plaintiff permission to go hunting, briefly instructed the boys about gun safety, transported them to the location, and dropped them off for the afternoon.

J.J. did not know of the hunting plans until he arrived at the plaintiff's house. J.J. did not inform his parents of the plans. J.J. had never gone hunting prior to the incident and had never completed a hunter safety course. J.J. had "no real experience" with weapons other than BB guns prior to the incident. The only training J.J. received from his father regarding firearms was "to not point guns at people and stuff like this." J.J. was aware that he was required to possess a hunter safety certificate in order to hunt on another person's property. J.J. did give the plaintiff $5 to buy a box of .22 shells.

J.J.'s father, Joe Mercer, knew that J.J. had not completed a hunter safety course and was also aware that a hunter safety certificate was required to hunt on another person's property. Joe Mercer did not require J.J. to ask for permission to use a firearm and J.J. could do so at his discretion. J.J. could also go hunting at J.J.'s discretion. However, Joe Mercer had no knowledge that J.J. had ever used a loaded firearm prior to the incident. Joe Mercer testified in his deposition that it came as no surprise to him that J.J. had gone hunting with the plaintiff without adult supervision and it was foreseeable to him that J.J. would decide to use a gun.

Joe Mercer testified that at some point he would want J.J. to have adequate training in firearms use. He also felt that he had a responsibility as a parent to make sure that J.J. was properly instructed on weapon safety before using a weapon. He did not know if he had ever told J.J. about the dangers involved in using a firearm. However, Joe Mercer did not foresee extraordinary danger in J.J. hunting without adult supervision.

Just before the accidental discharge of the weapon, the plaintiff was climbing up a creek bank. J.J. knew that William was carrying the loaded shotgun in the immediate area but he was not paying attention to William. J.J. gave no warning to the plaintiff regarding William's line of fire prior to the shooting. In fact, J.J. did not know the meaning of "line of fire." The shotgun held by William accidentally discharged, striking the plaintiff and resulting in a paralyzing injury.

The plaintiff filed suit against William and his father and stepmother, as well as plaintiff's mother, Lula O(Hara. The plaintiff also named J.J. and his parents as defendants in his action. Before summary judgment, the plaintiff settled with or dismissed all the defendants except J.J. and his parents. On the Mercers' motion, the trial court granted them summary judgment. The trial court concluded [that] Joe and LuElla Mercer owed no duty to the plaintiff and that J.J. breached no duty owed to the plaintiff. . . .

The plaintiff argues that J.J.'s failure to take a hunter safety course as required by K.S.A. 32-920 is negligence per se, subjecting J.J. to liability for the plaintiff's injury and damages. The plaintiff also argues that liability may be predicated upon a joint venture giving rise to the duty of each member of the hunting party to insure that proper safety precautions were followed by all members of the joint venture. . . .

The plaintiff identified the following theories of liability in his opposition to the defendants' motion for summary judgment: (1) J.J.'s failure to comply with K.S.A. 32-920 established negligence per se; and (2) J.J., as a member of the joint venture, assumed a duty of care to follow the tenets of hunter safety and to take safety precautions, a duty which he breached. We examined both contentions in accordance with our well-established standard of review on summary judgment. . . .

[The court first concluded that J.J.'s alleged violation of K.S.A. 32-920 (hunting without having completed a hunter safety course) was not the proximate cause of the plaintiff's injury.]

The other theory advanced by the plaintiff in his attempt to establish that J.J. owed a duty to him is the theory of joint venture. Under Kansas law, a joint venture occurs where two or more persons combine to engage in a single business enterprise for profit, such that liability is imputed to all participants. *See Stricklin v. Parsons Stockyard Co.,* 192 Kan. 360, 363, 388 P.2d 824 (1964). The essential elements to establish joint venture liability are (1) an agreement; (2) a common purpose; (3) a community of interest; and (4) an equal right to a voice accompanied by an equal right of control over the instrumentality causing the injury.

The plaintiff argues that he, William, and J.J. were involved in a joint hunting venture such that they owed duties to each other in furtherance of that venture. However, under Kansas law, the recreational hunting party in this case may not be considered a joint venture. A joint venture results when the enterprise is undertaken for profit. There is no evidence or allegation that the boys were engaged in a business enterprise.

Without articulating the difference between a joint venture and a joint enterprise, the plaintiff contends that liability arises out of the joint enterprise. In Kansas, the elements of joint ventures and joint enterprises are essentially the same, with the distinction that joint ventures apply to business ventures while joint enterprises do not. The elements of a joint enterprise are (1) an agreement, (2) a common purpose, (3) a community of interest, and (4) an equal right to a voice, accompanied by an equal right of control over the instrumentality. *See Scott v. McGaugh,* 211 Kan. 323, 327, 506 P.2d 1155 (1973). In *Scott,* the question was whether a passenger might be liable to a third person for the negligence of the driver. This court held that in situations where the passenger and driver were engaged in a joint enterprise, the passenger could be held liable to third persons for the negligence of the driver.

In this case, the uncontroverted facts do not establish a joint enterprise. It is doubtful whether the first three requirements of a joint enterprise are met even though there is some evidence that plaintiff, J.J., and William might have had an agreement to hunt, a common purpose in hunting, and a community of interest. However, there is no question that the fourth element, an equal right of control over the instrumentality, is lacking.

In *Delgado v. Lohmar,* 289 N.W.2d 479 (Minn. 1979), four young men decided to go grouse hunting on the plaintiff's land without his permission. When the plaintiff saw the hunters and came out to question them, one of the hunters, who was shooting at a bird, accidentally shot the plaintiff in the eye. The plaintiff sought to hold all the hunters liable under a joint enterprise theory. However, the Minnesota Supreme Court stated that as a matter of law, the hunters were not engaged in a joint enterprise because they were engaged in a recreational activity on a gratuitous and voluntary basis with no sharing of expenses or equipment, and, more importantly, each hunter had control of his or her own gun.

The facts are similar in this case. While there was some sharing in equipment in that the guns were provided by the plaintiff, the boys each had control of their own guns. J.J. had no right to control the instrumentality involved in the negligence, William's shotgun, or indeed to control William's actions in wielding the gun.

> "Where evidence of the relationship and understanding of the parties is undisputed and the facts and circumstances clearly show a passenger [alleged participant in a joint enterprise] does not have an equal privilege and right to control . . . the issue of joint enterprise to support vicarious liability becomes one of law for the court's determination. . . ." [972 P.2d at 783.]

We conclude under the uncontroverted facts of this case that not all of the elements of a joint enterprise are present. As a matter of law, the plaintiff's theory fails.

There is a second problem with the plaintiff's theory that liability arises out of a joint enterprise. While a joint enterprise makes each member of the enterprise liable for the actions of other members with regard to third persons who are not members, it does not establish a duty of care between its members. This is somewhat in contrast to a joint venture which has been held to impose a duty on all its members to engage in a full, fair, open, and honest disclosure of everything affecting the business relationship. Thus, even if the plaintiff could have established a joint enterprise, he cannot establish that such a relationship creates a duty among and to the members of the joint enterprise.

Nevertheless, the plaintiff argues that "[a] number of authorities support liability by one member of a joint enterprise to another who is injured." [None] are authority for the proposition which he alleges. Rather, each simply notes that in a joint venture the mere fact that each member of the venture might be jointly liable to third parties does not prevent them from suing each other. In this case, the plaintiff sued William, who carried and accidentally discharged the shotgun. Depending upon the circumstances, the tortious conduct of one member of a joint enterprise may be imputed to other members in an action brought by a third party, but the tortious conduct of one member of a joint enterprise is not imputed to the other members of the joint enterprise in an action between members of a joint enterprise.

Finally, the plaintiff argues that Kansas law has recognized joint liability when parties are involved in a joint enterprise, citing *Vetter v. Morgan*, 22 Kan. App. 2d 1, 913 P.2d 1200 (1995). *Vetter* provides little, if any, support for the plaintiff's argument. In *Vetter*, the driver of a van and his passenger intentionally verbally assaulted and swerved toward the plaintiff, causing an accident. In discussing the liability of the passenger, the Court of Appeals found that one person may be liable for the tortious conduct of another when they act in concert pursuant to a common design. 22 Kan. App. 2d at 7-8. In so doing, the Court of Appeals cited RESTATEMENT (SECOND) OF TORTS § 876 (1977), setting out the rules for tort liability of persons acting in concert:

> "'For harm resulting to a third person from the tortious conduct of another, one is subject to liability if he
>
> (a) does a tortious act in concert with the other or pursuant to a common design with him, or
>
> (b) knows that the other's conduct constitutes a breach of duty and gives substantial assistance or encouragement to the other so to conduct himself, or
>
> (c) gives substantial assistance to the other in accomplishing a tortious result and his own conduct, separately considered, constitutes a breach of duty to the third person.'"

22 Kan. App. 2d at 8.

Vetter does not apply to the facts of this case. *Vetter* has nothing to do with joint venture or joint enterprise law but instead speaks only of liability for concerted tortious action. More importantly, *Vetter* establishes only that persons acting in a concerted manner may be liable for injuries to third persons. In this case, the plaintiff was a member of the hunting party, not a third person. Further, the concerted action in *Vetter* was tortious. The Court of Appeals noted that the quoted Restatement passage "corresponds to the theories of civil conspiracy and aiding and abetting."

Under the uncontroverted facts of this case, the trial court did not err in finding that J.J. had no duty to the plaintiff. . . .

Affirmed.

ESQUIVEL v. MURRAY GUARD, INC.
992 S.W.2d 536 (Tex. App. 1999)

WANDA MCKEE FOWLER, Justice.

Appellants, Debbie Esquivel and Florida Residential Property & Casualty Joint Underwriters Association ("Esquivel"), appeal from the trial court's order granting summary judgment in favor of appellee, Murray Guard, Inc. ("Murray Guard"). Esquivel brings three points of error, contending the trial court erred in (1) granting summary judgment in favor of Murray Guard on her tort claim; (2) granting summary judgment in favor of Murray Guard on her contract claim; and (3) requiring her to file a supersedeas bond for taxable court costs. We affirm.

Background

On June 19, 1994, Debbie Esquivel rented a hotel room at the Baytown La Quinta. She asked the clerk where she could park a rented U-Haul moving van containing personal property and towing her car. A clerk told her to park on the street adjacent to the hotel and assured her the van would be safe "because of the security it provided." The next day, Esquivel's van and car were missing.

Esquivel sued La Quinta for negligence, breach of warranty, breach of contract, and violations of the Texas Deceptive Trade Practices Act (DTPA), believing La Quinta was the sole provider of security. During the course of discovery, Esquivel learned that Murray Guard provided security to the La Quinta in question. She joined Murray Guard on August 30, 1996, and Murray Guard filed a motion for summary judgment asserting that the statute of limitations had run and that the discovery rule did not apply. The court granted the motion and severed Murray Guard.

Esquivel argues the trial court erred in granting summary judgment for Murray Guard on her tort claim because "a genuine issue of material fact exists as to whether La Quinta and Murray Guard entered into a joint enterprise."

Joint Enterprise Rule

Esquivel argues that, under the joint enterprise rule, her joinder of Murray Guard relates back to the date she sued La Quinta. Under this rule, courts impute liability to one who was not an active wrongdoer but who is so closely connected to the wrongdoer to warrant the imposition of vicarious liability. To establish a joint enterprise, the plaintiff must prove (1) an express agreement; (2) a common purpose; (3) a common pecuniary interest; and (4) an equal right to control the enterprise.

As an initial matter, we note that the joint enterprise theory is a vehicle to impose vicarious liability, not, as Esquivel contends, a relation-back method. "The theory of joint enterprise is to make each party thereto the agent of the other and thereby to hold each responsible for the negligent act of the other." *Shoemaker*, 513 S.W.2d at 14; *see also* RESTATEMENT (SECOND) OF TORTS, § 491 (1965). Generally, an employer/employee relationship would not qualify as a joint enterprise because there is no mutuality of control-the employer has control over the employee and usually is responsible for the actions within the course and scope of his job, but the employee does not have the right to control the employer. *See Shoemaker*, 513 S.W.2d at 16 (rejecting the argument that a joint enterprise exists where one party occupies a position of authority and has overriding control over another).

In this case, the summary judgment proof establishes, as a matter of law, that there was no joint enterprise. Murray Guard's summary judgment proof included the contract between it and La Quinta. The contract requires Murray Guard to provide security services in exchange for an hourly rate of $7.66. The contract specifically states that Murray Guard will be a "contractor" and that La

Quinta "wishes to employ" Murray Guard. All security guards are employees of Murray Guard, and Murray Guard is exclusively responsible for their salaries, taxes, and expenses. Murray Guard agrees to indemnify La Quinta for any wrongful acts or negligence and to reimburse La Quinta for expenses it incurs due to defaults under the agreement. Murray Guard is obligated to maintain insurance. Murray Guard promises to use its "best effort" to honor a request from La Quinta with respect to the discharge of any employee whom La Quinta determines fails to meet required standards set forth in the agreement. Both parties have the right to cancel the contract, but only La Quinta may change or amend a document entitled "Guard Orders." Murray Guard is allowed to provide "some guest services" (emphasis in contract), but the Guard Orders specifically state that this is not routinely authorized. While La Quinta provides a radio for contact with the front desk, Murray Guard provides all other equipment. La Quinta issues keys to guards, which must be turned in at the end of the shift along with other La Quinta equipment. A second attachment, "Statement of Work," outlines rules and responsibilities. It uses mandatory language and includes items such as the guard's responsibility to report improper lighting and use only necessary force. This attachment states that a guard shall not admit liability on the part of La Quinta and that he should never hesitate to ask for assistance from the property manager.

The contract establishes that the relationship between La Quinta and Murray Guard is strictly employer and employee. La Quinta exercises significant control over Murray Guard, but Murray Guard does not have a reciprocal right to control La Quinta. In fact, Murray Guard is expressly limited in its ability to control La Quinta, as noted by the requirement that it may not render guest services and that it must return La Quinta keys at the end of a shift. This proof is germane to a right of control. Further, given the proof that Murray Guard received an hourly rate in return for the provision of security services, there is no common pecuniary interest. Thus, Murray Guard negated two elements of joint enterprise, and the burden shifted to Esquivel to raise a genuine issue of material fact as to these elements.

Esquivel argues she satisfied her burden with the deposition of Thomas K. Worley, a vice-president of Murray Guard. Worley testified that La Quinta approved the Murray Guard shifts, decided how many guards would be provided, prepared the Statement of Work and Guard Orders, and in consultation with Murray Guard, decided the scope of the security guards' duties. This proof does not establish an equal right to control the enterprise, it only supports a contention that La Quinta had a right to control Murray Guard. In addition, it does not raise a genuine issue of material fact as to a common pecuniary interest. In short, Esquivel did not meet her burden.

NOTES AND PROBLEMS

1. As the *Esquival* case demonstrates, whether a joint enterprise or joint venture exists may have several consequences. The primary focus of this chapter is the extent to which such relationships result in vicarious liability. However, a joint enterprise or joint venture also may affect questions such as the statute of limitations.

2. Courts in a majority of jurisdictions agree that in order to impute liability upon one member of a joint enterprise for tortious conduct committed by another member, the plaintiff must establish some variation of the following:

> a. *Common Purpose.* In *Salmeron v. Nava*, 694 A.2d 709, 712 (R.I. 1997), the plaintiff tenant sued the defendant lessor for injuries that he sustained while assisting in certain renovation work that was being performed on the leased premises. In response to the defendant's argument that the plaintiff's claim was barred because at the time of the accident he was participating with the defendant in the renovation activity as a joint enterprise, the court held that there was no "common purpose" between the parties. Pointing to the fact that the plaintiff tenant had been motivated to participate in the renovation project purely because of his personal gratitude to the defendant for having previously helped him move into this country and get a job, the court explained that under such circumstances the plaintiff's "purpose in participating in the renovation project was entirely different from [the defendant lessor's] purpose in renovating the apartment. . . ."

> b. *A Community of Interest.* This requirement is more commonly associated with a joint venture than with a joint enterprise. The difference is primarily based upon the fact that the participants in a joint venture usually share some common economic or commercial goal for which their venture was established. In a joint enterprise no such economic or commercial interest is required, and seldom is such an interest even present. The mere existence of a common economic interest among the participants does not in and of itself create a "community of interest."

3. The *Cullip* opinion seems to regard "joint enterprises" and "joint ventures" as synonymous. *Accord Estate of Hernandez v. Flavio*, 930 P.2d 1309 (Ariz. 1997) (reasoning that Arizona courts have used the terms "joint enterprise" and "joint venture" interchangably to identify either commercial or social partnerships). Although it is certainly true that in either a joint enterprise or a joint venture each member of the group can be held jointly liable (under principles of vicarious liability) for the tortious conduct of other members, there are significant differences between these two types of legal relationships. As observed in *Cullip*, each member of a joint venture, because of the unique economic or commercial purpose of such an association, owes a separate *fiduciary*

duty directly to each of the other members of the group. This duty does not exist with respect to the members of a joint enterprise. For an outstanding discussion of the differences between joint ventures and joint enterprises, as well as a comparison of those theories to other vicarious liability theories discussed in this chapter, *see St. Joseph Hospital v. Wolff*, 94 S.W.3d 513 (Tex. 2002).

4. *Partnerships.* A partnership is created "when persons join together their money, goods, labor or skill for the purpose of carrying on a trade, profession or business, and where there is a community of interest in the profits or losses." *See Pharmaceutical Sales & Consulting Corp. v. J.W.S. Delavau Co.*, 59 F. Supp. 2d 408, 415 (D.N.J. 1999) (applying New Jersey law). The Uniform Partnership Act defines a partnership as "an association of two or more persons to carry on as co-owners of a business for profit." *See* U.P.A. § 6 (1999). Although there is no specific requirement that a partnership be formally established in writing, most are. Likewise, where the participants do enter into a written agreement, the actual terms of the agreement itself generally govern, regardless of the intent of each individual partner. *See Creel v. Lilly*, 729 A.2d 385, 391 (Md. 1999).

In some respects the law treats a partnership as a legal entity, like a corporation. However, in most states a partnership is not a legal person for purposes of litigation. A party generally sues the partners, not the partnership itself, and any recovery comes from the assets of the general partners.

PROBLEMS

1. Asa and Ben are teenagers who meet one evening in the parking lot of their favorite fast food hangout. They become involved in a heated debate about which of them has the faster car, and Ben challenges Asa to a race to settle the issue once and for all. They agree that the winner will receive the title to the loser's car. Asa and Ben, together with a crowd of other teenagers, proceed to the starting line on a deserted stretch of rural highway. At the appointed time, Carl, a mutual friend, starts the race. Asa and Ben speed away, tires squealing and engines roaring. As they near the finish line the two contestants are in a dead heat. At the very last minute Asa's car hits some gravel, he loses control, and skids into Ben's car. Both cars flip over and crash, seriously injuring both drivers. Asa's car continues to roll until it comes to rest upside down in a ditch. Ben's car slams into Deb, a spectator near the finish line, cheering for both contestants. If Deb sues Asa to recover for her damages resulting from this incident, what is the most probable outcome?

2. Art, Bill, and Charlie were best friends and football fanatics. Since college they had attended every home game of their beloved Rockville Rockets, a minor league, semi-pro football team. Over the years they had almost "ritualized" their gameday activities. On the morning of every game they always met at The Rocket, a local sports bar, to begin their pre-game routine. First, they painted each other with green and orange body paint "the Rockets' team colors." Then,

after a few "warm-up drinks," they drove across town to Rocket Stadium. Each week, instead of sharing carpool expenses, each member of the trio simply took turns driving his own vehicle. While at the game, they also took turns buying beer and hot dogs for each other and, by prior agreement, whoever was in the "best condition" after each game would drive the trio home at the end of the game. One day, after an exciting overtime victory by the Rockets, all three friends were pretty well intoxicated. Art passed out in the back seat as soon as they reached his car that had been parked in the parking lot at the stadium. Charlie and Bill drew straws to determine who should drive home, and Charlie was selected. Bill agreed to help Charlie navigate through the heavy post-game traffic. Halfway home, after Bill fell asleep, Charlie ran off the road and struck Pedestrian who was standing in his own front yard. Can either Art or Bill (or both) be held vicariously liable under a theory of joint enterprise for Charlie's negligent driving?

Chapter 14

COMMON LAW STRICT LIABILITY

As we learned early in the course, American courts moved toward a fault-based tort regime during the nineteenth century. Pockets of no-fault liability, however, remained in existence. This chapter discusses two major examples — strict liability for harm caused by animals and strict liability for harm caused by the conduct of "abnormally dangerous" activities.

A. ANIMALS

One of the oldest forms of strict liability holds animal owners responsible for harm caused by their animals. The RESTATEMENT OF TORTS suggests different rules depending on whether the animal is "wild" or "domestic."

For injuries caused by wild animals (those not "by custom devoted to the service of mankind at the time and in the place in which [they are] kept"), courts apply strict liability broadly. In such cases, the owner must compensate an injured plaintiff in all cases where the harm resulted from an action of the animal that is characteristic of its class. *See* RESTATEMENT (SECOND) OF TORTS §§ 506-507 (1977); *see also Irvine v. Rare Feline Breeding Ctr., Inc.*, 685 N.E.2d 120 (Ind. Ct. App. 1997); *American States Insurance Co. v. Guillermin*, 671 N.E.2d 317 (Ohio Ct. App. 1996) (applying rule to case involving a lion); *Scorza v. Martinez*, 683 So. 2d 1115 (Fla. Dist. Ct. App. 1996) (applying rule to case involving a monkey).

For domestic animals ("an animal that is by custom devoted to the service of mankind at the time and in the place in which it is kept"), however, strict liability applies only where the owner knows or has reason to know that the animal has "dangerous propensities abnormal to its class." RESTATEMENT (SECOND) OF TORTS §§ 506, 509 (1977).

The majority of domestic animal strict liability cases involve dogs, although a handful of cases involve other types of animals. *See Blose v. Mactier*, 562 N.W.2d 363 (Neb. 1997) (horse); *Van Houten v. Pritchard*, 870 S.W.2d 377 (Ark. 1984) (cat).

One interesting question with respect to domestic animals is the point at which an owner should become aware that his animal had "dangerous propensities abnormal to its class." On this issue, consider the following case.

SINCLAIR v. OKATA
874 F. Supp. 1051 (D. Alaska 1994)

HOLLAND, CHIEF JUDGE.

Plaintiffs have moved for partial summary judgment on certain aspects of their complaint.

On June 4, 1993, Daniel Reinhard was bitten by Anchor, a two-and-a-half-year-old German Shepherd dog. Daniel was two years old when he was bitten. Daniel's five year old sister, Michelle Levshakoff, witnessed the attack. Katherine Sinclair [Daniel's mother], individually and on behalf of minors, Daniel and Michelle, filed suit asserting causes of action based on negligence [and] strict liability.

[It] is not genuinely disputed that the Okatas owned the dog, Anchor, at the time that Daniel Reinhard sustained his injuries. It is also undisputed that Daniel sustained his injuries when Anchor bit Daniel's face. Both sides to the dispute agree that on June 4, 1993, Yoshihide Okata, the 17-year-old son of Yoshitaka and Kazuyo Okata, arrived home without keys to enter the home he shared with his parents. With nothing else to do, Yoshihide decided to look through the owner's manuals to the new van his parents had recently purchased. While examining the manuals, Yoshihide heard the family's dog, Anchor, in the fenced backyard crying. Anchor was a two-and-a-half year old German Shepherd. Yoshihide brought Anchor into the unfenced driveway where the van was parked and ordered the dog to "stay." The dog was not leashed, but Yoshihide stated that he believed Anchor would obey his command to stay. Yoshihide fell asleep in the van, with the dog still unleashed in the driveway. Yoshihide did not awaken until he heard Daniel Reinhard crying. He then spoke to Katherine Sinclair, Daniel's mother, who told Yoshihide that the dog bit Daniel.

There is also no dispute as to the fact that Anchor was involved in at least four previous biting incidents. On the first occasion, a young boy, Shane Perrins, was bitten after he approached Anchor in the Okata's yard. Perrins did not require medical attention, as he received only minor scratches and a small cut on his head. On another occasion, Mina Iinuma was bitten on the arm. Ms. Iinuma's injuries consisted of one or two small holes in her elbow, which did not require medical attention. The third biting incident involved Mizutaka Azuma. According to Azuma's declaration, he was bitten as he entered the Okatas' car after eating dinner with the Okatas. Azuma went to a doctor and received three stitches to his ear. A fourth incident involved Yumiko Seifert, who was bitten on her buttocks while she was a guest at the Okatas' residence. Kazuyo Okata drove Seifert to receive medical treatment. The physician's examination revealed "multiple bite marks," but there was no bleeding. Finally, there is evidence of a fifth incident involving another child, Miwa Inoue, who sustained an injury to her face requiring one stitch.

Beyond the bare facts of the [prior] biting incidents, there is a marked dispute over the manner in which the incidents are characterized. Plaintiffs assert that the incidents establish that Anchor had "dangerous propensities" and that the Okatas had actual knowledge of Anchor's dangerousness. Defendants counter with evidence that each of the four admitted biting incidents were the result of natural instincts, not of any dangerous tendencies. They refer to the testimony of an expert who declared that each of the four biting incidents admitted to by defendants were the result of overstimulation, protective instincts and chase instincts.

Plaintiffs have moved for partial summary judgment on the issue of "liability" asserting that defendants are liable on a theory of strict liability

In *Hale v. O'Neill*, [492 P.2d 101 (Alaska 1971),] the Alaska Supreme Court referred to "the doctrine of strict liability for injuries caused by a domestic animal with known dangerous tendencies." [The] court first noted that "an owner of a domestic animal becomes liable, regardless of fault, for injuries caused by the animal which stem from a vicious propensity, known to the owner." In the same paragraph, the court described the elements of such an action as being: (1) the animal's owner knew or should have known of the animal's "dangerous tendency," and (2) that the dangerous tendency resulted in an injury to the claimant.

The first issue presented under this theory of strict liability is whether Anchor had a dangerous propensity. Plaintiffs point to what they believe are five prior biting incidents to establish Anchor's dangerous tendencies. Defendants' response to this point is ambiguous. On one hand, defendants seem to argue that Anchor was not dangerous because he never intended to injure any of the biting victims. Defendants also state or imply, incorrectly, that the jury decides dangerousness in a strict liability situation.

Defendants' argument fails on this point because it overstates the requirements for a finding that a dog is dangerous. A dog does not have to show a tendency to inflict grievous injury for it to be dangerous. Plaintiffs note that "[a]ny knowledge of the animal's propensity to bite or attack, whether in anger or play, is sufficient [knowledge]."

This is the position taken in the RESTATEMENT OF TORTS as well. If Anchor did have a dangerous propensity, then it is immaterial whether this propensity was driven by anger, playfulness, affection or curiosity.

Defendants make a second type of argument which successfully raises a genuine issue of material fact on the issue of dangerousness. Throughout most of their briefing, plaintiffs engage in a qualitative analysis of the dog's behavior to determine whether the behavior was dangerous. [However, a] possessor of a domestic animal is not subjected to liability for harm simply and solely because it resulted from a dangerous propensity of the domestic animal. To be strictly liable, the possessor must have known or had reason to know of a dangerous propensity or trait that was not characteristic of a domestic animal of like kind.

Here, defendants are able to present a genuine question of fact. Defendants' expert reviewed each of the four admitted biting incidents, and as to each one she concluded that Anchor's responses were "natural" or instinctive. Plaintiffs offer no evidence, through expert testimony or otherwise, to refute the opinion of defendants' expert. It may indeed be true that Anchor's reactions in the four or five incidents were abnormal in the sense that they were not reactions typical of domesticated dogs, but plaintiffs have not established that point beyond any reasonable dispute.

Summary judgment on [the strict liability count] of plaintiffs' complaint is denied.

NOTES

1. Many states have broadened the scope of dog owner liability through statutes and ordinances. Some jurisdictions, for example, permit plaintiffs who are harmed in a public place to recover regardless of whether the defendant knew that her dog had dangerous propensities. *See* CAL. CIV. CODE § 3342 (1997); DOBBS, THE LAW OF TORTS § 345 at 947 (2000). Other jurisdictions also have enacted leash laws or similar regulations requiring dog owners to keep their dogs under control to avoid liability.

2. Early cases of harm caused by animals often involved trespassing livestock. The common law rule, derived from England, imposed strict liability on the livestock owner for all property damage caused by such animals. As early as the 19th century, however, a number of American jurisdictions began to relax this rule, allowing livestock owners to avoid liability by "fencing in" their animals. On the other hand, some jurisdictions (most notably western jurisdictions where ranchers were a powerful constituency) applied "fencing out" rules, requiring crop-growers and other landowners to protect their own land before maintaining a lawsuit against a livestock owner. *See, e.g., Maguire v. Yanke*, 590 P.2d 85 (Idaho 1978). Strict liability, in any event, is generally limited to situations where an animal trespasses upon another's real property. So, for example, if a motorist collides with a cow who has roamed onto a public highway, the livestock owner's liability will be limited to negligence. *See Bryam v. Main*, 523 A.2d 1387 (Me. 1987).

3. As discussed in the note preceding the main case, the Second Restatement of Torts defines a "wild" animal as one "not by custom devoted to the service of mankind at the time and in the place in which it is kept." RESTATEMENT (SECOND) OF TORTS § 506 (1977). A preliminary draft of the Third Restatement of Torts would change the definition to include animals that belong "to a category which has not been generally domesticated and which is likely, unless restrained to cause physical injury." RESTATEMENT (THIRD) OF TORTS: GENERAL PRINCIPLES § 19(B) (Preliminary Draft No. 2 2000). Is there a significant difference in the two definitions?

PROBLEMS

1. Suppose that a plaintiff is stung by a group of bees maintained by a bee-keeper to produce honey. Is the beekeeper strictly liable?

2. Andy and Tom are neighbors in the suburban community of Hoosierville. Both Andy and Tom own dogs. Andy's dog is a gentle Collie, which has never harmed even a flea. Tom's dog is a ferocious Pit Bull, which regularly attacks squirrels and other small animals within its reach. One morning, Tom and Andy were walking together with their dogs on leash. Suddenly, a thunderclap sounded, startling both men and causing them to drop their leashes. Tom's Pit Bull bit Andy. Andy's Collie then bit Tom.

   a. Tom and Andy have sued one another for personal injury damages. Who is more likely to be successful? Why?

   b. Suppose that Andy's wife witnessed the incident through her kitchen window. Suppose further that the shock of seeing her husband attacked by the Pit Bull caused her to drop an expensive piece of china, which shattered on the floor. If Tom is *strictly liable* for Andy's personal injuries, is he also automatically responsible for the loss of the china?

   c. Suppose that Andy's neighbor witnessed the incident through her living room window. Suppose further that the neighbor suffered severe emotional distress as a result of seeing the Pit Bull attack Andy. If Tom is *strictly liable* for Andy's personal injuries, is he also automatically responsible for the neighbor's emotional distress damages?

3. Suppose that Mary, a newcomer to Hoosierville, saw Tom walking his Pit Bull on a leash. Without asking permission, Mary reached out to pet the Pit Bull on its nose. The Pit Bull responded by biting Mary's hand. Is Tom strictly liable to Mary? Can Tom raise comparative fault as a defense?

B. ABNORMALLY DANGEROUS ACTIVITIES

FLETCHER v. RYLANDS
Exchequer Chamber, 1866
4 H. & C. 263, S.C. 53 L.J. Ex. 154, L.R. 1 Ex. 265

[The plaintiff was engaged in coal mining operations under lease from the Earl of Wilton. From 1849 to 1855, plaintiff worked the Red House Colliery in the township of Ainsworth. Subsequently, the plaintiff worked an area north of the colliery, in the township of Radcliffe.

The defendants were proprieters of the Ainsworth Mill, situated near the Red House Colliery. To supply their mill with water, the defendants began construction of a reservoir to the northwest of the colliery. The defendants employed a competent engineer and contractors to plan their project. The engineer and contractors, however, failed to notice that they were constructing the reservoir on top of old coal workings from the plaintiff's mining operations.

The defendants completed building the reservoir in December 1860. When they began filling it with water, however, the mine shafts below gave way, and large quantities of water flowed into the passages and shafts below, eventually flooding the coal workings of the Red House Colliery. As a result of the flooding, the plaintiff was forced to suspend his operations.

The plaintiff brought an action against the defendant in 1861, and received a verdict in the Liverpool Summer Assizes in 1862. This verdict was reversed in the Exchequer. The plaintiff brought error to the Exchequer Chamber.]

BLACKBURN, J.

[P]laintiff was damaged by his property being flooded by water which, without any fault on his part, broke out of a reservoir constructed on the defendants' land by the defendants' orders, and maintained by the defendant.

It also appears from the statement in the case that the coal under the defendant's land had, at some remote period, been worked out; but that this was unknown at the time when the defendant gave directions to erect the reservoir, and the water in the reservoir would not have escaped from' the defendant's land, and no mischief would have been done to the plaintiff but for this latent defect in the defendant's subsoil. And it further appears that the defendant selected competent engineers and contractors to make his reservoir, and himself personally continued in total ignorance of what we have called the latent defect in the subsoil, but that those persons employed by him in the course of the work became aware of the existence of ancient shafts filled up with soil, though they did not know or suspect that they were shafts communicating with old workings.

The plaintiff, though free from all blame on his part, must bear the loss, unless he can establish that it was the consequence of some default for which the defendants are responsible. The question of law therefore arises, what is the obligation which the law casts on a person who, like the defendants, lawfully brings on his land something which though harmless whilst it remains there, will naturally do mischief if it escape out of his land.

We think that the true rule of law is, that the person who, for his own purposes, brings on his land and collects and keeps there anything likely to do mischief if it escapes, must keep it in at his peril, and if he does not do so, is prima facie answerable for all the damage which is the natural consequence of its escape. He can excuse himself by showing that the escape was owing to the plaintiff's default; or perhaps that the escape was the consequence of vis major or the act of God; but as nothing of this sort exists here, it is unnecessary to inquire what would be sufficient. The general rule as above stated seems on principle just. The person whose grass or corn is eaten down by the escaping cattle of his neighbour, or whose mine is flooded by the water from his neighbour's reservoir, or whose cellar is invaded by the filth of his neighbour's privy, or whose habitation is made unhealthy by the fumes and noisome vapours of his neighbour's alkali works, is damnified without any fault of his own; and it seems but reasonable and just that the neighbour who has brought something on his own property (which was not naturally there), harmless to others so long as it is confined to his own property, but which he knows will be mischievous if it gets on his neighbour's, should be obliged to make good the damage which ensues if he does not succeed in confining it to his own property. But for his act in bringing it there no mischief could have accrued, and it seems but just that he should at his peril keep it there so that no mischief may accrue; or answer for the natural and anticipated consequence. And upon authority this we think is established to be the law, whether the things so brought be beasts, or water, or filth, or stenches.

Judgment reversed.

RYLANDS v. FLETCHER
House of Lords, 1868
37 L.J. Ex. 161, S.C.L.R. 3 H.L. 300, 19 L.T.N.S. 220

THE LORD CHANCELLOR (LORD CAIRNS)

The principles on which this case must be determined appear to me to be extremely simple. The defendants, treating them as the owners or occupiers of the close on which the reservoir was constructed, might lawfully have used that close for any purpose for which it might in the ordinary course of the enjoyment of the land be used; and if, in what I may term the natural user of that land, there had been any accumulation of water either on the surface or under the ground, and if by the operation of the laws of nature that accumulation of water had passed off into the close occupied by the plaintiff, the plaintiff could not have complained that result had taken place.

On the other hand, if the defendants, not stopping at the natural use of their close, had desired to use it for any purpose which I may term a non-natural use, — for the purpose of introducing into the close that which, in its natural condition, was not in or upon it, — for the purpose of introducing water either above or below ground in quantities, and in a manner not the result of any natural work or operation on or under the land, and if, in consequence of their doing so, or in consequence of any imperfection in the mode of their doing so, the water came to escape and to pass off into the close of the plaintiff, then it appears to me that that which the defendants were doing they at their own peril, and if, in the course of their doing it, the evil arose to which I have referred, — the evil, namely, of the escape of the water and its passing away to the close of the plaintiff and injuring the plaintiff, — then for the consequence of that, in my opinion, the defendants would be liable.

Therefore, I have to move your Lordships that the judgment of the Court of Exchequer Chamber be affirmed, and that the present appeal be dismissed, with costs.

NOTES

1. Although the House of Lords affirmed the Exchequer Chamber's decision, note that Lord Cairns limited the scope of its rule. In particular, Lord Cairns stated that the strict liability rule only should apply to defendants who are not "natural users" of the land. Later courts interpreted this language as meaning "ordinary, appropriate, or customary, given the character of the defendant's and surrounding properties." This meant that the rule would only apply to extraordinary — or abnormal — activities. *See* Gerald W. Boston, *Strict Liability for Abnormally Dangerous Activity: The Negligence Barrier*, 36 SAN DIEGO L. REV. 597, 603 (1999). What is the justification for such a limitation? Does it make sense?

2. Despite some early adoptions, the *Rylands* rule did not face a warm reception in late 19th century American courts. In fact, by 1900, a majority of courts that had considered the rule rejected it. *Id.* at 604; *see Losee v. Buchanan*, 51 N.Y. 476 (1873). By the 1930s, however, judicial attitudes began to change, and about half of the states had adopted some form of the House of Lords decision. This was significant as the American Law Institute ("ALI") began work on the first RESTATEMENT OF TORTS in 1934. When the ALI promulgated the new RESTATEMENT in 1938, it contained two sections suggesting liability for the conduct of "ultrahazardous" activities:

> Section 519. Miscarriage of Ultrahazardous Activities Carefully Carried On
>
> Except as stated in §§ 521-4, one who carries on an ultrahazardous activity is liable to another whose person, land or chattels the actor should recognize as likely to be harmed by the unpreventable miscarriage of the activity for harm resulting thereto from that which makes the activity ultrahazardous, although the utmost care is exercised to prevent the harm.
>
> Section 520. Definition of Ultrahazardous Activity
>
> An activity is ultrahazardous if it necessarily involves a risk of serious harm to the person, land or chattels of others which cannot be eliminated by the exercise of the utmost care, and is not a matter of common usage.

How closely do the above provisions resemble the rule of *Rylands v. Fletcher*? Professor Boston explains some of the important differences:

First, even a cursory examination reveals that the Restatement went well beyond the holding in *Rylands*, especially that of the House of Lords, because it does not by its terms incorporate the "non-natural user" principle. Instead it incorporates a notion of an activity not being "a matter of common usage" — a much different and broader idea, since an activity might be compatible with its surroundings but not constitute a common usage, "normal to the average man." Second, the doctrine of ultrahazardous activities is not limited to adjacent land owners (the circumstances of *Rylands*). Third, [Francis Bohlen, the Reporter for the Restatement project,] cited English authorities for the proposition that, while the English cases spoke in terms of "land," the word "land" is used in the broader sense of any place where 'an abnormally dangerous instrumentality, physical condition or operation is used, created or carried on. Fourth, as Bohlen candidly admitted, apart from innumerable blasting cases, *"there are only a comparatively few cases . . . which support the rule stated in this Section."*

Boston, *Strict Liability*, 36 SAN DIEGO L. REV. at 605-06. Professor Boston further explains that the First Restatement's failure to incorporate a "locational appropriateness factor" led many courts to later criticize the Restatement provisions. *See id.* at 613-14; *Wheatland Irrigation Dist. v. McGuire*, 537 P.2d 1128 (Wyo. 1975); *Otero v. Burgess*, 505 P.2d 1251 (N.M. Ct. App. 1973); *Yommer v. McKenzie*, 257 A.2d 138 (Md. 1969).

3. A leading critic of the FIRST RESTATEMENT's ultrahazardous activity provisions was Dean William Prosser, who became Reporter for the SECOND RESTATEMENT OF TORTS when the ALI began work on the project in the 1950s. In 1964, the ALI approved a much different version of the strict liability rule, which it eventually published in 1977:

Section 519. General Principle

(1) One who carries on an abnormally dangerous activity is subject to liability for harm to the person, land or chattels of another resulting from the activity, although he has exercised the utmost care to prevent such harm.

(2) This strict liability is limited to the kind of harm, the possibility of which makes the activity abnormally dangerous.

Section 520. Abnormally Dangerous Activities

In determining whether an activity is abnormally dangerous, the following factors are to be considered:

(a) existence of a high degree of risk of some harm to the person, land or chattels of others;

(b) likelihood that the harm that results from it will be great;

(c) inability to eliminate the risk by the exercise of reasonable care;

(d) extent to which the activity is not a matter of common usage;

(e) inappropriateness of the activity to the place where it is carried on; and

(f) extent to which its value to the community is outweighed by its dangerous attributes.

Does the "factors" approach of the SECOND RESTATEMENT provide courts with sufficient guidance? Does the RESTATEMENT identify the right factors? The following cases provide examples of how courts have used the factors and applied the RESTATEMENT's rules.

SIEGLER v. KUHLMAN
502 P.2d 1181 (Wash. 1972)

HALE, ASSOCIATE JUSTICE.

Seventeen-year-old Carol J. House died in the flames of a gasoline explosion when her car encountered a pool of thousands of gallons of spilled gasoline. She was driving home from her after-school job in the early evening of November 22, 1967, along Capitol Lake Drive in Olympia; it was dark but dry; her car's headlamps were burning. There was a slight impact with some object, a muffled explosion, and then searing flames from gasoline pouring out of an overturned trailer tank engulfed her car. The result of the explosion is clear, but the real causes of what happened will remain something of an eternal mystery.

Aaron L. Kuhlman, [on the] evening of November 22nd, was scheduled to drive a gasoline truck and trailer unit, fully loaded with gasoline, from Tumwater to Port Angeles. Before leaving the Texaco plant, he inspected the trailer, checking the lights, hitch, air hoses and tires. Finding nothing wrong, he then set out, driving the fully loaded truck tank and trailer tank, stopping briefly at the Trail's End Café for a cup of coffee. It was just a few minutes after 6 p.m., and dark, but the roads were dry when he started the drive to deliver his cargo — 3,800 gallons of gasoline in the truck tank and 4,800 gallons of gasoline in the trailer tank. With all vehicle and trailer running lights on, he drove the truck and trailer onto Interstate Highway 5, proceeded north on that freeway at about 50 miles per hour, he said, and took the offramp about 1 mile later to enter Highway 101 at the Capitol Lake interchange. Running downgrade on the offramp, he felt a jerk, looked into his left-hand mirror and then his right-hand mirror to see that the trailer lights were not in place. The trailer was still moving but leaning over hard, he observed, onto its right side. The trailer then came loose. Realizing that the tank trailer had disengaged from his tank truck, he stopped the truck without skidding its tires. He got out and ran back to see that the tank trailer had crashed through a chain-link highway fence and had come to rest upside down on Capitol Lake Drive below. He heard a sound, he said, 'like somebody kicking an empty fifty-gallon drum and that is when the fire started.' The fire spread, he thought, about 100 feet down the road.

When the trailer landed upside down on Capitol Lake Drive, its lights were out, and it was unilluminated when Carol House's car in one way or another ignited the spilled gasoline.

Carol House was burned to death in the flames. There was no evidence of impact on the vehicle she had drive, Kuhlman said, except that the left front headlight was broken.

Why the tank trailer disengaged and catapulted off the freeway down through a chain-link fence to land upside down on Capitol Lake Drive below remains a mystery. What caused it to separate from the truck towing it, despite many theories offered in explanation, is still an enigma. Various theories as to the facts and cause were advanced in the trial. Plaintiff sought to prove both negligence on the part of the driver and owner of the vehicle and to bring the proven circumstances within the res ipsa loquitur doctrine. Defendants sought to obviate all inferences of negligence and the circumstances leading to the application of res ipsa loquitur by showing due care in inspection, maintenance and operation. Plaintiff argued negligence per se and requested a directed verdict on liability.

The jury apparently found that defendants had met and overcome the charges of negligence. . . . From a judgment entered upon a verdict for defendants, plaintiff appealed to the Court of Appeals which affirmed. We granted review and reverse.

In the Court of Appeals, the principal claim of error was directed to the trial court's refusal to give an instruction on res ipsa loquitur, and we think that claim of error well taken. [P]laintiff was entitled to an instruction permitting the jury to infer negligence from the occurrence.

But there exists here an even more impelling basis for liability[,] the proposition of strict liability arising as a matter of law from all of the circumstances of the event.

Strict liability is not a novel concept; it is at least as old as *Fletcher v. Rylands*, L.R. 1 Ex. 265, 278 (1866), affirmed, House of Lords, 3 H.L. 330 (1868). [The court then described the case.]

The basic principles supporting the *Fletcher* doctrine, we think, control the transportation of gasoline as freight along the public highways the same as it does the impounding of waters and for largely the same reasons. *See* Prosser, Torts, § 78 (4th ed. 1971).

In many respects, hauling gasoline as freight is no more unusual, but more dangerous, than collecting water. When gasoline is carried as cargo — as distinguished from fuel for the carrier vehicle — it takes on uniquely hazardous characteristics, as does water impounded in large quantities. Dangerous in itself, gasoline develops even greater potential for harm when carried as freight—extraordinary dangers deriving from sheer quantity, bulk and weight, which enormously multiply its hazardous properties. And the very hazards inhering from the size of the load, its bulk or quantity and its movement along the highways presents another reason for application of the *Fletcher v. Rylands* rule not present in the impounding of large quantities of water — the likely destruction of cogent evidence from which negligence or want of it may be proved or disproved. It is quite probable that the most important ingredients of proof will be lost in a gasoline explosion and fire. Gasoline is always dangerous whether kept in large or small quantities because of its volatility, inflammability and explosiveness. But when several thousand gallons of it are allowed to spill across a public highway — that is, if, while in transit as freight, it is not kept impounded — the hazards to third persons are so great as to be almost beyond calculation. As a consequence of its escape from impoundment and subsequent explosion and ignition, the evidence in a very high percentage of instances will be destroyed, and the reasons for and causes contributing to its escape will quite likely be lost in the searing flames and explosions.

The rule of strict liability rests not only upon the ultimate idea of rectifying a wrong and putting the burden where it should belong as a matter of abstract justice, that is, upon the one of the two innocent parties whose acts instigated or made the harm possible, but it also rests on problems of proof.

Thus, the reasons for applying a rule of strict liability obtain in this case. We have a situation where a highly flammable, volatile and explosive substance is being carried at a comparatively high rate of speed, in great and dangerous quantities as cargo upon the public highways, subject to all of the hazards of high-speed traffic, multiplied by the great dangers inherent in the volatile and explosive nature of the substance, and multiplied again by the quantity and size of the load. Then we have the added dangers of ignition and explosion generated when a load of this size, that is, about 5,000 gallons of gasoline, breaks its container and, cascading from it, spreads over the highway so as to release an invisible but highly volatile and explosive vapor above it.

The rule of strict liability, when applied to an abnormally dangerous activity, as stated in the RESTATEMENT (SECOND) OF TORTS § 519 (Tent.Draft No. 10, 1964), was adopted as the rule of decision in this state in *Pacific Northwest Bell Tel. Co. v. Port of Seattle, supra,* at 64, 491 P.2d, at 1039, 1040, as follows:

> (1) One who carries on an abnormally dangerous activity is subject to liability for harm to the person, land or chattels of another resulting from the activity, although he has exercised the utmost care to prevent such harm.

> (2) Such strict liability is limited to the kind of harm, the risk of which makes the activity abnormally dangerous.

As to what constitutes an abnormal activity, § 520 states:

> In determining whether an activity is abnormally dangerous, the following factors are to be considered:

> (a) Whether the activity involves a high degree of risk of some harm to the person, land or chattels of others;

(b) Whether the gravity of the harm which may result from it is likely to be great;

(c) Whether the risk cannot be eliminated by the exercise of reasonable care;

(d) Whether the activity is not a matter of common usage;

(e) Whether the activity is inappropriate to the place where it is carried on; and

(f) The value of the activity to the community.

[Consider] the activity of carrying gasoline as freight in quantities of thousands of gallons at freeway speeds along the public highway and even at lawful lesser speeds through cities and towns and on secondary roads in rural districts. [O]ne cannot escape the conclusion that hauling gasoline as cargo is undeniably an abnormally dangerous activity and on its face possesses all of the factors necessary for imposition of strict liability as set forth in the RESTATEMENT (SECOND) OF TORTS § 519 (Tent.Draft No. 10, 1964), above.

Transporting gasoline as freight by truck along the public highways and streets is obviously an activity involving a high degree of risk; it is a risk of great harm and injury; it creates dangers that cannot be eliminated by the exercise of reasonable care. That gasoline cannot be practicably transported except upon the public highways does not decrease the abnormally high risk arising from its transportation. Nor will the exercise of due and reasonable care assure protection to the public from the disastrous consequences of concealed or latent mechanical or metallurgical defects in the carrier's equipment, from the negligence of third parties, from latent defects in the highways and streets, and from all of the other hazards not generally disclosed or guarded against by reasonable care, prudence and foresight. Hauling gasoline in great quantities as freight, we think, is an activity that calls for the application of principles of strict liability.

The case is therefore reversed and remanded to the trial court for trial to the jury on the sole issue of damages.

NOTES

1. If the *Siegler* court had decided not to apply strict liability, might it have reached a decision favoring the plaintiff using a different theory? How about the doctrine of *res ipsa loquitur*?

2. Courts have applied strict liability for the conduct of abnormally dangerous activity to a variety of situations. Perhaps the most common factual scenario involves harm caused by blasting. *See, e.g., Saiz v. Belen School Dist.*, 827 P.2d 102 (N.M. 1992); *Spano v. Perini Corp.*, 250 N.E.2d 31 (N.Y. 1969). However, courts also have applied the doctrine to cases involving activities ranging from

fireworks (*Klein v. Pyrodyne Corp.*, 810 P.2d 917 (Wash. 1991)), to the operation of hazardous waste site (*Sterling v. Velsicol Chemical Corp.*, 855 F.2d 1188 (6th Cir. 1988)), to the firing a rocket motor device (*Smith v. Lockheed Propulsion Co.*, 56 Cal. Rptr. 128 (Cal. Ct. App. 1967)). On the other hand, courts fairly consistently have refused to apply the doctrine in several common fact patterns, including cases involving the manufacture and sale of firearms (*Burkett v. Freedom Arms, Inc.*, 704 P.2d 118 (Or. 1985)) and the use of uninsulated power lines (*Kent v. Gulf States Utilities*, 418 So. 2d 493 (La. 1982)).

3. One area of controversy involves the use of underground storage tanks at gas stations. Some courts have found the maintenance of such tanks abnormally dangerous, particularly when leakage might threaten drinking water supplies. *See City of North Glenn v. Chevron U.S.A., Inc.*, 519 F. Supp. 515 (D. Colo. 1981); *Yommer v. McKenzie*, 257 A.2d 139 (Md. 1969). Other courts, however, have concluded that the use of such tanks is not abnormally dangerous, given that so many people buy gasoline at the stations where the tanks are located. *See Davis Bros., Inc. v. Thornton Oil*, 12 F. Supp. 2d 1333 (M.D. Ga. 1998); *Arlington Forest Assocs. v. Exxon Corp.*, 774 F. Supp. 387 (E.D. Va. 1991). Which view is more convincing?

4. Factor (f) of § 520 of the Second Restatement of Torts (the "social value" factor) has engendered significant controversy. Even at the time of its promulgation, many leaders in the academic community criticized it as "destroying the whole purpose of the strict liability doctrine." *See* RESTATEMENT (THIRD) OF TORTS: GENERAL PRINCIPLES § 21 comment j (Preliminary Draft No. 2 2000) (quoting statement of Professor John Fleming in 41 A.L.I. Proc. 458 (1964)). Scholars continue to voice similar concerns. *See* DOBBS, THE LAW OF TORTS § 347 at 953 (2000) (application of factor (f) makes strict liability "a poorly designed negligence regime"). In actual case law, however, judges rarely rely on the social value factor as determinative in decisions about whether to apply strict liability. In fact, Professor Gerald W. Boston argues that factor (f) has turned out to be largely irrelevant to the development of the law in this area:

> It is my conclusion that section 520(f) is rarely outcome determinative on the question of abnormally dangerous activity. The analysis, if any is undertaken, reflects generalities and banalities, offered without any evidence [on] the issue, these seldom warranting much respect. [Professor Fleming's] apprehension that this factor would come to dominate the analysis . . . has not borne out in the decisions.

Boston, *Strict Liability*, 36 SAN DIEGO L. REV. at 667 (1999). The current preliminary draft of the Third Restatement of Torts contains no analogue to the social value factor. Is this a positive development?

5. While Professor Boston finds that section 520(f) has had little real life impact on the development of strict liability law, he concludes exactly the opposite with respect to section 520(c) which suggests that courts consider "[w]hether the risk cannot be eliminated by the exercise of reasonable care" in deciding

whether to apply strict liability. The following case is perhaps the most widely-cited case taking strong account of this factor.

INDIANA HARBOR BELT
RAILROAD CO. v. AMERICAN CYANAMID CO.
916 F.2d 1174 (7th Cir. 1990)

Posner, Circuit Judge.

American Cyanamid Company, the defendant in this diversity tort suit governed by Illinois law, is a major manufacturer of chemicals, including acrylonitrile, a chemical used in large quantities in making acrylic fibers, plastics, dyes, pharmaceutical chemicals, and other intermediate and final goods. On January 2, 1979, at its manufacturing plant in Louisiana, Cyanamid loaded 20,000 gallons of liquid acrylonitrile into a railroad tank car that it had leased from the North American Car Corporation. The next day, a train of the Missouri Pacific Railroad picked up the car at Cyanamid's siding. The car's ultimate destination was a Cyanamid plant in New Jersey served by Conrail rather than by Missouri Pacific. The Missouri Pacific train carried the car north to the Blue Island railroad yard of Indiana Harbor Belt Railroad, the plaintiff in this case, a small switching line that has a contract with Conrail to switch cars from other lines to Conrail, in this case for travel east. The Blue Island yard is in the Village of Riverdale, which is just south of Chicago and part of the Chicago metropolitan area.

The car arrived in the Blue Island yard on the morning of January 9, 1979. Several hours after it arrived, employees of the switching line noticed fluid gushing from the bottom outlet of the car. The lid on the outlet was broken. After two hours, the line's supervisor of equipment was able to stop the leak by closing a shut-off valve controlled from the top of the car. No one was sure at the time just how much of the contents of the car had leaked, but it was feared that all 20,000 gallons had, and since acrylonitrile is flammable at a temperature of 30 degrees Fahrenheit or above, highly toxic, and possibly carcinogenic[,] the local authorities ordered the homes near the yard evacuated. The evacuation lasted only a few hours, until the car was moved to a remote part of the yard and it was discovered that only about a quarter of the acrylonitrile had leaked. Concerned nevertheless that there had been some contamination of soil and water, the Illinois Department of Environmental Protection ordered the switching line to take decontamination measures that cost the line $981,022.75, which it sought to recover by this suit.

One count of the two-count complaint charges Cyanamid with having maintained the leased tank car negligently. The other count asserts that the transportation of acrylonitrile in bulk through the Chicago metropolitan area is an abnormally dangerous activity, for the consequences of which the shipper (Cyanamid) is strictly liable to the switching line, which bore the financial brunt of those consequences because of the decontamination measures that it was forced to take. [The trial court entered judgment of $981,022.75 against Cyanamid. Cyanamid appealed.]

The question whether the shipper of a hazardous chemical by rail should be strictly liable for the consequences of a spill or other accident to the shipment en route is a novel one in Illinois.

The parties agree [that] the Supreme Court of Illinois would treat as authoritative the provisions of the Restatement governing abnormally dangerous activities. The key provision is section 520, which sets forth six factors to be considered in deciding whether an activity is abnormally dangerous and the actor therefore strictly liable.

The roots of section 520 are in nineteenth-century cases. The most famous one is *Rylands v. Fletcher*, 1 Ex. 265, aff'd, L.R. 3 H.L. 300 (1868), but a more illuminating one in the present context is *Guille v. Swan*, 19 Johns. (N.Y.) 381 (1822). A man took off in a hot-air balloon and landed, without intending to, in a vegetable garden in New York City. A crowd that had been anxiously watching his involuntary descent trampled the vegetables in their endeavor to rescue him when he landed. The owner of the garden sued the balloonist for the resulting damage, and won. Yet the balloonist had not been careless. In the then state of ballooning it was impossible to make a pinpoint landing.

Guille is a paradigmatic case for strict liability. (a) The risk (probability) of harm was great, and (b) the harm that would ensue if the risk materialized could be, although luckily was not, great (the balloonist could have crashed into the crowd rather than into the vegetables). The confluence of these two factors established the urgency of seeking to prevent such accidents. (c) Yet such accidents could not be prevented by the exercise of due care; the technology of care in ballooning was insufficiently developed. (d) The activity was not a matter of common usage, so there was no presumption that it was a highly valuable activity despite its unavoidable riskiness. (e) The activity was inappropriate to the place in which it took place — densely populated New York City. The risk of serious harm to others (other than the balloonist himself, that is) could have been reduced by shifting the activity to the sparsely inhabited areas that surrounded the city in those days. (f) Reinforcing (d), the value to the community of the activity of recreational ballooning did not appear to be great enough to offset its unavoidable risks.

These are, of course, the six factors in section 520. They are related to each other in that each is a different facet of a common quest for a proper legal regime to govern accidents that negligence liability cannot adequately control. The interrelations might be more perspicuous if the six factors were reordered. One might for example start with (c), inability to eliminate the risk of accident by the exercise of due care. The baseline common law regime of tort liability is negligence. When it is a workable regime, because the hazards of an activity can be avoided by being careful (which is to say, nonnegligent), there is no need to switch to strict liability. Sometimes, however, a particular type of accident cannot be prevented by taking care but can be avoided, or its consequences minimized, by shifting the activity in which the accident occurs to another locale, where the risk or harm of an accident will be less (e), or by reducing the scale of the activity in order to minimize the number of accidents caused by it (f). By making the actor strictly liable — by denying him in other words an excuse based on his inability to avoid accidents by being more careful — we give him an incentive, missing in a negligence regime, to experiment with methods of preventing accidents that involve not greater exertions of care, assumed to be futile, but instead relocating, changing, or reducing (perhaps to the vanishing point) the activity giving rise to the accident. The greater the risk of an accident (a) and the costs of an accident if one occurs (b), the more we want the actor to consider the possibility of making accident-reducing activity changes; the stronger, therefore, is the case for strict liability. Finally, if an activity is extremely common (d), like driving an automobile, it is unlikely either that its hazards are perceived as great or that there is no technology of care available to minimize them; so the case for strict liability is weakened.

Against this background we turn to the particulars of acrylonitrile. Acrylonitrile is one of a large number of chemicals that are hazardous in the sense of being flammable, toxic, or both; acrylonitrile is both, as are many others. A table in the record contains a list of the 125 hazardous materials that are shipped in highest volume on the nation's railroads. Acrylonitrile is the fifty-third most hazardous on the list. The plaintiff's lawyer acknowledged at argument that the logic of the district court's opinion dictated strict liability for all 52 materials that rank higher than acrylonitrile on the list, and quite possibly for the 72 that rank lower as well, since all are hazardous if spilled in quantity while being shipped by rail. Every shipper of any of these materials would therefore be strictly liable for the consequences of a spill or other accident that occurred while the material was being shipped through a metropolitan area. The plaintiff's lawyer further acknowledged the irrelevance, on her view of the case, of the fact that Cyanamid had leased and filled the car that spilled the acrylonitrile; all she thought important is that Cyanamid introduced the product into the stream of commerce that happened to pass through the Chicago metropolitan area. Her concession may have been incautious. One might want to distinguish between the shipper who merely places his goods on his loading dock to be picked up by the carrier and the shipper who, as in this case, participates actively in the transportation. But the concession is illustrative of the potential scope of the district court's decision. . . . No cases recognize so sweeping a liability. Several reject it, though none has facts much like those of the present case.

So we can get little help from precedent, and might as well apply section 520 to the acrylonitrile problem from the ground up. To begin with, we have been given no reason [to believe] that a negligence regime is not perfectly adequate to remedy and deter, at reasonable cost, the accidental spillage of acrylonitrile from rail cars. Acrylonitrile could explode and destroy evidence, but of course did not here, making imposition of strict liability on the theory of [*Siegler v. Kuhlman*] premature. More important, although acrylonitrile is flammable even at relatively low temperatures, and toxic, it is not so corrosive or otherwise destructive that it will eat through or otherwise damage or weaken a tank car's valves although they are maintained with due (which essentially means, with average) care. No one suggests, therefore, that the leak in this case was caused by the inherent properties of acrylonitrile. It was caused by carelessness — whether that of the North American Car Corporation in failing to maintain or inspect the car properly, or that of Cyanamid in failing to maintain or inspect it, or that of the Missouri Pacific when it had custody of the car, or that of the switching line itself in failing to notice the ruptured lid, or some combination of these possible failures of care. Accidents that are due to a lack of care can be prevented by taking care; and when a lack of care can (unlike *Siegler*) be shown in court, such accidents are adequately deterred by the threat of liability for negligence.

The district judge and the plaintiff's lawyer make much of the fact that the spill occurred in a densely inhabited metropolitan area. Only 4,000 gallons spilled; what if all 20,000 had done so? Isn't the risk that this might happen even if everybody were careful sufficient to warrant giving the shipper an incentive to explore alternative routes? Strict liability would supply that incentive. But this argument overlooks the fact that, like other transportation networks, the railroad network is a hub-and-spoke system. And the hubs are in metropolitan areas. Chicago is one of the nation's largest railroad hubs. In 1983, the latest year for which we have figures, Chicago's railroad yards handled the third highest volume of hazardous-material shipments in the nation. East St. Louis, which is also in Illinois, handled the second highest volume. With most hazardous chemicals (by volume of shipments) being at least as hazardous as acrylonitrile, it is unlikely — and certainly not demonstrated by the plaintiff — that they can be rerouted around all the metropolitan areas in the country, except at prohibitive cost. Even if it were feasible to reroute them one would hardly expect shippers, as distinct from carriers, to be the firms best situated to do the rerouting.

The relevant activity is transportation, not manufacturing and shipping. This essential distinction the plaintiff ignores. But even if the plaintiff is treated as a transporter and not merely a shipper, it has not shown that the transportation of acrylonitrile in bulk by rail through populated areas is so hazardous an activity, even when due care is exercised, that the law should seek to create — perhaps quixotically — incentives to relocate the activity to nonpopulated areas, or to reduce the scale of the activity, or to switch to transporting acrylonitrile by road rather than by rail, perhaps to set the stage for a replay of *Siegler v. Kuhlman*. It is no more realistic to propose to reroute the shipment of all hazardous materials around Chicago than it is to propose the relocation of homes adjacent to the Blue Island switching yard to more distant suburbs. It may be less realistic. Brutal though it may seem to say it, the inappropriate use to which land is being put in the Blue Island yard and neighborhood may be, not the transportation of hazardous chemicals, but residential living. The analogy is to building your home between the runways at O'Hare.

The briefs hew closely to the Restatement, whose approach to the issue of strict liability is mainly allocative rather than distributive. By this we mean that the emphasis is on picking a liability regime (negligence or strict liability) that will control the particular class of accidents in question most effectively, rather than on finding the deepest pocket and placing liability there. At argument, however, the plaintiff's lawyer invoked distributive considerations by pointing out that Cyanamid is a huge firm and the Indiana Harbor Belt Railroad a fifty-mile-long switching line that almost went broke in the winter of 1979, when the accident occurred. Well, so what? A corporation is not a living person but a set of contracts the terms of which determine who will bear the brunt of liability. Tracing the incidence of a cost is a complex undertaking which the plaintiff sensibly has made no effort to assume, since its legal relevance would be dubious. We add only that however small the plaintiff may be, it has mighty parents: it is a jointly owned subsidiary of Conrail and the Soo line.

The case for strict liability has not been made. Not in this suit in any event.

The judgment is reversed (with no award of costs in this court) and the case remanded for further proceedings, consistent with this opinion, on the plaintiff's claim for negligence.

NOTES

1. *Indiana Harbor Belt* is representative of many recent opinions that place great reliance on the "inability to eliminate risk" factor in deciding whether to apply strict liability. *See* Boston, *Strict Liability*, 36 SAN DIEGO L. REV. at 667 ("[S]ection 520(c) — the inability to eliminate the risk with carefulness — has emerged as the dominant factor, normally being by itself outcome determinative"). But does Judge Posner go too far by essentially requiring a plaintiff to demonstrate that proof of negligence is impossible? Professor William K. Jones makes the case:

> Judge Posner correctly observes that the "baseline common law regime of tort liability is negligence" and then proceeds to apply strict liability to patch up deficiencies in the rule of negligence. But one of the common deficiencies of the negligence regime is unavailability of proof to the injured party. If a bystander had been injured in *Indiana Harbor*, she would have had to trace this carload of acrylonitrile from the supply of the railroad car by North American Car Corporation, to the loading of the car in Louisiana by American Cyanamid, to the movement of the car to Chicago by the Missouri Pacific Railroad, to the handling of the car in the yard of the switching road, Indiana Harbor. The court was of the opinion that the leak of acrylonitrile was caused by carelessness — whether that of the North American Car Corporation in failing to main-

tain or inspect the car properly, or that of Cyanamid in failing to maintain or inspect it, or that of the Missouri Pacific when it had custody of the car, or that of the switching line itself in failing to notice the ruptured lid, or some combination of these possible failures of care.

But the conclusion that negligence is possible or even probable is not the same as identifying or proving negligence in a litigated controversy. By contrast, strict liability assures more certain accountability for accidents, providing appropriate incentives for the control of risk in advance of any mishap. Under Judge Posner's approach, each party has an incentive to point a finger at the others in an effort to shift the blame for an accident. But by then the harm has been done.

William K. Jones, *Strict Liability for Hazardous Enterprises*, 92 COLUM. L. REV. 1705, 1752-53 (1992) (reprinted by permission).

2. Even if Professor Jones persuades you, it is important to understand that strict liability is not unlimited. Section 524A of the SECOND RESTATEMENT OF TORTS, for example, states that "[t]here is no strict liability for harm caused by an abnormally dangerous activity if the harm would not have resulted but for the abnormally sensitive character of the plaintiff's activity." Do you understand how this principle might apply? *See* Problem 5, below.

3. How about defenses? Traditionally, contributory negligence was not a defense to a strict liability claim. The theory behind this rule was that because strict liability was not founded on the defendant's fault, the plaintiff's fault should not be relevant on the defense side of the ledger. *See* DOBBS, THE LAW OF TORTS § 350 at 962 (citing RESTATEMENT (SECOND) OF TORTS § 515 comment b; § 524 comment a (1965)). Courts traditionally concluded that conduct amounting to implied assumption of the risk, however, was a defense to strict liability. This dichotomy became problematic as states adopted comparative fault principles and essentially subsumed implied assumption of the risk under the comparative fault rubric. *See* DOBBS, THE LAW OF TORTS § 350 at 963. We will cover the issue of defenses to strict liability in more detail in Chapter 16.

PROBLEMS

1. Hi-Way Construction Company stored a large amount of dynamite in a hut for the purpose of clearing rocks for a new road. The storage hut was located near a new subdivision built outside of Riverdale. When the dynamite accidentally exploded, Bob, a nearby resident, sustained injuries to his person and property. Would storage of dynamite be considered an abnormally dangerous activity? What other information might be helpful in making that decision?

2. Mary was injured when a shell from a Fourth-of-July fireworks display put on by the City of Littleville malfunctioned and exploded after landing in her yard. Mary was severely burned and is now deaf in one ear. Can Mary prevail on a theory of strict liability in her suit against the City?

3. Quick-n-Go operates a convenience store and gas station located near Bardstown. At some point in late 2002, some 10,000 gallons of gasoline leaked from underground tanks buried beneath Quick-n-Go's property, migrating onto land of several Bardstown residents. On December 21, 2002, the leaking gasoline caught fire, and produced an explosion in the home of Mr. and Mrs. Johnson. As a result, they were forced to evacuate their home for three months. Can the Johnsons maintain a strict liability action against Quick-n-Go?

4. Dave fires his gun at a shooting range. One of his shots misses the target and hits Peter, a visitor in the range area. Peter sues Dave for personal injury damages, arguing that the discharge of a firearm at a range is an abnormally dangerous activity. Should he succeed in this action? *See Miller v. Civil Constructors, Inc.*, 651 N.E.2d 239 (Ill. App. Ct. 1995).

5. Suppose Defendant was driving a truck containing a large quantity of gasoline (an abnormally dangerous activity according to the court in *Siegler v. Kuhlman*) when he hit a pedestrian and broke his leg. Is Defendant *strictly liable* for the pedestrian's harm? Why or why not?

CAMBRIDGE WATER CO. v. EASTERN COUNTIES LEATHER PLC.
House of Lords, 1994
2 A.C. 264, 1 All E.R. 53

LORD GOFF OF CHIEVELEY.

My Lords, this appeal is concerned with the question whether the appellant company, Eastern Counties Leather Plc. (E.C.L.), is liable to the respondent company, Cambridge Water Co. (C.W.C.), in damages in respect of damage suffered by reason of the contamination of water available for abstraction at C.W.C.'s borehole at Sawston Mill near Cambridge. The contamination was caused by a solvent known as perchloroethene (P.C.E.), used by E.C.L. in the process of degreasing pelts at its tanning works in Sawston, about 1.3 miles away from C.W.C.'s borehole, the P.C.E. having seeped into the ground beneath E.C.L.'s works and thence having been conveyed in percolating water in the direction of the borehole. C.W.C.'s claim against E.C.L. was based on three alternative grounds, viz. negligence, nuisance and the rule in *Rylands v. Fletcher* (1868) L.R. 3 H.L. 330. The judge, Ian Kennedy J., dismissed C.W.C.'s claim on all three grounds. . . . The Court of Appeal, however, allowed C.W.C.'s appeal from the decision of the judge, on the ground that E.C.L. was strictly liable for the contamination of the water percolating under C.W.C.'s land. It is against that decision that E.C.L. now appeals to your Lordships' House, with leave of this House.

[W]e are concerned with the scope of liability in nuisance and in *Rylands v. Fletcher*. In my opinion it is right to take as our starting point the fact that [the court in *Rylands*] was concerned in particular with the situation where the defendant collects things upon his land which are likely to do mischief if they escape, in which event the defendant will be strictly liable for damage resulting from any such escape. It follows that the essential basis of liability was the collection by the defendant of such things upon his land; and the consequence was a strict liability in the event of damage caused by their escape, even if the escape was an isolated event.

Of course, although liability for nuisance has generally been regarded as strict, at least in the case of a defendant who has been responsible for the creation of a nuisance, even so that liability has been kept under control by the principle of reasonable user — the principle of give and take as between neighbouring occupiers of land, under which 'those acts necessary for the common and ordinary use and occupation of land and houses may be done, if conveniently done, without subjecting those who do them to an action. The effect is that, if the user is reasonable, the defendant will not be liable for consequent harm to his neighbour's enjoyment of his land; but if the user is not reasonable, the defendant will be liable, even though he may have exercised reasonable care and skill to avoid it. Strikingly, a comparable principle has developed which limits liability under the rule in *Rylands v. Fletcher*.

It is not necessary for me to identify precise differences which may be drawn between this principle, and the principle of reasonable user as applied in the law of nuisance. It is enough for present purposes that I should draw attention to a similarity of function. The effect of this principle is that, where it applies, there will be no liability under the rule in *Rylands v. Fletcher*; but that where it does not apply, *i.e.*, where there is a non-natural use, the defendant will be liable for harm caused to the plaintiff by the escape, notwithstanding that he has exercised all reasonable care and skill to prevent the escape from occurring.

It is against this background that it is necessary to consider the question whether foreseeability of harm of the relevant type is an essential element of liability.

I start with the judgment of Blackburn J. in *Fletcher v. Rylands* (1866) L.R. 1 Ex. 265 itself. [Judge Blackburn] spoke of 'anything likely to do mischief if it escapes;' and later he spoke of something 'which he knows to be mischievous if it gets on his neighbour's [property],' and the liability to 'answer for the natural and anticipated consequences.' Furthermore, time and again he spoke of the strict liability imposed upon the defendant as being that he must keep the thing in at his peril; and, when referring to liability in actions for damage occasioned by animals, he referred to the established principle that 'it is quite immaterial whether the escape is by negligence or not.' The general tenor of his statement of principle is therefore that knowledge, or at least foreseeability of the risk, is a prerequisite of the recovery of damages under the principle; but that the principle is one of strict liability in the sense that the defendant may be held liable notwithstanding that he has exercised all due care to prevent the escape from occurring.

I incline to the opinion that, as a general rule, it is more appropriate for strict liability in respect of operations of high risk to be imposed by Parliament, than by the courts. If such liability is imposed by statute, the relevant activities can be identified, and those concerned can know where they stand. Furthermore, statute can where appropriate lay down precise criteria establishing the incidence and scope of such liability.

It is of particular relevance that the present case is concerned with environmental pollution. The protection and preservation of the environment is now perceived as being of crucial importance to the future of mankind; and public bodies, both national and international, are taking significant steps towards the establishment of legislation which will promote the protection of the environment, and make the polluter pay for damage to the environment for which he is responsible.

Having regard to these considerations, it appears to me to be appropriate now to take the view that foreseeability of damage of the relevant type should be regarded as a prerequisite of liability in damages under the rule. Such a conclusion can [be] derived from Blackburn J.'s original statement of the law; and I can see no good reason why this prerequisite should not be recognised under the rule.

Turning to the facts of the present case, it is plain that, at the time when the P.C.E. was brought onto E.C.L.'s land, and indeed when it was used in the tanning process there, nobody at E.C.L. could reasonably have foreseen the resultant damage which occurred at C.W.C.'s borehole at Sawston.

[F]or the reasons I have already given, I would allow E.C.L.'s appeal with costs before your Lordships' House and in the courts below.

NOTES

1. By requiring plaintiffs to prove foreseeability, has the House of Lord essentially eliminated the rule of *Rylands v. Fletcher* in England?

2. In the full opinion, Lord Goff spends a good deal of time discussing the overlap between the doctrine of strict liability and the law of nuisance. We will cover nuisance in the next chapter.

3. Debate over strict liability has generated a wealth of scholarly literature. Among the leading articles and book excerpts are Guido Calibresi & Jon T. Hirschoff, *Toward a Test for Strict Liability in Torts*, 81 YALE L.J. 1055 (1972); George Fletcher, *Fairness and Utility in Tort Theory*, 85 HARV. L. REV. 537 (1972); Richard Epstein, *A Theory of Strict Liability*, 2 J. LEGAL STUD. 151 (1973); Gary T. Schwartz, *The Vitality of Negligence and the Ethics of Strict Liability*, 15 GA. L. REV. 963 (1981); and RICHARD A. POSNER, ECONOMIC ANALYSIS OF THE LAW 175-79 (4th ed. 1992).

PROBLEM

Plaintiff Robbins operates a vinyl products plant in an industrial section of Martinsville. As part of its operations, Robbins uses highly toxic chemicals, most of which it purchased from Defendant Eastman. The sale and transportation of these chemicals took place as follows: Once Robbins placed an order with Eastman for a particular chemical to be delivered, Eastman contacted a carrier. Eastman informed the carrier of the amount and type of product and the time at which Robbins requested delivery. Upon arrival at Robbins, the driver of the truck was met by a Robbins employee who took a sample of the product to check its quality and made a determination as to whether Robbins's storage tank had enough capacity to store the product being delivered. The Robbins employee sent the driver to a storage tank to unload the chemicals. The driver would then connect hoses to the tank, unload the chemicals, and disconnect the hoses. The Robbins employee was not usually present during the unloading process. Robbins alleges that, during off-loading at the Site, chemicals spilled onto the property, resulting in contamination of the soil and possibly the groundwater at or near the plant. Robbins now seeks recovery for decontamination and cleanup costs under a strict liability theory, arguing that Eastman engaged in an abnormally dangerous activity. Using the cases in this chapter as precedent, make the best arguments for both parties. *See E.S. Robbins Corp. v. Eastman Chemical Co.*, 912 F. Supp. 1476 (N.D. Ala. 1995).

Chapter 15
NUISANCE

There are two types of nuisance: "public" nuisance and "private" nuisance. A "private" nuisance is one that unreasonably interferes with the use and enjoyment of nearby property. A "public" nuisance "is a species of catch-all criminal offense, consisting of an interference with the rights of the community at large, which may include anything from the obstruction of a highway to a public gaming-house or indecent exposure."

A. PRIVATE NUISANCE

1. General Principles of Liability

Private nuisance is like negligence in that courts weigh and balance a number of factors to decide whether a particular activity constitutes a nuisance. Consider the following case.

CLINIC & HOSPITAL, INC. v. McCONNELL
241 Mo. App. 223 (1951)

BOUR, Commissioner.

[Plaintiff] operates the McCleary Clinic and Hospital in Excelsior Springs, Missouri. . . . [Defendants operate] the "Tune In" music shop. . . . [The evidence shows that: defendants operate a] record player and loud speaker every day from 8:00 or 9:00 a.m. until 7:00 or 8:00 p.m.; that on many occasions the machine [operates] as late as 10:00 or 11:00 p.m.; and that during the hours mentioned the records [are] played almost continuously. The music [was] distinctly audible in plaintiff's main hospital and clinic buildings. . . .

[O]ne of plaintiff's surgeons, and two surgical nurses[,] testified that music [from] defendants' loud speaker disturbed patients in the recovery rooms, causing them to become very restless and nervous, and that it was necessary to give some of them additional sedatives. The nurses stated that the music was "loud" and could be heard "above the traffic." [Also affected were] patients suffering from gastro-intestinal disorders and diseases of the colon. "These patients are generally the nervous, tense type of individual, [and] need quiet, rest, and relaxation along with their treatment. . . . Some of the patients [stuffed their ears with cotton or checked out because they] couldn't take any more of the noise or music. . . .

[Plaintiff's president] testified that on two occasions he called on defendants and requested them to reduce the volume of the music and explained that it was disturbing the patients; that he "reasoned with them from the standpoint of business people, fair play, fair dealing, and not only the economic side of the clinic, but the inhuman side to suffering people"; that defendants continued to broadcast the music "just as they had always done," and on several occasions he complained to the city officials. . . .

A person has the right to the exclusive control of his property and the right to devote it to such uses as will best subserve his interests; but these rights are not absolute. There are certain uses to which property may be put which so seriously interfere with the use and enjoyment by others of their property or with the rights of the public that they must be forbidden. [A] court of equity may issue an injunction enjoining the use of property or a manner of carrying on a business if either constitutes a nuisance injuring another or his property. . . .

[A] business which is lawful in itself may become a nuisance where it is not operated in a fair and reasonable way with regard to the rights of others in the use and enjoyment of their property. [I]n every case the question is one of reasonableness. What is a reasonable use of one's property and whether a particular use is an unreasonable invasion of another's use and enjoyment of his property cannot be determined by exact rules, but must necessarily depend upon the circumstances of each case, such as locality and the character of the surroundings, the nature, utility and social value of the use, the extent and nature of the harm involved, the nature, utility and social value of the use or enjoyment invaded, and the like. *See* RESTATEMENT, TORTS, Vol. IV, secs. 822, 831, pp. 214, 265. The use of property for a particular purpose and in a particular way in one locality may be reasonable and lawful, but such use may be unreasonable, unlawful and a nuisance in another locality. [It] is true, of course, that persons who live or work in thickly populated communities or in business districts must necessarily endure the usual annoyances and discomforts incident to the conduct of those trades and businesses which are properly located and carried on in the neighborhood where they live or work. But these annoyances and discomforts must not be more than those ordinarily to be expected in the community or district, and which are incident to the lawful conduct of such trades and businesses. If they exceed what might be reasonably expected and cause unnecessary harm, then the court will grant relief.

The evidence shows that [defendants'] broadcast [are] substantially different from all other sounds and noises incident to the usual activities in that district. The record does not show that the other noises are harmful to the patients or that they interfere with the operation of the clinic and hospital. Under these circumstances, it cannot be said that plaintiff's business is unsuited to the character of the locality.

Furthermore, clinics and hospitals are essential to the functioning of society, and substantial interference with their operation under almost any circumstances is relatively serious. There can be no doubt that defendants have the right to operate their music shop in its present location so long as the business is conducted in a reasonable manner with regard to the rights of others. [However, the] broadcasting of the music in the manner described [is] an unusual, unreasonable, and unlawful use of defendants' property, in the particular location and under the conditions with which we are here confronted. . . . [P]laintiff is entitled to equitable relief.

[F]reedom of action on the part of one person ought not to be curtailed more than is necessary for the public welfare or the protection of the rights of some other person. In the present case, the chancellor should have entered a judgment perpetually enjoining the defendants, and each of them, from operating any loud speaker or sound amplifier, or any record player or phonograph, or permitting the same to be operated in or about their place of business, in such manner as to cause the music or sounds produced by any such device to be audible in any part of plaintiff's said clinic and hospital buildings devoted to the care and treatment of patients.

For the reasons stated, it is the recommendation of the Commissioner that the judgment be reversed and the cause remanded with directions to enter a judgment to the above effect.

PER CURIAM.

The foregoing opinion [is] adopted as the opinion of the court. . . . All concur.

NOTE

A variety of activities have been found to constitute nuisances. In *McCarty v. Natural Carbonic Gas Co.*, 81 N.E. 549 (N.Y. 1907), the court held that the burning of soft coal in a factory constituted a nuisance when the volume of discharge was so great as to envelop and discolor neighboring dwelling houses. *See also Baldwin v. McClendon*, 288 So. 2d 761 (Ala. 1974) (pig farm with massive lagoons); *Larsen v. McDonald*, 212 N.W.2d 505 (Iowa 1973) (defendants were maintaining more than 40 dogs on their property thereby creating noise and odors).

A few activities are routinely held to be nuisances including the location of a funeral home in a residential neighborhood: "A funeral home is not a nuisance per se. [However, t]he intrusion of a funeral home into an exclusively residential district would ordinarily constitute a nuisance. . . . If transition of the district from residential to business has so far progressed that the value of surrounding property would be enhanced as business property, rather than depreciated as residential property, the establishment of a funeral home would not constitute a nuisance." *Mitchell v. Bearden*, 503 S.W.2d 904 (Ark. 1974).

PROBLEMS

1. *The nature of nuisance.* Consider *Carpenter v. Double R. Cattle Co.*, 701 P.2d 222 (Idaho 1985), dissenting Justice Bistline found a nuisance:

> We have before [us] homeowners complaining of a nearby feedlot — not a small operation, but [one which holds] 9,000 cattle. The homeowners [claim] that [the] odor, manure, dust, insect infestation and increased concentration of birds [constituted] a nuisance. If the odoriferous quagmire created by 9,000 head of cattle is not a nuisance, it is difficult [to] imagine what is. . . . [W]hile it may be desirable to have a serious nuisance continue because the utility of the operation causing the nuisance is great, [those] directly impacted by the serious nuisance deserve some compensation for the invasion they suffer as a result of the continuation. . . . This is exactly what the more progressive provisions of § 826(b) of the RESTATEMENT (SECOND) OF TORTS address. . . . What § 826(b) adds is a method of compensating those who must suffer the invasion without putting out of business the source or cause of the invasion. [T]he fairness of it is overwhelming.

The majority disagreed and held that defendant's cattle feedlot did not constitute a nuisance. The majority rejected subsection (b), Section 826, of the RESTATEMENT (SECOND) OF TORTS, which permits a finding of nuisance even though the gravity of harm is outweighed by the utility of the conduct if the harm is "serious" and the payment of damages is "feasible" without forcing the business to discontinue. Do you agree with the majority or with Justice Bistline?

2. *The line between nuisance and annoyance.* Plaintiffs lived on the second floor of a 25-story building directly below the lobby. The lobby is uncarpeted and is covered with a terrazzo floor laid directly on the uninsulated concrete lobby flooring. The lobby is used by occupants of the apartments on the upper floors going to and from their apartments. The other corridors in the building are carpeted. Plaintiffs complain that the clicking of heels on the terrazo floor constitutes an unreasonable interference with the use and enjoyment of their condominium and have demanded that the association carpet the lobby. The association has refused to do so. Is this a nuisance? Should the noise be regarded as an incident of living in a condominium? Does the noise level matter? *See Baum v. Coronado Condominium Ass'n, Inc.*, 376 So. 2d 914 (Fla. Dist. Ct. App. 1979).

WINGET v. WINN-DIXIE STORES, INC.
130 S.E.2d 363 (S.C. 1963)

Lewis, Justice.

[Plaintiff's home is located adjacent] to a grocery supermarket operated by the defendant Winn-Dixie Stores, Inc. [Plaintiffs allege that] the supermarket [is] a nuisance because of both (1) its location and (2) the manner of its operation. . . .

Defendant's business is a lawful one and was located in an area which had been zoned [for] retail business and at a location which the Zoning Board determined to be suitable for a retail grocery. . . . The fact, however, that one had been issued a license or permit to conduct a business at a particular location cannot protect the licensee who operates the business in such a manner as to constitute a nuisance. An owner of property even in the conduct of a lawful business thereon is subject to reasonable limitations. [H]e must not unreasonably interfere with the health or comfort of neighbors or with their right to the enjoyment of their property. If a lawful business is operated in an unlawful or unreasonable manner so as to produce material injury or great annoyance to others or unreasonably interferes with the lawful use and enjoyment of their property, it will constitute a nuisance.

On the other hand, every annoyance or disturbance of a landowner from the use made of property by a neighbor does not constitute a nuisance. The question is not whether plaintiffs have been annoyed or disturbed by the operation of the business[,] but whether there has been an injury to their legal rights. People who live in organized communities must of necessity suffer some inconvenience and annoyance from their neighbors and must submit to annoyances consequent upon the reasonable use of property by others.

Whether a particular use of property is reasonable and whether such use constitutes a nuisance depends largely upon the facts and no definite rule can be laid down for the determination of the question. . . .

The plaintiffs, among other things complain that (1) the store has attracted crowds of people, and many automobiles which caused noise, unhealthy fumes, blocked traffic and generally disturbed the peace and quiet of the community, and (2) trash trucks and street sweepers operated on the premises at late night hours.

[I]t cannot be properly held that the normal traffic and noise caused by customers going to and from the supermarket would constitute a basis for declaring the operation of the business a nuisance. [T]he purpose of the business [is] to sell merchandise and in doing so to attract to their store as many customers as possible. It is a natural consequence and incident of the operation [that] there will be an increase in the number of people visiting the area. [The] store is operated only on week days, opening for business at 8:30 a.m. each day and never closing later than 7:30 p.m. While [the] operation of the supermarket has caused an increase in the number of people and automobiles coming into the area, there is nothing to show that there was any mass entrance to or exodus from the store at unreasonable hours. [T]he traffic [was] the normal traffic of patrons visiting such a grocery store over the usual business day. There is no basis for holding that [this] constituted a nuisance.

Neither do we think that the operation of trash trucks and street sweepers in connection with the removal of trash and garbage [can] form the basis of a finding of a nuisance. [The] noise complained of from [the City] trash trucks and mechanical street sweepers could not be charged to the defendants anymore than, generally, their operation by the City in collecting trash and garbage at any other business establishment could be attributed to those business owners.

[W]ith regard to other allegations of the complaint, [some issues should have been submitted to the jury.] [D]efendants erected fans on their building in connection with the air conditioning equipment. These fans were so directed as to blow against the trees and shrubbery on plaintiffs' property causing some damage and inconvenience. [Also, for a while,] the floodlights on defendants' lot caused a bright glare over the property of plaintiffs until late at night so as to disturb the plaintiffs in the enjoyment of their home, obnoxious odors were created from the garbage which accumulated at defendants' store, [and] paper and trash from the defendants' garbage was permitted to escape onto plaintiffs' lot to an unusual extent. The record gives rise to a reasonable inference that such acts were not normal or necessary incidents of the operation of the business. [T]he trial judge properly refused the defendants' motion for a directed verdict.

[The] acts which would form any basis for damages [have] been largely, if not entirely, discontinued. It was no doubt for this reason that the court ruled that no grounds existed for the issuance of an injunction. . . .

[Reversed] and remanded for a new trial.

NOTES

1. *Nuisance, Neglience and Trespass.* The same conduct can constitute nuisance, trespass and, possibly, negligence. For example, in *Smith v. New England Aircraft Co.*, 170 N.E. 385 (Mass. 1930), the court held that low-level flights over plaintiff's land constituted a trespass. Assuming that the flights also constituted an "unreasonable interference with the use and enjoyment" of plaintiff's land, they might constitute a private nuisance. *See also Martin v. Reynolds Metals Co.*, 342 P.2d 790 (Or. 1959) (emissions from defendant's aluminum reduction plant settled on plaintiff's land rendering it unfit to raise livestock). *Copart Industries, Inc. v. Consolidated Edison Co.*, 362 N.E.2d 968 (N.Y. 1977), is a case that analyzed the difference between nuisance and negligence. It concluded that the distinction between the two is primarily important to determine whether equitable defenses are available.

2. *Prescriptive Easement.* If a nuisance is maintained long enough, the operator may gain a prescriptive easement to continue it. In *Hoffman v. United Iron and Metal Co., Inc.*, 671 A.2d 55 (Md. Ct. Spec. App. 1996), defendants operated a scrap metal yard and automobile shredder operation for more than twenty years. During this period, there were more than 250 explosions. The court held that a prescriptive easement accrued after 20 years.

PROBLEMS

1. *Nursery next to Nursing Home.* Plaintiffs, the elderly proprietors of a guest house, allege that defendants' day nursery for young children constitutes a nuisance. Plaintiffs' guests complain about the noise and plaintiffs have seen a decline in business. Nearby are three filling stations, a thirty-room hotel, a doctor's office, an insurance agency, several guest houses, and a residence. A railway station and rail tracks are behind the properties. There was no zoning ordinance prohibiting either business. Children arrive at the nursery about 8:00 a.m. and leave about 5:00 p.m., taking a nap after being fed their lunch. The children play outside in a limited and supervised manner. Their actions and singing inside are supervised and actions were taken to minimize the noise. How would plaintiffs argue that the nursery constitutes a nuisance? How might defendants respond? If you were the judge, how would you rule? *See Beckman v. Marshall*, 85 So. 2d 552 (Fla. 1956).

2. *How Does a Court Determine the "Social Utility" of Each Party's Conduct?* Defendant ECS operates a center which provides free meals to indigent persons. Plaintiff, a corporation organized for the purpose of "improving, maintaining and insuring the quality of the neighborhood," sought a preliminary injunction prohibiting ECS from offering free meals. The area is primarily residential with only a few small businesses. When the center began operating, many transients crossed the neighborhood on their way to and from the center. Although the center is only open from 5:00 to 6:00 p.m., patrons line up well before 5:00 p.m. and often linger in the neighborhood long after finishing their meal. The center rented an adjacent fenced lot for a waiting area and organized neighborhood cleaning projects. Nevertheless transients frequently trespass on residents' yards, sometimes urinating, defecating, drinking and littering. A few have broken into storage areas and unoccupied homes, and some have begged residents for handouts. The number of arrests in the area has increased dramatically. Many residents are frightened or annoyed by the transients and have altered their lifestyles to avoid them. What arguments might the residents make on behalf of a request for treating the center as a nuisance? How might the Center respond? If you were the judge in this case, how would you rule? *See Armory Park Neighborhood Ass'n v. Episcopal Community Services*, 712 P.2d 914 (Ariz. 1985).

3. *Zoning laws.* The plaintiff, Ben Weaver, is a homeowner who lives in Great Falls, Montana. The defendant, Diversified Scientific Services (DSS),

has decided to build a hazardous waste incinerator on property across the street from the Weaver residence. Weaver fears that the incinerator will spew out hazardous waste thereby creating a nuisance. DSS disagrees noting that the incinerator is being built in compliance with all federal and state regulations, and therefore should not constitute a nuisance if operated properly. How should the court resolve these competing claims? If it is "possible" to operate the incinerator without creating a nuisance, is it appropriate for the court to issue the injunction before the incinerator is finished and operating? Would it matter whether the area was zoned residential so that the operation of an incinerator is illegal? *See Pace v. Diversified Scientific Services, Inc.*, 1993 Tenn. App. LEXIS 17; *Parker v. Ashford*, 661 So. 2d 213 (Ala. 1995).

4. *Church bells.* Plaintiff lives close to a Roman Catholic church which is located on a public street in a thickly-settled part of town. On Sunday mornings, the church rings a bell to call the faithful to worship. Plaintiff, whose mental and physical condition makes him painfully sensitive to noise, claims that the bell constitutes a nuisance. Others in the community have not complained. Does the bell ringing constitute a nuisance? *See Rogers v. Elliott*, 15 N.E. 768 (Mass. 1888).

5. *Lines of Customers.* Morrison's Cafeteria is located close to appellant's drug store. At mealtime, the cafeteria's customers form lines on the sidewalk which frequently block the entrances to appellant's drug store for long periods of time. Should this blockage be treated as a nuisance? How would you argue the case for plaintiff? How might Morrison's respond? *See Shamhart v. Morrison Cafeteria Co.*, 32 So. 2d 727 (Fla. 1947).

6. *Lights.* Plaintiff owns a drive-in theater. To shield his screen from cars on an adjoining highway, plaintiff built wing fences. In an effort to exclude moonlight, plaintiff built a shadow box around his screen. Later, defendant built a horse racing track next door. Plaintiff's screen faces directly toward the defendant's race track. To illuminate his track for night racing (the most profitable time), defendant installed 350 1500-watt lights in clusters on 80-foot poles at 250 foot intervals at a cost of $100,000. The flood lights were directed at the track, but adversely affected the quality of pictures on plaintiff's screen. Plaintiffs have suffered a loss of business including financial losses. The light from the race track when measured at plaintiff's screen approximated that of full moonlight. After the lights were installed, plaintiff immediately complained. Defendant denied liability, but tried to protect plaintiff by installing hoods on his lights, particularly those near plaintiff's property. He also installed thirty louvers to confine the light to his property. These efforts materially reduced, but did not eliminate the interference. How can plaintiff argue that defendant's lights constitute a nuisance? How would you argue the case on plaintiff's behalf? Who should win? *See Amphitheaters, Inc. v. Portland Meadows*, 198 P.2d 847 (Or. 1948).

7. *Parking.* Plaintiff, The Great Atlantic & Pacific Tea Co. (A&P), sued to enjoin construction of a drive-in bank facility in the parking lot of a shopping

center in which plaintiff maintains a store. A&P objected to the facility on the basis that it would interfere with A&P's business by depriving it of parking spaces, disrupting the pattern of customer travel, and affecting visibility of A&P's store. What would A&P have to prove in order to prevail? *See Great Atlantic & Pacific Tea Co., Inc. v. LaSalle National Bank*, 395 N.E.2d 1193 (Ill. App. Ct. 1979).

8. *The Relationship Between Negligence and Nuisance?* Plaintiff sued contending that an oil refinery was a private nuisance. Defendant refinery claimed that there was no evidence showing that the oil refinery was constructed or operated in a negligent manner, and that therefore the evidence did not establish the existence of either an actionable or an abatable private nuisance. Is a finding of "negligence" necessary in a nuisance action? If not, what is the basis of liability? If defendant "knows" that the refinery is interfering with plaintiff's property, is that "knowledge" sufficient to impose liability? *See Morgan v. High Penn Oil Co.*, 77 S.E.2d 682 (N.C. 1953).

2. Remedies

A variety of remedies are available against a private nuisance. One remedy is damages. Another remedy is fashioning an appropriate injunctive relief. Both issues are presented by the following case.

BOOMER v. ATLANTIC CEMENT COMPANY
257 N.E.2d 870 (N.Y. 1970)

BERGAN, Judge.

Defendant operates a large cement plant near Albany. These are actions for injunction and damages by neighboring land owners alleging injury to property from dirt, smoke and vibration emanating from the plant. A nuisance has been found after trial, temporary damages have been allowed; but an injunction has been denied.

The public concern with air pollution arising from many sources in industry and in transportation is currently accorded ever wider recognition accompanied by a growing sense of responsibility in State and Federal Governments to control it. Cement plants are obvious sources of air pollution in the neighborhoods where they operate.

But there is now before the court private litigation in which individual property owners have sought specific relief from a single plant operation. The threshold question raised by the division of view on this appeal is whether the court should resolve the litigation between the parties now before it as equitably as seems possible; or whether, seeking promotion of the general public welfare, it should channel private litigation into broad public objectives.

A court performs its essential function when it decides the rights of parties before it. Its decision of private controversies may sometimes greatly affect public issues. Large questions of law are often resolved by the manner in which private litigation is decided. But this is normally an incident to the court's main function to settle controversy. It is a rare exercise of judicial power to use a decision in private litigation as a purposeful mechanism to achieve direct public objectives greatly beyond the rights and interests before the court.

Effective control of air pollution is a problem presently far from solution even with the full public and financial powers of government. In large measure adequate technical procedures are yet to be developed and some that appear possible may be economically impracticable.

It seems apparent that the amelioration of air pollution will depend on technical research in great depth; on a carefully balanced consideration of the economic impact of close regulation; and of the actual effect on public health. It is likely to require massive public expenditure and to demand more than any local community can accomplish and to depend on regional and interstate controls.

A court should not try to do this on its own as a by-product of private litigation and it seems manifest that the judicial establishment is neither equipped in the limited nature of any judgment it can pronounce nor prepared to lay down and implement an effective policy for the elimination of air pollution. This is an area beyond the circumference of one private lawsuit. It is a direct responsibility for government and should not thus be undertaken as an incident to solving a dispute between property owners and a single cement plant — one of many — in the Hudson River valley.

The cement making operations of defendant have been found by the court of Special Term to have damaged the nearby properties of plaintiffs in these two actions. That court [found that] defendant maintained a [nuisance]. The total damage to plaintiffs' properties is, however, relatively small in comparison with the value of defendant's operation and with the consequences of the injunction which plaintiffs seek.

The ground for the denial of injunction, notwithstanding the finding both that there is a nuisance and that plaintiffs have been damaged substantially, is the large disparity in economic consequences of the nuisance and of the injunction. This theory cannot, however, be sustained without overruling a doctrine which has been consistently reaffirmed in several leading cases in this court and which has never been disavowed here, namely that where a nuisance has been found and where there has been any substantial damage shown by the party complaining an injunction will be granted.

The rule in New York has been that such a nuisance will be enjoined although marked disparity be shown in economic consequence between the effect of the injunction and the effect of the nuisance.

[Although] the court at Special Term and the Appellate Division held that injunction should be denied, it was found that plaintiffs had been damaged in various specific amounts up to the time of the trial and damages to the respective plaintiffs were awarded for those amounts. The effect of this was, injunction having been denied, plaintiffs could maintain successive actions at law for damages thereafter as further damage was incurred.

The court at Special Term also found the amount of permanent damage attributable to each plaintiff, for the guidance of the parties in the event both sides stipulated to the payment and acceptance of such permanent damage as a settlement of all the controversies among the parties. The total of permanent damages to all plaintiffs thus found was $185,000. This basis of adjustment has not resulted in any stipulation by the parties.

This result at Special Term and at the Appellate Division is a departure from a rule that has become settled; but to follow the rule literally in these cases would be to close down the plant at once. This court is fully agreed to avoid that immediately drastic remedy; the difference in view is how best to avoid it.

One alternative is to grant the injunction but postpone its effect to a specified future date to give opportunity for technical advances to permit defendant to eliminate the nuisance; another is to grant the injunction conditioned on the payment of permanent damages to plaintiffs which would compensate them for the total economic loss to their property present and future caused by defendant's operations. For reasons which will be developed the court chooses the latter alternative.

If the injunction were to be granted unless within a short period — *e.g.*, 18 months — the nuisance be abated by improved methods, there would be no assurance that any significant technical improvement would occur.

The parties could settle this private litigation at any time if defendant paid enough money and the imminent threat of closing the plant would build up the pressure on defendant. If there were no improved techniques found, there would inevitably be applications to the court at Special Term for extensions of time to perform on showing of good faith efforts to find such techniques.

Moreover, techniques to eliminate dust and other annoying by-products of cement making are unlikely to be developed by any research the defendant can undertake within any short period, but will depend on the total resources of the cement industry nationwide and throughout the world. The problem is universal wherever cement is made.

For obvious reasons the rate of the research is beyond control of defendant. If at the end of 18 months the whole industry has not found a technical solution a court would be hard put to close down this one cement plant if due regard be given to equitable principles.

On the other hand, to grant the injunction unless defendant pays plaintiffs such permanent damages as may be fixed by the court seems to do justice between the contending parties. All of the attributions of economic loss to the properties on which plaintiffs' complaints are based will have been redressed.

The nuisance complained of by these plaintiffs may have other public or private consequences, but these particular parties are the only ones who have sought remedies and the judgment proposed will fully redress them. The limitation of relief granted is a limitation only within the four corners of these actions and does not foreclose public health or other public agencies from seeking proper relief in a proper court.

It seems reasonable to think that the risk of being required to pay permanent damages to injured property owners by cement plant owners would itself be a reasonable effective spur to research for improved techniques to minimize nuisance.

The power of the court to condition on equitable grounds the continuance of an injunction on the payment of permanent damages seems undoubted.

[The] theory of damage is the "servitude on land" of plaintiffs imposed by defendant's nuisance. [This] judgment, by allowance of permanent damages imposing a servitude on land, [would] preclude future recovery by plaintiffs or their grantees.

This should be placed beyond debate by a provision of the judgment that the payment by defendant and the acceptance by plaintiffs of permanent damages found by the court shall be in compensation for a servitude on the land.

[The] orders should be reversed, without costs, and the cases remitted to Supreme Court, Albany County to grant an injunction which shall be vacated upon payment by defendant of such amounts of permanent damage to the respective plaintiffs as shall for this purpose be determined by the court.

JASEN, Judge (dissenting).

[T]he Legislature [has] enacted the Air Pollution Control Act declaring that it is the State policy to require the use of all available and reasonable methods to prevent and control air pollution.

The harmful nature and widespread occurrence of air pollution have been extensively documented. Congressional hearings have revealed that air pollution causes substantial property damage, as well as being a contributing factor to a rising incidence of lung cancer, emphysema, bronchitis and asthma.

The specific problem faced here is known as particulate contamination because of the fine dust particles emanating from defendant's cement plant. [It] is interesting to note that cement production has recently been identified as a significant source of particulate contamination in the Hudson Valley. This type of pollution, wherein very small particles escape and stay in the atmosphere, has been denominated as the type of air pollution which produces the greatest hazard to human health. We have thus a nuisance which not only is damaging to the plaintiffs, but also is decidedly harmful to the general public.

I see grave dangers in overruling our long-established rule of granting an injunction where a nuisance results in substantial continuing damage. In permitting the injunction to become inoperative upon the payment of permanent damages, the majority is, in effect, licensing a continuing wrong. It is the same as saying to the cement company, you may continue to do harm to your neighbors so long as you pay a fee for it. Furthermore, once such permanent damages are assessed and paid, the incentive to alleviate the wrong would be eliminated, thereby continuing air pollution of an area without abatement.

[This] kind of inverse condemnation may not be invoked by a private person or corporation for private gain or advantage. Inverse condemnation should only be permitted when the public is primarily served in the taking or impairment of property. The promotion of the interests of the polluting cement company has, in my opinion, no public use or benefit.

Nor is it constitutionally permissible to impose servitude on land, without consent of the owner, by payment of permanent damages where the continuing impairment of the land is for a private use. This is made clear by the State Constitution (art. I, § 7, subd. (a)) which provides that "[p]rivate property shall not be taken for *Public use* without just compensation". It is, of course, significant that the section makes no mention of taking for a *Private use*.

In sum, then, by constitutional mandate as well as by judicial pronouncement, the permanent impairment of private property for private purposes is not authorized in the absence of clearly demonstrated public benefit and use.

I would enjoin the defendant cement company from continuing the discharge of dust particles upon its neighbors' properties unless, within 18 months, the cement company abated this nuisance.

It is not my intention to cause the removal of the cement plant from the Albany area, but to recognize the urgency of the problem stemming from this stationary source of air pollution, and to allow the company a specified period of time to develop a means to alleviate this nuisance.

I am aware that the trial court found that the most modern dust control devices available have been installed in defendant's plant, but, I submit, this does not mean that *better* and more effective dust control devices could not be developed within the time allowed to abate the pollution.

Moreover, I believe it is incumbent upon the defendant to develop such devices, since the cement company, at the time the plant commenced production (1962), was well aware of the plaintiffs' presence in the area, as well as the probable consequences of its contemplated operation. Yet, it still chose to build and operate the plant at this site.

In a day when there is a growing concern for clean air, highly developed industry should not expect acquiescence by the courts, but should, instead, plan its operations to eliminate contamination of our air and damage to its neighbors.

Accordingly, the orders of the Appellate Division, insofar as they denied the injunction, should be reversed, and the actions remitted to Supreme Court, Albany County to grant an injunction to take effect 18 months hence, unless the nuisance is abated by improved techniques prior to said date. . . .

NOTES

1. As the *Boomer* case suggests, courts distinguish between "temporary" nuisances and "permanent" nuisances. When permanent damages are awarded, they impose a servitude on plaintiff's land. Such damages are calculated based on the diminution in value theory. Damages for temporary nuisances historically focused on diminution in rental value. Special damages were also available.

2. Since injunctions are equitable decrees, and therefore inherently discretionary, courts are free to shape their orders as required by the circumstances. In some cases, courts are moved by the balance of equities (including disproportionate economic consequences, the public interest, and other factors) to enter partial injunctions (a.k.a. experimental injunctions) or conditional injunctions. The following cases are illustrative.

SPUR INDUSTRIES, INC. v. DEL E. WEBB DEVELOPMENT CO.
1494 P.2d 700 (Ariz. 1972)

CAMERON, Vice Chief Justice.

From a judgment permanently enjoining the defendant, Spur Industries, Inc., from operating a cattle feedlot near the plaintiff Del E. Webb Development Company's Sun City, Spur appeals. Webb cross-appeals. Although numerous issues are raised, we feel that it is necessary to answer only two questions. They are: 1. Where the operation of a business, such as a cattle feedlot is lawful in the first instance, but becomes a nuisance by reason of a nearby residential area, may the feedlot operation be enjoined in an action brought by the developer of the residential area? 2. Assuming that the nuisance may be enjoined, may the developer of a completely new town or urban area in a previously agricultural area be required to indemnify the operator of the feedlot who must move or cease operation because of the presence of the residential area created by the developer?

[The] area in question is located in Maricopa County, Arizona, some 14 to 15 miles west of the urban area of Phoenix, on the Phoenix-Wickenburg Highway, also known as Grand Avenue. About two miles south of Grand Avenue is Olive Avenue which runs east and west. 111th Avenue runs north and south as does the Agua Fria River immediately to the west.

Farming started in this area about 1911. In 1929, with the completion of the Carl Pleasant Dam, gravity flow water became available to the property located to the west of the Agua Fria River, though land to the east remained dependent upon well water for irrigation. By 1950, the only urban areas in the vicinity were the agriculturally related communities of Peoria, El Mirage, and Surprise located along Grand Avenue. Along 111th Avenue, approximately one mile south of Grand Avenue and 1½ miles north of Olive Avenue, the community of Youngtown was commenced in 1954. Youngtown is a retirement community appealing primarily to senior citizens.

In 1956, Spur's predecessors in interest, H. Marion Welborn and the Northside Hay Mill and Trading Company, developed feed-lots, about ½ mile south of Olive Avenue, in an area between the confluence of the usually dry Agua Fria and New Rivers. The area is well suited for cattle feeding and in 1959, there were 25 cattle feeding pens or dairy operations within a 7 mile radius of the location developed by Spur's predecessors. In April and May of 1959, the Northside Hay Mill was feeding between 6,000 and 7,000 head of cattle and Welborn approximately 1,500 head on a combined area of 35 acres.

In May of 1959, Del Webb began to plan the development of an urban area to be known as Sun City. For this purpose, the Marinette and the Santa Fe Ranches, some 20,000 acres of farmland, were purchased for $15,000,000 or $750.00 per acre. This price was considerably less than the price of land located near the urban area of Phoenix, and along with the success of Youngtown was a factor influencing the decision to purchase the property in question.

By September 1959, Del Webb had started construction of a golf course south of Grand Avenue and Spur's predecessors had started to level ground for more feedlot area. In 1960, Spur purchased the property in question and began a rebuilding and expansion program extending both to the north and south of the original facilities. By 1962, Spur's expansion program was completed and had expanded from approximately 35 acres to 114 acres.

Accompanied by an extensive advertising campaign, homes were first offered by Del Webb in January 1960 and the first unit to be completed was south of Grand Avenue and approximately 2½ miles north of Spur. By 2 May 1960, there were 450 to 500 houses completed or under construction. At this time, Del Webb did not consider odors from the Spur feed pens a problem and Del Webb continued to develop in a southerly direction, until sales resistance became so great that the parcels were difficult if not impossible to sell. . . .

By December 1967, Del Webb's property had extended south to Olive Avenue and Spur was within 500 feet of Olive Avenue to the north. Del Webb filed its original complaint alleging that in excess of 1,300 lots in the southwest portion were unfit for development for sale as residential lots because of the operation of the Spur feedlot.

Del Webb's suit complained that the Spur feeding operation was a public nuisance because of the flies and the odor which were drifting or being blown by the prevailing south to north wind over the southern portion of Sun City. At the time of the suit, Spur was feeding between 20,000 and 30,000 head of cattle, and the facts amply support the finding of the trial court that the feed pens had become a nuisance to the people who resided in the southern part of Del Webb's development. The testimony indicated that cattle in a commercial feedlot will produce 35 to 40 pounds of wet manure per day, per head, or over a million pounds of wet manure per day for 30,000 head of cattle, and that despite the admittedly good feedlot management and good housekeeping practices by Spur, the resulting odor and flies produced an annoying if not unhealthy situation as far as the senior citizens of southern Sun City were concerned. There is no doubt that some of the citizens of Sun City were unable to enjoy the outdoor living which Del Webb had advertised and that Del Webb was faced with sales resistance from prospective purchasers as well as strong and persistent complaints from the people who had purchased homes in that area.

Trial was commenced before the court with an advisory jury. The advisory jury was later discharged and the trial was continued before the court alone. [In] one of the special actions before this court, Spur agreed to, and did, shut down its operation without prejudice to a determination of the matter on appeal. On appeal the many questions raised were extensively briefed.

It is noted, however, that neither the citizens of Sun City nor Youngtown are represented in this lawsuit and the suit is solely between Del E. Webb Development Company and Spur Industries, Inc.

MAY SPUR BE ENJOINED?

The difference between a private nuisance and a public nuisance is generally one of degree. A private nuisance is one affecting a single individual or a definite small number of persons in the enjoyment of private rights not common to the public, while a public nuisance is one affecting the rights enjoyed by citizens as a part of the public. To constitute a public nuisance, the nuisance must affect a considerable number of people or an entire community or neighborhood.

Where the injury is slight, the remedy for minor inconveniences lies in an action for damages rather than in one for an injunction. Moreover, some courts have held, in the "balancing of conveniences" cases, that damages may be the sole remedy.

Thus, it would appear from the admittedly incomplete record as developed in the trial court, that, at most, residents of Youngtown would be entitled to damages rather than injunctive relief.

We have no difficulty, however, in agreeing with the conclusion of the trial court that Spur's operation was an enjoinable public nuisance as far as the people in the southern portion of Del Webb's Sun City were concerned.

§ 36-601, subsec. A reads as follows:

"Public nuisances dangerous to public health A. The following conditions are specifically declared public nuisances dangerous to the public health:

1. Any condition or place in populous areas which constitutes a breeding place for flies, rodents, mosquitoes and other insects which are capable of carrying and transmitting disease-causing organisms to any person or persons."

By this statute, before an otherwise lawful (and necessary) business may be declared a public nuisance, there must be a "populous" area in which people are injured: "[I]t hardly admits a doubt that, in determining the question as to whether a lawful occupation is so conducted as to constitute a nuisance as a matter of fact, the locality and surroundings are of the first importance. (citations omitted) A business which is not per se a public nuisance may become such by being carried on at a place where the health, comfort, or convenience of a populous neighborhood is affected. [W]hat might amount to a serious nuisance in one locality by reason of the density of the population, or character of the neighborhood affected, may in another place and under different surroundings be deemed proper and [unobjectionable]." *MacDonald v. Perry*, 32 Ariz. 39, 49–50, 255 P. 494, 497 (1927).

It is clear that as to the citizens of Sun City, the operation of Spur's feedlot was both a public and a private nuisance. They could have successfully maintained an action to abate the nuisance. Del Webb, having shown a special injury in the loss of sales, had a standing to bring suit to enjoin the nuisance. The judgment of the trial court permanently enjoining the operation of the feedlot is affirmed.

MUST DEL WEBB INDEMNIFY SPUR?

A suit to enjoin a nuisance sounds in equity and the courts have long recognized a special responsibility to the public when acting as a court of equity:

§ 104. Where public interest is involved. "Courts of equity may, and frequently do, go much further both to give and withhold relief in furtherance of the public interest than they are accustomed to go when only private interests are involved. Accordingly, the granting or withholding of relief may properly be dependent upon considerations of public [interest]." § 27 Am.Jur.2d, Equity, page 626.

In addition to protecting the public interest, however, courts of equity are concerned with protecting the operator of a lawfully, albeit noxious, business from the result of a knowing and willful encroachment by others near his business.

In the so-called "coming to the nuisance" cases, the courts have held that the residential landowner may not have relief if he knowingly came into a neighborhood reserved for industrial or agricultural endeavors and has been damaged thereby: "Plaintiffs chose to live in an area uncontrolled by zoning laws or restrictive covenants and remote from urban development. In such an area plaintiffs cannot complain that legitimate agricultural pursuits are being carried on in the vicinity, nor can plaintiffs, having chosen to build in an agricultural area, complain that the agricultural pursuits carried on in the area depreciate the value of their homes. The area being primarily agricultural, and opinion reflecting the value of such property must take this factor into account. The standards affecting the value of residence property in an urban setting, subject to zoning controls and controlled planning techniques, cannot be the standards by which agricultural properties are judged. "People employed in a city who build their homes in suburban areas of the county beyond the limits of a city and zoning regulations do so for a reason. Some do so to avoid the high taxation rate imposed by cities, or to avoid special assessments for street, sewer and water projects. They usually build on improved or hard surface highways, which have been built either at state or county expense and thereby avoid special assessments for these improvements. It may be that they desire to get away from the congestion of traffic, smoke, noise, foul air and the many other annoyances of city life. But with all these advantages in going beyond the area which is zoned and restricted to protect them in their homes, they must be prepared to take the disadvantages." *Dill v. Excel Packing Company*, 183 Kan. 513, 525, 526, 331 P.2d 539, 548, 549 (1958). And: "[a] party cannot justly call upon the law to make that place suitable for his residence which was not so when he selected [it]." *Gilbert v. Showerman*, 23 Mich. 448, 455, 2 Brown 158 (1871). Were Webb the only party injured, we would feel justified in holding that the doctrine of "coming to the nuisance" would have been a bar to the relief asked by Webb, and, on the other hand, had Spur located the feedlot near the outskirts of a city and had the city grown toward the feedlot, Spur would have to suffer the cost of abating the nuisance as to those people locating within the growth pattern of the expanding city: "The case affords, perhaps, an example where a business established at a place remote from population is gradually surrounded and becomes part of a populous center, so that a business which formerly was not an interference with the rights of others has become so by the encroachment of the [population]." *City of Ft. Smith v. Western Hide & Fur Co.*, 153 Ark. 99, 103, 239 S.W. 724, 726 (1922).

We agree, however, with the Massachusetts court that: "The law of nuisance affords no rigid rule to be applied in all instances. It is elastic. It undertakes to require only that which is fair and reasonable under all the circumstances. In a commonwealth like this, which depends for its material prosperity so largely on the continued growth and enlargement of manufacturing of diverse varieties, 'extreme rights' cannot be [enforced]." *Stevens v. Rockport Granite Co.*, 216 Mass. 486, 488, 104 N.E. 371, 373 (1914).

There was no indication in the instant case at the time Spur and its predecessors located in western Maricopa County that a new city would spring up, full-blown, alongside the feeding operation and that the developer of that city would ask the court to order Spur to move because of the new city. Spur is required to move not because of any wrongdoing on the part of Spur, but because of a proper and legitimate regard of the courts for the rights and interests of the public.

Del Webb, on the other hand, is entitled to the relief prayed for (a permanent injunction), not because Webb is blameless, but because of the damage to the people who have been encouraged to purchase homes in Sun City. It does not equitable or legally follow, however, that Webb, being entitled to the injunction, is then free of any liability to Spur if Webb has in fact been the cause of the damage Spur has sustained. It does not seem harsh to require a developer, who has taken advantage of the lesser land values in a rural area as well as the availability of large tracts of land on which to build and develop a new town or city in the area, to indemnify those who are forced to leave as a result.

Having brought people to the nuisance to the foreseeable detriment of Spur, Webb must indemnify Spur for a reasonable amount of the cost of moving or shutting down. It should be noted that this relief to Spur is limited to a case wherein a developer has, with foreseeability, brought into a previously agricultural or industrial area the population which makes necessary the granting of an injunction against a lawful business and for which the business has no adequate relief.

It is therefore the decision of this court that the matter be remanded to the trial court for a hearing upon the damages sustained by the defendant Spur as a reasonable and direct result of the granting of the permanent injunction. Since the result of the appeal may appear novel and both sides have obtained a measure of relief, it is ordered that each side will bear its own costs.

Affirmed in part, reversed in part, and remanded for further proceedings consistent with this opinion.

NOTES

1. Conditional injunctions, such as the one granted in *Spur*, are also known as "compensated injunctions." *See* CALABRESI & MELAMED, *Property Rules, Liability Rules, and Inalienability: One View of the Cathedral*, 85 HARV. L. REV. 1089 (1972). Conditional injunctions allow courts to consider the following remedial options: 1) deny all relief (defendant wins); 2) grant an injunction permanently abating the nuisance (plaintiff wins); 3) award *Boomer*-style injunctive relief, but award plaintiff damages (partial win for each side); or 4) award *Spur*-style injunctive relief, but only if plaintiff pays for the cost of abatement (a win for both sides?).

2. The question of whether a remedy does more public harm than private good — and by how much — is often referred to as "balancing the equities" or "balancing the relative hardships." It is important not to confuse this balancing process with the balancing that occurs in deciding whether or not to grant provisional injunctive relief. Both *Boomer* and *Spur* are permanent injunction cases: the merits have been fully adjudicated, it is clear that defendant is a wrongdoer and that plaintiff has suffered irreparable harm. In other words, there is no uncertainty as to who is legally right. Accordingly, in the remedial

phase, should not the defendant be required to prove that the harm to it (and/or the public) far outweighs the harm to the plaintiff?

3. Presumably, the plaintiffs in *Boomer* were suffering depreciated real estate values, as well as health risks. In balancing the equities, how does a court assess such factors as the risk of respiratory disease, lung cancer, shortened life expectancy, and diminished quality of life. Why is economic harm the sole factor balanced? Is this the central fallacy of (or just a cheap shot at) law and economics? *See* Farber, *Reassessing Boomer: Justice, Efficiency, and Nuisance Law, in* PROPERTY LAW AND LEGAL EDUCATION: ESSAYS IN HONOR OF JOHN E. CRIBBETT (Hay & Hoeflich ed., 1988); Lewin, *Compensated Injunctions and the Evolution Nuisance Law*, 71 IOWA L. REV. 775 (1986).

PROBLEM

The Kansas City Airport Authority (KCAA) dramatically expanded Kansas City's airport. As part of its expansion plan, the KCAA condemned several nearby neighborhoods taking the land to build three new runways. These new runways gave the airport the capacity to handle twice as much air traffic as before.

Once the expansion project was complete, airplane traffic at the airport significantly increased. Several new airlines began flying out of Kansas City. Two of the airlines offered inexpensive fares that attracted many passengers. Also, a national parcel service expanded its Kansas City operations. The parcel service, an overnight delivery service, made numerous flights during the middle of the night.

KCAA officials, as well as City and County officials, were thrilled with the expansion's economic impact. In addition to the expansion's direct impact (new jobs created by the airlines and the parcel service), there was indirect impact which trickled through the entire community (jobs in hotels, car rental agencies, etc.).

The airport's expansion was not welcomed by everyone. Some nearby residential areas had always experienced noise disturbances from the airport's operations. After the expansion, the situation worsened. Moreover, some residential areas that had previously been unaffected by noise disturbances were now disturbed by new runways which created new traffic patterns. Noise disturbances in these areas became common.

Before the expansion, most of the noise disturbance was confined to daylight hours. Afterwards, because the parcel service operated at night, the noise disturbance was constant. Some neighbors complained that they were unable to sleep, or that they were unable to sleep well because of the constant flow of airplanes.

Over a period of months, a group, Citizens Against Airport Noise (CAAN), pressured KCAA to abate the noise. When KCAA refused to do so, citing the adverse economic effects that would result, CAAN filed suit. CAAN sought injunctive relief.

After a hearing, the judge has indicated that he plans to issue an injunction against the KCAA, but has asked the parties to make suggestions regarding the content of the order. What suggestions would you make on behalf of KCAA? What would you suggest on behalf of CAAN? How should the judge frame the order?

B. PUBLIC NUISANCE

In addition to the action for private nuisance, there is also an action for public nuisance. One way to distinguish the two is to look at whether there is standing for the state to bring suit. When someone or something has harmed the environment, it is also usually deemed to be a public nuisance.

STATE v. H. SAMUELS COMPANY, INC.
211 N.W.2d 417 (Wis. 1973)

HALLOWS, Chief Justice.

H. Samuels Company, Inc., has operated a salvage business in [the] city of Portage since the early 1900s. In 1948 the junk business was expanded to include the salvaging of metals from automobiles and other machinery. [T]he area was zoned commercial and light industry, but in 1966 the zoning was changed to heavy industrial. . . . The areas immediately adjacent to [this block] are zoned either residential, single-family homes or commercial and light industry.

[In] its operation, the defendant unloads scrap metal from railroad cars with a magnetized crane and drops the metal into a steel guillotine shears which snaps the metal and drops it onto an oscillating conveyor belt, which in turn drops it on a pile or to a sorting house. Other operations involve a two-ton magnet lifting a car engine to the height of four feet and dropping it onto a large piece of steel wedged into the ground. Air tools are used to dismantle the engines and the hammer mill is used to hammer metal into pieces in a large drum and to drop them on a conveyor belt where they are washed and sorted. The alleged nuisance consists of the air noise and ground vibrations created by the operation.

The city of Portage has an ordinance prescribing maximum permissible noise and vibration levels. The state contended the Samuels company has repeatedly violated this ordinance and will continue to do so to the injury of the public. [T]he state of Wisconsin [offered] the testimony of two expert witnesses who monitored the noise. . . . [Nearby] homeowners testified to their loss of sleep, domestic discord, added expense in remodeling their homes, suspension of home remodeling, moving from the neighborhood, rattling of windows, loss of hobbies such as working out of doors, loss of use of porches and yards for relaxation, shaking of pictures and furniture, shaking of beds and rattling of dishes. The two experts testified their tests showed that at various times the sounds caused by the operation exceeded the maximum permissible decibel levels and sound frequencies established by the city ordinance. . . . [T]he vibrations emanating from the salvage yard exceeded permissible displacement values prescribed by the ordinance for areas zoned heavy industrial.

[The] chief of police [related] that of the 32 complaints received in 1970, 24 were by one person and the rest by four persons; in 1971, of the 47 complaints, 38 were from one party and the balance from seven other persons. . . . The president of Samuels testified he has equipped his cranes with silencers, that he has reduced his operation, and intends to reduce the handling of automobiles in the future. In the area where defendant's plant is located, there are other industrial plants.

[T]he trial court stressed that an injunction to enjoin a public nuisance was a drastic remedy, that the city of Portage had never brought an action for the violation of the ordinance against the defendant and "the defendant had taken considerable steps to improve the situation" and was operating a legitimate business where it had been carried on for many years. The court acknowledged the operation of the defendant's plant "is obviously an annoyance to the immediate neighbors." However, the court was impressed by [the] concurring opinion in *State ex rel. Abbott v. House of Vision* (1951), 47 N.W.2d 321, to the effect that before an injunction will issue when a statute has been violated an effort must first be made to prosecute for the violation of the statute, as this remedy is presumably adequate. The court [also] commented that if an injunction to enjoin the nuisance required the defendant to stop operation, that would be the taking of defendant's property without adequate compensation and therefore unconstitutional. The court concluded the case did not [call for an] injunction.

We think the trial court was in error. [The] court questioned the accuracy of the tests performed by the state's experts by presuming noise from sources other than the Samuels' plant contributed to the result of the tests. The presumptions are contrary to the testimony and the evidence. The fact the defendant has made some efforts to cut down the amount of noise does not go to the question of the existence of a nuisance. A defendant may use all the means possible in the operation of a legitimate business and yet that operation can cause damage and constitute a nuisance. Neither the legitimacy of the business nor the length of time it has been in existence is controlling in determining whether a public nuisance exists. These factors are relevant to the question of whether the court should exercise its discretion to enjoin the nuisance. . . .

True, a court of equity will not enjoin a crime because it is a crime, *i.e.*, to enforce the criminal law, but the fact the acts complained of cause damage and also constitute a crime does not bar injunctional relief. The criminality of the act neither gives nor ousts the jurisdiction of equity. [E]quity grants relief, not because the acts are in violation of the statute, but because they constitute [a] nuisance.

This view must be distinguished from the doctrine that the repeated violation of a criminal statute constitutes per se a public nuisance. This doctrine justifies the issuance of an injunction not to enforce the criminal statute but to enjoin illegal conduct which, because of its repetition, constitutes a nuisance. . . .

The modern concept of injunctional relief is to use it when it is a superior or more effective remedy. . . . [Whether a] nuisance should be enjoined depends upon the amount of damages caused thereby and upon the application of the doctrine of the balancing of equities or comparative injury in which the relative harm which would be alleviated by the granting of the injunction is considered in balance with the harm to the defendant if the injunction is granted. If the public is injured in its civil or property rights or privileges or in respect to public health to any degree, that is sufficient to constitute a public nuisance; the degree of harm goes to whether or not the nuisance should be enjoined. . . .

It does not follow necessarily that the public nuisance resulting from the repeated violation of a statute or ordinance will be enjoined; this depends upon the degree of harm. In the instant case it may well be the amount of harm caused by the repeated violations during the normal working hours of the day is insufficient to call forth an injunction, but the same degree of violation impairing the public's right to the enjoyment of their homes after normal working hours causes a greater injury and ought to be enjoined. If we were to consider the facts in this case in relation to establishing a criminal-law nuisance, it might well be an operation less than that allowed by the ordinance would constitute a public nuisance which should be enjoined. However, the briefs ask for an injunction to limit the operation to what is permitted by the ordinance between 5:00 o'clock p.m. and 7:00 o'clock a.m. On the theory of our reversal, the injunction can only enjoin operations which constitute violations of the ordinance.

Judgment is reversed, with directions to enter a judgment enjoining the operation of the defendant from violating the city ordinance as to noise and ground vibration during the hours of 5:00 o'clock p.m. and 7:00 o'clock a.m. each day of the week.

NOTES

1. *Standing Requirements.* Both the "public nuisance" and the "private nuisance" actions are subject to standing requirements:

At common law, a citizen had no standing to sue for abatement or suppression of a public nuisance since such inconvenient or troublesome offences [sic], as annoy the whole community in general, and not merely some particular persons; and therefore are indictable only, and not actionable; as it would be unreasonable to multiply suits, by giving every man a separate right of action, by what danifies him in common only with the rest of his fellow subjects. IV BLACKSTONE COMMENTARIES 167 (1966). Today, a private individual can bring the action if he can show that his damage is different in kind or quality from that suffered by the public in common.

The rationale behind this limitation was two-fold. First, [it relieved] defendants and the courts of the multiple actions that might follow if every member of the public were allowed to sue for a common wrong. Second, it was believed that a harm which affected all members of the public equally should be handled by public officials. Considerable disagreement remains over the type of injury which the plaintiff must suffer in order to have standing to bring an action to enjoin a public nuisance. However, we have intimated in the past that an injury to plaintiff's interest in land is sufficient to distinguish plaintiff's injuries from those experienced by the general public and to give the plaintiff-landowner standing to bring the action.

Armory Park Neighborhood Ass'n v. Episcopal Community Services, 712 P.2d 914 (Ariz. 1985). In the *Armory Park* case, the court held that because the alleged nuisance "affected the residents' use and enjoyment of their real property, a damage special in nature and different in kind from that experienced by the residents of the city in general, the residents of the neighborhood could bring an action to recover damages for or enjoin the maintenance of a public nuisance."

2. In *State v. Kermit Lumber & Pressure Treating Co.*, 488 S.E.2d 901 (W. Va. Ct. App. 1997), defendant operated a lumber treatment plant which contaminated surrounding land with chromium and arsenic. The court concluded that defendant's actions constituted a public nuisance.

3. *Enjoining criminal activity. Benton v. City of Houston*, 605 S.W.2d 679 (Tex. Civ. App. 1980), involved a city's attempt to enjoin defendant from operating a house of prostitution. The court stated that: "Courts of equity [have] no jurisdiction [to] enjoin the commission of acts merely because such acts constitute crimes or penal offenses under penal laws. 'When the State [invokes] the jurisdiction of a court of equity to abate a nuisance, it must be shown either that the action is directly authorized by some constitutional or statutory law, or that such nuisance is an injury to the property or civil rights of the public at [large].'"

4. *Obscenity. Vance v. Universal Amusement Co., Inc.*, 445 U.S. 308 (1980), involved a Texas statute which allowed the state to abate "nuisances" defined to include "the commercial manufacturing, commercial distribution, or commercial exhibition of obscene material." The Court struck down the law:

> [The statute] authorizes prior restraints of indefinite duration on the exhibition of motion pictures that have not been finally adjudicated to be obscene. Presumably, an exhibitor would be required to obey such an order pending review of its merits and would be subject to contempt pro-

ceedings even if the film is ultimately found to be nonobscene. Such prior restraints would be more onerous and more objectionable than the threat of criminal sanctions after a film has been exhibited, since nonobscenity would be a defense to any criminal prosecution. . . . [That] a state trial judge might be thought more likely than an administrative censor to determine accurately that a work is obscene does not change the unconstitutional character of the restraint if erroneously entered. [T]he absence of any special safeguards governing the entry and review of orders restraining the exhibition of named or unnamed motion pictures, without regard to the context in which they are displayed, precludes the enforcement of these nuisance statutes against motion picture exhibitors.

Mr. Justice White dissented: "Prior restraints are distinct from, and more dangerous to free speech than, criminal statutes because, through caprice, mistake, or purpose, the censor may forbid speech which is constitutionally protected, and because the speaker may be punished for disobeying the censor even though his speech was protected. Those dangers are entirely absent here. An injunction against the showing of unnamed obscene motion pictures does not and cannot bar the exhibitor from showing protected material, nor can the exhibitor be punished, through contempt proceedings, for showing such material. . . ."

UNION OIL CO. v. OPPEN
501 F.2d 558 (C.A. Cal. 1974)

[The facts involved an oil spill of the coast of Santa Barbara. The plaintiffs were commercial fishermen, complaining that the defendants day-to-day operation was within the control and under the management of defendant Union Oil Company and that these defendants drilled for oil in the waters of the Santa Barbara Channel and vast quantities of raw crude oil were released and subsequently carried by wind, wave and tidal currents over vast stretches of the coastal waters of Southern California; and that as a consequence the plaintiffs have suffered various injuries for which damages are sought. To settle, Union Oil entered into a number of stipulations and agreed to pay compensatory damages for all legally cognizable claims (claims in negligence) but denied that though the fishers' had a economic right to fish in public waters' that their rights were legally compensable.]

Does the alleged diminution of the aquatic life of the Santa Barbara Channel claimed to have resulted from the occurrence constitute a legally compensable injury to the Commercial Fishermen claimants? As the district judge saw it, "the loss of a prospective economic advantage occasioned by the alleged diminishment of the quantities of available sea life formed a sufficient basis for the recovery under the law of negligence." We hold that the district court properly interpreted paragraph 3 of the Stipulation, and that its action in denying the defendants' motion was proper.

I. Applicable Law.

[The Court first held that admiralty law applied.] We are, however, not driven to the choice between maritime law and the law of California. So far as our research reveals, neither forum has made a definitive ruling on the precise issue before us.

II. Recovery for Pure Economic Loss in Negligence: The General Rule.

Defendants support their motion for partial summary judgment by pointing to the widely recognized principle that no cause of action lies against a defendant whose negligence prevents the plaintiff from obtaining a prospective pecuniary advantage. As the defendants see it, any diminution of the sea life in the Santa Barbara Channel caused by the occurrence, which, it must be remembered, is attributable to the defendants' negligence by reason of the parties' Stipulation, consists of no more than the loss of an economic advantage which is not a "legally cognizable injury" and thus not "legally" compensable.

Their argument has strength. It rests upon the proposition that a contrary rule, which would allow compensation for all losses of economic advantages caused by defendant's negligence, would subject the defendant to claims based upon remote and speculative injuries which he could not foresee in any practical sense of the term. Accordingly, in some cases it has been stated as the general rule that the negligent defendant owes no duty to plaintiffs seeking compensation for such injuries. In other of the cases, the courts have invoked the doctrine of proximate cause to reach the same result; and in yet a third class of cases the "remoteness" of the economic loss is relied upon directly to deny recovery. The consequence of these cases is that a defendant is normally relieved of the burden to defend against such claims, and the courts of a class of cases the resolution of which is particularly difficult.

Defendants in the present action rely heavily on California cases which indicate that no such recovery is possible.

Two things should be said concerning the court's reference to the scope of liability in negligence. The first is that it must be understood as having been made in the context of an unavoidable undertaking to fix the spheres in the field of products liability within which warranties and strict liability were to operate. Too much should not be made of a restraint imposed on the scope of liability for negligence when it has been developed for the purpose of preserving an area within which warranties can function. The second is that this restraint has been cogently criticized as being unnecessary to an appropriate accommodation of warranty and tort liability. *See* Franklin, *When Worlds Collide: Liability Theories and Disclaimers in Defective Product Cases*, 18 Stan. L. Rev. 974, 1002-03 (1966). The recovery of economic losses sustained by an ultimate consumer, even absent privity with a negligent manufacturer, may or may not be desirable; but its allowance, in any event, would not make warranty principles redundant.

III. Some Exceptions to the General Rule.

Doubt concerning the scope of *Seely* dictum is strengthened when the numerous exceptions or qualifications to the general rule are considered. Prosser recognizes that a recovery for pure economic losses in negligence has been permitted in instances in which there exists "some special relation between the parties." Prosser at 952.

The determination whether in a specific case the defendant will be held liable to a third person not in privity is a matter of policy and involves the balancing of various factors, among which are the extent to which the transaction was intended to affect the plaintiff, the foreseeability of harm to him, the degree of certainty that the plaintiff suffered injury, the closeness of the connection between the defendant's conduct and the injury suffered, the moral blame attached to the defendant's conduct, and the policy of preventing future harm. It is thus obvious that California does not blindly follow the general rule upon which the defendants here rely.

It is but a short step from these two California cases to a body of law existing both in this country and in the British Commonwealth in which defendants engaged in certain professions, businesses, or trades have been held liable for economic losses resulting from the negligent performance of tasks within the course of their callings. One Commonwealth scholar has stated that "in a proper case a person may recover economic loss caused by the negligence of persons such as bankers, commission agents, real estate agents, accountants, surveyors, valuers, analysts, insurance brokers, stock brokers, government employees, doctors, architects, car salesmen who undertake to have cars insured, car testers, and drawers of cheques." The American cases reflect a similar development. There are numerous cases indicating that economic losses may be recovered for the negligence of pension consultants, accountants, architects, attorneys, notaries public, test hole drillers, title abstractors, termite inspectors, soil engineers, surveyors, real estate brokers, drawers of checks, directors of corporations, trustees, bailees and public weighers.

Recovery for pure economic loss legally attributable to the defendant's negligence has also been recognized in traditional maritime settings. [Citing Scotish cases] Another instance in which a claim for economic loss, unaccompanied by any physical injury to the person or property of the claimant, has been recognized under admiralty law.

This much abridged catalogue of exceptions and qualifications to the general rule can be brought to a close for purposes of our analysis by calling attention to several cases in which pollution of a stream has enabled one whose business is injured thereby to recover his lost profits

Moreover, the plaintiffs' status as riparians does not make improper the classification of these cases as exceptions to, or qualifications of, the general rule which is relied upon by the defendants in the present action. The injury for which damages were sought in each case was the loss of anticipated profits —

a pure economic loss as that term is normally understood. To permit riparian-ship to transmute this loss into an ordinary property loss for the purpose of allowing recovery does no harm. However, harm would be done if the fact that the plaintiffs in this case are not riparian owners was held to deprive them of the comfort these authorities provide.

IV. The Instant Action.

It is thus apparent that we are not foreclosed by precedent from examining on its merits the issue presented by the defendants' motion for partial summary judgment. As we see it, the issue is whether the defendants owed a duty to the plaintiffs, commercial fishermen, to refrain from negligent conduct in their drilling operations, which conduct reasonably and foreseeably could have been anticipated to cause a diminution of the aquatic life in the Santa Barbara Chan-nel area and thus cause injury to the plaintiffs' business.

In finding that such a duty exists, we are influenced by the manner in which the Supreme Court of California has approached the duty issue in tort law. In holding that the mother of a child, killed by the defendant's negligent operation of an automobile, could recover for emotional disturbance and shock even though she was not within the zone of physical impact, the court in *Dillon v. Legg*, 441 P.2d 912, stated that:

> Defendant owes a duty, in the sense of a potential liability for dam-ages, only with respect to those risks or hazards whose likelihood made the conduct unreasonably dangerous, and hence negligent, in the first instance.

Harper and James state the prevailing view. The obligation turns on whether "the offending conduct foreseeably involved unreasonably great risk of harm to the interests of someone other than the actor. . . . The obligation to refrain from . . . particular conduct is owed only to those who are foreseeably endangered by the conduct and only with respect to those risks or hazards whose likelihood made the conduct unreasonably dangerous. Duty, in other words, is measured by the scope of the risk which negligent conduct foreseeably entails."

The same conclusion is reached when the issue before us is approached from the standpoint of economics. Recently a number of scholars have suggested that liability for losses occasioned by torts should be apportioned in a manner that will best contribute to the achievement of an optimum allocation of resources. *See, e.g.*, Calabresi, *The Cost of Accidents*, 69-73 (1970) (hereinafter Calabresi); Coase, *The Problem of Social Cost*, 3 J. Law & Econ. 1 (1960). This optimum, in theory, would be that which would be achieved by a perfect market system. In determining whether the cost of an accident should be borne by the injured party or be shifted, in whole or in part, this approach requires the court to fix the identity of the party who can avoid the costs most cheaply. Once fixed, this determination then controls liability.

It turns out, however, that fixing the identity of the best or cheapest cost-avoider is more difficult than might be imagined. In order to facilitate this determination, Calabresi suggests several helpful guidelines. The first of these would require a rough calculation designed to exclude as potential cost-avoiders those groups/activities which could avoid accident costs only at an extremely high expense. Calabresi at 140-43. While not easy to apply in any concrete sense, this guideline does suggest that the imposition of oil spill costs directly upon such groups as the consumers of staple groceries is not a sensible solution. Under this guideline, potential liability becomes resolved into a choice between, on an ultimate level, the consumers of fish and those of products derived from the defendants' total operations.

To refine this choice, Calabresi goes on to provide additional guidelines which, in this instance, have proven none too helpful. For example, he suggests an evaluation of the administrative costs which each party would be forced to bear in order to avoid the accident costs. He also states that an attempt should be made to avoid an allocation which will impose some costs on those groups or activities which neither consume fish nor utilize those products of the defendants derived from their operations in the Santa Barbara Channel. On the record before us, we have no way of evaluating the relative administrative costs involved. However, we do recognize that it is probable that by imposing liability on the defendants some portion of the accident costs in this case may be borne by those who neither eat fish nor use the petroleum products derived from the defendants' operations in Santa Barbara.

Calabresi's final guideline, however, unmistakably points to the defendants as the best cost-avoider. Under this guideline, the loss should be allocated to that party who can best correct any error in allocation, if such there be, by acquiring the activity to which the party has been made liable. The capacity "to buy out" the plaintiffs if the burden is too great is, in essence, the real focus of Calabresi's approach. On this basis there is no contest — the defendants' capacity is superior.

Our holding that the defendants are under a duty to commercial fisherman to conduct their drilling and production in a reasonably prudent manner so as to avoid the negligent diminution of aquatic life is not foreclosed by the fact that the defendants' negligence could constitute a public nuisance under California law. Contrary to the situation that existed [in a case where] the public's right of navigation in the navigable waters of California did not vest a private cause of action in those who lost the use of their private pleasure craft, in the case now before us the plaintiffs assert an injury to their commercial enterprises, not to their "occasional Sunday piscatorial pleasure." The right of commercial fishermen to recover for injuries to their businesses caused by pollution of public waters has been recognized on numerous occasions. The injury here asserted by the plaintiff is a pecuniary loss of a particular and special nature, limited to the class of commercial fishermen which they represent.

This injury must, of course, be established in the proceedings that will follow this appeal. To do this it must be shown that the oil spill did in fact diminish aquatic life, and that this diminution reduced the profits the plaintiffs would have realized from their commercial fishing in the absence of the spill. This reduction of profits must be established with certainty and must not be remote, speculative or conjectural. These are not small burdens, nor can they be eased by our abhorrence of massive oil spills. All that we do here is to permit the plaintiffs to attempt to prove their case, and to reject the idea urged upon us by the defendants that a barrier to such an effort exists in the form of the rule that negligent interference with an economic advantage is not actionable.

Chapter 16
PRODUCTS LIABILITY

Products liability deals with the problem of injuries accidentally inflicted on people by "defective" products. As will be seen in the following materials, injured parties have employed a number of legal theories in seeking a remedy for product harms. The most important of these are negligence, warranty, and strict liability.

A. HISTORICAL BACKGROUND: NEGLIGENCE ASSAULTS THE CITADEL OF PRIVITY

The development of products liability law was long hampered by the doctrine of privity of contract. The privity doctrine provided that a party who manufactured or sold a defective product owed a duty with respect to that product only to the immediate purchaser, the party with whom the seller was in privity of contract. If a third party were injured because of a defect in the product, the courts would hold that there could be no liability because no duty ran to the injured third party. We therefore begin our examination of products liability with the negligence cause of action, because here the law first began its assault on the "citadel" of privity.

THOMAS v. WINCHESTER
6 N.Y. 397 (1852)

RUGGLES, Ch. J. delivered the opinion of the court.

This is an action brought to recover damages from the defendant for negligently putting up, labeling and selling as and for the extract of *dandelion*, which is a simple and harmless medicine, a jar of the extract of *belladonna*, which is a deadly poison. . . .

The facts proved were briefly these: Mrs. Thomas being in ill health, her physician prescribed for her a dose of dandelion. Her husband purchased what was believed to be the medicine prescribed, at the store of Dr. Foord, a physician and druggist in Cazenovia, Madison county, where the plaintiffs reside.

A small quantity of the medicine thus purchased was administered to Mrs. Thomas, on whom it produced very alarming effects; such as coldness of the surface and extremities, feebleness of circulation, spasms of the muscles, giddiness of the head, dilation of the pupils of the eyes, and derangement of mind. She recovered however, after some time, from its effects, although for a short time her life was thought to be in great danger. The medicine administered was *belladonna, and not dandelion*. The jar from which it was taken was labeled *"1/2 lb. dandelion, prepared by A. Gilbert, No. 108, John-street, N. Y. Jar 8 oz."* It was sold for and believed by Dr. Foord to be the extract of dandelion as labeled. Dr. Foord purchased the article as the extract of dandelion from Jas. S. Aspinwall, a druggist at New York. Aspinwall bought it of the defendant as extract of dandelion, believing it to be such. The defendant was engaged at No. 108 John street, New York, in the manufacture and sale of certain vegetable extracts for medicinal purposes, and in the purchase and sale of others. The extracts manufactured by him were put up in jars for sale, and those which he purchased were put up by him in like manner. The jars containing extracts manufactured by himself and those containing extracts purchased by him from others, were labeled alike. Both were labeled like the jar in question, as "prepared by A. Gilbert." Gilbert was a person employed by the defendant at a salary, as an assistant in his business. The jars were labeled in Gilbert's name because he had been previously engaged in the same business on his own account at No. 108 John street, and probably because Gilbert's labels rendered the articles more salable. The extract contained in the jar sold to Aspinwall, and by him to Foord, was not manufactured by the defendant, but was purchased by him from another manufacturer or dealer. The extract of dandelion and the extract of belladonna resemble each other in color, consistence, smell and taste; but may on careful examination be distinguished the one from the other by those who are well acquainted with these articles. Gilbert's labels were paid for by Winchester and used in his business with his knowledge and assent.

The defendants' counsel moved for a nonsuit on the [ground that] the defendant was the remote vendor of the article in question: and there was no connection, transaction or privity between him and the plaintiffs, or either of them. . . . [T]he judge overruled the motion for a nonsuit, and the defendant's counsel excepted.

The judge among other things charged the jury, that if they should find from the evidence that either Aspinwall or Foord was guilty of negligence in vending as and for dandelion, the extract taken by Mrs. Thomas, or that the plaintiff Thomas, or those who administered it to Mrs. Thomas, were chargeable with negligence in administering it, the plaintiffs were not entitled to recover; but if they were free from negligence, and if the defendant Winchester was guilty of negligence in putting up and vending the extracts in question, the plaintiffs were entitled to recover, provided the extract administered to Mrs. Thomas was the same which was put up by the defendant and sold by him to Aspinwall and by Aspinwall to Foord. . . .

[T]he . . . question is, whether the defendant, being a remote vendor of the medicine, and there being no privity or connection between him and the plaintiffs, the action can be maintained.

If, in labeling a poisonous drug with the name of a harmless medicine, for public market, no duty was violated by the defendant, excepting that which he owed to Aspinwall, his immediate vendee, in virtue of his contract of sale, this action cannot be maintained. If A. build a wagon and sell it to B., who sells it to C., and C. hires it to D., who in consequence of the gross negligence of A. in building the wagon is overturned and injured, D. cannot recover damages against A., the builder. A.'s obligation to build the wagon faithfully, arises solely out of his contract with B. The public have nothing to do with it. Misfortune to third persons, not parties to the contract, would not be a natural and necessary consequence of the builder's negligence; and such negligence is not an act imminently dangerous to human life. . . .

This was the ground on which the case of *Winterbottom v. Wright*, (10 Mees. & Welsb. 109), was decided. A. contracted with the postmaster general to provide a coach to convey the mail bags along a certain line of road, and B. and others, also contracted to horse the coach along the same line. B. and his co-contractors hired C., who was the plaintiff, to drive the coach. The coach, in consequence of some latent defect, broke down; the plaintiff was thrown from his seat and lamed. It was held that C. could not maintain an action against A. for the injury thus sustained. . . . A.'s duty to keep the coach in good condition, was a duty to the postmaster general, with whom he made his contract, and not a duty to the driver employed by the owners of the horses.

But the case in hand stands on a different ground. The defendant was a dealer in poisonous drugs. Gilbert was his agent in preparing them for market. The death or great bodily harm of some person was the natural and almost inevitable consequence of the sale of belladonna by means of the false label. . . .

In respect to the wrongful and criminal character of the negligence complained of, this case differs widely from those put by the defendant's counsel. No such imminent danger existed in those cases. In the present case the sale of the poisonous article was made to a dealer in drugs, and not to a consumer. The injury therefore was not likely to fall on him, or on his vendee who was also a dealer; but much more likely to be visited on a remote purchaser, as actually happened. The defendant's negligence put human life in imminent danger. Can it be said that there was no duty on the part of the defendant, to avoid the creation of that danger by the exercise of greater caution? or that the exercise of that caution was a duty only to his immediate vendee, whose life was not endangered? The defendant's duty arose out of the nature of his business and the danger to others incident to its mismanagement. Nothing but mischief like that which actually happened could have been expected from sending the poison falsely labeled into the market; and the defendant is justly responsible for the probable consequences of the act. The duty of exercising caution in this respect did not arise out of the defendant's contract of sale to Aspinwall. The wrong done by the defendant was in putting the poison, mislabeled, into the hands of Aspinwall as an article of merchandise to be sold and afterwards used as the extract of dandelion, by some person then unknown. . . . The defendant's contract of sale to Aspinwall does not excuse the wrong done to the plaintiffs. It was a part of the means by which the wrong was effected. The plaintiffs' injury and their remedy would have stood on the same principle, if the defendant had given the belladonna to Dr. Foord without price, or if he had put it in his shop without his knowledge, under circumstances which would probably have led to its sale on the faith of the label.

In *Longmeid v. Holliday*, (6 Law and Eq. Rep. 562), the distinction is recognized between an act of negligence imminently dangerous to the lives of others, and one that is not so. In the former case, the party guilty of the negligence is liable to the party injured, whether there be a contract between them or not; in the latter, the negligent party is liable only to the party with whom he contracted, and on the ground that negligence is a breach of the contract. . . .

[I]t seems to me to be clear that the defendant cannot, in this case, set up as a defense, that Foord sold the contents of the jar as and for what the defendant represented it to be. The label conveyed the idea distinctly to Foord that the contents of the jar was the extract of dandelion; and that the defendant knew it to be such. So far as the defendant is concerned, Foord was under no obligation to test the truth of the representation. The charge of the judge in submitting to the jury the question in relation to the negligence of Foord and Aspinwall, cannot be complained of by the defendant. . . .

Judgment affirmed.

NOTES

1. *Winterbottom v. Wright*, cited in the main opinion, was the leading case establishing the rule of privity of contract; that is, that a duty owed by one party to another arising out of a contract between them did not create a duty in tort to anyone not a party to the contract. Under this rule, if one party to the contract did not perform, this would create a cause of action for breach of contract in the other contracting party, but would not create any cause of action in any third party who might also be injured by the failure to perform. The same rule also began to be applied in cases where the party to the contract performed, but did so in a negligent fashion, with the result that third parties were injured. Consider, for example, a contract to repair vehicles such as that involved in *Winterbottom* itself. On the facts of *Winterbottom* it appears that the defendant had not performed the contract at all — a form of nonfeasance. But suppose the work had been performed, but negligently, so that the brakes did not work. As *Winterbottom* was interpreted, passengers and bystanders injured by a brake failure would have no claim against the defendant, because they were not parties to the contract to repair the brakes. A number of concerns were put forward to justify this result. First, the courts feared that allowing actions by non-parties opened the contracting parties to limitless liability, via tort claims, that might be far beyond what they contemplated when they entered into the contract. This in turn raised the concern that allowing the action would let tort law and its legally imposed duties invade the realm of private ordering set up by contract law. The courts therefore tended to rule that injuries to third parties aris-

ing out of negligent performance of contracts would not be considered foreseeable. The facts of *Thomas* presented one of the earliest cases in which this rule was challenged, and it is worthwhile noting the reasons why the court believed *Thomas* presented a different case.

2. Following this decision, the courts developed further exceptions to the privity rule. *Huset v. J. I. Case Threshing Machine Co.*, 120 F. 865 (8th Cir. 1903), summarized the law at that time. The case involved a farm worker who lost a leg when he fell into the works of a threshing machine. The injured plaintiff claimed that the injury occurred because the sheet metal covering for the works of the machine, on which the operator was expected to stand, was not sturdy enough to support a person's weight. In reversing the trial court's judgment on the pleadings in favor of the manufacturer, the appellate court first acknowledged what it viewed to be the rationale behind the privity bar:

> So, when a manufacturer sells articles to the wholesale or retail dealers, or to those who are to use them, injury to third persons is not generally the natural or probable effect of negligence in their manufacture because (1) such a result cannot ordinarily be reasonably anticipated, and because (2) an independent cause — the responsible human agency of the purchaser — without which the injury to the third person would not occur, intervenes, and . . . 'insulates' the negligence of the manufacturer from the injury to the third person. . . . For the reason that in the cases of the character which have been mentioned the natural and probable effect of the negligence of the contractor or manufacturer will generally be limited to the party for whom the article is constructed, or to whom it is sold, and, perhaps more than all this, for the reason that a wise and conservative public policy has impressed the courts with the view that there must be a fixed and definite limitation to the liability of manufacturers and vendors for negligence in the construction and sale of complicated machines and structures which are to be operated or used by the intelligent and the ignorant, the skillful and the incompetent, the watchful and the careless, parties that cannot be known to the manufacturers or vendors, and who use the articles all over the country hundreds of miles distant from the place of their manufacture or original sale, a general rule has been adopted and has become established by repeated decisions of the courts of England and of this country that in these cases the liability of the contractor or manufacturer for negligence in the construction or sale of the articles which he makes or vends is limited to the persons to whom he is liable under his contracts of construction or sale.

The court then explained that a plaintiff could avoid the bar of privity by invoking one of the following exceptions:

> The first is that an act of negligence of a manufacturer or vendor which is imminently dangerous to the life or health of mankind, and which is committed in the preparation or sale of an article intended to preserve,

destroy, or affect human life, is actionable by third parties who suffer from the negligence. . . . The leading case upon this subject is *Thomas v. Winchester.* . . . In all these cases of sale the natural and probable result of the act of negligence — nay, the inevitable result of it — was not an injury to the party to whom the sales were made, but to those who, after the purchasers had disposed of the articles, should consume them. . . .

The second exception is that an owner's act of negligence which causes injury to one who is invited by him to use his defective appliance upon the owner's premises may form the basis of an action against the owner. . . .

The third exception to the rule is that one who sells or delivers an article which he knows to be imminently dangerous to life or limb to another without notice of its qualities is liable to any person who suffers an injury therefrom which might have been reasonably anticipated, whether there were any contractual relations between the parties or not. . . .

The court ruled that the plaintiff's complaint set forth facts that would bring the case within the third exception, although the court suggested that "[i]t is perhaps improbable that the defendant was possessed of the knowledge of the imminently dangerous character of this threshing machine when it delivered it. . . ."

PROBLEMS AND QUESTIONS

1. A wealthy individual hires Driver to act as his chauffeur. By a signed contract, Driver agrees always to drive with due care. However, Driver breaches the agreement, drives negligently, and runs over Pedestrian. Would the rule of *Winterbottom v. Wright* lead to the conclusion that Driver, by virtue of the contract, owes Pedestrian no duty to drive with due care? Why or why not? Is this situation different from the problem presented by *Winterbottom* and *Thomas*?

2. Why did the *Thomas* court find a duty of care existed? Note that the court focused, among other things, on the fact that the defendant sold to a middleman rather than directly to the consumer. Why does that affect the duty owed? Note also that the court bases its decision on the "imminent danger" created in this case. What does this phrase mean and why is it significant to the decision?

3. The court in the *Huset* case tried to link the contractual and tort arguments by asserting that in most cases, the defendant can foresee harm to the other contracting party, but cannot foresee harm to unknown third parties. This argument attempts to justify the privity of contract limitations on foreseeability grounds, but how successful is it? If *Thomas* and similar exceptions are based on the foreseeability of harm to third persons, how stable is the privity of contract rule likely to be?

4. The court then introduces a new argument by claiming that in cases involving a third party, the conduct of the third party is an independent cause that insulates the defendant from liability. Does this situation constitute what is today called an intervening cause? On the other hand, the court puts forth a policy argument in favor of the limitation, by noting that once a product leaves the control of the manufacturer it may be "operated or used by the intelligent and the ignorant, the skillful and the incompetent, the watchful and the careless, parties that cannot be known to the manufacturers or vendors, and who use the articles all over the country hundreds of miles distant from the place of their manufacture or original sale. . . ." Are these valid concerns that should limit manufacturer liability? What should be the responsibility of a company that makes a product that can be used safely by the skillful but is a thing of peril in the hands of the incompetent or untrained? Should the incompetent be protected? Should the skillful be forced to pay for safety features they do not need? Is a warning or instruction book sufficient

5. Consider *Huset*'s three exceptions to the no-liability rule. The first, of course, is based on *Thomas v. Winchester*. The second does not relate to the liability of the manufacturer at all. The third seems to be based on a kind of misrepresentation or breach of warranty theory. Are these exceptions consistent with the basic privity of contract rule? Are they consistent with the limited foreseeability of harm argued by the court in justifying that rule? In other words, if third party users are unforeseeable, or if the conduct of the user is an independent cause insulating the manufacturer from liability, why is the third exception proper?

MacPHERSON v. BUICK MOTOR CO.
111 N.E. 1050 (N.Y. 1916)

CARDOZO, J.

The defendant is a manufacturer of automobiles. It sold an automobile to a retail dealer. The retail dealer resold to the plaintiff. While the plaintiff was in the car, it suddenly collapsed. He was thrown out and injured. One of the wheels was made of defective wood, and its spokes crumbled into fragments. The wheel was not made by the defendant; it was bought from another manufacturer. There is evidence, however, that its defects could have been discovered by reasonable inspection, and that inspection was omitted. There is no claim that the defendant knew of the defect and willfully concealed it. . . . The charge is one, not of fraud, but of negligence. The question to be determined is whether the defendant owed a duty of care and vigilance to any one but the immediate purchaser.

The foundations of this branch of the law, at least in this state, were laid in *Thomas v. Winchester* (6 N.Y. 397). A poison was falsely labeled. The sale was made to a druggist, who in turn sold to a customer. The customer recovered damages from the seller who affixed the label. 'The defendant's negligence,' it was said, 'put human life in imminent danger.' A poison falsely labeled is likely to injure any one who gets it. Because the danger is to be foreseen, there is a duty to avoid the injury. Cases were cited by way of illustration in which manufacturers were not subject to any duty irrespective of contract. The distinction was said to be that their conduct, though, negligent, was not likely to result in injury to any one except the purchaser. We are not required to say whether the chance of injury was always as remote as the distinction assumes. Some of the illustrations might be rejected today. The *principle* of the distinction is for present purposes the important thing.

Thomas v. Winchester became quickly a landmark of the law. In the application of its principle there may at times have been uncertainty or even error. There has never in this state been doubt or disavowal of the principle itself. . . . [E]arly cases suggest a narrow construction of the rule. Later cases, however, evince a more liberal spirit. First in importance is *Devlin v. Smith* (89 N.Y. 470). The defendant, a contractor, built a scaffold for a painter. The painter's servants were injured. The contractor was held liable. He knew that the scaffold, if improperly constructed, was a most dangerous trap. He knew that it was to be used by the workmen. He was building it for that very purpose. Building it for their use, he owed them a duty, irrespective of his contract with their master, to build it with care.

[T]he latest case in this court in which *Thomas v. Winchester* was followed . . . is *Statler v. Ray Mfg. Co.* (195 N.Y. 478, 480). The defendant manufactured a large coffee urn. It was installed in a restaurant. When heated, the urn exploded and injured the plaintiff. We held that the manufacturer was liable. We said that the urn 'was of such a character inherently that, when applied to the purposes for which it was designed, it was liable to become a source of great danger to many people if not carefully and properly constructed.' It may be that *Devlin v. Smith* and *Statler v. Ray Mfg. Co.* have extended the rule of *Thomas v. Winchester*. If so, this court is committed to the extension. The defendant argues that things imminently dangerous to life are poisons, explosives, deadly weapons-things whose normal function it is to injure or destroy. But whatever the rule in *Thomas v. Winchester* may once have been, it has no longer that restricted meaning. A large coffee urn . . . may have within itself, if negligently made, the potency of danger, yet no one thinks of it as an implement whose normal function is destruction. . . .

We hold, then, that the principle of *Thomas v. Winchester* is not limited to poisons, explosives, and things of like nature, to things which in their normal operation are implements of destruction. If the nature of a thing is such that it is reasonably certain to place life and limb in peril when negligently made, it is then a thing of danger. Its nature gives warning of the consequences to be expected. If to the element of danger there is added knowledge that the thing will be used by persons other than the purchaser, and used without new tests then, irrespective of contract, the manufacturer of this thing of danger is under a duty to make it carefully. That is as far as we are required to go for the decision of this case. There must be knowledge of a danger, not merely possible, but probable. It is possible to use almost anything in a way that will make it dangerous if defective. That is not enough to charge the manufacturer with a duty independent of his contract. Whether a given thing is dangerous may be sometimes a question for the court and sometimes a question for the jury. There must also be knowledge that in the usual course of events the danger will be shared by others than the buyer. Such knowledge may often be inferred from the nature of the transaction. But it is possible that even knowledge of the danger and of the use will not always be enough. The proximity or remoteness of the relation is a factor to be considered. We are dealing now with the liability of the manufacturer of the finished product, who puts it on the market to be used without inspection by his customers. If he is negligent, where danger is to be foreseen, a liability will follow. We are not required at this time to say that it is legitimate to go back of the manufacturer of the finished product and hold the manufacturers of the component parts. To make their negligence a cause of imminent danger, an independent cause must often intervene; the manufacturer of the finished product must also fail in his duty of inspection. It may be that in those circumstances the negligence of the earlier members of the series as too remote to constitute, as to the ultimate user, an actionable wrong. . . . We shall have to deal with it when it arises. . . . There is here no break in the chain of cause and effect. In such circumstances, the presence of a known danger, attendant upon a known use, makes vigilance a duty. We have put aside the notion that the duty to safeguard life and limb, when the consequences of negligence may be foreseen, grows out of contract and nothing else. We have put the source of the obligation where it ought to be. We have put its source in the law.

From this survey of the decisions, there thus emerges a definition of the duty of a manufacturer which enables us to measure this defendant's liability. Beyond all question, the nature of an automobile gives warning of probable danger if its construction is defective. This automobile was designed to go fifty miles an hour. Unless its wheels were sound and strong, injury was almost certain. It was as much a thing of danger as a defective engine for a railroad. The defendant knew the danger. It knew also that the car would be used by persons other than the buyer. This was apparent from its size; there were seats for three persons. It was apparent also from the fact that the buyer was a dealer in cars, who bought to resell. The maker of this car supplied it for the use of purchasers from the dealer just as plainly as the contractor in *Devlin v. Smith* supplied the scaffold for use by the servants of the owner. The dealer was indeed the one person of whom it might be said with some approach to certainly that by him the car would not be used. Yet the defendant would have us say that he was the one person whom it was under a legal duty to protect. The law does not lead us to so inconsequent a conclusion. Precedents drawn from the days of travel by stage coach do not fit the conditions of travel today. The principle that the danger must be imminent does not change, but the things subject to the principle do change. They are whatever the needs of life in a developing civilization require them to be. . . .

[T]here is nothing anomalous in a rule which imposes upon A, who has contracted with B, a duty to C and D and others according as he knows or does not know that the subject matter of the contract is intended for their use. We may find an analogy in the law which measures the liability of landlords. If A leases to B a tumble-down house he is not liable, in the absence of fraud, to B's guests who enter it and are injured. This is because B is then under the duty to repair it, the lessor has the right to suppose that he will fulfill that duty, and if he omits to do so, his guests must look to him. . . . But if A leases a building to be used by the lessee at once as a place of public entertainment, the rule is different. There is injury to persons other than the lessee is to be foreseen, and foresight of the consequences involves the creation of a duty. . . .

[W]e think the defendant was not absolved from a duty of inspection because it bought the wheels from a reputable manufacturer. It was not merely a dealer in automobiles. It was a manufacturer of automobiles. It was responsible for the finished product. It was not at liberty to put the finished product on the market without subjecting the component parts to ordinary and simple tests. . . . Under the charge of the trial judge nothing more was required of it. The obligation to inspect must vary with the nature of the thing to be inspected. The more probable the danger, the greater the need of caution. . . . Other rulings complained of have been considered, but no error has been found on them.

Judgment affirmed.

NOTES AND QUESTIONS

1. Notice how the majority opinion handles the issue of foreseeability and links it to the question of what products are imminently dangerous. This is a classic example of "the exception swallowing the rule."

2. The case abolished the privity of contract doctrine for negligence cases, a result which now obtains in all jurisdictions.

PROBLEMS

1. The basis of liability remains negligence, however. Consider what evidence of negligence the plaintiff was able to produce in this case. How, in this or other cases, will the plaintiff be able to meet the burden of proving that the defect in the product resulted from the negligence of the defendant? How do we know, for example, that the wheel was defective when delivered to the Buick factory? How does the plaintiff prove that the failure to detect the defect was the result of Buick's negligence? Was the defect even detectable? Suppose Buick can put on evidence of due care, by demonstrating that it has a thorough quality control and inspection system in place; should this defeat the plaintiff's claim?

2. Could plaintiff assert a viable negligence claim by arguing that a car capable of going 50 miles per hour should not be equipped with wooden wheels? How does this claim differ from that actually put forward in the case? How could plaintiff demonstrate that the decision to use wooden wheels was negligent?

ESCOLA v. COCA COLA BOTTLING CO. OF FRESNO
150 P.2d 436 (Cal. 1944)

GIBSON, Chief Justice.

Plaintiff, a waitress in a restaurant, was injured when a bottle of Coca Cola broke in her hand. She alleged that defendant company, which had bottled and delivered the alleged defective bottle to her employer, was negligent in selling 'bottles containing said beverage which on account of excessive pressure of gas or by reason of some defect in the bottle was dangerous [and] likely to explode.' This appeal is from a judgment upon a jury verdict in favor of plaintiff.

Defendant's driver delivered several cases of Coca Cola to the restaurant, placing them on the floor, one on top of the other, under and behind the counter, where they remained at least thirty-six hours. Immediately before the accident, plaintiff picked up the top case and set it upon a near-by ice cream cabinet in front of and about three feet from the refrigerator. She then proceeded to take the bottles from the case with her right hand, one at a time, and put them into the refrigerator. Plaintiff testified that after she had placed three bottles in the refrigerator and had moved the fourth bottle about 18 inches from the case 'it exploded in my hand.' The bottle broke into two jagged pieces and inflicted a deep five-inch cut, severing blood vessels, nerves and muscles of the thumb and palm of the hand. Plaintiff further testified that when the bottle exploded, 'It made a sound similar to an electric light bulb that would have dropped. It made a loud pop.' Plaintiff's employer testified, 'I was about twenty feet from where it actually happened and I heard the explosion.' A fellow employee, on the opposite side of the counter, testified that plaintiff 'had the bottle, I should judge, waist high, and I know that it didn't bang either the case or the door or another bottle [when] it popped. It sounded just like a fruit jar would blow up[.]' The witness further testified that the contents of the bottle 'flew all over herself and myself and the walls and one thing and another.' . . .

Plaintiff . . . announced to the court that being unable to show any specific acts of negligence she relied completely on the doctrine of res ipsa loquitur.

Defendant contends that the doctrine of res ipsa loquitur does not apply in this case, and that the evidence is insufficient to support the judgment.

[The court then analyzed the plaintiff's case in terms of the elements of res ipsa loquitur, finding first that the defendant bottling company had exclusive control of the bottle at the time the negligent act must have occurred, that is, during the bottling process, provided the plaintiff shows that the bottle was not changed after it left the defendant's control. The plaintiff was also required to prove that she handled the bottle carefully, so as to negate her own conduct as the source of the accident. The court noted, however, that the plaintiff was not required to "eliminate every remote possibility of injury to the bottle after defendant lost control, and the requirement is satisfied if there is evidence permitting a reasonable inference that it was not accessible to extraneous harmful forces and that it was carefully handled by plaintiff or any third person who may have moved or touched it." Finally, the court reviewed the possible ways in which the accident could have occurred and concluded: "Although it is not clear in this case whether the explosion was caused by an excessive charge or a defect in the glass there is a sufficient showing that neither cause would ordinarily have been present if due care had been used. Further, defendant had exclusive control over both the charging and inspection of the bottles." The judgment was accordingly affirmed. Justice Traynor, however, wrote the following concurring opinion.]

TRAYNOR, Justice.

I concur in the judgment, but I believe the manufacturer's negligence should no longer be singled out as the basis of a plaintiff's right to recover in cases like the present one. In my opinion it should now be recognized that a manufacturer incurs an absolute liability when an article that he has placed on the market, knowing that it is to be used without inspection, proves to have a defect that causes injury to human beings. *MacPherson v. Buick Motor Co.* . . . established the principle, recognized by this court, that irrespective of privity of contract, the manufacturer is responsible for an injury caused by such an article to any person who comes in lawful contact with it. . . . In these cases the source of the manufacturer's liability was his negligence in the manufacturing process or in the inspection of component parts supplied by others. Even if there is no negligence, however, public policy demands that responsibility be fixed wherever it will most effectively reduce the hazards to life and health inherent in defective products that reach the market. It is evident that the manufacturer can anticipate some hazards and guard against the recurrence of others, as the public cannot. Those who suffer injury from defective products are unprepared to meet its consequences. The cost of an injury and the loss of time or health may be an overwhelming misfortune to the person injured, and a needless one, for the risk of injury can be insured by the manufacturer and distributed among the public as a cost of doing business. It is to the public interest to discourage the marketing of products having defects that are a menace to the public. If such products nevertheless find their way into the market it is to the public interest to place the responsibility for whatever injury they may cause upon the manufacturer, who, even if he is not negligent in the manufacture of the product, is responsible for its reaching the market. However intermittently such injuries may occur and however haphazardly they may strike, the risk of their occurrence is a constant risk and a general one. Against such a risk there should be general and constant protection and the manufacturer is best situated to afford such protection.

The injury from a defective product does not become a matter of indifference because the defect arises from causes other than the negligence of the manufacturer, such as negligence of a submanufacturer of a component part whose defects could not be revealed by inspection . . . or unknown causes that even by the device of res ipsa loquitur cannot be classified as negligence of the manufacturer. The inference of negligence may be dispelled by an affirmative showing of proper care. If the evidence against the fact inferred is 'clear, positive, uncontradicted, and of such a nature that it can not rationally be disbelieved, the court must instruct the jury that the nonexistence of the fact has been established as a matter of law.' . . . An injured person, however, is not ordinarily in a position to refute such evidence or identify the cause of the defect, for he can hardly be familiar with the manufacturing process as the manufacturer himself is. In leaving it to the jury to decide whether the inference has been dispelled, regardless of the evidence against it, the negligence rule approaches the rule of strict liability. It is needlessly circuitous to make negligence the basis of recovery and impose what is in reality liability without negligence. If public policy demands that a manufacturer of goods be responsible for their quality regardless of negligence there is no reason not to fix that responsibility openly. . . .

[I]t is to the public interest to prevent injury to the public from any defective goods by the imposition of civil liability generally.

The retailer, even though not equipped to test a product, is under an absolute liability to his customer, for the implied warranties of fitness for proposed use and merchantable quality include a warranty of safety of the product. . . . This warranty is not necessarily a contractual one . . . , for public policy requires that the buyer be insured at the seller's expense against injury. . . . The courts recognize, however, that the retailer cannot bear the burden of this warranty, and allow him to recoup any losses by means of the warranty of safety attending the wholesaler's or manufacturer's sale to him. . . . Such a procedure, however, is needlessly circuitous and engenders wasteful litigation. Much would be gained if the injured person could base his action directly on the manufacturer's warranty.

The liability of the manufacturer to an immediate buyer injured by a defective product follows without proof of negligence from the implied warranty of safety attending the sale. Ordinarily, however, the immediate buyer is a dealer who does not intend to use the product himself, and if the warranty of safety is to serve the purpose of protecting health and safety it must give rights to others than the dealer. In the words of Judge Cardozo in the *MacPherson* case: 'The dealer was indeed the one person of whom it might be said with some approach to certainty that by him the car would not be used. Yet the defendant would have us say that he was the one person whom it was under a legal duty to protect. The law does not lead us to so inconsequent a conclusion.' While the defendant's negligence in the *MacPherson* case made it unnecessary for the court to base liability on warranty, Judge Cardozo's reasoning recognized the injured person as the real party in interest and effectively disposed of the theory that the liability of the manufacturer incurred by his warranty should apply only to the immediate purchaser. It thus paves the way for a standard of liability that would make the manufacturer guarantee the safety of his product even when there is no negligence. . . .

In the food products cases the courts have resorted to various fictions to rationalize the extension of the manufacturer's warranty to the consumer: that a warranty runs with the chattel; that the cause of action of the dealer is assigned to the consumer; that the consumer is a third party beneficiary of the manufacturer's contract with the dealer. They have also held the manufacturer liable on a mere fiction of negligence: 'Practically he must know [the product] is fit, or take the consequences, if it proves destructive.' . . . Such fictions are not necessary to fix the manufacturer's liability under a warranty if the warranty is severed from the contract of sale between the dealer and the consumer and based on the law of torts . . . as a strict liability. . . . Warranties are not necessarily rights arising under a contract. An action on a warranty 'was, in its origin, a pure action of tort,' and only late in the historical development of warranties was an action in assumpsit allowed. . . . 'And it is still generally possible where a distinction of procedure is observed between actions of tort and of contract to frame the declaration for breach of warranty in tort.' . . . On the basis of the tort character of an action on a warranty, recovery has been allowed for wrongful death as it could not be in an action for breach of contract. . . . 'Though the action may be brought solely for the breach of the implied warranty, the breach is a wrongful act, a default, and, in its essential nature, a tort.' Even a seller's express warranty can arise from a noncontractual affirmation inducing a person to purchase the goods. . . . 'As an actual agreement to contract is not essential, the obligation of a seller in such a case is one imposed by law as distinguished from one voluntarily assumed. It may be called an obligation either on a quasi-contract or quasi-tort, because remedies appropriate to contract and also to tort are applicable.' . . .

As handicrafts have been replaced by mass production with its great markets and transportation facilities, the close relationship between the producer and consumer of a product has been altered. Manufacturing processes, frequently valuable secrets, are ordinarily either inaccessible to or beyond the ken of the general public. The consumer no longer has means or skill enough to investigate for himself the soundness of a product, even when it is not contained in a sealed package, and his erstwhile vigilance has been lulled by the steady efforts of manufacturers to build up confidence by advertising and marketing devices such as trade-marks. . . . Consumers no longer approach products warily but accept them on faith, relying on the reputation of the manufacturer or the trade-mark. . . . Manufacturers have sought to justify that faith by increasingly high standards of inspection and a readiness to make good on defective products by way of replacements and refunds. . . . The manufacturer's obligation to the consumer must keep pace with the changing relationship between them; it cannot be escaped because the marketing of a product has become so complicated as to require one or more intermediaries. Certainly there is greater reason to impose liability on the manufacturer than on the retailer who is but a conduit of a product that he is not himself able to test. . . .

The manufacturer's liability should, of course, be defined in terms of the safety of the product in normal and proper use, and should not extend to injuries that cannot be traced to the product as it reached the market.

NOTES AND QUESTIONS

1. The case illustrates the problems facing plaintiffs who had to prove that the negligence of the manufacturer caused their injuries. The plaintiff, remote from the moment at which the defect entered into the product, has a difficult time establishing any breach of duty. The defendant, on the other hand, will have ample evidence of its own due care to present. The case shows one common response to this problem, which was to invoke res ipsa loquitur and send the case to the jury. In effect, this allowed plaintiff to pursue a negligence case against the manufacturer (the privity rule having already been abrogated) without direct evidence of negligence. Is this really the same as strict liability? Is the majority's use of res ipsa justifiable on these facts?

2. The famous concurrence by Justice Traynor, on the other hand, argues for a frank adoption of strict liability. It is helpful to read carefully the reasons of policy put forward to support this change. What are the most compelling reasons for adopting strict liability?

3. We have now traced the development of the negligence cause of action for harms caused by product defects. From an initial position of no liability without privity of contract the law had developed so that the rule of privity had been abolished for this cause of action and proof of negligence could, at times, be finessed by means of res ipsa loquitur. Justice Traynor's opinion, however, also makes reference to another body of law that also provided remedies for injuries from defective products, including personal injuries of the sort usually remedied via tort: the law of warranty. Here, Justice Traynor is arguing in favor of employing the law of warranty as an alternative basis for imposing strict liability on the manufacturer. For liability under warranty is strict, but is often hedged around with limitations. These limitations mostly come from the contractual aspect of warranties, and include the privity of contract limitation (again), a requirement of prompt notice of the breach of warranty, and the ability of the parties to the contract to limit or disclaim the warranty. What should be done with these limitations? If one abolishes them, one is left with, again, strict liability. The next section of the chapter will trace the use of breach of warranty as an alternative cause of action for injuries caused by defective products.

B. THE NEXT ASSAULT ON THE CITADEL: BREACH OF WARRANTY

In recent times legislatures have codified the law of warranty in commercial and consumer transactions. One important codification of warranty was the Uniform Sales Act. This act was then largely replaced by the sales provisions of the Uniform Commercial Code (UCC). The following provisions outline the warranties recognized by the UCC.

§ 2-313. Express Warranties by Affirmation, Promise, Description, Sample.

(1) Express warranties by the seller are created as follows:

(a) Any affirmation of fact or promise made by the seller to the buyer which relates to the goods and becomes part of the basis of the bargain creates an express warranty that the goods shall conform to the affirmation or promise.

(b) Any description of the goods which is made part of the basis of the bargain creates an express warranty that the goods shall conform to the description.

(c) Any sample or model which is made part of the basis of the bargain creates an express warranty that the whole of the goods shall conform to the sample or model.

(2) It is not necessary to the creation of an express warranty that the seller use formal words such as "warrant" or "guarantee" or that he have a specific intention to make a warranty, but an affirmation merely of the value of the goods or a statement purporting to be merely the seller's opinion or commendation of the goods does not create a warranty.

§ 2-314. Implied Warranty: Merchantability; Usage of Trade.

(1) Unless excluded or modified (Section 2-316), a warranty that the goods shall be merchantable is implied in a contract for their sale if the seller is a merchant with respect to goods of that kind. Under this section the serving for value of food or drink to be consumed either on the premises or elsewhere is a sale.

(2) Goods to be merchantable must be at least such as

(a) pass without objection in the trade under the contract description; and

(b) in the case of fungible goods, are of fair average quality within the description; and

(c) are fit for the ordinary purposes for which such goods are used; and

(d) run, within the variations permitted by the agreement, of even kind, quality and quantity within each unit and among all units involved; and

(e) are adequately contained, packaged, and labeled as the agreement may require; and

(f) conform to the promises or affirmations of fact made on the container or label if any.

(3) Unless excluded or modified (Section 2-316) other implied warranties may arise from course of dealing or usage of trade.

§ 2-315. Implied Warranty: Fitness for Particular Purpose.

Where the seller at the time of contracting has reason to know any particular purpose for which the goods are required and that the buyer is relying on the seller's skill or judgment to select or furnish suitable goods, there is unless excluded or modified under the next section an implied warranty that the goods shall be fit for such purpose.

§ 2-316. Exclusion or Modification of Warranties.

(1) Words or conduct relevant to the creation of an express warranty and words or conduct tending to negate or limit warranty shall be construed wherever reasonable as consistent with each other; but subject to the provisions of this Article on parol or extrinsic evidence (Section 2-202) negation or limitation is inoperative to the extent that such construction is unreasonable.

(2) Subject to subsection (3), to exclude or modify the implied warranty of merchantability or any part of it the language must mention merchantability and in case of a writing must be conspicuous, and to exclude or modify any implied warranty of fitness the exclusion must be by a writing and conspicuous. Language to exclude all implied warranties of fitness is sufficient if it states, for example, that "There are no warranties which extend beyond the description on the face hereof."

(3) Notwithstanding subsection (2)

(a) unless the circumstances indicate otherwise, all implied warranties are excluded by expressions like "as is", "with all faults" or other language which in common understanding calls the buyer's attention to the exclusion of warranties and makes plain that there is no implied warranty; and

(b) when the buyer before entering into the contract has examined the goods or the sample or model as fully as he desired or has refused to examine the goods there is no implied warranty with regard to defects which an examination ought in the circumstances to have revealed to him; and

(c) an implied warranty can also be excluded or modified by course of dealing or course of performance or usage of trade.

(4) Remedies for breach of warranty can be limited in accordance with the provisions of this Article on liquidation or limitation of damages and on contractual modification of remedy (Sections 2-718 and 2-719).

§ 2-719. Contractual Modification or Limitation of Remedy.

(1) Subject to the provisions of subsections (2) and (3) of this section and of the preceding section on liquidation and limitation of damages,

(a) the agreement may provide for remedies in addition to or in substitution for those provided in this Article and may limit or alter the measure of damages recoverable under this Article, as by limiting the buyer's remedies to return of the goods and repayment of the price or to repair and replacement of non-conforming goods or parts; and

(b) resort to a remedy as provided is optional unless the remedy is expressly agreed to be exclusive, in which case it is the sole remedy.

(2) Where circumstances cause an exclusive or limited remedy to fail of its essential purpose, remedy may be had as provided in this Act.

(3) Consequential damages may be limited or excluded unless the limitation or exclusion is unconscionable. Limitation of consequential damages for injury to the person in the case of consumer goods is prima facie unconscionable but limitation of damages where the loss is commercial is not.

HENNINGSEN v. BLOOMFIELD MOTORS, INC.
161 A.2d 69 (N.J. 1960)

FRANCIS, J.

Plaintiff Clause H. Henningsen purchased a Plymouth automobile, manufactured by defendant Chrysler Corporation, from defendant Bloomfield Motors, Inc. His wife, plaintiff Helen Henningsen, was injured while driving it and instituted suit against both defendants to recover damages on account of her injuries. Her husband joined in the action seeking compensation for his consequential losses. The complaint was predicated upon breach of express and implied warranties and upon negligence. At the trial the negligence counts were dismissed by the court and the cause was submitted to the jury for determination solely on the issues of implied warranty of merchantability. Verdicts were returned against both defendants and in favor of the plaintiffs. Defendants appealed and plaintiffs cross-appealed from the dismissal of their negligence claim. The matter was certified by this court prior to consideration in the Appellate Division.

[Because the car was to be a gift for his wife, only Clause Henningsen signed the sales contract. This two page document contained, at the bottom of the first page, which is where he signed, a paragraph in tiny type incorporating the provisions on the back of the contract form. One of these provisions was a limited warranty which read as follows:

["It is expressly agreed that there are no warranties, express or implied, *made* by either the dealer or the manufacturer on the motor vehicle, chassis, or parts furnished hereunder except as follows.

["The manufacturer warrants each new motor vehicle (including original equipment placed thereon by the manufacturer except tires), chassis or parts manufactured by it to be free from defects in material or workmanship under normal use and service. Its obligation under this warranty being limited to making good at its factory any part or parts thereof which shall, within ninety (90) days after delivery of such vehicle *to the original purchaser* or before such vehicle has been driven 4,000 miles, whichever event shall first occur, be returned to it with transportation charges prepaid and which its examination shall disclose to its satisfaction to have been thus defective; *this warranty being expressly in lieu of all other warranties expressed or implied, and all other obligations or liabilities on its part*, and it neither assumes nor authorizes any other person to assume for it any other liability in connection with the sale of its vehicles. . . ."

[Shortly after the purchase, and with less than 500 miles on the odometer, Mrs. Henningsen was driving the car on the highway when the steering went out. The car swerved to the right and hit a brick wall, injuring Mrs. Henningsen and rendering the car a total loss. The Henningsens sued, as indicated, and the defendants argued the disclaimer of implied warranties in the contract and the lack of privity between the defendants and Mrs. Henningsen.]

The Claim of Implied Warranty against the Manufacturer.

In the ordinary case of sale of goods by description an implied warranty of merchantability is an integral part of the transaction. R.S. 46:30-20, N.J.S.A. If the buyer, expressly or by implication, makes known to the seller the particular purpose for which the article is required and it appears that he has relied on the seller's skill or judgment, an implied warranty arises of reasonable fitness for that purpose. R.S. 46:30-21(1), N.J.S.A. The former type of warranty simply means that the thing sold is reasonably fit for the general purpose for which it is manufactured and sold. . . .

The uniform act codified, extended and liberalized the common law of sales. The motivation in part was to ameliorate the harsh doctrine of *caveat emptor*, and in some measure to impose a reciprocal obligation on the seller to beware. The transcendent value of the legislation, particularly with respect to implied warranties, rests in the fact that obligations on the part of the seller were imposed by operation of law, and did not depend for their existence upon express agreement of the parties. And of tremendous significance in a rapidly expanding commercial society was the recognition of the right to recover damages on account of personal injuries arising from a breach of warranty. . . . The particular importance of this advance resides in the fact that under such circumstances strict liability is imposed upon the maker or seller of the product. Recovery of damages does not depend upon proof of negligence or knowledge of the defect. . . .

As the Sales Act and its liberal interpretation by the courts threw this protective cloak about the buyer, the decisions in various jurisdictions revealed beyond doubt that many manufacturers took steps to avoid these ever increasing warranty obligations. Realizing that the act governed the relationship of buyer and seller, they undertook to withdraw from actual and direct contractual contact with the buyer. They ceased selling products to the consuming public through their own employees and making contracts of sale in their own names. Instead, a system of independent dealers was established; their products were sold to dealers who in turn dealt with the buying public, ostensibly solely in their own personal capacity as sellers. In the past in many instances, manufacturers were able to transfer to the dealers burdens imposed by the act and thus achieved a large measure of immunity for themselves. But, as will be noted in more detail hereafter, such marketing practices, coupled with the advent of large scale advertising by manufacturers to promote the purchase of these goods from dealers by members of the public, provided a basis upon which the existence of express or implied warranties was predicated, even though the manufacturer was not a party to the contract of sale.

[The court then analyzed the rather minimal protections extended by the warranty, and the extent to which the warranty attempted to disclaim all other responsibility.] Chrysler points out that an implied warranty of merchantability is an incident of a contract of sale. It concedes, of course, the making of the original sale to Bloomfield Motors, Inc., but maintains that this transaction marked the terminal point of its contractual connection with the car. Then Chrysler urges that since it was not a party to the sale by the dealer to Henningsen, there is no privity of contract between it and the plaintiffs, and the absence of this privity eliminates any such implied warranty.

There is no doubt that under early common-law concepts of contractual liability only those persons who were parties to the bargain could sue for a breach of it. In more recent times a noticeable disposition has appeared in a number of jurisdictions to break through the narrow barrier of privity when dealing with sales of goods in order to give realistic recognition to a universally accepted fact.

The fact is that the dealer and the ordinary buyer do not, and are not expected to, buy goods, whether they be foodstuffs or automobiles, exclusively for their own consumption or use. Makers and manufacturers know this and advertise and market their products on that assumption; witness, the 'family' car, the baby foods, etc. The limitations of privity in contracts for the sale of goods developed their place in the law when marketing conditions were simple, when maker and buyer frequently met face to face on an equal bargaining plane and when many of the products were relatively uncomplicated and conducive to inspection by a buyer competent to evaluate their quality. . . . With the advent of mass marketing, the manufacturer became remote from the purchaser, sales were accomplished through intermediaries, and the demand for the product was created by advertising media. In such an economy it became obvious that the consumer was the person being cultivated. Manifestly, the connotation of 'consumer' was broader than that of 'buyer.' He signified such a person who, in the reasonable contemplation of the parties to the sale, might be expected to use the product. Thus, where the commodities sold are such that if defectively manufactured they will be dangerous to life or limb, then society's interests can only be protected by eliminating the requirement of privity between the maker and his dealers and the reasonably expected ultimate consumer. In that way the burden of losses consequent upon use of defective articles is borne by those who are in a position to either control the danger or make an equitable distribution of the losses when they do occur. . . .

Accordingly, we hold that under modern marketing conditions, when a manufacturer puts a new automobile in the stream of trade and promotes its purchase by the public, an implied warranty that it is reasonably suitable for use as such accompanies it into the hands of the ultimate purchaser. Absence of agency between the manufacturer and the dealer who makes the ultimate sale is immaterial.

II.

The Effect of the Disclaimer and Limitation of Liability Clauses on the
Implied Warranty of Merchantability.

[I]n the light of these matters, what effect should be given to the express warranty in question which seeks to limit the manufacturer's liability to replacement of defective parts, and which disclaims all other warranties, express or implied? In assessing its significance we must keep in mind the general principle that, in the absence of fraud, one who does not choose to read a contract before signing it, cannot later relieve himself of its burdens. . . . And in applying that principle, the basic tenet of freedom of competent parties to contract is a factor of importance. But in the framework of modern commercial life and business practices, such rules cannot be applied on a strict, doctrinal basis. The conflicting interests of the buyer and seller must be evaluated realistically and justly, giving due weight to the social policy evinced by the Uniform Sales Act, the progressive decisions of the courts engaged in administering it, the mass production methods of manufacture and distribution to the public, and the bargaining position occupied by the ordinary consumer in such an economy. . . .

[W]hat influence should these circumstances have on the restrictive effect of Chrysler's express warranty in the framework of the purchase contract? As we have said, warranties originated in the law to safeguard the buyer and not to limit the liability of the seller or manufacturer. It seems obvious in this instance that the motive was to avoid the warranty obligations which are normally incidental to such sales. The language gave little and withdrew much. In return for the delusive remedy of replacement of defective parts at the factory, the buyer is said to have accepted the exclusion of the maker's liability for personal injuries arising from the breach of the warranty, and to have agreed to the elimination of any other express or implied warranty. An instinctively felt sense of justice cries out against such a sharp bargain. But does the doctrine that a person is bound by his signed agreement, in the absence of fraud, stand in the way of any relief? . . .

[T]he traditional contract is the result of free bargaining of parties who are brought together by the play of the market, and who meet each other on a footing of approximate economic equality. In such a society there is no danger that freedom of contract will be a threat to the social order as a whole. But in present-day commercial life the standardized mass contract has appeared. It is used primarily by enterprises with strong bargaining power and position. 'The weaker party, in need of the goods or services, is frequently not in a position to shop around for better terms, either because the author of the standard contract has a monopoly (natural or artificial) or because all competitors use the same clauses. His contractual intention is but a subjection more or less voluntary to terms dictated by the stronger party, terms whose consequences are often understood in a vague way, if at all.' . . .

The warranty before us is a standardized form designed for mass use. It is imposed upon the automobile consumer. He takes it or leaves it, and he must take it to buy an automobile. No bargaining is engaged in with respect to it. In fact, the dealer through whom it comes to the buyer is without authority to alter it; his function is ministerial — simply to deliver it. The form warranty is not only standard with Chrysler but, as mentioned above, it is the uniform warranty of the Automobile Manufacturers Association. . . .

The gross inequality of bargaining position occupied by the consumer in the automobile industry is thus apparent. There is no competition among the car makers in the area of the express warranty. Where can the buyer go to negotiate for better protection? Such control and limitation of his remedies are inimical to the public welfare and, at the very least, call for great care by the courts to avoid injustice through application of strict common-law principles of freedom of contract. Because there is no competition among the motor vehicle manufacturers with respect to the scope of protection guaranteed to the buyer, there is no incentive on their part to stimulate good will in that field of public relations. Thus, there is lacking a factor existing in more competitive fields, one which tends to guarantee the safe construction of the article sold. Since all competitors operate in the same way, the urge to be careful is not so pressing. . . .

[T]he judicial process has recognized a right to recover damages for personal injuries arising from a breach of that warranty. The disclaimer of the implied warranty and exclusion of all obligations except those specifically assumed by the express warranty signify a studied effort to frustrate that protection. . . . In the framework of this case, illuminated as it is by the facts and the many decisions noted, we are of the opinion that Chrysler's attempted disclaimer of an implied warranty of merchantability and of the obligations arising therefrom is so inimical to the public good as to compel an adjudication of its invalidity. . . .

[The portion of the opinion in which the court held that the dealership could not disclaim the implied warranty of fitness is omitted.]

V.

The Defense of Lack of Privity Against Mrs. Henningsen.

Both defendants contend that since there was no privity of contract between them and Mrs. Henningsen, she cannot recover for breach of any warranty made by either of them. On the facts, as they were developed, we agree that she was not a party to the purchase agreement. . . . Her right to maintain the action, therefore, depends upon whether she occupies such legal status thereunder as to permit her to take advantage of a breach of defendants' implied warranties.

For the most part the cases that have been considered dealt with the right of the buyer or consumer to maintain an action against the manufacturer where the contract of sale was with a dealer and the buyer had no contractual relationship with the manufacturer. In the present matter, the basic contractual relationship is between Claus Henningsen, Chrysler, and Bloomfield Motors, Inc. The precise issue presented is whether Mrs. Henningsen, who is not a party to their respective warranties, may claim under them. In our judgment, the principles of those cases and the supporting texts are just as proximately applicable to her situation. We are convinced that the cause of justice in this area of the law can be served only by recognizing that she is such a person who, in the reasonable contemplation of the parties to the warranty, might be expected to become a user of the automobile. Accordingly, her lack of privity does not stand in the way of prosecution of the injury suit against the defendant Chrysler.

The context in which the problem of privity with respect to the dealer must be considered, is much the same. . . .

Under all of the circumstances outlined above, the judgments in favor of the plaintiffs and against the defendants are affirmed. . . .

NOTES AND QUESTIONS

1. Would this court recognize any circumstances in which a manufacturer or other seller could successfully limit or disclaim warranties? What circumstances might those be?

2. Should the rule be different today when many manufacturers do compete in offering warranties?

3. Consider the policy grounds put forward by the court. How do they compare with Justice Traynor's?

4. What effect does this case have on the more usual use of warranty in strictly commercial transactions, as in situations where a claim is made that a product has performed poorly? Are there reasons to retain the traditional warranty limitations in such cases?

5. With this case, warranty also moved close to a kind of strict tort liability. Warranty liability had always been strict, of course, but hedged about with limitations such as privity and the ability to disclaim or limit the warranty. With privity abolished and disclaimers at least severely limited in consumer cases, warranty, like negligence, began to appear, in some cases, to be a form of strict tort liability. It was not long after this case was decided that strict products liability finally came into its own as a frankly acknowledged tort doctrine. Two events triggered this change. The first was the decision of the California Supreme Court in *Greenman v. Yuba Power Products*, 377 P.2d 897 (Cal. 1963), in which Justice Traynor, his time come round at last, was able to adopt the doctrine he had argued for in *Escola*. The second, made possible by the first, was the promulgation by the American Law Institute of section 402A of the RESTATEMENT (SECOND) OF TORTS, which gave the ALI's imprimatur to the concept of strict products liability.

C. STRICT LIABILITY IN TORT

The plaintiff in *Greenman v. Yuba Power Products*, 377 P.2d 897 (Cal. 1963), was severely injured while working with a Shopsmith lathe manufactured by the defendant. The injury occurred when the piece of wood on which the plaintiff was working came loose and flew out of the machine, striking him in the forehead. The plaintiff demonstrated at trial that the piece of wood came loose because "inadequate set screws were used to hold parts of the machine together so that normal vibration caused the tailstock of the lathe to move away from the piece of wood being turned permitting it to fly out of the lathe." The plaintiff's experts also testified "that there were other more positive ways of fastening the parts of the machine together, the use of which would have prevented the accident." The court noted that this evidence could establish both negligence on the part of the manufacturer or breach of warranty. However, the defendant claimed that the warranty claim must fail because the plaintiff had not provided the notice called for by the sales act. Rather than placing the basis of liability in the breach of warranty, however, the court explicitly adopted strict liability in tort as the appropriate basis for liability of a manufacturer to a consumer injured by a defective product:

> A manufacturer is strictly liable in tort when an article he places on the market, knowing that it is to be used without inspection for defects, proves to have a defect that causes injury to a human being. Recognized first in the case of unwholesome food products, such liability has now been extended to a variety of other products that create as great or greater hazards if defective. . . .

> Although in these cases strict liability has usually been based on the theory of an express or implied warranty running from the manufacturer to the plaintiff, the abandonment of the requirement of a contract between them, the recognition that the liability is not assumed by agreement but imposed by law . . . and the refusal to permit the manufacturer to define the scope of its own responsibility for defective products . . . make clear that the liability is not one governed by the law of contract warranties but by the law of strict liability in tort. Accordingly, rules defining and governing warranties that were developed to meet the needs of commercial transactions cannot properly be invoked to govern the manufacturer's liability to those injured by their defective products unless those rules also serve the purposes for which such liability is imposed.

The adoption of section 402A as part of the SECOND RESTATEMENT OF TORTS sealed this development, as strict products liability quickly swept the nation, with many courts explicitly adopting the standards set forth by 402A. It is therefore important to become familiar with section 402A's formulation of strict products liability, both in the text of the section itself and in the accompanying "comments." It is equally important to recognize 402A's limitations, and to understand the ways in which the courts have had to expand on the outline of liability found there. The developments in the courts have recently led to a new attempt to restate the law of products liability, the THIRD RESTATEMENT OF TORTS. The relevant sections of the THIRD RESTATEMENT will be used to introduce the relevant topics as we address them.

402A. SPECIAL LIABILITY OF SELLER OF PRODUCT FOR PHYSICAL HARM TO USER OR CONSUMER

(1) One who sells any product in a defective condition unreasonably dangerous to the user or consumer or to his property is subject to liability for physical harm thereby caused to the ultimate user or consumer, or to his property, if

   (a) the seller is engaged in the business of selling such a product, and

(b) it is expected to and does reach the user or consumer without substantial change in the condition in which it is sold.

(2) The rule stated in Subsection (1) applies although

(a) the seller has exercised all possible care in the preparation and sale of his product, and

(b) the user or consumer has not bought the product from or entered into any contractual relation with the seller.

Caveat:

The Institute expresses no opinion as to whether the rules stated in this Section may not apply

(1) to harm to persons other than users or consumers;

(2) to the seller of a product expected to be processed or otherwise substantially changed before it reaches the user or consumer; or

(3) to the seller of a component part of a product to be assembled.

Comment:

a. This Section states a special rule applicable to sellers of products. The rule is one of strict liability, making the seller subject to liability to the user or consumer even though he has exercised all possible care in the preparation and sale of the product. The Section is inserted in the Chapter dealing with the negligence liability of suppliers of chattels, for convenience of reference and comparison with other Sections dealing with negligence. The rule stated here is not exclusive, and does not preclude liability based upon the alternative ground of negligence of the seller, where such negligence can be proved.

. . . .

f. Business of selling. The rule stated in this Section applies to any person engaged in the business of selling products for use or consumption. It therefore applies to any manufacturer of such a product, to any wholesale or retail dealer or distributor, and to the operator of a restaurant. It is not necessary that the seller be engaged solely in the business of selling such products. Thus the rule applies to the owner of a motion picture theatre who sells popcorn or ice cream, either for consumption on the premises or in packages to be taken home.

The rule does not, however, apply to the occasional seller of food or other such products who is not engaged in that activity as a part of his business. Thus it does not apply to the housewife who, on one occasion, sells to her neighbor a jar of jam or a pound of sugar. Nor does it apply to the owner of an automobile who, on one occasion, sells it to his neighbor, or even sells it to a dealer in used cars, and this even though he is fully aware that the dealer plans to resell it. The basis for the rule is the ancient one of the special responsibility for the safety of the public undertaken by one who enters into the business of supplying human beings with products which may endanger the safety of their persons and property, and the forced reliance upon that undertaking on the part of those who purchase such goods. This basis is lacking in the case of the ordinary individual who makes the isolated sale, and he is not liable to a third person, or even to his buyer, in the absence of his negligence. . . .

g. Defective condition. The rule stated in this Section applies only where the product is, at the time it leaves the seller's hands, in a condition not contemplated by the ultimate consumer, which will be unreasonably dangerous to him. The seller is not liable when he delivers the product in a safe condition, and subsequent mishandling or other causes make it harmful by the time it is consumed. The burden of proof that the product was in a defective condition at the time that it left the hands of the particular seller is upon the injured plaintiff; and unless evidence can be produced which will support the conclusion that it was then defective, the burden is not sustained.

Safe condition at the time of delivery by the seller will, however, include proper packaging, necessary sterilization, and other precautions required to permit the product to remain safe for a normal length of time when handled in a normal manner.

h. A product is not in a defective condition when it is safe for normal handling and consumption. If the injury results from abnormal handling, as where a bottled beverage is knocked against a radiator to remove the cap, or from abnormal preparation for use, as where too much salt is added to food, or from abnormal consumption, as where a child eats too much candy and is made ill, the seller is not liable. Where, however, he has reason to anticipate that danger may result from a particular use, as where a drug is sold which is safe only in limited doses, he may be required to give adequate warning of the danger (*See* Comment *j*), and a product sold without such warning is in a defective condition.

The defective condition may arise not only from harmful ingredients, not characteristic of the product itself either as to presence or quantity, but also from foreign objects contained in the product, from decay or deterioration before sale, or from the way in which the product is prepared or packed. No reason is apparent for distinguishing between the product itself and the container in which it is supplied; and the two are purchased by the user or consumer as an integrated whole. Where the container is itself dangerous, the product is sold in a defective condition. Thus a carbonated beverage in a bottle which is so weak, or cracked, or jagged at the edges, or bottled under such excessive pressure that it may explode or otherwise cause harm to the person who handles it, is in a defective and dangerous condition. The container cannot logically be separated from the contents when the two are sold as a unit, and the liability stated in this Section arises not only when the consumer drinks the beverage and is poisoned by it, but also when he is injured by the bottle while he is handling it preparatory to consumption.

i. Unreasonably dangerous. The rule stated in this Section applies only where the defective condition of the product makes it unreasonably dangerous to the user or consumer. Many products cannot possibly be made entirely safe for all consumption, and any food or drug necessarily involves some risk of harm, if only from over-consumption. Ordinary sugar is a deadly poison to diabetics, and castor oil found use under Mussolini as an instrument of torture. That is not what is meant by "unreasonably dangerous" in this Section. The article sold must be dangerous to an extent beyond that which would be contemplated by the ordinary consumer who purchases it, with the ordinary knowledge common to the community as to its characteristics. Good whiskey is not unreasonably dangerous merely because it will make some people drunk, and is especially dangerous to alcoholics; but bad whiskey, containing a dangerous amount of fuel oil, is unreasonably dangerous. Good tobacco is not unreasonably dangerous merely because the effects of smoking may be harmful; but tobacco containing something like marijuana may be unreasonably dangerous. Good butter is not unreasonably dangerous merely because, if such be the case, it deposits cholesterol in the arteries and leads to heart attacks; but bad butter, contaminated with poisonous fish oil, is unreasonably dangerous.

j. Directions or warning. In order to prevent the product from being unreasonably dangerous, the seller may be required to give directions or warning, on the container, as to its use. The seller may reasonably assume that those with common allergies, as for example to eggs or strawberries, will be aware of them, and he is not required to warn against them. Where, however, the product contains an ingredient to which a substantial number of the population are allergic, and the ingredient is one whose danger is not generally known, or if known is one which the consumer would reasonably not expect to find in the product, the seller is required to give warning against it, if he has knowledge, or by the application of reasonable, developed human skill and foresight should have knowledge, of the presence of the ingredient and the danger. Likewise in the case of poisonous drugs, or those unduly dangerous for other reasons, warning as to use may be required.

But a seller is not required to warn with respect to products, or ingredients in them, which are only dangerous, or potentially so, when consumed in excessive quantity, or over a long period of time, when the danger, or potentiality of danger, is generally known and recognized.

Again the dangers of alcoholic beverages are an example, as are also those of foods containing such substances as saturated fats, which may over a period of time have a deleterious effect upon the human heart.

Where warning is given, the seller may reasonably assume that it will be read and heeded; and a product bearing such a warning, which is safe for use if it is followed, is not in defective condition, nor is it unreasonably dangerous.

k. Unavoidably unsafe products. There are some products which, in the present state of human knowledge, are quite incapable of being made safe for their intended and ordinary use. These are especially common in the field of drugs. An outstanding example is the vaccine for the Pasteur treatment of rabies, which not uncommonly leads to very serious and damaging consequences when it is injected. Since the disease itself invariably leads to a dreadful death, both the marketing and the use of the vaccine are fully justified, notwithstanding the unavoidable high degree of risk which they involve. Such a product, properly prepared, and accompanied by proper directions and warning, is not defective, nor is it unreasonably dangerous. The same is true of many other drugs, vaccines, and the like, many of which for this very reason cannot legally be sold except to physicians, or under the prescription of a physician. It is also true in particular of many new or experimental drugs as to which, because of lack of time and opportunity for sufficient medical experience, there can be no assurance of safety, or perhaps even of purity of ingredients, but such experience as there is justifies the marketing and use of the drug notwithstanding a medically recognizable risk. The seller of such products, again with the qualification that they are properly prepared and marketed, and proper warning is given, where the situation calls for it, is not to be held to strict liability for unfortunate consequences attending their use, merely because he has undertaken to supply the public with an apparently useful and desirable product, attended with a known but apparently reasonable risk.

l. User or consumer. In order for the rule stated in this Section to apply, it is not necessary that the ultimate user or consumer have acquired the product directly from the seller, although the rule applies equally if he does so. He may have acquired it through one or more intermediate dealers. It is not even necessary that the consumer have purchased the product at all. He may be a member of the family of the final purchaser, or his employee, or a guest at his table, or a mere donee from the purchaser. The liability stated is one in tort, and does not require any contractual relation, or privity of contract, between the plaintiff and the defendant.

"Consumers" include not only those who in fact consume the product, but also those who prepare it for consumption; and the housewife who contracts tularemia while cooking rabbits for her husband is included within the rule stated in this Section, as is also the husband who is opening a bottle of beer for his wife to drink. Consumption includes all ultimate uses for which the product is intended, and the customer in a beauty shop to whose hair a permanent wave solution is applied by the shop is a consumer. "User" includes those who are passively enjoying the benefit of the product, as in the case of passengers in automobiles or airplanes, as well as those who are utilizing it for the purpose of doing work upon it, as in the case of an employee of the ultimate buyer who is making repairs upon the automobile which he has purchased.

. . . .

n. Contributory negligence. Since the liability with which this Section deals is not based upon negligence of the seller, but is strict liability, the rule applied to strict liability cases (*See* § 524) applies. Contributory negligence of the plaintiff is not a defense when such negligence consists merely in a failure to discover the defect in the product, or to guard against the possibility of its existence. On the other hand the form of contributory negligence which consists in voluntarily and unreasonably proceeding to encounter a known danger, and commonly passes under the name of assumption of risk, is a defense under this Section as in other cases of strict liability. If the user or consumer discovers the defect and is aware of the danger, and nevertheless proceeds unreasonably to make use of the product and is injured by it, he is barred from recovery.

. . . .

NOTE

It is not an exaggeration to say that the meaning of every phrase, if not of every word, in section 402A has been tested in litigation. In these contests, the policy concerns set out in the comments often lead courts to expand the literal meaning of the Restatement section itself.

PROBLEMS

1. Consider the phrases "one who sells" and "is in the business of selling." Comment *f* makes it clear that this does not apply to the casual seller, but should it apply to one in the business of *leasing* products, such as a car rental company? Suppose your doctor gives you a sample package of a drug to take — should section 402A apply to make the doctor strictly liable if the drug is defective? This issue is explored further in Section E, below

2. Consider the meaning of "product." Is a mobile home a product? What about an apartment in a large apartment complex? This issue is also explored below at Section F.

3. Section 402A says that it applies when the defective product causes "physical harm" to the user or consumer or to his or her property. Should it apply when the product does not perform properly and causes economic harm? For example, suppose a truck purchased for use in a business constantly breaks down, costing the business for both repairs and for lost income. Should the manufacturer be strictly liable for these losses under section 402A? *See* Section G, below

D. THE DEFINITION OF "DEFECTIVE"

The definition of "defective condition" found in Comment *g* to section 402A was written with manufacturing defects in mind. These are defects in which the product leaves the control of the manufacturer in a condition that is different from what the manufacturer intended. In other words, the product was not made correctly and the mistake escaped the manufacturer's quality control. When the mistake makes the product unreasonably dangerous, it is considered "defective" under section 402A. Comment *j* also recognized that a product could be defective if the manufacturer failed to provide the consumer with necessary warnings or instructions for use. The *Greenman* case itself imposed liability for a defect in the design of the product. Courts soon recognized that all three types of defect could result in strict liability under section 402A. Courts also recognized, however, that each different type of defect called for different standards for the imposition of liability. In dealing with manufacturing defects, for example, it was always possible to compare the product to the standard the manufacturer itself had established. With both design and warning defects, however, the product had to be compared to an external standard of "proper" design or warning. The establishment of different standards for each type of defect will be examined in the sections that follow. The new THIRD RESTATEMENT has recognized the development of these three types of defect, defining them as follows:

§ 2. CATEGORIES OF PRODUCT DEFECT

A product is defective when, at the time of sale or distribution, it contains a manufacturing defect, is defective in design, or is defective because of inadequate instructions or warnings. A product:

(a) contains a manufacturing defect when the product departs from its intended design even though all possible care was exercised in the preparation and marketing of the product;

(b) is defective in design when the foreseeable risks of harm posed by the product could have been reduced or avoided by the adoption of a reasonable alternative design by the seller or other distributor, or a predecessor in the commercial chain of distribution, and the omission of the alternative design renders the product not reasonably safe;

(c) is defective because of inadequate instructions or warnings when the foreseeable risks of harm posed by the product could have been reduced or avoided by the provision of reasonable instructions or warnings by the seller or other distributor, or a predecessor in the commercial chain of distribution, and the omission of the instructions or warnings renders the product not reasonably safe.

1. Manufacturing Defects

FORD MOTOR COMPANY v. GONZALEZ
9 S.W.3d 195 (Tex. App. 1999)

Opinion by: ALMA L. LOPEZ, Justice.

This is a products liability case stemming from a single car accident in Jim Wells County. Ford Motor challenges the legal and factual sufficiency of the evidence of causation supporting a jury verdict in favor of plaintiffs' claims of manufacturing defect, marketing defect, negligence, and deceptive trade practices concerning a 1989 Ford Escort. We find sufficient evidence of a causal link and affirm the judgment of the trial court.

FACTUAL BACKGROUND

Robert Gonzalez, Jr. purchased a new Ford Escort from the Ford dealership in Alice, Texas, in 1989, and over the next several months noticed excessive wear on the outer part of the right front tire. None of the other three tires on the vehicle exhibited unusual or uneven wear. Gonzalez returned to the dealer to have the car's front end checked. On this first of many such attempts to address the problem, Ford dealership mechanic, Frank Ruiz, checked the camber, caster, and toe-in measurements on the front-end wheel alignment and found a misalignment of the right front wheel. Ruiz adjusted the alignment by turning the tie rod ends to adjust the toe-in. The adjustment held for a time; however, when Gonzalez noticed that his right front tire was, again, showing uneven, outer-edge wear, he returned to the dealership several more times. He ultimately discussed the problem on four separate occasions with factory representatives and was reassured that "the problem would be corrected."

When the realignment did not hold, Ruiz next noted that the ball joint tie rod ends were worn and loose. He replaced them, reset the toe-in, and rotated the tires. When the uneven wear on the right front tire reoccurred, Gonzalez took the car to Sears Automotive Center for another realignment. The uneven wear problem continued. Gonzalez returned to the Ford dealership where Ruiz again adjusted the toe-in. Gonzalez brought his Escort in for such service between ten and fifteen times during the two years he owned the car.

Gonzalez used this car to drive to and from his work as a derrick hand for Blocker Drilling. On April 15, 1991, he had completed a 12-hour shift at a drilling site near Pearsall and slept for several hours before driving to his home in Alice, Texas. Traveling with him were his fiancee, plaintiff Nora Navin, and her son, Jordan. They were all wearing seatbelts. As they neared Alice, Gonzalez and Navin were conversing in the front seat, and Jordan was eating a snack in the back seat. Driving southward on Highway 281 at approximately 58 miles per hour, Gonzalez testified that the steering wheel suddenly jerked violently in his hands, the Escort swerved to the right, onto the shoulder, then as he steered back onto the pavement, it rolled over five times.

The accident was witnessed by Sam Rodriguez, who was driving in the opposite direction in the northbound lane. Rodriguez noticed the Escort approaching in a normal manner, then the right front wheel wobbled and leaned to the right. The left front tire was straight, but the right front tire was leaning in the two o'clock position. He could see Gonzalez fight with the steering wheel as the car approached the shoulder. When the car returned to the pavement, it rolled over. Rodriguez reported to the investigating officer, Trooper Caro, that a visible problem with the right front wheel occurred before Gonzalez lost control of the Escort. The trooper testified that Rodriguez's eye-witness account was consistent with his investigation of the tire tracks, gouge marks, and other evidence at the crash site. Appellees' expert, James Flanagan, M.E., agreed. Trooper Caro also testified that the tire marks on the roadway left by the right tires indicated to him that these tires were "at least upright enough" to be leaving tire marks. He thought they might be "yaw marks," indicating that the right front wheel was sliding sideways but still spinning when the car returned to the pavement after going off the shoulder, but he wasn't sure.

The Escort was unavailable for inspection by either party. The jury viewed photographs of the right front wheel and the suspension assembly taken after the accident which show that the right front MacPherson strut was disconnected from the wheel assembly.

Ford's mechanical engineering expert, Frederick Dahnke, stated that the repairs performed by the dealership were appropriate responses to the complaints Gonzalez brought and that in his opinion the repairs had corrected the problem each time. He also stated that he would expect the right front tire to show wear first because it receives the power of acceleration first. Another contributing factor to right front tire wear is the fact that the passenger seat is often unoccupied, causing the wheel with the lighter load to want to spin faster. The right front tire at the time of the accident did not show unusual wear; however, Gonzalez testified that he had to frequently rotate and replace his tires because of the misalignment problem. . . .

Ford's accident reconstructionist, Dr. Martinez, testified that the cause of the accident actually lay with Gonzalez. Calculating that Gonzalez was traveling approximately 70 miles per hour, he made a sharp steer to the right causing the Escort to go off the road, and then a sharp left steer to get back on the pavement which ultimately sent him into the roll.

The jury found Ford Motor Company liable for manufacturing defect, marketing defect, negligence, and violations of the DTPA. Comparative negligence findings were assessed at 80% liability to Ford Motor and 20% against Gonzalez. Based on this verdict, the trial court entered judgment in favor of Navin for $249,000.00 and in favor of Gonzalez for $361,400 plus pre- and post judgment interest. This appeal followed.

LEGAL SUFFICIENCY

Ford Motor's first issue complains there is no evidence that any defect in the Ford Escort or that Ford Motor, itself, caused the plaintiffs' accident. To review a no-evidence challenge to the verdict, we must consider all of the record evidence in the light most favorable to the party in whose favor the verdict has been rendered, and indulge every reasonable inference deducible from the evidence in that party's favor. . . . Under this standard our scope of review extends to all the evidence. Where there is any evidence of probative force to support the finding, we must overrule the challenge and uphold the finding.

Ford Motor asserts that the pivotal issue is whether the right front wheel disconnected as a result of the accident, or whether it occurred before and caused the accident. Ford Motor argues that the jury, having heard evidence of abnormal tire wear, drew an unsupported causal connection between tire wear and the strut coming out of the steering knuckle. Ford Motor asserts that there is no evidence that anything was wrong with the tire alignment or suspension camber or caster. To make this argument, however, Ford Motor ignores testimony supplied by the appellees' witnesses. While the jury did hear testimony that when the Escort returned to the pavement after veering on the shoulder, its right tires were still upright, it also heard Rodriguez state that the right front tire was leaning in the two o'clock position before the car left the pavement the first time. They also heard Trooper Caro opine that the tire marks made once the car returned to the pavement, although "upright," were in a sliding, spinning or yaw pattern. Flanagan testified that the relatively undamaged condition of the strut proved that the wheel came loose before the crash. Had the wheel torn off during the crash, as Ford suggests, he would have expected to see more damage to the strut.

The thrust of Ford Motor's argument is that appellees' expert witnesses did not offer sufficient explanation of the mechanical relation between the strut and wheel alignment, camber and caster, and off-roadtire marks to support a causal connection between misalignment and the resulting accident. Ford claims that the only evidence of this relation is Flanagan's "bare" expert opinion that "the wheel came off, came loose from the strut." Ford points out that Rodriguez, the eyewitness, offered no testimony as to why the wheel came loose, only that it leaned prior to the accident. Gonzalez and Navin testified about what they experienced inside the car. Only Flanagan attempts to link their testimony to a defect, and Ford attacks this effort as "totally deficient."

Naked expert opinion unsupported by fact can be said to have a "suspension problem" of its own because it carries no probative force in law. . . . However, [direct] proof of a defect is not required.

In this case, there was no opportunity for experts to [pore] over the wrecked car before testifying. Flanagan, instead had to piece together for the jury the evidence that something was wrong with the car from the beginning. Flanagan testified that the recurring problem of uneven wear on the outer edge of the Escort's right front tire was caused by a misalignment of the camber and castor, not by a misalignment of the toe-in. Both he and Ruiz testified that the Ford Escort's front-end suspension is designed so that the camber and castor are built-in at the factory — dealership readjustment is not intended.

Flanagan stated that the misalignment of camber and caster caused vibration in the ball joints which are bolted to the steering knuckle arm. He opined that this vibration from the factory-set misalignment damaged the ball joint by hammering the socket and ball. Such damage loosens the ball joint to the point that the wheel can be wobbled back and forth. He stated that this damage began when the Escort left the Ford factory and continued with the replacements until the day of the accident. He further testified that when the Escort was returned to the dealership several times with alignment problems, the factory representative should have acknowledged that there was a problem with the suspension system, replaced the front end, and that would have prevented the accident.

Ford also argues that there is no evidence to support an inference that tire alignment or tire wear caused the right front MacPherson strut to pull free from the steering knuckle. The only evidence offered, says Ford, is that Gonzalez testified he met with Ford factory representatives at least four times, and they assured him the problem would be corrected. Ruiz testified he did realign the wheels each time. Ford says this does not prove that alignment caused the strut to separate from the knuckle, therefore it does not prove a defect caused the accident. Unusual tire wear, however, was not touted as the cause of the accident, rather it evidenced a chronic symptom from which the jury could infer a defective suspension system. . . .

The jury [could] reasonably conclude that if Gonzalez experienced recurring problems with the right front tire and Rodriguez saw the right front wheel lean or bend in the two o'clock position before the Escort went off the pavement, that the separation between strut and knuckle occurred before the accident and caused the accident. The conflicting expert testimony was subject to a credibility call which the jury made.

Ford Motor Company's issues are overruled and the judgment of the trial court is affirmed.

NOTES AND QUESTIONS

1. As this case illustrates, manufacturing defect cases are fairly straightforward on the law but often difficult to prove. Did the plaintiff succeed in proving: a) that a manufacturing defect existed in the car and was present when the car left the hands of the manufacturer; and b) that more likely than not the defect caused the accident? Are the other possible explanations for the accident equally plausible? What are the most important pieces of evidence supporting the plaintiff's theory?

2. If a defect was present, did it render the car "unreasonably dangerous to the user or consumer"? Is the fact that the defect may have caused the accident sufficient to establish this point as well?

PROBLEMS

1. Plaintiff was driving her new car at night on an unlighted country road. Plaintiff naturally had turned on her headlights. In order to see better, the plaintiff toggled the switch for her high-beam headlights. Instead of high beams, however, the switch caused her headlights to go out completely. Plaintiff was now driving in total blackness. She tried to apply the brakes and turned the lights back on, but before she could stop she drove off the road and hit a tree. Inspection revealed that the switch that was supposed to turn on the high-beams was defectively manufactured. Research further revealed that the switch was not manufactured by the automobile maker itself, but was supplied to the auto-maker by another company. Should the automobile maker be strictly liable for the defect in the component part supplied by another company? Should plaintiff be required to sue the component part manufacturer? Should the plaintiff be allowed to sue the component part manufacturer? *Cf. Goldberg v. Kollsman Instrument Co.*, 191 N.E.2d 81 (N.Y. 1963); RESTATEMENT (THIRD) OF TORTS (Products Liability) § 5.

2. Plaintiff became ill after eating ground beef contaminated with the *E. Coli* bacteria. Plaintiff purchased the beef from Groceries, Inc., which purchased its ground beef from Grinder's Packing Co. Grinder's can trace the contaminated shipment of ground beef back to cows purchased from Rancher, who raised and fattened the cattle before shipping them to the packing plant. Should Plaintiff be able to sue Rancher? Is this case different from the situation presented by the problem above?

2. Design Defects

BARKER v. LULL ENGINEERING COMPANY, INC.
573 P.2d 443 (Cal. 1978)

TOBRINER, Acting Chief Justice.

In August 1970, plaintiff Ray Barker was injured at a construction site at the University of California at Santa Cruz while operating a high-lift loader manufactured by defendant Lull Engineering Co. and leased to plaintiff's employer by defendant George M. Philpott Co., Inc. Claiming that his injuries were proximately caused, inter alia, by the alleged defective design of the loader, Barker instituted the present tort action seeking to recover damages for his injuries. The jury returned a verdict in favor of defendants, and plaintiff appeals from the judgment entered upon that verdict, contending primarily that in view of this court's decision in *Cronin v. J. B. E. Olson Corp.* (1972) 8 Cal. 3d 121, 104 Cal. Rptr. 433, 501 P.2d 1153, the trial court erred in instructing the jury "that strict liability for a defect in design of a product is based on a finding that the product was unreasonably dangerous for its intended use. . . ."

As we explain, we agree with plaintiff's objection to the challenged instruction and conclude that the judgment must be reversed. . . . As numerous recent judicial decisions and academic commentaries have recognized, the formulation of a satisfactory definition of "design defect" has proven a formidable task; trial judges have repeatedly confronted difficulties in attempting to devise accurate and helpful instructions in design defect cases. [A]s we explain in more detail below, we have concluded from this review that a product is defective in design either (1) if the product has failed to perform as safely as an ordinary consumer would expect when used in an intended or reasonably foreseeable manner, or (2) if, in light of the relevant design factors discussed below, the benefits of the challenged design [are] outweigh[ed] [by] the risk of danger in such design. In addition, we explain how the burden of proof with respect to the latter "risk-benefit" standard should be allocated.

This dual standard for design defect assures an injured plaintiff protection from products that either fall below ordinary consumer expectations as to safety, or that, on balance, are not as safely designed as they should be. At the same time, the standard permits a manufacturer who has marketed a product which satisfies ordinary consumer expectations to demonstrate the relative complexity of design decisions and the trade-offs that are frequently required in the adoption of alternative designs. Finally, this test reflects our continued adherence to the principle that, in a product liability action, the trier of fact must focus on the *product*, not on the *manufacturer's conduct*, and that the plaintiff need not prove that the manufacturer acted unreasonably or negligently in order to prevail in such an action. . . .

[A]s we noted in *Cronin*, the Restatement draftsmen adopted the "unreasonably dangerous" language primarily as a means of confining the application of strict tort liability to an article which is "dangerous to an extent beyond that which would be contemplated by the ordinary consumer who purchases it, with the ordinary knowledge common to the community as to its characteristics." (Rest.2d Torts, § 402A, com. i.) In *Cronin*, however, we flatly rejected the suggestion that recovery in a products liability action should be permitted only if a product is more dangerous than contemplated by the average consumer, refusing to permit the low esteem in which the public might hold a dangerous product to diminish the manufacturer's responsibility for injuries caused by that product. As we pointedly noted in *Cronin*, even if the "ordinary consumer" may have contemplated that Shopsmith lathes posed a risk of loosening their grip and letting a piece of wood strike the operator, "another Greenman" should not be denied recovery. . . .

Thus, our rejection of the use of the "unreasonably dangerous" terminology in *Cronin* rested in part on a concern that a jury might interpret such an instruction, as the Restatement draftsman had indeed intended, as shielding a defendant from liability so long as the product did not fall below the ordinary consumer's expectations as to the product's safety. [T]he dangers posed by such a misconception by the jury extend to cases involving design defects as well as to actions involving manufacturing defects: indeed, the danger of confusion is perhaps more pronounced in design cases in which the manufacturer could frequently argue that its product satisfied ordinary consumer expectations since it was identical to other items of the same product line with which the consumer may well have been familiar.

Accordingly, contrary to defendants' contention, the reasoning of *Cronin* does not dictate that that decision be confined to the manufacturing defect context. Indeed, in *Cronin* itself we expressly stated that our holding applied to design defects as well as to manufacturing defects. . . . Consequently, we conclude that the design defect instruction given in the instant case was erroneous. . . .

[A]s this court has recognized on numerous occasions, the term defect as utilized in the strict liability context is neither self-defining nor susceptible to a single definition applicable in all contexts. . . .

In general, a manufacturing or production defect is readily identifiable because a defective product is one that differs from the manufacturer's intended result or from other ostensibly identical units of the same product line. For example, when a product comes off the assembly line in a substandard condition it has incurred a manufacturing defect. . . . A design defect, by contrast, cannot be identified simply by comparing the injury-producing product with the manufacturer's plans or with other units of the same product line, since by definition the plans and all such units will reflect the same design. Rather than applying any sort of deviation-from-the-norm test in determining whether a product is defective in design for strict liability purposes, our cases have employed two alternative criteria in ascertaining, in Justice Traynor's words, whether there is something "wrong, if not in the manufacturer's manner of production, at least in his product." . . .

First, our cases establish that a product may be found defective in design if the plaintiff demonstrates that the product failed to perform as safely as an ordinary consumer would expect when used in an intended or reasonably foreseeable manner. . . . When a product fails to satisfy such ordinary consumer expectations as to safety in its intended or reasonably foreseeable operation, a manufacturer is strictly liable for resulting injuries. . . .

As Professor Wade has pointed out, however, the expectations of the ordinary consumer cannot be viewed as the exclusive yardstick for evaluating design defectiveness because "(i)n many situations . . . the consumer would not know what to expect, because he would have no idea how safe the product could be made." (Wade, *On the Nature of Strict Tort Liability for Products, supra*, 44 MISS. L.J. 825, 829.) Numerous California decisions have implicitly recognized this fact and have made clear, through varying linguistic formulations, that a product may be found defective in design, even if it satisfies ordinary consumer expectations, if through hindsight the jury determines that the product's design embodies "excessive preventable danger," or, in other words, if the jury finds that the risk of danger inherent in the challenged design outweighs the benefits of such design. . . .

A review of past cases indicates that in evaluating the adequacy of a product's design pursuant to this latter standard, a jury may consider, among other relevant factors, the gravity of the danger posed by the challenged design, the likelihood that such danger would occur, the mechanical feasibility of a safer alternative design, the financial cost of an improved design, and the adverse consequences to the product and to the consumer that would result from an alternative design. . . .

Although our cases have thus recognized a variety of considerations that may be relevant to the determination of the adequacy of a product's design, past authorities have generally not devoted much attention to the appropriate allocation of the burden of proof with respect to these matters. . . . The allocation of such burden is particularly significant in this context inasmuch as this court's product liability decisions, from *Greenman* to *Cronin*, have repeatedly emphasized that one of the principal purposes behind the strict product liability doctrine is to relieve an injured plaintiff of many of the onerous evidentiary burdens inherent in a negligence cause of action. Because most of the evidentiary matters which may be relevant to the determination of the adequacy of a product's design under the "risk-benefit" standard, *e.g.*, the feasibility and cost of alternative designs are similar to issues typically presented in a negligent design case and involve technical matters peculiarly within the knowledge of the manufacturer, we conclude that once the plaintiff makes a prima facie showing that the injury was proximately caused by the product's design, the burden should appropriately shift to the defendant to prove, in light of the relevant factors, that the product is not defective. Moreover, inasmuch as this conclusion flows from our determination that the fundamental public policies embraced in *Greenman* dictate that a manufacturer who seeks to escape liability for an injury proximately caused by its product's design on a risk-benefit theory should bear the burden of persuading the trier of fact that its product should not be judged defective, the defendant's burden is one affecting the burden of proof, rather than simply the burden of producing evidence. . . .

[W]e hold that a trial judge may properly instruct the jury that a product is defective in design (1) if the plaintiff demonstrates that the product failed to perform as safely as an ordinary consumer would expect when used in an intended or reasonably foreseeable manner, or (2) if the plaintiff proves that the product's design proximately caused his injury and the defendant fails to prove, in light of the relevant factors discussed above, that on balance the benefits of the challenged design outweigh the risk of danger inherent in such design.

Because the jury may have interpreted the erroneous instruction given in the instant case as requiring plaintiff to prove that the high-lift loader was ultra-hazardous or more dangerous than the average consumer contemplated, and because the instruction additionally misinformed the jury that the defectiveness of the product must be evaluated in light of the product's "intended use" rather than its "reasonably foreseeable use", we cannot find that the error was harmless on the facts of this case. In light of this conclusion, we need not address plaintiff's additional claims of error, for such issues may not arise on retrial.

The judgment in favor of defendants is reversed.

NOTES AND QUESTIONS

1. Under the test set forth in *Barker*, would any product that did not incorporate every available safety feature be considered defective in design?

2. Consider how the consumer contemplation test might yield different results from the risk/utility balancing test.

3. In judging the design, should the court take into consideration whether a proposed design change was technologically feasible at the time that the product was manufactured? This is known as the "state of the art" problem. Even if a product had all available safety features when it was manufactured, should technological improvements impose any duty on the manufacturer to update its products after sale? To at least inform purchasers of possible upgrades that are available?

PROBLEMS

1. A passenger on a municipal bus sues the bus manufacturer to recover for injuries suffered in a fall on the bus. The evidence presented at trial is that the bus driver made a sudden stop to avoid a stalled car. The plaintiff, who was

seated in a center-facing seat at the front of the bus was thrown violently forward. She reached out with both arms but could not find a hand-hold to grab. As a result, she was thrown to the floor and injured. Under the test set forth in *Barker*, is this sufficient to satisfy the plaintiff's prima facie case? *Cf. Campbell v. General Motors Corp.*, 649 P.2d 224 (Cal. 1982)

2. Are small, inexpensive handguns defectively designed because they are easy to conceal and therefore useful for criminals? Would the victim of a shooting by a criminal using such a gun have a claim against the gun manufacturer?

3. Are small cars defective simply because they are small, and therefore, under the laws of physics, likely to sustain more damage in a collision with a larger vehicle? On the other hand, are giant sports-utility vehicles defective simply because they are large, and therefore likely to inflict greater harm on the occupants of other, smaller vehicles? How should such design decisions be judged?

4. Plaintiff drove a 1992 MoCo Shrimp, a small, lightly built, inexpensive, and fuel efficient automobile. Plaintiff was injured in a head-on collision with another vehicle. The Shrimp was not equipped with airbags. At the time MoCo manufactured the 1992 Shrimp, airbags were technologically feasible but expensive, and were not required by any government regulation. The evidence indicates, however, that Plaintiff's injuries would have been less severe if the Shrimp had been equipped with airbags. Does the lack of airbags mean that the Shrimp is defectively designed?

HERNANDEZ v. TOKAI CORPORATION
2 S.W.3d 251 (Tex. 1999)

Justice HECHT delivered the opinion of the Court.

The United States Court of Appeals for the Fifth Circuit has certified to us the following question:

> Under the Texas Products Liability Act of 1993, can the legal representative of a minor child injured as a result of the misuse of a product by another minor child maintain a defective-design products liability claim against the product's manufacturer where the product was intended to be used only by adults, the risk that children might misuse the product was obvious to the product's manufacturer and to its intended users, and a safer alternative design was available?

> In the context of this case, the question, more specifically, is whether a disposable butane lighter, intended only for adult use, can be found to be defectively designed if it does not have a child-resistant mechanism that would have prevented or substantially reduced the risk of injury from a child's foreseeable misuse of the lighter. As usual, the Circuit has disclaimed "any intention or desire that the Supreme Court of Texas con-

fine its reply to the precise form or scope of the question certified." Thus advised, we answer, in the factual setting presented, that:

- none of the conditions stated in the question precludes imposition of liability, but neither are they together enough to establish liability;

- proof of an available "safer alternative design", as defined by statute, is necessary but not sufficient for liability; the claimant must also show that the product was unreasonably dangerous as designed, taking into consideration the utility of the product and the risk involved in its use; and

- in determining whether a product is unreasonably dangerous, the product's utility to its intended market must be balanced against foreseeable risks associated with use by its intended users.

Our answer requires the following explanation and elaboration.

I

The factual circumstances in which the certified question comes to us are these.

Rita Emeterio bought disposable butane lighters for use at her bar. Her daughter, Gloria Hernandez, took lighters from the bar from time to time for her personal use. Emeterio and Hernandez both knew that it was dangerous for children to play with lighters. They also knew that some lighters were made with child-resistant mechanisms, but Emeterio chose not to buy them. On April 4, 1995, Hernandez's five-year-old daughter, Daphne, took a lighter from her mother's purse on the top shelf of a closet in a bedroom in her grandparents' home and started a fire in the room that severely burned her two-year-old brother, Ruben.

Hernandez, on Ruben's behalf, sued the manufacturers and distributors of the lighter, Tokai Corporation and Scripto-Tokai Corporation (collectively, "Tokai"), in the United States District Court for the Western District of Texas, San Antonio Division. Asserting strict liability and negligence claims, Hernandez alleged that the lighter was defectively designed and unreasonably dangerous because it did not have a child-resistant safety mechanism that would have prevented or substantially reduced the likelihood that a child could have used it to start a fire. . . .

Tokai moved for summary judgment on the grounds that a disposable lighter is a simple household tool intended for adult use only, and a manufacturer has no duty to incorporate child-resistant features into a lighter's design to protect unintended users — children — from obvious and inherent dangers. Tokai also noted that adequate warnings against access by children were provided with its lighters, even though that danger was obvious and commonly known. In response to Tokai's motion, Hernandez argued that, because an alternative design existed at the time the lighter at issue was manufactured and distributed that would have made the lighter safer in the hands of children, it remained for the jury to decide whether the lighter was defective under Texas' common-law risk-utility test.

The federal district court granted summary judgment for Tokai, and Hernandez appealed.

II

A

Although the certified question references a 1993 Act adopting several statutes pertaining to products liability, the parties confine their arguments to the effect of a portion of one such statute, section 82.005(a) and (b) of the Texas Civil Practice and Remedies Code, applicable to cases like this one that accrued on or after September 1, 1993. We therefore limit our discussion to those provisions, which are as follows:

> (a) In a products liability action in which a claimant alleges a design defect, the burden is on the claimant to prove by a preponderance of the evidence that:
>
>> (1) there was a safer alternative design; and
>>
>> (2) the defect was a producing cause of the personal injury, property damage, or death for which the claimant seeks recovery.
>
> (b) In this section, "safer alternative design" means a product design other than the one actually used that in reasonable probability:
>
>> (1) would have prevented or significantly reduced the risk of the claimant's personal injury, property damage, or death without substantially impairing the product's utility; and
>>
>> (2) was economically and technologically feasible at the time the product left the control of the manufacturer or seller by the application of existing or reasonably achievable scientific knowledge.

Section 82.005 does not attempt to state all the elements of a product liability action for design defect. It does not, for example, define design defect or negate the common law requirement that such a defect render the product unreasonably dangerous. Additionally, the statute was not intended to, and does not, supplant the risk-utility analysis Texas has for years employed in determining whether a defectively designed product is unreasonably dangerous. That analysis involves consideration of several factors, which we listed in *American Tobacco Co. v. Grinnell* as including:

> (1) the utility of the product to the user and to the public as a whole weighed against the gravity and likelihood of injury from its use; (2) the availability of a substitute product which would meet the same need and not be unsafe or unreasonably expensive; (3) the manufacturer's ability to eliminate the unsafe character of the product without seriously

impairing its usefulness or significantly increasing its costs; (4) the user's anticipated awareness of the dangers inherent in the product and their avoidability because of the general public knowledge of the obvious condition of the product, or of the existence of suitable warnings or instructions; and (5) the expectations of the ordinary consumer.

Rather, section 82.005 prescribes two elements — a safer alternative design and producing cause — that must be proved, but are not alone sufficient, to establish liability for a defectively designed product. Section 82.005 reflects the trend in our common-law jurisprudence of elevating the availability of a safer alternative design from a factor to be considered in the risk-utility analysis to a requisite element of a cause of action for defective design. The *Restatement (Third) of Torts: Products Liability* also makes a reasonable alternative design a prerequisite to design-defect liability, as does the law in most jurisdictions.

Whether a defective-design action can be maintained under the circumstances posed in the certified question does not, therefore, depend entirely on section 82.005. A claimant must not only meet the proof requirements of the statute but must show, under the common law, that the product was defectively designed so as to be unreasonably dangerous, taking into consideration the utility of the product and the risk involved in its use. To respond to the certified question, we must consider not only the requirements of section 82.005 but those of the common law as well.

B

The certified question inquires whether a defective-design action can be maintained under several conditions. . . .

2. *The injury was caused by a child's misuse of the product, the risk of which was obvious to the product manufacturer.* Implicit in the question is that it was also obvious to the manufacturer that an intended adult user would allow a child access to the product. Foreseeability of risk of harm is a requirement for liability for a defectively designed product; a product need not be designed to reduce or avoid unforeseeable risks of harm. Risk must be assessed in light of both the gravity and the likelihood of injury from a product's use. But the fact that the foreseeable risk of harm is due to a misuse of the product, rather than an intended use, is not an absolute bar to liability for that portion of an injury caused by a product's defective design. Instead, misuse of a product is a factor that must be considered in allocating responsibility for the injury. In this case, misuse of the lighter by Daphne, Hernandez, or Emeterio does not preclude Ruben from recovering damages caused by the lighter's allegedly defective design.

3. *The risk of injury from a child's misuse of the product was also obvious to the product's intended adult users.* The fact that a product user is or should be aware of the existence and avoidability of dangers inherent in a product's use that are obvious, commonly known, or warned against, is an important consid-

eration in determining whether the product is unreasonably dangerous. In the risk-utility analysis, that fact may even be decisive in a particular case. But in general, the obviousness of danger in and of itself is not an absolute bar — like certain affirmative defenses — to liability for a defective design. Thus, while Hernandez and Emeterio's acknowledged awareness of the dangers involved in allowing children access to lighters weighs against a finding that Tokai's lighter was unreasonably dangerous as designed, it is not, by itself, an absolute bar to recovery. Whether this factor is determinative in this case is a question that must be decided by applying the risk-utility analysis in the federal court proceeding.

4. A safer alternative was available. This is a prerequisite to liability under section 82.005(b), as it has come to be under the common law. The statute requires a claimant to prove that an alternative design (i) would in reasonable probability have prevented or significantly reduced the risk of the claimant's injury or damage (ii) without substantially impairing the product's utility, and (iii) was economically and technologically feasible when the product was manufactured or sold. The relevant risk of injury or damage under the statute is the risk to the claimant; in this case, that risk is that Ruben would be injured in a fire started by his minor sister with a disposable lighter obtained from their mother's purse. The relevant utility is to the intended users of the product, here all adults, according to the certified question. To prove a safer alternative design in the circumstances presented, Hernandez must prove, by a preponderance of the evidence that the child-resistant design available when the lighter was manufactured (the parties all agree that such a design was feasible then) would in reasonable probability have prevented or significantly reduced the risk of Ruben's being burned as a result of his sister's misuse of the lighter without substantially impairing the lighter's utility to the product's intended adult users. As we have already explained, however, proof of a safer alternative design under section 82.005 is necessary but not sufficient to maintain a defective-design claim. The claimant must also prove a design defect, which, under Texas common law, is a condition of the product that renders it "unreasonably dangerous as designed, taking into consideration the utility of the product and the risk involved in its use."

5. The product was intended to be used only by adults. A product's utility and risk under the common-law test must both be measured with reference to the product's intended users. A product intended for adults need not be designed to be safe for children solely because it is possible for the product to come into a child's hands. . . . A child may hurt himself or others with a hammer, a knife, an electrical appliance, a power tool, or a ladder; he may fall into a pool, or start a car. The manufacturers and sellers of such products need not make them child-proof merely because it is possible for children to cause harm with them and certain that some children will do so. The risk that adults, for whose use the products were intended, will allow children access to them, resulting in harm, must be balanced against the products' utility to their intended users.

We have not had occasion to consider the situation presented in this case — a child's misuse of a product intended only for adults — but we have applied the general principle that a product's safety must be assessed in the context of its intended use. In *Caterpillar Co. v. Shears*, [911 S.W.2d 379 (Tex. 1995)], we held that a product that is safe for its intended use is not defectively designed merely because it is unsafe in other circumstances. Shears was injured when the front-end loader he was operating was struck from behind by another loader. Shears would not have been injured had the protective canopy over the driver's seat not been removed by his employer. Shears claimed that the canopy should have been designed so that it was not removable. The canopy was designed to be removable so that the loader could be used in areas where there was low vertical clearance and little risk of rollover, the principal danger the canopy was meant to protect against. We concluded, as a matter of law, that the loader was not defectively designed merely because its canopy, which had to be removed for some work, could be removed when it should not have been. Caterpillar was not required to design the loader so that, to be safe in all situations, it could not be used at all in some.

Even if an alternative design does not restrict a product's utility as severely as in *Caterpillar*, it still may not be sufficient for defective-design liability if it overly restricts consumer choice. The *Restatement (Third) of Torts: Products Liability* offers two examples: a smaller car that is not as crashworthy as a larger car merely because it is not as large, and a bullet-proof vest that offers only front-and-back protection but is more flexible and comfortable and less expensive than a wrap-around model. Consumers are entitled to consider the risks and benefits of the different designs and choose among them. The briefs in this case suggest other examples: a chemistry set for teenagers that includes a Bunsen burner and chemicals that most younger children should not be allowed to use; a high-power nail gun that should be used only by experienced carpenters; and a sailboat designed for speed rather than stability that is safe only for more experienced sailors. . . . To make such products safe for the least apt, and unintended, user would hold other users hostage to the lowest common denominator.

A disposable lighter without a child-resistant mechanism is safe as long as its use is restricted to adults, as its manufacturer and users intend. Tokai makes lighters with and without child-resistant devices. Adults who want to minimize the possibility that their lighter may be misused by a child may purchase the child-resistant models. Adults who prefer the other model, as Hernandez and Emeterio did, may purchase it (although we note that the federal Consumer Product Safety Commission has adopted a safety standard banning the manufacture and importation of non-child-resistant disposable lighters after July 12, 1994). Whether adult users of lighters should be deprived of this choice of product design because of the risk that some children will obtain lighters that are not child-resistant and cause harm is the proper focus of the common-law risk-utility test.

The utility of disposable lighters must be measured with reference to the intended adult users. Consumer preference — that is, that users like Hernandez and Emeterio simply prefer lighters without child-resistant features — is one consideration. Tokai also argues that adults whose dexterity is impaired, such as by age or disease, cannot operate child-resistant lighters, but Hernandez disputes this. If Tokai were shown to be correct, then that would be an additional consideration in assessing the utility of non-child-resistant lighters.

The relevant risk includes consideration of both the likelihood that adults will allow children access to lighters and the gravity of the resulting harm. The risk is not that a child who plays with a lighter may harm himself. We assume that that risk is substantial. As Hernandez and Emeterio both acknowledged in this case, they would not allow a child to have a lighter and would discipline a child caught playing with one. Rather, the risk is that a lighter will come into a child's hands. The record before us suggests that children will almost certainly obtain access to lighters, that this will not happen often in comparison with the number of lighters sold, but that when it does happen the harm caused can be extreme. Each of these considerations is relevant in assessing the risk of non-child-resistant lighters.

In sum, a manufacturer's intention that its product be used only by adults does not insulate it from liability for harm caused by a child who gains access to the product, but liability standards must be applied in the context of the intended users. . . .

NOTES

1. To what extent must a manufacturer anticipate and guard against "misuse" of its products? And whose "misuse" must the manufacturer anticipate? Only intended users of the product? Or misuse by anyone who might come into contact with the product?

2. The misuse problem shades into the issue of whether or not contributory negligence (and what sort of contributory negligence) can be a defense to a strict products liability claim. The problem of the plaintiff's conduct as a defense is discussed in Section H of this chapter, below. The relationship between the two doctrines can be addressed by considering this question: Does a manufacturer have a duty to design a product so as to protect the user against the user's own carelessness? Such a duty is recognized, for example, in the obligation of automobile manufacturers to design cars that will protect the occupants in a crash, and in the obligation of manufacturers of industrial equipment to provide safety interlocks to prevent the operator from putting his or her hand in the machine while it is operating.

3. Why must the plaintiff prove the existence of an alternative safer design in order to recover? Is it possible for a product to be defective in design even if no alternative design that would have prevented the injury is feasible? That

would in effect be a declaration that the risks of the product so outweigh the benefits that it would be better not to have the product at all. Can you think of such any products?

PROBLEMS

1. Father parked his car in the street in front of a convenience store. He put the automatic transmission into Park and got out of the car, leaving the engine running, in order to run into the store and quickly buy a newspaper. Father left his seven-year-old son in the back seat while he did this. The boy was not wearing a seat belt. As soon as father left the car, the boy jumped into the front seat and got behind the wheel so he could play "driver." The boy grabbed the gearshift lever and put the car into Reverse. The car began to back up and turn into the traffic on the street. There it collided with another car. The force of the collision was sufficient to cause significant damage to both cars and minor personal injuries to the boy. A shift interlock that would prevent the operator of the car from shifting out of Park unless the foot brake was depressed would have prevented the accident. What are the significant factors that must be considered in determining whether the manufacturer is liable for this accident for failing to include such a safety device in its design of the automobile?

2. AutoCo manufactures a small convertible sports car. The car is equipped with a cloth convertible top and no roll-bar. For that reason, it provides less protection in the event of a roll-over than a traditional hard-top. The presence of the convertible top and the absence of a roll-bar are apparent to prospective purchasers. Is the car defective in design? What is the significance of the obviousness of the design defect, if such it be, and the role of consumer choice in purchasing a car with these features?

BROWN v. SUPERIOR COURT
751 P.2d 470 (Cal. 1988)

MOSK, Justice.

In current litigation several significant issues have arisen relating to the liability of manufacturers of prescription drugs for injuries caused by their products. Our first and broadest inquiry is whether such a manufacturer may be held strictly liable for a product that is defective in design. . . .

A number of plaintiffs filed actions in the San Francisco Superior Court against numerous drug manufacturers which allegedly produced DES, a substance plaintiffs claimed was used by their mothers to prevent miscarriage. They alleged that the drug was defective and they were injured in utero when their mothers ingested it. . . .

The trial court [determined] that defendants could not be held strictly liable for the alleged defect in DES but only for their failure to warn of known or knowable side effects of the drug. It held further that neither breach of warranty nor fraud will lie in an action based on the market share theory of *Sindell*. . . .

Plaintiff sought a writ of mandate or prohibition in the Court of Appeal to review the foregoing rulings. That court [upheld] the trial court's determination. . . . We granted review to examine the conclusions of the Court of Appeal [on] the issue of strict liability of a drug manufacturer for a defect in the design of a prescription drug. . . .

[E]ven before *Greenman* was decided, the members of the American Law Institute, in considering whether to adopt a rule of strict liability, pondered whether the manufacturer of a prescription drug should be subject to the doctrine. (38 ALI Proc. 19, 90-92, 98 (1961).). . . . A motion to exempt prescription drugs from the section was defeated on the suggestion of Dean Prosser that the problem could be dealt with in the comments to the section. However, a motion to state the exemption in a comment was also defeated. At the next meeting of the institute in 1962, section 402A was approved together with comment *k* thereto.

The comment provides that the producer of a properly manufactured prescription drug may be held liable for injuries caused by the product only if it was not accompanied by a warning of dangers that the manufacturer knew or should have known about. . . .

Comment *k* has been analyzed and criticized by numerous commentators. While there is some disagreement as to its scope and meaning, there is a general consensus that, although it purports to explain the strict liability doctrine, in fact the principle it states is based on negligence. . . . That is, comment *k* would impose liability on a drug manufacturer only if it failed to warn of a defect of which it either knew or should have known. This concept focuses not on a deficiency in the product — the hallmark of strict liability — but on the fault of the producer in failing to warn of dangers inherent in the use of its product that were either known or knowable — an idea which "rings of negligence," in the words of *Cronin*. . . .

Comment *k* has been adopted in the overwhelming majority of jurisdictions that have considered the matter. . . . We appear, then, to have three distinct choices: (1) to hold that the manufacturer of a prescription drug is strictly liable for a defect in its product because it was defectively designed, as that term is defined in Barker, or because of a failure to warn of its dangerous propensities even though such dangers were neither known nor scientifically knowable at the time of distribution; (2) to determine that liability attaches only if a manufacturer fails to warn of dangerous propensities of which it was or should have been aware, in conformity with comment k; or (3) to decide, . . . that strict liability for design defects should apply to prescription drugs unless the particular drug which caused the injury is found to be "unavoidably dangerous."

We shall conclude that (1) a drug manufacturer's liability for a defectively designed drug should not be measured by the standards of strict liability; (2) because of the public interest in the development, availability, and reasonable price of drugs, the appropriate test for determining responsibility is the test stated in comment k; and (3) for these same reasons of policy, we disapprove the holding . . . that only those prescription drugs found to be "unavoidably dangerous" should be measured by the comment k standard and that strict liability should apply to drugs that do not meet that description.

1. Design Defect

Barker, as we have seen, set forth two alternative tests to measure a design defect: first, whether the product performed as safely as the ordinary consumer would expect when used in an intended and reasonably foreseeable manner, and second, whether, on balance, the benefits of the challenged design outweighed the risk of danger inherent in the design. . . .

Defendants assert that neither of these tests is applicable to a prescription drug like DES. As to the "consumer expectation" standard, they claim, the "consumer" is not the plaintiff but the physician who prescribes the drug, and it is to him that the manufacturer's warnings are directed. A physician appreciates the fact that all prescription drugs involve inherent risks, known and unknown, and he does not expect that the drug is without such risks. We agree that the "consumer expectation" aspect of the *Barker* test is inappropriate to prescription drugs. While the "ordinary consumer" may have a reasonable expectation that a product such as a machine he purchases will operate safely when used as intended, a patient's expectations regarding the effects of such a drug are those related to him by his physician, to whom the manufacturer directs the warnings regarding the drug's properties. The manufacturer cannot be held liable if it has provided appropriate warnings and the doctor fails in his duty to transmit these warnings to the patient or if the patient relies on inaccurate information from others regarding side effects of the drug.

The second test, which calls for the balancing of risks and benefits, is inapposite to prescription drugs, according to defendants, because it contemplates that a safer alternative design is feasible. While the defective equipment in *Barker* and other cases involving mechanical devices might be "redesigned" by the addition of safety devices, there is no possibility for an alternative design for a drug like DES, which is a scientific constant compounded in accordance with a required formula.

We agree with defendants that *Barker* contemplates a safer alternative design is possible, but we seriously doubt their claim that a drug like DES cannot be "redesigned" to make it safer. For example, plaintiff might be able to demonstrate at trial that a particular component of DES rendered it unsafe as a miscarriage preventative and that removal of that component would not have affected the efficacy of the drug. Even if the resulting product, without the damaging component, would bear a name other than DES, it would do no violence to semantics to view it as a "redesign" of DES.

Or plaintiff might be able to prove that other, less harmful drugs were available to prevent miscarriage; the benefit of such alternate drugs could be weighed against the advantages of DES in making the risk/benefit analysis of *Barker*. . . .

Of course, the fact that a drug with dangerous side effects may be characterized as containing a defect in design does not necessarily mean that its producer is to be held strictly liable for the defect. The determination of that issue depends on whether the public interest would be served by the imposition of such liability. As we have seen, the fundamental reasons underlying the imposition of strict liability are to deter manufacturers from marketing products that are unsafe, and to spread the cost of injury from the plaintiff to the consuming public, which will pay a higher price for the product to reflect the increased expense of insurance to the manufacturer resulting from its greater exposure to liability. . . .

But there is an important distinction between prescription drugs and other products such as construction machinery, . . . a lawnmower, . . . or perfume, . . . the producers of which were held strictly liable. In the latter cases, the product is used to make work easier or to provide pleasure, while in the former it may be necessary to alleviate pain and suffering or to sustain life. Moreover, unlike other important medical products (wheelchairs, for example), harm to some users from prescription drugs is unavoidable. Because of these distinctions, the broader public interest in the availability of drugs at an affordable price must be considered in deciding the appropriate standard of liability for injuries resulting from their use.

Perhaps a drug might be made safer if it was withheld from the market until scientific skill and knowledge advanced to the point at which additional dangerous side effects would be revealed. But in most cases such a delay in marketing new drugs — added to the delay required to obtain approval for release of the product from the Food and Drug Administration — would not serve the public welfare. Public policy favors the development and marketing of beneficial new drugs, even though some risks, perhaps serious ones, might accompany their introduction, because drugs can save lives and reduce pain and suffering.

If drug manufacturers were subject to strict liability, they might be reluctant to undertake research programs to develop some pharmaceuticals that would prove beneficial or to distribute others that are available to be marketed, because of the fear of large adverse monetary judgments. Further, the additional expense of insuring against such liability — assuming insurance would be available — and of research programs to reveal possible dangers not detectable by available scientific methods could place the cost of medication beyond the reach of those who need it most.

The possibility that the cost of insurance and of defending against lawsuits will diminish the availability and increase the price of pharmaceuticals is far from theoretical. Defendants cite a host of examples of products which have greatly increased in price or have been withdrawn or withheld from the market because of the fear that their producers would be held liable for large judgments.

For example, according to defendant E.R. Squibb & Sons, Inc., Benedictin, the only antinauseant drug available for pregnant women, was withdrawn from sale in 1983 because the cost of insurance almost equaled the entire income from sale of the drug. Before it was withdrawn, the price of Benedictin increased by over 300 percent. . . .

Drug manufacturers refused to supply a newly discovered vaccine for influenza on the ground that mass inoculation would subject them to enormous liability. The government therefore assumed the risk of lawsuits resulting from injuries caused by the vaccine. . . . One producer of diphtheria-tetanus-pertussis vaccine withdrew from the market, giving as its reason "extreme liability exposure, cost of litigation and the difficulty of continuing to obtain adequate insurance." There are only two manufacturers of the vaccine remaining in the market, and the cost of each dose rose a hundredfold from 11 cents in 1982 to $11.40 in 1986, $8 of which was for an insurance reserve. The price increase roughly paralleled an increase in the number of lawsuits from one in 1978 to 219 in 1985. . . . Finally, a manufacturer was unable to market a new drug for the treatment of vision problems because it could not obtain adequate liability insurance at a reasonable cost. . . .

There is no doubt that, from the public's standpoint, these are unfortunate consequences. And they occurred even though almost all jurisdictions follow the negligence standard of comment k. It is not unreasonable to conclude in these circumstances that the imposition of a harsher test for liability would not further the public interest in the development and availability of these important products.

We decline to hold, therefore, that a drug manufacturer's liability for injuries caused by the defective design of a prescription drug should be measured by the standard set forth in *Barker*.

2. Failure to Warn

For these same reasons of policy, we reject plaintiff's assertion that a drug manufacturer should be held strictly liable for failure to warn of risks inherent in a drug even though it neither knew nor could have known by the application of scientific knowledge available at the time of distribution that the drug could produce the undesirable side effects suffered by the plaintiff. . . .

The judgment of the Court of Appeal is affirmed.

NOTES AND QUESTIONS

1. Compare the approach of the THIRD RESTATEMENT to the problem of liability for prescription drugs:

§ 6. LIABILITY OF COMMERCIAL SELLER OR DISTRIBUTOR FOR HARM CAUSED BY DEFECTIVE PRESCRIPTION DRUGS AND MEDICAL DEVICES

(a) A manufacturer of a prescription drug or medical device who sells or otherwise distributes a defective drug or medical device is subject to liability for harm to persons caused by the defect. A prescription drug or medical device is one that may be legally sold or otherwise distributed only pursuant to a health-care provider's prescription.

(b) For purposes of liability under Subsection (a), a prescription drug or medical device is defective if at the time of sale or other distribution the drug or medical device:

    (1) contains a manufacturing defect as defined in § 2(a); or

    (2) is not reasonably safe due to defective design as defined in Subsection (c); or

    (3) is not reasonably safe due to inadequate instructions or warnings as defined in Subsection (d).

(c) A prescription drug or medical device is not reasonably safe due to defective design if the foreseeable risks of harm posed by the drug or medical device are sufficiently great in relation to its foreseeable therapeutic benefits that reasonable health-care providers, knowing of such foreseeable risks and therapeutic benefits, would not prescribe the drug or medical device for any class of patients.

(d) A prescription drug or medical device is not reasonably safe due to inadequate instructions or warnings if reasonable instructions or warnings regarding foreseeable risks of harm are not provided to:

    (1) prescribing and other health-care providers who are in a position to reduce the risks of harm in accordance with the instructions or warnings; or

    (2) the patient when the manufacturer knows or has reason to know that health-care providers will not be in a position to reduce the risks of harm in accordance with the instructions or warnings.

(e) A retail seller or other distributor of a prescription drug or medical device is subject to liability for harm caused by the drug or device if:

    (1) at the time of sale or other distribution the drug or medical device contains a manufacturing defect as defined in § 2(a); or

(2) at or before the time of sale or other distribution of the drug or medical device the retail seller or other distributor fails to exercise reasonable care and such failure causes harm to persons.

2. Not all courts have accepted the reasoning of *Brown* and the THIRD RESTATEMENT and afforded more favorable treatment to prescription drugs than to other types of products. Is the reasoning of the *Brown* court convincing? The RESTATEMENT section quoted above makes the problem of prescription drugs into a warning issue except in the rare cases in which the risks of the drug outweigh the benefits for all classes of patients. What would be wrong with using an ordinary risk/utility analysis for prescription drugs? *Cf. Hill v. Searle Laboratories*, 884 F.2d 1064 (8th Cir. 1989). Or using the consumer expectation test? If the consumer expectation test is used, who is the relevant consumer?

3. If the problem of prescription drugs is to be dealt with as a warnings issue, then at least two other problems need to be addressed. First, what must the drug manufacturer warn about? The California Supreme Court in Brown suggested one answer in the final section of its opinion: the company must warn of risks of which it should have been aware. Second, to whom must the warning be directed? In the case of most prescription drugs, the courts apply what is known as the "learned intermediary" doctrine. Under this rule, the manufacturer's duty is to provide warnings and instructions to the physician who will prescribe the drug. The physician in turn is responsible for informing the patient of relevant risks so that the patient can give an informed consent to the treatment.

4. The same concerns have been raised in cases involving patients who contracted disease such as hepatitis and AIDS from blood transfusions. Courts and especially legislatures have been reluctant to impose strict liability when no tests were available at the time of the transfusion that could have detected the presence of the viruses that caused these diseases.

PROBLEMS

1. Plaintiff saw a television advertisement for a new prescription pain medication. The advertisement, of course, touted the drug's safety and effectiveness and included, at the end, a series of warnings about the most serious side effects. Additional warnings were provided with the literature sent to Plaintiff's doctor. The advertisement did not warn of a rare but potentially serious stomach problem that could accompany use of the drug, although this danger was disclosed in the more extensive warnings provided to the doctor. At Plaintiff's request, the doctor agreed to prescribe the drug for Plaintiff's sore back, but did so without conveying any warning about the rare stomach problems. Plaintiff did develop serious stomach problems but failed to inform her doctor about them until after the drug caused permanent damage to her stomach. Who should be liable for this failure to warn?

2. Plaintiff participated in a government sponsored mass immunization program. The vaccine presented a very slight risk of adverse effects, on the order of 1 problem in 1 million doses. No warning was provided to the participants, although the physicians administering the program were aware of risk. Given the size of the program, it was not thought possible for those administering the vaccine to patients to provide individualized warnings to each recipient. If Plaintiff is injured by the vaccine, could plaintiff sue the manufacturers of the vaccine? The doctors? Who should have the responsibility of providing a warning? Is there a causation problem for the plaintiff?

3. Warning Defects

LIVINGSTON v. MARIE CALLENDER'S, INC.
85 Cal. Rptr. 2d 528 (Cal. Ct. App. 1999)

TURNER, P.J.

I. INTRODUCTION

The question in this case is whether a restaurant offering vegetable soup "made from the freshest ingredients, from scratch, . . . every day," has an affirmative obligation to warn customers the soup contains monosodium glutamate (MSG). Plaintiff, David Livingston, alleges he suffered a severe adverse reaction after consuming a bowl of Marie Callender's vegetable soup. It is undisputed the soup contained MSG. Had plaintiff known the soup contained MSG, he would not have eaten it. The trial court dismissed plaintiff's strict liability claim on the ground, as a matter of law, there was nothing wrong with the soup, or the MSG in the soup. Plaintiff contends that, pursuant to section 402A of the Restatement Second of Torts, comment *j*, a cause of action for strict liability failure to warn exists where a product "contains an ingredient to which a substantial number of the population are allergic, and the ingredient is one whose danger is not generally known, or if known is one which the consumer would reasonably not expect to find in the product, [and the seller] has knowledge, or by the application of reasonable, developed human skill and foresight should have knowledge, of the presence of the ingredient and the danger." We agree. Accordingly, we remand for a limited retrial on that theory. We wish to emphasize that we are not holding that in every or any case there is a duty to warn restaurant customers of the presence of MSG; rather, we merely hold plaintiff is entitled to a limited retrial on his failure to warn contentions. Whether it can be held by an appellate court that there is a duty to warn of the presence of MSG must await a trial and later appeal.

II. SUBSTANTIVE AND PROCEDURAL HISTORY

In his third amended complaint, the operative pleading, plaintiff alleged that on July 12, 1993, he went to a Marie Callender's restaurant in Toluca Lake for lunch. He reviewed the menu and was interested in ordering a bowl of vegetable soup. He told the waitress he had asthma and he wanted to know if the soup contained MSG. The waitress assured plaintiff the soup did not contain MSG. Plaintiff ordered and consumed the soup. In fact, the soup did contain MSG. As a result of consuming the soup, plaintiff suffered MSG Symptom Complex including, but not limited to, respiratory arrest, hypoxia, cardiac arrest, and brain damage. In his first cause of action, for strict liability, plaintiff alleged the presence of MSG in the soup rendered it defective and unfit for human consumption. Plaintiff also asserted causes of action for negligence, breach of implied warranty, breach of express warranty, negligent misrepresentation, and intentional spoliation of evidence.

In June 1997, [the] trial court struck plaintiff's causes of action with the exception of his negligence claim and dismissed all defendants except Marie Callender's # 24, the restaurant. The trial court concluded "there was nothing wrong with the soup, or the MSG in the soup."

The case proceeded to trial on defendant's negligence cause of action against the restaurant. A special verdict form was submitted to the jury. The first question asked, "Was the defendant negligent?" The jury responded in the negative. A judgment was entered on the special verdict. This appeal followed.

III. DISCUSSION

[T]he present appeal involves an allegation that defendants failed to warn plaintiff of the presence of MSG in the soup. California's strict liability failure to warn jurisprudence was synthesized [as] follows: "We specifically addressed the issue 'whether knowledge, actual or constructive, is a component of strict liability on the failure-to-warn theory.' . . . We concluded that it is. 'The California courts, either expressly or by implication, have to date required knowledge, actual or constructive, of potential risk or danger before imposing strict liability for a failure to warn.' . . . We affirmed that 'California is well settled into the majority view [that] knowledge or knowability is a component of strict liability for failure to warn.' [Citing *Brown v. Superior Court*.] We concluded that the holding in *Brown* applied to all products, not only to prescription drugs: '*Brown*'s logic and common sense are not limited to drugs. In recognizing the extent to which the majority rule pervades California precedents in both drug and non-drug cases, *Brown* clearly implied that knowledge is also a component of strict liability for failure to warn in cases other than prescription drug cases.'" . . .

[T]he Supreme Court emphasized that strict liability failure to warn jurisprudence is different from negligence. [The] majority explained: "'[F]ailure to warn in strict liability differs markedly from failure to warn in the negligence context. Negligence law in a failure-to-warn case requires a plaintiff to prove that a manufacturer or distributor did not warn of a particular risk for reasons which fell below the acceptable standard of care, *i.e.*, what a reasonably prudent manufacturer would have known and warned about. Strict liability is not concerned with the standard of due care or the reasonableness of a manufacturer's conduct.

The rules of strict liability require a plaintiff to prove only that the defendant did not adequately warn of a particular risk that was known or knowable in light of the generally recognized and prevailing best scientific and medical knowledge available at the time of manufacture and distribution. Thus, in strict liability, as opposed to negligence, the reasonableness of the defendant's failure to warn is immaterial. Stated another way, a reasonably prudent manufacturer might reasonably decide that the risk of harm was such as not to require a warning as, for example, if the manufacturer's own testing showed a result contrary to that of others in the scientific community. Such a manufacturer might escape liability under negligence principles. In contrast, under strict liability principles the manufacturer has no such leeway; the manufacturer is liable if it failed to give warning of dangers that were known to the scientific community at the time it manufactured or distributed the product.' . . . We explained the policy behind our strict liability standard for failure to warn as follows: "'When, in a particular case, the risk qualitatively (*e.g.*, of death or major disability) as well as quantitatively, on balance with the end sought to be achieved, is such as to call for a true choice judgment, medical or personal, the warning must be given. . . ." Thus, the fact that a manufacturer acted as a reasonably prudent manufacturer in deciding not to warn, while perhaps absolving the manufacturer of liability under the negligence theory, will not preclude liability under strict liability principles if the trier of fact concludes that, based on the information scientifically available to the manufacturer, the manufacturer's failure to warn rendered the product unsafe to its users.' . . ."

Finally, the failure to warn contention in the present case arises in the context of a person with an allergy to a particular food additive, MSG. California has adopted the *Restatement Second of Torts*, section 402A, comment *j* application of strict tort liability failure to warn in the case of allergies. . . .

Restatement Second of Torts, section 402A, comment *j* states: "Directions or warning. In order to prevent the product from being unreasonably dangerous, the seller may be required to give directions or warning, on the container, as to its use. The seller may reasonably assume that those with common allergies, as for example to eggs or strawberries, will be aware of them, and he is not required to warn against them. Where, however, the product contains an ingredient to which a substantial number of the population are allergic, and the ingredient is one whose danger is not generally known, or if known is one which the consumer would reasonably not expect to find in the product, the seller is required to give warning against it, if he has knowledge, or by the application of reasonable, developed human skill and foresight should have knowledge, of the presence of the ingredient and the danger. Likewise in the case of poisonous drugs, or those unduly dangerous for other reasons, warning as to use may be required." The recently adopted *Restatement Third of Torts: Products Liability*, section 2, comment *k*, similarly states: "Cases of adverse allergic or idiosyncratic reactions involve a special subset of products that may be defective because of inadequate warnings. . . . The general rule in cases involving allergic reactions is that a warning is required when the harm-causing ingredient is one to which a substantial number of persons are allergic." . . .

[A]s discussed above, under the *Restatement Second of Torts*, section 402A, comment *j*, and California decisional authority, a defendant may be liable to a plaintiff who suffered an allergic reaction to a product on a strict liability failure to warn theory when: the defendant's product contained "an ingredient to which a substantial number of the population are allergic"; the ingredient "is one whose danger is not generally known, or if known is one which the consumer would reasonably not expect to find in the product"; and where the defendant knew or "by the application of reasonable, developed human skill and foresight should have know[n], of the presence of the ingredient and the danger." . . . Moreover, those issues are for the trier of fact to determine. . . . Further, issues of legal causation must be resolved. . . . Those issues not having been tried, it was error to strike plaintiff's strict liability cause of action. The trial court improperly based its order striking the claim on a finding, as a matter of law, that "there was nothing wrong with . . . the MSG in the soup." Plaintiff is entitled to a trial on the theory there was a failure to warn of an ingredient to which a substantial number of the population are allergic within the meaning of comment *j* to section 402A of the *Restatement Second of Torts*. . . .

NOTES AND QUESTIONS

1. The *Livingston* case involves what may be called a "risk" warning: Given the warning, the consumer can decide whether to meet the risk or avoid it altogether by not using the product. The risk, however, is intrinsic to the product and cannot be reduced by, for example, using the product carefully. In other words, if one is seriously allergic to MSG, there is no way to safely consume soup containing this chemical. Similar are warnings about the possible adverse side effects of prescription drugs: there is often no way to avoid them, and the patient must decide whether the expected benefits of the drug therapy are worth the risk of the possible side effects. This type of warning may be contrasted with that involved in the following case.

2. Are the rules governing negligence liability for failure to warn and strict products liability for failure to warn really distinct? How "strict" is liability for failure to warn, given that the risk must be one that is known or knowable given current scientific knowledge? What is the standard for deciding whether or not a warning must be given?

PROBLEMS

1. Must a product seller warn of dangers that are obvious? For example, should a seller of kitchen knives be required to warn consumers that the knives are sharp and can cause injury?

2. Many people are allergic to peanuts. Should a seller of peanut butter have to provide a warning about the possibility of an allergic reaction to peanuts? What about a seller of chocolate eclairs who uses peanut oil in the recipe? If a warning is required, what should it say?

3. Manufacturer builds and sells a table saw with a completely unguarded blade. Consumer, while using the saw to cut a rough piece of wood, accidentally put his hand near the blade and cut off one of his fingers. In a products liability suit, would this be better approached as a design or a warning defect? Suppose the manufacturer prints a warning on the table saw in large red letters: "Danger: Unguarded Blade — Use extreme caution!" Would such a warning preclude liability on either theory? Suppose the manufacturer argued that no warning was needed because the danger was obvious? Would that argument preclude liability on either theory?

JACKSON v. COAST PAINT AND LACQUER COMPANY
499 F.2d 809 (9th Cir. 1974)

MERRILL, Circuit Judge:

In this diversity case plaintiff seeks to recover from a manufacturer-seller of paint for personal injuries which he claims resulted from failure of the manufacturer to warn adequately of the product's dangerous characteristics. The case was presented to a jury on a theory of strict liability. The jury returned a general verdict for the defendant. On this appeal plaintiff challenges the correctness of the district court's instructions to the jury [on] the nature of the defendant's duty to warn. . . . Concluding that there was indeed error in these instructions, we reverse.

In 1964 plaintiff, a citizen of Utah, was a journeyman painter employed by a Utah painting contractor. His employer entered into a contract with a Montana manufacturing company to paint some railroad tank cars that were to be used for the shipment of bulk quantities of honey. Plaintiff was sent by his employer to Billings, Montana, to do the work.

The paint used to coat the inside of the tank cars, 'Copon EA9,' was manufactured and sold by defendant Reliance Universal, Inc., a Texas manufacturer of industrial paints and coatings. It is an epoxy paint which is highly flammable. While plaintiff was spray painting the inside of one of the tanks a fire occurred and he was very severely burned. The fuel of the fire consisted of the paint fumes which had accumulated in the tank. The cause of ignition is uncertain and was a disputed issue at trial. There was some evidence that it was caused by breakage of a light bulb used by plaintiff in the tank. This is the theory favored by defendant. There was other evidence, mainly expert testimony including an experiment-demonstration, to the effect that the fire could have been touched off by static electricity, perhaps generated by the friction of the rubber soles of plaintiff's shoes on the tank floor. This is the theory favored by plaintiff.

An officer of Reliance testified that Reliance was aware of the fact that Copon EA9 is hazardous if not properly used under proper conditions. Two hazards are recognized to be associated with use of the paint: breathing the toxic vapors, and fire.

The label on the paint used by plaintiff was introduced into evidence. It contains a warning which first refers to the toxicity of the paint if ingested, and then states:

> 'Keep away from heat, sparks, and open flame. USE WITH ADEQUATE VENTILATION. Avoid prolonged contact with skin and breathing of spray mist. Close container after each use. KEEP OUT OF REACH OF CHILDREN.'

Plaintiff testified that he and other painters of his acquaintance understood the warning regarding adequate ventilation to refer only to the danger of breathing toxic vapors. While painting the tanks he had contrived and used a tube and mask which enabled him to breathe fresh air from outside the tank. Otherwise plaintiff took no precautions in the nature of 'ventilation.' He testified that he had been unaware of the possibility that flammable vapors permitted to accumulate in a closed, inadequately ventilated area could be touched off by a spark resulting in a fire or explosion. There was, however, other evidence that some persons in plaintiff's company were aware that such a danger existed. . . .

1. The duty to warn instruction

[After quoting section 402A and comments *i* and *j*, the court continued:] The district court's instructions to the jury included the following:

> 'Defendant had a duty to supply plaintiff or his employer with proper and adequate directions for the use of the paint and proper and adequate warnings concerning the dangers inherent in the paint.

> 'If the defendant had reason to believe that plaintiff or his employer knew or would discover the hazards inherent in the paint, then defendant had no duty to warn plaintiff or his employer of these dangers.'

In our judgment this instruction was erroneous in three respects.

First. It suggests that liability is based on negligence rather than strict liability. (It is in fact patterned upon 388(b) of the Restatement, which sets forth the elements of liability on the part of a supplier of a chattel for negligent failure to warn of dangers known to the supplier.) In strict liability it is of no moment what defendant 'had reason to believe.' Liability arises from (sell(ing) any product in a defective condition unreasonably dangerous to the user or consumer.' It is the unreasonableness of the condition of the product, not of the conduct of the defendant, that creates liability.

Second. Plaintiff has contended that a more specific warning of the fire hazard ought to have been given, namely, that accumulated fumes or vapors in an inadequately ventilated area may be ignited by a spark resulting in a violent fire or explosion. His position is that the absence of such a specific warning rendered the paint as marketed by the defendant 'unreasonably dangerous to the user or consumer'; in other words, that there was a 'duty to warn' of the particular hazard. Defendant contends, in this regard, that it had no duty to warn of this particular hazard because, in the words of comment *j* to 402A, 'the danger, or potentiality of danger, is generally known and recognized.'

On the evidence presented, this was an issue for the jury. The challenged instruction, however, presents the wrong issue. It is not the knowledge actually possessed by the plaintiff, individually, that determines whether the absence of warning renders a product unreasonably dangerous. The subjective knowledge of the plaintiff becomes relevant upon the issue of contributory negligence, as we explain below. On the issue of duty to warn, however, the question to be put to the jury is whether 'the danger, or potentiality of danger, is generally known and recognized'; whether the product as sold was 'dangerous to an extent beyond that which would be contemplated by the ordinary consumer who purchases it, with the ordinary knowledge common to the community as to its characteristics.' Restatement § 402A, comments *j, i.*

Third. The most serious error in the challenged instruction is the statement that knowledge of the hazard on the part of plaintiff's employer would obviate any duty to warn plaintiff. Besides improperly focusing on the knowledge of an individual rather than general or common knowledge, this erroneously conceives the 'community' whose common knowledge the jury is to ascertain. The seller's duty under § 402A is to 'the ultimate user or consumer.' At least in the case of paint sold in labeled containers, the adequacy of warnings must be measured according to whatever knowledge and understanding may be common to painters who will actually open the containers and use the paints; the possibly superior knowledge and understanding of painting contractors is irrelevant. . . .

A distinction analogous to the one we draw here . . . was made in *Davis v. Wyeth Laboratories, Inc.*, 399 F.2d 121, 130-31 (9th Cir. 1968). There we noted that in the case of a prescription drug, normally a warning of dangers given to the physician is sufficient; but we held that when a drug was distributed 'to all comers at mass clinics without an individualized balancing by a physician of the risks involved,' a warning sufficient to apprise the patient himself of the risks was mandated.

Accordingly we hold that the duty to warn runs, on these facts, directly to the painter, and is not discharged when the employer alone is informed of the danger.

Reversed and remanded for new trial.

NOTES

1. The warning in this case consisted of instructions on the proper use of the product. Such warnings acknowledge that the product does pose certain risks which can be avoided if the user is instructed how to use the product safely. A familiar example is the ladder, which today is covered with instructions on how to properly set it up, where not to stand, and the like.

2. The ladder example illustrates an important problem with warnings. Warnings and instructions do no good unless they reach the person who is actually using the product. In the case of ladders, the manufacturer can solve this problem by pasting the warnings and instructions directly to the product. Where this approach is possible it is probably more effective than providing warnings in a brochure than will likely be separated from the product and lost. But often it is not possible to do this, because the instructions, for example, are simply too long to fit on the product.

3. Warnings tend to look like a cheap and effective way of preventing harm. In a cost/benefit analysis that weighs the cost of giving a warning against the benefit of preventing accidents, the balance almost always appears to favor the giving of warnings. More recently, however, at least some courts have questioned whether additional warnings will necessarily be effective. The concern is that an endless proliferation of warnings might cause users to ignore all the warnings, or at least that the volume of warnings will cause the really important ones to be less conspicuous. *Cf. Cotton v. Buckeye Gas Products Co.*, 840 F.2d 935 (D.C. Cir. 1988).

4. The *Jackson* case also involves the issue of the adequacy of the warning. Consider what the warning in this case should have said in order to meet the court's standards.

PROBLEMS

1. Bob, who was twelve years old, figured out a way to make his own hand-held flame-thrower. He got a can of spray paint and some stiff wire from his family's garage and some small (birthday-cake-type) candles and matches from the kitchen. He attached the candle to the top of the paint can with the wire in such a way that the paint would spray from the can over the top of the candle. He then lit the candle and pushed down the button. The paint sprayed over the lighted candle, producing a jet of flame. On his third attempt, unfortunately, the can of paint exploded, causing Bob severe burns. The paint can contained a warning that the paint was flammable ("Flammable: Do not use near open flame"), but no warning that it was explosive, nor was there any warning against using the paint can to construct a flame-thrower. Was the warning given adequate? If the warning given was inadequate, was the inadequacy of the warning the cause of Bob's injuries?

2. More fun with fire: Julia, who did not drink alcoholic beverages, was given a bottle of expensive bourbon whiskey by an important client. Not only was the whiskey expensive, it was also unusually strong, being 130 proof instead of the usual 80 or 90 proof. Not wishing to offend by refusing the gift, she took the whiskey home and used it for cooking. One dish she tried from her "Gracious Southern Cookin'" cookbook was called "Bourbon Chicken." This was basically roast chicken basted with bourbon whiskey. Julia put the chicken in a hot oven, poured a cup of the 130 proof whiskey around it and closed the oven door. The subsequent explosion blew the oven door off its hinges and started a damaging fire in Julia's kitchen. The whiskey bottle contained no warning of this danger. Is the seller liable for the damage to Julia's kitchen?

3. In the previous problem, was the cookbook defective for not warning of this danger?

4. Is the problem of burns caused by scalding hot coffee served from the drive-thru window of the local fast food chain caused by a design defect (the coffee is too hot)? A warning defect ("Contents Extremely Hot" your cup now warns)? Will warnings actually prevent many accidents of this type? Could you draft a warning that would be effective? Would government regulation of coffee temperature be more effective?

E. THE DEFINITION OF "ONE WHO SELLS"

ALLENBERG v. BENTLEY HEDGES TRAVEL SERV., INC.
22 P.3d 223 (Okla. 2001)

KAUGER, J.

The first impression question presented is whether manufacturers' products liability is applicable to the commercial seller of a used product if the alleged defect was not created by the seller, and if the product is sold in essentially the same condition as when it was acquired for resale. We have determined that it is not.

FACTS

On July 16, 1997, Bentley Hedges Travel arranged transportation to the airport for Ava Pattee Allenberg and her daughter, Gwinn Norman (passengers), in a used shuttle bus which it had purchased from the appellee, Arkansas Bus Exchange (Arkansas Bus). While en route to the airport, the driver of the bus ran a red light causing the bus to collide with other vehicles in an intersection. Both passengers were seated on the left side of the bus facing the center aisle. The bus was not equipped with seat belts, and the passengers were flung from their seats and injured in the collision. Ava Allenberg died a few days after the accident.

On February 19, 1998, Gwinn Norman, filed a lawsuit on her own behalf and another lawsuit as the personal representative of her mother's estate. She sued Bentley Hedges Travel and the driver of the bus alleging that they were negligent. She also sued Arkansas Bus alleging that it had distributed and sold a defective, unreasonably dangerous shuttle bus because the bus was not equipped with seat belts, adequate handholds, or secured luggage compartments. Bentley Hedges and the bus driver were later dismissed from the lawsuit.

Arkansas Bus filed answers in both causes, denying the allegations and asserting that it could not be liable because it did not manufacture, design, or produce the bus, nor did it alter, change or modify the bus in any way from its original condition. . . .

On July 17, 2000, Arkansas Bus again filed motions for summary judgment in both causes, arguing that the doctrine of manufacturers' products liability is inapplicable to commercial sellers of used products. [O]n September 27, 2000, the trial court entered judgment in favor of Arkansas Bus, finding that the shuttle bus was a used vehicle when the bus exchange purchased it and that it did not alter, modify, rebuild or restore the bus. . . .

The estate representatives appealed. [We] address the first impression question regarding the application of manufacturers' products liability to the seller of a used product if the alleged defect was not created by the seller, and if the product is sold in essentially the same condition as when it was acquired for resale.

MANUFACTURERS' PRODUCTS LIABILITY IS INAPPLICABLE TO THE COMMERCIAL SELLER OF A USED PRODUCT IF THE ALLEGED DEFECT WAS NOT CREATED BY THE SELLER, AND IF THE PRODUCT IS SOLD IN ESSENTIALLY THE SAME CONDITION AS WHEN IT WAS ACQUIRED FOR RESALE.

[A]rkansas Bus contends that the undisputed facts reveal that any defects were created by the manufacturer and that it purchased the shuttle bus in a used condition and, other than changing the oil and/or tires, it did not warrant, recondition, change, alter, modify, or rebuild the bus before it sold it to Bentley Hedges. It argues that, under these circumstances, commercial sellers of used goods are not subject to strict liability for injuries caused by defects which were present at the time of original distribution. It urges us to join the majority of jurisdictions which have considered the issue and which have determined that strict liability does not extend to commercial sellers of used products if the alleged defect was not created by the seller, and if the product is sold in essentially the same condition as when it was acquired for resale.

Oklahoma adopted the theory of manufacturers' products liability in *Kirkland v. General Motors Corp.,* 1974 Okla. 52, 521 P.2d 1353. . . . In *Kirkland,* we defined manufacturers as "processors, assemblers, and all other persons who are similarly situated in processing and distribution." We recognized that manufacturers' products liability is founded upon public interest in human safety and that the rationale for adopting the rule is that the manufacturer of the product is responsible for the product reaching its market, and the manufacturer is best situated to provide protection against the risk of injuries caused by a defective product.

We have not previously determined whether manufacturers' products liability should apply to commercial sellers of used products when the alleged defect was not created by the seller, and the product was sold in essentially the same condition as when it was acquired for resale. However, since *Kirkland,* and consistent with its rationale, manufacturers' products liability has been applied to various members of the manufacturers' marketing chain. For instance, it has been held applicable to retailers, dealers or distributors, importers, and lessors. . . .

In *Moss v. Polyco,* 1974 Okla. 53, 522 P.2d 622, we explained the rationale for holding non-manufacturer-suppliers to the same liability standard as manufacturers. Relying on cases from other jurisdictions, we noted that: 1) retailers like manufacturers, are engaged in the business of distributing goods to the public; 2) because they are an integral part of the overall producing and marketing enterprise, they should bear the cost of injuries resulting from defective products; 3) in some cases the retailer may be the only member of the marketing chain reasonably available to the public; and 4) in other cases the retailer may play a substantial part in insuring that the product is safe or may be in a position to exert pressure on the manufacturer to make the product safer.

Following the trend of other jurisdictions, [w]e expanded strict liability to include lessors engaged in the business of leasing chattels even when no sale is involved on the basis that such persons put products into the stream of commerce in a fashion not unlike a manufacturer or retailer. . . .

For three decades, courts from other jurisdictions have struggled with the question of whether or under what circumstances the commercial seller of used products should be liable for a defect attributable to the initial design or manufacturing of a used product. Their answers are as varied as the many different fact situations involved, resulting in a split in authority. The impact of the Third Restatement has yet to be seen in the courts, and it has been approached with considerable caution. . . . Despite conflicting results reached by these jurisdictions, the courts generally agree that resolution of the question hinges upon the policies which underpin strict liability and whether those policies are promoted by applying the doctrine to commercial sellers of used products if the alleged defect was not created by the seller, and if the product is sold in essentially the same condition as when it was acquired for resale.

Some courts have imposed strict liability on commercial sellers of used products because they conclude that the Restatement (Second) of Torts, § 402A is not limited by its terms to commercial sellers of new products. These courts have found that the same policy reasons for which we previously applied strict liability to manufacturers, retailers, dealers or distributors, importers and lessors, should also apply to dealers in used goods.

In contrast, courts which have declined to extend the strict liability to commercial sellers of used products have noted that the policy reasons which underlie strict liability are not fully applicable to commercial sellers of used products. For instance, in *Tillman v. Vance Equipment Co.,* 286 Or. 747, 596 P.2d 1299, 1301 (1979), the Oregon Supreme Court held that a commercial seller of a used crane was not strictly liable for a defect created by the manufacturer. [T]he *Tillman* Court reasoned that: 1) generally, used goods markets operate on the apparent understanding that the commercial seller makes no particular representation about the quality of the used goods simply by offering them for sale; 2) if the buyer wants assurances of quality, the buyer typically either bargains for it or seeks out dealers who routinely offer it; 3) the sale of a used product, without more, may not be found to generate the kind of expectations of safety that the courts have held are justifiably created by the introduction of a new product into the stream of commerce; 4) the position of the used-goods dealer is normally entirely outside the original chain of distribution of the product; 5) and there is typically no ready channel of communication by which the dealer and the manufacturer exchange information about possible dangerous defects in particular product lines or about actual and potential liability claims. . . .

Since *Tillman,* the majority of courts have either expressly or implicitly followed its rationale and have concluded that the doctrine of strict liability should not be extended to commercial sellers of used goods, at least when the alleged defects were not created by the seller, and/or the product was sold in essentially the same condition as when it was acquired for resale. Here, the undisputed facts reveal that any alleged defects were created by the manufacturer and Arkansas Bus purchased the shuttle bus in a used condition and, other than changing the oil and/or tires, it did not warrant, recondition, change, alter, modify, or rebuild the bus before it sold the bus to Bentley Hedges. Consequently, under the facts presented, we align ourselves with the majority view and refuse to extend manufacturers' products liability to the commercial seller of the used bus.

TRIAL COURT AFFIRMED.

NOTES

1. Compare the approach of the RESTATEMENT THIRD section 8, mentioned in the main case:

§ 8. LIABILITY OF COMMERCIAL SELLER OR DISTRIBUTOR OF DEFECTIVE USED PRODUCTS

One engaged in the business of selling or otherwise distributing used products who sells or distributes a defective used product is subject to liability for harm to persons or property caused by the defect if the defect:

  (a) arises from the seller's failure to exercise reasonable care; or

(b) is a manufacturing defect under § 2(a) or a defect that may be inferred under § 3 and the seller's marketing of the product would cause a reasonable person in the position of the buyer to expect the used product to present no greater risk of defect than if the product were new; or

(c) is a defect under § 2 or § 3 in a used product remanufactured by the seller or a predecessor in the commercial chain of distribution of the used product; or

(d) arises from a used product's noncompliance under § 4 with a product safety statute or regulation applicable to the used product.

A used product is a product that, prior to the time of sale or other distribution referred to in this Section, is commercially sold or otherwise distributed to a buyer not in the commercial chain of distribution and used for some period of time.

Under this section, would Arkansas Bus be liable?

2. Should a lending company that finances a sale or lease (or lease/purchase) of equipment be considered a "seller"? How do the policies of strict liability apply here?

PROBLEMS

1. Should strict liability apply if the commercial seller of used cars represents that the cars are "inspected?" What if the dealer represents that the car is "Certified", where that term suggests that the dealer has overhauled the used car before offering it for sale? What if the dealer offers a thirty day money back guarantee? Consider your answers under both the approach of the Oklahoma Court and of RESTATEMENT THIRD section 8.

2. On the other hand, if a jurisdiction adopts strict liability for sellers of used products, should the dealer be able to escape such liability by offering a used car "as is" or "with all defects"? What about a junk dealer offering the hulk of a wrecked automobile for sale for parts?

3. Plaintiff went to a bowling alley and rented shoes and a ball. Plaintiff did not notice that the ball she selected was chipped around the edge of one of the finger holes. When she attempted to bowl with the ball, she caught her finger on the chipped portion of the ball and severely cut herself. Should the bowling alley be strictly liable for the condition of the "defective" ball? Do you see any defenses that the bowling alley should argue?

4. Plaintiff buys a can of spinach, of a nationally advertised brand, from Supergrocery. Plaintiff prepares the spinach according to package directions and eats it for dinner. In doing so, Plaintiff breaks a tooth on a small stone hidden in the spinach, a stone that was in the spinach from the time it was canned.

Supergrocery did not cause the stone to be in the can, nor could it have inspected the contents before sale. On what policy basis would section 402A impose liability on the retailer in such a situation?

F. SALE OF PRODUCTS OR PROVISION OF SERVICES?

ROYER v. CATHOLIC MEDICAL CENTER
741 A.2d 74 (N.H. 1999)

BROCK, C.J.

The plaintiffs, Ira A. and Rachel M. Royer, appeal from an order of the Superior Court (Sullivan, J.) granting a motion to dismiss in favor of the defendant, Catholic Medical Center (CMC). We affirm.

The plaintiffs have pleaded the following facts. In September 1991, Ira Royer underwent total knee replacement surgery at CMC. As part of the procedure, a prosthetic knee, provided by CMC, was surgically implanted. In April 1993, Royer complained to his doctor that the pain in his knee was worse than it had been before the surgery. His doctors determined that the prosthesis was defective, and in June 1993 Royer underwent a second operation in which the prosthesis was removed, and a second prosthesis inserted.

Ira Royer initially brought suit against Dow Corning Corp., Dow Corning Wright, Inc., and Wright Medical Technologies, Inc., the companies that had allegedly designed and manufactured the defective prosthesis. Subsequently, Dow Corning commenced federal bankruptcy proceedings, and the plaintiffs filed a second writ against CMC, alleging that CMC was strictly liable to Ira because it had sold a prosthesis with a design defect that was in an unreasonably dangerous condition, and liable to Rachel who suffered a loss of consortium.

The defendant moved to dismiss, arguing, inter alia, that it was not a "seller of goods" for purposes of strict products liability, and that absent the strict liability claim, the loss of consortium claim could not stand. The trial court granted the motion, finding that CMC was not, as a matter of law, engaged in the business of selling prosthetic devices. On appeal, the plaintiffs contend that this finding was error. . . .

In New Hampshire, "[o]ne who sells any product in a defective condition unreasonably dangerous to the user or consumer or to his property is subject to [strict] liability for physical harm thereby caused" if, inter alia, "the seller is engaged in the business of selling such a product." Restatement (Second) of Torts § 402A (1965). . . . If the defendant merely provides a service, however, there is no liability absent proof of a violation of a legal duty. . . . In this case, we are asked to determine whether a health care provider that supplies a defective prosthesis in the course of delivering health care services is a "seller" of prosthetic devices, or is merely providing a professional service.

[T]he reasons for the development of strict liability in tort were the lack of privity between the manufacturer and the buyer, the difficulty of proving negligence against a distant manufacturer using mass production techniques, and the better ability of the mass manufacturer to spread the economic risks among consumers. . . . Particularly crucial to our adoption of strict liability in the context of defective products was the practical impossibility of proving legal fault in many products liability cases. . . .

A majority of the jurisdictions that have addressed whether a health care provider who supplies a defective prosthesis is subject to strict liability have declined to extend strict liability, . . . reasoning that the health care provider primarily renders a service, and that the provision of a prosthetic device is merely incidental to that service. . . .

The plaintiffs argue, however, that the distinction between selling products and providing services is a legal fiction. The defendant, according to the plaintiffs, acted both as a seller of the prosthetic knee and as a provider of professional services in the transaction. Because the defendant charged separately for the prosthesis and earned a profit on the "sale," the plaintiffs argue that the defendant should be treated no differently than any other distributor of a defective product. The defendant, according to the plaintiffs, primarily supplied a prosthesis, while the surgeon provided the professional "services."

Although a defendant may both provide a service and sell a product within the same transaction for purposes of strict liability, . . . the dispositive issue in this case is not whether the defendant "sold" or transferred a prosthetic knee, but whether the defendant was an entity "engaged in the business of selling" prosthetic knees so as to warrant the imposition of liability without proof of legal fault. . . .

[W]e cannot agree that this distinction is merely a legal fiction. "[T]he *essence* of the transaction between the retail seller and the consumer relates to the *article sold*. The seller is *in the business* of supplying the product to the consumer. It is that, and that alone, for which he is paid." *Hoff v. Zimmer, Inc.*, 746 F. Supp. 872, 875 (W.D. Wis. 1990) (quotation omitted) (construing Wisconsin law). A patient, by contrast, does not enter a hospital to "purchase" a prosthesis, "but to obtain a course of treatment in the hope of being cured of what ails him." . . . Indeed, "to ignore the ancillary nature of the association of product with activity is to posit surgery, or . . . any medical service requiring the use of a physical object, as a marketing device for the incorporated object."

We decline to ignore the reality of the relationship between Ira Royer and CMC, and to treat any services provided by CMC as ancillary to a primary purpose of selling a prosthetic knee. Rather, the record indicates that in addition to the prosthesis, Royer was billed for a hospital room, operating room services, physical therapy, a recovery room, pathology laboratory work, an EKG or ECG, X rays, and anesthesia. Thus, it is evident that Ira Royer entered CMC not to purchase a prosthesis, but to obtain health care services that included the implantation of the knee, with the overall objective of restoring his health. . . .

Moreover, the policy rationale underlying strict liability . . . does not support extension of the doctrine under the facts of this case. With respect to the inherent difficulty of proving negligence in many products liability cases, this rationale fails in the context of non-manufacturer cases alleging a design defect. Because "ordinarily there is no possibility that a distributor other than the manufacturer created a design defect[,] . . . strict liability would impose liability when there is no possibility of negligence." . . . The plaintiffs do not allege in this case that the defendant altered the prosthesis in any way. Further, holding health care providers strictly liable for defects in prosthetic devices necessary to the provision of health care would likely result in higher health care costs borne ultimately by all patients, . . . and "place an unrealistic burden on the physicians and hospitals of this state to test or guarantee the tens of thousands of products used in hospitals by doctors. . . ."

We conclude that where, as here, a health care provider in the course of rendering health care services supplies a prosthetic device to be implanted into a patient, the health care provider is not "engaged in the business of selling" prostheses for purposes of strict products liability. Accordingly, the trial court did not err in granting the defendant's motion to dismiss.

NOTES

1. Try to identify the policy reasons given by the court for treating the sale of a product differently from the provision of services. Try to develop a policy argument for treating them identically.

2. What distinguishes a sale of goods from a service? What factors are significant? Try to apply your test to the problems below.

3. What is the relationship between these rules and the ones governing liability for prescription drugs? Is the problem with medical services the same as the problem with unavoidably dangerous products?

PROBLEMS

Consider whether the following should be treated as a sale of goods or the provision of services:

   a. Plaintiff went to a hairdresser. As part of the hair styling services, the hairdresser applied a permanent wave solution to the Plaintiff's hair and scalp. Plaintiff suffered an allergic reaction which caused injury to the scalp and loss of hair. Should the hairdressing business be subjected to strict liability for selling the wave solution?

b. Plaintiff went to an auto repair shop. The shop installed a defective oil filter in the course of changing the oil in Plaintiff's car. Because of the defect the car lost oil and the engine was badly damaged. Should strict liability apply for the sale of the defective filter?

c. Plaintiff went to a plastic surgeon for breast implant surgery. The surgeon used defective implants which leaked and later had to be removed. Should the surgeon be held strictly liable for the sale of the defective implants?

G. THE TYPE OF HARM: THE ECONOMIC LOSS PROBLEM

MOORMAN MANUFACTURING COMPANY v. NATIONAL TANK COMPANY
435 N.E.2d 443 (Ill. 1982)

THOMAS J. MORAN, Justice.

[O]n July 26, 1978, plaintiff filed a . . . complaint containing the following allegations. Defendant designed, manufactured and sold storage tanks. In 1966, plaintiff purchased a bolted-steel grain-storage tank from defendant for use at its feed-processing plant in Alpha, Illinois. In the last few months of 1976 or the first months of 1977, a crack developed in one of the steel plates on the second ring of the tank. Count I alleged that the tank was not reasonably safe due to certain design and manufacturing defects. . . . [P]laintiff sought damages representing the cost of repairs and reinforcement as well as loss of use of the tank. The trial court granted defendant's motion to dismiss . . . concluding that the cost of repair and loss of profits or income were economic losses which could not be recovered under the tort theories named in the complaint. [The intermediate court of appeal reversed.]

[T]his State adopted the tort theory of strict liability in *Suvada v. White Motor Co.* (1965), 32 Ill.2d 612, 210 N.E.2d 182, to allow a plaintiff to recover from a manufacturer for personal injuries. *Suvada*, however, did not address the question of whether a consumer could recover under a strict liability in tort theory for solely economic loss. That issue was first addressed in *Santor v. A & M Karagheusian*, Inc. (1965), 44 N.J. 52, 207 A.2d 305. There, the plaintiff purchased, from a third-party seller, carpeting that had been manufactured by the defendant. After several months, unsightly lines began to appear on the surface of the carpeting. The Supreme Court of New Jersey held that the plaintiff could maintain a breach-of-warranty claim directly against the manufacturer despite the lack of privity between them. In dicta, the court went on to declare that although the strict liability in tort doctrine had been applied principally in connection with personal injuries, the responsibility of the manufacturer should be no different where damage to the article sold or to other property is involved.

Several months later, in *Seely v. White Motor Co.* (1965), 63 Cal.2d 9, 403 P.2d 145, 45 Cal.Rptr. 17, the Supreme Court of California rejected the rationale by which the court in Santor imposed strict liability in tort for economic loss. In *Seely*, plaintiff purchased a truck manufactured by defendant. After he took possession, Seely discovered that the truck bounced violently. Nine months later, the truck overturned after brake failure, causing damage to the truck but no personal injury to Seely. Plaintiff had the damage repaired and subsequently stopped making his installment payments. Defendant repossessed the truck, at which time plaintiff sued on theories of breach of express warranty and strict tort liability, and sought damages for the repair of the truck, for money paid on the purchase price, and for profits lost by virtue of the truck's unsuitability for normal use. The court affirmed the trial court's award to Seely for money paid on the purchase price and for lost profits on the basis of express warranty. The court, however, went on to state that these economic losses are not recoverable under strict liability in tort. The court also declared, in reference to *Santor*, "Only if someone had been injured because the rug was unsafe for use would there have been any basis for imposing strict liability in tort." Thus, the court refused to expand the scope of its opinion in *Greenman v. Yuba Power Products, Inc.* (1963), 59 Cal. 2d 57, 62, 377 P.2d 897, 900, 27 Cal. Rptr. 697, 700, which declared that a manufacturer is strictly liable in tort for a product that has a defect that causes injury to a person. . . .

Like the California Supreme Court in *Greenman* and *Seely*, this court, in adopting the strict liability in tort theory in *Suvada*, emphasized the unreasonably dangerous nature of the product. The focus upon the unreasonably dangerous condition of the product in cases involving strict liability has been consistently followed by this court. As noted by the dissenting opinion of the appellate court in this case, the unreasonably dangerous nature of a product has particular relevance when a personal injury results and to some degree when property damage occurs. It has little relevance to economic loss when neither personal injury nor property damage is involved. . . .

[F]irst, the law of sales has been carefully articulated to govern the economic relations between suppliers and consumers of goods. . . . Although warranty rules frustrate just compensation for physical injury, they function well in a commercial setting. These rules determine the quality of the product the manufacturer promises and thereby determine the quality he must deliver.

We note, for example, section 2-316 of the UCC, which permits parties to a sales contract to limit warranties in any reasonable manner, or to agree that the buyer possesses no warranty protection at all. The parties may even agree to exclude the implied warranties of merchantability and fitness if they do so in writing, and may modify the implied warranty by clear and conspicuous language. Yet, a manufacturer's strict liability for economic loss cannot be disclaimed because a manufacturer should not be permitted to define the scope of its own responsibility for defective products. Thus, adopting strict liability in tort for economic loss would effectively eviscerate section 2-316 of the UCC.

Further, application of the rules of warranty prevents a manufacturer from being held liable for damages of unknown and unlimited scope. If a defendant were held strictly liable in tort for the commercial loss suffered by a particular purchaser, it would be liable for business losses of other purchasers caused by the failure of the product to meet the specific needs of their business, even though these needs were communicated only to the dealer. Finally, a large purchaser, such as plaintiff in the instant case, can protect itself against the risk of unsatisfactory performance by bargaining for a warranty. Or, it may choose to accept a lower purchase price for the product in lieu of warranty protection. Subsequent purchasers may do likewise in bargaining over the price of the product. We believe it is preferable to relegate the consumer to the comprehensive scheme of remedies fashioned by the UCC, rather than requiring the consuming public to pay more for their products so that a manufacturer can insure against the possibility that some of his products will not meet the business needs of some of his customers.

A common argument advanced by those favoring imposition of strict liability in tort for solely economic loss is the arbitrariness in allowing one who has suffered a personal injury to recover for all types of harm, yet preventing one from recovering for economic loss because he fortuitously escaped personal injury. Although the argument has some appeal, we find Justice Traynor's response to that contention in his majority opinion in *Seely* more persuasive. Justice Traynor stated:

> "The distinction that the law has drawn between tort recovery for physical injuries and warranty recovery for economic loss is not arbitrary and does not rest on the 'luck' of one plaintiff in having an accident causing physical injury. The distinction rests, rather, on an understanding of the nature of the responsibility a manufacturer must undertake in distributing his products. He can appropriately be held liable for physical injuries caused by defects by requiring his goods to match a standard of safety defined in terms of conditions that create unreasonable risks of harm. He cannot be held for the level of performance of his products in the consumer's business unless he agrees that the product was designed to meet the consumer's demands. A consumer should not be charged at the will of the manufacturer with bearing the risk of physical injury when he buys a product on the market. He can, however, be fairly charged with the risk that the product will not match his economic expectations unless the manufacturer agrees that it will. Even in actions for negligence, a manufacturer's liability is limited to damages for physical injuries and there is no recovery for economic loss alone."

Our examination of the considerable number of arguments advanced on both sides of the issue leads us to reject imposition of a strict liability in tort theory for recovery of solely economic loss.

We do hold, however, that when a product is sold in a defective condition that is unreasonably dangerous to the user or consumer or to his property, strict liability in tort is applicable to physical injury to plaintiff's property, as well as to personal injury. When an unreasonably dangerous defect is present, such as the truck's nonfunctioning brakes in *Seely*, and physical injury does, in fact, result, then "(p)hysical injury to property is so akin to personal injury that there is no reason to distinguish them." This comports with the notion that the essence of a product liability tort case is not that the plaintiff failed to receive the quality of product he expected, but that the plaintiff has been exposed, through a hazardous product, to an unreasonable risk of injury to his person or property. On the other hand, contract law, which protects expectation interests, provides the proper standard when a qualitative defect is involved, *i.e.*, when a product is unfit for its intended use. . . .

[W]e follow the decisions of the majority of courts and commentators and hold that plaintiff cannot recover for solely economic loss under the tort theories of strict liability, negligence and innocent misrepresentation. Inasmuch as the alleged damages suffered by plaintiff in this case fall under the purview of economic loss, his remedy for the alleged defect must lie in the warranty provisions of the UCC.

For the reasons stated, we reverse the appellate court's judgment. . . .

NOTE

It is not always easy to distinguish economic loss and physical damage loss. Note in this case the damages that the plaintiff was seeking: the cost of repairs and loss of use of the tank. If the crack in the tank had resulted in the spilling and spoilage of a large quantity of grain, would that represent economic loss or physical damage?

PROBLEM

Pilot and Passenger took off one clear, dry, sunny day in a brand new private jet designed and manufactured by Belchfire Aviation. Shortly after take-off the plane developed engine trouble, and the Pilot turned around and attempted an emergency landing back at the Airport. The troublesome engine exploded just before the plane touched down on the runway, and Pilot lost control as the plane skidded towards the airport's maintenance facility. The skidding aircraft sideswiped and damaged two other planes that were parked at the maintenance shop. These two planes were not in flyable condition until they were finally repaired two weeks later. Mechanic, who was working on one of the damaged planes, was killed by the collision. Pilot and Passenger were able to escape from the plane when it finally came to rest. Pilot suffered cuts and bruises. Both Passenger and Pilot were severely shaken by their narrow escape. The Belchfire jet caught fire and was a total loss. Which of the losses and injuries in this scenario are compensible in a strict liability action? Which would be covered only by warranty or contract law? What justifies the distinction? *Cf. Midcontinent Aircraft Corp. v. Curry County Spraying Service, Inc.*, 572 S.W.2d 308 (Tex. 1978).

H. THE ISSUE OF PLAINTIFF'S CONDUCT

DALY v. GENERAL MOTORS CORPORATION
575 P.2d 1162 (Cal. 1978)

RICHARDSON, Justice.

The most important of several problems which we consider is whether the principles of comparative negligence expressed by us in *Li v. Yellow Cab Co.* (1975) 13 Cal.3d 804, 119 Cal.Rptr. 858, 532 P.2d 1226, apply to actions founded on strict products liability. We will conclude that they do. . . .

THE FACTS AND THE TRIAL

Although there were no eyewitnesses, the parties agree, generally, on the reconstruction of the accident in question. In the early hours of October 31, 1970, decedent Kirk Daly, a 36-year-old attorney, was driving his Opel southbound on the Harbor Freeway in Los Angeles. The vehicle, while traveling at a speed of 50-70 miles per hour, collided with and damaged 50 feet of metal divider fence. After the initial impact between the left side of the vehicle and the fence the Opel spun counterclockwise, the driver's door was thrown open, and Daly was forcibly ejected from the car and sustained fatal head injuries. It was equally undisputed that had the deceased remained in the Opel his injuries, in all probability, would have been relatively minor.

Plaintiffs, who are decedent's widow and three surviving minor children, sued General Motors Corporation, Boulevard Buick, Underwriter's Auto Leasing, and Alco Leasing Company, the successive links in the Opel's manufacturing and distribution chain. The sole theory of plaintiffs' complaint was strict liability for damages allegedly caused by a defective product, namely, an improperly designed door latch claimed to have been activated by the impact. It was further asserted that, but for the faulty latch, decedent would have been restrained in the vehicle and, although perhaps injured, would not have been killed. Thus, the case involves a so-called "second collision" in which the "defect" did not contribute to the original impact, but only to the "enhancement" of injury. . . .

Over plaintiffs' objections, defendants were permitted to introduce evidence indicating that: (1) the Opel was equipped with a seat belt-shoulder harness system, and a door lock, either of which if used, it was contended, would have prevented Daly's ejection from the vehicle; (2) Daly used neither the harness system nor the lock; (3) the 1970 Opel owner's manual contained warnings that seat belts should be worn and doors locked when the car was in motion for "accident security"; and (4) Daly was intoxicated at the time of collision, which evidence the jury was advised was admitted for the limited purpose of determining whether decedent had used the vehicle's safety equipment. After relatively brief deliberations the jury returned a verdict favoring all defendants, and plaintiffs appeal from the ensuing adverse judgment.

STRICT PRODUCTS LIABILITY AND COMPARATIVE FAULT

In response to plaintiffs' assertion that the "intoxication-nonuse" evidence was improperly admitted, defendants contend that the deceased's own conduct contributed to his death. Because plaintiffs' case rests upon strict products liability based on improper design of the door latch and because defendants assert a failure in decedent's conduct, namely, his alleged intoxication and nonuse of safety equipment, without which the accident and ensuing death would not have occurred, there is thereby posed the overriding issue in the case, should comparative principles apply in strict products liability actions? . . .

Those counseling against the recognition of comparative fault principles in strict products liability cases vigorously stress, perhaps equally, not only the conceptual, but also the semantic difficulties incident to such a course. The task of merging the two concepts is said to be impossible, that "apples and oranges" cannot be compared, that "oil and water" do not mix, and that strict liability, which is not founded on negligence or fault, is inhospitable to comparative principles. The syllogism runs, contributory negligence was only a defense to negligence, comparative negligence only affects contributory negligence, therefore comparative negligence cannot be a defense to strict liability. . . . While fully recognizing the theoretical and semantic distinctions between the twin principles of strict products liability and traditional negligence, we think they can be blended or accommodated. . . .

Furthermore, the "apples and oranges" argument may be conceptually suspect. It has been suggested that the term "contributory negligence," one of the vital building blocks upon which much of the argument is based, may indeed itself be a misnomer since it lacks the first element of the classical negligence formula, namely, a duty of care owing to another. A highly respected torts authority, Dean William Prosser, has noted this fact by observing, "It is perhaps unfortunate that contributory negligence is called negligence at all. 'Contributory fault' would be a more descriptive term. Negligence as it is commonly understood is conduct which creates an undue risk of harm to others. Contributory negligence is conduct which involves an undue risk of harm to the actor himself. Negligence requires a duty, an obligation of conduct to another person. Contributory negligence involves no duty, unless we are to be so ingenious as to say that the plaintiff is under an obligation to protect the defendant against liability for the consequences of his own negligence." (Prosser, Law of Torts, *supra*, § 65, p. 418.) . . .

We pause at this point to observe that where, as here, a consumer or user sues the manufacturer or designer alone, technically, neither fault nor conduct is really compared functionally. The conduct of one party in combination with the product of another, or perhaps the placing of a defective article in the stream of projected and anticipated use, may produce the ultimate injury. In such a case, as in the situation before us, we think the term "equitable apportionment or allocation of loss" may be more descriptive than "comparative fault."

Given all of the foregoing, we are . . . disinclined to resolve the important issue before us by the simple expedient of matching linguistic labels which have evolved either for convenience or by custom. Rather, we consider it more useful to examine the foundational reasons underlying the creation of strict products liability in California to ascertain whether the purposes of the doctrine would be defeated or diluted by adoption of comparative principles. We imposed strict liability against the manufacturer and in favor of the user or consumer in order to relieve injured consumers "from problems of proof inherent in pursuing negligence [and warranty] remedies. . . ." [A]s we have noted, we sought to place the burden of loss on manufacturers rather than ". . . injured persons *who are powerless to protect themselves. . . .*"

The foregoing goals, we think, will not be frustrated by the adoption of comparative principles. Plaintiffs will continue to be relieved of proving that the manufacturer or distributor was negligent in the production, design, or dissemination of the article in question. Defendant's liability for injuries caused by a defective product remains strict. The principle of protecting the defenseless is likewise preserved, for plaintiff's recovery will be reduced only to the extent that his own lack of reasonable care contributed to his injury. The cost of compensating the victim of a defective product, albeit proportionately reduced, remains on defendant manufacturer, and will, through him, be "spread among society." However, we do not permit plaintiff's own conduct relative to the product to escape unexamined, and as to that share of plaintiff's damages which flows from his own fault we discern no reason of policy why it should [be] borne by others. Such a result would directly contravene the principle [that] loss should be assessed equitably in proportion to fault.

We conclude, accordingly, that the expressed purposes which persuaded us in the first instance to adopt strict liability in California would not be thwarted were we to apply comparative principles. What would be forfeit is a degree of semantic symmetry. However, in this evolving area of tort law in which new remedies are judicially created, and old defenses judicially merged, impelled by strong considerations of equity and fairness we seek a larger synthesis. If a more just result follows from the expansion of comparative principles, we have no hesitancy in seeking it, mindful always that the fundamental and underlying purpose of *Li* was to promote the equitable allocation of loss among all parties legally responsible in proportion to their fault.

A second objection to the application of comparative principles in strict products liability cases is that a manufacturer's incentive to produce safe products will thereby be reduced or removed. While we fully recognize this concern we think, for several reasons, that the problem is more shadow than substance.

First, of course, the manufacturer cannot avoid its continuing liability for a defective product even when the plaintiff's own conduct has contributed to his injury. The manufacturer's liability, and therefore its incentive to avoid and correct product defects, remains; its exposure will be lessened only to the extent that the trier finds that the victim's conduct contributed to his injury. Second, as a practical matter a manufacturer, in a particular case, cannot assume that the user of a defective product upon whom an injury is visited will be blameworthy. Doubtless, many users are free of fault, and a defect is at least as likely as not to be exposed by an entirely innocent plaintiff who will obtain full recovery. In such cases the manufacturer's incentive toward safety both in design and production is wholly unaffected. Finally, we must observe that under the present law, which recognizes assumption of risk as a complete defense to products liability, the curious and cynical message is that it profits the manufacturer to make his product so defective that in the event of injury he can argue that the user had to be aware of its patent defects. To that extent the incentives are inverted. We conclude, accordingly, that no substantial or significant impairment of the safety incentives of defendants will occur by the adoption of comparative principles. . . .

A third objection to the merger of strict liability and comparative fault focuses on the claim that, as a practical matter, triers of fact, particularly jurors, cannot assess, measure, or compare plaintiff's negligence with defendant's strict liability. We are unpersuaded by the argument and are convinced that jurors are able to undertake a fair apportionment of liability. . . .

Having examined the principal objections and finding them not insurmountable, and persuaded by logic, justice, and fundamental fairness, we conclude that a system of comparative fault should be and it is hereby extended to actions founded on strict products liability. In such cases the separate defense of "assumption of risk," to the extent that it is a form of contributory negligence, is abolished. While, as we have suggested, on the particular facts before us, the term "equitable apportionment of loss" is more accurately descriptive of the process, nonetheless, the term "comparative fault" has gained such wide acceptance by courts and in the literature that we adopt its use herein.

GENERAL MOTORS CORPORATION v. SANCHEZ
997 S.W.2d 584 (Tex. 1999)

Justice GONZALES delivered the opinion for a unanimous Court.

The principal question in this case is when does the doctrine of comparative responsibility apply in a products-liability case. [T]he court of appeals held that the decedent's responsibility for the accident that resulted in his death should not be compared with the manufacturer's responsibility because the decedent's actions merely amounted to the failure to discover or guard against a product defect. We conclude that: (1) comparative responsibility applies in strict liability if a plaintiff's negligence is something other than the mere failure to discover or guard against a product defect, and (2) there was evidence here the decedent was negligent apart from the mere failure to discover or guard against a product defect. . . . Therefore, we reverse the court of appeals' judgment and render judgment for the plaintiffs' actual damages, as reduced by the jury's comparative responsibility finding.

Because there were no witnesses, relatively little is known first hand about the circumstances of the accident that is the basis of this litigation. Lee Sanchez, Jr. left his home to feed a pen of heifers in March 1993. The ranch foreman found his lifeless body the next morning and immediately called Sanchez's father. Apparently, Sanchez's 1990 Chevy pickup had rolled backward with the driver's side door open pinning Sanchez to the open corral gate in the angle between the open door and the cab of the truck. Sanchez suffered a broken right arm and damaged right knee where the gate crushed him against the door pillar, the vertical metal column to which the door is hinged. He bled to death from a deep laceration in his right upper arm.

The Sanchez family, his estate, and his wife sued General Motors Corporation and the dealership that sold the pickup for negligence, products liability, and gross negligence based on a defect in the truck's transmission and transmission-control linkage. The plaintiffs presented circumstantial evidence to support the following theory of how the accident happened. Sanchez drove his truck into the corral and stopped to close the gate. He mis-shifted into what he thought was Park, but what was actually an intermediate, "perched" position between Park and Reverse where the transmission was in "hydraulic neutral." Expert witnesses explained that hydraulic neutral exists at the intermediate positions between the denominated gears, Park, Reverse, Neutral, Drive, and Low, where no gear is actually engaged. Under this scenario, as Sanchez walked toward the gate, the gear shift slipped from the perched position of hydraulic neutral into Reverse and the truck started to roll backwards. It caught Sanchez at or near the gate and slammed him up against it, trapping his right arm and knee. He was pinned between the gate and the door pillar by the pressure the truck exerted while idling in Reverse. Struggling to free himself, Sanchez severed an artery in his right arm and bled to death after 45 to 75 minutes.

In the trial court, G.M. offered alternative theories explaining the cause of the accident, all of which directed blame at Sanchez. It suggested that Sanchez left his truck in Reverse either accidentally or in a conscious attempt to prevent cattle from escaping the corral. Alternatively, G.M. suggested that Sanchez simply left the truck in Neutral and it rolled down the five degree slope toward the gate. Finally, G.M. argued that even if the accident was caused by a mis-shift as alleged by the plaintiffs, the mis-shift was a result of operator error, and not a defect in design.

The jury rejected G.M.'s theories and found that G.M. was negligent, the transmission was defectively designed, and G.M.'s warning was so inadequate as to constitute a marketing defect. The jury also found that Sanchez was fifty percent responsible for the accident, but the trial court disregarded this finding.

The trial court rendered judgment for actual and punitive damages of $8.5 million for the plaintiffs. . . . [T]he court of appeals affirmed the trial court's judgment. . . .

[G.]M. challenges the trial court's refusal to apply the comparative responsibility statute. The plaintiffs respond that . . . Sanchez's negligence was nothing more than a failure to discover or guard against a product defect. Thus, they contend, comparative responsibility does not apply here as a defense to strict liability. . . .

[The majority in *Keen v. Ashot Ashkelon, Ltd.,* 748 S.W.2d 91 (Tex. 1988)] held that a negligent failure to discover or guard against a product defect is not a defense against strict liability. The Court characterized the plaintiff's conduct as a failure to discover or guard against a product defect, rather than an assumption of a known risk, thus implying that these were the only two choices. The Court therefore refused to apply the jury's comparative causation finding to reduce recoverable damages. . . . Both dissenting opinions fault the majority for considering only two types of plaintiff conduct: the failure to discover or guard against a product defect and assumption of the risk. Both dissents argued that the plaintiff in Keen was negligent without regard to any defect, and such negligence should be considered when apportioning responsibility. The *Keen* majority did not respond to this criticism, however. Thus [it] was unclear whether a plaintiff's negligence other than a failure to discover or guard against a product defect should be submitted as part of a comparative responsibility inquiry. . . .

Implicit in this Court's holding in *Keen* was that a consumer has no duty to discover or guard against a product defect. . . . Thus, *Keen*'s viability [depends] on whether a plaintiff in a strict liability case has a duty to take steps to discover and guard against product defects. . . . [The Court notes that the refusal to recognize such a duty is based on comment *n* to section 402A.]

We note that comment "*n*" was not carried forward in the *Restatement (Third)*. The position of *Restatement (Third),* section 17(a), is that a plaintiff's conduct should be considered to reduce a damages recovery if it fails to conform to applicable standards of care. . . . However, comment "d" to *Restatement (Third)* states:

> [W]hen the defendant claims that the plaintiff failed to discover a defect, there must be evidence that the plaintiff's conduct in failing to discover a defect did, in fact, fail to meet a standard of reasonable care. In general, a plaintiff has no reason to expect that a new product contains a defect and would have little reason to be on guard to discover it.

We believe that a duty to discover defects, and to take precautions in constant anticipation that a product might have a defect, would defeat the purposes of strict liability. Thus, we hold that a consumer has no duty to discover or guard against a product defect, but a consumer's conduct other than the mere failure to discover or guard against a product defect is subject to comparative responsibility. . . . Because we conclude that a consumer has no duty to discover or guard against a product defect, we next determine whether the decedent's conduct in this case was merely the failure to discover or guard against a product defect or some other negligence unrelated to a product defect.

The truck's owner's manual describes safety measures designed to ensure that the truck would not move when parked: (1) set the parking brake; (2) place the truck completely in Park; (3) turn off the engine; (4) remove the key from the ignition; and (5) check that Park is fully engaged by pulling down on the gear shift. Sanchez's father testified that his son probably read the entire owner's manual. The plaintiff's own experts agreed at trial that Sanchez failed to perform any of the safety measures described in the owner's manual and that performing any one of them would have prevented the accident. This evidence is sufficient to support the jury's negligence finding.

Regardless of any danger of a mis-shift, a driver has a duty to take reasonable precautions to secure his vehicle before getting out of it. The danger that it could roll, or move if the engine is running, exists independently of the possibility of a mis-shift. . . . [W]e . . . expect the reasonably prudent driver to take safety precautions to prevent a runaway car. Sanchez had a responsibility to operate his truck in a safe manner. The fact that the precautions demanded of a driver generally would have prevented this accident does not make Sanchez's negligence a mere failure to discover or guard against a mis-shift. . . .

Sanchez's actions amounted to conduct other than a mere failure to discover or guard against a product defect. We hold as a matter of law that such conduct must be scrutinized under the duty to use ordinary care or other applicable duty. We conclude that there was legally sufficient evidence to support the jury's verdict that Sanchez breached the duty to use ordinary care and was fifty percent responsible for the accident. . . .

Accordingly, we reverse the court of appeals judgment and render judgment that the plaintiffs recover their actual damages reduced by the jury's finding of fifty percent comparative responsibility.

NOTES

1. Compare the approach of the Supreme Court of Ohio in *Bowling v. Heil Company*, 511 N.E.2d 373 (Ohio 1987):

> The court of appeals below, construing Comment *n* to Section 402A, attempted to distinguish between negligent "affirmative action" by a plaintiff and negligent passive conduct by him in failing either to discover a defect or to guard against the possibility of its existence. The court held that although a plaintiff's passive contributory negligence provides no defense to a products liability action, his contributorily negligent "affirmative action" does provide a defense, and that such affirmative negligence should be compared by a jury to the fault of a strictly

liable manufacturer of a defective product, in a manner similar to the principles of comparative negligence. . . .

The court of appeals has carved out a middle ground, to wit: contributory negligence consisting of "affirmative action," theoretically located between a plaintiff's failure to discover or guard against a defect and his voluntary assumption of a known risk. There is no such middle ground. Comment n covers the entire spectrum of conduct which can be termed "contributory negligence," as applicable to products liability actions. That spectrum begins with a mere failure to discover a defect in a product, continues with a failure to guard against the existence of a defect, and concludes with an assumption of the risk of a known defect. "Affirmative action" by the plaintiff is not left uncovered. Failure to guard against a defect can be "affirmative action." Indeed such would describe the conduct of David Bowling in this case.

Under Comment n, either a plaintiff's contributory negligence amounts to a voluntary assumption of a known risk, or it does not. If it does, then that conduct provides an otherwise strictly liable defendant with a complete defense. If it does not, the contributory negligence of the plaintiff provides no defense.

In the case *sub judice*, the jury found that Bowling was contributorily negligent but that he had not assumed a known risk. Therefore, his contributory negligence did not provide Heil with a defense to appellant's strict liability claim.

Who has the better argument?

2. What is the relationship between a plaintiff's comparative fault or responsibility and the doctrine that requires the defendant to anticipate and protect against foreseeable misuse of the product?

PROBLEMS

1. The plaintiff in *Ford Motor Co. v. Gonzalez*, 9 S.W.3d 195 (Tex. App. 1999), *supra* p. 748, continued to drive the car in spite of continuing problems with the front end alignment, problems that repeated trips to the mechanic failed to correct. Should the plaintiff be charged with negligence or assumption of the risk for driving the car with knowledge of this problem?

2. Frog Motor Co. built a sport coupe designed to appeal to young drivers who like speed. The car was equipped with a powerful V-8 engine and could exceed 100 miles an hour. To save money and help keep the price low, the car was equipped with tires that were rated for safe operation only to 85 miles an hour. The owner's manual warned against prolonged operation in excess of 90 miles an hour, but did not inform the user of the low safe speed rating of the tires. Plaintiff drove the car on a rural highway in West Texas, where one can see for

about thirty miles in all directions. The road was straight, the weather was clear and dry. Plaintiff got the speed up to 100 miles an hour and held this speed for some time. Then the tread on the tires separated and plaintiff lost control of the car, which ran off the road and crashed, causing plaintiff severe injuries. Plaintiff sues for failure to warn. Should plaintiff's conduct limit or bar recovery? *Cf. LeBouef v. Goodyear Tire and Rubber Co.*, 623 F.2d 985 (5th Cir. 1980) (applying Louisiana law.)

Chapter 17

DEFAMATION

Defamation protects an individual's interest in reputation. At common law, defamation was both a crime and a tort. In a number of early cases, individuals were punished for "seditious libel." The most famous criminal libel case occurred in 1735 when John Peter Zenger was prosecuted in New York for criticizing the government. The case was aggravated by the fact that the Chief Justice of the Province of New York disbarred two lawyers who tried to represent Zenger. Andrew Hamilton ultimately represented Zenger and gained acquittal for him. 17 How. St. Tr. 675.

On the civil side, defamation was divided into "slander" and "libel." Slander included defamatory statements made orally while libel included written statements. As a general rule, libel was actionable without proof of damage. Slander required damage except when the communication constituted "slander per se": it carried the imputation that plaintiff had committed a criminal offense, suffered from a loathsome or venereal disease, engaged in conduct incompatible with one's profession, or — in the case of women — had engaged in acts of unchastity.

A. DEFAMATION DEFINED

LEGA SICILIANA SOCIAL CLUB v. ST. GERMAINE
77 Conn. App. 846, 825 A.2d 827 (2003)

BISHOP, J.

A review of the documents submitted in conjunction with the motion for summary judgment reveals the following undisputed facts. At some point in 1994, the plaintiff purchased from the city of Waterbury a former school building, Roosevelt School, for use as a private social club, whose regular membership is restricted to native born Sicilians or natural born Americans of Sicilian ancestry. Thereafter, it sought and received a zone change from the Waterbury zoning board, despite objection from the defendant, a resident of the Norton Heights neighborhood of Waterbury, and other residents.

Approximately five years later, in 1999, the plaintiff applied for and obtained a liquor license for the club. The defendant was unhappy that he was not provided with "adequate notice" that the club had applied for the liquor license. In the defendant's view, the granting of a liquor license along with other operations of the club led to increased traffic and noise, which adversely affected the residents by destroying the privacy, seclusion and quiet character of their residential community.

On or about October 24, 1999, well after the plaintiff had received approval of its liquor license, the defendant sent a letter to Nicholas Augelli, president of the board of aldermen of the city of Waterbury, in which the plaintiff detailed his concerns regarding the club. A copy of that letter was sent to the minority leader of the board of aldermen and the zoning board. At the time the letter was sent, there were no proceedings pertaining to the club pending before either the board of aldermen or the Waterbury zoning board.

On the basis of its belief that the letter contained defamatory statements, the plaintiff commenced this action. The statements in question are as follows:

> "The rumors with the elderly go from [members of the club] having political connections in both state and local, to Mafia connections to rubber stamp whatever they want. We wish to live out our lives without fear. They as Italians do have the ethnic [muscle] to influence policy in both state and city [department] on the side of what is in their best interest for their Social Club. . . .

> "Would Club Members allow another ethnic group to invade their [families'] quality of life as they are doing to us. . . .

> "Due to rumors of Mafia and political connections my own wife would not sign the petitions for fear of having someone setting our house on fire. . . ."

[D]efendant filed a motion for summary judgment in which he denied making the statements, claimed that the statements were not libelous per se and that the plaintiff had not shown any "cognizable damage or harm" to its reputation. The court granted the motion. This appeal followed.

The dispositive issue on appeal is whether, in granting the motion for summary judgment, the court properly concluded that the publication by the defendant of the subject letter did not constitute libel per se.

The court granted the defendant's motion for summary judgment on the ground that the allegedly defamatory statements did not constitute libel per se. The court further concluded that because the statements were not libelous per se, to prevail, the plaintiff had to show "cognizable damage or harm" to its reputation to survive a motion for summary judgment. On the basis of the documents filed in conjunction with the motion for summary judgment, the court concluded that the plaintiff had shown no "cognizable damage or harm" as a consequence of the defendant's allegedly libelous statements.

We begin our resolution of the plaintiff's first claim with a brief overview of the law of defamation. "Defamation is comprised of the torts of libel and slander. Defamation is that which tends to injure reputation in the popular sense;

to diminish the esteem, respect, goodwill or confidence in which the plaintiff is held, or to excite adverse, derogatory, or unpleasant feelings or opinions against him. . . . Slander is oral defamation." Libel, which we are concerned with in the present case, is written defamation

"While all libel was once actionable without proof of special damages, a distinction arose between libel per se and libel per quod. . . . A libel per quod is not libelous on the face of the communication, but becomes libelous in light of extrinsic facts known by the recipient of the communication. . . . When a plaintiff brings an action in libel per quod, he must plead and prove actual damages in order to recover. . . .

"Libel per se, on the other hand, is a libel the defamatory meaning of which is apparent on the face of the statement and is actionable without proof of actual damages. . . . The distinction between libel per se and libel per quod is important because [a] plaintiff may recover general damages where the defamation in question constitutes libel per se. . . . When the defamatory words are actionable per se, the law conclusively presumes the existence of injury to the plaintiff's reputation. He is required neither to plead nor to prove it. . . . The individual plaintiff is entitled to recover, as general damages, for the injury to his reputation and for the humiliation and mental suffering which the libel caused him. . . . Whether a publication is libelous per se is a question for the court." Because the plaintiff in the present case has not shown actual economic damages, the parties agree that to prevail, the plaintiff must prove that the defendant's statements constitute libel per se.

"Two of the general classes of libel which, it is generally recognized, are actionable per se are (1) libels charging crimes and (2) libels which injure a man in his profession and calling. . . . To fall within the category of libels that are actionable per se because they charge crime, the libel must be one which charges a crime which involves moral turpitude or to which an infamous penalty is attached."

"Moral turpitude, [our Supreme Court has] observed, is a vague and imprecise term to which no hard and fast definition can be given. . . . A general definition applicable to the case before us is that moral turpitude involves an act of inherent baseness, vileness or depravity in the private and social duties which man does to his fellow man or to society in general, contrary to the accepted rule of right and duty between man and law."

With those legal principles in mind, we turn to the plaintiff's allegations. The complaint alleges that the plaintiff's reputation in the community has been damaged as a consequence of defamatory statements contained in the subject letter. The plaintiff's claim is based largely on the defendant's assertion in the letter that the club has "political connections in both state and local, *to Mafia connections to rubber stamp whatever [it] want[s]*." (Emphasis added.)

[T]he plaintiff claims that the Mafia generally is known to be involved in criminal activities such as bribery, illegal gambling, manufacturing of narcotics and other acts. Those are crimes, many of which, involve moral turpitude and are punishable by imprisonment.

Moreover, the plaintiff claims that the allegedly libelous letter went beyond suggesting a mere affiliation with the Mafia because it stated that the plaintiff uses its Mafia connections to *rubber stamp whatever [it] want[s].*" (Emphasis added.) Finally, the plaintiff claims that on its face, the latter recitation amounts to a statement that the plaintiff approves of the Mafia's illegal tactics and that the club utilizes those tactics to its benefit because it is by using those illegal tactics that the club gets whatever it wants.

We agree with the plaintiff that the allegedly defamatory statement is of the type that will "diminish the esteem, respect, goodwill or confidence in which the plaintiff is held, or to excite adverse, derogatory, or unpleasant feelings or opinions against [it]." We therefore conclude that the statement linking the plaintiff to the Mafia was libelous per se and, consequently, that the plaintiff was required neither to plead nor to prove actual damages.

The judgment is reversed and the case is remanded for further proceedings in accordance with law.

In this opinion the other judges concurred.

NOTES

1. As noted in the introduction to this chapter, libel is normally actionable without proof of damages. The Bella Siciliana court, however, would require proof of damages in cases of "libel per quod" — communications that become "libelous in light of extrinsic facts known by the recipient of the communication." As we will see shortly, this is a minority position, rejected by most jurisdictions. *See Lent v. Huntoon, infra* at 814.

2. A dead person cannot be defamed. *See Bello v. Random House, Inc.*, 422 S.W.2d 339 (Mo. 1967):

> [No] right of action existed at common law for damages for the defamation of the dead, in favor of the surviving relatives who themselves are not defamed.
>
> One reason for the rule is that the action is personal. The injury must be to the reputation of the plaintiff. No action lies by a third person for a libel directed at another. "A party cannot support a charge of libel by showing that the same publication libeled another. To make a case, the publication must be libelous as to the plaintiff, not another. The malice supporting the charge must flow from defendant to plaintiff and be personal to him alone and not [another]."

The intent of the General Assembly [was not] to modify the common law by creating an entirely new cause of action for the recovery by surviving relatives and friends of damages for the defamation of a dead person. . . .

3. Corporations cannot sue for defamation. However, they can sue for commercial disparagement.

PROBLEMS

1. Plaintiff was a doctor of dental surgery who was a candidate for public office. Defendant printed an article on the front page of its newspaper which read as follows:

Red Paper Issues Election Extra

The San Francisco People's world, recognized throughout the state as the mouthpiece of the communist party, distributed a last-minute extra edition in Oakland yesterday, on the eve of the city election.

It verified reports that the paper is showing unusual interest in Oakland and its city election.

The Communist-line paper defended the proposal to revive ward politics in Oakland and printed a list of recommendations which included the names of council candidates John F. Quinn, John W. Holmdahl, and Dr. Grover H. MacLeod. It also listed recommendations against police reorganization measures which were endorsed by the Alameda County Grand Jury following its recent investigation.

The polls are open until 7 p.m. today.

Plaintiff claims that he was libeled when the paper stated that he was "recommended" by a communist-line paper (the "mouthpiece of the Communist Party") when, in fact, he had not been so recommended. Plaintiff claims that he did poorly in the election because of the libel. He also claims that his dental practice has suffered. Assuming that plaintiff was not "recommended" by the paper, was he defamed? *See MacLeod v. Tribune Publishing Co.*, 343 P.2d 36 (Cal. 1959).

2. *Defamation by omission?* The New York Times publishes a list of the best selling books. In the Times' own words, the list purports "to rank best selling books [based] on actual sales." The list has a substantial positive influence on the ordering and promotion of books by booksellers and on the purchase of books by consumers. Plaintiff, who has written a number of best sellers, published a book entitled "Legion." This book sold more than enough copies to be included on the list, and met all other criteria for inclusion, but was not included. Does the non-inclusion of "Legion" on the list constitute defamation?

How would you argue the case for the author? How might the New York Times respond? *See Blatty v. New York Times Co.*, 728 P.2d 1177 (Cal. 1986).

3. Is it defamatory to use the word "bastard" to refer to someone under circumstances where the person's parentage is not being questioned? Colonel T.B. Birdsong was Commander of the Mississippi Highway Patrol. In an article entitled "What Next in Mississippi?" a magazine described the events surrounding the registration of James Meredith as a student at the University of Mississippi at Oxford. The article, which commented on difficulties associated with the registration, criticized the Highway Patrol for inaction:

> A sizable portion of blame must go to the gray-uniformed men of the Mississippi Highway Patrol. "Those bastards just walked off and left us," said one top official of the Department of Justice.

Plaintiff claims that the use of the words "those bastards" are "obscene and fighting words of and concerning plaintiffs and reflecting on their personal reputation." As a result, plaintiff seeks damages for defamation. Should plaintiff be entitled to recover? *See Curtis Publishing Co. v. Birdsong*, 360 F.2d 344 (5th Cir. 1966).

4. Plaintiff, a medical doctor, agreed to testify for a drug company at a hearing before the Food and Drug Administration. In reporting about the plaintiff (as well as about other expert witnesses), defendant made the following statements:

> These expert witnesses [at the FDA hearing] included William McBride of the Women's Hospital in Sydney, Australia, who was paid $5,000 a day to testify in Orlando. In contrast, [Merrell Dow] pays witnesses $250 to $500 a day, and the most it has ever paid is $1,000 a day.

Assuming that the allegation that plaintiff was paid $1,000 a day is untrue, is it defamatory? Why? Why not? *See McBride v. Merrell Dow and Pharmaceuticals, Inc.*, 800 F.2d 1208 (D.C. Cir. 1986).

5. A public recreation area is used principally as a ski resort, but is also used for other recreational activities. Plaintiff was employed by and directly responsible to the county commissioners (three elected officials in charge of the county government) who oversaw the recreation area. During the 1950s, a public controversy developed over the way respondent and the commissioners operated the recreation area; some protested that respondent and the commissioners had not developed the Area's full potential, either as a resort for local residents or as a tourist attraction that might contribute to the county's taxes. The discussion culminated in 1959, when the New Hampshire Legislature enacted a law transferring control of the Area to a special five-man commission. At least in part to give this new regime a fresh start, plaintiff was discharged.

Defendant regularly contributed an unpaid column to the Laconia Evening Citizen. In it he frequently commented on political matters. As an outspoken proponent of the change in operations at the recreation area, defendant's views were often sharply stated, and he had indicated disagreement with the actions taken by respondent and the commissioners. In January 1960, during the first ski season under the new management, some six months after respondent's discharge, petitioner published the column that respondent alleges libeled him. In relevant part, it reads:

> Been doing a little listening and checking at Belknap Recreation Area and am thunderstruck by what am learning.
>
> This year, a year without snow till very late, a year with actually few very major changes in procedure; the difference in cash income simply fantastic, almost unbelievable.
>
> On any sort of comparative basis, the Area this year is doing literally hundreds of per cent BETTER than last year.
>
> When consider that last year was excellent snow year, that season started because of more snow, months earlier last year, one can only ponder following question:
>
> What happened to all the money last year? and every other year? What magic has Dana Beane (Chairman of the new commission) and rest of commission, and Mr. Warner (respondent's replacement as Supervisor) wrought to make such tremendous difference in net cash results?

Assuming that the allegations in the article are untrue, did they defame plaintiff? How might defendant argue that there was no defamation? *See Rosenblatt v. Baer*, 383 U.S. 75 (1966).

6. Are some plaintiffs "libel proof"? Plaintiffs were the Chief Deputy Sheriff and Chief of Detectives in a city in Louisiana. They were discharged for malfeasance in office, and ultimately convicted of the crime of malfeasance. For a while, they were held in the jail they formerly managed. After being released from jail, they "kept their noses clean." Six years later, untrue allegations were made about their honesty. Given plaintiffs' prior conduct and prior convictions, are plaintiffs "libel proof"? If plaintiffs can prove that they were defamed (and can meet other requirements to recover for defamation), how would they prove and measure their damages? *See Zerangue v. TSP Newspapers, Inc.*, 814 F.2d 1066 (5th Cir. 1987).

NEIMAN-MARCUS v. LAIT
13 F.R.D. 311 (S.D.N.Y. 1952)

IRVING R. KAUFMAN, District Judge.

[D]efendants are authors of a book entitled "U.S.A. Confidential." The plaintiffs are the Neiman-Marcus Company, a Texas corporation operating a department store at Dallas, Texas, and three groups of its employees. They allege that the following matter libeled and defamed them: "The telephone had come into its own. Whores are 'call girls,' 'party girls' or 'company girls.' Instead of your visiting them, they come to see you." "This resulted in a complete change in the economic set-up of the oldest profession. Since houses are not needed, neither are large investments. Without houses immovably located, pay-offs to blue-coats on the beat have become almost extinct and so, for that matter, have raids. Only the lowest streetwalkers are collared. Meanwhile, the price is up; the old 50-cent house girl is insulted with $10 for a quick visit to your hotel room. The younger, fresher and smarter talent asks $100 and frequently gets it."

"Some people call them call girls and others refer to them as party girls; because you call them when you want a party." "He [Stanley Marcus, president of plaintiff Neiman-Marcus Company] may not know that some Neiman models are call girls — the top babes in town. The guy who escorts one feels in the same league with the playboys who took out Ziegfeld's glorified. Price, a hundred bucks a night." "The salesgirls are good, too — pretty, and often much cheaper — twenty bucks on the average. They're more fun, too, not as snooty as the models. We got this confidential, from a Dallas wolf." "Neiman-Marcus also contributes to the improvement of the local breed when it imports New York models to make a flash at style shows. These girls are the cream of the crop. Oil millionaires toss around thousand-dollar bills for a chance to take them out." "Neiman's was a women's specialty shop until the old biddies who patronized it decided their husbands should get class, too. So Neiman's put in a men's store. Well, you should see what happened. You wonder how all the faggots got to the wild and wooly. You thought those with talent ended up in New York and Hollywood and the plodders got government jobs in Washington. Then you learn the nucleus of the Dallas fairy colony is composed of many Neiman dress and millinery designers, imported from New York and Paris, who sent for their boy friends when the men's store expanded. Now most of the sales staff are fairies, too." "Houston is faced with a serious homosexual problem. It is not as evident as Dallas, because there are no expensive imported faggots in town like those in the Neiman-Marcus set."

[The] individual plaintiffs [state] that they were employed by the Neiman-Marcus Company at the time the alleged libel was published and that the groups of individual plaintiffs are composed as follows:

(1) Nine individual models who constitute the entire group of models at the time of the publication;

(2) Fifteen salesmen of a total of twenty-five suing on their own behalf and on behalf of the others;

(3) Thirty saleswomen of a total of 382 suing on their own behalf and on behalf of the others.

The first part of defendants' motion is to dismiss the amended complaint as to the salesmen and saleswomen for failure to state a cause of action for libel since, it is alleged, no ascertainable person is identified by the words complained of.

[An] examination of the case and text law of libel reveals that the following propositions are rather widely accepted:

(1) Where the group or class libeled is large, none can sue even though the language used is inclusive.

(2) Where the group or class libeled is small, and each and every member of the group or class is referred to, then any individual member can sue.

Conflict arises when the publication complained of libels some or less than all of a designated small group. Some courts say no cause of action exists in any individual of the group. Other courts in other states would apparently allow such an action.

While no choice of law is made at this time, it appears from the complaint that Texas or New York law will be of greatest importance at the trial because of the many contacts with these states; not of small significance is the fact that the individual plaintiffs' community and place of livelihood is in Texas.

The courts of Texas do not seem to have spoken on the "some" allegation of libel. A reading of the New York cases indicates a trend towards submitting to the jury the question as to whether the "charge against several individuals, under some general description or general name [has] the personal application averred by the plaintiff."

The Court of Appeals for this Circuit has referred to the RESTATEMENT OF TORTS for the "general law." If we do so in this instance, we find that Illustration 2 of § 564, Comment (c) reads as follows: "A newspaper publishes the statement that some member of B's household has committed murder. In the absence of any circumstances indicating that some particular member of B's household was referred to, the newspaper has defamed each member of B's household."

Thus the Restatement of Torts would authorize suit by each member of a small group where the defamatory publication refers to but a portion of the group. This result seems to find support in logic and justice, as well as the case law mentioned above. An imputation of gross immorality to some of a small group casts suspicion upon all, where no attempt is made to exclude the innocent.

Applying the above principles to the case at bar, it is the opinion of this Court that the plaintiff salesmen, of whom it is alleged that "most [are] fairies" have a cause of action in New York and most likely other states; where the courts have specifically held to the contrary, a fortiori no cause exists. Defendants' motion to dismiss as to the salesmen for failure to state a claim upon which relief can be granted is denied.

The plaintiff saleswomen are in a different category. The alleged defamatory statement in defendants' book speaks of the saleswomen generally. While it does not use the word "all" or similar terminology, yet it stands unqualified.

However, the group of saleswomen is extremely large, consisting of 382 members at the time of publication. No specific individual is named in the alleged libelous statement. I am not cited to a single case which would support a cause of action by an individual member of any group of such magnitude. The courts have allowed suit where the group consisted of four coroners, twelve doctors composing the residential staff of a hospital, a posse, twelve radio editors, and in similar cases involving small groups.

But where the group or class disparaged is a large one, absent circumstances pointing to a particular plaintiff as the person defamed, no individual member of the group or class has a cause of action. RESTATEMENT OF TORTS, § 564(c). Thus actions for libel have failed where the groups libeled consisted of all officials of a state-wide union; all the taxicab drivers in Washington, D.C.; the parking lot owners in downtown Washington, D.C. (10 to 12 in number); or the members of a clan.

Giving the plaintiff saleswomen the benefit of all legitimate favorable inferences, the defendants' alleged libel cannot reasonably be said to concern more than the saleswomen as a class. There is no language referring to some ascertained or ascertainable person. Nor is the class so small that it follows that defamation of the class infects the individual of the class. This Court so holds as a matter of law since it is of the opinion that no reasonable man would take the writers seriously and conclude from the publication a reference to any individual saleswoman.

While it is generally recognized that even where the group is large, a member of the group may have a cause of action if some particular circumstances point to the plaintiff as the person defamed, no such circumstances are alleged in the amended complaint. This further exception is designed to apply only where a plaintiff can satisfy a jury that the words referred solely or especially to himself. The plaintiffs' general allegation that the alleged libelous and defamatory matter was written "of and concerning [each] of them" is insufficient to satisfy this requirement.

Accordingly it is the opinion of this Court that as a matter of law the individual saleswomen do not state a claim for libel upon which relief can be granted and the motion to dismiss their cause of action is granted.

[The] amended complaint is dismissed with leave to file separate complaints as to the two groups of individuals and the corporation, all in conformity with this opinion.

NOTE

As the primary case suggests, defamation must refer to the plaintiff to be actionable. However, if a company consists of Smith, Jones, and Doe, and a publication asserts that "Smith and Jones are the only honest members of the company," the publication specifically refers to Doe and accuses him of dishonesty by clear implication (even though he isn't named).

PROBLEMS

1. A cartoon book described a fictional six-year-old "Eloise" as "precocious, spoiled and lovable." Eloise purportedly lived at the Plaza Hotel in New York with her nanny, and the book mentioned a "Mr. Salamone" as the manager of the Plaza. Some years after "Eloise" came out, a group of women produced a "humor" book which showed the six-year-old later as an adult. The humor book alleged that Mr. Salamone was a child molester.

In fact, an actual person by the name of Salamone was the manager of the Plaza at the time Eloise was published. Eventually, he became a senior vice president of the Hilton Hotels Corporation and a managing director of the New York Hilton. The evidence revealed that the women who wrote the humor book were unaware that there was a real Mr. Salamone. Assuming that he has suffered embarrassment and anguish from the humorous parody, did the humor book refer to him so that he can recover for defamation? How would you argue the case for plaintiff? How might defendant respond? If Mr. Salamone was defamed, how would he prove damage? *See Salamone v. MacMillan Publishing Co., Inc.*, 97 Misc. 2d 346, 411 N.Y.S.2d 105 (Sup. Ct. 1978).

2. Defendant, a corporate officer, found money missing from the corporate till. Defendant approached three employees and uttered the following words:

> "Mr. Cohn, there is a hundred-dollar bill missing and only you three had access to it, Mr. Cohn, and I want that money returned or else I will fire you, you and you" and while looking directly at the plaintiff, the defendant, Nicholas Brecher, said "One of you is a crook."

Were all three of the employees defamed? What about any one employee? Would it matter whether defendant had said "all three of you are crooks"? *See Cohn v. Brecher*, 20 Misc. 2d 329, 192 N.Y.S.2d 877 (1959).

3. In a lounging room in the Helvetia Hotel in Portland, in which room there were about 20 or 25 men at the time sitting around, the following occurred:

> Mrs. Krattiger came out in the bar and she spoke to John Feurer and she says, "What do you think, John, there is a fellow in here stole about a thousand dollars worth of my jewelry, and the man is sitting right here in the office, and it is a Swiss. And I know the name of the fellow," she says, "and I just give that fellow a chance to bring that jewelry back to next Saturday." [She] says, "That son of a bitch is right in the room here."

Would it matter whether the allegations were uttered in a foreign language, and none of those in the room understood that language? What if the language was German and all of the Swiss in the room understood it? If the latter constitutes defamation, which of the 20-25 men were defamed? *See Blaser v. Krattiger*, 195 P. 359 (Or. 1921).

4. Plaintiff owned one of four businesses that sold trading stamps in Detroit. Defendant made disparaging remarks about the honesty of stamp trading businesses in general, *i.e.*, it referred to them as outlawed "get-rich-quick" schemes and as disreputable. Defendant alleged that these businesses:

> have as their chief element of attractiveness to uninformed persons a pretended offer to give something for nothing — that is, to give a greater value than that for which one may have paid. Both, too, are dependent for the enormous profits yielded to their promoters on the great percentage of "lapses" — that is, failures to carry out their original intention on the part of those who may be seduced by the promise of something for nothing to invest in the scheme. The result of the crusade against the tontine diamond fake is still fresh in the public mind. The chief promoter of the graft fled the city and the swindling enterprise was speedily broken up. The trading stamp concerns may struggle against the inevitable and resort to every technical obstruction which the civil courts may place at their command, but the result is already discernible.

Which of the four trading stamp businesses may sue for defamation? *See Watson v. Detroit Journal Co.*, 107 N.W. 81 (Mich. 1906).

5. Plaintiff Melanie Geisler is a petite and attractive young woman who worked as a publicity assistant for Mason Charter, Inc., a small publishing company. Defendant also worked for Mason Charter which was relatively small so that defendant must have known her.

After defendant left Mason Charter, he authored a book entitled "Match Set" concerning the odyssey of a female transsexual athlete in the allegedly corrupt and corrupting world of the women's professional tennis circuit. The book purports to be a work of fiction and contains a disclaimer that the book does not portray real persons or actual incidents. The book's plot centers upon the attempt by certain unscrupulous persons to manipulate the outcome of a tournament by sabotaging the efforts of certain favored players, thereby making possible an upset victory for the protagonist, whom they alone know to be transsexual.

This central character bears appellant's precise name, "Melanie Geisler" and is described as young, attractive and honey-blonde, "her body [firm] and compact, though heavier than she would like." Although she is initially portrayed as innocent and naive, during the course of the narrative she is induced to participate in the tennis fraud, and perhaps more to the author's point, lured into untoward sexual conduct which is graphically portrayed.

Plaintiff is concededly an upstanding individual and the mother of two. She claims that defendant's use of her exact name coupled with a commonality of physical traits and personal knowledge have reputedly caused reasonable people to understand that the character pictured in "Match Set" was appellant, acting as described. Is she right? Should plaintiff be able to recover for defamation? *See Geisler v. Petrocelli*, 616 F.2d 636 (2d Cir. 1979). *See also Springer v. Viking Press*, 458 N.E.2d 1256 (N.Y. 1983) (Chapter 10 of the fictional book "State of Grace" suggests that Lisa Blake is a whore. Plaintiff Lisa Blake, a real person, sues. She claims that the reference to "Lisa Blake" is "of and concerning" her because of the similarity in name, physical height, weight and build, incidental grooming habits and recreational activities of plaintiff as the fictional character portrayed in the novel.).

6. Penthouse magazine published an article about the Miss America contest and about a woman named "Charlene" who purportedly participated as "Miss Wyoming" in the contest. Charlene was described as a baton twirler. The story then switches to the contest as Charlene is about to perform her talent as a baton twirler:

> She is about to go on stage and her thoughts are described. She thinks of Wyoming and an incident there when she was with a football player from her school. It describes an act of fellatio whereby she causes him to levitate. The story returns to the Miss America stage where she goes on to perform her talent. She there performs a fellatio-like act on her baton which stops the orchestra. [She] did not reach the finals but she says or thinks she has a "real talent." The third incident is then described. She is at the edge of the stage during the finals while the finalists are at center stage and the finals are under way. Charlene's thoughts are again described and these are how she would have answered the questions put to the finalists had she been one. These thoughts were that she would "save the world" with her real talent with the "entire Soviet Central Committee to prevent a Third World War? Marshall Tito? Fidel Castro?" She would be the ambassador of love and peace. The article then describes an act of fellatio with her coach at the edge of the stage while the audience was applauding the new Miss America in center stage. This fellatio causes the levitation of her coach. It is described that the television cameras were not on the new Miss America but "remained" on Charlene and her coach who was then rising into the air, and the story ends.

Penthouse regarded the article as "black humor" — a spoof of the Miss America contest that no one would take literally. Plaintiff (the Miss Wyoming participant in the last Miss America contest) claims that the article conveys the suggestion that she committed fellatio on one Monty Applewhite and also upon her coach, Corky Corcoran, in the presence of a national television audience at the Miss America Pageant. The article also creates the impression that Plaintiff committed fellatio like acts upon her baton at the Miss America contest.

Who is correct? Does the Penthouse article contain actionable defamation? Would it matter whether community witnesses testified that the story could not possibly be about plaintiff as she would not do that? *See Pring v. Penthouse International, Ltd.*, 695 F.2d 438 (10th Cir. 1982).

LENT v. HUNTOON
470 A.2d 1162 (Vt. 1983)

UNDERWOOD, Justice.

[Plaintiff] worked for Huntoon Business Machines, Inc. (Huntoon Corporation) from 1964 until his employment was terminated in 1977 — a period of thirteen years. During that time he worked his way up to the position of service manager. At the time he was hired, in 1964, the plaintiff informed defendant H.J. Huntoon (Huntoon) that he was on probation for a criminal conviction and that he had once been confined to the base for a period of time for a minor offense during his service in the Air Force. Defendants hired plaintiff with full knowledge of these events.

In the early part of 1977, plaintiff informed Huntoon that he would be leaving his job at Huntoon Corporation as he was moving to Florida as soon as he and his wife could sell their house. He offered to stay on long enough to train his successor. Shortly thereafter, and without any prior notice, Huntoon told plaintiff that he was discharged.

Plaintiff was unable to sell his house and so decided to remain in Rutland. In August of 1977, he started his own business equipment sales and service business, Lent Business Machines. Early in March of 1978, plaintiff was awarded a cash register sales and service franchise formerly held by the Huntoon Corporation. Thus, plaintiff and Huntoon Corporation became direct competitors. About this same time, plaintiff became aware that defendants sent a letter to the cash register franchise customers who were formerly serviced by Huntoon Corporation and for whose business both the plaintiff and defendants were then vying. The letter, which indicated that plaintiff had been discharged for "sound business reasons," formed the basis of plaintiff's libel count. Plaintiff asserted that the letter, taken in its totality, was defamatory since it implied that he was fired because of some dishonesty or incompetence. There was evidence that the letter caused plaintiff to become estranged from some of his customers, to suffer physical and emotional malaise, and to neglect his business to the point where it nearly collapsed.

About this time, plaintiff became aware of numerous verbal statements made about him by Huntoon to customers sought after by both plaintiff and defendants. Testimony revealed that these statements asserted that plaintiff had a criminal "record a mile long," had stolen merchandise from the defendants, had stolen money from the cash register of Huntoon Corporation, was an incompetent serviceman, and was generally untrustworthy. Testimony indicated that most of these statements were made by Huntoon in competitive business situations. Plaintiff asked Huntoon to stop making the statements, apparently to no avail, as there was further testimony that some of the statements were made even after plaintiff's lawsuit was initiated. Some testimony indicated that the defendants were fully satisfied with plaintiff's work prior to termination and had never complained about any thefts by plaintiff prior to his leaving Huntoon

Corporation. Defendants also knew he intended to leave his job voluntarily and was not fired.

[Defamation] is comprised of the complementary torts of libel and slander. Although these torts evolved from different antecedents, both were eventually cognizable in the King's courts in England prior to reception of the common law in Vermont. Because of the permanence of the written word, libel was considered the more serious tort, with slander, or the spoken word, considered the less serious. The distinction between written and spoken defamation has resulted in a host of special rules with corresponding special legal terminology. Herein lies much of the confusion which abounds even today.

Libel is generally considered "actionable per se"; that is, the plaintiff need not allege nor prove that he or she suffered any "special damages" as a direct or proximate result of the libel. Special damages, in short, are presumed. Special damages have a unique connotation in the law of defamation. Special damages are those of a pecuniary nature, and historically they have included loss of customers or business, loss of contracts, or loss of employment. In addition,

> modern decisions have shown some tendency to liberalize the old rule, and to find pecuniary loss when the plaintiff has been deprived of benefit which has a more or less indirect financial value to him. Thus the loss of the society, companionship and association of friends may be sufficient when [it] can be found to have a money value.

RESTATEMENT (SECOND) OF TORTS § 575 comment b, at 198 (1977).

Slander, on the other hand, is generally not actionable per se; that is, special damages are not presumed and must be alleged and proven. Several kinds of slander, however, were identified at English common law as more serious than others and these were held to be actionable per se. Spoken defamation involving (1) imputation of a crime, (2) statements injurious to one's trade, business or occupation, or (3) charges of having a loathsome disease were deemed slander per se and were actionable without proof of special damages. The decisions of our Court are in accord with this common law exception. Most American jurisdictions added still a fourth exception: charging a woman to be unchaste. Thus "actionable per se" simply means special damages need not be proved in libel actions or in those slander actions which fall into one of the exceptions categorized as slander per se.

The general elements of a private action for defamation (libel and/or slander) are: (1) a false and defamatory statement concerning another; (2) some negligence, or greater fault, in publishing the statement; (3) publication to at least one third person; (4) lack of privilege in the publication; (5) special damages, unless actionable per se; and (6) some actual harm so as to warrant compensatory damages.

For reasons probably lost in history, a special rule of procedure developed for the trial of a defamation action. Once the plaintiff's evidence was in, the court had to determine whether the written or spoken words were defamatory as a matter of law. If the court was in doubt because the connotation of the written or spoken words was ambiguous, then the court had to submit the question to the jury to decide. In libel actions, when the court determined that the written words were libelous as a matter of law, the term "libel per se" was used. This unfortunate terminology when used in conjunction with such terms as "slander per se" and "actionable per se" has greatly confused courts and counsel. "Libel per se" simply means defamatory as a matter of law. Since all libel is actionable per se, it makes no difference whether the court rules that the written words are defamatory as a matter of law, or that the written words are ambiguous and the jury determines that there is defamation; in each instance special damages need not be proven.

A further complication in the semantics of defamation law arose when the courts embarked upon the "spurious" concept of a "libel per quod." This rule only served to compound an already confusing area of the law of torts. Being written, libel is generally evaluated by examining the four corners of the writing itself. A letter or newspaper article can be introduced at trial and its defamatory nature determined by judge or jury as appropriate. Some writings, however, are seemingly innocent in and of themselves, and resort must be had to extrinsic evidence to determine if they have defamatory qualities. If the writing together with the extrinsic evidence constitutes defamation, such a writing is referred to as "libel per quod" in several American jurisdictions. These jurisdictions require that special damages be proven for libel per quod, unless the libel falls into one of the exceptions we previously mentioned as constituting slander per se. Thus, under this rule, the simple fact that extrinsic evidence must be used to prove the defamatory nature of a libel prevents it from being "actionable per se" and special damages must be proven.

A scholarly debate concerning libel per quod took place before the Restatement (Second) of Torts was published. Thereafter, section 569 of the Restatement reflects the simpler rule and rejects any notion of libel per quod.

Vermont's reported decisions do not recognize libel per quod, and we adhere to the wisdom of that course today. We hold that libel, whether defamatory on the face of the writing alone or with the aid of extrinsic evidence, is actionable per se. Our previous use of the term libel per se in no way, directly or inferentially, encompasses the rule of libel per quod. In the appropriate circumstances we recognize that libel per se may be found either solely from the writing or from the writing together with extrinsic evidence. Similarly the question of whether an ambiguous writing is defamatory or not is a jury question under either set of circumstances.

Given the great confusion in this area, we urge the future use of the term "libel as a matter of law" in situations where "libel per se" has been used in the past. "Libel as a matter of law" and where appropriate "slander as a matter of law" accurately identify the issue as one of law for the preliminary determination of the trial court.

In the case before us the pleadings include one count sounding in libel and one count sounding in slander. Two defenses to these allegations of defamation are raised: truth and privilege. Truth, of course, defeats the action and is a complete defense to defamation. The privilege raised here is a conditional privilege which may be overcome by a showing of malice. The defendants allege a privilege to protect their legitimate business interests. This privilege is recognized in Restatement (Second) of Torts, supra, § 595 comment d, and we hold it to be applicable in Vermont. The burden of proving the privilege is on the defendants. RESTATEMENT, *supra*, § 613(2).

A showing of malice, however, may defeat the conditional privilege, but in such instance the plaintiff must show malice by clear and convincing proof. In this sense malice may be either actual or implied. The court will infer malice upon a showing that the defendant knew the statement was false or acted with reckless disregard of its truth. Actual malice includes spiteful or wanton conduct.

This case also raises the issue of general and punitive damages in defamation. [We] are persuaded and now hold that liability for defamation must logically be based on some showing of harm to the plaintiff. Thus, Vermont will require defamation plaintiffs to demonstrate some "actual harm" as a prerequisite to recovering general damages. In summary, defamation that is actionable per se will require some showing of actual harm, but not of special damages before recovery of general, or compensatory, damages. This sound rule is reflected in the Restatement, § 621.

Finally, this case raises the question of punitive damages. Once general (compensatory) damages are established, punitive damages may be awarded on a showing of actual malice, but actual malice may not be considered to enhance compensatory damages. "[Malice] may be shown by conduct manifesting personal ill will or carried out under circumstances evidencing insult or oppression, or even by conduct showing a reckless or wanton disregard of one's rights." Malice supporting punitive damages may be shown by proving that the defendant repeated the defamatory statement, especially when the repetition occurred after commencement of the lawsuit.

Once malice sufficient to entitle plaintiff to punitive damages has been shown, the plaintiff may present evidence of defendant's financial condition: "Where exemplary damages are awardable [the] defendant's pecuniary ability may be considered in order to determine what would be a just punishment for him."

[Our] review of the record reveals that there was ample evidence for the jury to have found actual malice on the part of the defendants; therefore, in the exercise of its discretion, the jury could have awarded punitive damages. The jury could have concluded that (1) defendants knew that plaintiff had not been fired "for sound business reasons" but had, in fact, voluntarily left, (2) Huntoon said that plaintiff had stolen money and merchandise knowing this to be false, (3) Huntoon knew that plaintiff did not have a "record a mile long," and (4) Huntoon repeated the alleged slanderous statements.

[The jury returned a verdict for the plaintiff of $15,000 in compensatory and $25,000 in punitive damages]. [W]e find no error when the trial court denied defendants' motion for judgment notwithstanding the verdict.

[Affirmed.]

NOTE

1. *Publication requirement.* In order to recover in defamation, the defamatory statements must be "published" to others. It is not enough that defendant make derogatory statements that are heard only by plaintiff. No reputational injury can occur unless others also hear the statements.

2. *Lent v. Huntoon* represents the majority position in rejecting the distinction between libel per quod and libel per se. As we saw in the *Lega Siciliana* case, *supra*, however, some courts still consider the difference significant. Does it make sense to distinguish between libel per se and libel per quod? What policies might support doing so, or not doing so?

PROBLEMS

1. Defendant wrote a letter to plaintiff which alleged that plaintiff obtained goods under false pretenses. The sealed letter was sent through the mail, addressed to plaintiff, but was opened by plaintiff's wife. Did defendant "publish" the defamation to plaintiff's wife? Would it matter whether defendant had reason to know that plaintiff's wife opens his mail? *See Roberts v. English Mfg. Co.*, 46 So. 752 (Ala. 1908).

2. *Self-publication.* In spring 1980, the company hired plaintiffs as dental claim approvers in its St. Paul office. Eventually, plaintiffs were dismissed for "gross insubordination." The company admitted that the production and performance of plaintiffs was at all times satisfactory and even commendable. Although plaintiffs were fired for insubordination (for their failure to amend expense reports), there was some dispute about whether the reports needed amending, about whether the company's written guidelines for expense reports had been explained to plaintiffs, and whether plaintiffs had been given proper guidelines prior to their departure on the trip related to the expense reports.

In seeking new employment, plaintiffs were requested by prospective employers to disclose their reasons for leaving their prior employer, and each indicated that she had been "terminated." When plaintiffs received interviews, they were asked to explain their terminations. Each stated that she had been terminated for "gross insubordination" and attempted to explain the situation. The company neither published nor stated to any prospective employer that plaintiffs had been terminated for gross insubordination. Its policy was to give only the dates of employment and the final job title of a former employee unless specifically authorized in writing to release additional information.

Is there publication of the defamation when plaintiffs revealed the reason for the dismissal to prospective employers? Should it matter that plaintiffs felt that they were ethically obligated to reveal the reason for the dismissal? *See Lewis v. Equitable Life Assurance Society*, 389 N.W.2d 876 (Minn. 1986).

3. *Publication by omission?* On the wall of the bathroom in defendant's tavern, someone printed allegations that plaintiff was an unchaste woman who engaged in "illicit amatory ventures." The statement then listed plaintiff's home telephone number and suggested that callers ask for "Isabelle" (plaintiff's name). A man saw plaintiff's name and number on the wall and called her (from the tavern). After plaintiff turned down the man's proposition, he explained what was written on the bathroom wall.

Plaintiff told her husband about the writing, and the husband called the bartender at the tavern. The bartender replied that he was busy and alone and would remove the writing when he got around to it. When plaintiff's husband arrived at the tavern, the allegations were still on the bathroom wall. Did the tavern "publish" the defamatory material by failing to remove it in a timely manner? *See Hellar v. Bianco*, 244 P.2d 757 (Cal. Ct. App. 1952).

4. *More on publication by omission.* Fracket, an employee of a factory, helped "S & T Specialties" secure a contract with the factory for 2,000 wooden boxes to be built by "S & F Specialties." The factory's union was upset about the contract because it involved the subcontracting out of work which the union believes that it could have done. Later, the union learned that the "S" was someone named Spearman who worked for the factory. The union suspected that the "F" stood for Fracket. Both Spearman and Fracket were suspended pending an investigation, but Fracket eventually returned to work. In the meantime, someone spray painted a sign on a factory wall which read "FRACKET FRACKET WHAT A RACKET." Plaintiff repeatedly complained to his supervisor and asked that the sign be removed. Nevertheless, the sign remained on the wall for seven to eight months until it was painted over. Assume that management did not create the sign. Have they published it by their failure to remove the sign within a reasonable amount of time? *See Tacket v. General Motors Corp.*, 836 F.2d 1042 (7th Cir. 1987).

5. *Is a bookstore a "publisher" of defamation for books that it sells?* In May of 1983, William J. Janklow, the present governor and former attorney general of South Dakota (Janklow), filed a complaint alleging that Peter Matthiessen (author) and Viking Penguin, Inc. (Viking), as author and publisher respectively, collaborated with the American Indian Movement (AIM), to publish and distribute a book "In the Spirit of Crazy Horse," containing numerous "false and unprivileged statements" about Janklow. The complaint further alleged that the statements were made "with actual malice or reckless disregard for the truth" and that all the libelous statements made against Janklow were "false and

untrue" and that the author and Viking "had to entertain serious doubts about the truth of the libelous statements." Janklow claimed that the author and Viking, in failing to examine evidence that was available to them and in failing to disclose the evidence in the book, recklessly disregarded the truth or acted maliciously toward him. Janklow also contended that the reckless disregard for the truth is evidenced by their failure to interview him regarding the veracity of the charges repeated in the book. According to Janklow's complaint, all references to him were edited "in order to present a false and defamatory picture of him."

Janklow's complaint also named a number of bookstore owners and operators, all residents of South Dakota, as defendants and alleged that they "willfully refused to remove the book from the [shelves]" even though he had notified them of its libelous nature. Janklow contends that the "writing, publication, dissemination, sale, distribution and promotion of the book constitutes a single libelous wrong" which holds him up to "public obloquy, ridicule and contempt" and has caused him extreme mental anguish, diminished his standing as a father and husband, and impaired his ability to seek and maintain public office or any other occupation. Janklow claimed actual damages of $4,000,000 and exemplary damages of $20,000,000 and requested a jury trial. *See Janklow v. Viking Press*, 378 N.W.2d 875 (S.D. 1985).

B. THE CONSTITUTIONALIZATION OF DEFAMATION

From the founding of this country until the early 1960s, the Court treated libel as speech that raised no First Amendment issues. As the Court stated in *Beauharnais v. Illinois*, 343 U.S. 250 (1952), "[l]ibellous utterances [are not] within the area of constitutionally protected speech" because they have "such slight social value as a step to truth that any benefit that may be derived from them is clearly outweighed by the social interest in order and morality." As a result, the states were free to define the tort of defamation and to determine the scope of recovery. Some states readily imposed liability for inaccurate statements.

NEW YORK TIMES CO. v. SULLIVAN
376 U.S. 254 (1964)

Mr. Justice BRENNAN delivered the opinion of the Court.

We are required in this case to determine for the first time the extent to which the constitutional protections for speech and press limit a State's power to award damages in a libel action brought by a public official against critics of his official conduct.

Respondent L.B. Sullivan is one [of] three elected Commissioners of the City of Montgomery, Alabama. [His duties involve] supervision of the Police Department, Fire Department, Department of Cemetery and Department of Scales." He brought this civil libel action against [petitioners], who are Negroes and Alabama clergymen, [and] the New York Times Company, a New York corporation which publishes the New York Times, a daily newspaper. [An Alabama jury] awarded him $500,000 [against] all the petitioners, and the Supreme Court of Alabama affirmed.

[Respondent alleges that he was] libeled by statements in a full-page advertisement [in] the New York Times. . . . Entitled "Heed Their Rising Voices," the advertisement began by stating that "As the whole world knows[,] thousands of Southern Negro students are engaged in widespread non-violent demonstrations in positive affirmation of the right to live in human dignity as guaranteed by the U.S. Constitution and the Bill of Rights." It went on to charge that "in their efforts to uphold these guarantees, they are being met by an unprecedented wave of terror by those who would deny and negate that document which the whole world looks upon as setting the pattern for modern [freedom]." Succeeding paragraphs [illustrate] the "wave of terror" by describing certain alleged events. The text concluded with an appeal for funds for three purposes: support of the student movement, "the struggle for the right-to-vote," and the legal defense of Dr. Martin Luther King, Jr., leader of the movement, against a perjury indictment then pending in Montgomery.

The text appeared over the names of 64 persons, many widely known for their activities in public affairs, religion, trade unions, and the performing arts. Below these names, and under a line reading "We in the south who are struggling daily for dignity and freedom warmly endorse this appeal," appeared the names of the four individual petitioners and of 16 other persons, all but two of whom were identified as clergymen in various Southern cities. The advertisement was signed at the bottom of the page by the "Committee to Defend Martin Luther King and the Struggle for Freedom in the South," and the officers of the Committee were listed.

[T]he third [paragraph] and a portion of the sixth were the basis of respondent's claim of libel. They read as follows: Third paragraph: "In Montgomery, Alabama, after students sang 'My Country, 'Tis of Thee' on the State Capitol steps, their leaders were expelled from school, and truckloads of police armed with shotguns and tear-gas ringed the Alabama State College Campus. When the entire student body protested to state authorities by refusing to re-register, their dining hall was padlocked in an attempt to starve them into submission." Sixth paragraph: "Again and again the Southern violators have answered Dr. King's peaceful protests with intimidation and violence. They have bombed his home almost killing his wife and child. They have assaulted his person. They have arrested him seven times — for 'speeding,' 'loitering' and similar 'offenses.' And now they have charged him with 'perjury' — a felony under which they could imprison him for ten [years]."

Although neither of these statements mentions respondent by name, he contended that the word "police" in the third paragraph referred to him as the

Montgomery Commissioner who supervised the Police Department, so that he was being accused of "ringing" the campus with police. He further claimed that the paragraph would be read as imputing to the police, and hence to him, the padlocking of the dining hall in order to starve the students into submission. As to the sixth paragraph, he contended that since arrests are ordinarily made by the police, the statement "They have arrested [Dr. King] seven times" would be read as referring to him; [and] that the "They" who did the arresting would be equated with the "They" who committed the other described acts and with the "Southern violators." Thus, he argued, the paragraph would be read as accusing the Montgomery police, and hence him, of answering Dr. King's protests with "intimidation and violence," bombing his home, assaulting his person, and charging him with perjury. Respondent and six other Montgomery residents testified that they read some or all of the statements as referring to him in his capacity as Commissioner.

It is uncontroverted that some of the statements contained in the two paragraphs were not accurate descriptions of events which occurred in Montgomery. Although Negro students staged a demonstration on the State Capital steps, they sang the National Anthem and not "My Country, 'Tis of Thee." Although nine students were expelled[,] this was not for leading the demonstration at the Capitol, but for demanding service at a lunch counter in the Montgomery County Courthouse on another day. Not the entire student body, but most of it, had protested the expulsion, not by refusing to register, but by boycotting classes on a single day; virtually all the students did register for the ensuing semester. The campus dining hall was not padlocked on any occasion, and the only students who may have been barred from eating there were the few who had neither signed a preregistration application nor requested temporary meal tickets. Although the police were deployed near the campus in large numbers on three occasions, they did [not] "ring" the campus, and they were not called to the campus in connection with the demonstration on the State Capitol steps[.] Dr. King had not been arrested seven times, but only four; and although he claimed to have been assaulted some years earlier in connection with his arrest for loitering outside a courtroom, one of the officers who made the arrest denied that there was such an assault.

On the premise that the charges in the sixth paragraph could be read as referring to him, respondent was allowed to prove that he had not participated in the events described. Although Dr. King's home had in fact been bombed twice when his wife and child were there, both of these occasions antedated respondent's tenure as Commissioner, and the police were not only not implicated in the bombings, but had made every effort to apprehend those who were. Three of Dr. King's four arrests took place before respondent became Commissioner. Although Dr. King had in fact been indicted (he was subsequently acquitted) on two counts of perjury, each of which carried a possible five-year sentence, respondent had nothing to do with procuring the indictment.

Respondent made no effort to prove that he suffered actual pecuniary loss as a result of the alleged libel. One of his witnesses, a former employer, testified that if he had believed the statements, he doubted whether he "would want to be associated with anybody who would be a party to such things that are stated in that ad," and that he would not re-employ respondent if he believed "that he allowed the Police Department to do the things that the paper say he did." But neither this witness nor any [other] testified that [he] actually believed the statements in their supposed reference to respondent.

The cost of the advertisement was approximately $4800, and it was published by the Times upon an order from a New York advertising agency acting for the signatory Committee. The agency submitted the advertisement with a letter [certifying] that the persons whose names appeared on the advertisement had given their [permission]. The manager of the Advertising [Department] testified that he had approved the advertisement [because] he knew nothing to cause him to believe that anything in it was false, and because it bore the endorsement of "a number of people who are well known and whose reputation" he "had no reason to question." Neither he nor anyone else at the Times made an effort to confirm the accuracy of the advertisement, either by checking it against recent Times news stories [or] by any other means.

[Because] of the importance of the constitutional issues involved, we granted [certiorari]. We reverse the judgment. . . .

II.

Under Alabama law[,] a publication is "libelous per se" if the words "tend to injure a person [in] his reputation" or to "bring [him] into public contempt" . . . . The jury must find that the words were published "of and concerning" the plaintiff, but where the plaintiff is a public official his place in the governmental hierarchy is sufficient evidence to support a finding that his reputation has been affected by statements that reflect upon the agency of which he is in charge. Once "libel per se" has been established, the defendant has no defense as to stated facts unless he can persuade the jury that they were true in all their particulars. His privilege of "fair comment" for expressions of opinion depends on the truth of the facts upon which the comment is based. Unless he can discharge the burden of proving truth, general damages are presumed, and may be awarded without proof of pecuniary injury. A showing of actual malice is apparently a prerequisite to recovery of punitive damages, [and] defendant may [forestall] a punitive award by a retraction meeting the statutory requirements. Good motives and belief in truth do not negate an inference of malice, but are relevant only in mitigation of punitive damages[.]

The question before us is whether this rule of liability, as applied to an action brought by a public official against critics of his official conduct, abridges the freedom of speech and of the press that is guaranteed by the First and Fourteenth Amendments.

Respondent relies heavily [on] statements of this Court to the effect that the Constitution does not protect libelous publications. Those statements do not foreclose our inquiry here. None of the cases sustained the use of libel laws to impose sanctions upon expression critical of the official conduct of public officials. We are compelled by neither precedent nor policy to give any more weight to the epithet "libel" than we have to other "mere labels" of state law. [L]ibel can claim no talismanic immunity from constitutional limitations. It must be measured by standards that satisfy the First Amendment.

The general proposition that freedom of expression upon public questions is secured by the First Amendment has long been settled by our decisions. The constitutional [safeguard] "was fashioned to assure unfettered interchange of ideas for the bringing about of political and social changes desired by the people." . . . Thus we consider this case against the background of a profound national commitment to the principle that debate on public issues should be uninhibited, robust, and wide-open, and that it may well include vehement, caustic, and sometimes unpleasantly sharp attacks on government and public officials. The present advertisement, as an expression of grievance and protest on one of the major public issues of our time, would seem clearly to qualify for the constitutional protection. The question is whether it forfeits that protection by the falsity of some of its factual statements and by its alleged defamation of respondent.

Authoritative interpretations of the First Amendment guarantees have consistently refused to recognize an exception for any test of truth — whether administered by judges, juries, or administrative officials — and especially one that puts the burden of proving truth on the speaker. The constitutional protection does not turn upon "the truth, popularity, or social utility of the ideas and beliefs which are offered." [E]rroneous statement is inevitable in free debate, and [it] must be protected if the freedoms of expression are to have the "breathing space" that they "need [to] survive," *N.A.A.C.P. v. Button*, 371 U.S. 415, 433. . . .

Injury to official reputation [affords] no more warrant for repressing speech that would otherwise be free than does factual error. Where judicial officers are involved, this Court has held that concern for the dignity and reputation of the courts does not justify the punishment as criminal contempt of criticism of the judge or his decision. This is true even though the utterance contains "half-truths" and "misinformation." Such repression can be justified, if at all, only by a clear and present danger of the obstruction of justice. If judges are to be treated as "men of fortitude, able to thrive in a hardy climate," surely the same must be true of other government officials, such as elected city commissioners. Criticism of their official conduct does not lose its constitutional protection merely because it is effective criticism and hence diminishes their official reputations.

If neither factual error nor defamatory content suffices to remove the constitutional shield from criticism of official conduct, the combination of the two elements is no less inadequate. This is the lesson to be drawn from the great controversy over the Sedition Act of 1798, which first crystallized a national awareness of the central meaning of the First Amendment. That statute made it a crime, punishable by a $5,000 fine and five years in prison, "if any person shall write, print, utter or publish [any] false, scandalous and malicious writing or writings against the government of the United States, or either house of the Congress[,] or the President[,] with intent to defame [or] to bring them, or either or any of them, into contempt or disrepute; or to excite against them, or either of any of them, the hatred of the good people of the United States." . . . Although the Sedition Act was never tested in this Court, the attack upon its validity has carried the day in the court of history. Fines levied in its prosecution were repaid by Act of Congress on the ground that it was unconstitutional. [There was] broad consensus that the Act, because of the restraint it imposed upon criticism of government and public officials, was inconsistent with the First Amendment. . . .

What a State may not constitutionally bring about by means of a criminal statute is likewise beyond the reach of its civil law of libel. The fear of damage awards under a rule such as that invoked by the Alabama courts here may be markedly more inhibiting than the fear of prosecution under a criminal statute. [The] judgment awarded in this case — without the need for any proof of actual pecuniary loss — was one thousand times greater than the maximum fine provided by the Alabama criminal [libel] statute, and one hundred times greater than that provided by the Sedition Act. And since there is no double-jeopardy limitation applicable to civil lawsuits, this is not the only judgment that may be awarded against petitioners for the same publication. Whether or not a newspaper can survive a succession of such judgments, the pall of fear and timidity imposed upon those who would give voice to public criticism is an atmosphere in which the First Amendment freedoms cannot survive. Plainly the Alabama law of civil libel is "a form of regulation that creates hazards to protected freedoms markedly greater than those that attend reliance upon the criminal law."

The state rule of law is not saved by its allowance of the defense of truth. [A] rule compelling the critic of official conduct to guarantee the truth of all his factual assertions — and to do so on pain of libel judgments virtually unlimited in amount — leads to a comparable "self-censorship." Allowance of the defense of truth, with the burden of proving it on the defendant, does not mean that only false speech will be deterred. Even courts accepting this defense as an adequate safeguard have recognized the difficulties of adducing legal proofs that the alleged libel was true in all its factual particulars. Under such a rule, would-be critics of official conduct may be deterred from voicing their criticism, even though it is believed to be true and even though it is in fact true, because of doubt whether it can be proved in court or fear of the expense of having to do so. They tend to make only statements which "steer far wider of the unlawful zone." The rule thus dampens the vigor and limits the variety of public debate. It is inconsistent with the First and Fourteenth Amendments.

The constitutional guarantees require, we think, a federal rule that prohibits a public official from recovering damages for a defamatory falsehood relating to his official conduct unless he proves that the statement was made with "actual malice" — that is, with knowledge that it was false or with reckless disregard of whether it was false or not. . . .

Such a privilege for criticism of official conduct is appropriately analogous to the protection accorded a public official when he is sued for libel by a private citizen. In *Barr v. Matteo*, 360 U.S. 564, 575, this Court held the utterance of a federal official to be absolutely privileged if made "within the outer perimeter" of his duties. [The] threat of damage suits would otherwise "inhibit the fearless, vigorous, and effective administration of policies of government" and "dampen the ardor of all but the most resolute, or the most irresponsible, in the unflinching discharge of their duties." Analogous considerations support the privilege for the citizen-critic of government. [It] would give public servants an unjustified preference over the public they serve, if critics of official conduct did not have a fair equivalent of the immunity granted to the officials themselves.

[We] conclude that such a privilege is required by the First and Fourteenth Amendments.

[While] Alabama law apparently requires proof of actual malice for an award of punitive damages, where general damages are concerned malice is "presumed." Such a presumption is inconsistent with the federal rule. . . .

Since respondent may seek a new trial, [considerations] of effective judicial administration require us to review the evidence in the present record to determine whether it could constitutionally support a judgment for [respondent]. We must "make an independent examination of the whole record," so as to assure ourselves that the judgment does not constitute a forbidden intrusion on the field of free expression.

Applying these standards, we consider that the proof presented to show actual malice lacks the convincing clarity which the constitutional standard demands, and hence [would] not constitutionally sustain the judgment for respondent under the proper rule of law. [Even] assuming that [the individual respondents authorized] the use of their names on the advertisement, there was no evidence [that] they were aware of any erroneous statements or were in any way reckless in that regard. The judgment against them is thus without constitutional support.

As to the Times, we similarly conclude that the facts do not support a finding of actual malice. The statement by the Times' Secretary [that] he thought the advertisement was "substantially correct," affords no [warrant] for the Alabama Supreme Court's conclusion [of bad faith and maliciousness]. The statement does not indicate malice at the time of the publication; even if the advertisement was not "substantially correct" [that] opinion was at least a reasonable one, and there was no evidence to impeach the witness' good faith in holding it. The Times' failure to retract upon respondent's demand [is] likewise not adequate evidence of malice. . . . Whether or not a failure to retract may ever constitute such evidence, there are two reasons why it does not here. First, the letter written by the Times reflected a reasonable doubt on its part as to whether the advertisement could reasonably be taken to refer to respondent at all. Second, it was not a final refusal, since it asked for [an] explanation — a request that respondent chose to ignore. . . .

[T]here is evidence that the Times published the advertisement without checking its accuracy against the news stories in the Times' own files. The mere presence of the stories in the files does not, of course, establish that the Times "knew" the advertisement was false, since the state of mind required for actual malice [involves] the persons [having] responsibility [for] publication of the advertisement. With respect to the failure of those persons to make the check, the record shows that they relied upon their knowledge of the good reputation of many of those whose names were listed as sponsors of the advertisement, and upon the letter from A. Philip Randolph, known to them as a responsible individual, certifying that the use of the names was authorized. There was testimony that the persons handling the advertisement saw nothing in it that would render it unacceptable under the Times' policy of rejecting advertisements containing "attacks of a personal character"; their failure to reject it on this ground was not unreasonable. We think the evidence against the Times supports at most a finding of negligence in failing to discover the misstatements, and is constitutionally insufficient to show the recklessness that is required for a finding of actual malice.

We also think the evidence was constitutionally defective in another respect: it was incapable of supporting the jury's finding that the allegedly libelous statements were made "of and concerning" respondent. [The Supreme Court of Alabama relied on the bare fact of respondent's official position. But that would transmute] criticism of government, however impersonal it may seem on its face, into personal criticism, and hence potential libel, of the officials of whom the government is composed.

[The] judgment of the Supreme Court of Alabama is reversed and the case is remanded to that court for further proceedings not inconsistent with this opinion.

Reversed and remanded.

Mr. Justice BLACK, with whom Mr. Justice DOUGLAS joins (concurring).

[T]he Federal Constitution has dealt with this deadly danger to the press in the only way possible without leaving the free press open to destruction — by granting the press an absolute immunity for criticism of the way public officials do their public duty. Stopgap measures like those the Court adopts are in my judgment not enough. . . . [S]ince the adoption of the Fourteenth Amendment a State has no more power than the Federal Government to use a civil libel law or any other law to impose damages for merely discussing public affairs and criticizing public officials. The power of the United States to do that [is] precisely nil. . . .

[Elected] officials are responsible to the people for the way they perform their [duties]. To punish the exercise of this right to discuss public affairs or to penalize it through libel judgments is to abridge or shut off discussion of the very kind most needed. This Nation, I suspect, can live in peace without libel suits based on public discussions of public affairs and public officials. But I doubt that a country can live in freedom where its people can be made to suffer physically or financially for criticizing their government, its actions, or its officials. [An] unconditional right to say what one pleases about public affairs is what I consider to be the minimum guarantee of the First Amendment. . . .

I regret that the Court has stopped short of this holding indispensable to preserve our free press from destruction.

Mr. Justice GOLDBERG, with whom Mr. Justice DOUGLAS joins (concurring in the result).

[In] a democratic society, one who assumes to act for the citizens in an executive, legislative, or judicial capacity must expect that his official acts will be commented upon and criticized. Such criticism cannot, in my opinion, be muzzled or deterred by the courts at the instance of public officials under the label of libel. [Our] national experience teaches that repressions breed hate and "that hate menaces stable government." *Whitney v. California*, 274 U.S. 357, 375 (Brandeis, J., concurring).

[It] may be urged that deliberately and maliciously false statements have no conceivable value as free speech. That argument, however, is not responsive to the real issue presented by this case, which is whether that freedom of speech [can] be effectively safeguarded by a rule allowing the imposition of liability upon a jury's evaluation of the speaker's state of mind. If individual citizens may be held liable in damages for strong words, which a jury finds false and maliciously motivated, there can be little doubt that public debate and advocacy will be constrained. And if newspapers, publishing advertisements dealing with public issues, thereby risk liability, there can also be little doubt that the ability of minority groups to secure publication of their views on public affairs and to seek support for their causes will be greatly diminished. . . .

[The] conclusion that the Constitution affords the citizen and the press an absolute privilege for criticism of official conduct does not leave the public official without defenses against unsubstantiated opinions or deliberate misstatements. "Under our system of government, counterargument and education are the weapons available to expose these matters, not abridgment [of free speech]." *Wood v. Georgia*, 370 U.S. 375, 389. . . .

NOTES AND QUESTIONS

1. In *Rinaldi v. Holt, Rinehart & Winston, Inc.*, 366 N.E.2d 1299 (N.Y. 1977), and *Curtis Publishing Co. v. Birdsong*, 360 F.2d 344 (5th Cir. 1966), a state court judge and the Commander of Mississippi Highway Patrol, respectively, were

subjected to the actual malice standard. Both were deemed to be public officials within the meaning of the *New York Times* standard.

2. *Injunctive relief and prior restraints.* In *Near v. Minnesota*, 283 U.S. 697 (1931), the county attorney of Hennepin county sued to enjoin publication of what was described as a "malicious, scandalous and defamatory newspaper." Although the trial court granted the injunction, the United States Supreme Court reversed establishing a broad rule against prior restraints: "Public officers, whose character and conduct remain open to debate and free discussion in the press, find their remedies for false accusations in actions under libel laws providing for redress and punishment, and not in proceedings to restrain the publication of newspapers and periodicals. . . ."

3. *Public Figures — Private Lives.* In *Monitor Patriot Co. v. Roy*, 401 U.S. 265 (1971), a newspaper published an article about a candidate for the U.S. Senate. The article referred to the candidate as a "former small-time bootlegger." The Court held that a candidate for public office must satisfy the actual malice standard even as to allegations relating to his personal life: "The principal activity of a candidate in our political system, his 'office,' so to speak, consists in putting before the voters every conceivable aspect of his public and private life that he thinks may lead the electorate to gain a good impression of him. [A] charge of criminal conduct, no matter how remote in time or place, can never be irrelevant to an official's or a candidate's fitness for office. . . ."

4. Does the *New York Times* decision give too much protection to the press? Consider Mr. Justice White's concurrence in *Dun & Bradstreet, Inc. v. Greenmoss Builders, Inc.*, 472 U.S. 749 (1985):

> [The] *New York Times* rule [leaves] the public official without [remedy] for the damage to his reputation. Yet [the] individual's right to the protection of his own good name is a basic consideration of our constitutional system, reflecting "'our basic concept of the essential dignity and worth of every human being — a concept at the root of any decent system of ordered liberty.'" The upshot is that the public official must suffer the injury, often cannot get a judgment identifying the lie for what it is, and has very little, if any, chance of countering that lie in the public press.
>
> We are not talking in these cases about mere criticism or opinion, but about misstatements of fact that seriously harm the reputation of another, by lowering him in the estimation of the community or to deter third persons from associating or dealing with him. The necessary breathing room for speakers can be ensured by limitations on recoverable damages; it does not also require depriving many public figures of any room to vindicate their reputations. . . . It could be suggested that even without the threat of large presumed and punitive damages awards, press defendants' communication will be unduly chilled by having to pay for the actual damages caused to those they defame. But other commercial enterprises in this country not in the business of dis-

seminating information must pay for the damage they cause as a cost of doing business, and it is difficult to argue that the United States did not have a free and vigorous press before the rule in *New York Times* was announced. . . .

5. *Is a "public interest" standard preferable to a "public figure" standard?* In *Rosenbloom v. Metromedia, Inc.*, 403 U.S. 29 (1971), a plurality held that: "[W]e think the time has come forthrightly to announce that the determinant whether the First Amendment applies to state libel actions is whether the utterance involved concerns an issue of public or general concern, albeit leaving the delineation of the reach of that term to future cases. . . ." *See Gertz v. Robert Welch, Inc.*, *infra*, for a discussion of the fate of the "public interest" standard.

6. *More concerns about the "actual malice" standard.* Recent studies suggest that libel litigation in the United States is on the increase, and that defamation awards occur more frequently and in much larger amounts. Consider Libel Defense Resource Center Press Release 1 (September 26, 1991): "The LDRC study documents a dramatic increase in the already-high average of damage awards against media defendants in libel (and related) cases. Compared to the prior two-year period, the average award increased ten-fold, from almost half-a-million [dollars] in 1987-88 . . . to just under $4.5 million in 1989-90. . . . This most recent average is more than 3 times larger than the average award for the 8 years prior to the most recent study period, which was just under $1.5 million. . . . Including the most recent data, the average media libel award for the decade, 1980-90, was nearly $2 million. . . ." These statistics prompted Professor Richard Epstein to observe that "the onslaught of defamation actions is greater in number and severity than it was in the 'bad old days' of common law libel [notwithstanding] *New York Times*." Richard A. Epstein, *Was New York Times v. Sullivan Wrong?*, 53 U. CHI. L. REV. 782, 783 (1986); *see also* Anthony Lewis, *New York Times v. Sullivan Reconsidered: Time to Return to "The Central Meaning of the First Amendment"*, 83 COLUM. L. REV. 603 (1983); Rodney A. Smolla, *Let The Author Beware: The Rejuvenation of The American Law of Libel*, 132 U. PA. L. REV. 1 (1983). Do these statistics suggest that the Court should provide even greater protection to newspapers and broadcasters including, possibly, a ban on libel suits by public officials? *See* Garbus, *25 Years After "Times v. Sullivan": What Remains to Be Done*, 201 N.Y.L.J. 2-3 (1989).

7. *Does* New York Times v. Sullivan *strike the right balance, or perhaps provide too much protection to the media?* The Libel Resource Defense Center's data is contradicted by empirical research conducted by professors Russell L. Weaver and Geoffrey J.G. Bennett during the 1990s. Professors Weaver and Bennett found that the U.S. media is generally unconcerned about the threat of defamation liability:

> [U.S.] editors are concerned about the threat of defamation actions and the possibility of adverse judgments, but they are far less concerned about this possibility than their British counterparts. . . . The reason U.S. newspapers and broadcasters are less concerned about

defamation is because they are threatened with suit, and actually sued, far less frequently than their British counterparts. . . . Editors and producers in the United States are not so relaxed that they ignore the possibility of defamation liability. But, because the threat of suit is much lower, they often tend to be more worried about other matters (*e.g.*, journalistic accuracy and integrity) than they are about the threat of liability. Producers and editors stated that for professional reasons, they want to report accurately. Even if there is no threat of liability, they want to avoid publishing something that is untrue or that cannot be supported by hard evidence. Thus, at times, they know things they do not report. But the primary reason for withholding such information is that the editors are concerned about the ethics of publishing it. They also fear that questionable allegations might diminish their credibility or harm their standing in the community.

[These] attitudes are reflected in the day-to-day functioning of U.S. newspapers and broadcasters. Unlike the British, U.S. newspapers and broadcasters do not have teams of lawyers that comb through copy searching for material that may be defamatory. Most papers and broadcasters allow editors and producers to decide for themselves whether material is potentially defamatory and whether to involve counsel. If an editor or producer feels comfortable with a piece, he may publish or air it without any input from counsel.

Thus, the possibility of defamation suits has some impact on reporting. But most interviewees indicated that the impact was minimal. Few editors or producers reported that they had ever killed a story for fear of defamation liability. Moreover, few indicated that they were unable to make a statement for fear of liability. They were often reluctant to rely entirely on confidential sources. In addition, if they had inadequate support for a piece, they might seek additional support. Alternatively, they might soften a statement or attempt to present it in a more balanced way. But there was a very good chance that the allegation would still be made.

Russell L. Weaver & Geoffrey J.G. Bennett, *Is the New York Times "Actual Malice" Standard Really Necessary? A Comparative Perspective*, 53 LA. L. REV. 1153 (1993).

8. In the United States, a number of commentators have expressed concerns about "irresponsible journalism." *See* Edward T. Fenno, *Public Figure Libel: The Premium on Ignorance and the Race to the Bottom*, 4 S. CAL. INTERDISC. L.J. 253, 265 (1995); Honorable Abner J. Mikva, *In My Opinion, Those Are Not Facts*, 11 GA. ST. U. L. REV. 291 (1995); Jeffrey A. Smith, *Prior Restraint: Original Intentions and Modern Interpretations*, 28 WM. & MARY L. REV. 439, 470 (1987). As the Honorable Abner J. Mikva stated, "a feeling is abroad among some judges that the Supreme Court has gone too far in protecting the media from

defamation actions resulting from instances of irresponsible [journalism]." Is Judge Mikva correct?

9. *A modified "actual malice" standard?* In *Theophanous v. The Herald & Weekly Times Ltd.*, (1994) 182 CLR 104, the Australian High Court adopted a modified version of the actual malice standard. The High Court began by expressing concerns about the "actual malice" standard: "[The actual malice] test [tilts] the balance unduly in favour of free speech against protection of individual reputation." Because of these concerns, the High Court adopted a modified version of that test: "[T]he defendant should be liable in damages unless it can establish that it was unaware of the falsity, that it did not publish recklessly (*i.e.*, not caring whether the matter was true or false), and that the publication was reasonable in the sense described. [D]efendant [must] establish that the publication falls within the constitutional protection." Is the High Court's approach (which was subsequently abandoned in favor of a common law privilege) preferable to the actual malice standard?

10. *Is there a better solution?* The UNIFORM CORRECTION OR CLARIFICATION OF DEFAMATION ACT encourages defamation plaintiffs to request, and defamation defendants to give, corrections or clarifications. It does so by limiting damages when a correction or clarification is made: "In limiting recovery of damages to provable economic loss as mitigated by the correction or clarification, the Act anticipates that any loss caused by the publication can be significantly reduced by publication of the correction or clarification. The burden of proving mitigation of economic loss, however, rests with the publisher." Is this approach preferable?

11. *Yet another solution?* In *Dun & Bradstreet*, *supra*, Mr. Justice White, concurring, suggested the following solution: "We entrust to juries and the courts the responsibility of decisions affecting the life and liberty of persons. It is perverse indeed to say that these bodies are incompetent to inquire into the truth of a statement of fact in a defamation case. [N]othing in the Constitution [forbids] a plaintiff to obtain a judicial decree that a statement is false — a decree he can then use in the community to clear his name and to prevent further damage from a defamation already published." Is it desirable to allow public officials and public figures to obtain declarations of falsity?

PROBLEMS

1. Suppose that you represent the mayor of a large city. The mayor is angry over an article in the local newspaper which suggests that the mayor is corrupt (allegedly, he gave city contracts to those who donated to his last campaign) and that he has had several extra-marital affairs. You are convinced that the allegations are untrue (as well as unfair), but you are not sure that you can satisfy the "actual malice" standard. What advice would you give to the mayor about his remedial options? How would you advise him to respond to the allegations?

2. It is well settled that the Fourteenth Amendment to the U.S. Constitution (which incorporates the First Amendment and applies it to the states) is directed against state action and not private action. If that is so, then how did the Constitution have any application to this lawsuit between private parties?

3. As we shall see in a later chapter, the Court treats "commercial speech" quite differently than "political speech." Should the Court have treated this advertisement as commercial speech and subjected the case to a lower standard of review?

4. *Does the "actual malice" standard apply to any public official?* Do *New York Times* and *Gertz* justify subjecting all public officials to the "actual malice" standard? Should it matter whether a low level official has the same opportunity to respond and to rebut allegations as do prominent officials like the President of the United States? Should it matter whether the allegations relate to a matter of "public interest"? For example, does the rationale of *New York Times* justify subjecting a judge or a highway patrolman to the "actual malice" standard? What about an ordinary police officer? *See Coughlin v. Westinghouse Broadcasting and Cable, Inc.,* 780 F.2d 340 (3d Cir. 1985). What about the supervisor of a recreation area? *See Rosenblatt v. Baer,* 383 U.S. 75 (1966).

5. Should the "actual malice" standard be applied to allegations made against a public official relating to matters in his private life (*i.e.*, the allegations made against President Bill Clinton regarding his various alleged affairs)?

6. *Is one still a "public official" for purposes of the* New York Times *decision after leaving office?* Suppose that a city's Chief Deputy Sheriff and Chief of Detectives were fired for malfeasance in office and ultimately convicted of a crime. Six years later, both were allegedly defamed by an article about a key witness in their trial. Should the "actual malice" standard apply to a former public official? *See Zerangue v. TSP Newspapers, Inc.*, 814 F.2d 1066 (5th Cir. 1987).

C. "PUBLIC FIGURES" AND "PRIVATE PLAINTIFFS"

In *Curtis Publishing Co. v. Butts*, 388 U.S. 130 (1967), the Court extended *New York Times* protections to defamatory statements made regarding public figures. The Saturday Evening Post alleged that Butts, the Athletic Director at the University of Georgia, had conspired to fix a football game. Butts had previously served as the University's head football coach and was a well-known and respected figure in coaching ranks. The jury returned a verdict of $60,000 in general damages and $3,000,000 in punitive damages. The companion case of *Associated Press v. Walker*, 388 U.S. 130 (1967), involved an eyewitness account of a riot on the University of Mississippi campus. The Associated Press article claimed that Walker, a private citizen who had been in the United States Army, had taken command of a violent crowd and had personally led a charge against federal marshals sent to enforce a court decree and to assist in preserving order. The article described Walker as encouraging rioters to use violence and giving them technical advice on combating the effects of tear gas. A verdict of $500,000 compensatory damages and $300,000 punitive damages was returned. In a plurality opinion written by Mr. Justice Harlan, the Court treated both Butts and Walker as public figures:

> [T]he public interest in the circulation of the materials here involved, and the publisher's interest in circulating them, is not less than that involved in *New York Times*. [B]oth Butts and Walker commanded a substantial amount of independent public interest at the time of the publications; both, in our opinion, would have been labeled "public figures" under ordinary tort rules. Butts may have attained that status by position alone and Walker by his purposeful activity amounting to a thrusting of his personality into the "vortex" of an important public controversy, but both commanded sufficient continuing public interest and had sufficient access to the means of counterargument to be able "to expose through discussion the falsehood and fallacies" of the defamatory statements. [L]ibel actions of the present kind cannot be left entirely to state libel laws, unlimited by any overriding constitutional safeguard.
> . . .

Mr. Chief Justice Warren concurred:

> [A]lthough they are not subject to the restraints of the political process, "public figures," like "public officials," often play an influential role in ordering society. And surely as a class these "public figures" have as ready access as "public officials" to mass media of communication, both to influence policy and to counter criticism of their views and activities. Our citizenry has a legitimate and substantial interest in the conduct of such persons, and freedom of the press to engage in uninhibited debate about their involvement in public issues and events is as crucial as it is in the case of "public officials." The fact that they are not amenable to the restraints of the political process only underscores the legitimate and substantial nature of the interest, since it means that public opinion may be the only instrument by which society can attempt to influence their conduct.

GERTZ v. ROBERT WELCH, INC.
418 U.S. 323 (1974)

Mr. Justice POWELL delivered the opinion of the Court.

[In] 1968 a Chicago policeman named Nuccio shot and killed a youth named Nelson. The state authorities prosecuted Nuccio for the homicide and ultimately obtained a conviction for murder in the second degree. The Nelson family retained petitioner Elmer Gertz, a reputable attorney, to represent them in civil litigation against Nuccio.

Respondent publishes American Opinion, a monthly outlet for the views of the John Birch Society. [I]n the 1960's the magazine began to warn of a nationwide conspiracy to discredit local law enforcement agencies and create [a] national police force capable of supporting a Communist dictatorship. [In an] effort to alert the public to this assumed danger, [the] American Opinion commissioned an article on the murder trial of Officer Nuccio. [In] 1969 respondent published the resulting article under the title "FRAME-UP: Richard Nuccio And The War On Police." The article purports to demonstrate that the testimony against Nuccio at his criminal trial was false and that his prosecution was part of the Communist campaign against the police.

[A]s counsel for the Nelson family in the civil litigation, petitioner attended the coroner's inquest into the boy's death and initiated actions for damages, but he neither discussed Officer Nuccio with the press nor played any part in the criminal proceeding. Notwithstanding petitioner's remote connection with the prosecution of Nuccio, respondent's magazine portrayed him as an architect of the "frame-up." According to the article, the police file on petitioner took "a big, Irish cop to lift." The article stated that petitioner had been an official of the "Marxist League for Industrial Democracy, originally known as the Intercollegiate Socialist Society, which has advocated the violent seizure of our government." It labeled Gertz a "Leninist" and a "Communist-fronter." It also stated that Gertz had been an officer of the National Lawyers Guild, described as a Communist organization that "probably did more than any other outfit to plan the Communist attack on the Chicago police during the 1968 Democratic Convention."

[The article] contained serious inaccuracies. The implication that petitioner had a criminal record was false. Petitioner had been a member and officer of the National Lawyers Guild some 15 years earlier, but there was no evidence that he or that organization had taken any part in planning the 1968 demonstrations in Chicago. There was also no basis for the charge that petitioner was a "Leninist" or a "Communist-fronter." And he had never been a member of the "Marxist League for Industrial Democracy" or the "Intercollegiate Socialist Society."

The managing editor of American Opinion made no effort to verify or substantiate the charges against petitioner. Instead, he appended [an] introduction stating that the author had "conducted extensive research into [the] Nuccio Case." And he included in the article a photograph of petitioner and wrote the caption that appeared under it: "Elmer Gertz of Red Guild harasses Nuccio." Respondent placed the [issue] containing the article on sale at newsstands throughout the country and distributed reprints of the article on the streets of Chicago.

[T]he District Court [entered] judgment for respondent. . . .

II

The principal issue [is] whether a newspaper or broadcaster that publishes defamatory falsehoods about an individual who is neither a public official nor a public figure may claim a constitutional privilege against liability for the injury inflicted by those statements. The Court considered this question on the rather different set of facts presented in *Rosenbloom v. Metromedia, Inc.*, 403 U.S. 29 (1971). Rosenbloom, a distributor of nudist magazines, was arrested for selling allegedly obscene material while making a delivery to a retail dealer. The police [seized] his entire inventory of 3,000 books and magazines. [He] obtained an injunction prohibiting further police interference with his business. He then sued a local radio station for failing to note in two of its newscasts that [the] items seized were only "reportedly" or "allegedly" obscene and for broadcasting references to "the smut literature racket" and to "girlie-book peddlers" in its coverage of the court proceeding for injunctive relief. He obtained a judgment against the radio station, but the Court of Appeals for the Third Circuit [reversed].

This Court affirmed the decision below, but no majority could agree on a controlling rationale. The eight Justices [announced] their views in five separate opinions, none of which commanded more than three votes. [The] several statements [reflect] divergent traditions of thought about the general problem of reconciling the law of defamation with the First Amendment. One approach has been to extend the *New York Times* test to an expanding variety of situations. Another has been to vary the level of constitutional privilege for defamatory falsehood with the status of the person defamed. And a third view would grant to the press and broadcast media absolute immunity from liability for defamation. . . . In his opinion for the plurality[,] Mr. Justice Brennan [concluded] that [the actual malice standard] should extend to defamatory falsehoods relating to private persons if the statements concerned matters of general or public interest. . . .

[Our] decisions recognize that a rule of strict liability that compels a publisher or broadcaster to guarantee the accuracy of his factual assertions may lead to intolerable self-censorship. [The] need to avoid self-censorship [is], however, not the only societal value at issue. If it were, this Court would have embraced [the] view that publishers and broadcasters enjoy an unconditional and indefeasible immunity from liability for defamation. [The] legitimate state interest underlying the law of libel is the compensation of individuals for the harm inflicted on them by defamatory falsehood. We would not lightly require the State to abandon this purpose, for, as Mr. Justice Stewart has reminded us, the individual's right to the protection of his own good name "reflects no more than our basic concept of the essential dignity and worth of every human being — a concept at the root of any decent system of ordered liberty." *Rosenblatt v. Baer*, 383 U.S. 75 (1966) (concurring opinion).

Some tension necessarily exists between the need for a vigorous and uninhibited press and the legitimate interest in redressing wrongful injury. [In] our continuing effort to define the proper accommodation between these competing concerns, we have been especially anxious to assure to the freedoms of speech and press that "breathing space" essential to their fruitful exercise. To that end this Court has extended a measure of strategic protection to defamatory falsehood.

The *New York Times* standard defines the level of constitutional protection appropriate to the context of defamation of a public person. Those who, by reason of the notoriety of their achievements or the vigor and success with which they seek the public's attention, are properly classed as public figures and those who hold governmental office. . . . This standard [exacts a] high price from the victims of defamatory falsehood. [M]any deserving plaintiffs, including some intentionally subjected to injury, will be unable to surmount the barrier of the *New York Times* test. [We] believe that the *New York Times* rule states an accommodation between this concern and the limited state interest present in the context of libel actions brought by public persons. [T]he state interest in compensating injury to the reputation of private individuals requires that a different rule should obtain with respect to them.

[W]e have no difficulty in distinguishing among defamation plaintiffs. The first remedy of any victim of defamation is self-help — using available opportunities to contradict the lie or correct the error and thereby to minimize its adverse impact on reputation. Public officials and public figures usually enjoy significantly greater access to the channels of effective communication and hence have a more realistic opportunity to counteract false statements then private individuals normally enjoy. Private individuals are therefore more vulnerable to injury, and the state interest in protecting them is correspondingly greater.

More important[,] there is a compelling normative consideration underlying the distinction between public and private defamation plaintiffs. An individual who decides to seek governmental office must accept certain necessary consequences of that involvement in public affairs. He runs the risk of closer public scrutiny than might otherwise be the case. And society's interest in the officers of government is not strictly limited to the formal discharge of official duties. [T]he public's interest extends to "anything which might touch on an official's fitness for [office]. Few personal attributes are more germane to fitness for office than dishonesty, malfeasance, or improper motivation, even though these characteristics may also affect the official's private character."

Those classed as public figures stand in a similar position. Hypothetically, it may be possible for someone to become a public figure through no purposeful action of his own, but the instances of truly involuntary public figures must be exceedingly rare. For the most part those who attain this status have assumed roles of especial prominence in the affairs of society. Some occupy positions of such persuasive power and influence that they are deemed public figures for all purposes. More commonly, those classed as public figures have thrust themselves to the forefront of particular public controversies in order to influence the resolution of the issues involved. In either event, they invite attention and comment.

Even if the foregoing generalities do not obtain in every instance, the communications media are entitled to act on the assumption that public officials and public figures have voluntarily exposed themselves to increased risk of injury from defamatory falsehood concerning them. No such assumption is justified with respect to a private individual. He has not accepted public office or assumed an "influential role in ordering society." He has relinquished no part of his interest in the protection of his own good name, and consequently he has a more compelling call on the courts for redress of injury inflicted by defamatory falsehood. Thus, private individuals are not only more vulnerable to injury than public officials and public figures; they are also more deserving of recovery.

For these reasons we conclude that the States should retain substantial latitude in their efforts to enforce a legal remedy for defamatory falsehood injurious to the reputation of a private individual. The extension of the *New York Times* test proposed by the *Rosenbloom* plurality would abridge this legitimate state interest to a degree that we find unacceptable. And it would occasion [the] difficulty of forcing [judges] to decide [which] publications address issues of "general or public interest" and which do not. . . . We doubt the wisdom of committing this task to the conscience of judges. [The] "public or general interest" test for determining the applicability of the *New York Times* standard to private defamation actions inadequately serves both of the competing values at stake. . . .

We hold that, so long as they do not impose liability without fault, the States may define for themselves the appropriate standard of liability for a publisher or broadcaster of defamatory falsehood injurious to a private individual. This approach provides a more equitable boundary between the competing concerns involved here. It recognizes the strength of the legitimate state interest in compensating private individuals for wrongful injury to reputation, yet shields the press and broadcast media from the rigors of strict liability for defamation. . . .

[The] strong and legitimate state interest in compensating private individuals for injury to reputation [extends] no further than compensation for actual injury. [W]e hold that the States may not permit recovery of presumed or punitive damages, at least when liability is not based on a showing of knowledge of falsity or reckless disregard for the truth.

The common law of defamation is an oddity of tort law, for it allows recovery of purportedly compensatory damages without evidence of actual loss. Under the traditional rules pertaining to actions for libel, the existence of injury is presumed from the fact of publication. Juries may award substantial sums as compensation for supposed damage to reputation without any proof that such harm actually occurred. The largely uncontrolled discretion of juries to award damages where there is no loss unnecessarily compounds the potential of any system of liability for defamatory falsehood to inhibit the vigorous exercise of First Amendment freedoms. Additionally, the doctrine of presumed damages invites juries to punish unpopular opinion rather than to compensate individuals for injury sustained by the publication of a false fact. [T]he States have no substantial interest in securing for plaintiffs such as this petitioner gratuitous awards of money damages far in excess of any actual injury.

[H]ere we are attempting to reconcile state law with a competing interest grounded in the constitutional command of the First Amendment. It is therefore appropriate to require that state remedies for defamatory falsehood reach no farther than is necessary to protect the legitimate interest involved. It is necessary to restrict defamation plaintiffs who do not prove knowledge of falsity or reckless disregard for the truth to compensation for actual injury [which] is not limited to out-of-pocket loss. [T]he more customary types of actual harm inflicted by defamatory falsehood include impairment of reputation and standing in the community, personal humiliation, and mental anguish and suffering. Of course, juries must be limited by appropriate instructions, and all awards must be supported by competent evidence concerning the injury, although there need be no evidence which assigns an actual dollar value to the injury.

We also find no justification for allowing awards of punitive damages against publishers and broadcasters. . . . [J]uries assess punitive damages in wholly unpredictable amounts bearing no necessary relation to the actual harm caused. And they remain free to use their discretion selectively to punish expressions of unpopular views. Like the doctrine of presumed damages, jury discretion to award punitive damages [exacerbates] the danger of media self-censorship, [but] punitive damages are wholly irrelevant to the state interest that justifies a negligence standard for private defamation actions. They are not compensation for injury. Instead, they are private fines levied by civil juries to punish reprehensible conduct and to deter its future occurrence. In short, the private defamation plaintiff who establishes liability under a less demanding standard than that stated by *New York Times* may recover only such damages as are sufficient to compensate him for actual injury.

[R]espondent contends that we should affirm [on] the ground that petitioner is either a public official or a public figure. There is little basis for the former assertion. Several years prior to the present incident, petitioner [served] briefly on housing committees appointed by the mayor of Chicago, but [he] never held any remunerative governmental position. Respondent [argues] that petitioner's appearance at the coroner's inquest rendered him a "de facto public official." Our cases recognized no such concept. Respondent's suggestion would sweep all lawyers under the *New York Times* rule as officers of the court and distort the plain meaning of the "public official" category beyond all recognition. We decline to follow it.

Respondent's characterization of petitioner as a public figure raises a different question. . . .

Petitioner has long been active in community and professional affairs. He has served as an officer of local civic groups and of various professional organizations, and he has published several books and articles on legal subjects. Although petitioner was consequently well known in some circles, he had achieved no general fame or notoriety in the community. [We] would not lightly assume that a citizen's participation in community and professional affairs rendered him a public figure for all purposes. Absent clear evidence of general fame or notoriety in the community, and pervasive involvement in the affairs of society, an individual should not be deemed a public personality for all aspects of his life. It is preferable to reduce the public-figure question to a more meaningful context by looking to the nature and extent of an individual's participation in the particular controversy giving rise to the defamation.

In this context it is plain that petitioner was not a public figure. He played a minimal role at the coroner's inquest, and his participation related solely to his representation of a private client. He took no part in the criminal prosecution of Officer Nuccio. Moreover, he never discussed either the criminal or civil litigation with the press and was never quoted as having done so. He plainly did not thrust himself into the vortex of this public issue, nor did he engage the public's attention in an attempt to influence its outcome. We are persuaded that the trial court did not err in refusing to characterize petitioner as a public figure for the purpose of this litigation.

[T]he trial court erred in entering judgment for respondent. [We] reverse and remand for further proceedings in accord with this opinion.

Mr. Chief Justice BURGER, dissenting.

[The] important public policy which underlies [the] right to counsel [would] be gravely jeopardized if every lawyer who takes an "unpopular" case, civil or criminal, would automatically become fair game for irresponsible reporters and editors who might, for example, describe the lawyer as a "mob mouthpiece" for representing a client with a serious prior criminal record. . . .

Mr. Justice DOUGLAS, dissenting.

[The] vehicle for publication in this case was the American Opinion, a most controversial periodical which disseminates the views of the John Birch Society, an organization which many deem to be quite offensive. The subject matter involved "Communist plots," "conspiracies against law enforcement agencies," and the killing of a private citizen by the police. With any such amalgam of controversial elements[,] a jury determination, unpredictable in the most neutral circumstances, becomes [a] virtual roll of the dice separating them from liability for often massive claims of damage. [It] is only the hardy publisher who will engage in discussion in the face of such risk, and the Court's preoccupation with proliferating standards [increases] the risks. [T]he First and Fourteenth Amendments prohibit the imposition of damages [for] this discussion of public affairs. . . .

Mr. Justice BRENNAN, dissenting.

[Matters] of public or general interest do not "suddenly become less so merely because a private individual is involved, or because in some sense the individual did not 'voluntarily' choose to become involved." [The] Court's broad-ranging examples of "actual injury," including impairment of reputation and stand-ing in the community, as well as personal humiliation, and mental anguish and suffering, inevitably allow a jury bent on punishing expression of unpopu-lar views a formidable weapon for doing so. . . . "It is not simply the possibility of a judgment for damages that results in self-censorship. The very possibility of having to engage in litigation, an expensive and protracted process, is threat enough to cause discussion and debate to 'steer far wider of the unlawful zone' thereby keeping protected discussion from public [cognizance]. . . ."

NOTES

1. In *Dun & Bradstreet, Inc. v. Greenmoss Builders, Inc.,* 472 U.S. 749 (1985), in a plurality opinion, the Court held that the states had even more latitude in cases involving private plaintiffs and matters of purely private concern. The case involved a credit reporting agency that inaccurately reported that plaintiff's business was in bankruptcy:

> [It] is speech on "matters of public concern" that is "at the heart of the First Amendment's protection." [In] contrast, speech on matters of purely private concern is of less First Amendment concern. [T]he role of the Constitution in regulating state libel law is far more limited when the concerns that activated *New York Times* and *Gertz* are absent. In such a case, "[t]here is no threat to the free and robust debate of public issues; there is no potential interference with a meaningful dialogue of ideas concerning self-government; and there is no threat of liability causing a reaction of self-censorship by the press. . . ."

> [C]ourts for centuries have allowed juries to presume that some dam-age occurred from many defamatory utterances and publications. This rule furthers the state interest in providing remedies for defamation by ensuring that those remedies are effective. In light of the reduced con-stitutional value of speech involving no matters of public concern, we hold that the state interest adequately supports awards of presumed and punitive damages — even absent a showing of "actual malice."

> "[W]hether [speech] addresses a matter of public concern must be determined by [the expression's] content, form, and context [as] revealed by the whole record." These factors indicate that petitioner's credit report concerns no public issue. It was speech solely in the individual interest of the speaker and its specific business audience. This partic-ular interest warrants no special protection when [the] speech is wholly false and clearly damaging to the victim's business reputation. More-over, since the credit report was made available to only five subscribers, who [could] not disseminate it further, it cannot be said that the report involves any "strong interest in the free flow of commercial information." There is simply no credible argument that this type of credit reporting

requires special protection to ensure that "debate on public issues [will] be uninhibited, robust, and wide-open."

[We] conclude that permitting recovery of presumed and punitive damages in defamation cases absent a showing of "actual malice" does not violate the First Amendment when the defamatory statements do not involve matters of public concern. . . .

Four justices dissented including Mr. Justice Brennan who stated: "Speech about commercial or economic matters [is] an important part [of] public discourse. . . . [It] is difficult to suggest that a bankruptcy is not a subject matter of public concern. . . ."

2. *Defining the Public Figure Concept.* In *Tavoulareas v. Piro*, 817 F.2d 762 (D.C. Cir. 1987), the court drew a distinction between "public figures" and "limited public figures," and held that the President of Mobil Oil Corporation qualified as a limited public figure:

[A] person becomes a general purpose public figure only if he or she is "a well-known 'celebrity,' his name a 'household word.'" Such persons have knowingly relinquished their anonymity in return for fame, fortune, or influence. They are frequently so famous that they "may be able to transfer their recognition and influence from one field to another." Thus, it is reasonable to attribute a public character to all aspects of their lives. William Tavoulareas is a highly prominent individual, especially in business circles, but his celebrity in society at large does not approach that of a well-known athlete or entertainer. . . . The standard as generally applied is a strict one; the Supreme Court has not found anyone to be a general public figure since *Butts*. . . .

[M]any individuals may be public figures for the more limited purpose of certain issues or situations. [We use] a three-step inquiry to identify these limited-purpose public figures. First, [the] controversy must be public both in the sense that "persons actually were discussing" it, and that "persons beyond the immediate participants in the dispute [are likely] to feel the impact of its resolution." Second, [plaintiff's] role in the controversy [must be] more than "trivial or tangential." An individual does not forfeit the full protection of the libel laws merely by stating a position on a controversial issue if he or she is not a principal participant in the debate or is unlikely to have much effect on its resolution. Finally, we determine if the alleged defamation was germane to the plaintiff's participation in the controversy. [T]he touchstone remains whether an individual has "assumed [a] role of especial prominence in the affairs of society [that] invite[s] attention and comment."

"[B]eing an executive within a prominent and influential company does not by itself make one a [limited purpose] public figure." [But] that is not to say that an individual's position as president and chief operating officer of one of the world's largest multinational corporations, with a quarter-million stockholders, is irrelevant to whether that person has "invite[d] attention and comment" with respect to public issues affecting his business dealings. This is especially true when that industry — and the company itself — is at the center of a vigorous public debate touching on a vital national interest. [Tavoulareas] avowedly attempted to "thrust [Mobil and himself] to the forefront" of the national controversy over the state of the oil industry. [Tavoulareas] was not "merely a boardroom president whose vision was limited to the balance sheet. He became an activist, projecting his own image and that of [Mobil] far beyond the dollars and cents aspects of marketing."

3. *More on defining the "public figure" concept.* In *Cole v. Westinghouse Broadcasting Co., Inc.*, 435 N.E.2d 1021 (Mass. 1982), a television reporter was deemed to be a public figure. However, in *Time, Inc. v. Firestone*, 424 U.S. 448 (1976), the Court rejected public figure status for a petitioner in a divorce proceeding: "Dissolution of a marriage through judicial proceedings is not the sort of 'public controversy' referred to in *Gertz*, even though the marital difficulties of extremely wealthy individuals may be of interest to some portion of the reading public. Nor did respondent freely choose to publicize issues as to the propriety of her married life. She was compelled to go to court by the State in order to obtain legal release from the bonds of matrimony. [Her] actions, both in instituting the litigation and in its conduct, were quite different from those of General Walker in *Curtis Publishing Co*. She assumed no 'special prominence in the resolution of public questions. We hold respondent was not a 'public figure'" Mr. Justice Brennan dissented: "[At] stake in the present case is the ability of the press to report to the citizenry the events transpiring in the Nation's judicial systems."

4. In *Lerman v. Flynt Distributing Co., Inc.*, 745 F.2d 123 (2d Cir. 1984), defendant published an article about plaintiff's husband's movie entitled "The World is Full of Married Men." The article contained photographs of an actress from the film who appeared topless in one picture and in an "orgy" scene in the other. The caption identifies the photos as being Ms. Lerman, who sued the magazine for defamation. The court found that she was a limited purpose public figure: "[Ms.] Lerman has achieved international renown as the author of nine novels. Her books are decidedly controversial in nature because of her firm conviction — made the focal point of her comments to the press — that there is a pervasive inequality in the treatment accorded to females vis-à-vis males. This topic greatly appeals to the public since her books sell in the millions, are full of descriptions of sex, including deviate sex and orgies, and are heavily laden with four-letter words."

5. In *Hutchinson v. Proxmire*, 443 U.S. 111 (1979), Senator William Proxmire awarded a research behavioral scientist his "Golden Fleece" award. The award was designed to publicize the most egregious examples of wasteful governmental spending. The second such award, in April 1975, went to the National Science Foundation, the National Aeronautics and Space Administration, and

the Office of Naval Research, for spending almost half a million dollars during the preceding seven years to fund Hutchinson's research involving monkeys. Senator Proxmire stated: "[i]n fact, the good doctor has made a fortune from his monkeys and in the process made a monkey out of the American taxpayer." The Court held that the scientist was not a public figure: "Hutchinson did not thrust himself or his views into public controversy to influence others. Respondents [point] to concern about general public expenditures. But that concern is shared by most and relates to most public expenditures. . . . Neither [Hutchinson's] applications for federal grants nor his publications in professional journals can be said to have invited that degree of public attention and comment on his receipt of federal grants essential to meet the public figure level. . . ."

PROBLEMS

1. *Does the wife of a public figure automatically become a public figure by virtue of her status as a wife?* Johnny Carson and his wife, Joanna Holland, sued Allied News Company and National Insider, Inc., for an article which alleged that "Johnny Carson Is Moving 'Tonight Show' To Hollywood So He Could Be Closer To The Woman Who Broke Up His Marriage." Johnny Carson was a public figure due to his status as an entertainer. Is the wife also a public figure, if she is not famous in her own right? *See Carson v. Allied News Co.*, 529 F.2d 206 (7th Cir. 1976).

2. *Belli v. Orlando Daily Newspapers, Inc.*, 393 U.S. 825 (1968), involved Melvin Belli, an attorney of national prominence, who was well known in the legal profession for his pioneering in the development of demonstrative evidence as a trial tactic and his success in obtaining large judgments for plaintiffs in personal injury suits. He is known to the general public because of his representation of Jack Ruby and others in the public eye. In light of *Gertz* and *Firestone*, would Belli be considered a "public figure" so that he would have to prove "actual malice" in order to recover?

3. Why wasn't Mrs. Firestone a "public figure" given her involvement in Palm Beach society? Consider Mr. Justice Marshall's dissent in *Firestone*:

> [Mrs.] Firestone [was] "prominent among the '400' of Palm Beach society," and an "active (member) of the sporting set," whose activities predictably attracted the attention of a sizable portion of the public. [Mrs.] Firestone's appearances in the press were [frequent] enough to warrant her subscribing to a press-clipping service. . . . Mr. and Mrs. Firestone's "marital difficulties [were] well-known," and the lawsuit became "a veritable cause celèbre in social circles across the country." The 17-month trial and related events attracted national news coverage, and elicited no fewer than [88] articles in [three local newspapers]. Far from shunning the publicity, Mrs. Firestone held several press conferences in the course of the proceedings. [These] facts [warrant] the conclusion that Mary Alice Firestone was a "public figure" for purposes of

reports on the judicial proceedings she initiated. . . . If these actions [fail] to establish [that she] "voluntarily exposed [herself] to increased risk of injury from defamatory falsehood," surely they are sufficient to entitle the press to act on the assumption that she did. . . .

Do you agree with the majority or with Mr. Justice Marshall?

4. *Does a doctor become a "limited public figure" by testifying at Food and Drug Administration (FDA) hearings on a drug?* In response to allegations that the pregnancy drug, Bendectin, caused birth defects, the FDA held hearings on the safety of the drug. Plaintiff, a medical doctor and an expert on birth defects, testified at the hearings. In reporting on the hearings, the journal Science ran an article entitled "How Safe Is Bendectin?" which contained the following statements about plaintiff (and other expert witnesses): "These expert witnesses [at the FDA hearing] included William McBride of the Women's Hospital in Sydney, Australia, who was paid $5,000 a day to testify in Orlando. In contrast, [Merrell Dow] pays witnesses $250 to $500 a day, and the most it has ever paid is $1,000 a day." Should the doctor be regarded as a "limited public figure"? *See McBride v. Merrell Dow and Pharmaceuticals, Inc.*, 800 F.2d 1208 (D.C. Cir. 1986).

5. *Is a former secret agent a "public figure" within the meaning of the* New York Times *test?* In 1974, respondent Reader's Digest Association, Inc., published a book entitled *KGB, the Secret Work of Soviet Agents* (KGB), written by respondent John Barron. The book describes the Soviet Union's espionage organization and chronicles its activities since World War II. In a passage referring to disclosures by "royal commissions in Canada and Australia, and official investigations in Great Britain and the United States," the book contains the following statements relating to petitioner Ilya Wolston: "Among Soviet agents identified in the United States were . . . Ilya Wolston." In addition, the index to KGB lists petitioner as follows: "Wolston, Ilya, Soviet agent in U.S." Is plaintiff one of those who have "thrust themselves to the forefront of particular public controversies in order to influence the resolution of the issues involved"? *See Wolston v. Reader's Digest Ass'n, Inc.*, 443 U.S. 157 (1979).

D. APPLICATION OF THE "ACTUAL MALICE" STANDARD

ST. AMANT v. THOMPSON
390 U.S. 727 (1968)

Mr. Justice WHITE delivered the opinion of the Court.

[P]etitioner St. Amant, a candidate for public office, made a televised speech in Baton Rouge, Louisiana. In the course of this speech, St. Amant read a series of questions which he had put to J.D. Albin, a member of a Teamsters Union local, and Albin's answers to those questions. The exchange concerned the allegedly nefarious activities of E.G. Partin, the president of the local, and the alleged relationship between Partin and St. Amant's political opponent. One of Albin's answers concerned his efforts to prevent Partin from secreting union records; in this answer Albin referred to Herman A. Thompson, an East Baton Rouge Parish deputy sheriff and respondent here:

> Now, we knew that this safe was gonna be moved that night, but imagine our predicament, knowing of Ed's connections with the Sheriff's office through Herman Thompson, who made recent visits to the Hall to see Ed. We also knew of money that had passed hands between Ed and Herman Thompson. . . . We also knew of his connections with State Trooper Lieutenant Joe Green. We knew we couldn't get any help from there and we didn't know how far that he was involved in the Sheriff's office or the State Police office through that, and it was out of the jurisdiction of the City Police.

Thompson promptly brought suit for defamation, claiming that the publication had "impute[d] gross misconduct" and "infer[red] conduct of the most nefarious nature." [In the case, tried prior to the decision in *New York Times*] the trial judge ruled in Thompson's favor and awarded $5,000 in damages. . . .

Purporting to apply the *New York Times* malice standard, the Louisiana Supreme Court ruled that St. Amant had broadcast false information about Thompson recklessly, though not knowingly. Several reasons were given for this conclusion. St. Amant had no personal knowledge of Thompson's activities; he relied solely on Albin's affidavit although the record was silent as to Albin's reputation for veracity; he failed to verify the information with those in the union office who might have known the facts; he gave no consideration to whether or not the statements defamed Thompson and went ahead heedless of the consequences; and he mistakenly believed he had no responsibility for the broadcast because he was merely quoting Albin's words.

These considerations fall short of proving St. Amant's reckless disregard for the accuracy of his statements about Thompson. "Reckless disregard," it is true, cannot be fully encompassed in one infallible definition. . . . Our cases, however, have furnished meaningful guidance. . . . [R]eckless conduct is not measured by whether a reasonably prudent man would have published, or would have investigated before publishing. There must be sufficient evidence to permit the conclusion that the defendant in fact entertained serious doubts as to the truth of his publication. Publishing with such doubts shows reckless disregard for truth or falsity and demonstrates actual malice.

It may be said that such a test puts a premium on ignorance, encourages the irresponsible publisher not to inquire, and permits the issue to be determined by the defendant's testimony that he published the statement in good faith and unaware of its probable falsity. Concededly the reckless disregard standard may permit recovery in fewer situations than would a rule that publishers must satisfy the standard of the reasonable man or the prudent publisher. But *New York Times* [emphasized] that the stake of the people in public business and the conduct of public officials is so great that neither the defense of truth nor the standard of ordinary care would protect against self-censorship and thus adequately implement First Amendment policies. Neither lies nor false communications serve the ends of the First Amendment, and no one suggests their desirability or further proliferation. But to insure the ascertainment and publication of the truth about public affairs, it is essential that the First Amendment protect some erroneous publications as well as true ones. We adhere to [the] line which our cases have drawn between false communications which are protected and those which are not.

The defendant in a defamation action brought by a public official cannot, however, automatically insure a favorable verdict by testifying that he published with a belief that the statements were true. The finder of fact must determine whether the publication was indeed made in good faith. Professions of good faith will be unlikely to prove persuasive, for example, where a story is fabricated by the defendant, is the product of his imagination, or is based wholly on an unverified anonymous telephone call. Nor will they be likely to prevail when the publisher's allegations are so inherently improbable that only a reckless man would have put them in circulation. Likewise, recklessness may be found where there are obvious reasons to doubt the veracity of the informant or the accuracy of his reports.

By no proper test of reckless disregard was St. Amant's broadcast a reckless publication about a public officer. Nothing [indicates] an awareness by St. Amant of the probable falsity of Albin's statement about Thompson. Failure to investigate does not in itself establish bad faith. St. Amant's mistake about his probable legal liability does not evidence a doubtful mind on his part. That he failed to realize the import of what he broadcast — and was thus "heedless" of the consequences for Thompson — is similarly colorless. Closer to the mark are considerations of Albin's reliability. However, the most the state court could say was that there was no evidence in the record of Albin's reputation for veracity, and this fact merely underlines the failure of Thompson's evidence to demonstrate a low community assessment of Albin's trustworthiness or unsatisfactory experience with him by St. Amant.

Other facts in this record support our view. St. Amant made his broadcast in June 1962. He had known Albin since October 1961, when he first met with members of the dissident Teamsters faction. St. Amant testified that he had verified other aspects of Albin's information and that he had affidavits from others. Moreover Albin swore to his answers, first in writing and later in the presence of newsmen. According to Albin, he was prepared to substantiate his charges. St. Amant knew that Albin was engaged in an internal struggle in the union; Albin seemed to St. Amant to be placing himself in personal danger by publicly airing the details of the dispute.

Because the state court misunderstood and misapplied the actual malice standard which must be observed in a public official's defamation action, the judgment is reversed and the case remanded for further proceedings not inconsistent with this opinion.

Reversed and remanded.

Mr. Justice FORTAS, dissenting.

[The] affidavit that petitioner broadcast contained a seriously libelous statement directed against respondent. [Petitioner's] casual, careless, callous use of the libel cannot be rationalized as resulting from the heat of a campaign. Under *New York Times*, this libel was broadcast by petitioner with "actual malice". . . .

[The] First Amendment is not a shelter for the character assassinator. [The] occupation of public officeholder does not forfeit one's membership in the human race. The public official should be subject to severe scrutiny and to free and open criticism. But if he is needlessly, heedlessly, falsely accused of crime, he should have a remedy in law. *New York Times* does not preclude this minimal standard of civilized living.

Petitioner had a duty here to check the reliability of the libelous statement about respondent. If he had made a good-faith check, [he] should be protected even if the statement were false, because the interest of public officials in their reputation must endure this degree of assault. But since he made no check, [*New York Times*] does not prohibit recovery.

NOTES

1. *Does the "actual malice" standard provide too little protection to the media?* In *Herbert v. Lando*, 441 U.S. 153 (1979), in an effort to prove that an article was published with "actual malice," plaintiff sought discovery of the following information relating to an article published by Lando:

   1. Lando's conclusions during his research and investigations regarding people or leads to be pursued, or not to be pursued, in connection with the '60 Minutes' segment and the Atlantic Monthly article;

   2. Lando's conclusions about facts imparted by interviewees and his state of mind with respect to the veracity of persons interviewed;

   3. The basis for conclusions where Lando testified that he did reach a conclusion concerning the veracity of persons, information or events;

   4. Conversations between Lando and Wallace about matter to be included or excluded from the broadcast publication; and

   5. Lando's intentions as manifested by his decision to include or exclude certain material.

Defendant objected to the discovery on the grounds that it would unduly intrude into a news gatherer's editorial processes. The Court overruled the objection: "[O]ur cases [contemplate] examination of the editorial process to prove the necessary awareness of probable falsehood. . . ." The Court rejected the notion that "frank discussion among reporters and editors will be dampened and sound editorial judgment endangered if such exchanges, oral or written, are subject to inquiry by defamation plaintiffs." "Lando's deposition [continued] intermittently for [a] year and filled 26 volumes containing nearly 3,000 pages and 240 exhibits. [T]here were substantial legal fees, and Lando and his associates were diverted from news gathering and reporting for a significant amount of time." In *Dun & Bradstreet*, Justice White offered the following thoughts about *Lando*: "[T]he burden that plaintiffs must meet invites long and complicated discovery involving detailed investigation of the workings of the press, how a news story is developed, and the state of mind of the reporter and publisher. That kind of litigation is very expensive. I suspect that the press would be no worse off financially if the common-law rules were to apply and if the judiciary was careful to insist that damages awards be kept within bounds. . . ." Do you agree with Justice White?

2. *Confidentiality of Sources. Desai v. Hersh*, 954 F.2d 1408 (7th Cir. 1992), held that a journalist could not protect the confidentiality of his sources in a defamation action: "[I]n defamation actions in which a plaintiff must establish 'malice' on the part of a defendant, [the] reporter's privilege must give way to disclosure."

3. *Burden of proof.* In *Philadelphia Newspapers, Inc. v. Hepps*, 475 U.S. 767 (1986), the Court held that, when a newspaper publishes matters of public concern, a private-figure plaintiff cannot recover damages without proving that the statements are false: "There will always be instances when the factfinding process will be unable to resolve conclusively whether the speech is true or false; it is in those cases that the burden of proof is dispositive. [W]here the scales are in [an] uncertain balance, we believe that the Constitution requires us to tip them in favor of protecting true speech. [T]he common-law presumption that defamatory speech is false cannot stand when a plaintiff seeks damages against a media defendant for speech of public concern." Mr. Justice Stevens dissented: "[T]he overriding concern for reliable protection of truthful statements must make room for "the compensation of individuals for the harm inflicted on them by defamatory falsehood."

PROBLEM

A prior problem focused on the mayor of a local city who was allegedly defamed by the local newspaper (which alleged corruption and extra-martial affairs). Notwithstanding the fact that the mayor will have to satisfy the "actual malice" standard, the mayor has decided to sue the newspaper. You know that the allegations are untrue. How will you go about proving that the newspaper acted with "actual malice"?

MASSON v. NEW YORKER MAGAZINE, INC.
501 U.S. 496 (1991)

Justice KENNEDY delivered the opinion of the Court.

[Petitioner Jeffrey Masson] came to know Dr. Kurt Eissler, head of the Sigmund Freud Archives, and Dr. Anna Freud, daughter of Sigmund Freud and a major psychoanalyst in her own right. The Sigmund Freud Archives [is] a repository for materials about Freud, including [his] writings, letters, and personal library. . . .

[Eissler] and Anna Freud hired petitioner as Projects Director of the Archives. After assuming his post, petitioner became disillusioned with Freudian psychology. In a 1981 lecture[,] he advanced his theories of Freud. Soon after, the Board of the Archives terminated petitioner as Projects Director.

Respondent Janet Malcolm is [a] contributor to respondent The New Yorker, a weekly magazine, [and did] a series of interviews with petitioner on his relationship with the Archives]. Based on the interviews and other sources, Malcolm wrote a lengthy article. One of Malcolm's narrative devices consists of enclosing lengthy passages in quotation marks. . . .

The New Yorker published Malcolm's piece in December 1983, as a two-part series. In 1984, [respondent] Alfred A. Knopf, Inc., published the entire work as a book, entitled In the Freud Archives. [The book portrayed Masson] in a most unflattering light. According to one reviewer, "Masson the promising psychoanalytic scholar emerges gradually, as a grandiose egotist — mean-spirited, self-serving, full of braggadocio, impossibly arrogant and, in the end, a self-destructive fool. But it is not Janet Malcolm who calls him such: his own words reveal this psychological profile — a self-portrait offered to us through the efforts of an observer and listener who is, surely, as wise as any in the psychoanalytic profession." Coles, *Freudianism Confronts Its Malcontents*, BOSTON GLOBE, May 27, 1984, pp. 58, 60. [Petitioner] brought an action for libel under California law in [federal district court].

Each passage before us purports to quote a statement made by petitioner during the interviews. Yet in each instance no identical statement appears in the more than 40 hours of taped interviews. Petitioner complains that Malcolm fabricated all but one passage; with respect to that passage, he claims Malcolm omitted a crucial portion, rendering the remainder misleading.

[In] general, quotation marks around a passage indicate to the reader that the passage reproduces the speaker's words verbatim. They inform the reader that he or she is reading the statement of the speaker, not a paraphrase or other indirect interpretation by an author. By providing this information, quotations add authority to the statement and credibility to the author's work. . . .

A fabricated quotation may injure reputation in at least two senses. . . . First, the quotation might injure because it attributes an untrue factual assertion to the speaker. An example would be a fabricated quotation of a public official admitting he had been convicted of a serious crime. . . . [Second,] regardless of the truth or falsity of the factual matters asserted[,] the attribution may result in injury [because] the manner of expression or even the fact that the statement was made indicates a negative personal trait or an attitude the speaker does not hold. [O]ne need not determine whether petitioner is or is not the greatest analyst who ever lived in order to determine that it might have injured his reputation to be reported as having so proclaimed. [A] self-condemnatory quotation may carry more force than criticism by another. . . .

Of course, quotations do not always convey that the speaker actually said or wrote the quoted material. [An] acknowledgment that the work is so-called docudrama or historical fiction, or that it recreates conversations from memory, not from recordings, might indicate that the quotations should not be interpreted as the actual statements of the speaker to whom they are attributed.

The work at issue here [provides] the reader no clue that the quotations are being used as a rhetorical device or to paraphrase the speaker's actual statements. To the contrary, the work purports to be nonfiction, the result of numerous interviews. [Further,] the work was published in The New Yorker, a magazine which at the relevant time seemed to enjoy a reputation for scrupulous factual accuracy. [A] trier of fact [could] find that the reasonable reader would understand the quotations to be nearly verbatim reports of statements made by the subject.

[In] some sense, any alteration of a verbatim quotation is false. But writers and reporters by necessity alter what people say, at the very least to eliminate grammatical and syntactical infelicities. If every alteration constituted the falsity required to prove actual malice, the practice of journalism [would] require a radical change, one inconsistent with our precedents and First Amendment principles. Petitioner concedes [that] "minor changes to correct for grammar or syntax" do not amount to falsity for purposes of proving actual malice. . . .

[Even] if a journalist has tape recorded the spoken statement of a public figure, the full and exact statement will be reported in only rare circumstances. [If] a speaker makes an obvious misstatement, for example by unconscious substitution of one name for another, a journalist might alter the speaker's words but preserve his intended meaning. And conversely, an exact quotation out of context can distort meaning, although the speaker did use each reported word.

[The] common law of libel takes but one approach to the question of falsity, regardless of the form of the communication. It overlooks minor inaccuracies and concentrates upon substantial truth. [The] burden is upon petitioner to prove falsity. [Minor] inaccuracies do not amount to falsity so long as "the substance, the gist, the sting, of the libelous charge be justified." [A] deliberate alteration of the words uttered by a plaintiff does not equate with knowledge of falsity [unless] the alteration results in a material change in the meaning conveyed by the statement. The use of quotations to attribute words not in fact spoken bears in a most important way on that inquiry, but it is not dispositive in every case.

[Q]uotations may be a devastating instrument for conveying false meaning. [R]eaders of In the Freud Archives may have found Malcolm's portrait of petitioner especially damning because [it] appeared to be a self-portrait, told by petitioner in his own words. And if the alterations of petitioner's words gave a different meaning to the statements, bearing upon their defamatory character, then the device of quotations might well be critical in finding the words actionable.

[The] protection for rational interpretation serves First Amendment principles by allowing an author the interpretive license that is necessary when relying upon ambiguous sources. Where, however, a writer uses a quotation, and where a reasonable reader would conclude that the quotation purports to be a verbatim repetition of a statement by the speaker, the quotation marks indicate that the author [is] attempting to convey what the speaker said. . . . Were we to assess quotations under a rational interpretation standard, we would give journalists the freedom to place statements in their subjects' mouths without fear of liability. [This standard] would diminish to a great degree the trustworthiness of the printed word, and eliminate the real meaning of quotations. . . . Newsworthy figures might become more wary of journalists, knowing that any comment could be transmuted and attributed to the subject, so long as some bounds of rational interpretation were not exceeded. We would ill serve the values of the First Amendment if we were to grant near absolute, constitutional protection for such a practice. . . .

We must determine whether the published passages differ materially in meaning from the tape recorded statements so as to create an issue of fact for a jury as to falsity.

(a) "Intellectual Gigolo." "[F]airly read, intellectual gigolo suggests someone who forsakes intellectual integrity in exchange for pecuniary or other gain." A reasonable jury could find a material difference between the meaning of this passage and petitioner's tape-recorded statement that he was considered "much too junior within the hierarchy of analysis, for these important training analysts to be caught dead with [him]." . . .

(b) "Sex, Women, Fun." This passage presents a closer question. The "sex, women, fun" quotation offers a very different picture of petitioner's plans for Maresfield Gardens than his remark that "Freud's library alone is priceless." Petitioner's other tape-recorded remarks did indicate that he and another analyst planned to have great parties at the Freud house and, [to] "pass women on to each other." We cannot conclude as a matter of law that these remarks bear the same substantial meaning as the quoted passage's suggestion that petitioner would make the Freud house a place of "sex, women, fun."

(c) "It Sounded Better." We agree [that] any difference between petitioner's tape-recorded statement that he "just liked" the name Moussaieff, and the quotation that "it sounded better" [is] immaterial. Although Malcolm did not include all of petitioner's lengthy explanation of his name change, she did convey the gist of that explanation [and] did not materially alter the meaning of his statement.

(d) "I Don't Know Why I Put It In." Malcolm quotes petitioner as saying that he "tacked on at the last minute" a "totally gratuitous" remark about the "sterility of psychoanalysis" in an academic paper, and that he did so for no particular reason. [Petitioner admits] that the remark was "possibly [a] gratuitously offensive way to end a paper to a group of analysts," but when asked why he included the remark, he answered "[because] it was [true]. I really believe it." Malcolm's version contains material differences from petitioner's statement, [and] the alteration results in a statement that could injure a scholar's reputation.

(e) "Greatest Analyst Who Ever Lived." While petitioner predict[ed] that his theories would do irreparable damage to the practice of psychoanalysis, and [suggested] that no other analyst shared his views, no tape-recorded statement appears to contain the substance or the arrogant and unprofessional tone apparent in this quotation. A material difference exists between the quotation and the tape-recorded statements, and a jury could find that the difference exposed petitioner to contempt, ridicule or obloquy.

(f) "He Had The Wrong Man." The quoted version makes it appear as if petitioner rejected a plea to remain in stoic silence and do "the honorable thing." The tape-recorded version indicates that petitioner rejected a plea supported by far more varied motives: Eissler told petitioner that not only would silence be "the honorable thing," but petitioner would "save face," and might be rewarded for that silence with eventual reinstatement. Petitioner described himself as willing to undergo a scandal in order to shine the light of publicity upon the actions of the Freud Archives, while Malcolm would have petitioner describe himself as a person who was "the wrong man" to do "the honorable thing." This difference is material, a jury might find it defamatory, and, [there] is evidence to support a finding of deliberate or reckless falsification.

[The] judgment of the Court of Appeals is reversed, and the case is remanded for further proceedings consistent with this opinion.

It is so ordered.

Justice WHITE, with whom Justice SCALIA joins, concurring in part and dissenting in part.

[T]he use of quotation marks [asserts] that the person spoke the words as quoted. [The] reporter, Malcolm, wrote that Masson said certain things that she knew Masson did not say. [W]e need to go no further to conclude that the defendants in this case were not entitled to summary judgment on the issue of malice with respect to any of the six erroneous quotations.

[T]he Court states that deliberate misquotation does not amount [to] malice unless it results in a material change in the meaning conveyed by the statement. This ignores the fact [that] reporting a known falsehood — here the knowingly false attribution — is sufficient proof of malice. The falsehood, apparently, must be substantial; the reporter may lie a little, but not too much.

[D]efendants' motion for summary judgment based on lack of malice should not have been granted on any of the six [quotations].

E. FACT VERSUS OPINION

Should a distinction be made between statements of "fact" and statements of "opinion"? Consider the next case.

MILKOVICH v. LORAIN JOURNAL CO.
497 U.S. 1 (1990)

Chief Justice REHNQUIST delivered the opinion of the Court.

Respondent J. Theodore Diadiun authored [a newspaper article which implied] that petitioner Michael Milkovich, [a] high school wrestling coach, lied under oath in a judicial proceeding about an incident involving [his] team which occurred at a wrestling match. Petitioner sued Diadiun and the newspaper for libel. . . .

[Respondents] would have us [recognize First Amendment protection] for defamatory statements which are categorized as "opinion" as opposed to "fact." For this proposition they rely principally on the following dictum from our opinion in *Gertz*: "Under the First Amendment there is no such thing as a false idea. However pernicious an opinion may seem, we depend for its correction not on the conscience of judges and juries but on the competition of other ideas. But there is no constitutional value in false statements of fact." [W]e do not think this passage [was] intended to create a wholesale [exemption] for anything that might be labeled "opinion." Not only would such an interpretation be contrary to the tenor and context of the passage, but it would also ignore the fact that expressions of "opinion" may often imply an assertion of objective fact. [If] a speaker says, "In my opinion John Jones is a liar," he implies a knowledge of facts which lead to the conclusion that Jones told an untruth. . . .

[W]e think the "'breathing space'" which "'[f]reedoms of expression require in order to survive'" is adequately secured by existing constitutional doctrine without the creation of an artificial dichotomy between "opinion" and fact. [A] statement on matters of public concern must be provable as false before there can be liability under state defamation law, at least [where] a media defendant is involved. . . . [Our] cases provide protection for statements that cannot "reasonably [be] interpreted as stating actual facts" about an individual. This provides assurance that public debate will not suffer for lack of "imaginative expression" or the "rhetorical hyperbole" which has traditionally added much to the discourse of our Nation.

The *New York Times* [culpability] requirements further ensure that debate on public issues remains "uninhibited, robust, and wide-open." [W]here a statement of "opinion" on a matter of public concern reasonably implies false and defamatory facts regarding public figures or officials, those individuals must show that such statements were made with knowledge of their false implications or with reckless disregard of their truth. Similarly, where [a] statement involves a private figure on a matter of public concern, a plaintiff must show that the false connotations were made with some level of fault as required by *Gertz*. [Enhanced] appellate review [provides] assurance that the foregoing determinations will be made [so] as not to "constitute a forbidden intrusion [into] free expression."

[T]he connotation that petitioner committed perjury is sufficiently factual to be susceptible of being proved true or false. A determination whether petitioner lied [can] be made on a core of objective evidence by comparing, inter alia, petitioner's testimony before the OHSAA board with his subsequent testimony before the trial court. . . .

[The] judgment of the Ohio Court of Appeals is reversed, and the case is remanded for further proceedings not inconsistent with this opinion.

Reversed.

Justice BRENNAN, with whom Justice MARSHALL joins, dissenting.

[No] reasonable reader could understand Diadiun to be impliedly asserting — as fact — that Milkovich had perjured himself. Nor could such a reader infer that Diadiun had further information about Milkovich's court testimony on which his belief was based. It is plain from the column that Diadiun did not attend the court hearing. Diadiun also clearly had no detailed second hand information about what Milkovich had said in court. Instead, what suffices for "detail" and "color" are quotations from the OHSAA hearing — old news compared to the court decision which prompted the column — and a vague quotation from an OHSAA commissioner. Readers could see that Diadiun was focused on the court's reversal of the OHSAA's decision and was angrily supposing what must have led to it.

Even the insinuation that Milkovich had repeated, in court, a more plausible version of the misrepresentations he had made at the OHSAA hearing is preceded by the cautionary term "apparently" — an unmistakable sign that Diadiun did not know what Milkovich had actually said in court. "[C]autionary language or interrogatories of this type put the reader on notice that what is being read is opinion and thus weaken any inference that the author possesses knowledge of damaging, undisclosed [facts]. In a word, when the reasonable reader encounters cautionary language, he tends to 'discount that which follows.'" . . .

Furthermore, the tone and format of the piece notify readers to expect speculation and personal judgment. The tone is pointed, exaggerated, and heavily laden with emotional rhetoric and moral outrage. Diadiun never says [that] Milkovich committed perjury. He says that "[a]nyone who attended the meet [knows] in his heart" that Milkovich lied — obvious hyperbole as Diadiun does not purport to have researched what everyone who attended the meet knows in his heart. [Punishing] such conjecture protects reputation only at the cost of expunging a genuinely useful mechanism for public debate. "In a society which takes seriously the principle that government rests upon the consent of the governed, freedom of the press must be the most cherished tenet."

NOTE

In *Buckley v. Littell*, 539 F.2d 882, 895 (2d Cir. 1976), *cert. denied*, 429 U.S. 1062 (1977), the court held that the use of the term "fascist" could not "be regarded as [a] statement of fact [because] of the tremendous imprecision of the meaning and usage of [this] term."

PROBLEMS

1. *Is it defamatory to allege that a real estate developer engaged in "blackmail"?* The plaintiff, a developer, negotiated with the Greenbelt City Council to obtain zoning variances that would allow the construction of high-density housing on his land. At the same time the city was attempting to acquire another tract of land owned by plaintiff for the construction of a new high school. Extensive litigation concerning compensation for the school site seemed imminent, and the concurrent negotiations obviously provided both parties considerable bargaining leverage. These joint negotiations evoked a great deal of controversy and produced several tumultuous city council meetings. Two news articles in consecutive weekly editions of the local paper stated that at the public meetings some people had characterized plaintiff's negotiating position as "blackmail." The word appeared several times, both with and without quotation marks, and was used once as a subheading within a news story. Were the remarks defamatory? How might defendant argue that they were not defamatory? *See Greenbelt Cooperative Publishing Ass'n, Inc. v. Bresler*, 398 U.S. 6 (1970).

2. Defendant Darrel "Mouse" Davis, in a statement to newspaper reporters, called the plaintiff a "sleaze-bag agent" who "slimed up from the bayou." Plaintiff is an agent for professional football players. Plaintiff sued seeking damages. Also named as defendants were a news editor and two newspaper companies whose papers published Davis' remarks. Do such statements constitute action-

able defamation under *Milkovoich*? *See Henderson v. Times Mirror Co.*, 669 F. Supp. 356 (D. Colo. 1987).

3. [Plaintiffs] and defendant owned separate condominium units at the Ocean Club in Atlantic City. They both attended a board meeting of the condominium association. Plaintiff husband briefly addressed the Board, and when his wife got up to speak, defendant said "Don't listen to those people. They don't like Jews. She's a bitch." Defendant's statements were wholly unrelated to plaintiffs' remarks to the Board (which focused on the condominium's business and did not implicate defendant). At trial, defendant testified that he had been told by another resident at Ocean Club that she had heard plaintiff husband make an anti-Semitic remark. Defendant could not remember the exact nature of the remark. Another witness stated that she had once heard plaintiff husband make a comment about Jews that she considered derogatory (although she could not remember the comment), and she told defendant about the comment. After *Milkovich*, are such statements actionable? *See Ward v. Zelikovsky*, 623 A.2d 285 (N.J. Super. Ct. App. Div. 1993).

Chapter 18

PRIVACY

In everyday speech, people often talk about "invasions of privacy." And as you might suspect, the law does recognize and protect people's legitimate privacy interests. Some acts that intrude upon the privacy of others, such as industrial espionage or the "Peeping Tom," are punished by the criminal law. However, the primary means of protecting privacy is tort law. A person whose privacy interests are invaded may, in certain situations, be able to recover from the offender.

The privacy tort has proven exceptionally difficult in practice. One of the problems is that the word "privacy" actually can mean several different things. In response, the courts have crafted a tort that can take several different forms.

A. OVERVIEW OF THE "RIGHT TO BE LEFT ALONE"

Deckle McLean
PRIVACY AND ITS INVASION 1-4 (1995)

Privacy has always been important, but it has always been taken for granted. As a result, very few people have singled it out for attention. It did not seem worth it. This is changing.

Prior to the twentieth century, privacy was a feature of privilege, owned by the wealthy, or a fringe benefit — or curse — of deep rural life. It entered conversation as light observation but not at depth: "They're a private family"; "She hardly needs any privacy at all"; "Leave me alone so that I can work this out in private." Famous philosophers did not address the subject. In fact, philosophers and religious figures everywhere ignored it.

Privacy and its invasion were features of other issues, but were not isolated from these other issues. . . .

While privacy was then an element embedded in other issues, in the twentieth century it has been pressed forward as a concept that demands individual attention. Probably, a combination of the following forces accounts for the change. First, some methods of violating privacy were refined during the twentieth century: Bureaucratic efficiency grew, and electronic data processing was perfected. Second, because progress was made in addressing such recognized issues as women's inequality, class conflict, caste formation, racial injustice, religious intolerance, local political tyranny, and child labor, privacy itself was left visible in the cleared underbrush. Third, aspirations for privacy increased in the industrially advanced countries as the general level of wealth rose. Many people began to think of themselves as higher in class than they had been and to demand a privilege that higher classes appeared always to have had. Fourth, the principal challenges facing large populations underwent a significant change from gross physical, economic, or political challenges to internal goals, such as self-improvement and service to others. . . .

Privacy is difficult to discuss for several reasons, one being that the concept of privacy will always be elusive. Another is that privacy has been a target of concentrated attention only for decades, and language has not caught up with the challenge of discussing it. Privacy also presents a valuational problem because many people are not confident that privacy is good, even as they know they want it. . . .

Any discussion of privacy is made more difficult by the newness of the subject. Privacy is about 100 years old as a legal or political issue. The article by Samuel Warren and Louis Brandeis that began the development of American privacy law was published in 1890 in the *Harvard Law Review*. . . . Comparable ideals — liberty, equality, representative government, truth as a defense to libel, free speech and press, religious freedom — took far longer than a century to evolve. . . .

STIEN v. MARRIOT OWNERSHIP RESORTS, INC.
944 P.2d 374 (Utah Ct. App. 1977)

The current formulation of privacy law has been influenced to a large degree by Dean William L. Prosser, who illuminated the law of privacy in a 1960 law review article. *See* William L. Prosser, *Privacy*, 48 CAL. L. REV. 383 (1960). Instead of just one tort, Dean Prosser wrote, the law of privacy

> comprises four distinct kinds of invasion of four different interests of the plaintiff, which are tied together by the common name, but otherwise have almost nothing in common except that each represents an interference with the right of the plaintiff, in the phrase coined by Judge Cooley, "to be let alone."

According to Dean Prosser, the four privacy torts are: (1) intrusion upon the plaintiff's seclusion or solitude, or into plaintiff's private affairs, (2) appropriation, for the defendant's advantage, of the plaintiff's name or likeness, (3) public disclosure of embarrassing private facts about the plaintiff, and (4) publicity which places the plaintiff in a false light in the public eye. This characterization of the privacy torts was later adopted by the Restatement, *see* RESTATEMENT (SECOND) OF TORTS §§ 652A-652E, as well as by a number of states. . . .

[I]n order to establish a claim of intrusion upon seclusion, the plaintiff must prove two elements by a preponderance of the evidence: (1) that there was "an intentional substantial intrusion, physically or otherwise, upon the solitude or seclusion of the complaining party," and (2) that the intrusion "would be highly offensive to the reasonable person." This holding comports with the view expressed in the Restatement. . . .

[In order to recover for appropriation of name or likeness, plaintiff must] establish three elements: (1) appropriation, (2) of another's name or likeness that has some "intrinsic value," (3) for the use or benefit of another. . . .

The third of the privacy torts is that of publicity given to private facts. Dean Prosser synthesized from the case law three elements for this tort:

(1) the disclosure of the private facts must be a public disclosure and not a private one;

(2) the facts disclosed to the public must be private facts, and not public ones; and

(3) the matter made public must be one that would be highly offensive and objectionable to a reasonable person of ordinary sensibilities.

The Restatement added to these requirements the notion that the public must not have a legitimate interest in having the information made available. "It is important to stress that this privacy tort permits recovery for truthful disclosures." . . .

The "false light" privacy tort provides that one is subject to liability to another for invasion of privacy if (1) he or she

gives publicity to a matter concerning another that places the other before the public in a false light[; (2)] the false light in which the other was placed would be highly offensive to a reasonable person[;] and [(3)] the actor had knowledge of or acted in reckless disregard as to the falsity of the publicized matter and the false light in which the other would be placed.

Russell v. Thomson Newspapers, Inc., 842 P.2d 896, 907 (Utah 1992) (quoting RESTATEMENT (SECOND) OF TORTS § 652E (1977)).

A false light claim is "closely allied" with an action for defamation, and "the same considerations apply to each." Under the law of defamation, "[a] parody or spoof that no reasonable person would read as a factual statement, or as anything other than a joke[,] . . . cannot be actionable as a defamation." Similarly, an action for "false light" invasion of privacy cannot survive when the publication or statement sued upon cannot be reasonably viewed as a factual claim and is nothing more than a joke or a spoof. . . .

NOTES

1. *Birth of the "Right" to Privacy.* As the excerpt and the case both emphasize, "privacy" is a relatively young concept, not only in the law but also in philosophical thought. Moreover, it has a distinctly American flavor. The 1890 War-

ren and Brandeis article cited by both sources was the first to argue that privacy is itself a discrete, cognizable legal right. Although that article resulted in a virtual explosion of legal and philosophical debate in the United States, it has had less of an effect elsewhere. Many legal systems do not recognize a right of privacy at all, and few have developed the right to the extent seen in the United States.

2. *Stien* is typical of the overwhelming majority of courts in that it divides "privacy" into four separate and independent torts. Even considering the relatively short life of the right to privacy, that division is a fairly recent development. The seminal Warren and Brandeis article actually dealt only with the "publication of private facts" branch. However, as courts in this century struggled to define the right to privacy, they soon began to include other types of cases within its ambit.

Dean Prosser's 1960 law review article canvassed the case law to see how the right to privacy had been interpreted. To him, the cases fell into four distinct categories. Prosser's four categories continue to dominate the case law today.

However, although the vast majority of courts recognize the four branches, not all states allow recovery in all four situations. See, for example, the *Cain* case on page 888.

3. *Do corporations have a right of privacy?* The overwhelming majority of courts limit the right to individuals. *See, e.g., United States v. Morton Salt Co.,* 338 U.S. 632 (1950); *Health Cent. v. Commissioner,* 393 N.W.2d 625 (Mich. Ct. App. 1986); *Warner-Lambert Co. v. Execuquest Corp.,* 691 N.E.2d 545 (Mass. 1998). But does this limitation make sense? Are the values protected by the four privacy torts limited to individuals? Or is a corporation — which owes its very existence to government — by its very nature a public entity that can have no private life?

Although a corporation cannot invoke any of the privacy torts, it may have other remedies for certain types of intrusions. The law of trade secrets allows businesses, including corporations, to recover if a competitor or employee wrongfully obtains or uses commercially valuable information. *See* Uniform Trade Secrets Act § 2; RESTATEMENT (THIRD) OF UNFAIR COMPETITION § 40. The tort of unfair competition, the subject of Chapter 22, may also be available in some cases, especially those involving "false light."

4. *The Constitutional Right to Privacy.* The discussion in this chapter focuses on the remedies that the law provides when a private individual or concern (such as a newspaper) intrudes upon the privacy of another individual. There are also a number of cases and statutes that deal with *government* invasions of privacy. Although there are similarities between the limitations on government and non-government actors, there are also enough important differences to make it dangerous to apply the lessons of this chapter to government invasions of privacy. Unlike the tort law set out in this chapter, the law dealing with government invasions of privacy is grounded at least in part in constitutional

law. Therefore, full discussion of the right of privacy as it pertains to government is best deferred to a course in Constitutional Law.

PROBLEMS

1. Do all four of the torts really involve considerations of "privacy"? Consider in particular the "false light" branch. Does a plaintiff's right to prevent the spread of false information about him really protect his private life? Similarly, how does the "appropriation" branch, which gives a right to prevent the use of one's picture or name, involve privacy?

2. Perhaps the problem that arises in the prior note stems from the fact that the term "privacy" was an unfortunate choice of labels. Can you identify a single unifying concept that binds all four of the "privacy" torts? Many courts and commentators speak generally of the right of privacy as a "right to be left alone." Is that a better way to think of the common theme of all four privacy torts?

3. How does the privacy tort apply in the case of cigarette or cigar smoking? Does a smoker have a right to light up at will, free from the criticism and demands of others? Or does tort law give rights to the non-smoker? For an interesting discussion, see Michele L. Tyler, *Blowing Smoke: Do Smokers Have a Right? Limiting the Privacy Rights of Cigarette Smokers*, 86 GEO. L.J. 783 (1998).

B. THE PRIVACY TORTS

For better or for worse, Dean Prosser's four-way division of the right to privacy has firmly established itself in the case law. This section focuses on each of these torts in turn, fleshing out their elements, their limitations, and the respective problems they engender.

1. Intrusion

The intrusion tort is most similar to what most lay people envision by the right of privacy. A party uses the intrusion tort when someone else has violated that person's personal or private space. But unlike the real property tort of trespass, no one has an absolute right to his or her own privacy. Balancing the interests of the individual with those of the intruder is one of the more difficult issues in intrusion.

PEOPLE FOR THE ETHICAL TREATMENT OF ANIMALS v. BEROSINI
895 P.2d 1269 (Nev. 1995)

SPRINGER, J.

In this litigation respondent Berosini claims that two animal rights organizations, People for the Ethical Treatment of Animals (PETA) and Performing Animal Welfare Society (PAWS), and three individuals defamed him and invaded his privacy. Judgment was entered by the trial court on jury verdicts on the libel and invasion of privacy claims in the aggregate amount of $4.2 million. This appeal followed. We conclude that the evidence was insufficient to support the jury's verdict and, accordingly, reverse the judgment. . . .

[This case arises from] a videotape which shows world-renowned animal trainer, Bobby Berosini, back-stage before the beginning of his show, shaking and punching his trained orangutans and hitting them with some kind of rod. . . .

Appellant Ottavio Gesmundo did the actual taping of Berosini. Gesmundo was a dancer in the Stardust Hotel's "Lido" floor show, at which Berosini's animal act was the principal attraction. Gesmundo claims that he was prompted to videotape Berosini's treatment of the animals because he had become aware of Berosini's conduct with the animals and thought that he would be in a better position to put an end to it if Berosini's actions were permanently recorded on tape. Gesmundo says that he had, on a number of occasions, heard the animals crying out in distress and that he had overheard "thumping noises" coming from the area backstage where the videotaping was eventually done. The area in question was demarked by curtains which kept backstage personnel from entering the staging area where Berosini made last-minute preparations before going on stage. By looking through the worn portions of the curtains, Gesmundo testified that backstage personnel were able to observe the manner in which Berosini disciplined his animals in the mentioned staging area. Berosini's position is that his actions depicted on the tape were a "proper" and "necessary" manner of treating these animals.

However motivated, Gesmundo did decide to record Berosini's treatment of the animals on his eight-millimeter home video recorder. From July 9 through July 16, 1989, Gesmundo placed his video camera in a place that would permit Berosini's actions to be recorded without Berosini's being aware of it. [The court concluded that the video was not libelous because what it showed was either true or constitutionally protected opinion.]

The jury in this case awarded two different species of privacy tort damage awards, each based on a different aspect of a charged invasion of Berosini's privacy. The first species of privacy tort is "intrusion on seclusion," for which Berosini was awarded $250,000.00 against Gesmundo alone. The second species of invasion of privacy upon which the jury returned a verdict in this case was for the appropriation of Berosini's name or likeness. For commission of this tort the jury awarded Berosini $500,000.00 against PETA and $250,000.00 against Jeanne Roush. For the sake of convenience we will refer to these two torts as the tort of intrusion and the tort of appropriation.

The law relating to a protectable "right to privacy" is an American invention, developing over a period of approximately the last one hundred years. . . .

Nevada has long recognized the existence of the right to privacy. A jurist noted some fifty years ago that "it may be conceded that the doctrine of privacy in general is still suffering the pains of its birth." It is still suffering; accordingly, we undertake in this opinion to offer some guidance on the right of privacy as it is recognized in Nevada, at least with regard to the two specific torts involved in this appeal: the tort of intrusion and the tort of appropriation. . . .

FIRST INVASION OF PRIVACY ACTION: Intrusion

You had to live — did live, from habit that became instinct — in the assumption that every sound you made was overheard and, except in darkness, every movement scrutinized.

George Orwell
1984

Berosini claims that one of the Stardust dancers, Ottavio Gesmundo, has intruded upon his "seclusion" backstage, before his act commenced. We support the need for vigilance in preventing unwanted intrusions upon our privacy and the need to protect ourselves against the Orwellian nightmare that our "every movement [be] scrutinized." The question now to be examined is whether Gesmundo's inquiring video camera gives cause for concern over privacy and gives rise to a tort action against Gesmundo for invasion of Berosini's privacy. . . .

To recover for the tort of intrusion, a plaintiff must prove the following elements: 1) an intentional intrusion (physical or otherwise); 2) on the solitude or seclusion of another; 3) that would be highly offensive to a reasonable person.

In order to have an interest in seclusion or solitude which the law will protect, a plaintiff must show that he or she had an actual expectation of seclusion or solitude and that that expectation was objectively reasonable. Thus, not every expectation of privacy and seclusion is protected by the law. "The extent to which seclusion can be protected is severely limited by the protection that must often be accorded to the freedom of action and expression of those who threaten that seclusion of others." For example, it is no invasion of privacy to photograph a person in a public place; or for the police, acting within their powers, to photograph and fingerprint a suspect. Bearing this in mind, let us examine Berosini's claimed "right to be left alone" in this case and, particularly, the nature of Berosini's claim to seclusion backstage at the Stardust Hotel. . . .

The focus, then, of Berosini's intrusion upon seclusion claim is Gesmundo's having "trespassed onto the Stardust Hotel with a video camera" and having "unlawfully filmed Plaintiff Berosini disciplining the orangutans without the Plaintiffs knowledge or consent." It is of no relevance to the intrusion tort that Gesmundo trespassed onto the Stardust Hotel, and it is of no moment that Gesmundo might have "unlawfully" filmed Berosini, unless at the same time he was violating a justifiable expectation of privacy on Berosini's part. The issue, then, is whether, when Gesmundo filmed Berosini "disciplining the orangutans without the Plaintiff's knowledge or consent," Gesmundo was intruding on "the solitude or seclusion" of Berosini.

The primary thrust of Berosini's expectation of privacy backstage at the Stardust was that he be left alone with his animals and trainers for a period of time immediately before going on stage. . . . Berosini's counsel asked him what his "purpose" was in requiring that he be "secured from the other cast members and people before [he] went on stage." Berosini's answer to this question was: "I have to have the attention . . . I have to know how they think. I cannot have them drift away with their mind. . . ."; and, further, "it is very important that before the show I have the orangutans' attention and I can see what they think before I take him on stage. . . ." Significantly, Berosini testified that his "concern for privacy was based upon the animals" and that his "main concern is that [he] have no problems going on stage and off stage," that is to say that no one interfere with his animals in any way immediately before going on stage. . . .

He never expressed any concern about backstage personnel merely seeing him or hearing him during these necessary final preparations before going on stage; his only expressed concern was about possible interference with his pre-act training procedures and the danger that such interference might create with respect to his control over the animals. Persons who were backstage at the Stardust could hear what was going on when "Berosini [was] disciplining his animals," and, without interfering with Berosini's activities, could, if they wanted to, get a glimpse of what Berosini was doing with his animals as he was going on stage.

What is perhaps most important in defining the breadth of Berosini's expectation of privacy is that in his own mind there was nothing wrong or untoward in the manner in which he disciplined the animals, as portrayed on the videotape, and he expressed no concern about merely being seen or heard carrying out these disciplinary practices. To Berosini all of his disciplinary activities were completely "justified." He had nothing to hide — nothing to be private about. Except to avoid possible distraction of the animals, he had no reason to exclude others from observing or listening to his activities with the animals. Berosini testified that he was not "ashamed of the way that [he] controlled [his] animals"; and he testified that he "would have done the same thing if people were standing there because if anybody would have been standing there, it was visible. It was correct. It was proper. It was necessary." . . .

Having testified that he would have done the same thing if people were standing there, he can hardly complain about a camera "standing there."

If Berosini's expectation was, as he says it is, freedom from distracting intrusion and interference with his animals and his pre-act disciplinary procedures, then Gesmundo's video "filming" did not invade the scope of this expectation. Gesmundo did not intrude upon Berosini's expected seclusion. For this reason the tort of intrusion cannot be maintained in this case.

On the question of whether Gesmundo's camera was highly offensive to a reasonable person, we first note that this is a question of first impression in this state. As might be expected, "the question of what kinds of conduct will be regarded as a 'highly offensive' intrusion is largely a matter of social conventions and expectations." For example, while questions about one's sexual activities would be highly offensive when asked by an employer, they might not be offensive when asked by one's closest friend. "While what is 'highly offensive to a reasonable person' suggests a standard upon which a jury would properly be instructed, there is a preliminary determination of 'offensiveness' which must be made by the court in discerning the existence of a cause of action for intrusion." A court considering whether a particular action is "highly offensive" should consider the following factors: "the degree of intrusion, the context, conduct and circumstances surrounding the intrusion as well as the intruder's motives and objectives, the setting into which he intrudes, and the expectations of those whose privacy is invaded."

Three of these factors are of particular significance here and, we conclude, militate strongly against Berosini's claim that Gesmundo's conduct was highly offensive to a reasonable person. These factors are: the degree of the alleged intrusion, the context in which the actions occurred, and the motive of the supposed intruder. First, we note the nonintrusive nature of the taping process in the instant case. Berosini was concerned with anyone or anything interfering with his animals prior to performance. The camera caused no such interference. Neither Berosini nor his animals were aware of the camera's presence. If Gesmundo had surprised Berosini and his animals with a film crew and had caused a great commotion, we might view this factor differently. On the contrary, it appears from these facts that any colorable privacy claims arose not from the actual presence of the video camera but from the subsequent use to which the video tape was put.

Secondly, as has been discussed fully above, the context in which this allegedly tortious conduct occurred was hardly a model of what we think of as "privacy." We must remember that the videotaping did not take place in a private bedroom, or in a hospital room, or in a restroom, or in a young ladies' dressing room, or in any other place traditionally associated with a legitimate expectation of privacy. Rather, Gesmundo filmed activities taking place backstage at the Stardust Hotel, an area where Gesmundo had every right to be, and the filming was of a subject that could be seen and heard by any number of persons. This was not, after all, Berosini's dressing room; it was a holding area for his orangutans.

Finally, with regard to Gesmundo's motives, we note that Gesmundo's purpose was not to eavesdrop or to invade into a realm that Berosini claimed for personal seclusion. Gesmundo was merely memorializing on tape what he and others could readily perceive. Unlike the typical intrusion claim, Gesmundo was not trying to pry, he was not trying to uncover the covered-up. . . . Furthermore, even if Gesmundo was conspiring to put an end to the use of animals in entertainment, this is not the kind of motive that would be considered highly offensive to a reasonable person. Many courts, and Professor Prosser, have found the inquiry into motive or purpose to be dispositive of this particular element of the tort. For example, in *Estate of Berthiaume*, 365 A.2d at 796, the court held that a doctor who photographed a dying patient against his will could be held liable for intrusion, in part because the doctor was not seeking to further the patient's treatment when he photographed him. . . .

While we could reverse Berosini's intrusion upon seclusion judgment solely on the absence of any intrusion upon his actual privacy expectation, we go on to conclude that even if Berosini had expected complete seclusion from prying eyes and ears, Gesmundo's camera was not "highly offensive to a reasonable person" because of the nonintrusive nature of the taping process, the context in which the taping took place, and Gesmundo's well-intentioned (and in the eyes of some, at least, laudable) motive. If Berosini suffered as a result of the videotaping, it was not because of any tortious intrusion, it was because of subsequent events that, if remediable, relate to other kinds of tort actions than the intrusion upon seclusion tort. . . .

NOTES

1. *Protecting Private Space.* As the court's discussion makes clear, a person can have a reasonable expectation of privacy in places that the person does not "own." Therefore, the tort of intrusion may be available in situations where the person cannot sue for trespass. *See, e.g., Harkey v. Abate*, 346 N.W.2d 74 (Mich. Ct. App. 1983) (public restroom); Annotation, *Retailer's Surveillance of Fitting or Dressing Rooms as Invasion of Privacy*, 38 A.L.R.4th 954 (1985). Conversely, not all cases of trespass give rise to intrusion. Unlike trespass, which occurs when a defendant enters real property without permission or privilege, intrusion exists only when the defendant's act is offensive. A number of courts have found intentional intrusions of personal space not to be offensive. *See, e.g., McLain v. Boise Cascade Corp.*, 533 P.2d 343 (Or. 1975); *Mark v. KING Broadcasting*, 635 P.2d 1081 (Wash. 1981), *cert. denied*, 457 U.S. 1124 (1982).

2. *The Intrusion.* As one might expect, there is a considerable range of opinions in the cases on the issue of whether a given intrusion is "offensive." The difference between the cases is more than a matter of degree. Although few discuss the issue, courts do not seem to agree on the way in which the intrusion must "offend." Some, like the court in *Berosini*, focus on whether defendant disrupted the plaintiff's solitude. Another well-known case upheld the right of a photographer to take photos of Jacqueline Kennedy Onassis as long as he acted in an unobtrusive manner. *Galella v. Onassis*, 487 F.2d 986 (2d Cir. 1973). Other

courts focus less on the means of intrusion and more on the event or activity that is observed. For example, in *Carter v. Innisfree Hotel, Inc.,* 661 So. 2d 1174 (Ala. 1995), hotel guests discovered a peephole in their room several hours after entering the room. Before they discovered the peephole, they had engaged in private acts. The court allowed the guests to recover against the hotel for intrusion even though they did not realize the intrusion was occurring, and even though they had no evidence that anyone had looked through the peephole. Apparently, the observation device was itself intrusive. *See also Hamberger v. Eastman,* 206 A.2d 239 (N.H. 1964) (listening device); *Harkey v. Abate,* 346 N.W.2d 74 (Mich. Ct. App. 1983).

3. Notwithstanding the tenor of the main case, defendants have fared relatively well in the intrusion cases. Most of the cases in which courts impose liability are those involving an actual trespass onto plaintiff's property. Media defendants have a particularly good record in these cases.

PROBLEMS

1. The interplay between privacy and trespass means that there are two torts — overlapping but not perfectly contiguous — that protect someone's "space." Is this a good idea? Which of the following statements do you find more convincing?

Statement 1. The intrusion tort causes more problems than it solves. Property law emphasizes *boundaries* that are clear, definable, and easily ascertainable. Because it borrows these well-established property law concepts, the law of trespass is fairly manageable. The intrusion tort, by contrast, requires that a court determine whether a person has a "reasonable expectation of privacy" and whether defendant's acts were "objectionable." These standards are so ambiguous as to lead to impossible confusion in the case law.

Statement 2. The law of trespass builds upon a legal fiction. It protects against intrusions onto a person's property. But property has no feelings. Instead, what we really ought to be concerned with are the feelings of the *owner* of that property. Those feelings can be injured by intrusions that do not involve property. The intrusion tort is in this sense more realistic, because it looks directly at the harm that intrusion causes to the plaintiff, ignoring the legal fiction of whether there is a property interest.

Moreover, the law of trespass is guilty of sublime, but quite real, class discrimination. Only people who own property can sue for trespass. Our legal system, however, has been trying to abolish the use of property as a way to establish social class. We no longer require people to own property as a condition of voting. In the same vein, it only seems fair that we should give people without significant property holdings the same right to privacy as we give to those wealthy enough to own land.

2. In *Berosini*, the court found it significant that other people who worked at the Stardust Hotel could observe plaintiff and his orangutans through the curtains. But unlike these others, defendant did more than just watch; it actually filmed plaintiff's activities. Should that make a difference? Although plaintiff may have anticipated being observed on occasion, did he anticipate being filmed on a regular basis? And concerning the issue of intrusiveness, isn't being filmed much more intrusive than casual observation?

3. The court also noted that plaintiff considered his acts of discipline justified. How is that relevant? Does the tort law of privacy only protect those engaged in dishonest, immoral, or illegal activities? Does a person have a greater expectation of privacy when involved in such acts? Could you argue that the nature of the observed activity affects the amount of *damages*, not whether the tort itself was committed?

4. Does a person have a reasonable expectation of privacy in garbage? For one author's view, *see* Comment, *Privacy in the Can:* State v. Boland *and the Right to Privacy in Garbage*, 28 GONZAGA L. REV. 159 (1992) (dealing with government searches, which involves the same issue of whether there was an expectation of privacy). With respect to the intrusion tort, even if there is no expectation of privacy, is searching someone's garbage offensive?

5. South Ward Elementary School has just completed a battery of interviews for a new art instructor. These interviews were conducted by a committee comprising of both faculty and parents. The clear favorite is Art Teacher, a 35-year-old man who currently teaches at a different elementary school in the city. Before extending an offer to Teacher, however, the committee decides to check his references. The committee assigns the task of checking references to the school principal. The committee plans to meet again in one week to hear the principal report on her findings.

Notwithstanding the committee's decision to have the principal contact references, Julie Parrent, a parent member of the committee, decides to do a little background check of her own. After an exhaustive investigation, she learns that everything Teacher represented to the committee on his résumé and in the interviews was completely true. However, she also discovers other information that changes her opinion of Teacher. First, she discovers that although Teacher is currently in what seems to be a stable marriage, he had been married twice before. Neither of these earlier marriages had lasted for more than three months. Second, she learns that while in college, Teacher had undergone extensive psychiatric counseling. Third, she learns that Teacher is a registered member of the Socialist Party.

Parrent debates what to do with this information. She knows that under the law of that state, it would have been illegal for the committee to ask Teacher about his current or prior marital status. On the other hand, she also knows that it is not illegal for the committee to consider that information in making its decision.

When the hiring committee reconvenes after a week, the principal gives a glowing report. Parrent says nothing. The committee then decides to take a vote. Everyone but Parrent votes to hire Teacher. Troubled by the lack of unanimity, the committee chair asks Parrent why she voted against Teacher. Parrent says merely, "I have my reasons." Given the majority vote in favor of Teacher, the committee extends him an offer.

Teacher later discovers that Parrent had been snooping into what he considers his private affairs. He therefore sues Parrent under the intrusion branch of the invasion of privacy. What is the likely outcome of the case?

2. Appropriation of Name or Likeness

The second branch of the privacy tort involves a fundamentally different interest than the intrusion tort. Indeed, some have argued that this branch really should be separated from the other privacy torts. As you read the cases and the notes, try to ascertain what interest or interests are protected by this branch, and why the courts have treated the tort of appropriation of name or likeness as a subset of the general privacy tort.

AINSWORTH v. CENTURY SUPPLY CO.
693 N.E.2d 510 (Ill. App. Ct. 1998)

Justice INGLIS delivered the opinion of the court:

Plaintiff, Charles H. Ainsworth, [was] hired to install tile at the house Tom Parks was building. Parks is also referred to as Thomas Poczatek. Parks was the sales manager for Century. Century is in the business of selling, among other things, ceramic tile. In October 1993, Century created a videotape that instructs customers how to install ceramic tile. Century asked plaintiff for permission to videotape him installing tile in Parks's house. Parks explained that the video would be distributed to Century's customers. Plaintiff consented to appear in the video. The video was completed and Century began providing it to the public.

In 1994, Century hired TCI to create a television commercial. The television commercial TCI created contained blank space into which short bits of videotape could be inserted, thus creating a number of different versions of the television commercial. One of the inserts was taken from the instructional video in which plaintiff participated. The television commercial with plaintiff's image was aired a number of times.

In November 1994, plaintiff called Parks and complained about his appearance in Century's television commercial, giving Century two weeks to respond.

Century asserted that it called TCI and requested that the commercial be discontinued.

Plaintiff's image appears in the television commercial for only a few seconds. Plaintiff concedes that there is nothing objectionable about his appearance or the way he is installing tile.

Plaintiff sued defendants for using his image in the television commercial. In his five-count first amended complaint, plaintiff alleged claims against Century for infringement to his right of publicity (count I); invasion of privacy by appropriating his likeness (counts II and IV); and for the establishment of a constructive trust and an accounting (count III). Count V alleged that TCI appropriated his likeness.

TCI filed a motion to dismiss plaintiff's claim. TCI claimed that count V did not state a claim for invasion of privacy and that TCI did not commercially benefit from the publication of plaintiff's image. The trial court agreed and dismissed count V of plaintiff's complaint.

Century filed a motion for summary judgment. Century alleged that plaintiff's consent to appear in the instructional video extended to the commercial and that plaintiff did not incur damages and was not entitled to punitive damages from Century. The trial court denied the motion as to the consent issue but granted summary judgment in favor of Century on the issue of damages, holding that plaintiff did not sustain actual damages and the lack of evidence of malice or reckless indifference to plaintiff's rights precluded an award of punitive damages. In addition, plaintiff voluntarily dismissed counts I and III. Plaintiff timely appeals.

Plaintiff first contends that the trial court erroneously dismissed count V of his complaint against TCI. Plaintiff argues that TCI was paid to create a television commercial for Century and thus received a commercial benefit. We agree. . . .

The tort of invasion of privacy consists of four branches: "(1) an unreasonable intrusion upon the seclusion of another; (2) an appropriation of another's name or likeness; (3) a public disclosure of private facts; and (4) publicity which reasonably places another in a false light before the public." The elements of an appropriation claim are "an appropriation, without consent, of one's name or likeness for another's use or benefit. This branch of the privacy doctrine is designed to protect a person from having his name or image used for commercial purposes without consent."

Here, plaintiff alleged that TCI was hired by Century to produce a television commercial and that Century paid TCI for completing the television commercial. Plaintiff further alleged that TCI used footage from the instructional video in which plaintiff appeared in creating the television commercial. Plaintiff alleged that he did not consent to the use of his image from the instructional video, but TCI nevertheless broadcast the television commercial. Plaintiff also alleged that TCI received further income from airing the television commercial. Plaintiff has sufficiently pleaded an appropriation claim against TCI.

TCI argues that plaintiff failed to allege that TCI used his image for its own benefit. TCI asserts that, because the television commercial touted Century's products, TCI's use of plaintiff's image in it conferred no commercial benefit on TCI. This misses the mark. TCI created a television commercial which used plaintiff's image and for which it was paid. We fail to see how TCI's use of plaintiff's image was for anything but TCI's commercial benefit. TCI's argument is without merit.

TCI also asserts that, as a media defendant, it should not be liable for appropriating plaintiff's likeness, citing *Berkos v. National Broadcasting Co.*, 515 N.E.2d 668 (1987). In *Berkos*, the defendant displayed the plaintiff's photograph during a news broadcast. The court determined that "[a] commercial appropriation claim cannot be stated where a plaintiff's name or likeness has been used as part of a 'vehicle of information,' such as the news media." The court also distinguished the situation in *Berkos* from the commercial use of a person's likeness in advertising as occurred in *Eick v. Perk Dog Food Co.*, 106 N.E.2d 742 (1952). Here, TCI made commercial use of plaintiff's likeness by including it in an advertisement it had been commissioned to create. Its use of plaintiff's likeness was not incidental to the transmission of news information, but rather it was central to the endeavor of advertising. *Berkos* is therefore inapposite. . . .

Plaintiff next contends that the trial court erroneously granted summary judgment in favor of Century. . . .

Plaintiff first contends that the trial court erred by finding that he had failed to demonstrate the existence of actual damages. We agree.

Century argues that, as a matter of law, plaintiff's allegations are insufficient to prove any actual damages. Century points to plaintiff's deposition, in which plaintiff stated that he was angry over the use of his image in Century's television commercial. Century overlooks, however, the venerable principle that the law will presume that damages exist for every infringement of a right. Here, plaintiff has alleged that Century appropriated his image from the instructional video, without his consent, for Century's own benefit. Accordingly, plaintiff has alleged the infringement of his legal right to the use of his image. It is proper to vindicate plaintiff's right to the use of his image against this deliberate violation, even if plaintiff cannot prove actual damages. In addition, we note that the courts in Illinois have long presumed that nominal damages are available for this tort.

The availability of nominal damages notwithstanding, Century maintains that plaintiff has failed to demonstrate the existence of any damages beyond an award of nominal damages. Century contends that plaintiff must experience severe emotional distress. Century misapprehends the nature of the tort with which it is charged. The appropriation of a plaintiff's image is more properly in the nature of a usurpation of a plaintiff's property rights in the exclusive use of his image. Thus, Century's contention that plaintiff must prove a significant level of mental distress is immaterial. Accordingly, plaintiff may prove, if he is able, the value of the use Century made of his image as well as any damages resulting from his alleged emotional distress.

Century rightly notes that a reviewing court may sustain a summary judgment on any ground justified by the record. As grounds supporting the summary judgment, Century first contends that, by consenting to appear in the instructional video, plaintiff also consented to appear in its television commercial. Century's reasoning is clearly flawed, as it amounts to the assertion that, by consenting to eat apples with dinner, one has also consented to eat oranges. The fact that both are fruit does not make them indistinguishable. Likewise, the fact that plaintiff consented to appear in the instructional video that was to be available to Century's customers does not mean that his consent extended to his appearance in a television commercial, broadcast to the television-watching public. We reject Century's consent argument.

Century next argues that it received no commercial benefit from the use of plaintiff's image in its television commercial. Century seems to advance the contention that plaintiff's image is fungible and that, by using plaintiff's image as opposed to any other, it received no commercial benefit. This argument fares little better, for, even if we accept that plaintiff's image was a fungible commodity, Century nevertheless chose plaintiff's image and no other. Plaintiff's image was integral to the concept of the advertisement. Century benefitted by airing the television commercial. Plaintiff's image, not one of the others, had some value to Century, even if it were merely ease of procurement. Because Century received a commercial benefit from its advertising, we cannot say that Century received no benefit from the use of plaintiff's image. Accordingly, we hold that the trial court erroneously granted summary judgment in favor of Century on the issue of actual damages.

Plaintiff next argues that the trial court erred by granting summary judgment in favor of Century on the issue of punitive damages. The purpose of punitive damages is to punish the offender and to deter others from committing similar actions.

Punitive [damages] may be awarded when torts are committed with fraud, actual malice, deliberate violence or oppression, or when the defendant acts wilfully or with such gross negligence as to indicate a wanton disregard for the rights of others [citation], or for conduct involving some element of outrage similar to that found in crime." . . .

Here, as proof of Century's culpable mental state, plaintiff points to the fact that Century did not bother to secure his consent. In his deposition, Tom Parks stated that he was "shocked" by plaintiff's complaint because plaintiff's "part was so small and I thought most people would be thrilled that they would be in a commercial." Additionally, in his deposition, plaintiff stated that, when he first confronted Century about the television commercial, Century denied he was in it. According to plaintiff, this demonstrates that Century intended to deceive him and deprive him of the benefit of the use of his image. Pointing to the various broadcast records of the stations airing the commercial, plaintiff also contends that Century continued to air the television commercial for months after he demanded that it be taken off the air. The records indicate there is some merit to plaintiff's contention. Viewing these contentions most favorably for the non-movant plaintiff, as we must, we conclude that plaintiff has demonstrated the existence of evidence from which the finder of fact could infer that Century acted with malice or reckless indifference to his rights. . . .

For the foregoing reasons, the judgment of the circuit court of Du Page County is reversed, and the cause is remanded for further proceedings consistent with our disposition.

Reversed and remanded.

PEOPLE FOR THE ETHICAL
TREATMENT OF ANIMALS v. BEROSINI
895 P.2d 1269 (Nev. 1995)

[The facts of this case, together with the court's discussion of the first right of privacy claim, are set out on page 866.]

SECOND INVASION OF PRIVACY ACTION: Appropriation

We now draw our attention to the other privacy tort pursued by Berosini in this case, namely, the tort of invasion of privacy based upon appropriation of name or likeness. There is considerable confusion in the cases and in the literature regarding this tort, primarily because the difference between the appropriation tort and the right of publicity tort is often obscured. The common law appropriation tort ordinarily involves the unwanted and unpermitted use of the name or likeness of an ordinary, uncelebrated person for advertising or other such commercial purposes, although it is possible that the appropriation tort might arise from the misuse of another's name for purposes not involving strictly monetary gain. The right of publicity tort, on the other hand, involves the appropriation of a celebrity's name or identity for commercial purposes. The distinction between these two torts is the interest each seeks to protect. The appropriation tort seeks to protect an individual's personal interest in privacy; the personal injury is measured in terms of the mental anguish that results from the appropriation of an ordinary individual's identity. The right to publicity seeks to protect the property interest that a celebrity has in his or her name; the injury is not to personal privacy, it is the economic loss a celebrity suffers when someone else interferes with the property interest that he or she has in his or her name. We consider it critical in deciding this case that recognition be given to the difference between the personal, injured-feelings quality involved in the appropriation privacy tort and the property, commercial value quality involved in the right of publicity tort.

As said, in the case of a private person, the invasion of privacy resulting from misuse or misappropriation of that person's name or identity is a personal injury, an injury that is redressable by general damages for the mental anguish and embarrassment suffered by reason of the unwanted public use of the private person's name. When, however, the name of a famous or celebrated person is used unauthorizedly, that person's main concern is not with bruised feelings, but rather, with the commercial loss inherent in the use by another of the celebrated name or identity. The commercial or property interest that celebrities have in the use of their names and identities is protected under what has been termed the "right of publicity." . . .

Berosini, a public figure and celebrity, has not sued for violation of his right of publicity. Berosini has prosecuted a common law appropriation tort action in this litigation. Even though he sues under the appropriation tort, it is apparent from Berosini's brief that tort damages for hurt feelings stemming from defendants' commission of the appropriation privacy tort is not what he is really interested in; rather, Berosini is (understandably) only interested in recovery of the "pecuniary gain sought by PETA through the use of Berosini's name and likeness. . . ."

Berosini, therefore, cannot recover on the "common law" tort, the appropriation privacy tort, for the reasons stated; and he cannot recover under the statutory tort, the right of publicity tort because he has not sought recovery under the statute. The "privacy" tort judgments against PETA and Roush must therefore be reversed.

NOTE

As *Berosini* indicates, a related tort, the right of "publicity," will often be available for the unauthorized use of a public figure's image or voice. Because both the genealogy and the current makeup of the right of publicity differ from appropriation, discussion of the right of publicity has been deferred to Chapter 22.

PROBLEMS

1. What purpose is served by allowing recovery in a case like *Ainsworth*? Certainly Ainsworth would have preferred to control the dissemination of his likeness. But the court acknowledges that he has no proof of any actual damages from the use of his picture. This fact does not bother the court, as it concludes that he might be able to prove the "value" of Century's use of the picture. How would one calculate that value? Given that plaintiff is not known beyond his family and friends, is there likely to be *any* value? On the other hand, even if Ainsworth lost nothing, did Century unfairly benefit?

2. The court also holds that even if Ainsworth cannot prove damages, he may receive nominal and possibly punitive damages. It supports that holding by reasoning that the tort of appropriation "is more properly in the nature of a usurpation of a plaintiff's property right in the exclusive use of his image." As you saw earlier, courts presume damages when there is an intentional encroachment on a "property" right, as in the case of trespass.

Is the analogy to the property torts accurate? Does a person really have a "property" right in his or her image? If so, consider the implications. Could a faculty member at your law school sue to prevent the use of her photograph in the school catalog or web page? How about the use of biographical data? Suppose that the same faculty member was a bystander at a parade, and the newspaper wanted to publish a picture of the parade in which the faculty member appeared?

3. Should punitive damages be available in an appropriation case? Is the use of a private person's photograph sufficiently egregious to call for deterrence?

4. Like *Berosini*, many courts do not allow "public figures" to invoke the appropriation privacy tort. What considerations underlie this exception? At one level, of course, it seems unfair to allow the public figure, who has profited from thrusting his persona into the public eye, to complain about a loss of "privacy". But is that reasoning too simplistic? Does the appropriation tort protect the same personal interest as the intrusion tort? In this regard, consider the discussion earlier in this chapter regarding the array of unique values reflected in the concept of privacy. If the appropriation tort protects different values, should it also be available to public figures?

5. Truth is indeed sometimes stranger than fiction. Consider the following facts, which were taken from an actual case:

> Plaintiff creates unique clothing designs and displays these designs at bikers' events. At a Chillicothe, Ohio, bikers' festival, Plaintiff wore one of her distinctive creations, which displayed her bottom through fishnet fabric that replaced cut out portions of her blue jeans. In May of 1993, Paisano Publications' ("Paisano's") *In the Wind* magazine published a picture of Plaintiff's backside as part of a photo essay of the Chillicothe festival. The picture does not identify Plaintiff. A year and a half later, in December of 1994, Paisano's *Easyriders* magazine published T-Shurte's advertisement for a T-shirt with a similarly-clad backside, which Plaintiff claims portrayed her likeness. T-Shurte's may have sold several hundred or more of the shirts.

Suppose (as happened in the actual case) that Plaintiff sues both Paisano and T-Shurte for appropriation. What type of evidence will she need to present at trial in order to recover for appropriation? Exactly what was appropriated? Assuming that she can proffer evidence, how will the court calculate her damages? After you have worked through the problem, you may want to consider how the court dealt with the case: *Cheatham v. Paisano Publications, Inc.*, 891 F. Supp. 381 (W.D. Ky. 1995).

3. Publication of Private Facts

Like the intrusion tort, the tort of publication of private facts fits easily into lay notions of "invasion of privacy." Both torts involve situations where the defendant has allegedly intruded, in some fashion, on something intensely personal to the plaintiff. And in fact, as the following case demonstrates, the same fact situation often gives rise to both claims.

GREEN v. CHICAGO TRIBUNE CO.
675 N.E.2d 249 (Ill. App. Ct. 1996)

JUSTICE O'BRIEN delivered the opinion of the court:

Plaintiff, Laura Green, filed an amended complaint against defendant, the Chicago Tribune Company (hereinafter Tribune), alleging invasion of privacy, intentional infliction of emotional distress, and battery. The trial court dismissed plaintiff's amended complaint against the Tribune pursuant to section 2-615 of the Code of Civil Procedure. Plaintiff appeals.

First, we address whether the trial court properly granted the Tribune's section 2-615 motion to dismiss plaintiff's claim for invasion of privacy. In the invasion of privacy count, plaintiff pleaded the following allegations which must be assumed true for purposes of the motion: Tribune staffers photographed her son, Calvin Green, on December 30, 1992, while he was undergoing emergency treatment at Cook County Hospital for a bullet wound. The Tribune never asked plaintiff's permission to photograph Calvin. After attempts to resuscitate Calvin failed, medical personnel moved him to a private hospital room to await the coroner. The coroner pronounced Calvin dead at 12:10 a.m. on December 31, 1992. Around that time, a reporter for the Tribune asked plaintiff for a statement regarding her son's death. She refused to make a statement. Meanwhile, Tribune staffers entered the private hospital room and took further unauthorized photographs of Calvin. While photographing Calvin, they prevented plaintiff from entering the room. When plaintiff did enter the room, the Tribune staffers listened to her statements to Calvin.

On January 1, 1993, the Tribune published a front-page article, about Chicago's record homicide rate. The article included the following quotes from plaintiff's statements to Calvin on December 31: "I love you, Calvin. I have been telling you for the longest time about this street thing." "I love you, sweetheart. That is my baby. The Lord has taken him, and I don't have to worry about him anymore. I accept it." "They took him out of this troubled world. The boy has been troubled for a long time. Let the Lord have him." The Tribune also published one of the unauthorized photographs taken of Calvin after he died. In a January 3, 1993, article, the Tribune published one of the unauthorized photographs taken of Calvin while undergoing medical treatment.

Plaintiff's complaint alleges the Tribune publicly disclosed private facts and thus invaded her privacy when it (a) "trespassed" into Calvin's room; (b) photographed Calvin without plaintiff's consent; (c) prevented plaintiff from entering Calvin's room while the Tribune took photographs of him; (d) "eavesdropped" on plaintiff's statements to Calvin; (e) published on January 1 the front-page article containing quotes from plaintiff's statements to Calvin and the photograph of Calvin lying dead; and (f) published on January 3 the photograph of Calvin undergoing medical treatment. The trial court dismissed plaintiff's action pursuant to section 2-615 of the Code of Civil Procedure. . . .

The public disclosure of private facts is one branch of the tort of invasion of privacy. To state a cause of action for the public disclosure of private facts, plaintiff must plead (1) the Tribune gave publicity; (2) to her private, not public, life; (3) the matter publicized was highly offensive to a reasonable person; and (4) the matter publicized was not of legitimate public concern. . . .

Plaintiff satisfied the publicity element of the tort by pleading a cause of action premised on the Tribune's publishing her statements and the photographs of her son in the January 1 and January 3 editions of the Chicago Tribune.

Next, we address whether plaintiff pleaded facts sufficient to assert the second prong of the tort: the facts disclosed in the Chicago Tribune were private. The circuit court found plaintiff failed to plead that the matter published was private, not public. The court stated "When you talk aloud in a public place, [how] can you say that you have an expectation of privacy? [The] reporting was of at least a semi-public statement of the plaintiff [said] aloud voluntarily with knowledge of [Tribune personnel] present."

We disagree with the trial court's finding as a matter of law that Calvin's hospital room was a "public place" and thus plaintiff's statements in that room could not be private. Plaintiff's complaint clearly pleads that Calvin was in a private room, and, as the court must accept all well-pleaded facts as true, the trial court's failure to accept that fact as true contributed to the error in its analysis. Further, Black's Law Dictionary defines "public place" as:

> A place to which the general public has a right to resort; not necessarily a place devoted solely to the uses of the public, but a place which is in point of fact public rather than private, a place visited by many persons and usually accessible to the neighboring public (*e.g.*, a park or public beach). Also, a place in which the public has an interest as affecting the safety, health, morals, and welfare of the community. A place exposed to the public, and where the public gather together or pass to and fro.

The general public surely had no right to resort in Calvin's private hospital room, nor did the public have an interest in that room that affected their safety, health, morals, or welfare. Thus, Calvin's hospital room was not a "public place."

We also disagree with the trial court's finding as a matter of law that plaintiff's statements were not private because she made them in front of Tribune personnel. . . .

[P]laintiff's allegation here that she spoke to her dead son in front of Tribune personnel in Cook County Hospital is not dispositive as to whether her statements were private or public. Rather, the analysis must focus on whether plaintiff alleged that she informed the Tribune personnel that she wished to keep the content of those statements private with respect to the general public. Plaintiff pleaded in her amended complaint that around the time of her son's death in Cook County Hospital, she informed the Tribune reporter who was in the hospital that she wished to make no statement to the Tribune regarding her son's death. Taking these well-pleaded facts as true for purposes of the section 2-615 motion to dismiss, we think a jury could find plaintiff's conversation with that reporter sufficient to put the Tribune on notice it was not to disclose to the general public the statements she made in the hospital to her son. Accordingly, plaintiff pleaded sufficient facts to allege her statements to her son were private, not public.

The Tribune argues, though, that we should affirm the trial court's dismissal order because plaintiff's complaint seeks to recover damages for the invasion of her son's privacy. The Tribune contends the right of privacy is purely personal and plaintiff must prove invasion of her own privacy before she can recover. . . .

In the present case, the complaint alleges the Tribune did substantially publicize plaintiff on January 1, 1993, by publishing a photograph of her dead son, Calvin, and by identifying her as Calvin's mother and publishing her statements to Calvin. Thus, plaintiff's cause of action for the January 1 publication can go forward because it is based on her privacy interest. However, plaintiff also pleaded an invasion of privacy for the January 3, 1993, publication that included the December 30 photograph of Calvin undergoing medical treatment. The January 3 publication never mentions plaintiff and thus does not invade her privacy. Accordingly, pursuant to Bradley, we hold plaintiff's complaint for invasion of privacy based on the January 3 publication must be dismissed.

Next, we address whether plaintiff's complaint pleaded facts sufficient to assert the third prong of the public disclosure of private facts tort: the matter published was highly offensive to a reasonable person. Having determined the January 3 publication cannot be the basis for plaintiff's privacy action, we examine only the January 1 publication. . . .

In determining whether plaintiff pleaded facts sufficient to assert that the January 1 publication was highly offensive to a reasonable person, we examine the allegations of the context, conduct and circumstances surrounding the publication as well as the publication itself. We are also mindful of the following comment to the Restatement (Second) of Torts:

> Complete privacy does not exist in this world except in a desert, and anyone who is not a hermit must expect and endure the ordinary inci-

dents of the community life of which he is a part. Thus he must expect the more or less casual observation of his neighbors as to what he does, and that his comings and goings and his ordinary daily activities, will be described in the press as a matter of casual interest to others. . . .

From the allegations in plaintiff's complaint, reasonable people could differ and could find that the Tribune's January 1 publication was not about an ordinary daily activity or incident in plaintiff's life; rather, the publication concerned an extraordinarily painful incident in plaintiff's life, when she first set eyes on her minor son after he had been shot to death. Further, reasonable people could differ and could find that the Tribune's publication was not a minor or moderate annoyance, especially since the photograph of Calvin it published on January 1 was taken while Tribune staffers prevented plaintiff from seeing Calvin, and its quotation from plaintiff's grief-stricken statements to Calvin came after plaintiff expressly told the Tribune reporter she wanted to make no public statement about her son's death. Because reasonable people could differ as to these facts, we believe a jury could find the Tribune's January 1 publication highly offensive to a reasonable person. Plaintiff therefore has pleaded facts sufficient to assert the third prong of the public disclosure of private facts tort.

Next, we address whether plaintiff pleaded facts sufficient to assert the fourth prong of the tort: the matter publicized was not of legitimate public concern. . . .

The Tribune argues the subject of the January 1 article was the death toll from guns and gang warfare, which, like the subject of drug use, is of legitimate public concern. In our view, however, the relevant inquiry is whether the photograph of plaintiff's dead son and her statements to him are of legitimate public concern.

The Tribune argues plaintiff's statements to her son, Calvin, and the photograph of him give "an identity and a voice to the victims" of gang violence, and therefore are of legitimate public interest. However, members of the public itself, a jury, could find the January 1 article, which reported Calvin's gang-related shooting as well as the futile attempts to revive him by opening his chest and massaging his heart, did not need plaintiff's intimate statements to Calvin or his photograph to convey the human suffering behind gang violence.

"[In] determining what is a matter of legitimate public interest, account must be taken of the customs and conventions of the community; and in the last analysis what is proper becomes a matter of the community mores. The line is to be drawn when the publicity ceases to be the giving of information to which the public is entitled, and becomes a morbid and sensational prying into private lives for its own sake, with which a reasonable member of the public, with decent standards, would say that he had no concern."

A jury could find that a reasonable member of the public has no concern with the statements a grieving mother makes to her dead son, or with what he looked like lying dead in the hospital, even though he died as the result of a gang shooting. Accordingly, plaintiff has pleaded sufficient facts to assert the fourth prong of the public disclosure of private facts tort.

In sum, we hold plaintiff's amended complaint states a cause of action for public disclosure of private facts with respect to the January 1, 1993, Tribune publication. It does not state a cause of action for the January 3, 1993, publication. . . .

[The court next held that plaintiff had also stated a claim for intentional infliction of emotional distress based on the publication, but not a claim for battery.]

Affirmed in part, reversed in part, and remanded for further proceedings consistent with this opinion.

JUSTICE CAHILL dissents:

I respectfully dissent from the majority conclusion that the complaint before us states a cause of action for invasion of privacy and intentional infliction of emotional distress based upon the January 1, 1993, edition of the Chicago Tribune. While I agree that the January 3, 1993, edition does not state a cause of action, I disagree with the reasoning of the majority in reaching that conclusion. I would affirm the trial court in all respects.

Three fundamental problems surface with the majority approach. To each point in turn:

First, count III of the complaint, directed at the Tribune for invasion of privacy, alleges five separate acts: entry of the hospital room without the consent of Green; preventing Green from entering the same room; photographing her son; eavesdropping on Green's words to her dead son; and publishing these words and a photograph of her dead son. The first four allegations have nothing to do with the tort of public disclosure of private facts. If they state a cause of action, it is under section 652B of the Restatement: an unreasonable intrusion upon the seclusion of another. Although plaintiff's complaint describes her cause of action as one of publication of private facts alone, it is the allegations that define the cause of action and not the name or title that may be used.

The tort of intrusion upon the plaintiff's seclusion and the tort of publication of private facts are treated as a single cause of action in the complaint and by the majority. They are separate torts, as recognized by Dean Prosser who first proposed them, the Restatement of Torts which adopts Prosser's categories, and almost all state and federal courts that track the Restatement in a privacy case.

This is more than a quibble over a distinction that does not amount to a significant difference. . . .

Intrusion does not implicate the First Amendment. Publication by a media defendant of facts alleged to be private triggers the First Amendment debate about the nature of the facts published, whether the plaintiff is an involuntary public figure, and whether the facts are of legitimate public concern. When the elements of the torts are mingled as they are here, we are led down an analytical path that ignores the distinction between the way information is gathered and its subsequent publication. If this photograph had been taken on the street where Calvin Green was slain, and his mother's tragic words recorded as she stood over him, I doubt I would be writing this dissent. That Calvin and his mother were tragic involuntary public figures in a story of grim but legitimate public interest is self-evident. The alleged intrusion cannot change their status or diminish the newsworthiness of the story. [Judge Cahill then discussed the tort of intrusion, and concluded that even if Illinois recognized the tort, plaintiff had not properly pled it in her complaint.]

The tort of giving publicity to the private life of a person may occur when the matter publicized "would be highly offensive to a reasonable person," but only when the matter publicized "is not of legitimate concern to the public." The jury is not called upon to decide what is "highly offensive" until a court has determined that the matter is first, private, and second, offensive. . . .

The majority finds that plaintiff states a cause of action based on the reasoning that "a jury could find" the article "did not need" the photo of Calvin and plaintiff's statements to him. That may well be, but it is not for a jury to decide how a news story should be edited. To question whether the newspaper should have omitted certain details from a story of legitimate public concern amounts to editorial second guessing rather than legal analysis. Where the general content of an article is newsworthy, editors must be allowed a measure of discretion to determine how the article will be written and what details will be included. . . .

Here, the article about deaths from gang violence and the photograph, charts, and statistics accompanying the article are matters of legitimate public concern. The statements by plaintiff to her son and his photo are closely related to the subject matter of the news story, which documented the fact and effect of gang violence on the offenders and the victims. The subject is of public interest. In the sense of serving an appropriate news function, the quotation and photograph contribute constructively to the impact of the article. They give a personalized frame of reference, allowing the reader to relate, perceive, and understand that the class of victims is not limited to gang members. They verify the article's message that victims include the community, friends, and family. They show Calvin Green was not only the 934th person to die from gang violence in 1992 — he was a young man with a loving parent who is also a victim of gang violence. The photograph and the statements heighten the impact and credibility of the article and prevent an impression that gangs are a remote or hypothetical problem. . . .

The right of privacy must give way when balanced against the publication of matters of public interest to insure the "uninhibited, robust and wide-open" discussion of legitimate public issues. *New York Times Co. v. Sullivan*, 376 U.S. 254, 270 (1964). . . .

There are, no doubt, cases in the pipeline where the phenomena of "infomercials," "info-entertainment," "docu-dramas" and "reenactments" blur the differences between legitimate news and pulp fiction. The shield of the First Amendment may develop cracks as courts respond to this trend and the insensitive aggressiveness of legitimate news gatherers who must compete with the purveyors of soft core "information" to supply market demands. This case is not one of them.

I respectfully dissent.

NOTES

1. As its name implies, the tort discussed in *Green* protects only against publication of *private* facts. Is it really possible to distinguish between one's public and private life? Do celebrities and other public figures have a smaller sphere of private facts? For some interesting discussions of the concepts of public and private, see JURGEN HABERMAS, THE STRUCTURAL TRANSFORMATION OF THE PUBLIC SPHERE 3-4 (1962); Howard B. Radest, *The Public and the Private: An American Fairy Tale*, 89 ETHICS 280 (1979).

2. The concept of "publication" is a term of art. Unlike other torts that turn on "publication," for purposes of the private facts tort merely disclosing the information to others is not enough. Rather, publication occurs only when the information is disseminated to a wide audience. Thus, in *Kuhn v. Account Control Technology, Inc.*, 865 F. Supp. 1443 (D. Nev. 1994), the court granted summary judgment to a defendant collection agency that revealed plaintiff's credit problems to his co-workers.

PROBLEMS

1. In 25 words or less, explain what the *Tribune* did wrong in *Green*. Does your statement of the reasoning include the fact that the reporters came into the room without permission? If so, is Justice Cahill correct when he says that this case is closer to one of intrusion than one of publication of private facts?

2. The late twentieth century could be dubbed the "Age of Merger." The last twenty years have been marked by the merger of several large corporations. The media is no stranger to this trend. Today, a few media giants dominate the dissemination of information. Suppose that one of these media giants decides to create a vast database on the American public. It includes in this database all information that it has in its archives on everyone. In addition, the company hires researchers to seek out additional information on the populace. The researchers limit their searches to public records, such as court files, marriage

license bureaus, and land title records, coupled with the archives of other media companies. Because the company's computer has a practically limitless capacity, the company stores all of this information without any attempt to weed out information of little relevance.

This database proves to be a real boon in reporting. Whenever a story arises involving a particular person, the media company can prepare an instant dossier on that person by searching the database. In one case, for example, a local newspaper controlled by the giant company was able to report that a candidate for mayor had been arrested (but acquitted) for embezzlement in a city located over a thousand miles away. Readers find the information sometimes helpful, but more often simply scintillating.

Of course, maintaining such a database is quite costly. The media conglomerate therefore decides to make computer-generated dossiers available to the public for a fee. That service proves to be an instant hit, especially among potential employers and lending institutions. Does the media conglomerate face tort liability for revealing truthful, but not widely know, information about a given person?

3. Even when a defendant has published facts that everyone agrees are private, the law imposes liability for publication of private facts only when the publication would be "highly offensive." Why do courts impose such a requirement? Compare the private facts tort with appropriation, discussed in the prior section. Liability for appropriation will be imposed for any use of a private person's name or likeness. The rationale is that a person has a property right in her image. Could you also argue that a person has a property right in information that he has chosen not to make public, so that any disclosure of that information should be actionable?

4. Note that the court would not impose liability if the matter in question involved a legitimate public concern. As this case involved the sufficiency of plaintiff's complaint, the court remanded that issue to the trial court. If you were the trial judge, would you conclude that the matter was one of legitimate public concern? Is the public concern anything more than a sordid interest in seeing how "the other half lives"?

Even more fundamentally, why should there be an exception for matters in which the public has an interest? Isn't the right of privacy *especially* important when the public is curious? Does it matter that *Green* involved a media defendant, the sort of entity upon which society relies for information? If the defendant had been a local busybody instead of Chicago's best-known paper, would the court consider whether the matter was of public concern?

5. The notes in the prior section discussed how public figures lost their right to sue for "appropriation" by purposefully drawing attention to themselves. The publication branch of the privacy tort contains an analogous concept: people who share their private lives with others cannot later complain when the information is published to third parties. *See, e.g., Schuler v. McGraw-Hill Co.,*

Inc., 989 F. Supp. 1377 (D.N.M. 1997) (corporate executive who had granted interviews about sex change operation could not sue when another magazine revealed the change; even though the interviews had occurred twenty years earlier). What about information in court records? Most courts find such information to be public. *See, e.g., Haynes v. Alfred A. Knopf, Inc.,* 1993 U.S. Dist. LEXIS 2880 (N.D. Ill. 1993). However, *see United States Department of Justice v. Reporters Committee for Freedom of the Press,* 489 U.S. 749 (1989), which found that a collection of public records invaded privacy. Can a third party turn private facts into public? For example, suppose that in *Green* the trial court, on remand, imposes liability on the *Tribune.* Is anyone now free to publicize the same information, on the theory that the facts are no longer private?

4. False Light

The publication of private facts tort discussed in the prior section involves the revelation of true information about the plaintiff. The false light tort, by contrast, arises only when the information is false or has the capacity to deceive. Because false information is of less value to a free society, there are fewer policy concerns with imposing liability in false light cases. Nevertheless, the false light tort is not without its problems, as the following case demonstrates.

CAIN v. HEARST CORP.
878 S.W.2d 577 (Tex. 1994)

JUSTICE GONZALEZ delivered the opinion of the Court, in which CHIEF JUSTICE PHILLIPS, JUSTICE HECHT, JUSTICE CORNYN and JUSTICE ENOCH join.

This case comes to us on certified questions from the United States Court of Appeals for the Fifth Circuit. We are asked to decide two issues: 1) whether Texas recognizes the tort of false light invasion of privacy, and 2) if Texas recognizes this tort, which statute of limitations governs that action. Because false light substantially duplicates the tort of defamation while lacking many of its procedural limitations, we answer the first question in the negative, thereby dispensing with the need to answer the second question.

Clyde Cain is a prison inmate in the Texas Department of Corrections serving a life sentence for murder. He sued the Hearst Corporation, d/b/a the Houston Chronicle Publishing Company, claiming that a newspaper article invaded his privacy by placing him in a false light. The article, which appeared in the Chronicle on June 30, 1991, referred to Cain as a burglar, thief, pimp, and killer. . . . Cain's sole complaint is that the article printed false information that he was a member of the "Dixie Mafia" and that he had killed as many as eight people. Cain asserted that these statements put him in a false light with the public. . . .

Hearst removed the case to the United States District Court for the Southern District of Texas. The court granted Hearst's motion for dismissal on the grounds that Cain's action lies in libel, and held that the one-year limitations period expired before Cain brought the suit. Determining that the above questions are unsettled under Texas precedent, the Fifth Circuit certified these questions to us.

Genesis of Invasion of Privacy

[Although] we acknowledged the Prosser categorization in [*Industrial Found. of the South v. Texas Indus. Accident Bd.*, 540 S.W.2d 668, 682 (Tex. 1976), *cert. denied*, 430 U.S. 931 (1977)], we have never embraced nor recognized the fourth and final type of invasion of privacy, the "false light" tort. We decline to do so today.

The Restatement (Second) of Torts, Section 652E defines false light invasion of privacy as follows:

> One who gives publicity to a matter concerning another that places the other before the public in a false light is subject to liability to the other for invasion of his privacy, if
>
> (a) the false light in which the other was placed would be highly offensive to a reasonable person, and
>
> (b) the actor had knowledge of or acted in reckless disregard as to the falsity of the publicized matter and the false light in which the other would be placed.

RESTATEMENT (SECOND) OF TORTS § 652E (1977). . . . Nevertheless, false light remains the least-recognized and most controversial aspect of invasion of privacy.

Today, we join those jurisdictions that do not recognize the false light invasion of privacy action. *Renwick v. News & Observer Publishing Co.*, 310 N.C. 312, *cert. denied*, 469 U.S. 858 (1984); *see Sullivan v. Pulitzer Broadcasting Co.*, 709 S.W.2d 475, 480-81 (Mo. 1986); *Arrington v. New York Times Co.*, 55 N.Y.2d 433 (N.Y. 1982), *cert. denied*, 459 U.S. 1146 (1983); *Yeager v. Local 20, Int'l Bhd. of Teamsters*, 6 Ohio St. 3d 369 (Ohio 1983); *Falwell v. Penthouse Int'l, Ltd.*, 521 F. Supp. 1204, 1206 (W.D. Va. 1981). . . .

We reject the false light invasion of privacy tort for two reasons: 1) it largely duplicates other rights of recovery, particularly defamation; and 2) it lacks many of the procedural limitations that accompany actions for defamation, thus unacceptably increasing the tension that already exists between free speech constitutional guarantees and tort law.

Duplication of Other Causes of Action

The false light action, as it has been defined by the Restatement, permits recovery for injuries caused by publicity that unreasonably places the plaintiff in a false light before the public. RESTATEMENT (SECOND) OF TORTS § 652A. Although not explicitly required by the Restatement definition, most jurisdictions [require] that a statement be false if it is to be cognizable under the false light doctrine. The falsity requirement is sensible, considering that the "revelation of private facts" invasion of privacy tort purports to grant relief for the disclosure of true statements that adversely affect the plaintiff.

If we were to recognize a false light tort in Texas, it would largely duplicate several existing causes of action, particularly defamation. . . . Recovery for defamation requires the communication of a false statement. . . .

Furthermore, the elements of damages that have been recognized in false light actions are similar to those awarded for defamation. The principal element of actual damages for false light claims is typically mental anguish, but physical illness and harm to the plaintiff's commercial interests have also been recognized. . . .

Freedom of Speech Considerations

As discussed above, the false light tort bears remarkable similarities to defamation. However, the torts are not wholly identical for two reasons: (1) defamation actions are subject to a number of procedural requirements to which invasion of privacy actions are not subject, and (2) certain publications not actionable under a defamation theory might be actionable under false light. Far from persuading us that these distinctions justify a separate tort, we believe they demonstrate that adopting a false light tort in this State would unacceptably derogate constitutional free speech rights under both the Texas and the United States Constitution.

1. Procedural and Substantive Differences

Actions for defamation in Texas are subject to numerous procedural and substantive hurdles. For example, accounts of governmental proceedings, public meetings dealing with a public purpose, or any "reasonable and fair comment on or criticism of an official act" are privileged under Texas Civil Practice & Remedies Code Section 73.002. Broadcasters are generally not liable in defamation for broadcasts made by third parties. Qualified privileges against defamation exist at common law when a communication is made in good faith and the author, the recipient or a third person, or one of their family members, has an interest that is sufficiently affected by the communication. A communication may also be conditionally privileged if it affects an important public interest. Damages awarded for defamatory statements may be mitigated by factors such as public apology, correction, or retraction.

These technical restrictions serve to safeguard the freedom of speech. Every defamation action that the law permits necessarily inhibits free speech. As the Supreme Court stated with respect to political speech in *New York Times v. Sullivan*, 376 U.S. 254, 272 (1964), "whatever is added to the field of libel is taken from the field of free debate." While less compelling, these same considerations are also at play in private, non-political expression. Thus, the defamation action has been narrowly tailored to limit free speech as little as possible. . . .

2. Non-Defamatory Speech

In theory, the false light action may provide a remedy for certain non-defamatory speech against which there may be no other remedy in tort law. *See* RESTATEMENT (SECOND) OF TORTS § 652E, cmt. b (1977). This rationale, however, does not persuade us to recognize the false light tort.

It is questionable whether a remedy for non-defamatory speech should exist at all. . . . The class of speech restricted by defamation is only that which defames. False light may be brought against any untruth to which the subject of the speech takes umbrage. Editors for the media may guard against defamation by being alert to facts which tend to diminish reputation; under false light, any fact in the story, no matter how seemingly innocuous, may prove to be the basis for liability.

The Restatement adds an element not associated with defamation, the requirement that the statement places the subject in a false light "highly offensive" to the reasonable person. The distinction fails to draw reasonably clear lines between lawful and unlawful conduct, however. . . .

Thus, the uncertainty of not knowing what speech may subject the speaker or writer to liability would have an unacceptable chilling effect on freedom of speech. Such liability is incongruent with the high priority this state has placed on freedom of expression. . . .

On balance, the marginal benefit to be achieved by permitting recovery against non-defamatory speech not addressed by any existing tort is outweighed by the probable chilling effect on speech and, in some cases, on freedom of the press, that would result from recognition of the false light tort. For the reasons expressed in this opinion, we expressly decline to recognize the tort of false light.

JUSTICE HIGHTOWER, joined by JUSTICE DOGGETT, JUSTICE GAMMAGE and JUSTICE SPECTOR, dissenting.

[That] the substance of communications constituting defamation will usually also constitute false light does not make the two torts coextensive. The scope of actionable conduct differs between the torts, and the torts are designed to protect different interests.

First, the court rightly notes, as do many courts and commentators, that there are communications which, based on their content, are not defamatory but may be false light violations of privacy because they are highly offensive. For example, an article which falsely reports that an individual suffers from a serious disease such as cancer would not be defamatory but could comprise a cause of action for false light.

Second, the torts protect different interests. Defamation preserves individuals' reputation interests, but false light invasion of privacy, as the other branches of the right of privacy, safeguards individuals' sensitivities about what people know and believe about them. . . .

That, in some cases, both torts allow mental anguish damages does not detract from these differing protections. For example, mental anguish damages are available in suits for medical malpractice, certain violations of the Deceptive Trade Practices Act, or personal injury, but that does not mean that the torts duplicate each other or the interests they serve.

Furthermore, the scopes of the torts differ with respect to the level of publicity required for the cause of action to arise. False light requires significantly broader publication than does defamation. Defamation only requires publication to a single individual, but false light requires widespread dissemination. . . .

The court's conclusion that many, if not all, of the injuries redressed by the false light tort are redressed by defamation is plainly wrong as a matter of logic. That false light covers some of the injuries covered by defamation in no way leads to the conclusion that defamation covers most of the injuries covered by false light.

Furthermore, overlap, by itself, is no reason to reject a cause of action for false light invasion of privacy. For example, in Texas, a citizen who feels cheated in a financial transaction has a variety of choices for a cause of action, including a claim for fraud, violation of the Deceptive Trade Practices Act, breach of warranty, or a combination of any and all of these claims. Moreover, although traditional theories such as actions for eavesdropping and wiretapping protected individuals from invasions into their private business and personal affairs, the availability of such actions did not preclude the court from adopting the right of privacy in the wiretapping context.

The court's only explanation of why it will tolerate no overlap in this arena is that free speech rights are implicated because the procedures attending defamation are lacking. Rather than assess and weigh the interests at stake in each right and add any procedures necessary to effectuate an even balance of the rights, the court simply concludes that false light invasion of privacy and free speech cannot coexist. . . .

I respectfully dissent.

NOTES

1. The false light tort is the most controversial of the four branches of invasion of privacy. Texas is one of at least sixteen states that do not recognize the tort.

2. Defendant's use of plaintiff's own words can give rise to a false light claim. For example, where a paper publishes excerpts from a speech, but those excerpts

grossly distort the plaintiff's message, plaintiff may be able to recover under a false light theory. Similarly, if a third party has spoken about the plaintiff, plaintiff may be able to recover against a defendant who reprints misleading excerpts of that statement. *See, e.g., Varnish v. Best Medium Publishing*, 405 F.2d 608 (2d Cir. 1968), *cert. denied*, 394 U.S. 987 (1969). In both of these situations the courts will treat defendant's publication of the other person's words as a statement by defendant.

PROBLEMS

1. As both the majority and the dissent recognize, the common-law false light action imposes liability even when the defendant's false statement does not defame the plaintiff. Thus, in the majority of states that recognize the false light tort, plaintiffs often join a false light claim with their defamation claim. The majority and dissent disagree on whether allowing these parallel causes of action is desirable. In your view who has the better of the argument?

2. Note that although the statement need not be defamatory, it must be "highly offensive" before a false light action will lie. The dissent gives one example of such a statement: one that falsely indicates that a person is suffering from cancer. Is that really highly offensive? Moreover, how many other statements of that sort are there? Won't most statements be highly offensive precisely *because* they are defamatory? If so, the practical differences between defamation and false light may not be that great.

3. May a plaintiff collect separate damages for false light and defamation? Most courts do not allow separate recovery because of the significant overlap between the two torts. But is this the correct result? Defamation deals with injury to a person's reputation. False light, by contrast, deals with damage to a person's sensitivities. Are these not separate injuries? In fact, from this perspective is the false light tort actually a closer cousin to the tort of emotional distress, discussed in Chapter 2, than it is to defamation?

C. REVISITING THE RIGHT TO PRIVACY

In the excerpt from the McLean book that led off this chapter, the author argues that one key feature of the twentieth century has been the development of privacy as a discrete, free-standing legal interest. Yet do the cases really bear out this conclusion? The majority in *Cain* (page 886) concluded that the "false light" branch of privacy largely duplicates another tort. And as noted in the second *Berosini* excerpt (page 875), there is little practical difference between the appropriation species of privacy and other actions, such as the right of publicity and the tort of general misappropriation (both of which are covered in Chapter 22). Likewise, many intrusion and private facts case will also present other torts, *e.g.*, trespass or intentional infliction of emotional distress.

Chapter 19
CIVIL RIGHTS

Tort actions can also be brought under the U.S. Constitution or under various federal civil rights statutes. In many instances, these cases are also actionable under state law. For example, assume that the police break into a man's home, beat him up, and arrest him. Assuming insufficient justifications for the officer's actions, the citizen can sue the officers for trespass, assault, battery and false imprisonment. But the same conduct may be actionable under the Fourth Amendment to the United States Constitution or under 42 U.S.C. § 1983. By suing under the Constitution or § 1983, the citizen is able to bring the case in federal court.

A. SECTION 1983

There are two types of constitutional violations brought under § 1983: substantive violations and procedural violations. Substantive violations involve abuse of specific provisions of the Bill of Rights or other constitutional guarantees such as the Equal Protection Clause of the Fourteenth Amendment. Many amendments have been incorporated into the Equal Protection Clause of the Fourteenth Amendment (First Amendment deprivation of speech and assembly, Fifth Amendment coerced confession, Sixth Amendment interference with attorney-client privilege, Eighth Amendment cruel and unusual punishment). Procedural violations, on the other hand, inlcude violation of the Due Process Clause of the Fourteenth Amendment, but are not based on any specific Constitutional provision. Most cases involve substantive violations, or combinations of substantive and procedural violations.

42 U.S.C. § 1983, the most widely used statute, provides as follows:

> Every person who, under color of any statute, ordinance, regulation, custom or usage, of any State or Territory, subjects, or causes to be subjected, any citizen of the United States or other person within the jurisdiction thereof to the deprivation of any rights, privileges, or immunities secured by the Constitution and laws, shall be liable to the party injured in an action at law, suit in equity, or other proper proceeding for redress.

In *Monroe v. Pape*, 365 U.S. 167 (1961), the Court explained the purposes of § 1983 as follows:

> [The legislation had] three main aims. First, it [overrode certain] state laws. . . . Second, it provided a remedy where state law was inadequate. [The] third aim was to provide a federal remedy where the state remedy, though adequate

897

in theory, was not available in practice. [While one main scourge] was the Ku Klux Klan, the remedy [was] not a remedy against it or its members but against [state officials who] were unable or unwilling to enforce a state law. . . . There [was] no quarrel with [the] laws on the books. [L]ack of enforcement [was the] difficulty. . . . Although the legislation was enacted because [of] conditions that existed in the South at that time, it is cast in general language and is as applicable to Illinois as it is to the States whose names were mentioned [in] the debates. . . . The federal remedy is supplementary to the state remedy, and the latter need not be first sought and refused. . . .

A § 1983 claim has two elements. "First, the plaintiff must show that someone has deprived him of a federal right, either statutory or Constitutional. Second, the plaintiff must prove that the individual acted under color of state or territorial law. . . ." *Barnier v. Szentmiklosi*, 565 F. Supp. 869 (E.D. Mich. 1983).

DAVIDSON v. CANNON
474 U.S. 344 (1986)

Justice REHNQUIST delivered the opinion of the Court.

Petitioner sued prison officials seeking damages under 42 U.S.C. § 1983 for injuries he suffered when they negligently failed to protect him from another inmate. On December 19, 1980, petitioner was threatened by one McMillian, a fellow inmate at the New Jersey State Prison at Leesburg. Petitioner sent a note reporting the incident that found its way to respondent Cannon, the Assistant Superintendent of the prison, who read the note and sent it on to respondent James, a Corrections Sergeant. Cannon subsequently testified that he did not view the situation as urgent because on previous occasions when petitioner had a serious problem he had contacted Cannon directly.

James received the note at about 2 p.m. on December 19, and was informed of its contents. James then attended to other matters, which he described as emergencies, and left the note on his desk unread. By the time he left the prison that evening James had forgotten about the note, and since neither he nor Cannon worked on December 20 or 21, the officers on duty at that time had not been informed of the threat. Petitioner took no steps other than writing the note to alert the authorities that he feared an attack, nor did he request protective custody. He testified that he did not foresee an attack, and that he wrote the note to exonerate himself in the event that McMillian started another fight. He also testified that he wanted officials to reprimand McMillian in order to forestall any future incident. On Sunday, December 21, McMillian attacked petitioner with a fork, breaking his nose and inflicting other wounds to his face, neck, head, and body.

Petitioner brought this § 1983 suit [claiming] that respondents had violated his constitutional rights under the Eighth and Fourteenth Amendments. [Finding] the principles enunciated in *Daniels* controlling here, we affirm. [Respondents'] lack of due care in this case led to serious injury, but that lack of care simply does not approach the sort of abusive government conduct that the Due Process Clause was designed to prevent. Far from abusing governmental power, or employing it as an instrument of oppression, respondent Cannon mistakenly believed that the situation was not particularly serious, and respondent James simply forgot about the note. The guarantee of due process has never been understood to mean that the State must guarantee due care on the part of its officials. . . .

Accordingly, the judgment of the Court of Appeals for the Third Circuit is affirmed.

It is so ordered.

Justice BLACKMUN, with whom Justice MARSHALL joins, dissenting.

[In] some cases, by any reasonable standard, governmental negligence is an abuse of power. This is one of those cases. [W]hen a State assumes sole responsibility for one's physical security and then ignores his call for help, the State cannot claim that it did not know a subsequent injury was likely to occur. Under such circumstances, the State should not automatically be excused from responsibility. [O]nce the State has taken away an inmate's means of protecting himself from attack by other inmates, a prison official's negligence in providing protection can amount to a deprivation of the inmate's liberty, at least absent extenuating circumstances. Such conduct by state officials [is] the "arbitrary action" against which the Due Process Clause protects [and] are not remote from the purpose of the Due Process Clause and § 1983.

[P]rison officials act recklessly when they disregard the potential for violence between a known violent inmate and a known likely victim. [Even] if respondents' conduct ordinarily would be considered only negligent, the forewarning here changes the constitutional complexion of the case. When officials have actual notice of a prisoner's need for physical protection, " 'administrative negligence can rise to the level of deliberate indifference to or reckless disregard for that prisoner's safety.' "

Respondents "had the responsibility to care for plaintiff's safety, actual notice of the threat by an inmate with a known history of violence, and an opportunity to prevent harm to plaintiff." Both respondents knew that McMillian had threatened Davidson after the fight and that Davidson had reported the threat immediately. Although Cannon knew that McMillian was a troublemaker, he nonetheless chose to think that the situation was not serious. Likewise, James decided to attend to other matters during the entire eight hours he worked after receiving the note. Cannon and James intentionally delayed protecting Davidson's personal security in the face of a real and known possibility of violence. Yet the risk that harm would occur was substantial and obvious. Respondents' behavior very well may have been sufficiently irresponsible to constitute reckless disregard of Davidson's safety.

[Recklessness] or deliberate indifference is all that a prisoner need prove to show that denial of essential medical care violated the Eighth Amendment's ban on cruel and unusual punishments. The Due Process Clause provides broader protection than does the Eighth Amendment, so a violation of the Due Process Clause certainly should not require a more culpable mental state. . . .

NOTES

1. *The 1983 Trend.* Section 1983 was not used much until recent decades. "Underlying [this] was the Supreme Court's desire [to] maintain the old federalism in which the central government [had] little responsibility [for] protecting civil liberties. . . . Section 1983 was largely limited to vindicating deprivations of voting rights. . . ." *Barnier v. Szentmiklosi*, 565 F. Supp. 869 (E.D. Mich. 1983). *Monroe v. Pape*, 365 U.S. 167 (1961), "ushered in the modern era of § 1983 jurisprudence." *Monroe* allowed a § 1983 suit for a violation of Fourth Amendment rights, and "[led] to an extraordinary increase in the civil rights caseload of the federal courts. In 1960, about 300 cases were filed. . . . [In 1982, there were] more than 17,000 cases [plus] 17,000 [petitions] filed by state and federal prisoners [for a total of 34,000 cases]." *Barnier v. Szentmiklosi*, 565 F. Supp. 869 (E.D. Mich. 1983).

2. *Mixed Motive Decisions.* In *Mt. Healthy City School District v. Doyle*, 429 U.S. 274 (1977), an untenured teacher sued the school board claiming that he had been wrongfully discharged for engaging in free speech, in violation of his First and Fourteenth Amendment rights. Although sympathetic to the teacher's right to free speech, the court noted that the existence of the protected conduct does not preclude the school board from firing him for other justifiable reasons.

> A borderline or marginal candidate should not have the employment question resolved against him because of constitutionally protected conduct. But that same candidate ought not to be able, by engaging in such conduct, to prevent his employer from assessing his performance record and reaching a decision not to rehire on the basis of that record, simply because the protected conduct makes the employer more certain of the correctness of its decision.

The Supreme Court remanded the case to the district court to determine whether the protected conduct was the "motivating factor" behind the school board's decision or whether "it would have reached the same decision as to respondent's re-employment even in the absence of the protected conduct." *Mt Healthy,* at 576, *appeal after remand*, 670 F.2d 59 (1982) (holding that the school board had met its burden).

3. *Daniels v. Williams*, 474 U.S. 327 (1986), referred to in *Davidson*, involved an inmate tripping over a pillow that a prison guard had negligently left on the stairs. Petitioner in that case brought a § 1983 action based on the Fourteenth Amendment and claimed a deprivation of his liberty interest in freedom from

bodily injury. The Supreme Court held that the injury did not amount to a deprivation within the meaning of the Fourteenth Amendment but rather amounted to a "lack of due care [suggesting] no more than a failure to measure up to the conduct of a reasonable person."

4. *Liability for omissions.* In *DeShaney*, a boy, Joshua, and his mother sued a county department of social services and several social workers under § 1983, alleging that respondents had deprived him of his liberty interest in bodily integrity, by failing to intervene to protect him against his father's violence. Although Joshua was repeatedly taken to the hospital for injuries resulting from child abuse and social services was aware of the abuse for over two years, Joshua was not removed from the home and was eventually beaten so severely as to inflict permanent brain damage.

Joshua claimed that the failure to act deprived him of his liberty in violation of the Due Process Clause of the Fourteenth Amendment to the United States Constitution. The Court disagreed:

> [Petitioners] argue that [h]aving actually undertaken to protect Joshua [from] danger — which [the] State played no part in creating — the State acquired an affirmative "duty," enforceable through the Due Process Clause, to do so in a reasonably competent fashion. . . . We reject this argument. . . . In *Estelle v. Gamble*, 429 U.S. 97 (1976), we recognized that the Eighth Amendment's prohibition against cruel and unusual punishment [requires] the State to provide adequate medical care to incarcerated prisoners. . . . In *Youngberg v. Romeo*, 457 U.S. 307 (1982), we [held] that the substantive component of the Fourteenth Amendment's Due Process Clause requires the State to provide involuntarily committed mental patients with such services as are necessary to ensure their "reasonable safety" from themselves and others. . . .

> [T]hese cases afford petitioners no help. [They stand] for the proposition that when the State takes a person into its custody and holds him there against his will, the Constitution imposes [a] corresponding duty to assume some responsibility for his safety and general well-being. . . . [T]he harms Joshua suffered occurred not while he was in the State's custody, but while he was in the custody of his natural father, who was in no sense a state actor. . . . That the State once took temporary custody of Joshua does not alter the analysis, for when it returned him to his father's custody, it placed him in no worse position than that in which he would have been had it not acted at all; the State does not become the permanent guarantor of an individual's safety by having once offered him shelter. Under these circumstances, the State had no constitutional duty to protect Joshua.

5. *The Deliberate Indifference Standard.* The Court in *City of Canton v. Harris*, 489 U.S. 378 (1989), held that, under the deliberate indifference standard, the lack of adequate police training did not amount to a violation under § 1983. In *City of Canton v. Harris*, Harris was arrested, but was later found sitting on

the floor of the paddy wagon incoherent. At the police station, Harris slumped to the floor on two occasions and the police left her there. No medical attention was summoned. When Harris was released from custody, her family took her by ambulance to a nearby hospital where she was diagnosed with several emotional ailments. She was hospitalized for a week and received outpatient treatment for an additional year. Harris sued claiming that the City failed to adequately train the officers, and that this failure caused her injury. In *City of Canton,* one of the Harris's claims was brought "under 42 U.S.C. § 1983 for its violation of [Mrs. Harris'] right, under the Due Process Clause of the Fourteenth Amendment, to receive necessary medical attention while in police custody." Under this claim the critical question to the court was: "Under what circumstances can inadequate training be found to be a 'policy' that is actionable under § 1983." It held that the inadequacy of police training may serve as the basis for § 1983 liability only where the failure to train amounts to *deliberate indifference* to the rights of persons with whom the police come into contact. "Only where a municipality's failure to train its employees in a relevant respect evidences a 'deliberate indifference' to the rights of its inhabitants can such a shortcoming be properly thought of as a city 'policy or custom' that is actionable under § 1983."

The court in *Farmer v. Brennan*, 511 U.S. 825 (1994), applying a deliberate indifference standard, held a prison liable for the harm done to a prisoner. The Court clarified the "deliberate indifference" standard. Petitioner, a transsexual, sued alleging that prison officials violated the Eighth Amendment by their deliberate indifference to his safety. Before being sentenced at age 18, petitioner, a biological male, wore women's clothing, underwent estrogen therapy, received silicone breast implants, and had unsuccessful testicle-removal surgery. Petitioner continued hormonal treatment while incarcerated using smuggled drugs, wore clothing in a feminine manner (i.e., draping a shirt "off the shoulder"), and "projected feminine characteristics." Federal prison authorities incarcerated preoperative transsexuals with prisoners of like biological sex. Within two weeks after being incarcerated, petitioner was beaten and raped by another inmate. Petitioner filed a *Bivens* complaint, alleging a violation of the Eighth Amendment. Petitioner claimed that respondents placed petitioner in its general population despite knowledge that the penitentiary had a violent environment and a history of inmate assaults, and despite knowledge that petitioner, as a transsexual who "projects feminine characteristics," would be particularly vulnerable to sexual attack. This allegedly amounted to a deliberately indifferent failure to protect petitioner's safety, and thus to a violation of petitioner's Eighth Amendment rights. Before remanding, the Court clarified the standard of liability:

> "[P]rison officials have a duty [to] protect prisoners from violence at the hands of other prisoners." Having [individuals in the same facility with] incarcerated "persons [with] demonstrated proclivit[ies] for anti-social criminal, and often violent, conduct," having stripped them of virtually every means of self-protection and foreclosed their access to

outside aid, the government and its officials are not free to let the state of nature take its course. . . .

[A] prison official violates the Eighth Amendment only when two requirements are met. [For a claim based] on a failure to prevent harm, the inmate must show that he is incarcerated under conditions posing a substantial risk of serious harm. [The] second requirement follows from the principle that "only the unnecessary and wanton infliction of pain implicates the Eighth Amendment." [A] prison official must have a "sufficiently culpable state of mind." In prison-conditions cases that state of mind is one of "deliberate indifference" to inmate health or safety. . . .

[The term "deliberate indifference"] describes a state of mind more blameworthy than negligence [but] something [less] than acts or omissions for the very purpose of causing harm or with knowledge that harm will result. [A]cting or failing to act with deliberate indifference to a substantial risk of serious harm to a prisoner is the equivalent of recklessly disregarding that risk.

[A] prison official cannot be found liable [unless] the official knows of and disregards an excessive risk to inmate health or safety; the official must both be aware of facts from which the inference could be drawn that a substantial risk of serious harm exists, and he must also draw the inference. . . . [A]n official's failure to alleviate a significant risk that he should have perceived but did not[, cannot] be condemned as the infliction of punishment.

[P]rison officials who actually knew of a substantial risk to inmate health or safety may be found free from liability if they responded reasonably to the risk, even if the harm ultimately was not averted. A prison official's duty under the Eighth Amendment is to ensure "'reasonable safety,'" a standard that incorporates due regard for prison officials' "unenviable task of keeping dangerous men in safe custody under humane conditions." Whether one puts it in terms of duty or deliberate indifference, prison officials who act reasonably cannot be found liable under the Cruel and Unusual Punishment Clause.

B. *BIVENS* ACTIONS

If the offending individual is a federal official, rather than a state or local official, a § 1983 action may not be available. As a result, some have tried to sue federal officials (and, for that matter, state officials) based on the Constitution itself. Does the Constitution provide a right of action to those injured by a violation of its provisions? Until 1971, the answer to this question was in doubt. Then, the Court decided the following case.

BIVENS v. SIX UNKNOWN NAMED AGENTS OF FEDERAL BUREAU OF NARCOTICS
403 U.S. 388 (1971)

Mr. Justice BRENNAN delivered the opinion of the Court.

The Fourth Amendment provides that:

> "The right of the people to be secure in their persons, houses, papers, and effects, against unreasonable searches and seizures, shall not be violated. . . ."

In *Bell v. Hood*, 327 U.S. 678 (1946), we reserved the question whether violation of that command by a federal agent acting under color of his authority gives rise to a cause of action for damages consequent upon his unconstitutional conduct. Today we hold that it does.

This case has its origin in an arrest and search carried out on the morning of November 26, 1965. [R]espondents, agents of the Federal Bureau of Narcotics acting under claim of federal authority, entered his apartment and arrested him for alleged narcotics violations. The agents manacled petitioner in front of his wife and children, and threatened to arrest the entire family. They searched the apartment from stem to stern. Thereafter, petitioner was taken to the federal courthouse [where] he was interrogated, booked, and subjected to a visual strip search.

[P]etitioner brought suit in Federal District Court [asserting] that the arrest and search were effected without a warrant, and that unreasonable force was employed in making the arrest; [it] alleges as well that the arrest was made without probable cause. Petitioner claimed to have suffered great humiliation, embarrassment, and mental suffering as a result of the agents' unlawful conduct, and sought $15,000 damages from each of them. [The District Court dismissed the complaint for failure to state a cause of action. The Court of Appeals affirmed. We] reverse.

[Respondents claim that] petitioner may obtain money damages [only] by an action in tort, under state law, in the state courts. In this scheme the Fourth Amendment would serve merely to limit the extent to which the agents could defend the state law tort suit by asserting that their actions were a valid exercise of federal power: if the agents were shown to have violated the Fourth Amendment, such a defense would be lost to them and they would stand before the state law merely as private individuals. . . .

Respondents seek to treat the relationship between a citizen and a federal agent unconstitutionally exercising his authority as no different from the relationship between two private citizens. . . . An agent acting — albeit unconstitutionally — in the name of the United States possesses a far greater capacity for harm than an individual trespasser exercising no authority other than his own. [The] Fourth Amendment [guarantees] to citizens of the United States the absolute right to be free from unreasonable searches and seizures carried out by virtue of federal authority. And "where federally protected rights have been invaded, it has been the rule from the beginning that courts will be alert to adjust their remedies so as to grant the necessary relief."

[T]he interests protected by state laws regulating trespass and the invasion of privacy, and those protected by the Fourth Amendment's guarantee against unreasonable searches and seizures, may be inconsistent or even hostile. . . . The mere invocation of federal power by a federal law enforcement official will normally render futile any attempt to resist an unlawful entry or arrest by resort to the local police; and a claim of authority to enter is likely to unlock the door as well. "In such cases there is no safety for the citizen, except [in] the judicial tribunals, for rights which have been invaded by the officers of the government, professing to act in its name. There remains to him but the alternative of resistance, which may amount to crime." . . .

That damages may be obtained for injuries consequent upon a violation of the Fourth Amendment by federal officials should hardly seem a surprising proposition. . . . "[I]t is well settled that where legal rights have been invaded, and a federal statute provides for a general right to sue for such invasion, federal courts may use any available remedy to make good the wrong done." *Bell v. Hood*, 327 U.S. at 684. . . .

Judgment reversed and case remanded.

Mr. Justice HARLAN, concurring in the judgment. [Justice Harlan reiterated that judicial action was a citizens only action in such a case.]

Mr. Chief Justice BURGER, dissenting.

I dissent from today's holding which judicially creates a damage remedy not provided for by the Constitution and not enacted by Congress. We would more surely preserve the important values of the doctrine of separation of powers [by] recommending a solution to the Congress as the branch of government in which the Constitution has vested the legislative power. Legislation is the business of the Congress, and it has the facilities and competence for that task — as we do not. . . .

[Congress] should develop an administrative or quasi-judicial remedy against the government itself to afford compensation and restitution for persons whose Fourth Amendment rights have been violated. The venerable doctrine of respondeat superior in our tort law provides an entirely appropriate conceptual basis for this remedy. [Such] a statutory scheme would have the added advantage of providing some remedy to the completely innocent persons who are sometimes the victims of illegal police conduct. . . .

NOTE

A *Bivens* action may be unavailable when the plaintiff has alternate remedies. In *Bush v. Lucas*, 462 U.S. 367 (1983), petitioner claimed that his First Amendment rights were violated when his supervisor demoted him, and sought recovery under *Bivens*. The Court concluded that a *Bivens* suit could be defeated when there was a congressional determination foreclosing the damages claim and making the Federal Tort Claims Act exclusive. *See also Schweiker v. Chilicky*, 487 U.S. 412 (1988) (improper denial of Social Security disability benefits was not actionable given elaborate remedial scheme devised by Congress).

C. IMMUNITY

Under both § 1983 and *Bivens*, governmental actors are protected by immunities from suit. Municipalities and other local governing bodies are not entitled to immunity.

MONELL v. DEPARTMENT OF SOCIAL SERVICES
436 U.S. 658 (1978)

Mr. Justice BRENNAN delivered the opinion of the Court.

Petitioners, a class of female employees of the Department of Social Services and of the Board of Education of the city of New York, commenced this action under 42 U.S.C. § 1983 in July 1971. The gravamen of the complaint was that the Board and the Department had as a matter of official policy compelled pregnant employees to take unpaid leaves of absence before such leaves were required for medical reasons. The suit sought injunctive relief and backpay for periods of unlawful forced leave. Named as defendants in the action were the Department and its Commissioner, the Board and its Chancellor, and the city of New York and its Mayor. . . .

[T]he District Court [concluded] that the acts complained of were unconstitutional. . . . Nonetheless plaintiffs' prayers for backpay were denied because any such damages would come ultimately from the City of New York and, therefore, to hold otherwise would be to "circumven[t]" the immunity conferred on municipalities by *Monroe v. Pape*, 365 U.S. 167 (1961). [In] *Monroe*, we held that "Congress did not undertake to bring municipal corporations within the ambit of [§ 1983]." The sole basis for this conclusion was an inference drawn from Congress' rejection of the "Sherman amendment" to the bill which became the Civil Rights Act of 1871, the precursor of § 1983. . . .

Our analysis of the legislative history of the Civil Rights Act of 1871 compels the conclusion that Congress did intend municipalities and other local government units to be included among those persons to whom § 1983 applies. Local governing bodies, therefore, can be sued directly under § 1983 for monetary, declaratory, or injunctive relief where [the action] alleged to be unconstitutional implements or executes a policy statement, ordinance, regulation, or decision officially adopted and promulgated by that body's officers. Moreover, although the touchstone of the § 1983 action against a government body is an allegation that official policy is responsible for a deprivation of rights protected by the Constitution, local governments, like every other § 1983 "person," by the very terms of the statute, may be sued for constitutional deprivations visited pursuant to governmental "custom" even though such a custom has not received formal approval through the body's official decisionmaking channels. As Mr. Justice Harlan, writing for the Court, said in *Adickes v. S.H. Kress & Co.*, 398 U.S. 144, 167-68 (1970): "Congress included customs and usages [in § 1983] because of the persistent and widespread discriminatory practices of state [officials]. Although not authorized by written law, such practices of state officials could well be so permanent and well settled as to constitute a 'custom or usage' with the force of law."

On the other hand, the language of § 1983, read against the background of the same legislative history, compels the conclusion that Congress did not intend municipalities to be held liable unless action pursuant to official municipal policy of some nature caused a constitutional tort. . . . [The language] plainly imposes liability on a government that, under color of some official policy, "causes" an employee to violate another's constitutional rights. At the same time, that language cannot be easily read to impose liability vicariously on governing bodies solely on the basis of the existence of an employer-employee relationship with a tortfeasor. [T]he fact that Congress did specifically provide that A's tort became B's liability if B "caused" A to subject another to a tort suggests that Congress did not intend § 1983 liability to attach where such causation was absent.

Equally important, creation of a federal law of respondeat superior would have raised all the constitutional problems associated with the obligation to keep the peace, an obligation Congress chose not to impose because it thought imposition of such an obligation unconstitutional. . . .

We conclude, therefore, that a local government may not be sued under § 1983 for an injury inflicted solely by its employees or agents. [I]t is when execution of a government's policy or custom, whether made by its lawmakers or by those whose edicts or acts may fairly be said to represent official policy, inflicts the injury that the government as an entity is responsible under § 1983. Since this case unquestionably involves official policy as the moving force of the constitutional violation found by the District Court, we must reverse the judgment below. . . .

[T]he judgment of the Court of Appeals is

Reversed.

Mr. Justice REHNQUIST, with whom THE CHIEF JUSTICE joins, dissenting.

[T]he Court abandons [a] long and consistent line of precedents, offering in justification only an elaborate canvass of the same legislative history which was before the Court in 1961. . . . None of the Members of this Court can foresee the practical consequences of today's [decision].

NOTES

1. *What constitutes government custom or policy?* In *Pembaur v. City of Cincinnati*, 475 U.S. 469 (1985), police officers had writs allowing them to search for and detain witnesses. When the officers attempted to serve the writs at a doctor's office, they were met with resistance. The County Prosecutor told his assistant to instruct the officers to "go in and get [the witnesses]," and the assistant passed these instructions along to the police. The police, after unsuccessfully trying to force the door, chopped it down with an axe. The Court held that the officers acted pursuant to municipal policy:

> [A] municipality may be liable under § 1983 for a single decision by its properly constituted legislative body [because] even a single decision by such a body unquestionably constitutes an act of official government policy. . . . Municipal liability attaches only where the decisionmaker possesses final authority to establish municipal policy with respect to the action ordered. . . . [M]unicipal liability under § 1983 attaches where [a] deliberate choice to follow a course of action is made from among various alternatives by the official or officials responsible for establishing final policy with respect to the subject matter in question. [T]he Deputy Sheriffs who attempted to serve the capiases at petitioner's clinic found themselves in a difficult situation. Unsure of the proper course of action[,] they sought instructions from their supervisors. The instructions [were] to follow the orders of the County Prosecutor. The Prosecutor made a considered decision based on his understanding of the law and commanded the officers forcibly to enter petitioner's clinic. That decision directly caused the violation of petitioner's Fourth Amendment rights. [T]he County Sheriff and the County Prosecutor could establish county policy under [these] circumstances. . . .

2. *The Eleventh Amendment.* In *Will v. Michigan Department of State Police*, 491 U.S. 58 (1989), the Supreme Court held that § 1983 actions were not available against a state or its subdivision. *See also Quern v. Jordan*, 440 U.S. 332 (1979), in which the Court reaffirmed the principle that a state could not be joined as a defendant in a § 1983 suit without violating the Eleventh Amendment. As for the availability of injunctive relief against the states, *see Hutto v. Finney*, 437 U.S. 678 (1978).

SIEGERT v. GILLEY
500 U.S. 226 (1991)

Chief Justice REHNQUIST delivered the opinion of the Court.

[Petitioner] Frederick A. Siegert, a clinical psychologist, was employed at St. Elizabeths Hospital, a Federal Government facility in Washington, D.C., from November 1979 to October 1985. He was a behavior therapy coordinator specializing in work with mentally retarded children and, to a lesser extent, with adults. In January 1985, respondent H. Melvyn Gilley became head of the division for which Siegert worked.

In August 1985, St. Elizabeths notified Siegert that it was preparing to terminate his employment. Siegert was informed that his "proposed removal was based upon his inability to report for duty in a dependable and reliable manner, his failure to comply with supervisory directives, and cumulative charges of absence without approved leave." After meeting with hospital officials, Siegert agreed to resign from the hospital and thereby avoid a termination that might damage his reputation.

Following his resignation from St. Elizabeths, Siegert began working as a clinical psychologist at a United States Army Hospital in Bremerhaven, West Germany. Because of the requirement that he be "credentialed" to work in hospitals operated by the Army, Siegert signed a "Credential Information Request Form" asking that St. Elizabeths Hospital provide to his prospective supervisor[,] "all information on job performance and the privileges" he had enjoyed while a member of its staff. Siegert's request was referred to Gilley because he had been Siegert's supervisor. . . . Gilley notified the Army by letter that "he could not recommend [Siegert] for privileges as a psychologist." [Gilley] wrote that he "consider[ed] Dr. Siegert to be both inept and unethical, perhaps the least trustworthy individual I have supervised in my thirteen years at [St. Elizabeths]." After receiving this letter, the Army Credentials Committee told Siegert that since "reports about him were 'extremely unfavorable' [the] committee [was] recommending that [Siegert] not be credentialed."

After being denied credentials by the committee, Siegert was turned down for a position he sought with an Army hospital in Stuttgart. Siegert then returned to Bremerhaven where he was given provisional credentials, limited to his work with adults. Siegert filed administrative appeals with the Office of the Surgeon General to obtain full credentials[, but was denied]. Soon thereafter, his "federal service employment [was] terminated."

Upon learning of Gilley's letter[,] Siegert filed suit. . . . Relying on *Bivens v. Six Unknown Fed. Narcotics Agents*, 403 U.S. 388 (1971), Siegert sought $4 million in damages [based on] an infringement of his "liberty interests" in violation of [the] Due Process Clause of the Fifth Amendment. Siegert also [asserted] state-law claims of defamation, intentional infliction of emotional distress, and interference with contractual relations. [Gilley asserted] the defense of qualified immunity under *Harlow v. Fitzgerald*, 457 U.S. 800 (1982), contending that Siegert's allegations did not state the violation of any "clearly established" constitutional right. . . . [We] granted certiorari [to] clarify the analytical structure under which a claim of qualified immunity should be addressed. . . .

[Qualified] immunity is a defense that must be pleaded by a defendant official. "[O]n summary judgment, the judge [may] determine, not only the currently applicable law, but whether that law was clearly established at the time an action occurred. . . . Until this threshold immunity question is resolved, discovery should not be allowed."

In this case, Siegert based his constitutional claim on the theory that Gilley's actions, undertaken with malice, deprived him of a "liberty interest" secured by the Fifth Amendment to the United States Constitution. He contended that the loss of his position at the Bremerhaven Hospital, followed by the refusal of the Army hospital in Stuttgart to consider his application for employment, and his general inability to find comparable work because of Gilley's letter, constituted such a deprivation. . . .

A necessary concomitant to the determination of whether the constitutional right asserted by a plaintiff is "clearly established" at the time the defendant acted is the determination of whether the plaintiff has asserted a violation of a constitutional right at all. Decision of this purely legal question permits courts expeditiously to weed out suits which fail the test without requiring a defendant who rightly claims qualified immunity to engage in expensive and time consuming preparation to defend the suit on its merits. One of the purposes of immunity, absolute or qualified, is to spare a defendant not only unwarranted liability, but unwarranted demands customarily imposed upon those defending a long drawn out lawsuit. . . .

[Siegert] failed not only to allege the violation of a constitutional right that was clearly established at the time of Gilley's actions, but also to establish the violation of any constitutional right at all.

In *Paul v. Davis*, 424 U.S. 693 (1976), the plaintiff's photograph was included by local police chiefs in a "flyer" of "active shoplifters," after petitioner had been arrested for shoplifting. The shoplifting charge was eventually dismissed, and the plaintiff filed suit under 42 U.S.C. § 1983 [alleging] that the officials' actions inflicted a stigma to his reputation that would seriously impair his future employment opportunities, and thus deprived him under color of state law of liberty interests protected by the Fourteenth Amendment. . . . We rejected the plaintiff's claim, holding that injury to reputation by itself was not a "liberty" interest protected under the Fourteenth Amendment. . . . Defamation, by itself, is a tort actionable under the laws of most States, but not a constitutional deprivation.

The facts alleged by Siegert cannot [state] a claim for denial of a constitutional right. . . . The alleged defamation was not uttered incident to the termination of Siegert's employment by the hospital, since he voluntarily resigned from his position at the hospital, and the letter was written [later]. The statements contained in the letter would undoubtedly damage the reputation of one in his position, and impair his future employment prospects. But the plaintiff in *Paul v. Davis* similarly alleged serious impairment of his future employment opportunities as well as other harm. Most defamation plaintiffs attempt to show some sort of special damage and out-of-pocket loss which flows from the injury to their reputation. But so long as such damage flows from injury caused by the defendant to a plaintiff's reputation, it may be recoverable under state tort law but it is not recoverable in a *Bivens* action. . . .

Affirmed.

Justice MARSHALL, with whom Justice BLACKMUN joins, and with whom Justice STEVENS joins as to Parts II and III, dissenting.

Paul holds that injury to reputation, standing alone, is not enough to demonstrate deprivation of a liberty interest. *Paul* also establishes, however, that injury to reputation does deprive a person of a liberty interest when the injury is combined with the impairment of "some more tangible" government benefit. It is enough [if] the plaintiff shows that the reputational injury causes the "loss of government employment," or the imposition of a legal disability. . . . This standard is met here because the injury to Siegert's reputation caused him to lose the benefit of eligibility for future government employment. . . . Gilley's letter caused him not to be credentialed, and thus effectively foreclosed his eligibility for future Government employment. . . .

[A]n individual suffers the loss of a protected liberty interest "'where government action has operated to bestow a badge of disloyalty or infamy, with an attendant foreclosure from other employment opportunity.'" [It] should have been [clear] to any reasonable governmental official that mailing stigmatizing letters [that] would severely impair or effectively foreclose a government employee from obtaining similar government employment in the future would deprive the individual of a constitutionally protected liberty interest. [The] loss in Siegert's case [is] tragic because his professional specialty [is] difficult to practice outside of government institutions. . . .

NOTES

1. In accord is *Pierson v. Ray*, 386 U.S. 547 (1967), where the Court recognized a qualified immunity for police officers in the conduct of their duties. In *Wood v. Strickland*, 420 U.S. 308 (1975), the Court explained this standard: "[T]he appropriate standard [contains elements of objectivity and subjectivity]. The official [must] be acting sincerely and with a belief that he is doing right, but an act violating [rights cannot be] justified by ignorance or disregard of settled, indisputable law." In *Malley v. Briggs*, 475 U.S. 335 (1986), the Court held that, in applying for a warrant, officers could be civilly liable if "no reasonably competent officer would have concluded that a warrant should issue." "[I]f offi-

cers of reasonable competence could disagree on this issue, immunity should be recognized."

2. *Judicial Immunity.* In *Forrester v. White*, 484 U.S. 219 (1988), the Court recognized that, while state court judges were absolutely immune from suit for "judicial functions," they can be sued for their non-judicial acts. In *Forrester*, the judge dismissed a subordinate employee because of her sex. The Court concluded that the dismissal did not constitute a judicial act.

3. *Prosecutorial Immunity.* In *Imbler v. Pachtman*, 424 U.S. 409 (1976), the Court held that a prosecutor who is sued for withholding evidence at trial was protected by an absolute immunity. However, in *Buckley v. Fitzsimmons*, 509 U.S. 259 (1993), the Court held that:

> When a prosecutor "functions as an administrator rather than as an officer of the court" he is entitled only to qualified immunity. . . . When a prosecutor performs the investigative functions normally performed by a detective or police officer, it is "neither appropriate nor justifiable [that] immunity should protect the one and not the other." . . .

> [S]tatements to the media are not entitled to absolute immunity. [W]hile prosecutors, like all attorneys, were entitled to absolute immunity from defamation liability for statements made during the course of judicial proceedings and relevant to them, most statements made out of court received only good-faith immunity. [Comments] to the media have no functional tie to the judicial process just because they are made by a prosecutor. . . .

4. *Municipal Immunity.* In *Owen v. City of Independence*, 445 U.S. 622 (1980), the Court held that "there is no tradition of immunity for municipal corporations, and neither history nor policy supports a construction of § 1983 that would justify the qualified immunity accorded [a city]. We hold, therefore, that the municipality may not assert the good faith of its officers or agents as a defense to liability under § 1983."

5. *Bivens Immunities. Butz v. Economu*, 438 U.S. 478 (1978), involved immunity claims by federal officials working in the Executive Branch who instituted an investigation and an administrative proceeding against plaintiff in retaliation for his criticism of the agency. The Court analogized to cases decided under § 1983: "[I]n the absence of congressional direction to the contrary, there is no basis for according to federal officials a higher degree of immunity from liability when sued for a constitutional infringement as authorized by *Bivens* than is accorded state officials when sued for the identical violation under § 1983. The constitutional injuries [are] of no greater magnitude than those for which federal officials may be responsible. . . ."

PROBLEMS

1. A prisoner in a city jail was in line in the jail cafeteria when he was attacked by another prisoner. A jail guard came to the prisoner's aid, but only after the prisoner's ear had been cut off in the attack. The jail's doctor treated the prisoner without anesthetic, informed him that the ear was not needed and threw it away. The prisoner is thinking about bringing a § 1983 which would allege that the guard failed to come to his aid in a reasonable amount of time resulting in the loss of the ear. In addition, the prisoner wants to sue the prison doctor for failing to provide him with medication, as well as for the doctor's decision to throw away the ear. Finally, the prisoner wants to sue the city for failure to adequately train the doctor. Would you advise the prisoner to bring the suit? What would he have to prove in order to prevail? Can he overcome any immunities the guard and doctor might raise? Is he likely to recover against the city itself? *See Williams v. Vincent*, 508 F.2d 541 (2d Cir. 1974).

2. A court held that overcrowding at a city jail violated the constitutional rights of pretrial detainees. The court was concerned about the practice of placing two inmates in cells designed for one ("double celling"). Because of crisis conditions at the jail, the court amended its order to permit double celling under tight restrictions: no pretrial detainee can be double-celled for more than 12 hours per day nor for more than 30 days. Later, the court held city officials in contempt for failing to comply with the restrictions. Shortly thereafter, some inmates set fire to one unit of the jail. Plaintiff inmates sued to recover damages for injuries for (1) the fire itself, which they alleged was caused by unconstitutional overcrowding of the jail, and (2) alleged violations of their constitutional rights arising from a delay in evacuating the cell block and extinguishing the fire, inadequate medical care after the fire, and the temporary denial of access to telephone calls, mail privileges, showers, clean linen and clothing, recreation, and attendance at religious services. Can plaintiffs recover under § 1983? Against which defendants might they recover? The city? The mayor? Jail officials? Guards? To what extent will qualified immunity protect the defendants? *See Marsh v. Barry*, 824 F.2d 1139 (D.C. Cir. 1987).

3. Police officers stopped plaintiff for a traffic violation near his parents' home. By law, the officers were entitled to stop plaintiff and to issue a summons, but were not entitled to arrest him. The officers pulled plaintiff from his vehicle, and beat and choked him with their flashlights and hands. Plaintiff's parents, who also sued, heard the commotion and ran outside where they saw their son being beaten. The officers threatened the parents with arrest, pushed and shoved plaintiff's mother, and partially broke the door to the home after chasing plaintiff's father inside. What do plaintiffs need to show in order to recover against the officers? Can they also recover against the city? *See Barnier v. Szentmiklosi*, 565 F. Supp. 869 (E.D. Mich. 1983).

Chapter 20
MISUSE OF LEGAL PROCESS

A. INTRODUCTION

In this chapter we will examine special tort actions that are designed to provide a remedy to persons who have been subjected to the expense, inconvenience,
and embarrassment of being forced to defend themselves from various types of
unjustified legal proceedings, involving both criminal and civil actions. There are
generally two basic types of these tort actions. The tort of "Malicious Prosecution" typically refers to actions that have been *wrongfully initiated* against the
complaining party (Section B, *infra*), whereas the tort of "Abuse of Process"
refers to those actions which, although properly initiated, nevertheless have
been maintained for some *improper purpose* not intended in the law (Section C,
infra).

As a general proposition, both of these types of tort actions are disfavored in
most jurisdictions. This is in large part due to American constitutional, as well
as common law history, that favor "open access" to the courts for all citizens with
respect to the resolution of their conflicts. Permitting any tort actions against
the unsuccessful parties involved in prior litigation has an obvious "chilling
effect" upon those who might otherwise wish to assert close or questionable
legal claims, for fear of being held liable in damages if the court or jury in that
prior case should disagree. Consequently, most courts have been fairly strict in
construing and applying the various requirements for imposing liability with
respect to these torts.

B. MALICIOUS PROSECUTION

The modern-day tort of "malicious prosecution" has long been recognized in
one form or another by the common law. Indeed, its origins may be traced all the
way back to tenth or eleventh century Anglo-Saxon courts where the unsuccessful litigant quite literally would lose his tongue. *See* Note, *Groundless Litigation and the Malicious Prosecution Debate: A Historical Analysis*, 88 YALE L.J.
1218, 1212 (1979). The original tort of "Malicious Prosecution" was intended
solely as a remedy for those persons who had been wrongfully subjected to
criminal prosecutions. As such, the specific requirements for the *prima facie*
cause of action originally required a *criminal* prosecution, initiated with malice
and *without probable cause*, which terminated in favor of the accused. Over time,
however, a majority of jurisdictions have expanded this tort to include *civil*
actions as well as criminal actions. Because of these developments, the specific
requirements of this tort may vary somewhat from one jurisdiction to another.
In the materials that follow, we will examine first the tort as it applies with

respect to a traditional criminal proceeding, and then we will look at how the individual requirements of this tort must be further adapted to accommodate the differences inherent in an underlying civil action.

1. Malicious Prosecution of a Criminal Action

BANKS v. NORDSTROM
787 P.2d 953 (Wash. Ct. App. 1990)

RINGOLD, J.

The plaintiff Lisa Banks appeals from a summary judgment dismissing her complaint against defendants Nordstrom, Inc., and several Nordstrom's employees (referred to collectively as Nordstrom). Finding that material factual issues remain regarding her claim for malicious prosecution, we reverse.

On December 26, 1987, Gail Smith, a Nordstrom security officer at the downtown Seattle Nordstrom store, observed five individuals shoplifting. Seattle police officers were called. The suspects were questioned by Smith and the police officers and then arrested. Two of the suspects were identified as Lisa Banks and her father John Banks. In actuality, the individuals arrested were Sharon Banks, Lisa's older sister, and Sharon's boyfriend. Sharon was carrying Lisa's driver's license. The suspects were taken to the police station, booked, and released.

On January 5, 1988, defendant Evelyn Dingman a/k/a Sevelette, Nordstrom's civil claims manager, sent a letter to Lisa demanding civil restitution totaling $889.70. This letter, received on January 6, 1988, was Lisa's first notice of the shoplifting incident. At about this time, Lisa also received a notice from the prosecuting attorney's office that she had been charged with first degree theft and was scheduled to be arraigned on January 11, 1988.

Lisa immediately telephoned Gail Smith and informed her of the error. At Smith's request, Lisa and her father went to the Nordstrom store later the same day. Smith confirmed that Lisa and John Banks were not the individuals arrested on December 26, 1987, and gave Lisa a handwritten note on Nordstrom stationery, dated January 6, 1988 stating that Lisa was not the same woman who was arrested on December 26. Lisa states that Smith also told her that she would get the charges dismissed.

Smith maintains that she called a "Detective Corbett" of the Seattle Police Department and told him that Lisa was not the woman arrested on December 26, 1987. The record does not disclose, however, who "Detective Corbett" is or when this call occurred. By affidavit, Detective Frank Kampsen, one of the investigating officers, stated that the Seattle Police Department's fingerprint system was inoperable on December 26, 1987, making it impossible to discover the false identification provided by the suspects. Kampsen further averred that the involvement of store security generally ceases at the time of arrest until trial and that Nordstrom "would not and could not" have prevented Banks's arraignment.

Lisa also contacted the prosecutor's office and was informed that the charges against her were still pending and that if she did not appear at the arraignment, a bench warrant for her arrest would be issued and she could go to jail. Lisa was unable to contact anyone at Nordstrom, except Ms. Sevelette on one occasion, who told her that she could not do anything because of "inventory." On January 11, 1988, Lisa appeared at arraignment. After entering her "not guilty" plea, Lisa was booked, fingerprinted, and released. The omnibus hearing was scheduled for January 22, 1988.

On the day after arraignment, Lisa retained counsel, who also was unable to contact either Ms. Smith or Ms. Sevelette. Counsel received a telephone call on January 21, 1988, from Mike Wargin, Nordstrom's security manager, who stated that "all efforts will be made to prevent a false arrest," but that he had not yet contacted Gail Smith or the prosecutor.

In response to a letter from Lisa's counsel, Ms. Sevelette sent a notarized statement by messenger to the prosecutor on January 22, 1988, indicating that Lisa and John Banks were not the shoplifting suspects. Based upon the affidavit, the charges against Lisa were dismissed just prior to the omnibus hearing. Both Smith and Sevelette assert that they heard nothing further from Lisa after she came to the store for identification until the receipt of the letter from Lisa's counsel on January 19.

On March 18, 1988, Lisa filed the instant action against Nordstrom, Evelyn Sevelette, and Gail Smith, alleging claims of malicious prosecution, outrage, invasion of privacy, negligent hiring and supervision, and violations of the Consumer Protection Act. Lisa sought damages for "personal, mental and emotional anguish, . . . embarrassment and humiliation." Lisa also sought recovery for legal expenses and triple damages. The trial court granted Nordstrom's motion for summary judgment dismissing the action. This appeal followed.

Malicious Prosecution

Malicious prosecution is the label attached to a tort violating one's freedom from wrongful prosecution. *See* W. KEETON, D. DOBBS, R. KEETON & D. OWEN, PROSSER AND KEETON ON TORTS § 119, at 870 (5th ed. 1984).

Banks first contends that there are material factual issues regarding her malicious prosecution claim. In order to maintain an action for malicious prosecution, the plaintiff must establish

> (1) that the prosecution claimed to have been malicious was instituted or continued by the defendant; (2) that there was want of probable cause for the institution or continuation of the prosecution; (3) that the proceedings were instituted or continued through malice; (4) that the proceedings terminated on the merits in favor of the plaintiff, or were

abandoned; and (5) that the plaintiff suffered injury or damage as a result of the prosecution.

Peasley v. Puget Sound Tug & Barge Co., 13 Wn.2d 485, 497, 125 P.2d 681 (1942). Nordstrom asserts that no material factual issues exist as to elements (1), (2), and (5).

1. Prosecution Instituted or Continued by the Defendant.

Nordstrom's primary argument is that it did not "institute" or "continue" the prosecution against Lisa but merely called the police and assisted in the apprehension of the shoplifting suspects. No authority supports such a narrow interpretation of the "institution" requirement in a malicious prosecution action. Moreover, the basis for Lisa's claim is not the institution of the prosecution, but rather Nordstrom's alleged malicious continuation of the prosecution between January 6, 1988, when Nordstrom became aware of the misidentification, and January 22, 1988, when the prosecution was dismissed. Consequently Detective Kampsen's assertion that Nordstrom could not have prevented Lisa's arraignment is essentially irrelevant.

Although Washington law has long recognized a cause of action for malicious prosecution or the malicious continuation of a prosecution, no reported Washington decision has directly addressed the circumstances here, in which a party that properly instituted or procured the institution of criminal proceedings subsequently became aware of the defendant's innocence. Potential liability under such circumstances is recognized by the Restatement (Second) of Torts § 655 (1977), which states:

§ 655. Continuing Criminal Proceedings

A private person who takes an active part in continuing or procuring the continuation of criminal proceedings initiated by himself or by another is subject to the same liability for malicious prosecution as if he had then initiated the proceedings.

As one commentator has observed:

Not only the instigation of criminal proceedings but continuing to prosecute such proceedings maliciously after learning of their groundless nature will result in liability, although they had been begun in good faith and with probable cause. Clearly, it is as much a wrong against the victim and as socially or morally unjustifiable to take an active part in a prosecution after knowledge that there is no factual foundation for it, as to instigate such proceedings in the first place. (Footnote omitted.)

1 F. HARPER & F. JAMES, TORTS § 4.4, at 307 (1956).

Whether a party has "continued" a criminal proceeding for purposes of malicious prosecution liability depends on the specific facts of the case. There is general agreement, however, that where the instigator loses control of the case once prosecution has commenced, his or her continued participation in the prosecution will not support liability for malicious prosecution. *Walsh v. Eberlein*, 114 Ariz. 342, 560 P.2d 1249, 1252 (Ct. App. 1977). "[A] malicious prosecution action will not lie where a prosecuting attorney is left to judge the propriety of proceeding with the charge and acts on his own initiative in doing so." *Walsh v. Eberlein, supra* at 345.

In *Walsh v. Eberlein, supra*, the plaintiff was arrested and charged with passing forged checks, based primarily on eyewitness identifications. Subsequently, the investigating detective became aware of exculpatory handwriting and polygraph evidence, as well as the existence of another suspect who had confessed to passing forged checks using the same name and identification as that allegedly used by the plaintiff. The detective informed the prosecuting attorney of only a portion of the exculpatory evidence. After the charges against her were dismissed just prior to trial, the plaintiff sued the investigating detective for malicious prosecution. After a judgment was entered in the plaintiff's favor, the detective appealed.

In reversing the judgment, the *Walsh* court rejected the plaintiff's contention that the detective had maliciously "continued" the prosecution by failing to notify the prosecutor of all of the exculpatory evidence. The court noted that the prosecutor was aware of all of the exculpatory evidence and independently decided to continue with the prosecution. *Walsh*, at 345. Moreover, the prosecutor had expressly testified that dismissal of the prosecution was "not [the investigating detective's] decision . . . ." *Walsh*, at 346. Resolution of the "continuation" issue in *Walsh* thus rested on a factual basis that is still disputed in the instant case.

Comment c to § 655 of the Restatement (Second) of Torts is misleading in suggesting that only affirmative conduct will sustain a cause of action for malicious prosecution.

As in all tort law inaction, failure to act, or an omission when there is a duty to act affirmatively (do something) may impose liability. The Restatement defines "tortious conduct" as follows:

> The word "tortious" is used throughout the Restatement of this Subject to denote the fact that conduct whether of act or omission is of such a character as to subject the actor to liability under the principles of the laws of Torts.

Restatement (Second) of Torts § 6 (1965).

We also decline to follow comment c to the extent it suggests that Nordstrom, after instituting the prosecution against the defendant, had no duty to inform the prosecutor once it learned of the mistake. Comment c would apply only if "the instigator of a proceeding loses control over the case once the prosecution has been initiated. . . ." *Walsh v. Eberlein*, 114 Ariz. 342, 345, 560 P.2d 1249, 1252 (Ct. App. 1977). No case has been cited, nor have we found any decision, in which a court has exculpated a defendant from liability by remaining passive when there is a duty to act affirmatively. Whether Nordstrom had a duty, by virtue of its conduct here and whether Nordstrom lost control are material issues of fact to be determined by the trier of fact.

Here, when viewing the following evidence in the light most favorable to Lisa, a trier of fact could find that Nordstrom caused the continuation or prolongation of the criminal proceedings: Gail Smith assured Lisa that Nordstrom would have the charge dismissed. Lisa called the prosecutor's office seeking to avoid her appearance at the arraignment. Although Smith contends that she contacted a detective at the Seattle Police Department, the record does not indicate when this occurred. As late as January 21, the day before the scheduled omnibus hearing, Nordstrom's security manager indicated to appellant's counsel that he had not yet contacted the prosecutor. Although Nordstrom maintains it had no influence over the matter once the police had arrested the shoplifters, it is undisputed that the prosecution was dismissed immediately after Nordstrom sent a notarized statement to the prosecutor.

2. Probable Cause.

Nordstrom next contends that there was probable cause to institute the criminal proceeding against Lisa, based upon the identification provided by the shoplifting suspect. Generally, the dismissal of criminal charges establishes a prima facie case of want of probable cause in favor of the plaintiff. *Peasley v. Puget Sound Tug & Barge Co., supra* at 498. Proof of probable cause is a complete defense to a malicious prosecution action. *Pace v. Brodie-National, Inc.*, 60 Wn.2d 654, 656, 374 P.2d 1000 (1962). A full and honest disclosure of all material facts to the prosecutor establishes probable cause as a matter of law. *Robertson v. Bell*, 57 Wn.2d 505, 510, 358 P.2d 149 (1961). Even if true, however, Nordstrom's assertion that there was probable cause to initiate the criminal proceeding is irrelevant; the issue is whether the defendant maliciously continued the prosecution. As set forth above, the circumstances surrounding the continuation of the proceeding against Lisa are disputed. Consequently, whether there was a want of probable cause is for the jury. *See Bender v. Seattle*, 99 Wn.2d 582, 593-94, 664 P.2d 492 (1983).

3. Malice.

Relying on its argument that it did not institute the prosecution and that, in any event, there was probable cause to support initiation of the prosecution, Nordstrom fails to address the malice requirements. This reliance is incorrect for two reasons. First, a dismissal or termination of the criminal proceeding may establish a prima facie case of malice. The rule is stated in *Pallett v. Thompkins*, 10 Wn.2d 697, 699-700, 118 P.2d 190 (1941):

> A prima facie case of want of probable cause (*from which malice may be inferred*) is made by proof that the criminal proceedings were dismissed or terminated in plaintiff's favor. But malice is not necessarily to be inferred from such prima facie showing of want of probable cause.

(Citations and italics omitted. Italics ours.) *See also Peasley v. Puget Sound Tug & Barge* Co., *supra* at 498 (malice may be inferred from lack of probable cause). Second, in a malicious prosecution action, malice

> takes on a more general meaning, so that the requirement that malice be shown as part of the plaintiff's case in an action for malicious prosecution may be satisfied by proving that the prosecution complained of was undertaken from improper or wrongful motives or in reckless disregard of the rights of the plaintiff.

Peasley v. Puget Sound Tug & Barge Co., supra at 502.

Whether Nordstrom's actions between January 6 and January 22 manifested "reckless disregard" for the appellant's rights is a factual question.

4. Damages.

Nordstrom next contends that Lisa's claimed injuries of legal fees and emotional distress are insufficient to support a malicious prosecution action as a matter of law. Nordstrom relies on the general rule that

> unless there is interference with the person or property by a provisional remedy such as arrest, injunction or attachment as an incident to the maintenance of an action, a suit for malicious prosecution will not lie despite the fact that the action was instituted maliciously and without probable cause. (Italics omitted.)

Petrich v. McDonald, 44 Wn.2d 211, 220, 266 P.2d 1047 (1954) (quoting *Adley Express Co. v. Corn Exch. Bank Trust Co.*, 99 F. Supp. 406 (S.D.N.Y. 1951)).

This principle was reaffirmed in *Gem Trading Co. v. Cudahy Corp.*, 92 Wn.2d 956, 965, 603 P.2d 828 (1979), which held that a malicious prosecution action requires both an arrest or seizure of property and some special injury. Legal fees and emotional distress are not the requisite type of injuries in a malicious prosecution action absent an arrest or seizure of property. *Fenner v. Lindsay*, 28 Wn. App. 626, 630, 625 P.2d 180 (1981).

Nordstrom maintains that Lisa has not suffered the requisite harm because it was her sister who was in fact "arrested" and because Lisa appeared at arraignment "voluntarily." This cramped characterization of "arrest" ignores the reality of a summons to appear for arraignment. Lisa not only appeared at arraignment, she entered a plea and was then fingerprinted, released on bail, and required to appear on January 22, 1988, for the omnibus hearing. This was sufficient "interference with the person" to support a malicious prosecution claim.

In decisions subsequent to *Gem Trading Co.*, our Supreme Court has deemphasized the arrest and special injury requirements in malicious prosecution actions. In *Bender v. Seattle, supra*, a jeweler was charged with grand larceny and arrested; his store was searched pursuant to a search warrant and he was booked and held in custody for a short time prior to release on bail. The charge was subsequently dismissed, and the jeweler sued the City of Seattle for, among other things, malicious prosecution. Although the plaintiff in Bender had been arrested, the court did not discuss any special injury and reinstated a jury award of $80,000 in unspecified damages.

The court, in *Turngren v. King Cy.*, 104 Wn.2d 293, 705 P.2d 258 (1985), reversed a summary judgment dismissing the plaintiffs' malicious prosecution claim. The plaintiffs had been required to leave their house and stand in the yard at gunpoint while their house was searched pursuant to a warrant. The area had also been cordoned off and neighbors had been told to leave. The plaintiffs were not arrested or booked and no charges were ever brought. The plaintiffs filed an action for damages. In holding that the plaintiffs had made out a prima facie case of malicious prosecution, the court focused on the issue of probable cause. There was no discussion of an arrest or seizure of property or of any special injury. . . .

The judgment of dismissal is reversed and the case remanded for further proceedings consistent with this opinion.

COLEMAN, C.J. (concurring in part, dissenting in part)

I agree with the majority that the trial court properly entered summary judgment on Banks' claims for outrage, invasion of privacy, [and] negligent hiring or supervision. . . . I disagree, however, with the majority's conclusion that material factual issues remain regarding her claim for malicious prosecution, and I therefore dissent from that portion of the opinion.

It is undisputed that the basis for Banks' claim of malicious prosecution is not the institution of the prosecution, which was clearly based upon probable cause, but rather Nordstrom's alleged malicious continuation of the prosecution between January 6, 1988, when Nordstrom became aware of the misidentification, and January 22, 1988, when the prosecution was dismissed. There is absolutely no evidence to support an inference that Nordstrom took any action in furtherance of the prosecution during this period. In fact, the uncontroverted evidence is that upon confirming that Banks was not the individual arrested on December 26, 1987, Gail Smith, a Nordstrom security officer, gave Banks a handwritten note on Nordstrom stationery dated January 6, 1988, stating that Banks was not the same woman who was arrested on December 26, 1987. For some inexplicable reason Banks did not show this document to any of the prosecuting authorities; nothing in the record indicates that she showed it to anyone at the arraignment or even raised the issue of the erroneous identification. Smith also filed an affidavit stating that she called "Detective Corbett" of the Seattle Police Department and told him that Banks was not the woman arrested on December 26, 1987. This statement, although uncorroborated, is not contradicted. The majority suggests that because Nordstrom arguably could have done more between January 6 and January 22, 1988, to obtain dismissal of the proceedings, it can be inferred that Nordstrom somehow continued the prosecution.

Contrary to the majority's assertion, potential liability under the circumstances presented by this record is not recognized by the Restatement (Second) of Torts § 655 (1977).

For liability to attach under the authority of this provision, an individual must take an active part in continuing or procuring the continuation of criminal proceedings initiated by himself or by another. The comments and illustration to section 655 repeatedly stress that liability for malicious prosecution depends upon the defendant taking some active role in the continuation of the prosecution; it is not enough that the defendant simply remain passive, even where the defendant possesses knowledge that the accused is innocent:

> b. The rule stated in this Section applies when the defendant has himself initiated criminal proceedings against another or procured their institution, upon probable cause and for a proper purpose, and thereafter takes an active part in pressing the proceedings after he has discovered that there is no probable cause for them. . . .
>
> Illustration:
>
> 1. A, by swearing out a complaint, initiates the criminal prosecution of B for theft of A's watch. Before trial A discovers that the watch was not stolen and he had merely mislaid it. He informs C of his discovery. For the purpose of compelling B to pay a debt owed to C, C persuades the prosecuting attorney to proceed with the trial. C is subject to liability to B for malicious prosecution.
>
> c. Active participation required. In order that there may be liability under the rule stated in this Section, the defendant must take an active part in their prosecution after learning that there is no probable cause for believing the accused guilty. It is not enough that he appears as a witness against the accused either under subpoena or voluntarily, and thereby aids in the prosecution of the charges which he knows to be groundless. His share in continuing the prosecution must be active, as by insisting upon or urging further prosecution. The fact that he initiated the proceedings does not make him liable under the rule stated in this Section merely because he intentionally refrains from informing a public prosecutor, into whose control the prosecution has passed, of subsequently discovered facts that clearly indicate the innocence of the accused, even though they have the effect of convincing him that this is the fact.

Restatement (Second) of Torts § 655, comments b, c (1977).

It is not necessary to determine if this court should follow comment c to section 655 of the Restatement (Second) of Torts to the extent that the comment suggests that Nordstrom had no duty to inform the prosecutor once it learned of the mistake. The restatement rule is clear that active participation in continuing the prosecution is required. In the record before us, Nordstrom did not in any sense actively participate in causing the continuation of this prosecution. Not only did Nordstrom not actively participate in the continuation of the prosecution, Nordstrom took affirmative steps to communicate to the authorities that there had been a misidentification. Moreover, in addition to the absence of any evidence of active participation, there is absolutely no evidence supporting any inference of malice. The majority suggests that because the criminal proceedings were dismissed in plaintiff's favor, that alone is sufficient to raise an inference of malice. The authorities relied upon by the majority do not support this proposition. In fact, as stated in *Peasley v. Puget Sound Tug & Barge Co.*, 13 Wn.2d 485, 502, 125 P.2d 681 (1942).

> [m]alice as a term of law has a broader significance than that which is applied to it in ordinary parlance. The word "malice" may simply denote ill will, spite, personal hatred, or vindictive motives according to the popular conception, but in its legal significance it includes something more. It takes on a more general meaning, so that the requirement that malice be shown as part of the plaintiff's case in an action for malicious prosecution may be satisfied by proving that the prosecution complained of was undertaken from improper or wrongful motives or in reckless disregard of the rights of the plaintiff. Impropriety of motive may be established in cases of this sort by proof that the defendant instituted the criminal proceedings against the plaintiff: (1) without believing him to be guilty, or (2) primarily because of hostility or ill will toward him, or (3) for the purpose of obtaining a private advantage as against him. Newell, Malicious Prosecution (1892), 237, § 3; 34 Am. Jur. 728, Malicious Prosecution, § 45; 38 C. J. 421-425, Malicious Prosecution, §§ 60-67; 3 Restatement, Torts (1938), § 668. We have recognized and applied this broader conception of the term in *Waring v. Hudspeth*, [75 Wash. 534, 135 P. 222 (1913)]. Compare *Ladd v. Miles*, [171 Wash. 44, 17 P.2d 875 (1932)].

In the instant case, the prosecution was not undertaken for "improper or wrongful motives", and there is absolutely nothing to suggest that Nordstrom took any action in furtherance of this prosecution in "reckless disregard of the rights of the plaintiff." Furthermore, actions for malicious prosecution are not favored in law and will be readily upheld only upon presentation of the proper elements. *Peasley*, at 496. For the reasons stated, I would affirm the summary judgment dismissal of Banks' claim for malicious prosecution.

NOTES

1. What is the basis for the disagreement between the majority and Chief Judge Coleman's opinions in *Banks*? Do they disagree as to the facts (or the legal interpretation of those facts) or does this disagreement relate to the legal inter-

pretation of the requirement that the defendant must actively participate in continuing the underlying prosecution?

General Requirements For a Malicious Prosecution Action

A. Prosecution Initiated or Continued by the Defendant

2. What does it mean to "initiate" a criminal prosecution? Does merely reporting a suspected crime to the proper authorities satisfy this requirement? What if a citizen demands that authorities act on his or her complaint?

3. In *Banks, supra*, the defendant was apparently justified in bringing the initial complaint against the accused. What, then, was the legal basis for the plaintiff's allegation that the defendant initiated criminal proceedings?

B. Absence of Probable Cause

4. What probable cause is necessary to sustain liability for the tort of malicious prosecution? Does this differ from the probable cause needed to maintain a traditional criminal prosecution?

5. Is probable cause for this tort determined on the basis of an objective or a subjective standard?

C. Malice

6. In the law, there are generally three distinct types of malice to which courts often refer. **Actual malice** may be defined as "[a]ny feeling of hatred, animosity, or ill will toward the plaintiff." *Keller v. Schwegmann Giant Supermarkets, Inc.*, 604 So. 2d 1058, 1061 (La. Ct. App. 1992). *Accord, Williams v. Kuppenheimer Mfg. Co.,* 105 N.C. 198, 202-03, 412 S.E.2d 897 (N.C. 1992). **Legal malice** is broader in scope than actual malice, and can include any improper or wrongful motive. *See, e.g., S.S. Kresge Co. v. Ruby*, 348 So. 2d 484, 489 (Ala. 1977); *Brodie v. Hawaii Automotive Retail Gasoline Dealers Ass'n*, 631 P.2d 600, 605 (Haw. Ct. App. 1981); *Owens v. Kroger Co.*, 430 So. 2d 843 (Miss. 1983); *Sanders v. Daniel International Corp.*, 682 S.W.2d 803, 808 (Mo. 1984). **Malice in law** may be defined generally as "a wrongful act done intentionally without just cause or excuse." *See Sanders v. Daniel International Corp.*, 682 S.W.2d 803, 808 (Mo. 1984). This type of malice does not require any proof as to the defendant's mental state, regardless of whether direct or indirect. Instead, the law simply *imputes* "malice in law" to any intentional wrongdoer who injures another person without just cause or legal excuse.

What type of malice is required for the tort of malicious prosecution? Which type of malice did the court in *Banks* apply?

D. Termination in Favor of the Accused

7. What does it mean to terminate the underlying criminal action "in favor of" the accused? If the original criminal charges are reduced to some lesser offense does this constitute a termination in favor of the accused?

E. Damages

8. Are special damages required for this tort, or are damages presumed? Can punitive damages be recovered?

Defenses to Malicious Prosecution

9. What if the defendant, before initiating criminal proceedings against the accused, seeks the advice of an attorney and only proceeds after receiving a favorable opinion from the attorney? What if the defendant only obtains such legal advice after first initiating the criminal proceedings without any regard to the law? Would this make any difference?

10. In *Birwood Paper Co. v. Damsky*, 229 So. 2d 514, 522 (Ala. 1969), the Alabama Supreme Court made the following comment as to the defendant's reliance upon the advice of counsel in a malicious prosecution lawsuit:

> Advice of counsel honestly sought and acted on in good faith is a complete defense to an action for malicious prosecution. Such advice, honestly sought and honestly acted on, supplies the indispensable element of probable cause.

According to the court in *Birwood*, is reliance upon the advice of counsel a defense to a malicious prosecution action in Alabama, or does it merely negate one of the *prima facie* requirements of the tort itself by supplying probable cause? Does it really make any difference which of these approaches the court chooses to follow? Isn't the ultimate outcome the same under either approach?

11. *Prosecutorial Immunity.* The public prosecutor who actually brings a criminal prosecution against the accused on behalf of the state (*i.e.*, prosecutor, district attorney, etc.) is *absolutely* immune from liability for the tort of malicious prosecution. *See, e.g., Powell v. Seay*, 553 P.2d 161 (Okla. 1976); *Rogers v. Hill*, 576 P.2d 328 (Or. 1978). *See also* RESTATEMENT (SECOND) OF TORTS § 656 (1977). What if the prosecutor's actions are proven to have been motivated by malice? *See* RESTATEMENT (SECOND) OF TORTS § 656 (1977), comment b.

Malicious Prosecution Distinguished from False Imprisonment

12. How is the tort of malicious prosecution different from the tort of false imprisonment? For an excellent discussion of the various distinctions between common law false imprisonment and malicious prosecution actions, see *Boose v. City of Rochester*, 421 N.Y.S.2d 740 (N.Y. App. Div. 1979).

2. Malicious Prosecution of a Civil Action

Arising as an outgrowth of the original common law action for malicious prosecution, some jurisdictions have long recognized as a separate tort the "malicious prosecution of a civil action." *See, e.g., Eastin v. Bank of Stockton*, 66 Cal. 123, 126-27, 4 P. 1106 (1884). In these jurisdictions, the major difference between the two types of actions lies in the defendant's initiation of a civil rather than a criminal proceeding, as well as in attempting to articulate precisely what constitutes the appropriate probable cause necessary for the filing of a civil complaint. Concerns over the constantly-expanding volume and scope of civil litigation in American courts have led some jurisdictions to simply reject this tort altogether. Other courts, while continuing to recognize the action, have nevertheless drastically restricted its scope, typically by declining to expand the definition of probable cause necessary to justify the filing of a civil complaint (*see, e.g., Wong v. Tabor*, 422 N.E.2d 1279 (Ind. Ct. App. 1981); *Friedman v. Dozorc*, 312 N.W.2d 585 (Mich. 1981)), or by refusing to abandon the traditional special injury rule with respect to such actions (*See, e.g., O'Toole v. Franklin*, 569 P.2d 561 (Or. 1977)). These courts generally justify their refusal to expand the scope of a separate malicious prosecution of a civil action tort by pointing to the existence of adequate existing remedies in favor of those who have been wrongfully accused in a civil case. (*See, e.g., Sheldon Appel Co. v. Albert & Oliker*, 765 P.2d 498 (Cal. 1989).) Such remedies include judicially-imposed sanctions against both litigants and their attorneys who file frivolous civil litigation, as well as various other procedural mechanisms that are generally designed to "weed out" unmerited civil claims.

For an example of non-tort responses to frivolous litigation, consider Federal Rule of Civil Procedure 11, a version of which is in force in approximately 35 states:

> Rule 11. Signing of Pleadings, Motions, and Other Papers; Representations to Court; Sanctions

> . . . .

> (b) Representations to Court.

> By presenting to the court (whether by signing, filing, submitting, or later advocating) a pleading, written motion, or other paper, an attorney or unrepresented party is certifying that to the best of the person's knowledge, information, and belief, formed after an inquiry reasonable under the circumstances, —

> (1) it is not being presented for any improper purpose, such as to harass or to cause unnecessary delay or needless increase in the cost of litigation; . . .

C. ABUSE OF PROCESS

Whereas the tort of "malicious prosecution" focuses entirely upon the defendant's wrongful conduct in *initiating* criminal or civil actions against the plaintiff, the separate tort of "abuse of process" concerns the wrongful *use* of such actions, even when otherwise properly initiated, to accomplish some ulterior purpose other than that for which such actions were designed. While these two torts are similar in that they both focus upon the defendant's subjective motive in acting, they differ significantly as to the focal point of the defendant's wrongful conduct. In malicious prosecution actions, there is no legal justification for the underlying claim. It simply never should have been brought at all, and it would not have been except for the defendant's wrongful motive. In abuse of process actions there is legal justification for the underlying claim against the plaintiff, regardless of the defendant's actual motive in bringing it. However, in abuse of process, even though the underlying claim may have been technically proper, criminal or civil process is abused for some purpose that clearly was never intended. Here, the defendant's motive is important in establishing the wrongful use of such a legal process against the plaintiff.

VITTANDS v. SUDDUTH
730 N.E.2d 325 (Mass. App. 2000)

LENK, J.

. . .

Facts and procedural history. At the heart of this case is lot 4A, apparently a quite desirably situated lot with ocean views, located on Hesperus Avenue in the Magnolia section of the city of Gloucester (city). Sudduth, as trustee of the Hesperus Avenue Realty Trust, purchased the six-lot subdivision containing lot 4A in 1985 and sought to develop the subdivision for residential use. By 1994, after approximately nine years of proceedings, Sudduth had obtained from the city and the Commonwealth all of the necessary building and sewage disposal permits that would allow construction of residences on the subdivision finally to go forward.

The plaintiffs are neighbors but not abutters to lot 4A. Sudduth alleges in affidavit form that several of the plaintiffs (the neighbors) confronted her from time to time, informing her that they would never allow anything to be built on lot 4A, that their children had always played on it, and that the neighbors considered it their "private park." According to Sudduth, one of the neighbors, Jekabs P. Vittands, told her in 1985 that he was going to "take" all her land and later told her that he would prevent the construction of anything on the Hesperus Avenue lots at all costs. The neighbors state that they had been "involved in a series of administrative proceedings and litigation involving the development of Lots 4A, 5A and 6A." Indeed, we had occasion several years ago to observe that the neighbors had been "actively opposing the development of the defendant's property for nine years." *See Vittands v. Sudduth*, 41 Mass.App.Ct. 515, 515 n. 3, 671 N.E.2d 527 (1996) (*Vittands I*).

In November, 1993, the neighbors' attorney, Brian Cassidy, allegedly discovered for the first time that the city board of health (board) had granted Sudduth an on-site sewage disposal permit in December, 1992. Cassidy had represented the neighbors in matters relating to Sudduth's property since 1989, including the litigation mentioned above. After his discovery, Cassidy sent a letter to the board on December 3, 1993, alleging that the sewage disposal system was in violation of board regulations and requesting a review of the situation. The board never responded to this letter.

On May 11, 1994, Sudduth entered into a purchase and sale agreement for lot 4A with Great Pond Builders. According to Sudduth's affidavit, the sale was to close on July 18, 1994, and the sale proceeds would be her only source of income at that time. Sudduth contends that Great Pond Builders informed her that the neighbors, aware of this pending sales agreement, had trespassed onto her land in order to harass individuals from Great Pond Builders as well as other potential buyers.

On May 31, 1994, approximately five and one-half months after his first letter, Cassidy again wrote to the board, itemizing the sewage disposal system's alleged violations of local and State environmental regulations. Cassidy's letter also stated that the disposal system required a variance and therefore the board's agent did not have the authority to approve the disposal permit issued to Sudduth.

On June 2, 1994, two of the neighbors, Vittands and David McArdle, observed the presence of an employee of a septic system installation company on lot 4A. Believing that the installation of the sewage disposal system was "imminent," the neighbors filed suit against Sudduth in Superior Court the next day, requesting relief in the form of a temporary restraining order and a preliminary injunction to prevent the construction of the disposal system. The neighbors also sought a declaratory judgment that Sudduth needed variances from the board and the Department of Environmental Protection (DEP) before the plans for the system could be approved by the board. The neighbors' complaint reiterated the allegations made in Cassidy's letters to the board. Curiously, neither the board, the city, nor the DEP were named as parties. The complaint further stated that disposal system variances had been required for other subdivision lots and were denied and that they had expected that lot 4A's system would also require variances pursuant to board regulations. In support of their allegations, the neighbors submitted an affidavit by Vittands, who is an environmental engineer, averring that his review of the sewage disposal system plans submitted by Sudduth showed numerous State and local environmental violations. On June 6, 1994, a hearing was held on the neighbors' motion for injunctive relief. Sudduth did not appear, since neither she nor her counsel apparently knew of the hearing in time to attend, although notice had been served at Sudduth's place of business. A Superior Court judge granted the motion for injunctive relief ex parte.

On Sudduth's subsequent motion, the same judge vacated the preliminary injunction without opinion on June 19. Shortly thereafter, on June 23, 1994, Sudduth filed four counterclaims against the neighbors, claiming abuse of process and intentional infliction of emotional distress, costs under G.L. c. 231, §§ 6 and 7, and requesting sanctions against Cassidy under Mass.R.Civ.P. 11(a). A trial on Sudduth's counterclaims was set for January, 1995.

On November 15, 1994, the judge entered summary judgment without opinion in favor of Sudduth on the neighbors' initial lawsuit. The neighbors did not appeal from this judgment. Meanwhile, Great Pond Builders had opted not to complete the purchase of lot 4A. According to Sudduth's affidavit, they had informed her that they would not close pursuant to the purchase and sale agreement while the neighbors' claims remained outstanding. In addition, Sudduth contends that the neighbors' action was an impediment to the value and marketability of the lot since no other buyers were interested in purchasing lot 4A due to the pending litigation.

Another round of legal dueling began in January, 1995, when the neighbors filed a special motion to dismiss Sudduth's counterclaims. . . . On March 28, 1995, a different Superior Court judge allowed the special motion and, pursuant to the statute, also awarded attorneys' fees to the neighbors in the amount of $3,255. Sudduth appealed this dismissal of her counterclaims to this court. While her appeal was pending, Sudduth received a summons in December, 1995, to appear for involuntary bankruptcy. The subdivision containing lot 4A was eventually sold to pay the accumulated taxes on the land.

On October 22, 1996, we reversed the dismissal of Sudduth's counterclaims, holding that the neighbors' [motion had been filed prematurely]. . . .

After remand, the neighbors filed a renewed special motion to dismiss . . . as well as a motion for summary judgment on Sudduth's counterclaims. On August 6, 1997, a third Superior Court judge heard and, on October 14, 1997, decided these motions. The judge denied the neighbors' special motion to dismiss, holding that Sudduth had met her statutory burden of establishing that the neighbors' complaint was devoid of factual or legal merit.

The judge also allowed the neighbors' motion for summary judgment on all of Sudduth's counterclaims. Both Sudduth and the neighbors appeal.

1. *Sudduth's counterclaims.* Summary judgment was granted in favor of the neighbors on all of Sudduth's counterclaims, namely abuse of process, intentional infliction of emotional distress, c. 231 costs, and rule 11 sanctions. Rule 56(c) of the Massachusetts Rules of Civil Procedure provides that summary judgment is appropriate "if the pleadings, depositions, answers to interrogatories, and admissions on file, together with the affidavits, if any, show that there is no genuine issue as to any material fact and that the moving party is entitled to a judgment as a matter of law." We view the evidence in the light most favorable to the nonmoving party. With these principles in mind, we review the granting of summary judgment on each of Sudduth's counterclaims.

a. *Abuse of process.* The essential elements of the tort of abuse of process are "(1) 'process' was used; (2) for an ulterior or illegitimate purpose; (3) resulting in damage."[1] *Kelley v. Stop & Shop Cos.*, 26 Mass.App.Ct. 557, 558, 530 N.E.2d

---

[1] "More precisely the word 'process' in the context of abuse of process means causing papers to be issued by a court 'to bring a party or property within its jurisdiction.'" *Silvia v. Building Inspector of W. Bridgewater*, 35 Mass.App.Ct. 451, 453 n. 4, 621 N.E.2d 686 (1993). The neighbors did not

190 (1988), quoting from *Datacomm Interface, Inc. v. Computerworld, Inc.*, 396 Mass. 760, 775-776, 489 N.E.2d 185 (1986). More specifically, abuse of process has been described as a "form of coercion to obtain a collateral advantage, not properly involved in the proceeding itself, such as the surrender of property or the payment of money." *Cohen v. Hurley*, 20 Mass.App.Ct. 439, 442, 480 N.E.2d 658 (1985), quoting from Prosser & Keeton, Torts § 121, at 898 (5th ed.1984). "It is immaterial that the process was properly issued, [or] that it was obtained in the course of proceedings that were brought with probable cause and for a proper purpose. . . . The subsequent misuse of the process, though properly obtained, constitutes the misconduct for which the liability is imposed. . . ." *Kelley*, *supra* at 558, 530 N.E.2d 190. Further, "[t]he ulterior motive may be shown by showing a direct demand for collateral advantage; or it may be inferred from what is said or done about the process." *Ladd v. Polidoro*, 424 Mass. 196, 198, 675 N.E.2d 382 (1997).

The Superior Court judge, in granting summary judgment to the neighbors on Sudduth's abuse of process claim, held that "the record is insufficient to warrant a fact-finder in concluding that the original complaint was brought for an 'ulterior purpose,'" the only element of Sudduth's claim that was challenged by the neighbors. To the contrary, we think the affidavits and attached documents supplied by Sudduth present a genuine issue of material fact whether the neighbors had an ulterior purpose in bringing suit against Sudduth.

Sudduth contends that the neighbors' ulterior, collateral purpose was to prevent her from building on lot 4A, thereby allowing them continued access to her property. In support of this, Sudduth attests in her affidavit that Vittands told her when she first purchased the property in 1985 that he "would take all her land" and that he would prevent the construction of anything on her lots "at all costs." She also attests that other neighbors told her that they considered lot 4A their own "private park." She states that she was subjected to nine years of litigation relating to lot 4A, a point essentially confirmed in the neighbors' own submissions to the court. Sudduth avers as well that the neighbors trespassed on her land and confronted potential buyers, including the individuals from Great Pond Builders. Finally, Sudduth attached materials to her affidavits indicating that she had secured all of the proper permits to begin construction, including the permit for the septic system that had been issued approximately one and one-half years before the neighbors filed their complaint contesting it.

Viewing this evidence in the light most favorable to Sudduth, a jury could reasonably infer that the neighbors served their complaint for an ulterior, illegitimate motive, namely to maintain their access to Sudduth's private property by involving the property in protracted litigation before the sale could be finalized. *See Powers v. Leno*, 24 Mass.App.Ct. 381, 384, 509 N.E.2d 46 (1987) (jury issue as to whether defendant's statement "if I don't get what I want, I'll make sure

---

dispute that "process" was utilized, stating in their memorandum in support of their motion for summary judgment that "[f]iling a [c]omplaint for injunctive and declaratory relief is clearly lawful process."

these condominiums are never built[,] I'll delay it in court forever, even if I have to spend one million dollars" evidences abutter defendant's ulterior motive of preventing sale to others of land that he sought to purchase). In their motion for summary judgment, the neighbors insist that their goal was instead to ensure that the septic system was legal. We note in this regard that even process that is obtained with probable cause and for a proper purpose does not necessarily preclude liability.

More significantly, the neighbors' true motivation for filing this action is in fact in dispute. In instances such as this, where state of mind is an essential element of the cause of action, summary judgment is disfavored. On this record, summary judgment should not have been granted on this claim.

[The court then determined, based on most of the same facts, that summary judgment also should not have been granted on the intentional infliction of emotional distress claim.]

Because summary judgment should not have entered on Sudduth's abuse of process and emotional distress claims, those claims are remanded for trial. We affirm the dismissal of all other claims and motions in this action.

NOTES

1. Did the court ever determine that the neighbors' claims about the need for a variance were legally unsupported? If they were supported by law, then how can they give rise to liability?

2. *Probable Cause and Abuse of Process.* In a majority of jurisdictions, proof as to the absence of probable cause is not essential to the maintenance of an action for abuse of process. As stated in RESTATEMENT (SECOND) OF TORTS § 682 (1977), comment a:

> [I]t is the misuse of process, no matter how properly obtained, for any purpose other than that which it was designed to accomplish. Therefore, it is immaterial that the process was properly issued, that it was obtained in the course of proceedings that were brought with probable cause and for a proper purpose, or even that the proceeding terminated in favor of the person instituting or initiating them.

3. *Ulterior Purpose.* Despite individual variations in the specific requirements for establishing liability for the tort of abuse of process, where this tort is recognized most courts do require some sort of ulterior purpose by the defendant with respect to the misuse of the underlying legal process. *See, e.g., Union Bank v. Kutait*, 312 Ark. 14, 17, 846 S.W.2d 652 (Ark. 1993); *Ladd v. Polidoro*, 675 N.E.2d 382, 384 (Mass. 1997). Generally, an ulterior purpose or motive requires the use of the legal process for some purpose other than that for which such process was intended. *See, e.g., Priest v. Union Agency*, 125 S.W.2d 142 (Tenn. 1939). *Accord, Volk v. Wisconsin Mortgage Assurance Co.*, 474 N.W.2d 40,

43 (N.D. 1991). *See generally* RESTATEMENT (SECOND) OF TORTS § 682 (1977). In many instances this ulterior purpose requirement has been likened to a motive of extortion or coercion. *See, e.g., Union Bank v. Kutait*, 312 Ark. 14, 16, 846 S.W.2d 652 (Ark. 1993).

4. What effect will this rule have on the public's willingness to help enforce zoning ordinances and environmental laws? If you were a competitor of a manufacturing concern, would you think twice before reporting any violations of such laws committed by your competitor? On the other hand, isn't a competitor one of the people in the best position to know of wrongdoing?

5. If the evidence clearly shows that a defendant's motive in initiating criminal charges against the plaintiff is solely to enable the defendant to collect a debt that is owed, is such evidence sufficient to establish tort liability against the defendant for an abuse of process? If not, then what else must the defendant do in order to create liability for such a tort? What would prevent an unscrupulous merchant from routinely filing criminal charges against every person who writes a bad check in payment to the merchant for merchandise sold, without first making any effort to call the person and attempt to collect the debt prior to bringing the criminal charges, in situations where it is also shown that the merchant's sole intent was to dismiss all charges as soon as the accused did in fact come forward and pay off the bad check?

6. *Historical Development of Abuse of Process.* The common law tort of abuse of process developed solely as a response to certain procedural inadequacies that existed with respect to the malicious prosecution tort that prevented certain tortious injuries from receiving any remedy under the malicious prosecution cause of action. *See* Getzoff, *Dazed and Confused in Colorado: The Relationship among Malicious Prosecution, Abuse of Process and the Noerr-Pennington Doctrine*, 67 U. COLO. L. REV. 675, 682 (1996).

7. *Merger of Malicious Prosecution and Abuse of Process.* Because of the close similarity between these two torts, courts often confused them in their application. Indeed, some courts have simply merged the two torts into a single cause of action. *See Yost v. Torok*, 344 S.E.2d 414, 417 (Ga. 1986). Other jurisdictions have achieved similar results by codifying these common law torts into a single statutory cause of action. For example, Pennsylvania has statutorily modified its original malicious prosecution tort by replacing the malice requirement with gross negligence, and by broadening the scope of the original malicious prosecution action to encompass the wrongful "continuation of civil proceedings . . . for a purpose other than that of securing the proper discovery, joinder of parties or adjudication of the claim in which the proceedings are based. . . ." 42 Pa. C.S.A. § 8351(a) (1999). Consider also the provisions of Federal Rule of Civil Procedure 11, quoted in the introductory text to part B.2 of this chapter.

PROBLEM

Darlene was a patron at Miguel's seafood restaurant. After ordering a fresh lobster dinner, she took a bite and spit it out, claiming that the lobster was cold and frozen in the middle. Darlene called Waitress to her table and complained about her dinner, whereupon Waitress offered to bring Darlene a fresh shrimp dinner instead, although explaining that she would have to pay for both meals. When Darlene refused to do this, Waitress then removed Darlene's lobster and advised her that she would return it to the kitchen and have it re-cooked. A few minutes later Waitress, accompanied by Miguel, returned to Darlene's table with her lobster. Darlene looked at the lobster and without trying to eat any of it, she loudly declared that it was "still cold!" Miguel claimed that it could not possibly be cold, since had personally "microwaved" the lobser for several minutes. Still, Darlene refused to eat the lobster, and she got up from her table and proceeded to leave the restaurant. Miguel stopped her and demanded that she pay for the dinner or he would call the police. Indignantly, Darlene said, "Well then, go ahead and call them!" Miguel immediately called the police to the restaurant, believing that once they arrived, Darlene would simply pay her bill and leave, just like his other customers had always done. Instead, when the police arrived Darlene stubbornly refused to pay for "a cold lobster dinner that was inedible!" Angry, Miguel demanded that Darlene be arrested for defrauding an innkeeper. He signed an arrest warrant and Darlene was handcuffed and taken to jail by the police. Later that same day, Darlene was released from police custody and the criminal charges were dropped. Does Darlene have an action against Miguel for malicious prosecution? What about abuse of process? *See Lashley v. Bowman*, 561 So. 2d 406 (Fla. Dist. Ct. App. 1990).

Chapter 21
MISREPRESENTATION

A. OVERVIEW

This chapter deals with injuries caused by false representations. At first glance, devoting a full chapter to that topic may seem redundant. After all, several of the other torts you have already considered, including products liability (Chapter 16) and defamation (Chapter 17), also frequently involve false statements. However, the conduct covered by this chapter is different in one crucial respect from what you have covered before. What ties the material in this chapter together is the type of *injury* for which the plaintiff seeks recovery. Unlike the earlier materials, which involve harm to a person's body or a distinctly personal interest such as reputation or privacy, the cases in this chapter involve purely economic loss. That difference is important. Historically, courts and legislatures have been hesitant to extend tort law to purely economic losses. That they have been willing to make an exception to this principle in the case of misrepresentations reflects a widely-held attitude as to how people should deal with each other.

Of course, misrepresentations may also cause bodily or reputational harm. This chapter does not deal with those cases, as they are already covered in the aforementioned chapters.

WEST v. GLADNEY
533 S.E.2d 334 (S.C. Ct. App. 2000)

Per Curiam:

[In] August 1996, West sold all of his shares in Am-Pro Protective Agency, Inc. to Gladney. In payment thereof, Gladney gave West $150,000 and executed a promissory note for $525,000. [When] Gladney failed to make the payments required by the note, West declared Gladney in default and accelerated all future payments.

West filed suit on June 3, 1997. Gladney answered and counterclaimed, complaining that a few months after the sale, Am-Pro filed for bankruptcy. [He] alleged West knew or should have known at the time of the sale about Am-Pro's financial condition and that the stock was essentially worthless. Gladney asserted that West's failure to fully inform him of Am-Pro's true financial status and West's failure to deliver the stock constituted failure of consideration, misrepresentation, or concealment of material facts or all three. Not only did Gladney contend these facts barred West from receiving any additional payments on the note, he also asserted they justified his recouping all funds already paid.

[The trial court] found West fully performed his obligations under the sales agreement and note and that Gladney failed to make the payments when [due]. The court further held West "neither misrepresented the value of the shares of stock . . . nor did he know or have reason to know at or prior to the time of the sale" that their value was "anything other than the sales price." Accordingly, it awarded West summary judgment. . . .

Gladney argues the trial court erred in granting West's motion for summary judgment because the record reveals that genuine issues of material fact exist as to whether West was guilty of making misrepresentations. We disagree.

Gladney contends his assertion of misrepresentation encompasses negligent as well as intentional misrepresentation. The elements of an action for fraud based on a representation include: "(1) a representation; (2) falsity; (3) its materiality; (4) knowledge of the falsity or a reckless disregard of its truth or falsity; (5) intent that the representation be acted upon; (6) the hearer's ignorance of its falsity; (7) the hearer's reliance upon the truth; (8) the hearer's right to rely thereon; and (9) the hearer's consequent and proximate injury." *Moorhead v. First Piedmont Bank & Trust Co.*, 273 S.C. 356, 359, 256 S.E.2d 414, 416 (1979). These elements must be established by clear, cogent, and convincing evidence.

In a claim for the common law tort of negligent misrepresentation where the damage alleged is a pecuniary loss, the plaintiff must allege and prove the following essential elements: (1) the defendant made a false representation to the plaintiff; (2) the defendant had a pecuniary interest in making the statement; (3) the defendant owed a duty of care to see that he communicated truthful information to the plaintiff; (4) the defendant breached that duty by failing to exercise due care; (5) the plaintiff justifiably relied on the representation; and (6) the plaintiff suffered a pecuniary loss as the proximate result of his reliance upon the representation. As part of his case, the plaintiff must establish that his reliance on the misrepresentation was reasonable. "There is no liability for casual statements, representations as to matters of law, or matters which plaintiff could ascertain on his own in the exercise of due diligence." Moreover, "there can be no reasonable reliance on a misstatement if the plaintiff knows the truth of the matter." A determination of justifiable reliance involves the evaluation of the totality of the circumstances, "including the positions and relations of the parties."

Fraud based on a misrepresentation and negligent misrepresentation both include a requirement that the plaintiff justifiably relied on the representation made by the defendant. In the case before us, John E. Brown, the chief executive officer of Am-Pro, negotiated the sale of West's stock as part of an agreement Gladney entered into with Am-Pro. According to West, Gladney and his representatives had been present at Am-Pro headquarters for a number of weeks prior to any meaningful negotiations with him. Gladney had extensive conferences with Brown, and West contends Gladney had more access to the financial records than did West. West also asserts Gladney was in a better position than he to know the financial status of Am-Pro as a result of Gladney's access to Brown and the corporation's books. West claims he never knew on or before the date of the sale that the value of his shares was anything other than the sales price negotiated with Gladney.

Gladney produced no evidence to refute West's statements. . . . We find Gladney failed to establish a genuine issue of material fact that his reliance on any alleged representation by West was justified. Accordingly, the trial court did not err in granting West's motion for summary judgment. . . .

NOTES

1. As *West* points out, the law of misrepresentation is divided into two broad categories. The first includes intentional misrepresentations. Historically, the action for intentional misrepresentation went by the monikers "fraud" or "deceit." The label "fraud" can prove confusing, because fraud is also a criminal offense. Nevertheless, you will still find frequent use of the term in intentional misrepresentation cases. The second category includes negligent representations, and variations on negligence such as gross negligence. The tort of negligent misrepresentation has been recognized only for a relatively short time, for reasons that should become apparent later in the chapter.

2. Compare the differences between the elements for intentional and negligent misrepresentations as set out in *West*. You will immediately notice that negligent misrepresentation is limited to "commercial" cases. What might explain that limitation?

3. An intentional misrepresentation is an intentional tort, raising the possibility of punitive damages. Negligent misrepresentation cases, by contrast, allow for only compensatory damages. What are the actual damages in a case like *West*?

4. The misrepresentation claim in *West* originally arose as a defense to the main claim. This is quite common. A party has bound itself by contract to another, and seeks to nullify that obligation based on a misstatement allegedly made by the other side during negotiation of that contract. Of course, in addition to allowing rescission of the contract, proof of a misrepresentation may also give rise to an affirmative counterclaim, as in *West*.

5. *Civil Procedure Issues.* The court in *West* indicates that a party alleging an intentional misrepresentation must prove the elements by "clear, cogent, and convincing evidence." This is a more difficult burden of persuasion than the "preponderance of the evidence" standard that typically applies in civil litigation. However, it is not as onerous as the "beyond a reasonable doubt" standard that applies in criminal cases. The higher burden applies only to intentional mis-

representations. A party suing for negligent misrepresentation need only prove her case by a preponderance of the evidence.

In addition to the higher burden of persuasion, many states impose an elevated pleading requirement in intentional misrepresentation cases. Federal Rule of Civil Procedure 9(b), which has counterparts in many state rules, provides:

> (b) Fraud, Mistake, Condition of the Mind. In all averments of fraud or mistake, the circumstances constituting fraud or mistake shall be stated with particularity. Malice, intent, knowledge, and other condition of mind may be averred generally.

This higher standard stands in stark contrast to the "notice" pleading that applies to most issues under Federal Rule 8. What explains these heightened requirements? Some have suggested that the requirements are a way to protect the speaker's reputation. A charge of fraud, after all, can create quite a stigma regardless of its ultimate resolution. But if that were the reason, then why does Rule 9(b) also encompass mistake? And why do the heightened requirements *not* apply to other sorts of intentional lies, such as those involved in defamation cases? In truth, the more rigorous pleading and evidence rules are merely a carryover from the past, when claims of fraud and mistake usually fell within the jurisdiction of courts of equity.

B. THE MISREPRESENTATION

Intentional and negligent misrepresentations are separate torts. However, there is considerable overlap in the elements. Aside from the obvious differences in state of mind, and the more subtle "commercial interest" limitation for negligent misrepresentations, a party seeking to recover for pecuniary losses caused by a false statement must prove roughly the same facts regardless of whether she proceeds under a theory of intentional or negligent misrepresentation.

Because of this overlap, this chapter will not distinguish between intentional and negligent misrepresentations when dealing with most of the elements. Only in part C will the difference be crucial. Nevertheless, it is essential that you always remember that there are two types of misrepresentation torts.

Regardless of whether the claim is for intentional or negligent misrepresentation, the party must prove that the other person made a false statement. Of course, as you have seen before, truth is not always simple to ascertain. Certain issues repeatedly crop up in the cases, as the following selections illustrate.

DELTA SCHOOL OF COMMERCE, INC. v. WOOD
766 S.W.2d 424 (Ark. 1989)

HOLT, Chief Justice.

Appellee Earlene Wood (Wood) filed suit against appellants Delta School of Commerce, Inc. (Delta), and Steve McCray (McCray), alleging that they fraudulently induced her to enter a course in nursing by making false representations that the course would lead her to a position of employment similar to that of a Licensed Practical Nurse. Delta and McCray denied making any false statements or fraudulently inducing Wood to enter a course of study. The jury found in favor of Wood and assessed compensatory damages of $3,064.00 and punitive damages of $50,000.00 against Delta and McCray. The trial court entered judgment accordingly. From this order, Delta and McCray appeal. We find no error and affirm.

Wood testified that in May or June of 1986, she read a newspaper article concerning a course of study at Delta leading to a diploma as a nursing assistant. Shortly thereafter, she made an appointment to talk with McCray, president of Delta, concerning the program. During their meeting, she asked him if a nursing assistant was the same thing as a nurse's aide. McCray replied that it was not. He also told her that "they are phasing out the LPNs (Licensed Practical Nurses) in the State of Arkansas, so the nursing assistants will be taking the place of the LPNs" and that "she would not get rich as a nursing assistant but that the pay would be comparable to that of an LPN." Based upon these statements, she enrolled at Delta the next day. In addition, she got a student loan for $3,064.00. After completing seven months of the eight or nine-month program, she dropped out because she discovered she was studying to be a nurse's aide. Wood further testified that the training for nursing assistants and LPNs is quite different: Nursing assistants learn to make beds, empty bed pans, and take vital signs; LPNs learn to assist in surgery and give medication and injections.

Although McCray denied that he told Wood "they are phasing out the LPNs in the State of Arkansas, so the nursing assistants will be taking the place of the LPNs," he acknowledged an awareness of the issue by stating that "the question that keeps coming up, whether or not LPNs are being phased out, I've heard before." Maxine Ottey, Director of Nursing Practice with the Arkansas Board of Nursing, testified that "a nursing assistant certainly cannot and does not take the place of an LPN." . . .

The appellants argue that the representations in question were expressions of opinion and predictions of future events, not representations of fact, and therefore not actionable. We disagree.

In general, an expression of opinion, *i.e.*, a statement concerning a matter not susceptible of accurate knowledge, cannot furnish the basis for a cause of action for deceit or fraud. However, an expression of opinion that is false and known to be false at the time it is made is actionable. The general rule only applies where the person expressing his or her opinion does so in good faith.

In *Grendell*, supra, we held that statements by the defendant that an oil investment was a "good thing" and would "make money" and that the wells would pump "fifty barrels a day" were in the nature of puffing and constituted mere expressions of opinion. In *Cannaday v. Cossey*, 228 Ark. 1119, 312 S.W.2d 442 (1958), we held that a statement by a vendor that he had a "good house" was also a statement of opinion.

In the case at bar, the statements made by McCray to Wood that "they are phasing out the LPNs in the State of Arkansas, so the nursing assistants will be taking the place of the LPNs" and that "she would not get rich as a nursing assistant but that the pay would compare to that of an LPN" were representations of fact, not expressions of opinion. Unlike the loose general statements made by sellers in commending their products which we found to be expressions of opinion in *Grendell* and *Cannaday*, the statements made by McCray were specific and definite.

Even if McCray's statements were construed to be expressions of opinion, it does not automatically follow, as appellants erroneously assume, that such expressions cannot form the basis of a cause of action for fraud or deceit. It is clear from *Anthony* and *Horn* that expressions of opinion which are false and known to be false when made are actionable. From the testimony and other evidence presented at trial, the jury reasonably could have concluded that the statements made by McCray were false and that he knew them to be false at the time he made them.

Appellants' contention that the statements made by McCray were predictions of future events is also without merit.

In general, an action for fraud or deceit may not be predicated on representations relating solely to future events. However, the general rule is inapplicable if the person making the representation or prediction knows it to be false at the time it is made.

The statements in question were not predictions of future events, but statements of existing situation. Moreover, even if the statements were considered to be predictions, the appellants would still be liable if McCray believed them to be false when he made them to Wood. Again, in light of the testimony and other evidence presented at trial, the jury reasonably could have concluded that McCray knew the statements were false at the time he made them. . . .

Affirmed.

NOTES

1. Carefully re-read the fifth paragraph of the opinion. Are the court's statements consistent? If a mere opinion is not actionable, why should it matter

that the speaker knew it was false? And more fundamentally, if an opinion is, as the court says, the assertion of something that is not "susceptible of actual knowledge," then how could the speaker ever "know" it is false?

Part of the problem may stem from some confusion as to the reason for the rule. Why is it that opinions are not actionable? Is it because they cannot be false? Or is it for some other reason? Consider the other elements of the tort, and see if you can come up with an alternate argument justifying the opinion exception.

2. The court distinguishes the *Grendell* case, in which the defendant claimed that the wells would pump fifty barrels a day. Is that statement not every bit as specific as the defendant's assertion in the main case? Is there any way to explain the difference? Consider the relationship between the parties in both cases. Should a different standard apply in buyer-seller cases like *Grendell* than in a case like *Delta School*? In this regard, you may want to refer to section 542 of the RESTATEMENT (SECOND) OF TORTS.

PROBLEM

Peters is interested in showing dogs. He contacts Daniels, a well-known breeder of Giant Schnauzers, to see if Daniels has any pups for sale. Daniels indicates that she does, and invites Peters to her kennel the next day. Because Peters has little expertise in the breed, he asks Edwards, the president of the local Giant Schnauzer club, to accompany him on this visit.

At the kennel, Daniels shows Peters a particular dog. Daniels then says, "This pup is absolutely great. I'm sure that this little fellow will rack up the ribbons in the dog shows."

Peters then turns to Edwards. Edwards nods and adds, "In my opinion this dog will be a real champion."

Relying on these representations, Peters buys the pup for $2500. Although quite friendly, the dog is no champion, and Peters has no success in the ring.

Peters later learns that Daniels and Edwards are related, and had talked to each other before Peters visited the kennel. Assuming Peters can prove the other elements, can he recover against either Daniels or Edwards for misrepresentation?

ROHM AND HAAS CO. v. CONTINENTAL CASUALTY CO.
781 A.2d 1172 (Pa. 2001)

FLAHERTY, Chief Justice:

[Appellants] are manufacturers of specialty chemicals headquartered in Philadelphia. In June 1964, appellants, through a wholly owned subsidiary, purchased Whitmoyer Laboratories, a small veterinary pharmaceuticals company, and continued operations. Shortly thereafter, appellants discovered that the site was extensively polluted with arsenic waste, a byproduct of Whitmoyer's and appellants' manufacturing processes. Although appellants undertook remedial measures to clean up the site, arsenic waste continued to be produced as a result of appellants' operations. In 1978, appellants sold the site to Smith-Kline Beecham.

In December 1964, appellants added the Whitmoyer site to existing CGL [comprehensive general liability] insurance coverage it held with appellee insurers. Appellants periodically purchased from appellees additional policies that covered Whitmoyer throughout the time that they operated the site and were aware of the contamination. Although appellants disclosed the problem to their primary coverage insurer and to their insurance broker as well as to the proper commonwealth authorities, there is no evidence that the excess insurers were ever notified of the pollution problem.

In 1980, Congress enacted the Comprehensive Environmental Response, Compensation, and Liability Act (CERCLA). This act retroactively imposes strict liability for environmental cleanup costs on present and former owners or operators of polluting facilities without regard to fault. Subsequently, the Environmental Protection Agency notified appellants that they were strictly liable for the cleanup costs associated with the Whitmoyer site. In 1988, twenty-four years after becoming aware of the severe pollution at Whitmoyer, appellants notified their excess insurers that they were asserting a claim to cover the Whitmoyer cleanup costs, more than twenty-one million dollars. Appellees denied the claim and appellants brought suit.

[The] jury, in response to the special verdict interrogatories, determined that no coverage existed as it found in favor of appellees on, inter alia, the following questions

> by answer to Jury Verdict Question No. 7: That Rohm & Haas failed to disclose material facts about the arsenic pollution at Whitmoyer when it purchased the excess policies [the fraud issue].

After post-trial motions were filed, the court entered JNOV on the jury's verdict with respect to [question] 7, among others. Superior Court reversed the trial court. . . .

We must decide whether JNOV was properly granted with respect to question no. 7, which reads:

> Do you find that, as to [the policies at issue], the insurer issuing the policy has proven the following facts by clear and convincing evidence:

> A. That in connection with buying the specific insurance policy, Rohm and Haas' employees or agents of Rohm and Haas who were in contact with the issuing insurer intentionally failed to disclose material information about Whitmoyer, and, if so,

B. That Rohm and Haas employees or agents deliberately concealed material information with the intent to deceive the CGL excess insurer; or, that other persons at Rohm and Haas, as part of an intentional plan to conceal and deceive, kept material information from the employees or agents in contact with the insurer so that the information would not be disclosed?

The jury answered affirmatively with respect to each policy. The trial court entered JNOV with respect to the three policies already in existence at the time Rohm & Haas acquired Whitmoyer on the basis that Rohm & Haas could not have been aware of the problem prior to acquiring Whitmoyer when it contracted for those policies, and thus, could not have had an intent to deceive or conceal material information from the insurers. That court further granted JNOV with respect to the remaining policies on the basis that the evidence presented at trial was insufficient for the jury to find a "deliberate, fraudulent intent to deceive."

When an insured secures an insurance policy by means of fraudulent misrepresentations, the insurer may avoid that policy. The burden of proving fraud must be established by clear and convincing evidence and rests with the party alleging it. The clear and convincing standard requires evidence that is "so clear, direct, weighty, and convincing as to enable the jury to come to a clear conviction, without hesitancy, of the truth of the precise facts of the issue." This court has previously observed that fraud "is never proclaimed from the housetops nor is it done otherwise than surreptitiously with every effort usually made to conceal the truth of what is being done. So fraud can rarely if ever be shown by direct proof. It must necessarily be largely inferred from the surrounding circumstances." *Shechter v. Shechter,* 366 Pa. 30, 76 A.2d 753, 755 (1950).

In an insurance fraud case, the insurer must prove that the fraudulent misrepresentations were material to the risk assumed by the insurer. When knowledge or ignorance of certain information would influence the decision of an insurer in the issuance of a policy, assessing the nature of the risk, or setting premium rates, that information is deemed material to the risk assumed by the insurer. Furthermore, "fraud consists of anything calculated to deceive, whether by single act or combination, or by suppression of truth, or suggestion of what is false, whether it be by direct falsehood or by innuendo, by speech or silence, word of mouth or look or gesture." *Moser v. DeSetta*, 527 Pa. 157, 589 A.2d 679, 682 (1991). That is, there must be a deliberate intent to deceive. Finally, "the concealment of a material fact can amount to a culpable misrepresentation no less than does an intentional false statement." *Moser, supra* at 682.

In the present case, evidence was adduced at trial regarding the calamitous nature of the pollution at Whitmoyer. It is undisputed that Rohm & Haas learned of this problem shortly after purchasing the site. Rohm & Haas did not disclose the problem to the insurers either when adding Whitmoyer to the policies in existence or when purchasing subsequent coverage. Indeed, the insurers were not made aware of the problem until some twenty-four years later when Rohm & Haas filed a claim for coverage. Furthermore, evidence was introduced at trial which showed that the pollution at Whitmoyer was material to the insurers' decision to provide coverage.

The insurers presented a chronology of events showing that as Rohm & Haas increasingly became aware of the pervasiveness of the problem, with its concomitant risk of liability, the company purchased increasing amounts of excess coverage. Evidence was also adduced of the company's awareness of the potential liability to its neighbors. Furthermore, while Rohm & Haas cooperated fully and openly with the appropriate commonwealth agencies to address the problems at Whitmoyer, the company also deliberately undertook to keep the situation from becoming public knowledge.

Examining this evidence under the standard required in a review of JNOV, we conclude that there is sufficient support for the jury's answer to question no. 7. . . . Here, the jury weighed the evidence and, drawing permissible inferences, concluded that the failure to disclose was not merely inadvertent and unrelated to Whitmoyer, but knowing and deliberate. The jury determined that at the times that Whitmoyer was added to existing policies or included in newly purchased policies Rohm & Haas deliberately withheld information it knew would be material to the insurers' decision to provide coverage. We therefore conclude that Superior Court appropriately reversed the entry of JNOV on this issue.

CASTILLE, Justice, dissenting.

Notwithstanding its overall factual complexity, the resolution of this case turns on the perceived legal consequences of a single fact crucial both to the insurers' argument and the majority's affirmance, and to a single federal statute crucial to appellants' argument. That fact consists of appellants' failure to volunteer information in the 1960s to their excess insurers concerning arsenic pollution at the Whitmoyer facility, which they purchased in 1964. It is undisputed that appellants made no misrepresentations in this regard: The insurers never asked about environmental pollution in approving and issuing the excess comprehensive liability policies, and appellants did not tell. The insurers' legal theory, accepted by the Superior Court, was that, notwithstanding the insurers' failure to condition their excess comprehensive liability coverage upon the disclosure of this particular kind of information, appellants should be charged with an extra-contractual, *de jure* obligation to volunteer it. . . .

In my view, as a matter of law, appellants' mere failure to volunteer unrequested information concerning the contamination at Whitmoyer when they secured excess comprehensive coverage against a risk of liability, such as the massive environmental cleanup costs that were retroactively mandated by the subsequent passage and interpretation of CERCLA, provides no basis for finding an extra-contractual forfeiture of coverage. The majority overlooks the insurers' failure to make the mere fact of contamination relevant to issuing the coverage and also fails to factor in the controlling importance of CERCLA. Because I disagree with the majority's approach here, and because I believe that a deeper inquiry commands a different result, I respectfully dissent. . . .

The very purpose of insurance is to protect against identifiable, known risks of varying degrees of predictability. Indeed, perception of a risk is an ineluctable element of the desire for insurance. Recognizing the risk of a specific peril, both the insurer and insured wager against an occurrence or nonoccurrence; the carrier is thus insuring against the risk of an occurrence, not the certainty thereof. This insurable risk is eliminated only where the insured knows and fails to disclose, when it purchases the policy, that it already "has suffered the threat of an immediate economic loss, as a result of some event, and that the reality of that loss occurring is a certainty." *Insurance Co. of North America v. Kayser-Roth Corp., et al.*, 770 A.2d 403, 415 (R.I. 2001).

It is undisputed that, as early as 1965, appellants voluntarily disclosed to Commonwealth authorities the arsenic contamination at Whitmoyer and conducted an extensive cleanup program at their own expense. Appellants also disclosed the contamination in 1965 to their primary insurance carrier and their insurance broker. Although it is unclear whether the environmental contamination, which was of public record, was specifically relayed to the excess carriers, it was indisputably not hidden by appellants. At the times appellants secured their excess coverage — with appellants failing to volunteer the fact of contamination and their insurers failing to ask about or condition the issuance of the policies upon the absence of contamination — appellants were not faced with any actual lawsuits or other existing bases of liability that threatened to trigger the various excess insurance policies. Nor was there any evidence to suggest that appellants had actual knowledge or "could be charged with knowledge" that the pollution they discovered was at that time remotely likely to result in third party liability that would exhaust their primary insurance coverage and trigger their various and escalating excess comprehensive liability policies. . . . The notion that the mere fact of pollution at Whitmoyer would inevitably lead to a legal liability reaching the excess carriers is so attenuated that it cannot be said that appellants "knew" of that "loss." . . . The majority simply fails to grasp that, under the law and state of affairs existing at the times of purchase, appellants had suffered no known relevant loss that would implicate their excess coverage. Passage of CERCLA was the controlling event.

The majority in essence "charges" appellants with knowledge of a revolutionary environmental statute that was not passed until many years later, and with knowledge that CERCLA not only would affect its potential liability for cleanup, but that it would also result in a liability of sufficient magnitude as to reach the substantial thresholds of the excess policies. . . .

Appellants accurately argue that the Superior Court imposed upon it an "unprecedented duty to volunteer unrequested information." They claim that has long been the law in Pennsylvania that "mere silence is not fraud absent a duty to speak." Appellants further cite cases from other jurisdictions recognizing, as a general proposition, that information not requested by the insurer is presumptively not material and, thus, need not be volunteered. . . .

It is inequitable to retroactively impose a duty upon appellants to disclose information concerning the contamination at Whitmoyer when such information of pollution or contamination was never requested by the insurer. Although appellants may be "sophisticated" purchasers of insurance, the insurers here certainly were no less sophisticated or powerful.

On the other hand, the prospective insured is, as a general matter, in no position to know with any kind of certainty what unidentified information an insurer might later deem relevant to its decision to insure. Hence, the insured should be under no extra-contractual, judicial obligation to speculate as to what its insurer might later deem relevant and to volunteer that information. . . .

In any event, even if I could agree with the majority's new requirement that insureds in this Commonwealth are now required to speculate as to what their insurers might someday claim is material, and then volunteer information relevant to those speculations, I would still hold that appellants were entitled to judgment as a matter of law on the fraud defense. In my view, the proof here does not support a finding, by clear and convincing evidence, that the failure to volunteer here concerned "material" information or was motivated by a "deliberate, fraudulent intent to deceive."

As the trial court noted, there was no direct evidence that appellants planned to deceive their insurers. "Notably, in the vast amount of documents produced throughout the over nine weeks of trial, there was not one exhibit introduced into evidence which demonstrated that any Rohm and Haas supervisory or executive employee was involved in a plan to deceive the . . . insurers." Trial Court Opinion, 36. Furthermore, the circumstantial evidence belied any claim of intent to deceive. Without external prompting, Rohm and Haas immediately disclosed the existence of the Whitmoyer contamination to Commonwealth authorities (who promptly made it public), to its neighbors, to its primary insurer and to its insurance broker who arranged the excess coverage with appellees. The fact that their primary insurer did not reject coverage after the disclosure is objective proof that appellants had no reason to believe that the fact of pollution was material to issuance of the excess coverage. Nor did appellants ever fail to answer accurately any question actually posed by their insurers respecting the facility; the insurers simply failed to ask. This objective evidence hardly constitutes conduct warranting a jury finding of clear and convincing evidence of an intent to deceive. . . .

All that is left is the *post hoc ergo propter hoc* (fallacy of false cause) inference arising from the equivocal fact that appellants increased their coverage as time went by. . . .

Justices CAPPY and SAYLOR join this dissenting opinion.

NOTES

1. *Concealment vs. Failure to Volunteer.* Like the main case, the RESTATEMENT (SECOND) OF TORTS draws a distinction between mere failure to disclose and active concealment of a fact. Under section 550, a party who conceals a fact is liable to the same extent that he would be liable had he affirmatively stated that the fact was not true. Section 551, by contrast, says that a party is not liable for failing to disclose a fact unless there is a duty to disclose the fact. A duty to disclose will exist, for example, when the parties are in a fiduciary relationship (§ 551(2)(a)), when a party has made a partial statement of the truth (§ 551(2)(b)), when a party later acquires information that makes an earlier statement untrue (§ 551(2)(c)), or when the case involves facts crucial to a transaction, and "the customs of the trade or other objective circumstances" lead the party injured by the failure to reveal reasonably to expect disclosure (§ 551(2)(e)).

Did *Rohm and Haas* involve concealment or a failure to disclose? What is the difference? If the case involved a mere failure to disclose, then why was the company under a duty to reveal the fact of pollution?

2. The case also involves an interesting policy issue. What exactly is the purpose of insurance? Isn't the dissenting justice right when he suggests that insurance deals with known risks? Although the insurance company needs to know the risk to set an appropriate premium, shouldn't it take it upon itself to ask the necessary questions? After all, anyone who has purchased automobile insurance has been subjected to a battery of questions.

3. *Additional Duties to Disclose.* In addition to the common-law duties to disclose listed in the Restatement, positive law may also create a duty to disclose certain information. A duty to disclose may be imposed by statute, *see, e.g., Binette v. Dyer Library Assoc.*, 688 A.2d 898 (Me. 1996) (statutory duty for seller of land to disclose presence of underground storage tanks to potential buyer), or by the rules of regulated professions, *see, e.g., In the Matter of Scahill*, 767 N.E.2d 976 (Ind.) (attorney); *Duman v. Campbell*, 2002 Ohio App. LEXIS 2279 (real estate agent).

PROBLEM

Buyer purchased a used computer from Seller through an internet auction site. Seller had posted a picture of the computer on the site. The picture showed the computer sitting in a clean, attractive room. In addition, the listing contained detailed information about the hardware, but said nothing about the software. Buyer and Seller agreed on a price, and signed an agreement pursuant to which the computer was sold "as is."

When Buyer received the computer, she was greatly disappointed. First, the computer was filthy. In fact, Seller had used the computer in a dusty shed, not the room revealed in the photo. Because of the limits of internet imaging, the picture on the auction site was too grainy to show the dirt.

Second, and even worse, the computer had absolutely no software installed . . . not even an operating system.

Has Seller made any statements that could result in liability for misrepresentation?

If you have taken a course in Sales, contrast Seller's potential liability for misrepresentation with his potential liability under the Uniform Commercial Code.

C. DEFENDANT'S STATE OF MIND

As indicated at the beginning of the chapter, one of the key differences between intentional and negligent misrepresentations concerns the speaker's state of mind. Part One of this section covers intentional misrepresentations; Part Two addresses negligent misrepresentations.

1. Intentional Misrepresentations

BRITT v. BRITT
359 S.E.2d 467 (N.C. 1987)

The plaintiff Betsy Britt brought this action, seeking to impose a parol trust on certain real property or for restitution for benefits bestowed by her on the defendants and for damages, including punitive damages, for fraud. Robert Dixon Britt was made a party plaintiff after the action was filed.

The plaintiffs' evidence showed that in 1977 the two plaintiffs were working as Amway distributors for Billy Britt. Robert or Bobby Britt and Billy Britt are brothers. In August 1977, Billy Britt purchased a farm in Orange County known as Magnolia Hill Farm which had been operated as a horse farm since 1972. It was agreed that Bobby and Betsy Britt would occupy the farm. Billy Britt promised Betsy and Bobby that when they "hit the diamond level" of Amway sales, he would convey the farm to them if they would repay to him his investment in the farm. It was agreed that Bobby and Betsy would "repair and maintain the farm . . . and operate the stable business to carry the farm." They were to live on the farm and retain any surplus income as compensation. Shortly after the plaintiffs went on the farm, Billy Britt delivered to Betsy Britt a payment book of the Orange Savings and Loan Association. According to the payment book monthly payments of $378.63 were due on a note secured by a deed of trust on the farm. Billy told Betsy that the payments on this debt were to be paid from the income from the farm. He also told her that she was to pay from the farm income $1,033.63 per month on a purchase money note secured by a second deed of trust on the farm.

After the plaintiffs had worked on the farm for approximately eighteen months, Betsy asked Billy to put their agreement in writing. She testified as follows:

> [H]e said that that wasn't necessary, he was a man of his word and that wasn't going to happen; and he said well maybe, I said, "I'm putting so much money in the farm and all and I'd like some kind of protection." He said, "Maybe we'll just make you an employee or something." And at that point, I had already put money in the farm and I didn't really want to be an employee from that point on; and I knew that the farm based on what the mortgage payments there was no way that I could be paid because everything I was making, I was putting back into the farm. So I said, "No, I don't want to do that." And he said, "Well we'll work it out." And I said, "How will we work it out?" He said, "Well," he said, "I'm forming a corporation and how would you feel about having accruing stock in the corporation each time you made a mortgage payment, then you would be accruing more stock?" So I thought well stock is paper, you know, and I assumed though that the stock was relative to the property, relative to the actual real estate. And I didn't know much about stock or anything; but I know there would be something on paper; and so I was satisfied with that. . . .
>
> Q. Did you trust him at that point?
>
> A. Yes.
>
> Q. Okay. So what did you do as a result of that conversation?
>
> A. I just kept making the mortgage payments and kept putting more, you know, money into the farm and just going about my usual routine.

No stock was issued to Betsy Britt. There was evidence that the plaintiffs made mortgage payments of $98,126.00. There was also evidence that they expended $40,469.95 in repairs and maintenance of the property. An expert witness was allowed to testify that the reasonable value of the personal labor and services that Betsy performed for the business ranged from $224,415.00 to $338,833.00. There was also evidence that during Betsy's tenure at Magnolia Hill the fair market value of the property increased from $175,000.00 to more than $337,500.00.

In 1983 the marriage of the plaintiffs deteriorated. They were separated and Billy demanded that Betsy leave the farm. She did so and filed this action.

The superior court submitted to the jury the claims for a parol trust, unjust enrichment and fraud. The jury answered the issue against the plaintiffs on their claim for a parol trust. The jury answered the issue favorably to the plaintiff Betsy Britt on her claim for unjust enrichment and awarded her $363,616.00. They answered the issue on the claim for fraud favorably to the plaintiff Betsy Britt and awarded her $1.00 in compensatory and $400,000.00 in punitive damages.

The defendants appealed from a judgment on the verdict and the Court of Appeals reversed. The Court of Appeals held there was not sufficient evidence to support a claim of unjust enrichment or fraud. It ordered the superior court to enter a judgment dismissing the case. This Court allowed discretionary review.

WEBB, Justice.

The plaintiffs did not appeal from the judgment dismissing their claim for a parol trust and that question is not before us.

[The] elements of fraud are: (1) the defendant's false representation of a past or existing fact, (2) defendant's knowledge that the representation was false when made or it was made recklessly without any knowledge of its truth and as a positive assertion, (3) defendant made the false representation with the intent it be relied on by the plaintiff, and (4) the plaintiff was injured by reasonably relying on the false representation. Evidence of a promise which is not fulfilled is not sufficient to support a finding of a false representation unless the evidence shows the promisor made the promise with no intention of fulfilling it.

The plaintiff Betsy Britt contends that in a conversation by telephone with her, Billy Britt made a promise to her that he had no intention of keeping, that he made this representation to keep her working on the farm and making the mortgage payments, and that she reasonably relied on this false representation to her injury. She contends the false promise was made when she asked Billy Britt to put their contract in writing and he told her he was forming a corporation and asked how she would like to be issued stock in the corporation each time she made a payment on the loan. She contends she relied on this promise and stayed on the farm to her injury.

Although the defendant Billy Britt did not specifically promise to put stock in a corporation in Betsy Britt's name if she stayed on the farm, the jury could infer that is what he meant when he said "how would you feel about accruing stock in the corporation each time you made a mortgage payment . . .?" If the defendant did not intend to keep this promise at the time it was made, this would be the misrepresentation of a material fact. The only evidence that he did not intend to keep the promise is that no stock was issued to Betsy Britt. . . . "Mere proof of nonperformance is not sufficient to establish the necessary fraudulent intent." . . . [T]he evidence fails to show that the promise by Billy Britt was a misrepresentation of a material fact. All Betsy has shown is nonperformance. . . .

Affirmed in part, reversed and remanded in part.

NOTES

1. Note that this case looks somewhat like a contract case. Billy's promise to issue stock, which was relied upon by Betsy, could be deemed a contract. The

problem is that this case involves rights in land, which means that the Statute of Frauds would prevent enforcement of the oral contract. Plaintiffs who find themselves barred by the Statute of Frauds often bring misrepresentation claims, seeking recovery for the loss occasioned by their reliance on the statement. However, as the case demonstrates, misrepresentation works only if the statement is false when made.

In fact, Betsy had brought an unjust enrichment claim in addition to her fraud claim. The court held that her unjust enrichment claim should have gone to trial.

2. At first glance, it might seem impossible for Betsy Britt to prove what she needed to prove. Unless Billy was careless enough to reveal his intent to others, after all, the crucial issue of his intent would be known only to Billy. However, do not confuse criminal and civil cases. Although a defendant in a criminal case cannot be forced to testify, defendants in civil cases can be deposed and called to the witness stand.

3. In addition, state of mind can be proven by circumstantial evidence. Suppose, for example, that Billy had conveyed title to the farm to someone else two hours after making the statement to Betsy. The fact of that conveyance would indicate that Billy had no intention of putting stock in her name.

PROBLEMS

1. Fly-By-Night Airlines is a new airline. Fly-By-Night offers extremely low fares. Two features of its operations allow the company to remain profitable. First, as its name implies, Fly-By-Night flies only at night, when landing slots at airports are much less costly. Second, Fly-By-Night always tries to make sure that its planes are completely full, which spreads the cost of the flight among more people.

To enable it to fill its planes, Fly-By-Night typically "overbooks" each flight by 30%. However, Fly-By-Night does not reveal that fact to those who purchase tickets.

A group of angry passengers has brought an intentional misrepresentation action against Fly-By-Night. All of these passengers were "bumped" from Fly-By-Night flights because the flights had been overbooked. The passengers claim that Fly-By-Night never intended to perform the contract represented by the ticket.

What is the passengers' chance of success? [NOTE: You should assume that there are no statutes or agency rules covering overbooking.]

2. You represent a seller who made a promise identical to that made by Billy Britt in the main case. However, there is one additional fact; on the eve of trial, your client has confided in you that she never had any intention of conveying stock to the person taking care of the farm. Your client also indicates that she

wants to get up on the witness stand and testify that she *did* intend to convey the stock at the time. What do you do? Do you allow your client to testify? Do you even continue representing your client?

2. Negligent Misrepresentations

SAIN v. CEDAR RAPIDS COMMUNITY SCHOOL DISTRICT
626 N.W.2d 115 (Iowa 2001)

CADY, Justice.

This appeal requires us to decide whether an action for negligence should be recognized based upon inaccurate information concerning the course requirements to compete in intercollegiate sports at a National Collegiate Athletic Association (NCAA) Division I university as a freshman allegedly given to a high school student by a guidance counselor. The district court found no cause of action existed as a matter of law and granted summary judgment. On review of the facts in the light most favorable to the student, we conclude summary judgment was improperly granted. We reverse the decision of the district court and remand for further proceedings.

Bruce Sain attended Jefferson High School in Cedar Rapids during his junior and senior years. . . . Sain was a member of the varsity basketball team at Jefferson and maintained aspirations of receiving a scholarship to play basketball for a major college. He received many basketball accolades and awards during high school, including selection to the all-state basketball team.

Sain's guidance counselor at Jefferson was Larry Bowen. Bowen was generally familiar with the high school credits and course requirements imposed by the NCAA for incoming student-athletes to be eligible to compete in sports as a freshman at those Division I institutions which maintain membership in the NCAA. One such rule requires a student to complete three years of English courses approved by the NCAA, as well as core courses in mathematics, science, and the social sciences. The NCAA maintains a list of high school courses for each school which satisfy the core course requirements for each discipline. This list is known as Form 48-H. A high school submits the courses it offers to students to the NCAA for approval. . . .

Sain began his senior year at Jefferson in the fall of 1995. During the first trimester he enrolled in and satisfactorily completed an English course entitled "World Literature." This course was included in the NCAA list of approved core English courses. He registered to take a course entitled "English Literature" during the second trimester. This class was also approved by the NCAA as a core English course. Sain, however, was dissatisfied with the class and met with Bowen to determine if he could drop it and add another English course. Bowen suggested Sain take a different English course entitled "Technical Communications." . . . Bowen believed the course would be compatible with Sain's interest in computers. Additionally, Bowen told Sain that the course would be approved by the NCAA as a core English course. Sain subsequently dropped "English Literature" from his schedule and enrolled in the "Technical Communications" course. He satisfactorily completed the course, as well as another English course during the final trimester.

The school failed to include the "Technical Communications" course on the list of classes submitted to the NCAA for approval. . . . Consequently, the course was not approved by the Clearinghouse and was not included on Form 48-H. . . .

During the final trimester of high school, Sain was offered and accepted a full five-year basketball scholarship at Northern Illinois University beginning in the fall semester of 1996. . . .

Sain graduated from Jefferson High School in the spring of 1996. Shortly after graduation, Sain received a letter from the NCAA Clearinghouse. The Clearinghouse informed Sain that the "Technical Communications" course he took during the second trimester did not satisfy the core English requirements. This meant only two of the three English courses taken by Sain during his senior year had been accepted by the NCAA Clearinghouse, and Sain fell one-third credit short of the core English requirements to participate in Division I basketball as a freshman. Sain and Northern Illinois University requested a waiver from the NCAA. The request was denied and Sain lost his scholarship. As a result, Sain was unable to attend Northern Illinois University during the 1996-97 school year and compete in basketball for the school.

Sain brought this action against the school district and the NCAA. The claim against the NCAA was later voluntarily dismissed.

The action against the school district was based on separate claims of negligence and negligent misrepresentation under the Restatement (Second) of Torts section 552(1). Sain claimed Bowen breached a duty to provide competent academic advice concerning the eligibility to participate in Division I sports as a freshman. He also claimed the school district was negligent in failing to submit the "Technical Communications" course to the NCAA for pre-approval.

The school district moved for summary judgment. The district court granted the motion. It found . . . the claim for negligent misrepresentation did not apply to an educational setting, but was limited to commercial or business transactions.

Sain appeals. He claims . . . the recognized tort of negligent misrepresentation is broad enough to hold a guidance counselor liable for providing specific information to a student pertaining to the required courses and credits necessary to pursue post-high school goals. . . .

[Discussion of the educational malpractice claim is omitted.]

IV. Negligent Misrepresentation — Providing Information

The tort of negligence has developed into a broad and open-ended cause of action. Unlike the intentional trespassory torts that are generally geared toward specific conduct, a cause of action for negligence may find support in most any conduct. Although the familiar elements of duty, breach of care, proximate cause, and damages must always be established, most any circumstances not exempted by a special rule or a statute can be used to prove these elements. Negligence has clearly emerged as "the central focus of modern tort law." The expansive nature of the tort has challenged courts in not only applying the principles of negligence to accommodate its growth into new areas of human interaction, but to properly limit the tort within certain boundaries as well.

Although misrepresentation is recognized as a distinct and separate cause of action, misrepresentation based on negligent conduct has typically been addressed within the framework of a claim for negligence when the conduct has caused personal injury or property damage. Courts have never found a need to treat negligent misrepresentation as a separate basis for liability when the interference consists of personal or property damage. On the other hand, when misrepresentation based on negligent acts results solely in an interference with intangible economic interests, more restrictive rules of recovery have been developed. This has been mainly due to the fear that liability for misinformation could be virtually unlimited and include unknown claimants under the traditional foreseeability limitation applicable to negligence claims. Thus, the tort of negligent misrepresentation has taken the form of limiting "the group of persons to whom [a] defendant may be liable, short of the foreseeability of possible harm."

We first recognized the tort of negligently giving misinformation with this limitation on the scope of liability in *Ryan v. Kanne*, 170 N.W.2d 395 (Iowa 1969). In that case, we permitted a third party who reasonably relied upon financial statements prepared by an accountant to maintain a negligence action against the accountant for misinformation in the statements when the accountant knew the information was intended for the benefit and guidance of the third party. *Ryan*, 170 N.W.2d at 403. We recognized professionals such as accountants, abstractors, and attorneys owe a duty of care in supplying information to foreseeable third parties as members of a limited class of persons who would be contemplated to use and rely upon the information. Thus, we joined the drafters of the tentative draft of the Restatement (Second) of Torts section 552 to the extent that they recognized "the right to recover for negligence to persons for whose benefit and guidance the accountant knows the information is intended." *Ryan*, 170 N.W.2d at 403. Instead of using foreseeability of harm to limit the scope of the duty of care, we relied upon a stricter standard of knowledge.

We have continued to recognize negligence claims for misinformation following *Ryan,* and continue to utilize the Restatement (Second) of Torts section 552 to help define the tort. . . .

As with all negligence actions, an essential element of negligent misrepresentation is that the defendant must owe a duty of care to the plaintiff. In the context of negligent misrepresentation, this means the person who supplies the information must owe a duty to the person to whom the information is provided. Although the Restatement supports a broader view, we have determined that this duty arises only when the information is provided by persons in the business or profession of supplying information to others. Thus, when deciding whether the tort of negligent misrepresentation imposes a duty of care in a particular case, we distinguish between those transactions where a defendant is in the business or profession of supplying information to others from those transactions that are arm's length and adversarial. We recognize the former circumstances justify the imposition of a duty of care because a transaction between a person in the business or profession of supplying information and a person seeking information is compatible to a special relationship. A special relationship, of course, is an important factor to support the imposition of a duty of care under a claim for negligence. Moreover, a person in the profession of supplying information for the guidance of others acts in an advisory capacity and is manifestly aware of the use that the information will be put, and intends to supply it for that purpose. Such a person is also in a position to weigh the use for the information against the magnitude and probability of the loss that might attend the use of the information if it is incorrect. Under these circumstances, the foreseeability of harm helps support the imposition of a duty of care. Additionally, the pecuniary interest which a person has in a business, profession, or employment which supplies information serves as an additional basis for imposing a duty of care. On the other hand, information given gratuitously or incidental to a different service imposes no such duty.

. . . Historically, those cases which were responsible for developing the tort arose from a business or financial setting, and the recognition of negligent misrepresentation as a separate tort has from the beginning been confined largely to financial or commercial harm in the course of business dealings. Consequently, the tort is generally thought to only apply to business transactions. On the other hand, we observe that some courts have applied the tort in other contexts, such as adoption. Yet, no jurisdiction has recognized a tort in the context of a school counselor and a student.

Our examination of both section 552 and our own cases reveals the business or commercial requirement for the tort does not actually concern the subject matter of the transaction between the plaintiff and the defendant, but requires the defendant to be in the business or profession of supplying information for the guidance of others. This is the fundamental requirement to support the imposition of a duty, which is essential for all negligence claims. Additionally, the language of section 552 requires the information to not only be supplied "for the guidance of others," but "for the guidance of others in their business transactions." Restatement (Second) of Torts § 552(1). Yet, this additional requirement also does not exist to restrict the subject of the information to business matters. Instead, the supplied "for the guidance of others in their business transactions" requirement recognizes that the tort predominantly applies to situations where the information supplied harmed the plaintiff in its relations with third parties, as opposed to harm to a plaintiff in its relations with the provider of the information. This means the tort does not apply when a defendant directly provides information to a plaintiff in the course of a transaction between the two parties, which information harms the plaintiff in the transaction with the defendant. This situation is compatible with our approach that there is no duty imposed on parties who deal at arm's length.

We conclude that the context of the transaction in this case does not draw the case outside the scope of the tort of negligent misrepresentation. Instead, our task, as in other cases which assert a claim of negligent misrepresentation, is to determine if the defendant — a high school counselor in this case — is in the profession of supplying information to others.

In deciding this question, we observe that those same characteristics which exist when a person is found to be in the business of supplying information to others also exist in the case of a high school counselor. The counselor and student have a relationship which extends beyond a relationship found in an arm's length transaction. It is advisory in nature and not adversarial. The school counselor does not act for his or her own benefit, but provides information for the benefit of students. Furthermore, in matters that involve matriculation from high school to college, a high school counselor clearly assumes an advisory role, is aware of the use for the information, and knows the student is relying upon the information provided. Additionally, the counselor is paid by the school system to provide such advice, and has an indirect financial interest in providing the information. Thus, the counselor does not provide gratuitous information that the counselor would not expect the student to rely upon. Furthermore, the information is not incidental to some more central function or service provided by the counselor.

Considering the rationale which supports the imposition of a duty of care on a person in the business or profession of supplying information, we discern no reason why a high school counselor should not fall within the category as a person in the profession of supplying information to others to support the imposition of a duty of reasonable care in the manner he or she provides information to students. We should not confine the tort to traditional commercial transactions when the rationale for the tort allows it to be applied beyond those factual circumstances which originally gave rise to the tort. . . . For the purposes of the tort of negligent misrepresentation, we conclude a high school counselor is also a person in the profession of supplying information to others.

We understand that our expansion of the tort of negligent misrepresentation to include a high school counselor and a student relationship will impose a greater burden on school counselors. There is a concern, of course, that this greater burden may have a chilling effect on school counselors, who may refrain from providing information because of the potential for liability. However, . . . liability for negligent misrepresentation is limited to harm suffered by a person for whose benefit and guidance the counselor intended to supply the information or knew the recipient intended to supply it and to loss suffered through reliance upon the information in a transaction the counselor intended the information to influence. Additionally, we observe that the tort applies only to false information and does not apply to personal opinions or statements of future intent. Finally, the standard imposed is only one of reasonableness, and the elements of proximate cause and damage must also be shown. Thus, these limitations will help to continue to promote the important public policy of encouraging interaction between high school counselors and students, and maintain the flow of necessary information to the students. We also observe that some states have enacted statutes giving schools and teachers immunity from any liability.

In this case, we find Sain has submitted sufficient facts to withstand summary judgment on the claim that the guidance counselor negligently told him that a specific English course would be certified by the NCAA Clearinghouse. The relationship between the high school counselor and the student, together with the activity engaged in by Sain and the counselor in this case, is sufficient to give rise to a duty for the counselor to use reasonable care when informing a student that a class will be approved by the NCAA. We continue to confine the tort of negligent misrepresentation to persons in the business or profession of supplying information to others, but find that a high school counselor falls within that language because the policies which support the imposition of a duty of care on such a person applies to a high school counselor.

V. Negligent Misrepresentation — Failure to Submit Class.

The second prong of Sain's negligence claim is based upon the failure of the school district to include the "Technical Communications" course on the list of courses submitted to the NCAA. Like the first claim, Sain asserts the school district had a duty of care to submit the course and breached the duty when it failed to do so. Sain asserts the internal policies of the school to submit all courses for approval by the NCAA Clearinghouse supports such a duty.

We begin by recognizing that the tort of negligent misrepresentation does not apply to the failure to provide information, but to the disclosure of information. Thus, the imposition of a duty to support a claim of providing false information does not support the imposition of a duty for not disclosing information.

A claim for negligence can be based on both actions and inactions. However, liability for the failure to act to protect another from harm is largely restricted to those situations where there is a special relationship between the parties. It is essentially based upon a relationship of dependence and an expectation of protection.

Nevertheless, a duty of care is imposed to protect against the foreseeable risk of harm. The failure of a school district to submit a course for approval by the NCAA Clearinghouse would not increase the hazard of a student taking an unapproved course. If a school fails to submit a course, the course would not be included on the approved list. The absence of the course from the list would not induce reliance, and would not make it foreseeable that harm would result to a student by taking an unapproved course under the belief that the course was in fact approved. Thus, there is no duty to students for a school district or a high school counselor to submit courses to the NCAA Clearinghouse. We conclude the district court properly granted summary judgment on this claim.

NOTES

1. *Sain* restates a crucial point made at the beginning of the chapter. Negligent misrepresentations can cause different types of harm. The law of misrepresentation as covered in this chapter, however, deals only with pecuniary harm. Misrepresentations that cause bodily harm or harm to one's reputation are typically labelled with other names, such as products liability or defamation.

2. *Sain* also points out that the tort of negligent misrepresentation is of fairly recent vintage. Iowa only recognized the tort in 1969, which is fairly typical. By contrast, courts have allowed recovery for intentional misrepresentations for a much longer period of time.

3. In most jurisdictions, negligent misrepresentation is limited by one important element — that the defendant have some sort of "commercial" motivation for making the statement. Without that motivation, there is no duty. Now that you are more familiar with misrepresentation in general, rethink a question posed at the beginning of this chapter. *Why* is negligent misrepresentation limited in this fashion? Do statements made by those without an economic interest somehow cause less harm? If people give advice, and that advice is foreseeably relied upon by others, why not impose liability?

Do courts limit negligent misrepresentation to the commercial world because they are concerned that a party with something to gain might have a greater motivation to distort the truth? But if a party intentionally distorts the truth, she has committed an intentional misrepresentation, where recovery is allowed even in non-commercial cases.

4. Note too that the commercial limitation contradicts to some extent the rules dealing with opinions. When two parties are dealing with each other at arm's length in a business transaction, a court is more likely to find a statement made by one an "opinion," and thereby deny recovery. Does this suggest that people rely on statements by people without commercial interests to an even greater degree? If so, isn't the case for liability even stronger?

5. Of course, the situation in *Sain* falls somewhere between these purely commercial and purely non-commercial poles. The counselor was not negotiating a business deal with the student. On the other hand, because of the relationship between the parties, reliance by the student is certainly justified. The court decides that, even though there was no transaction, the counselor meets the "commercial" requirement because he was "in the business" of providing

such advice. Does extending liability to the counselor really satisfy the policy underlying the commercial limitation?

6. What are the student's damages in *Sain*? Suppose that Northern Illinois University offers the student another scholarship the next year. Has there been any damage? Is the delay compensable? What if Northern does not extend a scholarship, but another university does?

3. Scienter and Intent

In addition to showing that the defendant knew or should have known that its representation was false, the plaintiff in an intentional misrepresentation case must demonstrate that the defendant intended to deceive the plaintiff. As the following case demonstrates, there can be some tension between those two elements.

MYERS & CHAPMAN, INC. v. THOMAS G. EVANS, INC.
374 S.E.2d 385 (N.C. 1988)

MEYER, Justice.

[Myers, a general contractor, entered into a subcontract with Evans. As the project continued, Evans would periodically make applications for payment. In one of its applications, Evans represented that it had purchased over $11,000 of equipment for use in the project. This equipment was never actually purchased. Myers therefore sued for fraud and gross negligence.

[The jury found that although the application was false, Evans did not actually know if its falsity. However, the jury also found that Evans was either reckless or grossly negligent in filing the erroneous application.]

[A]s the Court of Appeals correctly noted, although the jury found in answer to issue 2 that Thomas Evans had committed a fraud, the same jury found, in response to issue 4, that Thomas and Brenda Evans did not knowingly submit a false Application for Payment to plaintiff. In other words, the jury found no knowledge of the falsity of the statement made, which is an essential element of fraud.

Plaintiff argues that because it proved conscious and reckless ignorance of the truth, it has satisfied the "knowledge" element and has thus proved fraud. Plaintiff implies that in this circumstance, it is unnecessary to prove an intent to deceive because intent may be inferred by reckless indifference to the truth. This argument appears to be based on language in recent cases from this Court. *See, e.g., Britt v. Britt*, 320 N.C. 573, 579, 359 S.E.2d 467, 471 (1987) [note: *Britt* is set out on page 948 of this book]; *Johnson v. Insurance Co.*, 300 N.C. 247, 253, 266 S.E.2d 610, 615 (1980); *Odom v. Little Rock & I-85 Corp.*, 299 N.C. 86, 92,

261 S.E.2d 99, 103 (1980). In *Odom,* the essential elements of fraud were defined as follows:

> To make out an actionable case of fraud plaintiff must show: (a) that the defendant made a representation relating to some material past or existing fact; (b) that the representation was false; (c) that when he made it defendant knew it was false *or made it recklessly without any knowledge of its truth and as a positive assertion;* (d) that the defendant made the false representation with the intention that it should be acted on by the plaintiff; (e) that the plaintiff reasonably relied upon the representation and acted upon it; and (f) that the plaintiff suffered injury.

While the concept of a statement "made with reckless indifference as to its truth," or one "recklessly made without knowledge as a positive assertion" or words of like import, or the concept of "concealment of a material fact" have been held to satisfy the element of "false representation," those concepts do not satisfy the element of a statement "made with intent to deceive." Without the element of intent to deceive, the required scienter for *fraud* is not present. The term "scienter" embraces both knowledge *and* an intent to deceive, manipulate or defraud.

In *Myrtle Apartments,* the Court stated that in order to constitute fraud there must be false representation, known to be false, or made with reckless indifference as to its truth, *and it must be made with intent to deceive. Myrtle Apartments,* 258 N.C. 49, 52, 127 S.E.2d 759, 761 (emphasis added). . . .

Britt, Johnson and *Odom* may be interpreted to have expanded the definition of fraud to the point where the essential element of the defendant's intent to deceive is only implicitly recognized at best. To the extent that the statements of the elements of fraud in *Britt, Johnson, Odom* and other cases omit the essential element of the intent to deceive in a definition of fraud, they are hereby disavowed.

The record and transcript in the case *sub judice* reveal that Thomas Evans had neither knowledge *nor* intent to deceive plaintiff when he signed and swore to Applications for Payment Nos. 2 and 3. He had no scienter. We therefore affirm the Court of Appeals, but not for the reasons stated in its opinion. We hold that the evidence presented to the jury was insufficient to support a finding that Thomas Evans intentionally committed a fraud.

We are satisfied, however, that the same evidence was sufficient to support the submission of the issues to the jury based on Thomas Evans' gross negligence in subscribing and swearing to Applications for Payment Nos. 2 and 3. . . .

NOTE

Has North Carolina effectively eviscerated the cause of action for "reckless" misrepresentation? Although the plaintiff may still sue for a negligent misrepresentation in these cases, punitive damages are not available in negligent misrepresentation cases.

D. RELIANCE

As a reminder, this element is the same in misrepresentation cases whether the case is brought in negligence or in intentional tort.

FRANCIS v. STINSON
760 A.2d 209 (Me. 2000)

CLIFFORD, J.

The parties' statements of material fact establish the following: The Stinson Canning Company was established by Calvin Stinson Sr. many years ago. Between 1950 and the late 1970s, Calvin Sr. made gifts of stock in the company to his six children and his grandchildren such that by the late 1970s each of six families owned approximately one-sixth of the company. . . .

The Stinson Canning Company profited and grew in value between 1975 and 1980. Between 1978 and 1980, other businesses began to show interest in acquiring the company. One such company, Connors Brothers Ltd., offered $14 million for the company sometime prior to 1980. By late 1979, the company's assets were valued at more than $20 million, and Charles believed that the company could be sold for $18 million.

The present dispute arises out of the sale of Stinson Canning Company stock by two of the six families that had been given stock by Calvin Sr. Calvin Sr.'s daughter, Lou Ann Francis, her husband Arnold, and her children, Arnold G. and Marion Alley, made the first sale in February of 1980 for approximately $700,000. Three years later, another of Calvin Sr.'s daughters, Eva Wight, her husband Carl, and her daughters, Carla Intza and Jean Rakoske, sold their stock to the company for approximately $1.9 million. The facts set out below reflect a view of the evidence most favorable to the plaintiffs.

A. The Francis Family

In the fall of 1979, Calvin Jr. called his sister Lou Ann and suggested that her family sell its stock to the corporation. Later that fall, Lou Ann received another phone call, this time from Charles, inquiring as to whether Lou Ann had decided to sell her family's stock. Charles told Lou Ann that her family's stock was worth $300,000. Lou Ann was surprised at such a low offer and assumed that it was because the company was doing poorly.

Lou Ann and her husband Arnold met with Charles who, according to Lou Ann, told her that he was not getting along with Calvin Jr. and that the company was having a "financial problem." Charles advised Lou Ann to sell her stock now because if the company got a good buyer, it would probably be sold. Charles also informed her that if she died, her inheritance taxes might ruin her husband's business, and that if the company filed for bankruptcy protection, her family would be responsible for one-sixth of the company's debts. Lou Ann later reported at her deposition that she was aware of the estate tax problem but was not aware that the company had eliminated that problem by implementing the stock repurchase program.

Lou Ann and Arnold then visited with Calvin Jr., who acknowledged that he was not getting along well with Charles, and confirmed that "the company was rocky financially." Calvin Jr. added that Charles "and the rest of them wanted to sell the company," and that if he was in Lou Ann's position, he would sell his stock.

Lou Ann never participated in the management of the company and had no representation on its board of directors. As far as she was concerned Charles and Calvin Jr. "were the company . . . they ran Stinson Canning Company. They called all the shots." She trusted her two brothers and thought that they would only tell her what was "right or good." She even considered Charles to be her "little God" and said she "would never believe him to tell [her] a falsehood."

While Lou Ann and Arnold were considering the $300,000 offer, a friend of theirs, J.C. Strout, disclosed that he knew a third party who might be interested in purchasing the stock. A few days later, Strout made an offer on behalf of Shaw Mudge of $10,000 per share of common stock and $100 per share of preferred stock for the Francis family's stock in Stinson Canning (a total of approximately $2,170,000).

Lou Ann believed she was required by the by-laws of the company to inform it of the offer, so she wrote a letter to the company, signed by her entire family, which detailed the terms of Mudge's offer. After the company received the letter, Charles phoned Lou Ann and told her that her letter was a "joke" and that he "didn't have to pay [her] a goddamn thing." Charles then offered Lou Ann $700,000 for all of the Francis family stock.

Lou Ann discussed the offer with her family. Arnold feared the estate tax consequences and the possible family liability if the company were to file for bankruptcy protection. Lou Ann also wanted to keep the business in the family, and so she phoned Charles and accepted his offer. When asked why she would turn down a $2,170,000 offer to accept a $700,000 offer, Lou Ann responded that she believed in her brothers and that they would not "have allowed an outsider to buy [her] stock." Lou Ann and Arnold also relied on a statement made previously by Charles, in which he allegedly promised that, "if they sold [the company] and made a good profit out of it, then . . . they would make up the difference" if Lou Ann accepted the company's offer. She further alleges that

Charles also stated that if other family members sold their stock to the company at a higher price, the company would give the Francises the same amount. . . .

The sale of the Francis family stock to the company was held on February 4, 1980, at the company offices; the closing lasted approximately five minutes. With little discussion, the Francises signed the stock purchase agreements that the company presented to them. Lou Ann did not read the agreement because "my brothers and I had discussed this sale; and they're honorable people, so we just believed what they said. They wouldn't have me sign something I shouldn't be signing." . . .

Each member of the Francis family signed stock purchase agreements which included the following disclosure statement:

4. *Disclosure.*

(a) Inquiries and Offers. The Seller has been advised that the officers and directors of the Company have, from time to time, received inquiries with regard to the possible acquisition of the outstanding stock or assets of the Company and its subsidiaries. The written inquiries received since July 1, 1978, include those received from: [fourteen companies were listed]

In addition, the Seller is aware that the officers and directors of the Company have recently received two (2) offers to purchase the outstanding stock of the Company and its subsidiaries and one (1) offer to acquire the assets of the Company. . . .

(b) Seller's Representations. Seller hereby acknowledges and represents that:

(i) The Company, through its President and Treasurer, has made available to her the opportunity to ask questions of, and receive answers from, the Company concerning inquiries and/or offers from third parties with regard to the purchase of the outstanding stock or assets of the Company and its subsidiaries and to obtain any additional information, to the extent the Company possesses such information or can acquire it with reasonable effort or expense, necessary to verify the accuracy of the information given to her;

(ii) The purchase and sale contemplated by Section 1 was initiated by her and the price for her Common Stock and Preferred Stock, as well as the other terms of this Agreement, were determined as a result of good faith negotiation between the Board of Directors of the Company and her; . . .

Attachments referred to in the disclosure statements were not physically attached to the agreements, but were located in a manilla envelope on the table beside the agreements. The Francises, however, did not read the attachments before signing the agreements.

The attachments contained the company's financial statements for the years 1976-79. The financial statements contained information regarding the company's assets, gross profits, and net earnings per share during those years. . . .

B. The Wight Family

Eva Wight was also aware of the estate tax problem. She was told that the estate taxes could "wipe out" her family, and she was advised to consider selling the stock back to the company for a "minimal" amount. Unlike Lou Ann, Eva became suspicious that her brothers were trying to "grab" her stock in the corporation. At about the same time, her husband, Carl, told Eva that he had spoken with Calvin Jr., who did not appear to approve of the "pressure tactics" being applied by the company. . . .

In October of 1980, Eva and Carl separated. By early 1981, Eva was experiencing financial difficulty and began to investigate the possibility of selling her stock back to the company. Her family agreed and she began negotiating with the company. During the entire negotiation, Eva did not obtain any additional financial information regarding the company's performance after 1980.

On behalf of the company, Charles initially offered the Wights $700,000, the same amount the Francises had received. Eva rejected that offer and made a counteroffer of $2 million. The company rejected that offer and made three additional offers to Eva. She consulted her accountant regarding each offer from the company. He advised her to accept, and she did accept, an offer of $1.9 million ($8,883.18 per share of common stock and $50 per share of preferred stock) payable over a term of years at 13% interest.

Eva testified that she was told that the company was in financial trouble, but could not remember who gave her that information. . . .

In 1990, the company, comprising substantially the same assets as in 1980, was sold for $24 million. None of that money was paid to either the Francis family or the Wight family. A certified public accountant, Dennis Norton, concluded that, on the date it was sold back to the company, the fair market value of the Francis family stock was $2,254,591. Norton valued the Wight family stock at between $2,500,000 and $3,333,000 as of the date that stock was bought by the company. . . .

In October of 1995, the Francis family and the Wight family filed a complaint in the Superior Court naming Charles, Calvin Jr., and Camp Hills, Inc. as defendants. . . .

Count VII alleges "an intentional plan or course of conduct to defraud [p]laintiffs of their fair shares in the family company, and in their father's estate," and Count VIII alleges intentional or reckless misrepresentations that induced the plaintiffs to sign the stock purchase agreements. . . .

The court entered summary judgment on Count VI through VIII on the basis that the plaintiffs had presented insufficient evidence to support their claims. . . .

The trial court determined that the plaintiffs had failed to present sufficient evidence to sustain any action for fraud. We thus look to see whether the facts alleged are sufficient to survive a motion for summary judgment.

> [A] defendant is liable for fraud or deceit if he (1) makes a false representation (2) of a material fact (3) with knowledge of its falsity or in reckless disregard of whether it is true or false (4) for the purpose of inducing another to act or to refrain from acting in reliance upon it, and (5) the plaintiff justifiably relies upon the representation as true and acts upon it to [her] damage. . . . Reliance is unjustified only if the plaintiff knows the representation is false or its falsity is obvious to [her].

A claim for fraud must be proved by evidence that shows that the existence of fraud is "highly probable." *Barnes v. Zappia*, 658 A.2d 1086, 1089 (Me.1995). A person may justifiably rely on a representation without investigating the truth or falsity of the representation unless the person knows that the statement is false or the falsity is obvious.

A. The Francis Family's Fraud Claims

With respect to the Francis family, the statement of material facts alleges that Calvin Jr. and Charles told them that (1) potential estate taxes could destroy Arnold Francis's business; (2) if Stinson Canning Company declared bankruptcy, the Francises would be liable for one sixth of the debts; (3) the company was in financial trouble; and (4) they would receive their "fair share" of the proceeds from any future sale of the company.

The defendants point out, however, that the stock purchase agreement lists fourteen companies that had expressed interest in buying the company, and it also lists two companies that had made actual offers. The financial statements also contain recent balance sheets that make it clear that the company was not in financial trouble. Moreover, the defendants contend that it should have been obvious to the Francis family that any fair share promise was not enforceable because the stock purchase agreement stated explicitly that the Francises would receive no share of any future sale, and that any reliance on the representations was not reasonable.

As a matter of general contract law, parties to a contract are deemed to have read the contract and are bound by its terms. The terms of the stock purchase agreement signed by the Francis family so clearly spelled out the financial well being of the company that the falsity of any representations that the company was doing poorly, or that bankruptcy was likely, became obvious. Accordingly, any reliance on those representations is not reasonable.

Lou Ann argues, however, that she reasonably relied on the "fair share" promise made to her, and that she therefore justifiably disregarded the language in the agreement reflecting the strong financial state of the company. She relies on the admissibility of parol evidence to show that fraudulent fair share promise. Parol evidence may be introduced to show that a signed document does not bar all actions for fraud as a matter of law and that the contract does not reflect the intent of the parties.

This agreement, however, contained language that clearly contradicted the "fair share" promise. The agreement provided that payment to the Francis family for their shares of stock was accepted as "full payment," and further provided that other family members could sell their shares to the company at higher prices than the Francis family was realizing without an increased benefit to the Francises. There is no allegation that any representation was made to any member of the Francis family that such language could be disregarded, as there was in *Ferrell v. Cox,* 617 A.2d at 1006, and in *Harriman v. Maddocks,* 518 A.2d 1027 (Me. 1986), where the fraudulent inducement was directly related to the signing of the document. . . .

In this case, however, there is no evidence that any "fair share" assurance was made to Lou Ann after she became aware of the contract language that imposed no fair share distribution obligation on the defendants, and indeed, clearly stated that other family members could receive more money for the sale of their shares than the Francis family. Despite such language, Lou Ann signed the agreement without any further assurance from the defendants. Because Lou Ann cannot demonstrate that her reliance on an earlier promise of fair share distribution was reasonable, the trial court correctly concluded that the Francis family could not vary the terms of the contract, and properly entered a summary judgment against them.

B. The Wight Family's Fraud Claims

With respect to the Wights, the complaint alleges that, like Lou Ann, Eva Wight also relied on the defendants' intentional misrepresentations that the company was in financial trouble and that the family faced potentially "onerous estate tax consequences" if they continued holding the stock. The parties' Rule 7(d) statements of fact, however, even when viewed in the light most favorable to the Wights, reveal that Eva could not state with any real certainty that it was one of the defendants who told her that the company was in financial trouble. Nor could Eva identify any false financial information provided by the company or the defendants prior to her sale of stock to the company.

Moreover, the plaintiffs' own statement of material facts does not establish that the Wights, in making their decision to sell the stock, relied on the defendants' representations regarding the potential estate tax consequences of continuing to hold the stock. To the contrary, Eva alleged that, when she was informed of the estate tax consequences and encouraged to sell her stock at a low price, she "became suspicious . . . that her brothers were trying to grab her stock in the corporation." She added that she did not consider selling her stock until two years later, and then only because "she was in financial distress" and "because there was no income from the stock."

Because the Wights failed to develop sufficient facts to establish fraud to a "high probability," and because the evidence does not reveal that Eva reasonably relied on the allegedly fraudulent misrepresentations, summary judgment was properly entered on the Wights' claims for fraud and fraud in the inducement.

. . .

Judgments affirmed.

NOTES

1. The element of justified reliance can be one of the most problematic in representation cases. It may help to divide the issue into two parts. First, there must be *actual* reliance on the statement. This is really a question of causation. The statement must lead the plaintiff to act in a way that results in pecuniary harm. Second, that reliance must be justified under the circumstances. Which of these two parts was not met in *Francis*?

2. The court treats the sale of the stock essentially as an arm's length transaction. Is that realistic? While the sellers were armed with evidence that showed the statements were false, did they really have any reason to doubt their brother?

3. The court also places considerable weight in the disclosure statement that Charles provided in connection with the sale. Yet there is no evidence that Lou Ann even read the statement. Is a party under a duty to investigate the truth of a statement, at least when proof of veracity is right at hand, as in this case? If a close relative of yours gave you a similar statement, would you have read it?

PROBLEMS

1. Seller owns a parcel of land. He sells the north half first, for $10,000. He then sells the south half to Buyer for $50,000. During the negotiations with Buyer, Seller represents to Buyer that he had sold the north half for $50,000. When Buyer discovers the truth, she sues for misrepresentation. Should Buyer prevail?

2. Same as Problem 1, except that Buyer also talks to the party who purchased the north half before signing a contract with Seller. When Buyer asks whether it was true that this party had paid $50,000, the party refuses to answer. *See Smith v. Walden*, 549 S.E.2d 750 (Ga. Ct. App. 2001).

3. Same as Problem 1, except that the local paper regularly publishes the prices at which real estate is sold. Even though the sale of the north half of the property was published, Buyer never bothers to check the paper.

4. Same as Problem 1, except that Buyer also arranges for an independent appraisal of the property. Because of a serious error in calculation, this appraisal shows the value of the south parcel to be $70,000 instead of its true value of $10,000. Consider only the liability of Seller, not the appraiser.

E. DAMAGES

BURKE v. HARMAN
574 N.W.2d 156 (Neb. Ct. App. 1998)

SIEVERS, Judge.

A Navajo chief's blanket, first phase, Ute style, is a rare and beautiful object because of its historical and ethnographic significance, as well as its art; all of which add to the blanket's great value. Such blankets were handwoven by Navajo women before 1850. The plaintiff, John Burke, acquired such a blanket by purchase for $115 from an antique mall in Lincoln. He sold the blanket to the defendant, Kenneth Harman, for $1,000. Harman sold the blanket to an individual in New York for $290,000. Burke has sued Harman for $289,000, claiming that Harman falsely or negligently misrepresented the blanket as a substantially less valuable Mexican weaving.

John Burke resides in Ithaca, Nebraska, and his work is primarily wood carvings of Native Americans, mountainmen, early American historical figures, Civil War figures, and the like. In order to lend authenticity to his work, Burke engages in some collecting of historical artifacts involving his subject matter, which he studies and then typically sells or trades when he is finished with them. Burke teaches his wood-carving art throughout the United States and has published several how-to books on the subject.

Kenneth Harman holds a bachelor of arts degree in education and has taught first grade at Arnold Elementary School in Lincoln for over 23 years. Harman says that he has been a collector since he was 10 years old. . . .

Harman has a reference library of some consequence in his home dealing with collecting and collectibles. His library included at least two reference books which displayed pictures of Navajo chief's blankets, first phase, Ute style. . . .

The story of the particular Navajo chief's blanket involved in this case began before 1850, when it was handwoven in the Ute style by a Navajo woman. The Ute Indians, with whom the Navajos traded, preferred the ivory, chocolate brown (natural colors from the wool), and indigo (naturally dyed) stripe pattern seen on this blanket — hence the name "Ute style." The name indicates a particular and recognizable style of chief's blanket. According to Alexanian, the term "first phase" means that it was woven before there were white settlers in the Southwest.

The history of the blanket involved in this case, at least for us, begins on July 1, 1993, when Burke attended the opening of St. George's Antique Mall in Lincoln. Burke was the second customer in line to enter the business. There, he purchased the blanket for $115. It had a price tag of $115 on it from its owner, Tedd Whipple of Grand Island, who had placed it at the mall for sale. On the tag, Whipple described it as a "1930's Southwest wool handwoven throw." Burke testified that the blanket was placed on the floor in front of the fireplace at his home. On August 1, a houseguest, William Hackett, inquired about the rug. Burke indicated that he did not know anything of its background or origin. Burke and Hackett discussed the matter and concluded that some effort should be made to determine its age and origin, and in that regard, Harman's name occurred to Burke. Burke and Harman had known each other since early 1993, when Harman had called Burke about some items Burke had displayed for sale at the Antique Market in Lincoln. As a result, the two men met, and Harman purchased items from Burke.

Burke, Hackett, and the blanket proceeded to Harman's residence on August 1, 1993, after Burke had called Harman about looking at the blanket. . . .

Burke's version of the meeting is that after Harman rolled out the blanket for examination, Harman told Burke that it was Mexican and that in Santa Fe it was worth $1,500 to $2,000. Harman offered Burke $500 plus two Indian Skookum dolls for the weaving. When Burke refused that offer, Harman offered $1,000 cash, which Burke accepted. Burke had also brought an Indian basket along, which Burke sold to Harman for $250. Harman admits in his testimony that he was asked by Burke, "What do you think it is?" But he relates that he told Burke that it could be Mexican or Indian and that he gave no opinion as to its value except in reference to its condition in relation to the rug he had acquired from Deeds, Harman saying that Burke's weaving was in poorer condition. Harman testified that he liked the weaving and that he asked what Burke wanted for it, to which Burke responded with, "What will you give me?" Harman responded by offering Burke $500 in cash plus the two Indian Skookum dolls which he had lying on the table, preparing to pack them to take to Santa Fe. Harman related that Burke did not think the dolls were worth the $500 asserted by Harman. Harman testified that he then said, "I'll give you a thousand dollars for your blanket." According to Harman, Burke's response was, "Hell, yes. I'll sell it for $1,000." Harman paid Burke $1,250 in cash for the blanket and the basket, and Burke and Hackett left.

The blanket was identified as a Navajo chief's blanket, first phase, Ute style. Howard Grimmer, the former owner of Morning Star Gallery in Santa Fe, which handles valuable Indian artifacts, put the matter in perspective when he testified that even if a person had $500,000 in a checking account and wanted to buy a first phase blanket on a particular day, he did not think that anyone could do it, because the blankets are very rare, and there are only a "handful of them in public hands and those only move occasionally." Harman sold the blanket a year after he got it from Burke to an individual in New York for $290,000. The parties have stipulated that on August 1, 1993, the blanket Burke sold to Harman had a "fair market value of $290,000." . . .

[Burke sued, bringing a variety of claims, including a claim for negligent representation.]

At the close of Burke's case, Harman's counsel made a motion for a directed verdict on the ground that "the type of expectancy or loss [sic] profit damages which plaintiff seeks are not recoverable under Nebraska law under a theory of negligent misrepresentation." Following the motion, there was an extensive on-the-record discussion among counsel and the court about damages recoverable under negligent misrepresentation. Burke argued that under either negligent misrepresentation or fraudulent misrepresentation, the damages were the difference in value between what Harman paid for the blanket and the fair market value of the blanket at the time. The record establishes that the parties stipulated that $290,000 was the blanket's fair market value at the time of the sale by Burke to Harman.

Harman's position was that the Nebraska Supreme Court had adopted the Restatement (Second) of Torts § 552 (1977) with respect to negligent misrepresentation in *Gibb v. Citicorp Mortgage, Inc.*, 246 Neb. 355, 518 N.W.2d 910 (1994); that in fraudulent misrepresentation cases, one was entitled to profits, *i.e.*, expectancies; that in mere negligent misrepresentation cases, the law limits recovery to "out-of-pocket"; and that the plaintiff is "not going to get you the profits you would have made if you hadn't been injured." After ascertaining from Burke's counsel that there was no claim except diminimus for out-of-pocket expenses, the court granted Harman's motion for a directed verdict on the theory of negligent misrepresentation, and the case was submitted to the jury only on fraudulent misrepresentation. . . .

We have not found a Nebraska case which discusses the matter of the type of damages recoverable for the tort of negligent misrepresentation. However, the issue of recoverable damages under that theory is covered in the Restatement.

The matter of damages takes a bit of a tortured path through the Restatement. Section 552 outlines the basic requirements of the theory of recovery for negligent misrepresentation. . . . Harman clearly had a pecuniary interest in the transaction. Section 552B(1) at 140 sets forth the damages for negligent misrepresentation and provides:

(1) The damages recoverable for a negligent misrepresentation are those necessary to compensate the plaintiff for the pecuniary loss to him of which the misrepresentation is a legal cause, including

(a) the difference between the value of what he has received in the transaction and its purchase price or other value given for it; and

(b) pecuniary loss suffered otherwise as a consequence of the plaintiff's reliance upon the misrepresentation.

Section 552B(2) at 140 excludes damages for "the benefit of the plaintiff's contract with the defendant." In § 552B, comment *a.* at 141, we are referred to the Restatement (Second) of Torts § 549(1) (1977). . . .

Section 549 at 108, entitled "Measure of Damages for Fraudulent Misrepresentation," states:

(1) The recipient of a fraudulent misrepresentation is entitled to recover his damages in an action of deceit against the maker the pecuniary loss to him of which the misrepresentation is a legal cause, including

(a) the difference between the value of what he has received in the transaction and its purchase price or other value given for it; and

(b) pecuniary loss suffered otherwise as a consequence of the recipient's reliance upon the misrepresentation.

It is, of course, important to remember that although this section defines recoverable damages for fraudulent misrepresentation, § 552B "borrows" § 549(1) for the measure of damages for negligent misrepresentation.

Section 549(1), comment *a.* at 109, states that the most usual loss "is when the falsity of the representation causes the article bought, sold or exchanged to be regarded as of greater or less value than that which it would be regarded as having if the truth were known." In the context of negligent misrepresentation, it is not whether the truth is known, but, rather, whether reasonable care or competence was exercised in obtaining or communicating the information which forms the alleged misrepresentation. In this case, under Burke's evidence, the alleged misrepresentation is what Harman said the blanket was and what it was worth.

The fact that Burke is the seller and the alleged recipient of the fraudulent or negligent misrepresentation is not of consequence.

The commentary to § 552B of the Restatement adopts the out-of-pocket rule as the appropriate measure of damages for negligent misrepresentation and specifically excludes benefit of bargain damages. . . . W. Page Keeton et al., Prosser and Keeton on the Law of Torts § 10 (5th ed. 1984), [explains] the crucial difference between these different measurements of damages as follows: "The out-of-pocket rule 'looks to the loss which the plaintiff has suffered in the transaction, and gives him the difference between the value of what he has parted with and the value of what he has received.'" *W.K.T. Distributing Co. v. Sharp Electronics*, 746 F.2d 1333, 1337 (8th Cir. 1984), explained that "[t]he loss is usually measured as the difference between what the plaintiff parted with and what the plaintiff received." In contrast, the benefit of the bargain rule "gives the plaintiff the benefit of what he was promised, and allows recovery of the difference between the actual value of what he has received and the value that it would have had if it had been as represented." Keeton et al., *supra*, § 10 at 768.

Admittedly, the difference between "out-of-pocket" and "benefit of the bargain" may seem amorphous. . . .

Burke seeks $289,000, which is the difference between the value parted with at the time of the misrepresentation (it is crucial here to recall the parties' stipulation that on August 1, 1993, the blanket had a "fair market value of $290,000") and the value of what he received in return, $1,000 in cash. In fact, in this connection, we again observe that on the fraudulent misrepresentation claim, the court instructed the jury that if it found for Burke, it must return a verdict of $289,000. In short, the trial court directed what the amount of a verdict would be — a finding as a matter of law as to Burke's out-of-pocket damages — should liability on fraudulent misrepresentation be found. . . .

While applying these concepts to the instant case, and importantly remembering the stipulation that the blanket had a fair market value of $290,000 on August 1, 1993, it is clear to us that the damages sought are not benefit of the bargain, but, rather, are a real loss. Burke walked into Harman's house with a blanket, which, by stipulation, was worth $290,000. He left Harman's house with $1,000 because of a fraudulent or negligent misrepresentation, according to his evidence. Thus, under the parties' stipulation, there is a real loss of $289,000. As stated earlier by the Eighth Circuit in *W.K.T. Distributing Co. v. Sharp Electronics*, 746 F.2d 1333 (8th Cir. 1984), the loss is measured as the difference between what the plaintiff parted with (in this case, a $290,000 Navajo chief's blanket) and what he received ($1,000 cash). Thus, this is not an expectancy claim but a claim for out-of-pocket damage which is recoverable under the Restatement, *supra*, when § 552B (negligent misrepresentation) borrows the measure of damages from § 549(1).

Consequently, the district court erred in concluding that Burke's damages were not recoverable under negligent misrepresentation, and thereby, the trial court erred in directing a verdict on that claim and refusing to submit the theory of negligent misrepresentation to the jury. . . .

REVERSED AND REMANDED FOR A NEW TRIAL.

BRITT v. BRITT
359 S.E.2d 467 (N.C. 1987)

[The facts of this case are set out on page 948.]

We also hold there was not sufficient evidence that the plaintiff Betsy Britt was injured by relying on the representation. We have held that Betsy cannot recover in unjust enrichment for the value of her services in managing the farm because she was paid for those services pursuant to an express contract. By the same token, she cannot say she was injured by relying on a promise to her which caused her to continue working on the farm when she received compensation to which she had agreed for the employment. The plaintiff Betsy Britt also contends that she was injured by making the payments on the farm indebtedness and for the repairs and maintenance when she relied on Billy Britt's representation. We do not believe Betsy Britt has shown she was injured by making these payments. The funds to make these payments were generated by farm operations. If Betsy had not stayed on the farm she would not have had these funds. She has not shown a loss to her by staying on the farm after her conversation with Billy Britt.

The appellant contends she has been injured by not receiving the stock in the corporation Billy Britt told her he was forming. This argument raises the question of whether the plaintiff in a claim for fraud may recover damages for the loss of a bargain. As far as we can determine, this is a question of first impression in this jurisdiction. There have been cases from other states dealing with this problem. The plaintiff has not sued for breach of contract which she could have done for the failure of Billy Britt to have the stock issued to her. Her claim is for fraud. The gravamen of a claim for fraud is the damage to a person for a change in position based on the reliance on a false statement. The damage is caused by this change of position and not the lost bargain. There is a split among the jurisdictions which have decided this question. A majority allows damages for the lost bargain as well as for the change in position. A minority limits damages to that caused by a change in position.

We do not have to choose in this case between the majority and minority rules. All jurisdictions which have passed on the question hold that loss of bargain damages must be proved with reasonable certainty before they are allowed. In this case there is no evidence that Betsy Britt was damaged by not receiving stock. The evidence does not show for what purpose the corporation was to be organized or that it ever was organized. There is no evidence as to the value of the stock. Betsy Britt has not shown she was damaged by the failure to receive stock. . . .

AFFIRMED IN PART, REVERSED AND REMANDED IN PART.

NOTES

1. Note that the issue of expectations is another area in which there is a difference between intentional and negligent misrepresentations. Anticipated profits typically are allowed in intentional misrepresentation cases, but historically were not allowed in negligent misrepresentation cases. Do you understand why? If not, think of what you have learned in Contracts class. If one could recover the benefit of the bargain in a negligent misrepresentation case, what effect would that have on contract law?

2. As the court in *Britt* indicates, most jurisdictions no longer follow the Restatement (Second) rule. In these jurisdictions, a plaintiff can recover expectation damages even in negligent misrepresentation cases.

3. Of course, it is not always easy to distinguish between actual losses and benefit of the bargain. As the court recognizes in *Burke*, the difference can be

"amorphous." In *Burke*, the plaintiff had no idea of the real value of the blanket. Had defendant not come along, he may never have realized the $290,000 value. Do you nevertheless understand why the court indicates that $289,000 is an "out of pocket" expense?

4. In *Britt*, by contrast, it is easy to see why the stock is benefit of the bargain rather than an out-of-pocket expense. But the court also refuses to allow recovery for the mortgage payments and repairs that Betsy made. Why are these not out-of-pocket expenses?

5. The question of damages may also be affected by contract law. If you have studied Sales, you may remember that misrepresentations made in connection with the sale of goods are governed by the Uniform Commercial Code, which does not accord with the rule set out in the Restatement.

F. THIRD PARTY STATEMENTS

FISHER v. COMER PLANTATION, INC.
772 So. 2d 455 (Ala. 2000)

MADDOX, Justice.

[This] case arises out of a sale of real estate and requires us to examine the various duties owed to prospective buyers in real-estate transactions. [In] early 1995, Harry Fisher, a lawyer from Troy, North Carolina, developed an interest in Alabama real estate after going on numerous hunting trips throughout the State. Because Fisher knew nothing about Alabama real-estate markets, he contacted Locators for assistance. . . .

Tim Speaks, an agent for Locators, . . . sent Fisher information regarding various properties, including Comer Plantation, a 2600-acre antebellum plantation located in Barbour County. Speaks told Fisher that this property best accommodated Fisher's potential needs. . . .

Speaks provided him with a real-estate appraisal that had been prepared by Roger Pugh for the benefit of Paul Thomas, who was the owner of Locators and a stockholder in Comer Plantation, Inc. The report, addressed to SouthTrust Bank, estimated the value of Comer Plantation to be $919,000. Speaks advised Fisher to read the entire report and to bring it with him when he looked at the property.

The following morning, Speaks took Fisher on a tour of the property, and Fisher saw that the property needed extensive work in order to be usable. Many of the roads were impassable, primarily because of washouts and a need for culverts. Many of the structures on the property, including antiquated tenant houses, a windmill, a smokehouse, and other structures dating back to the antebellum period, were in complete disrepair. . . .

After a second day of inspecting the property, Speaks introduced Fisher to Paul Thomas. Speaks, however, never told Fisher that Thomas was also his employer.

The meeting was short and spirited. Fisher offered $500,000 for the property "as-is." Thomas refused to take the offer to the other owners. Fisher suggested that they should reduce the offer to writing, but Thomas abruptly said that there was no need to do so because the other owners would never consider it. When Thomas left, Speaks apologized for Thomas's conduct and said that he was going to talk with other owners who, he said, were more influential. Fisher responded by saying that he was no longer interested in the property, and he returned to North Carolina.

Days later, Billy Pritchard, a Birmingham lawyer who was also a stockholder in Comer Plantation, Inc., telephoned Fisher, apologized for Thomas's conduct, and told Fisher that he was the only true representative of the owners in regard to a sale. He told Fisher that he — Pritchard — would like to sell the property, but not "as-is," if Fisher was still interested.

Fisher soon began to negotiate with Pritchard. According to Fisher, Pugh's appraisal was the foundation for the negotiations. In arriving at an agreeable price, Fisher and Pritchard started at the full-appraisal figure, $919,000, and made deductions where both agreed deductions were appropriate. Fisher testified that he believed that $919,000 represented the true market value of Comer Plantation, and that because Pritchard clearly relied on that figure as the starting price, he thought that Pritchard also believed that it represented the true market value. . . .

Eventually, Fisher and Pritchard agreed on a price of $710,000. Pritchard sent Fisher a contract, which he signed and returned. Pursuant to the contract, Fisher tendered a check for $50,000 earnest money to be deposited in an escrow account maintained by Locators.

Days after the execution of the contract, Fisher sent Pugh's appraisal to Jimmy Preslar, his personal banker in North Carolina, to obtain financing. Preslar checked the arithmetic used in the appraisal and discovered an error in addition that had caused the estimate to be nearly $100,000 greater than the underlying numbers supported. Fisher immediately telephoned Pritchard, notified him of the error, and told him that he no longer wished to be bound by the contract because, he said, the negotiations had been premised on a faulty estimate. Fisher also demanded the return of his $50,000. Pritchard checked the appraisal, confirmed the error, and promised to investigate it.

. . . The error convinced Fisher that he should withdraw from the contract. He again demanded the return of his $50,000, but Speaks refused to return it. . . .

Subsequently, Fisher filed this lawsuit to recover the $50,000 down payment and to recover other damages, based on claims of fraudulent misrepresentation, suppression, breach of fiduciary duty, and negligence. Most of the issues presented in this case are affected by the relationship that Fisher, as a prospective purchaser of real estate, had with each defendant. . . .

Fisher's Claims Against Pugh

[The] threshold question we must consider appears to be one of first impression: When and under what circumstances can a real-estate appraiser be held liable to a third party for a negligent misrepresentation in an appraisal? Insofar as we can tell, that precise issue has not been addressed by Alabama courts, although this Court has held that accountants may be liable to third parties under a theory of negligent misrepresentation if certain circumstances exist.

In *Boykin v. Arthur Andersen & Co.*, this Court adopted *Restatement (Second) of Torts* § 552 (1977) as the law of this State in cases involving negligent misrepresentations relied upon by third parties, or parties who were not in privity of contract with the person making the misrepresentation. *Restatement* § 552 reads as follows:

(1) One who, in the course of his business, profession or employment, or in any other transaction in which he has a pecuniary interest, supplies false information for the guidance of others in their business transactions, is subject to liability for pecuniary loss caused to them by their justifiable reliance upon the information, if he fails to exercise reasonable care or competence in obtaining or communicating the information.

(2) Except as stated in Subsection (3), the liability stated in Subsection (1) is limited to loss suffered

(a) by the person or one of a limited group of persons for whose benefit and guidance he intends to supply the information or knows that the recipient intends to supply it; and

(b) through reliance upon it in a transaction that he intends the information to influence or knows that the recipient so intends or in a substantially similar transaction.

(3) The liability of one who is under a public duty to give the information extends to loss suffered by any of the class of persons for whose benefit the duty is created, in any of the transactions in which it is intended to protect them.

While we have applied this rule only to accountants, nothing in our prior cases should be understood as restricting our application of the *Restatement* approach to that one class of professionals. . . .

We now consider whether, based on the facts suggested by the record, Pugh owed Fisher a duty the breach of which would be actionable. We noted that the *Restatement*'s definition of "duty" in negligent-misrepresentation cases limits the defendant's liability to "specifically foreseen and limited groups of third parties for whose benefit and guidance the [defendant] supplied the financial information and who used it as the [defendant] intended it to be used." *Boykin*, 639 So. 2d at 510. Under the *Restatement* rule, as applied to the facts of this case, Fisher would have the burden of showing that Pugh, the appraiser, foresaw, or should have foreseen, that his appraisal would be relied upon by a limited class that included Fisher. The *Restatement* rule, if applied to appraisers generally, would impose on an appraiser a duty to third parties that the appraiser intended to influence, as well as any party that the appraiser knew his client intended to influence by means of the appraisal. The *Restatement* rule, however, does not require, for the imposition of a duty, that one making a representation through a report or appraisal contemplate the specific identity of the person who may rely on the representation.

Fisher argues that Pugh should have known that Locators would distribute the appraisal to prospective purchasers of Comer Plantation, given Pugh's extensive experience in the real-estate industry. . . .

These arguments, however, ignore the undisputed fact that the appraisal report was issued for the benefit of Thomas in his individual capacity rather than as a representative of his real-estate firm. Given that fact, we must conclude that Fisher's argument would impose on Pugh a duty that goes beyond that established by the *Restatement* rule and the cases interpreting it, and that Fisher failed to present evidence sufficient to support an inference that Pugh foresaw, or should have foreseen, that his appraisal would be used by prospective purchasers.

Pugh's report contains a statement, entitled "Assumptions and Limiting Conditions," that describes the intended use of the document. It expressly provides that the report may not be used for any purpose other than its "intended use" without the permission of the appraiser. "Intended use" has several meanings, depending on the context in which the report is provided, but based on the facts of this case, we cannot accept Fisher's argument that these facts satisfy the *Restatement* rule for the imposition of a duty to him. . . .

We must conclude that the evidence does not create a genuine issue of material fact as to whether Pugh owed Fisher a duty. "[B]ecause liability for negligence and wantonness is predicated upon the existence of a duty," *Colonial Bank of Alabama*, 551 So. 2d at 395, the trial court correctly granted Pugh's motion for summary judgment. Therefore, we need not address the question whether the appraisal contained a misrepresentation or, if it did, whether Fisher relied on it. The summary judgment is affirmed as to the claims against Pugh.

Fisher's Fraudulent Misrepresentation Claims Against Speaks, Locators, and the Owners

Fisher seeks damages from Speaks, alleging that Speaks, on behalf of, and as an agent for, Locators and the owners of Comer Plantation, fraudulently misrepresented the value of the property and the accuracy of Pugh's appraisal. . . .

In the present case, the faulty information was supplied by Pugh, who prepared the appraisal report that contained the alleged misrepresentations. No evidence in the record suggests that Thomas or Locators retained the right to direct the manner in which Pugh prepared the appraisal; thus, in making it, Pugh was acting as an independent contractor. The report was received from Pugh by Thomas, who was acting in an arm's-length relationship with Pugh. Thomas was a part-owner of Comer Plantation; he passed the report on to Locators, a real-estate agency he owned. Speaks, as an employee of Locators, ultimately received the report and relayed its contents on to Fisher; its contents included an attestation of accuracy. We can find no evidence in the record indicating that Speaks, Locators, or Thomas acted in bad faith. Therefore, under the authority of *Speigner*, we conclude that the trial court correctly entered the summary judgment as to Fisher's claims against Speaks and Thomas, because they were conduits passing information supplied by Pugh. Because the liability of Locators and the owners is premised on the liability of Speaks, an agent of Locators, we likewise conclude that the summary judgment was proper as to the claims against them. As to the fraudulent-misrepresentation claims against Speaks, Locators, and the owners, the summary judgment is affirmed. . . .

AFFIRMED IN PART; REVERSED IN PART; APPLICATIONS FOR REHEARING OVERRULED.

NOTES

1. The common-law rule was extremely narrow: if the fraudulent representation was made to someone other than the plaintiff, recovery was allowed only if the speaker *intended* that plaintiff also rely on the statement. As the case indicates, the RESTATEMENT (SECOND) broadens the action.

2. Under the RESTATEMENT, a person who makes a false statement in a commercial document is liable to anyone who justifiably relies on the statement. The document in *Fisher*, however, was not a commercial document. Instead, a commercial document is something that has its own legal effect, such as a negotiable instrument or deed.

3. If the representation is made by means other than a commercial document, then liability extends only to those people whose reliance can be reasonably foreseen. In these cases, as in *Fisher*, the purpose of the representation becomes crucial. The appraisal in *Fisher* was made only for the recipient. The court indicates that this made it unforeseeable that it would be distributed to anyone else. Is that realistic? Does a property owner usually have her property appraised just because she is curious? Isn't an appraisal always an attempt to convince someone *else* of the value of the property, whether it be a sale, refinance, or a dispute with the property tax authorities?

Would it affect your answer to know that appraisals almost always contain language indicating their intended use, and stating that only the recipient may rely on the information?

PROBLEM

The Gluttony Network ["TGN"] is a cable channel dedicated entirely to hawking goods. One day, TGN was selling a toaster oven. Several celebrities appeared on the segment, making all sorts of claims about the product. One of the celebrities claimed that the oven could make toast in less than thirty seconds.

Buyer's mother watched the segment. Excited, she called Buyer, and convinced him to buy a toaster oven. Rather than ordering from the notoriously high-priced TGN, Buyer went to the department store and purchased the identical make and model of toaster oven. When he discovered that the oven would in fact *not* make toast as quickly as the celebrity had claimed, he sued both the celebrity and TGN for misrepresentation. Does Buyer have a claim?

Chapter 22
COMPETITIVE TORTS

A. INTRODUCTION

To this point, you have been focusing almost exclusively on tort claims brought by individuals. Although corporations have been involved in many of these cases, they have been the defendants, not the plaintiffs. But tort law does not exist only to protect individuals. Instead, in certain types of situations, it will also afford protection to corporations and other sorts of business concerns.

Of course, a business cannot suffer a personal injury like a broken arm. The injuries that a business suffers are instead purely financial in nature. This chapter explores the situations in which tort law will protect a business's financial position from harm occasioned by other businesses.

Do not assume that this area of the law is completely divorced from the other torts. The field of competitive torts does share certain core principles with the torts you have studied so far. On the other hand, the field also has its own idiosyncratic policy concerns and practical features, both of which affect how the rules in this area have evolved.

B. COMPETITION AS A TORT

KATZ v. KAPPER
44 P.2d 1060 (Cal. Ct. App. 1935)

SHINN, Justice pro tem.

Plaintiff and defendants were rival wholesale fish dealers in the city of Los Angeles. The defendants Kapper, Isenberg, Baker, and Simon comprised a single firm doing business under the name of "Central Market." The action is for damages alleged to have been sustained to plaintiff's business by reasons of the acts of defendants, and for exemplary damages. The complaint alleges that plaintiff had a well-established wholesale fish business, the good will of which was valuable; that with the sole intention "to put the plaintiff out of business, ruin him, deprive him of his customers and custom, and to take away from him all of his business and trade, together with the good will, without any benefit to themselves," the defendants maliciously called meetings of the customers of plaintiff, threatened them that they would be driven out of business and ruined if they continued to purchase fish from plaintiff, but promised that if they purchased fish from defendants, they would be given substantial reductions in price, so that they could successfully compete with plaintiff and drive him out of business; that if said customers continued to buy from plaintiff, the defendants would open a retail store and would sell fish to the customers of plaintiff's customers at such low prices that plaintiff's customers would be driven out of business. It was further alleged that the defendants did open such a store, did widely advertise and sell fish at lower prices than either plaintiff or defendants could purchase the same, and at a loss to the defendants; that all of said acts were done for the purpose of driving plaintiff out of business; and that as a result thereof "a considerable number of said retailers and peddlers and customers ceased from doing business with plaintiff and made their purchases from these defendants to plaintiff's damage," etc.

To this complaint, defendants interposed a general and special demurrer. . . . [J]udgment of dismissal was entered. . . .

In deciding whether the conduct of defendants alleged in the complaint is actionable, it is necessary to apply certain well-settled rules relating to competition in business. These may be generally stated as follows:

> "Competition in business, though carried to the extent of ruining a rival, is not ordinarily actionable, but every trader is left to conduct his business in his own way, so long as the methods he employs do not involve wrongful conduct such as fraud, misrepresentation, intimidation, coercion, obstruction, or molestation of the rival or his servants or workmen, or the procurement of the violation of contractual relations. . . .

> "It has long been a rule of the common law that a man has the right to start a store, and to sell at such reduced prices that he is able in a short time to drive the other storekeepers in his vicinity out of business, when, having possession of the trade, he finds himself soon able to recover the loss sustained while ruining the others." . . .

There are cases relied upon by appellant, of which *Dunshee v. Standard Oil Co.*, 152 Iowa 618, is a leading one, in which interference with business is held actionable. In that case, the defendant pursued a policy of selling gasoline and oil to plaintiff's customers from tank wagons purchased and used solely for that purpose, initiating the practice for the purpose of driving the plaintiff out of business, and with the intention of discontinuing it when such purpose was accomplished. An action was held to lie because the object of the defendant was not to engage in real competition or to build up its own business but to ruin a business rival. The cases that follow this doctrine proceed on the theory that an act lawful in itself becomes unlawful if induced by a wrong motive. This principle is not generally recognized by English or American authorities. In California the Supreme Court in *Boyson v. Thorn*, 33 P. 492, adopted the rule that an act lawful in itself does not become unlawful because of a malicious or wrongful motive. *People v. Schmitz*, 94 P. 407, and *Parkinson Co. v. Building Trades Council*, 98 P. 1027, follow this principle. We may apply either rule to the facts of the present case with the same result because they both recognize the principle that detriment to business which is incidental to lawful competition is *damnum absque injuria.*

It very clearly appears from the allegations of the complaint that the primary purpose of the defendants was to acquire for themselves the business of plaintiff's customers, and that the detriment which would result to plaintiff's business from the accomplishment of defendants' purpose was incidental thereto. This view must be taken of the complaint, notwithstanding the allegation that the sole purpose was to drive plaintiff out of business. The defendants are not charged with making any effort to deprive plaintiff of his trade except by transferring the same to themselves. This is essentially business competition. The defendants did or threatened to do nothing other than to gain a business advantage proportionate to the losses sustained by plaintiff, and by the accomplishment of that end their purposes would have been satisfied. It cannot be said that the methods used by the defendants were unlawful. They threatened plaintiff's customers with the ruination of their businesses if they continued to trade with plaintiff, but a threat is not unlawful if it is to do a lawful thing. . . .

The threats alleged in general terms are identified and particularized by the allegations that the defendants threatened to and did undersell the plaintiff and his customers at retail prices less than the wholesale prices at which the commodities could be purchased. These must be taken as the only acts of coercion either threatened or done, since no others are alleged. They were not unlawful nor were they committed in an unlawful manner. They related solely to the aims of the defendants to engage in business competition with plaintiff for the resulting business advantage to themselves. The fact that the methods used were ruthless, or unfair, in a moral sense, does not stamp them as illegal. It has never been regarded as the duty or province of the courts to regulate practices in the business world beyond the point of applying legal or equitable remedies in cases involving acts of oppression or deceit which are unlawful. Any extension of this jurisdiction must come through legislative action. In this case no questions of statutory law are involved. The alleged acts of defendants do not fall within the category of business methods recognized as unlawful, and hence they are not actionable. The demurrer to the complaint was properly sustained.

The judgment is affirmed.

NOTES AND PROBLEMS

1. *The Competition "Exception."* Putting to one side for a moment the particulars of *Katz*, consider the basic premise of the court's opinion: competition is ordinarily not a tort. The proposition may seem unremarkable at first glance. But consider how it relates to other areas of tort law. Competition, after all, involves a party who knowingly and intentionally causes economic harm to another. Is that consistent with the general theory underlying intentional torts, where courts generally do allow recovery whenever one party intentionally

causes injury to another? Why do courts create an exception, sometimes phrased as a "defense," for competition?

2. *Scope of the Exception.* Of course, only "fair" competition qualifies for the competition exception. What factors determine if competition is fair? Consider whether the following variations on the facts of *Katz* would make a difference:

    a. Defendants threatened the plaintiff's customers with physical harm.

    b. Defendants intentionally lied about their fish, telling consumers that they were "caught that morning," when in actuality they were several days old.

    c. Defendants intended to sell their fish for far below cost until plaintiff went out of business, and then to raise prices to a level sufficient to recoup their losses.

    d. Plaintiff had evidence that the defendants intended to abandon their retail operations and concentrate solely on wholesale after successfully driving the plaintiff out of business.

3. *Unlawful Acts.* Situations (a) and (b) in Note 2 involve cases where the defendants' acts are independently tortious. Therefore, courts have universally concluded that such acts also give rise to a claim for unfair competition. But should courts automatically allow unfair competition claims in these circumstances? Consider situation (b). Even if there were no tort of unfair competition, defendants' acts could still give rise to liability. Customers, the true victims, would already have a right to recover from defendants under the tort of misrepresentation, or for breach of warranty. Given that defendants are already liable for their acts, should the law also afford a remedy to the plaintiff, a competitor? Isn't there a risk of "over-punishing" the defendants?

On the other hand, is the existing consumer cause of action for misrepresentation an adequate deterrent for this intentionally wrongful behavior? How many consumers will actually go to court over the purchase of a few smelly fish?

4. *Motive.* Situations (c) and (d) in Note 2 are somewhat more difficult, and there is accordingly less of a consensus in the courts. In those situations, defendants' acts, standing alone, are not tortious. Is the *Katz* court saying that motive is completely irrelevant, or merely that a motive to compete is *per se* acceptable? Would the court recognize liability in a case in which the defendant entered into a business venture with the sole purpose of harming plaintiff? What about in situation (d), where the defendants stand to lose money from their vendetta? But did plaintiff not allege precisely that in its complaint?

5. In situation (c), by contrast, defendants hope to gain money, at least in the long run. If defendants stand to make money by underselling plaintiff, most courts today do not allow recovery under the common law even if defendants' overriding goal is to injure plaintiff. Are the courts setting the right priorities? Are they saying that it is unacceptable to injure someone unless your acts also

let you take money that would ordinarily have gone to the victim? Should civilized society accept such a rule?

6. Not all courts agree that motive is irrelevant if the defendant stands to make a profit. Consider the views of the Iowa Supreme Court in *Dunshee*, a case cited in *Katz*:

> The laws of competition in business are harsh enough at best; but if the rule here suggested were to be carried to its logical and seemingly unavoidable extreme there is no practical limit to the wrongs which may be justified upon the theory that "it is business." Fortunately, we think, there has for many years been a distinct and growing tendency of the courts to look beneath the letter of the law and give some effect to its beneficent spirit, thereby preventing the perversion of the rules intended for the protection of human rights into engines of oppression and wrong. [T]here is [an] abundance of authority for saying that [an] act which is legally right when done without malice may become legally wrong when done maliciously, wantonly, or without reasonable cause.
> . . .
>
> But if competition be "war", in which "everything is fair", or if it be so regarded by those who participate therein, certainly the law will not give that doctrine its sanction.

Dunshee v. Standard Oil Co., 132 N.W. 371 (Iowa 1911). Is this just a fond remembrance of a bygone day?

C. UNLAWFUL MEANS: LYING, CHEATING, AND STEALING IN THE PROCESS OF COMPETITION

1. Lying: The Law of False Advertising

From almost the very beginning, courts have recognized that lying to customers constitutes a form of "unfair" competition. As the case law developed, courts began to distinguish between several categories of cases. The first, commonly called "passing off" or "palming off," involved a defendant who had represented to consumers that its product had actually been produced or approved by the plaintiff. In order to prevent a competitor from preying on the goodwill of a more established seller, courts routinely allowed plaintiff to recover in these cases.

The "passing off" branch of unfair competition law has evolved into the modern law of trademarks, service marks, and trade names. Most nations encourage the use of these commercial symbols by providing a registry. A party who registers its mark with the government typically receives a number of added benefits, such as a presumption that the registrant "owns" the symbol. Nevertheless, the basic principles of trademark law still reflect the common-law origins. A study of the fascinating but complex law of trademarks is best deferred to a specialized course.

The "lying" branch of unfair competition was not limited to cases where a defendant misrepresented the source of its product. Courts also routinely declared that it was unfair to allow a defendant to lie about the quality of goods being sold in the marketplace. However, the common-law tort of unfair competition proved much less effective in dealing with these types of misrepresentations.

Most common law courts distinguished two categories of cases, deception and disparagement. A defendant engaged in *deception* (sometimes called false advertising) when it lied to consumers about the quality or characteristics of its product. In a *disparagement* (sometimes called "trade libel") case, by contrast, defendant lied about *plaintiff's* goods.

Each of these common-law actions had a significant limitation that greatly limited its usefulness. In a case of deception, courts would afford relief to a plaintiff only if that plaintiff was the defendant's *sole* competitor. If third parties also sold the same product or service, none of the competitors could recover. At first, this requirement seems wholly arbitrary. After all, if the legal system disfavors monopolies, why should the common law give a cause of action only to the virtual monopolist? However, the limitation had a solid logical foundation. To understand why courts required plaintiff to show that it and defendant were the only sellers, answer the following questions:

> What is the harm that a defendant causes when it engages in unfair competition?
>
> How can plaintiff prove that such harm occurred?
>
> Can it make that showing when there are other competitors?

Once you understand the reason for the "monopoly" requirement, you will also understand why the courts did not impose a similar requirement in a case of passing off.

The limitation on the action for disparagement was the "special damages" rule. This rule denied any recovery to plaintiff unless it could provide specific evidence of actual economic harm caused by defendant's conduct. Unlike the rule that applied to deception, the "special damages" rule is not grounded in logic. The cause of action for disparagement has a somewhat murky ancestry, with roots both in the commercial tort of unfair competition and in the personal tort of defamation (discussed in Chapter 17). The special damages rule is a carryover from the law of defamation. At common law, certain types of defamatory statements required proof of special damages before they were actionable. Statements about the goods sold or services performed by a person were the sort that would require such a showing. Therefore, courts continued to invoke the special damages requirement in disparagement cases, even though the tort also descended from the tort of unfair competition. Some courts have recognized this historical accident and have accordingly abandoned the special damages rule, at least in a case where the plaintiff seeks only an injunction.

Because of these limitations, the common law was not terribly effective in policing false statements about the nature and quality of products. Congress responded to this problem in 1946 by enacting the Lanham Act § 43(a), a new federal law dealing with false advertising. In its current form, § 43(a) (which is codified at 15 U.S.C. § 1125(a)) provides in relevant part:

> (1) Any person who, on or in connection with any goods or services, or any container for goods, uses in commerce any word, term, name, symbol, or device, or any combination thereof, or any false designation of origin, false or misleading description of fact, or false or misleading representation of fact, which —
>
> (A) is likely to cause confusion, or to cause mistake, or to deceive as to the affiliation, connection, or association of such person with another person, or as to the origin, sponsorship, or approval of his or her goods, services, or commercial activities by another person, or
>
> (B) in commercial advertising or promotion, misrepresents the nature, characteristics, qualities, or geographic origin of his or her or another person's goods, services, or commercial activities,
>
> shall be liable in a civil action by any person who believes that he or she is or is likely to be damaged by such act.

Note how § 43(a) carries forward the common-law distinction between "passing off" (Subsection (A)) and misrepresentations as to quality (Subsection (B)).

Interestingly, § 43(a) may have been an accident. Taken as a whole, the Lanham Act deals almost exclusively with the law of trademarks. Although § 43(a) can also be used in cases of trademark infringement, it also contains broader language that makes it useful in other types of false advertising cases. Why Congress chose to include a provision like § 43(a) is not entirely clear. Regardless of Congress's motive, however, § 43(a) has proven to be a tremendously useful statute, as the following case illustrates.

UPJOHN COMPANY v. RIAHOM CORPORATION
641 F. Supp. 1209 (D. Del. 1986)

WRIGHT, Senior Judge.

The Upjohn Company filed this lawsuit against Riahom Corp. and its president, J. P. Utsick, asserting patent infringement under 15 U.S.C. § 271, and unfair competition under § 43(a) of the Lanham Act, 15 U.S.C. § 1125(a), in relation to a hair treatment product defendants market. This Opinion addresses the motion for a preliminary injunction which Upjohn filed simultaneously with its complaint on May 6, 1986.

This hair-raising saga began in the late 1960's, when Upjohn was conducting clinical investigations of a compound now known generically as minoxidil. . . . Upjohn eventually received approval from the Food & Drug Administration ("FDA") to market LONITEN tablets, a prescription antihypertensive drug product containing minoxidil. . . .

In 1968-71, Dr. Charles Chidsey, a cardiologist at the University of Colorado Medical School, conducted clinical investigations relating to the effects of oral administration of LONITEN to treat hypertension. . . . During these investigations, Chidsey observed that LONITEN, as a side effect in some patients, caused hirsutism, or the growth of excess facial and body hair. . . .

Although the FDA has not approved . . . REGAINE, Upjohn is now spending $35 million for plant and equipment for its commercial production. The company, as well as outside analysts, expect the market for REGAINE to be very substantial. Upjohn will satisfy this demand from its own facilities and will not issue licenses under the '619 patent.

Defendants' hair treatment product, RIVIXIL, was developed by Kemyos Bio Medical Research, of Binasco, Italy. Kemyos filed two patent applications in Italy in 1984 covering minoxidil compounds used for the stimulation of hair growth and treatment of baldness. It is unclear whether any patent has issued from either application. . . .

Riahom buys RIVIXIL concentrate from Kemyos in Italy, ships it to New York, and then transfers it to J. Coburn, Inc., an independent custom packager in Florida, which reformulates the concentrate and packages it for sale. Riahom markets RIVIXIL to hair salons and other independent dealers through regional sales managers, who solicit orders. . . .

Although Kemyos and several Italian universities conducted tests in Italy to determine the safety of RIVIXIL, Riahom has spent no funds on safety and efficacy testing for RIVIXIL in the United States and knows of no tests conducted in this country. Riahom conducts no quality control procedures on RIVIXIL. The independent packager in Florida conducts certain quality checks, but Riahom did not select the procedures and evidently does not know what they are.

Riahom is marketing RIVIXIL as a cosmetic, rather than a drug, so that they have not submitted the product to the FDA for testing and approval. The original advertising brochures for RIVIXIL described it as "Europe's Answer to Minoxidil". The brochures, among other things, stated that RIVIXIL contained "the patent molecule 'SKM005'" and "has been tested in many European universities and the tests conclude that it is non-toxic and safe to use." The brochure also stated that RIVIXIL is "[a] product proven safe and easy for your clients to use" and is "[a] product that has the most 'pre-sale' publicity of any hair product ever including coverage on 20/20 (TV) and articles in People Magazine, Newsweek, Time, Esquire, Science Digest and all major European publications."

An Upjohn employee posing as a hair salon operator visited the Riahom/RIV-IXIL exhibit at the All-Texas Beauty Show on April 7, 1986. Among the materials he received at the exhibit are the brochure described above and a letter from defendant Utsick to salon owners. The letter related how Utsick had seen in Italy a RIVIXIL package listing a minoxidil compound among the ingredients. Utsick's letter then stated: "From all the press generated in the United States about Minoxidil, I knew Minoxidil grew hair!!! About two-thirds of those tested in the United States grew hair to varying degrees of satisfaction. Well, any product that had that kind of proven record was worth a try for me, because the top of my head is 'losing it' very rapidly." Attached to the letter were numerous articles from such publications as People Magazine, Newsweek, and Esquire referring to minoxidil and Upjohn. A television monitor at the exhibit showed a videotape of a "20/20" broadcast relating to Upjohn and the use of minoxidil in treating persons with baldness.

[The] standards for granting a preliminary injunction under [§ 43(a) of] the Lanham Act are similar to those used in patent cases. The movant must show that it has a reasonable likelihood of success on the merits; it may suffer irreparable injury without injunctive relief; the balance of equities favors relief; and the public interest favors relief.

[Section 43(a)] clearly encompasses false and misleading statements in advertising and promoting a company's products. When the challenged claim is literally false, the court may grant relief without considering the impression that the advertising may have created on the buying public. When the challenged advertisement is literally true, but creates a deceptive impression about the product, the Court must find that the ad has a tendency to deceive the consumer and that the deceptive statement is likely to influence the purchasing decision.

a. COSMETIC

Defendants consistently claim in their advertising and promotional literature that RIVIXIL is a "cosmetic." This claim may be literally false. Both the FDA and Italian regulatory authorities have determined that any minoxidil compound promoted for hair growth is a drug, rather than a cosmetic. Defendants seek to escape this characterization by arguing that RIVIXIL, although containing minoxidil, does not promote hair growth so that it is a cosmetic.

As outlined in the earlier discussion of patent infringement, this Court has no direct proof that RIVIXIL promotes hair growth. There is a possibility, however, that RIVIXIL, if tested, may be shown to promote hair growth. Defendants have never tested RIVIXIL to determine its lack of efficacy for hair growth and thus have no basis to claim it is a cosmetic. Their characterization of RIVIXIL as a cosmetic therefore creates a deceptive impression about the product — regardless of its truth or falsity.

The Court finds that the claim has a tendency to deceive the consumer and is likely to influence the purchasing decision. Cosmetics are widely available for sale. If tests show RIVIXIL to be a drug, it would be unavailable for lawful sale except by physician's prescription. The necessity of getting a prescription definitely would influence a person's decision to purchase the product.

b. PATENTED

Defendants' promotional materials state that RIVIXIL and/or SKM005 is patented. Defendants do not claim that RIVIXIL and SKM005 are patented in the United States. Although Kemyos has filed two patent applications for minoxidil compounds in Italy, the Court has no evidence that a patent has resulted from the applications, and defendants do not claim that Kemyos has a patent. Even if a patent issued in Italy, there is no record of such a patent in the United States. Defendants' unqualified statement that their product is patented, when made to the American public in the United States, leaves the clear implication that RIVIXIL is patented in this country. It is possible that defendants' promotional materials allude to Upjohn's patents, but they contain no such acknowledgement.

False or misleading claims of patent protection clearly violate § 43(a). *See John Wright, Inc. v. Casper Corp.*, (E.D. Pa. 1976) (false claims that penny banks were patented constituted material misrepresentation of quality which tended to deceive ordinary purchaser).

c. CLINICALLY TESTED AND SAFE

Defendants' promotional materials state that RIVIXIL has been clinically tested and shown safe for use. Upjohn does not dispute that RIVIXIL may have been subjected to clinical testing; indeed, the Court received copies of a number of tests conducted in Italy. Upjohn does object to defendants' claims that those tests showed that RIVIXIL is non-toxic and safe to use, arguing that the "safety" of a drug is a determination that only the FDA can make. Defendants again respond that RIVIXIL is not a drug, so that it can claim the product is safe without FDA approval.

Assuming that the safety claim is literally true, the Court nonetheless finds that the claim creates a deceptive impression about the product which would influence a consumer's decision to purchase it. . . . American consumers who see a product claiming that clinical tests have shown it safe for use expect that the product has gone through extensive and rigorous testing by the manufacturer, the government or both before its general sale. Kemyos' minimal testing of RIVIXIL hardly meets these expectations. . . . The Court concludes that defendants' claim that clinical tests have shown the safety of RIVIXIL is a deceptive statement covered by the Lanham Act.

d. HAIR GROWTH

Some of defendants' early advertising explicitly promoted RIVIXIL as a hair growth product. Defendants' entire marketing approach left the unmistakable impression that their product promoted hair growth. Defendants now advise the Court that RIVIXIL does not grow hair, but that it only promotes a fuller, thicker head of hair and nourishes the scalp. They purportedly have removed all references to Upjohn's hair growth product and any representation that RIVIXIL grows hair. Nevertheless, defendants' dealers still say that RIVIXIL grows hair. Defendants' marketing materials still leave the unmistakable impression that their product promotes hair growth, and they contain no disclaimer regarding hair growth. The $150 price for a supply of RIVIXIL suggests that the product is supposed to do more than simply work as a hair conditioner.

In addition to literal falsehoods, § 43(a) of the Lanham Act "embraces 'innuendo, indirect intimations, and ambiguous suggestions' evidenced by the consuming public's misapprehension of the hard facts underlying an advertisement." The Court finds that the overall impression conveyed by defendants' advertising and promotional materials is that RIVIXIL grows hair. . . .

For all the foregoing reasons, the Court concludes that Upjohn has shown a reasonable likelihood of success on the merits of its unfair competition claim.

To prove irreparable injury under § 43(a), a plaintiff need only provide "a reasonable basis for the belief that [it] is likely to be damaged as a result of the false advertising." No proof of actual sales diversion is required.

Defendants' false and misleading claims about RIVIXIL definitely tend to induce consumers to purchase their product, thereby depriving Upjohn of potential customers and sales for REGAINE. In addition, consumers who purchase RIVIXIL because of defendants' false claims and who are dissatisfied with the product or injured by it may avoid REGAINE out of the assumption that all minoxidil-based hair products share the same shortcomings. Whatever the cause, defendants' deceptive claims will deny Upjohn part of the legitimate market for its patented discovery.

Defendants' use of publicity about Upjohn and REGAINE to promote RIVIXIL tends to make the public think that some association exists between Upjohn and RIVIXIL. Upjohn will be injured if consumers attribute RIVIXIL to it and "this injury is by its very nature irreparable, since no payment of money damages in itself can abate the confusion." The Court concludes that Upjohn has made a sufficient showing of irreparable injury.

The balance of equities greatly favors a grant of injunctive relief. Upjohn has spent approximately $100 million in research and development to prepare a topical minoxidil compound for the market. It spent at least $25 million over the last three years for clinical studies relating to its NDA for REGAINE, in an attempt to comply with the applicable legal requirements for marketing a pharmaceutical product.

In contrast, defendants have invested next to nothing in the discovery and development of their product. They merely import a minoxidil concentrate from Italy and pay an independent packager to reformulate it. Defendants are thumbing their nose at United States drug regulations. They impudently assert that RIVIXIL is a "cosmetic" not subject to FDA regulation without ever having conducted any tests to determine whether the product lacks the attributes of a drug. They may also be misleading the public. Although defendants claim that RIVIXIL does not cause hair growth (and indeed, it may not), their promotional materials implicitly dangle the prospect of renewed hair growth in front of every balding person who sees them. The product either grows hair or it does not. As an equitable matter, defendants cannot have it both ways. . . .

In light of the findings set out above regarding defendants' acts of unfair competition, the Court finds that several types of relief are appropriate. Defendants are enjoined in their packaging, advertising and promotional materials and in any other oral or written presentation from making the following representations either directly or by inference:

(a) that RIVIXIL or SKM005 is patented or that it contains a patented molecule;

(b) that RIVIXIL or SKM005 has been clinically or medically tested and proven safe and/or non-toxic for use;

(c) that RIVIXIL or SKM005 is a cosmetic;

(d) that RIVIXIL or SKM005 grows hair, retards hair loss, transforms one type of hair into another, or in any other way promotes hair growth.

Defendants also are prohibited, directly or by inference, from making any use of, or reference to, any publicity from television, periodicals or other sources about Upjohn, its REGAINE product, or the use of topical minoxidil compositions for the treatment of baldness. This prohibition shall include indirect references, such as those found in defendants' dealer sales manuals or brochures.

The Court has concluded that defendants' current promotional materials deceptively suggest that the product grows hair, although the product supposedly does not have that effect. The Court has the equitable power to require a defendant who has engaged in acts of unfair competition to take affirmative steps to eliminate possible consumer confusion. Accordingly, to eliminate the possibility of confusion, the Court will require that all packaging, brochures and other literature about RIVIXIL disseminated to the public and all material prepared for use by defendants' sales staff include language that RIVIXIL does not promote hair growth, does not retard hair loss and is ineffective for the treatment of baldness. This language should be clearly noticeable by persons reading the package or materials.

Finally, the Court finds that a cancellation of any outstanding orders for RIVIXIL and a recall of defendants' product and offending promotional materials, pending their revision to comply with this Court's order, are appropriate. Imposition of a recall requirement and cancellation of pending orders are both within the broad powers of this Court as a court of equity. Accordingly, defendants shall be required to recall all RIVIXIL and any packaging and promotional materials for RIVIXIL now in the possession of Riahom's packagers, national sales managers or regional sales managers. In addition, defendants shall send a written notice to each of the customers from whom it has an outstanding order for RIVIXIL notifying them that the orders have been cancelled because defendants are unable to supply the product. Defendants or their agents are prohibited from soliciting any new orders until new packaging and promotional materials for RIVIXIL have been prepared.

An Order will enter in conformity with this Opinion.

NOTE

The patent laws impose criminal fines on anyone who falsely implies that he or she has a United States patent. 25 U.S.C. § 292. The provision also allows "any person" to bring an action to recover the fine, in which case the fine is shared with the United States. Does the availability of this statutory remedy affect the issue of whether the Lanham Act also provides a claim? Partly because of these concerns, not all courts treat false statements about the existence of a patent or "patent pending" as actionable under the Lanham Act. *See, e.g., Sheldon Friedlich Mktg. Corp. v. Carol Wright Sales, Inc.*, 219 U.S.P.Q. 883 (S.D.N.Y. 1983). By contrast, most courts do not allow recovery for a false claim about a copyright. The Copyright Act has no counterpart to Patent Act § 292.

PROBLEMS

1. Consider each of the claims that defendant made about RIVIXIL. Were all of the claims really false? Given the language of § 43(a) of the Lanham Act, how can the court allow recovery for statements that are literally true? *Upjohn* is certainly not the only case in which the court found a literally true statement to be deceiving. Another influential case is *American Home Prods. Corp. v. Johnson & Johnson*, 577 F.2d 160 (2d Cir. 1978), which involved a clash between Anacin and Tylenol.

2. In some respects, the easiest claim for the court to resolve is defendant's assertion that RIVIXIL promoted hair growth. Defendant had in fact conceded that claim was false, and had actually removed it from its recent advertisements. But the court finds that defendant had not gone far enough, and orders it to take the extra step of including an affirmative statement that the product does not promote hair growth. Why does the court feel that this order is justified?

3. Why does the court order defendant to recall all of the product from consumers? In the more typical case, a court would simply have ordered the defendant to turn over the profits from those sales to plaintiff. Logically, which is

preferable? Can we assume that everyone who purchased defendant's product would have purchased from plaintiff had they known the truth?

4. Finally, consider defendant's claim that its product is "patented." This statement is clearly false. The court states the majority rule: "when the challenged claim is literally false, the court may grant relief without considering the impression that the advertising may have created on the buying public." But does that approach oversimplify things? By its terms, section § 43(a) allows recovery only if the plaintiff is likely to be damaged by the statement. Plaintiff would be damaged only if consumers, relying on defendant's statement, forego plaintiff's product for defendant's. Will defendant's statement that the product is patented have this effect?

To answer that question, it may be useful to consider what it actually means for a product to be patented. A patent is a government-granted monopoly. A person may obtain a patent by being the first to invent a useful product like a drug. However, the inventor need not show that the product is *better* than the current state of the art, merely that it is new and unanticipated. If that is so, how would defendant's false statement about a patent have any influence on purchasers?

Reread § 43(a), which is quoted just before *Upjohn*. Could you argue that a false statement about a patent falls under § 43(a)(1)(A) instead of (B)? The *John Wright* case cited by the *Upjohn* court took that tack.

5. In recent years, science has made great strides in developing ways to preserve fruits and vegetables for market. The most promising methods involve a chemical known as Zeta Omega. Dipping ripe fruits and vegetables in a bath of Zeta Omega and water significantly improves the shelf life of the produce. Even in its pure form, Zeta Omega has been tested by the FDA and found safe for human consumption. Therefore, consumers may treat fruits and vegetables themselves.

Because Zeta Omega is not patented and is relatively easy to produce, a number of companies begin marketing ready-made solutions made up of Zeta Omega and water. The companies sell these solutions directly to consumers for home use. Most firms sell a solution made up of 5% Zeta Omega and 95% water. A few companies, however, alter these proportions. The percentage of Zeta Omega in the solutions sold in the market varies from 2% to 35%.

Due to the intense competition, no single firm can realize much profit. Four of the competitors try to corner a larger share of the market by the use of new advertising campaigns.

Alpha Co. begins a series of advertisements that tout its product as "the most effective on the market." Unlike all its competitors, Alpha's solution is made up of 10% Zeta Omega and 90% water. Before commencing its campaign, Alpha conducted a series of rigorous tests of Zeta Omega solutions. These tests conclusively demonstrated that a 10% solution provided the best preservative effects, even beating out solutions of higher concentration. However, all of these tests were conducted in a laboratory in Sweden.

Beta, Inc. tries an entirely different tack. In its ads, Beta claims that "use of Beta-brand Zeta Omega significantly reduces the cholesterol levels of people who regularly consume treated fruits and vegetables." Beta has conducted no tests, and therefore had no idea whether this claim was true. Purely by chance, however, a university study conducted after Beta began its ad campaign demonstrates that produce treated in a Zeta Omega bath actually *does* significantly reduce cholesterol levels.

Gamma Corp. is a relatively new player in the market. Gamma's founder is an opportunist who invests in new fads. Having no expertise in the production of chemicals, Gamma simply purchases 5% Zeta Omega solution in large quantities from other companies, removes the other labels, and substitutes its own glitzy label. Because most companies offer tremendous quantity discounts, Gamma is able to eke out a profit from this operation. Gamma's advertising campaign makes no specific claims, but is simply designed to help purchasers remember the Gamma label.

Delta Ltd. decides to make its niche by appealing to the snob factor. Like the others, Delta sells a 5% Zeta Omega solution. However, while a gallon of 5% solution typically sells for approximately $25, Delta adds a new fancy label and raises its price to $80 a gallon. Its ads proclaim, "Buy Delta . . . we're more expensive, but we're worth it!"

Based upon the court's reasoning in *Upjohn*, each of these advertisements could be deemed false or misleading. Reconstruct the argument for each ad.

As the *Upjohn* case demonstrates, the question of whether a statement is false or misleading can often prove quite difficult. Truth depends on the context in which the statement is made. The following case applies that principle in a completely different venue.

CHICAGOLAND PROCESSING CORP. v. WHITE
714 F. Supp. 383 (N.D. Ill. 1989)

DUFF, District Judge.

When the rain poured from the Chicago skies on the night of August 8, 1988, it put to an early end the first baseball game played under the lights at Wrigley Field — so early, in fact, that the game never became official under major league baseball rules. The teams and the fans returned the next night, started anew and completed the game. Most people understood what the rainout meant; the plaintiff in this action apparently does not.

The plaintiff, you see, is the Chicagoland Processing Corporation, a manufacturer and marketer of commemorative medallions. Before the first night game, it contracted with the Major League Baseball Properties, Inc., to sell

39,012 medallions for the historic event. Each medallion depicted Wrigley Field and included the following legend:

FIRST NIGHT GAME
CHICAGO CUBS
PHILADELPHIA PHILLIES
A NIGHT TO REMEMBER

Chicagoland began advertising its medallion around July 17, 1988 in newspapers of general and interstate circulation, including the following advertisement in the Chicago Tribune:

1ST CHICAGO CUBS NIGHT GAME
AUGUST 8, 1988 — CUBS VS PHILLIES
WHERE WERE YOU WHEN THE LIGHTS WENT ON?

* * *

Officially Licensed by Major League Baseball

* * *

Individually Numbered
Edition limited to Wrigley Field seating
Capacity of 39,012

Though Chicagoland was the only company to receive Major League authorization for a medallion, defendant Fred White, president and sole owner of defendant Chicago Numismatic Foundation, also saw the potential for turning a profit on the sporting event. A few weeks before the game, he too began advertising a medal commemorating the event. An attorney for the Major Leagues visited him and warned against representing that his medal was sponsored or authorized by Major League Baseball; Mr. White complied.

After the first night game ended early, Mr. White had an idea. Why not make a medal commemorating the second game, the first official night game played at Wrigley Field? During May, 1989, he ran the following advertisements for this medal in the Chicago Sun-Times:

SPORTS FANS & COLLECTORS
FIRST OFFICIAL WRIGLEY FIELD NIGHT GAME
COMMEMORATIVE MEDAL

Now Available: The First Official Night Game in Wrigley Field, August 9, 1988, one ounce silver proof commemorative Medal. All medals are serial numbered, registered and come with a lifetime buy back guarantee. . . . There is a strict limited edition of 36,399, this represents the attendance of the game. This is the finest sport medal made to date.

Though Chicagoland had nearly sold out all of its medallions (and now apparently has done so), Chicagoland's counsel, by letter dated May 19, 1989, demanded that Mr. White cease these advertisements because they were false and misleading, and as such in violation of § 43(a) of the Lanham Act, 15 U.S.C. § 1125(a), as well as the Illinois Consumer Fraud and Deceptive Business Practices Act, Ill. Rev. Stat. ch. 121½ , § 261 et seq. When Mr. White refused, Chicagoland filed this lawsuit.

Chicagoland first came to bat before Judge Aspen, sitting as the emergency judge. It must have swung well, for on May 25, 1989, Judge Aspen issued a Temporary Restraining Order preventing Mr. White from advertising his medals for ten days. In return, Chicagoland posted a $5,000 bond as security.

On June 4, this court ordered expedited discovery, extended the TRO to June 9, and set an evidentiary hearing on Chicagoland's motion for that date. The parties completed their discovery, and agreed to consolidate the preliminary injunction hearing with the final hearing on the merits.

DISCUSSION

To prove a violation of either the Lanham Act or the Consumer Fraud Act, Chicagoland must first show that Mr. White falsely represented his medallion. Since it cannot do so, this court need not decide whether Mr. White's medallion has a tendency to deceive a substantial section of the baseball-loving public, nor whether any such deception would cause Chicagoland harm.

Chicagoland argues that Mr. White's advertisement is false because it represents that his is the first official medallion commemorating the first Chicago Cubs night game. Mr. White's medallion was neither the first, nor official, Chicagoland says.

Mr. White insists that his advertisement does not say what Chicagoland says it does. According to Mr. White, the advertisement represents that his is simply a medallion, neither the first nor official, commemorating the first official Chicago Cubs night game, a reading he supports by the fact that the second line of the advertisement states "FIRST OFFICIAL WRIGLEY FIELD NIGHT GAME", and the third "COMMEMORATIVE MEDAL".

In an advertisement lacking punctuation, it is difficult to say what the significance of a line break should be. In this case, however, it is also unnecessary, for Chicagoland's reading of the advertisement makes no sense. According to Chicagoland, "FIRST OFFICIAL" modifies "MEDAL", not "WRIGLEY FIELD NIGHT GAME", so that the sentence reads something like this: "FIRST OFFICIAL . . . WRIGLEY FIELD NIGHT GAME COMMEMORATIVE MEDAL", but that makes no sense. Mr. White is not selling a medal commemorating a Wrigley Field night game, he is selling a medal commemorating the first official Wrigley Field night game — the game played on August 9, 1988 — as the first line of small print in his advertisement explicitly says. Perhaps he could make this even clearer by advertising "A COMMEMORATIVE MEDAL FOR THE FIRST OFFICIAL WRIGLEY FIELD NIGHT GAME", but he need not do so. There is nothing false about his advertisement as it now reads, and thus this court has no grounds for preventing him from running it.

One issue remains. During the June 9 hearing, Mr. White moved for relief against the security Chicagoland posted in obtaining the TRO. Fed. R. Civ. P. 65.1 provides for precisely such a motion "without the necessity of an independent action." Mr. White says that he lost thirty sales, at nine dollars per sale, as a result of the TRO, and Chicagoland does not dispute this amount. This court therefore will award Mr. White $270 out of Chicagoland's surety bond.

Chicagoland's motion for preliminary and permanent injunctions is denied. Judgment is entered against Chicagoland. Chicagoland shall tender the defendants $270 out of the surety bond.

NOTE

Do you agree with the court that defendant's use of the word "OFFICIAL" in connection with its medallion was not deceptive? Note that the court assumes that consumers will ascribe the peculiar definition of official used in the context of baseball. Is that realistic? Why might consumers buy these medallions? Do they want the medallion because it is a product approved by Major League Baseball, or because it is a medallion, from any source, commemorating the first complete night game in Wrigley Field?

2. Cheating: The Limits of Competitive Behavior

Few would argue with the proposition that lying to customers constitutes a form of "unfair" competition. After all, lying is considered immoral in and of itself. Moreover, tort law already gives a cause of action to the consumer who is victimized by the defendant's lie. The false advertising branch of unfair competition law works in tandem with the consumers' claims to make the defendant pay for all of the harm occasioned by its false statement.

Aside from lying, what other sorts of activities exceed the limits of fair competition? The next two sections explore some of the more common acts that give rise to litigation. Because these other acts are not considered independently wrongful, there is less of a consensus here than in the area of false advertising.

a. Sales Below Cost

BARTHOLMEW COUNTY BEVERAGE CO., INC. v. BARCO BEVERAGE CORP.
524 N.E.2d 353 (Ind. Ct. App. 1988)

RATLIFF, Chief Judge.

Barco Beverage Corp., Inc. (hereinafter Barco) is a family owned beer whole-sale business located in Columbus, Indiana. Robert Welmer and his children operated the business. Welmer started the business in 1961. Over time, the business grew. Barco acquired a franchise to sell Lite beer by Miller and the brewery assigned the Bartholomew County area to Barco as a primary area of responsibility. When Miller Lite beer became a big seller, Barco's business expanded rapidly, and through Robert and his family's hard work and good will, Barco acquired almost all the Miller Lite beer accounts in Bartholomew County. By late 1983 Barco served seventy-two (72) of seventy-five (75) Miller Lite accounts in Bartholomew County. Barco's Miller Lite sales accounted for approximately seventy percent (70%) of Barco's total business. Due to the increased sales, Barco outgrew its original headquarters and had to build a new warehouse.

Bartholomew County Beverage Company, Inc. (hereinafter BCB) is owned and operated by Edna Howe and her children. BCB sells Budweiser, Bud Light, Busch products, Miller High Life, and Miller Lite. The record reveals that in the fall of 1983 BCB attempted to put Barco out of business by cutting the price of Miller Lite. In the fall of 1983, BCB began its attack on Barco by offering to sell Miller Lite to Barco's customers at a price that was five cents (5 cents) lower than Barco's price. This tactic failed as Barco retained its Miller Lite customers. Thereafter[,] BCB offered Miller Lite to Barco's customers in Columbus, Indiana, at a drastically reduced price. BCB dropped the price for a case of twenty-four twelve ounce cans from Eight Dollars and Ninety Cents ($8.90) to Six Dollars and Ninety Cents ($6.90). At the same time BCB retained the higher price per case for BCB's customers not located in Columbus, Indiana. Barco's customers could not ignore the drastic price reduction offered by BCB. Thus, Barco had to either meet the price or lose customers. However, because of a required sales quota, Barco had to keep the customer's accounts or risk loss of its Miller Lite franchise. Barco lowered its Miller Lite price. Barco's business was damaged as a result of the price cuts.

[Barco] filed a Verified Petition for Temporary Restraining Order alleging among other things that BCB was violating Indiana Code section 7.1-5-5-7 which prohibits price discrimination. On March 6, 1984, Barco filed an additional complaint for the damages caused by BCB's illegal pricing practices. . . . [A] jury returned a verdict in favor of Barco for Fifty-Seven Thousand Dollars ($57,000). BCB appeals this judgment. . . .

[The court first determined that even though the Indiana statute, § 7.1-5-5-7, was a criminal law, Barco could bring a civil claim for violation of the statute. This criminal statute prohibited price discrimination among various buyers, not sales below cost.]

This court notes also that even if Barco could not proceed based upon I.C. § 7.1-5-5-7, a common law cause of action existed. Barco sued BCB for unfair competition based upon predatory price cutting. A valid common law cause of action exists for the tort of unfair competition. Although the law of unfair competition has been defined as the palming off of ones [sic] goods or services as that of someone else, and the attempt thereof, the tort of unfair competition is much broader and also includes actions for the interference with a contract or business relationship, as well as for predatory price cutting. With regard to price cutting, although price cutting generally is considered a fair and welcomed part of vibrant competition, if prices are cut for the primary purpose of destroying a competing business then the price cutting is considered unfair competition. This form of unfair competition has been termed "predatory pricing", and was defined and examined by the United States Supreme Court, in *Cargill*, as follows:

> Predatory pricing may be defined as pricing below an appropriate measure of cost for the purpose of eliminating competitors in the short run and reducing competition in the long run. It is a practice that harms both competitors and competition. In contrast to price cutting aimed simply at increasing market share, predatory pricing has as its aim the elimination of competition. Predatory pricing is thus a practice 'inimical to the purposes of [the antitrust] laws, and one capable of inflicting antitrust injury.'

Since Barco alleged that BCB cut prices with the intent of putting Barco out of business, a valid common law cause of action for unfair competition existed. Therefore, the trial court could have allowed Barco to proceed to trial on either a statutory or common law cause of action.

[S]ufficient evidence exists to support the elements of the tort of unfair competition, and the judgment of the trial court is affirmed.

NOTE

Statutory Treatments of the Issue. Economic theory can prove quite useful in analyzing the law of unfair competition. In conditions of perfect competition, sales below cost would not be a problem, as no competitor could afford to take losses for any appreciable period. Moreover, even if a seller could absorb short-term losses, it would need some time after competition is destroyed to recoup those losses. During that recoupment period, the seller would need to sell at well above its cost. However, other companies could theoretically enter the market at that point and undercut the seller. That sales below cost (often called "dumping") do occur, then, is a sign that a "market imperfection" exists, *i.e.*, that there is not perfect competition.

In the "real world," large companies may have the wherewithal to operate at a loss for a significant period of time. The defendant in *Barco*, for example, could offset its losses in one market by its sales in other markets. In other cases, the start-up costs involved in marketing a particular good or service make it difficult for others to jump into the market once the seller raises its prices after the competition is destroyed. Although some commentators question whether these conditions will actually exist very often, *see, e.g.* ROBERT BORK, THE ANTITRUST PARADOX 145 (1978); and Easterbrook, *Predatory Strategies and Counterstrategies*, 48 U. CHI. L. REV. 263 (1981), there is no doubt that sales below cost occur often enough to present a real-world problem.

In recognition of this threat, both the federal government and some states have enacted statutes prohibiting, or at least limiting, sales below cost. At the national level, section 3 of the Robinson-Patman Act (part of the antitrust laws) makes it a crime to sell goods at "unreasonably low prices for the purpose of destroying competition or eliminating a competitor." 15 U.S.C. § 13. The criminal law involved in *Barco* is one example of a state response.

PROBLEMS

1. Compare the main case with *Katz v. Kapper* on page 981. Both cases involve a defendant who sells its product below cost, with the immediate aim of driving the plaintiff out of business. *Katz* found that such facts did not state a cause of action. This court, by contrast, allows recovery. Are the cases distinguishable? Or do they simply represent opposing views concerning whether sales below cost are fair?

2. In other unfair competition cases involving "unlawful means," the defendant's acts injure not only the plaintiff competitor, but also purchasers. One justification for giving the competitor a claim is that the competitor has a greater economic incentive to go to court than do consumers. Do sales below cost injure purchasers? If they do not, why should a court deem them unlawful merely because they injure a competitor? After all, a number of acts taken in the name of business, including comparative advertising, injure competitors.

b. Tortious Interference with Economic Relations

MAGNUM RADIO, INC. v. BRIESKE
577 N.W.2d 377 (Wis. Ct. App. 1998)

EICH, Chief Judge.

Magnum Radio sued Ronald Brieske, claiming, among other things, that Brieske had intentionally interfered with Magnum's contract to purchase two radio stations in Tomah, Wisconsin. The trial court dismissed the action for failure to state a claim upon which relief could be granted, and Magnum appeals. We agree with Magnum that its complaint states a claim. We also conclude that material issues of fact remain to be tried and we therefore reverse the order and remand to the circuit court for further proceedings.

The underlying facts are largely undisputed. When Brieske — who was admittedly interested in purchasing one of the two stations himself — learned of Magnum's proposed purchase of the stations, he wrote to the Federal Communications Commission to express opposition to the purchase. The FCC is the agency charged with the licensing and regulation of radio stations and, under federal law, must approve the transfer of any station's license. Brieske's letter was based on his concern that if Magnum were to purchase the stations it would not provide adequate local news and sports coverage in the Tomah area. "[T]his buyout," Brieske said, "is going to mean the isolation of the Tomah community from local activities."

After being notified of Brieske's objection, David Magnum, a Magnum owner, contacted Brieske, and while the parties dispute the precise nature of their conversation, it appears that Magnum told Brieske that local news and sports coverage would continue under his ownership of the stations and he attempted to persuade Brieske to withdraw his opposition. Brieske refused.

The FCC, taking the position that program formatting is not a material issue in license transfer approvals, ultimately rejected Brieske's opposition and approved the transfer. Magnum then brought this action, stating in its complaint that:

> [Brieske's] actions in objecting to the . . . sales and license transfers were done with the intent to knowingly, intentionally and willfully interfere with the business and economic relations between [Magnum] and the sellers. . . . While Brieske acted under the guise of a concerned citizen, his true intention was to quash the agreement . . . and . . . purchase the stations himself.

Magnum claimed that the delay in the FCC's approval of its purchase of the stations caused it to lose revenues and incur added legal expenses.

Brieske moved to dismiss Magnum's complaint, arguing that it failed to allege the facts necessary to state a claim for interference with contractual relations. He also contended that his opposition to the license transfers was a guaranteed First Amendment right. The circuit court held a hearing on the motion to dismiss, and both parties submitted affidavits for the court's consideration. The circuit court granted the motion, noting that Brieske had not attempted to "persuade the sellers [of the stations] to back out of the deal or in any way to sabotage the agreement," and concluding that "in this case . . . there is just no way under these facts that there is a cause of action." . . .

Wisconsin has long adhered to the basic interference-with-contract rule of RESTATEMENT (SECOND) OF TORTS § 766 (1979), which states: "One who intentionally and improperly interferes with the performance of a contract . . . by inducing or otherwise causing the third person not to perform the contract, is subject to liability." The question in this case is whether a person whose alleged interference with a contractual relationship results not in abandonment or nonperformance of the contract but only in making the plaintiff's performance of the contract more expensive or onerous may also be held liable for his or her actions.

The rule of RESTATEMENT (SECOND) OF TORTS § 766A (1979) answers the question in the affirmative: "One who intentionally and improperly interferes with the performance of a contract . . . between another and a third person, by preventing the other from performing the contract, or causing his [or her] performance to be more expensive or burdensome, is subject to liability to the other for the [resulting] pecuniary loss. . . ." The comments to § 766A indicate that the rule is complementary to § 766. . . .

We are satisfied, then, that a RESTATEMENT (SECOND) OF TORTS § 766A cause of action exists in Wisconsin: one who, not being privileged to do so, intentionally and improperly interferes with another's performance of a contract, which interference either prevents the performance of the contract, or causes the other's performance to be more expensive or burdensome, may be subject to liability for the pecuniary loss caused thereby.

We are equally satisfied that Magnum's complaint states a cause of action for interference. It alleges that, after receiving a copy of Brieske's letter to the FCC, David Magnum told Brieske that Magnum Radio would broadcast high school sports in the Tomah area, but Brieske refused to withdraw his objection because "he would be 'giving up his leverage' if he did." The complaint goes on to allege that Brieske refused to discuss the matter further with David Magnum, despite attempts on Magnum's part to do so, and that while Brieske was acting "under the guise of a concerned citizen, his true intention was to quash [Magnum Radio's purchase] agreement . . . and to allow Brieske to purchase the stations himself." We believe that, under Wisconsin's liberal pleading rules, the complaint states a claim for intentional interference with Magnum's contract to purchase the stations by making the performance of that contract more expensive or burdensome.

Brieske's answer denies the material factual allegations and raises several "affirmative defenses," among them that he had a "legally protected right" under federal law and the constitution to express his views to the FCC. We thus consider the parties' affidavits to determine: (1) whether Magnum has stated a prima facie case for recovery and, if so, (2) whether Brieske's affidavit raises a triable issue of fact.

David Magnum's affidavit reasserts the allegations in the complaint concerning Brieske's interest in purchasing the stations himself and his statement that, despite his assurances that Magnum Radio would broadcast local sports events, Brieske refused to withdraw his FCC opposition because he did not want to give up his "leverage." It also recounts that Brieske refused to discuss the matter further and that Brieske's opposition caused delay that resulted in financial and other damage to Magnum. Magnum's affidavit states a prima facie case for recovery.

Brieske argues that Magnum's action was properly dismissed for failure to state a claim because he (Brieske) had a "legally protected right" — *i.e.*, a privilege — to file his objection with the FCC, and he states in his affidavit that he learned about the proposed purchase of the stations from a public notice in a local newspaper and contacted the FCC only to express his concerns about coverage of local sports events. We recognized in *Liebe v. City Finance Co.* (Ct. App. 1980), that "transmission of truthful information" can be the type of privilege the supreme court discussed in *Gerke*, when it said that "one who, without a privilege to do so," interferes with a contract may be liable.

We see the affidavits as raising material factual issues as to both the impropriety of Brieske's actions — whether his letter to the FCC was "privileged" within the meaning of applicable case law — as well as whether his actions constituted a tortious interference with Magnum's contract resulting in pecuniary loss. Brieske's position is that he was simply acting as a concerned citizen, responding to the FCC's invitation to comment on the transfer. Magnum's position is that Brieske's interest was something else altogether: he acted as a potential, if not an actual, competitor who desired to squelch Magnum's purchase in order to acquire the stations himself. Those issues are rife with factual questions that should be resolved at trial, not on a pretrial motion.

Because Magnum's complaint states a cause of action, and because of the existence of genuine disputes as to the material facts, the action was not subject to dismissal, whether by order or summary judgment. We therefore remand this case for further proceedings consistent with this opinion.

THE SOAP COMPANY v. ECOLAB, INC.
646 So. 2d 1366 (Ala. 1994)

KENNEDY, Justice.

These appeals arise from a case involving allegations of tortious interference with business relations. The Soap Company and Andy Anderson appeal from a summary judgment in favor of the defendants, Ecolab, Inc., and Mike Todd. Ecolab and Todd appeal from a summary judgment in favor of the Soap Company and Anderson on Ecolab and Todd's counterclaim.

Andy Anderson is the president and principal shareholder of the Soap Company, an Alabama corporation that manufactures and sells laundry and dishwashing detergents to commercial businesses. Mike Todd is a salesman for Ecolab, which also manufactures and sells commercial detergents.

Before founding the Soap Company, Anderson was a service manager for Ecolab in Birmingham. The Soap Company began as a service company to repair commercial laundry and dishwashing machines. Later, it started manufacturing soap products for these machines. Initially, the Soap Company offered free service on the customer's equipment along with the purchase of detergents. The Soap Company attracted new customers, many of which were former customers of Ecolab.

According to the Soap Company, Ecolab set out on a deliberate and malicious plan to put the Soap Company out of business. The Soap Company presented memorandums written by employees of Ecolab developing a strategy to identify and acquire as many of the Soap Company accounts as possible. The memorandums also detailed a "mission" to remove $200,000 in business from the Soap Company, stating that a business of its size could not survive with such losses.

One of the memorandums was entitled "The Soap Company — First Assault." In it were statements from an Ecolab manager outlining a strategy:

> Personally, the existence of the Soap Company bothers me. The collective knowledge of all concerned estimates their volume around $800,000 with all but two identifiable accounts being within the State of Alabama. . . . Mission: To remove a minimum of $200,000 annualized business by October 31st. Any business that size cannot survive business losses of this magnitude. Those dollars directly impact the bottom line and any response by them also takes more dollars off the bottom line. Second step is to sell another $200,000 in annualized business between November 1st and December 31st one account at a time. Goal: Have one less competitor in the Alabama marketplace and a major part of the $800,000 volume carrying forward into 1990 as growth to us.

The memorandum identified one account in particular:

[W]e have sued [this particular business] twice in the past for payment and we have no assurances that we won't have another collection problem, but it's a risk we have to live with because the loss of a $50,000 account (presumably with money still owed to the Soap Co.) will kill them.

The assistant vice president of national accounts for Ecolab wrote, "[W]e have a situation in Birmingham, Alabama where a group of ex-EL [Ecolab] people are operating a competitor called the Soap Company. We are in a war at this time trying to put them out of business."

Ecolab's version of the facts is as follows: Anderson and his wife began a pattern and practice of entering premises shared by Ecolab and other companies after business hours in order to steal documents from a trash dumpster located on the premises. The type of documents that Anderson retrieved included proposals to specific customers, customer complaints, and price lists. Ecolab claims that the Soap Company was able to obtain a competitive edge in the market by obtaining this information and that Ecolab's actions were in response to the Soap Company's attempt to take Ecolab's customers.

The Soap Company and Anderson sued Ecolab and Todd, alleging tortious interference with business relations and claiming damages for financial loss and mental anguish to Anderson. Ecolab and Todd counterclaimed, alleging that the retrieval of Ecolab's documents from the trash dumpster was trespass, conversion, and a violation of the Alabama Trade Secrets Act, Ala.Code 1975, § 8-27-1 et seq.

The Soap Company and Anderson moved for a summary judgment on both their complaint and the counterclaim. In support of the motion, they presented memorandums and affidavits concerning Ecolab's plan to obtain the Soap Company's accounts. Ecolab and Todd also moved for a summary judgment on the complaint and on the counterclaim, claiming that they were entitled to a "competitor's privilege," which, they say, provides a business justification for interference with the Soap Company's customers. Additionally, Ecolab presented affidavits concerning Anderson's alleged trespass, conversion, and improper use of trade secrets.

The trial court entered a summary judgment in favor of Ecolab and Todd on the tortious interference with business relations claim. It also entered a summary judgment in favor of the Soap Company and Anderson on the trespass, conversion, and trade secrets claim.

Before discussing the appropriateness of the summary judgments entered in this case, this Court must decide whether to adopt the competitor's privilege as a defense to a claim of tortious interference with business relations. The competitor's privilege applies when the contract involved is terminable at will or when the defendant causes a third person not to enter into a prospective contract with another who is his competitor.

This Court has adopted the tort of tortious interference with business relations, based on § 767, RESTATEMENT (SECOND) OF TORTS. A companion doctrine to the tort of interference with business relations is the "competitor's privilege." Section 768, RESTATEMENT (SECOND) OF TORTS, states:

> One who intentionally causes a third person not to enter into a prospective contractual relation with another who is his competitor or not to continue in an existing contract terminable at will does not interfere improperly with the other's relation if
>
> > (a) the relation concerns a matter involved in the competition between the actor and the other, and
> >
> > (b) the actor does not employ wrongful means and
> >
> > (c) his action does not create or continue an unlawful restraint of trade and
> >
> > (d) his purpose is at least in part to advance his interest in competing with the other.
>
> (2) The fact that one is a competitor of another for the business of a third person does not prevent his causing a breach of an existing contract with the other from being an improper interference if the contract is not terminable at will.

Comment b to § 768 states:

> The rule stated in this Section is a special application of the factors determining whether an interference is improper or not, as stated in § 767. One's privilege to engage in business and to compete with others implies a privilege to induce third persons to do their business with him rather than with his competitors. In order not to hamper competition unduly, the rule stated in this Section entitles one not only to seek to divert business from his competitors generally but also from a particular competitor. And he may seek to do so directly by express inducement as well as indirectly by attractive offers of his own goods or services.

The element of the competitor's privilege requiring that the competitor not "employ wrongful means" is discussed in comment e to § 768:

> If the actor employs wrongful means, he is not justified under the rule stated in this Section. The predatory means discussed in § 767, Comment c, physical violence, fraud, civil suits and criminal prosecutions, are all wrongful in the situation covered by this Section. On the other hand, the actor may use persuasion and he may exert limited economic pressure. . . .

The rule stated in this Section rests on the belief that competition is a necessary or desirable incident of free enterprise. Superiority of power in the matters relating to competition is believed to flow from superiority in efficiency and service. If the actor succeeds in diverting business from his competitor by virtue of superiority in matters relating to their competition, he serves the purpose for which competition is encouraged.

We find persuasive this statement of the Seventh Circuit Court of Appeals with regard to what constitutes "wrongful means":

> We think these limitations by the various authorities on the tort of interference with prospective business relations are appropriate. Competitors and their allies are not necessarily gentlemen — or even scholars. Competition may be rough and tumble and even — within reasonable bounds — involve economic factors extraneous to the main competition itself. We do not believe a searching analysis only of motive is in most instances enough to send these cases to the jury. There must still under the Indiana cases be something 'illegal' about the means employed.

Great Escape, Inc. v. Union City Body Co. (7th Cir. 1986).

We note that other jurisdictions have adopted the competitor's privilege as a defense to tortious interference with contracts or business relations.

This Court expressly adopts the competitor's privilege as a defense to a claim of tortious interference with business relations. With this in mind, we turn to the summary judgments entered in this case. . . .

Did the trial court err in entering the summary judgment in favor of Ecolab and Todd based on the Soap Company and Anderson's claim of tortious interference with business relations? The elements of the tort of intentional interference with business relations are: 1) the existence of a contract or business relation; 2) the defendant's knowledge of the contract or business relation; 3) intentional interference by the defendant with the contract or business relation; 4) the absence of justification for the defendant's interference; and 5) damage to the plaintiff as a result of the interference.

We agree that, viewed in the light most favorable to the Soap Company and Anderson, the Ecolab memorandums and the affidavits from Ecolab employees present a jury question as to whether Ecolab and Todd tortiously interfered with the Soap Company's business relations.

As was noted in *Gross*, the fourth element of tortious interference with business relations, the absence of justification for the interference, really relates to an affirmative defense to be pleaded and proved by the defendant, namely, the defense of justification. Generally, whether the defendant is justified in the interference is a question to be resolved by the trier of fact.

The following factors should be considered in determining whether a defendant's interference was justified: (1) the nature of the actor's conduct; (2) the actor's motive; (3) the interests of the person in whose business the actor's conduct interferes; (4) the interests sought to be advanced by the actor; (5) the social interests in protecting the freedom of action of the actor and the contractual interests of the other; (6) the proximity or remoteness of the actor's conduct to the interference; and (7) the relations between the parties.

Legitimate economic motives and bona fide business competition qualify as justification for interfering with a competitor's business. This Court has held that "'competition in business, even though carried to the extent of ruining a rival, constitutes justifiable interference in another's business relations, and is not actionable, so long as it is carried on in furtherance of one's own interests.'"

We hold that Ecolab and Todd are entitled to present, in addition to the justification defense, the competitor's privilege defense discussed earlier. . . .

Based on the foregoing, the summary judgments are reversed and the cause is remanded for trial.

NOTES

1. As a close reading of §§ 766 and 767 demonstrates, parties other than competitors may be held liable for tortious interference with both contractual and business relations. For one example of a case involving interference by a non-competitor, see *Turner v. Halliburton Co.*, 722 P.2d 1106 (Kan. 1986). Of course, the "competitor's privilege" of § 768 will not apply to these defendants.

2. A few states also recognize a cause of action for tortious interference with a bequest. *See generally Liability in Damages for Interference with Expected Inheritance of Gift*, 22 A.L.R.4th 1229 (1983). Although this tort bears a superficial resemblance to tortious interference with contract, there is a crucial difference between a contract and a will; namely that the latter may be modified at will. Therefore, tortious interference with a bequest is actually more similar to interference with an ongoing business relation.

PROBLEMS

1. Factually, these two cases look quite similar. In both, one competitor is intentionally interfering with the business of another. Yet, there is a fundamental factual difference between the two situations, one that significantly affects the way the courts approach the cases. Can you identify that difference? A clue lies in the different Restatement provisions employed by the two courts.

2. Now that you have identified the factual difference between the two cases, review RESTATEMENT §§ 766 and 767. At first glance, they seem virtually identical. So why does the law differentiate between the two situations? The answer to this dilemma lies in the "competitor's privilege" set out in § 768. That privilege applies to § 767, but not to § 766.

3. Why does a competitor have a privilege to interfere with the sorts of business relations covered by § 767, but not in cases under § 766? Is there something more sacred about the type of relationship covered by § 766?

In fact, does the RESTATEMENT turn matters on its head? When defendant induces breach of a contract, the plaintiff can already recover its losses by suing the party who breached. Allowing a claim against the party inducing the breach simply gives the plaintiff two sources from which it can obtain damages. In the case of a non-contractual business relationship, however, a plaintiff has no such right. If it cannot recover against the competitor who induced the third party to quit dealing with the plaintiff, it cannot recover at all. Is that fair?

4. What sorts of acts are improper, and thereby go beyond the competitor's privilege? Consider the situation in the *Soap Company* case. Did defendant really do anything more than engage in vigorous, "rough and tumble" competition? Thinking back to the very beginning of this chapter, doesn't every competitor hope to corner the market?

5. From the viewpoint of the above note, some of the discussion in the *Magnum* case may appear somewhat puzzling. In the penultimate paragraph of its opinion, the court emphasizes that the defendant was not merely a concerned citizen, but was instead a "competitor." The clear implication of this statement is that the court would be more likely to impose liability for inducing breach on the defendant. Should that be the case? In this regard, consider both § 768 of the RESTATEMENT and the general competition exception discussed in the notes following *Katz v. Kapper*. Do these not demonstrate that the law of unfair competition usually holds competitors to a *lower* standard than non-competitors? Should we turn that general presumption on its head in the case where one competitor interferes with the contracts of another?

c. Refusals to Deal

RESTATEMENT OF TORTS, § 762 (1939):

Privilege of Selecting Persons for Business Relations

One who causes intended or unintended harm to another merely by refusing to enter into a business relation with the other or to continue a business relation terminable at will is not liable for that harm if the refusal is not

(a) a breach of the actor's duty to the other arising from the nature of the actor's business or from a legislative enactment, or

(b) a means of accomplishing an illegal effect on competition, or

(c) part of a concerted refusal by a combination of persons of which he is a member.

RESTATEMENT OF TORTS, § 764 (1939):

Refusal for Purpose of Monopoly

One who in his business refuses to deal with another in order to establish or maintain an illegal monopoly is liable to the other for the harm caused thereby.

NOTES

1. Although dated, the Restatement fairly closely reflects the current state of the law. Today, most cases involving a refusal to enter into a contract with another will be resolved under the federal antitrust laws. Like the RESTATEMENT, the antitrust laws distinguish between individual and concerted refusals to deal. Section 1 of the Sherman Act prohibits parties from entering into a "contract" or "conspiracy" in restraint of trade. An agreement among two or more parties to refuse to buy from or sell to another will often constitute such a contract or conspiracy, and therefore be unlawful *per se*.

Individual actions, of course, cannot constitute a contract or conspiracy. However, Sherman Act § 2, like RESTATEMENT § 764, prohibits individual actions that could destroy competition. Liability can be imposed under § 2 only if the actions have an actual, substantial effect on the market. Except in cases where one company dominates an industry, individual refusals to deal rarely have enough of an effect on the market to be actionable.

Although employing the same basic principles as the RESTATEMENT, the Sherman Act affords a number of advantages to a party who has been the victim of an unlawful refusal to deal. Most significantly, the statute allows for an award of treble damages. Violations of the Sherman Act are also crimes.

2. Of course, the Sherman Act is not the only law that touches upon the question of a refusal to deal. Because of longstanding problems with discrimination in housing, accommodations, and employment, both the federal and state governments have enacted laws that limit one's ability to refuse to enter into certain types of contracts with others. Therefore, for example, although a landlord may refuse to lease an apartment to a potential tenant for a good reason (such as inadequate income) or for no reason at all, she cannot refuse to lease because of the tenant's race.

3. Stealing: The Tort of Misappropriation

a. General Misappropriation

**AMERICAN TELEVISION AND
COMMUNICATIONS CORP. v. MANNING**
651 P.2d 440 (Colo. Ct. App. 1982)

ENOCH, Chief Judge.

[Evidence] introduced by plaintiffs at this stage of the proceedings is undisputed. ATC is engaged in the business of furnishing television programs to residents of the Denver Metropolitan Area. ATC purchases the exclusive rights to display the programs from Home Box Office, Inc., (HBO) and pays common carriers to deliver the programs via microwave from the point of origin. The microwave signal ordinarily travels by satellite to an earth receiving station in Denver, where it is relayed to a microwave antenna atop Lookout Mountain. From this antenna, a common carrier under agreement with ATC provides "multi-point distribution service," transmitting the signal to ATC's home subscribers.

ATC advertises the programming, installs and leases to each subscriber a special antenna and down converter which makes the signal capable of viewing on the ordinary television set, and services the equipment after installation. ATC finances its operation by charging each subscriber a refundable equipment deposit, an installation fee, and a monthly charge.

Defendants advertise, sell, and install antennas and down converters which are capable of receiving the HBO signal. The antennas are capable of receiving signals of various frequencies, but are designed such that the center of their receiving capability matches the HBO frequency.

Only plaintiff presented evidence during the hearing on the preliminary injunction, and it was undisputed that defendants advertised that the equipment they were selling was capable of receiving the HBO signal and that some defendants installed and adjusted the equipment for purchasers so that it would receive HBO. The "pirate" equipment is easily concealed, and some of it is visually indistinguishable from the equipment installed by ATC.

ATC sued defendants for damages, both actual and exemplary, and for injunctive relief. . . .

I. The denial of ATC's motion for Preliminary Injunction

The granting or denial of a preliminary injunction is a decision which lies within the trial court's sound discretion, and the trial court's ruling will be reversed only when there has been an abuse of that discretion. Factors to consider when deciding whether a preliminary injunction should be granted [include probability of success on the merits of the underlying claim].

ATC first contends that the trial court erred in finding that there was not a reasonable probability that it would succeed on the merits. We agree.

In resolving the problem of whether plaintiff is likely to succeed on the merits, we need address only plaintiff's third claim for relief, based on the common law tort of unfair competition. We are satisfied here that the undisputed facts presented at the hearing on the preliminary injunction establish the elements of the common law torts of unfair competition and misappropriation as recognized in *International News Service v. Associated Press*, 248 U.S. 215 (1918).

. . .

In *International News Service*, Associated Press (AP) sued International News Service (INS), a competing news service, alleging that INS was engaging in unfair competition by, among other things, copying AP's east coast press releases from posted bulletins and early edition newspapers, and wiring them to INS's west coast affiliate newspapers for publication. The news which INS "pirated" was gathered by AP at considerable cost, which AP recouped by collecting a fee for transmission of the news from each member newspaper. . . . The Supreme Court [characterized] INS's conduct as unfair competition because INS took material that was acquired by AP "as the result of organization and the expenditure of labor skill and money and which is saleable by [AP] for money," and, for commercial purposes, sold it, "endeavoring to reap where it has not sown." The court went on to state that:

> "Stripped of all disguises, the process amounts to an unauthorized interference with the normal operation of complainant's legitimate business precisely at the point where the profit is to be reaped, in order to divert a material portion of the profit from those who have earned it to those who have not; with special advantage to defendant in the competition because of the fact that it is not burdened with any part of the expense of gathering the news. The transaction speaks for itself, and a court of equity ought not to hesitate long in characterizing it as unfair competition in business."

Although some courts and commentators have attempted to limit the rule in *INS* to cases in which one competitor engaged in "palming off," *i.e.*, misrepresenting work of another as his own, we agree with those courts and commentators which have interpreted *INS* to prohibit unfair misappropriation and the exploitation of a competitor's business values.

Although it has not been decided in Colorado whether the principle in *INS* and its progeny is included within the Colorado common law of unfair competition, several opinions of our Supreme Court convince us that, contrary to the trial court's finding, there is a reasonable probability that such a cause of action is available. There has also been a trend in Colorado to increase the protection afforded commercial rights, such as trade names and trademarks.

We therefore hold that the facts presented established the elements of the common law tort of unfair competition and that there is reasonable probability that plaintiff would be successful under this claim.

In light of this holding we need not address the issue of whether there is a reasonable probability that ATC will succeed on the merits of its other claims. . . .

The judgment denying the preliminary injunction [is] reversed, and the cause is remanded for further proceedings. . . .

NOTES

1. The court states that "the general principle of *INS* and its progeny" applies in Colorado. Can you state that principle in 25 words or less?

2. Like most courts, the court in *American Television* uses the term "misappropriation" as a shorthand way to describe the plaintiff's claim. What precisely did the defendant "appropriate"? The television signal? But is there any evidence that defendant itself was receiving that signal? Should the plaintiff be suing the customers instead of defendant?

Perhaps defendant is liable for aiding and abetting the customers in their tortious acts. On the other hand, are the customers doing anything wrong? Is it even true that the customers "appropriated" anything? Did the customers who received plaintiff's signal using defendant's antenna deprive anyone else of use of the signal? If not, there was no appropriation, at least in the sense that term is usually employed in the law.

3. Even if no one appropriated plaintiff's actual signal, could you argue that defendant appropriated the *value* of that signal? Another way to restate "the principle of *INS* and its progeny" is to declare that it is improper for a person to compete with another by profiting from the creative activity of that other person. In other words, defendant is free to compete, but cannot "piggyback" on plaintiff's creative efforts.

The problem with that formulation of the "rule" is that it would prohibit much of what we consider legitimate competition. Consider 3M's POST-IT NOTES, a clever idea that proved to be an instant market hit. Other companies soon began to market their own versions of that product. Surely that copying, although blatant, does not give rise to liability. If it did, after all, then every firm that developed an original and profitable idea would automatically have a practical monopoly.

Of course, the law sometimes is willing to grant monopolies in innovations and other business values. The federal patent and copyright laws, and to a somewhat lesser extent the law of trade secrets, give an innovator a form of monopoly over the fruits of his creative activity. Similarly, the law of trademarks gives one competitor the exclusive right to use a given trade symbol in a market, although the goal in this latter case is to prevent customer confusion rather than encourage innovation.

Because the tort of misappropriation threatens to provide a monopoly independent of the patent and copyright laws, there is a real issue as to whether the common-law tort is preempted. This question is addressed below.

4. Note that the tort is called *mis*appropriation, not appropriation. Is that prefix significant? In other words, does it mean that courts will impose liability for an appropriation of a business value only when the means of appropriation is wrongful independent of the fact of appropriation? Limiting misappropriation in this fashion certainly makes the tort fit more closely with the other torts set out in this chapter. Except in the case of a contract, a party is generally free to appropriate the customers of a competitor. However, it cannot take those customers by using otherwise unlawful acts, such as lying or intimidation. Does it follow that a competitor should be free to "piggyback" on what other companies do as long as it commits no other wrong? Reconsider *American Television* from this perspective. Does the court limit the tort to cases where the act is independently tortious? Independently wrongful? What is wrong with building and selling an antenna?

PROBLEM

Gloria Jean operates a small coffee shop in which she serves high-quality coffee, together with pastries, cakes, and similar baked goods. Gloria's shop is situated in a small building in the downtown area. To increase business, Gloria adds a beautiful flower garden to the back of her building. This $50,000 investment bears immediate fruit, as Gloria's business increases substantially.

But Gloria's customers are not the only people interested in flowers. Raphael's Restaurant, a formal four-star restaurant, occupies the building immediately to Gloria's north. Soon after Gloria completes the flower garden, Raphael knocks out the entire south wall of his building, which was solid brick, and replaces it with floor-to-ceiling windows. This enables Raphael's customers to take in the views of Gloria's garden while dining. As a result of this renovation, Raphael's profits soar, more than offsetting the $30,000 cost of the construction work.

Gloria's southern neighbor is Tabatha's Tavern. For several years, Tabatha had an outdoor beer garden in the back of her tavern. Because it was run down, it was rarely used. After Gloria builds her flower garden, Tabatha spends $200 for some minor sprucing up, and renames the beer garden the "FLOWER TERRACE." The idea proves to be a hit, and Tabatha's profits soar.

Although Gloria has admittedly profited from her flower garden, she is upset that other firms are taking advantage of her work without offering to pick up some of the cost. Gloria has accordingly consulted you, a local attorney, for advice concerning her rights. What will you tell her?

b. The Right of Publicity

ATHANS v. CANADIAN ADVENTURE CAMPS LTD.
80 D.L.R.(3d) 583 (Ont. High Ct. Just. 1977)

ACTION for damages for passing off and for wrongful appropriation of personality.

HENRY, J. — The plaintiff is a professional athlete who has achieved the highest recognition for his prowess in water-skiing, both in Canada and internationally. He promotes his image, expertise, and personality commercially. . . .

After he won his first world title in 1971, Mr. Athans decided to promote and market himself commercially. . . . He purchased a photograph taken by a professional photographer in San Francisco showing himself in the act of making a turn around a ball on a slalom course. This photograph is an excellent dramatic black-and-white action shot of Mr. Athans, and is described in evidence not only as exhibiting perfect form, but also as characteristic of his personal style. One witness described it as the best-known water-skiing photograph in the world. Mr. Athans described it as his trademark. Since 1971, he has used it to promote himself commercially. It appears on his letterhead, on his business card, in his promotional packages, in magazines and other publications.

[Clearly,] the photograph and the representations of that photograph in various artistic forms were identified by knowledgeable people with George Athans, the outstanding Canadian and international champion.

In 1974, the defendant, C.A.C., was preparing to launch a boys' camp which was to open in the summer of 1975, featuring water-skiing as a major programme. [Defendant then approached Athans to ask if he might be interested in participating in and sponsoring the program. After some negotiations, Athans refused for 1975, because he was already committed elsewhere. However, in the meanwhile a marketing company had prepared a brochure for the camp with a "line drawing" of the famous photograph. This line drawing was a simplified, stylized rendition of the photograph. The court found that the line drawing and the photograph bore a "striking similarity." Defendant used the brochure with the line drawing to promote the camp. A similar line drawing was also used in magazine advertisements.]

The evidence, as a whole, satisfied me that the two defendants did not intend improperly to use the image of Mr. Athans as such for the purposes of their promotion. I accept Mr. Connett's explanation that there was no intention to injure or cause concern to Mr. Athans, and I accept the explanation of the witnesses, McCullough and Steventon, that their intention was to produce a stylized, or abstract, drawing of an interesting and attractive kind, depicting the sport of water-skiing without intending it to be a representation of any particular person. In this respect, their intention was innocent, but their judgment was faulty and misinformed.

I also find, on the evidence, that the sport of water-skiing, as it is competitively and professionally conducted, is characterized by limited public knowledge and support. It is not, for example, in the same class as professional football, hockey, tennis, or golf. . . . On the evidence, I cannot find that more than a relatively small number of very well-informed people would be likely to recognize the drawings as representations of Mr. Athans, without the addition of his name, to identify them. Apart from the drawings, there was no mention of Mr. Athans in the either the advertisement or the brochure.

I turn now to a consideration of the claim for passing off. Essentially, the action of passing off constitutes the sale of goods or the carrying on of a business under a name, mark, or description in such a manner as to mislead the public into believing that the merchandise or the business is that of another person. The law is designed to protect traders against a form of unfair competition, which consists of acquiring for oneself by means of false or misleading devices the benefit of the reputation already achieved by a rival trader. . . .

In my opinion, the plaintiff has not made a case for passing off, for the simple reason that, on the evidence as a whole, I am not able to find that the use of the line drawings in the advertisement and the brochure were, on the balance of probability, likely to give rise to confusion between the plaintiff's business and that of the defendant, C.A.C. . . . As I have said, there is no evidence that any but the most knowledgeable persons concerned in the sport of water-skiing would identify the drawings with Mr. Athans. It is obvious that the brochure and advertisement are designed to attract customers who wish to send their children to a summer camp where water-skiing is featured in the programme. There is no evidence, and experience suggests it is unlikely, that that segment of the public would be particularly knowledgeable about the sport of water-skiing, or would identify the drawings with Mr. Athans. It is not sufficient that persons having expert knowledge of the field would identify him and would connect him with defendant's camp. There is nothing in the explanatory material, either in the advertisement or the brochure, that either names or otherwise identifies Mr. Athans with the programme. . . .

I turn now to the second head of claim, namely, wrongful appropriation of the plaintiff's personality. I say at once that, on the basis of recent authority, it is clear that Mr. Athans has a proprietary right in the exclusive marketing for gain of his personality, image and name, and that the law entitles him to protect that right, if it is invaded. . . . It is only in recent years that the concept of appropriation of personality has moved from its place in the tort of defamation, as exemplified, by *Tolley v. J.S. Fry and Sons, Ltd.* [1931] A.C. 333, to a more broadly based common law tort. . . .

If the defendants, C.A.C., wished to derive commercial advantage by associating its activities with the sport of water-skiing, it would be natural and acceptable that it should adopt some device depicting an individual water-skier in action. But the defendants, out of, no doubt, a vast number of photographs of unknown water-skiers in action that must be available, chose the photograph of George Athans in a pose that was used and know as his "trademark" image, and deliberately incorporated a representation of it in the promotional material at a time when C.A.C., at least, knew that Mr. Athans would not be associated with the camp for the forthcoming season, and had undertaken not to use his name. Had the defendants identified the promotional drawings as representing George Athans, or incorporated in the printed copy language stating or imply-ing that he was endorsing, sponsoring, or participating in the camp's activities, I would unhesitatingly find that the defendants had appropriated his person-ality for commercial advantage. But, as I have stated earlier, the drawings are the only aspect of the material that could form any supposed connection between Mr. Athans and the defendant's camp. . . . On the basis of the drawings alone, it is not only improbable, but it is highly unlikely that potential customers of the camp would consider that George Athans, assuming they even knew who he was, had lent his personality to the camp, or had endorsed it, or was partici-pating in its programme. . . . On the evidence as a whole, I find that the action of the defendants does not amount to a wrongful appropriation of Mr. Athans' personality, as such. I further find, in case it should be necessary, that Mr. Athans has suffered no injury or damage (apart from what I shall say later) by the action of the defendants. . . .

This, however, does not dispose of the matter. The defendants have used the image of George Athans for their commercial advantage. . . . Mr. Athans had, as I find, adopted the photograph and the various representations of it, as his dis-tinctive *indicia*. He used them as an essential component in the marketing of his personality, which he had an exclusive right to do. The commercial use of his representation image by the defendants without his consent constituted an invasion and *pro tanto* an impairment of his exclusive right to market his per-sonality and this, in my opinion, constitutes an aspect of the tort of appropria-tion of personality. . . . In the circumstances, the reproduction of commercial advantage of the photograph in the form which it took, was an invasion of Mr. Athans' exclusive right to market his personality. For this he is entitled to com-pensation. No other injury having been proved, the measure of damages should be the amount he ought reasonably to have received in the market for permis-sion to publish the drawings.

It is difficult to assess damages on this basis on the evidence. [After a lengthy analysis the court awarded $500, which represented 10 cents for each "copy" that defendants had made of the photograph.]

Judgment for plaintiff.

NOTES AND QUESTIONS

1. There have been several cases in the United States in which celebrities have recovered against advertisers who used "look-alikes" or people with similar voices. *See, e.g., Midler v. Young & Rubicam, Inc.*, 944 F.2d 909 (9th Cir. 1991) (use of a Bette Midler sound-alike in voice over); *Waits v. Frito-Lay, Inc.*, 978 F.2d 1093 (9th Cir. 1992) (use of a Tom Waits sound-alike); *White v. Samsung Electronics America, Inc.*, 971 F.2d 1395 (9th Cir. 1992) (Vanna White recovered for an advertisement using a robot that vaguely resembled her). See also the case following these Notes and Questions.

2. The court analyzes two separate claims involving use of the drawing: "passing off" and "appropriation of plaintiff's personality." How do the two claims differ? Are the torts designed to protect the same values?

3. Suppose that defendant had used a photograph of a virtually unknown water skier. Would that person have been able to recover? Does it matter that the plaintiff in the actual case, Mr. Athans, had actually used the photograph in his own marketing campaign?

4. Were Athans and Canadian Adventure Camp in competition? Certainly Athans did not operate water-skiing camps. But could you argue that the two were in competition with respect to the drawing? On the other hand, did C.A.C.'s use of that drawing deprive Athans of any sales?

5. Suppose that the photograph of Athans also showed the logo of the manufacturer of Athans's bathing suit. Should that party also be able to recover against C.A.C.?

6. Does the right of publicity survive the death of the celebrity? The courts are split. For a general analysis, see Felcher & Rubin, *The Descendability of the Right of Publicity: Is There Commercial Life After Death?*, 89 YALE L.J. 1125 (1980). Tennessee apparently does allow the right to descend. *Tennessee ex rel. The Elvis Presley International Memorial Foundation v. Crowell*, 733 S.W.2d 89 (Tenn. Ct. App. 1987). Because Tennessee law usually governs the rights of the heirs of Elvis Presley, whose personality has been appropriated perhaps more often than any other celebrity, this ruling has proven important.

WENDT v. HOST INTERNATIONAL, INC.
123 F.3d 806 (9th Cir. 1997)

FLETCHER, J.

Actors George Wendt and John Ratzenberger appeal the district court's grant of summary judgment in favor of Host International, Inc. ("Host") and applicant in intervention Paramount Pictures Corporation ("Paramount"), dismissing their action for violations of the Lanham Act, 15 U.S.C. Section 1125(a), and California's statutory and common law right of publicity. We reverse.

Wendt and Ratzenberger argue that the district court erred in dismissing their action because they have raised issues of material fact as to whether Host violated their trademark and publicity rights by creating animatronic robotic figures (the "robots") based upon their likenesses without their permission and placing these robots in airport bars modeled upon the set from the television show Cheers. They also appeal the district court's orders excluding appellants' survey evidence, barring presentation of expert testimony, and awarding Host and Paramount attorney's fees. We have jurisdiction, 28 U.S.C. Section 1291, and we reverse and remand for trial.

[T]he district court granted summary judgment [after] an in-court inspection of the robots. It held that it could not "find, by viewing both the robotics and the live persons of Mr. Wendt and Mr. Ratzenberger, that there is any similarity at all . . . except that one of the robots, like one of the plaintiffs, is heavier than the other. . . . The facial features are totally different." The district court then awarded attorney's fees to Host and Paramount pursuant to Cal. Civ. Code Section 3344.

Appellants argue that despite the district court's comparison of the animatronic figures and the appellants, dismissal was inappropriate because material issues of fact remain as to the degree to which the animatronic figures appropriate the appellants' likenesses. Appellants claim that the district court erred in determining that the robots were not likenesses of the appellants because the "likeness" need not be identical or photographic. Further, they argue that the likeness determination is an issue for the jury to decide in this case. We agree.

III. ANALYSIS

We review a grant of summary judgment de novo. We must determine, viewing the evidence in the light most favorable to the nonmoving party, whether there are any genuine issues of material fact, and whether the district court correctly applied the relevant substantive law. We are not to weigh the evidence or determine the truth of the matter, but only to determine whether there is a genuine issue for trial. . . .

A. The Statutory Right of Publicity

California Civil Code Section 3344 provides in relevant part:

> [a]ny person who knowingly uses another's name, voice, signature, photograph, or likeness, in any manner, . . . for purposes of advertising or selling, . . . without such person's prior consent . . . shall be liable for any damages sustained by the person or persons injured as a result thereof.

[Despite] the district court's assertions that no reasonable jury could find that the robots are "similar in any manner whatsoever to Plaintiffs," we respectfully disagree. Without making any judgment about the ultimate similarity of the figures to the appellants, we conclude from our own inspection of the robots that material facts exist that might cause a reasonable jury to find them sufficiently "like" the appellants to violate Cal. Civ. Code Section 3344. . . .

B. Common-Law Right of Publicity

California recognizes a common law right of privacy that includes protection against appropriation for the defendant's advantage of the plaintiff's name or likeness. *Eastwood v. Super. Ct. for Los Angeles County*, 198 Cal. Rptr. 342, 347 (Cal. Ct. App. 1983). The right to be protected against such appropriations is also referred to as the "right of publicity." A common law cause of action for appropriation of name or likeness may be pleaded by alleging 1) the defendant's use of the plaintiff's identity; 2) the appropriation of plaintiff's name or likeness to defendant's advantage, commercially or otherwise; 3) lack of consent; and 4) resulting injury.

> The so-called right of publicity means in essence that the reaction of the public to name and likeness, which may be fortuitous or which may be managed and planned, endows the name and likeness of the person involved with commercially exploitable opportunities. The protection of name and likeness from unwarranted intrusion or exploitation is the heart of the law of privacy.

Lugosi v. Universal Pictures, 603 P.2d 425, 431(1979).

We have held that this common-law right of publicity protects more than the knowing use of a plaintiff's name or likeness for commercial purposes that is protected by Cal. Civ. Code Section 3344. It also protects against appropriations of the plaintiff's identity by other means. *See Motschenbacher v. R.J. Reynolds Tobacco Co.*, 498 F.2d 821, 827 (9th Cir. 1974) (concluding that there was a common-law claim from use of an identifiable race car in an advertisement, even though name or likeness of famous driver was not visible).

Appellees argue that the figures appropriate only the identities of the characters Norm and Cliff, to which Paramount owns the copyrights, and not the identities of Wendt and Ratzenberger, who merely portrayed those characters on television and retain no licensing rights to them. They argue that appellants may not claim an appropriation of identity by relying upon indicia, such as the Cheers Bar set, that are the property of, or licensee of, a copyright owner.

Appellants freely concede that they retain no rights to the characters Norm and Cliff; they argue that the figures, named "Bob" and "Hank," are not related to Paramount's copyright of the creative elements of the characters Norm and Cliff. They argue that it is the physical likeness to Wendt and Ratzenberger, not Paramount's characters, that has commercial value to Host.

While it is true that appellants' fame arose in large part through their participation in Cheers, an actor or actress does not lose the right to control the commercial exploitation of his or her likeness by portraying a fictional character.

Appellants have raised genuine issues of material fact concerning the degree to which the figures look like them. Because they have done so, appellants have also raised triable issues of fact as to whether or not appellees sought to appropriate their likenesses for their own advantage and whether they succeeded in doing so. The ultimate issue for the jury to decide is whether the defendants are commercially exploiting the likeness of the figures to Wendt and Ratzenberger intending to engender profits to their enterprises. We therefore reverse the grant of summary judgment on the common law right of publicity claim.

C. Unfair Competition

Section 43(a) of the Lanham Act (15 U.S.C. Section 1125(a)) prohibits, inter alia, the use of any symbol or device which is likely to deceive consumers as to the association, sponsorship, or approval of goods or services by another person. The appellants' claim is for false endorsement — that by using an imitation of their unique physical characteristics, Host misrepresented their association with and endorsement of the Cheers bars concept.

In *Waits*, 978 F.2d at 1110, we held such a claim actionable under Section 43(a):

> false endorsement claim based on the unauthorized use of a celebrity's identity . . . alleges the misuse of a trademark, *i.e.*, a symbol or device such as a visual likeness, vocal imitation, or other uniquely distinguishing characteristic, which is likely to confuse consumers as to the plaintiff's sponsorship or approval of the product. . . .

A reasonable jury could conclude that most of the factors weigh in appellants' favor and that Host's alleged conduct creates at least the likelihood of consumer confusion. Whether appellants' Lanham Act claim should succeed, of course, is a matter for the jury. Accordingly, we reverse the dismissal of the unfair competition claim and remand.

NOTES

1. Exactly what did the defendant do wrong? The robots did not look exactly like the actors. Instead, they simply reminded people of the actors. Is it now considered improper to remind people of a famous person? Apparently so, at least in the Ninth Circuit. In *White v. Samsung Electronics America, Inc.*, 971 F.2d 1395 (9th Cir. 1992), a case heavily relied upon in *Wendt*, the court allowed Vanna White to recover against Samsung based on a humorous ad that used a robot that only remotely resembled White. There was no evidence that any customer was confused into believing that White endorsed the product. Nevertheless, the court held that White had the exclusive right to profit from her persona. In his dissent, Judge Alcaron noted,

> Under the majority's view of the law, Gene Autrey could have brought an action for damages against all other singing cowboys. Clint Eastwood would be able to sue anyone who plays a tall, soft-spoken cowboy, unless, of course, Jimmy Stewart had not previously enjoined Clint Eastwood. Johnny Weismuller would have been able to sue each actor who played

the role of Tarzan. Sylvester Stallone could sue actors who play blue-collar boxers. Chuck Norris could sue all karate experts who display their skills in motion pictures. Arnold Schwarzenegger could sue body builders who are compensated for appearing in public.

2. Is the right of publicity recognized in *Wendt* limited to situations where the defendant uses plaintiff's image for commercial purposes? The new RESTATEMENT (THIRD) OF UNFAIR COMPETITION would limit the tort to such cases. Section 46 provides:

> One who appropriates the commercial value of a person's identity by using without consent the person's name, likeness, or other indicia of identity for purposes of trade is subject to liability for the relief appropriate under the rules stated in §§ 48 and 49.

3. As *Wendt* indicates, a few states have elected to codify the right of publicity, in an effort to resolve many of the difficult issues faced by courts in dealing with the common-law right. Other examples of codifications include FLA. STAT. ANN. § 540.08; KY. REV. STAT. § 391.170; NEB. REV. STAT. ANN. § 20-202; N.Y. CIV. RTS. LAW §§ 50-51; R.I. GEN. LAWS ANN. §§ 9-1-28, 9-1-28.1; TEX. PROP. CODE § 26.001 *et seq.*; and WIS. STAT. § 895.50.

PROBLEMS

1. In discussing the common-law right of publicity in Part B of its opinion, the court cites the right of *privacy*, which is discussed in Chapter 18. Like the tort of disparagement discussed earlier in this chapter, the right of publicity can be viewed as evolving both from the concept of privacy and from the competitive tort of unfair competition.

Is the right of publicity more like unfair competition or the right to privacy? Can either Wendt or Ratzenberger really claim a right to "privacy" with respect not to their personal lives, but to imaginary characters that they played for years on television? On the other hand, do the acts of the defendant really constitute "unfair" competition? Note that the court does not conclude that defendant's use of the image is unfair in and of itself. Rather, the court labels it unfair because it finds that defendant's acts tend to confuse the public into thinking that the actors were behind, or at least approved of, the use of the robots. Do you agree with the court that people will really be confused?

2. Fergus McTavish, a Cairn terrier, has won "best of show" awards in several prestigious dog shows. These victories have earned Karen, Fergus' owner, a considerable financial award. Karen herself, however, has diligently avoided any publicity for herself, focusing the media's attention completely on Fergus.

Because Cairn terriers are fairly photogenic, Paul Paparazzi, a free-lance photographer, shoots several rolls of film of Fergus. Some of these photographs are taken at public dog shows; others while Fergus is at play in Karen's back yard. Because Paul has a telephoto lens, he is able to avoid trespassing on Karen's property when taking the backyard photographs.

After developing the film, Paul approaches companies that sell canine-related products to see if they will buy the photographs. Paul's efforts pay off when he goes to Equus, a company that produces dog food. The president of Equus, an avid dog-show buff, instantly recognizes Fergus in the photos. With a wink, the president says to Paul, "I won't ask you where you got these." The president then purchases six photographs of Fergus: two taken at dog shows, and four in Karen's back yard. Equus uses the photos in advertising its dog food.

Karen is shocked when the pictures of Fergus appear in these advertisements. She accordingly sues both Paul and Equus for both general misappropriation and violation of the right of publicity. Will she prevail?

c. The Clash Between Misappropriation and the Federal Patent and Copyright Laws

Article I, section eight of the United States Constitution gives Congress the authority to enact patent and copyright laws. Pursuant to that power, Congress has enacted comprehensive federal statutes covering both areas. These statutes provide an alternative to the torts set out in this chapter for protecting the fruits of creative activity.

More importantly, however, the federal Patent and Copyright Acts can significantly limit the scope of the non-federal tort remedies. Patents and copyrights involve a tradeoff between the need to provide economic incentives to artists and inventors and the goal of ensuring that knowledge is fully disseminated to the public. Both federal acts resolve that tension by giving the author or inventor a legal monopoly that is limited both in scope and term. State tort remedies do not necessarily contain these same substantive limits, and can in theory last forever. Therefore, because the state-law torts threaten to upset Congress's careful balance, both the Patent and Copyright Acts *preempt* state laws that provide similar forms of protection.

Determining what laws are preempted and which survive can often be a difficult task. The United States Supreme Court decision in *Bonito Boats, Inc. v. Thunder Craft Boats*, 489 U.S. 141 (1989), illustrates the approach used for patent preemption. That case dealt with a Florida law that prohibited copying of boat hulls by making a mold of the original. The court held that the state law was preempted by the Patent Act. In essence, the state law flatly prohibited copying of a useful item (although the law barred only one method of copying, that method was apparently the cheapest and easiest way to make an exact copy). Because Congress intended that the patent laws were to be the only way an inventor could prevent the copying of useful items, the state law could not stand.

Do not conclude from this brief exposition that the Patent Act preempts all of the torts set forth in this chapter. In *Kewanee Oil Co. v. Bicron Corp.*, 416 U.S. 470 (1974), a case discussed with approval in *Bonito Boats*, the Supreme Court held that trade secret laws are generally not preempted. Unlike the Florida boat hull law, the protection afforded by the trade secret law differs from a patent in that trade secret law requires a "wrongful" taking or use of the secret. Although a state cannot create a legal regime that parallels the federal patent, it is free "to promote goals outside the contemplation of the federal patent scheme." *Bonito Boats*, 489 U.S. at 166. Therefore, any law that requires plaintiff to prove an independently tortious act should survive a preemption challenge, even if it involves an invention within the scope of the patent laws. Second, patent law only covers creative activity that results in a new and useful "invention," *i.e.*, a machine or process that performs a utilitarian function. States are therefore not barred by the Patent Act from protecting things other than inventions. Thus, the right of personality discussed in the prior case is not preempted by the Patent Act for the simple reason that personalities cannot be patented.

The rules governing the preemptive scope of the Copyright Act closely parallel the rules that apply in the case of patents. The main difference between copyright and patent preemption lies in the very different types of creations that are protected under the two legal regimes. Copyright protects expression of an idea, including not only books and paintings, but also works such as musical recordings and computer programs. Because of the wide range of works that fall within copyright, courts have wrestled with questions of copyright preemption in a number of cases involving various competitive torts. The outcome of any given case often turns on the facts and the scope of the state law. For a tiny sampling of cases finding preemption by the Copyright Act, see *National Basketball Assoc. v. Motorola, Inc.*, 105 F.3d 841 (2d Cir. 1997) (plaintiff sought recovery for misappropriation based on defendant's sale of hand-held pagers that displayed scores and statistics of basketball games); *Ahn v. Midway Mfg. Co.*, 965 F. Supp. 1134 (N.D. Ill. 1997) (right of publicity claim); *Balsamo/Olson Group, Inc. v. Bradley Place Ltd. Partnership*, 950 F. Supp. 896 (C.D. Ill. 1997) (tortious interference with a business advantage claim based on use of architect's design).

Earlier in this chapter, there was a brief discussion of the Lanham Act, which is the main federal law governing trademarks. Compared with the Patent and Copyright Acts, the Lanham Act has very little preemptive effect. Common-law trademark claims, then, remain quite common. In fact, many states even offer their own trademark registration systems.

D. REPRISE: THE WIDE RANGE OF COMPETITIVE TORTS

In one chapter, it is impossible to provide more than a cursory overview of the competitive torts. The catalog of torts set out in this chapter is by no means exhaustive. For example, the oft-litigated tort of trade secret misappropriation, and its close cousin breach of confidence, is beyond the scope of this chapter. Another claim that is growing in importance, the right to be named as the author or inventor of a creative work, also had to be omitted.

Moreover, the above discussion does not even deal fully with the nuances of the torts that are discussed. Perhaps more than in other areas of tort law, courts hold widely diverging views towards some of the competitive torts. For example, not all jurisdictions recognize a right of publicity. Similarly, there is an ongoing debate in the courts concerning the extent to which a party suing for disparagement under either the common law or § 43(a) must demonstrate that the defendant knew its statement was false.

Nevertheless, the material in this chapter should provide a taste of the world of commercial torts. As you have seen, these torts serve different purposes than the personal torts. As a result, although they are logically related to personal torts, they also involve certain unique considerations that make them a true subset of tort law.

Table of Cases

(Principal cases are in all caps; references are to pages.)

Index

References are to pages.